THE LIFE DIVINE

Sri Aurobindo

The Life Divine

Publisher:
Lotus Press
PO Box 325
Twin Lakes, WI 53181 USA

First published in the monthly review Arya 1914-1920
First Indian edition (revised and enlarged) 1939-1940
First American edition 1949, Reprinted 1951, 1965
Second American edition April 24, 1990
(American Edition) Second Impression 1994
Third Impression 2000
Fourth Impression 2006

© Sri Aurobindo Ashram Trust 1990

This edition is published and distributed in the United States
by Lotus Press, Box 325, Twin Lakes, WI 53181 USA
by arrangement with Sri Aurobindo Ashram Trust,
Publication Department, Pondicherry 605 002, India

ISBN for Paper Bound:
ISBN-13: 978-0-9415-2461-2
ISBN-10: 0-9415-2461-2

ISBN for Hard Bound:
ISBN-13: 978-0-9415-2462-9
ISBN-10: 0-9415-2462-0

Library of Congress Catalogue Card Number 89-63859

Printed at Sri Aurobindo Ashram Press,
Pondicherry, India

Printed in India

Publisher's Note

The Life Divine first appeared serially in the *Arya* from August 1914 to January 1919. Book I, revised and enlarged, was first published in book form in November 1939; Book II, recast and enlarged, followed in July 1940, in two parts. These were reprinted in 1943 and 1947. A single-volume edition under the imprint of the Sri Aurobindo International Centre of Education appeared in 1955 and was reprinted in 1960. In 1972 *The Life Divine* was published as volumes 18 and 19 of the Sri Aurobindo Birth Centenary Library. The text of the present edition follows that of the SABCL edition.

CONTENTS

CONTENTS

CONTENTS

CONTENTS

The Life Divine

Book I

Omnipresent Reality
and the Universe

Chapter I

The Human Aspiration

She follows to the goal of those that are passing on beyond,
she is the first in the eternal succession of the dawns that
are coming, — Usha widens bringing out that which lives,
awakening someone who was dead.... What is her scope when
she harmonises with the dawns that shone out before and
those that now must shine? She desires the ancient mornings
and fulfils their light; projecting forwards her illumination she
enters into communion with the rest that are to come.

Kutsa Angirasa — Rig Veda.[1]

Threefold are those supreme births of this divine force that is
in the world, they are true, they are desirable; he moves there
wide-overt within the Infinite and shines pure, luminous and
fulfilling.... That which is immortal in mortals and possessed
of the truth, is a god and established inwardly as an energy
working out in our divine powers.... Become high-uplifted,
O Strength, pierce all veils, manifest in us the things of the
Godhead. *Vamadeva — Rig Veda.*[2]

THE EARLIEST preoccupation of man in his awakened
thoughts and, as it seems, his inevitable and ultimate
preoccupation, — for it survives the longest periods of
scepticism and returns after every banishment, — is also the
highest which his thought can envisage. It manifests itself in
the divination of Godhead, the impulse towards perfection, the
search after pure Truth and unmixed Bliss, the sense of a secret immortality. The ancient dawns of human knowledge have
left us their witness to this constant aspiration; today we see

---

[1] I. 113. 8, 10.   [2] IV. 1. 7; IV. 2. 1; IV. 4. 5.

a humanity satiated but not satisfied by victorious analysis of
the externalities of Nature preparing to return to its primeval
longings. The earliest formula of Wisdom promises to be its last,
— God, Light, Freedom, Immortality.

These persistent ideals of the race are at once the contradiction of its normal experience and the affirmation of higher
and deeper experiences which are abnormal to humanity and
only to be attained, in their organised entirety, by a revolutionary individual effort or an evolutionary general progression. To
know, possess and be the divine being in an animal and egoistic
consciousness, to convert our twilit or obscure physical mentality into the plenary supramental illumination, to build peace
and a self-existent bliss where there is only a stress of transitory
satisfactions besieged by physical pain and emotional suffering,
to establish an infinite freedom in a world which presents itself
as a group of mechanical necessities, to discover and realise
the immortal life in a body subjected to death and constant
mutation, — this is offered to us as the manifestation of God in
Matter and the goal of Nature in her terrestrial evolution. To
the ordinary material intellect which takes its present organisation of consciousness for the limit of its possibilities, the direct
contradiction of the unrealised ideals with the realised fact is
a final argument against their validity. But if we take a more
deliberate view of the world's workings, that direct opposition
appears rather as part of Nature's profoundest method and the
seal of her completest sanction.

For all problems of existence are essentially problems of
harmony. They arise from the perception of an unsolved discord
and the instinct of an undiscovered agreement or unity. To rest
content with an unsolved discord is possible for the practical and
more animal part of man, but impossible for his fully awakened
mind, and usually even his practical parts only escape from
the general necessity either by shutting out the problem or by
accepting a rough, utilitarian and unillumined compromise. For
essentially, all Nature seeks a harmony, life and matter in their
own sphere as much as mind in the arrangement of its perceptions. The greater the apparent disorder of the materials offered

or the apparent disparateness, even to irreconcilable opposition, of the elements that have to be utilised, the stronger is the spur, and it drives towards a more subtle and puissant order than can normally be the result of a less difficult endeavour. The accordance of active Life with a material of form in which the condition of activity itself seems to be inertia, is one problem of opposites that Nature has solved and seeks always to solve better with greater complexities; for its perfect solution would be the material immortality of a fully organised mind-supporting animal body. The accordance of conscious mind and conscious will with a form and a life in themselves not overtly self-conscious and capable at best of a mechanical or sub-conscious will is another problem of opposites in which she has produced astonishing results and aims always at higher marvels; for there her ultimate miracle would be an animal consciousness no longer seeking but possessed of Truth and Light, with the practical omnipotence which would result from the possession of a direct and perfected knowledge. Not only, then, is the upward impulse of man towards the accordance of yet higher opposites rational in itself, but it is the only logical completion of a rule and an effort that seem to be a fundamental method of Nature and the very sense of her universal strivings.

We speak of the evolution of Life in Matter, the evolution of Mind in Matter; but evolution is a word which merely states the phenomenon without explaining it. For there seems to be no reason why Life should evolve out of material elements or Mind out of living form, unless we accept the Vedantic solution that Life is already involved in Matter and Mind in Life because in essence Matter is a form of veiled Life, Life a form of veiled Consciousness. And then there seems to be little objection to a farther step in the series and the admission that mental consciousness may itself be only a form and a veil of higher states which are beyond Mind. In that case, the unconquerable impulse of man towards God, Light, Bliss, Freedom, Immortality presents itself in its right place in the chain as simply the imperative impulse by which Nature is seeking to evolve beyond Mind, and appears to be as natural, true and just as the impulse towards Life which she has planted in certain forms of Matter or the impulse towards Mind which she has planted in certain forms of Life. As there, so here, the impulse exists more or less obscurely in her different vessels with an ever-ascending series in the power of its will-to-be; as there, so here, it is gradually evolving and bound fully to evolve the necessary organs and faculties. As the impulse towards Mind ranges from the more sensitive reactions of Life in the metal and the plant up to its full organisation in man, so in man himself there is the same ascending series, the preparation, if nothing more, of a higher and divine life. The animal is a living laboratory in which Nature has, it is said, worked out man. Man himself may well be a thinking and living laboratory in whom and with whose conscious co-operation she wills to work out the superman, the god. Or shall we not say, rather, to manifest God? For if evolution is the progressive manifestation by Nature of that which slept or worked in her, involved, it is also the overt realisation of that which she secretly is. We cannot, then, bid her pause at a given stage of her evolution, nor have we the right to condemn with the religionist as perverse and presumptuous or with the rationalist as a disease or hallucination any intention she may evince or effort she may make to go beyond. If it be true that Spirit is involved in Matter and apparent Nature is secret God, then the manifestation of the divine in himself and the realisation of God within and without are the highest and most legitimate aim possible to man upon earth.

Thus the eternal paradox and eternal truth of a divine life in an animal body, an immortal aspiration or reality inhabiting a mortal tenement, a single and universal consciousness representing itself in limited minds and divided egos, a transcendent, indefinable, timeless and spaceless Being who alone renders time and space and cosmos possible, and in all these the higher truth realisable by the lower term, justify themselves to the deliberate reason as well as to the persistent instinct or intuition of mankind. Attempts are sometimes made to have done finally with questionings which have so often been declared insoluble by logical thought and to persuade men to limit their mental activities to the practical and immediate problems of their material existence in the universe; but such evasions are never permanent in their effect. Mankind returns from them with a more vehement impulse of inquiry or a more violent hunger for an immediate solution. By that hunger mysticism profits and new religions arise to replace the old that have been destroyed or stripped of significance by a scepticism which itself could not satisfy because, although its business was inquiry, it was unwilling sufficiently to inquire. The attempt to deny or stifle a truth because it is yet obscure in its outward workings and too often represented by obscurantist superstition or a crude faith, is itself a kind of obscurantism. The will to escape from a cosmic necessity because it is arduous, difficult to justify by immediate tangible results, slow in regulating its operations, must turn out eventually to have been no acceptance of the truth of Nature but a revolt against the secret, mightier will of the great Mother. It is better and more rational to accept what she will not allow us as a race to reject and lift it from the sphere of blind instinct, obscure intuition and random aspiration into the light of reason and an instructed and consciously self-guiding will. And if there is any higher light of illumined intuition or self-revealing truth which is now in man either obstructed and inoperative or works with intermittent glancings as if from behind a veil or with occasional displays as of the northern lights in our material skies, then there also we need not fear to aspire. For it is likely that such is the next higher state of consciousness of which Mind is only a form and veil, and through the splendours of that light may lie the path of our progressive self-enlargement into whatever highest state is humanity's ultimate resting-place.

Chapter II

The Two Negations

I. The Materialist Denial

> He energised conscious-force (in the austerity of thought) and
> came to the knowledge that Matter is the Brahman. For from
> Matter all existences are born; born, by Matter they increase
> and enter into Matter in their passing hence. Then he went to
> Varuna, his father, and said, "Lord, teach me of the Brahman."
> But he said to him: "Energise (again) the conscious-energy in
> thee; for the Energy is Brahman."   *Taittiriya Upanishad.*[1]

THE AFFIRMATION of a divine life upon earth and an
immortal sense in mortal existence can have no base unless we recognise not only eternal Spirit as the inhabitant
of this bodily mansion, the wearer of this mutable robe, but
accept Matter of which it is made, as a fit and noble material
out of which He weaves constantly His garbs, builds recurrently
the unending series of His mansions.

Nor is this, even, enough to guard us against a recoil from
life in the body unless, with the Upanishads, perceiving behind
their appearances the identity in essence of these two extreme
terms of existence, we are able to say in the very language of
those ancient writings, "Matter also is Brahman", and to give its
full value to the vigorous figure by which the physical universe
is described as the external body of the Divine Being. Nor, —
so far divided apparently are these two extreme terms, — is that
identification convincing to the rational intellect if we refuse to
recognise a series of ascending terms (Life, Mind, Supermind
and the grades that link Mind to Supermind) between Spirit

---

[1] III. l, 2.

and Matter. Otherwise the two must appear as irreconcilable opponents bound together in an unhappy wedlock and their divorce the one reasonable solution. To identify them, to represent each in the terms of the other, becomes an artificial creation of Thought opposed to the logic of facts and possible only by an irrational mysticism.

If we assert only pure Spirit and a mechanical unintelligent substance or energy, calling one God or Soul and the other Nature, the inevitable end will be that we shall either deny God or else turn from Nature. For both Thought and Life, a choice then becomes imperative. Thought comes to deny the one as an illusion of the imagination or the other as an illusion of the senses; Life comes to fix on the immaterial and flee from itself in a disgust or a self-forgetting ecstasy, or else to deny its own immortality and take its orientation away from God and towards the animal. Purusha and Prakriti, the passively luminous Soul of the Sankhyas and their mechanically active Energy, have nothing in common, not even their opposite modes of inertia; their antinomies can only be resolved by the cessation of the inertly driven Activity into the immutable Repose upon which it has been casting in vain the sterile procession of its images. Shankara's wordless, inactive Self and his Maya of many names and forms are equally disparate and irreconcilable entities; their rigid antagonism can terminate only by the dissolution of the multitudinous illusion into the sole Truth of an eternal Silence.

The materialist has an easier field; it is possible for him by denying Spirit to arrive at a more readily convincing simplicity of statement, a real Monism, the Monism of Matter or else of Force. But in this rigidity of statement it is impossible for him to persist permanently. He too ends by positing an unknowable as inert, as remote from the known universe as the passive Purusha or the silent Atman. It serves no purpose but to put off by a vague concession the inexorable demands of Thought or to stand as an excuse for refusing to extend the limits of inquiry.

Therefore, in these barren contradictions the human mind cannot rest satisfied. It must seek always a complete affirmation; it can find it only by a luminous reconciliation. To reach that reconciliation it must traverse the degrees which our inner consciousness imposes on us and, whether by objective method of analysis applied to Life and Mind as to Matter or by subjective synthesis and illumination, arrive at the repose of the ultimate unity without denying the energy of the expressive multiplicity. Only in such a complete and catholic affirmation can all the multiform and apparently contradictory data of existence be harmonised and the manifold conflicting forces which govern our thought and life discover the central Truth which they are here to symbolise and variously fulfil. Then only can our Thought, having attained a true centre, ceasing to wander in circles, work like the Brahman of the Upanishad, fixed and stable even in its play and its world-wide coursing, and our life, knowing its aim, serve it with a serene and settled joy and light as well as with a rhythmically discursive energy.

But when that rhythm has once been disturbed, it is necessary and helpful that man should test separately, in their extreme assertion, each of the two great opposites. It is the mind's natural way of returning more perfectly to the affirmation it has lost. On the road it may attempt to rest in the intervening degrees, reducing all things into the terms of an original Life-Energy or of sensation or of Ideas; but these exclusive solutions have always an air of unreality. They may satisfy for a time the logical reason which deals only with pure ideas, but they cannot satisfy the mind's sense of actuality. For the mind knows that there is something behind itself which is not the Idea; it knows, on the other hand, that there is something within itself which is more than the vital Breath. Either Spirit or Matter can give it for a time some sense of ultimate reality; not so any of the principles that intervene. It must, therefore, go to the two extremes before it can return fruitfully upon the whole. For by its very nature, served by a sense that can perceive with distinctness only the parts of existence and by a speech that, also, can achieve distinctness only when it carefully divides and limits, the intellect is driven, having before it this multiplicity of elemental principles, to seek unity by reducing all ruthlessly to the terms of one. It attempts practically, in order to assert this one, to get rid of the others. To perceive the real source of their identity without this exclusive process, it must either have overleaped itself or must have completed the circuit only to find that all equally reduce themselves to That which escapes definition or description and is yet not only real but attainable. By whatever road we may travel, That is always the end at which we arrive and we can only escape it by refusing to complete the journey.

It is therefore of good augury that after many experiments and verbal solutions we should now find ourselves standing today in the presence of the two that have alone borne for long the most rigorous tests of experience, the two extremes, and that at the end of the experience both should have come to a result which the universal instinct in mankind, that veiled judge, sentinel and representative of the universal Spirit of Truth, refuses to accept as right or as satisfying. In Europe and in India, respectively, the negation of the materialist and the refusal of the ascetic have sought to assert themselves as the sole truth and to dominate the conception of Life. In India, if the result has been a great heaping up of the treasures of the Spirit, — or of some of them, — it has also been a great bankruptcy of Life; in Europe, the fullness of riches and the triumphant mastery of this world's powers and possessions have progressed towards an equal bankruptcy in the things of the Spirit. Nor has the intellect, which sought the solution of all problems in the one term of Matter, found satisfaction in the answer that it has received.

Therefore the time grows ripe and the tendency of the world moves towards a new and comprehensive affirmation in thought and in inner and outer experience and to its corollary, a new and rich self-fulfilment in an integral human existence for the individual and for the race.

From the difference in the relations of Spirit and Matter to the Unknowable which they both represent, there arises also a difference of effectiveness in the material and the spiritual negations. The denial of the materialist although more insistent and immediately successful, more facile in its appeal to the generality of mankind, is yet less enduring, less effective finally than the absorbing and perilous refusal of the ascetic. For it carries within itself its own cure. Its most powerful element is the Agnosticism which, admitting the Unknowable behind all manifestation, extends the limits of the unknowable until it comprehends all that is merely unknown. Its premise is that the physical senses are our sole means of Knowledge and that Reason, therefore, even in its most extended and vigorous flights, cannot escape beyond their domain; it must deal always and solely with the facts which they provide or suggest; and the suggestions themselves must always be kept tied to their origins; we cannot go beyond, we cannot use them as a bridge leading us into a domain where more powerful and less limited faculties come into play and another kind of inquiry has to be instituted.

A premise so arbitrary pronounces on itself its own sentence of insufficiency. It can only be maintained by ignoring or explaining away all that vast field of evidence and experience which contradicts it, denying or disparaging noble and useful faculties, active consciously or obscurely or at worst latent in all human beings, and refusing to investigate supraphysical phenomena except as manifested in relation to matter and its movements and conceived as a subordinate activity of material forces. As soon as we begin to investigate the operations of mind and of supermind, in themselves and without the prejudgment that is determined from the beginning to see in them only a subordinate term of Matter, we come into contact with a mass of phenomena which escape entirely from the rigid hold, the limiting dogmatism of the materialist formula. And the moment we recognise, as our enlarging experience compels us to recognise, that there are in the universe knowable realities beyond the range of the senses and in man powers and faculties which determine rather than are determined by the material organs through which they hold themselves in touch with the world of the senses, — that outer shell of our true and complete existence, — the premise of materialistic Agnosticism disappears. We are ready for a larger statement and an ever-developing enquiry.

But, first, it is well that we should recognise the enormous, the indispensable utility of the very brief period of rationalistic

Materialism through which humanity has been passing. For that vast field of evidence and experience which now begins to reopen its gates to us, can only be safely entered when the intellect has been severely trained to a clear austerity; seized on by unripe minds, it lends itself to the most perilous distortions and misleading imaginations and actually in the past encrusted a real nucleus of truth with such an accretion of perverting superstitions and irrationalising dogmas that all advance in true knowledge was rendered impossible. It became necessary for a time to make a clean sweep at once of the truth and its disguise in order that the road might be clear for a new departure and a surer advance. The rationalistic tendency of Materialism has done mankind this great service.

For the faculties that transcend the senses, by the very fact of their being immeshed in Matter, missioned to work in a physical body, put in harness to draw one car along with the emotional desires and nervous impulses, are exposed to a mixed functioning in which they are in danger of illuminating confusion rather than clarifying truth. Especially is this mixed functioning dangerous when men with unchastened minds and unpurified sensibilities attempt to rise into the higher domains of spiritual experience. In what regions of unsubstantial cloud and semi-brilliant fog or a murk visited by flashes which blind more than they enlighten, do they not lose themselves by that rash and premature adventure! An adventure necessary indeed in the way in which Nature chooses to effect her advance, — for she amuses herself as she works, — but still, for the Reason, rash and premature.

It is necessary, therefore, that advancing Knowledge should base herself on a clear, pure and disciplined intellect. It is necessary, too, that she should correct her errors sometimes by a return to the restraint of sensible fact, the concrete realities of the physical world. The touch of Earth is always reinvigorating to the son of Earth, even when he seeks a supraphysical Knowledge. It may even be said that the supraphysical can only be really mastered in its fullness — to its heights we can always reach — when we keep our feet firmly on the physical. "Earth is

His footing",[2] says the Upanishad whenever it images the Self that manifests in the universe. And it is certainly the fact that the wider we extend and the surer we make our knowledge of the physical world, the wider and surer becomes our foundation for the higher knowledge, even for the highest, even for the Brahmavidya.

In emerging, therefore, out of the materialistic period of human Knowledge we must be careful that we do not rashly condemn what we are leaving or throw away even one tittle of its gains, before we can summon perceptions and powers that are well grasped and secure, to occupy their place. Rather we shall observe with respect and wonder the work that Atheism has done for the Divine and admire the services that Agnosticism has rendered in preparing the illimitable increase of knowledge. In our world error is continually the handmaid and pathfinder of Truth; for error is really a half-truth that stumbles because of its limitations; often it is Truth that wears a disguise in order to arrive unobserved near to its goal. Well, if it could always be, as it has been in the great period we are leaving, the faithful handmaid, severe, conscientious, clean-handed, luminous within its limits, a half-truth and not a reckless and presumptuous aberration.

A certain kind of Agnosticism is the final truth of all knowledge. For when we come to the end of whatever path, the universe appears as only a symbol or an appearance of an unknowable Reality which translates itself here into different systems of values, physical values, vital and sensational values, intellectual, ideal and spiritual values. The more That becomes real to us, the more it is seen to be always beyond defining thought and beyond formulating expression. "Mind attains not there, nor speech."[3] And yet as it is possible to exaggerate, with the Illusionists, the unreality of the appearance, so it is possible to exaggerate the unknowableness of the Unknowable. When

---

[2] "*Padbhyām pṛthivī.*" — *Mundaka Upanishad.* II. 1. 4.
  "*Pṛthivī pājasyam.*" — *Brihadaranyaka Upanishad.* I. 1. 1.
[3] *Kena Upanishad.* I. 3.

we speak of It as unknowable, we mean, really, that It escapes the grasp of our thought and speech, instruments which proceed always by the sense of difference and express by the way of definition; but if not knowable by thought, It is attainable by a supreme effort of consciousness. There is even a kind of Knowledge which is one with Identity and by which, in a sense, It can be known. Certainly, that Knowledge cannot be reproduced successfully in the terms of thought and speech, but when we have attained to it, the result is a revaluation of That in the symbols of our cosmic consciousness, not only in one but in all the ranges of symbols, which results in a revolution of our internal being and, through the internal, of our external life. Moreover, there is also a kind of Knowledge through which That does reveal itself by all these names and forms of phenomenal existence which to the ordinary intelligence only conceal It. It is this higher but not highest process of Knowledge to which we can attain by passing the limits of the materialistic formula and scrutinising Life, Mind and Supermind in the phenomena that are characteristic of them and not merely in those subordinate movements by which they link themselves to Matter.

The Unknown is not the Unknowable;[4] it need not remain the unknown for us, unless we choose ignorance or persist in our first limitations. For to all things that are not unknowable, all things in the universe, there correspond in that universe faculties which can take cognisance of them, and in man, the microcosm, these faculties are always existent and at a certain stage capable of development. We may choose not to develop them; where they are partially developed, we may discourage and impose on them a kind of atrophy. But, fundamentally, all possible knowledge is knowledge within the power of humanity. And since in man there is the inalienable impulse of Nature towards self-realisation, no struggle of the intellect to limit the action of our capacities within a determined area can for ever prevail. When we have proved Matter and realised its secret capacities,

---

[4] Other is That than the Known; also it is above the Unknown.
— *Kena Upanishad*. 1. 3.

the very knowledge which has found its convenience in that temporary limitation, must cry to us, like the Vedic Restrainers, "Forth now and push forward also in other fields."[5]

If modern Materialism were simply an unintelligent acquiescence in the material life, the advance might be indefinitely delayed. But since its very soul is the search for Knowledge, it will be unable to cry a halt; as it reaches the barriers of sense-knowledge and of the reasoning from sense-knowledge, its very rush will carry it beyond and the rapidity and sureness with which it has embraced the visible universe is only an earnest of the energy and success which we may hope to see repeated in the conquest of what lies beyond, once the stride is taken that crosses the barrier. We see already that advance in its obscure beginnings.

Not only in the one final conception, but in the great line of its general results Knowledge, by whatever path it is followed, tends to become one. Nothing can be more remarkable and suggestive than the extent to which modern Science confirms in the domain of Matter the conceptions and even the very formulae of language which were arrived at, by a very different method, in the Vedanta, — the original Vedanta, not of the schools of metaphysical philosophy, but of the Upanishads. And these, on the other hand, often reveal their full significance, their richer contents only when they are viewed in the new light shed by the discoveries of modern Science, — for instance, that Vedantic expression which describes things in the Cosmos as one seed arranged by the universal Energy in multitudinous forms.[6] Significant, especially, is the drive of Science towards a Monism which is consistent with multiplicity, towards the Vedic idea of the one essence with its many becomings. Even if the dualistic appearance of Matter and Force be insisted on, it does not really stand in the way of this Monism. For it will be evident that essential Matter is a thing non-existent to the senses and only, like the Pradhana of the Sankhyas, a conceptual

[5] *Rig Veda.* I. 4. 5.
[6] *Swetaswatara Upanishad.* VI. 12.

form of substance; and in fact the point is increasingly reached where only an arbitrary distinction in thought divides form of substance from form of energy.

Matter expresses itself eventually as a formulation of some unknown Force. Life, too, that yet unfathomed mystery, begins to reveal itself as an obscure energy of sensibility imprisoned in its material formulation; and when the dividing ignorance is cured which gives us the sense of a gulf between Life and Matter, it is difficult to suppose that Mind, Life and Matter will be found to be anything else than one Energy triply formulated, the triple world of the Vedic seers. Nor will the conception then be able to endure of a brute material Force as the mother of Mind. The Energy that creates the world can be nothing else than a Will, and Will is only consciousness applying itself to a work and a result.

What is that work and result, if not a self-involution of Consciousness in form and a self-evolution out of form so as to actualise some mighty possibility in the universe which it has created? And what is its will in Man if not a will to unending Life, to unbounded Knowledge, to unfettered Power? Science itself begins to dream of the physical conquest of death, expresses an insatiable thirst for knowledge, is working out something like a terrestrial omnipotence for humanity. Space and Time are contracting to the vanishing-point in its works, and it strives in a hundred ways to make man the master of circumstance and so lighten the fetters of causality. The idea of limit, of the impossible begins to grow a little shadowy and it appears instead that whatever man constantly wills, he must in the end be able to do; for the consciousness in the race eventually finds the means. It is not in the individual that this omnipotence expresses itself, but the collective Will of mankind that works out with the individual as a means. And yet when we look more deeply, it is not any conscious Will of the collectivity, but a superconscious Might that uses the individual as a centre and means, the collectivity as a condition and field. What is this but the God in man, the infinite Identity, the multitudinous Unity, the Omniscient, the Omnipotent, who having made man in His own image, with the ego as a centre of working, with the race, the collective Narayana,[7] the *viśvamānava*[8] as the mould and circumscription, seeks to express in them some image of the unity, omniscience, omnipotence which are the self-conception of the Divine? "That which is immortal in mortals is a God and established inwardly as an energy working out in our divine powers."[9] It is this vast cosmic impulse which the modern world, without quite knowing its own aim, yet serves in all its activities and labours subconsciously to fulfil.

But there is always a limit and an encumbrance, — the limit of the material field in the Knowledge, the encumbrance of the material machinery in the Power. But here also the latest trend is highly significant of a freer future. As the outposts of scientific Knowledge come more and more to be set on the borders that divide the material from the immaterial, so also the highest achievements of practical Science are those which tend to simplify and reduce to the vanishing-point the machinery by which the greatest effects are produced. Wireless telegraphy is Nature's exterior sign and pretext for a new orientation. The sensible physical means for the intermediate transmission of the physical force is removed; it is only preserved at the points of impulsion and reception. Eventually even these must disappear; for when the laws and forces of the supraphysical are studied with the right starting-point, the means will infallibly be found for Mind directly to seize on the physical energy and speed it accurately upon its errand. There, once we bring ourselves to recognise it, lie the gates that open upon the enormous vistas of the future.

Yet even if we had full knowledge and control of the worlds immediately above Matter, there would still be a limitation and still a beyond. The last knot of our bondage is at that point where the external draws into oneness with the internal, the machinery of ego itself becomes subtilised to the vanishing-point and the law of our action is at last unity embracing and

---

[7] A name of Vishnu, who, as the God in man, lives constantly associated in a dual unity with Nara, the human being.
[8] The universal man.
[9] *Rig Veda*. IV. 2. 1.

possessing multiplicity and no longer, as now, multiplicity struggling towards some figure of unity. There is the central throne of cosmic Knowledge looking out on her widest dominion; there the empire of oneself with the empire of one's world;[10] there the life[11] in the eternally consummate Being and the realisation of His divine nature[12] in our human existence.

[10] *Svārājya* and *Sāmrājya*, the double aim proposed to itself by the positive Yoga of the ancients.
[11] *Sālokya-mukti*, liberation by conscious existence in one world of being with the Divine.
[12] *Sādharmya-mukti*, liberation by assumption of the Divine Nature.

Chapter III

The Two Negations

II. The Refusal of the Ascetic

All this is the Brahman; this Self is the Brahman and the Self
is fourfold.
Beyond relation, featureless, unthinkable, in which all is
still.   *Mandukya Upanishad.*[1]

AND STILL there is a beyond.
For on the other side of the cosmic consciousness
there is, attainable to us, a consciousness yet more transcendent, — transcendent not only of the ego, but of the Cosmos
itself, — against which the universe seems to stand out like a
petty picture against an immeasurable background. That supports the universal activity, — or perhaps only tolerates it; It
embraces Life with Its vastness, — or else rejects it from Its
infinitude.

If the materialist is justified from his point of view in insisting on Matter as reality, the relative world as the sole thing of
which we can in some sort be sure and the Beyond as wholly
unknowable, if not indeed non-existent, a dream of the mind,
an abstraction of Thought divorcing itself from reality, so also
is the Sannyasin, enamoured of that Beyond, justified from his
point of view in insisting on pure Spirit as the reality, the one
thing free from change, birth, death, and the relative as a creation of the mind and the senses, a dream, an abstraction in
the contrary sense of Mentality withdrawing from the pure and
eternal Knowledge.

What justification, of logic or of experience, can be asserted

[1] Verses 2, 7.

in support of the one extreme which cannot be met by an equally cogent logic and an equally valid experience at the other end? The world of Matter is affirmed by the experience of the physical senses which, because they are themselves unable to perceive anything immaterial or not organised as gross Matter, would persuade us that the suprasensible is the unreal. This vulgar or rustic error of our corporeal organs does not gain in validity by being promoted into the domain of philosophical reasoning. Obviously, their pretension is unfounded. Even in the world of Matter there are existences of which the physical senses are incapable of taking cognisance. Yet the denial of the suprasensible as necessarily an illusion or a hallucination depends on this constant sensuous association of the real with the materially perceptible, which is itself a hallucination. Assuming throughout what it seeks to establish, it has the vice of the argument in a circle and can have no validity for an impartial reasoning.

Not only are there physical realities which are suprasensible, but, if evidence and experience are at all a test of truth, there are also senses which are supraphysical[2] and can not only take cognisance of the realities of the material world without the aid of the corporeal sense-organs, but can bring us into contact with other realities, supraphysical and belonging to another world — included, that is to say, in an organisation of conscious experiences that are dependent on some other principle than the gross Matter of which our suns and earths seem to be made.

Constantly asserted by human experience and belief since the origins of thought, this truth, now that the necessity of an exclusive preoccupation with the secrets of the material world no longer exists, begins to be justified by new-born forms of scientific research. The increasing evidences, of which only the most obvious and outward are established under the name of telepathy with its cognate phenomena, cannot long be resisted except by minds shut up in the brilliant shell of the past, by intellects limited in spite of their acuteness through the limitation

---

[2] *Sūkṣma indriya*, subtle organs, existing in the subtle body (*sūkṣma deha*), and the means of subtle vision and experience (*sūkṣma dṛṣṭi*).

of their field of experience and inquiry, or by those who confuse enlightenment and reason with the faithful repetition of the formulas left to us from a bygone century and the jealous conservation of dead or dying intellectual dogmas.

It is true that the glimpse of supraphysical realities acquired by methodical research has been imperfect and is yet ill-affirmed; for the methods used are still crude and defective. But these rediscovered subtle senses have at least been found to be true witnesses to physical facts beyond the range of the corporeal organs. There is no justification, then, for scouting them as false witnesses when they testify to supraphysical facts beyond the domain of the material organisation of consciousness. Like all evidence, like the evidence of the physical senses themselves, their testimony has to be controlled, scrutinised and arranged by the reason, rightly translated and rightly related, and their field, laws and processes determined. But the truth of great ranges of experience whose objects exist in a more subtle substance and are perceived by more subtle instruments than those of gross physical Matter, claims in the end the same validity as the truth of the material universe. The worlds beyond exist: they have their universal rhythm, their grand lines and formations, their self-existent laws and mighty energies, their just and luminous means of knowledge. And here on our physical existence and in our physical body they exercise their influences; here also they organise their means of manifestation and commission their messengers and their witnesses.

But the worlds are only frames for our experience, the senses only instruments of experience and conveniences. Consciousness is the great underlying fact, the universal witness for whom the world is a field, the senses instruments. To that witness the worlds and their objects appeal for their reality and for the one world or the many, for the physical equally with the supraphysical we have no other evidence that they exist. It has been argued that this is no relation peculiar to the constitution of humanity and its outlook upon an objective world, but the very nature of existence itself; all phenomenal existence consists of an observing consciousness and an active objectivity, and the

Action cannot proceed without the Witness because the universe exists only in or for the consciousness that observes and has no independent reality. It has been argued in reply that the material universe enjoys an eternal self-existence; it was here before life and mind made their appearance: it will survive after they have disappeared and no longer trouble with their transient strivings and limited thoughts the eternal and inconscient rhythm of the suns. The difference, so metaphysical in appearance, is yet of the utmost practical import, for it determines the whole outlook of man upon life, the goal that he shall assign for his efforts and the field in which he shall circumscribe his energies. For it raises the question of the reality of cosmic existence and, more important still, the question of the value of human life.

If we push the materialist conclusion far enough, we arrive at an insignificance and unreality in the life of the individual and the race which leaves us, logically, the option between either a feverish effort of the individual to snatch what he may from a transient existence, to "live his life", as it is said, or a dispassionate and objectless service of the race and the individual, knowing well that the latter is a transient fiction of the nervous mentality and the former only a little more long-lived collective form of the same regular nervous spasm of Matter. We work or enjoy under the impulsion of a material energy which deceives us with the brief delusion of life or with the nobler delusion of an ethical aim and a mental consummation. Materialism like spiritual Monism arrives at a Maya that is and yet is not, — is, for it is present and compelling, is not, for it is phenomenal and transitory in its works. At the other end, if we stress too much the unreality of the objective world, we arrive by a different road at similar but still more trenchant conclusions, — the fictitious character of the individual ego, the unreality and purposelessness of human existence, the return into the Non-Being or the relationless Absolute as the sole rational escape from the meaningless tangle of phenomenal life.

And yet the question cannot be solved by logic arguing on the data of our ordinary physical existence; for in those data there is always a hiatus of experience which renders all argument inconclusive. We have, normally, neither any definitive experience of a cosmic mind or supermind not bound up with the life of the individual body, nor, on the other hand, any firm limit of experience which would justify us in supposing that our subjective self really depends upon the physical frame and can neither survive it nor enlarge itself beyond the individual body. Only by an extension of the field of our consciousness or an unhoped-for increase in our instruments of knowledge can the ancient quarrel be decided.

The extension of our consciousness, to be satisfying, must necessarily be an inner enlargement from the individual into the cosmic existence. For the Witness, if he exists, is not the individual embodied mind born in the world, but that cosmic Consciousness embracing the universe and appearing as an immanent Intelligence in all its works to which either world subsists eternally and really as Its own active existence or else from which it is born and into which it disappears by an act of knowledge or by an act of conscious power. Not organised mind, but that which, calm and eternal, broods equally in the living earth and the living human body and to which mind and senses are dispensable instruments, is the Witness of cosmic existence and its Lord.

The possibility of a cosmic consciousness in humanity is coming slowly to be admitted in modern Psychology, like the possibility of more elastic instruments of knowledge, although still classified, even when its value and power are admitted, as a hallucination. In the psychology of the East it has always been recognised as a reality and the aim of our subjective progress. The essence of the passage over to this goal is the exceeding of the limits imposed on us by the ego-sense and at least a partaking, at most an identification with the self-knowledge which broods secret in all life and in all that seems to us inanimate.

Entering into that Consciousness, we may continue to dwell, like It, upon universal existence. Then we become aware — for all our terms of consciousness and even our sensational experience begin to change, — of Matter as one existence and of bodies as its formations in which the one existence separates itself physically in the single body from itself in all others and again by physical means establishes communication between these multitudinous points of its being. Mind we experience similarly, and Life also, as the same existence one in its multiplicity, separating and reuniting itself in each domain by means appropriate to that movement. And, if we choose, we can proceed farther and, after passing through many linking stages, become aware of a supermind whose universal operation is the key to all lesser activities. Nor do we become merely conscious of this cosmic existence, but likewise conscious in it, receiving it in sensation, but also entering into it in awareness. In it we live as we lived before in the ego-sense, active, more and more in contact, even unified more and more with other minds, other lives, other bodies than the organism we call ourselves, producing effects not only on our own moral and mental being and on the subjective being of others, but even on the physical world and its events by means nearer to the divine than those possible to our egoistic capacity.

Real then to the man who has had contact with it or lives in it, is this cosmic consciousness, with a greater than the physical reality; real in itself, real in its effects and works. And as it is thus real to the world which is its own total expression, so is the world real to it; but not as an independent existence. For in that higher and less hampered experience we perceive that consciousness and being are not different from each other, but all being is a supreme consciousness, all consciousness is self-existence, eternal in itself, real in its works and neither a dream nor an evolution. The world is real precisely because it exists only in consciousness; for it is a Conscious Energy one with Being that creates it. It is the existence of material form in its own right apart from the self-illumined energy which assumes the form, that would be a contradiction of the truth of things, a phantasmagoria, a nightmare, an impossible falsehood.

But this conscious Being which is the truth of the infinite supermind, is more than the universe and lives independently in Its own inexpressible infinity as well as in the cosmic harmonies. World lives by That; That does not live by the world. And as we can enter into the cosmic consciousness and be one with all cosmic existence, so we can enter into the world-transcending consciousness and become superior to all cosmic existence. And then arises the question which first occurred to us, whether this transcendence is necessarily also a rejection. What relation has this universe to the Beyond?

For at the gates of the Transcendent stands that mere and perfect Spirit described in the Upanishads, luminous, pure, sustaining the world but inactive in it, without sinews of energy, without flaw of duality, without scar of division, unique, identical, free from all appearance of relation and of multiplicity, — the pure Self of the Adwaitins,[3] the inactive Brahman, the transcendent Silence. And the mind when it passes those gates suddenly, without intermediate transitions, receives a sense of the unreality of the world and the sole reality of the Silence which is one of the most powerful and convincing experiences of which the human mind is capable. Here, in the perception of this pure Self or of the Non-Being behind it, we have the starting-point for a second negation, — parallel at the other pole to the materialistic, but more complete, more final, more perilous in its effects on the individuals or collectivities that hear its potent call to the wilderness, — the refusal of the ascetic.

It is this revolt of Spirit against Matter that for two thousand years, since Buddhism disturbed the balance of the old Aryan world, has dominated increasingly the Indian mind. Not that the sense of the cosmic illusion is the whole of Indian thought; there are other philosophical statements, other religious aspirations. Nor has some attempt at an adjustment between the two terms been wanting even from the most extreme philosophies. But all have lived in the shadow of the great Refusal and the final end of life for all is the garb of the ascetic. The general conception of existence has been permeated with the Buddhistic theory of the chain of Karma and with the consequent antinomy of bondage and liberation, bondage by birth, liberation by cessation from birth. Therefore all voices are joined in one great consensus that not in this world of the dualities can there

---

[3] The Vedantic Monists.

be our kingdom of heaven, but beyond, whether in the joys of the eternal Vrindavan[4] or the high beatitude of Brahmaloka,[5] beyond all manifestations in some ineffable Nirvana[6] or where all separate experience is lost in the featureless unity of the indefinable Existence. And through many centuries a great army of shining witnesses, saints and teachers, names sacred to Indian memory and dominant in Indian imagination, have borne always the same witness and swelled always the same lofty and distant appeal, — renunciation the sole path of knowledge, acceptation of physical life the act of the ignorant, cessation from birth the right use of human birth, the call of the Spirit, the recoil from Matter.

For an age out of sympathy with the ascetic spirit — and throughout all the rest of the world the hour of the Anchorite may seem to have passed or to be passing — it is easy to attribute this great trend to the failing of vital energy in an ancient race tired out by its burden, its once vast share in the common advance, exhausted by its many-sided contribution to the sum of human effort and human knowledge. But we have seen that it corresponds to a truth of existence, a state of conscious realisation which stands at the very summit of our possibility. In practice also the ascetic spirit is an indispensable element in human perfection and even its separate affirmation cannot be avoided so long as the race has not at the other end liberated its intellect and its vital habits from subjection to an always insistent animalism.

We seek indeed a larger and completer affirmation. We perceive that in the Indian ascetic ideal the great Vedantic formula, "One without a second", has not been read sufficiently in the light of that other formula equally imperative, "All this is the Brahman". The passionate aspiration of man upward to the Divine has not been sufficiently related to the descending

---

[4] *Goloka*, the Vaishnava heaven of eternal Beauty and Bliss.

[5] The highest state of pure existence, consciousness and beatitude attainable by the soul without complete extinction in the Indefinable.

[6] Extinction, not necessarily of all being, but of being as we know it; extinction of ego, desire and egoistic action and mentality.

movement of the Divine leaning downward to embrace eternally Its manifestation. Its meaning in Matter has not been so
well understood as Its truth in the Spirit. The Reality which the
Sannyasin seeks has been grasped in its full height, but not, as
by the ancient Vedantins, in its full extent and comprehensiveness. But in our completer affirmation we must not minimise
the part of the pure spiritual impulse. As we have seen how
greatly Materialism has served the ends of the Divine, so we must
acknowledge the still greater service rendered by Asceticism to
Life. We shall preserve the truths of material Science and its real
utilities in the final harmony, even if many or even if all of its
existing forms have to be broken or left aside. An even greater
scruple of right preservation must guide us in our dealing with
the legacy, however actually diminished or depreciated, of the
Aryan past.

Chapter IV

Reality Omnipresent

If one knows Him as Brahman the Non-Being, he becomes merely the non-existent. If one knows that Brahman Is, then is he known as the real in existence.   *Taittiriya Upanishad.*[1]

SINCE, then, we admit both the claim of the pure Spirit to manifest in us its absolute freedom and the claim of universal Matter to be the mould and condition of our manifestation, we have to find a truth that can entirely reconcile these antagonists and can give to both their due portion in Life and their due justification in Thought, amercing neither of its rights, denying in neither the sovereign truth from which even its errors, even the exclusiveness of its exaggerations draw so constant a strength. For wherever there is an extreme statement that makes such a powerful appeal to the human mind, we may be sure that we are standing in the presence of no mere error, superstition or hallucination, but of some sovereign fact disguised which demands our fealty and will avenge itself if denied or excluded. Herein lies the difficulty of a satisfying solution and the source of that lack of finality which pursues all mere compromises between Spirit and Matter. A compromise is a bargain, a transaction of interests between two conflicting powers; it is not a true reconciliation. True reconciliation proceeds always by a mutual comprehension leading to some sort of intimate oneness. It is therefore through the utmost possible unification of Spirit and Matter that we shall best arrive at their reconciling truth and so at some strongest foundation for a reconciling practice in the inner life of the individual and his outer existence.

[1] II. 6.

We have found already in the cosmic consciousness a meeting-place where Matter becomes real to Spirit, Spirit becomes real to Matter. For in the cosmic consciousness Mind and Life are intermediaries and no longer, as they seem in the ordinary egoistic mentality, agents of separation, fomenters of an artificial quarrel between the positive and negative principles of the same unknowable Reality. Attaining to the cosmic consciousness Mind, illuminated by a knowledge that perceives at once the truth of Unity and the truth of Multiplicity and seizes on the formulae of their interaction, finds its own discords at once explained and reconciled by the divine Harmony; satisfied, it consents to become the agent of that supreme union between God and Life towards which we tend. Matter reveals itself to the realising thought and to the subtilised senses as the figure and body of Spirit, — Spirit in its self-formative extension. Spirit reveals itself through the same consenting agents as the soul, the truth, the essence of Matter. Both admit and confess each other as divine, real and essentially one. Mind and Life are disclosed in that illumination as at once figures and instruments of the supreme Conscious Being by which It extends and houses Itself in material form and in that form unveils Itself to Its multiple centres of consciousness. Mind attains its self-fulfilment when it becomes a pure mirror of the Truth of Being which expresses itself in the symbols of the universe; Life, when it consciously lends its energies to the perfect self-figuration of the Divine in ever-new forms and activities of the universal existence.

In the light of this conception we can perceive the possibility of a divine life for man in the world which will at once justify Science by disclosing a living sense and intelligible aim for the cosmic and the terrestrial evolution and realise by the transfiguration of the human soul into the divine the great ideal dream of all high religions.

But what then of that silent Self, inactive, pure, self-existent, self-enjoying, which presented itself to us as the abiding justification of the ascetic? Here also harmony and not irreconcilable opposition must be the illuminative truth. The silent and the active Brahman are not different, opposite and irreconcilable entities, the one denying, the other affirming a cosmic illusion; they are one Brahman in two aspects, positive and negative, and each is necessary to the other. It is out of this Silence that the Word which creates the worlds for ever proceeds; for the Word expresses that which is self-hidden in the Silence. It is an eternal passivity which makes possible the perfect freedom and omnipotence of an eternal divine activity in innumerable cosmic systems. For the becomings of that activity derive their energies and their illimitable potency of variation and harmony from the impartial support of the immutable Being, its consent to this infinite fecundity of its own dynamic Nature.

Man, too, becomes perfect only when he has found within himself that absolute calm and passivity of the Brahman and supports by it with the same divine tolerance and the same divine bliss a free and inexhaustible activity. Those who have thus possessed the Calm within can perceive always welling out from its silence the perennial supply of the energies that work in the universe. It is not, therefore, the truth of the Silence to say that it is in its nature a rejection of the cosmic activity. The apparent incompatibility of the two states is an error of the limited Mind which, accustomed to trenchant oppositions of affirmation and denial and passing suddenly from one pole to the other, is unable to conceive of a comprehensive consciousness vast and strong enough to include both in a simultaneous embrace. The Silence does not reject the world; it sustains it. Or rather it supports with an equal impartiality the activity and the withdrawal from the activity and approves also the reconciliation by which the soul remains free and still even while it lends itself to all action.

But, still, there is the absolute withdrawal, there is the Non-Being. Out of the Non-Being, says the ancient Scripture, Being appeared.[2] Then into the Non-Being it must surely sink again. If the infinite indiscriminate Existence permits all possibilities of discrimination and multiple realisation, does not the Non-Being at least, as primal state and sole constant reality, negate

---

2 In the beginning all this was the Non-Being. It was thence that Being was born.
— *Taittiriya Upanishad*. II. 7.

and reject all possibility of a real universe? The Nihil of certain
Buddhist schools would then be the true ascetic solution; the
Self, like the ego, would be only an ideative formation by an
illusory phenomenal consciousness.

But again we find that we are being misled by words, deceived by the trenchant oppositions of our limited mentality
with its fond reliance on verbal distinctions as if they perfectly
represented ultimate truths and its rendering of our supramental
experiences in the sense of those intolerant distinctions. Non-
Being is only a word. When we examine the fact it represents,
we can no longer be sure that absolute non-existence has any
better chance than the infinite Self of being more than an ideative
formation of the mind. We really mean by this Nothing something beyond the last term to which we can reduce our purest
conception and our most abstract or subtle experience of actual
being as we know or conceive it while in this universe. This
Nothing then is merely a something beyond positive conception. We erect a fiction of nothingness in order to overpass,
by the method of total exclusion, all that we can know and
consciously are. Actually when we examine closely the Nihil of
certain philosophies, we begin to perceive that it is a zero which
is All or an indefinable Infinite which appears to the mind a
blank, because mind grasps only finite constructions, but is in
fact the only true Existence.[3]

And when we say that out of Non-Being Being appeared,
we perceive that we are speaking in terms of Time about that
which is beyond Time. For what was that portentous date in the
history of eternal Nothing on which Being was born out of it
or when will come that other date equally formidable on which
an unreal all will relapse into the perpetual void? Sat and Asat,

---

[3] Another Upanishad rejects the birth of being out of Non-Being as an impossibility;
Being, it says, can only be born from Being. But if we take Non-Being in the sense, not
of an inexistent Nihil but of an *x* which exceeds our idea or experience of existence, —
a sense applicable to the Absolute Brahman of the Adwaita as well as the Void or Zero
of the Buddhists, — the impossibility disappears, for That may very well be the source
of being, whether by a conceptual or formative Maya or a manifestation or creation out
of itself.

if they have both to be affirmed, must be conceived as if they obtained simultaneously. They permit each other even though they refuse to mingle. Both, since we must speak in terms of Time, are eternal. And who shall persuade eternal Being that it does not really exist and only eternal Non-Being is? In such a negation of all experience how shall we find the solution that explains all experience?

Pure Being is the affirmation by the Unknowable of Itself as the free base of all cosmic existence. We give the name of Non-Being to a contrary affirmation of Its freedom from all cosmic existence, — freedom, that is to say, from all positive terms of actual existence which consciousness in the universe can formulate to itself, even from the most abstract, even from the most transcendent. It does not deny them as a real expression of Itself, but It denies Its limitation by all expression or any expression whatsoever. The Non-Being permits the Being, even as the Silence permits the Activity. By this simultaneous negation and affirmation, not mutually destructive, but complementary to each other like all contraries, the simultaneous awareness of conscious Self-being as a reality and the Unknowable beyond as the same Reality becomes realisable to the awakened human soul. Thus was it possible for the Buddha to attain the state of Nirvana and yet act puissantly in the world, impersonal in his inner consciousness, in his action the most powerful personality that we know of as having lived and produced results upon earth.

When we ponder on these things, we begin to perceive how feeble in their self-assertive violence and how confusing in their misleading distinctness are the words that we use. We begin also to perceive that the limitations we impose on the Brahman arise from a narrowness of experience in the individual mind which concentrates itself on one aspect of the Unknowable and proceeds forthwith to deny or disparage all the rest. We tend always to translate too rigidly what we can conceive or know of the Absolute into the terms of our own particular relativity. We affirm the One and Identical by passionately discriminating and asserting the egoism of our own opinions and partial experiences against the opinions and partial experiences of others. It is wiser to wait, to learn, to grow, and, since we are obliged for the sake of our self-perfection to speak of these things which no human speech can express, to search for the widest, the most flexible, the most catholic affirmation possible and found on it the largest and most comprehensive harmony.

We recognise, then, that it is possible for the consciousness in the individual to enter into a state in which relative existence appears to be dissolved and even Self seems to be an inadequate conception. It is possible to pass into a Silence beyond the Silence. But this is not the whole of our ultimate experience, nor the single and all-excluding truth. For we find that this Nirvana, this self-extinction, while it gives an absolute peace and freedom to the soul within is yet consistent in practice with a desireless but effective action without. This possibility of an entire motionless impersonality and void Calm within doing outwardly the works of the eternal verities, Love, Truth and Righteousness, was perhaps the real gist of the Buddha's teaching, — this superiority to ego and to the chain of personal workings and to the identification with mutable form and idea, not the petty ideal of an escape from the trouble and suffering of the physical birth. In any case, as the perfect man would combine in himself the silence and the activity, so also would the completely conscious soul reach back to the absolute freedom of the Non-Being without therefore losing its hold on Existence and the universe. It would thus reproduce in itself perpetually the eternal miracle of the divine Existence, in the universe, yet always beyond it and even, as it were, beyond itself. The opposite experience could only be a concentration of mentality in the individual upon Non-existence with the result of an oblivion and personal withdrawal from a cosmic activity still and always proceeding in the consciousness of the Eternal Being.

Thus, after reconciling Spirit and Matter in the cosmic consciousness, we perceive the reconciliation, in the transcendental consciousness, of the final assertion of all and its negation. We discover that all affirmations are assertions of status or activity in the Unknowable; all the corresponding negations are assertions of Its freedom both from and in that status or activity. The

Unknowable is Something to us supreme, wonderful and ineffable which continually formulates Itself to our consciousness and continually escapes from the formulation It has made. This it does not as some malicious spirit or freakish magician leading us from falsehood to greater falsehood and so to a final negation of all things, but as even here the Wise beyond our wisdom guiding us from reality to ever profounder and vaster reality until we find the profoundest and vastest of which we are capable. An omnipresent reality is the Brahman, not an omnipresent cause of persistent illusions.

If we thus accept a positive basis for our harmony — and on what other can harmony be founded? — the various conceptual formulations of the Unknowable, each of them representing a truth beyond conception, must be understood as far as possible in their relation to each other and in their effect upon life, not separately, not exclusively, not so affirmed as to destroy or unduly diminish all other affirmations. The real Monism, the true Adwaita, is that which admits all things as the one Brahman and does not seek to bisect Its existence into two incompatible entities, an eternal Truth and an eternal Falsehood, Brahman and not-Brahman, Self and not-Self, a real Self and an unreal yet perpetual Maya. If it be true that the Self alone exists, it must be also true that all is the Self. And if this Self, God or Brahman is no helpless state, no bounded power, no limited personality, but the self-conscient All, there must be some good and inherent reason in it for the manifestation, to discover which we must proceed on the hypothesis of some potency, some wisdom, some truth of being in all that is manifested. The discord and apparent evil of the world must in their sphere be admitted, but not accepted as our conquerors. The deepest instinct of humanity seeks always and seeks wisely wisdom as the last word of the universal manifestation, not an eternal mockery and illusion, — a secret and finally triumphant good, not an all-creative and invincible evil, — an ultimate victory and fulfilment, not the disappointed recoil of the soul from its great adventure.

For we cannot suppose that the sole Entity is compelled by something outside or other than Itself, since no such thing exists. Nor can we suppose that It submits unwillingly to something partial within Itself which is hostile to its whole Being, denied by It and yet too strong for It; for this would be only to erect in other language the same contradiction of an All and something other than the All. Even if we say that the universe exists merely because the Self in its absolute impartiality tolerates all things alike, viewing with indifference all actualities and all possibilities, yet is there something that wills the manifestation and supports it, and this cannot be something other than the All. Brahman is indivisible in all things and whatever is willed in the world has been ultimately willed by the Brahman. It is only our relative consciousness, alarmed or baffled by the phenomena of evil, ignorance and pain in the cosmos, that seeks to deliver the Brahman from responsibility for Itself and its workings by erecting some opposite principle, Maya or Mara, conscious Devil or self-existent principle of evil. There is one Lord and Self and the many are only His representations and becomings.

If then the world is a dream or an illusion or a mistake, it is a dream originated and willed by the Self in its totality and not only originated and willed, but supported and perpetually entertained. Moreover, it is a dream existing in a Reality and the stuff of which it is made is that Reality, for Brahman must be the material of the world as well as its base and continent. If the gold of which the vessel is made is real, how shall we suppose that the vessel itself is a mirage? We see that these words, dream, illusion, are tricks of speech, habits of our relative consciousness; they represent a certain truth, even a great truth, but they also misrepresent it. Just as Non-Being turns out to be other than mere nullity, so the cosmic Dream turns out to be other than mere phantasm and hallucination of the mind. Phenomenon is not phantasm; phenomenon is the substantial form of a Truth.

We start, then, with the conception of an omnipresent Reality of which neither the Non-Being at the one end nor the universe at the other are negations that annul; they are rather different states of the Reality, obverse and reverse affirmations. The highest experience of this Reality in the universe shows it to be not only a conscious Existence, but a supreme Intelligence and

Force and a self-existent Bliss; and beyond the universe it is still some other unknowable existence, some utter and ineffable Bliss. Therefore we are justified in supposing that even the dualities of the universe, when interpreted not as now by our sensational and partial conceptions, but by our liberated intelligence and experience, will be also resolved into those highest terms. While we still labour under the stress of the dualities, this perception must no doubt constantly support itself on an act of faith, but a faith which the highest Reason, the widest and most patient reflection do not deny, but rather affirm. This creed is given, indeed, to humanity to support it on its journey, until it arrives at a stage of development when faith will be turned into knowledge and perfect experience and Wisdom will be justified of her works.

Chapter V

The Destiny of the Individual

By the Ignorance they cross beyond Death and by the Knowledge enjoy Immortality.... By the Non-Birth they cross beyond Death and by the Birth enjoy Immortality.   *Isha Upanishad.*[1]

AN OMNIPRESENT Reality is the truth of all life and existence whether absolute or relative, whether corporeal or incorporeal, whether animate or inanimate, whether intelligent or unintelligent; and in all its infinitely varying and even constantly opposed self-expressions, from the contradictions nearest to our ordinary experience to those remotest antinomies which lose themselves on the verges of the Ineffable, the Reality is one and not a sum or concourse. From that all variations begin, in that all variations consist, to that all variations return. All affirmations are denied only to lead to a wider affirmation of the same Reality. All antinomies confront each other in order to recognise one Truth in their opposed aspects and embrace by the way of conflict their mutual Unity. Brahman is the Alpha and the Omega. Brahman is the One besides whom there is nothing else existent.

But this unity is in its nature indefinable. When we seek to envisage it by the mind we are compelled to proceed through an infinite series of conceptions and experiences. And yet in the end we are obliged to negate our largest conceptions, our most comprehensive experiences in order to affirm that the Reality exceeds all definitions. We arrive at the formula of the Indian sages, *neti neti,* "It is not this, It is not that", there is no experience by which we can limit It, there is no conception by which It can be defined.

[1] Verses 11, 14.

An Unknowable which appears to us in many states and attributes of being, in many forms of consciousness, in many activities of energy, this is what Mind can ultimately say about the existence which we ourselves are and which we see in all that is presented to our thought and senses. It is in and through those states, those forms, those activities that we have to approach and know the Unknowable. But if in our haste to arrive at a Unity that our mind can seize and hold, if in our insistence to confine the Infinite in our embrace we identify the Reality with any one definable state of being however pure and eternal, with any particular attribute however general and comprehensive, with any fixed formulation of consciousness however vast in its scope, with any energy or activity however boundless its application, and if we exclude all the rest, then our thoughts sin against Its unknowableness and arrive not at a true unity but at a division of the Indivisible.

So strongly was this truth perceived in the ancient times that the Vedantic Seers, even after they had arrived at the crowning idea, the convincing experience of Sachchidananda as the highest positive expression of the Reality to our consciousness, erected in their speculations or went on in their perceptions to an Asat, a Non-Being beyond, which is not the ultimate existence, the pure consciousness, the infinite bliss of which all our experiences are the expression or the deformation. If at all an existence, a consciousness, a bliss, it is beyond the highest and purest positive form of these things that here we can possess and other therefore than what here we know by these names. Buddhism, somewhat arbitrarily declared by the theologians to be an un-Vedic doctrine because it rejected the authority of the Scriptures, yet goes back to this essentially Vedantic conception. Only, the positive and synthetic teaching of the Upanishads beheld Sat and Asat not as opposites destructive of each other, but as the last antinomy through which we look up to the Unknowable. And in the transactions of our positive consciousness, even Unity has to make its account with Multiplicity; for the Many also are Brahman. It is by Vidya, the Knowledge of the Oneness, that we know God; without it Avidya, the relative and multiple consciousness, is a night of darkness and a disorder of Ignorance. Yet if we exclude the field of that Ignorance, if we get rid of Avidya as if it were a thing non-existent and unreal, then Knowledge itself becomes a sort of obscurity and a source of imperfection. We become as men blinded by a light so that we can no longer see the field which that light illumines.

Such is the teaching, calm, wise and clear, of our most ancient sages. They had the patience and the strength to find and to know; they had also the clarity and humility to admit the limitation of our knowledge. They perceived the borders where it has to pass into something beyond itself. It was a later impatience of heart and mind, vehement attraction to an ultimate bliss or high masterfulness of pure experience and trenchant intelligence which sought the One to deny the Many and because it had received the breath of the heights scorned or recoiled from the secret of the depths. But the steady eye of the ancient wisdom perceived that to know God really, it must know Him everywhere equally and without distinction, considering and valuing but not mastered by the oppositions through which He shines.

We will put aside then the trenchant distinctions of a partial logic which declares that because the One is the reality, the Many are an illusion, and because the Absolute is Sat, the one existence, the relative is Asat and non-existent. If in the Many we pursue insistently the One, it is to return with the benediction and the revelation of the One confirming itself in the Many.

We will guard ourselves also against the excessive importance that the mind attaches to particular points of view at which it arrives in its more powerful expansions and transitions. The perception of the spiritualised mind that the universe is an unreal dream can have no more absolute a value to us than the perception of the materialised mind that God and the Beyond are an illusory idea. In the one case the mind, habituated only to the evidence of the senses and associating reality with corporeal fact, is either unaccustomed to use other means of knowledge or unable to extend the notion of reality to a supra-physical experience. In the other case the same mind, passing beyond to the overwhelming experience of an incorporeal reality, simply transfers the same inability and the same consequent sense of dream or hallucination to the experience of the senses. But we perceive also the truth that these two conceptions disfigure. It is true that for this world of form in which we are set for our self-realisation, nothing is entirely valid until it has possessed itself of our physical consciousness and manifested on the lowest levels in harmony with its manifestation on the highest summits. It is equally true that form and matter asserting themselves as a self-existent reality are an illusion of Ignorance. Form and matter can be valid only as shape and substance of manifestation for the incorporeal and immaterial. They are in their nature an act of divine consciousness, in their aim the representation of a status of the Spirit.

In other words, if Brahman has entered into form and represented Its being in material substance, it can only be to enjoy self-manifestation in the figures of relative and phenomenal consciousness. Brahman is in this world to represent Itself in the values of Life. Life exists in Brahman in order to discover Brahman in itself. Therefore man's importance in the world is that he gives to it that development of consciousness in which its transfiguration by a perfect self-discovery becomes possible. To fulfil God in life is man's manhood. He starts from the animal vitality and its activities, but a divine existence is his objective.

But as in Thought, so in Life, the true rule of self-realisation is a progressive comprehension. Brahman expresses Itself in many successive forms of consciousness, successive in their relation even if coexistent in being or coeval in Time, and Life in its self-unfolding must also rise to ever-new provinces of its own being. But if in passing from one domain to another we renounce what has already been given us from eagerness for our new attainment, if in reaching the mental life we cast away or belittle the physical life which is our basis, or if we reject the mental and physical in our attraction to the spiritual, we do not fulfil God integrally, nor satisfy the conditions of His self-manifestation. We do not become perfect, but only shift the field of our imperfection or at most attain a limited altitude. However high we may climb, even though it be to the Non-Being itself, we climb ill if we forget our base. Not to abandon the lower to itself, but to transfigure it in the light of the higher to which we have attained, is true divinity of nature. Brahman is integral and unifies many states of consciousness at a time; we also, manifesting the nature of Brahman, should become integral and all-embracing.

Besides the recoil from the physical life, there is another exaggeration of the ascetic impulse which this ideal of an integral manifestation corrects. The nodus of Life is the relation between three general forms of consciousness, the individual, the universal and the transcendent or supracosmic. In the ordinary distribution of life's activities the individual regards himself as a separate being included in the universe and both as dependent upon that which transcends alike the universe and the individual. It is to this Transcendence that we give currently the name of God, who thus becomes to our conceptions not so much supracosmic as extracosmic. The belittling and degradation of both the individual and the universe is a natural consequence of this division: the cessation of both cosmos and individual by the attainment of the Transcendence would be logically its supreme conclusion.

The integral view of the unity of Brahman avoids these consequences. Just as we need not give up the bodily life to attain to the mental and spiritual, so we can arrive at a point of view where the preservation of the individual activities is no longer inconsistent with our comprehension of the cosmic consciousness or our attainment to the transcendent and supracosmic. For the World-Transcendent embraces the universe, is one with it and does not exclude it, even as the universe embraces the individual, is one with him and does not exclude him. The individual is a centre of the whole universal consciousness; the universe is a form and definition which is occupied by the entire immanence of the Formless and Indefinable.

This is always the true relation, veiled from us by our ignorance or our wrong consciousness of things. When we attain to knowledge or right consciousness, nothing essential in the eternal relation is changed, but only the inview and the outview

from the individual centre is profoundly modified and consequently also the spirit and effect of its activity. The individual is
still necessary to the action of the Transcendent in the universe
and that action in him does not cease to be possible by his
illumination. On the contrary, since the conscious manifestation
of the Transcendent in the individual is the means by which the
collective, the universal is also to become conscious of itself,
the continuation of the illumined individual in the action of the
world is an imperative need of the world-play. If his inexorable
removal through the very act of illumination is the law, then the
world is condemned to remain eternally the scene of unredeemed
darkness, death and suffering. And such a world can only be a
ruthless ordeal or a mechanical illusion.

It is so that ascetic philosophy tends to conceive it. But individual salvation can have no real sense if existence in the cosmos
is itself an illusion. In the Monistic view the individual soul is one
with the Supreme, its sense of separateness an ignorance, escape
from the sense of separateness and identity with the Supreme its
salvation. But who then profits by this escape? Not the supreme
Self, for it is supposed to be always and inalienably free, still,
silent, pure. Not the world, for that remains constantly in the
bondage and is not freed by the escape of any individual soul
from the universal Illusion. It is the individual soul itself which
effects its supreme good by escaping from the sorrow and the
division into the peace and the bliss. There would seem then to
be some kind of reality of the individual soul as distinct from
the world and from the Supreme even in the event of freedom
and illumination. But for the Illusionist the individual soul is
an illusion and non-existent except in the inexplicable mystery
of Maya. Therefore we arrive at the escape of an illusory non-
existent soul from an illusory non-existent bondage in an illusory
non-existent world as the supreme good which that non-existent
soul has to pursue! For this is the last word of the Knowledge,
"There is none bound, none freed, none seeking to be free."
Vidya turns out to be as much a part of the Phenomenal as
Avidya; Maya meets us even in our escape and laughs at the
triumphant logic which seemed to cut the knot of her mystery.

These things, it is said, cannot be explained; they are the initial and insoluble miracle. They are for us a practical fact and have to be accepted. We have to escape by a confusion out of a confusion. The individual soul can only cut the knot of ego by a supreme act of egoism, an exclusive attachment to its own individual salvation which amounts to an absolute assertion of its separate existence in Maya. We are led to regard other souls as if they were figments of our mind and their salvation unimportant, our soul alone as if it were entirely real and its salvation the one thing that matters. I come to regard my personal escape from bondage as real while other souls who are equally myself remain behind in the bondage!

It is only when we put aside all irreconcilable antinomy between Self and the world that things fall into their place by a less paradoxical logic. We must accept the many-sidedness of the manifestation even while we assert the unity of the Manifested. And is not this after all the truth that pursues us wherever we cast our eyes, unless seeing we choose not to see? Is not this after all the perfectly natural and simple mystery of Conscious Being that it is bound neither by its unity nor by its multiplicity? It is "absolute" in the sense of being entirely free to include and arrange in its own way all possible terms of its self-expression. There is none bound, none freed, none seeking to be free, — for always That is a perfect freedom. It is so free that it is not even bound by its liberty. It can play at being bound without incurring a real bondage. Its chain is a self-imposed convention, its limitation in the ego a transitional device that it uses in order to repeat its transcendence and universality in the scheme of the individual Brahman.

The Transcendent, the Supracosmic is absolute and free in itself beyond Time and Space and beyond the conceptual opposites of finite and infinite. But in cosmos it uses its liberty of self-formation, its Maya, to make a scheme of itself in the complementary terms of unity and multiplicity, and this multiple unity it establishes in the three conditions of the subconscient, the conscient and the superconscient. For actually we see that the Many objectivised in form in our material universe start with a subconscious unity which expresses itself openly enough in cosmic action and cosmic substance, but of which they are not themselves superficially aware. In the conscient the ego becomes the superficial point at which the awareness of unity can emerge; but it applies its perception of unity to the form and surface action and, failing to take account of all that operates behind, fails also to realise that it is not only one in itself but one with others. This limitation of the universal "I" in the divided ego-sense constitutes our imperfect individualised personality. But when the ego transcends the personal consciousness, it begins to include and be overpowered by that which is to us super-conscious; it becomes aware of the cosmic unity and enters into the Transcendent Self which here cosmos expresses by a multiple oneness.

The liberation of the individual soul is therefore the keynote of the definite divine action; it is the primary divine necessity and the pivot on which all else turns. It is the point of Light at which the intended complete self-manifestation in the Many begins to emerge. But the liberated soul extends its perception of unity horizontally as well as vertically. Its unity with the transcendent One is incomplete without its unity with the cosmic Many. And that lateral unity translates itself by a multiplication, a reproduc-tion of its own liberated state at other points in the Multiplicity. The divine soul reproduces itself in similar liberated souls as the animal reproduces itself in similar bodies. Therefore, whenever even a single soul is liberated, there is a tendency to an extension and even to an outburst of the same divine self-consciousness in other individual souls of our terrestrial humanity and, — who knows? — perhaps even beyond the terrestrial consciousness. Where shall we fix the limit of that extension? Is it altogether a legend which says of the Buddha that as he stood on the threshold of Nirvana, of the Non-Being, his soul turned back and took the vow never to make the irrevocable crossing so long as there was a single being upon earth undelivered from the knot of the suffering, from the bondage of the ego?

But we can attain to the highest without blotting ourselves out from the cosmic extension. Brahman preserves always Its two terms of liberty within and of formation without, of expression and of freedom from the expression. We also, being That, can attain to the same divine self-possession. The harmony of the two tendencies is the condition of all life that aims at being really divine. Liberty pursued by exclusion of the thing exceeded leads along the path of negation to the refusal of that which God has accepted. Activity pursued by absorption in the act and the energy leads to an inferior affirmation and the denial of the Highest. But what God combines and synthetises, wherefore should man insist on divorcing? To be perfect as He is perfect is the condition of His integral attainment.

Through Avidya, the Multiplicity, lies our path out of the transitional egoistic self-expression in which death and suffering predominate; through Vidya consenting with Avidya by the perfect sense of oneness even in that multiplicity, we enjoy integrally the immortality and the beatitude. By attaining to the Unborn beyond all becoming we are liberated from this lower birth and death; by accepting the Becoming freely as the Divine, we invade mortality with the immortal beatitude and become luminous centres of its conscious self-expression in humanity.

Chapter VI

Man in the Universe

The Soul of man, a traveller, wanders in this cycle of Brahman, huge, a totality of lives, a totality of states, thinking itself different from the Impeller of the journey. Accepted by Him, it attains its goal of Immortality.   *Swetaswatara Upanishad.*[1]

THE PROGRESSIVE revelation of a great, a transcendent, a luminous Reality with the multitudinous relativities of this world that we see and those other worlds that we do not see as means and material, condition and field, this would seem then to be the meaning of the universe, — since meaning and aim it has and is neither a purposeless illusion nor a fortuitous accident. For the same reasoning which leads us to conclude that world-existence is not a deceptive trick of Mind, justifies equally the certainty that it is no blindly and helplessly self-existent mass of separate phenomenal existences clinging together and struggling together as best they can in their orbit through eternity, no tremendous self-creation and self-impulsion of an ignorant Force without any secret Intelligence within aware of its starting-point and its goal and guiding its process and its motion. An existence, wholly self-aware and therefore entirely master of itself, possesses the phenomenal being in which it is involved, realises itself in form, unfolds itself in the individual.

That luminous Emergence is the dawn which the Aryan forefathers worshipped. Its fulfilled perfection is that highest step of the world-pervading Vishnu which they beheld as if an eye of vision extended in the purest heavens of the Mind. For it exists already as an all-revealing and all-guiding Truth of things which watches over the world and attracts mortal man, first without

---

[1] I. 6.

the knowledge of his conscious mind, by the general march of Nature, but at last consciously by a progressive awakening and self-enlargement, to his divine ascension. The ascent to the divine Life is the human journey, the Work of works, the acceptable Sacrifice. This alone is man's real business in the world and the justification of his existence, without which he would be only an insect crawling among other ephemeral insects on a speck of surface mud and water which has managed to form itself amid the appalling immensities of the physical universe.

This Truth of things that has to emerge out of the phenomenal world's contradictions is declared to be an infinite Bliss and self-conscious Existence, the same everywhere, in all things, in all times and beyond Time, and aware of itself behind all these phenomena by whose intensest vibrations of activity or by whose largest totality it can never be entirely expressed or in any way limited; for it is self-existent and does not depend for its being upon its manifestations. They represent it, but do not exhaust it; point to it, but do not reveal it. It is revealed only to itself within their forms. The conscious existence involved in the form comes, as it evolves, to know itself by intuition, by self-vision, by self-experience. It becomes itself in the world by knowing itself; it knows itself by becoming itself. Thus possessed of itself inwardly, it imparts also to its forms and modes the conscious delight of Sachchidananda. This becoming of the infinite Bliss-Existence-Consciousness in mind and life and body, — for independent of them it exists eternally, — is the transfiguration intended and the utility of individual existence. Through the individual it manifests in relation even as of itself it exists in identity.

The Unknowable knowing itself as Sachchidananda is the one supreme affirmation of Vedanta; it contains all the others or on it they depend. This is the one veritable experience that remains when all appearances have been accounted for negatively by the elimination of their shapes and coverings or positively by the reduction of their names and forms to the constant truth that they contain. For fulfilment of life or for transcendence of life, and whether purity, calm and freedom in the spirit be our aim or puissance, joy and perfection, Sachchidananda is the unknown, omnipresent, indispensable term for which the human consciousness, whether in knowledge and sentiment or in sensation and action, is eternally seeking.

The universe and the individual are the two essential appearances into which the Unknowable descends and through which it has to be approached; for other intermediate collectivities are born only of their interaction. This descent of the supreme Reality is in its nature a self-concealing; and in the descent there are successive levels, in the concealing successive veils. Necessarily, the revelation takes the form of an ascent; and necessarily also the ascent and the revelation are both progressive. For each successive level in the descent of the Divine is to man a stage in an ascension; each veil that hides the unknown God becomes for the God-lover and God-seeker an instrument of His unveiling. Out of the rhythmic slumber of material Nature unconscious of the Soul and the Idea that maintain the ordered activities of her energy even in her dumb and mighty material trance, the world struggles into the more quick, varied and disordered rhythm of Life labouring on the verges of self-consciousness. Out of Life it struggles upward into Mind in which the unit becomes awake to itself and its world, and in that awakening the universe gains the leverage it required for its supreme work, it gains self-conscious individuality. But Mind takes up the work to continue, not to complete it. It is a labourer of acute but limited intelligence who takes the confused materials offered by Life and, having improved, adapted, varied, classified according to its power, hands them over to the supreme Artist of our divine manhood. That Artist dwells in Supermind; for Supermind is Superman. Therefore our world has yet to climb beyond Mind to a higher principle, a higher status, a higher dynamism in which universe and individual become aware of and possess that which they both are and therefore stand explained to each other, in harmony with each other, unified.

The disorders of life and mind cease by discerning the secret of a more perfect order than the physical. Matter below life and mind contains in itself the balance between a perfect poise of tranquillity and the action of an immeasurable energy, but does not possess that which it contains. Its peace wears the dull mask of an obscure inertia, a sleep of unconsciousness or rather of a drugged and imprisoned consciousness. Driven by a force which is its real self but whose sense it cannot yet seize nor share, it has not the awakened joy of its own harmonious energies.

Life and mind awaken to the sense of this want in the form of a striving and seeking ignorance and a troubled and baffled desire which are the first steps towards self-knowledge and self-fulfilment. But where then is the kingdom of their self-fulfilling? It comes to them by the exceeding of themselves. Beyond life and mind we recover consciously in its divine truth that which the balance of material Nature grossly represented, — a tranquillity which is neither inertia nor a sealed trance of consciousness but the concentration of an absolute force and an absolute self-awareness, and an action of immeasurable energy which is at the same time an out-thrilling of ineffable bliss because its every act is the expression, not of a want and an ignorant straining, but of an absolute peace and self-mastery. In that attainment our ignorance realises the light of which it was a darkened or a partial reflection; our desires cease in the plenitude and fulfilment towards which even in their most brute material forms they were an obscure and fallen aspiration.

The universe and the individual are necessary to each other in their ascent. Always indeed they exist for each other and profit by each other. Universe is a diffusion of the divine All in infinite Space and Time, the individual its concentration within limits of Space and Time. Universe seeks in infinite extension the divine totality it feels itself to be but cannot entirely realise; for in extension existence drives at a pluralistic sum of itself which can neither be the primal nor the final unit, but only a recurring decimal without end or beginning. Therefore it creates in itself a self-conscious concentration of the All through which it can aspire. In the conscious individual Prakriti turns back to perceive Purusha, World seeks after Self; God having entirely become Nature, Nature seeks to become progressively God.

On the other hand, it is by means of the universe that the

individual is impelled to realise himself. Not only is it his foundation, his means, his field, the stuff of the divine Work; but also, since the concentration of the universal Life which he is takes place within limits and is not like the intensive unity of Brahman free from all conception of bound and term, he must necessarily universalise and impersonalise himself in order to manifest the divine All which is his reality. Yet is he called upon to preserve, even when he most extends himself in universality of consciousness, a mysterious transcendent something of which his sense of personality gives him an obscure and egoistic representation. Otherwise he has missed his goal, the problem set to him has not been solved, the divine work for which he accepted birth has not been done.

The universe comes to the individual as Life, — a dynamism the entire secret of which he has to master and a mass of colliding results, a whirl of potential energies out of which he has to disengage some supreme order and some yet unrealised harmony. This is after all the real sense of man's progress. It is not merely a restatement in slightly different terms of what physical Nature has already accomplished. Nor can the ideal of human life be simply the animal repeated on a higher scale of mentality. Otherwise, any system or order which assured a tolerable well-being and a moderate mental satisfaction would have stayed our advance. The animal is satisfied with a modicum of necessity; the gods are content with their splendours. But man cannot rest permanently until he reaches some highest good. He is the greatest of living beings because he is the most discontented, because he feels most the pressure of limitations. He alone, perhaps, is capable of being seized by the divine frenzy for a remote ideal.

To the Life-Spirit, therefore, the individual in whom its potentialities centre is pre-eminently Man, the Purusha. It is the Son of Man who is supremely capable of incarnating God. This Man is the Manu, the thinker, the Manomaya Purusha, mental person or soul in mind of the ancient sages. No mere superior mammal is he, but a conceptive soul basing itself on the animal body in Matter. He is conscious Name or Numen accepting and utilising form as a medium through which Person can deal with substance. The animal life emerging out of Matter is only the inferior term of his existence. The life of thought, feeling, will, conscious impulsion, that which we name in its totality Mind, that which strives to seize upon Matter and its vital energies and subject them to the law of its own progressive transformation, is the middle term in which he takes his effectual station. But there is equally a supreme term which Mind in man searches after so that having found he may affirm it in his mental and bodily existence. This practical affirmation of something essentially superior to his present self is the basis of the divine life in the human being.

Awakened to a profounder self-knowledge than his first mental idea of himself, Man begins to conceive some formula and to perceive some appearance of the thing that he has to affirm. But it appears to him as if poised between two negations of itself. If, beyond his present attainment, he perceives or is touched by the power, light, bliss of a self-conscious infinite existence and translates his thought or his experience of it into terms convenient for his mentality, — Infinity, Omniscience, Omnipotence, Immortality, Freedom, Love, Beatitude, God, — yet does this sun of his seeing appear to shine between a double Night, — a darkness below, a mightier darkness beyond. For when he strives to know it utterly, it seems to pass into something which neither any one of these terms nor the sum of them can at all represent. His mind at last negates God for a Beyond, or at least it seems to find God transcending Himself, denying Himself to the conception. Here also, in the world, in himself, and around himself, he is met always by the opposites of his affirmation. Death is ever with him, limitation invests his being and his experience, error, inconscience, weakness, inertia, grief, pain, evil are constant oppressors of his effort. Here also he is driven to deny God, or at least the Divine seems to negate or to hide itself in some appearance or outcome which is other than its true and eternal reality.

And the terms of this denial are not, like that other and remoter negation, inconceivable and therefore naturally mysterious, unknowable to his mind, but appear to be knowable, known, definite, — and still mysterious. He knows not what they are, why they exist, how they came into being. He sees their processes as they affect and appear to him; he cannot fathom their essential reality.

Perhaps they are unfathomable, perhaps they also are really unknowable in their essence? Or, it may be, they have no essential reality, — are an illusion, Asat, non-being. The superior Negation appears to us sometimes as a Nihil, a Non-Existence; this inferior negation may also be, in its essence, a Nihil, a nonexistence. But as we have already put away from us this evasion of the difficulty with regard to that higher, so also we discard it for this inferior Asat. To deny entirely its reality or to seek an escape from it as a mere disastrous illusion is to put away from us the problem and to shun our work. For Life, these things that seem to deny God, to be the opposites of Sachchidananda, are real, even if they turn out to be temporary. They and their opposites, good, knowledge, joy, pleasure, life, survival, strength, power, increase, are the very material of her workings.

It is probable indeed that they are the result or rather the inseparable accompaniments, not of an illusion, but of a wrong relation, wrong because it is founded on a false view of what the individual is in the universe and therefore a false attitude both towards God and Nature, towards self and environment. Because that which he has become is out of harmony both with what the world of his habitation is and what he himself should be and is to be, therefore man is subject to these contradictions of the secret Truth of things. In that case they are not the punishment of a fall, but the conditions of a progress. They are the first elements of the work he has to fulfil, the price he has to pay for the crown which he hopes to win, the narrow way by which Nature escapes out of Matter into consciousness; they are at once her ransom and her stock.

For out of these false relations and by their aid the true have to be found. By the Ignorance we have to cross over death. So too the Veda speaks cryptically of energies that are like women evil in impulse, wandering from the path, doing hurt to their Lord, which yet, though themselves false and unhappy, build up in the end "this vast Truth", the Truth that is the Bliss. It would be, then, not when he has excised the evil in Nature out of himself by an act of moral surgery or parted with life by an abhorrent recoil, but when he has turned Death into a more perfect life, lifted the small things of the human limitation into the great things of the divine vastness, transformed suffering into beatitude, converted evil into its proper good, translated error and falsehood into their secret truth that the sacrifice will be accomplished, the journey done and Heaven and Earth equalised join hands in the bliss of the Supreme.

Yet how can such contraries pass into each other? By what alchemy shall this lead of mortality be turned into that gold of divine Being? But if they are not in their essence contraries? If they are manifestations of one Reality, identical in substance? Then indeed a divine transmutation becomes conceivable.

We have seen that the Non-Being beyond may well be an inconceivable existence and perhaps an ineffable Bliss. At least the Nirvana of Buddhism which formulated one most luminous effort of man to reach and to rest in this highest Non-Existence, represents itself in the psychology of the liberated yet upon earth as an unspeakable peace and gladness; its practical effect is the extinction of all suffering through the disappearance of all ego-istic idea or sensation and the nearest we can get to a positive conception of it is that it is some inexpressible Beatitude (if the name or any name can be applied to a peace so void of contents) into which even the notion of self-existence seems to be swallowed up and disappear. It is a Sachchidananda to which we dare no longer apply even the supreme terms of Sat, of Chit and of Ananda. For all terms are annulled and all cognitive experience is overpassed.

On the other hand, we have hazarded the suggestion that since all is one Reality, this inferior negation also, this other contradiction or non-existence of Sachchidananda is none other than Sachchidananda itself. It is capable of being conceived by the intellect, perceived in the vision, even received through the sensations as verily that which it seems to deny, and such would it always be to our conscious experience if things were not falsified by some great fundamental error, some possessing and compelling Ignorance, Maya or Avidya. In this sense a solution might be sought, not perhaps a satisfying metaphysical solution for the logical mind, — for we are standing on the border-line of the unknowable, the ineffable and straining our eyes beyond, — but a sufficient basis in experience for the practice of the divine life.

To do this we must dare to go below the clear surfaces of things on which the mind loves to dwell, to tempt the vast and obscure, to penetrate the unfathomable depths of consciousness and identify ourselves with states of being that are not our own. Human language is a poor help in such a search, but at least we may find in it some symbols and figures, return with some just expressible hints which will help the light of the soul and throw upon the mind some reflection of the ineffable design.

Chapter VII

The Ego and the Dualities

The soul seated on the same tree of Nature is absorbed and deluded and has sorrow because it is not the Lord, but when it sees and is in union with that other self and greatness of it which is the Lord, then sorrow passes away from it.

Swetaswatara Upanishad.[1]

IF ALL is in truth Sachchidananda, death, suffering, evil, limitation can only be the creations, positive in practical effect, negative in essence, of a distorting consciousness which has fallen from the total and unifying knowledge of itself into some error of division and partial experience. This is the fall of man typified in the poetic parable of the Hebrew Genesis. That fall is his deviation from the full and pure acceptance of God and himself, or rather of God in himself, into a dividing consciousness which brings with it all the train of the dualities, life and death, good and evil, joy and pain, completeness and want, the fruit of a divided being. This is the fruit which Adam and Eve, Purusha and Prakriti, the soul tempted by Nature, have eaten. The redemption comes by the recovery of the universal in the individual and of the spiritual term in the physical consciousness. Then alone the soul in Nature can be allowed to partake of the fruit of the tree of life and be as the Divine and live for ever. For then only can the purpose of its descent into material consciousness be accomplished, when the knowledge of good and evil, joy and suffering, life and death has been accomplished through the recovery by the human soul of a higher knowledge which reconciles and identifies these opposites in the universal and transforms their divisions into the image of the divine Unity.

---

[1] IV. 7.

To Sachchidananda extended in all things in widest commonalty and impartial universality, death, suffering, evil and limitation can only be at the most reverse terms, shadow-forms of their luminous opposites. As these things are felt by us, they are notes of a discord. They formulate separation where there should be a unity, miscomprehension where there should be an understanding, an attempt to arrive at independent harmonies where there should be a self-adaptation to the orchestral whole. All totality, even if it be only in one scheme of the universal vibrations, even if it be only a totality of the physical consciousness without possession of all that is in movement beyond and behind, must be to that extent a reversion to harmony and a reconciliation of jarring opposites. On the other hand, to Sachchidananda transcendent of the forms of the universe the dual terms themselves, even so understood, can no longer be justly applicable. Transcendence transfigures; it does not reconcile, but rather transmutes opposites into something surpassing them that effaces their oppositions.

At first, however, we must strive to relate the individual again to the harmony of the totality. There it is necessary for us, — otherwise there is no issue from the problem, — to realise that the terms in which our present consciousness renders the values of the universe, though practically justified for the purposes of human experience and progress, are not the sole terms in which it is possible to render them and may not be the complete, the right, the ultimate formulas. Just as there may be sense-organs or formations of sense-capacity which see the physical world differently and it may well be better, because more completely, than our sense-organs and sense-capacity, so there may be other mental and supramental envisagings of the universe which surpass our own. States of consciousness there are in which Death is only a change in immortal Life, pain a violent backwash of the waters of universal delight, limitation a turning of the Infinite upon itself, evil a circling of the good around its own perfection; and this not in abstract conception only, but in actual vision and in constant and substantial experience. To arrive at such states of consciousness may, for the individual, be one of the most important and indispensable steps of his progress towards self-perfection.

Certainly, the practical values given us by our senses and by the dualistic sense-mind must hold good in their field and be accepted as the standard for ordinary life-experience until a larger harmony is ready into which they can enter and transform themselves without losing hold of the realities which they represent. To enlarge the sense-faculties without the knowledge that would give the old sense-values their right interpretation from the new standpoint might lead to serious disorders and incapacities, might unfit for practical life and for the orderly and disciplined use of the reason. Equally, an enlargement of our mental consciousness out of the experience of the egoistic dualities into an unregulated unity with some form of total consciousness might easily bring about a confusion and incapacity for the active life of humanity in the established order of the world's relativities. This, no doubt, is the root of the injunction imposed in the Gita on the man who has the knowledge not to disturb the life-basis and thought-basis of the ignorant; for, impelled by his example but unable to comprehend the principle of his action, they would lose their own system of values without arriving at a higher foundation.

Such a disorder and incapacity may be accepted personally and are accepted by many great souls as a temporary passage or as the price to be paid for the entry into a wider existence. But the right goal of human progress must be always an effective and synthetic reinterpretation by which the law of that wider existence may be represented in a new order of truths and in a more just and puissant working of the faculties on the life-material of the universe. For the senses the sun goes round the earth; that was for them the centre of existence and the motions of life are arranged on the basis of a misconception. The truth is the very opposite, but its discovery would have been of little use if there were not a science that makes the new conception the centre of a reasoned and ordered knowledge putting their right values on the perceptions of the senses. So also for the mental consciousness God moves round the personal ego and all His works and ways are brought to the judgment of our egoistic sensations, emotions and conceptions and are there given values and interpretations which, though a perversion and inversion of the truth of things, are yet useful and practically sufficient in a certain development of human life and progress. They are a rough practical systematisation of our experience of things valid so long as we dwell in a certain order of ideas and activities. But they do not represent the last and highest state of human life and knowledge. "Truth is the path and not the falsehood." The truth is not that God moves round the ego as the centre of existence and can be judged by the ego and its view of the dualities, but that the Divine is itself the centre and that the experience of the individual only finds its own true truth when it is known in the terms of the universal and the transcendent. Nevertheless, to substitute this conception for the egoistic without an adequate base of knowledge may lead to the substitution of new but still false and arbitrary ideas for the old and bring about a violent instead of a settled disorder of right values. Such a disorder often marks the inception of new philosophies and religions and initiates useful revolutions. But the true goal is only reached when we can group round the right central conception a reasoned and effective knowledge in which the egoistic life shall rediscover all its values transformed and corrected. Then we shall possess that new order of truths which will make it possible for us to substitute a more divine life for the existence which we now lead and to effectualise a more divine and puissant use of our faculties on the life-material of the universe.

That new life and power of the human integer must necessarily repose on a realisation of the great verities which translate into our mode of conceiving things the nature of the divine existence. It must proceed through a renunciation by the ego of its false standpoint and false certainties, through its entry into a right relation and harmony with the totalities of which it forms a part and with the transcendences from which it is a descent, and through its perfect self-opening to a truth and a law that exceed its own conventions, — a truth that shall be its fulfilment and a law that shall be its deliverance. Its goal must be the abolition of those values which are the creations of the egoistic view of things; its crown must be the transcendence of limitation, ignorance, death, suffering and evil.

The transcendence, the abolition are not possible here on earth and in our human life if the terms of that life are necessarily bound to our present egoistic valuations. If life is in its nature individual phenomenon and not representation of a universal existence and the breathing of a mighty Life-Spirit, if the dualities which are the response of the individual to its contacts are not merely a response but the very essence and condition of all living, if limitation is the inalienable nature of the substance of which our mind and body are formed, disintegration of death the first and last condition of all life, its end and its beginning, pleasure and pain the inseparable dual stuff of all sensation, joy and grief the necessary light and shade of all emotion, truth and error the two poles between which all knowledge must eternally move, then transcendence is only attainable by the abandonment of human life in a Nirvana beyond all existence or by attainment to another world, a heaven quite otherwise constituted than this material universe.

It is not very easy for the customary mind of man, always attached to its past and present associations, to conceive of an existence still human, yet radically changed in what are now our fixed circumstances. We are in respect to our possible higher evolution much in the position of the original Ape of the Darwinian theory. It would have been impossible for that Ape leading his instinctive arboreal life in primeval forests to conceive that there would be one day an animal on the earth who would use a new faculty called reason upon the materials of his inner and outer existence, who would dominate by that power his instincts and habits, change the circumstances of his physical life, build for himself houses of stone, manipulate Nature's forces, sail the seas, ride the air, develop codes of conduct, evolve conscious methods for his mental and spiritual development. And if such a conception had been possible for the Ape-mind, it would still have been difficult for him to imagine that by any progress of Nature or long effort of Will and tendency he himself could develop into that animal. Man, because he has acquired reason and still more because he has indulged his power of imagination and intuition, is able to conceive an existence higher than his own and even to envisage his personal elevation beyond his present state into that existence. His idea of the supreme state is an absolute of all that is positive to his own concepts and desirable to his own instinctive aspiration, — Knowledge without its negative shadow of error, Bliss without its negation in experience of suffering, Power without its constant denial by incapacity, purity and plenitude of being without the opposing sense of defect and limitation. It is so that he conceives his gods; it is so that he constructs his heavens. But it is not so that his reason conceives of a possible earth and a possible humanity. His dream of God and Heaven is really a dream of his own perfection; but he finds the same difficulty in accepting its practical realisation here for his ultimate aim as would the ancestral Ape if called upon to believe in himself as the future Man. His imagination, his religious aspirations may hold that end before him; but when his reason asserts itself, rejecting imagination and transcendent intuition, he puts it by as a brilliant superstition contrary to the hard facts of the material universe. It becomes then only his inspiring vision of the impossible. All that is possible is a conditioned, limited and precarious knowledge, happiness, power and good.

Yet in the principle of reason itself there is the assertion of a Transcendence. For reason is in its whole aim and essence the pursuit of Knowledge, the pursuit, that is to say, of Truth by the elimination of error. Its view, its aim is not that of a passage from a greater to a lesser error, but it supposes a positive, pre-existent Truth towards which through the dualities of right knowledge and wrong knowledge we can progressively move. If our reason has not the same instinctive certitude with regard to the other aspirations of humanity, it is because it lacks the same essential illumination inherent in its own positive activity. We can just conceive of a positive or absolute realisation of happiness, because the heart to which that instinct for happiness belongs has its own form of certitude, is capable of faith, and because our minds can envisage the elimination of unsatisfied want which is the apparent cause of suffering. But how shall we conceive of the elimination of pain from nervous sensation or of death from the life of the body? Yet the rejection of pain is a sovereign instinct of the sensations, the rejection of death a dominant claim inherent in the essence of our vitality. But these things present themselves to our reason as instinctive aspirations, not as realisable potentialities.

Yet the same law should hold throughout. The error of the practical reason is an excessive subjection to the apparent fact which it can immediately feel as real and an insufficient courage in carrying profounder facts of potentiality to their logical conclusion. What is, is the realisation of an anterior potentiality; present potentiality is a clue to future realisation. And here potentiality exists; for the mastery of phenomena depends upon a knowledge of their causes and processes and if we know the causes of error, sorrow, pain, death, we may labour with some hope towards their elimination. For knowledge is power and mastery.

In fact, we do pursue as an ideal, so far as we may, the elimination of all these negative or adverse phenomena. We seek constantly to minimise the causes of error, pain and suffering. Science, as its knowledge increases, dreams of regulating birth and of indefinitely prolonging life, if not of effecting the entire conquest of death. But because we envisage only external or secondary causes, we can only think of removing them to a distance and not of eliminating the actual roots of that against which we struggle. And we are thus limited because we strive towards secondary perceptions and not towards root-knowledge, because we know processes of things, but not their essence. We thus arrive at a more powerful manipulation of circumstances, but not at essential control. But if we could grasp the essential nature and the essential cause of error, suffering and death, we might hope to arrive at a mastery over them which should be not relative but entire. We might hope even to eliminate them altogether and justify the dominant instinct of our nature by the conquest of that absolute good, bliss, knowledge and immortality which our intuitions perceive as the true and ultimate condition of the human being.

The ancient Vedanta presents us with such a solution in the conception and experience of Brahman as the one universal and essential fact and of the nature of Brahman as Sachchidananda.

In this view the essence of all life is the movement of a universal and immortal existence, the essence of all sensation and emotion is the play of a universal and self-existent delight in being, the essence of all thought and perception is the radiation of a universal and all-pervading truth, the essence of all activity is the progression of a universal and self-effecting good.

But the play and movement embodies itself in a multiplicity of forms, a variation of tendencies, an interplay of energies. Multiplicity permits of the interference of a determinative and temporarily deformative factor, the individual ego; and the nature of the ego is a self-limitation of consciousness by a willed ignorance of the rest of its play and its exclusive absorption in one form, one combination of tendencies, one field of the movement of energies. Ego is the factor which determines the reactions of error, sorrow, pain, evil, death; for it gives these values to movements which would otherwise be represented in their right relation to the one Existence, Bliss, Truth and Good. By recovering the right relation we may eliminate the ego-determined reactions, reducing them eventually to their true values; and this recovery can be effected by the right participation of the individual in the consciousness of the totality and in the consciousness of the transcendent which the totality represents.

Into later Vedanta there crept and arrived at fixity the idea that the limited ego is not only the cause of the dualities, but the essential condition for the existence of the universe. By getting rid of the ignorance of the ego and its resultant limitations we do indeed eliminate the dualities, but we eliminate along with them our existence in the cosmic movement. Thus we return to the essentially evil and illusory nature of human existence and the vanity of all effort after perfection in the life of the world. A relative good linked always to its opposite is all that here we can seek. But if we adhere to the larger and profounder idea that the ego is only an intermediate representation of something beyond itself, we escape from this consequence and are able to apply Vedanta to fulfilment of life and not only to the escape from life. The essential cause and condition of universal existence is the Lord, Ishwara or Purusha, manifesting and occupying individual and universal forms. The limited ego is only an intermediate phenomenon of consciousness necessary for a certain line of development. Following this line the individual can arrive at that which is beyond himself, that which he represents, and can yet continue to represent it, no longer as an obscured and limited ego, but as a centre of the Divine and of the universal consciousness embracing, utilising and transforming into harmony with the Divine all individual determinations.

We have then the manifestation of the divine Conscious Being in the totality of physical Nature as the foundation of human existence in the material universe. We have the emergence of that Conscious Being in an involved and inevitably evolving Life, Mind and Supermind as the condition of our activities; for it is this evolution which has enabled man to appear in Matter and it is this evolution which will enable him progressively to manifest God in the body, — the universal Incarnation. We have in egoistic formation the intermediate and decisive factor which allows the One to emerge as the conscious Many out of that indeterminate totality general, obscure and formless which we call the subconscient, — *hṛdya samudra*, the ocean heart in things of the Rig Veda. We have the dualities of life and death, joy and sorrow, pleasure and pain, truth and error, good and evil as the first formations of egoistic consciousness, the natural and inevitable outcome of its attempt to realise unity in an artificial construction of itself exclusive of the total truth, good, life and delight of being in the universe. We have the dissolution of this egoistic construction by the self-opening of the individual to the universe and to God as the means of that supreme fulfilment to which egoistic life is only a prelude even as animal life was only a prelude to the human. We have the realisation of the All in the individual by the transformation of the limited ego into a conscious centre of the divine unity and freedom as the term at which the fulfilment arrives. And we have the outflowing of the infinite and absolute Existence, Truth, Good and Delight of being on the Many in the world as the divine result towards which the cycles of our evolution move. This is the supreme birth which maternal Nature holds in herself; of this she strives to be delivered.

Chapter VIII

The Methods of Vedantic Knowledge

This secret Self in all beings is not apparent, but it is seen by
means of the supreme reason, the subtle, by those who have
the subtle vision. *Katha Upanishad.*[1]

BUT WHAT then is the working of this Sachchidananda in
the world and by what process of things are the relations
between itself and the ego which figures it first formed,
then led to their consummation? For on those relations and
on the process they follow depend the whole philosophy and
practice of a divine life for man.

We arrive at the conception and at the knowledge of a divine
existence by exceeding the evidence of the senses and piercing
beyond the walls of the physical mind. So long as we confine
ourselves to sense-evidence and the physical consciousness, we
can conceive nothing and know nothing except the material
world and its phenomena. But certain faculties in us enable our
mentality to arrive at conceptions which we may indeed deduce
by ratiocination or by imaginative variation from the facts of
the physical world as we see them, but which are not warranted
by any purely physical data or any physical experience. The first
of these instruments is the pure reason.

Human reason has a double action, mixed or dependent,
pure or sovereign. Reason accepts a mixed action when it con-
fines itself to the circle of our sensible experience, admits its
law as the final truth and concerns itself only with the study
of phenomenon, that is to say, with the appearances of things
in their relations, processes and utilities. This rational action

[1] I. 3. 12.

is incapable of knowing what is, it only knows what appears to be, it has no plummet by which it can sound the depths of being, it can only survey the field of becoming. Reason, on the other hand, asserts its pure action, when accepting our sensible experiences as a starting-point but refusing to be limited by them it goes behind, judges, works in its own right and strives to arrive at general and unalterable concepts which attach themselves not to the appearances of things, but to that which stands behind their appearances. It may arrive at its result by direct judgment passing immediately from the appearance to that which stands behind it and in that case the concept arrived at may seem to be a result of the sensible experience and dependent upon it though it is really a perception of reason working in its own right. But the perceptions of the pure reason may also — and this is their more characteristic action — use the experience from which they start as a mere excuse and leave it far behind before they arrive at their result, so far that the result may seem the direct contrary of that which our sensible experience wishes to dictate to us. This movement is legitimate and indispensable, because our normal experience not only covers only a small part of universal fact, but even in the limits of its own field uses instruments that are defective and gives us false weights and measures. It must be exceeded, put away to a distance and its insistences often denied if we are to arrive at more adequate conceptions of the truth of things. To correct the errors of the sense-mind by the use of reason is one of the most valuable powers developed by man and the chief cause of his superiority among terrestrial beings.

The complete use of pure reason brings us finally from physical to metaphysical knowledge. But the concepts of metaphysical knowledge do not in themselves fully satisfy the demand of our integral being. They are indeed entirely satisfactory to the pure reason itself, because they are the very stuff of its own existence. But our nature sees things through two eyes always, for it views them doubly as idea and as fact and therefore every concept is incomplete for us and to a part of our nature almost unreal until it becomes an experience. But the truths which are now in question, are of an order not subject to our normal experience. They are, in their nature, "beyond the perception of the senses but seizable by the perception of the reason". Therefore, some other faculty of experience is necessary by which the demand of our nature can be fulfilled and this can only come, since we are dealing with the supraphysical, by an extension of psychological experience.

In a sense all our experience is psychological since even what we receive by the senses has no meaning or value to us till it is translated into the terms of the sense-mind, the Manas of Indian philosophical terminology. Manas, say our philosophers, is the sixth sense. But we may even say that it is the only sense and that the others, vision, hearing, touch, smell, taste are merely specialisations of the sense-mind which, although it normally uses the sense-organs for the basis of its experience, yet exceeds them and is capable of a direct experience proper to its own inherent action. As a result psychological experience, like the cognitions of the reason, is capable in man of a double action, mixed or dependent, pure or sovereign. Its mixed action takes place usually when the mind seeks to become aware of the external world, the object; the pure action when it seeks to become aware of itself, the subject. In the former activity, it is dependent on the senses and forms its perceptions in accordance with their evidence; in the latter it acts in itself and is aware of things directly by a sort of identity with them. We are thus aware of our emotions; we are aware of anger, as has been acutely said, because we become anger. We are thus aware also of our own existence; and here the nature of experience as knowledge by identity becomes apparent. In reality, all experience is in its secret nature knowledge by identity; but its true character is hidden from us because we have separated ourselves from the rest of the world by exclusion, by the distinction of ourself as subject and everything else as object, and we are compelled to develop processes and organs by which we may again enter into communion with all that we have excluded. We have to replace direct knowledge through conscious identity by an indirect knowledge which appears to be caused by physical contact and mental sympathy. This limitation is a fundamental creation of the ego and an instance of the manner in which it has proceeded throughout, starting from an original falsehood and covering over the true truth of things by contingent falsehoods which become for us practical truths of relation.

From this nature of mental and sense knowledge as it is at present organised in us, it follows that there is no inevitable necessity in our existing limitations. They are the result of an evolution in which mind has accustomed itself to depend upon certain physiological functionings and their reactions as its normal means of entering into relation with the material universe. Therefore, although it is the rule that when we seek to become aware of the external world, we have to do so indirectly through the sense-organs and can experience only so much of the truth about things and men as the senses convey to us, yet this rule is merely the regularity of a dominant habit. It is possible for the mind, — and it would be natural for it, if it could be persuaded to liberate itself from its consent to the domination of matter, — to take direct cognisance of the objects of sense without the aid of the sense-organs. This is what happens in experiments of hypnosis and cognate psychological phenomena. Because our waking consciousness is determined and limited by the balance between mind and matter worked out by life in its evolution, this direct cognisance is usually impossible in our ordinary waking state and has therefore to be brought about by throwing the waking mind into a state of sleep which liberates the true or subliminal mind. Mind is then able to assert its true character as the one and all-sufficient sense and free to apply to the objects of sense its pure and sovereign instead of its mixed and dependent action. Nor is this extension of faculty really impossible but only more difficult in our waking state, — as is known to all who have been able to go far enough in certain paths of psychological experiment.

The sovereign action of the sense-mind can be employed to develop other senses besides the five which we ordinarily use. For instance, it is possible to develop the power of appreciating accurately without physical means the weight of an object which we hold in our hands. Here the sense of contact and pressure is merely used as a starting-point, just as the data of sense-experience are used by the pure reason, but it is not really the sense of touch which gives the measure of the weight to the mind; that finds the right value through its own independent perception and uses the touch only in order to enter into relation with the object. And as with the pure reason, so with the sense-mind, the sense-experience can be used as a mere first point from which it proceeds to a knowledge that has nothing to do with the sense-organs and often contradicts their evidence. Nor is the extension of faculty confined only to outsides and superficies. It is possible, once we have entered by any of the senses into relation with an external object, so to apply the Manas as to become aware of the contents of the object, for example, to receive or to perceive the thoughts or feelings of others without aid from their utterance, gesture, action or facial expressions and even in contradiction of these always partial and often misleading data. Finally, by an utilisation of the inner senses, — that is to say, of the sense-powers, in themselves, in their purely mental or subtle activity as distinguished from the physical which is only a selection for the purposes of outward life from their total and general action, — we are able to take cognition of sense-experiences, of appearances and images of things other than those which belong to the organisation of our material environment. All these extensions of faculty, though received with hesitation and incredulity by the physical mind because they are abnormal to the habitual scheme of our ordinary life and experience, difficult to set in action, still more difficult to systematise so as to be able to make of them an orderly and serviceable set of instruments, must yet be admitted, since they are the invariable result of any attempt to enlarge the field of our superficially active consciousness whether by some kind of untaught effort and casual ill-ordered effect or by a scientific and well-regulated practice.

None of them, however, leads to the aim we have in view, the psychological experience of those truths that are "beyond perception by the sense but seizable by the perceptions of the reason", *buddhigrāhyam atīndriyam.*[2] They give us only a larger field of phenomena and more effective means for the observation of phenomena. The truth of things always escapes beyond the sense. Yet is it a sound rule inherent in the very constitution of universal existence that where there are truths attainable by the reason, there must be somewhere in the organism possessed of that reason a means of arriving at or verifying them by experience. The one means we have left in our mentality is an extension of that form of knowledge by identity which gives us the awareness of our own existence. It is really upon a self-awareness more or less conscient, more or less present to our conception that the knowledge of the contents of our self is based. Or to put it in a more general formula, the knowledge of the contents is contained in the knowledge of the continent. If then we can extend our faculty of mental self-awareness to awareness of the Self beyond and outside us, Atman or Brahman of the Upanishads, we may become possessors in experience of the truths which form the contents of the Atman or Brahman in the universe. It is on this possibility that Indian Vedanta has based itself. It has sought through knowledge of the Self the knowledge of the universe.

But always mental experience and the concepts of the reason have been held by it to be even at their highest a reflection in mental identifications and not the supreme self-existent identity. We have to go beyond the mind and the reason. The reason active in our waking consciousness is only a mediator between the subconscient All that we come from in our evolution upwards and the superconscient All towards which we are impelled by that evolution. The subconscient and the superconscient are two different formulations of the same All. The master-word of the subconscient is Life, the master-word of the superconscient is Light. In the subconscient knowledge or consciousness is involved in action, for action is the essence of Life. In the superconscient action re-enters into Light and no longer contains involved knowledge but is itself contained in a supreme

---

[2] *Gita*, VI. 21.

consciousness. Intuitional knowledge is that which is common between them and the foundation of intuitional knowledge is conscious or effective identity between that which knows and that which is known; it is that state of common self-existence in which the knower and the known are one through knowledge. But in the subconscient the intuition manifests itself in the action, in effectivity, and the knowledge or conscious identity is either entirely or more or less concealed in the action. In the superconscient, on the contrary, Light being the law and the principle, the intuition manifests itself in its true nature as knowledge emerging out of conscious identity, and effectivity of action is rather the accompaniment or necessary consequent and no longer masks as the primary fact. Between these two states reason and mind act as intermediaries which enable the being to liberate knowledge out of its imprisonment in the act and prepare it to resume its essential primacy. When the self-awareness in the mind applied, both to continent and content, to own-self and other-self, exalts itself into the luminous self-manifest identity, the reason also converts itself into the form of the self-luminous intuitional[3] knowledge. This is the highest possible state of our knowledge when mind fulfils itself in the supramental.

Such is the scheme of the human understanding upon which the conclusions of the most ancient Vedanta were built. To develop the results arrived at on this foundation by the ancient sages is not my object, but it is necessary to pass briefly in review some of their principal conclusions so far as they affect the problem of the divine Life with which alone we are at present concerned. For it is in those ideas that we shall find the best previous foundation of that which we seek now to rebuild and although, as with all knowledge, old expression has to be replaced to a certain extent by new expression suited to a later mentality and old light has to merge itself into new light

---

[3] I use the word "intuition" for want of a better. In truth, it is a makeshift and inadequate to the connotation demanded of it. The same has to be said of the word "consciousness" and many others which our poverty compels us to extend illegitimately in their significance.

as dawn succeeds dawn, yet it is with the old treasure as our initial capital or so much of it as we can recover that we shall most advantageously proceed to accumulate the largest gains in our new commerce with the ever-changeless and ever-changing Infinite.

Sad Brahman, Existence pure, indefinable, infinite, absolute, is the last concept at which Vedantic analysis arrives in its view of the universe, the fundamental Reality which Vedantic experience discovers behind all the movement and formation which constitute the apparent reality. It is obvious that when we posit this conception, we go entirely beyond what our ordinary consciousness, our normal experience contains or warrants. The senses and sense-mind know nothing whatever about any pure or absolute existence. All that our sense-experience tells us of, is form and movement. Forms exist, but with an existence that is not pure, rather always mixed, combined, aggregated, relative. When we go within ourselves, we may get rid of precise form, but we cannot get rid of movement, of change. Motion of Matter in Space, motion of change in Time seem to be the condition of existence. We may say indeed, if we like, that this is existence and that the idea of existence in itself corresponds to no discoverable reality. At the most in the phenomenon of self-awareness or behind it, we get sometimes a glimpse of something immovable and immutable, something that we vaguely perceive or imagine that we are beyond all life and death, beyond all change and formation and action. Here is the one door in us that sometimes swings open upon the splendour of a truth beyond and, before it shuts again, allows a ray to touch us, — a luminous intimation which, if we have the strength and firmness, we may hold to in our faith and make a starting-point for another play of consciousness than that of the sense-mind, for the play of Intuition.

For if we examine carefully, we shall find that Intuition is our first teacher. Intuition always stands veiled behind our mental operations. Intuition brings to man those brilliant messages from the Unknown which are the beginning of his higher knowledge. Reason only comes in afterwards to see what profit it can have of the shining harvest. Intuition gives us that idea of something behind and beyond all that we know and seem to be which pursues man always in contradiction of his lower reason and all his normal experience and impels him to formulate that formless perception in the more positive ideas of God, Immortality, Heaven and the rest by which we strive to express it to the mind. For Intuition is as strong as Nature herself from whose very soul it has sprung and cares nothing for the contradictions of reason or the denials of experience. It knows what is because it is, because itself it is of that and has come from that, and will not yield it to the judgment of what merely becomes and appears. What the Intuition tells us of, is not so much Existence as the Existent, for it proceeds from that one point of light in us which gives it its advantage, that sometimes opened door in our own self-awareness. Ancient Vedanta seized this message of the Intuition and formulated it in the three great declarations of the Upanishads, "I am He", "Thou art That, O Swetaketu", "All this is the Brahman; this Self is the Brahman".

But Intuition by the very nature of its action in man, working as it does from behind the veil, active principally in his more unenlightened, less articulate parts, served in front of the veil, in the narrow light which is our waking conscience, only by instruments that are unable fully to assimilate its messages, — Intuition is unable to give us the truth in that ordered and articulated form which our nature demands. Before it could effect any such completeness of direct knowledge in us, it would have to organise itself in our surface being and take possession there of the leading part. But in our surface being it is not the Intuition, it is the Reason which is organised and helps us to order our perceptions, thoughts and actions. Therefore the age of intuitive knowledge, represented by the early Vedantic thinking of the Upanishads, had to give place to the age of rational knowledge; inspired Scripture made room for metaphysical philosophy, even as afterwards metaphysical philosophy had to give place to experimental Science. Intuitive thought which is a messenger from the superconscient and therefore our highest faculty, was supplanted by the pure reason which is only a sort of deputy and belongs to the middle heights of our being; pure reason in its turn was supplanted for a time by the mixed action of the reason which lives on our plains and lower elevations and does not in its view exceed the horizon of the experience that the physical mind and senses or such aids as we can invent for them can bring to us. And this process which seems to be a descent, is really a circle of progress. For in each case the lower faculty is compelled to take up as much as it can assimilate of what the higher had already given and to attempt to re-establish it by its own methods. By the attempt it is itself enlarged in its scope and arrives eventually at a more supple and a more ample self-accommodation to the higher faculties. Without this succession and attempt at separate assimilation we should be obliged to remain under the exclusive domination of a part of our nature while the rest remained either depressed and unduly subjected or separate in its field and therefore poor in its development. With this succession and separate attempt the balance is righted; a more complete harmony of our parts of knowledge is prepared.

We see this succession in the Upanishads and the subsequent Indian philosophies. The sages of the Veda and Vedanta relied entirely upon intuition and spiritual experience. It is by an error that scholars sometimes speak of great debates or discussions in the Upanishad. Wherever there is the appearance of a controversy, it is not by discussion, by dialectics or the use of logical reasoning that it proceeds, but by a comparison of intuitions and experiences in which the less luminous gives place to the more luminous, the narrower, faultier or less essential to the more comprehensive, more perfect, more essential. The question asked by one sage of another is "What dost thou know?", not "What dost thou think?" nor "To what conclusion has thy reasoning arrived?" Nowhere in the Upanishads do we find any trace of logical reasoning urged in support of the truths of Vedanta. Intuition, the sages seem to have held, must be corrected by a more perfect intuition; logical reasoning cannot be its judge.

And yet the human reason demands its own method of satisfaction. Therefore when the age of rationalistic speculation began, Indian philosophers, respectful of the heritage of the past, adopted a double attitude towards the Truth they sought. They recognised in the Sruti, the earlier results of Intuition or, as they preferred to call it, of inspired Revelation, an authority superior to Reason. But at the same time they started from Reason and tested the results it gave them, holding only those conclusions to be valid which were supported by the supreme authority. In this way they avoided to a certain extent the besetting sin of metaphysics, the tendency to battle in the clouds because it deals with words as if they were imperative facts instead of symbols which have always to be carefully scrutinised and brought back constantly to the sense of that which they represent. Their speculations tended at first to keep near at the centre to the highest and profoundest experience and proceeded with the united consent of the two great authorities, Reason and Intuition. Nevertheless, the natural trend of Reason to assert its own supremacy triumphed in effect over the theory of its subordination. Hence the rise of conflicting schools each of which founded itself in theory on the Veda and used its texts as a weapon against the others. For the highest intuitive Knowledge sees things in the whole, in the large and details only as sides of the indivisible whole; its tendency is towards immediate synthesis and the unity of knowledge. Reason, on the contrary, proceeds by analysis and division and assembles its facts to form a whole; but in the assemblage so formed there are opposites, anomalies, logical incompatibilities, and the natural tendency of Reason is to affirm some and to negate others which conflict with its chosen conclusions so that it may form a flawlessly logical system. The unity of the first intuitional knowledge was thus broken up and the ingenuity of the logicians was always able to discover devices, methods of interpretation, standards of varying value by which inconvenient texts of the Scripture could be practically annulled and an entire freedom acquired for their metaphysical speculation.

Nevertheless, the main conceptions of the earlier Vedanta remained in parts in the various philosophical systems and efforts were made from time to time to recombine them into some image of the old catholicity and unity of intuitional thought. And behind the thought of all, variously presented, survived as the fundamental conception, Purusha, Atman or Sad Brahman, the pure Existent of the Upanishads, often rationalised into an idea or psychological state, but still carrying something of its old burden of inexpressible reality. What may be the relation of the movement of becoming which is what we call the world to this absolute Unity and how the ego, whether generated by the movement or cause of the movement, can return to that true Self, Divinity or Reality declared by the Vedanta, these were the questions speculative and practical which have always occupied the thought of India.

Chapter IX

The Pure Existent

One indivisible that is pure existence.

Chhandogya Upanishad.[1]

WHEN we withdraw our gaze from its egoistic preoccupation with limited and fleeting interests and look
upon the world with dispassionate and curious eyes
that search only for the Truth, our first result is the perception
of a boundless energy of infinite existence, infinite movement,
infinite activity pouring itself out in limitless Space, in eternal
Time, an existence that surpasses infinitely our ego or any ego or
any collectivity of egos, in whose balance the grandiose products
of aeons are but the dust of a moment and in whose incalculable sum numberless myriads count only as a petty swarm.
We instinctively act and feel and weave our life thoughts as if
this stupendous world movement were at work around us as
centre and for our benefit, for our help or harm, or as if the
justification of our egoistic cravings, emotions, ideas, standards
were its proper business even as they are our own chief concern.
When we begin to see, we perceive that it exists for itself, not for
us, has its own gigantic aims, its own complex and boundless
idea, its own vast desire or delight that it seeks to fulfil, its own
immense and formidable standards which look down as if with
an indulgent and ironic smile at the pettiness of ours. And yet
let us not swing over to the other extreme and form too positive
an idea of our own insignificance. That too would be an act of
ignorance and the shutting of our eyes to the great facts of the
universe.

[1] VI. 2. 1.

For this boundless Movement does not regard us as unimportant to it. Science reveals to us how minute is the care, how cunning the device, how intense the absorption it bestows upon the smallest of its works even as on the largest. This mighty energy is an equal and impartial mother, *samam Brahma*, in the great term of the Gita, and its intensity and force of movement is the same in the formation and upholding of a system of suns and the organisation of the life of an ant-hill. It is the illusion of size, of quantity that induces us to look on the one as great, the other as petty. If we look, on the contrary, not at mass of quantity but force of quality, we shall say that the ant is greater than the solar system it inhabits and man greater than all inanimate Nature put together. But this again is the illusion of quality. When we go behind and examine only the intensity of the movement of which quality and quantity are aspects, we realise that this Brahman dwells equally in all existences. Equally partaken of by all in its being, we are tempted to say, equally distributed to all in its energy. But this too is an illusion of quantity. Brahman dwells in all, indivisible, yet as if divided and distributed. If we look again with an observing perception not dominated by intellectual concepts, but informed by intuition and culminating in knowledge by identity, we shall see that the consciousness of this infinite Energy is other than our mental consciousness, that it is indivisible and gives, not an equal part of itself, but its whole self at one and the same time to the solar system and to the ant-hill. To Brahman there are no whole and parts, but each thing is all itself and benefits by the whole of Brahman. Quality and quantity differ, the self is equal. The form and manner and result of the force of action vary infinitely, but the eternal, primal, infinite energy is the same in all. The force of strength that goes to make the strong man is no whit greater than the force of weakness that goes to make the weak. The energy spent is as great in repression as in expression, in negation as in affirmation, in silence as in sound.

Therefore the first reckoning we have to mend is that between this infinite Movement, this energy of existence which is the world and ourselves. At present we keep a false account. We are infinitely important to the All, but to us the All is negligible; we alone are important to ourselves. This is the sign of the original ignorance which is the root of the ego, that it can only think with itself as centre as if it were the All, and of that which is not itself accepts only so much as it is mentally disposed to acknowledge or as it is forced to recognise by the shocks of its environment. Even when it begins to philosophise, does it not assert that the world only exists in and by its consciousness? Its own state of consciousness or mental standards are to it the test of reality; all outside its orbit or view tends to become false or non-existent. This mental self-sufficiency of man creates a system of false accountantship which prevents us from drawing the right and full value from life. There is a sense in which these pretensions of the human mind and ego repose on a truth, but this truth only emerges when the mind has learned its ignorance and the ego has submitted to the All and lost in it its separate self-assertion. To recognise that we, or rather the results and appearances we call ourselves, are only a partial movement of this infinite Movement and that it is that infinite which we have to know, to be consciously and to fulfil faithfully, is the commencement of true living. To recognise that in our true selves we are one with the total movement and not minor or subordinate is the other side of the account, and its expression in the manner of our being, thought, emotion and action is necessary to the culmination of a true or divine living.

But to settle the account we have to know what is this All, this infinite and omnipotent energy. And here we come to a fresh complication. For it is asserted to us by the pure reason and it seems to be asserted to us by Vedanta that as we are subordinate and an aspect of this Movement, so the movement is subordinate and an aspect of something other than itself, of a great timeless, spaceless Stability, *sthāṇu*, which is immutable, inexhaustible and unexpended, not acting though containing all this action, not energy, but pure existence. Those who see only this world-energy can declare indeed that there is no such thing: our idea of an eternal stability, an immutable pure existence is a fiction of our intellectual conceptions starting from a false idea of the stable: for there is nothing that is stable; all is movement and our conception of the stable is only an artifice of our mental consciousness by which we secure a standpoint for dealing practically with the movement. It is easy to show that this is true in the movement itself. There is nothing there that is stable. All that appears to be stationary is only a block of movement, a formulation of energy at work which so affects our consciousness that it seems to be still, somewhat as the earth seems to us to be still, somewhat as a train in which we are travelling seems to be still in the midst of a rushing landscape. But is it equally true that underlying this movement, supporting it, there is nothing that is moveless and immutable? Is it true that existence consists only in the action of energy? Or is it not rather that energy is an output of Existence?

We see at once that if such an Existence is, it must be, like the Energy, infinite. Neither reason nor experience nor intuition nor imagination bears witness to us of the possibility of a final terminus. All end and beginning presuppose something beyond the end or beginning. An absolute end, an absolute beginning is not only a contradiction in terms, but a contradiction of the essence of things, a violence, a fiction. Infinity imposes itself upon the appearances of the finite by its ineffugable self-existence.

But this is infinity with regard to Time and Space, an eternal duration, interminable extension. The pure Reason goes farther and looking in its own colourless and austere light at Time and Space points out that these two are categories of our consciousness, conditions under which we arrange our perception of phenomenon. When we look at existence in itself, Time and Space disappear. If there is any extension, it is not a spatial but a psychological extension; if there is any duration, it is not a temporal but a psychological duration; and it is then easy to see that this extension and duration are only symbols which represent to the mind something not translatable into intellectual terms, an eternity which seems to us the same all-containing ever-new moment, an infinity which seems to us the same all-containing all-pervading point without magnitude. And this conflict of terms, so violent, yet accurately expressive of something we do perceive, shows that mind and speech have passed beyond their natural limits and are striving to express a Reality in which their own conventions and necessary oppositions disappear into an ineffable identity.

But is this a true record? May it not be that Time and Space so disappear merely because the existence we are regarding is a fiction of the intellect, a fantastic Nihil created by speech, which we strive to erect into a conceptual reality? We regard again that Existence-in-itself and we say, No. There is something behind the phenomenon not only infinite but indefinable. Of no phenomenon, of no totality of phenomena can we say that absolutely it is. Even if we reduce all phenomena to one fundamental, universal irreducible phenomenon of movement or energy, we get only an indefinable phenomenon. The very conception of movement carries with it the potentiality of repose and betrays itself as an activity of some existence; the very idea of energy in action carries with it the idea of energy abstaining from action; and an absolute energy not in action is simply and purely absolute existence. We have only these two alternatives, either an indefinable pure existence or an indefinable energy in action and, if the latter alone is true, without any stable base or cause, then the energy is a result and phenomenon generated by the action, the movement which alone is. We have then no Existence, or we have the Nihil of the Buddhists with existence as only an attribute of an eternal phenomenon, of Action, of Karma, of Movement. This, asserts the pure reason, leaves my perceptions unsatisfied, contradicts my fundamental seeing, and therefore cannot be. For it brings us to a last abruptly ceasing stair of an ascent which leaves the whole staircase without support, suspended in the Void.

If this indefinable, infinite, timeless, spaceless Existence is, it is necessarily a pure absolute. It cannot be summed up in any quantity or quantities, it cannot be composed of any quality or combination of qualities. It is not an aggregate of forms or a formal substratum of forms. If all forms, quantities, qualities were to disappear, this would remain. Existence without quantity, without quality, without form is not only conceivable, but it is the one thing we can conceive behind these phenomena. Necessarily, when we say it is without them, we mean that it exceeds them, that it is something into which they pass in such a way as to cease to be what we call form, quality, quantity and out of which they emerge as form, quality and quantity in the movement. They do not pass away into one form, one quality, one quantity which is the basis of all the rest, — for there is none such, — but into something which cannot be defined by any of these terms. So all things that are conditions and appearances of the movement pass into That from which they have come and there, so far as they exist, become something that can no longer be described by the terms that are appropriate to them in the movement. Therefore we say that the pure existence is an Absolute and in itself unknowable by our thought although we can go back to it in a supreme identity that transcends the terms of knowledge. The movement, on the contrary, is the field of the relative and yet by the very definition of the relative all things in the movement contain, are contained in and are the Absolute. The relation of the phenomena of Nature to the fundamental ether which is contained in them, constitutes them, contains them and yet is so different from them that entering into it they cease to be what they now are, is the illustration given by the Vedanta as most nearly representing this identity in difference between the Absolute and the relative.

Necessarily, when we speak of things passing into that from which they have come, we are using the language of our temporal consciousness and must guard ourselves against its illusions. The emergence of the movement from the Immutable is an eternal phenomenon and it is only because we cannot conceive it in that beginningless, endless, ever-new moment which is the eternity of the Timeless that our notions and perceptions are compelled to place it in a temporal eternity of successive duration to which are attached the ideas of an always recurrent beginning, middle and end.

But all this, it may be said, is valid only so long as we accept the concepts of pure reason and remain subject to them. But the concepts of reason have no obligatory force. We must judge of

existence not by what we mentally conceive, but by what we see
to exist. And the purest, freest form of insight into existence as
it is shows us nothing but movement. Two things alone exist,
movement in Space, movement in Time, the former objective,
the latter subjective. Extension is real, duration is real, Space
and Time are real. Even if we can go behind extension in Space
and perceive it as a psychological phenomenon, as an attempt of
the mind to make existence manageable by distributing the indivisible whole in a conceptual Space, yet we cannot go behind the
movement of succession and change in Time. For that is the very
stuff of our consciousness. We are and the world is a movement
that continually progresses and increases by the inclusion of all
the successions of the past in a present which represents itself
to us as the beginning of all the successions of the future, — a
beginning, a present that always eludes us because it is not, for it
has perished before it is born. What is, is the eternal, indivisible
succession of Time carrying on its stream a progressive movement of consciousness also indivisible.[2] Duration then, eternally
successive movement and change in Time, is the sole absolute.
Becoming is the only being.

In reality, this opposition of actual insight into being to the
conceptual fictions of the pure Reason is fallacious. If indeed
intuition in this matter were really opposed to intelligence, we
could not confidently support a merely conceptual reasoning
against fundamental insight. But this appeal to intuitive experience is incomplete. It is valid only so far as it proceeds and
it errs by stopping short of the integral experience. So long as
the intuition fixes itself only upon that which we become, we see
ourselves as a continual progression of movement and change in
consciousness in the eternal succession of Time. We are the river,
the flame of the Buddhist illustration. But there is a supreme

---

[2] Indivisible in the totality of the movement. Each moment of Time or Consciousness
may be considered as separate from its predecessor and successor, each successive action
of Energy as a new quantum or new creation; but this does not abrogate continuity
without which there would be no duration of Time or coherence of consciousness. A
man's steps as he walks or runs or leaps are separate, but there is something that takes
the steps and makes the movement continuous.

experience and supreme intuition by which we go back behind our surface self and find that this becoming, change, succession are only a mode of our being and that there is that in us which is not involved at all in the becoming. Not only can we have the intuition of this that is stable and eternal in us, not only can we have the glimpse of it in experience behind the veil of continually fleeting becomings, but we can draw back into it and live in it entirely, so effecting an entire change in our external life, and in our attitude, and in our action upon the movement of the world. And this stability in which we can so live is precisely that which the pure Reason has already given us, although it can be arrived at without reasoning at all, without knowing previously what it is, — it is pure existence, eternal, infinite, indefinable, not affected by the succession of Time, not involved in the extension of Space, beyond form, quantity, quality, — Self only and absolute.

The pure existent is then a fact and no mere concept; it is the fundamental reality. But, let us hasten to add, the movement, the energy, the becoming are also a fact, also a reality. The supreme intuition and its corresponding experience may correct the other, may go beyond, may suspend, but do not abolish it. We have therefore two fundamental facts of pure existence and of world-existence, a fact of Being, a fact of Becoming. To deny one or the other is easy; to recognise the facts of consciousness and find out their relation is the true and fruitful wisdom.

Stability and movement, we must remember, are only our psychological representations of the Absolute, even as are oneness and multitude. The Absolute is beyond stability and movement as it is beyond unity and multiplicity. But it takes its eternal poise in the one and the stable and whirls round itself infinitely, inconceivably, securely in the moving and multitudinous. World-existence is the ecstatic dance of Shiva which multiplies the body of the God numberlessly to the view: it leaves that white existence precisely where and what it was, ever is and ever will be; its sole absolute object is the joy of the dancing.

But as we cannot describe or think out the Absolute in itself, beyond stability and movement, beyond unity and multitude, —

nor is that at all our business, — we must accept the double
fact, admit both Shiva and Kali and seek to know what is this
measureless Movement in Time and Space with regard to that
timeless and spaceless pure Existence, one and stable, to which
measure and measurelessness are inapplicable. We have seen
what pure Reason, intuition and experience have to say about
pure Existence, about Sat; what have they to say about Force,
about Movement, about Shakti?

And the first thing we have to ask ourselves is whether
that Force is simply force, simply an unintelligent energy of
movement or whether the consciousness which seems to emerge
out of it in this material world we live in, is not merely one of
its phenomenal results but rather its own true and secret nature.
In Vedantic terms, is Force simply Prakriti, only a movement
of action and process, or is Prakriti really power of Chit, in
its nature force of creative self-conscience? On this essential
problem all the rest hinges.

Chapter X

Conscious Force

They beheld the self-force of the Divine Being deep hidden by
its own conscious modes of working.
Swetaswatara Upanishad.[1]

This is he that is awake in those who sleep.
Katha Upanishad.[2]

ALL PHENOMENAL existence resolves itself into Force,
into a movement of energy that assumes more or less
material, more or less gross or subtle forms for self-
presentation to its own experience. In the ancient images by
which human thought attempted to make this origin and law
of being intelligible and real to itself, this infinite existence of
Force was figured as a sea, initially at rest and therefore free from
forms, but the first disturbance, the first initiation of movement
necessitates the creation of forms and is the seed of a universe.

Matter is the presentation of force which is most easily
intelligible to our intelligence, moulded as it is by contacts in
Matter to which a mind involved in material brain gives the
response. The elementary state of material Force is, in the view of
the old Indian physicists, a condition of pure material extension
in Space of which the peculiar property is vibration typified to
us by the phenomenon of sound. But vibration in this state of
ether is not sufficient to create forms. There must first be some
obstruction in the flow of the Force ocean, some contraction
and expansion, some interplay of vibrations, some impinging of
force upon force so as to create a beginning of fixed relations
and mutual effects. Material Force modifying its first ethereal

---

[1] I. 3.   [2] II. 2. 8.

status assumes a second, called in the old language the aerial, of which the special property is contact between force and force, contact that is the basis of all material relations. Still we have not as yet real forms but only varying forces. A sustaining principle is needed. This is provided by a third self-modification of the primitive Force of which the principle of light, electricity, fire and heat is for us the characteristic manifestation. Even then, we can have forms of force preserving their own character and peculiar action, but not stable forms of Matter. A fourth state characterised by diffusion and a first medium of permanent attractions and repulsions, termed picturesquely water or the liquid state, and a fifth of cohesion, termed earth or the solid state, complete the necessary elements.

All forms of Matter of which we are aware, all physical things even to the most subtle, are built up by the combination of these five elements. Upon them also depends all our sensible experience; for by reception of vibration comes the sense of sound; by contact of things in a world of vibrations of Force the sense of touch; by the action of light in the forms hatched, outlined, sustained by the force of light and fire and heat the sense of sight; by the fourth element the sense of taste; by the fifth the sense of smell. All is essentially response to vibratory contacts between force and force. In this way the ancient thinkers bridged the gulf between pure Force and its final modifications and satisfied the difficulty which prevents the ordinary human mind from understanding how all these forms which are to his senses so real, solid and durable can be in truth only temporary phenomena and a thing like pure energy, to the senses non-existent, intangible and almost incredible, can be the one permanent cosmic reality.

The problem of consciousness is not solved by this theory; for it does not explain how the contact of vibrations of Force should give rise to conscious sensations. The Sankhyas or analytic thinkers posited therefore behind these five elements two principles which they called Mahat and Ahankara, principles which are really non-material; for the first is nothing but the vast cosmic principle of Force and the other the divisional principle of Ego-formation. Nevertheless, these two principles, as also the principle of intelligence, become active in consciousness not by virtue of Force itself, but by virtue of an inactive Conscious-Soul or souls in which its activities are reflected and by that reflection assume the hue of consciousness.

Such is the explanation of things offered by the school of Indian philosophy which comes nearest to the modern materialistic ideas and which carried the idea of a mechanical or unconscious Force in Nature as far as was possible to a seriously reflective Indian mind. Whatever its defects, its main idea was so indisputable that it came to be generally accepted. However the phenomenon of consciousness may be explained, whether Nature be an inert impulse or a conscious principle, it is certainly Force; the principle of things is a formative movement of energies, all forms are born of meeting and mutual adaptation between unshaped forces, all sensation and action is a response of something in a form of Force to the contacts of other forms of Force. This is the world as we experience it and from this experience we must always start.

Physical analysis of Matter by modern Science has come to the same general conclusion, even if a few last doubts still linger. Intuition and experience confirm this concord of Science and Philosophy. Pure reason finds in it the satisfaction of its own essential conceptions. For even in the view of the world as essentially an act of consciousness, an act is implied and in the act movement of Force, play of Energy. This also, when we examine from within our own experience, proves to be the fundamental nature of the world. All our activities are the play of the triple force of the old philosophies, knowledge-force, desire-force, action-force, and all these prove to be really three streams of one original and identical Power, Adya Shakti. Even our states of rest are only equable state or equilibrium of the play of her movement.

Movement of Force being admitted as the whole nature of the Cosmos, two questions arise. And first, how did this movement come to take place at all in the bosom of existence? If we suppose it to be not only eternal but the very essence of all existence, the question does not arise. But we have negatived this theory. We are aware of an existence which is not compelled by the movement. How then does this movement alien to its eternal repose come to take place in it? by what cause? by what possibility? by what mysterious impulsion?

The answer most approved by the ancient Indian mind was that Force is inherent in Existence. Shiva and Kali, Brahman and Shakti are one and not two who are separable. Force inherent in existence may be at rest or it may be in motion, but when it is at rest, it exists none the less and is not abolished, diminished or in any way essentially altered. This reply is so entirely rational and in accordance with the nature of things that we need not hesitate to accept it. For it is impossible, because contradictory of reason, to suppose that Force is a thing alien to the one and infinite existence and entered into it from outside or was non-existent and arose in it at some point in Time. Even the Illusionist theory must admit that Maya, the power of self-illusion in Brahman, is potentially eternal in eternal Being and then the sole question is its manifestation or non-manifestation. The Sankhya also asserts the eternal coexistence of Prakriti and Purusha, Nature and Conscious-Soul, and the alternative states of rest or equilibrium of Prakriti and movement or disturbance of equilibrium.

But since Force is thus inherent in existence and it is the nature of Force to have this double or alternative potentiality of rest and movement, that is to say, of self-concentration in Force and self-diffusion in Force, the question of the how of the movement, its possibility, initiating impulsion or impelling cause does not arise. For we can easily, then, conceive that this potentiality must translate itself either as an alternative rhythm of rest and movement succeeding each other in Time or else as an eternal self-concentration of Force in immutable existence with a superficial play of movement, change and formation like the rising and falling of waves on the surface of the ocean. And this superficial play — we are necessarily speaking in inadequate images — may be either coeval with the self-concentration and itself also eternal or it may begin and end in Time and be resumed by a sort of constant rhythm; it is then not eternal in continuity but eternal in recurrence.

The problem of the how thus eliminated, there presents itself the question of the why. Why should this possibility of a play of movement of Force translate itself at all? why should not Force of existence remain eternally concentrated in itself, infinite, free from all variation and formation? This question also does not arise if we assume Existence to be non-conscious and consciousness only a development of material energy which we wrongly suppose to be immaterial. For then we can say simply that this rhythm is the nature of Force in existence and there is absolutely no reason to seek for a why, a cause, an initial motive or a final purpose for that which is in its nature eternally self-existent. We cannot put that question to eternal self-existence and ask it either why it exists or how it came into existence; neither can we put it to self-force of existence and its inherent nature of impulsion to movement. All that we can then inquire into is its manner of self-manifestation, its principles of movement and formation, its process of evolution. Both Existence and Force being inert, — inert status and inert impulsion, — both of them unconscious and unintelligent, there cannot be any purpose or final goal in evolution or any original cause or intention.

But if we suppose or find Existence to be conscious Being, the problem arises. We may indeed suppose a conscious Being which is subject to its nature of Force, compelled by it and without option as to whether it shall manifest in the universe or remain unmanifest. Such is the cosmic God of the Tantriks and the Mayavadins who is subject to Shakti or Maya, Purusha involved in Maya or controlled by Shakti. But it is obvious that such a God is not the supreme infinite Existence with which we have started. Admittedly, it is only a formulation of Brahman in the cosmos by the Brahman which is itself logically anterior to Shakti or Maya and takes her back into its transcendental being when she ceases from her works. In a conscious existence which is absolute, independent of its formations, not determined by its works, we must suppose an inherent freedom to manifest or not to manifest the potentiality of movement. A Brahman compelled by Prakriti is not Brahman, but an inert Infinite with an active content in it more powerful than the continent, a conscious holder of Force of whom his Force is master. If we say that it is compelled by itself as Force, by its own nature, we do not get rid of the contradiction, the evasion of our first postulate. We have got back to an Existence which is really nothing but Force, Force at rest or in movement, absolute Force perhaps, but not absolute Being.

It is then necessary to examine into the relation between Force and Consciousness. But what do we mean by the latter term? Ordinarily we mean by it our first obvious idea of a mental waking consciousness such as is possessed by the human being during the major part of his bodily existence, when he is not asleep, stunned or otherwise deprived of his physical and superficial methods of sensation. In this sense it is plain enough that consciousness is the exception and not the rule in the order of the material universe. We ourselves do not always possess it. But this vulgar and shallow idea of the nature of consciousness, though it still colours our ordinary thought and associations, must now definitely disappear out of philosophical thinking. For we know that there is something in us which is conscious when we sleep, when we are stunned or drugged or in a swoon, in all apparently unconscious states of our physical being. Not only so, but we may now be sure that the old thinkers were right when they declared that even in our waking state what we call then our consciousness is only a small selection from our entire conscious being. It is a superficies, it is not even the whole of our mentality. Behind it, much vaster than it, there is a subliminal or subconscient mind which is the greater part of ourselves and contains heights and profundities which no man has yet measured or fathomed. This knowledge gives us a starting-point for the true science of Force and its workings; it delivers us definitely from circumscription by the material and from the illusion of the obvious.

Materialism indeed insists that, whatever the extension of consciousness, it is a material phenomenon inseparable from our physical organs and not their utiliser but their result. This orthodox contention, however, is no longer able to hold the field against the tide of increasing knowledge. Its explanations are becoming more and more inadequate and strained. It is becoming always clearer that not only does the capacity of our total consciousness far exceed that of our organs, the senses, the nerves, the brain, but that even for our ordinary thought and consciousness these organs are only their habitual instruments and not their generators. Consciousness uses the brain which its upward strivings have produced, brain has not produced nor does it use the consciousness. There are even abnormal instances which go to prove that our organs are not entirely indispensable instruments, — that the heart-beats are not absolutely essential to life, any more than is breathing, nor the organised brain-cells to thought. Our physical organism no more causes or explains thought and consciousness than the construction of an engine causes or explains the motive-power of steam or electricity. The force is anterior, not the physical instrument.

Momentous logical consequences follow. In the first place we may ask whether, since even mental consciousness exists where we see inanimation and inertia, it is not possible that even in material objects a universal subconscient mind is present although unable to act or communicate itself to its surfaces for want of organs. Is the material state an emptiness of consciousness, or is it not rather only a sleep of consciousness — even though from the point of view of evolution an original and not an intermediate sleep? And by sleep the human example teaches us that we mean not a suspension of consciousness, but its gathering inward away from conscious physical response to the impacts of external things. And is not this what all existence is that has not yet developed means of outward communication with the external physical world? Is there not a Conscious Soul, a Purusha who wakes for ever even in all that sleeps?

We may go farther. When we speak of subconscious mind, we should mean by the phrase a thing not different from the outer mentality, but only acting below the surface, unknown to the waking man, in the same sense if perhaps with a deeper plunge and a larger scope. But the phenomena of the subliminal self far exceed the limits of any such definition. It includes an action not only immensely superior in capacity, but quite different in kind from what we know as mentality in our waking self. We have therefore a right to suppose that there is a superconscient in us as well as a subconscient, a range of conscious faculties and therefore an organisation of consciousness which rise high above that psychological stratum to which we give the name of mentality. And since the subliminal self in us thus rises in superconscience above mentality, may it not also sink in subconscience below mentality? Are there not in us and in the world forms of consciousness which are submental, to which we can give the name of vital and physical consciousness? If so, we must suppose in the plant and the metal also a force to which we can give the name of consciousness although it is not the human or animal mentality for which we have hitherto preserved the monopoly of that description.

Not only is this probable but, if we will consider things dispassionately, it is certain. In ourselves there is such a vital consciousness which acts in the cells of the body and the automatic vital functions so that we go through purposeful movements and obey attractions and repulsions to which our mind is a stranger. In animals this vital consciousness is an even more important factor. In plants it is intuitively evident. The seekings and shrinkings of the plant, its pleasure and pain, its sleep and its wakefulness and all that strange life whose truth an Indian scientist has brought to light by rigidly scientific methods, are all movements of consciousness, but, as far as we can see, not of mentality. There is then a sub-mental, a vital consciousness which has precisely the same initial reactions as the mental, but is different in the constitution of its self-experience, even as that which is superconscient is in the constitution of its self-experience different from the mental being.

Does the range of what we can call consciousness cease with the plant, with that in which we recognise the existence of a sub-animal life? If so, we must then suppose that there is a force of life and consciousness originally alien to Matter which has yet entered into and occupied Matter, — perhaps from another world.[3] For whence, otherwise, can it have come? The ancient thinkers believed in the existence of such other worlds, which perhaps sustain life and consciousness in ours or even call it out by their pressure, but do not create it by their entry. Nothing can evolve out of Matter which is not therein already contained.

But there is no reason to suppose that the gamut of life and consciousness fails and stops short in that which seems to us purely material. The development of recent research and thought seems to point to a sort of obscure beginning of life and perhaps a sort of inert or suppressed consciousness in the metal and in the earth and in other "inanimate" forms, or at least the first stuff of what becomes consciousness in us may be there. Only while in the plant we can dimly recognise and conceive the thing that I have called vital consciousness, the consciousness of Matter, of the inert form, is difficult indeed for us to understand or imagine, and what we find it difficult to understand or imagine we consider it our right to deny. Nevertheless, when one has pursued consciousness so far into the depths, it becomes incredible that there should be this sudden gulf in Nature. Thought has a right to suppose a unity where that unity is confessed by all other classes of phenomena and in one class only, not denied, but merely more concealed than in others. And if we suppose the unity to be unbroken, we then arrive at the existence of consciousness in all forms of the Force which is at work in the world. Even if there be no conscient or superconscient Purusha inhabiting all forms, yet is there in those forms a conscious force of being of which even their outer parts overtly or inertly partake.

Necessarily, in such a view, the word consciousness changes its meaning. It is no longer synonymous with mentality but indicates a self-aware force of existence of which mentality is a middle term; below mentality it sinks into vital and material movements which are for us subconscient; above, it rises into

---

[3] The curious speculation is now current that Life entered earth not from another world, but from another planet. To the thinker that would explain nothing. The essential question is how Life comes into Matter at all and not how it enters into the matter of a particular planet.

the supramental which is for us the superconscient. But in all it is one and the same thing organising itself differently. This is, once more, the Indian conception of Chit which, as energy, creates the worlds. Essentially, we arrive at that unity which materialistic Science perceives from the other end when it asserts that Mind cannot be another force than Matter, but must be merely development and outcome of material energy. Indian thought at its deepest affirms on the other hand that Mind and Matter are rather different grades of the same energy, different organisations of one conscious Force of Existence.

But what right have we to assume consciousness as the just description for this Force? For consciousness implies some kind of intelligence, purposefulness, self-knowledge, even though they may not take the forms habitual to our mentality. Even from this point of view everything supports rather than contradicts the idea of a universal conscious Force. We see, for instance, in the animal, operations of a perfect purposefulness and an exact, indeed a scientifically minute knowledge which are quite beyond the capacities of the animal mentality and which man himself can only acquire by long culture and education and even then uses with a much less sure rapidity. We are entitled to see in this general fact the proof of a conscious Force at work in the animal and the insect which is more intelligent, more purposeful, more aware of its intention, its ends, its means, its conditions than the highest mentality yet manifested in any individual form on earth. And in the operations of inanimate Nature we find the same pervading characteristic of a supreme hidden intelligence, "hidden in the modes of its own workings".

The only argument against a conscious and intelligent source for this purposeful work, this work of intelligence, of selection, adaptation and seeking is that large element in Nature's operations to which we give the name of waste. But obviously this is an objection based on the limitations of our human intellect which seeks to impose its own particular rationality, good enough for limited human ends, on the general operations of the World-Force. We see only part of Nature's purpose and all that does not subserve that part we call waste. Yet even our own human action is full of an apparent waste, so appearing from the individual point of view, which yet, we may be sure, subserves well enough the large and universal purpose of things. That part of her intention which we can detect, Nature gets done surely enough in spite of, perhaps really by virtue of her apparent waste. We may well trust to her in the rest which we do not yet detect.

For the rest, it is impossible to ignore the drive of set purpose, the guidance of apparent blind tendency, the sure eventual or immediate coming to the target sought, which characterise the operations of World-Force in the animal, in the plant, in inanimate things. So long as Matter was Alpha and Omega to the scientific mind, the reluctance to admit intelligence as the mother of intelligence was an honest scruple. But now it is no more than an outworn paradox to affirm the emergence of human consciousness, intelligence and mastery out of an unintelligent, blindly driving unconsciousness in which no form or substance of them previously existed. Man's consciousness can be nothing else than a form of Nature's consciousness. It is there in other involved forms below Mind, it emerges in Mind, it shall ascend into yet superior forms beyond Mind. For the Force that builds the worlds is a conscious Force, the Existence which manifests itself in them is conscious Being and a perfect emergence of its potentialities in form is the sole object which we can rationally conceive for its manifestation of this world of forms.

Chapter XI

Delight of Existence: The Problem

For who could live or breathe if there were not this delight of existence as the ether in which we dwell?

From Delight all these beings are born, by Delight they exist and grow, to Delight they return.

Taittiriya Upanishad.[1]

BUT EVEN if we accept this pure Existence, this Brahman, this Sat as the absolute beginning, end and continent of things and in Brahman an inherent self-consciousness inseparable from its being and throwing itself out as a force of movement of consciousness which is creative of forces, forms and worlds, we have yet no answer to the question "Why should Brahman, perfect, absolute, infinite, needing nothing, desiring nothing, at all throw out force of consciousness to create in itself these worlds of forms?" For we have put aside the solution that it is compelled by its own nature of Force to create, obliged by its own potentiality of movement and formation to move into forms. It is true that it has this potentiality, but it is not limited, bound or compelled by it; it is free. If, then, being free to move or remain eternally still, to throw itself into forms or retain the potentiality of form in itself, it indulges its power of movement and formation, it can be only for one reason, for delight.

This primary, ultimate and eternal Existence, as seen by the Vedantins, is not merely bare existence, or a conscious existence whose consciousness is crude force or power; it is a conscious existence the very term of whose being, the very term of whose consciousness is bliss. As in absolute existence there can be no

---

[1] II. 7; III. 6.

nothingness, no night of inconscience, no deficiency, that is to say, no failure of Force, — for if there were any of these things, it would not be absolute, — so also there can be no suffering, no negation of delight. Absoluteness of conscious existence is illimitable bliss of conscious existence; the two are only different phrases for the same thing. All illimitableness, all infinity, all absoluteness is pure delight. Even our relative humanity has this experience that all dissatisfaction means a limit, an obstacle, — satisfaction comes by realisation of something withheld, by the surpassing of the limit, the overcoming of the obstacle. This is because our original being is the absolute in full possession of its infinite and illimitable self-consciousness and self-power; a self-possession whose other name is self-delight. And in proportion as the relative touches upon that self-possession, it moves towards satisfaction, touches delight.

The self-delight of Brahman is not limited, however, by the still and motionless possession of its absolute self-being. Just as its force of consciousness is capable of throwing itself into forms infinitely and with an endless variation, so also its self-delight is capable of movement, of variation, of revelling in that infinite flux and mutability of itself represented by numberless teeming universes. To loose forth and enjoy this infinite movement and variation of its self-delight is the object of its extensive or creative play of Force.

In other words, that which has thrown itself out into forms is a triune Existence-Consciousness-Bliss, Sachchidananda, whose consciousness is in its nature a creative or rather a self-expressive Force capable of infinite variation in phenomenon and form of its self-conscious being and endlessly enjoying the delight of that variation. It follows that all things that exist are what they are as terms of that existence, terms of that conscious force, terms of that delight of being. Just as we find all things to be mutable forms of one immutable being, finite results of one infinite force, so we shall find that all things are variable self-expression of one invariable and all-embracing delight of self-existence. In everything that is, dwells the conscious force and it exists and is what it is by virtue of that conscious force; so also in everything that is there is the delight of existence and it exists and is what it is by virtue of that delight.

This ancient Vedantic theory of cosmic origin is immediately confronted in the human mind by two powerful contradictions, the emotional and sensational consciousness of pain and the ethical problem of evil. For if the world be an expression of Sachchidananda, not only of existence that is conscious-force, — for that can easily be admitted, — but of existence that is also infinite self-delight, how are we to account for the universal presence of grief, of suffering, of pain? For this world appears to us rather as a world of suffering than as a world of the delight of existence. Certainly, that view of the world is an exaggeration, an error of perspective. If we regard it dispassionately and with a sole view to accurate and unemotional appreciation, we shall find that the sum of the pleasure of existence far exceeds the sum of the pain of existence, — appearances and individual cases to the contrary notwithstanding, — and that the active or passive, surface or underlying pleasure of existence is the normal state of nature, pain a contrary occurrence temporarily suspending or overlaying that normal state. But for that very reason the lesser sum of pain affects us more intensely and often looms larger than the greater sum of pleasure; precisely because the latter is normal, we do not treasure it, hardly even observe it unless it intensifies into some acuter form of itself, into a wave of happiness, a crest of joy or ecstasy. It is these things that we call delight and seek and the normal satisfaction of existence which is always there regardless of event and particular cause or object, affects us as something neutral which is neither pleasure nor pain. It is there, a great practical fact, for without it there would not be the universal and overpowering instinct of self-preservation, but it is not what we seek and therefore we do not enter it into our balance of emotional and sensational profit and loss. In that balance we enter only positive pleasures on one side and discomfort and pain on the other; pain affects us more intensely because it is abnormal to our being, contrary to our natural tendency and is experienced as an outrage on our existence, an offence and external attack on what we are and seek to be.

Nevertheless the abnormality of pain or its greater or lesser sum does not affect the philosophical issue; greater or less, its mere presence constitutes the whole problem. All being Sachchidananda, how can pain and suffering at all exist? This, the real problem, is often farther confused by a false issue starting from the idea of a personal extracosmic God and a partial issue, the ethical difficulty.

Sachchidananda, it may be reasoned, is God, is a conscious Being who is the author of existence; how then can God have created a world in which He inflicts suffering on His creatures, sanctions pain, permits evil? God being All-Good, who created pain and evil? If we say that pain is a trial and an ordeal, we do not solve the moral problem, we arrive at an immoral or nonmoral God, — an excellent world-mechanist perhaps, a cunning psychologist, but not a God of Good and of Love whom we can worship, only a God of Might to whose law we must submit or whose caprice we may hope to propitiate. For one who invents torture as a means of test or ordeal, stands convicted either of deliberate cruelty or of moral insensibility and, if a moral being at all, is inferior to the highest instinct of his own creatures. And if to escape this moral difficulty, we say that pain is an inevitable result and natural punishment of moral evil, — an explanation which will not even square with the facts of life unless we admit the theory of Karma and rebirth by which the soul suffers now for antenatal sins in other bodies, — we still do not escape the very root of the ethical problem, — who created or why or whence was created that moral evil which entails the punishment of pain and suffering? And seeing that moral evil is in reality a form of mental disease or ignorance, who or what created this law or inevitable connection which punishes a mental disease or act of ignorance by a recoil so terrible, by tortures often so extreme and monstrous? The inexorable law of Karma is irreconcilable with a supreme moral and personal Deity, and therefore the clear logic of Buddha denied the existence of any free and all-governing personal God; all personality he declared to be a creation of ignorance and subject to Karma.

In truth, the difficulty thus sharply presented arises only if we assume the existence of an extracosmic personal God, not Himself the universe, one who has created good and evil, pain and suffering for His creatures, but Himself stands above and unaffected by them, watching, ruling, doing His will with a suffering and struggling world or, if not doing His will, if allowing the world to be driven by an inexorable law, unhelped by Him or inefficiently helped, then not God, not omnipotent, not all-good and all-loving. On no theory of an extracosmic moral God, can evil and suffering be explained, — the creation of evil and suffering, — except by an unsatisfactory subterfuge which avoids the question at issue instead of answering it or a plain or implied Manicheanism which practically annuls the Godhead in attempting to justify its ways or excuse its works. But such a God is not the Vedantic Sachchidananda. Sachchidananda of the Vedanta is one existence without a second; all that is, is He. If then evil and suffering exist, it is He that bears the evil and suffering in the creature in whom He has embodied Himself. The problem then changes entirely. The question is no longer how came God to create for His creatures a suffering and evil of which He is Himself incapable and therefore immune, but how came the sole and infinite Existence-Consciousness-Bliss to admit into itself that which is not bliss, that which seems to be its positive negation.

Half of the moral difficulty — that difficulty in its one unanswerable form disappears. It no longer arises, can no longer be put. Cruelty to others, I remaining immune or even participating in their sufferings by subsequent repentance or belated pity, is one thing; self-infliction of suffering, I being the sole existence, is quite another. Still the ethical difficulty may be brought back in a modified form; All-Delight being necessarily all-good and all-love, how can evil and suffering exist in Sachchidananda, since he is not mechanical existence, but free and conscious being, free to condemn and reject evil and suffering? We have to recognise that the issue so stated is also a false issue because it applies the terms of a partial statement as if they were applicable to the whole. For the ideas of good and of love which we thus bring into the concept of the All-Delight spring from a dualistic and divisional conception of things; they are based entirely on the relations between creature and creature, yet we persist in applying them to a problem which starts, on the contrary, from the assumption of One who is all. We have to see first how the problem appears or how it can be solved in its original purity, on the basis of unity in difference; only then can we safely deal with its parts and its developments, such as the relations between creature and creature on the basis of division and duality.

We have to recognise, if we thus view the whole, not limiting ourselves to the human difficulty and the human standpoint, that we do not live in an ethical world. The attempt of human thought to force an ethical meaning into the whole of Nature is one of those acts of wilful and obstinate self-confusion, one of those pathetic attempts of the human being to read himself, his limited habitual human self into all things and judge them from the standpoint he has personally evolved, which most effectively prevent him from arriving at real knowledge and complete sight. Material Nature is not ethical; the law which governs it is a co-ordination of fixed habits which take no cognisance of good and evil, but only of force that creates, force that arranges and preserves, force that disturbs and destroys impartially, non-ethically, according to the secret Will in it, according to the mute satisfaction of that Will in its own self-formations and self-dissolutions. Animal or vital Nature is also non-ethical, although as it progresses it manifests the crude material out of which the higher animal evolves the ethical impulse. We do not blame the tiger because it slays and devours its prey any more than we blame the storm because it destroys or the fire because it tortures and kills; neither does the conscious-force in the storm, the fire or the tiger blame or condemn itself. Blame and condemnation, or rather self-blame and self-condemnation, are the beginning of true ethics. When we blame others without applying the same law to ourselves, we are not speaking with a true ethical judgment, but only applying the language ethics has evolved for us to an emotional impulse of recoil from or dislike of that which displeases or hurts us.

This recoil or dislike is the primary origin of ethics, but is not itself ethical. The fear of the deer for the tiger, the rage of the strong creature against its assailant is a vital recoil of the individual delight of existence from that which threatens it. In the progress of the mentality it refines itself into repugnance, dislike, disapproval. Disapproval of that which threatens and hurts us, approval of that which flatters and satisfies refine into the conception of good and evil to oneself, to the community, to others than ourselves, to other communities than ours, and finally into the general approval of good, the general disapproval of evil. But, throughout, the fundamental nature of the thing remains the same. Man desires self-expression, self-development, in other words, the progressing play in himself of the conscious-force of existence; that is his fundamental delight. Whatever hurts that self-expression, self-development, satisfaction of his progressing self, is for him evil; whatever helps, confirms, raises, aggrandises, ennobles it is his good. Only, his conception of the self-development changes, becomes higher and wider, begins to exceed his limited personality, to embrace others, to embrace all in its scope.

In other words, ethics is a stage in evolution. That which is common to all stages is the urge of Sachchidananda towards self-expression. This urge is at first non-ethical, then infra-ethical in the animal, then in the intelligent animal even anti-ethical for it permits us to approve hurt done to others which we disapprove when done to ourselves. In this respect man even now is only half-ethical. And just as all below us is infra-ethical, so there may be that above us whither we shall eventually arrive, which is supra-ethical, has no need of ethics. The ethical impulse and attitude, so all-important to humanity, is a means by which it struggles out of the lower harmony and universality based upon inconscience and broken up by Life into individual discords towards a higher harmony and universality based upon conscient oneness with all existences. Arriving at that goal, this means will no longer be necessary or even possible, since the qualities and oppositions on which it depends will naturally dissolve and disappear in the final reconciliation.

If, then, the ethical standpoint applies only to a temporary though all-important passage from one universality to another, we cannot apply it to the total solution of the problem of the universe, but can only admit it as one element in that solution. To do otherwise is to run into the peril of falsifying all the facts of the universe, all the meaning of the evolution behind and beyond us in order to suit a temporary outlook and a half-evolved view of the utility of things. The world has three layers, infra-ethical, ethical and supra-ethical. We have to find that which is common to all; for only so can we resolve the problem.

That which is common to all is, we have seen, the satisfaction of conscious-force of existence developing itself into forms and seeking in that development its delight. From that satisfaction or delight of self-existence it evidently began; for it is that which is normal to it, to which it clings, which it makes its base; but it seeks new forms of itself and in the passage to higher forms there intervenes the phenomenon of pain and suffering which seems to contradict the fundamental nature of its being. This and this alone is the root-problem.

How shall we solve it? Shall we say that Sachchidananda is not the beginning and end of things, but the beginning and end is Nihil, an impartial void, itself nothing but containing all potentialities of existence or non-existence, consciousness or non-consciousness, delight or undelight? We may accept this answer if we choose; but although we seek thereby to explain everything, we have really explained nothing, we have only included everything. A Nothing which is full of all potentialities is the most complete opposition of terms and things possible and we have therefore only explained a minor contradiction by a major, by driving the self-contradiction of things to their maximum. Nihil is the void, where there can be no potentialities; an impartial indeterminate of all potentialities is Chaos, and all that we have done is to put Chaos into the Void without explaining how it got there. Let us return, then, to our original conception of Sachchidananda and see whether on that foundation a completer solution is not possible.

We must first make it clear to ourselves that just as when we speak of universal consciousness we mean something different

from, more essential and wider than the waking mental consciousness of the human being, so also when we speak of universal delight of existence we mean something different from,
more essential and wider than the ordinary emotional and sensational pleasure of the individual human creature. Pleasure,
joy and delight, as man uses the words, are limited and occasional movements which depend on certain habitual causes and
emerge, like their opposites pain and grief which are equally limited and occasional movements, from a background other than
themselves. Delight of being is universal, illimitable and self-
existent, not dependent on particular causes, the background of
all backgrounds, from which pleasure, pain and other more neutral experiences emerge. When delight of being seeks to realise
itself as delight of becoming, it moves in the movement of force
and itself takes different forms of movement of which pleasure
and pain are positive and negative currents. Subconscient in
Matter, superconscient beyond Mind this delight seeks in Mind
and Life to realise itself by emergence in the becoming, in the
increasing self-consciousness of the movement. Its first phenomena are dual and impure, move between the poles of pleasure
and pain, but it aims at its self-revelation in the purity of a
supreme delight of being which is self-existent and independent
of objects and causes. Just as Sachchidananda moves towards the
realisation of the universal existence in the individual and of the
form-exceeding consciousness in the form of body and mind,
so it moves towards the realisation of universal, self-existent
and objectless delight in the flux of particular experiences and
objects. Those objects we now seek as stimulating causes of a
transient pleasure and satisfaction; free, possessed of self, we
shall not seek but shall possess them as reflectors rather than
causes of a delight which eternally exists.

   In the egoistic human being, the mental person emergent out
of the dim shell of matter, delight of existence is neutral, semi-
latent, still in the shadow of the subconscious, hardly more than
a concealed soil of plenty covered by desire with a luxuriant
growth of poisonous weeds and hardly less poisonous flowers, the pains and pleasures of our egoistic existence. When the

divine conscious-force working secretly in us has devoured these growths of desire, when in the image of the Rig Veda the fire of God has burnt up the shoots of earth, that which is concealed at the roots of these pains and pleasures, their cause and secret being, the sap of delight in them, will emerge in new forms not of desire, but of self-existent satisfaction which will replace mortal pleasure by the Immortal's ecstasy. And this transformation is possible because these growths of sensation and emotion are in their essential being, the pains no less than the pleasures, that delight of existence which they seek but fail to reveal, — fail because of division, ignorance of self and egoism.

Chapter XII

Delight of Existence: The Solution

The name of That is the Delight; as the Delight we must worship and seek after It.   *Kena Upanishad.*[1]

IN THIS conception of an inalienable underlying delight of
existence of which all outward or surface sensations are a
positive, negative or neutral play, waves and foamings of
that infinite deep, we arrive at the true solution of the problem
we are examining. The self of things is an infinite indivisible
existence; of that existence the essential nature or power is an
infinite imperishable force of self-conscious being; and of that
self-consciousness the essential nature or knowledge of itself is,
again, an infinite inalienable delight of being. In formlessness
and in all forms, in the eternal awareness of infinite and indivisible being and in the multiform appearances of finite division
this self-existence preserves perpetually its self-delight. As in the
apparent inconscience of Matter our soul, growing out of its
bondage to its own superficial habit and particular mode of
self-conscious existence, discovers that infinite Conscious-Force
constant, immobile, brooding, so in the apparent non-sensation
of Matter it comes to discover and attune itself to an infinite
conscious Delight imperturbable, ecstatic, all-embracing. This
delight is its own delight, this self is its own self in all; but to our
ordinary view of self and things which awakes and moves only
upon surfaces, it remains hidden, profound, subconscious. And
as it is within all forms, so it is within all experiences whether
pleasant, painful or neutral. There too hidden, profound, subconscious, it is that which enables and compels things to remain

---

[1] IV. 6.

in existence. It is the reason of that clinging to existence, that overmastering will-to-be, translated vitally as the instinct of self-preservation, physically as the imperishability of matter, mentally as the sense of immortality which attends the formed existence through all its phases of self-development and of which even the occasional impulse of self-destruction is only a reverse form, an attraction to other state of being and a consequent recoil from present state of being. Delight is existence, Delight is the secret of creation, Delight is the root of birth, Delight is the cause of remaining in existence, Delight is the end of birth and that into which creation ceases. "From Ananda," says the Upanishad, "all existences are born, by Ananda they remain in being and increase, to Ananda they depart."

As we look at these three aspects of essential Being, one in reality, triune to our mental view, separable only in appearance, in the phenomena of the divided consciousness, we are able to put in their right place the divergent formulae of the old philosophies so that they unite and become one, ceasing from their agelong controversy. For if we regard world-existence only in its appearances and only in its relation to pure, infinite, indivisible, immutable Existence, we are entitled to regard it, describe it and realise it as Maya. Maya in its original sense meant a comprehending and containing consciousness capable of embracing, measuring and limiting and therefore formative; it is that which outlines, measures out, moulds forms in the formless, psychologises and seems to make knowable the Unknowable, geometrises and seems to make measurable the limitless. Later the word came from its original sense of knowledge, skill, intelligence to acquire a pejorative sense of cunning, fraud or illusion, and it is in the figure of an enchantment or illusion that it is used by the philosophical systems.

World is Maya. World is not unreal in the sense that it has no sort of existence; for even if it were only a dream of the Self, still it would exist in It as a dream, real to It in the present even while ultimately unreal. Nor ought we to say that world is unreal in the sense that it has no kind of eternal existence; for although particular worlds and particular forms may or do dissolve physically and return mentally from the consciousness of manifestation into the non-manifestation, yet Form in itself, World in itself are eternal. From the non-manifestation they return inevitably into manifestation; they have an eternal recurrence if not an eternal persistence, an eternal immutability in sum and foundation along with an eternal mutability in aspect and apparition. Nor have we any surety that there ever was or ever will be a period in Time when no form of universe, no play of being is represented to itself in the eternal Conscious-Being, but only an intuitive perception that the world that we know can and does appear from That and return into It perpetually.

Still world is Maya because it is not the essential truth of infinite existence, but only a creation of self-conscious being, — not a creation in the void, not a creation in nothing and out of nothing, but in the eternal Truth and out of the eternal Truth of that Self-being; its continent, origin and substance are the essential, real Existence, its forms are mutable formations of That to Its own conscious perception, determined by Its own creative conscious-force. They are capable of manifestation, capable of non-manifestation, capable of other-manifestation. We may, if we choose, call them therefore illusions of the infinite consciousness thus audaciously flinging back a shadow of our mental sense of subjection to error and incapacity upon that which, being greater than Mind, is beyond subjection to falsehood and illusion. But seeing that the essence and substance of Existence is not a lie and that all errors and deformations of our divided consciousness represent some truth of the indivisible self-conscious Existence, we can only say that the world is not essential truth of That, but phenomenal truth of Its free multiplicity and infinite superficial mutability and not truth of Its fundamental and immutable Unity.

If, on the other hand, we look at world-existence in relation to consciousness only and to force of consciousness, we may regard, describe and realise it as a movement of Force obeying some secret will or else some necessity imposed on it by the very existence of the Consciousness that possesses or regards it. It is then the play of Prakriti, the executive Force, to satisfy

Purusha, the regarding and enjoying Conscious-Being or it is the play of Purusha reflected in the movements of Force and with them identifying himself. World, then, is the play of the Mother of things moved to cast Herself for ever into infinite forms and avid of eternally outpouring experiences.

Again if we look at World-Existence rather in its relation to the self-delight of eternally existent being, we may regard, describe and realise it as Lila, the play, the child's joy, the poet's joy, the actor's joy, the mechanician's joy of the Soul of things eternally young, perpetually inexhaustible, creating and re-creating Himself in Himself for the sheer bliss of that self-creation, of that self-representation, — Himself the play, Himself the player, Himself the playground. These three generalisations of the play of existence in its relation to the eternal and stable, the immutable Sachchidananda, starting from the three conceptions of Maya, Prakriti and Lila and representing themselves in our philosophical systems as mutually contradictory philosophies, are in reality perfectly consistent with each other, complementary and necessary in their totality to an integral view of life and the world. The world of which we are a part is in its most obvious view a movement of Force; but that Force, when we penetrate its appearances, proves to be a constant and yet always mutable rhythm of creative consciousness casting up, projecting in itself phenomenal truths of its own infinite and eternal being; and this rhythm is in its essence, cause and purpose a play of the infinite delight of being ever busy with its own innumerable self-representations. This triple or triune view must be the starting-point for all our understanding of the universe.

Since, then, eternal and immutable delight of being moving out into infinite and variable delight of becoming is the root of the whole matter, we have to conceive one indivisible conscious Being behind all our experiences supporting them by its inalienable delight and effecting by its movement the variations of pleasure, pain and neutral indifference in our sensational existence. That is our real self; the mental being subject to the triple vibration can only be a representation of our real self put in front for the purposes of that sensational experience of things which is the first rhythm of our divided consciousness in its response and reaction to the multiple contacts of the universe. It is an imperfect response, a tangled and discordant rhythm preparing and preluding the full and unified play of the conscious Being in us; it is not the true and perfect symphony that may be ours if we can once enter into sympathy with the One in all variations and attune ourselves to the absolute and universal diapason.

If this view be right, then certain consequences inevitably impose themselves. In the first place, since in our depths we ourselves are that One, since in the reality of our being we are the indivisible All-Consciousness and therefore the inalienable All-Bliss, the disposition of our sensational experience in the three vibrations of pain, pleasure and indifference can only be a superficial arrangement created by that limited part of ourselves which is uppermost in our waking consciousness. Behind there must be something in us, — much vaster, profounder, truer than the superficial consciousness, — which takes delight impartially in all experiences; it is that delight which secretly supports the superficial mental being and enables it to persevere through all labours, sufferings and ordeals in the agitated movement of the Becoming. That which we call ourselves is only a trembling ray on the surface; behind is all the vast subconscient, the vast superconscient profiting by all these surface experiences and imposing them on its external self which it exposes as a sort of sensitive covering to the contacts of the world; itself veiled, it receives these contacts and assimilates them into the values of a truer, a profounder, a mastering and creative experience. Out of its depths it returns them to the surface in forms of strength, character, knowledge, impulsion whose roots are mysterious to us because our mind moves and quivers on the surface and has not learned to concentrate itself and live in the depths.

In our ordinary life this truth is hidden from us or only dimly glimpsed at times or imperfectly held and conceived. But if we learn to live within, we infallibly awaken to this presence within us which is our more real self, a presence profound, calm, joyous and puissant of which the world is not the master — a presence which, if it is not the Lord Himself, is the radiation of the Lord within. We are aware of it within supporting and helping the apparent and superficial self and smiling at its pleasures and pains as at the error and passion of a little child. And if we can go back into ourselves and identify ourselves, not with our superficial experience, but with that radiant penumbra of the Divine, we can live in that attitude towards the contacts of the world and, standing back in our entire consciousness from the pleasures and pains of the body, vital being and mind, possess them as experiences whose nature being superficial does not touch or impose itself on our core and real being. In the entirely expressive Sanskrit terms, there is an *ānandamaya* behind the *manomaya*, a vast Bliss-Self behind the limited mental self, and the latter is only a shadowy image and disturbed reflection of the former. The truth of ourselves lies within and not on the surface.

Again this triple vibration of pleasure, pain, indifference, being superficial, being an arrangement and result of our imperfect evolution, can have in it no absoluteness, no necessity. There is no real obligation on us to return to a particular contact, a particular response of pleasure, pain or neutral reaction, there is only an obligation of habit. We feel pleasure or pain in a particular contact because that is the habit our nature has formed, because that is the constant relation the recipient has established with the contact. It is within our competence to return quite the opposite response, pleasure where we used to have pain, pain where we used to have pleasure. It is equally within our competence to accustom the superficial being to return instead of the mechanical reactions of pleasure, pain and indifference that free reply of inalienable delight which is the constant experience of the true and vast Bliss-Self within us. And this is a greater conquest, a still deeper and more complete self-possession than a glad and detached reception in the depths of the habitual reactions on the surface. For it is no longer a mere acceptance without subjection, a free acquiescence in imperfect values of experience, but enables us to convert imperfect into perfect, false into true values, — the constant but veritable delight of the Spirit in things taking the place of the dualities experienced by the mental being.

In the things of the mind this pure habitual relativity of the reactions of pleasure and pain is not difficult to perceive. The nervous being in us, indeed, is accustomed to a certain fixedness, a false impression of absoluteness in these things. To it victory, success, honour, good fortune of all kinds are pleasant things in themselves, absolutely, and must produce joy as sugar must taste sweet; defeat, failure, disappointment, disgrace, evil fortune of all kinds are unpleasant things in themselves, absolutely, and must produce grief as wormwood must taste bitter. To vary these responses is to it a departure from fact, abnormal and morbid; for the nervous being is a thing enslaved to habit and in itself the means devised by Nature for fixing constancy of reaction, sameness of experience, the settled scheme of man's relations to life. The mental being on the other hand is free, for it is the means she has devised for flexibility and variation, for change and progress; it is subject only so long as it chooses to remain subject, to dwell in one mental habit rather than in another or so long as it allows itself to be dominated by its nervous instrument. It is not bound to be grieved by defeat, disgrace, loss: it can meet these things and all things with a perfect indifference; it can even meet them with a perfect gladness. Therefore man finds that the more he refuses to be dominated by his nerves and body, the more he draws back from implication of himself in his physical and vital parts, the greater is his freedom. He becomes the master of his own responses to the world's contacts, no longer the slave of external touches.

In regard to physical pleasure and pain, it is more difficult to apply the universal truth; for this is the very domain of the nerves and the body, the centre and seat of that in us whose nature is to be dominated by external contact and external pressure. Even here, however, we have glimpses of the truth. We see it in the fact that according to the habit the same physical contact can be either pleasurable or painful, not only to different individuals, but to the same individual under different conditions or at different stages of his development. We see it in the fact that men in periods of great excitement or high exaltation remain physically indifferent to pain or unconscious of pain under contacts which ordinarily would inflict severe torture or suffering. In many cases it is only when the nerves are able to reassert themselves and remind the mentality of its habitual obligation to suffer that the sense of suffering returns. But this return to the habitual obligation is not inevitable; it is only habitual. We see that in the phenomena of hypnosis not only can the hypnotised subject be successfully forbidden to feel the pain of a wound or puncture when in the abnormal state, but can be prevented with equal success from returning to his habitual reaction of suffering when he is awakened. The reason of this phenomenon is perfectly simple; it is because the hypnotiser suspends the habitual waking consciousness which is the slave of nervous habits and is able to appeal to the subliminal mental being in the depths, the inner mental being who is master, if he wills, of the nerves and the body. But this freedom which is effected by hypnosis abnormally, rapidly, without true possession, by an alien will, may equally be won normally, gradually, with true possession, by one's own will so as to effect partially or completely a victory of the mental being over the habitual nervous reactions of the body.

Pain of mind and body is a device of Nature, that is to say, of Force in her works, meant to subserve a definite transitional end in her upward evolution. The world is from the point of view of the individual a play and complex shock of multitudinous forces. In the midst of this complex play the individual stands as a limited constructed being with a limited amount of force exposed to numberless shocks which may wound, maim, break up or disintegrate the construction which he calls himself. Pain is in the nature of a nervous and physical recoil from a dangerous or harmful contact; it is a part of what the Upanishad calls *jugupsā*, the shrinking of the limited being from that which is not himself and not sympathetic or in harmony with himself, its impulse of self-defence against "others". It is, from this point of view, an indication by Nature of that which has to be avoided or, if not successfully avoided, has to be remedied. It does not come into being in the purely physical world so long as life does not enter into it; for till then mechanical methods are sufficient. Its office begins when life with its frailty and imperfect possession of Matter enters on the scene; it grows with the growth of Mind in life. Its office continues so long as Mind is bound in the life and body which it is using, dependent upon them for its knowledge and means of action, subjected to their limitations and to the egoistic impulses and aims which are born of those limitations. But if and when Mind in man becomes capable of being free, unegoistic, in harmony with all other beings and with the play of the universal forces, the use and office of suffering diminishes, its *raison d'être* must finally cease to be and it can only continue as an atavism of Nature, a habit that has survived its use, a persistence of the lower in the as yet imperfect organisation of the higher. Its eventual elimination must be an essential point in the destined conquest of the soul over subjection to Matter and egoistic limitation in Mind.

This elimination is possible because pain and pleasure themselves are currents, one imperfect, the other perverse, but still currents of the delight of existence. The reason for this imperfection and this perversion is the self-division of the being in his consciousness by measuring and limiting Maya and in consequence an egoistic and piecemeal instead of a universal reception of contacts by the individual. For the universal soul all things and all contacts of things carry in them an essence of delight best described by the Sanskrit aesthetic term, *rasa*, which means at once sap or essence of a thing and its taste. It is because we do not seek the essence of the thing in its contact with us, but look only to the manner in which it affects our desires and fears, our cravings and shrinkings that grief and pain, imperfect and transient pleasure or indifference, that is to say, blank inability to seize the essence, are the forms taken by the Rasa. If we could be entirely disinterested in mind and heart and impose that detachment on the nervous being, the progressive elimination of these imperfect and perverse forms of Rasa would be possible and the true essential taste of the inalienable delight of existence in all its variations would be within our reach. We attain to something of this capacity for variable but universal delight in the aesthetic reception of things as represented by

Art and Poetry, so that we enjoy there the Rasa or taste of the sorrowful, the terrible, even the horrible or repellent;[2] and the reason is because we are detached, disinterested, not thinking of ourselves or of self-defence (*jugupsā*), but only of the thing and its essence. Certainly, this aesthetic reception of contacts is not a precise image or reflection of the pure delight which is supramental and supra-aesthetic; for the latter would eliminate sorrow, terror, horror and disgust with their cause while the former admits them: but it represents partially and imperfectly one stage of the progressive delight of the universal Soul in things in its manifestation and it admits us in one part of our nature to that detachment from egoistic sensation and that universal attitude through which the one Soul sees harmony and beauty where we divided beings experience rather chaos and discord. The full liberation can come to us only by a similar liberation in all our parts, the universal aesthesis, the universal standpoint of knowledge, the universal detachment from all things and yet sympathy with all in our nervous and emotional being.

Since the nature of suffering is a failure of the conscious-force in us to meet the shocks of existence and a consequent shrinking and contraction and its root is an inequality of that receptive and possessing force due to our self-limitation by egoism consequent on the ignorance of our true Self, of Sachchidananda, the elimination of suffering must first proceed by the substitution of *titikṣā*, the facing, enduring and conquest of all shocks of existence for *jugupsā*, the shrinking and contraction: by this endurance and conquest we proceed to an equality which may be either an equal indifference to all contacts or an equal gladness in all contacts; and this equality again must find a firm foundation in the substitution of the Sachchidananda consciousness which is All-Bliss for the ego-consciousness which enjoys and suffers. The Sachchidananda consciousness may be transcendent of the universe and aloof from it, and to this state of distant Bliss the path is equal indifference; it is the path of the ascetic. Or the Sachchidananda consciousness may be at once transcendent

---

[2] So termed in Sanskrit Rhetoric, the *karuṇa*, *bhayānaka* and *bībhatsa* Rasas.

and universal; and to this state of present and all-embracing
Bliss the path is surrender and loss of the ego in the universal
and possession of an all-pervading equal delight; it is the path of
the ancient Vedic sages. But neutrality to the imperfect touches
of pleasure and the perverse touches of pain is the first direct
and natural result of the soul's self-discipline and the conversion
to equal delight can, usually, come only afterwards. The direct
transformation of the triple vibration into Ananda is possible,
but less easy to the human being.

Such then is the view of the universe which arises out of the
integral Vedantic affirmation. An infinite, indivisible existence
all-blissful in its pure self-consciousness moves out of its fundamental purity into the varied play of Force that is consciousness,
into the movement of Prakriti which is the play of Maya. The
delight of its existence is at first self-gathered, absorbed, subconscious in the basis of the physical universe; then emergent
in a great mass of neutral movement which is not yet what we
call sensation; then further emergent with the growth of mind
and ego in the triple vibration of pain, pleasure and indifference
originating from the limitation of the force of consciousness
in the form and from its exposure to shocks of the universal
Force which it finds alien to it and out of harmony with its own
measure and standard; finally, the conscious emergence of the
full Sachchidananda in its creations by universality, by equality,
by self-possession and conquest of Nature. This is the course
and movement of the world.

If it then be asked why the One Existence should take delight
in such a movement, the answer lies in the fact that all possibilities are inherent in Its infinity and that the delight of existence
— in its mutable becoming, not in its immutable being, — lies
precisely in the variable realisation of its possibilities. And the
possibility worked out here in the universe of which we are a
part, begins from the concealment of Sachchidananda in that
which seems to be its own opposite and its self-finding even
amid the terms of that opposite. Infinite being loses itself in
the appearance of non-being and emerges in the appearance of a
finite Soul; infinite consciousness loses itself in the appearance of

a vast indeterminate inconscience and emerges in the appearance of a superficial limited consciousness; infinite self-sustaining Force loses itself in the appearance of a chaos of atoms and emerges in the appearance of the insecure balance of a world; infinite Delight loses itself in the appearance of an insensible Matter and emerges in the appearance of a discordant rhythm of varied pain, pleasure and neutral feeling, love, hatred and indifference; infinite unity loses itself in the appearance of a chaos of multiplicity and emerges in a discord of forces and beings which seek to recover unity by possessing, dissolving and devouring each other. In this creation the real Sachchidananda has to emerge. Man, the individual, has to become and to live as a universal being; his limited mental consciousness has to widen to the superconscient unity in which each embraces all; his narrow heart has to learn the infinite embrace and replace its lusts and discords by universal love and his restricted vital being to become equal to the whole shock of the universe upon it and capable of universal delight; his very physical being has to know itself as no separate entity but as one with and sustaining in itself the whole flow of the indivisible Force that is all things; his whole nature has to reproduce in the individual the unity, the harmony, the oneness-in-all of the supreme Existence-Consciousness-Bliss.

Through all this play the secret reality is always one and the same delight of existence, — the same in the delight of the subconscious sleep before the emergence of the individual, in the delight of the struggle and all the varieties, vicissitudes, perversions, conversions, reversions of the effort to find itself amid the mazes of the half-conscious dream of which the individual is the centre, and in the delight of the eternal superconscient self-possession into which the individual must wake and there become one with the indivisible Sachchidananda. This is the play of the One, the Lord, the All as it reveals itself to our liberated and enlightened knowledge from the conceptive standpoint of this material universe.

Chapter XIII

The Divine Maya

By the Names of the Lord and hers they shaped and measured the force of the Mother of Light; wearing might after might of that Force as a robe the lords of Maya shaped out Form in this Being.

The Masters of Maya shaped all by His Maya; the Fathers who have divine vision set Him within as a child that is to be born.   *Rig Veda.*[1]

EXISTENCE that acts and creates by the power and from the pure delight of its conscious being is the reality that we are, the self of all our modes and moods, the cause, object and goal of all our doing, becoming and creating. As the poet, artist or musician when he creates does really nothing but develop some potentiality in his unmanifested self into a form of manifestation and as the thinker, statesman, mechanist only bring out into a shape of things that which lay hidden in themselves, was themselves, is still themselves when it is cast into form, so is it with the world and the Eternal. All creation or becoming is nothing but this self-manifestation. Out of the seed there evolves that which is already in the seed, pre-existent in being, predestined in its will to become, prearranged in the delight of becoming. The original plasm held in itself in force of being the resultant organism. For it is always that secret, burdened, self-knowing force which labours under its own irresistible impulse to manifest the form of itself with which it is charged. Only, the individual who creates or develops out of himself, makes a distinction between himself, the force that

---

[1] III. 38. 7; IX. 83. 3.

works in him and the material in which he works. In reality the force is himself, the individualised consciousness which it instrumentalises is himself, the material which it uses is himself, the resultant form is himself. In other words it is one existence, one force, one delight of being which concentrates itself at various points, says of each "This is I" and works in it by a various play of self-force for a various play of self-formation.

What it produces is itself and can be nothing other than itself; it is working out a play, a rhythm, a development of its own existence, force of consciousness and delight of being. Therefore whatever comes into the world, seeks nothing but this, to be, to arrive at the intended form, to enlarge its self-existence in that form, to develop, manifest, increase, realise infinitely the consciousness and the power that is in it, to have the delight of coming into manifestation, the delight of the form of being, the delight of the rhythm of consciousness, the delight of the play of force and to aggrandise and perfect that delight by whatever means is possible, in whatever direction, through whatever idea of itself may be suggested to it by the Existence, the Conscious-Force, the Delight active within its deepest being.

And if there is any goal, any completeness towards which things tend, it can only be the completeness, — in the individual and in the whole which the individuals constitute, — of its self-existence, of its power and consciousness and of its delight of being. But such completeness is not possible in the individual consciousness concentrated within the limits of the individual formation; absolute completeness is not feasible in the finite because it is alien to the self-conception of the finite. Therefore the only final goal possible is the emergence of the infinite consciousness in the individual; it is his recovery of the truth of himself by self-knowledge and by self-realisation, the truth of the Infinite in being, the Infinite in consciousness, the Infinite in delight repossessed as his own Self and Reality of which the finite is only a mask and an instrument for various expression.

Thus by the very nature of the world-play as it has been realised by Sachchidananda in the vastness of His existence extended as Space and Time, we have to conceive first of an involution and a self-absorption of conscious being into the density and infinite divisibility of substance, for otherwise there can be no finite variation; next, an emergence of the self-imprisoned force into formal being, living being, thinking being; and finally a release of the formed thinking being into the free realisation of itself as the One and the Infinite at play in the world and by the release its recovery of the boundless existence-consciousness-bliss that even now it is secretly, really and eternally. This triple movement is the whole key of the world-enigma.

It is so that the ancient and eternal truth of Vedanta receives into itself and illumines, justifies and shows us all the meaning of the modern and phenomenal truth of evolution in the universe. And it is so only that this modern truth of evolution which is the old truth of the Universal developing itself successively in Time, seen opaquely through the study of Force and Matter, can find its own full sense and justification, — by illuminating itself with the Light of the ancient and eternal truth still preserved for us in the Vedantic Scriptures. To this mutual self-discovery and self-illumination by the fusion of the old Eastern and the new Western knowledge the thought of the world is already turning.

Still, when we have found that all things are Sachchid-ananda, all has not yet been explained. We know the Reality of the universe, we do not yet know the process by which that Reality has turned itself into this phenomenon. We have the key of the riddle, we have still to find the lock in which it will turn. For this Existence, Conscious-Force, Delight does not work directly or with a sovereign irresponsibility like a magician building up worlds and universes by the mere fiat of its word. We perceive a process, we are aware of a Law.

It is true that this Law when we analyse it, seems to resolve itself into an equilibrium of the play of forces and a determination of that play into fixed lines of working by the accident of development and the habit of past realised energy. But this apparent and secondary truth is final to us only so long as we conceive of Force solely. When we perceive that Force is a self-expression of Existence, we are bound to perceive also that this line which Force has taken, corresponds to some self-truth of that Existence which governs and determines its constant curve and destination. And since consciousness is the nature of the original Existence and the essence of its Force, this truth must be a self-perception in Conscious-Being and this determination of the line taken by Force must result from a power of self-directive knowledge inherent in Consciousness which enables it to guide its own Force inevitably along the logical line of the original self-perception. It is then a self-determining power in universal consciousness, a capacity in self-awareness of infinite existence to perceive a certain Truth in itself and direct its force of creation along the line of that Truth, which has presided over the cosmic manifestation.

But why should we interpose any special power or faculty between the infinite Consciousness itself and the result of its workings? May not this Self-awareness of the Infinite range freely creating forms which afterwards remain in play so long as there is not the fiat that bids them cease, — even as the old Semitic Revelation tells us, "God said, Let there be Light, and there was Light"? But when we say, "God said, Let there be Light", we assume the act of a power of consciousness which determines light out of everything else that is not light; and when we say "and there was Light" we presume a directing faculty, an active power corresponding to the original perceptive power, which brings out the phenomenon and, working out Light according to the line of the original perception, prevents it from being overpowered by all the infinite possibilities that are other than itself. Infinite consciousness in its infinite action can produce only infinite results; to settle upon a fixed Truth or order of truths and build a world in conformity with that which is fixed, demands a selective faculty of knowledge commissioned to shape finite appearance out of the infinite Reality.

This power was known to the Vedic seers by the name of Maya. Maya meant for them the power of infinite consciousness to comprehend, contain in itself and measure out, that is to say, to form — for form is delimitation — Name and Shape out of the vast illimitable Truth of infinite existence. It is by Maya that static truth of essential being becomes ordered truth of active being, — or, to put it in more metaphysical language, out of the supreme being in which all is all without barrier of separative consciousness emerges the phenomenal being in which all is in each and each is in all for the play of existence with existence, consciousness with consciousness, force with force, delight with delight. This play of all in each and each in all is concealed at first from us by the mental play or the illusion of Maya which persuades each that he is in all but not all in him and that he is in all as a separated being not as a being always inseparably one with the rest of existence. Afterwards we have to emerge from this error into the supramental play or the truth of Maya where the "each" and the "all" coexist in the inseparable unity of the one truth and the multiple symbol. The lower, present and deluding mental Maya has first to be embraced, then to be overcome; for it is God's play with division and darkness and limitation, desire and strife and suffering in which He subjects Himself to the Force that has come out of Himself and by her obscure suffers Himself to be obscured. That other Maya concealed by this mental has to be overpassed, then embraced; for it is God's play of the infinities of existence, the splendours of knowledge, the glories of force mastered and the ecstasies of love illimitable where He emerges out of the hold of Force, holds her instead and fulfils in her illumined that for which she went out from Him at the first.

This distinction between the lower and the higher Maya is the link in thought and in cosmic Fact which the pessimistic and illusionist philosophies miss or neglect. To them the mental Maya, or perhaps an Overmind, is the creatrix of the world, and a world created by mental Maya would indeed be an inexplicable paradox and a fixed yet floating nightmare of conscious existence which could neither be classed as an illusion nor as a reality. We have to see that the mind is only an intermediate term between the creative governing knowledge and the soul imprisoned in its works. Sachchidananda, involved by one of His lower movements in the self-oblivious absorption of Force that is lost in the form of her own workings, returns towards Himself out of the self-oblivion; Mind is only one of His instruments in the descent and the ascent. It is an instrument of the descending creation, not the secret creatrix, — a transitional stage in the ascent, not our high original source and the consummate term of cosmic existence.

The philosophies which recognise Mind alone as the creator of the worlds or accept an original principle with Mind as the only mediator between it and the forms of the universe, may be divided into the purely noumenal and the idealistic. The purely noumenal recognise in the cosmos only the work of Mind, Thought, Idea: but Idea may be purely arbitrary and have no essential relation to any real Truth of existence; or such Truth, if it exists, may be regarded as a mere Absolute aloof from all relations and irreconcilable with a world of relations. The idealistic interpretation supposes a relation between the Truth behind and the conceptive phenomenon in front, a relation which is not merely that of an antinomy and opposition. The view I am presenting goes farther in idealism; it sees the creative Idea as Real-Idea, that is to say, a power of Conscious Force expressive of real being, born out of real being and partaking of its nature and neither a child of the Void nor a weaver of fictions. It is conscious Reality throwing itself into mutable forms of its own imperishable and immutable substance. The world is therefore not a figment of conception in the universal Mind, but a conscious birth of that which is beyond Mind into forms of itself. A Truth of conscious being supports these forms and expresses itself in them, and the knowledge corresponding to the truth thus expressed reigns as a supramental Truth-Consciousness[2] organising real ideas in a perfect harmony before they are cast into the mental-vital-material mould. Mind, Life and Body are an inferior consciousness and a partial expression which strives to arrive in the mould of a various evolution at that superior expression of itself already existent to the Beyond-Mind. That

---

[2] I take the phrase from the Rig Veda, — *rta-cit*, which means the consciousness of essential truth of being (*satyam*), of ordered truth of active being (*rtam*) and the vast self-awareness (*brhat*) in which alone this consciousness is possible.

which is in the Beyond-Mind is the ideal which in its own conditions it is labouring to realise.

From our ascending point of view we may say that the Real is behind all that exists; it expresses itself intermediately in an Ideal which is a harmonised truth of itself; the Ideal throws out a phenomenal reality of variable conscious-being which, inevitably drawn towards its own essential Reality, tries at last to recover it entirely whether by a violent leap or normally through the Ideal which put it forth. It is this that explains the imperfect reality of human existence as seen by the Mind, the instinctive aspiration in the mental being towards a perfectibility ever beyond itself, towards the concealed harmony of the Ideal, and the supreme surge of the spirit beyond the ideal to the transcendental. The very facts of our consciousness, its constitution and its necessity presuppose such a triple order; they negate the dual and irreconcilable antithesis of a mere Absolute to a mere relativity.

Mind is not sufficient to explain existence in the universe. Infinite Consciousness must first translate itself into infinite faculty of Knowledge or, as we call it from our point of view, omniscience. But Mind is not a faculty of knowledge nor an instrument of omniscience; it is a faculty for the seeking of knowledge, for expressing as much as it can gain of it in certain forms of a relative thought and for using it towards certain capacities of action. Even when it finds, it does not possess; it only keeps a certain fund of current coin of Truth — not Truth itself — in the bank of Memory to draw upon according to its needs. For Mind is that which does not know, which tries to know and which never knows except as in a glass darkly. It is the power which interprets truth of universal existence for the practical uses of a certain order of things; it is not the power which knows and guides that existence and therefore it cannot be the power which created or manifested it.

But if we suppose an infinite Mind which would be free from our limitations, that at least might well be the creator of the universe? But such a Mind would be something quite different from the definition of mind as we know it: it would be something

beyond mentality; it would be the supramental Truth. An infinite
Mind constituted in the terms of mentality as we know it could
only create an infinite chaos, a vast clash of chance, accident,
vicissitude wandering towards an indeterminate end after which
it would be always tentatively groping and aspiring. An infinite,
omniscient, omnipotent Mind would not be mind at all, but
supramental knowledge.

Mind, as we know it, is a reflective mirror which receives
presentations or images of a pre-existent Truth or Fact, either
external to or at least vaster than itself. It represents to itself
from moment to moment the phenomenon that is or has been.
It possesses also the faculty of constructing in itself possible
images other than those of the actual fact presented to it; that
is to say, it represents to itself not only phenomenon that has
been but also phenomenon that may be: it cannot, be it noted,
represent to itself phenomenon that assuredly will be, except
when it is an assured repetition of what is or has been. It has,
finally, the faculty of forecasting new modifications which it
seeks to construct out of the meeting of what has been and
what may be, out of the fulfilled possibility and the unfulfilled,
something that it sometimes succeeds in constructing more or
less exactly, sometimes fails to realise, but usually finds cast into
other forms than it forecasted and turned to other ends than it
desired or intended.

An infinite Mind of this character might possibly construct
an accidental cosmos of conflicting possibilities and it might
shape it into something shifting, something always transient,
something ever uncertain in its drift, neither real nor unreal,
possessed of no definite end or aim but only an endless succession
of momentary aims leading, — since there is no superior directing power of knowledge, — eventually nowhither. Nihilism or
Illusionism or some kindred philosophy is the only logical conclusion of such a pure noumenalism. The cosmos so constructed
would be a presentation or reflection of something not itself, but
always and to the end a false presentation, a distorted reflection;
all cosmic existence would be a Mind struggling to work out
fully its imaginations, but not succeeding, because they have no

imperative basis of self-truth; overpowered and carried forward
by the stream of its own past energies, it would be borne onward
indeterminately for ever without issue unless or until it can either
slay itself or fall into an eternal stillness. That traced to its roots is
Nihilism and Illusionism and it is the only wisdom if we suppose
that our human mentality or anything at all like it represents the
highest cosmic force and the original conception at work in the
universe.

But the moment we find in the original power of knowledge
a higher force than that which is represented by our human
mentality, this conception of the universe becomes insufficient
and therefore invalid. It has its truth but it is not the whole
truth. It is law of the immediate appearance of the universe,
but not of its original truth and ultimate fact. For we perceive
behind the action of Mind, Life and Body, something that is
not embraced in the stream of Force but embraces and controls
it; something that is not born into a world which it seeks to
interpret, but has created in its being a world of which it has the
omniscience; something that does not labour perpetually to form
something else out of itself while it drifts in the overmastering
surge of past energies it can no longer control, but has already
in its consciousness a perfect Form of itself and is here gradually
unfolding it. The world expresses a foreseen Truth, obeys a
predetermining Will, realises an original formative self-vision,
— it is the growing image of a divine creation.

So long as we work only through the mentality governed by
appearances, this something beyond and behind and yet always
immanent can be only an inference or a presence vaguely felt.
We perceive a law of cyclic progress and infer an ever-increasing
perfection of somewhat that is somewhere foreknown. For everywhere we see Law founded in self-being and, when we penetrate within into the rationale of its process, we find that Law
is the expression of an innate knowledge, a knowledge inherent
in the existence which is expressing itself and implied in the
force that expresses it; and Law developed by Knowledge so
as to allow of progression implies a divinely seen goal towards
which the motion is directed. We see too that our reason seeks to

emerge out of and dominate the helpless drift of our mentality and we arrive at the perception that Reason is only a messenger, a representative or a shadow of a greater consciousness beyond itself which does not need to reason because it is all and knows all that it is. And we can then pass to the inference that this source of Reason is identical with the Knowledge that acts as Law in the world. This Knowledge determines its own law sovereignly because it knows what has been, is and will be and it knows because it is eternally, and infinitely cognises itself. Being that is infinite consciousness, infinite consciousness that is omnipotent force, when it makes a world, — that is to say, a harmony of itself, — its object of consciousness, becomes seizable by our thought as a cosmic existence that knows its own truth and realises in forms that which it knows.

But it is only when we cease to reason and go deep into ourselves, into that secrecy where the activity of mind is stilled, that this other consciousness becomes really manifest to us — however imperfectly owing to our long habit of mental reaction and mental limitation. Then we can know surely in an increasing illumination that which we had uncertainly conceived by the pale and flickering light of Reason. Knowledge waits seated beyond mind and intellectual reasoning, throned in the luminous vast of illimitable self-vision.

Chapter XIV

The Supermind as Creator

All things are self-deployings of the Divine Knowledge.
Vishnu Purana.[1]

A PRINCIPLE of active Will and Knowledge superior to Mind and creatrix of the worlds is then the intermediary power and state of being between that self-possession of the One and this flux of the Many. This principle is not entirely alien to us; it does not belong solely and incommunicably to a Being who is entirely other than ourselves or to a state of existence from which we are mysteriously projected into birth, but also rejected and unable to return. If it seems to us to be seated on heights far above us, yet are they the heights of our own being and accessible to our tread. We can not only infer and glimpse that Truth, but we are capable of realising it. We may by a progressive expanding or a sudden luminous self-transcendence mount up to these summits in unforgettable moments or dwell on them during hours or days of greatest superhuman experience. When we descend again, there are doors of communication which we can keep always open or reopen even though they should constantly shut. But to dwell there permanently on this last and highest summit of the created and creative being is in the end the supreme ideal for our evolving human consciousness when it seeks not self-annulment but self-perfection. For, as we have seen, this is the original Idea and the final harmony and truth to which our gradual self-expression in the world returns and which it is meant to achieve.

Still, we may doubt whether it is possible, now or at all, to

___
[1] II. 12. 39.

give any account of this state to the human intellect or to utilise in any communicable and organisable way its divine workings for the elevation of our human knowledge and action. The doubt does not arise solely from the rarity or dubiety of any known phenomena that would betray a human working of this divine faculty, or from the remoteness which separates this action from the experience and verifiable knowledge of ordinary humanity; it is strongly suggested also by the apparent contradiction in both essence and operation between human mentality and the divine Supermind.

And certainly, if this consciousness had no relation at all to mind nor anywhere any identity with the mental being, it would be quite impossible to give any account of it to our human notions. Or, if it were in its nature only vision in knowledge and not at all dynamic power of knowledge, we could hope to attain by its contact a beatific state of mental illumination, but not a greater light and power for the works of the world. But since this consciousness is creatrix of the world, it must be not only state of knowledge, but power of knowledge, and not only a Will to light and vision, but a Will to power and works. And since Mind too is created out of it, Mind must be a development by limitation out of this primal faculty and this mediatory act of the supreme Consciousness and must therefore be capable of resolving itself back into it through a reverse development by expansion. For always Mind must be identical with Supermind in essence and conceal in itself the potentiality of Supermind, however different or even contrary it may have become in its actual forms and settled modes of operation. It may not then be an irrational or unprofitable attempt to strive by the method of comparison and contrast towards some idea of the Supermind from the standpoint and in the terms of our intellectual knowledge. The idea, the terms may well be inadequate and yet still serve as a finger of light pointing us onward on a way which to some distance at least we may tread. Moreover it is possible for Mind to rise beyond itself into certain heights or planes of consciousness which receive into themselves some modified light or power of the supramental consciousness and know that by an illumination, intuition or a direct contact or experience, although to live in it and see and act from it is a victory that has not yet been made humanly possible.

And first we may pause a moment and ask ourselves whether no light can be found from the past which will guide us towards these ill-explored domains. We need a name, and we need a starting-point. For we have called this state of consciousness the Supermind; but the word is ambiguous since it may be taken in the sense of mind itself super-eminent and lifted above ordinary mentality but not radically changed, or on the contrary it may bear the sense of all that is beyond mind and therefore assume a too extensive comprehensiveness which would bring in even the Ineffable itself. A subsidiary description is required which will more accurately limit its significance.

It is the cryptic verses of the Veda that help us here; for they contain, though concealed, the gospel of the divine and immortal Supermind and through the veil some illumining flashes come to us. We can see through these utterances the conception of this Supermind as a vastness beyond the ordinary firmaments of our consciousness in which truth of being is luminously one with all that expresses it and assures inevitably truth of vision, formulation, arrangement, word, act and movement and therefore truth also of result of movement, result of action and expression, in-fallible ordinance or law. Vast all-comprehensiveness; luminous truth and harmony of being in that vastness and not a vague chaos or self-lost obscurity; truth of law and act and knowledge expressive of that harmonious truth of being: these seem to be the essential terms of the Vedic description. The Gods, who in their highest secret entity are powers of this Supermind, born of it, seated in it as in their proper home, are in their knowledge "truth-conscious" and in their action possessed of the "seer-will". Their conscious-force turned towards works and creation is possessed and guided by a perfect and direct knowledge of the thing to be done and its essence and its law, — a knowledge which determines a wholly effective will-power that does not deviate or falter in its process or in its result, but expresses and fulfils spontaneously and inevitably in the act that which has been seen in the vision. Light is here one with Force, the vibrations of knowledge with the rhythm of the will and both are one, perfectly and without seeking, groping or effort, with the assured result. The divine Nature has a double power, a spontaneous self-formulation and self-arrangement which wells naturally out of the essence of the thing manifested and expresses its original truth, and a self-force of light inherent in the thing itself and the source of its spontaneous and inevitable self-arrangement.

There are subordinate, but important details. The Vedic seers seem to speak of two primary faculties of the "truth-conscious" soul; they are Sight and Hearing, by which is intended direct operations of an inherent Knowledge describable as truth-vision and truth-audition and reflected from far-off in our human mentality by the faculties of revelation and inspiration. Besides, a distinction seems to be made in the operations of the Supermind between knowledge by a comprehending and pervading consciousness which is very near to subjective knowledge by identity and knowledge by a projecting, confronting, apprehending consciousness which is the beginning of objective cognition. These are the Vedic clues. And we may accept from this ancient experience the subsidiary term "truth-consciousness" to delimit the connotation of the more elastic phrase, Supermind.

We see at once that such a consciousness, described by such characteristics, must be an intermediate formulation which refers back to a term above it and forward to another below it; we see at the same time that it is evidently the link and means by which the inferior develops out of the superior and should equally be the link and means by which it may develop back again towards its source. The term above is the unitarian or indivisible consciousness of pure Sachchidananda in which there are no separating distinctions; the term below is the analytic or dividing consciousness of Mind which can only know by separation and distinction and has at the most a vague and secondary apprehension of unity and infinity, — for, though it can synthetise its divisions, it cannot arrive at a true totality. Between them is this comprehensive and creative consciousness, by its power of pervading and comprehending knowledge the child of that self-awareness by identity which is the poise of the Brahman and by its power of projecting, confronting, apprehending knowledge parent of that awareness by distinction which is the process of the Mind.

Above, the formula of the One eternally stable and immutable; below, the formula of the Many which, eternally mutable, seeks but hardly finds in the flux of things a firm and immutable standing-point; between, the seat of all trinities, of all that is biune, of all that becomes Many-in-One and yet remains One-in-Many because it was originally One that is always potentially Many. This intermediary term is therefore the beginning and end of all creation and arrangement, the Alpha and the Omega, the starting-point of all differentiation, the instrument of all unification, originative, executive and consummative of all realised or realisable harmonies. It has the knowledge of the One, but is able to draw out of the One its hidden multitudes; it manifests the Many, but does not lose itself in their differentiations. And shall we not say that its very existence points back to Something beyond our supreme perception of the ineffable Unity, — Something ineffable and mentally inconceivable not because of its unity and indivisibility, but because of its freedom from even these formulations of our mind, — Something beyond both unity and multiplicity? That would be the utter Absolute and Real which yet justifies to us both our knowledge of God and our knowledge of the world.

But these terms are large and difficult to grasp; let us come to precisions. We speak of the One as Sachchidananda; but in the very description we posit three entities and unite them to arrive at a trinity. We say "Existence, Consciousness, Bliss", and then we say, "they are one." It is a process of the mind. But for the unitarian consciousness such a process is inadmissible. Existence is Consciousness and there can be no distinction between them; Consciousness is Bliss and there can be no distinction between them. And since there is not even this differentiation, there can be no world. If that is the sole reality, then world is not and never existed, can never have been conceived; for indivisible consciousness is undividing consciousness and cannot originate division and differentiation. But this is a *reductio ad absurdum*; we cannot admit it unless we are content to base everything upon an impossible paradox and an unreconciled antithesis.

On the other hand, Mind can conceive with precision divisions as real; it can conceive a synthetic totality or the finite extending itself indefinitely; it can grasp aggregates of divided things and the samenesses underlying them; but the ultimate unity and absolute infinity are to its conscience of things abstract notions and unseizable quantities, not something that is real to its grasp, much less something that is alone real. Here is therefore the very opposite term to the unitarian consciousness; we have, confronting the essential and indivisible unity, an essential multiplicity which cannot arrive at unity without abolishing itself and in the very act confessing that it could never really have existed. Yet it was; for it is this that has found unity and abolished itself. And again we have a *reductio ad absurdum* repeating the violent paradox which seeks to convince thought by stunning it and the irreconciled and irreconcilable antithesis.

The difficulty, in its lower term, disappears if we realise that Mind is only a preparatory form of our consciousness. Mind is an instrument of analysis and synthesis, but not of essential knowledge. Its function is to cut out something vaguely from the unknown Thing in itself and call this measurement or delimitation of it the whole, and again to analyse the whole into its parts which it regards as separate mental objects. It is only the parts and accidents that the Mind can see definitely and, after its own fashion, know. Of the whole its only definite idea is an assemblage of parts or a totality of properties and accidents. The whole not seen as a part of something else or in its own parts, properties and accidents is to the mind no more than a vague perception; only when it is analysed and put by itself as a separate constituted object, a totality in a larger totality, can Mind say to itself, "This now I know." And really it does not know. It knows only its own analysis of the object and the idea it has formed of it by a synthesis of the separate parts and properties that it has seen. There its characteristic power, its sure function ceases, and if we would have a greater, a profounder and a real knowledge, — a knowledge and not an intense but formless sentiment such as comes sometimes to certain deep but inarticulate parts of our mentality, — Mind has to make room for another consciousness which will fulfil Mind by transcending it or reverse and so rectify its operations after leaping beyond it: the summit of mental knowledge is only a vaulting-board from which that leap can be taken. The utmost mission of Mind is to train our obscure consciousness which has emerged out of the dark prison of Matter, to enlighten its blind instincts, random intuitions, vague perceptions till it shall become capable of this greater light and this higher ascension. Mind is a passage, not a culmination.

On the other hand, the unitarian consciousness or indivisible Unity cannot be that impossible entity, a thing without contents out of which all contents have issued and into which they disappear and become annihilated. It must be an original self-concentration in which all is contained but in another manner than in this temporal and spatial manifestation. That which has thus concentrated itself, is the utterly ineffable and inconceivable Existence which the Nihilist images to his mind as the negative Void of all that we know and are but the Transcendentalist with equal reason may image to his mind as the positive but indistinguishable Reality of all that we know and are. "In the beginning," says the Vedanta, "was the one Existence without a second", but before and after the beginning, now, for ever and beyond Time is that which we cannot describe even as the One, even when we say that nothing but That is. What we can be aware of is, first, its original self-concentration which we endeavour to realise as the indivisible One; secondly, the diffusion and apparent disintegration of all that was concentrated in its unity which is the Mind's conception of the universe; and thirdly, its firm self-extension in the Truth-consciousness which contains and upholds the diffusion and prevents it from being a real disintegration, maintains unity in utmost diversity and stability in utmost mutability, insists on harmony in the appearance of an all-pervading strife and collision, keeps eternal cosmos where Mind would arrive only at a chaos eternally attempting to form itself. This is the Supermind, the Truth-consciousness, the Real-Idea which knows itself and all that it becomes.

Supermind is the vast self-extension of the Brahman that contains and develops. By the Idea it develops the triune principle of existence, consciousness and bliss out of their indivisible unity. It differentiates them, but it does not divide. It establishes a Trinity, not arriving like the Mind from the three to the One, but manifesting the three out of the One, — for it manifests and develops, — and yet maintaining them in the unity, — for it knows and contains. By the differentiation it is able to bring forward one or other of them as the effective Deity which contains the others involved or explicit in itself and this process it makes the foundation of all other differentiations. And it acts by the same operation on all the principles and possibilities which it evolves out of this all-constituent trinity. It possesses the power of development, of evolution, of making explicit, and that power carries with it the other power of involution, of envelopment, of making implicit. In a sense, the whole of creation may be said to be a movement between two involutions, Spirit in which all is involved and out of which all evolves downward to the other pole of Matter, Matter in which also all is involved and out of which all evolves upwards to the other pole of Spirit.

Thus the whole process of differentiation by the Real-Idea creative of the universe is a putting forward of principles, forces, forms which contain for the comprehending consciousness all the rest of existence within them and front the apprehending consciousness with all the rest of existence implicit behind them. Therefore all is in each as well as each in all. Therefore every seed of things implies in itself all the infinity of various possibilities, but is kept to one law of process and result by the Will, that is to say, by the Knowledge-Force of the Conscious-Being who is manifesting himself and who, sure of the Idea in himself, predetermines by it his own forms and movements. The seed is the Truth of its own being which this Self-Existence sees in itself, the resultant of that seed of self-vision is the Truth of self-action, the natural law of development, formation and functioning which follows inevitably upon the self-vision and keeps to the processes involved in the original Truth. All Nature is simply, then, the Seer-Will, the Knowledge-Force of the Conscious-Being at work to evolve in force and form all the inevitable truth of the Idea into which it has originally thrown itself.

This conception of the Idea points us to the essential contrast between our mental consciousness and the Truth-Consciousness. We regard thought as a thing separate from existence, abstract, unsubstantial, different from reality, something which appears one knows not whence and detaches itself from objective reality in order to observe, understand and judge it; for so it seems and therefore is to our all-dividing, all-analysing mentality. The first business of Mind is to render "discrete", to make fissures much more than to discern, and so it has made this paralysing fissure between thought and reality. But in Supermind all being is consciousness, all consciousness is of being, and the idea, a pregnant vibration of consciousness, is equally a vibration of being pregnant of itself; it is an initial coming out, in creative self-knowledge, of that which lay concentrated in uncreative self-awareness. It comes out as Idea that is a reality, and it is that reality of the Idea which evolves itself, always by its own power and consciousness of itself, always self-conscious, always self-developing by the will inherent in the Idea, always self-realising by the knowledge ingrained in its every impulsion. This is the truth of all creation, of all evolution.

In Supermind being, consciousness of knowledge and consciousness of will are not divided as they seem to be in our mental operations; they are a trinity, one movement with three effective aspects. Each has its own effect. Being gives the effect of substance, consciousness the effect of knowledge, of the self-guiding and shaping idea, of comprehension and apprehension; will gives the effect of self-fulfilling force. But the idea is only the light of the reality illumining itself; it is not mental thought nor imagination, but effective self-awareness. It is Real-Idea.

In Supermind knowledge in the Idea is not divorced from will in the Idea, but one with it — just as it is not different from being or substance, but is one with the being, luminous power of the substance. As the power of burning light is not different from the substance of the fire, so the power of the Idea is not different from the substance of the Being which works itself out in the Idea and its development. In our mentality all are different. We have an idea and a will according to the idea or an impulsion of will and an idea detaching itself from it; but we differentiate effectually the idea from the will and both from ourselves. I am; the idea is a mysterious abstraction that appears in me, the will is another mystery, a force nearer to concreteness, though not concrete, but always something that is not myself, something that I have or get or am seized with, but am not. I make a gulf also between my will, its means and the effect, for these I regard as concrete realities outside and other than myself. Therefore neither myself nor the idea nor the will in me are self-effective. The idea may fall away from me, the will may fail, the means may be lacking, I myself by any or all of these lacunae may remain unfulfilled.

But in the Supermind there is no such paralysing division, because knowledge is not self-divided, force is not self-divided, being is not self-divided as in the mind; they are neither broken in themselves, nor divorced from each other. For the Supermind is the Vast; it starts from unity, not division, it is primarily comprehensive, differentiation is only its secondary act. Therefore whatever be the truth of being expressed, the idea corresponds to it exactly, the will-force to the idea, — force being only power of the consciousness, — and the result to the will. Nor does the idea clash with other ideas, the will or force with other will or force as in man and his world; for there is one vast Consciousness which contains and relates all ideas in itself as its own ideas, one vast Will which contains and relates all energies in itself as its own energies. It holds back this, advances that other, but according to its own preconceiving Idea-Will.

This is the justification of the current religious notions of the omnipresence, omniscience and omnipotence of the Divine Being. Far from being an irrational imagination they are perfectly rational and in no way contradict either the logic of a comprehensive philosophy or the indications of observation and experience. The error is to make an unbridgeable gulf between God and man, Brahman and the world. That error elevates an actual and practical differentiation in being, consciousness and force into an essential division. But this aspect of the question we shall touch upon afterwards. At present we have arrived at an affirmation and some conception of the divine and creative Supermind in which all is one in being, consciousness, will and delight, yet with an infinite capacity of differentiation that deploys but does not destroy the unity, — in which Truth is the substance and Truth rises in the Idea and Truth comes out in the form and there is one truth of knowledge and will, one truth of self-fulfilment and therefore of delight; for all self-fulfilment is satisfaction of being. Therefore, always, in all mutations and combinations a self-existent and inalienable harmony.

Chapter XV

The Supreme Truth-Consciousness

One seated in the sleep of Superconscience, a massed Intelligence, blissful and the enjoyer of Bliss.... This is the omnipotent, this is the omniscient, this is the inner control, this is the source of all.   *Mandukya Upanishad.*[1]

WE HAVE to regard therefore this all-containing, all-originating, all-consummating Supermind as the nature of the Divine Being, not indeed in its absolute self-existence, but in its action as the Lord and Creator of its own worlds. This is the truth of that which we call God. Obviously this is not the too personal and limited Deity, the magnified and supernatural Man of the ordinary occidental conception; for that conception erects a too human Eidolon of a certain relation between the creative Supermind and the ego. We must not indeed exclude the personal aspect of the Deity, for the impersonal is only one face of existence; the Divine is All-existence, but it is also the one Existent, — it is the sole Conscious-Being, but still a Being. Nevertheless, with this aspect we are not concerned at present; it is the impersonal psychological truth of the divine Consciousness that we are seeking to fathom: it is this that we have to fix in a large and clarified conception.

The Truth-Consciousness is everywhere present in the universe as an ordering self-knowledge by which the One manifests the harmonies of its infinite potential multiplicity. Without this ordering self-knowledge the manifestation would be merely a shifting chaos, precisely because the potentiality is infinite which by itself might lead only to a play of uncontrolled unbounded Chance. If there were only infinite potentiality without any law

---

[1] Verses 5,6

of guiding truth and harmonious self-vision, without any predetermining Idea in the very seed of things cast out for evolution,
the world could be nothing but a teeming, amorphous, confused
uncertainty. But the knowledge that creates, because what it
creates or releases are forms and powers of itself and not things
other than itself, possesses in its own being the vision of the
truth and law that governs each potentiality, and along with
that an intrinsic awareness of its relation to other potentialities
and the harmonies that are possible between them; it holds all
this prefigured in the general determining harmony which the
whole rhythmic Idea of a universe must contain in its very birth
and self-conception and which must therefore inevitably work
out by the interplay of its constituents. It is the source and
keeper of Law in the world; for that law is nothing arbitrary
— it is the expression of a self-nature which is determined by
the compelling truth of the real idea that each thing is in its
inception. Therefore from the beginning the whole development
is predetermined in its self-knowledge and at every moment in
its self-working: it is what it must be at each moment by its own
original inherent Truth; it moves to what it must be at the next,
still by its own original inherent Truth; it will be at the end that
which was contained and intended in its seed.

This development and progress of the world according to
an original truth of its own being implies a succession of Time,
a relation in Space and a regulated interaction of related things
in Space to which the succession of Time gives the aspect of
Causality. Time and Space, according to the metaphysician, have
only a conceptual and not a real existence; but since all things
and not these only are forms assumed by Conscious-Being in
its own consciousness, the distinction is of no great importance.
Time and Space are that one Conscious-Being viewing itself in
extension, subjectively as Time, objectively as Space. Our mental
view of these two categories is determined by the idea of measure
which is inherent in the action of the analytical dividing movement of Mind. Time is for the Mind a mobile extension measured
out by the succession of the past, present and future in which
Mind places itself at a certain standpoint whence it looks before

and after. Space is a stable extension measured out by divisibility of substance; at a certain point in that divisible extension Mind places itself and regards the disposition of substance around it.

In actual fact Mind measures Time by event and Space by Matter; but it is possible in pure mentality to disregard the movement of event and the disposition of substance and realise the pure movement of Conscious-Force which constitutes Space and Time; these two are then merely two aspects of the universal force of Consciousness which in their intertwined interaction comprehend the warp and woof of its action upon itself. And to a consciousness higher than Mind which should regard our past, present and future in one view, containing and not contained in them, not situated at a particular moment of Time for its point of prospection, Time might well offer itself as an eternal present. And to the same consciousness not situated at any particular point of Space, but containing all points and regions in itself, Space also might well offer itself as a subjective and indivisible extension, — no less subjective than Time. At certain moments we become aware of such an indivisible regard upholding by its immutable self-conscious unity the variations of the universe. But we must not now ask how the contents of Time and Space would present themselves there in their transcendent truth; for this our mind cannot conceive, — and it is even ready to deny to this Indivisible any possibility of knowing the world in any other way than that of our mind and senses.

What we have to realise and can to a certain extent conceive is the one view and all-comprehending regard by which the Supermind embraces and unifies the successions of Time and the divisions of Space. And first, if there were not this factor of the successions of Time, there would be no change or progression; a perfect harmony would be perpetually manifest, coeval with other harmonies in a sort of eternal moment, not successive to them in the movement from past to future. We have instead the constant succession of a developing harmony in which one strain rises out of another that preceded it and conceals in itself that which it has replaced. Or, if the self-manifestation were to exist without the factor of divisible Space, there would be no mutable relation of forms or intershock of forces; all would exist and not be worked out, — a spaceless self-consciousness purely subjective would contain all things in an infinite subjective grasp as in the mind of a cosmic poet or dreamer, but would not distribute itself through all in an indefinite objective self-extension. Or again, if Time alone were real, its successions would be a pure development in which one strain would rise out of another in a subjective free spontaneity as in a series of musical sounds or a succession of poetical images. We have instead a harmony worked out by Time in terms of forms and forces that stand related to one another in an all-containing spatial extension; an incessant succession of powers and figures of things and happenings in our vision of existence.

Different potentialities are embodied, placed, related in this field of Time and Space, each with its powers and possibilities fronting other powers and possibilities, and as a result the successions of Time become in their appearance to the mind a working out of things by shock and struggle and not a spontaneous succession. In reality, there is a spontaneous working out of things from within and the external shock and struggle are only the superficial aspect of this elaboration. For the inner and inherent law of the one and whole, which is necessarily a harmony, governs the outer and processive laws of the parts or forms which appear to be in collision; and to the supramental vision this greater and profounder truth of harmony is always present. That which is an apparent discord to the mind because it considers each thing separately in itself, is an element of the general ever-present and ever-developing harmony to the Supermind because it views all things in a multiple unity. Besides, the mind sees only a given time and space and views many possibilities pell-mell as all more or less realisable in that time and space; the divine Supermind sees the whole extension of Time and Space and can embrace all the mind's possibilities and very many more not visible to the mind, but without any error, groping or confusion; for it perceives each potentiality in its proper force, essential necessity, right relation to the others and the time, place and circumstance both of its gradual and its ultimate realisation. To see things steadily and see them whole is not possible to the mind; but it is the very nature of the transcendent Supermind.

This Supermind in its conscious vision not only contains all the forms of itself which its conscious force creates, but it pervades them as an indwelling Presence and a self-revealing Light. It is present, even though concealed, in every form and force of the universe; it is that which determines sovereignly and spontaneously form, force and functioning; it limits the variations it compels; it gathers, disperses, modifies the energy which it uses; and all this is done in accord with the first laws[2] that its self-knowledge has fixed in the very birth of the form, at the very starting-point of the force. It is seated within everything as the Lord in the heart of all existences, — he who turns them as on an engine by the power of his Maya;[3] it is within them and embraces them as the divine Seer who variously disposed and ordained objects, each rightly according to the thing that it is, from years sempiternal.[4]

Each thing in Nature, therefore, whether animate or inanimate, mentally self-conscious or not self-conscious, is governed in its being and in its operations by an indwelling Vision and Power, to us subconscient or inconscient because we are not conscious of it, but not inconscient to itself, rather profoundly and universally conscient. Therefore each thing seems to do the works of intelligence, even without possessing intelligence, because it obeys, whether subconsciously as in the plant and animal or half-consciously as in man, the real-idea of the divine Supermind within it. But it is not a mental Intelligence that informs and governs all things; it is a self-aware Truth of being in which self-knowledge is inseparable from self-existence: it is this Truth-Consciousness which has not to think out things but works them out with knowledge according to the impeccable self-vision and the inevitable force of a sole and self-fulfilling

---

[2] A Vedic expression. The gods act according to the first laws, original and therefore supreme, which are the law of the truth of things.
[3] *Gita*, XVIII. 61.
[4] *Isha Upanishad,* Verse 8.

Existence. Mental intelligence thinks out because it is merely
a reflecting force of consciousness which does not know, but
seeks to know; it follows in Time step by step the working of
a knowledge higher than itself, a knowledge that exists always,
one and whole, that holds Time in its grasp, that sees past,
present and future in a single regard.

This, then, is the first operative principle of the divine Supermind; it is a cosmic vision which is all-comprehensive, all-
pervading, all-inhabiting. Because it comprehends all things in
being and static self-awareness, subjective, timeless, spaceless,
therefore it comprehends all things in dynamic knowledge and
governs their objective self-embodiment in Space and Time.

In this consciousness the knower, knowledge and the known
are not different entities, but fundamentally one. Our mentality
makes a distinction between these three because without distinctions it cannot proceed; losing its proper means and fundamental
law of action, it becomes motionless and inactive. Therefore,
even when I regard myself mentally, I have still to make this
distinction. I am, as the knower; what I observe in myself, I
regard as the object of my knowledge, myself yet not myself;
knowledge is an operation by which I link the knower to the
known. But the artificiality, the purely practical and utilitarian
character of this operation is evident; it is evident that it does
not represent the fundamental truth of things. In reality, I the
knower am the consciousness which knows; the knowledge is
that consciousness, myself, operating; the known is also myself,
a form or movement of the same consciousness. The three are
clearly one existence, one movement, indivisible though seeming
to be divided, not distributed between its forms although appearing to distribute itself and to stand separate in each. But this is
a knowledge which the mind can arrive at, can reason out, can
feel, but cannot readily make the practical basis of its intelligent
operations. And with regard to objects external to the form of
consciousness which I call myself, the difficulty becomes almost
insuperable; even to feel unity there is an abnormal effort and to
retain it, to act upon it continually would be a new and foreign
action not properly belonging to the Mind. Mind can at most

hold it as an understood truth so as to correct and modify by it its own normal activities which are still based upon division, somewhat as we know intellectually that the earth moves round the sun and are able to correct by it but not abolish the artificial and physically practical arrangement by which the senses persist in regarding the sun as in motion round the earth.

But the Supermind possesses and acts always, fundamentally, on this truth of unity which to the mind is only a secondary or acquired possession and not the very grain of its seeing. Supermind sees the universe and its contents as itself in a single indivisible act of knowledge, an act which is its life, which is the very movement of its self-existence. Therefore this comprehensive divine consciousness in its aspect of Will does not so much guide or govern the development of cosmic life as consummate it in itself by an act of power which is inseparable from the act of knowledge and from the movement of self-existence, is indeed one and the same act. For we have seen that universal force and universal consciousness are one, — cosmic force is the operation of cosmic consciousness. So also divine Knowledge and divine Will are one; they are the same fundamental movement or act of existence.

This indivisibility of the comprehensive Supermind which contains all multiplicity without derogating from its own unity, is a truth upon which we have always to insist, if we are to understand the cosmos and get rid of the initial error of our analytic mentality. A tree evolves out of the seed in which it is already contained, the seed out of the tree; a fixed law, an invariable process reigns in the permanence of the form of manifestation which we call a tree. The mind regards this phenomenon, this birth, life and reproduction of a tree, as a thing in itself and on that basis studies, classes and explains it. It explains the tree by the seed, the seed by the tree; it declares a law of Nature. But it has explained nothing; it has only analysed and recorded the process of a mystery. Supposing even that it comes to perceive a secret conscious force as the soul, the real being of this form and the rest as merely a settled operation and manifestation of that force, still it tends to regard the form as a separate existence with its separate law of nature and process of development. In the animal and in man with his conscious mentality this separative tendency of the Mind induces it to regard itself also as a separate existence, the conscious subject, and other forms as separate objects of its mentality. This useful arrangement, necessary to life and the first basis of all its practice, is accepted by the mind as an actual fact and thence proceeds all the error of the ego.

But the Supermind works otherwise. The tree and its process would not be what they are, could not indeed exist, if it were a separate existence; forms are what they are by the force of the cosmic existence, they develop as they do as a result of their relation to it and to all its other manifestations. The separate law of their nature is only an application of the universal law and truth of all Nature; their particular development is determined by their place in the general development. The tree does not explain the seed, nor the seed the tree; cosmos explains both and God explains cosmos. The Supermind, pervading and inhabiting at once the seed and the tree and all objects, lives in this greater knowledge which is indivisible and one though with a modified and not an absolute indivisibility and unity. In this comprehensive knowledge there is no independent centre of existence, no individual separated ego such as we see in ourselves; the whole of existence is to its self-awareness an equable extension, one in oneness, one in multiplicity, one in all conditions and everywhere. Here the All and the One are the same existence; the individual being does not and cannot lose the consciousness of its identity with all beings and with the One Being; for that identity is inherent in supramental cognition, a part of the supramental self-evidence.

In that spacious equality of oneness the Being is not divided and distributed; equally self-extended, pervading its extension as One, inhabiting as One the multiplicity of forms, it is everywhere at once the single and equal Brahman. For this extension of the Being in Time and Space and this pervasion and indwelling is in intimate relation with the absolute Unity from which it has proceeded, with that absolute Indivisible in which there is no centre or circumference but only the timeless and spaceless One.

That high concentration of unity in the unextended Brahman must necessarily translate itself in the extension by this equal pervasive concentration, this indivisible comprehension of all things, this universal undistributed immanence, this unity which no play of multiplicity can abrogate or diminish. "Brahman is in all things, all things are in Brahman, all things are Brahman", is the triple formula of the comprehensive Supermind, a single truth of self-manifestation in three aspects which it holds together and inseparably in its self-view as the fundamental knowledge from which it proceeds to the play of the cosmos.

But what then is the origin of mentality and the organisation of this lower consciousness in the triple terms of Mind, Life and Matter which is our view of the universe? For since all things that exist must proceed from the action of the all-efficient Supermind, from its operation in the three original terms of Existence, Conscious-Force and Bliss, there must be some faculty of the creative Truth-Consciousness which so operates as to cast them into these new terms, into this inferior trio of mentality, vitality and physical substance. This faculty we find in a secondary power of the creative knowledge, its power of a projecting, confronting and apprehending consciousness in which knowledge centralises itself and stands back from its works to observe them. And when we speak of centralisation, we mean, as distinguished from the equable concentration of consciousness of which we have hitherto spoken, an unequal concentration in which there is the beginning of self-division, — or of its phenomenal appearance.

First of all, the Knower holds himself concentrated in knowledge as subject and regards his Force of consciousness as if continually proceeding from him into the form of himself, continually working in it, continually drawing back into himself, continually issuing forth again. From this single act of self-modification proceed all the practical distinctions upon which the relative view and the relative action of the universe is based. A practical distinction has been created between the Knower, Knowledge and the Known, between the Lord, His force and the children and works of the Force, between the Enjoyer, the

Enjoyment and the Enjoyed, between the Self, Maya and the becomings of the Self.

Secondly, this conscious Soul concentrated in knowledge, this Purusha observing and governing the Force that has gone forth from him, his Shakti or Prakriti, repeats himself in every form of himself. He accompanies, as it were, his Force of consciousness into its works and reproduces there the act of self-division from which this apprehending consciousness is born. In each form this Soul dwells with his Nature and observes himself in other forms from that artificial and practical centre of consciousness. In all it is the same Soul, the same divine Being; the multiplication of centres is only a practical act of consciousness intended to institute a play of difference, of mutuality, mutual knowledge, mutual shock of force, mutual enjoyment, a difference based upon essential unity, a unity realised on a practical basis of difference.

We can speak of this new status of the all-pervading Supermind as a further departure from the unitarian truth of things and from the indivisible consciousness which constitutes inalienably the unity essential to the existence of the cosmos. We can see that pursued a little farther it may become truly Avidya, the great Ignorance which starts from multiplicity as the fundamental reality and in order to travel back to real unity has to commence with the false unity of the ego. We can see also that once the individual centre is accepted as the determining standpoint, as the knower, mental sensation, mental intelligence, mental action of will and all their consequences cannot fail to come into being. But also we have to see that so long as the soul acts in the Supermind, Ignorance has not yet begun; the field of knowledge and action is still the Truth-Consciousness, the basis is still the unity.

For the Self still regards itself as one in all and all things as becomings in itself and of itself; the Lord still knows his Force as himself in act and every being as himself in soul and himself in form; it is still his own being that the Enjoyer enjoys, even though in a multiplicity. The one real change has been an unequal concentration of consciousness and a multiple distribution of force. There is a practical distinction in consciousness, but there is no essential difference of consciousness or true division in its vision of itself. The Truth-Consciousness has arrived at a position which prepares our mentality, but is not yet that of our mentality. And it is this that we must study in order to seize Mind at its origin, at the point where it makes its great lapse from the high and vast wideness of the Truth-Consciousness into the division and the ignorance. Fortunately, this apprehending Truth-Consciousness[5] is much more facile to our grasp by its nearness to us, by its foreshadowing of our mental operations than the remoter realisation that we have hitherto been struggling to express in our inadequate language of the intellect. The barrier that has to be crossed is less formidable.

[5] *Prajñāna.*

Chapter XVI

The Triple Status of Supermind

My self is that which supports all beings and constitutes their
existence.... I am the self which abides within all beings.
Gita.[1]

Three powers of Light uphold three luminous worlds divine.
Rig Veda.[2]

BEFORE we pass to this easier understanding of the world
we inhabit from the standpoint of an apprehending Truth-
Consciousness which sees things as would an individual
soul freed from the limitations of mentality and admitted to
participate in the action of the Divine Supermind, we must pause
and resume briefly what we have realised or can yet realise of the
consciousness of the Lord, the Ishwara as He develops the world
by His Maya out of the original concentrated unity of His being.

We have started with the assertion of all existence as one Being whose essential nature is Consciousness, one Consciousness
whose active nature is Force or Will; and this Being is Delight,
this Consciousness is Delight, this Force or Will is Delight. Eternal and inalienable Bliss of Existence, Bliss of Consciousness,
Bliss of Force or Will whether concentrated in itself and at rest
or active and creative, this is God and this is ourselves in our
essential, our non-phenomenal being. Concentrated in itself, it
possesses or rather is the essential, eternal, inalienable Bliss;
active and creative, it possesses or rather becomes the delight
of the play of existence, the play of consciousness, the play of
force and will. That play is the universe and that delight is the
sole cause, motive and object of cosmic existence. The Divine

---

[1] IX. 5; X. 20.   [2] V. 29. 1.

Consciousness possesses that play and delight eternally and in-alienably; our essential being, our real self which is concealed from us by the false self or mental ego, also enjoys that play and delight eternally and inalienably and cannot indeed do otherwise since it is one in being with the Divine Consciousness. If we aspire therefore to a divine life, we cannot attain to it by any other way than by unveiling this veiled self in us, by mounting from our present status in the false self or mental ego to a higher status in the true self, the Atman, by entering into that unity with the Divine Consciousness which something superconscient in us always enjoys, — otherwise we could not exist, — but which our conscious mentality has forfeited.

But when we thus assert this unity of Sachchidananda on the one hand and this divided mentality on the other, we posit two opposite entities one of which must be false if the other is to be held as true, one of which must be abolished if the other is to be enjoyed. Yet it is in the mind and its form of life and body that we exist on earth and, if we must abolish the consciousness of mind, life and body in order to reach the one Existence, Consciousness and Bliss, then a divine life here is impossible. We must abandon cosmic existence utterly as an illusion in order to enjoy or re-become the Transcendent. From this solution there is no escape unless there be an intermediate link between the two which can explain them to each other and establish between them such a relation as will make it possible for us to realise the one Existence, Consciousness, Delight in the mould of the mind, life and body.

The intermediate link exists. We call it the Supermind or the Truth-Consciousness, because it is a principle superior to mentality and exists, acts and proceeds in the fundamental truth and unity of things and not like the mind in their appearances and phenomenal divisions. The existence of the Supermind is a logical necessity arising directly from the position with which we have started. For in itself Sachchidananda must be a spaceless and timeless absolute of conscious existence that is bliss; but the world is, on the contrary, an extension in Time and Space and a movement, a working out, a development of relations and possibilities by causality — or what so appears to us — in Time and Space. The true name of this Causality is Divine Law and the essence of that Law is an inevitable self-development of the truth of the thing that is, as Idea, in the very essence of what is developed; it is a previously fixed determination of relative movements out of the stuff of infinite possibility. That which thus develops all things must be a Knowledge-Will or Conscious-Force; for all manifestation of universe is a play of the Conscious-Force which is the essential nature of existence. But the developing Knowledge-Will cannot be mental; for mind does not know, possess or govern this Law, but is governed by it, is one of its results, moves in the phenomena of the self-development and not at its root, observes as divided things the results of the development and strives in vain to arrive at their source and reality. Moreover this Knowledge-Will which develops all must be in possession of the unity of things and must out of it manifest their multiplicity; but mind is not in possession of that unity, it has only an imperfect possession of a part of the multiplicity.

Therefore there must be a principle superior to the Mind which satisfies the conditions in which Mind fails. No doubt, it is Sachchidananda itself that is this principle, but Sachchidananda not resting in its pure infinite invariable consciousness, but proceeding out of this primal poise, or rather upon it as a base and in it as a continent, into a movement which is its form of Energy and instrument of cosmic creation. Conscious-ness and Force are the twin essential aspects of the pure Power of existence; Knowledge and Will must therefore be the form which that Power takes in creating a world of relations in the extension of Time and Space. This Knowledge and this Will must be one, infinite, all-embracing, all-possessing, all-forming, holding eternally in itself that which it casts into movement and form. The Supermind then is Being moving out into a deter-minative self-knowledge which perceives certain truths of itself and wills to realise them in a temporal and spatial extension of its own timeless and spaceless existence. Whatever is in its own being, takes form as self-knowledge, as Truth-Consciousness, as

Real-Idea, and, that self-knowledge being also self-force, fulfils or realises itself inevitably in Time and Space.

This, then, is the nature of the Divine Consciousness which creates in itself all things by a movement of its conscious-force and governs their development through a self-evolution by inherent knowledge-will of the truth of existence or real-idea which has formed them. The Being that is thus conscient is what we call God; and He must obviously be omnipresent, omniscient, omnipotent. Omnipresent, for all forms are forms of His conscious being created by its force of movement in its own extension as Space and Time; omniscient, for all things exist in His conscious-being, are formed by it and possessed by it; omnipotent, for this all-possessing consciousness is also an all-possessing Force and all-informing Will. And this Will and Knowledge are not at war with each other as our will and knowledge are capable of being at war with each other, because they are not different but are one movement of the same being. Nor can they be contradicted by any other will, force or consciousness from outside or within; for there is no consciousness or force external to the One, and all energies and formations of knowledge within are not other than it, but are merely play of the one all-determining Will and the one all-harmonising Knowledge. What we see as a clash of wills and forces, because we dwell in the particular and divided and cannot see the whole, the Supermind envisages as the conspiring elements of a predetermined harmony which is always present to it because the totality of things is eternally subject to its gaze.

Whatever be the poise or form its action takes, this will always be the nature of the divine Consciousness. But, its existence being absolute in itself, its power of existence is also absolute in its extension, and it is not therefore limited to one poise or one form of action. We, human beings, are phenomenally a particular form of consciousness, subject to Time and Space, and can only be, in our surface consciousness which is all we know of ourselves, one thing at a time, one formation, one poise of being, one aggregate of experience; and that one thing is for us the truth of ourselves which we acknowledge; all the rest is either not true or no longer true, because it has disappeared into the past out

of our ken, or not yet true, because it is waiting in the future
and not yet in our ken. But the Divine Consciousness is not so
particularised, nor so limited; it can be many things at a time
and take more than one enduring poise even for all time. We find
that in the principle of Supermind itself it has three such general
poises or sessions of its world-founding consciousness. The first
founds the inalienable unity of things, the second modifies that
unity so as to support the manifestation of the Many in One
and One in Many; the third further modifies it so as to support
the evolution of a diversified individuality which, by the action
of Ignorance, becomes in us at a lower level the illusion of the
separate ego.

We have seen what is the nature of this first and primary
poise of the Supermind which founds the inalienable unity of
things. It is not the pure unitarian consciousness; for that is
a timeless and spaceless concentration of Sachchidananda in
itself, in which Conscious Force does not cast itself out into any
kind of extension and, if it contains the universe at all, contains
it in eternal potentiality and not in temporal actuality. This,
on the contrary, is an equal self-extension of Sachchidananda
all-comprehending, all-possessing, all-constituting. But this all
is one, not many; there is no individualisation. It is when the
reflection of this Supermind falls upon our stilled and purified self that we lose all sense of individuality; for there is no
concentration of consciousness there to support an individual
development. All is developed in unity and as one; all is held
by this Divine Consciousness as forms of its existence, not as in
any degree separate existences. Somewhat as the thoughts and
images that occur in our mind are not separate existences to
us, but forms taken by our consciousness, so are all names and
forms to this primary Supermind. It is the pure divine ideation
and formation in the Infinite, — only an ideation and formation
that is organised not as an unreal play of mental thought, but
as a real play of conscious being. The divine soul in this poise
would make no difference between Conscious-Soul and Force-
Soul, for all force would be action of consciousness, nor between
Matter and Spirit since all mould would be simply form of Spirit.

In the second poise of the Supermind the Divine Consciousness stands back in the idea from the movement which it contains, realising it by a sort of apprehending consciousness, following it, occupying and inhabiting its works, seeming to distribute itself in its forms. In each name and form it would realise itself as the stable Conscious-Self, the same in all; but also it would realise itself as a concentration of Conscious-Self following and supporting the individual play of movement and upholding its differentiation from other play of movement, — the same everywhere in soul-essence, but varying in soul-form. This concentration supporting the soul-form would be the individual Divine or Jivatman as distinguished from the universal Divine or one all-constituting self. There would be no essential difference, but only a practical differentiation for the play which would not abrogate the real unity. The universal Divine would know all soul-forms as itself and yet establish a different relation with each separately and in each with all the others. The individual Divine would envisage its existence as a soul-form and soul-movement of the One and, while by the comprehending action of consciousness it would enjoy its unity with the One and with all soul-forms, it would also by a forward or frontal apprehending action support and enjoy its individual movement and its relations of a free difference in unity both with the One and with all its forms. If our purified mind were to reflect this secondary poise of Supermind, our soul could support and occupy its individual existence and yet even there realise itself as the One that has become all, inhabits all, contains all, enjoying even in its particular modification its unity with God and its fellows. In no other circumstance of the supramental existence would there be any characteristic change; the only change would be this play of the One that has manifested its multiplicity and of the Many that are still one, with all that is necessary to maintain and conduct the play.

A third poise of the Supermind would be attained if the supporting concentration were no longer to stand at the back, as it were, of the movement, inhabiting it with a certain superiority to it and so following and enjoying, but were to project itself into the movement and to be in a way involved in it. Here, the character of the play would be altered, but only in so far as the individual Divine would so predominantly make the play of relations with the universal and with its other forms the practical field of its conscious experience that the realisation of utter unity with them would be only a supreme accompaniment and constant culmination of all experience; but in the higher poise unity would be the dominant and fundamental experience and variation would be only a play of the unity. This tertiary poise would be therefore that of a sort of fundamental blissful dualism in unity — no longer unity qualified by a subordinate dualism — between the individual Divine and its universal source, with all the consequences that would accrue from the maintenance and operation of such a dualism.

It may be said that the first consequence would be a lapse into the ignorance of Avidya which takes the Many for the real fact of existence and views the One only as a cosmic sum of the Many. But there would not necessarily be any such lapse. For the individual Divine would still be conscious of itself as the result of the One and of its power of conscious self-creation, that is to say, of its multiple self-centration conceived so as to govern and enjoy manifoldly its manifold existence in the extension of Time and Space; this true spiritual individual would not arrogate to itself an independent or separate existence. It would only affirm the truth of the differentiating movement along with the truth of the stable unity, regarding them as the upper and lower poles of the same truth, the foundation and culmination of the same divine play; and it would insist on the joy of the differentiation as necessary to the fullness of the joy of the unity.

Obviously, these three poises would be only different ways of dealing with the same Truth; the Truth of existence enjoyed would be the same, the way of enjoying it or rather the poise of the soul in enjoying it would be different. The delight, the Ananda would vary, but would abide always within the status of the Truth-Consciousness and involve no lapse into the Falsehood and the Ignorance. For the secondary and tertiary Supermind would only develop and apply in the terms of the divine multiplicity what the primary Supermind had held in the terms of the divine unity. We cannot stamp any of these three poises with the stigma of falsehood and illusion. The language of the Upanishads, the supreme ancient authority for these truths of a higher experience, when they speak of the Divine existence which is manifesting itself, implies the validity of all these experiences. We can only assert the priority of the oneness to the multiplicity, a priority not in time but in relation of consciousness, and no statement of supreme spiritual experience, no Vedantic philosophy denies this priority or the eternal dependence of the Many on the One. It is because in Time the Many seem not to be eternal but to manifest out of the One and return into it as their essence that their reality is denied; but it might equally be reasoned that the eternal persistence or, if you will, the eternal recurrence of the manifestation in Time is a proof that the divine multiplicity is an eternal fact of the Supreme beyond Time no less than the divine unity; otherwise it could not have this characteristic of inevitable eternal recurrence in Time.

It is indeed only when our human mentality lays an exclusive emphasis on one side of spiritual experience, affirms that to be the sole eternal truth and states it in the terms of our all-dividing mental logic that the necessity for mutually destructive schools of philosophy arises. Thus, emphasising the sole truth of the unitarian consciousness, we observe the play of the divine unity, erroneously rendered by our mentality into the terms of real difference, but, not satisfied with correcting this error of the mind by the truth of a higher principle, we assert that the play itself is an illusion. Or, emphasising the play of the One in the Many, we declare a qualified unity and regard the individual soul as a soul-form of the Supreme, but would assert the eternity of this qualified existence and deny altogether the experience of a pure consciousness in an unqualified oneness. Or, again, emphasising the play of difference, we assert that the Supreme and the human soul are eternally different and reject the validity of an experience which exceeds and seems to abolish that difference. But the position that we have now firmly taken absolves us from the necessity of these negations and exclusions: we see that there is a truth behind all these affirmations, but at the same time an excess which leads to an ill-founded negation. Affirming, as we have done, the absolute absoluteness of That, not limited by our ideas of unity, not limited by our ideas of multiplicity, affirming the unity as a basis for the manifestation of the multiplicity and the multiplicity as the basis for the return to oneness and the enjoyment of unity in the divine manifestation, we need not burden our present statement with these discussions or undertake the vain labour of enslaving to our mental distinctions and definitions the absolute freedom of the Divine Infinite.

Chapter XVII

The Divine Soul

He whose self has become all existences, for he has the knowledge, how shall he be deluded, whence shall he have grief, he
who sees everywhere oneness?   *Isha Upanishad.*[1]

BY THE conception we have formed of the Supermind,
by its opposition to the mentality on which our human
existence is based, we are able not only to form a precise
instead of a vague idea of divinity and the divine life, — expressions which we are otherwise condemned to use with looseness
and as the vague wording of a large but almost impalpable
aspiration, — but also to give these ideas a firm basis of philosophical reasoning, to put them into a clear relation with the
humanity and the human life which is all we at present enjoy
and to justify our hope and aspiration by the very nature of the
world and of our own cosmic antecedents and the inevitable
future of our evolution. We begin to grasp intellectually what
is the Divine, the eternal Reality, and to understand how out
of it the world has come. We begin also to perceive how inevitably that which has come out of the Divine must return
to the Divine. We may now ask with profit and a chance of
clearer reply how we must change and what we must become
in order to arrive there in our nature and our life and our relations with others and not only through a solitary and ecstatic
realisation in the profundities of our being. Certainly, there is
still a defect in our premisses; for we have so far been striving
to define for ourselves what the Divine is in its descent towards
limited Nature, whereas what we ourselves actually are is the

[1] Verse 7.

Divine in the individual ascending back out of limited Nature to its own proper divinity. This difference of movement must involve a difference between the life of the gods who have never known the fall and the life of man redeemed, conqueror of the lost godhead and bearing within him the experience and it may be the new riches gathered by him from his acceptance of the utter descent. Nevertheless, there can be no difference of essential characteristics, but only of mould and colouring. We can already ascertain on the basis of the conclusions at which we have arrived the essential nature of the divine life towards which we aspire.

What then would be the existence of a divine soul, not descended into the ignorance by the fall of Spirit into Matter and the eclipse of soul by material Nature? What would be its consciousness, living in the original Truth of things, in the inalienable unity, in the world of its own infinite being, like the Divine Existence itself, but able by the play of the Divine Maya and by the distinction of the comprehending and apprehending Truth-Consciousness to enjoy also difference from God at the same time as unity with Him and to embrace difference and yet oneness with other divine souls in the infinite play of the self-multiplied Identical?

Obviously, the existence of such a soul would be always self-contained in the conscious play of Sachchidananda. It would be pure and infinite self-existence in its being; in its becoming it would be a free play of immortal life uninvaded by death and birth and change of body because unclouded by ignorance and not involved in the darkness of our material being. It would be a pure and unlimited consciousness in its energy, poised in an eternal and luminous tranquillity as its foundation, yet able to play freely with forms of knowledge and forms of conscious power, tranquil, unaffected by the stumblings of mental error and the misprisions of our striving will because it never departs from truth and oneness, never falls from the inherent light and the natural harmony of its divine existence. It would be, finally, a pure and inalienable delight in its eternal self-experience and in Time a free variation of bliss unaffected by our perversions

0008747471405

of dislike, hatred, discontent and suffering because undivided in being, unbaffled by erring self-will, unperverted by the ignorant stimulus of desire.

Its consciousness would not be shut out from any part of the infinite truth, nor limited by any poise or status that it might assume in its relations with others, nor condemned to any loss of self-knowledge by its acceptance of a purely phenomenal individuality and the play of practical differentiation. It would in its self-experience live eternally in the presence of the Absolute. To us the Absolute is only an intellectual conception of indefinable existence. The intellect tells us simply that there is a Brahman higher than the highest,[2] an Unknowable that knows itself in other fashion than that of our knowledge; but the intellect cannot bring us into its presence. The divine soul living in the Truth of things would, on the contrary, always have the conscious sense of itself as a manifestation of the Absolute. Its immutable existence it would be aware of as the original "self-form"[3] of that Transcendent, — Sachchidananda; its play of conscious being it would be aware of as manifestation of That in forms of Sachchidananda. In its every state or act of knowledge it would be aware of the Unknowable cognising itself by a form of variable self-knowledge; in its every state or act of power, will or force aware of the Transcendence possessing itself by a form of conscious power of being and knowledge; in its every state or act of delight, joy or love aware of the Transcendence embracing itself by a form of conscious self-enjoyment. This presence of the Absolute would not be with it as an experience occasionally glimpsed or finally arrived at and held with difficulty or as an addition, acquisition or culmination superimposed on its ordinary state of being: it would be the very foundation of its being both in the unity and the differentiation; it would be present to it in all its knowing, willing, doing, enjoying; it would be absent neither from its timeless self nor from any moment of Time, neither from its spaceless being

---

[2] *parātpara.*
[3] *svarūpa.*

nor from any determination of its extended existence, neither
from its unconditioned purity beyond all cause and circumstance
nor from any relation of circumstance, condition and causality.
This constant presence of the Absolute would be the basis of its
infinite freedom and delight, ensure its security in the play and
provide the root and sap and essence of its divine being.

Moreover, such a divine soul would live simultaneously in
the two terms of the eternal existence of Sachchidananda, the
two inseparable poles of the self-unfolding of the Absolute which
we call the One and the Many. All being does really so live; but
to our divided self-awareness there is an incompatibility, a gulf
between the two driving us towards a choice, to dwell either in
the multiplicity exiled from the direct and entire consciousness
of the One or in the unity repellent of the consciousness of the
Many. But the divine soul would not be enslaved to this divorce
and duality. It would be aware in itself at once of the infinite
self-concentration and the infinite self-extension and diffusion.
It would be aware simultaneously of the One in its unitarian
consciousness holding the innumerable multiplicity in itself as
if potential, unexpressed and therefore to our mental experience of that state non-existent and of the One in its extended
consciousness holding the multiplicity thrown out and active as
the play of its own conscious being, will and delight. It would
equally be aware of the Many ever drawing down to themselves
the One that is the eternal source and reality of their existence
and of the Many ever mounting up attracted to the One that
is the eternal culmination and blissful justification of all their
play of difference. This vast view of things is the mould of
the Truth-Consciousness, the foundation of the large Truth and
Right hymned by the Vedic seers; this unity of all these terms
of opposition is the real Adwaita, the supreme comprehending
word of the knowledge of the Unknowable.

The divine soul will be aware of all variation of being, consciousness, will and delight as the outflowing, the extension,
the diffusion of that self-concentrated Unity developing itself,
not into difference and division, but into another, an extended
form of infinite oneness. It will itself always be concentrated in

oneness in the essence of its being, always manifested in variation in the extension of its being. All that takes form in itself will be the manifested potentialities of the One, the Word or Name vibrating out of the nameless Silence, the Form realising the formless essence, the active Will or Power proceeding out of the tranquil Force, the ray of self-cognition gleaming out from the sun of timeless self-awareness, the wave of becoming rising up into shape of self-conscious existence out of the eternally self-conscious Being, the joy and love welling for ever out of the eternal still Delight. It will be the Absolute biune in its self-unfolding, and each relativity in it will be absolute to itself because aware of itself as the Absolute manifested but without that ignorance which excludes other relativities as alien to its being or less complete than itself.

In the extension the divine soul will be aware of the three grades of the supramental existence, not as we are mentally compelled to regard them, not as grades, but as a triune fact of the self-manifestation of Sachchidananda. It will be able to embrace them in one and the same comprehensive self-realisation, — for a vast comprehensiveness is the foundation of the truth-conscious Supermind. It will be able divinely to conceive, perceive and sense all things as the Self, its own self, one self of all, one Self-being and Self-becoming, but not divided in its becomings which have no existence apart from its own self-consciousness. It will be able divinely to conceive, perceive and sense all existences as soul-forms of the One which have each its own being in the One, its own standpoint in the One, its own relations with all the other existences that people the infinite unity, but all dependent on the One, conscious form of Him in His own infinity. It will be able divinely to conceive, perceive and sense all these existences in their individuality, in their separate standpoint living as the individual Divine, each with the One and Supreme dwelling in it and each therefore not altogether a form or eidolon, not really an illusory part of a real whole, a mere foaming wave on the surface of an immobile Ocean, — for these are after all no more than inadequate mental images, — but a whole in the whole, a truth that repeats the infinite Truth, a wave that is all the sea, a relative that proves to be the Absolute itself when we look behind form and see it in its completeness.

For these three are aspects of the one Existence. The first is based upon that self-knowledge which, in our human realisation of the Divine, the Upanishad describes as the Self in us becoming all existences; the second on that which is described as seeing all existences in the Self; the third on that which is described as seeing the Self in all existences. The Self becoming all existences is the basis of our oneness with all; the Self containing all existences is the basis of our oneness in difference; the Self inhabiting all is the basis of our individuality in the universal. If the defect of our mentality, if its need of exclusive concentration compels it to dwell on any one of these aspects of self-knowledge to the exclusion of the others, if a realisation imperfect as well as exclusive moves us always to bring in a human element of error into the very Truth itself and of conflict and mutual negation into the all-comprehending unity, yet to a divine supramental being, by the essential character of the Supermind which is a comprehending oneness and infinite totality, they must present themselves as a triple and indeed a triune realisation.

If we suppose this soul to take its poise, its centre in the consciousness of the individual Divine living and acting in distinct relation with the "others", still it will have in the foundation of its consciousness the entire unity from which all emerges and it will have in the background of that consciousness the extended and the modified unity and to any of these it will be capable of returning and of contemplating from them its individuality. In the Veda all these poises are asserted of the gods. In essence the gods are one existence which the sages call by different names; but in their action founded in and proceeding from the large Truth and Right Agni or another is said to be all the other gods, he is the One that becomes all; at the same time he is said to contain all the gods in himself as the nave of a wheel contains the spokes, he is the One that contains all; and yet as Agni he is described as a separate deity, one who helps all the others, exceeds them in force and knowledge, yet is inferior to them in cosmic position and is employed by them as messenger, priest and worker, — the creator of the world and father, he is yet the son born of our works, he is, that is to say, the original and the manifested indwelling Self or Divine, the One that inhabits all.

All the relations of the divine soul with God or its supreme Self and with its other selves in other forms will be determined by this comprehensive self-knowledge. These relations will be relations of being, of consciousness and knowledge, of will and force, of love and delight. Infinite in their potentiality of variation, they need exclude no possible relation of soul with soul that is compatible with the preservation of the inalienable sense of unity in spite of every phenomenon of difference. Thus in its relations of enjoyment the divine soul will have the delight of all its own experience in itself; it will have the delight of all its experience of relation with others as a communion with other selves in other forms created for a varied play in the universe; it will have too the delight of the experiences of its other selves as if they were its own — as indeed they really are. And all this capacity it will have because it will be aware of its own experiences, of its relations with others and of the experiences of others and their relations with itself as all the joy or Ananda of the One, the supreme Self, its own self, differentiated by its separate habitation of all these forms comprehended in its own being but still one in difference. Because this unity is the basis of all its experience, it will be free from the discords of our divided consciousness, divided by ignorance and a separatist egoism; all these selves and their relations will play consciously into each other's hands; they will part and melt into each other as the numberless notes of an eternal harmony.

And the same rule will apply to the relations of its being, knowledge, will with the being, knowledge and will of others. For all its experience and delight will be the play of a self-blissful conscious force of being in which, by obedience to this truth of unity, will cannot be at strife with knowledge nor either of them with delight. Nor will the knowledge, will and delight of one soul clash with the knowledge, will and delight of another, because by their awareness of their unity what is clash and strife and discord in our divided being will be there the meeting, entwining and mutual interplay of the different notes of one infinite harmony.

In its relations with its supreme Self, with God, the divine soul will have this sense of the oneness of the transcendent and universal Divine with its own being. It will enjoy that oneness of God with itself in its own individuality and with its other selves in the universality. Its relations of knowledge will be the play of the divine omniscience, for God is Knowledge, and what is ignorance with us will be there only the holding back of knowledge in the repose of conscious self-awareness so that certain forms of that self-awareness may be brought forward into activity of Light. Its relations of will will be there the play of the divine omnipotence, for God is Force, Will and Power, and what with us is weakness and incapacity will be the holding back of will in tranquil concentrated force so that certain forms of divine conscious-force may realise themselves brought forward into form of Power. Its relations of love and delight will be the play of the divine ecstasy, for God is Love and Delight, and what with us would be denial of love and delight will be the holding back of joy in the still sea of Bliss so that certain forms of divine union and enjoyment may be brought in front in an active upwelling of waves of the Bliss. So also all its becoming will be formation of the divine being in response to these activities and what is with us cessation, death, annihilation will be only rest, transition or holding back of the joyous creative Maya in the eternal being of Sachchidananda. At the same time this oneness will not preclude relations of the divine soul with God, with its supreme Self, founded on the joy of difference separating itself from unity to enjoy that unity otherwise; it will not annul the possibility of any of those exquisite forms of God-enjoyment which are the highest rapture of the God-lover in his clasp of the Divine.

But what will be the conditions in which and by which this nature of the life of the divine soul will realise itself? All experience in relation proceeds through certain forces of being formulating themselves by an instrumentation to which we give the name of properties, qualities, activities, faculties. As, for instance, Mind throws itself into various forms of mind-power, such as judgment, observation, memory, sympathy, proper to its own being, so must the Truth-Consciousness or Supermind effect the relations of soul with soul by forces, faculties, functionings proper to supramental being; otherwise there would be no play of differentiation. What these functionings are, we shall see when we come to consider the psychological conditions of the divine Life; at present we are only considering its metaphysical foundations, its essential nature and principles. Suffice it at present to observe that the absence or abolition of separatist egoism and of effective division in consciousness is the one essential condition of the divine Life, and therefore their presence in us is that which constitutes our mortality and our fall from the Divine. This is our "original sin", or rather let us say in a more philosophical language, the deviation from the Truth and Right of the Spirit, from its oneness, integrality and harmony that was the necessary condition for the great plunge into the Ignorance which is the soul's adventure in the world and from which was born our suffering and aspiring humanity.

Chapter XVIII

Mind and Supermind

He discovered that Mind was the Brahman.

Taittiriya Upanishad.[1]

Indivisible, but as if divided in beings.

Gita.[2]

THE CONCEPTION which we have so far been striving to form is that of the essence only of the supramental life which the divine soul possesses securely in the being of Sachchidananda, but which the human soul has to manifest in this body of Sachchidananda formed here into the mould of a mental and physical living. But so far as we have been able yet to envisage this supramental existence, it does not seem to have any connection or correspondence with life as we know it, life active between the two terms of our normal existence, the two firmaments of mind and body. It seems rather to be a state of being, a state of consciousness, a state of active relation and mutual enjoyment such as disembodied souls might possess and experience in a world without physical forms, a world in which differentiation of souls had been accomplished but not differentiation of bodies, a world of active and joyous infinities, not of form-imprisoned spirits. Therefore it might reasonably be doubted whether such a divine living would be possible with this limitation of bodily form and this limitation of form-imprisoned mind and form-trammelled force which is what we now know as existence.

In fact, we have striven to arrive at some conception of that supreme infinite being, conscious-force and self-delight of

[1] III. 4.   [2] XIII. 17.

which our world is a creation and our mentality a perverse figure; we have tried to give ourselves an idea of what this divine Maya may be, this Truth-Consciousness, this Real-Idea by which the conscious force of the transcendent and universal Existence conceives, forms and governs the universe, the order, the cosmos of its manifested delight of being. But we have not studied the connections of these four great and divine terms with the three others with which our human experience is alone familiar, — mind, life and body. We have not scrutinised this other and apparently undivine Maya which is the root of all our striving and suffering or seen how precisely it develops out of the divine reality or the divine Maya. And till we have done this, till we have woven the missing cords of connection, our world is still unexplained to us and the doubt of a possible unification between that higher existence and this lower life has still a basis. We know that our world has come forth from Sachchidananda and subsists in His being; we conceive that He dwells in it as the Enjoyer and Knower, Lord and Self; we have seen that our dual terms of sensation, mind, force, being can only be representations of His delight, His conscious force, His divine existence. But it would seem that they are actually so much the opposite of what He really and supernally is that we cannot while dwelling in the cause of these opposites, cannot while contained in the lower triple term of existence attain to the divine living. We must either exalt this lower being into that higher status or exchange body for that pure existence, life for that pure condition of conscious-force, sensation and mentality for that pure delight and knowledge which live in the truth of the spiritual reality. And must not this mean that we abandon all earthly or limited mental existence for something which is its opposite, — either for some pure state of the Spirit or else for some world of the Truth of things, if such exists, or other worlds, if such exist, of divine Bliss, divine Energy, divine Being? In that case the perfection of humanity is elsewhere than in humanity itself; the summit of its earthly evolution can only be a fine apex of dissolving mentality whence it takes the great leap either into formless being or into worlds beyond the reach of embodied Mind.

But in reality all that we call undivine can only be an action of the four divine principles themselves, such action of them as was necessary to create this universe of forms. Those forms have been created not outside but in the divine existence, conscious-force and bliss, not outside but in and as a part of the working of the divine Real-Idea. There is therefore no reason to suppose that there cannot be any real play of the higher divine consciousness in a world of forms or that forms and their immediate supports, mental consciousness, energy of vital force and formal substance, must necessarily distort that which they represent. It is possible, even probable that mind, body and life are to be found in their pure forms in the divine Truth itself, are there in fact as subordinate activities of its consciousness and part of the complete instrumentation by which the supreme Force always works. Mind, life and body must then be capable of divinity; their form and working in that short period out of possibly only one cycle of the terrestrial evolution which Science reveals to us, need not represent all the potential workings of these three principles in the living body. They work as they do because they are by some means separated in consciousness from the divine Truth from which they proceed. Were this separation once abrogated by the expanding energy of the Divine in humanity, their present functioning might well be converted, would indeed naturally be converted by a supreme evolution and progression into that purer working which they have in the Truth-Consciousness.

In that case not only would it be possible to manifest and maintain the divine consciousness in the human mind and body but, even, that divine consciousness might in the end, increasing its conquests, remould mind, life and body themselves into a more perfect image of its eternal Truth and realise not only in soul but in substance its kingdom of heaven upon earth. The first of these victories, the internal, has certainly been achieved in a greater or less degree by some, perhaps by many, upon earth; the other, the external, even if never more or less realised in past aeons as a first type for future cycles and still held in the subconscious memory of the earth-nature, may yet be intended as a coming victorious achievement of God in humanity. This earthly life need not be necessarily and for ever a wheel of half-joyous half-anguished effort; attainment may also be intended and the glory and joy of God made manifest upon earth.

What Mind, Life and Body are in their supreme sources and what therefore they must be in the integral completeness of the divine manifestation when informed by the Truth and not cut off from it by the separation and the ignorance in which presently we live, — this then is the problem that we have next to consider. For there they must have already their perfection towards which we here are growing, — we who are only the first shackled movement of the Mind which is evolving in Matter, we who are not yet liberated from the conditions and effects of that involution of spirit in form, that plunge of Light into its own shadow by which the darkened material consciousness of physical Nature was created. The type of all perfection towards which we grow, the terms of our highest evolution must already be held in the divine Real-Idea; they must be there formed and conscious for us to grow towards and into them: for that pre-existence in the divine knowledge is what our human mentality names and seeks as the Ideal. The Ideal is an eternal Reality which we have not yet realised in the conditions of our own being, not a non-existent which the Eternal and Divine has not yet grasped and only we imperfect beings have glimpsed and mean to create.

Mind, first, the chained and hampered sovereign of our human living. Mind in its essence is a consciousness which measures, limits, cuts out forms of things from the indivisible whole and contains them as if each were a separate integer. Even with what exists only as obvious parts and fractions, Mind establishes this fiction of its ordinary commerce that they are things with which it can deal separately and not merely as aspects of a whole. For, even when it knows that they are not things in themselves, it is obliged to deal with them as if they were things in themselves; otherwise it could not subject them to its own characteristic activity. It is this essential characteristic of Mind which conditions the workings of all its operative powers, whether conception, perception, sensation or the dealings of creative thought. It conceives, perceives, senses things as if rigidly cut out from a background or a mass and employs them as fixed units of the material given to it for creation or possession. All its action and enjoyment deal thus with wholes that form part of a greater whole, and these subordinate wholes again are broken up into parts which are also treated as wholes for the particular purposes they serve. Mind may divide, multiply, add, subtract, but it cannot get beyond the limits of this mathematics. If it goes beyond and tries to conceive a real whole, it loses itself in a foreign element; it falls from its own firm ground into the ocean of the intangible, into the abysms of the infinite where it can neither perceive, conceive, sense nor deal with its subject for creation and enjoyment. For if Mind appears sometimes to conceive, to perceive, to sense or to enjoy with possession the infinite, it is only in seeming and always in a figure of the infinite. What it does thus vaguely possess is simply a formless Vast and not the real spaceless infinite. The moment it tries to deal with that, to possess it, at once the inalienable tendency to delimitation comes in and the Mind finds itself again handling images, forms and words. Mind cannot possess the infinite, it can only suffer it or be possessed by it; it can only lie blissfully helpless under the luminous shadow of the Real cast down on it from planes of existence beyond its reach. The possession of the infinite cannot come except by an ascent to those supramental planes, nor the knowledge of it except by an inert submission of Mind to the descending messages of the Truth-Conscious Reality.

This essential faculty and the essential limitation that accompanies it are the truth of Mind and fix its real nature and action, *svabhāva* and *svadharma*; here is the mark of the divine fiat assigning it its office in the complete instrumentation of the supreme Maya, — the office determined by that which it is in its very birth from the eternal self-conception of the Self-existent. That office is to translate always infinity into the terms of the finite, to measure off, limit, depiece. Actually it does this in our consciousness to the exclusion of all true sense of the infinite; therefore Mind is the nodus of the great Ignorance, because it is that which originally divides and distributes, and it has even been mistaken for the cause of the universe and for the whole of the divine Maya. But the divine Maya comprehends Vidya as well as Avidya, the Knowledge as well as the Ignorance. For it is obvious that since the finite is only an appearance of the infinite, a result of its action, a play of its conception and cannot exist except by it, in it, with it as a background, itself form of that stuff and action of that force, there must be an original consciousness which contains and views both at the same time and is intimately conscious of all the relations of the one with the other. In that consciousness there is no ignorance, because the infinite is known and the finite is not separated from it as an independent reality; but still there is a subordinate process of delimitation, — otherwise no world could exist, — a process by which the ever dividing and reuniting consciousness of Mind, the ever divergent and convergent action of Life and the infinitely divided and self-aggregating substance of Matter come, all by one principle and original act, into phenomenal being. This subordinate process of the eternal Seer and Thinker, perfectly luminous, perfectly aware of Himself and all, knowing well what He does, conscious of the infinite in the finite which He is creating, may be called the divine Mind. And it is obvious that it must be a subordinate and not really a separate working of the Real-Idea, of the Supermind, and must operate through what we have described as the apprehending movement of the Truth-Consciousness.

That apprehending consciousness, the Prajnana, places, as we have seen, the working of the indivisible All, active and formative, as a process and object of creative knowledge before the consciousness of the same All, originative and cognisant as the possessor and witness of its own working, — somewhat as a poet views the creations of his own consciousness placed before him in it as if they were things other than the creator and his creative force, yet all the time they are really no more than the play of self-formation of his own being in itself and are indivisible there from their creator. Thus Prajnana makes the fundamental division which leads to all the rest, the division of the Purusha, the conscious soul who knows and sees and by his vision creates and ordains, and the Prakriti, the Force-Soul or Nature-Soul which is his knowledge and his vision, his creation and his all-ordaining power. Both are one Being, one existence, and the forms seen and created are multiple forms of that Being which are placed by Him as Knowledge before Himself as Knower, by Himself as Force before Himself as Creator. The last action of this apprehending consciousness takes place when the Purusha pervading the conscious extension of his being, present at every point of himself as well as in his totality, inhabiting every form, regards the whole as if separately, from each of the standpoints he has taken; he views and governs the relations of each soul-form of himself with other soul-forms from the standpoint of will and knowledge appropriate to each particular form.

Thus the elements of division have come into being. First, the infinity of the One has translated itself into an extension in conceptual Time and Space; secondly, the omnipresence of the One in that self-conscious extension translates itself into a multiplicity of the conscious soul, the many Purushas of the Sankhya; thirdly, the multiplicity of soul-forms has translated itself into a divided habitation of the extended unity. This divided habitation is inevitable the moment these multiple Purushas do not each inhabit a separate world of its own, do not each possess a separate Prakriti building a separate universe, but rather all enjoy the same Prakriti, — as they must do, being only soul-forms of the One presiding over the multiple creations of His power, — yet have relations with each other in the one world of being created by the one Prakriti. The Purusha in each form actively identifies himself with each; he delimits himself in that and sets off his other forms against it in his consciousness as containing his other selves which are identical with him in being but different in relation, different in the various extent, various range of movement and various view of the one substance, force, consciousness, delight which each is actually deploying at any given moment of Time or in any given field of Space. Granted that in the divine Existence, perfectly aware of itself, this is not a binding limitation, not an identification to which the soul becomes enslaved and which it cannot exceed as we are enslaved to our self-identification with the body and unable to exceed the limitation of our conscious ego, unable to escape from a particular movement of our consciousness in Time determining our particular field in Space; granted all this, still there is a free identification from moment to moment which only the inalienable self-knowledge of the divine soul prevents from fixing itself in an apparently rigid chain of separation and Time succession such as that in which our consciousness seems to be fixed and chained.

Thus the depiecing is already there; the relation of form with form as if they were separate beings, of will-of-being with will-of-being as if they were separate forces, of knowledge-of-being with knowledge-of-being as if they were separate consciousnesses has already been founded. It is as yet only "as if"; for the divine soul is not deluded, it is aware of all as phenomenon of being and keeps hold of its existence in the reality of being; it does not forfeit its unity: it uses mind as a subordinate action of the infinite knowledge, a definition of things subordinate to its awareness of infinity, a delimitation dependent on its awareness of essential totality — not that apparent and pluralistic totality of sum and collective aggregation which is only another phenomenon of Mind. Thus there is no real limitation; the soul uses its defining power for the play of well-distinguished forms and forces and is not used by that power.

A new factor, a new action of conscious force is therefore needed to create the operation of a helplessly limited as opposed to a freely limiting mind, — that is to say, of mind subject to its own play and deceived by it as opposed to mind master of its own play and viewing it in its truth, the creature mind as opposed to the divine. That new factor is Avidya, the self-ignoring faculty which separates the action of mind from the action of the Supermind that originated and still governs it from behind the veil. Thus separated, Mind perceives only the particular and not the universal, or conceives only the particular in an unpossessed universal and no longer both particular and universal as phenomena of the Infinite. Thus we have the limited mind which

views every phenomenon as a thing-in-itself, separate part of a
whole which again exists separately in a greater whole and so
on, enlarging always its aggregates without getting back to the
sense of a true infinity.

Mind, being an action of the Infinite, depieces as well as
aggregates *ad infinitum*. It cuts up being into wholes, into ever
smaller wholes, into atoms and those atoms into primal atoms,
until it would, if it could, dissolve the primal atom into nothingness. But it cannot, because behind this dividing action is
the saving knowledge of the supramental which knows every
whole, every atom to be only a concentration of all-force, of
all-consciousness, of all-being into phenomenal forms of itself.
The dissolution of the aggregate into an infinite nothingness at
which Mind seems to arrive, is to the Supermind only the return
of the self-concentrating conscious-being out of its phenomenon
into its infinite existence. Whichever way its consciousness proceeds, by the way of infinite division or by the way of infinite
enlargement, it arrives only at itself, at its own infinite unity and
eternal being. And when the action of the mind is consciously
subordinate to this knowledge of the Supermind, the truth of the
process is known to it also and not at all ignored; there is no real
division but only an infinitely multiple concentration into forms
of being and into arrangements of the relation of those forms of
being to each other in which division is a subordinate appearance
of the whole process necessary to their spatial and temporal play.
For divide as you will, get down to the most infinitesimal atom
or form the most monstrous possible aggregate of worlds and
systems, you cannot get by either process to a thing-in-itself; all
are forms of a Force which alone is real in itself while the rest
are real only as self-imagings or manifesting self-forms of the
eternal Force-Consciousness.

Whence then does the limiting Avidya, the fall of mind
from Supermind and the consequent idea of real division originally proceed? exactly from what perversion of the supramental
functioning? It proceeds from the individualised soul viewing
everything from its own standpoint and excluding all others;
it proceeds, that is to say, by an exclusive concentration of

consciousness, an exclusive self-identification of the soul with a particular temporal and spatial action which is only a part of its own play of being; it starts from the soul's ignoring the fact that all others are also itself, all other action its own action and all other states of being and consciousness equally its own as well as the action of the one particular moment in Time and one particular standing-point in Space and the one particular form it presently occupies. It concentrates on the moment, the field, the form, the movement so as to lose the rest; it has then to recover the rest by linking together the succession of moments, the succession of points of Space, the succession of forms in Time and Space, the succession of movements in Time and Space. It has thus lost the truth of the indivisibility of Time, the indivisibility of Force and Substance. It has lost sight even of the obvious fact that all minds are one Mind taking many standpoints, all lives one Life developing many currents of activity, all body and form one substance of Force and Consciousness concentrating into many apparent stabilities of force and consciousness; but in truth all these stabilities are really only a constant whorl of movement repeating a form while it modifies it; they are nothing more. For the Mind tries to clamp everything into rigidly fixed forms and apparently unchanging or unmoving external factors, because otherwise it cannot act; it then thinks it has got what it wants: in reality all is a flux of change and renewal and there is no fixed form-in-itself and no unchanging external factor. Only the eternal Real-Idea is firm and maintains a certain ordered constancy of figures and relations in the flux of things, a constancy which the Mind vainly attempts to imitate by attributing fixity to that which is always inconstant. These truths Mind has to rediscover; it knows them all the time, but only in the hidden back of its consciousness, in the secret light of its self-being; and that light is to it a darkness because it has created the ignorance, because it has lapsed from the dividing into the divided mentality, because it has become involved in its own workings and in its own creations.

This ignorance is farther deepened for man by his self-identification with the body. To us mind seems to be determined by the body, because it is preoccupied with that and devoted to the physical workings which it uses for its conscious superficial action in this gross material world. Employing constantly that operation of the brain and nerves which it has developed in the course of its own development in the body, it is too absorbed in observing what this physical machinery gives to it to get back from it to its own pure workings; those are to it mostly subconscious. Still we can conceive a life mind or life being which has got beyond the evolutionary necessity of this absorption and is able to see and even experience itself assuming body after body and not created separately in each body and ending with it; for it is only the physical impress of mind on matter, only the corporeal mentality that is so created, not the whole mental being. This corporeal mentality is merely our surface of mind, merely the front which it presents to physical experience. Behind, even in our terrestrial being, there is this other, subconscious or subliminal to us, which knows itself as more than the body and is capable of a less materialised action. To this we owe immediately most of the larger, deeper and more forceful dynamic action of our surface mind; this, when we become conscious of it or of its impress on us, is our first idea or our first realisation of a soul or inner being, Purusha.[3]

But this life mentality also, though it may get free from the error of body, does not make us free from the whole error of mind; it is still subject to the original act of ignorance by which the individualised soul regards everything from its own standpoint and can see the truth of things only as they present themselves to it from outside or else as they rise up to its view from its separate temporal and spatial consciousness, forms and results of past and present experience. It is not conscious of its other selves except by the outward indications they give of their existence, indications of communicated thought, speech, action, result of actions, or subtler indications — not felt directly by the physical being — of vital impact and relation. Equally is it ignorant of itself; for it knows of its self only through a movement in

---

[3] Perceived as the life being or vital being, *prāṇamaya puruṣa*.

Time and a succession of lives in which it has used its variously embodied energies. As our physical instrumental mind has the illusion of the body, so this subconscious dynamic mind has the illusion of life. In that it is absorbed and concentrated, by that it is limited, with that it identifies its being. Here we do not yet get back to the meeting-place of mind and Supermind and the point at which they originally separated.

But there is still another clearer reflective mentality behind the dynamic and vital which is capable of escaping from this absorption in life and views itself as assuming life and body in order to image out in active relations of energy that which it perceives in will and thought. It is the source of the pure thinker in us; it is that which knows mentality in itself and sees the world not in terms of life and body but of mind; it is that[4] which, when we get back to it, we sometimes mistake for the pure spirit as we mistake the dynamic mind for the soul. This higher mind is able to perceive and deal with other souls as other forms of its pure self; it is capable of sensing them by pure mental impact and communication and no longer only by vital and nervous impact and physical indications; it conceives too a mental figure of unity, and in its activity and its will it can create and possess more directly — not only indirectly as in the ordinary physical life — and in other minds and lives as well as its own. But still even this pure mentality does not escape from the original error of mind. For it is still its separate mental self which it makes the judge, witness and centre of the universe and through it alone strives to arrive at its own higher self and reality; all others are "others" grouped to it around itself: when it wills to be free, it has to draw back from life and mind in order to disappear into the real unity. For there is still the veil created by Avidya between the mental and supramental action; an image of the Truth gets through, not the Truth itself.

It is only when the veil is rent and the divided mind over-powered, silent and passive to a supramental action that mind itself gets back to the Truth of things. There we find a luminous

---

[4] The mental being, *manomaya puruṣa*.

mentality reflective, obedient and instrumental to the divine
Real-Idea. There we perceive what the world really is; we know
in every way ourselves in others and as others, others as ourselves and all as the universal and self-multiplied One. We lose
the rigidly separate individual standpoint which is the source
of all limitation and error. Still, we perceive also that all that
the ignorance of Mind took for the truth was in fact truth but
truth deflected, mistaken and falsely conceived. We still perceive
the division, the individualising, the atomic creation, but we
know them and ourselves for what they and we really are. And
so we perceive that the Mind was really a subordinate action
and instrumentation of the Truth-Consciousness. So long as it
is not separated in self-experience from the enveloping Master-
Consciousness and does not try to set up house for itself, so
long as it serves passively as an instrumentation and does not
attempt to possess for its own benefit, Mind fulfils luminously
its function which is in the Truth to hold forms apart from each
other by a phenomenal, a purely formal delimitation of their
activity behind which the governing universality of the being
remains conscious and untouched. It has to receive the truth of
things and distribute it according to the unerring perception of
a supreme and universal Eye and Will. It has to uphold an individualisation of active consciousness, delight, force, substance
which derives all its power, reality and joy from an inalienable
universality behind. It has to turn the multiplicity of the One into
an apparent division by which relations are defined and held off
against each other so as to meet again and join. It has to establish
the delight of separation and contact in the midst of an eternal
unity and intermiscence. It has to enable the One to behave as if
He were an individual dealing with other individuals but always
in His own unity, and this is what the world really is. The mind
is the final operation of the apprehending Truth-Consciousness
which makes all this possible, and what we call the Ignorance
does not create a new thing and absolute falsehood but only
misrepresents the Truth. The Ignorance is the Mind separated
in knowledge from its source of knowledge and giving a false
rigidity and a mistaken appearance of opposition and conflict

to the harmonious play of the supreme Truth in its universal manifestation.

The fundamental error of the Mind is, then, this fall from self-knowledge by which the individual soul conceives of its individuality as a separate fact instead of as a form of Oneness and makes itself the centre of its own universe instead of knowing itself as one concentration of the universal. From that original error all its particular ignorances and limitations are contingent results. For, viewing the flux of things only as it flows upon and through itself, it makes a limitation of being from which proceeds a limitation of consciousness and therefore of knowledge, a limitation of conscious force and will and therefore of power, a limitation of self-enjoyment and therefore of delight. It is conscious of things and knows them only as they present themselves to its individuality and therefore it falls into an ignorance of the rest and thereby into an erroneous conception even of that which it seems to know: for since all being is interdependent, the knowledge either of the whole or of the essence is necessary for the right knowledge of the part. Hence there is an element of error in all human knowledge. Similarly our will, ignorant of the rest of the all-will, must fall into error of working and a greater or less degree of incapacity and impotence; the soul's self-delight and delight of things, ignoring the all-bliss and by defect of will and knowledge unable to master its world, must fall into incapacity of possessive delight and therefore into suffering. Self-ignorance is therefore the root of all the perversity of our existence, and that perversity stands fortified in the self-limitation, the egoism which is the form taken by that self-ignorance.

Yet is all ignorance and all perversity only the distortion of the truth and right of things and not the play of an absolute falsehood. It is the result of Mind viewing things in the division it makes, *avidyāyām antare*, instead of viewing itself and its divisions as instrumentation and phenomenon of the play of the truth of Sachchidananda. If it gets back to the truth from which it fell, it becomes again the final action of the Truth-Consciousness in its apprehensive operation, and the relations it helps to create in that light and power will be relations of the Truth and not of the perversity. They will be the straight things and not the crooked, to use the expressive distinction of the Vedic Rishis, — Truths, that is to say, of divine being with its self-possessive consciousness, will and delight moving harmoniously in itself. Now we have rather the warped and zigzag movement of mind and life, the contortions created by the struggle of the soul once grown oblivious of its true being to find itself again, to resolve back all error into the truth which both our truth and our error, our right and our wrong limit or distort, all incapacity into the strength which both our power and our weakness are a struggle of force to grasp, all suffering into the delight which both our joy and our pain are a convulsive effort of sensation to realise, all death into the immortality to which both our life and our death are a constant effort of being to return.

Chapter XIX

Life

Pranic energy is the life of creatures; for that is said to be the
universal principle of life.   *Taittiriya Upanishad.*[1]

W E PERCEIVE, then, what Mind is in its divine origin
and how it is related to the Truth-Consciousness, —
Mind, the highest of the three lower principles which
constitute our human existence. It is a special action of the divine
consciousness or rather, it is the final strand of its whole creative
action. It enables the Purusha to hold apart the relations of
different forms and forces of himself to each other; it creates
phenomenal differences which to the individual soul fallen from
the Truth-Consciousness take the appearance of radical divisions, and is by that original perversion the parent of all the
resultant perversions which impress us as the contrary dualities
and oppositions proper to the life of the Soul in the Ignorance.
But so long as it is not separated from the Supermind, it supports,
not perversions and falsehoods, but the various working of the
universal Truth.

Mind thus appears as a creative cosmic agency. This is not
the impression which we normally have of our mentality; rather
we regard it primarily as a perceptive organ, perceptive of things
already created by Force working in Matter, and the only origination we allow to it is a secondary creation of new combined
forms from those already developed by Force in Matter. But
the knowledge we are now recovering, aided by the last discoveries of Science, begins to show us that in this Force and
in this Matter there is a subconscious Mind at work which is

[1] II. 3.

certainly responsible for its own emergence, first in the forms
of life and secondly in the forms of mind itself, first in the
nervous consciousness of plant-life and the primitive animal,
secondly in the ever-developing mentality of the evolved animal
and of man. And as we have already discovered that Matter is
only substance-form of Force, so we shall discover that material
Force is only energy-form of Mind. Material force is, in fact, a
subconscious operation of Will; Will that works in us in what
seems to be light, though it is in truth no more than a half-
light, and material Force that works in what to us seems to be
a darkness of unintelligence, are yet really and in essence the
same, as materialistic thought has always instinctively felt from
the wrong or lower end of things and as spiritual knowledge
working from the summit had long ago discovered. We may say,
therefore, that it is a subconscious Mind or Intelligence which,
manifesting Force as its driving-power, its executive Nature, its
Prakriti, has created this material world.

But since, as we have now found, Mind is no independent
and original entity but only a final operation of the Truth-
Consciousness or Supermind, therefore wherever Mind is, there
Supermind must be. Supermind or the Truth-Consciousness is
the real creative agency of the universal Existence. Even when
Mind is in its own darkened consciousness separated from its
source, yet is that larger movement always there in the workings
of Mind; forcing them to preserve their right relation, evolving
from them the inevitable results they bear in themselves, producing the right tree from the right seed, it compels even the
operations of so brute, inert and darkened a thing as material
Force to result in a world of Law, of order, of right relation and
not, as it would otherwise be, of hurtling chance and chaos. Obviously, this order and right relation can only be relative and not
the supreme order and supreme right which would reign if Mind
were not in its own consciousness separated from Supermind;
it is an arrangement, an order of the results right and proper
to the action of dividing Mind and its creation of separative
oppositions, its dual contrary sides of the one Truth. The Divine
Consciousness, having conceived and thrown into operation the

Idea of this dual or divided representation of itself, deduces from it in real-idea and educes practically from it in substance of life, by the governing action of the whole Truth-Consciousness behind it, its own inferior truth or inevitable result of various relation. For this is the nature of Law or Truth in the world that it is the just working and bringing out of that which is contained in being, implied in the essence and nature of the thing itself, latent in its self-being and self-law, *svabhāva* and *svadharma*, as seen by the divine Knowledge. To use one of those wonderful formulas of the Upanishad[2] which contain a world of knowledge in a few revealing words, it is the Self-existent who as the seer and thinker becoming everywhere has arranged in Himself all things rightly from years eternal according to the truth of that which they are.

Consequently, the triple world that we live in, the world of Mind-Life-Body, is triple only in its actual accomplished evolution. Life involved in Matter has emerged in the form of thinking and mentally conscious life. But with Mind, involved in it and therefore in Life and Matter, is the Supermind, which is the origin and ruler of the other three, and this also must emerge. We seek for an intelligence at the root of the world, because intelligence is the highest principle of which we are aware and that which seems to us to govern and explain all our own action and creation and, therefore, if there is a Consciousness at all in the universe, we presume that it must be an Intelligence, a mental Consciousness. But intelligence only perceives, reflects and uses within the measure of its capacity the work of a Truth of being superior to itself; the power behind that works must therefore be another and superior form of Consciousness proper to that Truth. We have, accordingly, to mend our conception and affirm that not a subconscious Mind or Intelligence, but an involved Supermind, which puts Mind in front of it as the immediately active special form of its knowledge-will subconscious in Force and uses material Force or Will subconscious in substance of being as its executive Nature or Prakriti, has created this material universe.

---

[2] *Kavir manīṣī paribhūḥ svayambhūr yāthātathyato'rthān vyadadhāt śāśvatībhyaḥ samābhyaḥ.* — *Isha Upanishad*, Verse 8.

But we see that here Mind is manifested in a specialisation of Force to which we give the name of Life. What then is Life? and what relation has it to Supermind, to this supreme trinity of Sachchidananda active in creation by means of the Real-Idea or Truth-Consciousness? From what principle in the Trinity does it take its birth? or by what necessity, divine or undivine, of the Truth or the illusion, does it come into being? Life is an evil, rings down the centuries the ancient cry, a delusion, a delirium, an insanity from which we have to flee into the repose of eternal being. Is it so? and why then is it so? Why has the Eternal wantonly inflicted this evil, brought this delirium or insanity upon Himself or else upon the creatures brought into being by His terrible all-deluding Maya? Or is it rather some divine principle that thus expresses itself, some power of the Delight of eternal being that had to express and has thus thrown itself into Time and Space in this constant outburst of the million and million forms of life which people the countless worlds of the universe?

When we study this Life as it manifests itself upon earth with Matter as its basis, we observe that essentially it is a form of the one cosmic Energy, a dynamic movement or current of it positive and negative, a constant act or play of the Force which builds up forms, energises them by a continual stream of stimulation and maintains them by an unceasing process of disintegration and renewal of their substance. This would tend to show that the natural opposition we make between death and life is an error of our mentality, one of those false oppositions — false to inner truth though valid in surface practical experience — which, deceived by appearances, it is constantly bringing into the universal unity. Death has no reality except as a process of life. Disintegration of substance and renewal of substance, maintenance of form and change of form are the constant process of life; death is merely a rapid disintegration subservient to life's necessity of change and variation of formal experience. Even in the death of the body there is no cessation of Life, only the material of one form of life is broken up to serve as material for other forms of life. Similarly we may be sure, in the uniform law of Nature, that if there is in the bodily form a mental or psychic energy, that also is not destroyed but only breaks out from one form to assume others by some process of metempsychosis or new ensouling of body. All renews itself, nothing perishes.

It could be affirmed as a consequence that there is one all-pervading Life or dynamic energy — the material aspect being only its outermost movement — that creates all these forms of the physical universe, Life imperishable and eternal which, even if the whole figure of the universe were quite abolished, would itself still go on existing and be capable of producing a new universe in its place, must indeed, unless it be held back in a state of rest by some higher Power or hold itself back, inevitably go on creating. In that case Life is nothing else than the Force that builds and maintains and destroys forms in the world; it is Life that manifests itself in the form of the earth as much as in the plant that grows upon the earth and the animals that support their existence by devouring the life-force of the plant or of each other. All existence here is a universal Life that takes form of Matter. It might for that purpose hide life-process in physical process before it emerges as submental sensitivity and mentalised vitality, but still it would be throughout the same creative Life-principle.

It will be said, however, that this is not what we mean by life; we mean a particular result of universal force with which we are familiar and which manifests itself only in the animal and the plant, but not in the metal, the stone, the gas, operates in the animal cell but not in the pure physical atom. We must, therefore, in order to be sure of our ground, examine in what precisely consists this particular result of the play of Force which we call life and how it differs from that other result of the play of Force in inanimate things which, we say, is not life. We see at once that there are here on earth three realms of the play of Force, the animal kingdom of the old classification to which we belong, the vegetable, and lastly the mere material void, as we pretend, of life. How does life in ourselves differ from the life of the plant, and the life of the plant from the not-life, say, of the metal, the mineral kingdom of the old phraseology, or that new chemical kingdom which Science has discovered?

Ordinarily, when we speak of life, we have meant animal life, that which moves, breathes, eats, feels, desires, and, if we speak of the life of plants, it has been almost as a metaphor rather than a reality, for plant life was regarded as a purely material process rather than a biological phenomenon. Especially we have associated life with breathing; the breath is life, it was said in every language, and the formula is true if we change our conception of what we mean by the Breath of Life. But it is evident that spontaneous motion or locomotion, breathing, eating are only processes of life and not life itself; they are means for the generation or release of that constantly stimulating energy which is our vitality and for that process of disintegration and renewal by which it supports our substantial existence; but these processes of our vitality can be maintained in other ways than by our respiration and our means of sustenance. It is a proved fact that even human life can remain in the body and can remain in full consciousness when breathing and the beating of the heart and other conditions formerly deemed essential to it have been temporarily suspended. And new evidence of phenomena has been brought forward to establish that the plant, to which we can still deny any conscious reaction, has at least a physical life identical with our own and even organised essentially like our own though different in its apparent organisation. If that is proved true, we will have to make a clean sweep of our old facile and false conceptions and get beyond symptoms and externalities to the root of the matter.

In some recent discoveries[3] which, if their conclusions are

---

[3] These considerations drawn from recent scientific researches are brought in here as illustrative, not probative of the nature and process of Life in Matter as they are developed here. Science and metaphysics (whether founded on pure intellectual speculation or, as in India, ultimately on a spiritual vision of things and spiritual experience) have each its own province and method of inquiry. Science cannot dictate its conclusions to metaphysics any more than metaphysics can impose its conclusions on Science. Still if we accept the reasonable belief that Being and Nature in all their states have a system of correspondences expressive of a common Truth underlying them, it is permissible to suppose that truths of the physical universe can throw some light on the nature as well as the process of the Force that is active in the universe — not a complete light, for physical Science is necessarily incomplete in the range of its inquiry and has no clue to the occult movements of the Force.

accepted, must throw an intense light on the problem of Life in Matter, a great Indian physicist has pointed attention to the response to stimulus as an infallible sign of the existence of life. It is especially the phenomenon of plant-life that has been illumined by his data and illustrated in all its subtle functionings; but we must not forget that in the essential point the same proof of vitality, the response to stimulus, the positive state of life and its negative state which we call death, have been affirmed by him in metals as in the plant. Not indeed with the same abundance, not indeed so as to show an essentially identical organisation of life; but it is possible that, could instruments of the right nature and sufficient delicacy be invented, more points of similarity between the metal and plant life could be discovered; and even if it prove not to be so, this might mean that the same or any life organisation is absent, but the beginnings of vitality could still be there. But if life, however rudimentary in its symptoms, exists in the metal, it must be admitted as present, involved perhaps or elementary and elemental in the earth or other material existences akin to the metal. If we can pursue our inquiries farther, not obliged to stop short where our immediate means of investigation fail us, we may be sure from our unvarying experience of Nature that investigations thus pursued will in the end prove to us that there is no break, no rigid line of demarcation between the earth and the metal formed in it or between the metal and the plant and, pursuing the synthesis farther, that there is none either between the elements and atoms that constitute the earth or metal and the metal or earth that they constitute. Each step of this graded existence prepares the next, holds in itself what appears in that which follows it. Life is everywhere, secret or manifest, organised or elemental, involved or evolved, but universal, all-pervading, imperishable; only its forms and organisings differ.

We must remember that the physical response to stimulus is only an outward sign of life, even as are breathing and loco-motion in ourselves. An exceptional stimulus is applied by the experimenter and vivid responses are given which we can at once recognise as indices of vitality in the object of the experiment.

But during its whole existence the plant is responding constantly
to a constant mass of stimulation from its environment; that is to
say, there is a constantly maintained force in it which is capable
of responding to the application of force from its surroundings.
It is said that the idea of a vital force in the plant or other living
organism has been destroyed by these experiments. But when we
say that a stimulus has been applied to the plant, we mean that an
energised force, a force in dynamic movement has been directed
on that object, and when we say that a response is given, we
mean that an energised force capable of dynamic movement and
of sensitive vibration answers to the shock. There is a vibrant
reception and reply, as well as a will to grow and be, indicative of
a submental, a vital-physical organisation of consciousness-force
hidden in the form of being. The fact would seem to be, then,
that as there is a constant dynamic energy in movement in the
universe which takes various material forms more or less subtle
or gross, so in each physical body or object, plant or animal
or metal, there is stored and active the same constant dynamic
force; a certain interchange of these two gives us the phenomena
which we associate with the idea of life. It is this action that we
recognise as the action of Life-Energy and that which so energises itself is the Life-Force. Mind-Energy, Life-Energy, material
Energy are different dynamisms of one World-Force.

Even when a form appears to us to be dead, this force still
exists in it in potentiality although its familiar operations of vitality are suspended and about to be permanently ended. Within
certain limits that which is dead can be revived; the habitual
operations, the response, the circulation of active energy can be
restored; and this proves that what we call life was still there
in the body, latent, that is to say, not active in its usual habits,
its habits of ordinary physical functioning, its habits of nervous
play and response, its habits in the animal of conscious mental
response. It is difficult to suppose that there is a distinct entity
called life which has gone entirely out of the body and gets into
it again when it feels — how, since there is nothing to connect
it with the body? — that somebody is stimulating the form. In
certain cases, such as catalepsy, we see that the outward physical

signs and operations of life are suspended, but the mentality is there self-possessed and conscious although unable to compel the usual physical responses. Certainly, it is not the fact that the man is physically dead but mentally alive or that life has gone out of the body while mind still inhabits it, but only that the ordinary physical functioning is suspended, while the mental is still active.

So also, in certain forms of trance, both the physical functionings and the outward mental are suspended, but afterwards resume their operation, in some cases by external stimulation, but more normally by a spontaneous return to activity from within. What has really happened is that the surface mind-force has been withdrawn into subconscious mind and the surface life-force into sub-active life and either the whole man has lapsed into the subconscious existence or else he has withdrawn his outer life into the subconscious while his inner being has been lifted into the superconscient. But the main point for us at present is that the Force, whatever it be, that maintains dynamic energy of life in the body, has indeed suspended its outer operations, but still informs the organised substance. A point comes, however, at which it is no longer possible to restore the suspended activities; and this occurs when either such a lesion has been inflicted on the body as makes it useless or incapable of the habitual functionings or, in the absence of such lesion, when the process of disintegration has begun, that is to say, when the Force that should renew the life-action becomes entirely inert to the pressure of the environing forces with whose mass of stimulation it was wont to keep up a constant interchange. Even then there is Life in the body, but a Life that is busy only with the process of disintegrating the formed substance so that it may escape in its elements and constitute with them new forms. The Will in the universal force that held the form together, now withdraws from constitution and supports instead a process of dispersion. Not till then is there the real death of the body.

Life then is the dynamic play of a universal Force, a Force in which mental consciousness and nervous vitality are in some form or at least in their principle always inherent and therefore they appear and organise themselves in our world in the forms of Matter. The life-play of this Force manifests itself as an interchange of stimulation and response to stimulation between the different forms it has built up and in which it keeps up its constant dynamic pulsation; each form is constantly taking into itself and giving out again the breath and energy of the common Force; each form feeds upon that and nourishes itself with it by various means, whether indirectly by taking in other forms in which the energy is stored or directly by absorbing the dynamic discharges it receives from outside. All this is the play of Life; but it is chiefly recognisable to us where the organisation of it is sufficient for us to perceive its more outward and complex movements and especially where it partakes of the nervous type of vital energy which belongs to our own organisation. It is for this reason that we are ready enough to admit life in the plant because obvious phenomena of life are there, — and this becomes still easier if it can be shown that it manifests symptoms of nervosity and has a vital system not very different from our own, — but are unwilling to recognise it in the metal and the earth and the chemical atom where these phenomenal developments can with difficulty be detected or do not apparently at all exist.

Is there any justification for elevating this distinction into an essential difference? What, for instance, is the difference between life in ourselves and life in the plant? We see that they differ, first, in our possession of the power of locomotion which has evidently nothing to do with the essence of vitality, and, secondly, in our possession of conscious sensation which is, so far as we know, not yet evolved in the plant. Our nervous responses are largely, though by no means always or in their entirety, attended with the mental response of conscious sensation; they have a value to the mind as well as to the nerve-system and the body agitated by the nervous action. In the plant it would seem that there are symptoms of nervous sensation, including those which would be in us rendered as pleasure and pain, waking and sleep, exhilaration, dullness and fatigue, and the body is inwardly agitated by the nervous action, but there is no sign of the actual presence of mentally conscious sensation. But sensation is sensation whether mentally conscious or vitally sensitive, and sensation is a form of consciousness. When the sensitive plant shrinks from a contact, it appears that it is nervously affected, that something in it dislikes the contact and tries to draw away from it; there is, in a word, a subconscious sensation in the plant, just as there are, as we have seen, subconscious operations of the same kind in ourselves. In the human system it is quite possible to bring these subconscious perceptions and sensations to the surface long after they have happened and have ceased to affect the nervous system; and an ever-increasing mass of evidence has irrefutably established the existence of a subconscious mentality in us much vaster than the conscious. The mere fact that the plant has no superficially vigilant mind which can be awakened to the valuation of its subconscious sensations, makes no difference to the essential identity of the phenomena. The phenomena being the same, the thing they manifest must be the same, and that thing is a subconscious mind. And it is quite possible that there is a more rudimentary life operation of the subconscious sense-mind in the metal, although in the metal there is no bodily agitation corresponding to the nervous response; but the absence of bodily agitation makes no essential difference to the presence of vitality in the metal any more than the absence of bodily locomotion makes an essential difference to the presence of vitality in the plant.

What happens when the conscious becomes subconscious in the body or the subconscious becomes conscious? The real difference lies in the absorption of the conscious energy in part of its work, its more or less exclusive concentration. In certain forms of concentration, what we call the mentality, that is to say, the Prajnana or apprehensive consciousness almost or quite ceases to act consciously, yet the work of the body and the nerves and the sense-mind goes on unnoticed but constant and perfect; it has all become subconscious and only in one activity or chain of activities is the mind luminously active. While I write, the physical act of writing is largely or sometimes entirely done by the subconscious mind; the body makes, unconsciously as we say, certain nervous movements; the mind is awake only to the thought with which it is occupied. The whole man indeed may sink into the subconscious, yet habitual movements implying the action of mind may continue, as in many phenomena of sleep; or he may rise into the superconscient and yet be active with the subliminal mind in the body, as in certain phenomena of *samādhi* or Yoga trance. It is evident, then, that the difference between plant sensation and our sensation is simply that in the plant the conscious Force manifesting itself in the universe has not yet fully emerged from the sleep of Matter, from the absorption which entirely divides the worker Force from its source of work in the superconscient knowledge, and therefore does subconsciously what it will do consciously when it emerges in man from its absorption and begins to wake, though still indirectly, to its knowledge-self. It does exactly the same things but in a different way and with a different value in terms of consciousness.

It is becoming possible now to conceive that in the very atom there is something that becomes in us a will and a desire, there is an attraction and repulsion which, though phenomenally other, are essentially the same thing as liking and disliking in ourselves, but are, as we say, inconscient or subconscient. This essence of will and desire are evident everywhere in Nature and, though this is not yet sufficiently envisaged, they are associated with and indeed the expression of a subconscient or, if you will, inconscient or quite involved sense and intelligence which are equally pervasive. Present in every atom of Matter all this is necessarily present in everything which is formed by the aggregation of those atoms; and they are present in the atom because they are present in the Force which builds up and constitutes the atom. That Force is fundamentally the Chit-Tapas or Chit-Shakti of the Vedanta, consciousness-force, inherent conscious force of conscious-being, which manifests itself as nervous energy full of submental sensation in the plant, as desire-sense and desire-will in the primary animal forms, as self-conscious sense and force in the developing animal, as mental will and knowledge topping all the rest in man. Life is a scale of the universal Energy in which the transition from inconscience to consciousness is managed; it is an intermediary power of it latent or submerged in Matter, delivered by its own force into submental being, delivered finally by the emergence of Mind into the full possibility of its dynamis.

Apart from all other considerations, this conclusion imposes itself as a logical necessity if we observe even the surface process of the emergence in the light of the evolutionary theme. It is self-evident that Life in the plant, even if otherwise organised than in the animal, is yet the same power, marked by birth and growth and death, propagation by the seed, death by decay or malady or violence, maintenance by indrawing of nourishing elements from without, dependence on light and heat, productiveness and sterility, even states of sleep and waking, energy and depression of life-dynamism, passage from infancy to maturity and age; the plant contains, moreover, the essences of the force of life and is therefore the natural food of animal existences. If it is conceded that it has a nervous system and reaction to stimuli, a beginning or undercurrent of submental or purely vital sensations, the identity becomes closer; but still it remains evidently a stage of life evolution intermediate between animal existence and "inanimate" Matter. This is precisely what must be expected if Life is a force evolving out of Matter and culminating in Mind, and, if it is that, then we are bound to suppose that it is already there in Matter itself submerged or latent in the material subconsciousness or inconscience. For from where else can it emerge? Evolution of Life in matter supposes a previous involution of it there, unless we suppose it to be a new creation magically and unaccountably introduced into Nature. If it is that, it must either be a creation out of nothing or a result of material operations which is not accounted for by anything in the operations themselves or by any element in them which is of a kindred nature; or, conceivably, it may be a descent from above, from some supraphysical plane above the material universe. The two first suppositions can be dismissed as arbitrary conceptions; the last explanation is possible and it is quite conceivable and in the occult view of things true that a pressure from some plane of Life above the material universe has assisted the emergence of life here. But this does not exclude the origin of life from Matter itself as a primary and necessary movement; for the existence of a Life-world or Life-plane above the material does not of itself lead to the emergence of Life in matter unless that Life-plane exists as a formative stage in a descent of Being through several grades or powers of itself into the Inconscience with the result of an involution of itself with all these powers in Matter for a later evolution and emergence. Whether signs of this submerged life are discoverable, unorganised yet or rudimentary, in material things or there are no such signs, because this involved Life is in a full sleep, is not a question of capital importance. The material Energy that aggregates, forms and disaggregates[4] is the same Power in another grade of itself as that Life-Energy which expresses itself in birth, growth and death, just as by its doing of the works of Intelligence in a somnambulist subconscience it betrays itself as the same Power that in yet another grade attains the status of Mind; its very character shows that it contains in itself, though not yet in their characteristic organisation or process, the yet undelivered powers of Mind and Life.

Life then reveals itself as essentially the same everywhere from the atom to man, the atom containing the subconscious stuff and movement of being which are released into consciousness in the animal, with plant life as a midway stage in the evolution. Life is really a universal operation of Conscious-Force acting subconsciously on and in Matter; it is the operation that creates, maintains, destroys and re-creates forms or bodies and attempts by play of nerve-force, that is to say, by currents of interchange of stimulating energy to awake conscious sensation in those bodies. In this operation there are three stages; the lowest is that in which the vibration is still in the sleep of Matter, entirely subconscious so as to seem wholly mechanical; the middle stage is that in which it becomes capable of a response still submental but on the verge of what we know as consciousness;

---

[4] Birth, growth and death of life are in their outward aspect the same process of aggregation, formation and disaggregation, though more than that in their inner process and significance. Even the ensoulment of the body by the psychic being follows, if the occult view of these things is correct, a similar outward process, for the soul as nucleus draws to itself for birth and aggregates the elements of its mental, vital and physical sheaths and their contents, increases these formations in life, and in its departing drops and disaggregates again these aggregates, drawing back into itself its inner powers, till in rebirth it repeats the original process.

the highest is that in which life develops conscious mentality in the form of a mentally perceptible sensation which in this transition becomes the basis for the development of sense-mind and intelligence. It is in the middle stage that we catch the idea of Life as distinguished from Matter and Mind, but in reality it is the same in all the stages and always a middle term between Mind and Matter, constituent of the latter and instinct with the former. It is an operation of Conscious-Force which is neither the mere formation of substance nor the operation of mind with substance and form as its object of apprehension; it is rather an energising of conscious being which is a cause and support of the formation of substance and an intermediate source and support of conscious mental apprehension. Life, as this intermediate energising of conscious being, liberates into sensitive action and reaction a form of the creative force of existence which was working subconsciently or inconsciently, absorbed in its own substance; it supports and liberates into action the apprehensive consciousness of existence called mind and gives it a dynamic instrumentation so that it can work not only on its own forms but on forms of life and matter; it connects too, and supports, as a middle term between them, the mutual commerce of the two, mind and matter. This means of commerce Life provides in the continual currents of her pulsating nerve-energy which carry force of the form as a sensation to modify Mind and bring back force of Mind as will to modify Matter. It is therefore this nerve-energy which we usually mean when we talk of Life; it is the Prana or Life-force of the Indian system. But nerve-energy is only the form it takes in the animal being; the same Pranic energy is present in all forms down to the atom, since everywhere it is the same in essence and everywhere it is the same operation of Conscious-Force, — Force supporting and modifying the substantial existence of its own forms, Force with sense and mind secretly active but at first involved in the form and preparing to emerge, then finally emerging from their involution. This is the whole significance of the omnipresent Life that has manifested and inhabits the material universe.

Chapter XX

Death, Desire and Incapacity

In the beginning all was covered by Hunger that is Death; that made for itself Mind so that it might attain to possession of self.   *Brihadaranyaka Upanishad.*[1]

This is the Power discovered by the mortal that has the multitude of its desires so that it may sustain all things; it takes the taste of all foods and builds a house for the being.

Rig Veda.[2]

IN OUR last chapter we have considered Life from the point of view of the material existence and the appearance and working of the vital principle in Matter and we have reasoned from the data which this evolutionary terrestrial existence offers. But it is evident that wherever it may appear and however it may work, under whatsoever conditions, the general principle must be everywhere the same. Life is universal Force working so as to create, energise, maintain and modify, even to the extent of dissolving and reconstructing, substantial forms with mutual play and interchange of an overtly or secretly conscious energy as its fundamental character. In the material world we inhabit Mind is involved and subconscious in Life, just as Supermind is involved and subconscious in Mind, and this Life instinct with an involved subconscious Mind is again itself involved in Matter. Therefore Matter is here the basis and the apparent beginning; in the language of the Upanishads, Prithivi, the Earth-principle, is our foundation. The material universe starts from the formal atom surcharged with energy, instinct with the unformed stuff of a subconscious desire, will, intelligence. Out of this Matter

[1] I.2.1.   [2] V.7.6.

apparent Life manifests and it delivers out of itself by means of the living body the Mind it contains imprisoned within it; Mind also has still to deliver out of itself the Supermind concealed in its workings. But we can conceive a world otherwise constituted in which Mind is not involved at the start but consciously uses its innate energy to create original forms of substance and is not, as here, only subconscious in the beginning. Still though the working of such a world would be quite different from ours, the intermediate vehicle of operation of that energy would always be Life. The thing itself would be the same, even if the process were entirely reversed.

But then it appears immediately that as Mind is only a final operation of Supermind, so Life is only a final operation of the Consciousness-Force of which Real-Idea is the determinative form and creative agent. Consciousness that is Force is the nature of Being and this conscious Being manifested as a creative Knowledge-Will is the Real-Idea or Supermind. The supramental Knowledge-Will is Consciousness-Force rendered operative for the creation of forms of united being in an ordered harmony to which we give the name of world or universe; so also Mind and Life are the same Consciousness-Force, the same Knowledge-Will, but operating for the maintenance of distinctly individual forms in a sort of demarcation, opposition and interchange in which the soul in each form of being works out its own mind and life as if they were separate from the others, though in fact they are never separate but are the play of the one Soul, Mind, Life in different forms of its single reality. In other words, as Mind is the final individualising operation of the all-comprehending and all-apprehending Supermind, the process by which its consciousness works individualised in each form from the standpoint proper to it and with the cosmic relations which proceed from that standpoint, so Life is the final operation by which the Force of Conscious-Being acting through the all-possessing and all-creative Will of the universal Supermind maintains and energises, constitutes and reconstitutes individual forms and acts in them as the basis of all the activities of the soul thus embodied. Life is the energy of the Divine continually generating itself in forms as in a dynamo and not only playing with the outgoing battery of its shocks on surrounding forms of things but receiving itself the incoming shocks of all life around as they pour in upon and penetrate the form from outside, from the environing universe.

In this view Life appears as a form of energy of consciousness intermediary and appropriate to the action of Mind on Matter; in a sense, it may be said to be an energy aspect of Mind when it creates and relates itself no longer to ideas, but to motions of force and to forms of substance. But it must immediately be added that just as Mind is not a separate entity, but has all Supermind behind it and it is Supermind that creates with Mind only as its final individualising operation, so Life also is not a separate entity or movement, but has all Conscious-Force behind it in every one of its workings and it is that Conscious-Force alone which exists and acts in created things. Life is only its final operation intermediary between Mind and Body. All that we say of Life must therefore be subject to the qualifications arising from this dependence. We do not really know Life whether in its nature or its process unless and until we are aware and grow conscious of that Conscious-Force working in it of which it is only the external aspect and instrumentation. Then only can we perceive and execute with knowledge, as individual soul-forms and mental and bodily instruments of the Divine, the will of God in Life; then only can Life and Mind proceed in paths and movements of an ever-increasing straightness of the truth in ourselves and things by a constant diminishing of the crooked perversions of the Ignorance. Just as Mind has to unite itself consciously with the Supermind from which it is separated by the action of Avidya, so Life has to become aware of the Conscious-Force which operates in it for ends and with a meaning of which the life in us, because it is absorbed in the mere process of living as our mind is absorbed in the mere process of mentalising life and matter, is unconscious in its darkened action so that it serves them blindly and ignorantly and not, as it must and will in its liberation and fulfilment, luminously or with a self-fulfilling knowledge, power and bliss.

In fact, our Life, because it is subservient to the darkened and dividing operation of Mind, is itself darkened and divided and undergoes all that subjection to death, limitation, weakness, suffering, ignorant functioning of which the bound and limited creature-Mind is the parent and cause. The original source of the perversion was, we have seen, the self-limitation of the individual soul bound to self-ignorance because it regards itself by an exclusive concentration as a separate self-existent individuality and regards all cosmic action only as it presents itself to its own individual consciousness, knowledge, will, force, enjoyment and limited being instead of seeing itself as a conscious form of the One and embracing all consciousness, all knowledge, all will, all force, all enjoyment and all being as one with its own. The universal life in us, obeying this direction of the soul imprisoned in mind, itself becomes imprisoned in an individual action. It exists and acts as a separate life with a limited insufficient capacity undergoing and not freely embracing the shock and pressure of all the cosmic life around it. Thrown into the constant cosmic interchange of Force in the universe as a poor, limited, individual existence, Life at first helplessly suffers and obeys the giant interplay with only a mechanical reaction upon all that attacks, devours, enjoys, uses, drives it. But as consciousness develops, as the light of its own being emerges from the inert darkness of the involutionary sleep, the individual existence becomes dimly aware of the power in it and seeks first nervously and then mentally to master, use and enjoy the play. This awakening to the Power in it is the gradual awakening to self. For Life is Force and Force is Power and Power is Will and Will is the working of the Master-Consciousness. Life in the individual becomes more and more aware in its depths that it too is the Will-Force of Sachchidananda which is master of the universe and it aspires itself to be individually master of its own world. To realise its own power and to master as well as to know its world is therefore the increasing impulse of all individual life; that impulse is an essential feature of the growing self-manifestation of the Divine in cosmic existence.

But though Life is Power and the growth of individual life

means the growth of the individual Power, still the mere fact of its being a divided individualised life and force prevents it from really becoming master of its world. For that would mean to be master of the All-Force, and it is impossible for a divided and individualised consciousness with a divided, individualised and therefore limited power and will to be master of the All-Force; only the All-Will can be that and the individual only, if at all, by becoming again one with the All-Will and therefore with the All-Force. Otherwise, the individual life in the individual form must be always subject to the three badges of its limitation, Death, Desire and Incapacity.

Death is imposed on the individual life both by the conditions of its own existence and by its relations to the All-Force which manifests itself in the universe. For the individual life is a particular play of energy specialised to constitute, maintain, energise and finally to dissolve when its utility is over, one of the myriad forms which all serve, each in its own place, time and scope, the whole play of the universe. The energy of life in the body has to support the attack of the energies external to it in the universe; it has to draw them in and feed upon them and is itself being constantly devoured by them. All Matter according to the Upanishad is food, and this is the formula of the material world that "the eater eating is himself eaten". The life organised in the body is constantly exposed to the possibility of being broken up by the attack of the life external to it or, its devouring capacity being insufficient or not properly served or there being no right balance between the capacity of devouring and the capacity or necessity of providing food for the life outside, it is unable to protect itself and is devoured or is unable to renew itself and therefore wasted away or broken; it has to go through the process of death for a new construction or renewal.

Not only so but, again in the language of the Upanishad, the life-force is the food of the body and the body the food of the life-force; in other words, the life-energy in us both supplies the material by which the form is built up and constantly maintained and renewed and is at the same time constantly using up the substantial form of itself which it thus creates and keeps in existence.

If the balance between these two operations is imperfect or is disturbed or if the ordered play of the different currents of life-force is thrown out of gear, then disease and decay intervene and commence the process of disintegration. And the very struggle for conscious mastery and even the growth of mind make the maintenance of the life more difficult. For there is an increasing demand of the life-energy on the form, a demand which is in excess of the original system of supply and disturbs the original balance of supply and demand and, before a new balance can be established, many disorders are introduced inimical to the harmony and to the length of maintenance of the life; in addition the attempt at mastery creates always a corresponding reaction in the environment which is full of forces that also desire fulfilment and are therefore intolerant of, revolt against and attack the existence which seeks to master them. There too a balance is disturbed, a more intense struggle is generated; however strong the mastering life, unless either it is unlimited or else succeeds in establishing a new harmony with its environment, it cannot always resist and triumph but must one day be overcome and disintegrated.

But, apart from all these necessities, there is the one fundamental necessity of the nature and object of embodied life itself, which is to seek infinite experience on a finite basis, and since the form, the basis by its very organisation limits the possibility of experience, this can only be done by dissolving it and seeking new forms. For the soul, having once limited itself by concentrating on the moment and the field, is driven to seek its infinity again by the principle of succession, by adding moment to moment and thus storing up a Time-experience which it calls its past; in that Time it moves through successive fields, successive experiences or lives, successive accumulations of knowledge, capacity, enjoyment, and all this it holds in subconscious or superconscious memory as its fund of past acquisition in Time. To this process change of form is essential, and for the soul involved in individual body change of form means dissolution of the body in subjection to the law and compulsion of the All-life in the material universe, to its law of supply of the material of form and demand on the material, to its principle of constant intershock and the struggle of the embodied life to exist in a world of mutual devouring. And this is the law of Death.

This then is the necessity and justification of Death, not as a denial of Life, but as a process of Life; death is necessary because eternal change of form is the sole immortality to which the finite living substance can aspire and eternal change of experience the sole infinity to which the finite mind involved in living body can attain. This change of form cannot be allowed to remain merely a constant renewal of the same form-type such as constitutes our bodily life between birth and death; for unless the form-type is changed and the experiencing mind is thrown into new forms in new circumstances of time, place and environment, the necessary variation of experience which the very nature of existence in Time and Space demands, cannot be effectuated. And it is only the process of Death by dissolution and by the devouring of life by Life, it is only the absence of freedom, the compulsion, the struggle, the pain, the subjection to something that appears to be Not-Self which makes this necessary and salutary change appear terrible and undesirable to our mortal mentality. It is the sense of being devoured, broken up, destroyed or forced away which is the sting of Death and which even the belief in personal survival of death cannot wholly abrogate.

But this process is a necessity of that mutual devouring which we see to be the initial law of Life in Matter. Life, says the Upanishad, is Hunger which is Death, and by this Hunger which is Death, *aśanāyāmṛtyuḥ*, the material world has been created. For Life here assumes as its mould material substance, and material substance is Being infinitely divided and seeking infinitely to aggregate itself; between these two impulses of in-finite division and infinite aggregation the material existence of the universe is constituted. The attempt of the individual, the living atom, to maintain and aggrandise itself is the whole sense of Desire; a physical, vital, moral, mental increase by a more and more all-embracing experience, a more and more all-embracing possession, absorption, assimilation, enjoyment is the inevitable, fundamental, ineradicable impulse of Existence, once divided and individualised, yet ever secretly conscious of its all-embracing, all-possessing infinity. The impulse to realise that secret consciousness is the spur of the cosmic Divine, the lust of the embodied Self within every individual creature; and it is inevitable, just, salutary that it should seek to realise it first in the terms of life by an increasing growth and expansion. In the physical world this can only be done by feeding on the environment, by aggrandising oneself through the absorption of others or of what is possessed by others; and this necessity is the universal justification of Hunger in all its forms. Still what devours must also be devoured; for the law of interchange, of action and reaction, of limited capacity and therefore of a final exhaustion and succumbing governs all life in the physical world.

In the conscious mind that which was still only a vital hunger in subconscious life, transforms itself into higher forms; hunger in the vital parts becomes craving of Desire in the mentalised life, straining of Will in the intellectual or thinking life. This movement of desire must and ought to continue until the individual has grown sufficiently so that he can now at last become master of himself and by increasing union with the Infinite possessor of this universe. Desire is the lever by which the divine Life-principle effects its end of self-affirmation in the universe and the attempt to extinguish it in the interests of inertia is a denial of the divine Life-principle, a Will-not-to-be which is necessarily ignorance; for one cannot cease to be individually except by being infinitely. Desire too can only cease rightly by becoming the desire of the infinite and satisfying itself with a supernal fulfilment and an infinite satisfaction in the all-possessing bliss of the Infinite. Meanwhile it has to progress from the type of a mutually devouring hunger to the type of a mutual giving, of an increasingly joyous sacrifice of interchange; — the individual gives himself to other individuals and receives them back in exchange; the lower gives itself to the higher and the higher to the lower so that they may be fulfilled in each other; the human gives itself to the Divine and the Divine to the human; the All in the individual gives itself to the All in the universe and receives its realised universality as a divine recompense. Thus the law of Hunger must give place progressively to the law of Love, the

law of Division to the law of Unity, the law of Death to the law
of Immortality. Such is the necessity, such the justification, such
the culmination and self-fulfilment of the Desire that is at work
in the universe.

As this mask of Death which Life assumes results from the
movement of the finite seeking to affirm its immortality, so Desire is the impulse of the Force of Being individualised in Life to
affirm progressively in the terms of succession in Time and of
self-extension in Space, in the framework of the finite, its infinite
Bliss, the Ananda of Sachchidananda. The mask of Desire which
that impulse assumes comes directly from the third phenomenon
of Life, its law of incapacity. Life is an infinite Force working in
the terms of the finite; inevitably, throughout its overt individualised action in the finite its omnipotence must appear and act as
a limited capacity and a partial impotence, although behind every act of the individual, however weak, however futile, however
stumbling, there must be the whole superconscious and subconscious presence of infinite omnipotent Force; without that presence behind it no least single movement in the cosmos can happen; into its sum of universal action each single act and movement falls by the fiat of the omnipotent omniscience which works
as the Supermind inherent in things. But the individualised life-
force is to its own consciousness limited and full of incapacity;
for it has to work not only against the mass of other environing
individualised life-forces, but also subject to control and denial
by the infinite Life itself with whose total will and trend its own
will and trend may not immediately agree. Therefore limitation
of force, phenomenon of incapacity is the third of the three
characteristics of individualised and divided Life. On the other
hand, the impulse of self-enlargement and all-possession remains
and it does not and is not meant to measure or limit itself by the
limit of its present force or capacity. Hence from the gulf between
the impulse to possess and the force of possession desire arises;
for if there were no such discrepancy, if the force could always
take possession of its object, always attain securely its end, desire
would not come into existence but only a calm and self-possessed
Will without craving such as is the Will of the Divine.

If the individualised force were the energy of a mind free from ignorance, no such limitation, no such necessity of desire would intervene. For a mind not separated from Supermind, a mind of divine knowledge would know the intention, scope and inevitable result of its every act and would not crave or struggle but put forth an assured force self-limited to the immediate object in view. It would, even in stretching beyond the present, even in undertaking movements not intended to succeed immediately, yet not be subject to desire or limitation. For the failures also of the Divine are acts of its omniscient omnipotence which knows the right time and circumstance for the incipience, the vicissitudes, the immediate and the final results of all its cosmic undertakings. The mind of knowledge, being in unison with the divine Supermind, would participate in this omniscience and this all-determining power. But, as we have seen, individualised life-force here is an energy of individualising and ignorant Mind, Mind that has fallen from the knowledge of its own Supermind. Therefore incapacity is necessary to its relations in Life and inevitable in the nature of things; for the practical omnipotence of an ignorant force even in a limited sphere is unthinkable, since in that sphere such a force would set itself against the working of the divine and omniscient omnipotence and unfix the fixed purpose of things, — an impossible cosmic situation. The struggle of limited forces increasing their capacity by that struggle under the driving impetus of instinctive or conscious desire is therefore the first law of Life. As with desire, so with this strife; it must rise into a mutually helpful trial of strength, a conscious wrestling of brother forces in which the victor and vanquished or rather that which influences by action from above and that which influences by retort of action from below must equally gain and increase. And this again has eventually to become the happy shock of divine interchange, the strenuous clasp of Love replacing the convulsive clasp of strife. Still, strife is the necessary and salutary beginning. Death, Desire and Strife are the trinity of divided living, the triple mask of the divine Life-principle in its first essay of cosmic self-affirmation.

Chapter XXI

The Ascent of Life

Let the path of the Word lead to the godheads, towards the Waters by the working of the Mind....[1] O Flame, thou goest to the ocean of Heaven, towards the gods; thou makest to meet together the godheads of the planes, the waters that are in the realm of light above the sun and the waters that abide below.[2]

The Lord of Delight conquers the third status; he maintains and governs according to the Soul of universality; like a hawk, a kite he settles on the vessel and uplifts it, a finder of the Light he manifests the fourth status and cleaves to the ocean that is the billowing of those waters.[3]

Thrice Vishnu paced and set his step uplifted out of the primal dust; three steps he has paced, the Guardian, the Invincible, and from beyond he upholds their laws. Scan the workings of Vishnu and see from whence he has manifested their laws. That is his highest pace which is seen ever by the seers like an eye extended in heaven; that the illumined, the awakened kindle into a blaze, even Vishnu's step supreme....[4]

Rig Veda.

W E HAVE seen that as the divided mortal Mind, parent of limitation and ignorance and the dualities, is only a dark figure of the Supermind, of the self-luminous divine Consciousness in its first dealings with the apparent negation of itself from which our cosmos commences, so also Life as it emerges in our material universe, an energy of the dividing Mind subconscious, submerged, imprisoned in Matter, Life as

[1] X. 30. 1.   [2] III. 22. 3.   [3] IX. 96. 18, 19.   [4] I. 22. 17-21.

the parent of death, hunger and incapacity, is only a dark figure of the divine superconscient Force whose highest terms are immortality, satisfied delight and omnipotence. This relation fixes the nature of that great cosmic processus of which we are a part; it determines the first, the middle and the ultimate terms of our evolution. The first terms of Life are division, a force-driven subconscient will, apparent not as will but as dumb urge of physical energy, and the impotence of an inert subjection to the mechanical forces that govern the interchange between the form and its environment. This inconscience and this blind but potent action of Energy are the type of the material universe as the physical scientist sees it and this his view of things extends and turns into the whole of basic existence; it is the consciousness of Matter and the accomplished type of material living. But there comes a new equipoise, there intervenes a new set of terms which increase in proportion as Life delivers itself out of this form and begins to evolve towards conscious Mind; for the middle terms of Life are death and mutual devouring, hunger and conscious desire, the sense of a limited room and capacity and the struggle to increase, to expand, to conquer and to possess. These three terms are the basis of that status of evolution which the Darwinian theory first made plain to human knowledge. For the phenomenon of death involves in itself a struggle to survive, since death is only the negative term in which Life hides from itself and tempts its own positive being to seek for immortality. The phenomenon of hunger and desire involves a struggle towards a status of satisfaction and security, since desire is only the stimulus by which Life tempts its own positive being to rise out of the negation of unfulfilled hunger towards the full possession of the delight of existence. The phenomenon of limited capacity involves a struggle towards expansion, mastery and possession, the possession of the self and the conquest of the environment, since limitation and defect are only the negation by which Life tempts its own positive being to seek for the perfection of which it is eternally capable. The struggle for life is not only a struggle to survive, it is also a struggle for possession and perfection, since only by taking hold of the environment whether more or less, whether by self-adaptation to it or by adapting it to oneself either by accepting and conciliating it or by conquering and changing it, can survival be secured, and equally is it true that only a greater and greater perfection can assure a continuous permanence, a lasting survival. It is this truth that Darwinism sought to express in the formula of the survival of the fittest.

But as the scientific mind sought to extend to Life the mechanical principle proper to the existence and concealed mechanical consciousness in Matter, not seeing that a new principle has entered whose very reason of being is to subject to itself the mechanical, so the Darwinian formula was used to extend too largely the aggressive principle of Life, the vital selfishness of the individual, the instinct and process of self-preservation, self-assertion and aggressive living. For these two first states of Life contain in themselves the seeds of a new principle and another state which must increase in proportion as Mind evolves out of matter through the vital formula into its own law. And still more must all things change when as Life evolves upward towards Mind, so Mind evolves upward towards Supermind and Spirit. Precisely because the struggle for survival, the impulse towards permanence is contradicted by the law of death, the individual life is compelled, and used, to secure permanence rather for its species than for itself; but this it cannot do without the co-operation of others; and the principle of co-operation and mutual help, the desire of others, the desire of the wife, the child, the friend and helper, the associated group, the practice of association, of conscious joining and interchange are the seeds out of which flowers the principle of love. Let us grant that at first love may only be an extended selfishness and that this aspect of extended selfishness may persist and dominate, as it does still persist and dominate, in higher stages of the evolution: still as mind evolves and more and more finds itself, it comes by the experience of life and love and mutual help to perceive that the natural individual is a minor term of being and exists by the universal. Once this is discovered, as it is inevitably discovered by man the mental being, his destiny is determined; for he has reached the point at which Mind can begin to open to the truth that there is something beyond itself; from that moment his evolution, however obscure and slow, towards that superior something, towards Spirit, towards Supermind, towards Supermanhood is inevitably predetermined.

Therefore Life is predestined by its own nature to a third status, a third set of terms of its self-expression. If we examine this ascent of Life we shall see that the last terms of its actual evolution, the terms of that which we have called its third status, must necessarily be in appearance the very contradiction and opposite but in fact the very fulfilment and transfiguration of its first conditions. Life starts with the extreme divisions and rigid forms of Matter, and of this rigid division the atom, which is the basis of all material form, is the very type. The atom stands apart from all others even in its union with them, rejects death and dissolution under any ordinary force and is the physical type of the separate ego defining its existence against the principle of fusion in Nature. But unity is as strong a principle in Nature as division; it is indeed the master principle of which division is only a subordinate term, and to the principle of unity every divided form must therefore subordinate itself in one fashion or another by mechanical necessity, by compulsion, by assent or inducement. Therefore, if Nature for her own ends, in order principally to have a firm basis for her combinations and a fixed seed of forms, allows the atom ordinarily to resist the process of fusion by dissolution, she compels it to subserve the process of fusion by aggregation; the atom, as it is the first aggregate, is also the first basis of aggregate unities.

When Life reaches its second status, that which we recognise as vitality, the contrary phenomenon takes the lead and the physical basis of the vital ego is obliged to consent to dissolution. Its constituents are broken up so that the elements of one life can be used to enter into the elemental formation of other lives. The extent to which this law reigns in Nature has not yet been fully recognised and indeed cannot be until we have a science of mental life and spiritual existence as sound as our present science of physical life and the existence of Matter. Still we can see broadly that not only the elements of our physical body, but those of our subtler vital being, our life-energy, our desire-energy, our powers, strivings, passions enter both during our life and after our death into the life-existence of others. An ancient occult knowledge tells us that we have a vital frame as well as a physical and this too is after death dissolved and lends itself to the constitution of other vital bodies; our life energies while we live are continually mixing with the energies of other beings. A similar law governs the mutual relations of our mental life with the mental life of other thinking creatures. There is a constant dissolution and dispersion and a reconstruction effected by the shock of mind upon mind with a constant interchange and fusion of elements. Interchange, intermixture and fusion of being with being, is the very process of life, a law of its existence.

We have then two principles in Life, the necessity or the will of the separate ego to survive in its distinctness and guard its identity and the compulsion imposed upon it by Nature to fuse itself with others. In the physical world she lays much stress on the former impulse; for she needs to create stable separate forms, since it is her first and really her most difficult problem to create and maintain any such thing as a separative survival of individuality and a stable form for it in the incessant flux and motion of Energy and in the unity of the infinite. In the atomic life therefore the individual form persists as the basis and secures by its aggregation with others the more or less prolonged existence of aggregate forms which shall be the basis of vital and mental individualisations. But as soon as Nature has secured a sufficient firmness in this respect for the safe conduct of her ulterior operations, she reverses the process; the individual form perishes and the aggregate life profits by the elements of the form that is thus dissolved. This, however, cannot be the last stage; that can only be reached when the two principles are harmonised, when the individual is able to persist in the consciousness of his individuality and yet fuse himself with others without disturbance of preservative equilibrium and interruption of survival.

The terms of the problem presuppose the full emergence of Mind; for in vitality without conscious mind there can be no equation, but only a temporary unstable equilibrium ending in the death of the body, the dissolution of the individual and the dispersal of its elements into the universality. The nature of physical Life forbids the idea of an individual form possessing the same inherent power of persistence and therefore of continued individual existence as the atoms of which it is composed. Only a mental being, supported by the psychic nodus within which expresses or begins to express the secret soul, can hope to persist by his power of linking on the past to the future in a stream of continuity which the breaking of the form may break in the physical memory but need not destroy in the mental being itself and which may even by an eventual development bridge over the gap of physical memory created by death and birth of the body. Even as it is, even in the present imperfect development of embodied mind, the mental being is conscious in the mass of a past and a future extending beyond the life of the body; he becomes aware of an individual past, of individual lives that have created his and of which he is a development and modified reproduction and of future individual lives which his is creating out of itself; he is conscious also of an aggregate life past and future through which his own continuity runs as one of its fibres. This which is evident to physical Science in the terms of heredity, becomes otherwise evident to the developing soul behind the mental being in the terms of persistent personality. The mental being expressive of this soul-consciousness is therefore the nodus of the persistent individual and the persistent aggregate life; in him their union and harmony become possible.

Association with love as its secret principle and its emergent summit is the type, the power of this new relation and therefore the governing principle of the development into the third status of life. The conscious preservation of individuality along with the consciously accepted necessity and desire of interchange, self-giving and fusion with other individuals, is necessary for the working of the principle of love; for if either is abolished, the working of love ceases, whatever may take its place. Fulfilment of love by entire self-immolation, even with an illusion of self-annihilation, is indeed an idea and an impulse in the mental being, but it points to a development beyond this third status of

Life. This third status is a condition in which we rise progressively beyond the struggle for life by mutual devouring and the survival of the fittest by that struggle; for there is more and more a survival by mutual help and a self-perfectioning by mutual adaptation, interchange and fusion. Life is a self-affirmation of being, even a development and survival of ego, but of a being that has need of other beings, an ego that seeks to meet and include other egos and to be included in their life. The individuals and the aggregates who develop most the law of association and the law of love, of common help, kindliness, affection, comradeship, unity, who harmonise most successfully survival and mutual self-giving, the aggregate increasing the individual and the individual the aggregate, as well as individual increasing individual and aggregate aggregate by mutual interchange, will be the fittest for survival in this tertiary status of the evolution.

This development is significant of the increasing predominance of Mind[5] which progressively imposes its own law more and more upon the material existence. For mind by its greater subtlety does not need to devour in order to assimilate, possess and grow; rather the more it gives, the more it receives and grows; and the more it fuses itself into others, the more it fuses others into itself and increases the scope of its being. Physical life exhausts itself by too much giving and ruins itself by too much devouring; but though Mind in proportion as it leans on the law of Matter suffers the same limitation, yet, on the other hand, in proportion as it grows into its own law it tends to overcome this limitation, and in proportion as it overcomes the material limitation giving and receiving become one. For in its upward ascent it grows towards the rule of conscious unity in differentiation which is the divine law of the manifest Sachchidananda.

The second term of the original status of life is subconscious will which in the secondary status becomes hunger and

---

[5] What is spoken of here is mind as it acts directly in life, in the vital being, through the heart. Love — the relative principle, not its absolute — is a principle of life, not of mind, but it can possess itself and move towards permanence only when taken up by the mind into its own light. What is called love in the body and the vital parts is mostly a form of hunger without permanence.

conscious desire, — hunger and desire, the first seed of conscious mind. The growth into the third status of life by the principle of association, the growth of love, does not abolish the law of desire, but rather transforms and fulfils it. Love is in its nature the desire to give oneself to others and to receive others in exchange; it is a commerce between being and being. Physical life does not desire to give itself, it desires only to receive. It is true that it is compelled to give itself, for the life which only receives and does not give must become barren, wither and perish, — if indeed such life in its entirety is possible at all here or in any world; but it is compelled, not willing, it obeys the subconscious impulse of Nature rather than consciously shares in it. Even when love intervenes, the self-giving at first still preserves to a large extent the mechanical character of the subconscious will in the atom. Love itself at first obeys the law of hunger and enjoys the receiving and the exacting from others rather than the giving and surrendering to others which it admits chiefly as a necessary price for the thing that it desires. But here it has not yet attained to its true nature; its true law is to establish an equal commerce in which the joy of giving is equal to the joy of receiving and tends in the end to become even greater; but that is when it is shooting beyond itself under the pressure of the psychic flame to attain to the fulfilment of utter unity and has therefore to realise that which seemed to it not-self as an even greater and dearer self than its own individuality. In its life-origin, the law of love is the impulse to realise and fulfil oneself in others and by others, to be enriched by enriching, to possess and be possessed because without being possessed one does not possess oneself utterly.

The inert incapacity of atomic existence to possess itself, the subjection of the material individual to the not-self belongs to the first status of life. The consciousness of limitation and the struggle to possess, to master both self and the not-self is the type of the secondary status. Here, too, the development to the third status brings a transformation of the original terms into a fulfilment and a harmony which repeat the terms while seeming to contradict them. There comes about through association and through love a recognition of the not-self as a greater self and therefore a consciously accepted submission to its law and need which fulfils the increasing impulse of aggregate life to absorb the individual; and there is a possession again by the individual of the life of others as his own and of all that it has to give him as his own which fulfils the opposite impulse of individual possession. Nor can this relation of mutuality between the individual and the world he lives in be expressed or complete or secure unless the same relation is established between individual and individual and between aggregate and aggregate. All the difficult effort of man towards the harmonisation of self-affirmation and freedom, by which he possesses himself, with association and love, fraternity, comradeship, in which he gives himself to others, his ideals of harmonious equilibrium, justice, mutuality, equality by which he creates a balance of the two opposites, are really an attempt inevitably predetermined in its lines to solve the original problem of Nature, the very problem of Life itself, by the resolution of the conflict between the two opposites which present themselves in the very foundations of Life in Matter. The resolution is attempted by the higher principle of Mind which alone can find the road towards the harmony intended, even though the harmony itself can only be found in a Power still beyond us.

For, if the data with which we have started are correct, the end of the road, the goal itself can only be reached by Mind passing beyond itself into that which is beyond Mind, since of That the Mind is only an inferior term and an instrument first for descent into form and individuality and secondly for reascension into that reality which the form embodies and the individuality represents. Therefore the perfect solution of the problem of Life is not likely to be realised by association, interchange and accommodations of love alone or through the law of the mind and the heart alone. It must come by a fourth status of life in which the eternal unity of the many is realised through the spirit and the conscious foundation of all the operations of life is laid no longer in the divisions of body, nor in the passions and hungers of the vitality, nor in the groupings and the imperfect harmonies of the mind, nor in a combination of all these, but in the unity and freedom of the Spirit.

Chapter XXII

The Problem of Life

This it is that is called the universal Life.

Taittiriya Upanishad.[1]

The Lord is seated in the heart of all beings turning all beings mounted upon a machine by his Maya. *Gita.*[2]

He who knows the Truth, the Knowledge, the Infinity that is Brahman shall enjoy with the all-wise Brahman all objects of desire. *Taittiriya Upanishad.*[3]

LIFE IS, we have seen, the putting forth, under certain cosmic circumstances, of a Conscious-Force which is in its own nature infinite, absolute, untrammelled, inalienably possessed of its own unity and bliss, the Conscious-Force of Sachchidananda. The central circumstance of this cosmic process, in so far as it differs in its appearances from the purity of the infinite Existence and the self-possession of the undivided Energy, is the dividing faculty of the Mind obscured by ignorance. There results from this divided action of an undivided Force the apparition of dualities, oppositions, seeming denials of the nature of Sachchidananda which exist as an abiding reality for the mind, but only as a phenomenon misrepresenting a manifold Reality for the divine cosmic Consciousness concealed behind the veil of mind. Hence the world takes on the appearance of a clash of opposing truths each seeking to fulfil itself, each having the right to fulfilment, and therefore of a mass of problems and mysteries which have to be solved because behind all this confusion there is the hidden Truth and unity pressing for the solution and

---

[1] II. 3.   [2] XVIII. 61.   [3] II. 1.

by the solution for its own unveiled manifestation in the world.

This solution has to be sought by the mind, but not by the mind alone; it has to be a solution in Life, in act of being as well as in consciousness of being. Consciousness as Force has created the world-movement and its problems; consciousness as Force has to solve the problems it has created and carry the world-movement to the inevitable fulfilment of its secret sense and evolving Truth. But this Life has taken successively three appearances. The first is material, — a submerged consciousness is concealed in its own superficial expressive action and representative forms of force; for the consciousness itself disappears from view in the act and is lost in the form. The second is vital, — an emerging consciousness is half-apparent as power of life and process of the growth, activity and decay of form, it is half-delivered out of its original imprisonment, it has become vibrant in power, as vital craving and satisfaction or repulsion, but at first not at all and then only imperfectly vibrant in light as knowledge of its own self-existence and its environment. The third is mental, — an emerged consciousness reflects fact of life as mental sense and responsive perception and idea while as new idea it tries to become fact of life, modifies the internal and attempts to modify conformably the external existence of the being. Here, in mind, consciousness is delivered out of its imprisonment in the act and form of its own force; but it is not yet master of the act and form because it has emerged as an individual consciousness and is aware therefore only of a fragmentary movement of its own total activities.

The whole crux and difficulty of human life lies here. Man is this mental being, this mental consciousness working as mental force, aware in a way of the universal force and life of which he is part but, because he has not knowledge of its universality or even of the totality of his own being, unable to deal either with life in general or with his own life in a really effective and victorious movement of mastery. He seeks to know Matter in order to be master of the material environment, to know Life in order to be master of the vital existence, to know Mind in order to be master of the great obscure movement of mentality in which he is not only a jet of light of self-consciousness like the animal, but also more and more a flame of growing knowledge. Thus he seeks to know himself in order to be master of himself, to know the world in order to be master of the world. This is the urge of Existence in him, the necessity of the Consciousness he is, the impulsion of the Force that is his life, the secret will of Sachchidananda appearing as the individual in a world in which He expresses and yet seems to deny Himself. To find the conditions under which this inner impulsion is satisfied is the problem man must strive always to resolve and to that he is compelled by the very nature of his own existence and by the Deity seated within him; and until the problem is solved, the impulse satisfied, the human race cannot rest from its labour. Either man must fulfil himself by satisfying the Divine within him or he must produce out of himself a new and greater being who will be more capable of satisfying it. He must either himself become a divine humanity or give place to Superman.

This results from the very logic of things because, the mental consciousness of man not being the completely illumined consciousness entirely emerged out of the obscuration of Matter but only a progressive term in the great emergence, the line of evolutionary creation in which he has appeared cannot stop where he now is, but must go either beyond its present term in him or else beyond him if he himself has not the force to go forward. Mental idea trying to become fact of life must pass on till it becomes the whole Truth of existence delivering itself out of its successive wrappings, revealed and progressively fulfilled in light of consciousness and joyously fulfilled in power; for in and through these two terms of power and light Existence manifests itself, because existence is in its nature Consciousness and Force: but the third term in which these, its two constituents, meet, become one and are ultimately fulfilled, is satisfied Delight of self-existence. For an evolving life like ours this inevitable culmination must necessarily mean the finding of the self that was contained in the seed of its own birth and, with that self-finding, the complete working out of the potentialities deposited in the movement of Conscious-Force from which this life took its rise. The potentiality thus contained in our human existence is Sachchidananda realising Himself in a certain harmony and unification of the individual life and the universal so that mankind shall express in a common consciousness, common movement of power, common delight the transcendent Something which has cast itself into this form of things.

All life depends for its nature on the fundamental poise of its own constituting consciousness; for as the Consciousness is, so will the Force be. Where the Consciousness is infinite, one, transcendent of its acts and forms even while embracing and informing, organising and executing them, as is the consciousness of Sachchidananda, so will be the Force, infinite in its scope, one in its works, transcendent in its power and self-knowledge. Where the Consciousness is like that of material Nature, submerged, self-oblivious, driving along in the drift of its own Force without seeming to know it, even though by the very nature of the eternal relation between the two terms it really determines the drift which drives it, so will be the Force: it will be a monstrous movement of the Inert and Inconscient, unaware of what it contains, seeming mechanically to fulfil itself by a sort of inexorable accident, an inevitably happy chance, even while all the while it really obeys faultlessly the law of the Right and Truth fixed for it by the will of the supernal Conscious-Being concealed within its movement. Where the Consciousness is divided in itself, as in Mind, limiting itself in various centres, setting each to fulfil itself without knowledge of what is in other centres and of its relation to others, aware of things and forces in their apparent division and opposition to each other but not in their real unity, such will be the Force: it will be a life like that we are and see around us; it will be a clash and intertwining of individual lives seeking each its own fulfilment without knowing its relation to others, a conflict and difficult accommodation of divided and opposing or differing forces and, in the mentality, a mixing, a shock and wrestle and insecure combination of divided and opposing or divergent ideas which cannot arrive at the knowledge of their necessity to each other or grasp their place as elements of that Unity behind which is expressing itself through them and in which their discords must cease. But where the Consciousness is in possession of both the diversity and the unity and the latter contains and governs the former, where it is aware at once of the Law, Truth and Right of the All and the Law, Truth and Right of the individual and the two become consciously harmonised in a mutual unity, where the whole nature of the consciousness is the One knowing itself as the Many and the Many knowing themselves as the One, there the Force also will be of the same nature: it will be a Life that consciously obeys the law of Unity and yet fulfils each thing in the diversity according to its proper rule and function; it will be a life in which all the individuals live at once in themselves and in each other as one conscious Being in many souls, one power of Consciousness in many minds, one joy of Force working in many lives, one reality of Delight fulfilling itself in many hearts and bodies.

The first of these four positions, the source of all this progressive relation between Consciousness and Force, is their poise in the being of Sachchidananda where they are one; for there the Force is consciousness of being working itself out without ever ceasing to be consciousness and the Consciousness is similarly luminous Force of being eternally aware of itself and of its own Delight and never ceasing to be this power of utter light and self-possession. The second relation is that of material Nature; it is the poise of being in the material universe which is the great denial of Sachchidananda by Himself: for here there is the utter apparent separation of Force from Consciousness, the specious miracle of the all-governing and infallible Inconscient which is only the mask but which modern knowledge has mistaken for the real face of the cosmic Deity. The third relation is the poise of being in Mind and in the Life which we see emerging out of this denial, bewildered by it, struggling — without any possibility of cessation by submission, but also without any clear knowledge or instinct of a victorious solution — against the thousand and one problems involved in this perplexing apparition of man the half-potent conscient being out of the omnipotent Inconscience of the material universe. The fourth relation is the poise of being in Supermind: it is the fulfilled existence which will eventually solve all this complex problem created by the partial affirmation emerging out of the total denial; and it must needs solve it in the only possible way, by the complete affirmation fulfilling all that was secretly there contained in potentiality and intended in fact of evolution behind the mask of the great denial. That is the real life of the real Man towards which this partial life and partial unfulfilled manhood is striving forward with a perfect knowledge and guidance in the so-called Inconscient within us, but in our conscient parts with only a dim and struggling prevision, with fragments of realisation, with glimpses of the ideal, with flashes of revelation and inspiration in the poet and the prophet, the seer and the transcendentalist, the mystic and the thinker, the great intellects and the great souls of humanity.

From the data we have now before us we can see that the difficulties which arise from the imperfect poise of Consciousness and Force in man in his present status of mind and life are principally three. First, he is aware only of a small part of his own being: his surface mentality, his surface life, his surface physical being is all that he knows and he does not know even all of that; below is the occult surge of his subconscious and his subliminal mind, his subconscious and his subliminal life-impulses, his subconscious corporeality, all that large part of himself which he does not know and cannot govern, but which rather knows and governs him. For, existence and consciousness and force being one, we can only have some real power over so much of our existence as we are identified with by self-awareness; the rest must be governed by its own consciousness which is subliminal to our surface mind and life and body. And yet, the two being one movement and not two separate movements, the larger and more potent part of ourselves must govern and determine in the mass the smaller and less powerful; therefore we are governed by the subconscient and subliminal even in our conscious existence and in our very self-mastery and self-direction we are only instruments of what seems to us the Inconscient within us.

This is what the old wisdom meant when it said that man imagines himself to be the doer of the work by his free will, but in reality Nature determines all his works and even the wise are compelled to follow their own Nature. But since Nature is the creative force of consciousness of the Being within us who is masked by His own inverse movement and apparent denial of Himself, they called that inverse creative movement of His consciousness the Maya or Illusion-power of the Lord and said that all existences are turned as upon a machine through His Maya by the Lord seated within the heart of all existences. It is evident then that only by man so far exceeding mind as to become one in self-awareness with the Lord can he become master of his own being. And since this is not possible in the inconscience or in the subconscient itself, since profit cannot come by plunging down into our depths back towards the Inconscient, it can only be by going inward where the Lord is seated and by ascending into that which is still superconscient to us, into the Supermind, that this unity can be wholly established. For there in the higher and divine Maya is the conscious knowledge, in its law and truth, of that which works in the subconscient by the lower Maya under the conditions of the Denial which seeks to become the Affirmation. For this lower Nature works out what is willed and known in that higher Nature. The Illusion-Power of the divine knowledge in the world which creates appearances is governed by the Truth-Power of the same knowledge which knows the truth behind the appearances and keeps ready for us the Affirmation towards which they are working. The partial and apparent Man here will find there the perfect and real Man capable of an entirely self-aware being by his full unity with that Self-existent who is the omniscient lord of His own cosmic evolution and procession.

The second difficulty is that man is separated in his mind, his life, his body from the universal and therefore, even as he does not know himself, is equally and even more incapable of knowing his fellow-creatures. He forms by inferences, theories, observations and a certain imperfect capacity of sympathy a rough mental construction about them; but this is not knowledge. Knowledge can only come by conscious identity, for that is the only true knowledge, — existence aware of itself. We know what we are so far as we are consciously aware of ourself, the rest is hidden; so also we can come really to know that with which we become one in our consciousness, but only so far as we can become one with it. If the means of knowledge are indirect and imperfect, the knowledge attained will also be indirect and imperfect. It will enable us to work out with a certain precarious clumsiness but still perfectly enough from our mental standpoint certain limited practical aims, necessities, conveniences, a certain imperfect and insecure harmony of our relations with that which we know; but only by a conscious unity with it can we arrive at a perfect relation. Therefore we must arrive at a conscious unity with our fellow-beings and not merely at the sympathy created by love or the understanding created by mental knowledge, which will always be the knowledge of their superficial existence and therefore imperfect in itself and subject to denial and frustration by the uprush of the unknown and unmastered from the subconscient or the subliminal in them and us. But this conscious oneness can only be established by entering into that in which we are one with them, the universal; and the fullness of the universal exists consciently only in that which is superconscient to us, in the Supermind: for here in our normal being the greater part of it is subconscient and therefore in this normal poise of mind, life and body it cannot be possessed. The lower conscious nature is bound down to ego in all its activities, chained triply to the stake of differentiated individuality. The Supermind alone commands unity in diversity.

The third difficulty is the division between force and consciousness in the evolutionary existence. There is, first, the division which has been created by the evolution itself in its three successive formations of Matter, Life and Mind, each with its own law of working. The Life is at war with the body; it attempts to force it to satisfy life's desires, impulses, satisfactions and demands from its limited capacity what could only be possible to an immortal and divine body; and the body, enslaved and tyrannised over, suffers and is in constant dumb revolt against the demands made upon it by the Life. The Mind is at war with both: sometimes it helps the Life against the Body, sometimes restrains the vital urge and seeks to protect the corporeal frame from life's desires, passions and over-driving energies; it also seeks to possess the Life and turn its energy to the mind's own ends, to the utmost joys of the mind's own activity, to the satisfaction of mental, aesthetic, emotional aims and their fulfilment in human existence; and the Life too finds itself enslaved and misused and is in frequent insurrection against the ignorant half-wise tyrant seated above it. This is the war of our members which the mind cannot satisfactorily resolve because it has to deal with a problem insoluble to it, the aspiration of an immortal being in a mortal life and body. It can only arrive at a long succession of compromises or end in an abandonment of the problem either by submission with the materialist to the mortality of our apparent being or with the ascetic and the religionist by the rejection and condemnation of the earthly life and withdrawal to happier and easier fields of existence. But the true solution lies in finding the principle beyond Mind of which Immortality is the law and in conquering by it the mortality of our existence.

But there is also that fundamental division within between force of Nature and the conscious being which is the original cause of this incapacity. Not only is there a division between the mental, the vital and the physical being, but each of them is also divided against itself. The capacity of the body is less than the capacity of the instinctive soul or conscious being, the physical Purusha within it, the capacity of the vital force less than the capacity of the impulsive soul, the vital conscious being or Purusha within it, the capacity of the mental energy less than the capacity of the intellectual and emotional soul, the mental Purusha within it. For the soul is the inner consciousness which aspires to its own complete self-realisation and therefore always exceeds the individual formation of the moment, and the Force which has taken its poise in the formation is always pushed by its soul to that which is abnormal to the poise, transcendent of it; thus constantly pushed it has much trouble in answering, more in evolving from the present to a greater capacity. In trying to fulfil the demands of this triple soul it is distracted and driven to set instinct against instinct, impulse against impulse, emotion against emotion, idea against idea, satisfying this, denying that, then repenting and returning on what it has done, adjusting, compensating, readjusting *ad infinitum*, but not arriving at any principle of unity. And in the mind again the conscious-power that should harmonise and unite is not only limited in its knowledge and in its will, but the knowledge and the will are disparate and often at discord. The principle of unity is above in the Supermind: for there alone is the conscious unity of all diversities; there alone will and knowledge are equal and in perfect harmony; there alone Consciousness and Force arrive at their divine equation.

Man, in proportion as he develops into a self-conscious and truly thinking being, becomes acutely aware of all this discord and disparateness in his parts and he seeks to arrive at a harmony of his mind, life and body, a harmony of his knowledge and will and emotion, a harmony of all his members. Sometimes this desire stops short at the attainment of a workable compromise which will bring with it a relative peace; but compromise can only be a halt on the way, since the Deity within will not be satisfied eventually with less than a perfect harmony combining in itself the integral development of our many-sided potentialities. Less than this would be an evasion of the problem, not its solution, or else only a temporary solution provided as a resting-place for the soul in its continual self-enlargement and ascension. Such a perfect harmony would demand as essential terms a perfect mentality, a perfect play of vital force, a perfect physical existence. But where in the radically imperfect shall we find the principle and power of perfection? Mind rooted in division and limitation cannot provide it to us nor can life and the body which are the energy and the frame of dividing and limiting mind. The principle and power of perfection are there in the subconscient but wrapped up in the tegument or veil of the lower Maya, a mute premonition emerging as an unrealised ideal; in the superconscient they await open, eternally realised, but still separated from us by the veil of our self-ignorance. It is above, then, and not either in our present poise nor below it that we must seek for the reconciling power and knowledge.

Equally, man, as he develops, becomes acutely aware of

the discord and ignorance that governs his relations with the world, acutely intolerant of it, more and more set upon finding a principle of harmony, peace, joy and unity. This too can only come to him from above. For only by developing a mind which shall have knowledge of the mind of others as of itself, free from our mutual ignorance and misunderstanding, a will that feels and makes itself one with the will of others, an emotional heart that contains the emotions of others as its own, a life-force that senses the energies of others and accepts them for its own and seeks to fulfil them as its own, and a body that is not a wall of imprisonment and defence against the world, but all this under the law of a Light and Truth that shall transcend the aberrations and errors, the much sin and falsehood of our and others' minds, wills, emotions, life-energies, — only so can the life of man spiritually and practically become one with that of his fellow-beings and the individual recover his own universal self. The subconscient has this life of the All and the superconscient has it, but under conditions which necessitate our motion upwards. For not towards the Godhead concealed in the "inconscient ocean where darkness is wrapped within darkness",[4] but towards the Godhead seated in the sea of eternal light,[5] in the highest ether of our being, is the original impetus which has carried upward the evolving soul to the type of our humanity.

Unless therefore the race is to fall by the wayside and leave the victory to other and new creations of the eager travailing Mother, it must aspire to this ascent, conducted indeed through love, mental illumination and the vital urge to possession and self-giving, but leading beyond to the supramental unity which transcends and fulfils them; in the founding of human life upon the supramental realisation of conscious unity with the One and with all in our being and in all its members humanity must seek its final good and salvation. And this is what we have described as the fourth status of Life in its ascent towards the Godhead.

---

[4] *Rig Veda*, X. 129. 3.
[5] The Waters which are in the realm of light above the Sun and those which abide below. — *Rig Veda*, III. 22. 3.

Chapter XXIII

The Double Soul in Man

The Purusha, the inner Self, no larger than the size of a man's thumb.   *Katha Upanishad.*[1]

Swetaswatara Upanishad.[2]

He who knows this Self who is the eater of the honey of existence and the lord of what is and shall be, has thenceforward no shrinking.   *Katha Upanishad.*[3]

Whence shall he have grief, how shall he be deluded who sees everywhere the Oneness?   *Isha Upanishad.*[4]

He who has found the bliss of the Eternal has no fear from any quarter.   *Taittiriya Upanishad.*[5]

THE FIRST status of Life we found to be characterised by a dumb inconscient drive or urge, a force of some involved will in the material or atomic existence, not free and possessor of itself or its works or their results, but entirely possessed by the universal movement in which it arises as the obscure unformed seed of individuality. The root of the second status is desire, eager to possess but limited in capacity; the bud of the third is Love which seeks both to possess and be possessed, to receive and to give itself; the fine flower of the fourth, its sign of perfection, we conceive as the pure and full emergence of the original will, the illumined fulfilment of the intermediate desire, the high and deep satisfaction of the conscious interchange of Love by the unification of the state of the possessor and possessed in the divine unity of souls which is the foundation of the supramental existence. If we scrutinise these terms carefully we

[1] II. 1. 12. 13.; II. 3. 17.   [2] III. 13.   [3] II. 1. 5.   [4] Verse 7.   [5] II. 9.

shall see that they are shapes and stages of the soul's seeking for the individual and universal delight of things; the ascent of Life is in its nature the ascent of the divine Delight in things from its dumb conception in Matter through vicissitudes and opposites to its luminous consummation in Spirit.

The world being what it is, it could not be otherwise. For the world is a masked form of Sachchidananda, and the nature of the consciousness of Sachchidananda and therefore the thing in which His force must always find and achieve itself is divine Bliss, an omnipresent self-delight. Since Life is an energy of His conscious-force, the secret of all its movements must be a hidden delight inherent in all things which is at once cause, motive and object of its activities; and if by reason of egoistic division that delight is missed, if it is held back behind a veil, if it is represented as its own opposite, even as being is masked in death, consciousness figures as the inconscient and force mocks itself with the guise of incapacity, then that which lives cannot be satisfied, cannot either rest from the movement or fulfil the movement except by laying hold on this universal delight which is at once the secret total delight of its own being and the original, all-encompassing, all-informing, all-upholding delight of the transcendent and immanent Sachchidananda. To seek for delight is therefore the fundamental impulse and sense of Life; to find and possess and fulfil it is its whole motive.

But where in us is this principle of Delight? through what term of our being does it manifest and fulfil itself in the action of the cosmos as the principle of Conscious-Force manifests and uses Life for its cosmic term and the principle of Supermind manifests and uses Mind? We have distinguished a fourfold principle of divine Being creative of the universe, — Existence, Conscious-Force, Bliss and Supermind. Supermind, we have seen, is omnipresent in the material cosmos, but veiled; it is behind the actual phenomenon of things and occultly expresses itself there, but uses for effectuation its own subordinate term, Mind. The divine Conscious-Force is omnipresent in the material cosmos, but veiled, operative secretly behind the actual phenomenon of things, and it expresses itself there characteristically through its own subordinate term, Life. And, though we have not yet examined separately the principle of Matter, yet we can already see that the divine All-existence also is omnipresent in the material cosmos, but veiled, hidden behind the actual phenomenon of things, and manifests itself there initially through its own subordinate term, Substance, Form of being or Matter. Then, equally, the principle of divine Bliss must be omnipresent in the cosmos, veiled indeed and possessing itself behind the actual phenomenon of things, but still manifested in us through some subordinate principle of its own in which it is hidden and by which it must be found and achieved in the action of the universe.

That term is something in us which we sometimes call in a special sense the soul, — that is to say, the psychic principle which is not the life or the mind, much less the body, but which holds in itself the opening and flowering of the essence of all these to their own peculiar delight of self, to light, to love, to joy and beauty and to a refined purity of being. In fact, however, there is a double soul or psychic term in us, as every other cosmic principle in us is also double. For we have two minds, one the surface mind of our expressed evolutionary ego, the superficial mentality created by us in our emergence out of Matter, another a subliminal mind which is not hampered by our actual mental life and its strict limitations, something large, powerful and luminous, the true mental being behind that superficial form of mental personality which we mistake for ourselves. So also we have two lives, one outer, involved in the physical body, bound by its past evolution in Matter, which lives and was born and will die, the other a subliminal force of life which is not cabined between the narrow boundaries of our physical birth and death, but is our true vital being behind the form of living which we ignorantly take for our real existence. Even in the matter of our being there is this duality; for behind our body we have a subtler material existence which provides the substance not only of our physical but of our vital and mental sheaths and is therefore our real substance supporting this physical form which we erroneously imagine to be the whole body of our spirit. So too we have a double psychic entity in us, the surface desire-soul which works in our vital cravings, our emotions, aesthetic faculty and mental seeking for power, knowledge and happiness, and a subliminal psychic entity, a pure power of light, love, joy and refined essence of being which is our true soul behind the outer form of psychic existence we so often dignify by the name. It is when some reflection of this larger and purer psychic entity comes to the surface that we say of a man, he has a soul, and when it is absent in his outward psychic life that we say of him, he has no soul.

The external forms of our being are those of our small egoistic existence; the subliminal are the formations of our larger true individuality. Therefore are these that concealed part of our being in which our individuality is close to our universality, touches it, is in constant relation and commerce with it. The subliminal mind in us is open to the universal knowledge of the cosmic Mind, the subliminal life in us to the universal force of the cosmic Life, the subliminal physicality in us to the universal force-formation of cosmic Matter; the thick walls which divide from these things our surface mind, life, body and which Nature has to pierce with so much trouble, so imperfectly and by so many skilful-clumsy physical devices, are there, in the subliminal, only a rarefied medium at once of separation and communication. So too is the subliminal soul in us open to the universal delight which the cosmic soul takes in its own existence and in the existence of the myriad souls that represent it and in the operations of mind, life and matter by which Nature lends herself to their play and development; but from this cosmic delight the surface soul is shut off by egoistic walls of great thickness which have indeed gates of penetration, but in their entry through them the touches of the divine cosmic Delight become dwarfed, distorted or have to come in masked as their own opposites.

It follows that in this surface or desire-soul there is no true soul-life, but a psychic deformation and wrong reception of the touch of things. The malady of the world is that the individual cannot find his real soul, and the root-cause of this malady is again that he cannot meet in his embrace of things outward the real soul of the world in which he lives. He seeks to find there the essence of being, the essence of power, the essence of conscious-existence, the essence of delight, but receives instead a crowd of contradictory touches and impressions. If he could find that essence, he would find also the one universal being, power, conscious existence and delight even in this throng of touches and impressions; the contradictions of what seems would be reconciled in the unity and harmony of the Truth that reaches out to us in these contacts. At the same time he would find his own true soul and through it his self, because the true soul is his self's delegate and his self and the self of the world are one. But this he cannot do because of the egoistic ignorance in the mind of thought, the heart of emotion, the sense which responds to the touch of things not by a courageous and whole-hearted embrace of the world, but by a flux of reachings and shrinkings, cautious approaches or eager rushes and sullen or discontented or panic or angry recoils according as the touch pleases or displeases, comforts or alarms, satisfies or dissatisfies. It is the desire-soul that by its wrong reception of life becomes the cause of a triple misinterpretation of the *rasa*, the delight in things, so that, instead of figuring the pure essential joy of being, it comes rendered unequally into the three terms of pleasure, pain and indifference.

We have seen, when we considered the Delight of Existence in its relations to the world, that there is no absoluteness or essential validity in our standards of pleasure and pain and in-difference, that they are entirely determined by the subjectivity of the receiving consciousness and that the degree of either plea-sure and pain can be heightened to a maximum or depressed to a minimum or even effaced entirely in its apparent nature. Pleasure can become pain or pain pleasure because in their secret reality they are the same thing differently reproduced in the sensations and emotions. Indifference is either the inattention of the surface desire-soul in its mind, sensations, emotions and cravings to the *rasa* of things, or its incapacity to receive and respond to it, or its refusal to give any surface response or, again, its driving and crushing down of the pleasure or the pain by the will into the neutral tint of unacceptance. In all these cases what happens is that either there is a positive refusal or a negative unreadiness or incapacity to render or in any way represent positively on the surface something that is yet subliminally active.

For, as we now know by psychological observation and experiment that the subliminal mind receives and remembers all those touches of things which the surface mind ignores, so also we shall find that the subliminal soul responds to the *rasa*, or essence in experience, of these things which the surface desire-soul rejects by distaste and refusal or ignores by neutral unacceptance. Self-knowledge is impossible unless we go behind our surface existence, which is a mere result of selective outer experiences, an imperfect sounding-board or a hasty, incompetent and fragmentary translation of a little out of the much that we are, — unless we go behind this and send down our plummet into the subconscient and open ourself to the superconscient so as to know their relation to our surface being. For between these three things our existence moves and finds in them its totality. The superconscient in us is one with the self and soul of the world and is not governed by any phenomenal diversity; it possesses therefore the truth of things and the delight of things in their plenitude. The subconscient, so called,[6] in that luminous head of itself which we call the subliminal, is, on the contrary, not a true possessor but an instrument of experience; it is not practically one with the soul and self of the world, but it is open to it through its world-experience. The subliminal soul is conscious inwardly of the *rasa* of things and has an equal delight in all contacts; it is conscious also of the values and standards of the surface desire-soul and receives on its own surface corresponding touches of pleasure, pain and indifference, but takes an equal delight in all. In other words, our real soul within takes joy of all its experiences, gathers from them strength, pleasure and knowledge, grows by them in its store and its plenty. It is this

---

[6] The real subconscious is a nether diminished consciousness close to the Inconscient; the subliminal is a consciousness larger than our surface existence. But both belong to the inner realm of our being of which our surface is unaware, so both are jumbled together in our common conception and parlance.

real soul in us which compels the shrinking desire-mind to bear
and even to seek and find a pleasure in what is painful to it,
to reject what is pleasant to it, to modify or even reverse its
values, to equalise things in indifference or to equalise them in
joy, the joy of the variety of existence. And this it does because
it is impelled by the universal to develop itself by all kinds of
experience so as to grow in Nature. Otherwise, if we lived only
by the surface desire-soul, we could no more change or advance
than the plant or stone in whose immobility or in whose routine
of existence, because life is not superficially conscious, the secret
soul of things has as yet no instrument by which it can rescue
the life out of the fixed and narrow gamut into which it is born.
The desire-soul left to itself would circle in the same grooves for
ever.

In the view of old philosophies pleasure and pain are inseparable like intellectual truth and falsehood and power and
incapacity and birth and death; therefore the only possible escape from them would be a total indifference, a blank response
to the excitations of the world-self. But a subtler psychological
knowledge shows us that this view which is based on the surface
facts of existence only, does not really exhaust the possibilities
of the problem. It is possible by bringing the real soul to the
surface to replace the egoistic standards of pleasure and pain
by an equal, an all-embracing personal-impersonal delight. The
lover of Nature does this when he takes joy in all the things
of Nature universally without admitting repulsion or fear or
mere liking and disliking, perceiving beauty in that which seems
to others mean and insignificant, bare and savage, terrible and
repellent. The artist and the poet do it when they seek the *rasa*
of the universal from the aesthetic emotion or from the physical
line or from the mental form of beauty or from the inner sense
and power alike of that from which the ordinary man turns away
and of that to which he is attached by a sense of pleasure. The
seeker of knowledge, the God-lover who finds the object of his
love everywhere, the spiritual man, the intellectual, the sensuous,
the aesthetic all do this in their own fashion and must do it if
they would find embracingly the Knowledge, the Beauty, the Joy

or the Divinity which they seek. It is only in the parts where the little ego is usually too strong for us, it is only in our emotional or physical joy and suffering, our pleasure and pain of life, before which the desire-soul in us is utterly weak and cowardly, that the application of the divine principle becomes supremely difficult and seems to many impossible or even monstrous and repellent. Here the ignorance of the ego shrinks from the principle of impersonality which it yet applies without too much difficulty in Science, in Art and even in a certain kind of imperfect spiritual living because there the rule of impersonality does not attack those desires cherished by the surface soul and those values of desire fixed by the surface mind in which our outward life is most vitally interested. In the freer and higher movements there is demanded of us only a limited and specialised equality and impersonality proper to a particular field of consciousness and activity while the egoistic basis of our practical life remains to us; in the lower movements the whole foundation of our life has to be changed in order to make room for impersonality, and this the desire-soul finds impossible.

The true soul secret in us, — subliminal, we have said, but the word is misleading, for this presence is not situated below the threshold of waking mind, but rather burns in the temple of the inmost heart behind the thick screen of an ignorant mind, life and body, not subliminal but behind the veil, — this veiled psychic entity is the flame of the Godhead always alight within us, inextinguishable even by that dense unconsciousness of any spiritual self within which obscures our outward nature. It is a flame born out of the Divine and, luminous inhabitant of the Ignorance, grows in it till it is able to turn it towards the Knowledge. It is the concealed Witness and Control, the hidden Guide, the Daemon of Socrates, the inner light or inner voice of the mystic. It is that which endures and is imperishable in us from birth to birth, untouched by death, decay or corruption, an indestructible spark of the Divine. Not the unborn Self or Atman, for the Self even in presiding over the existence of the individual is aware always of its universality and transcendence, it is yet its deputy in the forms of Nature, the individual soul, *caitya puruṣa,* supporting mind, life and body, standing behind the mental, the vital, the subtle-physical being in us and watching and profiting by their development and experience. These other person-powers in man, these beings of his being, are also veiled in their true entity, but they put forward temporary personalities which compose our outer individuality and whose combined superficial action and appearance of status we call ourselves: this inmost entity also, taking form in us as the psychic Person, puts forward a psychic personality which changes, grows, develops from life to life; for this is the traveller between birth and death and between death and birth, our nature parts are only its manifold and changing vesture. The psychic being can at first exercise only a concealed and partial and indirect action through the mind, the life and the body, since it is these parts of Nature that have to be developed as its instruments of self-expression, and it is long confined by their evolution. Missioned to lead man in the Ignorance towards the light of the Divine Consciousness, it takes the essence of all experience in the Ignorance to form a nucleus of soul-growth in the nature; the rest it turns into material for the future growth of the instruments which it has to use until they are ready to be a luminous instrumentation of the Divine. It is this secret psychic entity which is the true original Conscience in us deeper than the constructed and conventional conscience of the moralist, for it is this which points always towards Truth and Right and Beauty, towards Love and Harmony and all that is a divine possibility in us, and persists till these things become the major need of our nature. It is the psychic personality in us that flowers as the saint, the sage, the seer; when it reaches its full strength, it turns the being towards the Knowledge of Self and the Divine, towards the supreme Truth, the supreme Good, the supreme Beauty, Love and Bliss, the divine heights and largenesses, and opens us to the touch of spiritual sympathy, universality, oneness. On the contrary, where the psychic personality is weak, crude or ill-developed, the finer parts and movements in us are lacking or poor in character and power, even though the mind may be forceful and brilliant, the heart of vital emotions hard and strong and masterful, the life-force dominant and successful, the bodily existence rich and fortunate and an apparent lord and victor. It is then the outer desire-soul, the pseudo-psychic entity, that reigns and we mistake its misinterpretations of psychic suggestion and aspiration, its ideas and ideals, its desires and yearnings for true soul-stuff and wealth of spiritual experience.[7] If the secret psychic Person can come forward into the front and, replacing the desire-soul, govern overtly and entirely and not only partially and from behind the veil this outer nature of mind, life and body, then these can be cast into soul images of what is true, right and beautiful and in the end the whole nature can be turned towards the real aim of life, the supreme victory, the ascent into spiritual existence.

But it might seem then that by bringing this psychic entity, this true soul in us, into the front and giving it there the lead and rule we shall gain all the fulfilment of our natural being that we can seek for and open also the gates of the kingdom of the Spirit. And it might well be reasoned that there is no need for any intervention of a superior Truth-Consciousness or principle of Supermind to help us to attain to the divine status or the divine perfection. Yet, although the psychic transformation is one necessary condition of the total transformation of our existence, it is not all that is needed for the largest spiritual change. In the first place, since this is the individual soul in Nature, it can open to the hidden diviner ranges of our being and receive and reflect their light and power and experience, but another, a spiritual transformation from above is needed for us to possess our self in its universality and transcendence. By itself the psychic being at a certain stage might be content to create a

---

[7] The word "psychic" in our ordinary parlance is more often used in reference to this desire-soul than to the true psychic. It is used still more loosely of psychological and other phenomena of an abnormal or supernormal character which are really connected with the inner mind, inner vital, subtle physical being subliminal in us and are not at all direct operations of the psyche. Even such phenomena as materialisation and dematerialisation are included, though, if established, they evidently are not soul-action and would not shed any light upon the nature or existence of the psychic entity, but would rather be an abnormal action of an occult subtle physical energy intervening in the ordinary status of the gross body of things, reducing it to its own subtle condition and again reconstituting it in the terms of gross matter.

formation of truth, good and beauty and make that its station; at a farther stage it might become passively subject to the world-self, a mirror of the universal existence, consciousness, power, delight, but not their full participant or possessor. Although more nearly and thrillingly united to the cosmic consciousness in knowledge, emotion and even appreciation through the senses, it might become purely recipient and passive, remote from mastery and action in the world; or, one with the static self behind the cosmos, but separate inwardly from the world-movement, losing its individuality in its Source, it might return to that Source and have neither the will nor the power any further for that which was its ultimate mission here, to lead the nature also towards its divine realisation. For the psychic being came into Nature from the Self, the Divine, and it can turn back from Nature to the silent Divine through the silence of the Self and a supreme spiritual immobility. Again, an eternal portion of the Divine[8], this part is by the law of the Infinite inseparable from its Divine Whole, this part is indeed itself that Whole, except in its frontal appearance, its frontal separative self-experience; it may awaken to that reality and plunge into it to the apparent extinction or at least the merging of the individual existence. A small nucleus here in the mass of our ignorant Nature, so that it is described in the Upanishad as no bigger than a man's thumb, it can by the spiritual influx enlarge itself and embrace the whole world with the heart and mind in an intimate communion or oneness. Or it may become aware of its eternal Companion and elect to live for ever in His presence, in an imperishable union and oneness as the eternal lover with the eternal Beloved, which of all spiritual experiences is the most intense in beauty and rapture. All these are great and splendid achievements of our spiritual self-finding, but they are not necessarily the last end and entire consummation; more is possible.

For these are achievements of the spiritual mind in man; they are movements of that mind passing beyond itself, but on its own plane, into the splendours of the Spirit. Mind, even at

---

[8] *Gita,* XV. 7.

its highest stages far beyond our present mentality, acts yet in its nature by division; it takes the aspects of the Eternal and treats each aspect as if it were the whole truth of the Eternal Being and can find in each its own perfect fulfilment. Even it erects them into opposites and creates a whole range of these opposites, the Silence of the Divine and the divine Dynamis, the immobile Brahman aloof from existence, without qualities, and the active Brahman with qualities, Lord of existence, Being and Becoming, the Divine Person and an impersonal pure Existence; it can then cut itself away from the one and plunge itself into the other as the sole abiding Truth of existence. It can regard the Person as the sole Reality or the Impersonal as alone true; it can regard the Lover as only a means of expression of eternal Love or love as only the self-expression of the Lover; it can see beings as only personal powers of an impersonal Existence or impersonal existence as only a state of the one Being, the Infinite Person. Its spiritual achievement, its road of passage towards the supreme aim will follow these dividing lines. But beyond this movement of spiritual Mind is the higher experience of the Supermind Truth-Consciousness; there these opposites disappear and these partialities are relinquished in the rich totality of a supreme and integral realisation of eternal Being. It is this that is the aim we have conceived, the consummation of our existence here by an ascent to the supramental Truth-Consciousness and its descent into our nature. The psychic transformation after rising into the spiritual change has then to be completed, integralised, exceeded and uplifted by a supramental transformation which lifts it to the summit of the ascending endeavour.

Even as between the other divided and opposed terms of manifested Being, so also a supramental consciousness-energy could alone establish a perfect harmony between these two terms, — apparently opposite only because of the Ignorance, — of spirit status and world dynamism in our embodied existence. In the Ignorance Nature centres the order of her psychological movements, not around the secret spiritual self, but around its substitute, the ego-principle: a certain ego-centrism is the basis on which we bind together our experiences and relations in the midst of the complex contacts, contradictions, dualities, incoherences of the world in which we live; this ego-centrism is our rock of safety against the cosmic and the infinite, our defence. But in our spiritual change we have to forego this defence; ego has to vanish, the person finds itself dissolved into a vast impersonality, and in this impersonality there is at first no key to an ordered dynamism of action. A very usual result is that one is divided into two parts of being, the spiritual within, the natural without; in one there is the divine realisation seated in a perfect inner freedom, but the natural part goes on with the old action of Nature, continues by a mechanical movement of past energies her already transmitted impulse. Even, if there is an entire dissolution of the limited person and the old ego-centric order, the outer nature may become the field of an apparent incoherence, although all within is luminous with the Self. Thus we become outwardly inert and inactive, moved by circumstance or forces but not self-mobile,[9] even though the consciousness is enlightened within, or as a child though within is a plenary self-knowledge,[10] or as one inconsequent in thought and impulse though within is an utter calm and serenity,[11] or as the wild and disordered soul though inwardly there is the purity and poise of the Spirit.[12] Or if there is an ordered dynamism in the outward nature, it may be a continuation of superficial ego-action witnessed but not accepted by the inner being, or a mental dynamism that cannot be perfectly expressive of the inner spiritual realisation; for there is no equipollence between action of mind and status of spirit. Even at the best where there is an intuitive guidance of Light from within, the nature of its expression in dynamism of action must be marked with the imperfections of mind, life and body, a King with incapable ministers, a Knowledge expressed in the values of the Ignorance. Only the descent of the Supermind with its perfect unity of Truth-Knowledge and Truth-Will can establish in the outer as in the inner existence the harmony of the Spirit; for it alone can turn the values of the Ignorance entirely into the values of the Knowledge.

---

[9] *jaḍavat.*   [10] *bālavat.*   [11] *unmattavat.*   [12] *piśācavat.*

In the fulfilment of our psychic being as in the consummation of our parts of mind and life, it is the relating of it to its divine source, to its correspondent truth in the Supreme Reality, that is the indispensable movement; and, here too as there, it is by the power of the Supermind that it can be done with an integral completeness, an intimacy that becomes an authentic identity; for it is the Supermind which links the higher and the lower hemispheres of the One Existence. In Supermind is the integrating Light, the consummating Force, the wide entry into the supreme Ananda: the psychic being uplifted by that Light and Force can unite itself with the original Delight of existence from which it came: overcoming the dualities of pain and pleasure, delivering from all fear and shrinking the mind, life and body, it can recast the contacts of existence in the world into terms of the Divine Ananda.

Chapter XXIV

Matter

He arrived at the knowledge that Matter is Brahman.
Taittiriya Upanishad.[1]

WE HAVE now the rational assurance that Life is neither an inexplicable dream nor an impossible evil that has yet become a dolorous fact, but a mighty pulsation of the divine All-Existence. We see something of its foundation and its principle, we look upward to its high potentiality and ultimate divine out-flowering. But there is one principle below all the others which we have not yet sufficiently considered, the principle of Matter upon which Life stands as upon a pedestal or out of which it evolves like the form of a many-branching tree out of its encasing seed. The mind, life and body of man depend upon this physical principle, and if the out-flowering of Life is the result of Consciousness emerging into Mind, expanding, elevating itself in search of its own truth in the largeness of the supramental existence, yet it seems also to be conditioned by this case of body and by this foundation of Matter. The importance of the body is obvious; it is because he has developed or been given a body and brain capable of receiving and serving a progressive mental illumination that man has risen above the animal. Equally, it can only be by developing a body or at least a functioning of the physical instrument capable of receiving and serving a still higher illumination that he will rise above himself and realise, not merely in thought and in his internal being but in life, a perfectly divine manhood. Otherwise either the promise of Life is cancelled, its meaning annulled and earthly being can

[1] III. 2.

only realise Sachchidananda by abolishing itself, by shedding from it mind, life and body and returning to the pure Infinite, or else man is not the divine instrument, there is a destined limit to the consciously progressive power which distinguishes him from all other terrestrial existences and as he has replaced them in the front of things, so another must eventually replace him and assume his heritage.

It seems indeed that the body is from the beginning the soul's great difficulty, its continual stumbling-block and rock of offence. Therefore the eager seeker of spiritual fulfilment has hurled his ban against the body and his world-disgust selects this world-principle above all other things as an especial object of loathing. The body is the obscure burden that he cannot bear; its obstinate material grossness is the obsession that drives him for deliverance to the life of the ascetic. To get rid of it he has even gone so far as to deny its existence and the reality of the material universe. Most of the religions have put their curse upon Matter and have made the refusal or the resigned temporary endurance of the physical life the test of religious truth and of spirituality. The older creeds, more patient, more broodingly profound, not touched with the torture and the feverish impatience of the soul under the burden of the Iron Age, did not make this formidable division; they acknowledged Earth the Mother and Heaven the Father and accorded to them an equal love and reverence; but their ancient mysteries are obscure and unfathomable to our gaze who, whether our view of things be materialistic or spiritual, are alike content to cut the Gordian knot of the problem of existence with one decisive blow and to accept an escape into an eternal bliss or an end in an eternal annihilation or an eternal quietude.

The quarrel does not really commence with our awakening to our spiritual possibilities; it begins from the appearance of life itself and its struggle to establish its activities and its permanent aggregations of living form against the force of inertia, against the force of inconscience, against the force of atomic disaggregation which are in the material principle the knot of the great Denial. Life is at constant war with Matter and the battle seems always to end in the apparent defeat of Life and in that collapse downward to the material principle which we call death. The discord deepens with the appearance of Mind; for Mind has its own quarrel with both Life and Matter: it is at constant war with their limitations, in constant subjection to and revolt against the grossness and inertia of the one and the passions and sufferings of the other; and the battle seems to turn eventually, though not very surely, towards a partial and costly victory for the Mind in which it conquers, represses or even slays the vital cravings, impairs the physical force and disturbs the balance of the body in the interests of a greater mental activity and a higher moral being. It is in this struggle that the impatience of Life, the disgust of the body and the recoil from both towards a pure mental and moral existence take their rise. When man awakens to an existence beyond Mind, he carries yet farther this principle of discord. Mind, Body and Life are condemned as the trinity of the world, the flesh and the devil. Mind too is banned as the source of all our malady; war is declared between the spirit and its instruments and the victory of the spiritual Inhabitant is sought for in an evasion from its narrow residence, a rejection of mind, life and body and a withdrawal into its own infinitudes. The world is a discord and we shall best solve its perplexities by carrying the principle of discord itself to its extreme possibility, a cutting away and a final severance.

But these defeats and victories are only apparent, this solution is not a solution but an escape from the problem. Life is not really defeated by Matter; it makes a compromise by using death for the continuance of life. Mind is not really victorious over Life and Matter, but has only achieved an imperfect development of some of its potentialities at the cost of others which are bound up with the unrealised or rejected possibilities of its better use of life and body. The individual soul has not conquered the lower triplicity, but only rejected their claim upon it and fled from the work which spirit had undertaken when it first cast itself into form of universe. The problem continues because the labour of the Divine in the universe continues, but without any satisfying solution of the problem or any victorious accomplishment of the labour. Therefore, since our own standpoint is that

Sachchidananda is the beginning and the middle and the end and that struggle and discord cannot be eternal and fundamental principles in His being but by their very existence imply labour towards a perfect solution and a complete victory, we must seek that solution in a real victory of Life over Matter through the free and perfect use of body by Life, in a real victory of Mind over Life and Matter through a free and perfect use of life-force and form by Mind and in a real victory of Spirit over the triplicity through a free and perfect occupation of mind, life and body by conscious spirit; in the view we have worked out this last conquest can alone make the others really possible. To the end, then, that we may see how these conquests can be at all or wholly possible, we must find out the reality of Matter just as, seeking the fundamental knowledge, we have found out the reality of Mind and Soul and Life.

In a certain sense Matter is unreal and non-existent; that is to say, our present knowledge, idea and experience of Matter is not its truth, but merely a phenomenon of particular relation between our senses and the all-existence in which we move. When Science discovers that Matter resolves itself into forms of Energy, it has hold of a universal and fundamental truth; and when philosophy discovers that Matter only exists as substantial appearance to the consciousness and that the one reality is Spirit or pure conscious Being, it has hold of a greater and completer, a still more fundamental truth. But still the question remains why Energy should take the form of Matter and not of mere force-currents or why that which is really Spirit should admit the phenomenon of Matter and not rest in states, velleities and joys of the spirit. This, it is said, is the work of Mind or else, since evidently Thought does not directly create or even perceive the material form of things, it is the work of Sense; the sense-mind creates the forms which it seems to perceive and the thought-mind works upon the forms which the sense-mind presents to it. But, evidently, the individual embodied mind is not the creator of the phenomenon of Matter; earth-existence cannot be the result of the human mind which is itself the result of earth-existence. If we say that the world exists only in our own minds, we express a non-fact and a confusion; for the material world existed before man was upon the earth and it will go on existing if man disappears from the earth or even if our individual mind abolishes itself in the Infinite. We must conclude then that there is a universal Mind,[2] subconscious to us in the form of the universe or superconscious in its spirit, which has created that form for its habitation. And since the creator must have preceded and must exceed its creation, this really implies a superconscient Mind which by the instrumentality of a universal sense creates in itself the relation of form with form and constitutes the rhythm of the material universe. But this also is no complete solution; it tells us that Matter is a creation of Consciousness, but it does not explain how Consciousness came to create Matter as the basis of its cosmic workings.

We shall understand better if we go back at once to the original principle of things. Existence is in its activity a Conscious-Force which presents the workings of its force to its consciousness as forms of its own being. Since Force is only the action of one sole-existing Conscious-Being, its results can be nothing else but forms of that Conscious-Being; Substance or Matter, then, is only a form of Spirit. The appearance which this form of Spirit assumes to our senses is due to that dividing action of Mind from which we have been able to deduce consistently the whole phenomenon of the universe. We know now that Life is an action of Conscious-Force of which material forms are the result; Life involved in those forms, appearing in them first as inconscient force, evolves and brings back into manifestation as Mind the consciousness which is the real self of the force and which never ceased to exist in it even when unmanifest. We know also that Mind is an inferior power of the original conscious Knowledge

---

[2] Mind, as we know it, creates only in a relative and instrumental sense; it has an unlimited power of combination, but its creative motives and forms come to it from above: all created forms have their base in the Infinite above Mind, Life and Matter and are here represented, reconstructed — very usually misconstructed — from the infinitesimal. Their foundation is above, their branchings downwards, says the Rig Veda. The superconscient Mind of which we speak might rather be called an Overmind and inhabits in the hierarchical order of the powers of the Spirit, a zone directly dependent on the supramental consciousness.

or Supermind, a power to which Life acts as an instrumental energy; for, descending through Supermind, Consciousness or Chit represents itself as Mind, Force of consciousness or Tapas represents itself as Life. Mind, by its separation from its own higher reality in Supermind, gives Life the appearance of division and, by its farther involution in its own Life-Force, becomes subconscious in Life and thus gives the outward appearance of an inconscient force to its material workings. Therefore, the inconscience, the inertia, the atomic disaggregation of Matter must have their source in this all-dividing and self-involving action of Mind by which our universe came into being. As Mind is only a final action of Supermind in the descent towards creation and Life an action of Conscious-Force working in the conditions of the Ignorance created by this descent of Mind, so Matter, as we know it, is only the final form taken by conscious-being as the result of that working. Matter is substance of the one Conscious-Being phenomenally divided within itself by the action of a universal Mind,[3] — a division which the individual mind repeats and dwells in, but which does not abrogate or at all diminish the unity of Spirit or the unity of Energy or the real unity of Matter.

But why this phenomenal and pragmatic division of an indivisible Existence? It is because Mind has to carry the principle of multiplicity to its extreme potential which can only be done by separativeness and division. To do that it must, precipitating itself into Life to create forms for the Multiple, give to the universal principle of Being the appearance of a gross and material substance instead of a pure or subtle substance. It must, that is to say, give it the appearance of substance which offers itself to the contact of Mind as stable thing or object in an abiding multiplicity of objects and not of substance which offers itself to the contact of pure consciousness as something of its own eternal pure existence and reality or to subtle sense as a principle of plastic form

---

[3] Mind is here used in its widest sense including the operation of an Overmind power which is nearest to the supramental Truth-Consciousness and which is the first fountain of the creation of the Ignorance.

freely expressive of the conscious being. The contact of mind with its objects creates what we call sense, but here it has to be an obscure externalised sense which must be assured of the reality of what it contacts. The descent of pure substance into material substance follows, then, inevitably on the descent of Sachchidananda through Supermind into mind and life. It is a necessary result of the will to make multiplicity of being and an awareness of things from separate centres of consciousness the first method of this lower experience of existence. If we go back to the spiritual basis of things, substance in its utter purity resolves itself into pure conscious being, self-existent, inherently self-aware by identity, but not yet turning its consciousness upon itself as object. Supermind preserves this self-awareness by identity as its substance of self-knowledge and its light of self-creation, but for that creation presents Being to itself as the subject-object one and multiple of its own active consciousness. Being as object is held there in a supreme knowledge which can, by comprehension, see it both as an object of cognition within itself and subjectively as itself, but can also and simultaneously, by apprehension, project it as an object (or objects) of cognition within the circumference of its consciousness, not other than itself, part of its being, but a part (or parts) put away from itself, — that is to say, from the centre of vision in which Being concentrates itself as the Knower, Witness or Purusha. We have seen that from this apprehending consciousness arises the movement of Mind, the movement by which the individual knower regards a form of his own universal being as if other than he; but in the divine Mind there is immediately or rather simultaneously another movement or reverse side of the same movement, an act of union in being which heals this phenomenal division and prevents it from becoming even for a moment solely real to the knower. This act of conscious union is that which is represented otherwise in dividing Mind obtusely, ignorantly, quite externally as contact in consciousness between divided beings and separate objects, and with us this contact in divided consciousness is primarily represented by the principle of sense. On this basis of sense, on this contact of union subject to division, the action of the thought-mind founds itself and prepares for the return to a higher principle of union in which division is made subject to unity and subordinate. Substance, then, as we know it, material substance, is the form in which Mind acting through sense contacts the Conscious Being of which it is itself a movement of knowledge.

But Mind by its very nature tends to know and sense substance of conscious-being, not in its unity or totality but by the principle of division. It sees it, as it were, in infinitesimal points which it associates together in order to arrive at a totality, and into these viewpoints and associations cosmic Mind throws itself and dwells in them. So dwelling, creative by its inherent force as the agent of Real-Idea, bound by its own nature to convert all its perceptions into energy of life, as the All-Existent converts all His self-aspectings into various energy of His creative Force of consciousness, cosmic Mind turns these, its multiple viewpoints of universal existence, into standpoints of universal Life; it turns them in Matter into forms of atomic being instinct with the life that forms them and governed by the mind and will that actuate the formation. At the same time, the atomic existences which it thus forms must by the very law of their being tend to associate themselves, to aggregate; and each of these aggregates also, instinct with the hidden life that forms and the hidden mind and will that actuate them, bears with it a fiction of a separated individual existence. Each such individual object or existence is supported, according as the mind in it is implicit or explicit, unmanifest or manifest, by its mechanical ego of force, in which the will-to-be is dumb and imprisoned but none the less powerful, or by its self-aware mental ego in which the will-to-be is liberated, conscious, separately active.

Thus not any eternal and original law of eternal and original Matter, but the nature of the action of cosmic Mind is the cause of atomic existence. Matter is a creation, and for its creation the infinitesimal, an extreme fragmentation of the Infinite, was needed as the starting-point or basis. Ether may and does exist as an intangible, almost spiritual support of Matter, but as a phenomenon it does not seem, to our present knowledge at least, to be materially detectable. Subdivide the visible aggregate or the formal atom into essential atoms, break it up into the most infinitesimal dust of being, we shall still, because of the nature of the Mind and Life that formed them, arrive at some utmost atomic existence, unstable perhaps but always reconstituting itself in the eternal flux of force, phenomenally, and not at a mere unatomic extension incapable of contents. Unatomic extension of substance, extension which is not an aggregation, coexistence otherwise than by distribution in space are realities of pure existence, pure substance; they are a knowledge of Supermind and a principle of its dynamism, not a creative concept of the dividing Mind, though Mind can become aware of them behind its workings. They are the reality underlying Matter, but not the phenomenon which we call Matter. Mind, Life, Matter itself can be one with that pure existence and conscious extension in their static reality, but not operate by that oneness in their dynamic action, self-perception and self-formation.

Therefore we arrive at this truth of Matter that there is a conceptive self-extension of being which works itself out in the universe as substance or object of consciousness and which cosmic Mind and Life in their creative action represent through atomic division and aggregation as the thing we call Matter. But this Matter, like Mind and Life, is still Being or Brahman in its self-creative action. It is a form of the force of conscious Being, a form given by Mind and realised by Life. It holds within it as its own reality consciousness concealed from itself, involved and absorbed in the result of its own self-formation and therefore self-oblivious. And, however brute and void of sense it seems to us, it is yet, to the secret experience of the consciousness hidden within it, delight of being offering itself to this secret consciousness as object of sensation in order to tempt that hidden godhead out of its secrecy. Being manifest as substance, force of Being cast into form, into a figured self-representation of the secret self-consciousness, delight offering itself to its own consciousness as an object, — what is this but Sachchidananda? Matter is Sachchidananda represented to His own mental experience as a formal basis of objective knowledge, action and delight of existence.

Chapter XXV

The Knot of Matter

I cannot travel to the Truth of the luminous Lord by force or
by the duality.... Who are they that protect the foundation of
the falsehood? Who are the guardians of the unreal word?

Then existence was not nor non-existence, the mid-world was
not nor the Ether nor what is beyond. What covered all? where
was it? in whose refuge? what was that ocean dense and deep?
Death was not nor immortality nor the knowledge of day and
night. That One lived without breath by his self-law, there was
nothing else nor aught beyond it. In the beginning Darkness
was hidden by darkness, all this was an ocean of inconscience.
When universal being was concealed by fragmentation, then
by the greatness of its energy That One was born. That moved
at first as desire within, which was the primal seed of mind.
The seers of Truth discovered the building of being in non-
being by will in the heart and by the thought; their ray was
extended horizontally; but what was there below, what was
there above? There were Casters of the seed, there were Great-
nesses; there was self-law below, there was Will above.

Rig Veda.[1]

IF THEN the conclusion at which we have arrived is correct,
— and there is no other possible on the data upon which
we are working, — the sharp division which practical experience and long habit of mind have created between Spirit and
Matter has no longer any fundamental reality. The world is a
differentiated unity, a manifold oneness, not a constant attempt
at compromise between eternal dissonances, not an everlasting

---

[1] V. 12. 2, 4; X. 129. 1-5.

struggle between irreconcilable opposites. An inalienable oneness generating infinite variety is its foundation and beginning;
a constant reconciliation behind apparent division and struggle
combining all possible disparates for vast ends in a secret Consciousness and Will which is ever one and master of all its own
complex action, appears to be its real character in the middle;
we must assume therefore that a fulfilment of the emerging Will
and Consciousness and a triumphant harmony must be its conclusion. Substance is the form of itself on which it works, and of
that substance if Matter is one end, Spirit is the other. The two
are one: Spirit is the soul and reality of that which we sense as
Matter; Matter is a form and body of that which we realise as
Spirit.

Certainly, there is a vast practical difference and on that
difference the whole indivisible series and ever-ascending degrees
of the world-existence are founded. Substance, we have said, is
conscious existence presenting itself to the sense as object so that,
on the basis of whatever sense-relation is established, the work
of world-formation and cosmic progression may proceed. But
there need not be only one basis, only one fundamental principle
of relation immutably created between sense and substance; on
the contrary, there is an ascending and developing series. We
are aware of another substance in which pure mind works as
its natural medium and which is far subtler, more flexible, more
plastic than anything that our physical sense can conceive of as
Matter. We can speak of a substance of mind because we become
aware of a subtler medium in which forms arise and action takes
place; we can speak also of a substance of pure dynamic life-
energy other than the subtlest forms of material substance and its
physically sensible force-currents. Spirit itself is pure substance
of being presenting itself as an object no longer to physical, vital
or mental sense, but to a light of a pure spiritual perceptive
knowledge in which the subject becomes its own object, that is
to say, in which the Timeless and Spaceless is aware of itself in
a pure spiritually self-conceptive self-extension as the basis and
primal material of all existence. Beyond this foundation is the
disappearance of all conscious differentiation between subject

and object in an absolute identity, and there we can no longer speak of Substance.

Therefore it is a purely conceptive — a spiritually, not a mentally conceptive difference ending in a practical distinction, which creates the series descending from Spirit through Mind to Matter and ascending again from Matter through Mind to Spirit. But the real oneness is never abrogated, and, when we get back to the original and integral view of things, we see that it is never even truly diminished or impaired, not even in the grossest densities of Matter. Brahman is not only the cause and supporting power and indwelling principle of the universe, he is also its material and its sole material. Matter also is Brahman and it is nothing other than or different from Brahman. If indeed Matter were cut off from Spirit, this would not be so; but it is, as we have seen, only a final form and objective aspect of the divine Existence with all of God ever present in it and behind it. As this apparently brute and inert Matter is everywhere and always instinct with a mighty dynamic force of Life, as this dynamic but apparently unconscious Life secretes within it an ever-working unapparent Mind of whose secret dealings it is the overt energy, as this ignorant, unillumined and groping Mind in the living body is supported and sovereignly guided by its own real self, the Supermind, which is there equally in unmentalised Matter, so all Matter as well as all Life, Mind and Supermind are only modes of the Brahman, the Eternal, the Spirit, Sachchidananda, who not only dwells in them all, but is all these things though no one of them is His absolute being.

But still there is this conceptive difference and practical distinction, and in that, even if Matter is not really cut off from Spirit, yet it seems with such a practical definiteness to be so cut off, it is so different, even so contrary in its law, the material life seems so much to be the negation of all spiritual existence that its rejection might well appear to be the one short cut out of the difficulty, — as undoubtedly it is; but a short cut or any cut is no solution. Still, there, in Matter undoubtedly lies the crux; that raises the obstacle: for because of Matter Life is gross and limited and stricken with death and pain, because of

Matter Mind is more than half blind, its wings clipped, its feet tied to a narrow perch and held back from the vastness and freedom above of which it is conscious. Therefore the exclusive spiritual seeker is justified from his viewpoint if, disgusted with the mud of Matter, revolted by the animal grossness of Life or impatient of the self-imprisoned narrowness and downward vision of Mind, he determines to break from it all and return by inaction and silence to the Spirit's immobile liberty. But that is not the sole viewpoint, nor, because it has been sublimely held or glorified by shining and golden examples, need we consider it the integral and ultimate wisdom. Rather, liberating ourselves from all passion and revolt, let us see what this divine order of the universe means, and, as for this great knot and tangle of Matter denying the Spirit, let us seek to find out and separate its strands so as to loosen it by a solution and not cut through it by a violence. We must state the difficulty, the opposition first, entirely, trenchantly, with exaggeration, if need be, rather than with diminution, and then look for the issue.

First, then, the fundamental opposition Matter presents to Spirit is this that it is the culmination of the principle of Ignorance. Here Consciousness has lost and forgotten itself in a form of its works, as a man might forget in extreme absorption not only who he is but that he is at all and become momentarily only the work that is being done and the force that is doing it. The Spirit self-luminous, infinitely aware of itself behind all workings of force and their master, seems here to have disappeared and not to be at all; somewhere He is perhaps, but here He seems to have left only a brute and inconscient material Force which creates and destroys eternally without knowing itself or what it creates or why it creates at all or why it destroys what once it has created: it does not know, for it has no mind; it does not care, for it has no heart. And if that is not the real truth even of the material universe, if behind all this false phenomenon there is a Mind, a Will and something greater than Mind or mental Will, yet it is this dark semblance that the material universe itself presents as a truth to the consciousness which emerges in it out of its night; and if it be no truth but a lie, yet is it a most effective lie, for it determines the conditions of our phenomenal existence and besieges all our aspiration and effort.

For this is the monstrous thing, the terrible and pitiless miracle of the material universe that out of this no-Mind a mind or, at least, minds emerge and find themselves struggling feebly for light, helpless individually, only less helpless when in self-defence they associate their individual feeblenesses in the midst of the giant Ignorance which is the law of the universe. Out of this heartless Inconscience and within its rigorous jurisdiction hearts have been born and aspire and are tortured and bleed under the weight of the blind and insentient cruelty of this iron existence, a cruelty which lays its law upon them and becomes sentient in their sentience, brutal, ferocious, horrible. But what after all, behind appearances, is this seeming mystery? We can see that it is the Consciousness which had lost itself returning again to itself, emerging out of its giant self-forgetfulness, slowly, painfully, as a Life that is would-be sentient, half-sentient, dimly sentient, wholly sentient and finally struggles to be more than sentient, to be again divinely self-conscious, free, infinite, immortal. But it works towards this under a law that is the opposite of all these things, under the conditions of Matter, that is to say, against the grasp of the Ignorance. The movements it has to follow, the instruments it has to use are set and made for it by this brute and divided Matter and impose on it at every step ignorance and limitation.

For the second fundamental opposition that Matter offers to Spirit, is this that it is the culmination of bondage to mechanic Law and opposes to all that seeks to liberate itself a colossal Inertia. Not that Matter itself is inert; it is rather an infinite motion, an inconceivable force, a limitless action, whose grandiose movements are a subject for our constant admiration. But while Spirit is free, master of itself and its works, not bound by them, creator of law and not its subject, this giant Matter is rigidly chained by a fixed and mechanical Law which is imposed on it, which it does not understand nor has ever conceived but works out inconsciently as a machine works and knows not who created it, by what process or to what end. And when Life awakes and seeks to impose itself on physical form and material force and to use all things at its own will and for its own need, when Mind awakes and seeks to know the who, the why, the how of itself and all things and above all to use its knowledge for the imposition of its own freer law and self-guiding action upon things, material Nature seems to yield, even to approve and aid, though after a struggle, reluctantly and only up to a certain point. But beyond that point it presents an obstinate inertia, obstruction, negation and even persuades Life and Mind that they cannot go farther, cannot pursue to the end their partial victory. Life strives to enlarge and prolong itself and succeeds; but when it seeks utter wideness and immortality, it meets the iron obstruction of Matter and finds itself bound to narrowness and death. Mind seeks to aid life and to fulfil its own impulse to embrace all knowledge, to become all light, to possess truth and be truth, to enforce love and joy and be love and joy; but always there is the deviation and error and grossness of the material life-instincts and the denial and obstruction of the material sense and the physical instruments. Error ever pursues its knowledge, darkness is inseparably the companion and background of its light; truth is successfully sought and yet, when grasped, it ceases to be truth and the quest has to continue; love is there but it cannot satisfy itself, joy is there but it cannot justify itself, and each of them drags as if its chain or casts as if its shadow its own opposites, anger and hatred and indifference, satiety and grief and pain. The inertia with which Matter responds to the demands of the Mind and Life, prevents the conquest of the Ignorance and of the brute Force that is the power of the Ignorance.

And when we seek to know why this is so, we see that the success of this inertia and obstruction is due to a third power of Matter; for the third fundamental opposition which Matter offers to Spirit is this that it is the culmination of the principle of division and struggle. Indivisible indeed in reality, divisibility is its whole basis of action from which it seems forbidden ever to depart; for its only two methods of union are either the aggregation of units or an assimilation which involves the destruction of one unit by another; and both of these methods of union are a confession of eternal division, since even the first associates rather than unifies and by its very principle admits the constant possibility and therefore the ultimate necessity of dissociation, of dissolution. Both methods repose on death, one as a means, the other as a condition of life. And both presuppose as the condition of world-existence a constant struggle of the divided units with each other, each striving to maintain itself, to maintain its associations, to compel or destroy what resists it, to gather in and devour others as its food, but itself moved to revolt against and flee from compulsion, destruction and assimilation by devouring. When the vital principle manifests its activities in Matter, it finds there this basis only for all its activities and is compelled to bow itself to the yoke; it has to accept the law of death, desire and limitation and that constant struggle to devour, possess, dominate which we have seen to be the first aspect of Life. And when the mental principle manifests in Matter, it has to accept from the mould and material in which it works the same principle of limitation, of seeking without secure finding, the same constant association and dissociation of its gains and of the constituents of its works, so that the knowledge gained by man, the mental being, seems never to be final or free from doubt and denial and all his labour seems condemned to move in a rhythm of action and reaction and of making and unmaking, in cycles of creation and brief preservation and long destruction with no certain and assured progress.

Especially and most fatally, the ignorance, inertia and division of Matter impose on the vital and mental existence emerging in it the law of pain and suffering and the unrest of dissatisfaction with its status of division, inertia and ignorance. Ignorance would indeed bring no pain of dissatisfaction if the mental consciousness were entirely ignorant, if it could halt satisfied in some shell of custom, unaware of its own ignorance or of the infinite ocean of consciousness and knowledge by which it lives surrounded; but precisely it is to this that the emerging consciousness in Matter awakes, first, to its ignorance of the world in which it lives and which it has to know and master in order to be happy, secondly, to the ultimate barrenness and limitation of this knowledge, to the meagreness and insecurity of the power and happiness it brings and to the awareness of an infinite consciousness, knowledge, true being in which alone is to be found a victorious and infinite happiness. Nor would the obstruction of inertia bring with it unrest and dissatisfaction if the vital sentience emerging in Matter were entirely inert, if it were kept satisfied with its own half-conscient limited existence, unaware of the infinite power and immortal existence in which it lives as part of and yet separated from it, or if it had nothing within driving it towards the effort really to participate in that infinity and immortality. But this is precisely what all life is driven to feel and seek from the first, its insecurity and the need and struggle for persistence, for self-preservation; it awakes in the end to the limitation of its existence and begins to feel the impulsion towards largeness and persistence, towards the infinite and the eternal.

And when in man life becomes wholly self-conscious, this unavoidable struggle and effort and aspiration reach their acme and the pain and discord of the world become finally too keenly sensible to be borne with contentment. Man may for a long time quiet himself by seeking to be satisfied with his limitations or by confining his struggle to such mastery as he can gain over this material world he inhabits, some mental and physical triumph of his progressive knowledge over its inconscient fixities, of his small, concentrated conscious will and power over its inertly-driven monstrous forces. But here, too, he finds the limitation, the poor inconclusiveness of the greatest results he can achieve and is obliged to look beyond. The finite cannot remain permanently satisfied so long as it is conscious either of a finite greater than itself or of an infinite beyond itself to which it can yet aspire. And if the finite could be so satisfied, yet the apparently finite being who feels himself to be really an infinite or feels merely the presence or the impulse and stirring of an infinite within, can never be satisfied till these two are reconciled, till that is possessed by him and he is possessed by it in whatever degree or manner. Man is such a finite-seeming infinity and cannot fail to arrive at a seeking after the Infinite. He is the first son of earth who becomes vaguely aware of God within him, of his immortality or of his need of immortality, and the knowledge is a whip that drives and a cross of crucifixion until he is able to turn it into a source of infinite light and joy and power.

This progressive development, this growing manifestation of the divine Consciousness and Force, Knowledge and Will that had lost itself in the ignorance and inertia of Matter, might well be a happy efflorescence proceeding from joy to greater and at last to infinite joy if it were not for the principle of rigid division from which Matter has started. The shutting up of the individual in his own personal consciousness of separate and limited mind, life and body prevents what would otherwise be the natural law of our development. It brings into the body the law of attraction and repulsion, of defence and attack, of discord and pain. For each body being a limited conscious-force feels itself exposed to the attack, impact, forceful contact of other such limited conscious-force or of universal forces and, where it feels itself broken in upon or unable to harmonise the contacting and the recipient consciousness, it suffers discomfort and pain, is attracted or repelled, has to defend itself or to assail; it is constantly called upon to undergo what it is unwilling or unable to suffer. Into the emotional and the sense-mind the law of division brings the same reactions with the higher values of grief and joy, love and hatred, oppression and depression, all cast into terms of desire, and by desire into straining and effort, and by the straining into excess and defect of force, incapacity, the rhythm of attainment and disappointment, possession and recoil, a constant strife and trouble and unease. Into the mind as a whole, instead of a divine law of narrower truth flowing into greater truth, lesser light taken up into wider light, lower will surrendered to higher transforming will, pettier satisfaction progressing towards nobler and more complete satisfaction, it brings similar dualities of truth pursued by error, light by darkness, power by incapacity, pleasure of pursuit and attainment by pain of repulse and of dissatisfaction with what is attained; mind takes up its own affliction along with the affliction of life and body and becomes aware of the triple defect and insufficiency of our natural being. All this means the denial of Ananda, the negation of the trinity of Sachchidananda and therefore, if the negation be insuperable, the futility of existence; for existence in throwing itself out in the play of consciousness and force must seek that movement not merely for itself, but for satisfaction in the play, and if in the play no real satisfaction can be found, it must obviously be abandoned in the end as a vain attempt, a colossal mistake, a delirium of the self-embodying spirit.

This is the whole basis of the pessimist theory of the world, — optimist, it may be, as to worlds and states beyond, but pessimist as to the earthly life and the destiny of the mental being in his dealings with the material universe. For it affirms that since the very nature of material existence is division and the very seed of embodied mind is self-limitation, ignorance and egoism, to seek satisfaction of the spirit upon earth or to seek an issue and divine purpose and culmination for the world-play is a vanity and delusion; only in a heaven of the Spirit and not in the world, or only in the Spirit's true quietude and not in its phenomenal activities can we reunite existence and consciousness with the divine self-delight. The Infinite can only recover itself by rejecting as an error and a false step its attempt to find itself in the finite. Nor can the emergence of mental consciousness in the material universe bring with it any promise of a divine fulfilment. For the principle of division is not proper to Matter, but to Mind; Matter is only an illusion of Mind into which Mind brings its own rule of division and ignorance. Therefore within this illusion Mind can only find itself; it can only travel between the three terms of the divided existence it has created: it cannot find there the unity of the Spirit or the truth of the spiritual existence.

Now it is true that the principle of division in Matter can be only a creation of the divided Mind which has precipitated itself into material existence; for that material existence has no self-being, is not the original phenomenon but only a form created by an all-dividing Life-force which works out the conceptions of an all-dividing Mind. By working out being into these appearances of the ignorance, inertia and division of Matter the dividing

Mind has lost and imprisoned itself in a dungeon of its own building, is bound with chains which it has itself forged. And if it be true that the dividing Mind is the first principle of creation, then it must be also the ultimate attainment possible in the creation, and the mental being struggling vainly with Life and Matter, overpowering them only to be overpowered by them, repeating eternally a fruitless cycle must be the last and highest word of cosmic existence. But no such consequence ensues if, on the contrary, it is the immortal and infinite Spirit that has veiled itself in the dense robe of material substance and works there by the supreme creative power of Supermind, permitting the divisions of Mind and the reign of the lowest or material principle only as initial conditions for a certain evolutionary play of the One in the Many. If, in other words, it is not merely a mental being who is hidden in the forms of the universe, but the infinite Being, Knowledge, Will which emerges out of Matter first as Life, then as Mind, with the rest of it still unrevealed, then the emergence of consciousness out of the apparently Inconscient must have another and completer term; the appearance of a supramental spiritual being who shall impose on his mental, vital, bodily workings a higher law than that of the dividing Mind is no longer impossible. On the contrary, it is the natural and inevitable conclusion of the nature of cosmic existence.

Such a supramental being would, as we have seen, liberate the mind from the knot of its divided existence and use the individualisation of mind as merely a useful subordinate action of the all-embracing Supermind; and he would liberate the life also from the knot of its divided existence and use the individualisation of life as merely a useful subordinate action of the one Conscious-Force fulfilling its being and joy in a diversified unity. Is there any reason why he should not also liberate the bodily existence from the present law of death, division and mutual devouring and use individualisation of body as merely a useful subordinate term of the one divine Conscious-Existence made serviceable for the joy of the Infinite in the finite? or why this spirit should not be free in a sovereign occupation of form, consciously immortal even in the changing of his robe of Matter, possessed of his self-delight in a world subjected to the law of unity and love and beauty? And if man be the inhabitant of terrestrial existence through whom that transformation of the mental into the supramental can at last be operated, is it not possible that he may develop, as well as a divine mind and a divine life, also a divine body? or, if the phrase seem to be too startling to our present limited conceptions of human potentiality, may he not in his development of his true being and its light and joy and power arrive at a divine use of mind and life and body by which the descent of Spirit into form shall be at once humanly and divinely justified?

The one thing that can stand in the way of that ultimate terrestrial possibility is if our present view of Matter and its laws represent the only possible relation between sense and substance, between the Divine as knower and the Divine as object, or if, other relations being possible, they are yet not in any way possible here, but must be sought on higher planes of existence. In that case, it is in heavens beyond that we must seek our entire divine fulfilment, as the religions assert, and their other assertion of the kingdom of God or the kingdom of the perfect upon earth must be put aside as a delusion. Here we can only pursue or attain an internal preparation or victory and, having liberated the mind and life and soul within, must turn from the unconquered and unconquerable material principle, from an unregenerated and intractable earth to find elsewhere our divine substance. There is, however, no reason why we should accept this limiting conclusion. There are, quite certainly, other states even of Matter itself; there is undoubtedly an ascending series of the divine gradations of substance; there is the possibility of the material being transfiguring itself through the acceptation of a higher law than its own which is yet its own because it is always there latent and potential in its own secrecies.

Chapter XXVI

The Ascending Series of Substance

There is a self that is of the essence of Matter — there is another inner self of Life that fills the other — there is another inner self of Mind — there is another inner self of Truth-Knowledge — there is another inner self of Bliss.

Taittiriya Upanishad.[1]

They climb Indra like a ladder. As one mounts peak after peak, there becomes clear the much that has still to be done. Indra brings consciousness of That as the goal.

Like a hawk, a kite He settles on the Vessel and upbears it; in His stream of movement He discovers the Rays, for He goes bearing his weapons: He cleaves to the ocean surge of the waters; a great King, He declares the fourth status. Like a mortal purifying his body, like a war-horse galloping to the conquest of riches He pours calling through all the sheath and enters these vessels. *Rig Veda.*[2]

IF WE consider what it is that most represents to us the materiality of Matter, we shall see that it is its aspects of solidity, tangibility, increasing resistance, firm response to the touch of Sense. Substance seems more truly material and real in proportion as it presents to us a solid resistance and by virtue of that resistance a durability of sensible form on which our consciousness can dwell; in proportion as it is more subtle, less densely resistant and enduringly seizable by the sense, it appears to us less material. This attitude of our ordinary consciousness towards Matter is a symbol of the essential object for which Matter has been created. Substance passes into the material status

---

[1] II. 1-5.   [2] I. 10. 1, 2; IX. 96. 19, 20.

in order that it may present to the consciousness which has to
deal with it durable, firmly seizable images on which the mind
can rest and base its operations and which the Life can handle
with at least a relative surety of permanence in the form upon
which it works. Therefore in the ancient Vedic formula Earth,
type of the more solid states of substance, was accepted as the
symbolic name of the material principle. Therefore, too, touch
or contact is for us the essential basis of Sense; all other physical
senses, taste, smell, hearing, sight are based upon a series of more
and more subtle and indirect contacts between the percipient
and the perceived. Equally, in the Sankhya classification of the
five elemental states of Substance from ether to earth, we see
that their characteristic is a constant progression from the more
subtle to the less subtle so that at the summit we have the subtle
vibrations of the ethereal and at the base the grosser density of
the earthly or solid elemental condition. Matter therefore is the
last stage known to us in the progress of pure substance towards
a basis of cosmic relation in which the first word shall be not
spirit but form, and form in its utmost possible development
of concentration, resistance, durably gross image, mutual im-
penetrability, — the culminating point of distinction, separation
and division. This is the intention and character of the material
universe; it is the formula of accomplished divisibility.

And if there is, as there must be in the nature of things, an
ascending series in the scale of substance from Matter to Spirit, it
must be marked by a progressive diminution of these capacities
most characteristic of the physical principle and a progressive
increase of the opposite characteristics which will lead us to
the formula of pure spiritual self-extension. This is to say that
they must be marked by less and less bondage to the form,
more and more subtlety and flexibility of substance and force,
more and more interfusion, interpenetration, power of assimilation, power of interchange, power of variation, transmutation,
unification. Drawing away from durability of form, we draw
towards eternity of essence; drawing away from our poise in
the persistent separation and resistance of physical Matter, we
draw near to the highest divine poise in the infinity, unity and

indivisibility of Spirit. Between gross substance and pure spirit substance this must be the fundamental antinomy. In Matter Chit or Conscious-Force masses itself more and more to resist and stand out against other masses of the same Conscious-Force; in substance of Spirit pure consciousness images itself freely in its sense of itself with an essential indivisibility and a constant unifying interchange as the basic formula even of the most diversifying play of its own Force. Between these two poles there is the possibility of an infinite gradation.

These considerations become of great importance when we consider the possible relation between the divine life and the divine mind of the perfected human soul and the very gross and seemingly undivine body or formula of physical being in which we actually dwell. That formula is the result of a certain fixed relation between sense and substance from which the material universe has started. But as this relation is not the only possible relation, so that formula is not the only possible formula. Life and mind may manifest themselves in another relation to substance and work out different physical laws, other and larger habits, even a different substance of body with a freer action of the sense, a freer action of the life, a freer action of the mind. Death, division, mutual resistance and exclusion between embodied masses of the same conscious life-force are the formula of our physical existence; the narrow limitation of the play of the senses, the determination within a small circle of the field, duration and power of the life-workings, the obscuration, lame movement, broken and bounded functioning of the mind are the yoke which that formula expressed in the animal body has imposed upon the higher principles. But these things are not the sole possible rhythm of cosmic Nature. There are superior states, there are higher worlds, and if the law of these can by any progress of man and by any liberation of our substance from its present imperfections be imposed on this sensible form and instrument of our being, then there may be even here a physical working of divine mind and sense, a physical working of divine life in the human frame and even the evolution upon earth of something that we may call a divinely human body. The body of man also may some day come by its transfiguration; the Earth-Mother too may reveal in us her godhead.

Even within the formula of the physical cosmos there is an ascending series in the scale of Matter which leads us from the more to the less dense, from the less to the more subtle. Where we reach the highest term of that series, the most supra-ethereal subtlety of material substance or formulation of Force, what lies beyond? Not a Nihil, not a void; for there is no such thing as absolute void or real nullity and what we call by that name is simply something beyond the grasp of our sense, our mind or our most subtle consciousness. Nor is it true that there is nothing beyond, or that some ethereal substance of Matter is the eternal beginning; for we know that Matter and material Force are only a last result of a pure Substance and pure Force in which consciousness is luminously self-aware and self-possessing and not as in Matter lost to itself in an inconscient sleep and an inert motion. What then is there between this material substance and that pure substance? For we do not leap from the one to the other, we do not pass at once from the inconscient to absolute consciousness. There must be and there are grades between inconscient substance and utterly self-conscious self-extension, as between the principle of Matter and the principle of Spirit.

All who have at all sounded those abysses are agreed and bear witness to this fact that there are a series of subtler and subtler formulations of substance which escape from and go beyond the formula of the material universe. Without going deeply into matters which are too occult and difficult for our present inquiry, we may say, adhering to the system on which we have based ourselves, that these gradations of substance, in one important aspect of their formulation in series, can be seen to correspond to the ascending series of Matter, Life, Mind, Supermind and that other higher divine triplicity of Sachchidananda. In other words, we find that substance in its ascension bases itself upon each of these principles and makes itself successively a characteristic vehicle for the dominating cosmic self-expression of each in their ascending series.

Here in the material world everything is founded upon the

formula of material substance. Sense, Life, Thought found themselves upon what the ancients called the Earth-Power, start from it, obey its laws, accommodate their workings to this fundamental principle, limit themselves by its possibilities and, if they would develop others, have even in that development to take account of the original formula, its purpose and its demand upon the divine evolution. The sense works through physical instruments, the life through a physical nerve-system and vital organs, the mind has to build its operations upon a corporeal basis and use a material instrumentation, even its pure mental workings have to take the data so derived as a field and as the stuff upon which it works. There is no necessity in the essential nature of mind, sense, life that they should be so limited: for the physical sense-organs are not the creators of sense-perceptions, but themselves the creation, the instruments and here a necessary convenience of the cosmic sense; the nervous system and vital organs are not the creators of life's action and reaction, but themselves the creation, the instruments and here a necessary convenience of the cosmic Life-force; the brain is not the creator of thought, but itself the creation, the instrument and here a necessary convenience of the cosmic Mind. The necessity then is not absolute, but teleological; it is the result of a divine cosmic Will in the material universe which intends to posit here a physical relation between sense and its object, establishes here a material formula and law of Conscious-Force and creates by it physical images of Conscious-Being to serve as the initial, dominating and determining fact of the world in which we live. It is not a fundamental law of being, but a constructive principle necessitated by the intention of the Spirit to evolve in a world of Matter.

In the next grade of substance the initial, dominating, determining fact is no longer substantial form and force, but life and conscious desire. Therefore the world beyond this material plane must be a world based upon a conscious cosmic vital Energy, a force of vital seeking and a force of Desire and their self-expression and not upon an inconscient or subconscient will taking the form of a material force and energy. All the forms, bodies, forces, life-movements, sense-movements, thought-movements, developments, culminations, self-fulfilments of that world must be dominated and determined by this initial fact of Conscious-Life to which Matter and Mind must subject themselves, must start from that, base themselves upon that, be limited or enlarged by its laws, powers, capacities, limitations; and if Mind there seeks to develop yet higher possibilities, still it must then too take account of the original vital formula of desire-force, its purpose and its demand upon the divine manifestation.

So too with the higher gradations. The next in the series must be governed by the dominating and determining factor of Mind. Substance there must be subtle and flexible enough to assume the shapes directly imposed upon it by Mind, to obey its operations, to subordinate itself to its demand for self-expression and self-fulfilment. The relations of sense and substance too must have a corresponding subtlety and flexibility and must be determined, not by the relations of physical organ with physical object, but of Mind with the subtler substance upon which it works. The life of such a world would be the servant of Mind in a sense of which our weak mental operations and our limited, coarse and rebellious vital faculties can have no adequate conception. There Mind dominates as the original formula, its purpose prevails, its demand overrides all others in the law of the divine manifestation. At a yet higher reach Supermind — or, intermediately, principles touched by it — or, still higher, a pure Bliss, a pure Conscious Power or pure Being replace Mind as the dominant principle, and we enter into those ranges of cosmic existence which to the old Vedic seers were the worlds of illuminated divine existence and the foundation of what they termed Immortality and which later Indian religions imaged in figures like the Brahmaloka or Goloka, some supreme self-expression of the Being as Spirit in which the soul liberated into its highest perfection possesses the infinity and beatitude of the eternal Godhead.

The principle which underlies this continually ascending experience and vision uplifted beyond the material formulation of things is that all cosmic existence is a complex harmony and does not finish with the limited range of consciousness in which the ordinary human mind and life is content to be imprisoned. Being, consciousness, force, substance descend and ascend a many-runged ladder on each step of which being has a vaster self-extension, consciousness a wider sense of its own range and largeness and joy, force a greater intensity and a more rapid and blissful capacity, substance gives a more subtle, plastic, buoyant and flexible rendering of its primal reality. For the more subtle is also the more powerful, — one might say, the more truly concrete; it is less bound than the gross, it has a greater permanence in its being along with a greater potentiality, plasticity and range in its becoming. Each plateau of the hill of being gives to our widening experience a higher plane of our consciousness and a richer world for our existence.

But how does this ascending series affect the possibilities of our material existence? It would not affect them at all if each plane of consciousness, each world of existence, each grade of substance, each degree of cosmic force were cut off entirely from that which precedes and that which follows it. But the opposite is the truth; the manifestation of the Spirit is a complex weft and in the design and pattern of one principle all the others enter as elements of the spiritual whole. Our material world is the result of all the others, for the other principles have all descended into Matter to create the physical universe, and every particle of what we call Matter contains all of them implicit in itself; their secret action, as we have seen, is involved in every moment of its existence and every movement of its activity. And as Matter is the last word of the descent, so it is also the first word of the ascent; as the powers of all these planes, worlds, grades, degrees are involved in the material existence, so are they all capable of evolution out of it. It is for this reason that material being does not begin and end with gases and chemical compounds and physical forces and movements, with nebulae and suns and earths, but evolves life, evolves mind, must evolve eventually Supermind and the higher degrees of the spiritual existence. Evolution comes by the unceasing pressure of the supra-material planes on the material compelling it to deliver out of itself their principles and powers which might conceivably otherwise have slept imprisoned in the rigidity of the material formula. This would even so have been improbable, since their presence there implies a purpose of deliverance; but still this necessity from below is actually very much aided by a kindred superior pressure.

Nor can this evolution end with the first meagre formulation of life, mind, Supermind, spirit conceded to these higher powers by the reluctant power of Matter. For as they evolve, as they awake, as they become more active and avid of their own potentialities, the pressure on them of the superior planes, a pressure involved in the existence and close connection and interdependence of the worlds, must also increase in insistence, power and effectiveness. Not only must these principles manifest from below in a qualified and restricted emergence, but also from above they must descend in their characteristic power and full possible efflorescence into the material being; the material creature must open to a wider and wider play of their activities in Matter, and all that is needed is a fit receptacle, medium, instrument. That is provided for in the body, life and consciousness of man.

Certainly, if that body, life and consciousness were limited to the possibilities of the gross body which are all that our physical senses and physical mentality accept, there would be a very narrow term for this evolution, and the human being could not hope to accomplish anything essentially greater than his present achievement. But this body, as ancient occult science discovered, is not the whole even of our physical being; this gross density is not all of our substance. The oldest Vedantic knowledge tells us of five degrees of our being, the material, the vital, the mental, the ideal, the spiritual or beatific and to each of these grades of our soul there corresponds a grade of our substance, a sheath as it was called in the ancient figurative language. A later psychology found that these five sheaths of our substance were the material of three bodies, gross physical, subtle and causal, in all of which the soul actually and simultaneously dwells, although here and now we are superficially conscious only of the material vehicle.

But it is possible to become conscious in our other bodies as well and it is in fact the opening up of the veil between them and consequently between our physical, psychical and ideal personalities which is the cause of those "psychic" and "occult" phenomena that are now beginning to be increasingly though yet too little and too clumsily examined, even while they are far too much exploited. The old Hathayogins and Tantriks of India had long ago reduced this matter of the higher human life and body to a science. They had discovered six nervous centres of life in the dense body corresponding to six centres of life and mind faculty in the subtle, and they had found out subtle physical exercises by which these centres, now closed, could be opened up, the higher psychical life proper to our subtle existence entered into by man, and even the physical and vital obstructions to the experience of the ideal and spiritual being could be destroyed. It is significant that one prominent result claimed by the Hathayogins for their practices and verified in many respects was a control of the physical life-force which liberated them from some of the ordinary habits or so-called laws thought by physical science to be inseparable from life in the body.

Behind all these terms of ancient psycho-physical science lies the one great fact and law of our being that whatever be its temporary poise of form, consciousness, power in this material evolution, there must be behind it and there is a greater, a truer existence of which this is only the external result and physically sensible aspect. Our substance does not end with the physical body; that is only the earthly pedestal, the terrestrial base, the material starting-point. As there are behind our waking mentality vaster ranges of consciousness subconscient and superconscient to it of which we become sometimes abnormally aware, so there are behind our gross physical being other and subtler grades of substance with a finer law and a greater power which support the denser body and which can by our entering into the ranges of consciousness belonging to them be made to impose that law and power on our dense matter and substitute their purer, higher, intenser conditions of being for the grossness and limitation of our present physical life and impulses and habits. If that be so, then the evolution of a nobler physical existence not limited by the ordinary conditions of animal birth and life and death, of difficult alimentation and facility of disorder and disease and subjection to poor and unsatisfied vital cravings ceases to have the appearance of a dream and chimera and becomes a possibility founded upon a rational and philosophic truth which is in accordance with all the rest that we have hitherto known, experienced or been able to think out about the overt and secret truth of our existence.

So it should rationally be; for the uninterrupted series of the principles of our being and their close mutual connection is too evident for it to be possible that one of them should be condemned and cut off while the others are capable of a divine liberation. The ascent of man from the physical to the supramental must open out the possibility of a corresponding ascent in the grades of substance to that ideal or causal body which is proper to our supramental being, and the conquest of the lower principles by Supermind and its liberation of them into a divine life and a divine mentality must also render possible a conquest of our physical limitations by the power and principle of supramental substance. And this means the evolution not only of an untrammelled consciousness, a mind and sense not shut up in the walls of the physical ego or limited to the poor basis of knowledge given by the physical organs of sense, but a life-power liberated more and more from its mortal limitations, a physical life fit for a divine inhabitant and, — in the sense not of attachment or of restriction to our present corporeal frame but an exceeding of the law of the physical body, — the conquest of death, an earthly immortality. For from the divine Bliss, the original Delight of existence, the Lord of Immortality comes pouring the wine of that Bliss, the mystic Soma, into these jars of mentalised living matter; eternal and beautiful, he enters into these sheaths of substance for the integral transformation of the being and nature.

Chapter XXVII

The Sevenfold Chord of Being

In the ignorance of my mind, I ask of these steps of the Gods
that are set within. The all-knowing Gods have taken the
Infant of a year and they have woven about him seven threads
to make this weft.   *Rig Veda.*[1]

WE HAVE now, by our scrutiny of the seven great terms
of existence which the ancient seers fixed on as the
foundation and sevenfold mode of all cosmic existence, discerned the gradations of evolution and involution and
arrived at the basis of knowledge towards which we were striving. We have laid down that the origin, the continent, the initial
and the ultimate reality of all that is in the cosmos is the triune
principle of transcendent and infinite Existence, Consciousness
and Bliss which is the nature of divine being. Consciousness has
two aspects, illuminating and effective, state and power of self-
awareness and state and power of self-force, by which Being
possesses itself whether in its static condition or in its dynamic
movement; for in its creative action it knows by omnipotent
self-consciousness all that is latent within it and produces and
governs the universe of its potentialities by an omniscient self-
energy. This creative action of the All-Existent has its nodus in
the fourth, the intermediate principle of Supermind or Real-Idea,
in which a divine Knowledge one with self-existence and self-
awareness and a substantial Will which is in perfect unison with
that knowledge, because it is itself in its substance and nature
that self-conscious self-existence dynamic in illumined action,
develop infallibly the movement and form and law of things in

---

[1] I. 164. 5.

right accordance with their self-existent Truth and in harmony with the significances of its manifestation.

The creation depends on and moves between the biune principle of unity and multiplicity; it is a manifoldness of idea and force and form which is the expression of an original unity, and it is an eternal oneness which is the foundation and reality of the multiple worlds and makes their play possible. Supermind therefore proceeds by a double faculty of comprehensive and apprehensive knowledge; proceeding from the essential oneness to the resultant multiplicity, it comprehends all things in itself as itself the One in its manifold aspects and it apprehends separately all things in itself as objects of its will and knowledge. While to its original self-awareness all things are one being, one consciousness, one will, one self-delight and the whole movement of things a movement one and indivisible, it proceeds in its action from the unity to the multiplicity and from multiplicity to unity, creating an ordered relation between them and an appearance but not a binding reality of division, a subtle unseparating division, or rather a demarcation and determination within the indivisible. The Supermind is the divine Gnosis which creates, governs and upholds the worlds: it is the secret Wisdom which upholds both our Knowledge and our Ignorance.

We have discovered also that Mind, Life and Matter are a triple aspect of these higher principles working, so far as our universe is concerned, in subjection to the principle of Ignorance, to the superficial and apparent self-forgetfulness of the One in its play of division and multiplicity. Really, these three are only subordinate powers of the divine quaternary: Mind is a subordinate power of Supermind which takes its stand in the standpoint of division, actually forgetful here of the oneness behind though able to return to it by reillumination from the supramental; Life is similarly a subordinate power of the energy aspect of Sachchidananda, it is Force working out form and the play of conscious energy from the standpoint of division created by Mind; Matter is the form of substance of being which the existence of Sachchidananda assumes when it subjects itself to this phenomenal action of its own consciousness and force.

In addition, there is a fourth principle which comes into manifestation at the nodus of mind, life and body, that which we call the soul; but this has a double appearance, in front the desire-soul which strives for the possession and delight of things, and, behind and either largely or entirely concealed by the desire-soul, the true psychic entity which is the real repository of the experiences of the spirit. And we have concluded that this fourth human principle is a projection and an action of the third divine principle of infinite Bliss, but an action in the terms of our consciousness and under the conditions of soul-evolution in this world. As the existence of the Divine is in its nature an infinite consciousness and the self-power of that consciousness, so the nature of its infinite consciousness is pure and infinite Bliss; self-possession and self-awareness are the essence of its self-delight. The cosmos also is a play of this divine self-delight and the delight of that play is entirely possessed by the Universal; but in the individual owing to the action of ignorance and division it is held back in the subliminal and the superconscient being; on our surface it lacks and has to be sought for, found and possessed by the development of the individual consciousness towards universality and transcendence.

We may, therefore, if we will, pose eight[2] principles instead of seven, and then we perceive that our existence is a sort of refraction of the divine existence, in inverted order of ascent and descent, thus ranged, —

Existence	Matter
Consciousness-Force	Life
Bliss	Psyche
Supermind	Mind.

The Divine descends from pure existence through the play of Consciousness-Force and Bliss and the creative medium of Supermind into cosmic being; we ascend from Matter through a developing life, soul and mind and the illuminating medium of Supermind towards the divine being. The knot of the two, the

---

[2] The Vedic Seers speak of the seven Rays, but also of eight, nine, ten or twelve.

higher and the lower hemisphere,[3] is where mind and Supermind meet with a veil between them. The rending of the veil is the condition of the divine life in humanity; for by that rending, by the illumining descent of the higher into the nature of the lower being and the forceful ascent of the lower being into the nature of the higher, mind can recover its divine light in the all-comprehending Supermind, the soul realise its divine self in the all-possessing all-blissful Ananda, life repossess its divine power in the play of omnipotent Conscious-Force and Matter open to its divine liberty as a form of the divine Existence. And if there be any goal to the evolution which finds here its present crown and head in the human being, other than an aimless circling and an individual escape from the circling, if the infinite potentiality of this creature, who alone here stands between Spirit and Matter with the power to mediate between them, has any meaning other than an ultimate awakening from the delusion of life by despair and disgust of the cosmic effort and its complete rejection, then even such a luminous and puissant transfiguration and emergence of the Divine in the creature must be that high-uplifted goal and that supreme significance.

But before we can turn to the psychological and practical conditions under which such a transfiguration may be changed from an essential possibility into a dynamic potentiality, we have much to consider; for we must discern not only the essential principles of the descent of Sachchidananda into cosmic existence, which we have already done, but the large plan of its order here and the nature and action of the manifested power of Conscious-Force which reigns over the conditions under which we now exist. At present, what we have first to see is that the seven or the eight principles we have examined are essential to all cosmic creation and are there, manifested or as yet unmanifested, in ourselves, in this "Infant of a year" which we still are, — for we are far yet from being the adults of evolutionary Nature. The higher Trinity is the source and basis of all existence and play of existence, and all cosmos must be an expression and

---

[3] *Parārdha* and *Aparārdha*.

action of its essential reality. No universe can be merely a form of being which has sprung up and outlined itself in an absolute nullity and void and remains standing out against a non-existent emptiness. It must be either a figure of existence within the infinite Existence who is beyond all figure or it must be itself the All-Existence. In fact, when we unify our self with cosmic being, we see that it is really both of these things at once; that is to say, it is the All-Existent figuring Himself out in an infinite series of rhythms in His own conceptive extension of Himself as Time and Space. Moreover we see that this cosmic action or any cosmic action is impossible without the play of an infinite Force of Existence which produces and regulates all these forms and movements; and that Force equally presupposes or is the action of an infinite Consciousness, because it is in its nature a cosmic Will determining all relations and apprehending them by its own mode of awareness, and it could not so determine and apprehend them if there were no comprehensive Consciousness behind that mode of cosmic awareness to originate as well as to hold, fix and reflect through it the relations of Being in the developing formation or becoming of itself which we call a universe.

Finally, Consciousness being thus omniscient and omnipotent, in entire luminous possession of itself, and such entire luminous possession being necessarily and in its very nature Bliss, for it cannot be anything else, a vast universal self-delight must be the cause, essence and object of cosmic existence. "If there were not," says the ancient seer, "this all-encompassing ether of Delight of existence in which we dwell, if that delight were not our ether, then none could breathe, none could live." This self-bliss may become subconscient, seemingly lost on the surface, but not only must it be there at our roots, all existence must be essentially a seeking and reaching out to discover and possess it, and in proportion as the creature in the cosmos finds himself, whether in will and power or in light and knowledge or in being and wideness or in love and joy itself, he must awaken to something of the secret ecstasy. Joy of being, delight of realisation by knowledge, rapture of possession by will and power or creative force, ecstasy of union in love and joy are the highest terms of expanding life because they are the essence of existence itself in its hidden roots as on its yet unseen heights. Wherever, then, cosmic existence manifests itself, these three must be behind and within it.

But infinite Existence, Consciousness and Bliss need not throw themselves out into apparent being at all or, doing so, it would not be cosmic being, but simply an infinity of figures without fixed order or relation, if they did not hold or develop and bring out from themselves this fourth term of Supermind, of the divine Gnosis. There must be in every cosmos a power of Knowledge and Will which out of infinite potentiality fixes determined relations, develops the result out of the seed, rolls out the mighty rhythms of cosmic Law and views and governs the worlds as their immortal and infinite Seer and Ruler.[4] This power indeed is nothing else than Sachchidananda Himself; it creates nothing which is not in its own self-existence, and for that reason all cosmic and real Law is a thing not imposed from outside, but from within, all development is self-development, all seed and result are seed of a Truth of things and result of that seed determined out of its potentialities. For the same reason no Law is absolute, because only the infinite is absolute, and everything contains within itself endless potentialities quite beyond its determined form and course, which are only determined through a self-limitation by Idea proceeding from an infinite liberty within. This power of self-limitation is necessarily inherent in the boundless All-Existent. The Infinite would not be the Infinite if it could not assume a manifold finiteness; the Absolute would not be the Absolute if it were denied in knowledge and power and will and manifestation of being a boundless capacity of self-determination. This Supermind then is the Truth or Real-Idea, inherent in all cosmic force and existence, which is necessary, itself remaining infinite, to determine and combine and uphold relation and order and the great lines of the manifestation. In the language of the Vedic Rishis, as infinite Existence,

---

[4] The Seer, the Thinker, He who becomes everywhere, the Self-existent. — *Isha Upanishad.* 8.

Consciousness and Bliss are the three highest and hidden Names of the Nameless, so this Supermind is the fourth Name[5] — fourth to That in its descent, fourth to us in our ascension.

But Mind, Life and Matter, the lower trilogy, are also indispensable to all cosmic being, not necessarily in the form or with the action and conditions which we know upon earth or in this material universe, but in some kind of action, however luminous, however puissant, however subtle. For Mind is essentially that faculty of Supermind which measures and limits, which fixes a particular centre and views from that the cosmic movement and its interactions. Granted that in a particular world, plane or cosmic arrangement, mind need not be limited, or rather that the being who uses mind as a subordinate faculty need not be incapable of seeing things from other centres or standpoints or even from the real Centre of all or in the vastness of a universal self-diffusion, still if he is not capable of fixing himself normally in his own firm standpoint for certain purposes of the divine activity, if there is only the universal self-diffusion or only infinite centres without some determining or freely limiting action for each, then there is no cosmos but only a Being musing within Himself infinitely as a creator or poet may muse freely, not plastically, before he proceeds to the determining work of creation. Such a state must exist somewhere in the infinite scale of existence, but it is not what we understand by a cosmos. Whatever order there may be in it, must be a sort of unfixed, unbinding order such as Supermind might evolve before it had proceeded to the work of fixed development, measurement and interaction of relations. For that measurement and interaction Mind is necessary, though it need not be aware of itself as anything but a subordinate action of Supermind nor develop the interaction of relations on the basis of a self-imprisoned egoism such as we see active in terrestrial Nature.

Mind once existent, Life and Form of substance follow; for life is simply the determination of force and action, of

---

[5] *Turīyam svid*, "a certain Fourth", also called *turīyam dhāma*, the fourth placing or poise of existence.

relation and interaction of energy from many fixed centres of consciousness, — fixed, not necessarily in place or time, but in a persistent coexistence of beings or soul-forms of the Eternal supporting a cosmic harmony. That life may be very different from life as we know or conceive it, but essentially it would be the same principle at work which we see here figured as vitality, — the principle to which the ancient Indian thinkers gave the name of Vayu or Prana, the life-stuff, the substantial will and energy in the cosmos working out into determined form and action and conscious dynamis of being. Substance too might be very different from our view and sense of material body, much more subtle, much less rigidly binding in its law of self-division and mutual resistance, and body or form might be an instrument and not a prison, yet for the cosmic interaction some determination of form and substance would always be necessary, even if it be only a mental body or something yet more luminous, subtle and puissantly and freely responsive than the freest mental body.

It follows that wherever Cosmos is, there, even if only one principle be initially apparent, even if at first that seem to be the sole principle of things and everything else that may appear afterwards in the world seem to be no more than its forms and results and not in themselves indispensable to cosmic existence, such a front presented by being can only be an illusory mask or appearance of its real truth. Where one principle is manifest in Cosmos, there all the rest must be not merely present and passively latent, but secretly at work. In any given world its scale and harmony of being may be openly in possession of all seven at a higher or lower degree of activity; in another they may be all involved in one which becomes the initial or fundamental principle of evolution in that world, but evolution of the involved there must be. The evolution of the sevenfold power of being, the realisation of its septuple Name, must be the destiny of any world which starts apparently from the involution of all in one power.[6] Therefore the material universe

---

[6] In any given world there need not be an involution but only a subordination of the other principles to one or their inclusion in one; then evolution is not a necessity of that world-order.

was bound in the nature of things to evolve from its hidden life apparent life, from its hidden mind apparent mind, and it must in the same nature of things evolve from its hidden Supermind apparent Supermind and from the concealed Spirit within it the triune glory of Sachchidananda. The only question is whether the earth is to be a scene of that emergence or the human creation on this or any other material scene, in this or any other cycle of the large wheelings of Time, its instrument and vehicle. The ancient seers believed in this possibility for man and held it to be his divine destiny; the modern thinker does not even conceive of it or, if he conceived, would deny or doubt. If he sees a vision of the Superman, it is in the figure of increased degrees of mentality or vitality; he admits no other emergence, sees nothing beyond these principles, for these have traced for us up till now our limit and circle. In this progressive world, with this human creature in whom the divine spark has been kindled, real wisdom is likely to dwell with the higher aspiration rather than with the denial of aspiration or with the hope that limits and circumscribes itself within those narrow walls of apparent possibility which are only our intermediate house of training. In the spiritual order of things, the higher we project our view and our aspiration, the greater the Truth that seeks to descend upon us, because it is already there within us and calls for its release from the covering that conceals it in manifested Nature.

Chapter XXVIII

Supermind, Mind and the Overmind Maya

There is a Permanent, a Truth hidden by a Truth where the Sun unyokes his horses. The ten hundreds (of his rays) came together — That One. I saw the most glorious of the Forms of the Gods.   *Rig Veda.*[1]

The face of Truth is hidden by a golden lid; that remove, O Fostering Sun, for the Law of the Truth, for sight. O Sun, O sole Seer, marshal thy rays, gather them together, — let me see of thee thy happiest form of all; that Conscious Being everywhere, He am I.   *Isha Upanishad.*[2]

The Truth, the Right, the Vast.   *Atharva Veda.*[3]

It became both truth and falsehood. It became the Truth, even all this that is.   *Taittiriya Upanishad.*[4]

ONE POINT remains to be cleared which we have till now left in obscurity, the process of the lapse into the Ignorance; for we have seen that nothing in the original nature of Mind, Life or Matter necessitates a fall from Knowledge. It has been shown indeed that division of consciousness is the basis of the Ignorance, a division of individual consciousness from the cosmic and the transcendent of which yet it is an intimate part, in essence inseparable, a division of Mind from the supramental Truth of which it should be a subordinate action, of Life from the original Force of which it is one energism, of Matter from the original Existence of which it is one form of

[1] V. 62. 1.   [2] Verses 15, 16.   [3] XII. 1. 1.   [4] II. 6.

substance. But it has still to be made clear how this division came about in the Indivisible, by what peculiar self-diminishing or self-effacing action of Consciousness-Force in the Being: for since all is a movement of that Force, only by some such action obscuring its own plenary light and power can there have arisen the dynamic and effective phenomenon of the Ignorance. But this problem can be left over to be treated in a more close examination of the dual phenomenon of Knowledge-Ignorance which makes our consciousness a blend of light and darkness, a half-light between the full day of the supramental Truth and the night of the material Inconscience. All that is necessary to note at present is that it must be in its essential character an exclusive concentration on one movement and status of Conscious Being, which puts all the rest of consciousness and being behind and veils it from that one movement's now partial knowledge.

Still there is one aspect of this problem which must be immediately considered; it is the gulf created between Mind as we know it and the supramental Truth-Consciousness of which we have found Mind in its origin to be a subordinate process. For this gulf is considerable and, if there are no gradations between the two levels of consciousness, a transition from one to the other, either in the descending involution of Spirit into Matter or the corresponding evolution in Matter of the concealed grades leading back to the Spirit, seems in the highest degree improbable, if not impossible. For Mind as we know it is a power of the Ignorance seeking for Truth, groping with difficulty to find it, reaching only mental constructions and representations of it in word and idea, in mind formations, sense formations, — as if bright or shadowy photographs or films of a distant Reality were all that it could achieve. Supermind, on the contrary, is in actual and natural possession of the Truth and its formations are forms of the Reality, not constructions, representations or indicative figures. No doubt, the evolving Mind in us is hampered by its encasement in the obscurity of this life and body, and the original Mind principle in the involutionary descent is a thing of greater power to which we have not fully reached, able to act with freedom in its own sphere or province, to build

more revelatory constructions, more minutely inspired formations, more subtle and significant embodiments in which the
light of Truth is present and palpable. But still that too is not
likely to be essentially different in its characteristic action, for
it too is a movement into the Ignorance, not a still unseparated
portion of the Truth-Consciousness. There must be somewhere
in the descending and ascending scale of Being an intermediate
power and plane of consciousness, perhaps something more than
that, something with an original creative force, through which
the involutionary transition from Mind in the Knowledge to
Mind in the Ignorance was effected and through which again the
evolutionary reverse transition becomes intelligible and possible.
For the involutionary transition this intervention is a logical imperative, for the evolutionary it is a practical necessity. For in the
evolution there are indeed radical transitions, from indeterminate Energy to organised Matter, from inanimate Matter to Life,
from a subconscious or submental to a perceptive and feeling
and acting Life, from primitive animal mentality to conceptive
reasoning Mind observing and governing Life and observing
itself also, able to act as an independent entity and even to seek
consciously for self-transcendence; but these leaps, even when
considerable, are to some extent prepared by slow gradations
which make them conceivable and feasible. There can be no
such immense hiatus as seems to exist between supramental
Truth-Consciousness and the Mind in the Ignorance.

But if such intervening gradations exist, it is clear that they
must be superconscient to human mind which does not seem
to have in its normal state any entry into these higher grades of
being. Man is limited in his consciousness by mind and even by a
given range or scale of mind: what is below his mind, submental
or mental but nether to his scale, readily seems to him subconscious or not distinguishable from complete inconscience; what
is above it is to him superconscious and he is almost inclined to
regard it as void of awareness, a sort of luminous Inconscience.
Just as he is limited to a certain scale of sounds or of colours
and what is above or below that scale is to him inaudible and
invisible or at least indistinguishable, so is it with his scale of

mental consciousness, confined at either extremity by an incapacity which marks his upper and his nether limit. He has no sufficient means of communication even with the animal who is his mental congener, though not his equal, and he is even capable of denying mind or real consciousness to it because its modes are other and narrower than those with which in himself and his kind he is familiar; he can observe submental being from outside but cannot at all communicate with it or enter intimately into its nature. Equally the superconscious is to him a closed book which may well be filled only with empty pages. At first sight, then, it would appear as if he had no means of contact with these higher gradations of consciousness: if so, they cannot act as links or bridges and his evolution must cease with his accomplished mental range and cannot exceed it; Nature in drawing these limits has written finis to his upward endeavour.

But when we look more closely, we perceive that this normality is deceptive and that in fact there are several directions in which human mind reaches beyond itself, tends towards self-exceeding; these are precisely the necessary lines of contact or veiled or half-veiled passages which connect it with higher grades of consciousness of the self-manifesting Spirit. First, we have noted the place Intuition occupies in the human means of knowledge, and Intuition is in its very nature a projection of the characteristic action of these higher grades into the mind of Ignorance. It is true that in human mind its action is largely hidden by the interventions of our normal intelligence; a pure intuition is a rare occurrence in our mental activity: for what we call by the name is usually a point of direct knowledge which is immediately caught and coated over with mental stuff, so that it serves only as an invisible or a very tiny nucleus of a crystallisation which is in its mass intellectual or otherwise mental in character; or else the flash of intuition is quickly replaced or intercepted, before it has a chance of manifesting itself, by a rapid imitative mental movement, insight or quick perception or some swift-leaping process of thought which owes its appearance to the stimulus of the coming intuition but obstructs its entry or covers it with a substituted mental suggestion true or erroneous but in either case not the authentic intuitive movement. Nevertheless, the fact of this intervention from above, the fact that behind all our original thinking or authentic perception of things there is a veiled, a half-veiled or a swift unveiled intuitive element is enough to establish a connection between mind and what is above it; it opens a passage of communication and of entry into the superior spirit-ranges. There is also the reaching out of mind to exceed the personal ego limitation, to see things in a certain impersonality and universality. Impersonality is the first character of cosmic self; universality, non-limitation by the single or limiting point of view, is the character of cosmic perception and knowledge: this tendency is therefore a widening, however rudimentary, of these restricted mind areas towards cosmicity, towards a quality which is the very character of the higher mental planes, — towards that superconscient cosmic Mind which, we have suggested, must in the nature of things be the original mind-action of which ours is only a derivative and inferior process. Again, there is not an entire absence of penetration from above into our mental limits. The phenomena of genius are really the result of such a penetration, — veiled, no doubt, because the light of the superior consciousness not only acts within narrow limits, usually in a special field, without any regulated separate organisation of its characteristic energies, often indeed quite fitfully, erratically and with a supernormal or abnormal irresponsible governance, but also in entering the mind it subdues and adapts itself to mind substance so that it is only a modified or diminished dynamis that reaches us, not all the original divine luminosity of what might be called the overhead consciousness beyond us. Still the phenomena of inspiration, of revelatory vision or of intuitive perception and intuitive discernment, surpassing our less illumined or less powerful normal mind-action, are there and their origin is unmistakable. Finally, there is the vast and multitudinous field of mystic and spiritual experience, and here the gates already lie wide open to the possibility of extending our consciousness beyond its present limits, — unless, indeed, by an obscurantism that refuses to inquire or an attachment to our boundaries of mental normality we shut them or turn

away from the vistas they open before us. But in our present
investigation we cannot afford to neglect the possibilities which
these domains of mankind's endeavour bring near to us, or the
added knowledge of oneself and of the veiled Reality which is
their gift to human mind, the greater light which arms them
with the right to act upon us and is the innate power of their
existence.

There are two successive movements of consciousness, difficult but well within our capacity, by which we can have access
to the superior gradations of our conscious existence. There
is first a movement inward by which, instead of living in our
surface mind, we break the wall between our external and our
now subliminal self; this can be brought about by a gradual
effort and discipline or by a vehement transition, sometimes
a forceful involuntary rupture, — the latter by no means safe
for the limited human mind accustomed to live securely only
within its normal limits, — but in either way, safe or unsafe,
the thing can be done. What we discover within this secret part
of ourselves is an inner being, a soul, an inner mind, an inner
life, an inner subtle-physical entity which is much larger in its
potentialities, more plastic, more powerful, more capable of a
manifold knowledge and dynamism than our surface mind, life
or body; especially, it is capable of a direct communication with
the universal forces, movements, objects of the cosmos, a direct
feeling and opening to them, a direct action on them and even
a widening of itself beyond the limits of the personal mind, the
personal life, the body, so that it feels itself more and more a
universal being no longer limited by the existing walls of our
too narrow mental, vital, physical existence. This widening can
extend itself to a complete entry into the consciousness of cosmic
Mind, into unity with the universal Life, even into a oneness with
universal Matter. That, however, is still an identification either
with a diminished cosmic truth or with the cosmic Ignorance.

But once this entry into the inner being is accomplished,
the inner Self is found to be capable of an opening, an ascent
upwards into things beyond our present mental level; that is the
second spiritual possibility in us. The first most ordinary result is

a discovery of a vast static and silent Self which we feel to be our real or our basic existence, the foundation of all else that we are. There may be even an extinction, a Nirvana both of our active being and of the sense of self into a Reality that is indefinable and inexpressible. But also we can realise that this self is not only our own spiritual being but the true self of all others; it presents itself then as the underlying truth of cosmic existence. It is possible to remain in a Nirvana of all individuality, to stop at a static realisation or, regarding the cosmic movement as a superficial play or illusion imposed on the silent Self, to pass into some supreme immobile and immutable status beyond the universe. But another less negative line of supernormal experience also offers itself; for there takes place a large dynamic descent of light, knowledge, power, bliss or other supernormal energies into our self of silence, and we can ascend too into higher regions of the Spirit where its immobile status is the foundation of those great and luminous energies. It is evident in either case that we have risen beyond the mind of Ignorance into a spiritual state; but, in the dynamic movement, the resultant greater action of Consciousness-Force may present itself either simply as a pure spiritual dynamis not otherwise determinate in its character or it may reveal a spiritual mind-range where mind is no longer ignorant of the Reality, — not yet a supermind level, but deriving from the supramental Truth-Consciousness and still luminous with something of its knowledge.

It is in the latter alternative that we find the secret we are seeking, the means of the transition, the needed step towards a supramental transformation; for we perceive a graduality of ascent, a communication with a more and more deep and immense light and power from above, a scale of intensities which can be regarded as so many stairs in the ascension of Mind or in a descent into Mind from That which is beyond it. We are aware of a sealike downpour of masses of a spontaneous knowledge which assumes the nature of Thought but has a different character from the process of thought to which we are accustomed; for there is nothing here of seeking, no trace of mental construction, no labour of speculation or difficult discovery; it is an automatic and spontaneous knowledge from a Higher Mind that seems to be in possession of Truth and not in search of hidden and withheld realities. One observes that this Thought is much more capable than the mind of including at once a mass of knowledge in a single view; it has a cosmic character, not the stamp of an individual thinking. Beyond this Truth-Thought we can distinguish a greater illumination instinct with an increased power and intensity and driving force, a luminosity of the nature of Truth-Sight with thought formulation as a minor and dependent activity. If we accept the Vedic image of the Sun of Truth, — an image which in this experience becomes a reality, — we may compare the action of the Higher Mind to a composed and steady sunshine, the energy of the Illumined Mind beyond it to an outpouring of massive lightnings of flaming sun-stuff. Still beyond can be met a yet greater power of the Truth-Force, an intimate and exact Truth-vision, Truth-thought, Truth-sense, Truth-feeling, Truth-action, to which we can give in a special sense the name of Intuition; for though we have applied that word for want of a better to any supra-intellectual direct way of knowing, yet what we actually know as intuition is only one special movement of self-existent knowledge. This new range is its origin; it imparts to our intuitions something of its own distinct character and is very clearly an intermediary of a greater Truth-Light with which our mind cannot directly communicate. At the source of this Intuition we discover a superconscient cosmic Mind in direct contact with the supramental Truth-Consciousness, an original intensity determinant of all movements below it and all mental energies, — not Mind as we know it, but an Overmind that covers as with the wide wings of some creative Oversoul this whole lower hemisphere of Knowledge-Ignorance, links it with that greater Truth-Consciousness while yet at the same time with its brilliant golden Lid it veils the face of the greater Truth from our sight, intervening with its flood of infinite possibilities as at once an obstacle and a passage in our seeking of the spiritual law of our existence, its highest aim, its secret Reality. This then is the occult link we were looking for; this is the Power that at once connects and divides the supreme Knowledge and the cosmic Ignorance.

In its nature and law the Overmind is a delegate of the Supermind Consciousness, its delegate to the Ignorance. Or we might speak of it as a protective double, a screen of dissimilar similarity through which Supermind can act indirectly on an Ignorance whose darkness could not bear or receive the direct impact of a supreme Light. Even, it is by the projection of this luminous Overmind corona that the diffusion of a diminished light in the Ignorance and the throwing of that contrary shadow which swallows up in itself all light, the Inconscience, became at all possible. For Supermind transmits to Overmind all its realities, but leaves it to formulate them in a movement and according to an awareness of things which is still a vision of Truth and yet at the same time a first parent of the Ignorance. A line divides Supermind and Overmind which permits a free transmission, allows the lower Power to derive from the higher Power all it holds or sees, but automatically compels a transitional change in the passage. The integrality of the Supermind keeps always the essential truth of things, the total truth and the truth of its individual self-determinations clearly knit together; it maintains in them an inseparable unity and between them a close interpenetration and a free and full consciousness of each other: but in Overmind this integrality is no longer there. And yet the Overmind is well aware of the essential Truth of things; it embraces the totality; it uses the individual self-determinations without being limited by them: but although it knows their oneness, can realise it in a spiritual cognition, yet its dynamic movement, even while relying on that for its security, is not directly determined by it. Overmind Energy proceeds through an illimitable capacity of separation and combination of the powers and aspects of the integral and indivisible all-comprehending Unity. It takes each Aspect or Power and gives to it an independent action in which it acquires a full separate importance and is able to work out, we might say, its own world of creation. Purusha and Prakriti, Conscious Soul and executive Force of Nature, are in the supramental harmony a two-aspected single truth, being and dynamis of the Reality; there can be no disequilibrium or predominance of one over the other. In Overmind we have the origin of the cleavage, the trenchant distinction made by the philosophy of the Sankhyas in which they appear as two independent entities, Prakriti able to dominate Purusha and cloud its freedom and power, reducing it to a witness and recipient of her forms and actions, Purusha able to return to its separate existence and abide in a free self-sovereignty by rejection of her original overclouding material principle. So with the other aspects or powers of the Divine Reality, One and Many, Divine Personality and Divine Impersonality, and the rest; each is still an aspect and power of the one Reality, but each is empowered to act as an independent entity in the whole, arrive at the fullness of the possibilities of its separate expression and develop the dynamic consequences of that separateness. At the same time in Overmind this separateness is still founded on the basis of an implicit underlying unity; all possibilities of combination and relation between the separated Powers and Aspects, all interchanges and mutualities of their energies are freely organised and their actuality always possible.

If we regard the Powers of the Reality as so many Godheads, we can say that the Overmind releases a million Godheads into action, each empowered to create its own world, each world capable of relation, communication and interplay with the others. There are in the Veda different formulations of the nature of the Gods: it is said they are all one Existence to which the sages give different names; yet each God is worshipped as if he by himself is that Existence, one who is all the other Gods together or contains them in his being; and yet again each is a separate Deity acting sometimes in unison with companion deities, sometimes separately, sometimes even in apparent opposition to other Godheads of the same Existence. In the Supermind all this would be held together as a harmonised play of the one Existence; in the Overmind each of these three conditions could be a separate action or basis of action and have its own principle of development and consequences and yet each keep the power to combine with the others in a more composite harmony. As

with the One Existence, so with its Consciousness and Force.
The One Consciousness is separated into many independent
forms of consciousness and knowledge; each follows out its own
line of truth which it has to realise. The one total and many-
sided Real-Idea is split up into its many sides; each becomes
an independent Idea-Force with the power to realise itself. The
one Consciousness-Force is liberated into its million forces, and
each of these forces has the right to fulfil itself or to assume, if
needed, a hegemony and take up for its own utility the other
forces. So too the Delight of Existence is loosed out into all
manner of delights and each can carry in itself its independent
fullness or sovereign extreme. Overmind thus gives to the One
Existence-Consciousness-Bliss the character of a teeming of infinite possibilities which can be developed into a multitude of
worlds or thrown together into one world in which the endlessly
variable outcome of their play is the determinant of the creation,
of its process, its course and its consequence.

Since the Consciousness-Force of the eternal Existence is the
universal creatrix, the nature of a given world will depend on
whatever self-formulation of that Consciousness expresses itself
in that world. Equally, for each individual being, his seeing or
representation to himself of the world he lives in will depend on
the poise or make which that Consciousness has assumed in him.
Our human mental consciousness sees the world in sections cut
by the reason and sense and put together in a formation which is
also sectional; the house it builds is planned to accommodate one
or another generalised formulation of Truth, but excludes the
rest or admits some only as guests or dependents in the house.
Overmind Consciousness is global in its cognition and can hold
any number of seemingly fundamental differences together in a
reconciling vision. Thus the mental reason sees Person and the
Impersonal as opposites: it conceives an impersonal Existence
in which person and personality are fictions of the Ignorance or
temporary constructions; or, on the contrary, it can see Person as
the primary reality and the impersonal as a mental abstraction
or only stuff or means of manifestation. To the Overmind intelligence these are separable Powers of the one Existence which

can pursue their independent self-affirmation and can also unite together their different modes of action, creating both in their independence and in their union different states of consciousness and being which can be all of them valid and all capable of coexistence. A purely impersonal existence and consciousness is true and possible, but also an entirely personal consciousness and existence; the Impersonal Divine, Nirguna Brahman, and the Personal Divine, Saguna Brahman, are here equal and coexistent aspects of the Eternal. Impersonality can manifest with person subordinated to it as a mode of expression; but, equally, Person can be the reality with impersonality as a mode of its nature: both aspects of manifestation face each other in the infinite variety of conscious Existence. What to the mental reason are irreconcilable differences present themselves to the Overmind intelligence as coexistent correlatives; what to the mental reason are contraries are to the Overmind intelligence complementaries. Our mind sees that all things are born from Matter or material Energy, exist by it, go back into it; it concludes that Matter is the eternal factor, the primary and ultimate reality, Brahman. Or it sees all as born of Life-Force or Mind, existing by Life or by Mind, going back into the universal Life or Mind, and it concludes that this world is a creation of the cosmic Life-Force or of a cosmic Mind or Logos. Or again it sees the world and all things as born of, existing by and going back to the Real-Idea or Knowledge-Will of the Spirit or to the Spirit itself and it concludes on an idealistic or spiritual view of the universe. It can fix on any of these ways of seeing, but to its normal separative vision each way excludes the others. Overmind consciousness perceives that each view is true of the action of the principle it erects; it can see that there is a material world-formula, a vital world-formula, a mental world-formula, a spiritual world-formula, and each can predominate in a world of its own and at the same time all can combine in one world as its constituent powers. The self-formulation of Conscious Force on which our world is based as an apparent Inconscience that conceals in itself a supreme Conscious-Existence and holds all the powers of Being together in its inconscient secrecy, a world of universal

Matter realising in itself Life, Mind, Overmind, Supermind, Spirit, each of them in its turn taking up the others as means of its self-expression, Matter proving in the spiritual vision to have been always itself a manifestation of the Spirit, is to the Overmind view a normal and easily realisable creation. In its power of origination and in the process of its executive dynamis Overmind is an organiser of many potentialities of Existence, each affirming its separate reality but all capable of linking themselves together in many different but simultaneous ways, a magician craftsman empowered to weave the multicoloured warp and woof of manifestation of a single entity in a complex universe.

In this simultaneous development of multitudinous independent or combined Powers or Potentials there is yet — or there is as yet — no chaos, no conflict, no fall from Truth or Knowledge. The Overmind is a creator of truths, not of illusions or falsehoods: what is worked out in any given overmental energism or movement is the truth of the Aspect, Power, Idea, Force, Delight which is liberated into independent action, the truth of the consequences of its reality in that independence. There is no exclusiveness asserting each as the sole truth of being or the others as inferior truths: each God knows all the Gods and their place in existence; each Idea admits all other ideas and their right to be; each Force concedes a place to all other forces and their truth and consequences; no delight of separate fulfilled existence or separate experience denies or condemns the delight of other existence or other experience. The Overmind is a principle of cosmic Truth and a vast and endless catholicity is its very spirit; its energy is an all-dynamism as well as a principle of separate dynamisms: it is a sort of inferior Supermind, — although it is concerned predominantly not with absolutes, but with what might be called the dynamic potentials or pragmatic truths of Reality, or with absolutes mainly for their power of generating pragmatic or creative values, although, too, its comprehension of things is more global than integral, since its totality is built up of global wholes or constituted by separate independent realities uniting or coalescing together, and although the essential unity is grasped by it and felt to be basic of things and pervasive in their manifestation, but no longer as in the Supermind their intimate and ever-present secret, their dominating continent, the overt constant builder of the harmonic whole of their activity and nature.

If we would understand the difference of this global Overmind Consciousness from our separative and only imperfectly synthetic mental consciousness, we may come near to it if we compare the strictly mental with what would be an overmental view of activities in our material universe. To the Overmind, for example, all religions would be true as developments of the one eternal religion, all philosophies would be valid each in its own field as a statement of its own universe-view from its own angle, all political theories with their practice would be the legitimate working out of an Idea Force with its right to application and practical development in the play of the energies of Nature. In our separative consciousness, imperfectly visited by glimpses of catholicity and universality, these things exist as opposites; each claims to be the truth and taxes the others with error and falsehood, each feels impelled to refute or destroy the others in order that itself alone may be the Truth and live: at best, each must claim to be superior, admit all others only as inferior truth-expressions. An overmental Intelligence would refuse to entertain this conception or this drift to exclusiveness for a moment; it would allow all to live as necessary to the whole or put each in its place in the whole or assign to each its field of realisation or of endeavour. This is because in us consciousness has come down completely into the divisions of the Ignorance; Truth is no longer either an Infinite or a cosmic whole with many possible formulations, but a rigid affirmation holding any other affirmation to be false because different from itself and entrenched in other limits. Our mental consciousness can indeed arrive in its cognition at a considerable approach towards a total comprehensiveness and catholicity, but to organise that in action and life seems to be beyond its power. Evolutionary Mind, manifest in individuals or collectivities, throws up a multiplicity of divergent viewpoints, divergent lines of action and lets them work themselves out side by side or in collision or in a certain intermixture; it can make selective harmonies, but it cannot arrive at the harmonic control of a true totality. Cosmic Mind must have even in the evolutionary Ignorance, like all totalities, such a harmony, if only of arranged accords and discords; there is too in it an underlying dynamism of oneness: but it carries the completeness of these things in its depths, perhaps in a supermind-overmind substratum, but does not impart it to individual Mind in the evolution, does not bring it or has not yet brought it from the depths to the surface. An Overmind world would be a world of harmony; the world of Ignorance in which we live is a world of disharmony and struggle.

And still we can recognise at once in the Overmind the original cosmic Maya, not a Maya of Ignorance but a Maya of Knowledge, yet a Power which has made the Ignorance possible, even inevitable. For if each principle loosed into action must follow its independent line and carry out its complete consequences, the principle of separation must also be allowed its complete course and arrive at its absolute consequence; this is the inevitable descent, *facilis descensus*, which Consciousness, once it admits the separative principle, follows till it enters by obscuring infinitesimal fragmentation, *tucchyena*,[5] into the material Inconscience, — the Inconscient Ocean of the Rig Veda, — and if the One is born from that by its own greatness, it is still at first concealed by a fragmentary separative existence and consciousness which is ours and in which we have to piece things together to arrive at a whole. In that slow and difficult emergence a certain semblance of truth is given to the dictum of Heraclitus that War is the father of all things; for each idea, force, separate consciousness, living being by the very necessity of its ignorance enters into collision with others and tries to live and grow and fulfil itself by independent self-assertion, not by harmony with the rest of existence. Yet there is still the unknown underlying Oneness which compels us to strive slowly towards some form of harmony, of interdependence, of concording of

[5] *Rig Veda*, X. 129. 3.

discords, of a difficult unity. But it is only by the evolution in us
of the concealed superconscient powers of cosmic Truth and of
the Reality in which they are one that the harmony and unity
we strive for can be dynamically realised in the very fibre of
our being and all its self-expression and not merely in imperfect
attempts, incomplete constructions, ever-changing approxima-
tions. The higher ranges of spiritual Mind have to open upon
our being and consciousness and also that which is beyond even
spiritual Mind must appear in us if we are to fulfil the divine
possibility of our birth into cosmic existence.

Overmind in its descent reaches a line which divides the
cosmic Truth from the cosmic Ignorance; it is the line at which
it becomes possible for Consciousness-Force, emphasising the
separateness of each independent movement created by Overmind and hiding or darkening their unity, to divide Mind by
an exclusive concentration from the overmental source. There
has already been a similar separation of Overmind from its
supramental source, but with a transparency in the veil which
allows a conscious transmission and maintains a certain luminous kinship; but here the veil is opaque and the transmission
of the Overmind motives to the Mind is occult and obscure.
Mind separated acts as if it were an independent principle,
and each mental being, each basic mental idea, power, force
stands similarly on its separate self; if it communicates with
or combines or contacts others, it is not with the catholic universality of the overmind movement, on a basis of underlying
oneness, but as independent units joining to form a separate
constructed whole. It is by this movement that we pass from
the cosmic Truth into the cosmic Ignorance. The cosmic Mind
on this level, no doubt, comprehends its own unity, but it is
not aware of its own source and foundation in the Spirit or
can only comprehend it by the intelligence, not in any enduring
experience; it acts in itself as if by its own right and works
out what it receives as material without direct communication
with the source from which it receives it. Its units also act in
ignorance of each other and of the cosmic whole except for the
knowledge that they can get by contact and communication,

—the basic sense of identity and the mutual penetration and understanding that comes from it are no longer there. All the actions of this Mind Energy proceed on the opposite basis of the Ignorance and its divisions and, although they are the results of a certain conscious knowledge, it is a partial knowledge, not a true and integral self-knowledge, nor a true and integral world-knowledge. This character persists in Life and in subtle Matter and reappears in the gross material universe which arises from the final lapse into the Inconscience.

Yet, as in our subliminal or inner Mind, so in this Mind also a larger power of communication and mutuality still remains, a freer play of mentality and sense than human mind possesses, and the Ignorance is not complete; a conscious harmony, an interdependent organisation of right relations is more possible: mind is not yet perturbed by blind Life forces or obscured by irresponsive Matter. It is a plane of Ignorance, but not yet of falsehood or error, — or at least the lapse into falsehood and error is not yet inevitable; this Ignorance is limitative but not necessarily falsificative. There is limitation of knowledge, an organisation of partial truths, but not a denial or opposite of truth or knowledge. This character of an organisation of partial truths on a basis of separative knowledge persists in Life and subtle Matter, for the exclusive concentration of Consciousness-Force which puts them into separative action does not entirely sever or veil Mind from Life or Mind and Life from Matter. The complete separation can take place only when the stage of Inconscience has been reached and our world of manifold Ignorance arises out of that tenebrous matrix. These other still conscient stages of the involution are indeed organisations of Conscious Force in which each lives from his own centre, follows out his own possibilities, and the predominant principle itself, whether Mind, Life or Matter, works out things on its own independent basis; but what is worked out are truths of itself, not illusions or a tangle of truth and falsehood, knowledge and ignorance. But when by an exclusive concentration on Force and Form Consciousness-Force seems phenomenally to separate Consciousness from Force, or when it absorbs Consciousness in a blind sleep lost in Form and Force, then Consciousness has to struggle back to itself by a fragmentary evolution which necessitates error and makes falsehood inevitable. Nevertheless, these things too are not illusions that have sprung out of an original Non-Existence; they are, we might say, the unavoidable truths of a world born out of Inconscience. For the Ignorance is still in reality a knowledge seeking for itself behind the original mask of Inconscience; it misses and finds; its results, natural and even inevitable on their own line, are the true consequence of the lapse, — in a way, even, the right working of the recovery from the lapse. Existence plunging into an apparent Non-Existence, Consciousness into an apparent Inconscience, Delight of existence into a vast cosmic insensibility are the first result of the fall and, in the return from it by a struggling fragmentary experience, the rendering of Consciousness into the dual terms of truth and falsehood, knowledge and error, of Existence into the dual terms of life and death, of Delight of existence into the dual terms of pain and pleasure are the necessary process of the labour of self-discovery. A pure experience of Truth, Knowledge, Delight, imperishable existence would here be itself a contradiction of the truth of things. It could only be otherwise if all beings in the evolution were quiescently responsive to the psychic elements within them and to the Supermind underlying Nature's operations; but here there comes in the Overmind law of each Force working out its own possibilities. The natural possibilities of a world in which an original Inconscience and a division of consciousness are the main principles, would be the emergence of Forces of Darkness impelled to maintain the Ignorance by which they live, an ignorant struggle to know originative of falsehood and error, an ignorant struggle to live engendering wrong and evil, an egoistic struggle to enjoy, parent of fragmentary joys and pains and sufferings; these are therefore the inevitable first-imprinted characters, though not the sole possibilities of our evolutionary existence. Still, because the Non-Existence is a concealed Existence, the Inconscience a concealed Consciousness, the insensibility a masked and dormant Ananda, these secret realities must emerge; the hidden Overmind and Supermind too must in the end fulfil themselves in this apparently opposite organisation from a dark Infinite.

Two things render that culmination more facile than it would otherwise be. Overmind in the descent towards material creation has originated modifications of itself, — Intuition especially with its penetrative lightning flashes of truth lighting up local points and stretches of country in our consciousness, — which can bring the concealed truth of things nearer to our comprehension, and, by opening ourselves more widely first in the inner being and then as a result in the outer surface self also to the messages of these higher ranges of consciousness, by growing into them, we can become ourselves also intuitive and overmental beings, not limited by the intellect and sense, but capable of a more universal comprehension and a direct touch of truth in its very self and body. In fact flashes of enlightenment from these higher ranges already come to us, but this intervention is mostly fragmentary, casual or partial; we have still to begin to enlarge ourselves into their likeness and organise in us the greater Truth activities of which we are potentially capable. But, secondly, Overmind, Intuition, even Supermind not only must be, as we have seen, principles inherent and involved in the Inconscience from which we arise in the evolution and inevitably destined to evolve, but are secretly present, occult actively with flashes of intuitive emergence in the cosmic activity of Mind, Life and Matter. It is true that their action is concealed and, even when they emerge, it is modified by the medium, material, vital, mental in which they work and not easily recognisable. Supermind cannot manifest itself as the Creator Power in the universe from the beginning, for if it did, the Ignorance and Inconscience would be impossible or else the slow evolution necessary would change into a rapid transformation scene. Yet at every step of the material energy we can see the stamp of inevitability given by a supramental creator, in all the development of life and mind the play of the lines of possibility and their combination which is the stamp of Overmind intervention. As Life and Mind have been released in Matter, so too must in their time these greater powers of the concealed Godhead emerge from the involution and their supreme Light descend into us from above.

A divine Life in the manifestation is then not only possible as the high result and ransom of our present life in the Ignorance but, if these things are as we have seen them, it is the inevitable outcome and consummation of Nature's evolutionary endeavour.

END OF THE FIRST BOOK

Book II

The Knowledge and the Ignorance —
The Spiritual Evolution

Part I

The Infinite Consciousness
and the Ignorance

Chapter I

Indeterminates,
Cosmic Determinations
and the Indeterminable

The Unseen with whom there can be no pragmatic relations, unseizable, featureless, unthinkable, undesignable by name, whose substance is the certitude of One Self, in whom world-existence is stilled, who is all peace and bliss — that is the Self, that is what must be known.   *Mandukya Upanishad.*[1]

One sees it as a mystery or one speaks of it or hears of it as a mystery, but none knows it.   *Gita.*[2]

When men seek after the Immutable, the Indeterminable, the Unmanifest, the All-Pervading, the Unthinkable, the Summit Self, the Immobile, the Permanent, — equal in mind to all, intent on the good of all beings, it is to Me that they come.
                                                            Gita.[3]

High. beyond the Intelligence is the Great Self, beyond the Great Self is the Unmanifest, beyond the Unmanifest is the Conscious Being. There is nothing beyond the Being, — that is the extreme ultimate, that the supreme goal.
                                                 Katha Upanishad.[4]

Rare is the great of soul to whom all is the Divine Being.
                                                            Gita.[5]

A CONSCIOUSNESS-FORCE, everywhere inherent in Existence, acting even when concealed, is the creator of the worlds, the occult secret of Nature. But in our material world and in our own being consciousness has a double aspect;

---

[1] Verse 7.   [2] II. 29.   [3] XII. 3, 4.   [4] III. 10, 1l.   [5] *vāsudevaḥ sarvamiti...* VII. 19.

there is a force of Knowledge, there is a force of Ignorance. In the infinite consciousness of a self-aware infinite Existence knowledge must be everywhere implicit or operative in the very grain of its action; but we see here at the beginning of things, apparent as the base or the nature of the creative world-energy, an Inconscience, a total Nescience. This is the stock with which the material universe commences: consciousness and knowledge emerge at first in obscure infinitesimal movements, at points, in little quanta which associate themselves together; there is a tardy and difficult evolution, a slowly increasing organisation and ameliorated mechanism of the workings of consciousness, more and more gains are written on the blank slate of the Nescience. But still these have the appearance of gathered acquisitions and constructions of a seeking Ignorance which tries to know, to understand, to discover, to change slowly and strugglingly into knowledge. As Life here establishes and maintains its operations with difficulty on a foundation and in an environment of general Death, first in infinitesimal points of life, in quanta of life-form and life-energy, in increasing aggregates that create more and more complex organisms, an intricate life-machinery, Consciousness also establishes and maintains a growing but precarious light in the darkness of an original Nescience and a universal Ignorance.

Moreover the knowledge gained is of phenomena, not of the reality of things or of the foundations of existence. Wherever our consciousness meets what seems to be a foundation, that foundation wears the appearance of a blank, — when it is not a void, — an original state which is featureless and a multitude of consequences which are not inherent in the origin and which nothing in it seems to justify or visibly to necessitate; there is a mass of superstructure which has no clear native relation to the fundamental existence. The first aspect of cosmic existence is an Infinite which is to our perception an indeterminate, if not indeterminable. In this Infinite the universe itself, whether in its aspect of Energy or its aspect of structure, appears as an indeterminate determination, a "boundless finite", — paradoxical but necessary expressions which would seem to indicate that we are face to face with a suprarational mystery as the base of things; in that universe arise — from where? — a vast number and variety of general and particular determinates which do not appear to be warranted by anything perceptible in the nature of the Infinite, but seem to be imposed, — or, it may be, self-imposed, — upon it. We give to the Energy which produces them the name of Nature, but the word conveys no meaning unless it is that the nature of things is what it is by virtue of a Force which arranges them according to an inherent Truth in them; but the nature of that Truth itself, the reason why these determinates are what they are is nowhere visible. It has been possible indeed for human Science to detect the process or many processes of material things, but this knowledge does not throw any light on the major question; we do not know even the rationale of the original cosmic processes, for the results do not present themselves as their necessary but only their pragmatic and actual consequence. In the end we do not know how these determinates came into or out of the original Indeterminate or Indeterminable on which they stand forth as on a blank and flat background in the riddle of their ordered occurrence. At the origin of things we are faced with an Infinite containing a mass of unexplained finites, an Indivisible full of endless divisions, an Immutable teeming with mutations and differentiae. A cosmic paradox is the beginning of all things, a paradox without any key to its significance.

It is possible indeed to question the need of positing an Infinite which contains our formed universe, although this conception is imperatively demanded by our mind as a necessary basis to its conceptions, — for it is unable to fix or assign a limit whether in Space or Time or essential existence beyond which there is nothing or before or after which there is nothing, — although too the alternative is a Void or Nihil which can be only an abyss of the Infinite into which we refuse to look; an infinite mystic zero of Non-Existence would replace an infinite x as a necessary postulate, a basis for our seeing of all that is to us existence. But even if we refuse to recognise anything as real except the limitless expanding finite of the material universe and its teeming determinations, the enigma remains the same. Infinite existence, infinite non-being or boundless finite, all are to us original indeterminates or indeterminables; we can assign to them no distinct characters or features, nothing which would predetermine their determinations. To describe the fundamental character of the universe as Space or Time or Space-Time does not help us; for even if these are not abstractions of our intelligence which we impose by our mental view on the cosmos, the mind's necessary perspective of its picture, these too are indeterminates and carry in themselves no clue to the origin of the determinations that take place in them; there is still no explanation of the strange process by which things are determined or of their powers, qualities and properties, no revelation of their true nature, origin and significance.

Actually to our Science this infinite or indeterminate Existence reveals itself as an Energy, known not by itself but by its works, which throws up in its motion waves of energism and in them a multitude of infinitesimals; these, grouping themselves to form larger infinitesimals, become a basis for all the creations of the Energy, even those farthest away from the material basis, for the emergence of a world of organised Matter, for the emergence of Life, for the emergence of Consciousness, for all the still unexplained activities of evolutionary Nature. On the original process are erected a multitude of processes which we can observe, follow, can take advantage of many of them, utilise; but they are none of them, fundamentally, explicable. We know now that different groupings and a varying number of electric infinitesimals can produce or serve as the constituent occasion — miscalled the cause, for here there seems to be only a necessary antecedent condition, — for the appearance of larger atomic infinitesimals of different natures, qualities, powers; but we fail to discover how these different dispositions can come to constitute these different atoms, — how the differentiae in the constituent occasion or cause necessitate the differentiae in the constituted outcome or result. We know also that certain combinations of certain invisible atomic infinitesimals produce or occasion new and visible determinations quite different in nature, quality and power from the constituent infinitesimals; but we fail to discover, for instance, how a fixed formula for the combination of oxygen and hydrogen comes to determine the appearance of water which is evidently something more than a combination of gases, a new creation, a new form of substance, a material manifestation of a quite new character. We see that a seed develops into a tree, we follow the line of the process of production and we utilise it; but we do not discover how a tree can grow out of a seed, how the life and form of the tree come to be implied in the substance or energy of the seed or, if that be rather the fact, how the seed can develop into a tree. We know that genes and chromosomes are the cause of hereditary transmissions, not only of physical but of psychological variations; but we do not discover how psychological characteristics can be contained and transmitted in this inconscient material vehicle. We do not see or know, but it is expounded to us as a cogent account of Nature-process, that a play of electrons, of atoms and their resultant molecules, of cells, glands, chemical secretions and physiological processes manages by their activity on the nerves and brain of a Shakespeare or a Plato to produce or could be perhaps the dynamic occasion for the production of a *Hamlet* or a *Symposium* or a *Republic*; but we fail to discover or appreciate how such material movements could have composed or necessitated the composition of these highest points of thought and literature: the divergence here of the determinants and the determination becomes so wide that we are no longer able to follow the process, much less understand or utilise. These formulae of Science may be pragmatically correct and infallible, they may govern the practical how of Nature's processes, but they do not disclose the intrinsic how or why; rather they have the air of the formulae of a cosmic Magician, precise, irresistible, automatically successful each in its field, but their rationale is fundamentally unintelligible.

There is more to perplex us; for we see the original indeterminate Energy throwing out general determinates of itself, — we might equally in their relation to the variety of their products call them generic indeterminates, — with their appropriate states of substance and determined forms of that substance: the latter are

numerous, sometimes innumerable variations on the substance-
energy which is their base: but none of these variations seems
to be predetermined by anything in the nature of the general
indeterminate. An electric Energy produces positive, negative,
neutral forms of itself, forms that are at once waves and parti-
cles; a gaseous state of energy-substance produces a considerable
number of different gases; a solid state of energy-substance from
which results the earth principle develops into different forms
of earth and rock of many kinds and numerous minerals and
metals; a life principle produces its vegetable kingdom teeming
with a countless foison of quite different plants, trees, flowers; a
principle of animal life produces an enormous variety of genus,
species, individual variations: so it proceeds into human life
and mind and its mind-types towards the still unwritten end
or perhaps the yet occult sequel of that unfinished evolutionary
chapter. Throughout there is the constant rule of a general sameness in the original determinate and, subject to this substantial
sameness of basic substance and nature, a profuse variation in
the generic and individual determinates; an identical law obtains
of sameness or similarity in the genus or species with numerous
variations often meticulously minute in the individual. But we do
not find anything in any general or generic determinate necessi-
tating the variant determinations that result from it. A necessity
of immutable sameness at the base, of free and unaccountable
variations on the surface seems to be the law; but who or what
necessitates or determines? What is the rationale of the determination, what is its original truth or its significance? What
compels or impels this exuberant play of varying possibilities
which seem to have no aim or meaning unless it be the beauty
or delight of creation? A Mind, a seeking and curious inventive
Thought, a hidden determining Will might be there, but there is
no trace of it in the first and fundamental appearance of material
Nature.

   A first possible explanation points to a self-organising dynamic Chance that is at work, — a paradox necessitated by the
appearance of inevitable order on one side, of unaccountable
freak and fantasy on the other side of the cosmic phenomenon

we call Nature. An inconscient and inconsequent Force, we may say, that acts at random and creates this or that by a general chance without any determining principle, — determinations coming in only as the result of a persistent repetition of the same rhythm of action and succeeding because only this repetitive rhythm could succeed in keeping things in being, — this is the energy of Nature. But this implies that somewhere in the origin of things there is a boundless Possibility or a womb of innumerable possibilities that are manifested out of it by the original Energy, — an incalculable Inconscient which we find some embarrassment in calling either an Existence or a Non-Existence; for without some such origin and basis the appearance and the action of the Energy is unintelligible. Yet an opposite aspect of the nature of the cosmic phenomenon as we see it appears to forbid the theory of a random action generating a persistent order. There is too much of an iron insistence on order, on a law basing the possibilities. One would be justified rather in supposing that there is an inherent imperative Truth of things unseen by us, but a Truth capable of manifold manifestation, throwing out a multitude of possibilities and variants of itself which the creative Energy by its action turns into so many realised actualities. This brings us to a second explanation, — a mechanical necessity in things, its workings recognisable by us as so many mechanical laws of Nature; — the necessity, we might say, of some such secret inherent Truth of things as we have supposed, governing automatically the processes we observe in action in the universe. But a theory of mechanical Necessity by itself does not elucidate the free play of the endless unaccountable variations which are visible in the evolution: there must be behind the Necessity or in it a law of unity associated with a co-existent but dependent law of multiplicity, both insisting on manifestation; but the unity of what, the multiplicity of what? Mechanical Necessity can give no answer. Again the emergence of consciousness out of the Inconscient is a stumbling-block in the way of this theory; for it is a phenomenon which can have no place in an all-pervading truth of inconscient mechanical Necessity. If there is a necessity which compels the emergence, it can be only this, that there is already a consciousness concealed in the Inconscient, waiting for evolution and when all is ready breaking out from its prison of apparent Nescience. We may indeed get rid of the difficulty of the imperative order of things by supposing that it does not exist, that determinism in Nature is imposed on it by our thought which needs such an imperative order to enable it to deal with its surroundings, but in reality there is no such thing; there is only a Force experimenting in a random action of infinitesimals which build up in their general results different determinations by a repetitive persistence operative in the sum of their action; thus we go back from Necessity to Chance as the basis of our existence. But what then is this Mind, this Consciousness which differs so radically from the Energy that produced it that for its action it has to impose its idea and need of order on the world she has made and in which it is obliged to live? There would then be the double contradiction of consciousness emerging from a fundamental Inconscience and of a Mind of order and reason manifesting as the brilliant final consequence of a world created by inconscient Chance. These things may be possible, but they need a better explanation than any yet given before we can accord to them our acceptance.

This opens the way for other explanations which make Consciousness the creator of this world out of an apparent original Inconscience. A Mind, a Will seems to have imagined and organised the universe, but it has veiled itself behind its creation; its first erection has been this screen of an inconscient Energy and a material form of substance, at once a disguise of its presence and a plastic creative basis on which it could work as an artisan uses for his production of forms and patterns a dumb and obedient material. All these things we see around us are then the thoughts of an extra-cosmic Divinity, a Being with an omnipotent and omniscient Mind and Will, who is responsible for the mathematical law of the physical universe, for its artistry of beauty, for its strange play of samenesses and variations, of concordances and discords, of combining and intermingling opposites, for the drama of consciousness struggling to exist and seeking to affirm itself in an inconscient universal order. The fact

that this Divinity is invisible to us, undiscoverable by our mind
and senses, offers no difficulty, since self-evidence or direct sign
of an extra-cosmic Creator could not be expected in a cosmos
which is void of his presence: the patent signals everywhere of
the works of an Intelligence, of law, design, formula, adaptation
of means to end, constant and inexhaustible invention, fantasy
even but restrained by an ordering Reason might be considered
sufficient proof of this origin of things. Or if this Creator is not
entirely supracosmic, but is also immanent in his works, even
then there need be no other sign of him, — except indeed to some
consciousness evolving in this inconscient world, but only when
its evolution reached a point at which it could become aware
of the indwelling Presence. The intervention of this evolving
consciousness would not be a difficulty, since there would be
no contradiction of the basic nature of things in its appearance;
an omnipotent Mind could easily infuse something of itself into
its creatures. One difficulty remains; it is the arbitrary nature of
the creation, the incomprehensibility of its purpose, the crude
meaninglessness of its law of unnecessary ignorance, strife and
suffering, its ending without denouement or issue. A play? But
why this stamp of so many undivine elements and characters in
the play of One whose nature must be supposed to be divine?
To the suggestion that what we see worked out in the world
is the thoughts of God, the retort can be made that God could
well have had better thoughts and the best thought of all would
have been to refrain from the creation of an unhappy and unintelligible universe. All theistic explanations of existence starting
from an extra-cosmic Deity stumble over this difficulty and can
only evade it; it would disappear only if the Creator were, even
though exceeding the creation, yet immanent in it, himself in
some sort both the player and the play, an Infinite casting infinite
possibilities into the set form of an evolutionary cosmic order.

On that hypothesis, there must be behind the action of the
material Energy a secret involved Consciousness, cosmic, infinite, building up through the action of that frontal Energy its
means of an evolutionary manifestation, a creation out of itself
in the boundless finite of the material universe. The apparent

inconscience of the material Energy would be an indispensable
condition for the structure of the material world-substance in
which this Consciousness intends to involve itself so that it may
grow by evolution out of its apparent opposite; for without some
such device a complete involution would be impossible. If there
is such a creation by the Infinite out of itself, it must be the manifestation, in a material disguise, of truths or powers of its own
being: the forms or vehicles of these truths or powers would be
the basic general or fundamental determinates we see in Nature;
the particular determinates, which otherwise are unaccountable
variations that have emerged from the vague general stuff in
which they originate, would be the appropriate forms or vehicles of the possibilities that the truths or powers residing in these
fundamentals bore within them. The principle of free variation
of possibilities natural to an infinite Consciousness would be the
explanation of the aspect of inconscient Chance of which we are
aware in the workings of Nature, — inconscient only in appearance and so appearing because of the complete involution in
Matter, because of the veil with which the secret Consciousness
has disguised its presence. The principle of truths, real powers of the Infinite imperatively fulfilling themselves would be
the explanation of the opposite aspect of a mechanical Necessity which we see in Nature, — mechanical in appearance only
and so appearing because of the same veil of Inconscience. It
would then be perfectly intelligible why the Inconscient does its
works with a constant principle of mathematical architecture,
of design, of effective arrangement of numbers, of adaptation of
means to ends, of inexhaustible device and invention, one might
almost say, a constant experimental skill and an automatism of
purpose. The appearance of consciousness out of an apparent
Inconscience would also be no longer inexplicable.

All the unexplained processes of Nature would find their
meaning and their place if this hypothesis proved to be tenable.
Energy seems to create substance, but, in reality, as existence
is inherent in Consciousness-Force, so also substance would be
inherent in Energy, — the Energy a manifestation of the Force,
substance a manifestation of the secret Existence. But as it is a

spiritual substance, it would not be apprehended by the material sense until it is given by Energy the forms of Matter seizable by that sense. One begins to understand also how arrangement of design, quantity and number can be a base for the manifestation of quality and property; for design, quantity and number are powers of existence-substance, quality and property are powers of the consciousness and its force that reside in the existence; they can then be made manifest and operative by a rhythm and process of substance. The growth of the tree out of the seed would be accounted for, like all other similar phenomena, by the indwelling presence of what we have called the Real-Idea; the Infinite's self-perception of the significant form, the living body of its power of existence that has to emerge from its own self-compression in energy-substance, would be carried internally in the form of the seed, carried in the occult consciousness involved in that form, and would naturally evolve out of it. There would be no difficulty either in understanding on this principle how infinitesimals of a material character like the gene and the chromosome can carry in them psychological elements to be transmitted to the physical form that has to emerge from the human seed; it would be at bottom on the same principle in the objectivity of Matter as that which we find in our subjective experience, — for we see that the subconscient physical carries in it a mental psychological content, impressions of past events, habits, fixed mental and vital formations, fixed forms of character, and sends them up by an occult process to the waking consciousness, thus originating or influencing many activities of our nature.

On the same basis there would be no difficulty in understanding why the physiological functionings of the body help to determine the mind's psychological actions: for the body is not mere unconscious Matter: it is a structure of a secretly conscious Energy that has taken form in it. Itself occultly conscious, it is, at the same time, the vehicle of expression of an overt Consciousness that has emerged and is self-aware in our physical energy-substance. The body's functionings are a necessary machinery or instrumentation for the movements of this mental Inhabitant; it is only by setting the corporeal instrument in motion that the Conscious Being emerging, evolving in it can transmit its mind formations, will formations and turn them into a physical manifestation of itself in Matter. The capacity, the processes of the instrument must to a certain extent reshape the mind formations in their transition from mental shape into physical expression; its workings are necessary and must exercise their influence before that expression can become actual. The bodily instrument may even in some directions dominate its user; it may too by a force of habit suggest or create involuntary reactions of the consciousness inhabiting it before the working Mind and Will can control or interfere. All this is possible because the body has a "subconscient" consciousness of its own which counts in our total self-expression; even, if we look at this outer instrumentation only, we can conclude that body determines mind, but this is only a minor truth and the major Truth is that mind determines body. In this view a still deeper Truth becomes conceivable; a spiritual entity ensouling the substance that veils it is the original determinant of both mind and body. On the other side, in the opposite order of process, — that by which the mind can transmit its ideas and commands to the body, can train it to be an instrument for new action, can even so impress it with its habitual demands or orders that the physical instinct carries them out automatically even when the mind is no longer consciously willing them, those also more unusual but well attested by which to an extraordinary and hardly limitable extent the mind can learn to determine the reactions of the body even to the overriding of its normal law or conditions of action, — these and other otherwise unaccountable aspects of the relation between these two elements of our being become easily understandable: for it is the secret consciousness in the living matter that receives from its greater companion; it is this in the body that in its own involved and occult fashion perceives or feels the demand on it and obeys the emerged or evolved consciousness which presides over the body. Finally, the conception of a divine Mind and Will creating the cosmos becomes justifiable, while at the same time the perplexing elements in it which our reasoning mentality refuses to ascribe to an arbitrary fiat of the Creator, find their explanation as inevitable phenomena of a Consciousness emerging with difficulty out of its opposite — but with the mission to override these contrary phenomena and manifest by a slow and difficult evolution its greater reality and true nature.

But an approach from the material end of Existence cannot give us any certitude of validity for this hypothesis or for that matter for any other explanation of Nature and her procedure: the veil cast by the original Inconscience is too thick for the Mind to pierce and it is behind this veil that is hidden the secret origination of what is manifested; there are seated the truths and powers underlying the phenomena and processes that appear to us in the material front of Nature. To know with greater certitude we must follow the curve of evolving consciousness until it arrives at a height and largeness of self-enlightenment in which the primal secret is self-discovered; for presumably it must evolve, must eventually bring out what was held from the beginning by the occult original Consciousness in things of which it is a gradual manifestation. In Life it would be clearly hopeless to seek for the truth; for Life begins with a formulation in which consciousness is still submental and therefore to us as mental beings appears as inconscient or at most subconscious, and our own investigation into this stage of life studying it from outside cannot be more fruitful of the secret truth than our examination of Matter. Even when mind develops in life, its first functional aspect is a mentality involved in action, in vital and physical needs and preoccupations, in impulses, desires, sensations, emotions, unable to stand back from these things and observe and know them. In the human mind there is the first hope of understanding, discovery, a free comprehension; here we might seem to be coming to the possibility of self-knowledge and world-knowledge. But in fact our mind can at first only observe facts and processes and for the rest it has to make deductions and inferences, to construct hypotheses, to reason, to speculate. In order to discover the secret of Consciousness it would have to know itself and determine the reality of its own being and process; but as in animal life the emerging Consciousness is involved in vital action and movement, so in the human being mind-consciousness is involved in its own whirl of thoughts, an activity in which it is carried on without rest and in which its very reasonings and speculations are determined in their tendency, trend, conditions by its own temperament, mental turn, past formation and line of energy, inclination, preference, an inborn natural selection, — we do not freely determine our thinking according to the truth of things, it is determined for us by our nature. We can indeed stand back with a certain detachment and observe the workings of the mental Energy in us; but it is still only its process that we see and not any original source of our mental determinations: we can build theories and hypotheses of the process of Mind, but a veil is still there over the inner secret of ourselves, our consciousness, our total nature.

It is only when we follow the yogic process of quieting the mind itself that a profounder result of our self-observation becomes possible. For first we discover that mind is a subtle substance, a general determinate — or generic indeterminate — which mental energy when it operates throws into forms or particular determinations of itself, thoughts, concepts, percepts, mental sentiments, activities of will and reactions of feeling, but which, when the energy is quiescent, can live either in an inert torpor or in an immobile silence and peace of self-existence. Next we see that the determinations of our mind do not all proceed from itself; for waves and currents of mental energy enter into it from outside: these take form in it or appear already formed from some universal Mind or from other minds and are accepted by us as our own thinking. We can perceive also an occult or subliminal mind in ourselves from which thoughts and perceptions and will-impulses and mental feelings arise; we can perceive too higher planes of consciousness from which a superior mind energy works through us or upon us. Finally we discover that that which observes all this is a mental being supporting the mind substance and mind energy; without this presence, their upholder and source of sanctions, they could not exist or operate. This mental being or Purusha first appears as a silent witness and, if that were all, we would have to accept the determinations of mind as a phenomenal activity imposed upon the being by Nature, by Prakriti, or else as a creation presented to it by Prakriti, a world of thought which Nature constructs and offers to the observing Purusha. But afterwards we find that the Purusha, the mental being, can depart from its posture of a silent or accepting Witness; it can become the source of reactions, accept, reject, even rule and regulate, become the giver of the command, the knower. A knowledge also arises that this mind-substance manifests the mental being, is its own expressive substance and the mental energy is its own consciousness-force, so that it is reasonable to conclude that all mind determinations arise from the being of the Purusha. But this conclusion is complicated by the fact that from another viewpoint our personal mind seems to be little more than a formation of universal Mind, an engine for the reception, modification, propagation of cosmic thought-waves, idea-currents, will-suggestions, waves of feeling, sense-suggestions, form-suggestions. It has no doubt its own already realised expression, predispositions, propensities, personal temperament and nature; what comes from the universal can only find a place there if it is accepted and assimilated into the self-expression of the individual mental being, the personal Prakriti of the Purusha. But still, in view of these complexities, the question remains entire whether all this evolution and action is a phenomenal creation by some universal Energy presented to the mental being or an activity imposed by Mind-Energy on the Purusha's indeterminate, perhaps indeterminable existence, or whether the whole is something predetermined by some dynamic truth of Self within and only manifested on the mind surface. To know that we would have to touch or to enter into a cosmic state of being and consciousness to which the totality of things and their integral principle would be better manifest than to our limited mind experience.

Overmind consciousness is such a state or principle beyond individual mind, beyond even universal mind in the Ignorance; it carries in itself a first direct and masterful cognition of cosmic truth: here then we might hope to understand something of the original working of things, get some insight into the fundamental movements of cosmic Nature. One thing indeed becomes clear; it is self-evident here that both the individual and the cosmos come from a transcendent Reality which takes form in them: the mind and life of the individual being, its self in nature must therefore be a partial self-expression of the cosmic Being and, both through that and directly, a self-expression of the transcendent Reality, — a conditional and half-veiled expression it may be, but still that is its significance. But also we see that what the expression shall be is also determined by the individual himself: only what he can in his nature receive, assimilate, formulate, his portion of the cosmic being or of the Reality, can find shape in his mind and life and physical parts; something that derives from Reality, something that is in the cosmos he expresses, but in the terms of his own self-expression, in the terms of his own nature. But the original question set out for us by the phenomenon of the universe is not solved by the overmind knowledge, — the question, in this case, whether the building of thought, experience, world of perceptions of the mental Person, the mind Purusha, is truly a self-expression, a self-determination proceeding from some truth of his own spiritual being, a manifestation of that truth's dynamic possibilities, or whether it is not rather a creation or construction presented to him by Nature, by Prakriti, and only in the sense of being individualised in his personal formation of that Nature can it be said to be his own or dependent on him; or, again, it might be a play of a cosmic Imagination, a fantasia of the Infinite imposed on the blank indeterminable of his own eternal pure existence. These are the three views of creation that seem to have an equal chance of being right, and mind is incapable of definitely deciding between them; for each view is armed with its own mental logic and its appeal to intuition and experience. Overmind seems to add to the perplexity, for the overmental view of things allows each possibility to formulate itself in its own independent right and realise its own existence in cognition, in dynamic self-presentation, in substantiating experience.

In Overmind, in all the higher ranges of the mind, we find recurring the dichotomy of a pure silent self without feature or qualities or relations, self-existent, self-poised, self-sufficient, and the mighty dynamis of a determinative knowledge-power, of a creative consciousness and force which precipitates itself into the forms of the universe. This opposition which is yet a collocation, as if these two were correlatives or complementaries, although apparent contradictions of each other, sublimates itself into the co-existence of an impersonal Brahman without qualities, a fundamental divine Reality free from all relations or determinates, and a Brahman with infinite qualities, a fundamental divine Reality who is the source and container and master of all relations and determinations — Nirguna, Saguna. If we pursue the Nirguna into a farthest possible self-experience, we arrive at a supreme Absolute void of all relations and determinations, the ineffable first and last word of existence. If we enter through the Saguna into some ultimate possible of experience, we arrive at a divine Absolute, a personal supreme and omnipresent Godhead, transcendent as well as universal, an infinite Master of all relations and determinations who can uphold in his being a million universes and pervade each with a single ray of his self-light and a single degree of his ineffable existence. The overmind consciousness maintains equally these two truths of the Eternal which face the mind as mutually exclusive alternatives; it admits both as supreme aspects of one Reality: somewhere, then, behind them there must be a still greater Transcendence which originates them or upholds them both in its supreme Eternity. But what can that be of which such opposites are equal truths, unless it be an original indeterminable Mystery of which any knowledge, any understanding by the mind is impossible? We can know it indeed to some degree, in some kind of experience or realisation, by its aspects, powers, constant series of fundamental negatives and positives through which we have to pursue it, independently in either or integrally in both together; but in the last resort it seems to escape even from the highest mentality and remain unknowable.

But if the supreme Absolute is indeed a pure Indeterminable, then no creation, no manifestation, no universe is possible. And yet the universe exists. What then is it that creates this contradiction, is able to effect the impossible, bring this insoluble riddle of self-division into existence? A Power of some kind it must be, and since the Absolute is the sole reality, the one origin of all things, this Power must proceed from it, must have some relation with it, a connection, a dependence. For if it is quite other than the supreme Reality, a cosmic Imagination imposing its determinations on the eternal blank of the Indeterminable, then the sole existence of an absolute Parabrahman is no longer admissible; there is then a dualism at the source of things, — not substantially different from the Sankhya dualism of Soul and Nature. If it is a Power, the sole Power indeed, of the Absolute, we have this logical impossibility that the existence of the Supreme Being and the Power of his existence are entirely opposite to each other, two supreme contradictories; for Brahman is free from all possibility of relations and determinations, but Maya is a creative Imagination imposing these very things upon it, an originator of relations and determinations of which Brahman must necessarily be the supporter and witness, — to the logical reason an inadmissible formula. If it is accepted, it can only be as a suprarational mystery, something neither real nor unreal, inexplicable in its nature, *anirvacanīya*. But the difficulties are so great that it can be accepted only if it imposes itself irresistibly as the inevitable ultimate, the end and summit of metaphysical inquiry and spiritual experience. For even if all things are illusory creations, they must have at least a subjective existence and they can exist nowhere except in the consciousness of the Sole Existence; they are then subjective determinations of the Indeterminable. If, on the contrary, the determinations of this Power are real creations, out of what are they determined, what is their substance? It is not possible that they are made out of a Nothing, a Non-Existence other than the Absolute; for that will erect a new dualism, a great positive Zero over against the greater indeterminable x we have supposed to be the one Reality. It is evident therefore that the Reality cannot be a rigid Indeterminable. Whatever is created must be of it and in it, and what is of the substance of the utterly Real must itself be real: a vast baseless negation of reality purporting to be real cannot be the sole outcome of the eternal Truth, the Infinite Existence. It is perfectly understandable that the Absolute is and must be indeterminable in the sense that it cannot be limited by any determination or any sum of possible determinations, but not in the sense that it is incapable of self-determination. The Supreme Existence cannot be incapable of creating true self-determinations of its being, incapable of upholding a real self-creation or manifestation in its self-existent infinite.

Overmind, then, gives us no final and positive solution; it is in a supramental cognition beyond it that we are left to seek for an answer. A supramental Truth-Consciousness is at once the self-awareness of the Infinite and Eternal and a power of self-determination inherent in that self-awareness; the first is its foundation and status, the second is its power of being, the dynamis of its self-existence. All that a timeless eternity of self-awareness sees in itself as truth of being, the conscious power of its being manifests in Time-eternity. To Supermind therefore the Supreme is not a rigid Indeterminable, an all-negating Absolute; an infinite of being complete to itself in its own immutable purity of existence, its sole power a pure consciousness able only to dwell on the being's changeless eternity, on the immobile delight of its sheer self-existence, is not the whole Reality. The Infinite of Being must also be an Infinite of Power; containing in itself an eternal repose and quiescence, it must also be capable of an eternal action and creation: but this too must be an action in itself, a creation out of its own self eternal and infinite, since there could be nothing else out of which it could create; any basis of creation seeming to be other than itself must be still really in itself and of itself and could not be something foreign to its existence. An infinite Power cannot be solely a Force resting in a pure inactive sameness, an immutable quiescence; it must have in it endless powers of its being and energy: an infinite Consciousness must hold within it endless truths of its own self-awareness. These in action would appear to our cognition as aspects of its being, to our spiritual sense as powers and movements of its dynamis, to our aesthesis as instruments and formulations of its delight of existence. Creation would then be a self-manifestation: it would be an ordered deploying of the infinite possibilities of the Infinite. But every possibility implies a truth of being behind it, a reality in the Existent; for without that supporting truth there could not be any possibles. In manifestation a fundamental reality of the Existent would appear to our cognition as a fundamental spiritual aspect of the Divine Absolute; out of it would emerge all its possible manifestations, its innate dynamisms: these again must create or rather bring out of a non-manifest latency their own significant forms, expressive powers, native processes; their own being would develop their own becoming, *svarūpa, svabhāva.* This then would be the complete process of creation: but in our mind we do not see the complete process, we see only possibilities that determine themselves into actualities and, though we infer or conjecture, we are not sure of a necessity, a predetermining truth, an imperative behind them which capacitates the possibilities, decides the actualities. Our mind is an observer of actuals, an inventor or discoverer of possibilities, but not a seer of the occult imperatives that necessitate the movements and forms of a creation: for in the front of universal existence there are only forces determining results by some balance of the meeting of their powers; the original Determinant or determinants, if it or they exist, are veiled from us by our ignorance. But to the supramental Truth-Consciousness these imperatives would be apparent, would be the very stuff of its seeing and experience: in the supramental creative process the imperatives, the nexus of possibilities, the resultant actualities would be a single whole, an indivisible movement; the possibilities and actualities would carry in themselves the inevitability of their originating imperative, — all their results, all their creation would be the body of the Truth which they manifest in predetermined significant forms and powers of the All-Existence.

Our fundamental cognition of the Absolute, our substantial spiritual experience of it is the intuition or the direct experience of an infinite and eternal Existence, an infinite and eternal Consciousness, an infinite and eternal Delight of Existence. In overmental and mental cognition it is possible to make discrete and even to separate this original unity into three self-existent aspects: for we can experience a pure causeless eternal Bliss so intense that we are that alone; existence, consciousness seem to be swallowed up in it, no longer ostensibly in presence; a similar experience of pure and absolute consciousness and a similar exclusive identity with it is possible, and there can be too a like identifying experience of pure and absolute existence. But to a supermind cognition these three are always an inseparable Trinity, even though one can stand in front of the others and manifest its own spiritual determinates; for each has its primal aspects or its inherent self-formations, but all of these together are original to the triune Absolute. Love, Joy and Beauty are the fundamental determinates of the Divine Delight of Existence, and we can see at once that these are of the very stuff and nature of that Delight: they are not alien impositions on the being of the Absolute or creations supported by it but outside it; they are truths of its being, native to its consciousness, powers of its force of existence. So too is it with the fundamental determinates of the absolute consciousness, — knowledge and will; they are truths and powers of the original Consciousness-Force and are inherent in its very nature. This authenticity becomes still more evident when we regard the fundamental spiritual determinates of the absolute Existence; they are its triune powers, necessary first postulates for all its self-creation or manifestation, — Self, the Divine, the Conscious Being; Atman, Ishwara, Purusha.

If we pursue the process of self-manifestation farther, we shall see that each of these aspects or powers reposes in its first action on a triad or trinity; for Knowledge inevitably takes its stand in a trinity of the Knower, the Known and Knowledge; Love finds itself in a trinity of the Lover, the Beloved and Love; Will is self-fulfilled in a trinity of the Lord of the Will, the object of the Will and the executive Force; Joy has its original and utter gladness in a trinity of the Enjoyer, the Enjoyed and the Delight that unites them; Self as inevitably appears and founds its manifestation in a trinity of Self as subject, Self as object and self-awareness holding together Self as subject-object. These and other primal powers and aspects assume their status among the fundamental spiritual self-determinations of the Infinite; all others are determinates of the fundamental spiritual determinates, significant relations, significant powers, significant forms of being, consciousness, force, delight, — energies, conditions, ways, lines of the truth-process of the Consciousness-Force of the Eternal, imperatives, possibilities, actualities of its manifestation. All this deploying of powers and possibilities and their inherent consequences is held together by supermind cognition in an intimate oneness; it keeps them founded consciously on the original Truth and maintained in the harmony of the truths they manifest and are in their nature. There is here no imposition of imaginations, no arbitrary creation, neither is there any division, fragmentation, irreconcilable contrariety or disparateness. But in Mind of Ignorance these phenomena appear; for there a limited consciousness sees and deals with everything as if all were separate objects of cognition or separate existences and it seeks so to know, possess and enjoy them and gets mastery over them or suffers their mastery: but, behind its ignorance, what the soul in it is seeking for is the Reality, the Truth, the Consciousness, the Power, the Delight by which they exist; the mind has to learn to awaken to this true seeking and true knowledge veiled within itself, to the Reality from which all things hold their truth, to the Consciousness of which all consciousnesses are entities, to the Power from which all get what force of being they have within them, to the Delight of which all delights are partial figures. This limitation of consciousness and this awakening to the integrality of consciousness are also a process of self-manifestation, are a self-determination of the Spirit; even when contrary to the Truth in their appearances, the things of the limited consciousness have in their deeper sense and reality a divine significance; they too bring out a truth or a possibility of the Infinite. Of some such nature, as far as it can be expressed in mental formulas, would be the supramental cognition of things which sees the one Truth everywhere and would so arrange its account to us of our existence, its report of the secret of creation and the significance of the universe.

At the same time indeterminability is also a necessary element in our conception of the Absolute and in our spiritual experience: this is the other side of the supramental regard on being and on things. The Absolute is not limitable or definable by any one determination or by any sum of determinations; on the other side, it is not bound down to an indeterminable vacancy of pure existence. On the contrary, it is the source of all determinations: its indeterminability is the natural, the necessary condition both of its infinity of being and its infinity of power of being; it can be infinitely all things because it is no thing in particular and exceeds any definable totality. It is this essential indeterminability of the Absolute that translates itself into our consciousness through the fundamental negating positives of our spiritual experience, the immobile immutable Self, the Nirguna Brahman, the Eternal without qualities, the pure featureless One Existence, the Impersonal, the Silence void of activities, the Non-being, the Ineffable and the Unknowable. On the other side it is the essence and source of all determinations, and this dynamic essentiality manifests to us through the fundamental affirming positives in which the Absolute equally meets us; for it is the Self that becomes all things, the Saguna Brahman, the Eternal with infinite qualities, the One who is the Many, the infinite Person who is the source and foundation of all persons and personalities, the Lord of creation, the Word, the Master of all works and action; it is that which being known all is known: these affirmatives correspond to those negatives. For it is not possible in a supramental cognition to split asunder the two sides of the One Existence, — even to speak of them as sides is excessive, for they are in each other, their co-existence or one-existence is eternal and their powers sustaining each other found the self-manifestation of the Infinite.

But neither is the separate cognition of them entirely an illusion or a complete error of the Ignorance; this too has its validity for spiritual experience. For these primary aspects of the Absolute are fundamental spiritual determinates or inde-terminates answering at this spiritual end or beginning to the general determinates or generic indeterminates of the material end or inconscient beginning of the descending and ascending Manifestation. Those that seem to us negative carry in them the freedom of the Infinite from limitation by its own determinations; their realisation disengages the spirit within, liberates us and enables us to participate in this supremacy: thus, when once we pass into or through the experience of immutable self, we are no longer bound and limited in the inner status of our being by the determinations and creations of Nature. On the other, the dynamic side, this original freedom enables the Consciousness to create a world of determinations without being bound by it: it enables it also to withdraw from what it has created and re-create in a higher truth-formula. It is on this freedom that is based the spirit's power of infinite variation of the truth-possibilities of existence and also its capacity to create, without tying itself to its workings, any and every form of Necessity or system of order: the individual being too by experience of these negating absolutes can participate in that dynamic liberty, can pass from one order of self-formulation to a higher order. At the stage when from the mental it has to move towards its supramental status, one most liberatingly helpful, if not indispensable experience that may intervene is the entry into a total Nirvana of mentality and mental ego, a passage into the silence of the Spirit. In any case, a realisation of the pure Self must always precede the transition to that mediating eminence of the consciousness from which a clear vision of the ascending and descending stairs of manifested existence is commanded and the possession of the free power of ascent and descent becomes a spiritual prerogative. An independent completeness of identity with each of the primal aspects and powers — not narrowing as in the mind into a sole engrossing experience seeming to be final and integral, for that would be incompatible with the realisation of the unity of all aspects and powers of existence — is a capacity inherent in consciousness in the Infinite; that indeed is the base and justification of the overmind cognition and its will to carry each aspect, each power, each possibility to its independent fullness. But the Supermind keeps always and in every status or condition the spiritual realisation of the Unity of all; the intimate presence of that unity is there even within the completest grasp of each thing, each state given its whole delight of itself, power and value: there is thus no losing sight of the affirmative aspects even when there is the full acceptance of the truth of the negative. The Overmind keeps still the sense of this underlying Unity; that is for it the secure base of the independent experience. In Mind the knowledge of the unity of all aspects is lost on the surface, the consciousness is plunged into engrossing, exclusive separate affirmations; but there too, even in the Mind's ignorance, the total reality still remains behind the exclusive absorption and can be recovered in the form of a profound mental intuition or else in the idea or sentiment of an underlying truth of integral oneness; in the spiritual mind this can develop into an ever-present experience.

All aspects of the omnipresent Reality have their fundamental truth in the Supreme Existence. Thus even the aspect or power of Inconscience, which seems to be an opposite, a negation of the eternal Reality, yet corresponds to a Truth held in itself by the self-aware and all-conscious Infinite. It is, when we look closely at it, the Infinite's power of plunging the consciousness into a trance of self-involution, a self-oblivion of the Spirit veiled in its own abysses where nothing is manifest but all inconceivably is and can emerge from that ineffable latency. In the heights of Spirit this state of cosmic or infinite trance-sleep appears to our cognition as a luminous uttermost Superconscience: at the other end of being it offers itself to cognition as the Spirit's potency of presenting to itself the opposites of its own truths of being, — an abyss of non-existence, a profound Night of inconscience, a fathomless swoon of insensibility from which yet all forms of being, consciousness and delight of existence can manifest themselves, — but they appear in limited terms, in slowly emerging and increasing self-formulations, even in contrary terms of themselves; it is the play of a secret all-being, all-delight, all-knowledge, but it observes the rules of its own self-oblivion, self-opposition, self-limitation until it is ready to surpass it. This is the Inconscience and Ignorance that we see at work in the material universe. It is not a denial, it is one term, one formula of the infinite and eternal Existence.

It is important to observe here the sense that is acquired

in such a total cognition of cosmic being by the phenomenon
of the Ignorance, its assigned place in the spiritual economy
of the universe. If all that we experience were an imposition,
an unreal creation in the Absolute, both cosmic and individual
existence would be in their very nature an Ignorance; the sole
real knowledge would be the indeterminable self-awareness of
the Absolute. If all were the erection of a temporal and phenomenal creation over against the reality of the witnessing timeless
Eternal and if the creation were not a manifestation of the Reality but an arbitrary self-effective cosmic construction, that too
would be a sort of imposition. Our knowledge of the creation
would be the knowledge of a temporary structure of evanescent
consciousness and being, a dubious Becoming that passes across
the vision of the Eternal, not a knowledge of Reality; that too
would be an Ignorance. But if all is a manifestation of the Reality
and itself real by the constituting immanence, the substantiating
essence and presence of the Reality, then the awareness of individual being and world-being would be in its spiritual origin and
nature a play of the infinite self-knowledge and all-knowledge:
ignorance could be only a subordinate movement, a suppressed
or restricted cognition or a partial and imperfect evolving knowledge with the true and total self-awareness and all-awareness
concealed both in it and behind it. It would be a temporary phenomenon, not the cause and essence of cosmic existence; its inevitable consummation would be a return of the spirit, not out of
the cosmos to a sole supracosmic self-awareness, but even in the
cosmos itself to an integral self-knowledge and all-knowledge.

It might be objected that the supramental cognition is, after
all, not the final truth of things. Beyond the supramental plane of
consciousness which is an intermediate step from overmind and
mind to the complete experience of Sachchidananda, are the
greatest heights of the manifested Spirit: here surely existence
would not at all be based on the determination of the One in
multiplicity, it would manifest solely and simply a pure identity
in oneness. But the supramental Truth-Consciousness would not
be absent from these planes, for it is an inherent power of Sachchidananda: the difference would be that the determinations

would not be demarcations, they would be plastic, interfused, each a boundless finite. For there all is in each and each is in all radically and integrally, — there would be to the utmost a fundamental awareness of identity, a mutual inclusion and interpenetration of consciousness: knowledge as we envisage it would not exist, because it would not be needed, since all would be direct action of consciousness in being itself, identical, intimate, intrinsically self-aware and all-aware. But still relations of consciousness, relations of mutual delight of existence, relations of self-power of being with self-power of being would not be excluded; these highest spiritual planes would not be a field of blank indeterminability, a vacancy of pure existence.

It might be said again that, even so, in Sachchidananda itself at least, above all worlds of manifestation, there could be nothing but the self-awareness of pure existence and consciousness and a pure delight of existence. Or, indeed, this triune being itself might well be only a trinity of original spiritual self-determinations of the Infinite; these too, like all determinations, would cease to exist in the ineffable Absolute. But our position is that these must be inherent truths of the supreme being; their utmost reality must be pre-existent in the Absolute even if they are ineffably other there than what they are in the spiritual mind's highest possible experience. The Absolute is not a mystery of infinite blankness nor a supreme sum of negations; nothing can manifest that is not justified by some self-power of the original and omnipresent Reality.

Chapter II

Brahman, Purusha, Ishwara —
Maya, Prakriti, Shakti

It is there in beings indivisible and as if divided. *Gita.*[1]

Brahman, the Truth, the Knowledge, the Infinite.
Taittiriya Upanishad.[2]

Know Purusha and Prakriti to be both eternal without beginning. *Gita.*[3]

One must know Maya as Prakriti and the Master of Maya as the great Lord of all. *Swetaswatara Upanishad.*[4]

It is the might of the Godhead in the world that turns the wheel of Brahman. Him one must know, the supreme Lord of all lords, the supreme Godhead above all godheads. Supreme too is his Shakti and manifold the natural working of her knowledge and her force. One Godhead, occult in all beings, the inner Self of all beings, the all-pervading, absolute without qualities, the overseer of all actions, the witness, the knower.
Swetaswatara Upanishad.[5]

THERE is then a supreme Reality eternal, absolute and infinite. Because it is absolute and infinite, it is in its essence indeterminable. It is indefinable and inconceivable by finite and defining Mind; it is ineffable by a mind-created speech; it is describable neither by our negations, *neti neti*, — for we cannot limit it by saying it is not this, it is not that, — nor by our affirmations, for we cannot fix it by saying it is this, it is that, *iti iti*. And yet, though in this way unknowable to

---

[1] XIII. 17.   [2] II. 1.   [3] XIII. 20.   [4] IV. 10.   [5] VI. 1, 7, 8, 11.

us, it is not altogether and in every way unknowable; it is self-evident to itself and, although inexpressible, yet self-evident to a knowledge by identity of which the spiritual being in us must be capable; for that spiritual being is in its essence and its original and intimate reality not other than this Supreme Existence.

But although thus indeterminable to Mind, because of its absoluteness and infinity, we discover that this Supreme and Eternal Infinite determines itself to our consciousness in the universe by real and fundamental truths of its being which are beyond the universe and in it and are the very foundation of its existence. These truths present themselves to our conceptual cognition as the fundamental aspects in which we see and experience the omnipresent Reality. In themselves they are seized directly, not by intellectual understanding but by a spiritual intuition, a spiritual experience in the very substance of our consciousness; but they can also be caught at in conception by a large and plastic idea and can be expressed in some sort by a plastic speech which does not insist too much on rigid definition or limit the wideness and subtlety of the idea. In order to express this experience or this idea with any nearness a language has to be created which is at once intuitively metaphysical and revealingly poetic, admitting significant and living images as the vehicle of a close, suggestive and vivid indication, — a language such as we find hammered out into a subtle and pregnant massiveness in the Veda and the Upanishads. In the ordinary tongue of metaphysical thought we have to be content with a distant indication, an approximation by abstractions, which may still be of some service to our intellect, for it is this kind of speech which suits our method of logical and rational understanding; but if it is to be of real service, the intellect must consent to pass out of the bounds of a finite logic and accustom itself to the logic of the Infinite. On this condition alone, by this way of seeing and thinking, it ceases to be paradoxical or futile to speak of the ineffable: but if we insist on applying a finite logic to the Infinite, the omnipresent Reality will escape us and we shall grasp instead an abstract shadow, a dead form petrified into speech or a hard incisive graph which speaks of the Reality but does not express it. Our way of knowing must be appropriate to that which is to be known; otherwise we achieve only a distant speculation, a figure of knowledge and not veritable knowledge.

The supreme Truth-aspect which thus manifests itself to us is an eternal and infinite and absolute self-existence, self-awareness, self-delight of being; this founds all things and secretly supports and pervades all things. This Self-existence reveals itself again in three terms of its essential nature, — Self, Conscious Being or Spirit, and God or the Divine Being. The Indian terms are more satisfactory, — Brahman the Reality is Atman, Purusha, Ishwara; for these terms grew from a root of Intuition and, while they have a comprehensive preciseness, are capable of a plastic application which avoids both vagueness in the use and the rigid snare of a too limiting intellectual concept. The Supreme Brahman is that which in Western metaphysics is called the Absolute: but Brahman is at the same time the omnipresent Reality in which all that is relative exists as its forms or its movements; this is an Absolute which takes all relativities in its embrace. The Upanishads affirm that all this is the Brahman; Mind is Brahman, Life is Brahman, Matter is Brahman; addressing Vayu, the Lord of Air, of Life, it is said "O Vayu, thou art manifest Brahman"; and, pointing to man and beast and bird and insect, each separately is identified with the One, — "O Brahman, thou art this old man and boy and girl, this bird, this insect." Brahman is the Consciousness that knows itself in all that exists; Brahman is the Force that sustains the power of God and Titan and Demon, the Force that acts in man and animal and the forms and energies of Nature; Brahman is the Ananda, the secret Bliss of existence which is the ether of our being and without which none could breathe or live. Brahman is the inner Soul in all; it has taken a form in correspondence with each created form which it inhabits. The Lord of Beings is that which is conscious in the conscious being, but he is also the Conscious in inconscient things, the One who is master and in control of the many that are passive in the hands of Force-Nature. He is the Timeless and Time; he is Space and all that is in Space; he is Causality and the cause and the effect: He is the thinker and his thought, the warrior and his courage, the gambler and his dice-throw. All realities and all aspects and all semblances are the Brahman; Brahman is the Absolute, the transcendent and incommunicable, the Supracosmic Existence that sustains the cosmos, the Cosmic Self that upholds all beings, but It is too the self of each individual: the soul or psychic entity is an eternal portion of the Ishwara; it is his supreme Nature or Consciousness-Force that has become the living being in a world of living beings. The Brahman alone is, and because of It all are, for all are the Brahman; this Reality is the reality of everything that we see in Self and Nature. Brahman, the Ishwara, is all this by his Yoga-Maya, by the power of his Consciousness-Force put out in self-manifestation: he is the Conscious Being, Soul, Spirit, Purusha, and it is by his Nature, the force of his conscious self-existence that he is all things; he is the Ishwara, the omniscient and omnipotent All-ruler, and it is by his Shakti, his conscious Power, that he manifests himself in Time and governs the universe. These and similar statements taken together are all-comprehensive: it is possible for the mind to cut and select, to build a closed system and explain away all that does not fit within it; but it is on the complete and many-sided statement that we must take our stand if we have to acquire an integral knowledge.

An absolute, eternal and infinite Self-existence, Self-aware-ness, Self-delight of being that secretly supports and pervades the universe even while it is also beyond it, is, then, the first truth of spiritual experience. But this truth of being has at once an impersonal and a personal aspect; it is not only Existence, it is the one Being absolute, eternal and infinite. As there are three fundamental aspects in which we meet this Reality, — Self, Conscious Being or Spirit and God, the Divine Being, or to use the Indian terms, the absolute and omnipresent Reality, Brahman, manifest to us as Atman, Purusha, Ishwara, — so too its power of Consciousness appears to us in three aspects: it is the self-force of that consciousness conceptively creative of all things, Maya; it is Prakriti, Nature or Force made dynamically executive, working out all things under the witnessing eye of the Conscious Being, the Self or Spirit; it is the conscious Power of the Divine Being, Shakti, which is both conceptively creative and dynamically executive of all the divine workings. These three aspects and their powers base and comprise the whole of existence and all Nature and, taken together as a single whole, they reconcile the apparent disparateness and incompatibility of the supracosmic Transcendence, the cosmic universality and the separativeness of our individual existence; the Absolute, cosmic Nature and ourselves are linked in oneness by this triune aspect of the one Reality. For taken by itself the existence of the Absolute, the Supreme Brahman, would be a contradiction of the relative universe and our own real existence would be incompatible with its sole incommunicable Reality. But the Brahman is at the same time omnipresent in all relativities; it is the Absolute independent of all relatives, the Absolute basing all relatives, the Absolute governing, pervading, constituting all relatives; there is nothing that is not the omnipresent Reality. In observing the triple aspect and the triple power we come to see how this is possible.

If we look at this picture of the Self-Existence and its works as a unitary unlimited whole of vision, it stands together and imposes itself by its convincing totality: but to the analysis of the logical intellect it offers an abundance of difficulties, such as all attempts to erect a logical system out of a perception of an illimitable Existence must necessarily create; for any such endeavour must either effect consistency by an arbitrary sectioning of the complex truth of things or else by its comprehensiveness become logically untenable. For we see that the Indeterminable determines itself as infinite and finite, the Immutable admits a constant mutability and endless differences, the One becomes an innumerable multitude, the Impersonal creates or supports personality, is itself a Person; the Self has a nature and is yet other than its nature; Being turns into becoming and yet it is always itself and other than its becomings; the Universal individualises itself and the Individual universalises himself; Brahman is at once void of qualities and capable of infinite qualities, the Lord and

Doer of works, yet a non-doer and a silent witness of the workings of Nature. If we look carefully at these workings of Nature, once we put aside the veil of familiarity and our unthinking acquiescence in the process of things as natural because so they always happen, we discover that all she does in whole or in parts is a miracle, an act of some incomprehensible magic. The being of the Self-existence and the world that has appeared in it are, each of them and both together, a suprarational mystery. There seems to us to be a reason in things because the processes of the physical finite are consistent to our view and their law determinable, but this reason in things, when closely examined, seems to stumble at every moment against the irrational or infrarational and the suprarational: the consistency, the determinability of process seems to lessen rather than increase as we pass from matter to life and from life to mentality; if the finite consents to some extent to look as if it were rational, the infinitesimal refuses to be bound by the same laws and the infinite is unseizable. As for the action of the universe and its significance, it escapes us altogether; if Self, God or Spirit there be, his dealings with the world and us are incomprehensible, offer no clue that we can follow. God and Nature and even ourselves move in a mysterious way which is only partially and at points intelligible, but as a whole escapes our comprehension. All the works of Maya look like the production of a suprarational magical Power which arranges things according to its wisdom or its phantasy, but a wisdom which is not ours and a phantasy which baffles our imagination. The Spirit that manifests things or manifests itself in them so obscurely, looks to our reason like a Magician and his power or Maya a creative magic: but magic can create illusions or it can create astounding realities, and we find it difficult to decide which of these suprarational processes faces us in this universe.

But, in fact, the cause of this impression must necessarily be sought not in anything illusory or fantastic in the Supreme or the universal Self-existence, but in our own inability to seize the supreme clue to its manifold existence or discover the secret plan and pattern of its action. The Self-existent is the Infinite and its way of being and of action must be the way of the Infinite, but our consciousness is limited, our reason built upon things finite: it is irrational to suppose that a finite consciousness and reason can be a measure of the Infinite; this smallness cannot judge that Immensity; this poverty bound to a limited use of its scanty means cannot conceive the opulent management of those riches; an ignorant half-knowledge cannot follow the motions of an All-Knowledge. Our reasoning is based upon our experience of the finite operations of physical Nature, on an incomplete observation and uncertain understanding of something that acts within limits; it has organised on that basis certain conceptions which it seeks to make general and universal, and whatever contradicts or departs from these conceptions it regards as irrational, false or inexplicable. But there are different orders of the reality and the conceptions, measures, standards suitable to one need not be applicable to another order. Our physical being is built first upon an aggregate of infinitesimals, electrons, atoms, molecules, cells; but the law of action of these infinitesimals does not explain all the physical workings even of the human body, much less can they cover all the law and process of action of man's supraphysical parts, his life movements and mind movements and soul movements. In the body finites have been formed with their own habits, properties, characteristic ways of action; the body itself is a finite which is not a mere aggregate of these smaller finites which it uses as parts, organs, constituent instruments of its operations; it has developed a being and has a general law which surpasses its dependence upon these elements or constituents. The life and mind again are supraphysical finites with a different and more subtle mode of operation of their own, and no dependence on the physical parts for instrumentation can annul their intrinsic character; there is something more and other in our vital and mental being and vital and mental forces than the functioning of a physical body. But, again, each finite is in its reality or has behind it an Infinite which has built and supports and directs the finite it has made as its self-figure; so that even the being and law and process of the finite cannot be totally understood without a knowledge of that which is occult within or behind it: our finite knowledge, conceptions, standards may be valid within their limits, but they are incomplete and relative. A law founded upon an observation of what is divided in Space and Time cannot be confidently applied to the being and action of the Indivisible; not only it cannot be applied to the spaceless and timeless Infinite, but it cannot be applied even to a Time Infinite or a Space Infinite. A law and process binding for our superficial being need not be binding on what is occult within us. Again, our intellect, founding itself on reason, finds it difficult to deal with what is infrarational; life is infrarational and we find that our intellectual reason applying itself to life is constantly forcing upon it a control, a measure, an artificial procrustean rule that either succeeds in killing or petrifying life or constrains it into rigid forms and conventions that lame and imprison its capacity or ends by a bungle, a revolt of life, a decay or disruption of the systems and superstructures built upon it by our intelligence. An instinct, an intuition is needed which the intellect has not at its command and does not always listen to when it comes in of itself to help the mental working. But still more difficult must it be for our reason to understand and deal with the suprarational; the suprarational is the realm of the spirit, and in the largeness, subtlety, profundity, complexity of its movement the reason is lost; here intuition and inner experience alone are the guide, or, if there is any other, it is that of which intuition is only a sharp edge, an intense projected ray, — the final enlightenment must come from the suprarational Truth-Consciousness, from a supramental vision and knowledge.

But the being and action of the Infinite must not be therefore regarded as if it were a magic void of all reason; there is, on the contrary, a greater reason in all the operations of the Infinite, but it is not a mental or intellectual, it is a spiritual and supramental reason: there is a logic in it, because there are relations and connections infallibly seen and executed; what is magic to our finite reason is the logic of the Infinite. It is a greater reason, a greater logic because it is more vast, subtle, complex in its operations: it comprehends all the data which our observation fails to seize, it deduces from them results which neither our deduction nor

induction can anticipate, because our conclusions and inferences
have a meagre foundation and are fallible and brittle. If we observe a happening, we judge and explain it from the result and
from a glimpse of its most external constituents, circumstances
or causes; but each happening is the outcome of a complex nexus
of forces which we do not and cannot observe, because all forces
are to us invisible, — but they are not invisible to the spiritual
vision of the Infinite: some of them are actualities working to
produce or occasion a new actuality, some are possibles that are
near to the pre-existent actuals and in a way included in their
aggregate; but there can intervene always new possibilities that
suddenly become dynamic potentials and add themselves to the
nexus, and behind all are imperatives or an imperative which
these possibilities are labouring to actualise. Moreover, out of
the same nexus of forces different results are possible; what
will come out of them is determined by a sanction which was no
doubt waiting and ready all the time but seems to come in rapidly
to intervene and alter everything, a decisive divine imperative.
All this our reason cannot grasp because it is the instrument of
an ignorance with a very limited vision and a small stock of
accumulated and not always very certain or reliable knowledge
and because too it has no means of direct awareness; for this
is the difference between intuition and intellect, that intuition is
born of a direct awareness while intellect is an indirect action
of a knowledge which constructs itself with difficulty out of the
unknown from signs and indications and gathered data. But
what is not evident to our reason and senses, is self-evident to
the Infinite Consciousness, and, if there is a Will of the Infinite,
it must be a Will that acts in this full knowledge and is the
perfect spontaneous result of a total self-evidence. It is neither a
hampered evolutionary Force bound by what it has evolved nor
an imaginative Will acting in the void upon a free caprice; it is
the truth of the Infinite affirming itself in the determinations of
the finite.

It is evident that such a Consciousness and Will need not
act in harmony with the conclusions of our limited reason or
according to a procedure familiar to it and approved of by our

constructed notions or in subjection to an ethical reason working for a limited and fragmentary good; it might and does admit things deemed by our reason irrational and unethical because that was necessary for the final and total Good and for the working out of a cosmic purpose. What seems to us irrational or reprehensible in relation to a partial set of facts, motives, desiderata might be perfectly rational and approvable in relation to a much vaster motive and totality of data and desiderata. Reason with its partial vision sets up constructed conclusions which it strives to turn into general rules of knowledge and action and it compels into its rule by some mental device or gets rid of what does not suit with it: an infinite Consciousness would have no such rules, it would have instead large intrinsic truths governing automatically conclusion and result, but adapting them differently and spontaneously to a different total of circumstances, so that by this pliability and free adaptation it might seem to the narrower faculty to have no standards whatever. In the same way, we cannot judge of the principle and dynamic operation of infinite being by the standards of finite existence, — what might be impossible for the one would be normal and self-evidently natural states and motives for the greater freer Reality. It is this that makes the difference between our fragmentary mind consciousness constructing integers out of its fractions and an essential and total consciousness, vision and knowledge. It is not indeed possible, so long as we are compelled to use reason as our main support, for it to abdicate altogether in favour of an undeveloped or half-organised intuition; but it is imperative on us in a consideration of the Infinite and its being and action to enforce on our reason an utmost plasticity and open it to an awareness of the larger states and possibilities of that which we are striving to consider. It will not do to apply our limited and limiting conclusions to That which is illimitable. If we concentrate only on one aspect and treat it as the whole, we illustrate the story of the blind men and the elephant; each of the blind inquirers touched a different part and concluded that the whole animal was some object resembling the part of which he had had the touch. An experience of some one aspect of the

Infinite is valid in itself; but we cannot generalise from it that the Infinite is that alone, nor would it be safe to view the rest of the Infinite in the terms of that aspect and exclude all other viewpoints of spiritual experience. The Infinite is at once an essentiality, a boundless totality and a multitude; all these have to be known in order to know truly the Infinite. To see the parts alone and the totality not at all or only as a sum of the parts is a knowledge, but also at the same time an ignorance; to see the totality alone and ignore the parts is also a knowledge and at the same time an ignorance, for a part may be greater than the whole because it belongs to the transcendence; to see the essence alone because it takes us back straight towards the transcendence and negate the totality and the parts is a penultimate knowledge, but here too there is a capital ignorance. A whole knowledge must be there and the reason must become plastic enough to look at all sides, all aspects and seek through them for that in which they are one.

Thus too, if we see only the aspect of Self, we may concentrate on its static silence and miss the dynamic truth of the Infinite; if we see only the Ishwara, we may seize the dynamic truth but miss the eternal status and the infinite silence, become aware of only dynamic being, dynamic consciousness, dynamic delight of being, but miss the pure existence, pure consciousness, pure bliss of being. If we concentrate on Purusha-Prakriti alone, we may see only the dichotomy of Soul and Nature, Spirit and Matter, and miss their unity. In considering the action of the Infinite we have to avoid the error of the disciple who thought of himself as the Brahman, refused to obey the warning of the elephant-driver to budge from the narrow path and was taken up by the elephant's trunk and removed out of the way; "You are no doubt the Brahman," said the master to his bewildered disciple, "but why did you not obey the driver Brahman and get out of the path of the elephant Brahman?" We must not commit the mistake of emphasising one side of the Truth and concluding from it or acting upon it to the exclusion of all other sides and aspects of the Infinite. The realisation "I am That" is true, but we cannot safely proceed on it unless we realise also that all is

That; our self-existence is a fact, but we must also be aware of other selves, of the same Self in other beings and of That which exceeds both own-self and other-self. The Infinite is one in a multiplicity and its action is only seizable by a supreme Reason which regards all and acts as a one-awareness that observes itself in difference and respects its own differences, so that each thing and each being has its form of essential being and its form of dynamic nature, *svarūpa*, *svadharma*, and all are respected in the total working. The knowledge and action of the Infinite is one in an unbound variability: it would be from the point of view of the infinite Truth equally an error to insist either on a sameness of action in all circumstances or on a diversity of action without any unifying truth and harmony behind the diversity. In our own principle of conduct, if we sought to act in this greater Truth, it would be equally an error to insist on our self alone or to insist on other selves alone; it is the Self of all on which we have to found a unity of action and a total, infinitely plastic yet harmonious diversity of action; for that is the nature of the working of the Infinite.

If we look from this viewpoint of a larger more plastic reason, taking account of the logic of the Infinite, at the difficulties which meet our intelligence when it tries to conceive the absolute and omnipresent Reality, we shall see that the whole difficulty is verbal and conceptual and not real. Our intelligence looks at its concept of the Absolute and sees that it must be indeterminable and at the same time it sees a world of determinations which emanates from the Absolute and exists in it, — for it can emanate from nowhere else and can exist nowhere else; it is further baffled by the affirmation, also hardly disputable on the premises, that all these determinates are nothing else than this very indeterminable Absolute. But the contradiction disappears when we understand that the indeterminability is not in its true sense negative, not an imposition of incapacity on the Infinite, but positive, a freedom within itself from limitation by its own determinations and necessarily a freedom from all external determination by anything not itself, since there is no real possibility of such a not-self coming into existence. The Infinite is illimitably free, free to determine itself infinitely, free from all restraining effect of its own creations. In fact the Infinite does not create, it manifests what is in itself, in its own essence of reality; it is itself that essence of all reality and all realities are powers of that one Reality. The Absolute neither creates nor is created, — in the current sense of making or being made; we can speak of creation only in the sense of the Being becoming in form and movement what it already is in substance and status. Yet we have to emphasise its indeterminability in that special and positive sense, not as a negation but as an indispensable condition of its free infinite self-determination, because without that the Reality would be a fixed eternal determinate or else an indeterminate fixed and bound to a sum of possibilities of determination inherent within it. Its freedom from all limitation, from any binding by its own creation cannot be itself turned into a limitation, an absolute incapacity, a denial of all freedom of self-determination; it is this that would be a contradiction, it would be an attempt to define and limit by negation the infinite and illimitable. Into the central fact of the two sides of the nature of the Absolute, the essential and the self-creative or dynamic, no real contradiction enters; it is only a pure infinite essence that can formulate itself in infinite ways. One statement is complementary to the other, there is no mutual cancellation, no incompatibility; it is only the dual statement of a single inescapable fact by human reason in human language.

The same conciliation occurs everywhere, when we look with a straight and accurate look on the truth of the Reality. In our experience of it we become aware of an Infinite essentially free from all limitation by qualities, properties, features; on the other hand, we are aware of an Infinite teeming with innumerable qualities, properties, features. Here again the statement of illimitable freedom is positive, not negative; it does not negate what we see, but on the contrary provides the indispensable condition for it, it makes possible a free and infinite self-expression in quality and feature. A quality is the character of a power of conscious being; or we may say that the consciousness of being expressing what is in it makes the power it brings out recognisable by a native stamp on it which we call quality or character. Courage as a quality is such a power of being, it is a certain character of my consciousness expressing a formulated force of my being, bringing out or creating a definite kind of force of my nature in action. So too the power of a drug to cure is its property, a special force of being native to the herb or mineral from which it is produced, and this speciality is determined by the Real-Idea concealed in the involved consciousness which dwells in the plant or mineral; the idea brings out in it what was there at the root of its manifestation and has now come out thus empowered as the force of its being. All qualities, properties, features are such powers of conscious being thus put forth from itself by the Absolute; It has everything within It, It has the free power to put all forth;[6] yet we cannot define the Absolute as a quality of courage or a power of healing, we cannot even say that these are a characteristic feature of the Absolute, nor can we make up a sum of qualities and say "that is the Absolute". But neither can we speak of the Absolute as a pure blank incapable of manifesting these things; on the contrary, all capacity is there, the powers of all qualities and characters are there inherent within it. The mind is in a difficulty because it has to say, "The Absolute or Infinite is none of these things, these things are not the Absolute or Infinite" and at the same time it has to say, "The Absolute is all these things, they are not something else than That, for That is the sole existence and the all-existence." Here it is evident that it is an undue finiteness of thought conception and verbal expression which creates the difficulty, but there is in reality none; for it would be evidently absurd to say that the Absolute is courage or curing-power, or to say that courage and curing-power are the Absolute, but it would be equally absurd to deny the capacity of the Absolute to put forth courage or curing-power as self-expressions in its manifestation. When the logic of the finite fails us, we have to see with a direct and unbound vision what is behind in the logic

---

[6] The word for creation in Sanskrit means a loosing or putting forth of what is in the being.

of the Infinite. We can then realise that the Infinite is infinite in quality, feature, power, but that no sum of qualities, features, powers can describe the Infinite.

We see that the Absolute, the Self, the Divine, the Spirit, the Being is One; the Transcendental is one, the Cosmic is one: but we see also that beings are many and each has a self, a spirit, a like yet different nature. And since the spirit and essence of things is one, we are obliged to admit that all these many must be that One, and it follows that the One is or has become many; but how can the limited or relative be the Absolute and how can man or beast or bird be the Divine Being? But in erecting this apparent contradiction the mind makes a double error. It is thinking in the terms of the mathematical finite unit which is sole in limitation, the one which is less than two and can become two only by division and fragmentation or by addition and multiplication; but this is an infinite Oneness, it is the essential and infinite Oneness which can contain the hundred and the thousand and the million and billion and trillion. Whatever astronomic or more than astronomic figures you heap and multiply, they cannot overpass or exceed that Oneness; for, in the language of the Upanishad, it moves not, yet is always far in front when you would pursue and seize it. It can be said of it that it would not be the infinite Oneness if it were not capable of an infinite multiplicity; but that does not mean that the One is plural or can be limited or described as the sum of the Many: on the contrary, it can be the infinite Many because it exceeds all limitation or description by multiplicity and exceeds at the same time all limitation by finite conceptual oneness. Pluralism is an error because, though there is the spiritual plurality, the many souls are dependent and interdependent existences; their sum also is not the One nor is it the cosmic totality; they depend on the One and exist by its Oneness: yet the plurality is not unreal, it is the One Soul that dwells as the individual in these many souls and they are eternal in the One and by the one Eternal. This is difficult for the mental reason which makes an opposition between the Infinite and the finite and associates finiteness with plurality and infinity with oneness; but in the logic of the Infinite there is no such opposition and the eternity of the Many in the One is a thing that is perfectly natural and possible.

Again, we see that there is an infinite pure status and immobile silence of the Spirit; we see too that there is a boundless movement of the Spirit, a power, a dynamic spiritual all-containing self-extension of the Infinite. Our conceptions foist upon this perception, in itself valid and accurate, an opposition between the silence and status and the dynamis and movement, but to the reason and the logic of the Infinite there can be no such opposition. A solely silent and static Infinite, an Infinite without an infinite power and dynamis and energy is inadmissible except as the perception of an aspect; a powerless Absolute, an impotent Spirit is unthinkable: an infinite energy must be the dynamis of the Infinite, an all-power must be the potency of the Absolute, an illimitable force must be the force of the Spirit. But the silence, the status are the basis of the movement, an eternal immobility is the necessary condition, field, essence even, of the infinite mobility, a stable being is the condition and foundation of the vast action of the Force of being. It is when we arrive at something of this silence, stability, immobility that we can base on it a force and energy which in our superficial restless state would be inconceivable. The opposition we make is mental and conceptual; in reality, the silence of the Spirit and the dynamis of the Spirit are complementary truths and inseparable. The immutable silent Spirit may hold its infinite energy silent and immobile within it, for it is not bound by its own forces, is not their subject or instrument, but it does possess them, does release them, is capable of an eternal and infinite action, does not weary or need to stop, and yet all the time its silent immobility inherent in its action and movement is not for a moment shaken or disturbed or altered by its action and movement; the witness silence of the Spirit is there in the very grain of all the voices and workings of Nature. These things may be difficult for us to understand because our own surface finite capacity in either direction is limited and our conceptions are based on our limitations; but it should be easy to see that these relative and finite conceptions do not apply to the Absolute and Infinite.

Our conception of the Infinite is formlessness, but everywhere we see form and forms surrounding us and it can be and is affirmed of the Divine Being that he is at once Form and the Formless. For here too the apparent contradiction does not correspond to a real opposition; the Formless is not a negation of the power of formation, but the condition for the Infinite's free formation: for otherwise there would be a single Form or only a fixity or sum of possible forms in a finite universe. The formlessness is the character of the spiritual essence, the spirit-substance of the Reality; all finite realities are powers, forms, self-shapings of that substance: the Divine is formless and nameless, but by that very reason capable of manifesting all possible names and shapes of being. Forms are manifestations, not arbitrary inventions out of nothing; for line and colour, mass and design which are the essentials of form carry always in them a significance, are, it might be said, secret values and significances of an unseen reality made visible; it is for that reason that figure, line, hue, mass, composition can embody what would be otherwise unseen, can convey what would be otherwise occult to the sense. Form may be said to be the innate body, the inevitable self-revelation of the formless, and this is true not only of external shapes, but of the unseen formations of mind and life which we seize only by our thought and those sensible forms of which only the subtle grasp of the inner consciousness can become aware. Name in its deeper sense is not the word by which we describe the object, but the total of power, quality, character of the reality which a form of things embodies and which we try to sum up by a designating sound, a knowable name, *Nomen*. *Nomen* in this sense, we might say, is *Numen*; the secret Names of the Gods are their power, quality, character of being caught up by the consciousness and made conceivable. The Infinite is nameless, but in that namelessness all possible names, Numens of the gods, the names and forms of all realities, are already envisaged and prefigured, because they are there latent and inherent in the All-Existence.

It becomes clear from these considerations that the co-existence of the Infinite and the finite, which is the very nature of universal being, is not a juxtaposition or mutual inclusion of two opposites, but as natural and inevitable as the relation of the principle of Light and Fire with the suns. The finite is a frontal aspect and a self-determination of the Infinite; no finite can exist in itself and by itself, it exists by the Infinite and because it is of one essence with the Infinite. For by the Infinite we do not mean solely an illimitable self-extension in Space and Time, but something that is also spaceless and timeless, a self-existent Indefinable and Illimitable which can express itself in the infinitesimal as well as in the vast, in a second of time, in a point of space, in a passing circumstance. The finite is looked upon as a division of the Indivisible, but there is no such thing: for this division is only apparent; there is a demarcation, but no real separation is possible. When we see with the inner vision and sense and not with the physical eye a tree or other object, what we become aware of is an infinite one Reality constituting the tree or object, pervading its every atom and molecule, forming them out of itself, building the whole nature, process of becoming, operation of indwelling energy; all of these are itself, are this infinite, this Reality: we see it extending indivisibly and uniting all objects so that none is really separate from it or quite separate from other objects. "It stands," says the Gita, "undivided in beings and yet as if divided." Thus each object is that Infinite and one in essential being with all other objects that are also forms and names, — powers, numens, — of the Infinite.

This incoercible unity in all divisions and diversities is the mathematics of the Infinite, indicated in a verse of the Upanishads, — "This is the complete and That is the complete; subtract the complete from the complete, the complete is the remainder." For so too it may be said of the infinite self-multiplication of the Reality that all things are that self-multiplication; the One becomes Many, but all these Many are That which was already and is always itself and in becoming the Many remains the One. There is no division of the One by the appearance of the finite, for it is the one Infinite that appears to us as the many finite: the creation adds nothing to the Infinite; it remains after creation what it was before. The Infinite is not a sum of

things, it is That which is all things and more. If this logic of
the Infinite contradicts the conceptions of our finite reason, it
is because it exceeds it and does not base itself on the data of
the limited phenomenon, but embraces the Reality and sees the
truth of all phenomena in the truth of the Reality; it does not
see them as separate beings, movements, names, forms, things;
for that they cannot be, since they could be that only if they
were phenomena in the Void, things without a common basis or
essence, fundamentally unconnected, connected only by coexistence and pragmatic relation, not realities which exist by their
root of unity and, so far as they can be considered independent,
are secured in their independence of outer or inner figure and
movement only by their perpetual dependence on their parent
Infinite, their secret identity with the one Identical. The Identical
is their root, their cause of form, the one power of their varying
powers, their constituting substance.

The Identical to our notions is the Immutable; it is ever the
same through eternity, for if it is or becomes subject to mutation or if it admits of differences, it ceases to be identical; but
what we see everywhere is an infinitely variable fundamental
oneness which seems the very principle of Nature. The basic
Force is one, but it manifests from itself innumerable forces;
the basic substance is one, but it develops many different sub-
stances and millions of unlike objects; mind is one but differentiates itself into many mental states, mind-formations, thoughts,
perceptions differing from each other and entering into harmony
or into conflict; life is one, but the forms of life are unlike and
innumerable; humanity is one in nature, but there are different
race types and every individual man is himself and in some way
unlike others; Nature insists on tracing lines of difference on the
leaves of one tree; she drives differentiation so far that it has
been found that the lines on one man's thumb are different from
the lines of every other man's thumb so that he can be identified
by that differentiation alone, — yet fundamentally all men are
alike and there is no essential difference. Oneness or sameness is
everywhere, differentiation is everywhere; the indwelling Reality
has built the universe on the principle of the development of one

seed into a million different fashions. But this again is the logic of the Infinite; because the essence of the Reality is immutably the same, it can assume securely these innumerable differences of form and character and movement, for even if they were multiplied a trillionfold, that would not affect the underlying immutability of the eternal Identical. Because the Self and Spirit in things and beings is one everywhere, therefore Nature can afford this luxury of infinite differentiation: if there were not this secure basis which brings it about that nothing changes yet all changes, all her workings and creations would in this play collapse into disintegration and chaos; there would be nothing to hold her disparate movements and creations together. The immutability of the Identical does not consist in a monotone of changeless sameness incapable of variation; it consists in an unchangeableness of being which is capable of endless formation of being, but which no differentiation can destroy or impair or minimise. The Self becomes insect and bird and beast and man, but it is always the same Self through these mutations because it is the One who manifests himself infinitely in endless diversity. Our surface reason is prone to conclude that the diversity may be unreal, an appearance only, but if we look a little deeper we shall see that a real diversity brings out the real Unity, shows it as it were in its utmost capacity, reveals all that it can be and is in itself, delivers from its whiteness of hue the many tones of colour that are fused together there; Oneness finds itself infinitely in what seems to us to be a falling away from its oneness, but is really an inexhaustible diverse display of unity. This is the miracle, the Maya of the universe, yet perfectly logical, natural and a matter of course to the self-vision and self-experience of the Infinite.

For the Maya of Brahman is at once the magic and the logic of an infinitely variable Oneness; if, indeed, there were only a rigid monotone of limited oneness and sameness, there would be no place for reason and logic, for logic consists in the right perception of relations: the highest work of reason is to find the one substance, the one law, the cementing latent reality connecting and unifying the many, the different, the discordant and disparate. All universal existence moves between these two terms, a diversification of the One, a unification of the many and diverse, and that must be because the One and the Many are fundamental aspects of the Infinite. For what the divine Self-knowledge and All-knowledge brings out in its manifestation must be a truth of its being and the play of that truth is its Lila.

This, then, is the logic of the way of universal being of Brahman and the basic working of the reason, the infinite intelligence of Maya. As with the being of Brahman, so with its consciousness, Maya: it is not bound to a finite restriction of itself or to one state or law of its action; it can be many things simultaneously, have many co-ordinated movements which to the finite reason may seem contradictory; it is one but innumerably manifold, infinitely plastic, inexhaustibly adaptable. Maya is the supreme and universal consciousness and force of the Eternal and Infinite and, being by its very nature unbound and illimitable, it can put forth many states of consciousness at a time, many dispositions of its Force, without ceasing to be the same consciousness-force for ever. It is at once transcendental, universal and individual; it is the supreme supracosmic Being that is aware of itself as All-Being, as the Cosmic Self, as the Consciousness-Force of cosmic Nature, and at the same time experiences itself as the individual being and consciousness in all existences. The individual consciousness can see itself as limited and separate, but can also put off its limitations and know itself as universal and again as transcendent of the universe; this is because there is in all these states or positions or underlying them the same triune consciousness in a triple status. There is then no difficulty in the One thus seeing or experiencing itself triply, whether from above in the Transcendent Existence or from between in the Cosmic Self or from below in the individual conscious being. All that is necessary for this to be accepted as natural and logical is to admit that there can be different real statuses of consciousness of the One Being, and that cannot be impossible for an Existence which is free and infinite and cannot be tied to a single condition; a free power of self-variation must be natural to a consciousness that is infinite. If the possibility of a manifold status of consciousness is admitted, no limit can be put to the ways of its variation of status, provided the One is aware of itself simultaneously in all of them; for the One and Infinite must be thus universally conscious. The only difficulty, which a further consideration may solve, is to understand the connections between a status of limited or constructed consciousness like ours, a status of ignorance, and the infinite self-knowledge and all-knowledge.

A second possibility of the Infinite Consciousness that must be admitted is its power of self-limitation or secondary self-formation into a subordinate movement within the integral illimitable consciousness and knowledge; for that is a necessary consequence of the power of self-determination of the Infinite. Each self-determination of the self-being must have its own awareness of its self-truth and its self-nature; or, if we prefer so to put it, the Being in that determination must be so self-aware. Spiritual individuality means that each individual self or spirit is a centre of self-vision and all-vision; the circumference, — the boundless circumference, as we may say, — of this vision may be the same for all, but the centre may be different, — not located as in a spatial point in a spatial circle, but a psychological centre related with others through a co-existence of the diversely conscious Many in the universal being. Each being in a world will see the same world, but see it from its own self-being according to its own way of self-nature: for each will manifest its own truth of the Infinite, its own way of self-determination and of meeting the cosmic determinations; its vision by the law of unity in variety will no doubt be fundamentally the same as that of others, but it will still develop its own differentiation, — as we see all human beings conscious in the one human way of the same cosmic things, yet always with an individual difference. This self-limitation would be, not fundamental, but an individual specialisation of a common universality or totality; the spiritual individual would act from his own centre of the one Truth and according to his self-nature, but on a common basis and not with any blindness to other-self and other-nature. It would be consciousness limiting its action with full knowledge, not a movement of ignorance. But apart from this individualising

self-limitation, there must also be in the consciousness of the
Infinite a power of cosmic limitation; it must be able to limit its
action so as to base a given world or universe and to keep it in its
own order, harmony, self-building: for the creation of a universe
necessitates a special determination of the Infinite Consciousness
to preside over that world and a holding back of all that is not
needed for that movement. In the same way the putting forth of
an independent action of some power like Mind, Life or Matter
must have as its support a similar principle of self-limitation. It
cannot be said that such a movement must be impossible for the
Infinite, because it is illimitable; on the contrary, this must be
one of its many powers, for its powers too are illimitable: but
this also, like other self-determinations, other finite buildings,
would not be a separation or a real division, for all the Infinite
Consciousness would be around and behind it and supporting it
and the special movement itself would be intrinsically aware not
only of itself, but, in essence, of all that was behind it. This would
be so, inevitably, in the integral consciousness of the Infinite:
but we can suppose also that an intrinsic though not an active
awareness of this kind, demarcating itself, yet indivisible, might
be there too in the total self-consciousness of the movement
of the Finite. This much cosmic or individual conscious self-
limitation would evidently be possible to the Infinite and can be
accepted by a larger reason as one of its spiritual possibilities;
but so far, on this basis, any division or ignorant separation or
binding and blinding limitation such as is apparent in our own
consciousness would be unaccountable.

But a third power or possibility of the Infinite Consciousness can be admitted, its power of self-absorption, of plunging
into itself, into a state in which self-awareness exists but not
as knowledge and not as all-knowledge; the all would then be
involved in pure self-awareness, and knowledge and the inner
consciousness itself would be lost in pure being. This is, luminously, the state which we call the Superconscience in an
absolute sense, — although most of what we call superconscient
is in reality not that but only a higher conscient, something that
is conscious to itself and only superconscious to our own limited

level of awareness. This self-absorption, this trance of infinity is again, no longer luminously but darkly, the state which we call the Inconscient; for the being of the Infinite is there though by its appearance of inconscience it seems to us rather to be an infinite non-being: a self-oblivious intrinsic consciousness and force are there in that apparent non-being, for by the energy of the Inconscient an ordered world is created; it is created in a trance of self-absorption, the force acting automatically and with an apparent blindness as in a trance, but still with the inevitability and power of truth of the Infinite. If we take a step further and admit that a special or a restricted and partial action of self-absorption is possible to the Infinite, an action not always of its infinity concentrated limitlessly in itself, but confined to a special status or to an individual or cosmic self-determination, we have then the explanation of the concentrated condition or status by which it becomes aware separately of one aspect of its being. There can then be a fundamental double status such as that of the Nirguna standing back from the Saguna and absorbed in its own purity and immobility, while the rest is held back behind a veil and not admitted within that special status. In the same way we could account for the status of consciousness aware of one field of being or one movement of it, while the awareness of all the rest would be held behind and veiled or, as it were, cut off by a waking trance of dynamic concentration from the specialised or limited awareness occupied only with its own field or movement. The totality of the infinite consciousness would be there, not abolished, recoverable, but not evidently active, active only by implication, by inherence or by the instrumentality of the limited awareness, not in its own manifest power and presence. It will be evident that all these three powers can be accepted as possible to the dynamics of the Infinite Consciousness, and it is by considering the many ways in which they can work that we may get a clue to the operations of Maya.

This throws light incidentally on the opposition made by our minds between pure consciousness, pure existence, pure bliss and the abundant activity, the manifold application, the endless vicissitudes of being, consciousness and delight of being that take place in the universe. In the state of pure consciousness and pure being we are aware of that only, simple, immutable, self-existent, without form or object, and we feel that to be alone true and real. In the other or dynamic state we feel its dynamism to be perfectly true and natural and are even capable of thinking that no such experience as that of pure consciousness is possible. Yet it is now evident that to the Infinite Consciousness both the static and the dynamic are possible; these are two of its statuses and both can be present simultaneously in the universal awareness, the one witnessing the other and supporting it or not looking at it and yet automatically supporting it; or the silence and status may be there penetrating the activity or throwing it up like an ocean immobile below throwing up a mobility of waves on its surface. This is also the reason why it is possible for us in certain conditions of our being to be aware of several different states of consciousness at the same time. There is a state of being experienced in Yoga in which we become a double consciousness, one on the surface, small, active, ignorant, swayed by thoughts and feelings, grief and joy and all kinds of reactions, the other within calm, vast, equal, observing the surface being with an immovable detachment or indulgence or, it may be, acting upon its agitation to quiet, enlarge, transform it. So too we can rise to a consciousness above and observe the various parts of our being, inner and outer, mental, vital and physical and the subconscient below all, and act upon one or other or the whole from that higher status. It is possible also to go down from that height or from any height into any of these lower states and take its limited light or its obscurity as our place of working while the rest that we are is either temporarily put away or put behind or else kept as a field of reference from which we can get support, sanction or light and influence or as a status into which we can ascend or recede and from it observe the inferior movements. Or we can plunge into trance, get within ourselves and be conscious there while all outward things are excluded; or we can go beyond even this inner awareness and lose ourselves in some deeper other consciousness or some high superconscience. There is also a pervading equal consciousness into which we can enter and see all ourselves with one enveloping glance or omnipresent awareness one and indivisible. All this which looks strange and abnormal or may seem fantastic to the surface reason acquainted only with our normal status of limited ignorance and its movements divided from our inner higher and total reality, becomes easily intelligible and admissible in the light of the larger reason and logic of the Infinite or by the admission of the greater illimitable powers of the Self, the Spirit in us which is of one essence with the Infinite.

Brahman the Reality is the self-existent Absolute and Maya is the Consciousness and Force of this self-existence; but with regard to the universe Brahman appears as the Self of all existence, Atman, the cosmic Self, but also as the Supreme Self transcendent of its own cosmicity and at the same time individual-universal in each being; Maya can then be seen as the self-power, Atma-Shakti, of the Atman. It is true that when we first become aware of this aspect, it is usually in a silence of the whole being or at the least in a silence within which draws back or stands away from the surface action; this Self is then felt as a status in silence, an immobile immutable being, self-existent, pervading the whole universe, omnipresent in all, but not dynamic or active, aloof from the ever mobile energy of Maya. In the same way we can become aware of it as the Purusha, separate from Prakriti, the Conscious Being standing back from the activities of Nature. But this is an exclusive concentration which limits itself to a spiritual status and puts away from it all activity in order to realise the freedom of Brahman the self-existent Reality from all limitation by its own action and manifestation: it is an essential realisation, but not the total realisation. For we can see that the Conscious-Power, the Shakti that acts and creates, is not other than the Maya or all-knowledge of Brahman; it is the Power of the Self; Prakriti is the working of the Purusha, Conscious Being active by its own Nature: the duality then of Soul and World-Energy, silent Self and the creative Power of the Spirit, is not really something dual and separate, it is biune. As we cannot separate Fire and the power of Fire, it has been said, so we cannot separate the Divine Reality and its Consciousness-

Force, Chit-Shakti. This first realisation of Self as something intensely silent and purely static is not the whole truth of it, there can also be a realisation of Self in its power, Self as the condition of world-activity and world-existence. However, the Self is a fundamental aspect of Brahman, but with a certain stress on its impersonality; therefore the Power of the Self has the appearance of a Force that acts automatically with the Self sustaining it, witness and support and originator and enjoyer of its activities but not involved in them for a moment. As soon as we become aware of the Self, we are conscious of it as eternal, unborn, unembodied, uninvolved in its workings: it can be felt within the form of being, but also as enveloping it, as above it, surveying its embodiment from above, *adhyakṣa*; it is omnipresent, the same in everything, infinite and pure and intangible for ever. This Self can be experienced as the Self of the individual, the Self of the thinker, doer, enjoyer, but even so it always has this greater character; its individuality is at the same time a vast universality or very readily passes into that, and the next step to that is a sheer transcendence or a complete and ineffable passing into the Absolute. The Self is that aspect of the Brahman in which it is intimately felt as at once individual, cosmic, transcendent of the universe. The realisation of the Self is the straight and swift way towards individual liberation, a static universality, a Nature-transcendence. At the same time there is a realisation of Self in which it is felt not only sustaining and pervading and enveloping all things, but constituting everything and identified in a free identity with all its becomings in Nature. Even so, freedom and impersonality are always the character of the Self. There is no appearance of subjection to the workings of its own Power in the universe, such as the apparent subjection of the Purusha to Prakriti. To realise the Self is to realise the eternal freedom of the Spirit.

The Conscious Being, Purusha, is the Self as originator, witness, support and lord and enjoyer of the forms and works of Nature. As the aspect of Self is in its essential character transcendental even when involved and identified with its universal and individual becomings, so the Purusha aspect is characteristically universal-individual and intimately connected with Nature even when separated from her. For this conscious Spirit while retaining its impersonality and eternity, its universality, puts on at the same time a more personal aspect;[7] it is the impersonal-personal being in Nature from whom it is not altogether detached, for it is always coupled with her: Nature acts for the Purusha and by its sanction, for its will and pleasure; the Conscious Being imparts its consciousness to the Energy we call Nature, receives in that consciousness her workings as in a mirror, accepts the forms which she, the executive cosmic Force, creates and imposes on it, gives or withdraws its sanction from her movements. The experience of Purusha-Prakriti, the Spirit or Conscious Being in its relations to Nature, is of immense pragmatic importance; for on these relations the whole play of the consciousness depends in the embodied being. If the Purusha in us is passive and allows Nature to act, accepting all she imposes on him, giving a constant automatic sanction, then the soul in mind, life, body, the mental, vital, physical being in us, becomes subject to our nature, ruled by its formation, driven by its activities; that is the normal state of our ignorance. If the Purusha in us becomes aware of itself as the Witness and stands back from Nature, that is the first step to the soul's freedom; for it becomes detached, and it is possible then to know Nature and her processes and in all independence, since we are no longer involved in her works, to accept or not to accept, to make the sanction no longer automatic but free and effective; we can choose what she shall do or not do in us, or we can stand back altogether from her works and withdraw easily into the Self's spiritual silence, or we can reject her present formations and rise to a spiritual level of existence and from there re-create our existence. The Purusha can cease to be subject, *aniśa*, and become lord of its nature, *īśvara*.

In the philosophy of the Sankhyas we find developed most thoroughly the metaphysical idea of Purusha-Prakriti.

---

[7] The Sankhya philosophy stresses this personal aspect, makes the Purusha many, plural, and assigns universality to Nature; in this view each soul is an independent existence although all souls experience a common universal Nature.

These two are eternally separate entities, but in relation to each other. Prakriti is Nature-power, an executive Power, it is Energy apart from Consciousness; for Consciousness belongs to the Purusha, Prakriti without Purusha is inert, mechanical, inconscient. Prakriti develops as its formal self and basis of action primal Matter and in it manifests life and sense and mind and intelligence; but intelligence too, since it is part of Nature and its product in primal Matter, is also inert, mechanical, inconscient, — a conception which sheds a certain light on the order and perfectly related workings of the Inconscient in the material universe: it is the light of the soul, the Spirit, that is imparted to the mechanical workings of sense-mind and intelligence, they become conscious by its consciousness, even as they become active only by the assent of the spirit. The Purusha becomes free by drawing back from Prakriti; it becomes master of her by refusing to be involved in Matter. Nature acts by three principles, modes or qualities of its stuff and its action, which in us become the fundamental modes of our psychological and physical substance and its workings, the principle of inertia, the principle of kinesis and the principle of balance, light and harmony: when these are in unequal motion, her action takes place; when they fall into equilibrium she passes into quiescence. Purusha, conscious being, is plural, not one and single, while Nature is one: it would seem to follow that whatever principle of oneness we find in existence belongs to Nature, but each soul is independent and unique, sole to itself and separate whether in its enjoyment of Nature or its liberation from Nature. All these positions of the Sankhya we find to be perfectly valid in experience when we come into direct inner contact with the realities of individual soul and universal Nature; but they are pragmatic truths and we are not bound to accept them as the whole or the fundamental truth either of self or of Nature. Prakriti presents itself as an inconscient Energy in the material world, but, as the scale of consciousness rises, she reveals herself more and more as a conscious force and we perceive that even her inconscience concealed a secret consciousness; so too conscious being is many in its individual souls, but in its self we can experience it as one in all and one in its own essential existence. Moreover, the experience of soul and Nature as dual is true, but the experience of their unity has also its validity. If Nature or Energy is able to impose its forms and workings on Being, it can only be because it is Nature or Energy of Being and so the Being can accept them as its own; if the Being can become lord of Nature, it must be because it is its own Nature which it has passively watched doing its work, but can control and master; even in its passivity its consent is necessary to the action of Prakriti and this relation shows sufficiently that the two are not alien to each other. The duality is a position taken up, a double status accepted for the operations of the self-manifestation of the being; but there is no eternal and fundamental separateness and dualism of Being and its Consciousness-Force, of the Soul and Nature.

It is the Reality, the Self, that takes the position of the Conscious Being regarding and accepting or ruling the works of its own Nature. An apparent duality is created in order that there may be a free action of Nature working itself out with the support of the Spirit and again a free and masterful action of the Spirit controlling and working out Nature. This duality is also necessary that the Spirit may be at any time at liberty to draw back from any formation of its Nature and dissolve all formation or accept or enforce a new or a higher formation. These are very evident possibilities of the Spirit in its dealings with its own Force and they can be observed and verified in our own experience; they are logical results of the powers of the Infinite Consciousness, powers which we have seen to be native to its infinity. The Purusha aspect and the Prakriti aspect go always together and whatever status Nature or Consciousness-Force in action assumes, manifests or develops, there is a corresponding status of the Spirit. In its supreme status the Spirit is the supreme Conscious Being, Purushottama, and the Consciousness-Force is his supreme Nature, Para-Prakriti. In each status of the gradations of Nature, the Spirit takes a poise of its being proper to that gradation; in Mind-Nature it becomes the mental being, in Life-Nature it becomes the vital being, in nature of Matter it becomes the physical being, in Supermind it becomes the Being of Knowledge; in the supreme spiritual status it becomes the Being of Bliss and pure Existence. In us, in the embodied individual, it stands behind all as the psychic Entity, the inner Self supporting the other formulations of our consciousness and spiritual existence. The Purusha, individual in us, is cosmic in the cosmos, transcendent in the transcendence: the identity with the Self is apparent, but it is the Self in its pure impersonal-personal status of a Spirit in things and beings, — impersonal because undifferentiated by personal quality, personal because it presides over the individualisations of self in each individual, — which deals with the works of its Consciousness-Force, its executive force of self-nature, in whatever poise is necessary for that purpose.

But it is evident that whatever the posture taken or relation formed in any individual nodus of Purusha-Prakriti, the Being is in a fundamental cosmic relation lord or ruler of its nature: for even when it allows Nature to have its own way with it, its consent is necessary to support her workings. This comes out in its fullest revelation in the third aspect of the Reality, the Divine Being who is the master and creator of the universe. Here the supreme Person, the Being in its transcendental and cosmic consciousness and force, comes to the front, omnipotent, omniscient, the controller of all energies, the Conscious in all that is conscient or inconscient, the Inhabitant of all souls and minds and hearts and bodies, the Ruler or Overruler of all works, the Enjoyer of all delight, the Creator who has built all things in his own being, the All-Person of whom all beings are personalities, the Power from whom are all powers, the Self, the Spirit in all, by his being the Father of all that is, in his Consciousness-Force the Divine Mother, the Friend of all creatures, the All-blissful and All-beautiful of whom beauty and joy are the revelation, the All-Beloved and All-Lover. In a certain sense, so seen and understood, this becomes the most comprehensive of the aspects of the Reality, since here all are united in a single formulation; for the Ishwara is supracosmic as well as intracosmic; He is that which exceeds and inhabits and supports all individuality;

He is the supreme and universal Brahman, the Absolute, the supreme Self, the supreme Purusha.[8] But, very clearly, this is not the personal God of popular religions, a being limited by his qualities, individual and separate from all others; for all such personal gods are only limited representations or names and divine personalities of the one Ishwara. Neither is this the Saguna Brahman active and possessed of qualities, for that is only one side of the being of the Ishwara; the Nirguna immobile and without qualities is another aspect of His existence. Ishwara is Brahman the Reality, Self, Spirit, revealed as possessor, enjoyer of his own self-existence, creator of the universe and one with it, Pantheos, and yet superior to it, the Eternal, the Infinite, the Ineffable, the Divine Transcendence.

The sharp opposition made between personality and impersonality by our mental way of thinking is a creation of the mind based on the appearances of the material world; for here in terrestrial existence the Inconscient from which everything takes its origin appears as something entirely impersonal; Nature, the inconscient Energy, is entirely impersonal in her manifest essence and dealings; all Forces wear this mask of impersonality, all qualities and powers, Love and Delight and Consciousness itself, have this aspect. Personality makes its apparition as a creation of consciousness in an impersonal world; it is a limitation by a restricted formation of powers, qualities, habitual forces of the nature-action, an imprisonment in a limited circle of self-experience which we have to transcend, — to lose personality is necessary if we are to gain universality, still more necessary if we are to rise into the Transcendence. But what we thus call personality is only a formation of superficial consciousness; behind it is the Person who takes on various personalities, who can have at the same time many personalities but is himself one, real, eternal. If we look at things from a larger point of view, we might say that what is impersonal is only a power of the Person: existence itself has no meaning without an Existent, consciousness has no standing-place if there is none who is conscious, delight is useless

and invalid without an enjoyer, love can have no foundation or
fulfilment if there is no lover, all-power must be otiose if there is
not an Almighty. For what we mean by Person is conscious being;
even if this emerges here as a term or product of the Inconscient,
it is not that in reality: for it is the Inconscient itself that is a term
of the secret Consciousness; what emerges is greater than that
in which it emerges, as Mind is greater than Matter, Soul than
Mind; Spirit, most secret of all, the supreme emergence, the last
revelation, is the greatest of all, and Spirit is the Purusha, the
All-Person, the omnipresent Conscious Being. It is the mind's
ignorance of this true Person in us, its confusion of person with
our experience of ego and limited personality, the misleading
phenomenon of the emergence of limited consciousness and personality in an inconscient existence that have made us create
an opposition between these two aspects of the Reality, but in
truth there is no opposition. An eternal infinite self-existence is
the supreme reality, but the supreme transcendent eternal Being,
Self and Spirit, — an infinite Person, we may say, because his
being is the essence and source of all personality, — is the reality
and meaning of self-existence: so too the cosmic Self, Spirit,
Being, Person is the reality and meaning of cosmic existence; the
same Self, Spirit, Being or Person manifesting its multiplicity is
the reality and meaning of individual existence.

   If we admit the Divine Being, the supreme Person and All-
Person as the Ishwara, a difficulty arises in understanding his
rule or government of world-existence, because we immediately
transfer to him our mental conception of a human ruler; we picture him as acting by the mind and mental will in an omnipotent
arbitrary fashion upon a world on which he imposes his mental
conceptions as laws, and we conceive of his will as a free caprice
of his personality. But there is no need for the Divine Being to
act by an arbitrary will or idea as an omnipotent yet ignorant
human being, — if such an omnipotence were possible, — might
do: for he is not limited by mind; he has an all-consciousness
in which he is aware of the truth of all things and aware of
his own all-wisdom working them out according to the truth
that is in them, their significance, their possibility or necessity,

the imperative selfness of their nature. The Divine is free and not bound by laws of any making, but still he acts by laws and processes because they are the expression of the truth of things, — not their mechanical, mathematical or other outward truth alone, but the spiritual reality of what they are, what they have become and have yet to become, what they have it within themselves to realise. He is himself present in the working, but he also exceeds and can overrule it; for on one side Nature works according to her limited complex of formulas and is informed and supported in their execution by the Divine Presence, but on the other side there is an overseeing, a higher working and determination, even an intervention, free but not arbitrary, often appearing to us magical and miraculous because it proceeds and acts upon Nature from a divine Supernature: Nature here is a limited expression of that Supernature and open to intervention or mutation by its light, its force, its influence. The mechanical, mathematical, automatic law of things is a fact, but within it there is a spiritual law of consciousness at work which gives to the mechanical steps of Nature's forces an inner turn and value, a significant rightness and a secretly conscious necessity, and above it there is a spiritual freedom that knows and acts in the supreme and universal truth of the Spirit. Our view of the divine government of the world or of the secret of its action is either incurably anthropomorphic or else incurably mechanical; both the anthropomorphism and mechanism have their elements of truth, but they are only a side, an aspect, and the real truth is that the world is governed by the One in all and over all who is infinite in his consciousness and it is according to the law and logic of an infinite consciousness that we ought to understand the significance and building and movement of the universe.

If we regard this aspect of the one Reality and put it in close connection with the other aspects, we can get a complete view of the relation between the eternal Self-Existence and the dynamics of the Consciousness-Force by which it manifests the universe. If we place ourselves in a silent Self-existence immobile, static, inactive, it will appear that a conceptive Consciousness-Force, Maya, able to effectuate all its conceptions, a dynamic consort of the Self of silence, is doing everything; it takes its stand on the fixed unmoving eternal status and casts the spiritual substance of being into all manner of forms and movements to which its passivity consents or in which it takes its impartial pleasure, its immobile delight of creative and mobile existence. Whether this be a real or an illusory existence, that must be its substance and significance. Consciousness is at play with Being, Force of Nature does what it wills with Existence and makes it the stuff of her creations, but secretly the consent of the Being must be there at every step to make this possible. There is an evident truth in this perception of things; it is what we see happening everywhere in us and around us; it is a truth of the universe and must answer to a fundamental truth-aspect of the Absolute. But when we step back from the outer dynamic appearances of things, not into a witness Silence, but into an inner dynamic participating experience of the Spirit, we find that this Consciousness-Force, Maya, Shakti, is itself the power of the Being, the Self-Existent, the Ishwara. The Being is lord of her and of all things, we see him doing everything in his own sovereignty as the creator and ruler of his own manifestation; or, if he stands back and allows freedom of action to the forces of Nature and her creatures, his sovereignty is still innate in the permission, at every step his tacit sanction, "Let it be so", *tathāstu*, is there implicit; for otherwise nothing could be done or happen. Being and its Consciousness-Force, Spirit and Nature cannot be fundamentally dual: what Nature does, is really done by the Spirit. This too is a truth that becomes evident when we go behind the veil and feel the presence of a living Reality which is everything and determines everything, is the All-powerful and the All-ruler; this too is a fundamental truth-aspect of the Absolute.

Again, if we remain absorbed in the Silence, the creative Consciousness and her works disappear into the Silence; Nature and the creation for us cease to exist or be real. On the other hand, if we look exclusively at the Being in its aspect of the sole-existent Person and Ruler, the Power or Shakti by which he does all things disappears into his uniqueness or becomes an attribute of His cosmic personality; the absolute monarchy of the one Being becomes our perception of the universe. Both these experiences create many difficulties for the mind due to its non-perception of the reality of the Self-Power whether in quiescence or in action, or to a too exclusively negative experience of the Self, or to the too anthropomorphic character our conceptions attach to the Supreme Being as Ruler. It is evident that we are looking at an Infinite of which the Self-Power is capable of many movements, all of them valid. If we look again more largely and take account of both the impersonal and the personal truth of things as one truth, if in that light, the light of personality in impersonality, we see the biune aspect of Self and Self-Power, then in the Person Aspect a dual Person emerges, Ishwara-Shakti, the Divine Self and Creator and the Divine Mother and Creatrix of the universe; there becomes apparent to us the mystery of the masculine and feminine cosmic Principles whose play and inter-action are necessary for all creation. In the superconscient truth of the Self-Existence these two are fused and implied in each other, one and indistinguishable, but in the spiritual-pragmatic truth of the dynamism of the universe, they emerge and be-come active; the Divine Mother-Energy as the universal creatrix, Maya, Para-Prakriti, Chit-Shakti, manifests the cosmic Self and Ishwara and her own self-power as a dual principle; it is through her that the Being, the Self, the Ishwara, acts and he does nothing except by her; though his Will is implicit in her, it is she who works out all as the supreme Consciousness-Force who holds all souls and beings within her and as executive Nature; all exists and acts according to Nature, all is the Consciousness-Force manifesting and playing with the Being in millions of forms and movements into which she casts his existence. If we draw back from her workings, then all can fall into quiescence and we can enter into the silence, because she consents to cease from her dynamic activity; but it is in her quiescence and silence that we are quiescent and cease. If we would affirm our independence of Nature, she reveals to us the supreme and omnipresent power of the Ishwara and ourselves as beings of his being, but that power is herself and we are that in her supernature. If we would realise a higher formation or status of being, then it is still through

her, through the Divine Shakti, the Consciousness-Force of the
Spirit that it has to be done; our surrender must be to the Divine
Being through the Divine Mother: for it is towards or into the
supreme Nature that our ascension has to take place and it can
only be done by the supramental Shakti taking up our mentality
and transforming it into her supramentality. Thus we see that
there is no contradiction or incompatibility between these three
aspects of Existence, or between them in their eternal status and
the three modes of its Dynamis working in the universe. One
Being, one Reality as Self bases, supports, informs, as Purusha
or Conscious Being experiences, as Ishwara wills, governs and
possesses its world of manifestation created and kept in motion
and action by its own Consciousness-Force or Self-Power, —
Maya, Prakriti, Shakti.

A certain difficulty arises for our mind in reconciling these
different faces or fronts of the One Self and Spirit, because we
are obliged to use abstract conceptions and defining words and
ideas for something that is not abstract, something that is spiritually living and intensely real. Our abstractions get fixed into
differentiating concepts with sharp lines between them: but the
Reality is not of that nature; its aspects are many but shade
off into each other. Its truth could only be rendered by ideas
and images metaphysical and yet living and concrete, — images
which might be taken by the pure Reason as figures and symbols but are more than that and mean more to the intuitive
vision and feeling, for they are realities of a dynamic spiritual
experience. The impersonal truth of things can be rendered into
the abstract formulas of the pure reason, but there is another
side of truth which belongs to the spiritual or mystic vision and
without that inner vision of realities the abstract formulation of
them is insufficiently alive, incomplete. The mystery of things
is the true truth of things; the intellectual presentation is only
truth in representation, in abstract symbols, as if in a cubist
art of thought-speech, in geometric figure. It is necessary in a
philosophic inquiry to confine oneself mostly to this intellectual
presentation, but it is as well to remember that this is only the
abstraction of the Truth and to seize it completely or express

it completely there is needed a concrete experience and a more living and full-bodied language.

Here it becomes opportune to see how in this aspect of the Reality we must regard the relation we have discovered between the One and the Many; this amounts to a determination of the true connection between the individual and the Divine Being, between the Soul and the Ishwara. In the normal theistic conception the Many are created by God; made by him as a potter might make a vessel, they are dependent on him as are creatures on their creator. But in this larger view of the Ishwara the Many are themselves the Divine One in their inmost reality, individual selves of the supreme and universal Self-Existence, eternal as he is eternal but eternal in his being: our material existence is indeed a creation of Nature, but the soul is an immortal portion of the Divinity and behind it is the Divine Self in the natural creature. Still the One is the fundamental Truth of existence, the Many exist by the One and there is therefore an entire dependence of the manifested being on the Ishwara. This dependence is concealed by the separative ignorance of the ego which strives to exist in its own right, although at every step it is evidently dependent on the cosmic Power that created it, moved by it, a part of its cosmic being and action; this effort of the ego is clearly a misprision, an erroneous reflection of the truth of the self-existence that is within us. It is true that there is something in us, not in the ego but in the self and inmost being, that surpasses cosmic Nature and belongs to the Transcendence. But this too finds itself independent of Nature only by dependence on a higher Reality; it is through self-giving or surrender of soul and nature to the Divine Being that we can attain to our highest self and supreme Reality, for it is the Divine Being who is that highest self and that supreme Reality, and we are self-existent and eternal only in his eternity and by his self-existence. This dependence is not contradictory of the Identity, but is itself the door to the realisation of the Identity, — so that here again we meet that phenomenon of duality expressing unity, proceeding from unity and opening back into unity, which is the constant secret and fundamental operation of the universe. It is this truth of the consciousness of the Infinite that creates the possibility of all relations between the Many and the One, among which the realisation of oneness by the mind, the presence of oneness in the heart, the existence of oneness in all the members is a highest peak, and yet it does not annul but confirms all the other personal relations and gives them their fullness, their complete delight, their entire significance. This too is the magiç, but also the logic of the Infinite.

One problem still remains to be solved, and it can be solved on the same basis; it is the problem of the opposition between the Non-Manifest and the manifestation. For it might be said that all that has been advanced hitherto may be true of the manifestation, but the manifestation is a reality of an inferior order, a partial movement derived from the Non-Manifest Reality and, when we enter into that which is supremely Real, these truths of the universe cease to have any validity. The Non-Manifest is the timeless, the utterly eternal, an irreducible absolute self-existence to which the manifestation and its limitations can give no clue or only a clue that by its insufficiency is illusory and deceptive. This raises the problem of the relation of Time to the timeless Spirit; for we have supposed on the contrary that what is in unmanifestation in the Timeless Eternal is manifested in Time-Eternity. If that is so, if the temporal is an expression of the Eternal, then however different the conditions, however partial the expression, yet what is fundamental in the Time-expression must be in some way pre-existent in the Transcendence and drawn from the timeless Reality. For if not, these fundamentals must come into it direct from an Absolute which is other than Time or Timelessness, and the Timeless Spirit must be a supreme spiritual negation, an indeterminable basing the Absolute's freedom from limitation by what is formulated in Time, — it must be the negative to the Time positive, in the same relation to it as the Nirguna to the Saguna. But, in fact, what we mean by the Timeless is a spiritual status of existence not subject to the time movement or to the successive or the relative time-experience of a past, present and future. The timeless Spirit is not necessarily a blank; it may hold all in itself, but in essence, without reference to time or form or relation or circumstance, perhaps in an eternal unity. Eternity is the common term between Time and the Timeless Spirit. What is in the Timeless unmanifested, implied, essential, appears in Time in movement, or at least in design and relation, in result and circumstance. These two then are the same Eternity or the same Eternal in a double status; they are a twofold status of being and consciousness, one an eternity of immobile status, the other an eternity of motion in status.

The original status is that of the Reality timeless and spaceless; Space and Time would be the same Reality self-extended to contain the deployment of what was within it. The difference would be, as in all the other oppositions, the Spirit looking at itself in essence and principle of being and the same Spirit looking at itself in the dynamism of its essence and principle. Space and Time are our names for this self-extension of the one Reality. We are apt to see Space as a static extension in which all things stand or move together in a fixed order; we see Time as a mobile extension which is measured by movement and event: Space then would be Brahman in self-extended status; Time would be Brahman in self-extended movement. But this may be only a first view and inaccurate: Space may be really a constant mobile, the constancy and the persistent time-relation of things in it creating the sense of stability of Space, the mobility creating the sense of time-movement in stable Space. Or, again, Space would be Brahman extended for the holding together of forms and objects; Time would be Brahman self-extended for the deployment of the movement of self-power carrying forms and objects; the two would then be a dual aspect of one and the same self-extension of the cosmic Eternal.

A purely physical Space might be regarded as in itself a property of Matter; but Matter is a creation of Energy in movement. Space therefore in the material world could be either a fundamental self-extension of material Energy or its self-formed existence-field, its representation of the Inconscient Infinity in which it is acting, a figure in which it accommodates the formulas and movements of its own action and self-creation. Time would be itself the course of that movement or else an impression created by it, an impression of something that presents itself to us as regularly successive in its appearance, — a division or a continuum upholding the continuity of movement and yet marking off its successions, — because the movement itself is regularly successive. Or else Time could be a dimension of Space necessary for the complete action of the Energy, but not understood by us as such because it is seen by our conscious subjectivity as something itself subjective, felt by our mind, not perceived by our senses, and therefore not recognised as a dimension of space which has to us the appearance of a sense-created or sense-perceived objective extension.

In any case, if Spirit is the fundamental reality, Time and Space must either be conceptive conditions under which the Spirit sees its own movement of energy or else they must be fundamental conditions of the Spirit itself which assume a different appearance or status according to the status of consciousness in which they manifest. In other words there is a different Time and Space for each status of our consciousness and even different movements of Time and Space within each status; but all would be renderings of a fundamental spiritual reality of Time-Space. In fact, when we go behind physical space, we become aware of an extension on which all this movement is based and this extension is spiritual and not material; it is Self or Spirit containing all action of its own Energy. This origin or basic reality of Space begins to become apparent when we draw back from the physical: for then we become aware of a subjective Space-extension in which mind itself lives and moves and which is other than physical Space-Time, and yet there is an interpenetration; for our mind can move in its own space in such a way as to effectuate a movement also in space of Matter or act upon something distant in space of Matter. In a still deeper condition of consciousness we are aware of a pure spiritual Space; in this awareness Time may no longer seem to exist, because all movement ceases, or, if there is a movement or happening, it can take place independent of any observable Time sequence.

If we go behind Time by a similar inward motion, drawing back from the physical and seeing it without being involved in it, we discover that Time observation and Time movement are relative, but Time itself is real and eternal. Time observation depends not only on the measures used, but on the consciousness and the position of the observer: moreover, each state of consciousness has a different Time relation; Time in Mind consciousness and Mind Space has not the same sense and measure of its movements as in physical Space; it moves there quickly or slowly according to the state of the consciousness. Each state of consciousness has its own Time and yet there can be relations of Time between them; and when we go behind the physical surface, we find several different Time statuses and Time movements co-existent in the same consciousness. This is evident in dream Time where a long sequence of happenings can occur in a period which corresponds to a second or a few seconds of physical Time. There is then a certain relation between different Time statuses but no ascertainable correspondence of measure. It would seem as if Time had no objective reality, but depends on whatever conditions may be established by action of consciousness in its relation to status and motion of being: Time would seem to be purely subjective. But, in fact, Space also would appear by the mutual relation of Mind-Space and Matter-Space to be subjective; in other words, both are the original spiritual extension, but it is rendered by mind in its purity into a subjective mind-field and by sense-mind into an objective field of sense-perception. Subjectivity and objectivity are only two sides of one consciousness, and the cardinal fact is that any given Time or Space or any given Time-Space as a whole is a status of being in which there is a movement of the consciousness and force of the being, a movement that creates or manifests events and happenings; it is the relation of the consciousness that sees and the force that formulates the happenings, a relation inherent in the status, which determines the sense of Time and creates our awareness of Time-movement, Time-relation, Time-measure. In its fundamental truth the original status of Time behind all its variations is nothing else than the eternity of the Eternal, just as the fundamental truth of Space, the original sense of its reality, is the infinity of the Infinite.

The Being can have three different states of its consciousness with regard to its own eternity. The first is that in which there is the immobile status of the Self in its essential existence, self-absorbed or self-conscious, but in either case without development of consciousness in movement or happening; this is what we distinguish as its timeless eternity. The second is its whole-consciousness of the successive relations of all things belonging to a destined or an actually proceeding manifestation, in which what we call past, present and future stand together as if in a map or settled design or very much as an artist or painter or architect might hold all the detail of his work viewed as a whole, intended or reviewed in his mind or arranged in a plan for execution; this is the stable status or simultaneous integrality of Time. This seeing of Time is not at all part of our normal awareness of events as they happen, though our view of the past, because it is already known and can be regarded in the whole, may put on something of this character; but we know that this consciousness exists because it is possible in an exceptional state to enter into it and see things from the view-point of this simultaneity of Time-vision. The third status is that of a processive movement of Consciousness-Force and its successive working out of what has been seen by it in the static vision of the Eternal; this is the Time movement. But it is in one and the same Eternity that this triple status exists and the movement takes place; there are not really two eternities, one an eternity of status, another an eternity of movement, but there are different statuses or positions taken by Consciousness with regard to the one Eternity. For it can see the whole Time development from outside or from above the movement; it can take a stable position within the movement and see the before and the after in a fixed, determined or destined succession; or it can take instead a mobile position in the movement, itself move with it from moment to moment and see all that has happened receding back into the past and all that has to happen coming towards it from the future; or else it may concentrate on the moment it occupies and see nothing but what is in that moment and immediately around or behind it. All these positions can be taken by the being of the Infinite in a simultaneous vision or experience. It can see Time from above and inside Time, exceeding it and not within it; it can see the Timeless develop the Time-movement without ceasing to be timeless, it can embrace the whole movement in a static and a dynamic vision and put out at the same time something of itself into the moment-vision. This simultaneity may seem to the finite consciousness tied to the moment-vision a magic of the Infinite, a magic of Maya; to its own way of perception which needs to limit, to envisage one status only at a time in order to harmonise, it would give a sense of confused and inconsistent unreality. But to an infinite consciousness such an integral simultaneity of vision and experience would be perfectly logical and consistent; all could be elements of a whole-vision capable of being closely related together in a harmonious arrangement, a multiplicity of view bringing out the unity of the thing seen, a diverse presentation of concomitant aspects of the One Reality.

If there can be this simultaneous multiplicity of self-presentation of one Reality, we see that there is no impossibility in the co-existence of a Timeless Eternal and a Time Eternity. It would be the same Eternity viewed by a dual self-awareness and there could be no opposition between them; it would be a correlation of two powers of the self-awareness of the infinite and eternal Reality, — a power of status and non-manifestation, a power of self-effecting action and movement and manifestation. Their simultaneity, however contradictory and difficult to reconcile it might seem to our finite surface seeing, would be intrinsic and normal to the Maya or eternal self-knowledge and all-knowledge of Brahman, the eternal and infinite knowledge and wisdom-power of the Ishwara, the consciousness-force of the self-existent Sachchidananda.

Chapter III

The Eternal and the Individual

He am I.   *Isha Upanishad.*[1]

It is an eternal portion of Me that has become the living being
in a world of living beings.... The eye of knowledge sees the
Lord abiding in the body and enjoying and going forth from
it.   *Gita.*[2]

Two birds beautiful of wing, friends and comrades, cling to a
common tree, and one eats the sweet fruit, the other regards
him and eats not.... Where winged souls cry the discoveries of
knowledge over their portion of immortality, there the Lord
of all, the Guardian of the World took possession of me, he
the Wise, me the ignorant.   *Rig Veda.*[3]

THERE is then a fundamental truth of existence, an Omnipresent Reality, omnipresent above the cosmic manifestation and in it and immanent in each individual. There
is also a dynamic power of this Omnipresence, a creative or self-
manifesting action of its infinite Consciousness-Force. There is
as a phase or movement of the self-manifestation a descent into
an apparent material inconscience, an awakening of the individual out of the Inconscience and an evolution of his being into
the spiritual and supramental consciousness and power of the
Reality, into his own universal and transcendent Self and source
of existence. It is on this foundation that we have to base our
conception of a truth in our terrestrial being and the possibility
of a divine Life in material Nature. There our chief need is to
discover the origin and nature of the Ignorance which we see

---

[1] Verse 16.   [2] XV. 7, 10.   [3] I. 164. 20, 21.

emerging out of the inconscience of matter or disclosing itself within a body of matter and the nature of the Knowledge that has to replace it, to understand too the process of Nature's self-unfolding and the soul's recovery. For in fact the Knowledge is there concealed in the Ignorance itself; it has rather to be unveiled than acquired: it reveals itself rather than is learned, by an inward and upward self-unfolding. But first it will be convenient to meet and get out of the way one difficulty that inevitably arises, the difficulty of admitting that, even given the immanence of the Divine in us, even given our individual consciousness as a vehicle of progressive evolutionary manifestation, the individual is in any sense eternal or that there can be any persistence of individuality after liberation has been attained by unity and self-knowledge.

This is a difficulty of the logical reason and must be met by a larger and more catholic enlightening reason. Or if it is a difficulty of spiritual experience, it can only be met by a wider resolving experience. It can indeed be met also by a dialectical battle, a logomachy of the logical mind; but that by itself is an artificial method, often a futile combat in the clouds and always inconclusive. Logical reasoning is useful and indispensable in its own field in order to give the mind a certain clearness, precision and subtlety in dealing with its own ideas and word-symbols, so that our perception of the truths which we arrive at by observation and experience or which physically, psychologically or spiritually we have seen, may be as little as possible obscured by the confusions of our average human intelligence, its proneness to take appearance for fact, its haste to be misled by partial truth, its exaggerated conclusions, its intellectual and emotional partialities, its incompetent bunglings in that linking of truth to truth by which alone we can arrive at a complete knowledge. We must have a clear, pure, subtle and flexible mind in order that we may fall as little as possible into that ordinary mental habit of our kind which turns truth itself into a purveyor of errors. That clarification, the habit of clear logical reasoning culminating in the method of metaphysical dialectics, does help to accomplish and its part in the preparation of knowledge is therefore very great. But by itself it cannot arrive either at the knowledge of the world or the knowledge of God, much less reconcile the lower and the higher realisation. It is much more efficiently a guardian against error than a discoverer of truth, — although by deduction from knowledge already acquired it may happen upon new truths and indicate them for experience or for the higher and larger truth-seeing faculties to confirm. In the more subtle field of synthetical or unifying knowledge the logical habit of mind may even become a stumbling-block by the very faculty which gives it its peculiar use; for it is so accustomed to making distinctions and dwelling upon distinctions and working by distinctions that it is always a little at sea when distinctions have to be overriden and overpassed. Our object, then, in considering the difficulties of the normal mind when face to face with the experience of cosmic and transcendental unity by the individual, must be solely to make more clear to ourselves, first, the origin of the difficulties and the escape from them and by that, what is more important, the real nature of the unity at which we arrive and of the culmination of the individual when he becomes one with all creatures and dwells in the oneness of the Eternal.

The first difficulty for the reason is that it has always been accustomed to identify the individual self with the ego and to think of it as existing only by the limitations and exclusions of the ego. If that were so, then by the transcendence of the ego the individual would abolish his own existence; our end would be to disappear and dissolve into some universality of matter, life, mind or spirit or else some indeterminate from which our egoistic determinations of individuality have started. But what is this strongly separative self-experience that we call ego? It is nothing fundamentally real in itself but only a practical constitution of our consciousness devised to centralise the activities of Nature in us. We perceive a formation of mental, physical, vital experience which distinguishes itself from the rest of being, and that is what we think of as ourselves in nature — this individualisation of being in becoming. We then proceed to conceive of ourselves as something which has thus individualised itself and only exists so long as it is individualised, — a temporary or at least a temporal becoming; or else we conceive of ourselves as someone who supports or causes the individualisation, an immortal being perhaps but limited by its individuality. This perception and this conception constitute our ego-sense. Normally, we go no farther in our knowledge of our individual existence.

But in the end we have to see that our individualisation is only a superficial formation, a practical selection and limited conscious synthesis for the temporary utility of life in a particular body, or else it is a constantly changing and developing synthesis pursued through successive lives in successive bodies. Behind it there is a consciousness, a Purusha, who is not determined or limited by his individualisation or by this synthesis but on the contrary determines, supports and yet exceeds it. That which he selects from in order to construct this synthesis, is his total experience of the world-being. Therefore our individualisation exists by virtue of the world-being, but also by virtue of a consciousness which uses the world-being for experience of its possibilities of individuality. These two powers, Person and his world-material, are both necessary for our present experience of individuality. If the Purusha with his individualising syntheses of consciousness were to disappear, to merge, to annul himself in any way, our constructed individuality would cease because the Reality that supported it would no longer be in presence; if, on the other hand, the world-being were to dissolve, merge, disappear, then also our individualisation would cease, for the material of experience by which it effectuates itself would be wanting. We have then to recognise these two terms of our existence, a world-being and an individualising consciousness which is the cause of all our self-experience and world-experience.

But we see farther that in the end this Purusha, this cause and self of our individuality, comes to embrace the whole world and all other beings in a sort of conscious extension of itself and to perceive itself as one with the world-being. In its conscious extension of itself it exceeds the primary experience and abolishes the barriers of its active self-limitation and individualisation; by its perception of its own infinite universality it goes beyond all consciousness of separative individuality or limited

soul-being. By that very fact the individual ceases to be the self-
limiting ego; in other words, our false consciousness of existing
only by self-limitation, by rigid distinction of ourselves from the
rest of being and becoming is transcended; our identification of
ourselves with our personal and temporal individualisation in a
particular mind and body is abolished. But is all truth of individuality and individualisation abolished? does the Purusha cease
to exist or does he become the world-Purusha and live intimately
in innumerable minds and bodies? We do not find it to be so.
He still individualises and it is still he who exists and embraces
this wider consciousness while he individualises: but the mind
no longer thinks of a limited temporary individualisation as all
ourselves but only as a wave of becoming thrown up from the
sea of its being or else as a form or centre of universality. The
soul still makes the world-becoming the material for individual
experience, but instead of regarding it as something outside and
larger than itself on which it has to draw, by which it is affected,
with which it has to make accommodations, it is aware of it subjectively as within itself; it embraces both its world-material and
its individualised experience of spatial and temporal activities
in a free and enlarged consciousness. In this new consciousness
the spiritual individual perceives its true self to be one in being
with the Transcendence and seated and dwelling within it, and
no longer takes its constructed individuality as anything more
than a formation for world-experience.

Our unity with the world-being is the consciousness of a
Self which at one and the same time cosmicises in the world and
individualises through the individual Purusha, and both in that
world-being and in this individual being and in all individual
beings it is aware of the same Self manifesting and experiencing
its various manifestations. That then is a Self which must be
one in its being, — otherwise we could not have this experience
of unity, — and yet must be capable in its very unity of cosmic
differentiation and multiple individuality. The unity is its being,
— yes, but the cosmic differentiation and the multiple individuality are the power of its being which it is constantly displaying
and which it is its delight and the nature of its consciousness to

display. If then we arrive at unity with that, if we even become entirely and in every way that being, why should the power of its being be excised and why at all should we desire or labour to excise it? We should then only diminish the scope of our unity with it by an exclusive concentration accepting the divine being but not accepting our part in the power and consciousness and infinite delight of the Divine. It would in fact be the individual seeking peace and rest of union in a motionless identity, but rejecting delight and various joy of union in the nature and act and power of the divine Existence. That is possible, but there is no necessity to uphold it as the ultimate aim of our being or as our ultimate perfection.

Or the one possible reason would be that in the power, the act of consciousness there is not real union and that only in the status of consciousness is there perfect undifferentiated unity. Now in what we may call the waking union of the individual with the Divine, as opposed to a falling asleep or a concentration of the individual consciousness in an absorbed identity, there is certainly and must be a differentiation of experience. For in this active unity the individual Purusha enlarges its active experience also as well as its static consciousness into a way of union with this Self of his being and of the world-being, and yet individualisation remains and therefore differentiation. The Purusha is aware of all other individuals as selves of himself; he may by a dynamic union become aware of their mental and practical action as occurring in his universal consciousness, just as he is aware of his own mental and practical action; he may help to determine their action by subjective union with them: but still there is a practical difference. The action of the Divine in himself is that with which he is particularly and directly concerned; the action of the Divine in his other selves is that with which he is universally concerned, not directly, but through and by his union with them and with the Divine. The individual therefore exists though he exceeds the little separative ego; the universal exists and is embraced by him but it does not absorb and abolish all individual differentiation, even though by his universalising himself the limitation which we call the ego is overcome.

Now we may get rid of this differentiation by plunging into the absorption of an exclusive unity, but to what end? For perfect union? But we do not forfeit that by accepting the differentiation any more than the Divine forfeits His oneness by accepting it. We have the perfect union in His being and can absorb ourselves in it at any time, but we have also this other differentiated unity and can emerge into it and act freely in it at any time without losing oneness: for we have merged the ego and are absolved from the exclusive stresses of our mentality. Then for peace and rest? But we have the peace and rest by virtue of our unity with Him, even as the Divine possesses for ever His eternal calm in the midst of His eternal action. Then for the mere joy of getting rid of all differentiation? But that differentiation has its divine purpose: it is a means of greater unity, not as in the egoistic life a means of divisions; for we enjoy by it our unity with our other selves and with God in all, which we exclude by our rejection of his multiple being. In either experience it is the Divine in the individual possessing and enjoying in one case the Divine in His pure unity or in the other the Divine in that and in the unity of the cosmos; it is not the absolute Divine recovering after having lost His unity. Certainly, we may prefer the absorption in a pure exclusive unity or a departure into a supracosmic transcendence, but there is in the spiritual truth of the Divine Existence no compelling reason why we should not participate in this large possession and bliss of His universal being which is the fulfilment of our individuality.

But we see farther that it is not solely and ultimately the cosmic being into which our individual being enters but something in which both are unified. As our individualisation in the world is a becoming of that Self, so is the world too a becoming of that Self. The world-being includes always the individual being; therefore these two becomings, the cosmic and the individual, are always related to each other and in their practical relation mutually dependent. But we find that the individual being also comes in the end to include the world in its consciousness, and since this is not by an abolition of the spiritual individual, but by his coming to his full, large and perfect self-consciousness, we must suppose that the individual always included the cosmos, and it is only the surface consciousness which by ignorance failed to possess that inclusion because of its self-limitation in ego. But when we speak of the mutual inclusion of the cosmic and the individual, the world in me, I in the world, all in me, I in all, — for that is the liberated self-experience, — we are evidently travelling beyond the language of the normal reason. That is because the words we have to use were minted by mind and given their values by an intellect bound to the conceptions of physical Space and circumstance and using for the language of a higher psychological experience figures drawn from the physical life and the experience of the senses. But the plane of consciousness to which the liberated human being arises is not dependent upon the physical world, and the cosmos which we thus include and are included in is not the physical cosmos, but the harmonically manifest being of God in certain great rhythms of His conscious-force and self-delight. Therefore this mutual inclusion is spiritual and psychological; it is a translation of the two forms of the Many, all and individual, into a unifying spiritual experience, — a translation of the eternal unity of the One and the Many; for the One is the eternal unity of the Many differentiating and undifferentiating itself in the cosmos. This means that cosmos and individual are manifestations of a transcendent Self who is indivisible being although he seems to be divided or distributed; but he is not really divided or distributed but indivisibly present everywhere. Therefore all is in each and each is in all and all is in God and God in all; and when the liberated soul comes into union with this Transcendent, it has this self-experience of itself and cosmos which is translated psychologically into a mutual inclusion and a persistent existence of both in a divine union which is at once a oneness and a fusion and an embrace.

The normal experience of the reason therefore is not applicable to these higher truths. In the first place the ego is the individual only in the ignorance; there is a true individual who is not the ego and still has an eternal relation with all other individuals which is not egoistic or self-separative, but of which the essential character is practical mutuality founded in essential unity. This mutuality founded in unity is the whole secret of the divine existence in its perfect manifestation; it must be the basis of anything to which we can give the name of a divine life. But, secondly, we see that the whole difficulty and confusion into which the normal reason falls is that we are speaking of a higher and illimitable self-experience founded on divine infinites and yet are applying to it a language formed by this lower and limited experience which founds itself on finite appearances and the separative definitions by which we try to distinguish and classify the phenomena of the material universe. Thus we have to use the word individual and speak of the ego and the true individual, just as we speak sometimes of the apparent and the real Man. Evidently, all these words, man, apparent, real, individual, true, have to be taken in a very relative sense and with a full awareness of their imperfection and inability to express the things that we mean. By individual we mean normally something that separates itself from everything else and stands apart, though in reality there is no such thing anywhere in existence; it is a figment of our mental conceptions useful and necessary to express a partial and practical truth. But the difficulty is that the mind gets dominated by its words and forgets that the partial and practical truth becomes true truth only by its relation to others which seem to the reason to contradict it, and that taken by itself it contains a constant element of falsity. Thus when we speak of an individual we mean ordinarily an individualisation of mental, vital, physical being separate from all other beings, incapable of unity with them by its very individuality. If we go beyond these three terms of mind, life and body, and speak of the soul or individual self, we still think of an individualised being separate from all others, incapable of unity and inclusive mutuality, capable at most of a spiritual contact and soul-sympathy. It is therefore necessary to insist that by the true individual we mean nothing of the kind, but a conscious power of being of the Eternal, always existing by unity, always capable of mutuality. It is that being which by self-knowledge enjoys liberation and immortality.

But we have to carry still farther the conflict between the

normal and the higher reason. When we speak of the true individual as a conscious power of being of the Eternal, we are still using intellectual terms, — we cannot help it, unless we plunge into a language of pure symbols and mystic values of speech, — but, what is worse, we are, in the attempt to get away from the idea of the ego, using a too abstract language. Let us say, then, a conscious being who is for our valuations of existence a being of the Eternal in his power of individualising self-experience; for it must be a concrete being, — and not an abstract power, — who enjoys immortality. And then we get to this that not only am I in the world and the world in me, but God is in me and I am in God; by which yet it is not meant that God depends for His existence on man, but that He manifests Himself in that which He manifests within Himself; the individual exists in the Transcendent, but all the Transcendent is there concealed in the individual. Further I am one with God in my being and yet I can have relations with Him in my experience. I, the liberated individual, can enjoy the Divine in His transcendence, unified with Him, and enjoy at the same time the Divine in other individuals and in His cosmic being. Evidently we have arrived at certain primary relations of the Absolute and they can only be intelligible to the mind if we see that the Transcendent, the individual, the cosmic being are the eternal powers of consciousness, — we fall again, this time without remedy, into a wholly abstract language, — of an absolute existence, a unity yet more than a unity, which so expresses itself to its own consciousness in us, but which we cannot adequately speak of in human language and must not hope to describe either by negative or positive terms to our reason, but can only hope to indicate it to the utmost power of our language.

But the normal mind, which has no experience of these things that are so powerfully real to the liberated consciousness, may well revolt against what may seem to it nothing more than a mass of intellectual contradictions. It may say, "I know very well what the Absolute is; it is that in which there are no relations. The Absolute and the relative are irreconcilable opposites; in the relative there is nowhere anything absolute, in the Absolute there can be nothing relative. Anything which contradicts these first data of my thought, is intellectually false and practically impossible. These other statements also contradict my law of contradictions which is that two opposing and conflicting affirmations cannot both be true. It is impossible that there should be oneness with God and yet a relation with Him such as this of the enjoyment of the Divine. In oneness there is no one to enjoy except the One and nothing to be enjoyed except the One. God, the individual and the cosmos must be three different actualities, otherwise there could be no relations between them. Either they are eternally different or they are different in present time, although they may have originally been one undifferentiated existence and may eventually re-become one undifferentiated existence. Unity was perhaps and will be perhaps, but it is not now and cannot be so long as cosmos and the individual endure. The cosmic being can only know and possess the transcendent unity by ceasing to be cosmic; the individual can only know and possess the cosmic or the transcendent unity by ceasing from all individuality and individualisation. Or if unity is the one eternal fact, then cosmos and individual are non-existent; they are illusions imposed on itself by the Eternal. That may well involve a contradiction or an unreconciled paradox; but I am willing to admit a contradiction in the Eternal which I am not compelled to think out, rather than a contradiction here of my primary conceptions which I am compelled to think out logically and to practical ends. I am on this supposition able either to take the world as practically real and think and act in it or to reject it as an unreality and cease to think and act; I am not compelled to reconcile contradictions, not called on to be conscious of and conscious in something beyond myself and world and yet deal from that basis, as God does, with a world of contradictions. The attempt to be as God while I am still an individual or to be three things at a time seems to me to involve a logical confusion and a practical impossibility." Such might well be the attitude of the normal reason, and it is clear, lucid, positive in its distinctions; it involves no extraordinary gymnastics of the reason trying to exceed itself and losing itself in shadows and half-lights or any kind of mysticism, or at least there is only one original and comparatively simple mysticism free from all other difficult complexities. Therefore it is the reasoning which is the most satisfactory to the simply rational mind. Yet is there here a triple error, the error of making an unbridgeable gulf between the Absolute and the relative, the error of making too simple and rigid and extending too far the law of contradictions and the error of conceiving in terms of Time the genesis of things which have their origin and first habitat in the Eternal.

We mean by the Absolute something greater than ourselves, greater than the cosmos which we live in, the supreme reality of that transcendent Being which we call God, something without which all that we see or are conscious of as existing, could not have been, could not for a moment remain in existence. Indian thought calls it Brahman, European thought the Absolute because it is a self-existent which is absolved of all bondage to relativities. For all relatives can only exist by something which is the truth of them all and the source and continent of their powers and properties and yet exceeds them all; it is something of which not only each relativity itself, but also any sum we can make of all relatives that we know, can only be, — in all that we know of them, — a partial, inferior or practical expression. We see by reason that such an Absolute must exist; we become by spiritual experience aware of its existence: but even when we are most aware of it, we cannot describe it because our language and thought can deal only with the relative. The Absolute is for us the Ineffable.

So far there need be no real difficulty nor confusion. But we readily go on, led by the mind's habit of oppositions, of thinking by distinctions and pairs of contraries, to speak of it as not only not bound by the limitations of the relative, but as if it were bound by its freedom from limitations, inexorably empty of all power for relations and in its nature incapable of them, something hostile in its whole being to relativity and its eternal contrary. By this false step of our logic we get into an impasse. Our own existence and the existence of the universe become not only a mystery, but logically inconceivable. For we get by that to

an Absolute which is incapable of relativity and exclusive of all
relatives and yet the cause or at least the support of relativity and
the container, truth and substance of all relatives. We have then
only one logical-illogical way of escape out of the impasse; we
have to suppose the imposition of the world as a self-effective
illusion or an unreal temporal reality, on the eternity of the
formless relationless Absolute. This imposition is made by our
misleading individual consciousness which falsely sees Brahman
in the figure of the cosmos, — as a man mistakes a rope for a
serpent; but since either our individual consciousness is itself a
relative supported by the Brahman and only existent by it, not a
real reality, or since in its reality it is itself the Brahman, it is the
Brahman after all which imposes on itself in us this delusion and
mistakes in some figure of its own consciousness an existent rope
for a non-existent snake, imposes on its own indeterminable pure
Reality the semblance of a universe, or if it does not impose it on
its own consciousness, it is on a consciousness derived from it
and dependent on it, a projection of itself into Maya. By this explanation nothing is explained; the original contradiction stands
where it was, unreconciled, and we have only stated it over again
in other terms. It looks as if, by attempting to arrive at an explanation by means of intellectual reasoning, we have only befogged
ourselves by the delusion of our own uncompromising logic: we
have imposed on the Absolute the imposition which our too
presumptuous reasoning has practised on our own intelligence;
we have transformed our mental difficulty in understanding the
world-manifestation into an original impossibility for the Absolute to manifest itself in world at all. But the Absolute, obviously,
finds no difficulty in world-manifestation and no difficulty either
in a simultaneous transcendence of world-manifestation; the difficulty exists only for our mental limitations which prevent us
from grasping the supramental rationality of the co-existence
of the infinite and the finite or seizing the nodus of the unconditioned with the conditioned. For our intellectual rationality
these are opposites; for the absolute reason they are interrelated
and not essentially conflicting expressions of one and the same
reality. The consciousness of infinite Existence is other than our

mind-consciousness and sense-consciousness, greater and more capacious, for it includes them as minor terms of its workings, and the logic of infinite Existence is other than our intellectual logic. It reconciles in its great primal facts of being what to our mental view, concerned as it is with words and ideas derived from secondary facts, are irreconcilable contraries.

Our mistake is that in trying to define the indefinable we think we have succeeded when we have described by an all-exclusive negation this Absolute which we are yet compelled to conceive of as a supreme positive and the cause of all positives. It is not surprising that so many acute thinkers, with their eye on the facts of being and not on verbal distinctions, should be driven to infer that the Absolute is a fiction of the intelligence, an idea born of words and verbal dialectics, a zero, non-existent, and to conclude that an eternal Becoming is the only truth of our existence. The ancient sages spoke indeed of Brahman negatively, — they said of it, *neti neti*, it is not this, it is not that, — but they took care also to speak of it positively; they said of it too, it is this, it is that, it is all: for they saw that to limit it either by positive or negative definitions was to fall away from its truth. Brahman, they said, is Matter, is Life, is Mind, is Supermind, is cosmic Delight, is Sachchidananda; yet it cannot really be defined by any of these things, not even by our largest conception of Sachchidananda. In the world as we see it, for our mental consciousness however high we carry it, we find that to every positive there is a negative. But the negative is not a zero, — indeed whatever appears to us a zero is packed with force, teeming with power of existence, full of actual or potential contents. Neither does the existence of the negative make its corresponding positive non-existent or an unreality; it only makes the positive an incomplete statement of the truth of things and even, we may say, of the positive's own truth. For the positive and the negative exist not only side by side, but in relation to each other and by each other; they complete and would to the all-view, which a limited mind cannot reach, explain one another. Each by itself is not really known; we only begin to know it in its deeper truth when we can read into it the suggestions of its apparent opposite. It is through such a profounder catholic intuition and not by exclusive logical oppositions that our intelligence ought to approach the Absolute.

The positives of the Absolute are its various statements of itself to our consciousness; its negatives bring in the rest of its absolute positivity by which its limitation to these first statements is denied. We have, to begin with, its large primary relations such as the infinite and the finite, the conditioned and unconditioned, the qualitied and unqualitied; in each pair the negative conceals the whole power of the corresponding positive which is contained in it and emerges from it: there is no real opposition. We have, in a less subtle order of truths, the transcendent and the cosmic, the universal and the individual; here we have seen that each member of these pairs is contained in its apparent opposite. The universal particularises itself in the individual; the individual contains in himself all the generalities of the universal. The universal consciousness finds all itself by the variations of numberless individuals, not by suppressing variations; the individual consciousness fulfils all itself when it is universalised into sympathy and identity with the cosmic, not by limiting itself in the ego. So too the cosmic contains in all itself and in each thing in it the complete immanence of the transcendent; it maintains itself as the world-being by the consciousness of its own transcendent reality, it finds itself in each individual being by the realisation of the divine and transcendent in that being and in all existences. The transcendent contains, manifests, constitutes the cosmos and by manifesting it manifests or discovers, as we may say in the old poetic sense of that word, its own infinite harmonic varieties. But even in the lower orders of the relative we find this play of negative and positive, and through the divine reconciliation of its terms, not by excising them or carrying their opposition to the bitter end, we have to arrive at the Absolute. For there in the Absolute all this relativity, all this varying rhythmic self-statement of the Absolute, finds, not its complete denial, but its reason for existence and its justification, not its conviction as a lie, but the source and principle of its truth. Cosmos and individual go back to something in the Absolute which is the true truth of individuality, the true truth of cosmic being and not their denial and conviction of their falsity. The Absolute is not a sceptical logician denying the truth of all his own statements and self-expressions, but an existence so utterly and so infinitely positive that no finite positive can be formulated which can exhaust it or bind it down to its definitions.

It is evident that if such is the truth of the Absolute, we cannot bind it either by our law of contradictions. That law is necessary to us in order that we may posit partial and practical truths, think out things clearly, decisively and usefully, classify, act, deal with them effectively for particular purposes in our divisions of Space, distinctions of form and property, moments of Time. It represents a formal and strongly dynamic truth of existence in its practical workings which is strongest in the most outward term of things, the material, but becomes less and less rigidly binding as we go upward in the scale, mount on the more subtle rungs of the ladder of being. It is especially necessary for us in dealing with material phenomena and forces; we have to suppose them to be one thing at a time, to have one power at a time and to be limited by their ostensible and practically effective capacities and properties; otherwise we cannot deal with them. But even there, as human thought is beginning to realise, the distinctions made by the intellect and the classifications and practical experiments of Science, while perfectly valid in their own field and for their own purpose, do not represent the whole or the real truth of things, whether of things in the whole or of the thing by itself which we have classified and set artificially apart, isolated for separate analysis. By that isolation we are indeed able to deal with it very practically, very effectively, and we think at first that the effectiveness of our action proves the entire and sufficient truth of our isolating and analysing knowledge. Afterwards we find that by getting beyond it we can arrive at a greater truth and a greater effectivity.

The isolation is certainly necessary for first knowledge. A diamond is a diamond and a pearl a pearl, each thing of its own class, existing by its distinction from all others, each distinguished by its own form and properties. But each has also

properties and elements which are common to both and others which are common to material things in general. And in
reality each does not exist only by its distinctions, but much
more essentially by that which is common to both; and we get
back to the very basis and enduring truth of all material things
only when we find that all are the same thing, one energy, one
substance or, if you like, one universal motion which throws
up, brings out, combines, realises these different forms, these
various properties, these fixed and harmonised potentialities of
its own being. If we stop short at the knowledge of distinctions,
we can deal only with diamond and pearl as they are, fix their
values, uses, varieties, make the best ordinary use and profit of
them; but if we can get to the knowledge and control of their
elements and the common properties of the class to which they
belong, we may arrive at the power of making either a diamond
or pearl at our pleasure: go farther still and master that which all
material things are in their essence and we may arrive even at the
power of transmutation which would give the greatest possible
control of material Nature. Thus the knowledge of distinctions
arrives at its greatest truth and effective use when we arrive at
the deeper knowledge of that which reconciles distinctions in
the unity behind all variations. That deeper knowledge does not
deprive the other and more superficial of effectivity nor convict
it of vanity. We cannot conclude from our ultimate material
discovery that there is no original substance or Matter, only
energy manifesting substance or manifesting as substance, —
that diamond and pearl are non-existent, unreal, only true to
the illusion of our senses of perception and action, that the one
substance, energy or motion is the sole eternal truth and that
therefore the best or only rational use of our science would be
to dissolve diamond and pearl and everything else that we can
dissolve into this one eternal and original reality and get done
with their forms and properties for ever. There is an essentiality
of things, a commonalty of things, an individuality of things; the
commonalty and individuality are true and eternal powers of the
essentiality: that transcends them both, but the three together
and not one by itself are the eternal terms of existence.

This truth which we can see, though with difficulty and under considerable restrictions, even in the material world where the subtler and higher powers of being have to be excluded from our intellectual operations, becomes clearer and more powerful when we ascend in the scale. We see the truth of our classifications and distinctions, but also their limits. All things, even while different, are yet one. For practical purposes plant, animal, man are different existences; yet when we look deeper we see that the plant is only an animal with an insufficient evolution of self-consciousness and dynamic force; the animal is man in the making; man himself is that animal and yet the something more of self-consciousness and dynamic power of consciousness that make him man; and yet again he is the something more which is contained and repressed in his being as the potentiality of the divine, — he is a god in the making. In each of these, plant, animal, man, god, the Eternal is there containing and repressing himself as it were in order to make a certain statement of his being. Each is the whole Eternal concealed. Man himself, who takes up all that went before him and transmutes it into the term of manhood, is the individual human being and yet he is all mankind, the universal man acting in the individual as a human personality. He is all and yet he is himself and unique. He is what he is, but he is also the past of all that he was and the potentiality of all that he is not. We cannot understand him if we look only at his present individuality, but we cannot understand him either if we look only at his commonalty, his general term of manhood, or go back by exclusion from both to an essentiality of his being in which his distinguishing manhood and his particularising individuality seem to disappear. Each thing is the Absolute, all are that One, but in these three terms always the Absolute makes its statement of its developed self-existence. We are not, because of the essential unity, compelled to say that all God's various action and workings are vain, worthless, unreal, phenomenal, illusory, and that the best and only rational or super-rational use we can make of our knowledge is to get away from them, dissolve our cosmic and individual existence into the essential being and get rid of all becoming as a futility for ever.

In our practical dealings with life we have to arrive at the same truth. For certain practical ends we have to say that a thing is good or bad, beautiful or ugly, just or unjust and act upon that statement; but if we limit ourselves by it, we do not get at real knowledge. The law of contradictions here is only valid in so far as two different and opposite statements cannot be true of the same thing at the same time, in the same field, in the same respect, from the same point of view and for the same practical purpose. A great war, destruction or violent all-upheaving revolution, for example, may present itself to us as an evil, a virulent and catastrophic disorder, and it is so in certain respects, results, ways of looking at it; but from others, it may be a great good, since it rapidly clears the field for a new good or a more satisfying order. No man is simply good or simply bad; every man is a mixture of contraries: even we find these contraries often inextricably mixed up in a single feeling, a single action. All kinds of conflicting qualities, powers, values meet together and run into each other to make up our action, life, nature. We can only understand entirely if we get to some sense of the Absolute and yet look at its workings in all the relativities which are being manifested, — look not only at each by itself, but each in relation to all and to that which exceeds and reconciles them all. In fact we can only know by getting to the divine view and purpose in things and not merely looking at our own, though our own limited human view and momentary purpose have their validity in the cadre of the All. For behind all relativities there is this Absolute which gives them their being and their justification. No particular act or arrangement in the world is by itself absolute justice; but there is behind all acts and arrangements something absolute which we call justice, which expresses itself through their relativities and which we would realise if our view and knowledge were comprehensive instead of being as they are partial, superficial, limited to a few ostensible facts and appearances. So too there is an absolute good and an absolute beauty: but we can only get a glimpse of it if we embrace all things impartially and get beyond their appearances to some sense of that which, between them, all and each are by their complex terms trying to state and work out; not an indeterminate, — for the indeterminate, being only the original stuff or perhaps the packed condition of determinations, would explain by itself nothing at all, — but the Absolute. We can indeed follow the opposite method of breaking up all things and refusing to look at them as a whole and in relation to that which justifies them and so create an intellectual conception of absolute evil, absolute injustice, the absolute hideousness, painfulness, triviality, vulgarity or vanity of all things; but that is to pursue to its extreme the method of the Ignorance whose view is based upon division. We cannot rightly so deal with the divine workings. Because the Absolute expresses itself through relativities the secret of which we find it difficult to fathom, because to our limited view everything appears to be a purposeless play of oppositions and negatives or a mass of contradictions, we cannot conclude that our first limited view is right or that all is a vain delusion of the mind and has no reality. Nor can we solve all by an original unreconciled contradiction which is to explain all the rest. The human reason is wrong in attaching a separate and definitive value to each contradiction by itself or getting rid of one by altogether denying the other; but it is right in refusing to accept as final and as the last word the coupling of contradictions which have in no way been reconciled together or else found their source and significance in something beyond their opposition.

We cannot, either, effect a reconciliation or explanation of the original contradictions of existence by taking refuge in our concept of Time. Time, as we know or conceive it, is only our means of realising things in succession, it is a condition and cause of conditions, varies on different planes of existence, varies even for beings on one and the same plane: that is to say, it is not an Absolute and cannot explain the primary relations of the Absolute. They work themselves out in detail by Time and seem to our mental and vital being to be determined by it; but that seeming does not carry us back to their sources and principles. We make the distinction of conditioned and unconditioned and we imagine that the unconditioned became conditioned, the Infinite became finite at some date in Time, and may cease to be finite at some other date in Time, because it so appears to us in details, particulars or with regard to this or that system of things. But if we look at existence as a whole, we see that infinite and finite co-exist and exist in and by each other. Even if our universe were to disappear and reappear rhythmically in Time, as was the old belief, that too would be only a large detail and would not show that at a particular time all condition ceases in the whole range of infinite existence and all Being becomes the unconditioned, at another it again takes on the reality or the appearance of conditions. The first source and the primary relations lie beyond our mental divisions of Time, in the divine timelessness or else in the indivisible or eternal Time of which our divisions and successions are only figures in a mental experience.

There we see that all meets and all principles, all persistent realities of existence, — for the finite as a principle of being is as persistent as the infinite, — stand in a primary relation to each other in a free, not an exclusive unity of the Absolute, and that the way they present themselves to us in a material or a mental world is only a working out of them in secondary, tertiary or yet lower relativities. The Absolute has not become the contrary of itself and assumed at a certain date real or unreal relativities of which it was originally incapable, nor has the One become by a miracle the Many, nor the unconditioned deviated into the conditioned, nor the unqualitied sprouted out into qualities. These oppositions are only the conveniences of our mental consciousness, our divisions of the indivisible. The things they represent are not fictions, they are realities, but they are not rightly known if they are set in irreconcilable opposition to or separation from each other; for there is no such irreconcilable opposition or separation of them in the all-view of the Absolute. This is the weakness not only of our scientific divisions and metaphysical distinctions, but of our exclusive spiritual realisations which are only exclusive because to arrive at them we have to start from our limiting and dividing mental consciousness. We have to make the metaphysical distinctions in order to help our intelligence towards a truth which exceeds it, because it is only so that it can escape from the confusions of our first undistinguishing mental view of things; but if we bind ourselves by them to the end, we make chains of what should only have been first helps. We have to make use too of distinct spiritual realisations which may at first seem contrary to each other, because as mental beings it is difficult or impossible for us to seize at once largely and completely what is beyond our mentality; but we err if we intellectualise them into sole truths, — as when we assert that the Impersonal must be the one ultimate realisation and the rest creation of Maya or declare the Saguna, the Divine in its qualities, to be that and thrust away the impersonality from our spiritual experience. We have to see that both these realisations of the great spiritual seekers are equally valid in themselves, equally invalid against each other; they are one and the same Reality experienced on two sides which are both necessary for the full knowledge and experience of each other and of that which they both are. So is it with the One and the Many, the finite and the infinite, the transcendent and the cosmic, the individual and the universal; each is the other as well as itself and neither can be entirely known without the other and without exceeding their appearance of contrary oppositions.

We see then that there are three terms of the one existence, transcendent, universal and individual, and that each of these always contains secretly or overtly the two others. The Transcendent possesses itself always and controls the other two as the basis of its own temporal possibilities; that is the Divine, the eternal all-possessing God-consciousness, omnipotent, omniscient, omnipresent, which informs, embraces, governs all existences. The human being is here on earth the highest power of the third term, the individual, for he alone can work out at its critical turning-point that movement of self-manifestation which appears to us as the involution and evolution of the divine consciousness between the two terms of the Ignorance and the Knowledge. The power of the individual to possess in his consciousness by self-knowledge his unity with the Transcendent and the universal, with the One Being and all beings and to live in that knowledge and transform his life by it, is that which makes the working out of the divine self-manifestation through the individual possible; and the arrival of the individual, — not in one but in all, — at the divine life is the sole conceivable object of the movement. The existence of the individual is not an error in some self of the Absolute which that self afterwards discovers; for it is impossible that the absolute self-awareness or anything that is one with it should be ignorant of its own truth and its own capacities and betrayed by that ignorance either into a false idea of itself which it has to correct or an impossible venture which it has to renounce. Neither is the individual existence a subordinate circumstance in a divine play or Lila, a play which consists in a continual revolution through unending cycles of pleasure and suffering without any higher hope in the Lila itself or any issue from it except the occasional escape of a few from time to time out of their bondage to this ignorance. We might be compelled to hold that ruthless and disastrous view of God's workings if man had no power of self-transcendence or no power of transforming by self-knowledge the conditions of the play nearer and nearer to the truth of the divine Delight. In that power lies the justification of individual existence; the individual and the universal unfolding in themselves the divine light, power, joy of transcendent Sachchidananda always manifest above them, always secret behind their surface appearances, this is the secret intention, the ultimate significance of the divine play, the Lila. But it is in themselves, in their transformation but also their persistence and perfect relations, not in their self-annihilation that that must be unfolded. Otherwise there would be no reason for their ever having existed; the possibility of the Divine's unfolding in the individual is the secret of the enigma, his presence there and this intention of self-unfolding the key to the world of Knowledge-Ignorance.

Chapter IV

The Divine and the Undivine

The Seer, the Thinker, the Self-existent who becomes everywhere has ordered perfectly all things from years sempiternal.
Isha Upanishad.[1]

Many purified by knowledge have come to My state of being....
They have reached likeness in their law of being to Me.
Gita.[2]

Know That for the Brahman and not this which men cherish
here. *Kena Upanishad.*[3]

One controlling inner Self of all beings.... As the Sun, the eye
of the world, is not touched by the external faults of vision,
so this inner Self in beings is not touched by the sorrow of the
world. *Katha Upanishad.*[4]

The Lord abides in the heart of all beings. *Gita.*[5]

THE UNIVERSE is a manifestation of an infinite and eternal All-Existence: the Divine Being dwells in all that is; we
ourselves are that in our self, in our own deepest being;
our soul, the secret indwelling psychic entity, is a portion of
the Divine Consciousness and Essence. This is the view we have
taken of our existence; but at the same time we speak of a divine
life as the culmination of the evolutionary process, and the use
of the phrase implies that our present life is undivine and all the
life too that is below us. At the first glance this looks like a self-
contradiction; instead of making a distinction between the divine
life we aspire for and a present undivine existence, it would be

---

[1] Verse 8.   [2] IV. 10; XIV. 2.   [3] I. 4.   [4] II. 2. 12, 11.   [5] XVIII. 61.

more logical to speak of an ascent from level to higher level of
a divine manifestation. It may be admitted that essentially, if
we look at the inner reality alone and discount the suggestions
of the outer figure, such might be the nature of the evolution,
the change we have to undergo in Nature; so it would appear
perhaps to the impartial eye of a universal vision untroubled
by our dualities of knowledge and ignorance, good and evil,
happiness and suffering and participating in the untrammelled
consciousness and delight of Sachchidananda. And yet, from
the practical and relative point of view as distinguished from
an essential vision, the distinction between the divine and the
undivine has an insistent value, a very pressing significance. This
then is an aspect of the problem which it is necessary to bring
into the light and assess its true importance.

The distinction between the divine and the undivine life
is in fact identical with the root distinction between a life of
Knowledge lived in self-awareness and in the power of the Light
and a life of Ignorance, — at any rate it so presents itself in
a world that is slowly and with difficulty evolving out of an
original Inconscience. All life that has still this Inconscience for
its basis is stamped with the mark of a radical imperfection;
for even if it is satisfied with its own type, it is a satisfaction
with something incomplete and inharmonious, a patch-work of
discords: on the contrary, even a purely mental or vital life might
be perfect within its limits if it were based on a restricted but
harmonious self-power and self-knowledge. It is this bondage
to a perpetual stamp of imperfection and disharmony that is
the mark of the undivine; a divine life, on the contrary, even
if progressing from the little to the more, would be at each
stage harmonious in its principle and detail: it would be a secure ground upon which freedom and perfection could naturally
flower or grow towards their highest stature, refine and expand
into their most subtle opulence. All imperfections, all perfections
have to be taken into view in our consideration of the difference
between an undivine and a divine existence: but ordinarily, when
we make the distinction, we do it as human beings struggling
under the pressure of life and the difficulties of our conduct

amidst its immediate problems and perplexities; most of all we are thinking of the distinction we are obliged to make between good and evil or of that along with its kindred problem of the duality, the blend in us of happiness and suffering. When we seek intellectually for a divine presence in things, a divine origin of the world, a divine government of its workings, the presence of evil, the insistence on suffering, the large, the enormous part offered to pain, grief and affliction in the economy of Nature are the cruel phenomena which baffle our reason and overcome the instinctive faith of mankind in such an origin and government or in an all-seeing, all-determining and omnipresent Divine Immanence. Other difficulties we could solve more easily and happily and make some shift to be better satisfied with the ready conclusiveness of our solutions. But this standard of judgment is not sufficiently comprehensive and it is supported upon a too human point of view; for to a wider outlook evil and suffering appear only as a striking aspect, they are not the whole defect, not even the root of the matter. The sum of the world's imperfections is not made up only of these two deficiencies; there is more than the fall, if fall there was, of our spiritual or material being from good and from happiness or our nature's failure to overcome evil and suffering. Besides the deficiency of the ethical and hedonistic satisfactions demanded by our being, the paucity of Good and Delight in our world-experience, there is also the deficiency of other divine degrees: for Knowledge, Truth, Beauty, Power, Unity are, they too, the stuff and elements of a divine life, and these are given to us in a scanty and grudging measure; yet all are, in their absolute, powers of the Divine Nature.

It is not possible then to limit the description of our and the world's undivine imperfection solely to moral evil or sensational suffering; there is more in the world-enigma than their double problem, — for they are only two strong results of a common principle. It is the general principle of imperfection that we have to admit and consider. If we look closely at this general imperfection, we shall see that it consists first in a limitation in us of the divine elements which robs them of their divinity, then in a various many-branching distortion, a perversion, a contrary turn, a falsifying departure from some ideal Truth of being. To our minds which do not possess that Truth but can conceive it, this departure presents itself either as a state from which we have lapsed spiritually or as a possibility or promise which we cannot fulfil, cannot realise because it exists only as an ideal. There has been either a lapse of the inner spirit from a greater consciousness and knowledge, delight, love and beauty, power and capacity, harmony and good, or else there is a failure of our struggling nature, an impotence to achieve what we instinctively see to be divine and desirable. If we penetrate to the cause of the fall or the failure, we shall find that all proceeds from the one primal fact that our being, consciousness, force, experience of things represent, — not in their very self, but in their surface pragmatic nature, — a principle or an effective phenomenon of division or rupture in the unity of the Divine Existence. This division becomes in its inevitable practical effect a limitation of the divine consciousness and knowledge, the divine delight and beauty, the divine power and capacity, the divine harmony and good: there is a limitation of completeness and wholeness, a blindness in our vision of these things, a lameness in our following of them, in our experience of them a fragmentation, a diminution of power and intensity, a lowering of quality, — the mark of a descent from spiritual heights or else of a consciousness emerging from the insensible neutral monotone of the Inconscience; the intensities which are normal and natural on higher ranges are in us lost or toned down so as to harmonise with the blacks and greys of our material existence. There arises too by a secondary ulterior effect a perversion of these highest things; in our limited mentality unconsciousness and wrong consciousness intervene, ignorance covers our whole nature and, — by the misapplication or misdirection of an imperfect will and knowledge, by automatic reactions of our diminished consciousness-force and the inept poverty of our substance, — contradictions of the divine elements are formed, incapacity, inertia, falsehood, error, pain and grief, wrong-doing, discord, evil. There is too, always, somewhere hidden in our selves, nursed in our recesses, even when not overtly felt in the conscious nature, even when rejected by the parts of us which these things torture, an attachment to this experience of division, a clinging to the divided way of being which prevents the excision of these unhappinesses or their rejection and removal. For since the principle of Consciousness-Force and Ananda is at the root of all manifestation, nothing can endure if it has not a will in our nature, a sanction of the Purusha, a sustained pleasure in some part of the being, even though it be a secret or a perverse pleasure, to keep it in continuance.

When we say that all is a divine manifestation, even that which we call undivine, we mean that in its essentiality all is divine even if the form baffles or repels us. Or, to put it in a formula to which it is easier for our psychological sense of things to give its assent, in all things there is a presence, a primal Reality, — the Self, the Divine, Brahman, — which is for ever pure, perfect, blissful, infinite: its infinity is not affected by the limitations of relative things; its purity is not stained by our sin and evil; its bliss is not touched by our pain and suffering; its perfection is not impaired by our defects of consciousness, knowledge, will, unity. In certain images of the Upanishads the divine Purusha is described as the one Fire which has entered into all forms and shapes itself according to the form, as the one Sun which illumines all impartially and is not affected by the faults of our seeing. But this affirmation is not enough; it leaves the problem unsolved, why that which is in itself ever pure, perfect, blissful, infinite, should not only tolerate but seem to maintain and encourage in its manifestation imperfection and limitation, impurity and suffering and falsehood and evil: it states the duality that constitutes the problem, but does not solve it.

If we simply leave these two dissonant facts of existence standing in each other's presence, we are driven to conclude that there is no reconciliation possible; all we can do is to cling as much as we can to a deepening sense of the joy of the pure and essential Presence and do the best we may with the discordant externality, until we can impose in its place the law of its divine contrary. Or else we have to seek for an escape rather than a solution. For we can say that the inner Presence alone is a Truth and the discordant externality is a falsehood or illusion created by a mysterious principle of Ignorance; our problem is to find some way of escape out of the falsehood of the manifested world into the truth of the hidden Reality. Or we may hold with the Buddhist that there is no need of explanation, since there is this one practical fact of the imperfection and impermanence of things and no Self, Divine or Brahman, for that too is an illusion of our consciousness: the one thing that is necessary for liberation is to get rid of the persistent structure of ideas and persistent energy of action which maintain a continuity in the flux of the impermanence. On this road of escape we achieve self-extinction in Nirvana; the problem of things gets itself extinguished by our own self-extinction. This is a way out, but it does not look like the true and only way, nor are the other solutions altogether satisfactory. It is a fact that by excluding the discordant manifestation from our inner consciousness as a superficial externality, by insisting only on the pure and perfect Presence, we can achieve individually a deep and blissful sense of this silent Divinity, can enter into the sanctuary, can live in the light and the rapture. An exclusive inner concentration on the Real, the Eternal is possible, even a self-immersion by which we can lose or put away the dissonances of the universe. But there is too somewhere deep down in us the need of a total consciousness, there is in Nature a secret universal seeking for the whole Divine, an impulsion towards some entire awareness and delight and power of existence; this need of a whole being, a total knowledge, this integral will in us is not fully satisfied by these solutions. So long as the world is not divinely explained to us, the Divine remains imperfectly known; for the world too is That and, so long as it is not present to our consciousness and possessed by our powers of consciousness in the sense of the divine being, we are not in possession of the whole Divinity.

It is possible to escape from the problem otherwise; for, admitting always the essential Presence, we can endeavour to justify the divinity of the manifestation by correcting the human view of perfection or putting it aside as a too limited mental standard. We may say that not only is the Spirit in things absolutely perfect and divine, but each thing also is relatively perfect and divine in itself, in its expression of what it has to express of the possibilities of existence, in its assumption of its proper place in the complete manifestation. Each thing is divine in itself because each is a fact and idea of the divine being, knowledge and will fulfilling itself infallibly in accordance with the law of that particular manifestation. Each being is possessed of the knowledge, the force, the measure and kind of delight of existence precisely proper to its own nature; each works in the gradations of experience decreed by a secret inherent will, a native law, an intrinsic power of the self, an occult significance. It is thus perfect in the relation of its phenomena to the law of its being; for all are in harmony with that, spring out of it, adapt themselves to its purpose according to the infallibility of the divine Will and Knowledge at work within the creature. It is perfect and divine also in relation to the whole, in its proper place in the whole; to that totality it is necessary and in it it fulfils a part by which the perfection actual and progressive of the universal harmony, the adaptation of all in it to its whole purpose and its whole sense is helped and completed. If to us things appear undivine, if we hasten to condemn this or that phenomenon as inconsistent with the nature of a divine being, it is because we are ignorant of the sense and purpose of the Divine in the world in its entirety. Because we see only parts and fragments, we judge of each by itself as if it were the whole, judge also the external phenomena without knowing their secret sense; but by doing so we vitiate our valuation of things, put on it the stamp of an initial and fundamental error. Perfection cannot reside in the thing in its separateness, for that separateness is an illusion; perfection is the perfection of the total divine harmony.

All this may be true up to a certain point and so far as it goes; but this also is a solution incomplete by itself and it cannot give us an entire satisfaction. It takes insufficient account of the human consciousness and the human view from which we have to start; it does not give us the vision of the harmony it alleges, and so it cannot meet our demand or convince, but only contradicts by a cold intellectual conception our acute human sense of the reality of evil and imperfection; it gives too no lead to the psychic element in our nature, the soul's aspiration towards light and truth and towards a spiritual conquest, a victory over imperfection and evil. By itself, this view of things amounts to little more than the facile dogma which tells us that all that is is right, because all is perfectly decreed by the divine Wisdom. It supplies us with nothing better than a complacent intellectual and philosophic optimism: no light is turned on the disconcerting facts of pain, suffering and discord to which our human consciousness bears constant and troubling witness; at most there is a suggestion that in the divine reason of things there is a key to these things to which we have no access. This is not a sufficient answer to our discontent and our aspiration which, however ignorant in their reactions, however mixed their mental motives, must correspond to a divine reality deeper down in our being. A Divine Whole that is perfect by reason of the imperfection of its parts, runs the risk of itself being only perfect in imperfection, because it fulfils entirely some stage in an unaccomplished purpose; it is then a present but not an ultimate Totality. To it we could apply the Greek saying *Theos ouk estin alla gignetai*, the Divine is not yet in being, but is becoming. The true Divine would then be secret within us and perhaps supreme above us; to find the Divine within us and above us would be the real solution, to become perfect as That is perfect, to attain liberation by likeness to it or by attaining to the law of its nature, *sādṛśya, sādharmya*.

If the human consciousness were bound to the sense of imperfection and the acceptance of it as the law of our life and the very character of our existence, — a reasoned acceptance that could answer in our human nature to the blind animal acceptance of the animal nature, — then we might say that what we are marks the limit of the divine self-expression in us; we might believe too that our imperfections and sufferings worked for the general harmony and perfection of things and console ourselves with this philosophic balm offered for our wounds, satisfied to move among the pitfalls of life with as much rational prudence or as much philosophic sagacity and resignation as our incomplete mental wisdom and our impatient vital parts permitted. Or else, taking refuge in the more consoling fervours of religion, we might submit to all as the will of God in the hope or the faith of recompense in a Paradise beyond where we shall enter into a happier existence and put on a more pure and perfect nature. But there is an essential factor in our human consciousness and its workings which, no less than the reason, distinguishes it entirely from the animal; there is not only a mental part in us which recognises the imperfection, there is a psychic part which rejects it. Our soul's dissatisfaction with imperfection as a law of life upon earth, its aspiration towards the elimination of all imperfections from our nature, not only in a heaven beyond where it would be automatically impossible to be imperfect, but here and now in a life where perfection has to be conquered by evolution and struggle, are as much a law of our being as that against which they revolt; they too are divine, — a divine dissatisfaction, a divine aspiration. In them is the inherent light of a power within which maintains them in us so that the Divine may not only be there as a hidden Reality in our spiritual secrecies but unfold itself in the evolution of Nature.

In this light we can admit that all works perfectly towards a divine end by a divine wisdom and therefore each thing is in that sense perfectly fitted in its place; but we say that that is not the whole of the divine purpose. For what is is only justifiable, finds its perfect sense and satisfaction by what can and will be. There is, no doubt, a key in the divine reason that would justify things as they are by revealing their right significance and true secret as other, subtler, deeper than their outward meaning and phenomenal appearance which is all that can normally be caught by our present intelligence: but we cannot be content with that belief, to search for and find the spiritual key of things is the law of our being. The sign of the finding is not a philosophic intellectual recognition and a resigned or sage acceptance of things as they are because of some divine sense and purpose in them which is beyond us; the real sign is an elevation towards the spiritual knowledge and power which will transform the law and phenomena and external forms of our life nearer to a true image of that divine sense and purpose. It is right and reasonable to endure with equanimity suffering and subjection to defect as the immediate will of God, a present law of imperfection laid on our members, but on condition that we recognise it also as the will of God in us to transcend evil and suffering, to transform imperfection into perfection, to rise into a higher law of Divine Nature. In our human consciousness there is the image of an ideal truth of being, a divine nature, an incipient godhead: in relation to that higher truth our present state of imperfection can be relatively described as an undivine life and the conditions of the world from which we start as undivine conditions; the imperfections are the indication given to us that they are there as first disguises, not as the intended expression of the divine being and the divine nature. It is a Power within us, the concealed Divinity, that has lit the flame of aspiration, pictures the image of the ideal, keeps alive our discontent and pushes us to throw off the disguise and to reveal or, in the Vedic phrase, to form and disclose the Godhead in the manifest spirit, mind, life and body of this terrestrial creature. Our present nature can only be transitional, our imperfect status a starting-point and opportunity for the achievement of another higher, wider and greater that shall be divine and perfect not only by the secret spirit within it but in its manifest and most outward form of existence.

But these conclusions are only first reasonings or primary intuitions founded on our inner self-experience and the apparent facts of universal existence. They cannot be entirely validated unless we know the real cause of ignorance, imperfection and suffering and their place in the cosmic purpose or cosmic order. There are three propositions about God and the world, — if we admit the Divine Existence, — to which the general reason and consciousness of mankind bear witness; but, one of the three, — which is yet necessitated by the character of the world we live in, — does not harmonise with the two others, and by this disharmony the human mind is thrown into great perplexities of contradiction and driven to doubt and denial. For, first, we find affirmed an omnipresent Divinity and Reality pure, perfect and blissful, without whom, apart from whom nothing could exist, since all exists only by him and in his being. All thinking on the subject that is not atheistic or materialistic or else primitive and anthropomorphic, has to start from this admission or to arrive at this fundamental concept. It is true that certain religions seem to suppose an extracosmic Deity who has created a world outside and apart from his own existence; but when they come to construct a theology or spiritual philosophy, these too admit omnipresence or immanence, — for this omnipresence imposes itself, is a necessity of spiritual thinking. If there is such a Divinity, Self or Reality, it must be everywhere, one and indivisible, nothing can possibly exist apart from its existence; nothing can be born from another than That; there can be nothing unsupported by That, independent of It, unfilled by the breath and power of Its being. It has been held indeed that the ignorance, the imperfection, the suffering of this world are not supported by the Divine Existence; but we have then to suppose two Gods, an Ormuzd of the good and an Ahriman of the evil or, perhaps, a perfect supracosmic and immanent Being and an imperfect cosmic Demiurge or separate undivine Nature. This is a possible conception but improbable to our highest intelligence, — it can only be at most a subordinate aspect, not the original truth or the whole truth of things; nor can we suppose that the one Self and Spirit in all and the one Power creator of all are different, contrary in the character of their being, separate in their will and purpose. Our reason tells us, our intuitive consciousness feels, and their witness is confirmed by spiritual experience, that the one pure and absolute Existence exists in all things and beings even as all things and beings exist in It and by It, and nothing can be or happen without this indwelling and all-supporting Presence.

A second affirmation, which our mind naturally accepts as the consequence of the first postulate, is that by the supreme consciousness and the supreme power of this omnipresent Divinity in its perfect universal knowledge and divine wisdom all things are ordered and governed in their fundamental relations and their process. But, on the other hand, the actual process of things, the actual relations which we see are, as presented to our human consciousness, relations of imperfection, of limitation; there appears a disharmony, even a perversion, something that is the contrary of our conception of the Divine Existence, a very apparent denial or at least a disfigurement or disguise of the Divine Presence. There arises then a third affirmation of the Divine Reality and the world reality as different in essence or in order, so different that we have to draw away from one to reach the other; if we would find the Divine Inhabitant, we must reject the world he inhabits, governs, has created or manifested in his own existence. The first of these three propositions is inevitable; the second also must stand if the omnipresent Divine has anything at all to do with the world he inhabits and with its manifestation, building, maintenance and government: but the third seems also self-evident and yet it is incompatible with its precedents, and this dissonance confronts us with a problem which appears to be incapable of satisfactory solution.

It is not difficult by some construction of the philosophic reason or of theological reasoning to circumvent the difficulty. It is possible to erect a fainéant Deity, like the gods of Epicurus, blissful in himself, observing but indifferent to a world conducted or misconducted by a mechanical law of Nature. It is open to us to posit a Witness Self, a silent Soul in things, a Purusha who allows Nature to do what she will and is content to reflect all her order and all her disorders in his passive and stainless consciousness, — or a supreme Self absolute, inactive, free from all relations, unconcerned with the works of the cosmic Illusion or Creation which has mysteriously or paradoxically originated from It or over against It to tempt and afflict a world of temporal creatures. But all these solutions do no more than reflect the apparent dissonance of our twofold experience; they do not attempt to reconcile, neither do they solve or explain it, but only reaffirm it by an open or covert dualism and an essential division of the Indivisible. Practically, there is affirmed a dual Godhead, Self or Soul and Nature: but Nature, the Power in things, cannot be anything else than a power of the Self, the Soul, the essential Being of things; her works cannot be altogether independent of Soul or Self, cannot be her own contrary result and working unaffected by its consent or refusal or a violence of mechanical Force imposed on an inertia of mechanical Passivity. It is possible again to posit an observing inactive Self and an active creating Godhead; but this device cannot serve us, for in the end these two must really be one in a dual aspect, — the Godhead the active aspect of the observing Self, the Self a witness of its own Godhead in action. A discord, a gulf between the Self in knowledge and the same Self in its works needs explanation, but it presents itself as unexplained and inexplicable. Or, again, we can posit a double consciousness of Brahman the Reality, one static and one dynamic, one essential and spiritual in which it is Self perfect and absolute, another formative, pragmatic, in which it becomes not-self and with which its absoluteness and perfection have no concern of participation; for it is only a temporal formation in the timeless Reality. But to us who even if only half-existent, half-conscious, yet inhabit the Absolute's half-dream of living and are compelled by Nature to have in it a terrible and insistent concern and to deal with it as real, this wears the appearance of an obvious mystification; for this temporal consciousness and its formations are also in the end a Power of the one Self, depend upon it, can exist only by it; what exists by the power of the Reality cannot be unrelated to It or That unrelated to the world of its own Power's making. If the world exists by the supreme Spirit, so also its ordering and relations must exist by the power of the Spirit; its law must be according to some law of the spiritual consciousness and existence. The Self, the Reality must be aware of and aware in the world-consciousness which exists in its being; a power of the Self, the Reality must be constantly determining or at least sanctioning its phenomena and operations: for there can be no independent power, no Nature not derived from the original and eternal Self-Existence. If it does no more, it must still be originating or determining the universe through the mere fact of its conscious omnipresence. It is, no doubt, a truth of spiritual experience that there is a status of peace and silence in the Infinite behind the cosmic activity, a Consciousness that is the immobile Witness of the creation; but this is not the whole of spiritual experience, and we cannot hope to find in one side only of knowledge a fundamental and total explanation of the Universe.

Once we admit a divine government of the universe, we must conclude that the power to govern is complete and absolute; for otherwise we are obliged to suppose that a being and consciousness infinite and absolute has a knowledge and will limited in their control of things or hampered in their power of working. It is not impossible to concede that the supreme and immanent Divinity may leave a certain freedom of working to something that has come into being in his perfection but is itself imperfect and the cause of imperfection, to an ignorant or inconscient Nature, to the action of the human mind and will, even to a conscious Power or Forces of darkness and evil that take their stand upon the reign of a basic Inconscience. But none of these things are independent of Its own existence, nature and consciousness and none of them can act except in Its presence and by Its sanction or allowance. Man's freedom is relative and he cannot be held solely responsible for the imperfection of his nature. Ignorance and inconscience of Nature have arisen, not independently, but in the one Being; the imperfection of her workings cannot be entirely foreign to some will of the Immanence. It may be conceded that forces set in motion are allowed to work themselves out according to the law of their movement; but what divine Omniscience and Omnipotence has allowed to arise and act in Its omnipresence, Its all-existence, we must consider It to have originated and decreed, since without the fiat of the Being they could not have been, could not remain in existence. If the Divine is at all concerned with the world he has manifested, there is no other Lord than He and from that necessity of His original and universal being there can eventually be no escape or departure. It is on the foundation of this self-evident consequence of our first premiss, without any evasion of its implications, that we have to consider the problem of imperfection, suffering and evil.

And first we must realise that the existence of ignorance,

error, limitation, suffering, division and discord in the world need not by itself, as we too hastily imagine, be a denial or a disproof of the divine being, consciousness, power, knowledge, will, delight in the universe. They can be that if we have to take them by themselves separately, but need not be so taken if we get a clear vision of their place and significance in a complete view of the universal workings. A part broken off from the whole may be imperfect, ugly, incomprehensible; but when we see it in the whole, it recovers its place in the harmony, it has a meaning and a use. The Divine Reality is infinite in its being; in this infinite being, we find limited being everywhere, — that is the apparent fact from which our existence here seems to start and to which our own narrow ego and its ego-centric activities bear constant witness. But, in reality, when we come to an integral self-knowledge, we find that we are not limited, for we also are infinite. Our ego is only a face of the universal being and has no separate existence; our apparent separative individuality is only a surface movement and behind it our real individuality stretches out to unity with all things and upward to oneness with the transcendent Divine Infinity. Thus our ego, which seems to be a limitation of existence, is really a power of infinity; the boundless multiplicity of beings in the world is a result and signal evidence, not of limitation or finiteness, but of that illimitable Infinity. Apparent division can never erect itself into a real separateness; there is supporting and overriding it an indivisible unity which division itself cannot divide. This fundamental world-fact of ego and apparent division and their separative workings in the world existence is no denial of the Divine Nature of unity and indivisible being; they are the surface results of an infinite multiplicity which is a power of the infinite Oneness.

There is then no real division or limitation of being, no fundamental contradiction of the omnipresent Reality; but there does seem to be a real limitation of consciousness: there is an ignorance of self, a veiling of the inner Divinity, and all imperfection is its consequence. For we identify ourselves mentally, vitally, physically with this superficial ego-consciousness which

is our first insistent self-experience; this does impose on us, not
a fundamentally real, but a practical division with all the untoward consequences of that separateness from the Reality. But
here again we have to discover that from the point of view of
God's workings, whatever be our reactions or our experience
on the surface, this fact of ignorance is itself an operation of
knowledge and not a true ignorance. Its phenomenon of ignorance is a superficial movement; for behind it is an indivisible
all-consciousness: the ignorance is a frontal power of that all-
consciousness which limits itself in a certain field, within certain
boundaries to a particular operation of knowledge, a particular
mode of conscious working, and keeps back all the rest of its
knowledge in waiting as a force behind it. All that is thus hidden
is an occult store of light and power for the All-Consciousness
to draw upon for the evolution of our being in Nature; there
is a secret working which fills up all the deficiencies of the
frontal Ignorance, acts through its apparent stumblings, prevents
them from leading to another final result than that which the
All-Knowledge has decreed, helps the soul in the Ignorance to
draw from its experience, even from the natural personality's
sufferings and errors, what is necessary for its evolution and to
leave behind what is no longer utilisable. This frontal power
of Ignorance is a power of concentration in a limited working,
much like that power in our human mentality by which we
absorb ourselves in a particular object and in a particular work
and seem to use only so much knowledge, only such ideas as
are necessary for it, — the rest, which are alien to it or would
interfere with it, are put back for the moment: yet, in reality, all
the time it is the indivisible consciousness which we are that has
done the work to be done, seen the thing that has to be seen,
— that and not any fragment of consciousness or any exclusive
ignorance in us is the silent knower and worker: so is it too with
this frontal power of concentration of the All-Consciousness
within us.

In our valuation of the movements of our consciousness
this ability of concentration is rightly held to be one of the
greatest powers of the human mentality. But equally the power

of putting forth what seems to be an exclusive working of limited knowledge, that which presents itself to us as ignorance, must be considered one of the greatest powers of the divine Consciousness. It is only a supreme self-possessing Knowledge which can thus be powerful to limit itself in the act and yet work out perfectly all its intentions through that apparent ignorance. In the universe we see this supreme self-possessing Knowledge work through a multitude of ignorances, each striving to act according to its own blindness, yet through them all it constructs and executes its universal harmonies. More, the miracle of its omniscience appears most strikingly of all in what seems to us the action of an Inconscient, when through the complete or the partial nescience, — more thick than our ignorance, — of the electron, atom, cell, plant, insect, the lowest forms of animal life, it arranges perfectly its order of things and guides the instinctive impulse or the inconscient impetus to an end possessed by the All-Knowledge but held behind a veil, not known by the instrumental form of existence, yet perfectly operative within the instinct or the impetus. We may say then that this action of the ignorance or nescience is no real ignorance, but a power, a sign, a proof of an omniscient self-knowledge and all-knowledge. If we need any personal and inner witness to this indivisible All-Consciousness behind the ignorance, — all Nature is its external proof, — we can get it with any completeness only in our deeper inner being or larger and higher spiritual state when we draw back behind the veil of our own surface ignorance and come into contact with the divine Idea and Will behind it. Then we see clearly enough that what we have done by ourselves in our ignorance was yet overseen and guided in its result by the invisible Omniscience; we discover a greater working behind our ignorant working and begin to glimpse its purpose in us: then only can we see and know what now we worship in faith, recognise wholly the pure and universal Presence, meet the Lord of all being and all Nature.

As with the cause, — the Ignorance, — so is it with the consequences of the Ignorance. All this that seems to us incapacity, weakness, impotence, limitation of power, our will's hampered struggle and fettered labour, takes from the point of view of the Divine in his self-workings the aspect of a just limitation of an omniscient power by the free will of that Power itself so that the surface energy shall be in exact correspondence with the work that it has to do, with its attempt, its allotted success or its destined because necessary failure, with the balance of the sum of forces in which it is a part and with the larger result of which its own results are an indivisible portion. Behind this limitation of power is the All-Power and in the limitation that All-Power is at work; but it is through the sum of many limited workings that the indivisible Omnipotence executes infallibly and sovereignly its purposes. This power to limit its force and to work through that self-limitation, by what we call labour, struggle, difficulty, by what seems to us a series of failures or half-baulked successes and through them to achieve its secret intention, is not therefore a sign, proof or reality of weakness, but a sign, proof, reality, — the greatest possible, — of an absolute omnipotence.

As to the suffering, which is so great a stumbling-block to our understanding of the universe, it is evidently a consequence of the limitation of consciousness, the restriction of force which prevents us from mastering or assimilating the touch of what is to us other-force: the result of this incapacity and disharmony is that the delight of the touch cannot be seized and it affects our sense with a reaction of discomfort or pain, a defect or excess, a discord resultant in inner or outer injury, born of division between our power of being and the power of being that meets us. Behind in our self and spirit is the All-Delight of the universal being which takes its account of the contact, a delight first in the enduring and then in the conquest of the suffering and finally in its transmutation that shall come hereafter; for pain and suffering are a perverse and contrary term of the delight of existence and they can turn into their opposite, even into the original All-Delight, Ananda. This All-Delight is not present in the universal alone, but it is here secret in ourselves, as we discover when we go back from our outward consciousness into the Self within us; the psychic being in us takes its account even of its most perverse or contrary as well as its more benign experiences and grows by the rejection of them or acceptance; it extracts a divine meaning and use from our most poignant sufferings, difficulties, misfortunes. Nothing but this All-Delight could dare or bear to impose such experiences on itself or on us; nothing else could turn them thus to its own utility and our spiritual profit. So too nothing but an inalienable harmony of being inherent in an inalienable unity of being would throw out so many harshest apparent discords and yet force them to its purpose so that in the end they are unable to do anything else but to serve and secure, and even themselves change into elements that constitute, a growing universal rhythm and ultimate harmony. At every turn it is the divine Reality which we can discover behind that which we are yet compelled by the nature of the superficial consciousness in which we dwell to call undivine and in a sense are right in using that appellation; for these appearances are a veil over the Divine Perfection, a veil necessary for the present, but not at all the true and complete figure.

But even when we thus regard the universe, we cannot and ought not to dismiss as entirely and radically false and unreal the values that are given to it by our own limited human consciousness. For grief, pain, suffering, error, falsehood, ignorance, weakness, wickedness, incapacity, non-doing of what should be done and wrong-doing, deviation of will and denial of will, egoism, limitation, division from other beings with whom we should be one, all that makes up the effective figure of what we call evil, are facts of the world-consciousness, not fictions and unrealities, although they are facts whose complete sense or true value is not that which we assign to them in our ignorance. Still our sense of them is part of a true sense, our values of them are necessary to their complete values. One side of the truth of these things we discover when we get into a deeper and larger consciousness; for we find then that there is a cosmic and individual utility in what presents itself to us as adverse and evil. For without experience of pain we would not get all the infinite value of the divine delight of which pain is in travail, all ignorance is a penumbra which environs an orb of knowledge, every error is significant of the possibility and the effort of a discovery of truth; every weakness and failure is a first sounding of gulfs of power and potentiality; all division is intended to enrich by an experience of various sweetness of unification the joy of realised unity. All this imperfection is to us evil, but all evil is in travail of the eternal good; for all is an imperfection which is the first condition, — in the law of life evolving out of Inconscience, — of a greater perfection in the manifesting of the hidden divinity. But at the same time our present feeling of this evil and imperfection, the revolt of our consciousness against them is also a necessary valuation; for if we have first to face and endure them, the ultimate command on us is to reject, to overcome, to transform the life and the nature. It is for that end that their insistence is not allowed to slacken; the soul must learn the results of the Ignorance, must begin to feel their reactions as a spur to its endeavour of mastery and conquest and finally to a greater endeavour of transformation and transcendence. It is possible, when we live inwardly in the depths, to arrive at a state of vast inner equality and peace which is untouched by the reactions of the outer nature, and that is a great but incomplete liberation, — for the outer nature too has a right to deliverance. But even if our personal deliverance is complete, still there is the suffering of others, the world travail, which the great of soul cannot regard with indifference. There is a unity with all beings which something within us feels and the deliverance of others must be felt as intimate to its own deliverance.

This then is the law of the manifestation, the reason of the imperfection here. True, it is a law of manifestation only and, even, a law special to this movement in which we live, and we may say that it need not have been, — if there were no movement of manifestation or not this movement; but, the manifestation and the movement being given, the law is necessary. It is not enough simply to say that the law and all its circumstances are an unreality created by the mental consciousness, non-existent in God, and to be indifferent to these dualities or to get out of the manifestation into God's pure being is the only wisdom. It is true they are creations of mind Consciousness, but Mind is only secondarily responsible; in a deeper reality they are, as we have seen already, creations of the Divine Consciousness projecting mind away from its all-knowledge so as to realise these opposite or contrary values of its all-power, all-knowledge, all-delight, all-being and unity. Obviously, this action and these fruits of the Divine Consciousness can be called by us unreal in the sense of not being the eternal and fundamental truth of being or can be taxed with falsehood because they contradict what is originally and eventually the truth of being; but, all the same, they have their persistent reality and importance in our present phase of the manifestation, nor can they be a mere mistake of the Divine Consciousness without any meaning in the divine wisdom, without any purpose of the divine joy, power and knowledge to justify their existence. Justification there must be even if it reposes for us upon a mystery which may confront us, so long as we live in a surface experience, as an insoluble riddle.

But if, accepting this side of Nature, we say that all things are fixed in their statutory and stationary law of being, and man too must be fixed in his imperfections, his ignorance and sin and weakness and vileness and suffering, our life loses its true significance. Man's perpetual attempt to arise out of the darkness and insufficiency of his nature can then have no issue in the world itself, in life itself; its one issue, if there is any, must be by an escape out of life, out of the world, out of his human existence and therefore out of its eternally unsatisfactory law of imperfect being, either into a heaven of the gods or of God or into the pure ineffability of the Absolute. If so, man can never really deliver out of the ignorance and falsehood the truth and knowledge, out of the evil and ugliness the good and beauty, out of the weakness and vileness the power and glory, out of the grief and suffering the joy and delight which are contained in the Spirit behind them and of which these contradictions are the first adverse and contrary conditions of emergence. All he can do is to cut the imperfections away from him and overpass too their balancing opposites, imperfect also, — leave with the ignorance the human knowledge, with the evil the human good, with the weakness the human strength and power, with the strife and suffering the human love and joy; for these are in our present nature inseparably entwined together, look like conjoint dualities, negative pole and positive pole of the same unreality, and since they cannot be elevated and transformed, they must be both abandoned: humanity cannot be fulfilled in divinity; it must cease, be left behind and rejected. Whether the result will be an individual enjoyment of the absolute divine nature or of the Divine Presence or a Nirvana in the featureless Absolute, is a point on which religions and philosophies differ: but in either case human existence on earth must be taken as condemned to eternal imperfection by the very law of its being; it is perpetually and unchangeably an undivine manifestation in the Divine Existence. The soul by taking on manhood, perhaps by the very fact of birth itself, has fallen from the Divine, has committed an original sin or error which it must be man's spiritual aim, as soon as he is enlightened, thoroughly to cancel, unflinchingly to eliminate.

In that case, the only reasonable explanation of such a paradoxical manifestation or creation is that it is a cosmic game, a Lila, a play, an amusement of the Divine Being. It may be he pretends to be undivine, wears that appearance like the mask or make-up of an actor for the sole pleasure of the pretence or the drama. Or else he has created the undivine, created ignorance, sin and suffering just for the joy of a manifold creation. Or, perhaps, as some religions curiously suppose, he has done this so that there may be inferior creatures who will praise and glorify Him for his eternal goodness, wisdom, bliss and omnipotence and try feebly to come an inch nearer to the goodness in order to share the bliss, on pain of punishment, — by some supposed eternal, — if, as the vast majority must by their very imperfection, they fail in their endeavour. But to the doctrine of such a Lila so crudely stated there is always possible the retort that a God, himself all-blissful, who delights in the suffering of creatures or imposes such suffering on them for the faults of his own imperfect creation, would be no Divinity and against him the moral being and intelligence of humanity must revolt or deny his existence. But if the human soul is a portion of the Divinity, if it is a divine Spirit in man that puts on this imperfection and in the form of humanity consents to bear this suffering, or if the soul in humanity is meant to be drawn to the Divine Spirit and is his associate in the play of imperfection here, in the delight of perfect being otherwhere, the Lila may still remain a paradox, but it ceases to be a cruel or revolting paradox; it can at most be regarded as a strange mystery and to the reason inexplicable. To explain it there must be two missing elements, a conscious assent by the soul to this manifestation and a reason in the All-Wisdom that makes the play significant and intelligible.

The strangeness of the play diminishes, the paradox loses its edge of sharpness if we discover that, although fixed grades exist each with its appropriate order of nature, they are only firm steps for a progressive ascent of the souls embodied in forms of matter, a progressive divine manifestation which rises from the inconscient to the superconscient or all-conscient status with the human consciousness as its decisive point of transition. Imperfection becomes then a necessary term of the manifestation: for, since all the divine nature is concealed but present in the Inconscient, it must be gradually delivered out of it; this graduation necessitates a partial unfolding, and this partial character or incompleteness of the unfolding necessitates imperfection. An evolutionary manifestation demands a mid-stage with gradations above and under it, — precisely such a stage as the mental consciousness of man, part knowledge, part ignorance, a middle power of being still leaning on the Inconscient but slowly rising towards the all-conscious Divine Nature. A partial unfolding implying imperfection and ignorance may take as its inevitable companion, perhaps its basis for certain movements, an apparent perversion of the original truth of being. For the ignorance or imperfection to endure there must be a seeming contrary of all that characterises the divine nature, its unity, its all-consciousness, its all-power, its all-harmony, its all-good, its all-delight; there must appear limitation, discord, unconsciousness, disharmony, incapacity, insensibility and suffering, evil. For without that perversion imperfection could have no strong standing-ground, could not so freely manifest and maintain its nature as against the presence of the underlying Divinity. A partial knowledge is imperfect knowledge and imperfect knowledge is to that extent ignorance, a contrary of the divine nature: but in its outlook on what is beyond its knowledge, this contrary negative becomes a contrary positive; it originates error, wrong knowledge, wrong dealing with things, with life, with action; the wrong knowledge becomes a wrong will in the nature, at first, it may be, wrong by mistake, but afterwards wrong by choice, by attachment, by delight in the falsehood, — the simple contrary turns into a complex perversion. Inconscience and ignorance once admitted, these form a natural result in a logical sequence and have to be admitted also as necessary factors. The only question is the reason why this kind of progressive manifestation was itself necessary; that is the sole point left obscure to the intelligence.

A manifestation of this kind, self-creation or Lila, would not seem justifiable if it were imposed on the unwilling creature; but it will be evident that the assent of the embodied spirit must be there already, for Prakriti cannot act without the assent of the Purusha. There must have been not only the will of the Divine Purusha to make the cosmic creation possible, but the assent of the individual Purusha to make the individual manifestation possible. But it may be said that the reason for the Divine Will and delight in such a difficult and tormented progressive manifestation and the reason for the soul's assent to it is still a mystery. But it is not altogether a mystery if we look at our own nature and can suppose some kindred movement of being in the beginning as its cosmic origin. On the contrary, a play of self-concealing and self-finding is one of the most strenuous joys that conscious being can give to itself, a play of extreme attractiveness. There is no greater pleasure for man himself than a victory which is in its very principle a conquest over difficulties, a victory in knowledge, a victory in power, a victory in creation over the impossibilities of creation, a delight in the conquest over an anguished toil and a hard ordeal of suffering. At the end of separation is the intense joy of union, the joy of a meeting with a self from which we were divided. There is an attraction in ignorance itself because it provides us with the joy of discovery, the surprise of new and unforeseen creation, a great adventure of the soul; there is a joy of the journey and the search and the finding, a joy of the battle and the crown, the labour and the reward of labour. If delight of existence be the secret of creation, this too is one delight of existence; it can be regarded as the reason or at least one reason of this apparently paradoxical and contrary Lila. But, apart from this choice of the individual Purusha, there is a deeper truth inherent in the original Existence which finds its expression in the plunge into Inconscience; its result is a new affirmation of Sachchidananda in its apparent opposite. If the Infinite's right of various self-manifestation is granted, this too as a possibility of its manifestation is intelligible and has its profound significance.

Chapter V

The Cosmic Illusion;
Mind, Dream and Hallucination

Thou who hast come to this transient and unhappy world,
turn to Me. *Gita.*[1]

This Self is a self of Knowledge, an inner light in the heart; he
is the conscious being common to all the states of being and
moves in both worlds. He becomes a dream-self and passes beyond this world and its forms of death.... There are two planes
of this conscious being, this and the other worlds; a third state
is their place of joining, the state of dream, and when he
stands in this place of their joining, he sees both planes of his
existence, this world and the other world. When he sleeps, he
takes the substance of this world in which all is and himself
undoes and himself builds by his own illumination, his own
light; when this conscious being sleeps, he becomes luminous
with his self-light.... There are no roads nor chariots, nor joys
nor pleasures, nor tanks nor ponds nor rivers, but he creates
them by his own light, for he is the maker. By sleep he casts off
his body and unsleeping sees those that sleep; he preserves by
his life-breath this lower nest and goes forth, immortal, from
his nest; immortal, he goes where he wills, the golden Purusha,
the solitary Swan. They say, "the country of waking only is
his, for the things which he sees when awake, these only he
sees when asleep"; but there he is his own self-light.

Brihadaranyaka Upanishad.[2]

What is seen and what is not seen, what is experienced and
what is not experienced, what is and what is not, — all it sees,
it is all and sees. *Prasna Upanishad.*[3]

---

[1] IX. 33.   [2] IV. 3. 7, 9-12,14.   [3] IV. 5.

ALL HUMAN thought, all mental man's experience moves between a constant affirmation and negation; there is for his mind no truth of idea, no result of experience that cannot be affirmed, none that cannot be negated. It has negated the existence of the individual being, negated the existence of the cosmos, negated the existence of any immanent or underlying Reality, negated any Reality beyond the individual and the cosmos; but it is also constantly affirming these things, — sometimes one of them solely or any two or all of them together. It has to do so because our thinking mind is in its very nature an ignorant dealer in possibilities, not possessing the truth behind any of them, but sounding and testing each in turn or many together if so perchance it may get at some settled belief or knowledge about them, some certitude; yet, living in a world of relativities and possibilities, it can arrive at no final certainty, no absolute and abiding conviction. Even the actual, the realised can present itself to our mentality as a "may be or may not be", *syād vā na syād vā*, or as an "is" under the shadow of the "might not have been" and wearing the aspect of that which will not be hereafter. Our life-being is also afflicted by the same incertitude; it can rest in no aim of living from which it can derive a sure or final satisfaction or to which it can assign an enduring value. Our nature starts from facts and actualities which it takes for real; it is pushed beyond them into a pursuit of uncertain possibilities and led eventually to question all that it took as real. For it proceeds from a fundamental ignorance and has no hold on assured truth; all the truths on which it relies for a time are found to be partial, incomplete and questionable.

At the outset man lives in his physical mind which perceives the actual, the physical, the objective and accepts it as fact and this fact as self-evident truth beyond question; whatever is not actual, not physical, not objective it regards as unreal or unrealised, only to be accepted as entirely real when it has succeeded in becoming actual, becoming a physical fact, becoming objective: its own being too it regards as an objective fact, warranted to be real by its existence in a visible and sensible body; all other subjective beings and things it accepts on the same evidence in so far as they can become objects of our external consciousness or acceptable to that part of the reason which builds upon the data supplied by that consciousness and relies upon them as the one solid basis of knowledge. Physical Science is a vast extension of this mentality: it corrects the errors of the sense and pushes beyond the first limitations of the sense-mind by discovering means of bringing facts and objects not seizable by our corporeal organs into the field of objectivity; but it has the same standard of reality, the objective, the physical actuality; its test of the real is possibility of verification by positive reason and objective evidence.

But man also has a life-mind, a vital mentality which is an instrument of desire: this is not satisfied with the actual, it is a dealer in possibilities; it has the passion for novelty and is seeking always to extend the limits of experience for the satisfaction of desire, for enjoyment, for an enlarged self-affirmation and aggrandisement of its terrain of power and profit. It desires, enjoys, possesses actualities, but it hunts also after unrealised possibilities, is ardent to materialise them, to possess and enjoy them also. It is not satisfied with the physical and objective only, but seeks too a subjective, an imaginative, a purely emotive satisfaction and pleasure. If there were not this factor, the physical mind of man left to itself would live like the animal, accepting his first actual physical life and its limits as his whole possibility, moving in material Nature's established order and asking for nothing beyond it. But this vital mind, this unquiet life-will comes in with its demands and disturbs this inert or routine satisfaction which lives penned within the bounds of actuality; it enlarges always desire and craving, creates a dissatisfaction, an unrest, a seeking for something more than what life seems able to give it: it brings about a vast enlargement of the field of physical actuality by the actualisation of our unrealised possibilities, but also a constant demand for more and always more, a quest for new worlds to conquer, an incessant drive towards an exceeding of the bounds of circumstance and a self-exceeding. To add to this cause of unrest and incertitude there comes in a thinking mind that inquires into everything, questions everything, builds up affirmations and unbuilds them, erects systems of certitude but finally accepts none of them as certain, affirms and questions the evidence of the senses, follows out the conclusions of the reason but undoes them again to arrive at different or quite opposite conclusions, and continues indefinitely if not *ad infinitum* this process. This is the history of human thought and human endeavour, a constant breaking of bounds only to move always in the same spirals enlarged perhaps but following the same or constantly similar curves of direction. The mind of humanity, ever seeking, ever active, never arrives at a firmly settled reality of life's aims and objects or at a settled reality of its own certitudes and convictions, an established foundation or firm formation of its idea of existence.

At a certain point of this constant unrest and travail even the physical mind loses its conviction of objective certitude and enters into an agnosticism which questions all its own standards of life and knowledge, doubts whether all this is real or else whether all, even if real, is not futile; the vital mind, baffled by life and frustrated or else dissatisfied with all its satisfactions, overtaken by a deep disgust and disappointment, finds that all is vanity and vexation of spirit and is ready to reject life and existence as an unreality, all that it hunted after as an illusion, Maya; the thinking mind, unbuilding all its affirmations, discovers that all are mere mental constructions and there is no reality in them or else that the only reality is something beyond this existence, something that has not been made or constructed, something Absolute and Eternal, — all that is relative, all that is of time is a dream, a hallucination of the mind or a vast delirium, an immense cosmic Illusion, a delusive figure of apparent existence. The principle of negation prevails over the principle of affirmation and becomes universal and absolute. Thence arise the great world-negating religions and philosophies; thence too a recoil of the life-motive from itself and a seeking after a life elsewhere flawless and eternal or a will to annul life itself in an immobile Reality or an original Non-Existence. In India the philosophy of world-negation has been given formulations of supreme power and value by two of the greatest of her thinkers, Buddha and Shankara. There have been, intermediate or later in time, other philosophies of considerable importance, some of them widely accepted, formulated with much acumen of thought by men of genius and spiritual insight, which disputed with more or less force and success the conclusions of these two great metaphysical systems, but none has been put forward with an equal force of presentation or drive of personality or had a similar massive effect. The spirit of these two remarkable spiritual philosophies, — for Shankara in the historical process of India's philosophical mind takes up, completes and replaces Buddha, — has weighed with a tremendous power on her thought, religion and general mentality: everywhere broods its mighty shadow, everywhere is the impress of the three great formulas, the chain of Karma, escape from the wheel of rebirth, Maya. It is necessary therefore to look afresh at the Idea or Truth behind the negation of cosmic existence and to consider, however briefly, what is the value of its main formulations or suggestions, on what reality they stand, how far they are imperative to the reason or to experience. For the present it will be enough to throw a regard on the principal ideas which are grouped around the conception of the great cosmic Illusion, Maya, and to set against them those that are proper to our own line of thought and vision; for both proceed from the conception of the One Reality, but one line leads to a universal Illusionism, the other to a universal Realism, — an unreal or real-unreal universe reposing on a transcendent Reality or a real universe reposing on a Reality at once universal and transcendent or absolute.

In itself and by itself the vital being's aversion, the life-mind's recoil from life cannot be taken as valid or conclusive. Its strongest motive is a sense of disappointment and an acceptance of frustration which has no greater claim to conclusiveness than the idealist's opposite motive of invariable hope and his faith and will to realise. Nevertheless there is a certain validity in the mental support of this sense of frustration, in the perception at which the thinking mind arrives that there is an illusion behind all human effort and terrestrial endeavour, the illusion of his political and social gospels, the illusion of his ethical efforts at perfection, the illusion of philanthropy and service, the illusion of works, the illusion of fame, power, success, the illusion of all achievement. Human, social and political endeavour turns always in a circle and leads nowhere; man's life and nature remain always the same, always imperfect, and neither laws nor institutions nor education nor philosophy nor morality nor religious teachings have succeeded in producing the perfect man, still less a perfect humanity, — straighten the tail of the dog as you will, it has been said, it always resumes its natural curve of crookedness. Altruism, philanthropy and service, Christian love or Buddhist compassion have not made the world a whit happier, they only give infinitesimal bits of momentary relief here and there, throw drops on the fire of the world's suffering. All aims are in the end transitory and futile, all achievements unsatisfying or evanescent; all works are so much labour of effort and success and failure which consummate nothing definitive: whatever changes are made in human life are of the form only and these forms pursue each other in a futile circle; for the essence of life, its general character remains the same for ever. This view of things may be exaggerated, but it has an undeniable force; it is supported by the experience of man's centuries and it carries in itself a significance which at one time or another comes upon the mind with an overwhelming air of self-evidence. Not only so, but if it is true that the fundamental laws and values of terrestrial existence are fixed or that it must always turn in repeated cycles, — and this has been for long a very prevalent notion, — then this view of things in the end is hardly escapable. For imperfection, ignorance, frustration and suffering are a dominant factor of the existing world-order, the elements contrary to them, knowledge, happiness, success, perfection are constantly found to be deceptive or inconclusive: the two opposites are so inextricably mixed that, if this state of things is not a motion towards a greater fulfilment, if this is the permanent character of the world-order, then it is hard to avoid the conclusion that all here is either the creation of an inconscient Energy, which would account for the incapacity of an apparent consciousness to arrive at anything, or intentionally a world of ordeal and failure, the issue being not here but elsewhere, or even a vast and aimless cosmic Illusion.

Among these alternative conclusions the second, as it is usually put before us, offers no ground for the philosophic reason, since we have no satisfying indication of the connection between the here and the elsewhere which are posited against each other but not explained in the inevitability of their relations, and there is no light cast on the necessity or fundamental significance of the ordeal and failure. It could only be intelligible, — except as the mysterious will of an arbitrary Creator, — if there was a choice by immortal spirits to try the adventure of the Ignorance and a necessity for them to learn the nature of a world of Ignorance in order that they might reject it. But such a creative motive, necessarily incidental and quite temporary in its incidence, with the earth as its casual field of experience, could hardly by itself account for the immense and enduring phenomenon of this complex universe. It can become an operative part of a satisfactory explanation if this world is the field for the working out of a greater creative motive, if it is a manifestation of a divine Truth or a divine Possibility in which under certain conditions an initiating Ignorance must intervene as a necessary factor, and if the arrangement of this universe contains in it a compulsion of the Ignorance to move towards Knowledge, of the imperfect manifestation to grow into perfection, of the frustration to serve as steps towards a final victory, of the suffering to prepare an emergence of the divine Delight of Being. In that case the sense of disappointment, frustration, illusion and the vanity of all things would not be valid; for the aspects that seem to justify it would be only the natural circumstances of a difficult evolution: all the stress of struggle and effort, success and failure, joy and suffering, the mixture of ignorance and knowledge would be the experience needed for the soul, mind, life and physical part to grow into the full light of a spiritual perfected being. It would reveal itself as the process of an evolutionary manifestation; there would be no need to bring in the fiat of an arbitrary Omnipotence or a cosmic Illusion, a phantasy of meaningless Maya.

But there is too a higher mental and spiritual basis for the philosophy of world-negation and here we are on more solid ground: for it can be contended that the world is in its very nature an illusion and no reasoning from the features and circumstances of an Illusion could justify it or raise it into a Reality, — there is only one Reality, the transcendent, the supracosmic: no divine fulfilment, even if our life were to grow into the life of gods, could nullify or cancel the original unreality which is its fundamental character; for that fulfilment would be only the bright side of an Illusion. Or even if not absolutely an illusion, it would be a reality of an inferior order and must come to an end by the soul's recognition that the Brahman alone is true, that there is nothing but the transcendent and immutable Absolute. If this is the one Truth, then all ground is cut away from under our feet; the divine Manifestation, the victory of the soul in Matter, its mastery over existence, the divine life in Nature would itself be a falsehood or at least something not altogether real imposed for a time on the sole true Reality. But here all turns on the mind's conception or the mental being's experience of Reality and how far that conception is valid or how far that experience is imperative, — even if it is a spiritual experience, how far it is absolutely conclusive, solely imperative.

The cosmic Illusion is sometimes envisaged, — though that is not the accepted position, — as something that has the character of an unreal subjective experience; it is then, — or may be, — a figure of forms and movements that arises in some eternal sleep of things or in a dream-consciousness and is temporarily imposed on a pure and featureless self-aware Existence; it is a dream that takes place in the Infinite. In the philosophies of the Mayavadins, — for there are several systems alike in their basis but not altogether and at every point coincident with each other, — the analogy of dream is given, but as an analogy only, not as the intrinsic character of the world-illusion. It is difficult for the positive physical mind to admit the idea that ourselves, the world and life, the sole thing to which our consciousness bears positive witness, are inexistent, a cheat imposed on us by that consciousness: certain analogies are brought forward,

the analogies especially of dream and hallucination, in order to
show that it is possible for the experiences of the consciousness
to seem to it real and yet prove to be without any basis or
without a sufficient basis in reality; as a dream is real to the
dreamer so long as he sleeps but waking shows it to be unreal,
so our experience of world seems to us positive and real but,
when we stand back from the illusion, we shall find that it had
no reality. But it may be as well to give the dream-analogy its
full value and see whether our sense of world-experience has in
any way a similar basis. For the idea of the world as a dream,
whether it be a dream of the subjective mind or a dream of
the soul or a dream in the Eternal, is often entertained and it
powerfully enforces the illusionist tendency in human feeling
and thinking. If it has no validity, we must definitely see that
and the reasons of its inapplicability and set it aside well out of
the way; if it has some validity, we must see what it is and how
far it goes. If the world is an illusion, but not a dream-illusion,
that distinction too must be put on a secure basis.

Dream is felt to be unreal, first, because it ceases and has no
farther validity when we pass from one status of consciousness
to another which is our normal status. But this is not by itself a
sufficient reason: for it may well be that there are different states
of consciousness each with its own realities; if the consciousness
of one state of things fades back and its contents are lost or,
even when caught in memory, seem to be illusory as soon as we
pass into another state, that would be perfectly normal, but it
would not prove the reality of the state in which we now are
and the unreality of the other which we have left behind us. If
earth circumstances begin to seem unreal to a soul passing into
a different world or another plane of consciousness, that would
not prove their unreality; similarly, the fact that world-existence
seems unreal to us when we pass into the spiritual silence or
into some Nirvana, does not of itself prove that the cosmos was
all the time an illusion. The world is real to the consciousness
dwelling in it, an unconditioned existence is real to the consciousness absorbed in Nirvana; that is all that is established.
But the second reason for refusing credit to our sleep experience

is that a dream is something evanescent without antecedents and without a sequel; ordinarily, too, it is without any sufficient coherence or any significance intelligible to our waking being. If our dreams wore like our waking life an aspect of coherence, each night taking up and carrying farther a past continuous and connected sleep-experience as each day takes up again our waking world-experience, then dreams would assume to our mind quite another character. There is therefore no analogy between a dream and waking life; these are experiences quite different in their character, validity, order. Our life is accused of evanescence and often it is accused too, as a whole, of a lack of inner coherence and significance; but its lack of complete significance may be due to our lack or limitation of understanding: actually, when we go within and begin to see it from within, it assumes a complete connected significance; at the same time whatever lack of inner coherence was felt before disappears and we see that it was due to the incoherence of our own inner seeing and knowledge and was not at all a character of life. There is no surface incoherence in life, it rather appears to our minds as a chain of firm sequences, and, if that is a mental delusion, as is sometimes alleged, if the sequence is created by our minds and does not actually exist in life, that does not remove the difference of the two states of consciousness. For in dream the coherence given by an observing inner consciousness is absent, and whatever sense of sequence there is seems to be due to a vague and false imitation of the connections of waking life, a subconscious mimesis, but this imitative sequence is shadowy and imperfect, fails and breaks always and is often wholly absent. We see too that the dream-consciousness seems to be wholly devoid of that control which the waking consciousness exercises to a certain extent over life-circumstances; it has the Nature-automatism of a subconscient construction and nothing of the conscious will and organising force of the evolved mind of the human being. Again the evanescence of a dream is radical and one dream has no connection with another; but the evanescence of the waking life is of details, — there is no evidence of evanescence in the connected totality of world-experience. Our bodies perish but souls proceed from birth to birth through the ages: stars and planets may disappear after a lapse of aeons or of many light-cycles, but universe, cosmic existence may well be a permanent as it is certainly a continuous activity; there is nothing to prove that the Infinite Energy which creates it has an end or a beginning either of itself or of its action. So far there is too great a disparateness between dream-life and waking life to make the analogy applicable.

But it may be questioned whether our dreams are indeed totally unreal and without significance, whether they are not a figure, an image-record or a symbolic transcript or representation of things that are real. For that we have to examine, however summarily, the nature of sleep and of dream-phenomena, their process of origination and their provenance. What happens in sleep is that our consciousness withdraws from the field of its waking experiences; it is supposed to be resting, suspended or in abeyance, but that is a superficial view of the matter. What is in abeyance is the waking activities, what is at rest is the surface mind and the normal conscious action of the bodily part of us; but the inner consciousness is not suspended, it enters into new inner activities, only a part of which, a part happening or recorded in something of us that is near to the surface, we remember. There is maintained in sleep, thus near the surface, an obscure subconscious element which is a receptacle or passage for our dream experiences and itself also a dream-builder; but behind it is the depth and mass of the subliminal, the totality of our concealed inner being and consciousness which is of quite another order. Normally it is a subconscient part in us, intermediate between consciousness and pure inconscience, that sends up through this surface layer its formations in the shape of dreams, constructions marked by an apparent inconsequence and incoherence. Many of these are fugitive structures built upon circumstances of our present life selected apparently at random and surrounded with a phantasy of variation; others call back the past, or rather selected circumstances and persons of the past, as a starting-point for similar fleeting edifices. There are other dreams of the subconscious which seem to be pure phantasy without any such initiation or basis; but the new method of psycho-analysis, trying to look for the first time into our dreams with some kind of scientific understanding, has established in them a system of meanings, a key to things in us which need to be known and handled by the waking consciousness; this of itself changes the whole character and value of our dream-experience. It begins to look as if there were something real behind it and as if too that something were an element of no mean practical importance.

But the subconscious is not our sole dream-builder. The subconscious in us is the extreme border of our secret inner existence where it meets the Inconscient, it is a degree of our being in which the Inconscient struggles into a half consciousness; the surface physical consciousness also, when it sinks back from the waking level and retrogresses towards the Inconscient, retires into this intermediate subconscience. Or, from another viewpoint, this nether part of us may be described as the antechamber of the Inconscient through which its formations rise into our waking or our subliminal being. When we sleep and the surface physical part of us, which is in its first origin here an output from the Inconscient, relapses towards the originating inconscience, it enters into this subconscious element, antechamber or substratum, and there it finds the impressions of its past or persistent habits of mind and experiences, — for all have left their mark on our subconscious part and have there a power of recurrence. In its effect on our waking self this recurrence often takes the form of a reassertion of old habits, impulses dormant or suppressed, rejected elements of the nature, or it comes up as some other not so easily recognisable, some peculiar disguised or subtle result of these suppressed or rejected but not erased impulses or elements. In the dream-consciousness the phenomenon is an apparently fanciful construction, a composite of figures and movements built upon or around the buried impressions with a sense in them that escapes the waking intelligence because it has no clue to the subconscient's system of significances. After a time this subconscious activity appears to sink back into complete inconscience and we speak of this state as deep dreamless sleep;

thence we emerge again into the dream-shallows or return to the waking surface.

But, in fact, in what we call dreamless sleep, we have gone into a profounder and denser layer of the subconscient, a state too involved, too immersed or too obscure, dull and heavy to bring to the surface its structures, and we are dreaming there but unable to grasp or retain in the recording layer of subconscience these more obscure dream-figures. Or else, it may be, the part of our mind which still remains active in the sleep of the body has entered into the inner domains of our being, the subliminal mental, the subliminal vital, the subtle-physical, and is there lost to all active connection with the surface parts of us. If we are still in the nearer depths of these regions, the surface subconscient which is our sleep-wakefulness records something of what we experience in these depths; but it records it in its own transcription, often marred by characteristic incoherences and always, even when most coherent, deformed or cast into figures drawn from the world of waking experience. But if we have gone deeper inward, the record fails or cannot be recovered and we have the illusion of dreamlessness; but the activity of the inner dream consciousness continues behind the veil of the now mute and inactive subconscient surface. This continued dream activity is revealed to us when we become more inwardly conscious, for then we get into connection with the heavier and deeper subconscient stratum and can be aware, — at the time or by a retracing or recovering through memory, — of what happened when we sank into these torpid depths. It is possible too to become conscious deeper within our subliminal selves and we are then aware of experiences on other planes of our being or even in supraphysical worlds to which sleep gives us a right of secret entry. A transcript of such experiences reaches us; but the transcriber here is not the subconscious, it is the subliminal, a greater dream-builder.

If the subliminal thus comes to the front in our dream-consciousness, there is sometimes an activity of our subliminal intelligence, — dream becomes a series of thoughts, often strangely or vividly figured, problems are solved which our waking consciousness could not solve, warnings, premonitions, indications of the future, veridical dreams replace the normal subconscious incoherence. There can come also a structure of symbol-images, some of a mental character, some of a vital nature: the former are precise in their figures, clear in their significance; the latter are often complex and baffling to our waking consciousness, but, if we can seize the clue, they reveal their own sense and peculiar system of coherence. Finally, there can come to us the records of happenings seen or experienced by us on other planes of our own being or of universal being into which we enter: these have sometimes, like the symbolic dreams, a strong bearing on our own inner and outer life or the life of others, reveal elements of our or their mental being and life-being or disclose influences on them of which our waking self is totally ignorant; but sometimes they have no such bearing and are purely records of other organised systems of consciousness independent of our physical existence. The subconscious dreams constitute the bulk of our most ordinary sleep-experience and they are those which we usually remember; but sometimes the subliminal builder is able to impress our sleep consciousness sufficiently to stamp his activities on our waking memory. If we develop our inner being, live more inwardly than most men do, then the balance is changed and a larger dream-consciousness opens before us; our dreams can take on a subliminal and no longer a subconscious character and can assume a reality and significance.

It is even possible to become wholly conscious in sleep and follow throughout from beginning to end or over large stretches the stages of our dream-experience; it is found that then we are aware of ourselves passing from state after state of consciousness to a brief period of luminous and peaceful dreamless rest, which is the true restorer of the energies of the waking nature, and then returning by the same way to the waking consciousness. It is normal, as we thus pass from state to state, to let the previous experiences slip away from us; in the return only the more vivid or those nearest to the waking surface are remembered: but this can be remedied, — a greater retention is possible or the power can be developed of going back in memory from dream to dream, from state to state, till the whole is once more before us. A coherent knowledge of sleep-life, though difficult to achieve or to keep established, is possible.

Our subliminal self is not, like our surface physical being, an outcome of the energy of the Inconscient; it is a meeting-place of the consciousness that emerges from below by evolution and the consciousness that has descended from above for involution. There is in it an inner mind, an inner vital being of ourselves, an inner or subtle-physical being larger than our outer being and nature. This inner existence is the concealed origin of almost all in our surface self that is not a construction of the first inconscient World-Energy or a natural developed functioning of our surface consciousness or a reaction of it to impacts from the outside universal Nature, — and even in this construction, these functionings, these reactions the subliminal takes part and exercises on them a considerable influence. There is here a consciousness which has a power of direct contact with the universal unlike the mostly indirect contacts which our surface being maintains with the universe through the sense-mind and the senses. There are here inner senses, a subliminal sight, touch, hearing; but these subtle senses are rather channels of the inner being's direct consciousness of things than its informants: the subliminal is not dependent on its senses for its knowledge, they only give a form to its direct experience of objects; they do not, so much as in waking mind, convey forms of objects for the mind's documentation or as the starting-point or basis for an indirect constructive experience. The subliminal has the right of entry into the mental and vital and subtle-physical planes of the universal consciousness, it is not confined to the material plane and the physical world; it possesses means of communication with the worlds of being which the descent towards involution created in its passage and with all corresponding planes or worlds that may have arisen or been constructed to serve the purpose of the re-ascent from Inconscience to Superconscience. It is into this large realm of interior existence that our mind and vital being retire when they withdraw from the surface activities whether by sleep or inward-drawn concentration or by the inner plunge of trance.

Our waking state is unaware of its connection with the subliminal being, although it receives from it, — but without any knowledge of the place of origin, — the inspirations, intuitions, ideas, will-suggestions, sense-suggestions, urges to action that rise from below or from behind our limited surface existence. Sleep like trance opens the gate of the subliminal to us; for in sleep, as in trance, we retire behind the veil of the limited waking personality and it is behind this veil that the subliminal has its existence. But we receive the records of our sleep experience through dream and in dream figures and not in that condition which might be called an inner waking and which is the most accessible form of the trance state, nor through the supernormal clarities of vision and other more luminous and concrete ways of communication developed by the inner subliminal cognition when it gets into habitual or occasional conscious connection with our waking self. The subliminal, with the subconscious as an annexe of itself, — for the subconscious is also part of the behind-the-veil entity, — is the seer of inner things and of supraphysical experiences; the surface subconscious is only a transcriber. It is for this reason that the Upanishad describes the subliminal being as the Dream Self because it is normally in dreams, visions, absorbed states of inner experience that we enter into and are part of its experiences, — just as it describes the superconscient as the Sleep Self because normally all mental or sensory experiences cease when we enter this superconscience. For in the deeper trance into which the touch of the superconscient plunges our mentality, no record from it or transcript of its contents can normally reach us; it is only by an especial or an unusual development, in a supernormal condition or through a break or rift in our confined normality, that we can be on the surface conscious of the contacts or messages of the Superconscience. But, in spite of these figurative names of dream-state and sleep-state, the field of both these states of consciousness was clearly regarded as a field of reality no less than that of the waking state in which our movements of perceptive consciousness are a record or transcript of physical things and of our contacts with the physical universe. No doubt, all the three states can be classed as parts of an illusion, our experiences of them can be ranked together as constructions of an illusory consciousness, our waking state no less illusory than our dream state or sleep-state, since the only true truth or real reality is the incommunicable Self or One-Existence (Atman, Adwaita) which is the fourth state of the Self described by the Vedanta. But it is equally possible to regard and rank them together as three different orders of one Reality or as three states of consciousness in which is embodied our contact with three different grades of self-experience and world-experience.

If this is a true account of dream-experience, dreams can no longer be classed as a mere unreal figure of unreal things temporarily imposed upon our half-unconsciousness as a reality; the analogy therefore fails even as an illustrative support for the theory of the cosmic Illusion. It may be said, however, that our dreams are not themselves realities but only a transcript of reality, a system of symbol-images, and our waking experience of the universe is similarly not a reality but only a transcript of reality, a series of collection of symbol-images. It is quite true that primarily we see the physical universe only through a system of images impressed or imposed on our senses and so far the contention is justified; it may also be admitted that in a certain sense and from one viewpoint our experiences and activities can be considered as symbols of a truth which our lives are trying to express but at present only with a partial success and an imperfect coherence. If that were all, life might be described as a dream-experience of self and things in the consciousness of the Infinite. But although our primary evidence of the objects of the universe consists of a structure of sense-images, these are completed, validated, set in order by an automatic intuition in the consciousness which immediately relates the image with the thing imaged and gets the tangible experience of the object, so that we are not merely regarding or reading a translation or sense-transcript of the reality but looking through the sense-image to the reality. This adequacy is amplified too by the action of a reason which fathoms and understands the law of things sensed and can observe scrupulously the sense-transcript and correct its errors. Therefore we may conclude that we experience a real universe through our imaged sense-transcript by the aid of the intuition and the reason, — an intuition which gives us the touch of things and a reason which investigates their truth by its conceptive knowledge. But we must note also that even if our image view of the universe, our sense-transcript, is a system of symbol-images and not an exact reproduction or transcription, a literal translation, still a symbol is a notation of something that is, a transcript of realities. Even if our images are incorrect, what they endeavour to image are realities, not illusions; when we see a tree or a stone or an animal, it is not a non-existent figure, a hallucination that we are seeing; we may not be sure that the image is exact, we may concede that other-sense might very well see it otherwise, but still there is something there that justifies the image, something with which it has more or less correspondence. But in the theory of Illusion the only reality is an indeterminable featureless pure Existence, Brahman, and there is no possibility of its being translated or mistranslated into a system of symbol-figures, for that could only be if this Existence had some determinate contents or some unmanifested truths of its being which could be transcribed into the forms or names given to them by our consciousness: a pure Indeterminable cannot be rendered by a transcript, a multitude of representative differentiae, a crowd of symbols or images; for there is in it only a pure Identity, there is nothing to transcribe, nothing to symbolise, nothing to image. Therefore the dream-analogy fails us altogether and is better put out of the way; it can always be used as a vivid metaphor of a certain attitude our mind can take towards its experiences, but it has no value for a metaphysical inquiry into the reality and fundamental significances or the origin of existence.

If we take up the analogy of hallucination, we find it hardly more helpful for a true understanding of the theory of cosmic Illusion than the dream-analogy. Hallucinations are of two kinds, mental or ideative and visual or in some way sensory. When we see an image of things where those things are not, it is an erroneous construction of the senses, a visual hallucination; when we take for an objective fact a thing which is a subjective structure of the mind, a constructive mental error or an objectivised imagination or a misplaced mental image, it is a mental hallucination. An example of the first is the mirage, an example of the second is the classic instance of a rope taken for a snake. In passing we may note that there are many things called hallucinations which are not really that but symbol-images sent up from the subliminal or experiences in which the subliminal consciousness or sense comes to the surface and puts us into contact with supraphysical realities; thus the cosmic consciousness which is our entry by a breaking down of our mental limitations into the sense of a vast reality, has been classed, even in admitting it, as a hallucination. But, taking only the common hallucination, mental or visual, we observe that it seems to be at first sight a true example of what is called imposition in the philosophic theory; it is the placement of an unreal figure of things on a reality, of a mirage upon the bare desert air, of the figure of a non-present snake on the present and real rope. The world, we may contend, is such a hallucination, an imposition of a non-existent unreal figure of things on the bare ever-present sole reality of the Brahman. But then we note that in each case the hallucination, the false image is not of something quite non-existent; it is an image of something existent and real but not present in the place on which it has been imposed by the mind's error or by a sense-error. A mirage is the image of a city, an oasis, running water or of other absent things, and if these things did not exist, the false image of them, whether raised up by the mind or reflected in the desert air, would not be there to delude the mind with a false sense of reality. A snake exists and its existence and form are known to the victim of the momentary hallucination: if it had not been so, the delusion would not have been created; for it is a form-resemblance of the seen reality to another reality previously known elsewhere that is the origin of the error. The analogy therefore is unhelpful; it would be valid only if our image of the universe were a falsity reflecting a true universe which is not here but elsewhere or else if it were a false imaged manifestation of the Reality replacing in the mind or covering with its distorted resemblance a true manifestation. But here the world is a non-existent form of things, an illusory construction imposed on the bare Reality, on the sole Existent which is for ever empty of things and formless: there would be a true analogy only if our vision constructed in the void air of the desert a figure of things that exist nowhere, or else if it imposed on a bare ground both rope and snake and other figures that equally existed nowhere.

It is clear that in this analogy two quite different kinds of illusion not illustrative of each other are mistakenly put together as if they were identical in nature. All mental or sense-hallucinations are really misrepresentations or misplacements or impossible combinations or false developments of things that are in themselves existent or possible or in some way within or allied to the province of the real. All mental errors and illusions are the result of an ignorance which miscombines its data or proceeds falsely upon a previous or present or possible content of knowledge. But the cosmic Illusion has no basis of actuality, it is an original and all-originating illusion; it imposes names, figures, happenings that are pure inventions on a Reality in which there never were and never will be any happenings, names or figures. The analogy of mental hallucination would only be applicable if we admit a Brahman without names, forms or relations and a world of names, forms and relations as equal realities imposed one upon the other, the rope in the place of the snake, or the snake in the place of the rope, — an attribution, it might be, of the activities of the Saguna to the quiescence of the Nirguna. But if both are real, both must be either separate aspects of the Reality or co-ordinate aspects, positive and negative poles of the one Existence. Any error or confusion of Mind between them would not be a creative cosmic Illusion, but only a wrong perception of realities, a wrong relation created by the Ignorance.

If we scrutinise other illustrations or analogies that are offered to us for a better understanding of the operation of Maya, we detect in all of them an inapplicability that deprives them of their force and value. The familiar instance of mother-of-pearl and silver turns also, like the rope and snake analogy, upon an error due to a resemblance between a present real and another and absent real; it can have no application to the imposition of a multiple and mutable unreality upon a sole and unique immutable Real. In the example of an optical illusion duplicating or multiplying a single object, as when we see two moons instead of one, there are two or more identical forms of the one object, one real, one — or the rest — an illusion: this does not illustrate the juxtaposition of world and Brahman; for in the operation of Maya there is a much more complex phenomenon, — there is indeed an illusory multiplication of the Identical imposed upon its one and ever-unalterable Identity, the One appearing as many, but upon that is imposed an immense organised diversity in nature, a diversity of forms and movements which have nothing to do with the original Real. Dreams, visions, the imagination of the artist or poet can present such an organised diversity which is not real; but it is an imitation, a mimesis of a real and already existent organised diversity, or it starts from such a mimesis and even in the richest variation or wildest invention some mimetic element is observable. There is here no such thing as the operation attributed to Maya in which there is no mimesis but a pure and radically original creation of unreal forms and movements that are non-existent anywhere and neither imitate nor reflect nor alter and develop anything discoverable in the Reality. There is nothing in the operations of Mind-illusion that throws light upon this mystery; it is, as a stupendous cosmic Illusion of this kind must be, *sui generis*, without parallel. What we see in the universe is that a diversity of the identical is everywhere the fundamental operation of cosmic Nature; but here it presents itself, not as an illusion, but as a various real formation out of a one original substance. A Reality of Oneness manifesting itself in a reality of numberless forms and powers of its being is what we confront everywhere. There is no doubt in its process a mystery, even a magic, but there is nothing to show that it is a magic of the unreal and not a working of a Consciousness and Force of being of the omnipotent Real, a self-creation operated by an eternal self-knowledge.

This at once raises the question of the nature of Mind, the parent of these illusions, and its relation to the original Existence. Is mind the child and instrument of an original Illusion, or is it itself a primal miscreating Force or Consciousness? or is the mental ignorance a misprision of the truths of Existence, a deviation from an original Truth-Consciousness which is the real world-builder? Our own mind, at any rate, is not an original and primary creative power of Consciousness; it is, and all mind of the same character must be, derivative, an instrumental demiurge, an intermediary creator. It is likely then that analogies from the errors of mind, which are the outcome of an intermediate Ignorance, may not truly illustrate the nature or action of an original creative Illusion, an all-inventing and all-constructing Maya. Our mind stands between a superconscience and an inconscience and receives from both these opposite powers: it stands between an occult subliminal existence and an outward cosmic phenomenon; it receives inspirations, intuitions, imaginations, impulses to knowledge and action, figures of subjective realities or possibilities from the unknown inner source; it receives the figures of realised actualities and their suggestions of further possibility from the observed cosmic phenomenon. What it receives are truths essential, possible or actual; it starts from the realised actualities of the physical universe and it brings out from them in its subjective action the unrealised possibilities which they contain or suggest or to which it can arrive by proceeding from them as a starting-point: it selects some out of these possibilities for a subjective action and plays with imagined or inwardly constructed forms of them; it chooses others for objectivisation and attempts to realise them. But it receives inspirations also from above and within, from invisible sources and not only from the impacts of the visible cosmic phenomenon; it sees truths other than those suggested by the actual physicality around it, and here too it plays subjectively with transmitted or constructed forms of these truths or it selects for objectivisation, attempts to realise.

Our mind is an observer and user of actualities, a diviner or recipient of truths not yet known or actualised, a dealer in possibilities that mediate between the truth and actuality. But it has not the omniscience of an infinite Consciousness; it is limited in knowledge and has to supplement its restricted knowledge by imagination and discovery. It does not, like the infinite Consciousness, manifest the known, it has to discover the unknown; it seizes the possibilities of the Infinite, not as results or variations of forms of a latent Truth, but as constructions or creations, figments of its own boundless imagination. It has not the omnipotence of an infinite conscious Energy; it can only realise or actualise what the cosmic Energy will accept from it or what it has the strength to impose or introduce into the sum of things because the secret Divinity, superconscient or subliminal, which uses it intends that that should be expressed in Nature. Its limitation of Knowledge constitutes by incompleteness, but also by openness to error, an Ignorance. In dealing with actualities it may misobserve, misuse, miscreate; in dealing with possibilities it may miscompose, miscombine, misapply, misplace; in its dealings with truths revealed to it it may deform, misrepresent, disharmonise. It may also make constructions of its own which have no correspondence with the things of actual existence, no potentiality of realisation, no support from the truth behind them; but still these constructions start from an illegitimate extension of actualities, catch at unpermitted possibilities, or turn truths to an application which is not applicable. Mind creates, but it is not an original creator, not omniscient or omnipotent, not even an always efficient demiurge. Maya, the Illusive Power, on the contrary, must be an original creator, for it creates all things out of nothing unless we suppose that it creates out of the substance of the Reality, but then the things it creates must be in some way real; it has a perfect knowledge of what it wishes to create, a perfect power to create whatever it chooses, omniscient and omnipotent though only over its own illusions, harmonising them and linking them together with a magical sureness and sovereign energy, absolutely effective in imposing its own formations or figments passed off as truths, possibilities, actualities on the creature intelligence.

Our mind works best and with a firm confidence when it

is given a substance to work on or at least to use as a basis for its operations, or when it can handle a cosmic force of which it has acquired the knowledge, — it is sure of its steps when it has to deal with actualities; this rule of dealing with objectivised or discovered actualities and proceeding from them for creation is the reason of the enormous success of physical Science. But here there is evidently no creation of illusions, no creation of non-existence *in vacuo* and turning them into apparent actualities such as is attributed to the cosmic Illusion. For Mind can only create out of substance what is possible to the substance, it can only do with the force of Nature what is in accordance with her realisable energies; it can only invent or discover what is already contained in the truth and potentiality of Nature. On the other side, it receives inspirations for creation from within itself or from above: but these can only take form if they are truths or potentials, not by the mind's own right of invention; for if the mind erects what is neither true nor potential, that cannot be created, cannot become actual in Nature. Maya, on the contrary, if it creates on the basis of the Reality, yet erects a superstructure which has nothing to do with the Reality, is not true or potential in it; if it creates out of the substance of the Reality, it makes out of it things that are not possible to it or in accordance with it, — for it creates forms and the Reality is supposed to be a Formless incapable of form, it creates determinations and the Reality is supposed to be absolutely indeterminable.

But our mind has the faculty of imagination; it can create and take as true and real its own mental structures: here, it might be thought, is something analogous to the action of Maya. Our mental imagination is an instrument of Ignorance; it is the resort or device or refuge of a limited capacity of knowledge, a limited capacity of effective action. Mind supplements these deficiencies by its power of imagination: it uses it to extract from things obvious and visible the things that are not obvious and visible; it undertakes to create its own figures of the possible and the impossible; it erects illusory actuals or draws figures of a conjectured or constructed truth of things that are not true to outer experience. That is at least the appearance of its operation; but, in reality, it is the mind's way or one of its ways of summoning out of Being its infinite possibilities, even of discovering or capturing the unknown possibilities of the Infinite. But, because it cannot do this with knowledge, it makes experimental constructions of truth and possibility and a yet unrealised actuality: as its power of receiving inspirations of Truth is limited, it imagines, hypothetises, questions whether this or that may not be truths; as its force to summon real potentials is narrow and restricted, it erects possibilities which it hopes to actualise or wishes it could actualise; as its power to actualise is cramped and confined by the material world's oppositions, it figures subjective actualisations to satisfy its will of creation and delight of self-presentation. But it is to be noted that through the imagination it does receive a figure of truth, does summon possibilities which are afterwards realised, does often by its imagination exercise an effective pressure on the world's actualities. Imaginations that persist in the human mind, like the idea of travel in the air, end often by self-fulfilment; individual thought-formations can actualise themselves if there is sufficient strength in the formation or in the mind that forms it. Imaginations can create their own potentiality, especially if they are supported in the collective mind, and may in the long run draw on themselves the sanction of the cosmic Will. In fact all imaginations represent possibilities: some are able one day to actualise in some form, perhaps a very different form of actuality; more are condemned to sterility because they do not enter into the figure or scheme of the present creation, do not come within the permitted potentiality of the individual or do not accord with the collective or the generic principle or are alien to the nature or destiny of the containing world-existence.

Thus the mind's imaginations are not purely and radically illusory: they proceed on the basis of its experience of actualities or at least set out from that, are variations upon actuality, or they figure the "may-be"s or "might-be"s of the Infinite, what could be if other truths had manifested, if existing potentials had been otherwise arranged or other possibilities than those already admitted became potential. Moreover, through this faculty forms and powers of other domains than that of the physical actuality communicate with our mental being. Even when the imaginations are extravagant or take the form of hallucinations or illusions, they proceed with actuals or possibles for their basis. The mind creates the figure of a mermaid, but the phantasy is composed of two actualities put together in a way that is outside the earth's normal potentiality; angels, griffins, chimeras are constructed on the same principle: sometimes the imagination is a memory of former actualities as in the mythical figure of the dragon, sometimes it is a figure or a happening that is real or could be real on other planes or in other conditions of existence. Even the illusions of the maniac are founded on an extravagant misfitting of actuals, as when the lunatic combines himself, kingship and England and sits in imagination on the throne of the Plantagenets and Tudors. Again, when we look into the origin of mental error, we find normally that it is a miscombination, misplacement, misuse, misunderstanding or misapplication of elements of experience and knowledge. Imagination itself is in its nature a substitute for a truer consciousness's faculty of intuition of possibility: as the mind ascends towards the Truth-Consciousness, this mental power becomes a truth-imagination which brings the colour and light of the higher truth into the limited adequacy or inadequacy of the knowledge already achieved and formulated and, finally, in the transforming light above it gives place wholly to higher truth-powers or itself turns into intuition and inspiration; the Mind in that uplifting ceases to be a creator of delusions and an architect of error. Mind then is not a sovereign creator of things non-existent or erected in a void: it is an ignorance trying to know; its very illusions start from a basis of some kind and are the results of a limited knowledge or a half-ignorance. Mind is an instrument of the cosmic Ignorance, but it does not seem to be or does not act like a power or an instrument of a cosmic Illusion. It is a seeker and discoverer or a creator or would-be creator of truths, possibilities and actualities, and it would be rational to suppose that the original Consciousness and Power, from which mind must be a derivation, is also a creator of truths, possibilities and actualities, not limited like mind but cosmic in its scope, not open to error, because free from all ignorance, a sovereign instrument or a self-power of a supreme Omniscience and Omnipotence, an eternal Wisdom and Knowledge.

This then is the dual possibility that arises before us. There is, we may suppose, an original consciousness and power creative of illusions and unrealities with mind as its instrument or medium in the human and animal consciousness, so that the differentiated universe we see is unreal, a fiction of Maya, and only some indeterminable and undifferentiated Absolute is real. Or there is, we may equally suppose, an original, a supreme or cosmic Truth-Consciousness creative of a true universe, but with mind acting in that universe as an imperfect consciousness, ignorant, partly knowing, partly not knowing, — a consciousness which is by its ignorance or limitation of knowledge capable of error, mispresentation, mistaken or misdirected development from the known, of uncertain gropings towards the unknown, of partial creations and buildings, a constant half-position between truth and error, knowledge and nescience. But this ignorance in fact proceeds, however stumblingly, upon knowledge and towards knowledge; it is inherently capable of shedding the limitation, the mixture, and can turn by that liberation into the Truth-Consciousness, into a power of the original Knowledge. Our inquiry has so far led rather in the second direction; it points towards the conclusion that the nature of our consciousness is not of a character that would justify the hypothesis of a Cosmic Illusion as the solution of its problem. A problem exists, but it consists in the mixture of Knowledge with Ignorance in our cognition of self and things, and it is the origin of this imperfection that we have to discover. There is no need of bringing in an original power of Illusion always mysteriously existent in the eternal Reality or else intervening and imposing a world of non-existent forms on a Consciousness or Superconscience that is for ever pure, eternal and absolute.

Chapter VI

Reality and the Cosmic Illusion

The Eternal is true; the world is a lie.   *Vivekachudamani.*[1]

The Master of Maya creates this world by his Maya and within it is confined another; one should know his Maya as Nature and the Master of Maya as the great Lord of all.

                Swetaswatara Upanishad.[2]

The Purusha is all this that is, what has been and what is yet to be; he is the master of Immortality and he is whatever grows by food.   *Rig Veda.*[3]

                Swetaswatara Upanishad.[4]

All is the Divine Being.   *Gita.*[5]

BUT SO far we have only cleared a part of the foreground of the field of inquiry; in the background the problem remains unsolved and entire. It is the problem of the nature of the original Consciousness or Power that has created or conceptively constructed or manifested the universe, and the relation to it of our world-cognition, — in sum, whether the universe is a figment of consciousness imposed on our mind by a supreme force of Illusion or a true formation of being experienced by us with a still ignorant but an increasing knowledge. And the true question is not of Mind alone or of a cosmic dream or a cosmic hallucination born of Mind, but of the nature of the Reality, the validity of the creative action that takes place in it or is imposed upon it, the presence or absence of a real content in its or our consciousness and its or our regard on the universe. On behalf of Illusionism it can be answered to the position put

---

[1] Verse 20.   [2] IV. 9, 10.   [3] X. 90. 2.   [4] III. 15.   [5] VII. 19.

forward by us with regard to the truth of existence that all this might be valid within the bounds of the cosmic Illusion; it is the system, the pragmatic machinery by which Maya works and maintains herself in the Ignorance: but the truths, possibilities, actualities of the cosmic system are true and actual only within the Illusion, outside that magic circle they have no validity; they are not abiding and eternal realities; all are temporary figures, the works of Knowledge no less than the works of Ignorance. It can be conceded that knowledge is a useful instrument of the Illusion of Maya, for escaping from herself, for destroying herself in the Mind; spiritual knowledge is indispensable: but the one true truth, the only abiding reality beyond all duality of knowledge and ignorance is the eternal relationless Absolute or the Self, the eternal pure Existence. All here turns on the mind's conception and the mental being's experience of reality; for according to the mind's experience or conception of reality will be its interpretation of data otherwise identical, the facts of the Cosmos, individual experience, the realisation of the supreme Transcendence. All mental cognition depends on three elements, the percipient, the perception and the thing perceived or percept. All or any of these three can be affirmed or denied reality; the question then is which of these, if any, are real and to what extent or in what manner. If all three are rejected as instruments of a cosmic Illusion, the farther and consequent question arises: is there then a reality outside them and, if so, what is the relation between the Reality and the Illusion?

It is possible to affirm the reality of the percept, of the objective universe, and deny or diminish the reality of the percipient individual and his perceptive consciousness. In the theory of the sole reality of Matter, consciousness is only an operation of Matter-energy in Matter, a secretion or vibration of the brain-cells, a physical reception of images and a brain-response, a reflex action or a reaction of Matter to the contacts of Matter. Even if the rigidity of this affirmation is relaxed and consciousness otherwise accounted for, still it is no more than a temporary and derivative phenomenon, not the enduring Reality. The percipient individual is himself only a body and brain capable of the

mechanical reactions we generalise under the name of consciousness: the individual has only a relative value and a temporary
reality. But if Matter turns out to be itself unreal or derivative and
simply a phenomenon of Energy, as seems now to be the probability, then Energy remains as the sole Reality; the percipient, his
perception, the perceived object are only phenomena of Energy.
But an Energy without a Being or Existence possessing it or a
Consciousness supplying it, an Energy working originally in the
void, — for the material field in which we see it at work is itself
a creation, — looks itself very much like a mental construction,
an unreality: or it might be a temporary inexplicable outbreak of
motion which might cease at any time to create phenomena; the
Void of the Infinite alone would be enduring and real. The Buddhist theory of the percipient and the perception and the percept
as a construction of Karma, the process of some cosmic fact of
Action, gave room to such a conclusion; for it led logically to the
affirmation of the Non-Being, Void or Nihil. It is possible indeed
that what is at work is not an Energy, but a Consciousness; as
Matter reduces itself to Energy seizable by us not in itself but in
its results and workings, so Energy could be reduced to action
of a Consciousness seizable by us not in itself but in its results
and workings. But if this Consciousness is supposed to work
similarly in a Void, we are exposed to the same conclusion, that
it is a creator of temporary phenomenal illusions and itself illusory; Void, an infinite Zero, an original Non-Existence is alone
the enduring Reality. But these conclusions are not binding; for
behind this Consciousness seizable in its works only there may
be an invisible original Existence: a Conscious-Energy of that
Existence could then be a reality; its creations too, made out
of an infinitesimal substance of being impalpable to the senses
but revealed to them at a certain stage of the action of Energy
as Matter, would be real, as also the individual emerging as a
conscious being of the original Existence in a world of Matter.
This original Reality might be a cosmic spiritual Existence, a
Pantheos, or it might have some other status; but in any case
there would be, not a universal illusion or mere phenomenon,
but a true universe.

In the classical theory of Illusionism a sole and supreme spiritual Existence is accepted as the one Reality: it is by its essentiality the Self, yet the natural beings of which it is the Self are only temporary appearances; it is in its absoluteness the substratum of all things, but the universe erected on the substratum is either a non-existence, a semblance, or else in some way unreally real; it is a cosmic illusion. For the Reality is one without a second, it is immutable in eternity, it is the sole Existence; there is nothing else, there are no true becomings of this Being: it is and must for ever remain void of name, feature, formation, relation, happening; if it has a Consciousness, it can only be a pure consciousness of its own absolute being. But what then is the relation between the Reality and the Illusion? By what miracle or mystery does the Illusion come to be or how does it manage to appear or to abide in Time for ever?

As only Brahman is real, only a consciousness or a power of Brahman could be a real creator and a creator of realities. But since there can be no other reality than Brahman pure and absolute, there can be no true creative power of Brahman. A Brahman-consciousness aware of real beings, forms and happenings would signify a truth of the Becoming, a spiritual and material reality of the universe, which the experience of the supreme Truth negates and nullifies and with which its sole existence is logically incompatible. Maya's creation is a presentation of beings, names, forms, happenings, things, impossible to accept as true, contradictory of the indeterminable purity of the One Existence. Maya then is not real, it is non-existent: Maya is itself an illusion, the parent of numberless illusions. But still this illusion and its works have some kind of existence and so must in some way be real: moreover, the universe does not exist in a Void but stands because it is imposed on Brahman, it is based in a way on the one Reality; we ourselves in the Illusion attribute its forms, names, relations, happenings to the Brahman, become aware of all things as the Brahman, see the Reality through these unrealities. There is then a reality in Maya; it is at the same time real and unreal, existent and non-existent; or, let us say, it is neither real nor unreal: it is a paradox, a suprarational enigma.

But what then is this mystery, or is it insoluble? how comes this illusion to intervene in Brahman-existence? what is the nature of this unreal reality of Maya?

At first sight one is compelled to suppose that Brahman must be in some way the percipient of Maya, — for Brahman is the sole Reality, and if he is not the percipient, who then perceives the Illusion? Any other percipient is not in existence; the individual who is in us the apparent witness is himself phenomenal and unreal, a creation of Maya. But if Brahman is the percipient, how is it possible that the illusion can persist for a moment, since the true consciousness of the percipient is consciousness of self, an awareness solely of its own pure self-existence? If Brahman perceives the world and things with a true consciousness, then they must all be itself and real; but since they are not the pure self-existence, but at best are forms of it and are seen through a phenomenal Ignorance, this realistic solution is not possible. Yet we have to accept, provisionally at least, the universe as a fact, an impossibility as a thing that is, since Maya is there and her works persist and obsess the spirit with the sense, however false, of their reality. It is on this basis that we have, then, to face and solve the dilemma.

If Maya is in some way real, the conclusion imposes itself that Brahman the Reality is in that way the percipient of Maya. Maya may be his power of differentiating perception, for the power of Maya consciousness which distinguishes it from the true consciousness of sole spiritual Self is its creative perception of difference. Or Maya must be at least, if this creation of difference is considered to be only a result and not the essence of Maya-force, some power of Brahman's consciousness, — for it is only a consciousness that can see or create an illusion and there cannot be another original or originating consciousness than that of Brahman. But since Brahman is also self-aware for ever, there must be a double status of Brahman-Consciousness, one conscious of the sole Reality, the other conscious of the un-realities to which by its creative perception of them it gives some kind of apparent existence. These unrealities cannot be made of the substance of the Reality, for then they also must be real. In

this view one cannot accept the assertion of the Upanishads that
the world is made out of the supreme Existence, is a becoming,
an outcome or product of the eternal Being. Brahman is not the
material cause of the universe: our nature, — as opposed to our
self, — is not made of its spiritual substance; it is constructed out
of the unreal reality of Maya. But, on the contrary, our spiritual
being is of that substance, is indeed the Brahman; Brahman is
above Maya, but he is also the percipient of his creations both
from above and from within Maya. This dual consciousness
offers itself as the sole plausible explanation of the riddle of a
real eternal Percipient, an unreal Percept, and a Perception that
is a half-real creator of unreal percepts.

If there is not this dual consciousness, if Maya is the sole
conscious power of Brahman, then one of two things must be
true: either the reality of Maya as a power is that it is a subjective
action of Brahman-consciousness emerging out of its silence and
superconscient immobility and passing through experiences that
are real because they are part of the consciousness of Brahman
but unreal because they are not part of its being, or else Maya
is Brahman's power of cosmic Imagination inherent in his eternal being creating out of nothing names, forms and happenings
that are not in any way real. In that case Maya would be real,
but her works entirely fictitious, pure imaginations: but can we
affirm Imagination as the sole dynamic or creative power of the
Eternal? Imagination is a necessity for a partial being with an
ignorant consciousness; for it has to supplement its ignorance by
imaginations and conjectures: there can be no place for such a
movement in the sole consciousness of a sole Reality which has
no reason to construct unrealities, for it is ever pure and self-
complete. It is difficult to see what in its own being could impel or
induce such a Sole Existence complete in its very essence, blissful
in its eternity, containing nothing to be manifested, timelessly
perfect, to create an unreal Time and Space and people it to all
eternity with an interminable cosmic show of false images and
happenings. This solution is logically untenable.

The other solution, the idea of a purely subjective unreal
reality, starts from the distinction made by the mind in physical

Nature between its subjective and objective experiences; for it is the objective alone of which it is sure as entirely and solidly real. But such a distinction could hardly exist in Brahman-consciousness since here there is either no subject and no object or Brahman itself is the sole possible subject of its consciousness and the sole possible object; there could be nothing externally objective to Brahman, since there is nothing else than Brahman. This idea, then, of a subjective action of consciousness creating a world of fictions other than or distorting the sole true object looks like an imposition on the Brahman by our mind; it imposes on the pure and perfect Reality a feature of its own imperfection, not truly attributable to the perception of a Supreme Being. On the other hand, the distinction between the consciousness and the being of Brahman could not be valid, unless Brahman-being and Brahman-consciousness are two distinct entities, — the consciousness imposing its experiences on the pure existence of the being but unable to touch or affect or penetrate it. Brahman, then, whether as the supreme sole Self-Existence or the Self of the real-unreal individual in Maya, would be aware by his true consciousness of the illusions imposed on him and would know them as illusions; only some energy of Maya-nature or something in it would be deluded by its own inventions, — or else, not being really deluded, still persist in behaving and feeling as if it were deluded. This duality is what happens to our consciousness in the Ignorance when it separates itself from the works of Nature and is aware within of the Self as the sole truth and the rest as not-self and not-real, but has on the surface to act as if the rest too were real. But this solution negates the sole and indivisible pure existence and pure awareness of the Brahman; it creates a dualism within its featureless unity which is not other in its purport than the dualism of the double Principle in the Sankhya view of things, Purusha and Prakriti, Soul and Nature. These solutions then must be put aside as untenable, unless we modify our first view of the Reality and concede to it a power of manifold status of consciousness or a power of manifold status of existence.

But, again, the dual consciousness, if we admit it, cannot

be explained as a dual power of Knowledge-Ignorance valid for the Supreme Existence as it is for us in the universe. For we cannot suppose that Brahman is at all subject to Maya, since that would mean a principle of Ignorance clouding the Eternal's self-awareness; it would be to impose the limitations of our own consciousness on the eternal Reality. An Ignorance which occurs or intervenes in the course of manifestation as a result of a subordinate action of Consciousness and as part of a divine cosmic plan and its evolutionary meaning, is one thing and is logically conceivable; a meaningless ignorance or illusion eternal in the original consciousness of the Reality is another thing and not easily conceivable; it appears as a violent mental construction which has no likelihood of validity in the truth of the Absolute. The dual consciousness of Brahman must be in no way an ignorance, but a self-awareness co-existent with a voluntary will to erect a universe of illusions which are held in a frontal perception aware at once of self and the illusory world, so that there is no delusion, no feeling of its reality. The delusion takes place only in the illusory world itself, and the Self or Brahman in the world either enjoys with a free participation or witnesses, itself separate and intangible, the play which lays its magical spell only upon the Nature-mind created for her action by Maya. But this would seem to signify that the Eternal, not content with its pure absolute existence, has the need to create, to occupy itself throughout Time with a drama of names and forms and happenings; it needs, being sole, to see itself as many, being peace and bliss and self-knowledge to observe an experience or representation of mingled knowledge and ignorance, delight and suffering, unreal existence and escape from unreal existence. For the escape is for the individual being constructed by Maya; the Eternal does not need to escape and the play continues its cycle for ever. Or if not the need, there is the will to so create, or there is the urge or the automatic action of these contraries: but, if we consider the sole eternity of pure existence attributed to the Reality, all alike, need, will, urge or automatism, are equally impossible and incomprehensible. This is an explanation of a sort, but it is an explanation which leaves the mystery still beyond logic or comprehension; for this dynamic consciousness of the Eternal is a direct contradiction of its static and real nature. A Will or Power to create or manifest is undoubtedly there: but, if it is a will or power of the Brahman, it can only be for a creation of realities of the Real or a manifestation of the timeless process of its being in Time-eternity; for it seems incredible that the sole power of the Reality should be to manifest something contrary to itself or to create non-existent things in an illusory universe.

There is so far no satisfying answer to the riddle: but it may be that we err in attributing any kind of reality, however illusory at bottom, to Maya or her works: the true solution lies in facing courageously the mystery of its and their utter unreality. This absolute unreality seems to be envisaged by certain formulations of Illusionism or by certain arguments put forward in its favour. This side then of the problem has to pass under consideration before we can examine with confidence the solutions that rest on a relative or partial reality of the universe. There is indeed a line of reasoning which gets rid of the problem by excluding it; it affirms that the question how the Illusion generated, how the universe manages to be there in the pure existence of Brahman, is illegitimate: the problem does not exist, because the universe is non-existent, Maya is unreal, Brahman is the sole truth, alone and self-existent for ever. Brahman is not affected by any illusory consciousness, no universe has come into existence within its timeless reality. But this evasion of the difficulty is either a sophism which means nothing, an acrobacy of verbal logic, the logical reason hiding its head in the play of words and ideas and refusing to see or to solve a real and baffling difficulty, or else it means too much, since in effect it gets rid of all relation of Maya to Brahman by affirming her as an independent absolute non-reality along with the universe created by her. If a real universe does not exist, a cosmic Illusion exists and we are bound to inquire how it came into being or how it manages to exist, what is its relation or non-relation to the Reality, what is meant by our own existence in Maya, by our subjugation to her cycles, by our liberation from her. For in this view we have to suppose that Brahman is not the percipient of Maya or her works, Maya herself is not a power of Brahman-consciousness: Brahman is superconscient, immersed in its own pure being or is conscious only of its own absoluteness; it has nothing to do with Maya. But in that case either Maya cannot exist even as an illusion or there would be a dual Entity or two entities, a real Eternal super- conscious or conscious only of itself and an illusive Power that creates and is conscious of a false universe. We are back on the horns of the dilemma and with no prospect of getting free from our impalement on it, unless we escape by concluding that since all philosophy is part of Maya, all philosophy is also an illusion, problems abound but no conclusion is possible. For what we are confronted with is a pure static and immutable Reality and an illusory dynamism, the two absolutely contradictory of each other, with no greater Truth beyond them in which their secret can be found and their contradictions discover a reconciling issue.

If Brahman is not the percipient, then the percipient must be the individual being: but this percipient is created by the Illusion and unreal; the percept, the world, is an illusion created by an Illusion and unreal; the perceiving consciousness is itself an illusion and therefore unreal. But this deprives everything of significance, our spiritual existence and our salvation from Maya no less than our temporal existence and our immersion in Maya; all are of an equal unreality and unimportance. It is possible to take a less rigid stand-point and hold that Brahman as Brahman has nothing to do with Maya, is eternally free from all illusion or any commerce with illusion, but Brahman as the individual percipient or as the Self of all being here has entered into Maya and can in the individual withdraw from it, and this withdrawal is for the individual an act of supreme importance. But here a dual being is imposed on Brahman and a reality attributed to something that belongs to the cosmic Illusion, — to the individual being of Brahman in Maya, for Brahman as the Self of all is not even phenomenally bound and does not need to escape from her: moreover, salvation cannot be of importance if bondage is unreal and bondage cannot be real unless Maya and her world are real. The absolute unreality of Maya disappears and gives place to a very comprehensive even if perhaps only a practical and temporal reality. To avoid this conclusion it may be said that our individuality is unreal, it is Brahman who withdraws from a reflection of itself in the figment of individuality and its extinction is our release, our salvation: but Brahman, always free, cannot suffer by bondage or profit by salvation, and a reflection, a figment of individuality is not a thing that can need salvation. A reflection, a figment, a mere image in the deceptive mirror of Maya cannot suffer a real bondage or profit by a real salvation. If it be said that it is a conscious reflection or figment and therefore can really suffer and enter into the bliss of release, the question arises whose is the consciousness that so suffers in this fictitious existence, — for there can be no real consciousness except that of the One Existence; so that once more there is established a dual consciousness for Brahman, a consciousness or superconscience free from the illusion and a consciousness subject to the illusion, and we have again substantiated a certain reality of our existence and experience in Maya. For if our being is that of the Brahman, our consciousness something of the consciousness of the Brahman, with whatever qualification, it is to that extent real, — and if our being, why not the being of the universe?

It may finally be put forward as a solution that the percipient individual and the percept universe are unreal, but Maya by imposing itself on Brahman acquires a certain reality, and that reality lends itself to the individual and to its experience in the cosmic Illusion which endures so long as it is subject to the illusion. But, again, for whom is the experience valid, the reality acquired while it endures, and for whom does it cease by liberation, extinction or withdrawal? For an illusory unreal being cannot put on reality and suffer from a real bondage or escape from it by a real act of evasion or self-extinction; it can only seem to some real self or being to exist, but in that case this real self must in some way or in some degree have become subject to Maya. It must either be the consciousness of Brahman that projects itself into a world of Maya and issues from Maya or it must be the being of Brahman that puts forth

something of itself, its reality, into Maya and withdraws it again
from Maya. Or what again is this Maya that imposes itself
on Brahman? from where does it come if it is not already in
Brahman, an action of the eternal Consciousness or the eternal
Superconscience? It is only if a being or a consciousness of the
Reality undergoes the consequences of the Illusion that the cycles
of the Illusion can put on any reality or have any importance
except as a dance of phantasmagoric marionettes with which the
Eternal amuses himself, a puppet-show in Time. We are driven
back to the dual being of Brahman, the dual consciousness of
Brahman involved in the Illusion and free from the Illusion, and
a certain phenomenal truth of being for Maya: there can be no
solution of our existence in the universe if that existence and the
universe itself have no reality, — even though the reality be only
partial, restricted, derivative. But what can be the reality of an
original universal and fundamentally baseless Illusion? The only
possible answer is that it is a suprarational mystery, inexplicable
and ineffable, — *anirvacanīya*.

There are, however, two possible replies to the difficulty, if
we get rid of the idea of absolute unreality and admit a qualification or compromise. A basis can be created for a subjective
illusion-consciousness which is yet part of Being, if we accept in
the sense of an illusory subjective world-awareness the account
of sleep and dream creation given to us in the Upanishads. For
the affirmation there is that Brahman as Self is fourfold; the Self
is Brahman and all that is is the Brahman, but all that is is the
Self seen by the Self in four states of its being. In the pure self-
status neither consciousness nor unconsciousness as we conceive
it can be affirmed about Brahman; it is a state of superconscience
absorbed in its self-existence, in a self-silence or a self-ecstasy, or
else it is the status of a free Superconscient containing or basing
everything but involved in nothing. But there is also a luminous
status of sleep-self, a massed consciousness which is the origin
of cosmic existence; this state of deep sleep in which yet there
is the presence of an omnipotent Intelligence is the seed state
or causal condition from which emerges the cosmos; — this and
the dream-self which is the continent of all subtle, subjective

or supraphysical experience, and the self of waking which is the support of all physical experience, can be taken as the whole field of Maya. As a man in deep sleep passes into dreams in which he experiences self-constructed unstable structures of name, form, relation, happenings, and in the waking state externalises himself in the more apparently stable but yet transient structures of the physical consciousness, so the Self develops out of a state of massed consciousness its subjective and its objective cosmic experience. But the waking state is not a true waking from this original and causal sleep; it is only a full emergence into a gross external and objective sense of the positive reality of objects of consciousness as opposed to the subtle subjective dream-awareness of those objects: the true waking is a withdrawal from both objective and subjective consciousness and from the massed causal Intelligence into the superconscience superior to all consciousness; for all consciousness and all unconsciousness is Maya. Here, we may say, Maya is real because it is the self's experience of the Self, something of the Self enters into it, is affected by its happenings because it accepts them, believes in them, they are to it real experiences, creations out of its conscious being; but it is unreal because it is a sleep state, a dream state, an eventually transient waking state, not the true status of the superconscient Reality. Here there is no actual dichotomy of being itself, but there is a multiplicity of status of the one Being; there is no original dual consciousness implying a Will in the Uncreated to create illusory things out of non-existence, but there is One Being in states of superconscience and consciousness each with its own nature of self-experience. But the lower states, although they have a reality, are yet qualified by a building and seeing of subjective self-constructions which are not the Real. The One Self sees itself as many, but this multiple existence is subjective; it has a multiplicity of its states of consciousness, but this multiplicity also is subjective; there is a reality of subjective experience of a real Being, but no objective universe.

It may be noted, however, that nowhere in the Upanishads is it actually laid down that the threefold status is a condition of illusion or the creation of an unreality; it is constantly affirmed that all this that is, — this universe we are now supposing to have been constructed by Maya, — is the Brahman, the Reality. The Brahman becomes all these beings; all beings must be seen in the Self, the Reality, and the Reality must be seen in them, the Reality must be seen as being actually all these beings; for not only the Self is Brahman, but all is the Self, all this that is is the Brahman, the Reality. That emphatic asseveration leaves no room for an illusory Maya; but still the insistent denial that there is anything other than or separate from the experiencing self, certain phrases used and the description of two of the states of consciousness as sleep and dream may be taken as if they annulled the emphasis on the universal Reality; these passages open the gates to the illusionist idea and have been made the foundation for an uncompromising system of that nature. If we take this fourfold status as a figure of the Self passing from its superconscient state, where there is no subject or object, into a luminous trance in which superconscience becomes a massed consciousness out of which the subjective status of being and the objective come into emergence, then we get according to our view of things either a possible process of illusionary creation or a process of creative Self-knowledge and All-knowledge.

In fact, if we can judge from the description of the three lower states of Self as the all-wise Intelligence,[6] the Seer of the subtle and the Seer of the gross material existence, this sleep state and this dream state seem to be figurative names for the superconscient and the subliminal which are behind and beyond our waking status; they are so named and figured because it is through dream and sleep, — or trance which can be regarded

6 *prajñā.* Yajnavalkya in the Brihadaranyaka Upanishad states very positively that there are two planes or states of the being which are two worlds and that in the dream state one can see both worlds for the dream state is intermediate between them, it is their joining-plane. This makes it clear that he is speaking of a subliminal condition of the consciousness which can carry in it communications between the physical and the supraphysical worlds. The description of the dreamless sleep-state applies both to deep sleep and to the condition of trance in which one enters into a massed consciousness containing in it all the powers of being but all compressed within itself and concentrated solely on itself and, when active, then active in a consciousness where all is the self; this is, clearly, a state admitting us into the higher planes of the spirit normally now superconscient to our waking being.

as a kind of dream or sleep, — that the surface mental consciousness normally passes out of the perception of objective
things into the inner subliminal and the superior supramental
or overmental status. In that inner condition it sees the supraphysical realities in transcribing figures of dream or vision or,
in the superior status, it loses itself in a massed consciousness
of which it can receive no thought or image. It is through this
subliminal and this superconscient condition that we can pass
into the supreme superconscience of the highest state of self-
being. If we make the transition, not through dream-trance or
sleep-trance, but through a spiritual awakening into these higher
states, we become aware in all of them of the one omnipresent
Reality; there need be no perception of an illusionary Maya,
there is only an experience of the passage from Mind to what is
beyond it so that our mental structure of the universe ceases to
be valid and another reality of it is substituted for the ignorant
mental knowledge. In this transition it is possible to be awake
to all the states of being together in a harmonised and unified
experience and to see the Reality everywhere. But if we plunge
by a trance of exclusive concentration into a mystic sleep-state
or pass abruptly in waking Mind into a state belonging to the
Superconscient, then the mind can be seized in the passage by
a sense of the unreality of the cosmic Force and its creations;
it passes by a subjective abolition of them into the supreme
superconscience. This sense of unreality and this sublimating
passage are the spiritual justification for the idea of a world
created by Maya; but this consequence is not conclusive, since a
larger and more complete conclusion superseding it is possible
to spiritual experience.

All these and other solutions of the nature of Maya fail to
satisfy because they have no conclusiveness: they do not establish the inevitability of the illusionist hypothesis which, to be
accepted, needs to be inevitable; they do not bridge the chasm
between the presumed true nature of the eternal Reality and
the paradoxical and contrary character of the cosmic Illusion.
At the most a process is indicated that claims to make the co-
existence of the two opposites conceivable and intelligible; but

it has no such force of certitude or illuminating convincingness effectively curing the improbability that its acceptance would be obligatory on the intelligence. The theory of the cosmic Illusion gets rid of an original contradiction, a problem and mystery which may be otherwise soluble, by erecting another contradiction, a new problem and mystery which is irreconcilable in its terms and insoluble. For we start with the conception or experience of an absolute Reality which is in its nature eternally one, supracosmic, static, immobile, immutable, self-aware of its pure existence, and a phenomenon of cosmos, dynamism, motion, mutability, modifications of the original pure existence, differentiation, infinite multiplicity. This phenomenon is got rid of by declaring it to be a perpetual Illusion, Maya. But this brings in, in effect, a self-contradictory dual status of consciousness of the One to annul a self-contradictory dual status of being of the One. A phenomenal truth of multiplicity of the One is annulled by setting up a conceptual falsehood in the One creating an unreal multiplicity. The One for ever self-aware of its pure existence entertains a perpetual imagination or illusory construction of itself as an infinite multiplicity of ignorant and suffering beings unaware of self who have to wake one by one to awareness of self and cease individually to be.

In face of this solution of a perplexity by a new perplexity we begin to suspect that our original premiss must have been somewhere incomplete, — not an error, but only a first statement and indispensable foundation. We begin to envisage the Reality as an eternal oneness, status, immutable essence of pure existence supporting an eternal dynamis, motion, infinite multiplicity and diversity of itself. The immutable status of oneness brings out of itself the dynamis, motion and multiplicity, — the dynamis, motion and multiplicity not abrogating but bringing into relief the eternal and infinite oneness. If the consciousness of Brahman can be dual in status or action or even manifold, there seems to be no reason why Brahman should be incapable of a dual status or a manifold real self-experience of its being. The cosmic consciousness would then be, not a creative Illusion, but an experience of some truth of the Absolute. This explanation, if worked out, might prove to be more comprehensive and spiritually fecund, more harmonic in its juncture of the two terms of our self-experience, and it would be at least as logically tenable as the idea of an eternal Reality supporting in perpetuity an eternal illusion real only to an infinite multiplicity of ignorant and suffering beings who escape one by one from the obscurity and pain of Maya, each one by a separate extinction of itself in Maya.

In a second possible answer on the illusionist basis to the problem, in the philosophy of Shankara which may be described as a qualified Illusionism, an answer which is presented with a force and comprehensiveness that are extraordinarily impressive, we make a first step towards this solution. For this philosophy affirms a qualified reality for Maya; it characterises it indeed as an ineffable and unaccountable mystery, but at the same time it does present us with a rational solution, at first sight thoroughly satisfactory, of the opposition which afflicts our mind; it accounts for our sense of the persistent and pressing reality of the universe and our sense of the inconclusiveness, insufficiency, vanity, evanescence, a certain unreality of life and phenomena. For we find a distinction made between two orders of reality, transcendental and pragmatic, absolute and phenomenal, eternal and temporal, — the former the reality of the pure being of Brahman, absolute and supracosmic and eternal, the latter the reality of Brahman in Maya, cosmic, temporal and relative. Here we get a reality for ourselves and the universe: for the individual self is really Brahman; it is Brahman who within the field of Maya seems phenomenally to be subjected to her as the individual and in the end releases the relative and phenomenal individual into his eternal and true being. In the temporal field of relativities our experience of the Brahman who has become all beings, the Eternal who has become universal and individual, is also valid; it is indeed a middle step of the movement in Maya towards liberation from Maya. The universe too and its experiences are real for the consciousness in Time and that consciousness is real. But the question of the nature and extent of this reality at once arises: for the universe and ourselves may be a true reality though of a lesser order, or they may be partly real, partly unreal, or they may be an unreal reality. If they are at all a true reality, there is no place for any theory of Maya; there is no illusory creation. If they are partly real, partly unreal, the fault must lie in something wrong either in the cosmic self-awareness or in our own seeing of ourselves and the universe which produces an error of being, an error of knowledge, an error in the dynamis of existence. But that error can amount only to an ignorance or a mixed knowledge and ignorance, and what needs to be explained then is not an original Cosmic Illusion but the intervention of Ignorance in the creative consciousness or in the dynamic action of the Eternal and Infinite. But if universe and ourselves are an unreal reality, if to a transcendental consciousness all this has no truth of existence and its apparent reality ceases once we step out of the field proper to Maya, then the concession accorded with one hand is taken away by the other; for what was conceded as a truth turns out to have been all the time an illusion. Maya and cosmos and ourselves are both real and unreal, — but the reality is an unreal reality, real only to our ignorance, unreal to any true knowledge.

It is difficult to see why, once any reality is conceded to ourselves and to the universe, it should not be a true reality within its limits. It may be admitted that the manifestation must be on its surface a more restricted reality than the Manifested; our universe is, we may say, one of the rhythms of Brahman and not, except in its essential being, the whole reality: but that is not a sufficient reason for it to be set aside as unreal. It is no doubt so felt by mind withdrawing from itself and its structures: but this is only because the mind is an instrument of Ignorance and, when it withdraws from its constructions, from its ignorant and imperfect picture of the universe, it is impelled to regard them as nothing more than its own fictions and formations, unfounded, unreal; the gulf between its ignorance and the supreme Truth and Knowledge disables it from discovering the true connections of the transcendent Reality and the cosmic Reality. In a higher status of consciousness the difficulty disappears, the connection is established; the sense of unreality recedes and a theory of illusion becomes superfluous and inapplicable. It cannot be the final truth that the Supreme Consciousness has no regard upon the universe or that it regards it as a fiction which its self in Time upholds as real. The cosmic can only exist by dependence on the supracosmic, Brahman in Time must have some significance for Brahman in timeless eternity; otherwise there could be no self and spirit in things and therefore no basis for the temporal existence.

But the universe is condemned as ultimately unreal because it is temporary and not eternal, a perishable form of being imposed on the Formless and Imperishable. This relation can be illustrated by the analogy of earth and the pot made out of earth: the pot and other forms so created perish and go back to the reality, earth, they are only evanescent forms; when they disappear there is left the formless and essential earth and nothing else. But this analogy can tell more convincingly the other way; for the pot is real by right of its being made out of the substance of earth which is real; it is not an illusion and, even when it is dissolved into the original earth, its past existence cannot be thought to have been unreal or an illusion. The relation is not that of an original reality and a phenomenal unreality, but of an original, — or, if we go back from earth to the invisible substratum and constituent ether, an eternal and non-manifest, — to a resultant and dependent, a temporal and manifested reality. Moreover, the pot form is an eternal possibility of earth substance, or ethereal substance, and while the substance exists the form can always be manifested. A form may disappear, but it only passes out of manifestation into non-manifestation; a world may disappear, but there is no proof that world-existence is an evanescent phenomenon: on the contrary, we may suppose that the power of manifestation is inherent in Brahman and continues to act either continuously in Time-eternity or in an eternal recurrence. The cosmic is a different order of the Real from the supracosmic Transcendence, but there is no need to take it as in any way non-existent or unreal to that Transcendence. For the purely intellectual conception that only the Eternal is real, whether we take it in the sense that reality depends on perpetual duration or that the timeless only is true, is an ideative distinction, a mental construction; it is not binding on a substantial and integral experience. Time is not necessarily cancelled out of existence by timeless Eternity; their relation is only verbally a relation of contradiction; in fact, it is more likely to be a relation of dependence.

Similarly, the reasoning which cancels the dynamics of the Absolute, the imposition of the stigma of unreal reality on the pragmatic truth of things because it is pragmatic, is difficult to accept; for the pragmatic truth is after all not something quite other, quite separate and unconnected with spiritual truth, it is a result of the energy or a motion of the dynamic activity of the Spirit. A distinction must, no doubt, be made between the two, but the idea of an entire opposition can rest only on the postulate that a silent and quiescent status is the Eternal's true and whole being; but in that case we must conclude that there is nothing dynamic in the Absolute and all dynamism is a contradiction of the supreme nature of the Divine and Eternal. But if a temporal or cosmic reality of any kind exists, there must be a power, an inherent dynamic force of the Absolute which brought it into being, and there is no reason to suppose that the power of the Absolute can do nothing but create illusions. On the contrary, the Power that creates must be the force of an omnipotent and omniscient Consciousness; the creations of the absolutely Real should be real and not illusions, and since it is the One Existence, they must be self-creations, forms of a manifestation of the Eternal, not forms of Nothing erected out of the original Void, — whether a void being or a void consciousness, — by Maya.

At the basis of the refusal to recognise the universe as real is the concept or experience of the Reality as immutable, featureless, non-active and realised through a consciousness that has itself fallen into a status of silence and is immobile. The universe is a result of dynamis in movement, it is force of being throwing itself out in action, energy at work, whether that energy be conceptive or mechanical or a spiritual, mental, vital or material dynamis; it can thus be regarded as a contradiction, — or a derogation from self, — of the static and immobile eternal Reality, therefore unreal. But as a concept this position of the thought has no inevitability; there is no reason why we should not conceive of the Reality as at once static and dynamic. It is perfectly rational to suppose that the eternal status of being of the Reality contains in it an eternal force of being, and this dynamis must necessarily carry in itself a power of action and movement, a kinesis; both status of being and movement of being can be real. There is no reason either why they should not be simultaneous; on the contrary, simultaneity is demanded, — for all energy, all kinetic action has to support itself on status or by status if it is to be effective or creative; otherwise there will be no solidity of anything created, only a constant whirl without any formation: status of being, form of being are necessary to kinesis of being. Even if energy be the primal reality, as it seems to be in the material world, still it has to create status of itself, lasting forms, duration of beings in order to have a support for its action: the status may be temporary, it may be only a balance or equilibrium of substance created and maintained by a constant kinesis, but while it endures it is real and, after it ceases, we still regard it as something that was real. The principle of a supporting status for action is a permanent principle, and its action is constant in Time-eternity. When we discover the stable Reality underlying all this movement of energy and this creation of forms, we do indeed perceive that the status of created forms is only temporary; there is a stability of repetition of the kinesis in a same persistent action and figure of movement which maintains substance of being in stable form of itself: but this stability is created, and the one permanent and self-existent status is that of the eternal Being whose Energy erected the forms. But we need not therefore conclude that the temporary forms are unreal; for the energy of the being is real and the forms made by it are forms of the being. In any case the status of the being and the eternal dynamis of the being are both real, and they are simultaneous; the status admits of action of dynamis and the action does not abrogate the status. We must therefore conclude that eternal status and eternal dynamis are both true of the Reality which itself surpasses both status and dynamis; the immobile and the mobile Brahman are both the same Reality.

But in experience we find that for us it is, normally, a quiescence that brings in the stable realisation of the eternal and the infinite: it is in silence or quietude that we feel most firmly the Something that is behind the world shown to us by our mind and senses. Our cognitive action of thought, our action of life and being seem to overlay the truth, the reality; they grasp the finite but not the infinite, they deal with the temporal and not the eternal Real. It is reasoned that this is so because all action, all creation, all determining perception limits; it does not embrace or grasp the Reality, and its constructions disappear when we enter into the indivisible and indeterminable consciousness of the Real: these constructions are unreal in eternity, however real they may seem or be in Time. Action leads to ignorance, to the created and finite; kinesis and creation are a contradiction of the immutable Reality, the pure uncreated Existence. But this reasoning is not wholly valid because it is looking at perception and action only as they are in our mental cognition of the world and its movement; but that is the experience of our surface being regarding things from its shifting motion in Time, a regard itself superficial, fragmentary and delimited, not total, not plunging into the inner sense of things. In fact we find that action need not bind or limit, if we get out of this moment-cognition into a status of cognition of the eternal proper to the true consciousness. Action does not bind or limit the liberated man; action does not bind or limit the Eternal: but we can go farther and say that action does not bind or limit our own true being at all. Action has no such effect on the spiritual Person or Purusha or on the psychic entity within us, it binds or limits only the surface constructed personality. This personality is a temporary expression of our self-being, a changing form of it, empowered to exist by it, dependent on it for substance and endurance, — temporary, but not unreal. Our thought and action are means for this expression of ourselves and, as the expression is incomplete and evolutive, as it is a development of our natural being in Time, thought and action help it to develop, to change, to alter and expand its limits, but at the same time to maintain limits; in that sense they are limiting and binding; they are themselves an incomplete mode of self-revelation. But when we go back into ourselves, into the true self and person, there is no longer a binding or limitation by the limits of action or perception; both arise as expressions of consciousness and expressions of force of the self operative for a free self-determination of its nature-being, for the self-unrolling, the becoming in time of something that is itself illimitable. The limitation, which is a necessary circumstance of an evolutive self-determination, might be an abrogation of self or derogation from self, from Reality, and therefore itself unreal, if it altered the essentiality or totality of the being; it would be a bondage of the spirit and therefore illegitimate if it obscured, by an alien imposition proceeding from a force that is not-self, the Consciousness that is the inmost witness and creator of our world-existence, or if it constructed something contrary to the Being's consciousness of self or will of becoming. But the essence of being remains the same in all action and formation, and the limitations freely accepted do not take from the being's totality; they are accepted and self-imposed, not imposed from outside, they are a means of expression of our totality in the movement of Time, an order of things imposed by our inner spiritual being on our outer nature-being, not a bondage inflicted on the ever-free spirit. There is therefore no reason to conclude from the limitations of perception and action that the movement is unreal or that the expression, formation or self-creation of the Spirit is unreal. It is a temporal order of reality, but it is still a reality of the Real, not something else. All that is in the kinesis, the movement, the action, the creation, is the Brahman; the becoming is a movement of the being; Time is a manifestation of the Eternal. All is one Being, one Consciousness, one even in infinite multiplicity, and there is no need to bisect it into an opposition of transcendent Reality and unreal cosmic Maya.

In the philosophy of Shankara one feels the presence of a conflict, an opposition which this powerful intellect has stated with full force and masterfully arranged rather than solved with any finality, — the conflict of an intuition intensely aware of an absolute transcendent and inmost Reality and a strong intellectual reason regarding the world with a keen and vigorous rational intelligence. The intellect of the thinker regards the phenomenal world from the standpoint of the reason; reason is there the judge and the authority and no suprarational authority can prevail against it: but behind the phenomenal world is a transcendent Reality which the intuition alone can see; there reason, — at least a finite dividing limited reason, — cannot prevail against the intuitive experience, it cannot even relate the two, it cannot therefore solve the mystery of the universe. The reason has to affirm the reality of the phenomenal existence, to affirm its truths as valid; but they are valid only in that phenomenal existence. This phenomenal existence is real because it is a temporal phenomenon of the eternal Existence, the Reality: but it is not itself that Reality and, when we pass beyond the phenomenon to the Real, it still exists but is no longer valid to our consciousness; it is therefore unreal. Shankara takes up this contradiction, this opposition which is normal to our mental consciousness when it becomes aware of both sides of existence and stands between them; he resolves it by obliging the reason to recognise its limits, in which its unimpaired sovereignty is left to it within its own cosmic province, and to acquiesce in the soul's intuition of the transcendent Reality and to support, by a dialectic which ends by dissolving the whole cosmic phenomenal and rational-practical edifice of things, its escape from the limitations constructed and imposed on the mind by Maya. The explanation of cosmic existence by which this is brought about seems to be, — or so we may translate it to our understanding, for there have been different expositions of this profound and subtle philosophy, — that there is a Transcendence which is for ever self-existent and immutable and a world which is only phenomenal and temporal. The eternal Reality manifests itself in regard to the phenomenal world as Self and Ishwara. The Ishwara by his Maya, his power of phenomenal creation, constructs this world as a temporal phenomenon, and this phenomenon of things which do not exist in the utterly Real is imposed by Maya through our conceptive and perceptive consciousness on the superconscient or purely self-conscient Reality. Brahman the Reality appears in the phenomenal existence as the Self of the living individual; but when the individuality of the individual is dissolved by intuitive knowledge, the phenomenal being is released into self-being: it is no longer subject to Maya and by its release from the appearance of individuality it is extinguished in the Reality; but the world continues to exist without beginning or end as the Mayic creation of the Ishwara.

This is an arrangement which puts into relation with each other the data of the spiritual intuition and the data of the reason and sense, and it opens to us a way out from their contradiction, a spiritual and practical issue: but it is not a solution, it does not resolve the contradiction. Maya is real and unreal; the world is not a mere illusion, for it exists and is real in Time, but eventually and transcendentally it turns out to be unreal. This creates an ambiguity which extends beyond itself and touches all that is not the pure self-existence. Thus the Ishwara, though he is undeluded by Maya and the creator of Maya, seems himself to be a phenomenon of Brahman and not the ultimate Reality, he is real only with regard to the Time-world he creates; the individual self has the same ambiguous character. If Maya were to cease altogether from its operations, Ishwara, the world and the individual would no longer be there; but Maya is eternal, Ishwara and the world are eternal in Time, the individual endures so long as he does not annul himself by knowledge. Our thought on these premises has to take refuge in the conception of an ineffable suprarational mystery which is to the intellect insoluble. But, faced with this ambiguity, this admission of an insoluble mystery at the commencement of things and at the end of the process of thought, we begin to suspect that there is a link missing. Ishwara is not himself a phenomenon of Maya, he is real; he must then be the manifestation of a truth of the Transcendence, or he must be the Transcendent itself dealing with a cosmos manifested in his own being. If the world is at all real, it also must be the manifestation of a truth of the Transcendence; for only that can have any reality. If the individual has the power of self-discovery and entrance into the transcendent eternity and his liberation has so great an importance, it must be because he too is a reality of the Transcendence; he has to discover himself individually, because his individuality also has some truth of itself in the Transcendence which is veiled from it and which it has to recover. It is an ignorance of self and world that has to be overcome and not an illusion, a figment of individuality and world-existence.

It becomes evident that as the Transcendence is suprarational and seizable only by an intuitive experience and realisation, so also the mystery of the universe is suprarational. It has to be so since it is a phenomenon of the transcendent Reality, and it would not, if it were otherwise, be insoluble by the intellectual reason. But if so, we have to pass beyond the intellect in order to bridge the gulf and penetrate the mystery; to leave an unsolved contradiction cannot be the final solution. It is the intellectual reason that crystallises and perpetuates an apparent contradiction by creating its opposite or dividing concepts of the Brahman, the Self, the Ishwara, the individual being, the supreme consciousness or superconscience and the Mayic world-consciousness. If Brahman alone exists, all these must be Brahman, and in Brahman-consciousness the division of these concepts must disappear in a reconciling self-vision; but we can arrive at their true unity only by passing beyond the intellectual Reason and finding out through spiritual experience where they meet and become one and what is the spiritual reality of their apparent divergence. In fact, in the Brahman-consciousness the divergences cannot exist, they must by our passage into it converge into unity; the divisions of the intellectual reason may correspond to a reality, but it must be then the reality of a manifold Oneness. The Buddha applied his penetrating rational intellect supported by an intuitive vision to the world as our mind and sense see it and discovered the principle of its construction and the way of release from all constructions, but he refused to go farther. Shankara took the farther step and regarded the suprarational Truth, which Buddha kept behind the veil as realisable by cancellation of the constructions of consciousness but beyond the scope of the reason's discovery. Shankara, standing between the world and the eternal Reality, saw that the mystery of the world must be ultimately suprarational, not conceivable or expressible by our reason, *anirvacanīya*; but he maintained the world as seen by the reason and sense as valid and had therefore to posit an unreal reality, because he did not take one step still farther. For to know the real truth of the world, its reality, it must be seen from the suprarational awareness, from the view of the Superconscience that maintains and surpasses and by surpassing knows it in its truth, and no longer from the view of the consciousness that is maintained by it and surpassed by it and therefore does not know it or knows it only by its appearance. It cannot be that to that self-creative supreme consciousness the world is an incomprehensible mystery or that it is to it an illusion that is yet not altogether an illusion, a reality that is yet unreal. The mystery of the universe must have a divine sense to the Divine; it must have a significance or a truth of cosmic being that is luminous to the Reality that upholds it with its transcending and yet immanent superconscience.

If the Reality alone exists and all is the Reality, the world also cannot be excluded from that Reality; the universe is real. If it does not reveal to us in its forms and powers the Reality that it is, if it seems only a persistent and yet changing movement in Space and Time, this must be not because it is unreal or because it is not at all That, but because it is a progressive self-expression, a manifestation, an evolving self-development of That in Time which our consciousness cannot yet see in its total or its essential significance. In this sense we can say that it is That and not That, — because it does not disclose all the Reality through any form or sum of its forms of self-expression; but still all its forms are forms of the substance and being of that Reality. All finites are in their spiritual essence the Infinite and, if we look deep enough into them, manifest to intuition the Identical and Infinite. It is contended indeed that the universe cannot be a manifestation because the Reality has no need of manifestation, since it is for ever manifest to itself; but so equally it can be said that the Reality has no need of self-illusion or illusion of any kind, no need to create a Mayic universe. The Absolute can have no need of anything; but still there can be, — not coercive of its freedom, not binding on it, but an expression of its self-force, the

result of its Will to become, — an imperative of a supreme self-
effectuating Force, a necessity of self-creation born of the power
of the Absolute to see itself in Time. This imperative represents
itself to us as a Will to create, a Will of self-expression; but it may
be better represented as a force of being of the Absolute which
displays itself as a power of itself in action. If the Absolute is
self-evident to itself in eternal Timelessness, it can also be self-
manifest to itself in eternal motion of Time. Even if the universe
is only a phenomenal reality, still it is a manifestation or phenomenon of Brahman; for since all is Brahman, phenomenon
and manifestation must be the same thing: the imputation of
unreality is a superfluous conception, otiose and unnecessarily
embarrassing, since whatever distinction is needed is already
there in the concept of Time and the timeless Eternal and the
concept of manifestation.

The one thing that can be described as an unreal reality is our
individual sense of separativeness and the conception of the finite
as a self-existent object in the Infinite. This conception, this sense
are pragmatically necessary for the operations of the surface
individuality and are effective and justified by their effects; they
are therefore real to its finite reason and finite self-experience:
but once we step back from the finite consciousness into the
consciousness of the essential and infinite, from the apparent
to the true Person, the finite or the individual still exists but
as being and power and manifestation of the Infinite; it has no
independent or separate reality. Individual independence, entire
separativeness are not necessary for individual reality, do not
constitute it. On the other hand, the disappearance of these
finite forms of the manifestation is evidently a factor in the
problem, but does not by itself convict them of unreality; the
disappearance may be only a withdrawal from manifestation.
The cosmic manifestation of the Timeless takes place in the successions of Time: its forms must therefore be temporary in their
appearance on the surface, but they are eternal in their essential
power of manifestation; for they are held always implicit and
potential in the essence of things and in the essential consciousness from which they emerge: timeless consciousness can always

turn their abiding potentiality into terms of time-actuality. The world would be unreal only if itself and its forms were images without substance of being, figments of consciousness presented to itself by the Reality as pure figments and then abolished for ever. But if manifestation or the power of manifestation is eternal, if all is the being of Brahman, the Reality, then this unreality or illusoriness cannot be the fundamental character of things or of the cosmos in which they make their appearance.

A theory of Maya in the sense of illusion or the unreality of cosmic existence creates more difficulties than it solves; it does not really solve the problem of existence, but rather renders it for ever insoluble. For, whether Maya be an unreality or a non-real reality, the ultimate effects of the theory carry in them a devastating simplicity of nullification. Ourselves and the universe fade away into nothingness or else keep for a time only a truth which is little better than a fiction. In the thesis of the pure unreality of Maya, all experience, all knowledge as well as all ignorance, the knowledge that frees us no less than the ignorance that binds us, world-acceptance and world-refusal, are two sides of an illusion; for there is nothing to accept or refuse, nobody to accept or refuse it. All the time it was only the immutable superconscient Reality that at all existed; the bondage and release were only appearances, not a reality. All attachment to world-existence is an illusion, but the call for liberation is also a circumstance of the illusion; it is something that was created in Maya which by its liberation is extinguished in Maya. But this nullification cannot be compelled to stop short in its devastating advance at the boundary fixed for it by a spiritual Illusionism. For if all other experiences of the individual consciousness in the universe are illusions, then what guarantee is there that its spiritual experiences are not illusions, including even its absorbed self-experience of the supreme Self which is conceded to us as utterly real?' For if cosmos is untrue, our experience of the cosmic consciousness, of the universal Self, of Brahman as all these beings or as the self of all these beings, the One in all, all in the One has no secure foundation, since it reposes in one of its terms on an illusion, on a construction of Maya. That term, the cosmic term, has to crumble, for all these beings which we saw as the Brahman were illusions; then what is our assurance of our experience of the other term, the pure Self, the silent, static or absolute Reality, since that too comes to us in a mind moulded of delusion and formed in a body created by an Illusion? An overwhelming self-evident convincingness, an experience of absolute authenticity in the realisation or experience is not an unanswerable proof of sole reality or sole finality: for other spiritual experiences such as that of the omnipresent Divine Person, Lord of a real Universe, have the same convincing, authentic and final character. It is open to the intellect which has once arrived at the conviction of the unreality of all other things, to take a farther step and deny the reality of Self and of all existence. The Buddhists took this last step and refused reality to the Self on the ground that it was as much as the rest a construction of the mind; they cut not only God but the eternal Self and impersonal Brahman out of the picture.

An uncompromising theory of Illusion solves no problem of our existence; it only cuts the problem out for the individual by showing him a way of exit: in its extreme form and effect, our being and its action become null and without sanction, its experience, aspiration, endeavour lose their significance; all, the one incommunicable relationless Truth excepted and the turning away to it, become equated with illusion of being, are part of a universal Illusion and themselves illusions. God and ourselves and the universe become myths of Maya; for God is only a reflection of Brahman in Maya, ourselves are only a reflection of Brahman in illusory individuality, the world is only an imposition on the Brahman's incommunicable self-existence. There is a less drastic nullification if a certain reality is admitted for the being even within the illusion, a certain validity for the experience and knowledge by which we grow into the spirit: but this is only if the temporal has a valid reality and the experience in it has a real validity, and in that case what we are in front of is not an illusion taking the unreal for real but an ignorance misapprehending the real. Otherwise if the beings of whom Brahman is the self are illusory, its selfhood is not valid, it is part of an illusion; the experience of self is also an illusion: the experience "I am That" is vitiated by an ignorant conception, for there is no I, only That; the experience "I am He" is doubly ignorant, for it assumes a conscious Eternal, a Lord of the universe, a Cosmic Being, but there can be no such thing if there is no reality in the universe. A real solution of existence can only stand upon a truth that accounts for our existence and world-existence, reconciles their truth, their right relation and the truth of their relation to whatever transcendent Reality is the source of everything. But this implies some reality of individual and cosmos, some true relation of the One Existence and all existences, of relative experience and of the Absolute.

The theory of Illusion cuts the knot of the world problem, it does not disentangle it; it is an escape, not a solution: a flight of the spirit is not a sufficient victory for the being embodied in this world of the becoming; it effects a separation from Nature, not a liberation and fulfilment of our nature. This eventual outcome satisfies only one element, sublimates only one impulse of our being; it leaves the rest out in the cold to perish in the twilight of the unreal reality of Maya. As in Science, so in metaphysical thought, that general and ultimate solution is likely to be the best which includes and accounts for all so that each truth of experience takes its place in the whole: that knowledge is likely to be the highest knowledge which illumines, integralises, harmonises the significance of all knowledge and accounts for, finds the basic and, one might almost say, the justifying reason of our ignorance and illusion while it cures them; this is the supreme experience which gathers together all experience in the truth of a supreme and all-reconciling oneness. Illusionism unifies by elimination; it deprives all knowledge and experience, except the one supreme merger, of reality and significance.

But this debate belongs to the domain of the pure reason and the final test of truths of this order is not reason but spiritual illumination verified by abiding fact of spirit; a single decisive spiritual experience may undo a whole edifice of reasonings and conclusions erected by the logical intelligence. Here the theory of Illusionism is in occupation of a very solid ground; for, although it is in itself no more than a mental formulation, the experience it formulates into a philosophy accompanies a most powerful and apparently final spiritual realisation. It comes upon us with a great force of awakening to reality when the thought is stilled, when the mind withdraws from its constructions, when we pass into a pure selfhood void of all sense of individuality, empty of all cosmic contents: if the spiritualised mind then looks at individual and cosmos, they may well seem to it to be an illusion, a scheme of names and figures and movements falsely imposed on the sole reality of the Self-Existent. Or even the sense of self becomes inadequate; both knowledge and ignorance disappear into sheer Consciousness and consciousness is plunged into a trance of pure superconscient existence. Or even existence ends by becoming too limiting a name for that which abides solely for ever; there is only a timeless Eternal, a spaceless Infinite, the utterness of the Absolute, a nameless peace, an overwhelming single objectless Ecstasy. There can certainly be no doubt of the validity, — complete within itself, — of this experience; there can be no denial of the overwhelming decisive convincingness, — *ekātma-pratyaya-sāram*, — with which this realisation seizes the consciousness of the spiritual seeker. But still all spiritual experience is experience of the Infinite and it takes a multitude of directions; some of them, — and not this alone, — are so close to the Divine and the Absolute, so penetrated with the reality of Its presence or with the ineffable peace and power of the liberation from all that is less than It, that they carry with them this overwhelming sense of finality complete and decisive. There are a hundred ways of approaching the Supreme Reality and, as is the nature of the way taken, so will be the nature of the ultimate experience by which one passes into That which is ineffable, That of which no report can be given to the mind or expressed by any utterance. All these definitive culminations may be regarded as penultimates of the one Ultimate; they are steps by which the soul crosses the limits of Mind into the Absolute. Is then this realisation of passing into a pure immobile self-existence or this Nirvana of the individual and the universe one among these penultimates, or is it itself the final and absolute realisation which is at the end of every journey and transcends and eliminates all lesser experience? It claims to stand behind and supersede, to sublate and to eliminate every other knowledge; if that is really so, then its finality must be accepted as conclusive. But, against this pretension, it has been claimed that it is possible to travel beyond by a greater negation or a greater affirmation, — to extinguish self in Non-Being or to pass through the double experience of cosmic consciousness and Nirvana of world-consciousness in the One Existence to a greater Divine Union and Unity which holds both these realisations in its vast integral Reality. It is said that beyond the duality and the non-duality there is That in which both are held together and find their truth in a Truth which is beyond them. A consummating experience which proceeds by the exceeding and elimination of all other possible but lesser experiences is, as a step towards the Absolute, admissible. A supreme experience which affirms and includes the truth of all spiritual experience, gives to each its own absolute, integralises all knowledge and experience in a supreme reality, might be the one step farther that is at once a largest illuminating and transforming Truth of all things and a highest infinite Transcendence. The Brahman, the supreme Reality, is That which being known all is known; but in the illusionist solution it is That, which being known, all becomes unreal and an incomprehensible mystery: in this other experience, the Reality being known, all assumes its true significance, its truth to the Eternal and Absolute.

All truths, even those which seem to be in conflict, have their validity, but they need a reconciliation in some largest Truth which takes them into itself; all philosophies have their value, — if for nothing else, then because they see the Self and the universe from a point of view of the spirit's experience of the many-sided Manifestation and in doing so shed light on something that has to be known in the Infinite. All spiritual experiences are true, but they point towards some highest and widest reality which admits their truth and exceeds it. This is, we may say, a sign of the relativity of all truth and all experience, since both vary with the outlook and the inlook of the knowing and experiencing mind and being; each man is said to have his own religion according to his own nature, but so too each man may be said to have his own philosophy, his own way of seeing and experience of existence, though only a few can formulate it. But from another point of view this variety testifies rather to the infinity of aspects of the Infinite; each catches a partial glimpse or a whole glimpse of one or more aspects or contacts or enters into it in his mental or his spiritual experience. To the mind at a certain stage all these viewpoints begin to lose their definitiveness in a large catholicity or a complex tolerant incertitude, or all the rest may fall away from it and yield place to an ultimate truth or a single absorbing experience. It is then that it is liable to feel the unreality of all that it has seen and thought and taken as part of itself or its universe. This "all" becomes to it a universal unreality or a many-sided fragmental reality without a principle of unification; as it passes into the negativing purity of an absolute experience, all falls away from it and there remains only a silent and immobile Absolute. But the consciousness might be called to go farther and see again all it has left in the light of a new spiritual vision: it may recover the truth of all things in the truth of the Absolute; it may reconcile the negation of Nirvana and the affirmation of the cosmic consciousness in a single regard of That of which both are the self-expressions. In the passage from mental to overmind cognition this many-sided unity is the leading experience; the whole manifestation assumes the appearance of a singular and mighty harmony which reaches its greatest completeness when the soul stands on the border between Overmind and Supermind and looks back with a total view upon existence.

This is at least a possibility that we have to explore and pursue this view of things to its ultimate consequence. A consideration of the possibility of a great cosmic Illusion as the explanation of the enigma of being had to be undertaken because this view and experience of things presents itself powerfully at the end of the mental spiral where that reaches its point of breaking or point of cessation; but once it is ascertained that it is not the obligatory end of a scrupulous enquiry into the ultimate truth, we can leave it aside or refer to it only when needed in connection with some line of a more plastic course of thought and reasoning. Our regard can now be concentrated on the problem that is left by the exclusion of the illusionist solution, the problem of the Knowledge and the Ignorance.

All turns round the question "What is Reality?" Our cognitive consciousness is limited, ignorant, finite; our conceptions of reality depend on our way of contact with existence in this limited consciousness and may be very different from the way in which an original and ultimate Consciousness sees it. It is necessary to distinguish between the essential Reality, the phenomenal reality dependent upon it and arising out of it, and the restricted and often misleading experience or notion of either that is created by our sense-experience and our reason. To our sense the earth is flat and, for most immediate practical purposes, within a limit, we have to follow the sense reality and deal with the flatness as if it were a fact; but in true phenomenal reality the flatness of the earth is unreal, and Science seeking for the truth of the phenomenal reality in things has to treat it as approximately round. In a host of details Science contradicts the evidence of the senses as to the real truth of phenomena; but, still, we have to accept the cadre provided by our senses because the practical relations with things which they impose on us have validity as an effect of reality and cannot be disregarded. Our reason, relying on the senses and exceeding them, constructs its own canons or notions of the real and unreal, but these canons vary according to the standpoint taken by the reasoning observer. The physical scientist probing into phenomena erects formulas and standards based on the objective and phenomenal reality and its processes: to his view mind may appear as a subjective result of Matter and self and spirit as unreal; at any rate he has to act as if matter and energy alone existed and mind were only an observer of an independent physical reality which is unaffected by any mental processes[7] or any presence or intervention of a cosmic Intelligence. The psychologist, probing independently into mind consciousness and mind unconsciousness, discovers

---

[7] This position has been shaken by the theory of Relativity, but it must hold as a pragmatic basis for experiment and affirmation of the scientific fact.

another domain of realities, subjective in its character, which
has its own law and process; to him Mind may even come to
appear as the key of the real, Matter as only a field for mind,
and spirit apart from mind as something unreal. But there is a
farther probing which brings up the truth of self and spirit and
establishes a greater order of the real in which there is a reversal
of our view both of the subjective mind realities and objective
physical realities so that they are seen as things phenomenal,
secondary, dependent upon the truth of self and the realities
of the spirit. In this deeper search into things mind and matter
begin to wear the appearance of a lesser order of the real and
may easily come to appear unreal.

But it is the reason accustomed to deal with the finite that
makes these exclusions; it cuts the whole into segments and can
select one segment of the whole as if it were the entire reality.
This is necessary for its action since its business is to deal with
the finite as finite, and we have to accept for practical purposes
and for the reason's dealings with the finite the cadre it gives us,
because it is valid as an effect of reality and so cannot be disregarded. When we come to the experience of the spiritual which
is itself the whole or contains the whole in itself, our mind carries
there too its segmenting reason and the definitions necessary to
a finite cognition; it cuts a line of section between the infinite
and the finite, the spirit and its phenomena or manifestations,
and dubs those as real and these as unreal. But an original and
ultimate consciousness embracing all the terms of existence in a
single integral view would see the whole in its spiritual essential
reality and the phenomenon as a phenomenon or manifestation
of that reality. If this greater spiritual consciousness saw in things
only unreality and an entire disconnection with the truth of the
spirit, it could not have — if it were itself a Truth-Consciousness
— any reason for maintaining them in continuous or recurrent
existence through all Time: if it so maintains them, it is because
they are based on the realities of the spirit. But, necessarily,
when thus integrally seen, the phenomenal reality would take
on another appearance than when it is viewed by the reason and
sense of the finite being; it would have another and deeper reality,

another and greater significance, another and more subtle and complex process of its movements of existence. The canons of reality and all the forms of thought created by the finite reason and sense would appear to the greater consciousness as partial constructions with an element of truth in them and an element of error; these constructions might therefore be described as at once real and unreal, but the phenomenal world itself would not become either unreal or unreal-real by that fact: it would put on another reality of a spiritual character; the finite would reveal itself as a power, a movement, a process of the Infinite.

An original and ultimate consciousness would be a consciousness of the Infinite and necessarily unitarian in its view of diversity, integral, all-accepting, all-embracing, all-discriminating because all-determining, an indivisible whole-vision. It would see the essence of things and regard all forms and movements as phenomenon and consequence of the essential Reality, motions and formations of its power of being. It is held by the reason that truth must be empty of any conflict of contradictions: if so, since the phenomenal universe is or seems to be the contrary of the essential Brahman it must be unreal; since individual being is the contrary of both transcendence and universality, it must be unreal. But what appear as contradictions to a reason based on the finite may not be contradictions to a vision or a larger reason based on the infinite. What our mind sees as contraries may be to the infinite consciousness not contraries but complementaries: essence and phenomenon of the essence are complementary to each other, not contradictory, — the phenomenon manifests the essence; the finite is a circumstance and not a contradiction of the infinite; the individual is a self-expression of the universal and the transcendent, — it is not a contradiction or something quite other than it, it is the universal concentrated and selective, it is one with the Transcendent in its essence of being and its essence of nature. In the view of this unitarian comprehensive seeing there is nothing contradictory in a formless Essence of being that carries a multitude of forms, or in a status of the Infinite supporting a kinesis of the Infinite, or in an infinite Oneness expressing itself in a multiplicity of beings and aspects and powers and movements, for they are beings and aspects and powers and movements of the One. A world-creation on this basis is a perfectly natural and normal and inevitable movement which in itself raises no problem, since it is exactly what one must expect in an action of the Infinite. All the intellectual problem and difficulty is raised by the finite reason cutting, separating, opposing the power of the Infinite to its being, its kinesis to its status, its natural multiplicity to its essential oneness, segmenting self, opposing Spirit to Nature. To understand truly the world-process of the Infinite and the Time-process of the Eternal, the consciousness must pass beyond this finite reason and the finite sense to a larger reason and spiritual sense in touch with the consciousness of the Infinite and responsive to the logic of the Infinite which is the very logic of being itself and arises inevitably from its self-operation of its own realities, a logic whose sequences are not the steps of thought but the steps of existence.

But what has been thus described, it may be said, is only a cosmic consciousness and there is the Absolute: the Absolute cannot be limited; since universe and individual limit and divide the Absolute, they must be unreal. It is self-evident indeed that the Absolute cannot be limited; it can be limited neither by formlessness nor by form, neither by unity nor by multiplicity, neither by immobile status nor by dynamic mobility. If it manifests form, form cannot limit it; if it manifests multiplicity, multiplicity cannot divide it; if it manifests motion and becoming, motion cannot perturb nor becoming change it: it cannot be limited any more than it can be exhausted by self-creation. Even material things have this superiority to their manifestation; earth is not limited by the vessels made from it, nor air by the winds that move in it, nor the sea by the waves that rise on its surface. This impression of limitation belongs only to the mind and sense which see the finite as if it were an independent entity separating itself from the Infinite or something cut out of it by limitation: it is this impression that is illusory, but neither the infinite nor the finite is an illusion; for neither exists by the impressions of the sense or the mind, they depend for their existence on the Absolute.

The Absolute is in itself indefinable by reason, ineffable to the speech; it has to be approached through experience. It can be approached through an absolute negation of existence, as if it were itself a supreme Non-Existence, a mysterious infinite Nihil. It can be approached through an absolute affirmation of all the fundamentals of our own existence, through an absolute of Light and Knowledge, through an absolute of Love or Beauty, through an absolute of Force, through an absolute of peace or silence. It can be approached through an inexpressible absolute of being or of consciousness, or of power of being, or of delight of being, or through a supreme experience in which these things become inexpressibly one; for we can enter into such an ineffable state and, plunged into it as if into a luminous abyss of existence, we can reach a superconscience which may be described as the gate of the Absolute. It is supposed that it is only through a negation of individual and cosmos that we can enter into the Absolute. But in fact the individual need only deny his own small separate ego-existence; he can approach the Absolute through a sublimation of his spiritual individuality taking up the cosmos into himself and transcending it; or he may negate himself altogether, but even so it is still the individual who by self-exceeding enters into the Absolute. He may enter also by a sublimation of his being into a supreme existence or super-existence, by a sublimation of his consciousness into a supreme consciousness or super-conscience, by a sublimation of his and all delight of being into a super-delight or supreme ecstasy. He can make the approach through an ascension in which he enters into cosmic consciousness, assumes it into himself and raises himself and it into a state of being in which oneness and multiplicity are in perfect harmony and unison in a supreme status of manifestation where all are in each and each in all and all in the one without any determining individuation, — for the dynamic identity and mutuality have become complete; on the path of affirmation it is this status of the manifestation that is nearest to the Absolute. This paradox of an Absolute which can be realised through an absolute negation and through an absolute affirmation, in many ways, can only be accounted for to the reason if it is a supreme

Existence which is so far above our notion and experience of existence that it can correspond also to our negation of it, to our notion and experience of non-existence, but also, since all that exists is That, whatever its degree of manifestation, it is itself the supreme of all things and can be approached through supreme affirmations as through supreme negations. The Absolute is the ineffable *x* overtopping and underlying and immanent and essential in all that we can call existence or non-existence.

It is our first premiss that the Absolute is the supreme reality; but the issue is whether all else that we experience is real or unreal. A distinction is sometimes made between being and existence, and it is supposed that being is real but existence or what manifests as such is unreal. But this can stand only if there is a rigid distinction, a cut and separation between the uncreated Eternal and created existences; the uncreated Being can then be taken as alone real. This conclusion does not follow if what exists is form of Being and substance of Being; it would be unreal only if it were a form of Non-Being, *asat,* created out of the Void, *śūnya.* The states of existence through which we approach and enter into the Absolute must have their truth, for the untrue and unreal cannot lead into the Real: but also what issues from the Absolute, what the Eternal supports and informs and manifests in itself, must have a reality. There is the unmanifest and there is the manifestation, but a manifestation of the Real must itself be real; there is the Timeless and there is the process of things in Time, but nothing can appear in Time unless it has a basis in the timeless Reality. If my self and spirit are real, my thoughts, feelings, powers of all kinds, which are its expressions, cannot be unreal; my body, which is the form it puts out in itself and which at the same time it inhabits, cannot be a nothing or a mere unsubstantial shadow. The only reconciling explanation is that timeless eternity and time eternity are two aspects of the Eternal and Absolute and both are real, but in a different order of reality: what is unmanifest in the Timeless manifests itself in Time; each thing that exists is real in its own degree of the manifestation and is so seen by the consciousness of the Infinite.

All manifestation depends upon being, but also upon consciousness and its power or degree; for as is the status of consciousness, so will be the status of being. Even the Inconscient is a status and power of involved consciousness in which being is plunged into an other and opposite state of non-manifestation resembling non-existence so that out of it all in the material universe may be manifested; so too the superconscient is consciousness taken up into an absolute of being. For there is a superconscient status in which consciousness seems to be luminously involved in being and as if unaware of itself; all consciousness of being, all knowledge, self-vision, force of being, seem to emerge from that involved state or to appear in it: this emergence, in our view of it, may appear to be an emergence into a lesser reality, but in fact both the superconscience and the consciousness are and regard the same Real. There is also a status of the Supreme in which no distinction can be made between being and consciousness, — for they are too much one there to be thus differentiated, — but this supreme status of being is also a supreme status of the power of being and therefore of the power of consciousness; for the force of being and the force of its consciousness are one there and cannot be separated: it is this unification of eternal Being with the eternal Consciousness-Force that is the status of the supreme Ishwara, and its force of being is the dynamis of the Absolute. This status is not a negation of cosmos; it carries in itself the essence and power of all cosmic existence.

But still unreality is a fact of cosmic existence, and if all is the Brahman, the Reality, we have to account for this element of unreality in the Real. If the unreal is not a fact of being, it must be an act or a formation of consciousness, and is there not then a status or degree of consciousness in which its acts and formations are wholly or partly unreal? If this unreality cannot be attributed to an original cosmic Illusion, to Maya, there is still in the universe itself a power of illusion of Ignorance. It is in the power of the Mind to conceive things that are not real, it is in its power even to create things that are not real or not wholly real; its very view of itself and universe is a construction that is not wholly real or wholly unreal. Where does this element of unreality begin and where does it stop, and what is its cause and what ensues on the removal of both the cause and the consequence? Even if all cosmic existence is not in itself unreal, cannot that description be applied to the world of Ignorance in which we live, this world of constant change and birth and death and frustration and suffering, and does not the removal of the Ignorance abolish for us the reality of the world which it creates, or is not a departure out of it the natural and only issue? This would be valid, if our ignorance were a pure ignorance without any element of truth or knowledge in it. But in fact our consciousness is a mixture of the true and the false; its acts and creations are not a pure invention, a baseless structure. The structure it builds, its form of things or form of the universe, is not a mixture of reality and the unreal so much as a half comprehension, a half expression of the real, and, since all consciousness is force and therefore potentially creative, our ignorance has the result of wrong creation, wrong manifestation, wrong action or misconceived and misdirected energy of the being. All world-existence is manifestation, but our ignorance is the agent of a partial, limited and ignorant manifestation, — in part an expression but in part also a disguise of the original being, consciousness and delight of existence. If this state of things is permanent and unalterable, if our world must always move in this circle, if some Ignorance is the cause of all things and all action here and not a condition and circumstance, then indeed the cessation of individual ignorance could only come by an escape of the individual from world-being, and a cessation of the cosmic ignorance would be the destruction of world-being. But if this world has at its root an evolutionary principle, if our ignorance is a half-knowledge evolving towards knowledge, another account and another issue and spiritual result of our existence in material Nature, a greater manifestation here becomes possible.

A farther distinction has to be made in our conceptions of unreality, so as to avoid a possible confusion in our dealings with this problem of the Ignorance. Our mind, or a part of it, has a pragmatic standard of reality; it insists on a standard of fact, of actuality. All that is fact of existence is to it real, but for it this factuality or reality of the actual is limited to the phenomena of this terrestrial existence in the material universe. But terrestrial or material existence is only a part manifestation, it is a system of actualised possibilities of the Being which does not exclude all other possibilities not yet actualised or not actualised here. In a manifestation in Time new realities can emerge, truths of being not yet realised can put forth their possibilities and become actual in the physical and terrestrial existence; other truths of being there may be that are supraphysical and belong to another domain of manifestation, not realised here but still real. Even what is nowhere actual in any universe, may be a truth of being, a potential of being, and cannot, because it is not yet expressed in form of existence, be taxed as unreal. But our mind or this part of it still insists on its pragmatic habit or conception of the real which admits only the factual and actual as true and is prone to regard all else as unreal. There is then for this mind an unreality which is of a purely pragmatic nature: it consists in the formulation of things which are not necessarily unreal in themselves but are not realised or perhaps cannot be realised by ourselves or in present circumstances or in our actual world of being; this is not a true unreality, it is not an unreal but an unrealised, not an unreal of being but only an unreal of present or known fact. There is, again, an unreality which is conceptual and perceptive and is caused by an erroneous conception and perception of the real: this too is not or need not be an unreality of being, it is only a false construction of consciousness due to limitation by Ignorance. These and other secondary movements of our ignorance are not the heart of the problem, for that turns upon a more general affliction of our consciousness and the world-consciousness here; it is the problem of the cosmic Ignorance. For our whole view and experience of existence labours under a limitation of consciousness which is not ours alone but seems to be at the basis of the material creation. Instead of the original and ultimate Consciousness which sees reality as a whole, we see active here a limited consciousness and either a

partial and unfinished creation or a cosmic kinesis that moves in
a perpetual circle of meaningless change. Our consciousness sees
a part and parts only of the Manifestation, — if manifestation it
be, — and treats it or them as if they were separate entities; all
our illusions and errors arise from a limited separative awareness which creates unrealities or misconceives the Real. But the
problem becomes still more enigmatic when we perceive that our
material world seems to arise directly, not out of any original
Being and Consciousness, but out of a status of Inconscience
and apparent Non-Existence, our ignorance itself is something
that has appeared as if with difficulty and struggle out of the
Inconscience.

   This then is the mystery, — how did an illimitable consciousness and force of integral being enter into this limitation and
separativeness? how could this be possible and, if its possibility
has to be admitted, what is its justification in the Real and its
significance? It is the mystery not of an original Illusion, but of
the origin of the Ignorance and Inconscience and of the relations
of Knowledge and Ignorance to the original Consciousness or
Superconscience.

Chapter VII

The Knowledge and the Ignorance

Let the Knower distinguish the Knowledge and the Ignorance.

Rig Veda.[1]

Two are there, hidden in the secrecy of the Infinite, the Knowledge and the Ignorance; but perishable is the Ignorance, immortal is the Knowledge; another than they is He who rules over both the Knowledge and the Ignorance.

Swetaswatara Upanishad.[2]

Two Unborn, the Knower and one who knows not, the Lord and one who has not mastery: one Unborn and in her are the object of enjoyment and the enjoyer.

Swetaswatara Upanishad.[3]

Two are joined together, powers of Truth, powers of Maya, — they have built the Child and given him birth and they nourish his growth.

Rig Veda.[4]

IN OUR scrutiny of the seven principles of existence it was found that they are one in their essential and fundamental reality: for if even the matter of the most material universe is nothing but a status of being of Spirit made an object of sense, envisaged by the Spirit's own consciousness as the stuff of its forms, much more must the life-force that constitutes itself into form of Matter, and the mind-consciousness that throws itself out as Life, and the Supermind that develops Mind as one of its powers, be nothing but Spirit itself modified in apparent substance and in dynamism of action, not modified in real essence. All are powers of one Power of being and not other

---

[1] IV. 2. 11.   [2] V. 1.   [3] I. 9.   [4] X. 5. 3.

than that All-Existence, All-Consciousness, All-Will, All-Delight
which is the true truth behind every appearance. And they are
not only one in their reality, but also inseparable in the sevenfold
variety of their action. They are the seven colours of the light of
the divine consciousness, the seven rays of the Infinite, and by
them the Spirit has filled in on the canvas of his self-existence
conceptually extended, woven of the objective warp of Space
and the subjective woof of Time, the myriad wonders of his self-
creation great, simple, symmetrical in its primal laws and vast
framings, infinitely curious and intricate in its variety of forms
and actions and the complexities of relation and mutual effect
of all upon each and each upon all. These are the seven Words
of the ancient sages; by them have been created and in the light
of their meaning are worked out and have to be interpreted the
developed and developing harmonies of the world we know and
the worlds behind of which we have only an indirect knowledge.
The Light, the Sound is one; their action is sevenfold.

But here there is a world based upon an original Inconscience; here consciousness has formulated itself in the figure of
an ignorance labouring towards knowledge. We have seen that
there is no essential reason either in the nature of Being itself or
in the original character and fundamental relations of its seven
principles for this intrusion of Ignorance, of discord into the
harmony, of darkness into the light, of division and limitation
into the self-conscious infinity of the divine creation. For we can
conceive, and since we can, the Divine can still more conceive,
— and since there is the conception, there must somewhere be
the execution, the creation actual or intended, — a universal
harmony into which these contrary elements do not enter. The
Vedic seers were conscious of such a divine self-manifestation
and looked on it as the greater world beyond this lesser, a freer
and wider plane of consciousness and being, the truth-creation
of the Creator which they described as the seat or own home of
the Truth, as the vast Truth, or the Truth, the Right, the Vast,[5] or
again as a Truth hidden by a Truth where the Sun of Knowledge

---

[5] *sadanam ṛtasya, sve dame ṛtasya, ṛtasya bṛhate, ṛtam satyam bṛhat.*

finishes his journey and unyokes his horses, where the thousand rays of consciousness stand together so that there is That One, the supreme form of the Divine Being. But this world in which we live seemed to them to be a mingled weft in which truth is disfigured by an abundant falsehood, *anṛtasya bhūreḥ*,[6] here the one light has to be born by its own vast force out of an initial darkness or sea of Inconscience;[7] immortality and godhead have to be built up out of an existence which is under the yoke of death, ignorance, weakness, suffering and limitation. This self-building they figured as the creation by man in himself of that other world or high ordered harmony of infinite being which already exists perfect and eternal in the Divine Infinite. The lower is for us the first condition of the higher; the darkness is the dense body of the light, the Inconscient guards in itself all the concealed Superconscient, the powers of the division and falsehood hold from us but also for us and to be conquered from them the riches and substance of the unity and the truth in their cave of subconscience. This was in their view, expressed in the highly figured enigmatic language of the early mystics, the sense and justification of man's actual existence and his conscious or unconscious Godward effort, his conception so paradoxical at first sight in a world which seems its very opposite, his aspiration so impossible to a superficial view in a creature so ephemeral, weak, ignorant, limited, towards a plenitude of immortality, knowledge, power, bliss, a divine and imperishable existence.

For, as a matter of fact, while the very keyword of the ideal creation is a plenary self-consciousness and self-possession in the infinite Soul and a perfect oneness, the keyword of the creation of which we have present experience is the very opposite; it is an original inconscience developing in life into a limited and divided self-consciousness, an original inert subjection to the drive of a blind self-existent Force developing in life into a struggle of the self-conscious being to possess himself and all things and

---

[6] *Rig Veda*, VII. 60. 5.
[7] *apraketam salilam.*

to establish in the kingdom of this unseeing mechanic Force the reign of an enlightened Will and Knowledge. And because the blind mechanic Force, — we know now really that it is no such thing, — confronts us everywhere, initial, omnipresent, the fundamental law, the great total energy, and because the only enlightened will we know, our own, appears as a subsequent phenomenon, a result, a partial, subordinate, circumscribed, sporadic energy, the struggle seems to us at the best a very precarious and doubtful venture. The Inconscient to our perceptions is the beginning and the end; the self-conscious soul seems hardly more than a temporary accident, a fragile blossom upon this great, dark and monstrous Ashwattha-tree of the universe. Or if we suppose the soul to be eternal, it appears at least as a foreigner, an alien and not over well-treated guest in the reign of this vast Inconscience. If not an accident in the Inconscient Darkness, it is perhaps a mistake, a stumble downwards of the superconscient Light.

If this view of things had a complete validity, then only the absolute idealist, sent perhaps out of some higher existence, unable to forget his mission, stung into indomitable enthusiasm by a divine oestrus or sustained in a calm and infinite fortitude by the light and force and voice of the unseen Godhead, could persist under such circumstances in holding up before himself, much more before an incredulous or doubting world, the hope of a full success for the human endeavour. Actually, for the most part, men either reject it from the beginning or turn away from it eventually, after some early enthusiasm, as a proved impossibility. The consistent materialist seeks a partial and short-lived power, knowledge, happiness, so much only as the dominant inconscient order of Nature will allow to the struggling self-consciousness of man if he accepts his limitations, obeys her laws and makes as good a use of them by his enlightened will as their inexorable mechanism will tolerate. The religionist seeks his reign of enlightened will, love or divine being, his kingdom of God, in that other world where they are unalloyed and eternal. The philosophic mystic rejects all as a mental illusion and aspires to self-extinction in some Nirvana or else an immersion in the featureless Absolute; if the soul or mind of the illusion-driven individual has dreamed of a divine realisation in this ephemeral world of the Ignorance, it must in the end recognise its mistake and renounce its vain endeavour. But still, since there are these two sides of existence, the ignorance of Nature and the light of the Spirit, and since there is behind them the One Reality, the reconciliation or at any rate the bridging of the gulf forecast in the mystic parables of the Veda ought to be possible. It is a keen sense of this possibility which has taken different shapes and persisted through the centuries, — the perfectibility of man, the perfectibility of society, the Alwar's vision of the descent of Vishnu and the Gods upon earth, the reign of the saints, *sādhūnām rājyam*, the city of God, the millennium, the new heaven and earth of the Apocalypse. But these intuitions have lacked a basis of assured knowledge and the mind of man has remained swinging between a bright future hope and a grey present certitude. But the grey certitude is not so certain as it looks and a divine life evolving or preparing in earth-Nature need not be a chimera. All acceptations of our defeat or our limitation start from the implied or explicit recognition, first, of an essential dualism and, then, of an irreconcilable opposition between the dual principles, between the Conscient and the Inconscient, between Heaven and Earth, between God and the World, between the limitless One and the limited Many, between the Knowledge and the Ignorance. We have arrived by the train of our reasoning at the conclusion that this need be no more than an error of the sense-mind and the logical intellect founded upon a partial experience. We have seen that there can be and is a perfectly rational basis for the hope of our victory; for the lower term of being in which we now live contains in itself the principle and intention of that which exceeds it and it is by its own self-exceeding and transformation into that that it can find and develop into a complete form its own real essence.

But there is one point in the reasoning which till now we have left somewhat obscure, and it is precisely in this matter of the co-existence of the Knowledge and the Ignorance. Admittedly, we start here from conditions which are the opposite of

the ideal divine Truth and all the circumstances of that opposition are founded upon the being's ignorance of himself and of
the Self of all, outcome of an original cosmic Ignorance whose
result is self-limitation and the founding of life on division in
being, division in consciousness, division in will and force, division in the light, division and limitation in knowledge, power,
love with, as consequence, the positive opposite phenomena of
egoism, obscuration, incapacity, misuse of knowledge and will,
disharmony, weakness and suffering. We have found that this
Ignorance, although shared by Matter and Life, has its roots in
the nature of Mind whose very office it is to measure off, limit,
particularise and thereby divide. But Mind also is a universal
principle, is One, is Brahman, and therefore it has a tendency to
a unifying and universalising knowledge as well as to that which
marks off and particularises. The particularising faculty of Mind
only becomes Ignorance when it separates itself from the higher
principles of which it is a power and acts not only with its
characteristic tendency, but also with a tendency to exclude the
rest of knowledge, to particularise first and foremost and always
and to leave unity as a vague concept to be approached only
afterwards, when particularisation is complete, and through
the sum of particulars. This exclusiveness is the very soul of
Ignorance.

   We must then seize hold on this strange power of Consciousness which is the root of our ills, examine the principle
of its operation and detect not only its essential nature and
origin, but its power and process of operation and its last end
and means of removal. How is it that the Ignorance exists?
How has any principle or power in the infinite self-awareness
been able to put self-knowledge behind it and exclude all but
its own characteristic limited action? Certain thinkers[8] have

---

[8] Buddha refused to consider the metaphysical problem; the process by which our
unreal individuality is constructed and a world of suffering maintained in existence and
the method of escape from it is all that is of importance. Karma is a fact; the construction
of objects, of an individuality not truly existent is the cause of suffering: to get rid of
Karma, individuality and suffering must be our one objective; by that elimination we
shall pass into whatever may be free from these things, permanent, real: the way of
liberation alone matters.

declared that the problem is insoluble, it is an original mystery and is intrinsically incapable of explanation; only the fact and the process can be stated: or else the question of the nature of the supreme original Existence or Non-existence is put aside as either unanswerable or unnecessary to answer. One can say that Maya with its fundamental principle of ignorance or illusion simply is, and this power of Brahman has the double force of Knowledge and Ignorance inherently potential in it; all we have to do is to recognise the fact and find a means of escape out of the Ignorance, — through the Knowledge, but into what is beyond both Knowledge and Ignorance, — by renunciation of life, by recognition of the universal impermanency of things and the vanity of cosmic existence.

But our mind cannot remain satisfied, — the mind of Buddhism itself did not remain satisfied, — with this evasion at the very root of the whole matter. In the first place, these philosophies, while thus putting aside the root question, do actually make far-reaching assertions that assume, not only a certain operation and symptoms, but a certain fundamental nature of the Ignorance from which their prescription of remedies proceeds; and it is obvious that without such a radical diagnosis no prescription of remedies can be anything but an empiric dealing. But if we are to evade the root-question, we have no means of judging whether the assertions advanced are correct or the remedies prescribed the right ones, or whether there are not others which without being so violent, destructively radical or of the nature of a surgical mutilation or extinction of the patient may yet bring a more integral and natural cure. Secondly, it is always the business of man the thinker to know. He may not be able by mental means to know the essentiality of the Ignorance or of anything in the universe in the sense of defining it, because the mind can only know things in that sense by their signs, characters, forms, properties, functionings, relations to other things, not in their occult self-being and essence. But we can pursue farther and farther, clarify more and more accurately our observation of the phenomenal character and operation of the Ignorance until we get the right revealing word, the right indicating sense of the thing and so come to know it, not by intellect but by vision and experience of the truth, by realising the truth in our own being. The whole process of man's highest intellectual knowledge is through this mental manipulation and discrimination to the point where the veil is broken and he can see; at the end spiritual knowledge comes in to help us to become what we see, to enter into the Light in which there is no Ignorance.

It is true that the first origin of the Ignorance is beyond us as mental beings because our intelligence lives and moves within the Ignorance itself and does not reach up to the point or ascend on to the plane where that separation took place of which the individual mind is the result. But this is true of the first origin and fundamental truth of all things, and on this principle we should have to rest satisfied with a general agnosticism. Man has to work in the Ignorance, to learn under its conditions, to know it up to its farthest point so that he may arrive at its borders where it meets the Truth, touch its final lid of luminous obscuration and develop the faculties which enable him to overstep that powerful but really unsubstantial barrier.

We have then to scrutinise more closely than we have yet done the character and operation of this principle or this power of Ignorance and arrive at a clearer conception of its nature and origin. And first we must fix firmly in our minds what we mean by the word itself. The distinction between the Knowledge and the Ignorance begins with the hymns of the Rig Veda. Here knowledge appears to signify a consciousness of the Truth, the Right, *satyam ṛtam*, and of all that is of the order of the Truth and Right; ignorance is an unconsciousness, *acitti*, of the Truth and Right, an opposition to its workings and a creation of false or adverse workings. Ignorance is the absence of the divine eye of perception which gives us the sight of the supramental Truth; it is the non-perceiving principle in our consciousness as opposed to the truth-perceiving conscious vision and knowledge.[9] In its actual operation this non-perceiving is not an entire inconscience,

---

[9] *acitti* and *citti*.

the inconscient sea from which this world has arisen,[10] but either a limited or a false knowledge, a knowledge based on the division of undivided being, founded upon the fragmentary, the little, opposed to the opulent, vast and luminous completeness of things; it is a cognition which by the opportunity of its limitations is turned into falsehood and supported in that aspect by the Sons of Darkness and Division, enemies of the divine endeavour in man, the assailants, robbers, coverers of his light of knowledge. It was therefore regarded as an undivine Maya,[11] that which creates false mental forms and appearances, — and hence the later significance of this word which seems to have meant originally a formative power of knowledge, the true magic of the supreme Mage, the divine Magician, but was also used for the adverse formative power of a lower knowledge, the deceit, illusion and deluding magic of the Rakshasa. The divine Maya is the knowledge of the Truth of things, its essence, law, operation, which the gods possess and on which they found their own eternal action and creation[12] and their building of their powers in the human being. This idea of the Vedic mystics can in a more metaphysical thought and language be translated into the conception that the Ignorance is in its origin a dividing mental knowledge which does not grasp the unity, essence, self-law of things in their one origin and in their universality, but works rather upon divided particulars, separate phenomena, partial relations, as if they were the truth we had to seize or as if they could really be understood at all without going back behind the division to the unity, behind the dispersion to the universality. The Knowledge is that which tends towards unification and, attaining to the supramental faculty, seizes the oneness, the essence, the self-law of existence and views and deals with the multiplicity of things out of that light and plenitude, in some sort as does the Divine Himself from the highest height whence He embraces the world. It must be noted, however, that the Ignorance in this conception

---

[10] *apraketam salilam.*
[11] *adevī māyā.*
[12] *devānām adabdhā vratāni.*

of it is still a kind of knowledge, but, because it is limited, it is
open at any point to the intrusion of falsehood and error; it turns
into a wrong conception of things which stands in opposition to
the true Knowledge.

In the Vedantic thought of the Upanishad we find the original Vedic terms replaced by the familiar antinomy of Vidya and
Avidya, and with the change of terms there has come a certain
development of significance: for since the nature of the Knowledge is to find the Truth and the fundamental Truth is the One,
— the Veda speaks repeatedly of it as "That Truth" and "That
One", — Vidya, Knowledge in its highest spiritual sense, came to
mean purely and trenchantly the knowledge of the One, Avidya,
Ignorance, purely and trenchantly the knowledge of the divided
Many divorced, as in our world it is divorced, from the unifying
consciousness of the One Reality. The complex associations, the
rich contents, the luminous penumbra of varied and corollary
ideas and significant figures which belonged to the conception
of the Vedic words, were largely lost in a language more precise
and metaphysical, less psychological and flexible. Still the later
exaggerated idea of absolute separation from the true truth of
Self and Spirit, of an original illusion, of a consciousness that
can be equated with dream or with hallucination, did not at
first enter into the Vedantic conception of the Ignorance. If in
the Upanishads it is declared that the man who lives and moves
within the Ignorance, wanders about stumbling like a blind man
led by the blind and returns ever to the net of Death which is
spread wide for him, it is also affirmed elsewhere in the Upanishads that he who follows after the Knowledge only, enters as if
into a blinder darkness than he who follows after the Ignorance
and that the man who knows Brahman as both the Ignorance
and the Knowledge, as both the One and the Many, as both
the Becoming and the Non-Becoming, crosses by the Ignorance,
by the experience of the Multiplicity, beyond death and by the
Knowledge takes possession of Immortality. For the Self-existent
has really become these many existences; the Upanishad can say
to the Divine Being, in all solemnity and with no thought to
mislead, "Thou *art* this old man walking with his staff, yonder

boy and girl, this blue-winged bird, that red of eye", not "Thou seemest to be these things" to the self-deluding mind of the Ignorance. The status of becoming is inferior to the status of Being, but still it is the Being that becomes all that is in the universe.

But the development of the separative distinction could not stop here; it had to go to its logical extreme. Since the knowledge of the One is Knowledge and the knowledge of the Many is Ignorance, there can be, in a rigidly analytic and dialectical view, nothing but pure opposition between the things denoted by the two terms; there is no essential unity between them, no reconciliation possible. Therefore Vidya alone is Knowledge, Avidya is pure Ignorance; and, if pure Ignorance takes a positive form, it is because it is not merely a not-knowing of Truth, but a creation of illusions and delusions, of seemingly real unrealities, of temporarily valid falsehoods. Obviously then, the object matter of Avidya can have no true and abiding existence; the Many are an illusion, the world has no real being. Undoubtedly it has a sort of existence while it lasts, as a dream has or the long-continued hallucination of a delirious or a demented brain, but no more. The One has not become and can never become Many; the Self has not and cannot become all these existences; Brahman has not manifested and cannot manifest a real world in itself: it is only the Mind or some principle of which Mind is a result that thrusts names and forms upon the featureless unity which is alone real and, being essentially featureless, cannot manifest real feature and variation; or else, if it manifests these things, then that is a temporal and temporary reality which vanishes and is convicted of unreality by the illumination of true knowledge.

Our view of the ultimate Reality and of the true nature of Maya has compelled us to depart from these later fine excesses of the dialectical intellect and return to the original Vedantic conception. While giving every tribute to the magnificent fearlessness of these extreme conclusions, to the uncompromising logical force and acuity of these speculations, inexpugnable so long as the premisses are granted, admitting the truth of two of the main contentions, the sole Reality of the Brahman and the fact that our normal conceptions about ourselves and world-existence are stamped with ignorance, are imperfect, are misleading, we are obliged to withdraw from the hold so powerfully laid by this conception of Maya on the intelligence. But the obsession of this long-established view of things cannot be removed altogether so long as we do not fathom the true nature of the Ignorance and the true and total nature of the Knowledge. For if these two are independent, equal and original powers of the Consciousness, then the possibility of a cosmic Illusion pursues us. If Ignorance is the very character of cosmic existence, then our experience of the universe, if not the universe itself, becomes illusory. Or, if Ignorance is not the very grain of our natural being, but still an original and eternal power of Consciousness, then, while there can be a truth of cosmos, it may be impossible for a being in the universe, while he is in it, to know its truth: he can only arrive at real knowledge by passing beyond mind and thought, beyond this world-formation, and viewing all things from above in some supracosmic or super-cosmic consciousness like those who have become of one nature with the Eternal and dwell in Him, unborn in the creation and unafflicted by the cataclysmic destruction of the worlds below them.[13] But the solution of this problem cannot be satisfactorily pursued and reached on the basis of an examination of words and ideas or a dialectical discussion; it must be the result of a total observation and penetration of the relevant facts of consciousness, — both those of the surface and those below or above our surface level or behind our frontal surface, — and a successful fathoming of their significance.

For the dialectical intellect is not a sufficient judge of essential or spiritual truths; moreover, very often, by its propensity to deal with words and abstract ideas as if they were binding realities, it wears them as chains and does not look freely beyond them to the essential and total facts of our existence. Intellectual statement is an account to our intelligence and a justification by reasoning of a seeing of things which pre-exists in our turn of

[13] *Gita.*

mind or temperament or in some tendency of our nature and secretly predetermines the very reasoning that claims to lead to it. That reasoning itself can be conclusive only if the perception of things on which it rests is both a true and a whole seeing. Here what we have to see truly and integrally is the nature and validity of our consciousness, the origin and scope of our mentality; for then alone can we know the truth of our being and nature and of world-being and world-nature. Our principle in such an inquiry must be to see and know; the dialectical intellect is to be used only so far as it helps to clarify our arrangement and justify our expression of the vision and the knowledge, but it cannot be allowed to govern our conceptions and exclude truth that does not fall within the rigid frame of its logic. Illusion, knowledge and ignorance are terms or results of our consciousness, and it is only by looking deeply into our consciousness that we can discover and determine the character and relations of the Knowledge and the Ignorance or of the Illusion, if it exists, and the Reality. Being is no doubt the fundamental object of inquiry, things in themselves and things in their nature; but it is only through consciousness that we can approach Being. Or if it be maintained that we can only reach Being, enter into the Real, because it is superconscient, through extinction or transcendence of consciousness or through its self-transcendence and self-transformation, it is still through consciousness that we must arrive at the knowledge of this necessity and the process or power of execution of this extinction or this self-transcendence, this transformation: then, through consciousness, to know of the Superconscient Truth becomes the supreme need and to discover the power and process of consciousness by which it can pass into superconscience, the supreme discovery.

But in ourselves consciousness seems to be identical with Mind; in any case Mind is so dominant a factor of our being that to examine its fundamental movements is the first necessity. In fact, however, Mind is not the whole of us; there is also in us a life and a body, a subconscience and an inconscience; there is a spiritual entity whose origin and secret truth carry us into an occult inward consciousness and a superconscience. If Mind were all or if the nature of the original Consciousness in things were of the nature of Mind, Illusion or Ignorance might conceivably be regarded as the source of our natural existence: for limitation of knowledge and obscuration of knowledge by Mind-nature create error and illusion, illusions created by Mind-action are among the first facts of our consciousness. It might therefore be conceivably held that Mind is the matrix of an Ignorance which makes us create or represent to ourselves a false world, a world that is nothing more than a subjective construction of the consciousness. Or else Mind might be the matrix in which some original Illusion or Ignorance, Maya or Avidya, cast the seed of a false impermanent universe; Mind would still be the mother, — a "barren mother" since the child would be unreal, — and Maya or Avidya could be looked at as a sort of grandmother of the universe; for Mind itself would be a production or reproduction of Maya. But it is difficult to discern the physiognomy of this obscure and enigmatic ancestress; for we have then to impose a cosmic imagination or an illusion-consciousness on the eternal Reality; Brahman the Reality must itself either be or have or support a constructing Mind or some constructive consciousness greater than Mind but of an analogous nature, must be by its activity or its sanction the creator and even perhaps in some sort by participation a victim, like Mind, of its own illusion and error. It would not be less perplexing if Mind were simply a medium or mirror in which there falls the reflection of an original illusion or a false image or shadow of the Reality. For the origin of this medium of reflection would be inexplicable and the origin also of the false image cast upon it would be inexplicable. An indeterminable Brahman could only be reflected as something indeterminable, not as a manifold universe. Or if it be the inequality of the reflecting medium, its nature as of rippling and restless water that creates broken images of the Reality, still it would be broken and distorted reflections of the Truth that would appear there, not a pullulation of false names and images of things that had no source or basis of existence in the Reality. There must be some manifold truth of the one Reality which is reflected, however falsely or imperfectly, in the manifold images of the mind's universe. It could then very well be that the world might be a reality and only the mind's construction of it or picture of it erroneous or imperfect. But this would imply that there is a Knowledge, other than our mental thought and perception which is only an attempt at knowing, a true cognition which is aware of the Reality and aware also in it of the truth of a real universe.

For if we found that the highest Reality and an ignorant Mind alone exist, we might have no choice but to admit the Ignorance as an original power of the Brahman and to accept as the source of all things Avidya or Maya. Maya would be an eternal power of the self-aware Brahman to delude itself or rather to delude something that seems to be itself, something created by Maya; Mind would be the ignorant consciousness of a soul that exists only as a part of Maya. Maya would be the Brahman's power to foist name and form upon itself, Mind its power to receive them and take them for realities. Or Maya would be Brahman's power to create illusions knowing them to be illusions, Mind its power to receive illusions forgetting that they are illusions. But if Brahman is essentially and always one in self-awareness, this trick would not be possible. If Brahman can divide itself in that fashion, at once knowing and not knowing or one part knowing and the other not knowing, or even if it can put something of itself into Maya, then Brahman must be capable of a double, — or a manifold, — action of consciousness, one a consciousness of Reality, the other a consciousness of illusion, or one an ignorant consciousness and the other a superconscience. This duality or manifoldness seems at first sight logically impossible, yet it must be on this hypothesis the crucial fact of existence, a spiritual mystery, a suprarational paradox. But once we admit the origin of things as a suprarational mystery, we can equally or preferably accept this other crucial fact of the One becoming or being always many and the Many being or becoming the One; this too is at first view dialectically impossible, a suprarational paradox, yet it presents itself to us as an eternal fact and law of existence. But if that is accepted, there is then no longer any need for the intervention of an illusive Maya. Or, equally, we can accept, as we have accepted, the conception of an Infinite and Eternal which is capable, by the infinite power of its consciousness, of manifesting the fathomless and illimitable Truth of its being in many aspects and processes, in innumerable expressive forms and movements; these aspects, processes, forms, movements could be regarded as real expressions, real consequences of its infinite Reality; even the Inconscience and Ignorance could then be accepted among them as reverse aspects, as powers of an involved consciousness and a self-limited knowledge brought forward because necessary to a certain movement in Time, a movement of involution and evolution of the Reality. If suprarational in its basis, this total conception is not altogether a paradox; it only demands a change, an enlargement in our conceptions of the Infinite.

But the real world cannot be known and none of these possibilities can be put to the test if we consider Mind alone or only Mind's power for ignorance. Mind has a power also for truth; it opens its thought-chamber to Vidya as well as to Avidya, and if its starting-point is Ignorance, if its passage is through crooked ways of error, still its goal is always Knowledge: there is in it an impulse of truth-seeking, a power, — even though secondary and limited, — of truth-finding and truth-creation. Even if it is only images or representations or abstract expressions of truth that it can show us, still these are in their own manner truth-reflections or truth-formations, and the realities of which they are forms are present in their more concrete truth in some deeper depth or on some higher level of power of our consciousness. Matter and Life may be the form of realities of which Mind touches only an incomplete figure; Spirit may have secret and supernal realities of which Mind is only a partial and rudimentary receiver, transcriber or transmitter. It would then be only by an examination of other supramental and inframental as well as higher and deeper mental powers of consciousness that we can arrive at the whole reality. And in the end all depends on the truth of the supreme Consciousness — or the Superconscience — that belongs to the highest Reality and the relation to it of Mind, Supermind, Infra-Mind and the Inconscience.

All indeed changes when we penetrate the lower and the higher depths of consciousness and unite them in the one omnipresent Reality. If we take the facts of our and the world's being, we find existence to be one always, — a unity governs even its utmost multiplicity; but the multiplicity is also on the face of things undeniable. We have found unity pursuing us everywhere: even, when we go below the surface, we find that there is no binding dualism; the contradictories and oppositions which the intellect creates exist only as aspects of the original Truth; oneness and multiplicity are poles of the same Reality; the dualities that trouble our consciousness are contrasted truths of one and the same Truth of being. All multiplicity resolves itself into a manifoldness of the one Being, the one Consciousness of Being, the one Delight of Being. Thus in the duality of pleasure and pain, we have seen that pain is a contrary effect of the one delight of existence resulting from the weakness of the recipient, his inability to assimilate the force that meets him, his incapacity to bear the touch of delight that would otherwise be felt in it; it is a perverse reaction of Consciousness to Ananda, not itself a fundamental opposite of Ananda: this is shown by the significant fact that pain can pass into pleasure and pleasure into pain and both resolve into the original Ananda. So too every form of weakness is really a particular working of the one divine Will-Force or the one Cosmic Energy; weakness in that Force means its power to hold back, measure, relate in a particular way its action of Force; incapacity or weakness is the Self's withholding of its force-completeness or an insufficient reaction of Force, not its fundamental opposite. If this is so, then also it may be, and should be in the nature of things, that what we call Ignorance is not really anything else than a power of the one divine Knowledge-Will or Maya; it is the capacity of the One Consciousness similarly to regulate, to hold back, measure, relate in a particular way the action of its Knowledge. Knowledge and Ignorance will then be, not two irreconcilable principles, one creative of world-existence, the other intolerant and destructive of it, but two co-existent powers both present in the universe itself, diversely operating in the conduct of its processes but one in their essence and able to pass by a natural transmutation into each other. But in their fundamental relation Ignorance would not be an equal co-existent, it would be dependent on Knowledge, a limitation or a contrary action of Knowledge.

To know, we have always to dissolve the rigid constructions of the ignorant and self-willed intellect and look freely and flexibly at the facts of existence. Its fundamental fact is consciousness which is power, and we actually see that this power has three ways of operating. First, we find that there is a consciousness behind all, embracing all, within all, which is eternally, universally, absolutely aware of itself whether in unity or multiplicity or in both simultaneously or beyond both in its sheer absolute. This is the plenitude of the supreme divine self-knowledge; it is also the plenitude of the divine all-knowledge. Next, at the other pole of things, we see this consciousness dwelling upon apparent oppositions in itself, and the most extreme antinomy of all reaches its acme in what seems to us to be a complete nescience of itself, an effective, dynamic, creative Inconscience, though we know that this is merely a surface appearance and that the divine Knowledge works with a sovereign security and sureness within the operations of the Inconscient. Between these two oppositions and as a mediary term we see Consciousness working with a partial, limited self-awareness which is equally superficial, for behind it and acting through it is the divine All-Knowledge. Here in its intermediate status, it seems to be a standing compromise between the two opposites, between the supreme Consciousness and the Nescience, but may prove rather in a larger view of our data to be an incomplete emergence of the Knowledge to the surface. This compromise or imperfect emergence we call the Ignorance, from our own point of view, because ignorance is our own characteristic way of the soul's self-withholding of complete self-knowledge. The origin of these three poises of the power of consciousness and their exact relation is what we have, if possible, to discover.

If we discovered that Ignorance and Knowledge were two independent powers of Consciousness, it might then be that we would have to pursue their difference up to the highest point of Consciousness where they would cease only in an Absolute from which both of them had issued together.[14] It might then be concluded that the only real knowledge is the truth of the superconscient Absolute and that truth of consciousness, truth of cosmos, truth of ourselves in cosmos is at best a partial figure burdened always with a concomitant presence, an encircling penumbra, a pursuing shadow of Ignorance. It might even be that an absolute Knowledge establishing truth, harmony, order and an absolute Inconscience basing a play of fantasy, disharmony and disorder, supporting inexorably its extreme of falsehood, wrong and suffering, a Manichean double principle of conflicting and intermingling light and darkness, good and evil, stand at the root of cosmic existence. The idea of certain thinkers that there is an absolute good but also an absolute evil, both of them an approach to the Absolute, might assume consistence. But if we find that Knowledge and Ignorance are light and shadow of the same consciousness, that the beginning of Ignorance is a limitation of Knowledge, that it is the limitation that opens the door to a subordinate possibility of partial illusion and error, that this possibility takes full body after a purposeful plunge of Knowledge into a material Inconscience but that Knowledge too emerges along with an emerging Consciousness out of the Inconscience, then we can be sure that this fullness of Ignorance is by its own evolution changing back into a limited Knowledge and can feel the assurance that the limitation itself will be removed and the full truth of things become apparent, the cosmic Truth free itself from the cosmic Ignorance. In fact, what is happening is that the Ignorance is seeking and preparing to transform itself by a progressive illumination of its darknesses into the Knowledge that is already concealed within it; the cosmic truth manifested in its real essence and figure would

---

[14] In the Upanishads Vidya and Avidya are spoken of as eternal in the supreme Brahman; but this can be accepted in the sense of the consciousness of the multiplicity and the consciousness of the Oneness which by co-existence in the supreme self-awareness became the basis of the Manifestation; they would there be two sides of an eternal self-knowledge.

by that transformation reveal itself as essence and figure of the supreme omnipresent Reality. It is from this interpretation of existence that we have started, but to verify it we must observe the structure of our surface consciousness and its relation to what is within it and above and below it; for so best we can distinguish the nature and scope of the Ignorance. In that process there will appear the nature and scope also of that of which the Ignorance is a limitation and deformation, the Knowledge, — in its totality the spiritual being's abiding self-knowledge and world-knowledge.

Chapter VIII

Memory, Self-Consciousness and the Ignorance

Some speak of the self-nature of things, others say that it is
Time.   *Swetaswatara Upanishad.*[1]

Two are the forms of Brahman, Time and the Timeless.
                                         Maitrayani Upanishad.[2]

Night was born and from Night the flowing ocean of being
and on the ocean Time was born to whom is subjected every
seeing creature.   *Rig Veda.*[3]

Memory is greater: without memory men could think and
know nothing.... As far as goes the movement of Memory,
there he ranges at will.   *Chhandogya Upanishad.*[4]

This is he who is that which sees, touches, hears, smells, tastes,
thinks, understands, acts in us, a conscious being, a self of
knowledge.   *Prasna Upanishad.*[5]

IN ANY survey of the dual character of our consciousness we
have first to look at the Ignorance, — for Ignorance trying to
turn into Knowledge is our normal status. To begin with, it
is necessary to consider some of the essential movements of this
partial awareness of self and things which works in us as a mediator between the complete self-knowledge and all-knowledge
and the complete Inconscience, and, from that starting-point,
find its relation to the greater Consciousness below our surface.
There is a line of thought in which great stress is laid upon the
action of memory: it has even been said that Memory is the

---

[1] VI. 1.   [2] VI. 15.   [3] X. 190. 1, 2.   [4] VII. 13. 1, 2.   [5] IV. 9.

man, — it is memory that constitutes our personality and holds cemented the foundation of our psychological being; for it links together our experiences and relates them to one and the same individual entity. This is an idea which takes its stand on our existence in the succession of Time and accepts process as the key to essential Truth, even when it does not regard the whole of existence as process or as cause and effect in the development of some kind of self-regulating Energy, as Karma. But process is merely a utility; it is a habitual adoption of certain effective relations which might in the infinite possibility of things have been arranged otherwise, for the production of effects which might equally have been quite different. The real truth of things lies not in their process, but behind it, in whatever determines, effects or governs the process; not in effectuation so much as in the Will or Power that effects, and not so much in Will or Power as in the Consciousness of which Will is the dynamic form and in the Being of which Power is the dynamic value. But memory is only a process of consciousness, a utility; it cannot be the substance of being or the whole of our personality: it is simply one of the workings of consciousness as radiation is one of the workings of Light. It is Self that is the man: or, if we regard only our normal surface existence, Mind is the man, — for man is the mental being. Memory is only one of the many powers and processes of the Mind, which is at present the chief action of Consciousness-Force in our dealings with self, world and Nature.

Nevertheless, it is as well to begin with this phenomenon of memory when we consider the nature of the Ignorance in which we dwell; for it may give the key to certain important aspects of our conscious existence. We see that there are two applications which the mind makes of its faculty or process of memory, memory of self, memory of experience. First, radically, it applies memory to the fact of our conscious-being and relates that to Time. It says, "I am now, I was in the past, I shall therefore be in the future, it is the same I in all the three ever unstable divisions of Time." Thus it tries to render to itself in the terms of Time an account of that which it feels to be the fact, but cannot know or prove to be true, the eternity of the conscious being. By memory Mind can only know of itself in the past, by direct self-awareness only in the moment of the present, and it is only by extension of and inference from this self-awareness and from the memory which tells us that for some time awareness has been continuously existent that mind can conceive of itself in the future. The extent of the past and the future it cannot fix; it can only carry back the past to the limit of its memory and infer from the evidence of others and the facts of life it observes around it that the conscious being already was in times which it can no longer remember. It knows that it existed in an infant unreasoning state of the mind to which memory has lost its link; whether it existed before physical birth, the mortal mind owing to the gap of memory cannot determine. Of the future it knows nothing at all; of its existing in the next moment it can only have a moral certainty which some happening of that moment can prove to be an error because what it saw was no more than a dominant probability; much less can it know whether or no physical dissolution is the end of the conscious being. Yet it has this sense of a persistent continuity which easily extends itself into a conviction of eternity.

This conviction may be either the reflection in the mind of an endless past which it has forgotten but of which something in it retains the formless impression, or it may be the shadow of a self-knowledge which comes to the mind from a higher or a deeper plane of our being where we are really aware of our eternal self-existence. Or, conceivably, it might be a hallucination; just as we cannot sense or realise in our foreseeing consciousness the fact of death and can only live in the feeling of continued existence, cessation being to us an intellectual conception we can hold with certainty, even imagine with vividness, but never actually realise because we live only in the present, yet death, cessation or interruption at least of our actual mode of being is a fact and the sense or prevision of continued existence in the future in the physical body becomes beyond a point we cannot now fix a hallucination, a false extension or a misapplication of our present mental impression of conscious being, — so conceivably it might be with this mental idea or impression of conscious eternity. Or it might be a false transference to ourselves of the perception of a real eternity conscient or inconscient other than ourselves, the eternity of the universe or of something which exceeds the universe. The mind seizing this fact of eternity may falsely transfer it to our own conscious being which may be nothing more than a transient phenomenon of that only true eternal.

These questions our surface mind by itself has no means of solving; it can only speculate upon them endlessly and arrive at more or less well-reasoned opinions. The belief in our immortality is only a faith, the belief in our mortality is only a faith. It is impossible for the materialist to prove that our consciousness ends with the death of the body; for he may indeed show that there is as yet no convincing proof that anything in us consciously survives, but equally there is and there can be in the nature of things no proof that our conscious self does not outlast the physical dissolution. Survival of the body by the human personality may hereafter be proved even to the satisfaction of the sceptic; but even then what will be established will only be a greater continuity and not the eternity of the conscious being.

In fact, if we look at the mind's concept of this eternity, we see that it comes only to a continuous succession of moments of being in an eternal Time. Therefore it is Time that is eternal and not the continuously momentary conscious being. But, on the other hand, there is nothing in mind-evidence to show that eternal Time really exists or that Time itself is anything more than the conscious being's way of looking at some uninterrupted continuity or, it may be, eternity of existence as an indivisible flow which it conceptually measures by the successions and simultaneities of the experiences through which alone that existence is represented to it. If there is an eternal Existence which is a conscious being, it must be beyond Time which it contains, timeless as we say; it must be the Eternal of the Vedanta who, we may then conjecture, uses Time only as a conceptual perspective for His view of His self-manifestation. But the timeless self-knowledge of this Eternal is beyond mind; it is a supramental knowledge superconscient to us and only to be acquired by the stilling or transcending of the temporal activity of our conscious mind, by an entry into Silence or a passage through Silence into the consciousness of eternity.

From all this the one great fact emerges that the very nature of our mind is Ignorance; not an absolute nescience, but a limited and conditioned knowledge of being, limited by a realisation of its present, a memory of its past, an inference of its future, conditioned therefore by a temporal and successive view of itself and its experiences. If real existence is a temporal eternity, then the mind has not the knowledge of real being: for even its own past it loses in the vague of oblivion except for the little that memory holds; it has no possession of its future which is withheld from it in a great blank of ignorance; it has only a knowledge of its present changing from moment to moment in a helpless succession of names, forms, happenings, the march or flux of a cosmic kinesis which is too vast for its control or its comprehension. On the other hand, if real existence is a time-transcending eternity, the mind is still more ignorant of it; for it only knows the little of it that it can itself seize from moment to moment by fragmentary experience of its surface self-manifestation in Time and Space.

If, then, mind is all or if the apparent mind in us is the index of the nature of our being, we can never be anything more than an Ignorance fleeting through Time and catching at knowledge in a most scanty and fragmentary fashion. But if there is a power of self-knowledge beyond mind which is timeless in essence and can look on Time, perhaps with a simultaneous all-relating view of past, present and future, but in any case as a circumstance of its own timeless being, then we have two powers of consciousness, Knowledge and Ignorance, the Vedantic Vidya and Avidya. These two must be, then, either different and unconnected powers, separately born as well as diverse in their action, separately self-existent in an eternal dualism, or else, if there is a connection between them, it must be this that consciousness as Knowledge knows its timeless self and sees Time within itself, while consciousness as Ignorance is a partial and superficial action of the same Knowledge which sees rather itself in Time, veiling itself in its own conception of temporal being, and can only by the removal of the veil return to eternal self-knowledge.

For it would be irrational to suppose that the superconscient Knowledge is so aloof and separate as to be incapable of knowing Time and Space and Causality and their works; for then it would be only another kind of Ignorance, the blindness of the absolute being answering to the blindness of the temporal being as positive pole and negative pole of a conscious existence which is incapable of knowing all itself, but either knows only itself and does not know its works or knows only its works and does not know itself, — an absurdly symmetrical equipollence in mutual rejection. From the larger point of view, the ancient Vedantic, we must conceive of ourselves not as a dual being, but as one conscious existence with a double phase of consciousness: one of them is conscient or partly conscient in our mind, the other superconscient to mind; one, a knowledge situated in Time, works under its conditions and for that purpose puts its self-knowledge behind it, the other, timeless, works out with mastery and knowledge its own self-determined conditions of Time; one knows itself only by its growth in Time-experience, the other knows its timeless self and consciously manifests itself in Time-experience.

We realise now what the Upanishad meant when it spoke of Brahman as being both the Knowledge and the Ignorance and of the simultaneous knowledge of Brahman in both as the way to immortality. Knowledge is the inherent power of consciousness of the timeless, spaceless, unconditioned Self which shows itself in its essence as a unity of being; it is this consciousness that alone is real and complete knowledge because it is an eternal transcendence which is not only self-aware but holds in itself, manifests, originates, determines, knows the temporally eternal successions of the universe. Ignorance is the consciousness of being in the successions of Time, divided in its knowledge by dwelling in the moment, divided in its conception of self-being by dwelling in the divisions of Space and the relations of circumstance, self-prisoned in the multiple working of the unity. It is called the Ignorance because it has put behind it the knowledge of unity and by that very fact is unable to know truly or completely either itself or the world, either the transcendent or the universal reality. Living within the Ignorance, from moment to moment, from field to field, from relation to relation, the conscious soul stumbles on in the error of a fragmentary knowledge.[6] It is not a nescience, but a view and experience of the reality which is partly true and partly false, as all knowledge must be which ignores the essence and sees only fugitive parts of the phenomenon. On the other hand, to be shut up in a featureless consciousness of unity, ignorant of the manifest Brahman, is described as itself also a blind darkness. In truth, neither is precisely darkness, but one is the dazzling by a concentrated Light, the other the illusive proportions of things seen in a dispersed, hazy and broken light, half mist, half seeing. The divine consciousness is not shut up in either, but holds the immutable One and the mutable Many in one eternal all-relating, all-uniting self-knowledge.

Memory, in the dividing consciousness, is a crutch upon which mind supports itself as it stumbles on driven helplessly, without possibility of stay or pause, in the rushing speed of Time. Memory is a poverty-stricken substitute for an integral direct abiding consciousness of self and a direct integral or global perception of things. Mind can only have the direct consciousness of self in the moment of its present being; it can only have some half-direct perception of things as they are offered to it in the present moment of time and the immediate field of space and seized by the senses. It makes up for its deficiency by memory, imagination, thought, idea-symbols of various kinds. Its senses are devices by which it lays hold on the appearances of things in the present moment and in the immediate space; memory, imagination, thought are devices by which it represents to itself,

---

[6] *avidyāyām antare vartamānāḥ.... janghanyamānāḥ pariyanti mūḍhāḥ andhenaiva nīyamānāḥ yathāndhāḥ.* "Living and moving within the Ignorance,... they go round and round stumbling and battered, men deluded, like the blind led by one who is blind."
— *Mundaka Upanishad*, I. 2. 8.

still less directly, the appearances of things beyond the present moment and the immediate space. The one thing which is not a device is its direct self-consciousness in the present moment. Therefore through that it can most easily lay hold on the fact of eternal being, on the reality; all the rest it is tempted, when it considers things narrowly, to look on not merely as phenomenon, but as, possibly, error, ignorance, illusion, because they no longer appear to it directly real. So the Illusionist considers them; the only thing he holds to be truly real is that eternal self which lies behind the mind's direct present self-consciousness. Or else, like the Buddhist, one comes to regard even that eternal self as an illusion, a representation, a subjective image, a mere imagination or false sensation and false idea of being. Mind becomes to its own view a fantastic magician, its works and itself at once strangely existent and non-existent, a persistent reality and yet a fleeting error which it accounts for or does not account for, but in any case is determined to slay and get done with both itself and its works so that it may rest, may cease in the timeless repose of the Eternal from the vain representation of appearances.

But, in truth, our sharp distinctions made between the without and the within, the present and the past self-consciousness are tricks of the limited unstable action of mind. Behind the mind and using it as its own surface activity there is a stable consciousness in which there is no binding conceptual division between itself in the present and itself in the past and future; and yet it knows itself in Time, in the present, past and future, but at once, with an undivided view which embraces all the mobile experiences of the Time-self and holds them on the foundation of the immobile timeless self. This consciousness we can become aware of when we draw back from the mind and its activities or when these fall silent. But we see first its immobile status, and if we regard only the immobility of the self, we may say of it that it is not only timeless, but actionless, without movement of idea, thought, imagination, memory, will, self-sufficient, self-absorbed and therefore void of all action of the universe. That then becomes alone real to us and the rest a vain symbolising in non-existent forms, — or forms corresponding to nothing truly existent, — and therefore a dream. But this self-absorption is only an act and resultant state of our consciousness, just as much as was the self-dispersion in thought and memory and will. The real self is the eternal who is obviously capable of both the mobility in Time and the immobility basing Time, — simultaneously, otherwise they could not both exist; nor, even, could one exist and the other create seemings. This is the supreme Soul, Self and Being[7] of the Gita who upholds both the immobile and the mobile being as the self and lord of all existence.

So far we arrive by considering mind and memory mainly in regard to the primary phenomenon of mental self-consciousness in Time. But if we consider them with regard to self-experience as well as consciousness and other-experience as well as self-experience, we shall find that we arrive at the same result with richer contents and a still clearer light on the nature of the Ignorance. At present, let us thus express what we have seen, — an eternal conscious being who supports the mobile action of mind on a stable immobile self-consciousness free from the action of Time and who, while with a knowledge superior to mind he embraces all the movement of Time, dwells by the action of mind in that movement. As the surface mental entity moving from moment to moment, not observing his essential self but only his relation to his experiences of the Time-movement, in that movement keeping the future from himself in what appears to be a blank of Ignorance and non-existence but is an unrealised fullness, grasping knowledge and experience of being in the present, putting it away in the past which again appears to be a blank of Ignorance and non-existence partly lighted, partly saved and stored up by memory, he puts on the aspect of a thing fleeting and uncertain seizing without stability upon things fleeting and uncertain. But in reality, we shall find, he is always the same Eternal who is for ever stable and self-possessed in His supramental knowledge and what he seizes on is also for ever stable and eternal; for it is himself that he is mentally experiencing in the succession of Time.

---

[7] *para puruṣa, paramātman, parabrahman.*

Time is the great bank of conscious existence turned into values of experience and action: the surface mental being draws upon the past (and the future also) and coins it continually into the present; he accounts for and stores up the gains he has gathered in what we call the past, not knowing how ever-present is the past in us; he uses as much of it as he needs as coin of knowledge and realised being and pays it out as coin of mental, vital and physical action in the commerce of the present which creates to his view the new wealth of the future. Ignorance is a utilisation of the Being's self-knowledge in such a way as to make it valuable for Time-experience and valid for Time-activity; what we do not know is what we have not yet taken up, coined and used in our mental experience or have ceased to coin or use. Behind, all is known and all is ready for use according to the will of the Self in its dealings with Time and Space and Causality. One might almost say that our surface being is only the deeper eternal Self in us throwing itself out as the adventurer in Time, a gambler and speculator in infinite possibilities, limiting itself to the succession of moments so that it may have all the surprise and delight of the adventure, keeping back its self-knowledge and complete self-being so that it may win again what it seems to have lost, reconquering all itself through the chequered joy and pain of an aeonic passion and seeking and endeavour.

Chapter IX

Memory, Ego and Self-Experience

Here this God, the Mind, in its dream experiences again and
again what once was experienced, what has been seen and
what has not been seen, what has been heard and what has
not been heard; what has been experienced and what has not
been experienced, what is and what is not, all it sees, it is all
and sees.   *Prasna Upanishad.*[1]

To dwell in our true being is liberation; the sense of ego is a
fall from the truth of our being.   *Mahopanishad.*[2]

One in many births, a single ocean holder of all streams of
movement, sees our hearts.   *Rig Veda.*[3]

THE DIRECT self-consciousness of the mental being, that
by which it becomes aware of its own nameless and
formless existence behind the flow of a differentiated
self-experience, of its eternal soul-substance behind the mental
formations of that substance, of its self behind the ego, goes
behind mentality to the timelessness of an eternal present; it is
that in it which is ever the same and unaffected by the mental
distinction of past, present and future. It is also unaffected by
the distinctions of space or of circumstance; for if the mental
being ordinarily says of itself, "I am in the body, I am here, I am
there, I shall be elsewhere", yet when it learns to fix itself in this
direct self-consciousness, it very soon perceives that this is the
language of its changing self-experience which only expresses
the relations of its surface consciousness to the environment
and to externalities. Distinguishing these, detaching itself from

[1] IV. 5.   [2] V. 2.   [3] X. 5. 1.

these, it perceives that the self of which it is directly conscious does not in any way change by these outward changes, but is always the same, unaffected by the mutations of the body or of the mentality or of the field in which these move and act. It is in its essence featureless, relationless, without any other character than that of pure conscious existence self-sufficient and eternally satisfied with pure being, self-blissful. Thus we become aware of the stable Self, the eternal "Am", or rather the immutable "Is" without any category of personality or Time.

But this consciousness of Self, as it is timeless, so is capable also of freely regarding Time as a thing reflected in it and as either the cause or the subjective field of a changing experience. It is then the eternal "I am", the unchanging consciousness on whose surface changes of conscious experience occur in the process of Time. The surface consciousness is constantly adding to its experience or rejecting from its experience, and by every addition it is modified and by every rejection also it is modified; although that deeper self which supports and contains this mutation remains unmodified, the outer or superficial self is constantly developing its experience so that it can never say of itself absolutely, "I am the same that I was a moment ago." Those who live in this surface Time-self and have not the habit of drawing back inward towards the immutable or the capacity of dwelling in it, are even incapable of thinking of themselves apart from this ever self-modifying mental experience. That is for them their self and it is easy for them, if they look with detachment at its happenings, to agree with the conclusion of the Buddhist Nihilists that this self is in fact nothing but a stream of idea and experience and mental action, the persistent flame which is yet never the same flame, and to conclude that there is no such thing as a real self, but only a flow of experience and behind it Nihil: there is experience of knowledge without a Knower, experience of being without an Existent; there are simply a number of elements, parts of a flux without a real whole, which combine to create the illusion of a Knower and Knowledge and the Known, the illusion of an Existent and existence and the experience of existence. Or they can conclude that Time is the only real existence and they themselves are its creatures. This conclusion of an illusory existent in a real or unreal world is as inevitable to this kind of withdrawal as is the opposite conclusion of a real Existence but an illusory world to the thinker who, dwelling on the immobile self, observes everything else as a mutable not-self; he comes eventually to regard the latter as the result of a deluding trick of consciousness.

But let us look a little at this surface consciousness without theorising, studying it only in its facts. We see it first as a purely subjective phenomenon. There is a constant rapid shifting of Time-point which it is impossible to arrest for a moment. There is a constant changing, even when there is no shifting of Space-circumstance, a change both in the body or form of itself which the consciousness directly inhabits and the environing body or form of things in which it less directly lives. It is equally affected by both, though more vividly, because directly, by the smaller than by the larger habitation, by its own body than by the body of the world, because only of the changes in its own body is it directly conscious and of the body of the world only indirectly through the senses and the effects of the macrocosm on the microcosm. This change of the body and the surroundings is not so insistently obvious or not so obviously rapid as the swift mutation of Time; yet it is equally real from moment to moment and equally impossible to arrest. But we see that the mental being only regards all this mutation so far as it produces effects upon its own mental consciousness, generates impressions and changes in its mental experience and mental body, because only through the mind can it be aware of its changing physical habitation and its changing world-experience. Therefore there is, as well as a shifting or change of Time-point and Space-field, a constant modifying change of the sum of circumstances experienced in Time and Space and as the result a constant modification of the mental personality which is the form of our superficial or apparent self. All this change of circumstance is summed up in philosophical language as causality; for in this stream of the cosmic movement the antecedent state seems to be the cause of a subsequent state, or else this subsequent state seems to be the result of a previous action of persons, objects or forces: yet in fact what we call cause may very well be only circumstance. Thus the mind has over and above its direct self-consciousness a more or less indirect mutable self-experience which it divides into two parts, its subjective experience of the ever-modified mental states of its personality and its objective experience of the ever-changing environment which seems partly or wholly to cause and is yet at the same time itself affected by the workings of that personality. But all this experience is at bottom subjective; for even the objective and external is only known to mind in the form of subjective impressions.

Here the part played by Memory increases greatly in importance; for while all that it can do for the mind with regard to its direct self-consciousness is to remind it that it existed and was the same in the past as in the present, it becomes in our differentiated or surface self-experience an important power linking together past and present experiences, past and present personality, preventing chaos and dissociation and assuring the continuity of the stream in the surface mind. Still even here we must not exaggerate the function of memory or ascribe to it that part of the operations of consciousness which really belongs to the activity of other power-aspects of the mental being. It is not the memory alone which constitutes the ego-sense; memory is only a mediator between the sense-mind and the co-ordinating intelligence: it offers to the intelligence the past data of experience which the mind holds somewhere within but cannot carry with it in its running from moment to moment on the surface.

A little analysis will make this apparent. We have in all functionings of the mentality four elements, the object of mental consciousness, the act of mental consciousness, the occasion and the subject. In the self-experience of the self-observing inner being, the object is always some state or movement or wave of the conscious being, anger, grief or other emotion, hunger or other vital craving, impulse or inner life-reaction or some form of sensation, perception or thought activity. The act is some kind of mental observation and conceptual valuation of this movement or wave or else a mental sensation of it in which observation and valuation may be involved and even lost, — so that in this act the mental person may either separate the act and the object by a distinguishing perception or confuse them together indistinguishably. That is to say, he may either simply become a movement, let us put it, of angry consciousness, not at all standing back from that activity, not reflecting or observing himself, not controlling the feeling or the accompanying action, or he may observe what he becomes and reflect on it, with this seeing or perception in his mind "I am angry". In the former case the subject or mental person, the act of conscious self-experience and the substantial angry becoming of the mind which is the object of the self-experience, are all rolled up into one wave of conscious-force in movement; but in the latter there is a certain rapid analysis of its constituents and the act of self-experience partly detaches itself from the object. Thus by this act of partial detachment we are able not only to experience ourselves dynamically in the becoming, in the process of movement of conscious-force itself, but to stand back, perceive and observe ourselves and, if the detachment is sufficient, to control our feeling and action, control to some extent our becoming.

However, there is usually a defect even in this act of self-observation; for there is indeed a partial detachment of the act from the object, but not of the mental person from the mental act: the mental person and the mental action are involved or rolled up in each other; nor is the mental person sufficiently detached or separated either from the emotional becoming. I am aware of myself in an angry becoming of my conscious stuff of being and in a thought-perception of this becoming: but all thought-perception also is a becoming and not myself, and this I do not yet sufficiently realise; I am identified with my mental activities or involved in them, not free and separate. I do not yet directly become aware of myself apart from my becomings and my perception of them, apart from the forms of active consciousness which I assume in the waves of the sea of conscious force which is the stuff of my mental and life nature. It is when I entirely detach the mental person from his act of self-experience that I become fully aware first, of the sheer ego and, in the end, of the witness self or the thinking mental Person, the something or someone who becomes angry and observes it but is not limited or determined in his being by the anger or the perception. He is, on the contrary, a constant factor aware of an unlimited succession of conscious movements and conscious experiences of movements and aware of his own being in that succession; but he can be aware of it also behind that succession, supporting it, containing it, always the same in fact of being and force of being beyond the changing forms or arrangements of his conscious force. He is thus the Self that is immutably and at the same time the Self that becomes eternally in the succession of Time.

It is evident that there are not really two selves, but one conscious being which throws itself up in the waves of conscious force so as to experience itself in a succession of changing movements of itself, by which it is not really changed, increased or diminished, — any more than the original stuff of Matter or Energy in the material world is increased or diminished by the constantly changing combinations of the elements, — although it seems to be changed to the experiencing consciousness so long as it lives only in the knowledge of the phenomenon and does not get back to the knowledge of the original being, substance or Force. When it does get back to that deeper knowledge, it does not condemn the observed phenomenon as unreal, but it perceives an immutable being, energy or real substance not phenomenal, not subject in itself to the senses; it sees at the same time a becoming or real phenomenon of that being, energy or substance. This becoming we call phenomenon because, actually, as things are with us now, it manifests itself to the consciousness under the conditions of sense-perception and sense-relation and not directly to the consciousness itself in its pure and unconditioned embracing and totally comprehending knowledge. So with the Self, — it is, immutably, to our direct self-consciousness; it manifests itself mutably in various becomings to the mind-sense and the mental experience — therefore, as things are with us now, not directly to the pure unconditioned knowledge of the consciousness, but to it under the conditions of our mentality.

It is this succession of experiences and it is this fact of an indirect or secondary action of the experiencing consciousness under the conditions of our mentality that bring in the device of Memory. For a primary condition of our mentality is division by the moments of Time; there is an inability to get its experience or to hold its experiences together except under the conditions of this self-division by the moments of Time. In the immediate mental experience of a wave of becoming, a conscious movement of being, there is no action or need of memory; I become angry, — it is an act of sensation, not of memory; I observe that I am angry, — it is an act of perception, not of memory. Memory only comes in when I begin to relate my experience to the successions of Time, when I divide my becoming into past, present and future, when I say, "I was angry a moment ago", or "I have become angry and am still in anger", or "I was angry once and will be again if there is the same occasion". Memory may indeed come immediately and directly into the becoming, if the occasion of the movement of consciousness is itself wholly or partly a thing of the past, — for example, if there is a recurrence of emotion, such as grief or anger, caused by memory of past wrong or suffering and not by any immediate occasion in the present or else caused by an immediate occasion reviving the memory of a past occasion. Because we cannot keep the past in us on the surface of the consciousness, — though it is always there behind, within, subliminally present and often even active, — therefore we have to recover it as something that is lost or is no longer existent, and this we do by that repetitive and linking action of the thought-mind which we call memory, — just as we summon things which are not within the actual field of our limited superficial mind-experience by the action of the thought-mind which we call imagination, that greater power in us and high summoner of all possibilities realisable or unrealisable into the field of our ignorance.

Memory is not the essence of persistent or continuous experience even in the succession of Time and would not be necessary at all if our consciousness were of an undivided movement, if it had not to run from moment to moment with a loss of direct grasp on the last and an entire ignorance or non-possession of the next. All experience or substance of becoming in Time is a flowing stream or sea not divided in itself, but only divided in the observing consciousness by the limited movement of the Ignorance which has to leap from moment to moment like a dragon-fly darting about on the surface of the stream: so too all substance of being in Space is a flowing sea not divided in itself, but only divided in the observing consciousness because our sense-faculty is limited in its grasp, can see only a part and is therefore bound to observe forms of substance as if they were separate things in themselves, independent of the one substance. There is indeed an arrangement of things in Space and Time, but no gap or division except to our ignorance, and it is to bridge the gaps and connect the divisions created by the ignorance of Mind that we call in the aid of various devices of the mind-consciousness, of which memory is only one device.

There is then in me this flowing stream of the world-sea, and anger or grief or any other inner movement can occur as a long-continued wave of the continuous stream. This continuity is not constituted by force of memory, although memory may help to prolong or repeat the wave when by itself it would have died away into the stream; the wave simply occurs and continues as a movement of conscious-force of my being carried forward by its own original impulsion of disturbance. Memory comes in to prolong the disturbance by a recurrence of the thinking mind to the occasion of anger or of the feeling mind to the first impulse of anger by which it justifies itself in a repetition of the disturbance; otherwise the perturbation would spend itself and only recur when the occasion itself was actually repeated. The natural recurrence of the wave, the same or a similar occasion causing the same disturbance, is not any more than its isolated occurrence a result of memory, although memory may help to fortify it and make the mind more subject to it. There is rather the same relation of repeated occasion and repeated result and movement in the more fluid energy and variable substance of mind as that we see presented mechanically by the repetition of the same cause and effect in the less variable operations of the energy and substance of the material world. We may say, if we like, that there is a subconscious memory in all energy of Nature which repeats invariably the same relation of energy and result; but then we enlarge illimitably the connotation of the word. In reality, we can only state a law of repetition in the action of the waves of conscious-force by which it regularises these movements of its own substance. Memory, properly speaking, is merely the device by which the witnessing Mind helps itself to link together these movements and their occurrence and recurrences in the successions of Time for Time-experience, for increasing use by a more and more co-ordinating will and for a constantly developing valuation by a more and more co-ordinating reason. It is a great, an indispensable but not the only factor in the process by which the Inconscience from which we start develops full self-consciousness, and by which the Ignorance of the mental being develops conscious knowledge of itself in its becomings. This development continues until the co-ordinating mind of knowledge and mind of will are fully able to possess and use all the material of self-experience. Such at least is the process of evolution as we see it governing the development of Mind out of the self-absorbed and apparently mindless energy in the material world.

The ego-sense is another device of mental Ignorance by which the mental being becomes aware of himself, — not only of the objects, occasions and acts of his activity, but of that which experiences them. At first it might seem as if the ego-sense were actually constituted by memory, as if it were memory that told us, "It is the same I who was angry some time ago and am again or still angry now." But, in reality, all that the memory can tell us by its own power is that it is the same limited field of conscious activity in which the same phenomenon has occurred. What happens is that there is a repetition of the mental phenomenon, of that wave of becoming in the mind-substance of which the mind-sense is immediately aware; memory comes in to link these repetitions together and enables the mind-sense to realise that it is the same mind-substance which is taking the same dynamic form and the same mind-sense which is experiencing it. The ego-sense is not a result of memory or built by memory, but already and always there as a point of reference or as something in which the mind-sense concentrates itself so as to have a co-ordinant centre instead of sprawling incoherently all over the field of experience; ego-memory reinforces this concentration and helps to maintain it, but does not constitute it. Possibly, in the lower animal the sense of ego, the sense of individuality would not, if analysed, go much farther than a sensational imprecise or less precise realisation of continuity and identity and separateness from others in the moments of Time. But in man there is in addition a co-ordinating mind of knowledge which, basing itself on the united action of the mind-sense and the memory, arrives at the distinct idea, — while it retains also the first constant intuitive perception, — of an ego which senses, feels, remembers, thinks, and which is the same whether it remembers or does not remember. This conscious mind-substance, it says, is always that of one and the same conscious person who feels, ceases to feel, remembers, forgets, is superficially conscious, sinks back from superficial consciousness into sleep; he is the same before the organisation of memory and after it, in the infant and in the dotard, in sleep and in waking, in apparent consciousness and apparent unconsciousness; he and no other did the acts which he forgets as well as the acts which he remembers; he is persistently the same behind all changes of his becoming or his personality. This action of knowledge in man, this co-ordinating intelligence, this formulation of self-consciousness and self-experience is higher than the memory-ego and sense-ego of the animal and therefore, we may suppose, nearer to real self-knowledge. We may even come to realise, if we study the veiled as well as the uncovered action of Nature, that all ego-sense, all ego-memory has at its back, is in fact a pragmatic contrivance of a secret co-ordinating power or mind of knowledge, present in the universal conscious-force, of which the reason in man is the overt form at which our evolution arrives, — a form still limited and imperfect in its modes of action and constituting principle. There is a subconscious knowledge even in the Inconscient, a greater intrinsic Reason in things which impose co-ordination, that is to say, a certain rationality, upon the wildest movements of the universal becoming.

The importance of Memory becomes apparent in the well-observed phenomenon of double personality or dissociation of personality in which the same man has two successive or alternating states of his mind and in each remembers and co-ordinates perfectly only what he was or did in that state of mind and not what he was or did in the other. This can be associated with an organised idea of different personality, for he thinks in one state that he is one person and in the other that he is quite another with a different name, life and feelings. Here it would seem that memory is the whole substance of personality. But, on the other side, we must see that dissociation of memory occurs also without dissociation of personality, as when a man in the state of hypnosis takes up a range of memories and experiences to which his waking mind is a stranger but does not therefore think himself another person, or as when one who has forgotten the past events of his life and perhaps even his name, still does not change his ego-sense and personality. And there is possible too a state of consciousness in which, although there is no gap of memory, yet by a rapid development the whole being feels itself changed in every mental circumstance and the man feels born into a new personality, so that, if it were not for the co-ordinating mind, he would not at all accept his past as belonging to the person he now is, although he remembers perfectly well that it was in the same form of body and same field of mind-substance that it occurred. Mind-sense is the basis, memory the thread on which experiences are strung by the self-experiencing mind: but it is the co-ordinating faculty of mind which, relating together all the material that memory provides and all its linkings of past, present and future, relates them also to an "I" who is the same in all the moments of Time and in spite of all the changes of experience and personality.

The ego-sense is only a preparatory device and a first basis for the development of real self-knowledge in the mental being. Developing from inconscience to self-conscience, from nescience of self and things to knowledge of self and things, the Mind in forms arrives thus far that it is aware of all its superficially conscious becoming as related to an "I" which it always is. That "I" it partly identifies with the conscious becoming, partly thinks of it as something other than the becoming and superior to it, even perhaps eternal and unchanging. In the last resort, by the aid of its reason which distinguishes in order to co-ordinate, it may fix its self-experience on the becoming only, on the constantly changing self and reject the idea of something other than it as a fiction of the mind; there is then no being, only becoming. Or it may fix its self-experience into a direct consciousness of its own eternal being and reject the becoming, even when it is compelled to be aware of it, as a fiction of the mind and the senses or the vanity of a temporary inferior existence.

But it is evident that a self-knowledge based on the separative ego-sense is imperfect and that no knowledge founded upon it alone or primarily or on a reaction against it can be secure or assured of completeness. First, it is a knowledge of our superficial mental activity and its experiences and, with regard to all the large rest of our becoming that is behind, it is an Ignorance. Secondly, it is a knowledge only of being and becoming as limited to the individual self and its experiences; all the rest of the world is to it not-self, something, that is to say, which it does not realise as part of its own being but as some outside existence presented to its separate consciousness. This happens because it has no direct conscious knowledge of this larger existence and nature such as the individual has of his own being and becoming. Here too there is a limited knowledge asserting itself in the midst of a vast Ignorance. Thirdly, the true relation between the being and the becoming has not been worked out on the basis of perfect self-knowledge but rather by the Ignorance, by a partial knowledge. As a consequence the mind in its impetus towards an ultimate knowledge attempts through the co-ordinating and dissociating will and reason on the basis of our present experience and possibilities to drive at a trenchant conclusion which cuts away one side of existence. All that has been established is that the mental being can on one side absorb himself in direct self-consciousness to the apparent exclusion of all becoming and can on the other side absorb himself in the becoming to the apparent exclusion of all stable self-consciousness. Both sides of the mind, separating as antagonists, condemn what they reject as unreal or else as only a play of the conscious mind; to one or the other, either the Divine, the Self, or the world is only relatively real so long as the mind persists in creating them, the world an effective dream of Self, or God and Self a mental construction or an effective hallucination. The true relation has not been seized, because these two sides of existence must always appear discordant and unreconciled to our intelligence so long as there is only a partial knowledge. An integral knowledge is the aim of the conscious evolution; a clean cut of the consciousness shearing apart one side and leaving the other cannot be the whole truth of self and things. For if some immobile Self were all, there could be no possibility of world-existence; if mobile Nature were all, there might be a cycle of universal becoming, but no spiritual foundation for the evolution of the Conscient out of the Inconscient and for the persistent aspiration of our partial Consciousness or Ignorance to exceed itself and arrive at the whole conscious Truth of its being and the integral conscious knowledge of all Being.

Our surface existence is only a surface and it is there that there is the full reign of the Ignorance; to know we have to go within ourselves and see with an inner knowledge. All that is formulated on the surface is a small and diminished representation of our secret greater existence. The immobile self in us is found only when the outer mental and vital activities are quieted; for since it is seated deep within and is represented on the surface only by the intuitive sense of self-existence and misrepresented by the mental, vital, physical ego-sense, its truth has to be experienced in the mind's silence. But also the dynamic parts of our surface being are similarly diminished figures of greater things that are there in the depths of our secret nature. The surface memory itself is a fragmentary and ineffective action pulling out details from an inner subliminal memory which receives and records all our world-experience, receives and records even what the mind has not observed, understood or noticed. Our

surface imagination is a selection from a vaster more creative
and effective subliminal image-building power of consciousness.
A mind with immeasurably wider and more subtle perceptions, a
life-energy with a greater dynamism, a subtle-physical substance
with a larger and finer receptivity are building out of themselves
our surface evolution. A psychic entity is there behind these occult activities which is the true support of our individualisation;
the ego is only an outward false substitute: for it is this secret
soul that supports and holds together our self-experience and
world-experience; the mental, vital, physical, external ego is a
superficial construction of Nature. It is only when we have seen
both our self and our nature as a whole, in the depths as well as
on the surface, that we can acquire a true basis of knowledge.

Chapter X

Knowledge by Identity and Separative Knowledge

They see the Self in the Self by the Self.   *Gita.*[1]

Where there is duality, there other sees other, other hears, touches, thinks of, knows other. But when one sees all as the Self, by what shall one know it? it is by the Self that one knows all this that is.... All betrays him who sees all elsewhere than in the Self; for all this that is is the Brahman, all beings and all this that is are this Self.   *Brihadaranyaka Upanishad.*[2]

The Self-Existent has pierced the doors of sense outward, therefore one sees things outwardly and sees not in one's inner being. Rarely a sage desiring immortality, his sight turned inward, sees the Self face to face.   *Katha Upanishad.*[3]

There is no annihilation of the seeing of the seer, the speaking of the speaker... the hearing of the hearer... the knowing of the knower, for they are indestructible; but it is not a second or other than and separate from himself that he sees, speaks to, hears, knows.   *Brihadaranyaka Upanishad.*[4]

OUR SURFACE cognition, our limited and restricted mental way of looking at our self, at our inner movements and at the world outside us and its objects and happenings, is so constituted that it derives in different degrees from a fourfold order of knowledge. The original and fundamental way of knowing, native to the occult self in things, is a knowledge by identity; the second, derivative,

---

[1] VI. 20.   [2] IV. 5. 15, 7.   [3] II. 1. 1.   [4] IV. 3. 23-30.

is a knowledge by direct contact associated at its roots with a secret knowledge by identity or starting from it, but actually separated from its source and therefore powerful but incomplete in its cognition; the third is a knowledge by separation from the object of observation, but still with a direct contact as its support or even a partial identity; the fourth is a completely separative knowledge which relies on a machinery of indirect contact, a knowledge by acquisition which is yet, without being conscious of it, a rendering or bringing up of the contents of a pre-existent inner awareness and knowledge. A knowledge by identity, a knowledge by intimate direct contact, a knowledge by separative direct contact, a wholly separative knowledge by indirect contact are the four cognitive methods of Nature.

The first way of knowing in its purest form is illustrated in the surface mind only by our direct awareness of our own essential existence: it is a knowledge empty of any other content than the pure fact of self and being; of nothing else in the world has our surface mind the same kind of awareness. But in the knowledge of the structure and movements of our subjective consciousness some element of awareness by identity does enter; for we can project ourselves with a certain identification into these movements. It has already been noted how this can happen in the case of an uprush of wrath which swallows us up so that for the moment our whole consciousness seems to be a wave of anger: other passions, love, grief, joy have the same power to seize and occupy us; thought also absorbs and occupies, we lose sight of the thinker and become the thought and the thinking. But very ordinarily there is a double movement; a part of our selves becomes the thought or the passion, another part of us either accompanies it with a certain adherence or follows it closely and knows it by an intimate direct contact which falls short of identification or entire self-oblivion in the movement.

This identification is possible, and also this simultaneous separation and partial identification, because these things are becomings of our being, determinations of our mind stuff and mind energy, of our life stuff and life energy; but, since they are only a small part of us, we are not bound to be identified and occupied, — we can detach ourselves, separate the being from its temporary becoming, observe it, control it, sanction or prevent its manifestation: we can, in this way, by an inner detachment, a mental or spiritual separateness, partially or even fundamentally liberate ourselves from the control of mind nature or vital nature over the being and assume the position of the witness, knower and ruler. Thus we have a double knowledge of the subjective movement: there is an intimate knowledge, by identity, of its stuff and its force of action, more intimate than we could have by any entirely separative and objective knowledge such as we get of things outside us, things that are to us altogether not-self; there is at the same time a knowledge by detached observation, detached but with a power of direct contact, which frees us from engrossment by the Nature-energy and enables us to relate the movement to the rest of our own existence and world existence. If we are without this detachment, we lose our self of being and mastering knowledge in the nature self of becoming and movement and action and, though we know intimately the movement, we do not know it dominatingly and fully. This would not be the case if we carried into our identification with the movement our identity with the rest of our subjective existence, — if, that is to say, we could plunge wholly into the wave of becoming and at the same time be in the very absorption of the state or act the mental witness, observer, controller; but this we cannot easily do, because we live in a divided consciousness in which the vital part of us, — our life nature of force and desire and passion and action, — tends to control or swallow up the mind, and the mind has to avoid this subjection and control the vital, but can only succeed in the effort by keeping itself separate; for if it identifies itself, it is lost and hurried away in the life movement. Nevertheless a kind of balanced double identity by division is possible, though it is not easy to keep the balance; there is a self of thought which observes and permits the passion for the sake of the experience, — or is obliged by some life-stress to permit it, — and there is a self of life which allows itself to be carried along in the movement of Nature. Here, then, in our subjective experience, we have a field of the action of consciousness in which three movements of cognition can meet together, a certain kind of knowledge by identity, a knowledge by direct contact and, dependent upon them, a separative knowledge.

In thought separation of the thinker and the thinking is more difficult. The thinker is plunged and lost in the thought or carried in the thought current, identified with it; it is not usually at the time of or in the very act of thinking that he can observe or review his thoughts, — he has to do that in retrospect and with the aid of memory or by a critical pause of corrective judgment before he proceeds further: but still a simultaneity of thinking and conscious direction of the mind's action can be achieved partially when the thought does not engross, entirely when the thinker acquires the faculty of stepping back into the mental self and standing apart there from the mental energy. Instead of being absorbed in the thought with at most a vague feeling of the process of thinking, we can see the process by a mental vision, watch our thoughts in their origination and movement and, partly by a silent insight, partly by a process of thought upon thought, judge and evaluate them. But whatever the kind of identification, it is to be noted that the knowledge of our internal movements is of a double nature, separation and direct contact: for even when we detach ourselves, this close contact is maintained; our knowledge is always based on a direct touch, on a cognition by direct awareness carrying in it a certain element of identity. The more separative attitude is ordinarily the method of our reason in observing and knowing our inner movements; the more intimate is the method of our dynamic part of mind associating itself with our sensations, feelings and desires: but in this association too the thinking mind can intervene and exercise a separative dissociated observation and control over both the dynamic self-associating part of mind and the vital or physical movement. All the observable movements of our physical being also are known and controlled by us in both these ways, the separative and the intimate; we feel the body and what it is doing intimately as part of us, but the mind is separate from it and can exercise a detached control over its movements. This gives to our normal knowledge of our subjective being and nature, incomplete and largely superficial though it still is, yet, so far as it goes, a certain intimacy, immediacy and directness. That is absent in our knowledge of the world outside us and its movements and objects: for there, since the thing seen or experienced is not-self, not experienced as part of us, no entirely direct contact of consciousness with the object is possible; an instrumentation of sense has to be used which offers us, not immediate intimate knowledge of it, but a figure of it as a first datum for knowledge.

In the cognition of external things, our knowledge has an entirely separative basis; its whole machinery and process are of the nature of an indirect perception. We do not identify ourselves with external objects, not even with other men though they are beings of our own nature; we cannot enter into their existence as if it were our own, we cannot know them and their movements with the directness, immediateness, intimacy with which we know, — even though incompletely, — ourselves and our movements. But not only identification lacks, direct contact also is absent; there is no direct touch between our consciousness and their consciousness, our substance and their substance, our self of being and their self-being. The only seemingly direct contact with them or direct evidence we have of them is through the senses; sight, hearing, touch seem to initiate some kind of a direct intimacy with the object of knowledge: but this is not so really, not a real directness, a real intimacy, for what we get by our sense is not the inner or intimate touch of the thing itself, but an image of it or a vibration or nerve message in ourselves through which we have to learn to know it. These means are so ineffective, so exiguous in their poverty that, if that were the whole machinery, we could know little or nothing or only achieve a great blur of confusion. But there intervenes a sense-mind intuition which seizes the suggestion of the image or vibration and equates it with the object, a vital intuition which seizes the energy or figure of power of the object through another kind of vibration created by the sense contact, and an intuition of the perceptive mind which at once forms a right idea of the object from all this evidence. Whatever is deficient in the interpretation of the image thus constructed is filled up by the intervention of the reason or the total understanding intelligence. If the first composite intuition were the result of a direct contact or if it summarised the action of a total intuitive mentality master of its perceptions, there would be no need for the intervention of the reason except as a discoverer or organiser of knowledge not conveyed by the sense and its suggestions: it is, on the contrary, an intuition working on an image, a sense document, an indirect evidence, not working upon a direct contact of consciousness with the object. But since the image or vibration is a defective and summary documentation and the intuition itself limited and communicated through an obscure medium, acting in a blind light, the accuracy of our intuitional interpretative construction of the object is open to question or at least likely to be incomplete. Man has had perforce to develop his reason in order to make up for the deficiencies of his sense instrumentation, the fallibility of his physical mind's perceptions and the paucity of its interpretation of its data.

Our world-knowledge is therefore a difficult structure made up of the imperfect documentation of the sense-image, an intuitional interpretation of it by perceptive mind, life-mind and sense-mind, and a supplementary filling up, correction, addition of supplementary knowledge, co-ordination, by the reason. Even so our knowledge of the world we live in is narrow and imperfect, our interpretations of its significances doubtful: imagination, speculation, reflection, impartial weighing and reasoning, inference, measurement, testing, a further correction and amplification of sense evidence by Science, — all this apparatus had to be called in to complete the incompleteness. After all that the result still remains a half-certain, half-dubious accumulation of acquired indirect knowledge, a mass of significant images and ideative representations, abstract thought-counters, hypotheses, theories, generalisations, but also with all that a mass of doubts and a never-ending debate and inquiry. Power has come with knowledge, but our imperfection of knowledge leaves us without any idea of the true use of the power, even of the aim towards which our utilisation of knowledge and power should be turned and made effective. This is worsened by the imperfection of our self-knowledge which, such as it is, meagre and pitifully insufficient, is of our surface only, of our apparent phenomenal self and nature and not of our true self and the true meaning of our existence. Self-knowledge and self-mastery are wanting in the user, wisdom and right will in his use of world-power and world-knowledge.

It is evident that our state on the surface is indeed a state of knowledge, so far as it goes, but a limited knowledge enveloped and invaded by ignorance and, to a very large extent, by reason of its limitation, itself a kind of ignorance, at best a mixed knowledge-ignorance. It could not be otherwise since our awareness of the world is born of a separative and surface observation with only an indirect means of cognition at its disposal; our knowledge of ourselves, though more direct, is stultified by its restriction to the surface of our being, by an ignorance of our true self, the true sources of our nature, the true motive-forces of our action. It is quite evident that we know ourselves with only a superficial knowledge, — the sources of our consciousness and thought are a mystery; the true nature of our mind, emotions, sensations is a mystery; our cause of being and our end of being, the significance of our life and its activities are a mystery: this could not be if we had a real self-knowledge and a real world-knowledge.

If we look for the reason of this limitation and imperfection, we shall find first that it is because we are concentrated on our surface; the depths of self, the secrets of our total nature are shut away from us behind a wall created by our externalising consciousness, — or created for it so that it can pursue its activity of egocentric individualisation of the mind, life and body uninvaded by the deeper and wider truth of our larger existence: through this wall we can look into our inner self and reality only through crevices and portholes and we see little there but a mysterious dimness. At the same time our consciousness has to defend its ego-centric individualisation, not only against its own deeper self of oneness and infinity, but against the cosmic infinite; it builds up a wall of division here also and shuts out all that is not centred round its ego, excludes it as the not-self. But since it has to live with this not-self, — for it belongs to it, depends upon it, is an inhabitant within it, — it must maintain some means of communication; it has too to make excursions out of its wall of ego and wall of self-restriction within the body in order to cater for those needs which the not-self can supply to it: it must learn to know in some way all that surrounds it so as to be able to master it and make it as far as possible a servant to the individual and collective human life and ego. The body provides our consciousness with the gates of the senses through which it can establish the necessary communication and means of observation and action upon the world, upon the not-self outside it; the mind uses these means and invents others that supplement them and it succeeds in establishing some construction, some system of knowledge which serves its immediate purpose or its general will to master partially and use this huge alien environmental existence or deal with it where it cannot master it. But the knowledge it gains is objective; it is mainly a knowledge of the surface of things or of what is just below the surface, pragmatic, limited and insecure. Its defence against the invasion of the cosmic energy is equally insecure and partial: in spite of its notice of no entry without permission, it is subtly and invisibly invaded by the world, enveloped by the not-self and moulded by it; its thought, its will, its emotional and its life energy are penetrated by waves and currents of thought, will, passion, vital impacts, forces of all kinds from others and from universal Nature. Its wall of defence becomes a wall of obscuration which prevents it from knowing all this interaction; it knows only what comes through the gates of sense or through mental perceptions of which it cannot be sure or through what it can infer or build up from its gathered sense-data; all the rest is to it a blank of nescience.

It is, then, this double wall of self-imprisonment, this self-fortification in the bounds of a surface ego, that is the cause of our limited knowledge or ignorance, and if this self-imprisonment were the whole character of our existence, the ignorance would be irremediable. But, in fact, this constant outer ego-building is only a provisional device of the Consciousness-Force in things so that the secret individual, the spirit within, may establish a representative and instrumental formation of itself in physical nature, a provisional individualisation in the nature of the Ignorance, which is all that can at first be done in a world emerging out of a universal Inconscience. Our self-ignorance and our world-ignorance can only grow towards integral self-knowledge and integral world-knowledge in proportion as our limited ego and its half-blind consciousness open to a greater inner existence and consciousness and a true self-being and become aware too of the not-self outside it also as self, — on one side a Nature constituent of our own nature, on the other an Existence which is a boundless continuation of our own self-being. Our being has to break the walls of ego-consciousness which it has created, it has to extend itself beyond its body and inhabit the body of the universe. In place of its knowledge by indirect contact, or in addition to it, it must arrive at a knowledge by direct contact and proceed to a knowledge by identity. Its limited finite of self has to become a boundless finite and an infinite.

But the first of these two movements, the awakening to our inner realities, imposes itself as the prior necessity because it is by this inward self-finding that the second, — the cosmic self-finding, — can become entirely possible: we have to go into our inner being and learn to live in it and from it; the outer mind and life and body must become for us only an antechamber. All that we are on the outside is indeed conditioned by what is within, occult, in our inner depths and recesses; it is thence that come the secret initiatives, the self-effective formations; our inspirations, our intuitions, our life-motives, our mind's preferences, our will's selections are actuated from there, — in so far as they are not shaped or influenced by an insistence, equally hidden, of a surge of cosmic impacts: but the use we make of these emergent powers and these influences is conditioned, largely determined and, above all, very much limited by our outermost nature. It is then the knowledge of this inner initiating self coupled with the

accurate perception of the outer instrumental self and the part
played by both of them in our building that we have to discover.

On the surface we know only so much of our self as is
formulated there and of even this only a portion; for we see our
total surface being in a general vagueness dotted and sectioned
by points or figures of precision: even what we discover by a
mental introspection is only a sum of sections; the entire figure
and sense of our personal formation escapes our notice. But there
is also a distorting action which obscures and disfigures even this
limited self-knowledge; our self-view is vitiated by the constant
impact and intrusion of our outer life-self, our vital being, which
seeks always to make the thinking mind its tool and servant: for
our vital being is not concerned with self-knowledge but with
self-affirmation, desire, ego. It is therefore constantly acting on
mind to build for it a mental structure of apparent self that
will serve these purposes; our mind is persuaded to present to
us and to others a partly fictitious representative figure of ourselves which supports our self-affirmation, justifies our desires
and actions, nourishes our ego. This vital intervention is not
indeed always in the direction of self-justification and assertion;
it turns sometimes towards self-depreciation and a morbid and
exaggerated self-criticism: but this too is an ego-structure, a
reverse or negative egoism, a poise or pose of the vital ego. For
in this vital ego there is frequently a mixture of the charlatan
and mountebank, the poser and actor; it is constantly taking
up a role and playing it to itself and to others as its public.
An organised self-deception is thus added to an organised self-
ignorance; it is only by going within and seeing these things at
their source that we can get out of this obscurity and tangle.

For a larger mental being is there within us, a larger inner
vital being, even a larger inner subtle-physical being other than
our surface body-consciousness, and by entering into this or
becoming it, identifying ourselves with it, we can observe the
springs of our thoughts and feelings, the sources and motives
of our action, the operative energies that build up our surface
personality. For we discover and can know the inner being that
secretly thinks and perceives in us, the vital being that secretly

feels and acts upon life through us, the subtle-physical being that
secretly receives and responds to the contacts of things through
our body and its organs. Our surface thought, feeling, emotion
is a complexity and confusion of impulsions from within and
impacts from outside us; our reason, our organising intelligence
can impose on it only an imperfect order: but here within we find
the separate sources of our mental, our vital and our physical
energisms and can see clearly the pure operations, the distinct
powers, the composing elements of each and their interplay in
a clear light of self-vision. We find that the contradictions and
the struggles of our surface consciousness are largely due to the
contrary or mutually discordant tendencies of our mental, vital
and physical parts opposing and unreconciled with each other
and these again to the discord of many different inner possibilities of our being and even of different personalities on each level
in us which are behind the intermixed disposition and differing
tendencies of our surface nature. But while on the surface their
action is mixed together, confused and conflicting, here in our
depths they can be seen and worked upon in their independent
and separate nature and action and a harmonisation of them by
the mental being in us, leader of the life and body,[5] — or, better,
by the central psychic entity, — is not so difficult, provided we
have the right psychic and mental will in the endeavour: for if
it is with the vital-ego motive that we make the entry into the
subliminal being, it may result in serious dangers and disaster or
at the least an exaggeration of ego, self-affirmation and desire,
an enlarged and more powerful ignorance instead of an enlarged
and more powerful knowledge. Moreover, we find in this inner
or subliminal being the means of directly distinguishing between
what rises from within and what comes to us from outside, from
others or from universal Nature, and it becomes possible to exercise a control, a choice, a power of willed reception, rejection
and selection, a clear power of self-building and harmonisation
which we do not possess or can operate very imperfectly in our
composed surface personality but which is the prerogative of

[5] *manomayaḥ prāṇaśarīranetā* — *Mundaka Upanishad,* 2. 2. 7.

our inner Person. For by this entry into the depths the inner being, no longer quite veiled, no longer obliged to exercise a fragmentary influence on its outer instrumental consciousness, is able to formulate itself more luminously in our life in the physical universe.

In its essence the inner being's knowledge has the same elements as the outer mind's surface knowledge, but there is between them the difference between a half blindness and a greater clarity of consciousness and vision due to a more direct and powerful instrumentation and a better arrangement of the elements of knowledge. Knowledge by identity, on the surface a vague inherent sense of our self-existence and a partial identification with our inner movements, can here deepen and enlarge itself from that indistinct essential perception and limited sensation to a clear and direct intrinsic awareness of the whole entity within: we can enter into possession of our whole conscious mental being and life being and arrive at a close intimacy of direct penetrating and enveloping contact with the total movements of our mental and vital energy; we meet clearly and closely and are, — but more freely and understandingly, — all the becomings of ourself, the whole self-expression of the Purusha on the present levels of our nature. But also there is or can be along with this intimacy of knowledge a detached observation of the actions of the nature by the Purusha and a great possibility, through this double status of knowledge, of a complete control and understanding. All the movements of the surface being can be seen with a complete detachment, but also with a direct sight in the consciousness by which the self-delusions and mistakes of self of the outer consciousness can be dispelled; there is a keener mental vision, a clearer and more accurate mental feeling of our subjective becoming, a vision which at once knows, commands and controls the whole nature. If the psychic and mental parts in us are strong, the vital comes under mastery and direction to an extent hardly possible to the surface mentality; even the body and the physical energies can be taken up by the inner mind and will and turned into a more plastic instrumentation of the soul, the psychic being. On the other hand, if the mental and psychic parts are weak and the vital strong and unruly, power is increased by entry into the inner vital, but discrimination and detached vision are deficient; the knowledge, even if increased in force and range, remains turbid and misleading; intelligent self-control may give place to a vast undisciplined impetus or a rigidly disciplined but misguided egoistic action. For the subliminal is still a movement of the Knowledge-Ignorance; it has in it a greater knowledge, but the possibility also of a greater because more self-affirming ignorance. This is because, though an increased self-knowledge is normal here, it is not at once an integral knowledge: an awareness by direct contact, which is the principal power of the subliminal, is not sufficient for that; for it may be contact with greater becomings and powers of Knowledge, but also with greater becomings and powers of the Ignorance.

But the subliminal being has also a larger direct contact with the world; it is not confined like the surface Mind to the interpretation of sense-images and sense-vibrations supplemented by the mental and vital intuition and the reason. There is indeed an inner sense in the subliminal nature, a subtle sense of vision, hearing, touch, smell and taste; but these are not confined to the creation of images of things belonging to the physical environment, — they can present to the consciousness visual, auditory, tactual and other images and vibrations of things beyond the restricted range of the physical senses or belonging to other planes or spheres of existence. This inner sense can create or present images, scenes, sounds that are symbolic rather than actual or that represent possibilities in formation, suggestions, thoughts, ideas, intentions of other beings, image-forms also of powers or potentialities in universal Nature; there is nothing that it cannot image or visualise or turn into sensory formations. It is the subliminal in reality and not the outer mind that possesses the powers of telepathy, clairvoyance, second sight and other supernormal faculties whose occurrence in the surface consciousness is due to openings or rifts in the wall erected by the outer personality's unseeing labour of individualisation and interposed between itself and the inner domain of our being.

It should be noted, however, that owing to this complexity the action of the subliminal sense can be confusing or misleading, especially if it is interpreted by the outer mind to which the secret of its operations is unknown and its principles of sign-construction and symbolic figure-languages foreign; a greater inner power of intuition, tact, discrimination is needed to judge and interpret rightly its images and experiences. It is still the fact that they add immensely to our possible scope of knowledge and widen the narrow limits in which our sense-bound outer physical consciousness is circumscribed and imprisoned.

But more important is the power of the subliminal to enter into a direct contact of consciousness with other consciousness or with objects, to act without other instrumentation, by an essential sense inherent in its own substance, by a direct mental vision, by a direct feeling of things, even by a close envelopment and intimate penetration and a return with the contents of what is enveloped or penetrated, by a direct intimation or impact on the substance of mind itself, not through outward signs or figures, — a revealing intimation or a self-communicating impact of thoughts, feelings, forces. It is by these means that the inner being achieves an immediate, intimate and accurate spontaneous knowledge of persons, of objects, of the occult and to us intangible energies of world-Nature that surround us and impinge upon our own personality, physicality, mind-force and life-force. In our surface mentality we are sometimes aware of a consciousness that can feel or know the thoughts and inner reactions of others or become aware of objects or happenings without any observable sense-intervention or otherwise exercise powers supernormal to our ordinary capacity; but these capacities are occasional, rudimentary, vague. Their possession is proper to our concealed subliminal self and, when they emerge, it is by a coming to the surface of its powers or operations. These emergent operations of the subliminal being or some of them are now fragmentarily studied under the name of psychic phenomena, — although they have ordinarily nothing to do with the *psyche*, the soul, the inmost entity in us, but only with the inner mind, the inner vital, the subtle-physical parts of our subliminal being; but the results cannot be conclusive or sufficiently ample because they are sought for by methods of inquiry and experiment and standards of proof proper to the surface mind and its system of knowledge by indirect contact. Under these conditions they can be investigated only in so far as they are able to manifest in that mind to which they are exceptional, abnormal or supernormal, and therefore comparatively rare, difficult, incomplete in their occurrence. It is only if we can open up the wall between the outer mind and the inner consciousness to which such phenomena are normal, or if we can enter freely within or dwell there, that this realm of knowledge can be truly explained and annexed to our total consciousness and included in the field of operation of our awakened force of nature.

In our surface mind we have no direct means of knowing even other men who are of our own kind and have a similar mentality and are vitally and physically built on the same model. We can acquire a general knowledge of the human mind and the human body and apply it to them with the aid of the many constant and habitual outer signs of the human inner movements with which we are familiar; these summary judgments can be farther eked out by our experience of personal character and habits, by instinctive application of what self-knowledge we have to our understanding and judgment of others, by inference from speech and conduct, by insight of observation and insight of sympathy. But the results are always incomplete and very frequently deceptive: our inferences are as often as not erroneous constructions, our interpretation of the outward signs a mistaken guess-work, our application of general knowledge or our self-knowledge baffled by elusive factors of personal difference, our very insight uncertain and unreliable. Human beings therefore live as strangers to each other, at best tied by a very partial sympathy and mutual experience; we do not know enough, do not know as well as we know ourselves, — and that itself is little, — even those nearest to us. But in the subliminal inner consciousness it is possible to become directly aware of the thoughts and feelings around us, to feel their impact, to see their movements; to read a mind and a heart becomes less difficult, a less uncertain venture. There is a constant mental, vital, subtle-physical interchange going on between all who meet or live together, of which they are themselves unaware except in so far as its impacts and interpenetrations touch them as sensible results of speech and action and outer contact: for the most part it is subtly and invisibly that this interchange takes place; for it acts indirectly, touching the subliminal parts and through them the outer nature. But when we grow conscious in these subliminal parts, that brings consciousness also of all this interaction and subjective interchange and intermingling, with the result that we need no longer be involuntary subjects of their impact and consequence, but can accept or reject, defend ourselves or isolate. At the same time, our action on others need no longer be ignorant or involuntary and often unintentionally harmful; it can be a conscious help, a luminous interchange and a fruitful accommodation, an approach towards an inner understanding or union, not as now a separative association with only a limited intimacy or unity, restricted by much non-understanding and often burdened or endangered by a mass of misunderstanding, of mutual misinterpretation and error.

Equally important would be the change in our dealings with the impersonal forces of the world that surround us. These we know only by their results, by the little that we can seize of their visible action and consequence. Among them it is mostly the physical world-forces of which we have some knowledge, but we live constantly in the midst of a whirl of unseen mind-forces and life-forces of which we know nothing, we are not even aware of their existence. To all this unseen movement and action the subliminal inner consciousness can open our awareness, for it has a knowledge of it by direct contact, by inner vision, by a psychic sensitiveness; but at present it can only enlighten our obtuse superficiality and outwardness by unexplained warnings, premonitions, attractions and repulsions, ideas, suggestions, obscure intuitions, the little it can get through imperfectly to the surface. The inner being not only contacts directly and concretely the immediate motive and movement of these universal forces and feels the results of their present action, but it can to a certain extent forecast or see ahead their farther action; there is a greater power in our subliminal parts to overcome the time barrier, to have the sense or feel the vibration of coming events, of distant happenings, even to look into the future. It is true that this knowledge proper to the subliminal being is not complete; for it is a mixture of knowledge and ignorance and it is capable of erroneous as well as of true perception, since it works not by knowledge by identity, but by a knowledge through direct contact and this is also a separative knowledge, though more intimate even in separation than anything that is commanded by our surface nature. But the mixed capacity of the inner mental and vital nature for a greater ignorance as well as a greater knowledge can be cured by going still deeper behind it to the psychic entity which supports our individual life and body. There is indeed a soul-personality, representative of this entity, already built up within us, which puts forward a fine psychic element in our natural being: but this finer factor in our normal make-up is not yet dominant and has only a limited action. Our soul is not the overt guide and master of our thought and acts; it has to rely on the mental, vital, physical instruments for self-expression and is constantly overpowered by our mind and life-force: but if once it can succeed in remaining in constant communion with its own larger occult reality, — and this can only happen when we go deep into our subliminal parts, — it is no longer dependent, it can become powerful and sovereign, armed with an intrinsic spiritual perception of the truth of things and a spontaneous discernment which separates that truth from the falsehood of the Ignorance and Inconscience, distinguishes the divine and the undivine in the manifestation and so can be the luminous leader of our other parts of nature. It is indeed when this happens that there can be the turning-point towards an integral transformation and an integral knowledge.

These are the dynamic functionings and pragmatic values of the subliminal cognition; but what concerns us in our present inquiry is to learn from its way of action the exact character of this deeper and larger cognition and how it is related to true knowledge. Its main character is a knowledge by the direct contact of consciousness with its object or of consciousness with other consciousness; but in the end we discover that this power is an outcome of a secret knowledge by identity, a translation of it into a separative awareness of things. For as in the indirect contact proper to our normal consciousness and surface cognition it is the meeting or friction of the living being with the existence outside it that awakens the spark of conscious knowledge, so here it is some contact that sets in action a pre-existent secret knowledge and brings it to the surface. For consciousness is one in the subject and the object, and in the contact of existence with existence this identity brings to light or awakens in the self the dormant knowledge of this other self outside it. But while this pre-existent knowledge comes up in the surface mind as a knowledge acquired, it arises in the subliminal as a thing seen, caught from within, remembered as it were, or, when it is fully intuitive, self-evident to the inner awareness; or it is taken in from the object contacted but with an immediate response as to something intimately recognisable. In the surface consciousness knowledge represents itself as a truth seen from outside, thrown on us from the object, or as a response to its touch on the sense, a perceptive reproduction of its objective actuality. Our surface mind is obliged to give to itself this account of its knowledge, because the wall between itself and the outside world is pierced by the gates of sense and it can catch through these gates the surface of outward objects though not what is within them, but there is no such ready-made opening between itself and its own inner being: since it is unable to see what is within its deeper self or observe the process of the knowledge coming from within, it has no choice but to accept what it does see, the external object, as the cause of its knowledge. Thus all our mental knowing of things represents itself to us as objective, a truth imposed on us from outside; our knowledge is a reflection or responsive construction reproducing in us a figure or picture or a mental scheme of something that is not in our own being. In fact, it is a hidden deeper response to the contact, a response coming from within that throws up from there an inner knowledge of the object, the object being itself part of our larger self; but owing to the double veil, the veil between our inner self and our ignorant surface self and the veil between that surface self and the object contacted, it is only an imperfect figure or representation of the inner knowledge that is formed on the surface.

This affiliation, this concealed method of our knowledge, obscure and non-evident to our present mentality, becomes clear and evident when the subliminal inner being breaks its boundaries of individuality and, carrying our surface mind with it, enters into the cosmic consciousness. The subliminal is separated from the cosmic through a limitation by the subtler sheaths of our being, its mental, vital, subtle-physical sheaths, just as the surface nature is separated from universal Nature by the gross physical sheath, the body; but the circumscribing wall around it is more transparent, is indeed less a wall than a fence. The subliminal has besides a formation of consciousness which projects itself beyond all these sheaths and forms a circumconscient, an environing part of itself, through which it receives the contacts of the world and can become aware of them and deal with them before they enter. The subliminal is able to widen indefinitely this circumconscient envelope and more and more enlarge its self-projection into the cosmic existence around it. A point comes where it can break through the separation altogether, unite, identify itself with cosmic being, feel itself universal, one with all existence. In this freedom of entry into cosmic self and cosmic nature there is a great liberation of the individual being; it puts on a cosmic consciousness, becomes the universal individual. Its first result, when it is complete, is the realisation of the cosmic spirit, the one self inhabiting the universe, and this union may even bring about a disappearance of the sense of individuality, a merger of the ego into the world-being. Another common result is an entire openness to the universal Energy so that it is felt acting through the mind and life and body and the sense of individual action ceases. But more usually there are results of less amplitude; there is a direct awareness of universal being and nature, there is a greater openness of the mind to the cosmic Mind and its energies, to the cosmic Life and its energies, to cosmic Matter and its energies. A certain sense of unity of the individual with the cosmic, a perception of the world held within one's consciousness as well as of one's own intimate inclusion in the world consciousness can become frequent or constant in this opening; a greater feeling of unity with other beings is its natural consequence. It is then that the existence of the cosmic Being becomes a certitude and a reality and is no longer an ideative perception.

But the cosmic consciousness of things is founded upon knowledge by identity; for the universal Spirit knows itself as the Self of all, knows all as itself and in itself, knows all nature as part of its nature. It is one with all that it contains and knows it by that identity and by a containing nearness; for there is at the same time an identity and an exceeding, and, while from the point of view of the identification there is a oneness and complete knowledge, so from the point of view of the exceeding there is an inclusion and a penetration, an enveloping cognition of each thing and all things, a penetrating sense and vision of each thing and all things. For the cosmic Spirit inhabits each and all, but is more than all; there is therefore in its self-view and world-view a separative power which prevents the cosmic consciousness from being imprisoned in the objects and beings in which it dwells: it dwells within them as an all-pervading spirit and power; whatever individualisation takes place is proper to the person or object, but is not binding on the cosmic Being. It becomes each thing without ceasing from its own larger all-containing existence. Here then is a large universal identity containing smaller identities; for whatever separative cognition exists in or enters into the cosmic consciousness must stand on this double identity and does not contradict it. If there is any need of a drawing back and a knowledge by separation plus contact, it is yet a separateness in identity, a contact in identity; for the object contained is part of the self of that which contains it. It is only when a more drastic separativeness intervenes, that the identity veils itself and throws up a lesser knowledge, direct or indirect, which is unaware of its source; yet is it always the sea of identity which throws up to the surface the waves or the spray of a direct or an indirect knowledge.

This is on the side of consciousness; on the side of action, of the cosmic energies, it is seen that they move in masses, waves, currents constantly constituting and reconstituting beings and objects, movements and happenings, entering into them, passing through them, forming themselves in them, throwing themselves out from them on other beings and objects. Each natural individual is a receptacle of these cosmic forces and a dynamo for their propagation; there passes from each to each a constant stream of mental and vital energies, and these run too in cosmic waves and currents no less than the forces of physical Nature. All this action is veiled from our surface mind's direct sense and knowledge, but it is known and felt by the inner being, though only through a direct contact; when the being enters into the cosmic consciousness, it is still more widely, inclusively, intimately aware of this play of cosmic forces. But although the knowledge is then more complete, the dynamisation of this knowledge can only be partial; for while a fundamental or static unification with the cosmic self is possible, the active dynamic unification with cosmic Nature must be incomplete. On the level of mind and life, even with the loss of the sense of a separate self-existence, the energisms must be in their very nature a selection through individualisation; the action is that of the cosmic Energy, but the individual formation of it in the living dynamo remains the method of its working. For the very use of the dynamo of individuality is to select, to concentrate and formulate selected energies and throw them out in formed and canalised currents: the flow of a total energy would mean that this dynamo had no further use, could be abolished or put out of action; instead of an activity of individual mind, life, body there would be only an individual but impersonal centre or channel through which the universal forces would flow unimpeded and unselective. This can happen, but it would imply a higher spiritualisation far exceeding the normal mental level. In the static seizure of the cosmic knowledge by identity, the subliminal universalised may feel itself one with the cosmic self and the secret self of all others: but the dynamisation of that knowledge would not go farther than a translation of this sense of identity into a greater power and intimacy of direct contact of consciousness with all, a greater, more intimate, more powerful and efficient impact of the force of consciousness on things and persons, a capacity too of an effective inclusion and penetration, of a dynamised intimate vision and feeling and other powers of cognition and action proper to this larger nature.

In the subliminal, therefore, even enlarged into the cosmic consciousness, we get a greater knowledge but not the complete and original knowledge. To go farther and see what the knowledge by identity is in its purity and in what way and to what extent it originates, admits or uses the other powers of knowledge, we have to go beyond the inner mind and life and subtle-physical to the two other ends of the subliminal, interrogate the subconscient and contact or enter into the superconscient. But in the subconscient all is blind, an obscure universalism such as is seen in the mass consciousness, an obscure individualism either abnormal to us or ill-formed and instinctive: here, in the subconscient, a dark knowledge by identity, such as we find already in the Inconscience, is the basis, but it does not reveal itself and its secret. The superior superconscient ranges are based upon the spiritual consciousness free and luminous, and it is there that we can trace the original power of knowledge and perceive the origin and difference of the two distinct orders, knowledge by identity and separative knowledge.

In the supreme timeless Existence, as far as we know it by reflection in spiritual experience, existence and consciousness are one. We are accustomed to identify consciousness with certain operations of mentality and sense and, where these are absent or quiescent, we speak of that state of being as unconscious. But consciousness can exist where there are no overt operations, no signs revealing it, even where it is withdrawn from objects and absorbed in pure existence or involved in the appearance of non-existence. It is intrinsic in being, self-existent, not abolished by quiescence, by inaction, by veiling or covering, by inert absorption or involution; it is there in the being, even when its state seems to be dreamless sleep or a blind trance or an annulment of awareness or an absence. In the supreme timeless status where consciousness is one with being and immobile, it is not a separate reality, but simply and purely the self-awareness inherent in existence. There is no need of knowledge nor is there any operation of knowledge. Being is self-evident to itself: it does not need to look at itself in order to know itself or learn that it is. But if this is evidently true of pure existence, it is also true of the primal All-Existence; for just as spiritual Self-existence is intrinsically aware of its self, so it is intrinsically aware of all that is in its being: this is not by an act of knowledge formulated in a self-regard, a self-observation, but by the same inherent awareness; it is intrinsically all-conscious of all that is by the very fact that all is itself. Thus conscious of its timeless self-existence, the Spirit, the Being is aware in the same way, — intrinsically, absolutely, totally, without any need of a look or act of knowledge, because it is all, — of Time-Existence and of all that is in Time. This is the essential awareness by identity; if applied to cosmic existence, it would mean an essential self-evident automatic consciousness of universe by the Spirit because it is everything and everything is its being.

But there is another status of spiritual awareness which seems to us to be a development from this state and power of pure self-consciousness, perhaps even a first departure, but is in fact normal and intimate to it; for the awareness by identity is always the very stuff of all the Spirit's self-knowledge, but it admits within itself, without changing or modifying its own eternal nature, a subordinate and simultaneous awareness by inclusion and by indwelling. The Being, the Self-existent sees all existences in its one existence; it contains them all and knows them as being of its being, consciousness of its consciousness, power of its power, bliss of its bliss; it is at the same time, necessarily, the Self in them and knows all in them by its pervadingly indwelling selfness: but still all this awareness exists intrinsically, self-evidently, automatically, without the need of any act, regard or operation of knowledge; for knowledge here is not an act, but a state pure, perpetual and inherent. At the base of all spiritual knowledge is this consciousness of identity and by identity, which knows or is simply aware of all as itself. Translated into our way of consciousness this becomes the triple knowledge thus formulated in the Upanishad, "He who sees all existences in the Self", "He who sees the Self in all existences", "He in whom the Self has become all existences", — inclusion, indwelling and identity: but in the fundamental consciousness this seeing is a spiritual self-sense, a seeing that is self-light of being, not a separative regard or a regard upon self turning that self into object. But in this fundamental self-experience a regard of consciousness can manifest which, though inherently possible, an inevitably self-contained power of spirit, is not a first active element of the absorbed intrinsic self-luminousness and self-evidence of the supreme consciousness. This regard belongs to or brings in another status of the supreme spiritual consciousness, a status in which knowledge as we know it begins; there is a state of consciousness and in it, intimate to it there is an act of knowing: the Spirit regards itself, it becomes the knower and the known, in a way the subject and object, — or rather the subject-object in one, — of its own self-knowledge. But this regard, this knowledge is still intrinsic, still self-evident, an act of identity; there is no beginning of what we experience as separative knowledge.

But when the subject draws a little back from itself as object, then certain tertiary powers of spiritual knowledge, of knowledge by identity, take their first origin. There is a spiritual intimate vision, a spiritual pervasive entry and penetration, a spiritual feeling in which one sees all as oneself, feels all as oneself, contacts all as oneself. There is a power of spiritual perception of the object and all that it contains or is, perceived in an enveloping and pervading identity, the identity itself constituting the perception. There is a spiritual conception that is the original substance of thought, not the thought that discovers the unknown, but that which brings out the intrinsically known from oneself and places it in self-space, in an extended being of self-awareness, as an object of conceptual self-knowledge. There is a spiritual emotion, a spiritual sense, there is an intermingling of oneness with oneness, of being with being, of consciousness with consciousness, of delight of being with delight of being. There is a joy of intimate separateness in identity, of relations of love joined with love in a supreme unity, a delight of the many powers, truths, beings of the eternal oneness, of the forms of the Formless; all the play of the becoming in the being founds its self-expression upon these powers of the consciousness of the Spirit. But in their spiritual origin all these powers are essential, not instrumental, not organised, devised or created; they are the luminous self-aware substance of the spiritual Identical made active on itself and in itself, spirit made sight, spirit vibrant as feeling, spirit self-luminous as perception and conception. All is in fact the knowledge by identity, self-powered, self-moving in its multitudinous selfhood of one-awareness. The Spirit's infinite self-experience moves between sheer identity and a multiple identity, a delight of intimately differentiated oneness and an absorbed self-rapture.

A separative knowledge arises when the sense of differentiation overpowers the sense of identity; the self still cognises its identity with the object but pushes to its extreme the play of intimate separateness. At first there is not a sense of self and not-self, but only of self and other-self. A certain knowledge of identity and by identity is still there, but it tends to be first overstructured, then submerged, then so replaced by knowledge through interchange and contact that it figures as a secondary awareness, as if it were a result and no longer the cause of the mutual contact, the still pervasive and enveloping touch, the interpenetrating intimacy of the separate selves. Finally, identity disappears behind the veil and there is the play of being with other beings, consciousness with other consciousness: an underlying identity is still there, but it is not experienced; its place is taken by a direct seizing and penetrating contact, intermingling, interchange. It is by this interaction that a more or less intimate knowledge, mutual awareness or awareness of the object remains possible. There is no feeling of self meeting self, but there is a mutuality; there is not yet an entire separateness, a complete otherness and ignorance. This is a diminished consciousness, but it retains some power of the original knowledge curtailed by division, by the loss of its primal and essential completeness, operating by division, effecting closeness but not oneness. The power of inclusion of the object in the consciousness, of an enveloping awareness and knowledge is there; but it is the inclusion of a now externalised existence which has to be made an element of our self by an attained or recovered knowledge, by a dwelling of consciousness upon the object, a concentration, a taking possession of it as part of the existence. The power of penetration is there, but it has no natural pervasiveness and does not lead to identity; it gathers what it can, takes what is thus acquired and carries the contents of the object of knowledge to the subject. There can still be a direct and penetrating contact of consciousness with consciousness creating a vivid and intimate knowledge, but it is confined to the points or to the extent of the contact. There is still a direct sense, consciousness-sight, consciousness-feeling which can see and feel what is within the object as well as its outside and surface. There is still a mutual penetration and interchange between being and being, between consciousness and consciousness, waves of thought, of feeling, of energy of all kinds which may be a movement of sympathy and union or of opposition and struggle. There can be an attempt at unification by possession of others or through one's own acceptance of possession by other consciousness or other being; or there can be a push towards union by reciprocal inclusion, pervasion, mutual possession. Of all this action and interaction the knower by direct contact is aware and it is on this basis that he arranges his relations with the world around him. This is the origin of knowledge by direct contact of consciousness with its object, which is normal to our inner being but foreign or only imperfectly known to our surface nature.

This first separative ignorance is evidently still a play of knowledge but of a limited separative knowledge, a play of divided being working upon a reality of underlying unity and arriving only at an imperfect result or outcome of the concealed oneness. The complete intrinsic awareness of identity and the act of knowledge by identity belong to the higher hemisphere of existence: this knowledge by direct contact is the main character of the highest supraphysical mental planes of consciousness, those to which our surface being is closed in by a wall of ignorance; in a diminished and more separative form it is a property of the lesser supraphysical planes of mind; it is or can be an element in all that is supraphysical. It is the main instrumentation of our subliminal self, its central means of awareness; for the subliminal self or inner being is a projection from these higher planes to meet the subconscience and it inherits the character of consciousness of its planes of origin with which it is intimately associated and in touch by kinship. In our outer being we are children of the Inconscience; our inner being makes us inheritors of the higher heights of mind and life and spirit: the more we open inwards, go inwards, live inwards, receive from within, the more we draw away from subjection to our inconscient origin and move towards all which is now superconscient to our ignorance.

Ignorance becomes complete with the entire separation of being from being: the direct contact of consciousness with consciousness is then entirely veiled or heavily overlaid, even though it still goes on within our subliminal parts, just as there is also, though wholly concealed and not directly operative, the underlying secret identity and oneness. There is on the surface a complete separateness, a division into self and not-self; there is the necessity of dealing with the not-self, but no direct means of knowing it or mastering it. Nature then creates indirect means, a contact by physical organs of sense, a penetration of outside impacts through the nerve currents, a reaction of mind and its co-ordinations acting as an aid and supplement to the activity of the physical organs, — all of them methods of an indirect knowledge; for the consciousness is forced to rely on these instruments and cannot act directly on the object. To these means is added a reason, intelligence and intuition which seize on the communications thus indirectly brought to them, put all in order and utilise their data to get as much knowledge and mastery and possession of the not-self or as much partial unity with it as the original division allows to the separated being.

These means are obviously insufficient and often inefficient, and the indirect basis of the mind's operations afflicts knowledge with a fundamental incertitude; but this initial insufficiency is inherent in the very nature of our material existence and of all still undelivered existence that emerges from the Inconscience.

The Inconscience is an inverse reproduction of the supreme superconscience: it has the same absoluteness of being and automatic action, but in a vast involved trance; it is being lost in itself, plunged in its own abyss of infinity. Instead of a luminous absorption in self-existence there is a tenebrous involution in it, the darkness veiled within darkness of the Rig Veda, *tama āsīt tamasā gūḍham*, which makes it look like Non-Existence; instead of a luminous inherent self-awareness there is a consciousness plunged into an abyss of self-oblivion, inherent in being but not awake in being. Yet is this involved consciousness still a concealed knowledge by identity; it carries in it the awareness of all the truths of existence hidden in its dark infinite and, when it acts and creates, — but it acts first as Energy and not as Consciousness, — everything is arranged with the precision and perfection of an intrinsic knowledge. In all material things reside a mute and involved Real-Idea, a substantial and self-effective intuition, an eyeless exact perception, an automatic intelligence working out its unexpressed and unthought conceptions, a blindly seeing sureness of sight, a dumb infallible sureness of suppressed feeling coated in insensibility, which effectuate all that has to be effected. All this state and action of the Inconscient corresponds very evidently with the same state and action of the pure Superconscience, but translated into terms of self-darkness in place of the original self-light. Intrinsic in the material form, these powers are not possessed by the form, but yet work in its mute subconscience.

We can, in this knowledge, understand more clearly the stages of the emergence of consciousness from involution to its evolved appearance, of which we have already attempted some general conception. The material existence has only a physical, not a mental individuality, but there is a subliminal Presence in it, the one Conscious in unconscious things, that determines the operation of its indwelling energies. If, as has been affirmed, a material object receives and retains the impression of the contacts of things around it and energies emanate from it, so that an occult knowledge can become aware of its past, can make us conscious of these emanating influences, the intrinsic unorganised Awareness pervading the form but not yet enlightening it must be the cause of this receptivity and these capacities. What we see from outside is that material objects like plants and minerals have their powers, properties and inherent influences, but as there is no faculty or means of communication, it is only by being brought into contact with person or object or by a conscious utilisation by living beings that their influences can become active, — such a utilisation is the practical side of more than one human science. But still these powers and influences are attributes of Being, not of mere indeterminate substance, they are forces of the Spirit emerging by Energy from its self-absorbed Inconscience. This first crude mechanical action of an inherent absorbed conscious energy opens in the primary forms of life into submental life-vibrations that imply an involved sensation; there is a seeking for growth, light, air, life-room, a blind feeling out, which is still internal and confined within the immobile being, unable to formulate its instincts, to communicate, to externalise itself. An immobility not organised to establish living relations, it endures and absorbs contacts, involuntarily inflicts but cannot voluntarily impose them; the inconscience is still dominant, still works out everything by the secret involved knowledge by identity, it has not yet developed the surface contactual means of a conscious knowledge. This further development begins with overtly conscious life; what we see in it is the imprisoned consciousness struggling out to the surface: it is under the compulsion of this struggle that the separated living being strives, however blindly at first and within narrow limits, to enter into conscious relations with the rest of the world-being outside it. It is by the growing amount of contacts that it can receive and respond to and by the growing amount of contacts that it can put out from itself or impose in order to satisfy its needs and impulsions that the being of living matter develops its consciousness, grows from inconscience or subconscience into a limited separative knowledge.

We see then all the powers inherent in the original self-existent spiritual Awareness slowly brought out and manifested in this growing separative consciousness; they are activities suppressed but native to the secret and involved knowledge by identity and they now emerge by degrees in a form strangely diminished and tentative. First, there emerges a crude or veiled sense which develops into precise sensations aided by a vital instinct or concealed intuition; then a life-mind perception manifests and at its back an obscure consciousness-sight and feeling of things; emotion vibrates out and seeks an interchange with others; last arises to the surface conception, thought, reason comprehending and apprehending the object, combining its data of knowledge. But all are incomplete, still maimed by the separative ignorance and the first obscuring inconscience; all are dependent on the outward means, not empowered to act in their own right: consciousness cannot act directly on consciousness; there is a constructive envelopment and penetration of things by the mind consciousness, but not a real possession; there is no knowledge by identity. Only when the subliminal is able to force upon the frontal mind and sense some of its secret activities pure and untranslated into the ordinary forms of mental intelligence, does a rudimentary action of the deeper methods lift itself to the surface; but such emergences are still an exception, they strike across the normality of our acquired and learned knowledge with a savour of the abnormal and the supernormal. It is only by an opening to our inner being or an entry into it that a direct intimate awareness can be added to the outer indirect awareness. It is only by our awakening to our inmost soul or superconscient self that there can be a beginning of the spiritual knowledge with identity as its basis, its constituent power, its intrinsic substance.

Chapter XI

The Boundaries of the Ignorance

One who thinks there is this world and no other...
Katha Upanishad.[1]

Extended within the Infinite... headless and footless, concealing his two ends.[2]
Rig Veda.[3]

He who has the knowledge "I am Brahman" becomes all this that is; but whoever worships another divinity than the One Self and thinks, "Other is he and I am other", he knows not.
Brihadaranyaka Upanishad.[4]

This Self is fourfold, — the Self of Waking who has the outer intelligence and enjoys external things, is its first part; the Self of Dream who has the inner intelligence and enjoys things subtle, is its second part; the Self of Sleep, unified, a massed intelligence, blissful and enjoying bliss, is the third part... the lord of all, the omniscient, the inner Control. That which is unseen, indefinable, self-evident in its one selfhood, is the fourth part: this is the Self, this is that which has to be known.
Mandukya Upanishad.[5]

A conscious being, no larger than a man's thumb, stands in the centre of our self; he is master of the past and the present... he is today and he is tomorrow.
Katha Upanishad.[6]

IT IS now possible to review in its larger lines this Ignorance, or this separative knowledge labouring towards identical knowledge, which constitutes our human mentality and, in an obscurer form, all consciousness that has evolved below our

---

[1] I. 2. 6.   [2] Head and feet, the superconscient and the inconscient.
[3] IV. I. 7, 11.   [4] I. 4. 10.   [5] Verses 2-7.   [6] II. 1. 12, 13.

level. We see that in us it consists of a succession of waves of being and force, pressing from outside and rising from within, which become stuff of consciousness and formulate in a mental cognition and mentalised sensation of self and things in Time and Space. Time presents itself to us as a flow of dynamic movement, Space as an objective field of contents for the experience of this imperfect and developing awareness. By immediate awareness the mental being mobile in Time lives perpetually in the present; by memory he saves a certain part of his experience of self and things from streaming away from him entirely into the past; by thought and will and action, by mind energy, life energy, body energy he utilises it for what he becomes in the present and is yet to become hereafter; the force of being in him that has made him what he is works to prolong, develop and amplify his becoming in the future. All this insecurely held material of self-expression and experience of things, this partial knowledge accumulated in the succession of Time, is co-ordinated for him by perception, memory, intelligence and will to be utilised for an ever-new or ever-repeated becoming and for the mental, vital, physical action which helps him to grow into what he is to be and to express what he already is. The present totality of all this experience of consciousness and output of energy is co-ordinated for relation to his being, gathered into consistency around an ego-sense which formulates the habit of response of self-experience to the contacts of Nature in a persistent limited field of conscious being. It is this ego-sense that gives a first basis of coherence to what otherwise might be a string or mass of floating impressions: all that is so sensed is referred to a corresponding artificial centre of mental consciousness in the understanding, the ego-idea. This ego-sense in the life stuff and this ego-idea in the mind maintain a constructed symbol of self, the separative ego, which does duty for the hidden real self, the spirit or true being. The surface mental individuality is, in consequence, always ego-centric; even its altruism is an enlargement of its ego: the ego is the lynch-pin invented to hold together the motion of our wheel of nature. The necessity of centralisation around the ego continues until there is no longer need of any such device or contrivance because there has emerged the true self, the spiritual being, which is at once wheel and motion and that which holds all together, the centre and the circumference.

But the moment we study ourselves, we find that the self-experience which we thus co-ordinate and consciously utilise for life, is a small part even of our waking individual consciousness. We fasten only upon a very limited number of the mental sensations and perceptions of self and things which come up into our surface consciousness in our continual present: of these again memory saves up only a scanty part from the oblivious gulf of the past; of the storings of memory our intelligence utilises only a small portion for co-ordinated knowledge, our will utilises a smaller percentage for action. A narrow selection, a large rejection or reservation, a miserly-spendthrift system of waste of material and unemployment of resources and a scanty and disorderly modicum of useful spending and utilisable balance seems to be the method of Nature in our conscious becoming even as it is in the field of the material universe. But this is only in appearance, for it would be a wholly untrue account to say that all that is not thus saved up and utilised is destroyed, becomes null and has passed away ineffectually and in vain. A great part of it has been quietly used by Nature herself to form us and actuates that sufficiently large mass of our growth and becoming and action for which our conscious memory, will and intelligence are not responsible. A still greater part is used by her as a store from which she draws and which she utilises, while we ourselves have utterly forgotten the origin and provenance of this material which we find ourselves employing with a deceptive sense of creation; for we imagine we are creating this new material of our work, when we are only combining results out of that which we have forgotten but Nature in us has remembered. If we admit rebirth as part of her system, we shall realise that all experience has its use; for all experience counts in this prolonged building and nothing is rejected except what has exhausted its utility and would be a burden on the future. A judgment from what appears now in our conscious surface is fallacious: for when we study and understand, we perceive that only a little of her action and growth in us is conscious; the bulk of it is carried on subconsciously as in the rest of her material life. We are not only what we know of ourselves but an immense more which we do not know; our momentary personality is only a bubble on the ocean of our existence.

A superficial observation of our waking consciousness shows us that of a great part of our individual being and becoming we are quite ignorant; it is to us the Inconscient, just as much as the life of the plant, the metal, the earth, the elements. But if we carry our knowledge farther, pushing psychological experiment and observation beyond their normal bounds, we find how vast is the sphere of this supposed Inconscient or this subconscient in our total existence, — the subconscient, so seeming and so called by us because it is a concealed consciousness, — and what a small and fragmentary portion of our being is covered by our waking self-awareness. We arrive at the knowledge that our waking mind and ego are only a superimposition upon a submerged, a subliminal self, — for so that self appears to us, — or, more accurately, an inner being, with a much vaster capacity of experience; our mind and ego are like the crown and dome of a temple jutting out from the waves while the great body of the building is submerged under the surface of the waters.

This concealed self and consciousness is our real or whole being, of which the outer is a part and a phenomenon, a selective formation for a surface use. We perceive only a small number of the contacts of things which impinge upon us; the inner being perceives all that enters or touches us and our environment. We perceive only a part of the workings of our life and being; the inner being perceives so much that we might almost suppose that nothing escapes its view. We remember only a small selection from our perceptions, and of these even we keep a great part in a store-room where we cannot always lay our hand upon what we need; the inner being retains everything that it has ever received and has it always ready to hand. We can form into co-ordinated understanding and knowledge only so much of our perceptions and memories as our trained intelligence and mental capacity can grasp in their sense and appreciate in their relations: the intelligence of the inner being needs no training, but preserves the accurate form and relations of all its perceptions and memories and, — though this is a proposition which may be considered doubtful or difficult to concede in its fullness, — can grasp immediately, when it does not possess already, their significance. And its perceptions are not confined, as are ordinarily those of the waking mind, to the scanty gleanings of the physical senses, but extend far beyond and use, as telepathic phenomena of many kinds bear witness, a subtle sense the limits of which are too wide to be easily fixed. The relations between the surface will or impulsion and the subliminal urge, mistakenly described as unconscious or subconscious, have not been properly studied except in regard to unusual and unorganised manifestations and to certain morbidly abnormal phenomena of the diseased human mind; but if we pursue our observation far enough, we shall find that the cognition and will or impulsive force of the inner being really stand behind the whole conscious becoming; the latter represents only that part of its secret endeavour and achievement which rises successfully to the surface of our life. To know our inner being is the first step towards a real self-knowledge.

If we undertake this self-discovery and enlarge our knowledge of the subliminal self, so conceiving it as to include in it our lower subconscient and upper superconscient ends, we shall discover that it is really this which provides the whole material of our apparent being and that our perceptions, our memories, our effectuations of will and intelligence are only a selection from its perceptions, memories, activities and relations of will and intelligence; our very ego is only a minor and superficial formulation of its self-consciousness and self-experience. It is, as it were, the urgent sea out of which the waves of our conscious becoming arise. But what are its limits? how far does it extend? what is its fundamental nature? Ordinarily, we speak of a subconscious existence and include in this term all that is not on the waking surface. But the whole or the greater part of the inner or subliminal self can hardly be characterised by that epithet; for when we say subconscious, we think readily of an obscure unconsciousness or half-consciousness or else a submerged consciousness below and in a way inferior to and less than our organised waking awareness or, at least, less in possession of itself. But we find, when we go within, that somewhere in our subliminal part, — though not co-extensive with it since it has also obscure and ignorant regions, — there is a consciousness much wider, more luminous, more in possession of itself and things than that which wakes upon our surface and is the percipient of our daily hours; that is our inner being, and it is this which we must regard as our subliminal self and set apart the subconscient as an inferior, a lowest occult province of our nature. In the same way there is a superconscient part of our total existence in which there is what we discover to be our highest self, and this too we can set apart as a higher occult province of our nature.

But what then is the subconscient and where does it begin and how is it related to our surface being or to the subliminal of which it would seem more properly to be a province? We are aware of our body and know that we have a physical existence, even very largely identify ourselves with it, and yet most of its operations are really subconscious to our mental being; not only does the mind take no part in them but, as we suppose, our most physical being has no awareness of its own hidden operations or, by itself, of its own existence; it knows or rather feels only so much of itself as is enlightened by mind-sense and observable by intelligence. We are aware of a vitality working in this bodily form and structure as in the plant or lower animal, a vital existence which is also for the most part subconscious to us, for we only observe some of its movements and reactions. We are partly aware of its operations, but not by any means of all or most of them, and rather of those which are abnormal than those which are normal; its wants impress themselves more forcibly upon us than its satisfactions, its diseases and disorders than its health and its regular rhythm, its death is more poignant to us than its life is vivid; we know as much of it as we can consciously observe and use or as much as forces itself upon us by pain and pleasure and other sensations or as a cause of nervous or physical reaction and disturbance, but no more. Accordingly, we suppose that this vital-physical part of us also is not conscious of its own operations or has only a suppressed consciousness or no-consciousness like the plant or an inchoate consciousness like the incipient animal; it becomes conscious only so far as it is enlightened by mind and observable by intelligence.

This is an exaggeration and a confusion due to our identification of consciousness with mentality and mental awareness. Mind identifies itself to a certain extent with the movements proper to physical life and body and annexes them to its mentality, so that all consciousness seems to us to be mental. But if we draw back, if we separate the mind as witness from these parts of us, we can discover that life and body, — even the most physical parts of life, — have a consciousness of their own, a consciousness proper to an obscurer vital and to a bodily being, even such an elemental awareness as primitive animal forms may have, but in us partly taken up by the mind and to that extent mentalised. Yet it has not, in its independent motion, the mental awareness which we enjoy; if there is mind in it, it is mind involved and implicit in the body and in the physical life: there is no organised self-consciousness, but only a sense of action and reaction, movement, impulse and desire, need, necessary activities imposed by Nature, hunger, instinct, pain, insensibility and pleasure. Although thus inferior, it has this awareness obscure, limited and automatic; but since it is less in possession of itself, void of what to us is the stamp of mentality, we may justly call it the submental, but not so justly the subconscious part of our being. For when we stand back from it, when we can separate our mind from its sensations, we perceive that this is a nervous and sensational and automatically dynamic mode of consciousness, a gradation of awareness different from the mind: it has its own separate reactions to contacts and is sensitive to them in its own power of feeling; it does not depend for that on the mind's perception and response. The true subconscious is other than this vital or physical substratum; it is the Inconscient vibrating on the borders of consciousness, sending up its motions to be changed into conscious stuff, swallowing into its depths

impressions of past experience as seeds of unconscious habit and
returning them constantly but often chaotically to the surface
consciousness, missioning upwards much futile or perilous stuff
of which the origin is obscure to us, in dream, in mechanical
repetitions of all kinds, in untraceable impulsions and motives,
in mental, vital, physical perturbations and upheavals, in dumb
automatic necessities of our obscurest parts of nature.

But the subliminal self has not at all this subconscious character: it is in full possession of a mind, a life-force, a clear
subtle-physical sense of things. It has the same capacities as
our waking being, a subtle sense and perception, a comprehensive extended memory and an intensive selecting intelligence,
will, self-consciousness; but even though the same in kind, they
are wider, more developed, more sovereign. And it has other
capacities which exceed those of our mortal mind because of a
power of direct awareness of the being, whether acting in itself or
turned upon its object, which arrives more swiftly at knowledge,
more swiftly at effectivity of will, more deeply at understanding
and satisfaction of impulse. Our surface mind is hardly a true
mentality, so involved, bound, hampered, conditioned is it by the
body and bodily life and the limitations of the nerve-system and
the physical organs. But the subliminal self has a true mentality
superior to these limitations; it exceeds the physical mind and
physical organs although it is aware of them and their works
and is, indeed, in a large degree their cause or creator. It is only
subconscious in the sense of not bringing all or most of itself
to the surface, it works always behind the veil: it is rather a
secret intraconscient and circumconscient than a subconscient;
for it envelops quite as much as it supports the outer nature.
This description is no doubt truest of the deeper parts of the
subliminal; in other layers of it nearer to our surface there is a
more ignorant action and those who, penetrating within, pause
in the zones of lesser coherence or in the No-man's-land between
the subliminal and the surface, may fall into much delusion and
confusion: but that too, though ignorant, is not of the nature of
the subconscious; the confusion of these intermediate zones has
no kinship to the Inconscience.

We might say then that there are three elements in the totality of our being: there is the submental and the subconscient which appears to us as if it were inconscient, comprising the material basis and a good part of our life and body; there is the subliminal, which comprises the inner being, taken in its entirety of inner mind, inner life, inner physical with the soul or psychic entity supporting them; there is this waking consciousness which the subliminal and the subconscient throw up on the surface, a wave of their secret surge. But even this is not an adequate account of what we are; for there is not only something deep within behind our normal self-awareness, but something also high above it: that too is ourselves, other than our surface mental personality, but not outside our true self; that too is a country of our spirit. For the subliminal proper is no more than the inner being on the level of the Knowledge-Ignorance luminous, powerful and extended indeed beyond the poor conception of our waking mind, but still not the supreme or the whole sense of our being, not its ultimate mystery. We become aware, in a certain experience, of a range of being superconscient to all these three, aware too of something, a supreme highest Reality sustaining and exceeding them all, which humanity speaks of vaguely as Spirit, God, the Oversoul: from these superconscient ranges we have visitations and in our highest being we tend towards them and to that supreme Spirit. There is then in our total range of existence a superconscience as well as a subconscience and inconscience, overarching and perhaps enveloping our subliminal and our waking selves, but unknown to us, seemingly unattainable and incommunicable.

But with the extension of our knowledge we discover what this Spirit or Oversoul is: it is ultimately our own highest deepest vastest Self, it is apparent on its summits or by reflection in ourselves as Sachchidananda creating us and the world by the power of His divine Knowledge-Will, spiritual, supramental, truth-conscious, infinite. That is the real Being, Lord and Creator, who, as the Cosmic Self veiled in Mind and Life and Matter, has descended into that which we call the Inconscient and constitutes and directs its subconscient existence by His supramental will and knowledge, has ascended out of the Inconscient and dwells in the inner being constituting and directing its subliminal existence by the same will and knowledge, has cast up out of the subliminal our surface existence and dwells secretly in it overseeing with the same supreme light and mastery its stumbling and groping movements. If the subliminal and subconscient may be compared to a sea which throws up the waves of our surface mental existence, the superconscience may be compared to an ether which constitutes, contains, overroofs, inhabits and determines the movements of the sea and its waves. It is there in this higher ether that we are inherently and intrinsically conscious of our self and spirit, not as here below by a reflection in silent mind or by acquisition of the knowledge of a hidden Being within us; it is through it, through that ether of superconscience, that we can pass to a supreme status, knowledge, experience. Of this superconscient existence through which we can arrive at the highest status of our real, our supreme Self, we are normally even more ignorant than of the rest of our being; yet is it into the knowledge of it that our being emerging out of the involution in Inconscience is struggling to evolve. This limitation to our surface existence, this unconsciousness of our highest as of our inmost self, is our first, our capital ignorance.

We exist superficially by a becoming in Time; but here again out of that becoming in Time the surface mind, which we call ourselves, is ignorant of all the long past and the long future, aware only of the little life which it remembers and not of all even of that; for much of it is lost to its observation, much to its memory. We readily believe, — for the simple and compelling but insufficient reason that we do not remember, have not perceived, are not informed of anything else, — that we came into existence first by our physical birth into this life and shall cease to exist by the death of this body and the cessation of this brief physical activity. But while this is true of our physical mentality and physical vitality, our corporeal sheath, for they have been constituted at our birth and are dissolved by death, it is not true of our real becoming in Time. For our real self in the cosmos is the Superconscient which becomes the subliminal self and throws up this apparent surface self to act out the brief and limited part assigned to it between birth and death as a present living and conscious self-formation of the being in the stuff of a world of inconscient Nature. The true being which we are no more dies by the cessation of one life than the actor ceases to exist when he has finished one of his parts or the poet when he has poured out something of himself in one of his poems; our mortal personality is only such a role or such a creative self-expression. Whether or no we accept the theory of many births of the same soul or psychic being in various human bodies upon this earth, certain it is that our becoming in Time goes far back into the past and continues far on into the future. For neither the superconscient nor the subliminal can be limited by a few moments of Time: the one is eternal and Time is only one of its modes; to the other, to the subliminal, it is an infinite field of various experience and the very existence of the being presupposes all the past for its own and equally all the future. Yet of this past which alone explains our present being, our mind knows, if knowledge it can be called, only this actual physical existence and its memories: of the future which alone explains the constant trend of our becoming, it knows nothing. So fixed are we in the experience of our ignorance that we even insist that the one can be known only by its vestiges and the other cannot be known, because the future is not yet and the past is no longer in existence; yet are they both here in us, the past involved and active, the future ready to evolve in the continuity of the secret spirit. This is another limiting and frustrating ignorance.

But even here the self-ignorance of man does not end; for not only is he ignorant of his superconscient Self, of his subliminal self, of his subconscient self, he is ignorant of his world in which he presently lives, which constantly acts on and through him and on which and by which he has to act. And the stamp of his ignorance is this, that he regards it as something quite separate from him, as not-self because it is other than his individual nature-formation and his ego. So too when he confronts his superconscient Self, he thinks of it first as something quite other than he, an external, even extracosmic God; when he confronts and becomes aware of his subliminal self, it seems to him at first another greater person or another consciousness than his own which can support and guide him. Of the world he regards only one little foam-bubble, his life and body, as himself. But when we get into our subliminal consciousness, we find it extending itself to be commensurate with its world; when we get into our superconscient Self, we find that the world is only its manifestation and that all in it is the One, all in it is our self. We see that there is one indivisible Matter of which our body is a knot, one indivisible Life of which our life is an eddy, one indivisible Mind of which our mind is a receiving and recording, forming or translating and transmitting station, one indivisible Spirit of which our soul and individual being are a portion or a manifestation. It is the ego-sense which clinches the division and in which the ignorance we superficially are finds its power to maintain the strong though always permeable walls it has created to be its own prison. Ego is the most formidable of the knots which keep us tied to the Ignorance.

As we are ignorant of our existence in Time except the small hour which we remember, so we are ignorant of ourselves in Space except the small span of which we are mentally and sensationally conscious, the single body that moves there and the mind and life which are identified with it, and we regard the environment as a not-self we have to deal with and use: it is this identification and this conception that form the life of the ego. Space according to one view is only the co-existence of things or of souls; the Sankhya affirms the plurality of souls and their independent existence, and their co-existence is then only possible by the unity of Nature-force, their field of experience, Prakriti: but, even granting this, the co-existence is there and it is in the end co-existence in one Being. Space is the self-conceptive extension of that one Being; it is the one spiritual Existence displaying the field of movement of its Conscious-Force in its own self as Space. Because that Conscious-Force concentrates in manifold bodies, lives, minds and the soul presides over one of them, therefore our mentality is concentrated in this and regards this as itself and all the rest as not-self, just as it regards its one life on which it concentrates by a similar ignorance as its whole term of existence cut off from the past and the future. Yet we cannot really know our own mentality without knowing the one Mind, our own vitality without knowing the one Life, our own body without knowing the one Matter; for not only is their nature determined by the nature of that, but by that their activities are at every moment being influenced and determined. But, with all this sea of being flowing in on us, we do not participate in its consciousness, but know of it only so much as can be brought into the surface of our minds and co-ordinated there. The world lives in us, thinks in us, forms itself in us; but we imagine that it is we who live, think, become separately by ourselves and for ourselves. As we are ignorant of our timeless, of our superconscient, of our subliminal and subconscient selves, so are we ignorant of our universal self. This alone saves us that ours is an ignorance which is full of the impulse and strives irresistibly, eternally, by the very law of its being towards the realisation of self-possession and self-knowledge. A many-sided Ignorance striving to become an all-embracing Knowledge is the definition of the consciousness of man the mental being, — or, looking at it from another side, we may say equally that it is a limited separate awareness of things striving to become an integral consciousness and an integral Knowledge.

Chapter XII

The Origin of the Ignorance

By energism of consciousness[1] Brahman is massed; from that
Matter is born and from Matter Life and Mind and the worlds.

Mundaka Upanishad.[2]

He desired, "May I be Many", he concentrated in Tapas,
by Tapas he created the world; creating, he entered into it;
entering, he became the existent and the beyond-existence, he
became the expressed and the unexpressed, he became knowledge and ignorance, he became the truth and the falsehood:
he became the truth, even all this whatsoever that is. "That
Truth" they call him. *Taittiriya Upanishad.*[3]

Energism of consciousness[4] is Brahman.

Taittiriya Upanishad.[5]

IT BECOMES necessary and possible, now that so much has
been fixed, to consider at close quarters the problem of the
Ignorance from the point of view of its pragmatic origin, the
process of consciousness which brought it into existence. It is
on the basis of an integral Oneness as the truth of existence that
we have to consider the problem and see how far the different
possible solutions are on this basis applicable. How could this
manifold ignorance or this narrowly self-limiting and separative
knowledge arise and come into action or maintain itself in action in an absolute Being who must be absolute consciousness
and therefore cannot be subject to ignorance? How is even an
apparent division effectively operated and kept in continuance
in the Indivisible? The Being, integrally one, cannot be ignorant
of itself; and since all things are itself, conscious modifications,

[1] Tapas.   [2] I. 1. 8.   [3] II. 6.   [4] Tapas.   [5] III. 2-5.

determinations of its being, it cannot either be ignorant of things, of their true nature, of their true action. But though we say that we are That, that the Jivatman or individual self is no other than the Paramatman, no other than the Absolute, yet we are certainly ignorant both of ourselves and things, from which this contradiction results that what must be in its very grain incapable of ignorance is yet capable of it, and has plunged itself into it by some will of its being or some necessity or possibility of its nature. We do not ease the difficulty if we plead that Mind, which is the seat of ignorance, is a thing of Maya, non-existent, not-Brahman, and that Brahman, the Absolute, the sole Existence cannot in any way be touched by the ignorance of mind which is part of the illusory being, Asat, the Non-Existence. This is an escape which is not open to us if we admit an integral Oneness: for then it is evident that, in making so radical a distinction and at the same time cancelling it by terming it illusory, we are using the magic or Maya of thought and word in order to conceal from ourselves the fact that we are dividing and denying the unity of the Brahman; for we have erected two opposite powers, Brahman incapable of illusion and self-illusive Maya, and pitchforked them into an impossible unity. If Brahman is the sole existence, Maya can be nothing but a power of Brahman, a force of his consciousness or a result of his being; and if the Jivatman, one with Brahman, is subject to its own Maya, the Brahman in it is subject to Maya. But this is not intrinsically or fundamentally possible: the subjection can only be a submission of something in Nature to an action of Nature which is part of the conscious and free movement of the Spirit in things, a play of its own self-manifesting Omniscience. Ignorance must be part of the movement of the One, a development of its consciousness knowingly adopted, to which it is not forcibly subjected but which it uses for its cosmic purpose.

It is not open to us to get rid of the whole difficulty by saying that the Jivatman and the Supreme are not One, but eternally different, the one subject to ignorance, the other absolute in being and consciousness and therefore in knowledge; for this contradicts the supreme experience and the whole experience which is that of unity in being, whatever difference there may be in the action of Nature. It is easier to accept the fact of unity in difference which is so evident and pervasive in all the building of the universe and satisfy ourselves with the statement that we are one, yet different, one in essential being and therefore in essential nature, different in soul-form and therefore in active nature. But we thereby only state the fact, leaving the difficulty raised by the fact unsolved, how that which belongs in the essence of its being to the unity of the Absolute and should therefore be one with it and with all in consciousness, comes to be divided in its dynamic form of self and its activity and subject to Ignorance. It is also to be noted that the statement would not be wholly true, since it is possible for the Jivatman to enter into unity with the active nature of the One and not only into a static essential oneness. Or we may escape the difficulty by saying that beyond or above existence and its problems there is the Unknowable which is beyond or above our experience, and that the action of Maya has already begun in the Unknowable before the world began and therefore is itself unknowable and inexplicable in its cause and its origin. This would be a sort of idealistic as opposed to a materialistic Agnosticism. But all Agnosticism is subject to this objection that it may be nothing but our refusal to know, a too ready embracing of an apparent and present restriction or constriction of consciousness, a sense of impotence which may be permitted to the immediate limitations of the mind but not to the Jivatman who is one with the Supreme. The Supreme must surely know himself and the cause of ignorance, and therefore the Jivatman has no ground to despair of any knowledge or deny his capacity of knowing the integral Supreme and the original cause of his own present ignorance.

The Unknowable, if it is at all, may be a supreme state of Sachchidananda beyond our highest conceptions of existence, consciousness and bliss; that is what was evidently meant by the Asat, the Non-Existent of the Taittiriya Upanishad, which alone was in the beginning and out of which the existent was born, and possibly too it may be the inmost sense of the Nirvana of the Buddha: for the dissolution of our present state by Nirvana may be a reaching to some highest state beyond all notion or experience of self even, an ineffable release from our sense of existence. Or it may be the Upanishad's absolute and unconditioned bliss which is beyond expression and beyond understanding, because it surpasses all that we can conceive of or describe as consciousness and existence. This is the sense in which we have already accepted it; for the acceptation commits us only to a refusal to put a limit to the ascension of the Infinite. Or, if it is not this, if it is something quite different from existence, even from an unconditioned existence, it must be the absolute Non-Being of the nihilistic thinker.

But out of absolute Nothingness nothing can come, not even anything merely apparent, not even an illusion; and if the absolute Non-Existence is not that, then it can only be an absolute eternally unrealised Potentiality, an enigmatic zero of the Infinite out of which relative potentialities may at any time emerge, but only some actually succeed in emerging into phenomenal appearance. Out of this Non-Existence anything may arise, and there is no possibility of saying what or why; it is for all practical purposes a seed of absolute chaos out of which by some happy, — or rather unhappy, — accident there has emerged the order of a universe. Or we may say that there is no real order of the universe; what we take for such is a persistent habit of the senses and the life and a figment of the mind and it is useless to seek for an ultimate reason of things. Out of an absolute chaos all paradox and absurdity can be born, and the world is such a paradox, a mysterious sum of contraries and puzzles, or, it may be, in effect, as some have felt or thought, a huge error, a monstrous, an infinite delirium. Of such a universe not an absolute Consciousness and Knowledge, but an absolute Inconscience and Ignorance may be the source. Anything may be true in such a cosmos: everything may have been born out of nothing; thinking mind may be only a disease of unthinking Force or inconscient Matter; dominant order, which we suppose to be existence according to the truth of things, may be really the mechanical law of an eternal self-ignorance and not the self-evolution of a supreme self-ruling conscious

Will; perpetual existence may be the constant phenomenon of an eternal Nihil. All opinions about the origins of things become of an equal force, since all are equally valid or invalid; for all become equally possible where there is no sure starting-point and no ascertainable goal of the revolutions of the becoming. All these opinions have been held by the human mind and in all there has been profit, even if we regard them as errors; for errors are permitted to the mind because they open doors upon truth, negatively by destroying opposite errors, positively by preparing an element in a new constructive hypothesis. But, pushed too far, this view of things leads to the negation of the whole aim of philosophy, which seeks for knowledge and not for chaos and which cannot fulfil itself if the last word of knowledge is the Unknowable, but only if it is something, to use the words of the Upanishad, which being known all is known. The Unknowable, — not absolutely unknowable, but beyond mental knowledge, — can only be a higher degree in the intensity of being of that Something, a degree beyond the loftiest summit attainable by mental beings, and, if it were known as it must be known to itself, that discovery would not destroy entirely what is given us by our supreme possible knowledge but rather carry it to a higher fulfilment and larger truth of what it has already gained by self-vision and self-experience. It is then this Something, an Absolute which can be so known that all truths can stand in it and by it and find there their reconciliation, that we must discover as our starting-point and keep as our constant base of thinking and seeing and by it find a solution of the problem; for it is That alone that can carry in it a key to the paradoxes of the universe.

This Something is, as Vedanta insists and as we have throughout insisted, in its manifest nature Sachchidananda, a trinity of absolute existence, consciousness and bliss. It is from this primal truth that we must start in approaching the problem, and it is evident then that the solution must be found in an action of consciousness manifesting itself as knowledge and yet limiting that knowledge in such a way as to create the phenomenon of the Ignorance, — and since the Ignorance is a phenomenon of the dynamic action of Force of Consciousness, not an essential fact but a creation, a consequence of that action, it is this Force aspect of Consciousness that it will be fruitful to consider. Absolute consciousness is in its nature absolute power; the nature of Chit is Shakti: Force or Shakti concentrated and energised for cognition or for action in a realising power effective or creative, the power of conscious being dwelling upon itself and bringing out, as it were, by the heat of its incubation[6] the seed and development of all that is within it or, to use a language convenient to our minds, of all its truths and potentialities, has created the universe. If we examine our own consciousness, we shall see that this power of its energy applying itself to its object is really the most positive dynamic force it has; by that it arrives at all its knowledge and its action and its creation. But for us there are two objects on which the dynamism within can act, ourselves, the internal world, and others, whether creatures or things, the external world around us. To Sachchidananda this distinction with its effective and operative consequences does not apply in the same way as for us, because all is himself and within himself and there is no such division as we make by the limitations of our mind. Secondly, in us only a part of the force of our being is identified with our voluntary action, with our will engaged in mental or other activity, the rest is to our surface mental awareness involuntary in its action or subconscient or superconscient, and from this division also a great number of important practical consequences emerge: but in Sachchidananda this division too and its consequences do not apply, since all is his one indivisible self and all action and result

---

[6] Tapas means literally heat, afterwards any kind of energism, askesis, austerity of conscious force acting upon itself or its object. The world was created by Tapas in the form, says the ancient image, of an egg which being broken, again by Tapas, heat of incubation of conscious force, the Purusha emerged, Soul in Nature, like a bird from the egg. It may be observed that the usual translation of the word *tapasyā* in English books, "penance", is quite misleading, — the idea of penance entered rarely into the austerity practised by Indian ascetics. Nor was mortification of the body the essence even of the most severe and self-afflicting austerities; the aim was rather an overpassing of the hold of the bodily nature on the consciousness or else a supernormal energising of the consciousness and will to gain some spiritual or other object.

are movements of his one indivisible will, his consciousness-force in dynamic operation. Tapas is the nature of action of his consciousness as of ours, but it is the integral Tapas of an integral consciousness in an indivisible Existence.

But here a question may arise, since there is a passivity in Existence and in Nature as well as an activity, immobile status as well as kinesis, what is the place and role of this Force, this power and its concentration in regard to a status where there is no play of energy, where all is immobile. In ourselves we habitually associate our Tapas, our conscious force, with active consciousness, with energy in play and in internal or external act and motion. That which is passive in us produces no action or only an involuntary or mechanical action, and we do not associate it with our will or conscious force; still, since there too there is the possibility of action or the emergence of an automatic activity, it must have at least a passively responsive or automatic conscious force in it; or there is in it either a secretly positive or a negative and inverse Tapas. It may also be that there is a larger conscious force, power or will in our being unknown to us which is behind this involuntary action, — if not a will, at least a force of some kind which itself initiates action or else responds to the contacts, suggestions, stimulations of the universal Energy. In Nature also we know that things stable, inert or passive are yet maintained in their energy by a secret and unceasing motion, an energy in action upholding the apparent immobility. Here too, then, all is due to the presence of Shakti, to the action of its power in concentration, its Tapas. But beyond this, beyond this relative aspect of status and kinesis, we find that we have the power to arrive at what seems to us an absolute passivity or immobility of our consciousness in which we cease from all mental and physical activity. There seem, then, to be an active consciousness in which consciousness works as an energy throwing up knowledge and activity out of itself and of which therefore Tapas is the character, and a passive consciousness in which consciousness does not act as an energy, but only exists as a status and of which therefore absence of Tapas or force in action is the character. Is the apparent absence of Tapas in this state real, or is there such an effective distinction in Sachchid-ananda? It is affirmed that there is: the dual status of Brahman, quiescent and creative, is indeed one of the most important and fruitful distinctions in Indian philosophy; it is besides a fact of spiritual experience.

Here let us observe, first, that by this passivity in ourselves we arrive from particular and broken knowledge at a greater, a one and a unifying knowledge; secondly, that if, in the state of passivity, we open ourselves entirely to what is beyond, we can become aware of a Power acting upon us which we feel to be not our own in the limited egoistic sense, but universal or transcendental, and that this Power works through us for a greater play of knowledge, a greater play of energy, action and result, which also we feel to be not our own, but that of the Divine, of Sachchidananda, ourselves only its field or channel. The result happens in both cases because our individual con-sciousness rests from an ignorant limited action and opens itself to the supreme status or to the supreme action. In the latter, the more dynamic opening, there is power and play of knowledge and action, and that is Tapas; but in the former also, in the static consciousness, there is evidently a power for knowledge and a concentration of knowledge or at least a concentration of consciousness in immobility and a self-realisation, and that too is Tapas. Therefore it would seem that Tapas, concentration of power of consciousness, is the character of both the passive and the active consciousness of Brahman, and that our own passivity also has a certain character of an unseen supporting or instrumentalising Tapas. It is a concentration of energy of consciousness that sustains, while it lasts, all creation, all action and kinesis; but it is also a concentration of power of conscious-ness that supports inwardly or informs all status, even the most immobile passivity, even an infinite stillness or an eternal silence.

But still, it may be said, these are in the end two different things, and this is shown by their difference of opposite results; for a resort to the passivity of Brahman leads to the cessation of this existence and a resort to the active Brahman leads to its continuance. But here too, let us observe that this distinction arises by a movement of the individual soul from one poise to another, from the poise of Brahman-consciousness in the world, where it is a fulcrum for the universal action, to or towards the poise of Brahman-consciousness beyond the world, where it is a power for the withholding of energy from the universal action. Moreover, if it is by energy of Tapas that the dispensing of force of being in the world-action is accomplished, it is equally by the energy of Tapas that the drawing back of that force of being is accomplished. The passive consciousness of Brahman and its active consciousness are not two different, conflicting and incompatible things; they are the same consciousness, the same energy, at one end in a state of self-reservation, at the other cast into a motion of self-giving and self-deploying, like the stillness of a reservoir and the coursing of the channels which flow from it. In fact, behind every activity there is and must be a passive power of being from which it arises, by which it is supported, which even, we see in the end, governs it from behind without being totally identified with it, — in the sense at least of being itself all poured out into the action and indistinguishable from it. Such a self-exhausting identification is impossible; for no action, however vast, exhausts the original power from which it proceeds, leaving nothing behind it in reserve. When we get back into our own conscious being, when we stand back from our own action and see how it is done, we discover that it is our whole being which stands behind any particular act or sum of activities, passive in the rest of its integrality, active in its limited dispensation of energy; but that passivity is not an incapable inertia, it is a poise of self-reserved energy. A similar truth must apply still more completely to the conscious being of the Infinite, whose power, in silence of status as in creation, must also be infinite.

It is immaterial for the moment to inquire whether the passivity out of which all emerges is absolute or only relative to the observable action from which it holds back. It is enough to note that, though we make the distinction for the convenience of our minds, there is not a passive Brahman and an active Brahman, but one Brahman, an Existence which reserves Its Tapas in what we call passivity and gives Itself in what we call Its activity. For the purposes of action, these are two poles of one being or a double power necessary for creation; the action proceeds on its circuit from the reservation and returns to it, presumably, the energies that were derived, to be again thrown out in a fresh circuit. The passivity of Brahman is Tapas or concentration of Its being dwelling upon Itself in a self-absorbed concentration of Its immobile energy; the activity is Tapas of Its being releasing what It held out of that incubation into mobility and travelling in a million waves of action, dwelling still upon each as It travels and liberating in it the being's truths and potentialities. There too is a concentration of force, but a multiple concentration, which seems to us a diffusion. But it is not really a diffusion, but a deploying; Brahman does not cast Its energy out of Itself to be lost in some unreal exterior void, but keeps it at work within Its being, conserving it unabridged and undiminished in all its continual process of conversion and transmutation. The passivity is a great conservation of Shakti, of Tapas supporting a manifold initiation of movement and transmutation into forms and happenings; the activity is a conservation of Shakti, of Tapas in the movement and transmutation. As in ourselves, so in Brahman, both are relative to each other, both simultaneously co-exist, pole and pole in the action of one Existence.

The Reality then is neither an eternal passivity of immobile Being nor an eternal activity of Being in movement, nor is It an alternation in Time between these two things. Neither in fact is the sole absolute truth of Brahman's reality; their opposition is only true of It in relation to the activities of Its consciousness. When we perceive Its deployment of the conscious energy of Its being in the universal action, we speak of It as the mobile active Brahman; when we perceive Its simultaneous reservation of the conscious energy of Its being kept back from the action, we speak of It as the immobile passive Brahman, — Saguna and Nirguna, Kshara and Akshara: otherwise the terms would have no meaning; for there is one reality and not two independent realities, one immobile, the other mobile. In the ordinary view of the soul's evolution into the action, *pravṛtti*, and its involution into the passivity, *nivṛtti*, it is supposed that in the action the individual soul becomes ignorant, nescient of its passive which is supposed to be its true being, and in the passivity it becomes finally nescient of its active which is supposed to be its false or only apparent being. But this is because these two movements take place alternately for us, as in our sleep and waking; we pass in waking into nescience of our sleeping condition, in sleep into nescience of our waking being. But this happens because only part of our being performs this alternative movement and we falsely think of ourselves as only that partial existence: but we can discover by a deeper psychological experience that the larger being in us is perfectly aware of all that happens even in what is to our partial and superficial being a state of unconsciousness; it is limited neither by sleep nor by waking. So it is in our relations with Brahman who is our real and integral being. In the ignorance we identify ourselves with only a partial consciousness, mental or spiritual-mental in its nature, which becomes nescient of its self of status by movement; in this part of us, when we lose the movement, we lose at the same time our hold on our self of action by entering into passivity. By an entire passivity the mind falls asleep or enters into trance or else is liberated into a spiritual silence; but though it is a liberation from the ignorance of the partial being in its flux of action, it is earned by putting on a luminous nescience of the dynamic Reality or a luminous separation from it: the spiritual-mental being remains self-absorbed in a silent essential status of existence and becomes either incapable of active consciousness or repugnant to all activity; this release of silence is a status through which the soul passes in its journey towards the Absolute. But there is a greater fulfilment of our true and integral being in which both the static and the dynamic sides of the self are liberated and fulfilled in That which upholds both and is limited neither by action nor by silence.

For Brahman does not pass alternately from passivity to activity and back to passivity by cessation of Its dynamic force of being. If that were really true of the integral Reality, then, while the universe continued, there would be no passive Brahman in existence, all would be action, and, if our universe were dissolved, there would be no active Brahman, all would become cessation and immobile stillness. But this is not so, for we can become aware of an eternal passivity and self-concentrated calm penetrating and upholding all the cosmic activity and all its multiple concentrated movement, — and this could not be if, so long as any activity continued, the concentrated passivity did not exist supporting it and within it. Integral Brahman possesses both the passivity and the activity simultaneously and does not pass alternately from one to the other as from a sleep to a waking: it is only some partial activity in us which seems to do that, and we by identifying ourselves with that partial activity have the appearance of this alternation from one nescience to another nescience; but our true, our integral being is not subject to these opposites and it does not need to become unaware of its dynamic self in order to possess its self of silence. When we get the integral knowledge and the integral liberation of both soul and nature free from the disabilities of the restricted partial and ignorant being, we too can possess the passivity and the activity with a simultaneous possession, exceeding both these poles of the universality, limited by neither of these powers of the Self in its relation or non-relation to Nature.

The Supreme, it has been declared in the Gita, exceeds both the immobile self and the mobile being; even put together they do not represent all he is. For obviously we do not mean, when we speak of his possessing them simultaneously, that he is the sum of a passivity and an activity, an integer made of those two fractions, passive with three fourths of himself, active with one fourth of his existence. In that case, Brahman might be a sum of nescinces, the passive three fourths not only indifferent to but quite ignorant of all that the activity is doing, the active one fourth quite unaware of the passivity and unable to possess it except by ceasing from action. Even, Brahman the sum might amount to something quite different from his two fractions, something, as it were, up and aloof, ignorant of and irresponsible for anything which some mystic Maya was at once obstinately doing and rigidly abstaining from doing in the two fractions of his existence. But it is clear that Brahman the Supreme Being must be aware both of the passivity and the activity and regard them not as his absolute being, but as opposite, yet, mutually satisfying terms of his universalities. It cannot be true that Brahman, by an eternal passivity, is unaware, entirely separated from his own activities; free, he contains them in himself, supports them with his eternal power of calm, initiates them from his eternal poise of energy. It must be equally untrue that Brahman in his activity is unaware of or separated from his passivity; omnipresent, he is there supporting the action, possesses it always in the heart of the movement and is eternally calm and still and free and blissful in all the whirl of its energies. Nor in either silence or action can he be at all unaware of his absolute being, but knows that all he expresses through them draws its value and power from the power of that absolute existence. If it seems otherwise to our experience, it is because we identify with one aspect and by that exclusiveness fail to open ourselves to the integral Reality.

There necessarily follows an important first result, already arrived at from other viewpoints, that the Ignorance cannot have the origin of its existence or the starting-point of its dividing activities in the absolute Brahman or in integral Sachchidananda; it belongs only to a partial action of the being with which we identify ourselves, just as in the body we identify ourselves with that partial and superficial consciousness which alternates between sleep and waking: it is indeed this identification putting aside all the rest of the Reality behind us that is the constituting cause of the Ignorance. And if Ignorance is not an element or power proper to the absolute nature of the Brahman or to Its integrality, there can be no original and primal Ignorance. Maya, if it be an original power of the consciousness of the Eternal, cannot itself be an ignorance or in any way akin to the nature of ignorance, but must be a transcendent and universal power of self-knowledge and all-knowledge; ignorance can only intervene as a minor and subsequent movement, partial and relative. Is it then something inherent in the multiplicity of souls? Does it come into being immediately Brahman views himself in the multiplicity, and does that multiplicity consist of a sum of souls each in its very nature fractional and divided from all the others in consciousness, unable to become aware of them at all except as things external to it, linked at most by communication from body to body or mind to mind, but incapable of unity? But we have seen that this is only what we seem to be in our most superficial layer of consciousness, the external mind and the physical; when we get back into a subtler, deeper, larger action of our consciousness, we find the walls of division becoming thinner and in the end there is left no wall of division, no Ignorance.

Body is the outward sign and lowest basis of the apparent division which Nature plunging into ignorance and self-nescience makes the starting-point for the recovery of unity by the individual soul, unity even in the midst of the most exaggerated forms of her multiple consciousness. Bodies cannot communicate with each other except by external means and through a gulf of externality; cannot penetrate each other except by division of the penetrated body or by taking advantage of some gap in it, some pre-existent division; cannot unite except by a breaking up and devouring, a swallowing and absorption and so an assimilation, or at most a fusion in which both forms disappear. Mind too, when identified with body, is hampered by its limitations; but in itself it is more subtle and two minds can penetrate each other without hurt or division, can interchange their substance without mutual injury, can in a way become parts of each other: still mind too has its own form which is separative of it from other minds and is apt to take its stand on this separateness. When we get back to soul-consciousness, the obstacles to unity lessen and finally cease to exist altogether. The soul can in its consciousness identify itself with other souls, can contain them and enter into and be contained by them, can realise its unity with them; and this can take place, not in a featureless and indistinguishable sleep, not in a Nirvana in which all distinctions and individualities of soul and mind and body are lost, but in a perfect waking which observes and takes account of all distinctions but exceeds them.

Therefore ignorance and self-limiting division are not inherent and insuperable in the multiplicity of souls, are not the very nature of the multiplicity of Brahman. Brahman, as he exceeds the passivity and the activity, so too exceeds the unity and multiplicity. He is one in himself, but not with a self-limiting unity exclusive of the power of multiplicity, such as is the separated unity of the body and the mind; he is not the mathematical integer, one, which is incapable of containing the hundred and is therefore less than the hundred. He contains the hundred, is one in all the hundred. One in himself, he is one in the many and the many are one in him. In other words, Brahman in his unity of spirit is aware of his multiplicity of souls and in the consciousness of his multiple souls is aware of the unity of all souls. In each soul he, the immanent Spirit, the Lord in each heart, is aware of his oneness. The Jivatman illumined by him, aware of its unity with the One, is also aware of its unity with the many. Our superficial consciousness, identified with body and with divided life and dividing mind, is ignorant; but that also can be illumined and made aware. Multiplicity, then, is not the necessary cause of the ignorance.

Ignorance, as we have already stated, comes in at a later stage, as a later movement, when mind is separated from its spiritual and supramental basis, and culminates in this earth-life where the individual consciousness in the many identifies itself by dividing mind with the form, which is the only safe basis of division. But what is the form? It is, at least as we see it here, a formation of concentrated energy, a knot of the force of consciousness in its movement, a knot maintained in being by a constant whirl of action; but whatever transcendent truth or reality it proceeds from or expresses, it is not in any part of itself in manifestation durable or eternal. It is not eternal in its integrality, nor in its constituting atoms; for they can be disintegrated by dissolving the knot of energy in constant concentrated action which is the sole thing that maintains their apparent stability. It is a concentration of Tapas in movement of force on the form maintaining it in being which sets up the physical basis of division. But all things in the activity are, we have seen, a concentration of Tapas in movement of force upon its object. The origin of the Ignorance must then be sought for in some self-absorbed concentration of Tapas, of Conscious-Force in action on a separate movement of the Force; to us this takes the appearance of mind identifying itself with the separate movement and identifying itself also in the movement separately with each of the forms resulting from it. So it builds a wall of separation which shuts out the consciousness in each form from awareness of its own total self, of other embodied consciousnesses and of universal being. It is here that we must look for the secret of the apparent ignorance of the embodied mental being as well as of the great apparent inconscience of physical Nature. We have to ask ourselves what is the nature of this absorbing, this separating, this self-forgetful concentration which is the obscure miracle of the universe.

Chapter XIII

Exclusive Concentration of Consciousness-Force and the Ignorance

From the kindled fire of Energy of Consciousness, Truth was born and the Law of Truth; from that the Night, from the Night the flowing ocean of being.   *Rig Veda.*[1]

SINCE Brahman is in the essentiality of its universal being a unity and a multiplicity aware of each other and in each other and since in its reality it is something beyond the One and the Many, containing both, aware of both, Ignorance can only come about as a subordinate phenomenon by some concentration of consciousness absorbed in a part knowledge or a part action of the being and excluding the rest from its awareness. There may be either a concentration of the One in itself to the exclusion of the Many or of the Many in their own action to the exclusion of the all-awareness of the One, or of the individual being in himself to the exclusion both of the One and the rest of the Many who are then to him separated units not included in his direct awareness. Or again there may be or there may intervene at a certain point some general rule of exclusive concentration, operative in all these three directions, a concentration of separative active consciousness in a separative movement; but this takes place not in the true self, but in the force of active being, in Prakriti.

This hypothesis we adopt in preference to the others, because none of the others taken by itself will hold or will square with all the facts of existence. Integral Brahman cannot be in

[1] X. 190. 1.

its integrality the source of the Ignorance, because its integrality is in its very nature all-consciousness. The One cannot in its integral conscious being exclude the Many from itself, because the Many would not then at all exist; at most it can stand back somewhere in its consciousness from the cosmic play so as to enable a similar movement in the individual being. The Many in the integrality or in each self of the Many cannot be really ignorant of the One or of others, because by the Many we mean the same divine Self in all, individualised indeed, but still one in conscious being with all in a single universality and one too with the original and transcendent Being. Ignorance is therefore not the natural character of the consciousness of the soul, even of the individual soul; it is the outcome of some particularising action in the executive Conscious-Force when it is absorbed in its works and forgetful of self and of the total reality of the nature. This action cannot be that of the whole being or of the whole force of being, — for the character of that completeness is whole consciousness and not partial consciousness, — it must be a superficial or partial movement absorbed in a superficial or partial action of the consciousness and the energy, concentrated in its formation, oblivious of all else that is not included in the formation or not there overtly operative. Ignorance is Nature's purposeful oblivion of the Self and the All, leaving them aside, putting them behind herself in order to do solely what she has to do in some outer play of existence.

In the infinity of being and its infinite awareness concentration of consciousness, Tapas, is always present as an inherent power of Consciousness-Force: it is a self-held or self-gathered dwelling of the eternal Awareness in itself and on itself or on its object; but the object is always in some way itself, its own being or a manifestation and movement of its being. The concentration may be essential; it may be even a sole indwelling or an entire absorption in the essence of its own being, a luminous or else a self-oblivious self-immersion. Or it may be an integral or else a total-multiple or a part-multiple concentration. Or it may be a single separative regard on one field of its being or movement, a single-pointed concentration in one centre or an absorption in one objective form of its self-existence. The first, the essential, is at one end the superconscient Silence and at the other end the Inconscience; the second, the integral, is the total consciousness of Sachchidananda, the supramental concentration; the third, the multiple, is the method of the totalising or global overmental awareness; the fourth, the separative, is the characteristic nature of the Ignorance. The supreme integrality of the Absolute holds all these states or powers of its consciousness together as a single indivisible being looking at all itself in manifestation with a simultaneous self-vision.

Concentration in this sense of self-held dwelling in itself or on itself as object may be said then to belong to the very nature of conscious being. For, although there is an infinite extension of consciousness and a diffusion of consciousness, it is a self-held self-contained extension or a self-held self-contained diffusion. Although there may seem to be a dispersion of its energies, that is in reality a form of distribution, and is only possible in a superficial field because it is supported by an underlying self-held concentration. An exclusive concentration on or in a single subject or object or domain of being or movement is not a denial or departure from the Spirit's awareness, it is one form of the self-gathering of the power of Tapas. But when the concentration is exclusive, it brings about a holding back behind it of the rest of self-knowledge. It may be aware of the rest all the time, yet act as if it were not aware of it; that would not be a state or act of Ignorance: but if the consciousness erects by the concentration a wall of exclusion limiting itself to a single field, domain or habitation in the movement so that it is aware only of that or aware of all the rest as outside itself, then we have a principle of self-limiting knowledge which can result in a separative knowledge and culminate in a positive and effective ignorance.

We can get some glimpse of what this means, to what it amounts in action, when we look at the nature of exclusive concentration in mental man, in our own consciousness. First of all, we must note that what we mean ordinarily by the man is not his inner self, but only a sum of apparent continuous movement of consciousness and energy in past, present and future to which we give this name. It is this that in appearance does all the works of the man, thinks all his thoughts, feels all his emotions. This energy is a movement of Consciousness-Force concentrated on a temporal stream of inward and outward workings. But we know that behind this stream of energy there is a whole sea of consciousness which is aware of the stream, but of which the stream is unaware; for this sum of surface energy is a selection, an outcome from all the rest that is invisible. That sea is the subliminal self, the superconscient, the subconscient, the intraconscient and circumconscient being, and holding it all together the soul, the psychic entity. The stream is the natural, the superficial man. In this superficial man Tapas, the being's dynamic force of consciousness, is concentrated on the surface in a certain mass of superficial workings; all the rest of itself it has put behind and may be vaguely aware of it there in the unformulated back of its conscious existence, but is not aware of it in this superficial absorbed movement in front. It is not precisely, at any rate in that back or in the depths, ignorant of itself in any essential sense of the word, but for the purposes of its superficial movement and within that movement only it is oblivious of its real, its greater self, by absorption, by exclusive concentration on what it is superficially doing. Yet it is really the hidden sea and not the superficial stream which is doing all the action: it is the sea that is the source of this movement, not the conscious wave it throws up, whatever the consciousness of the wave, absorbed in its movement, living in that, seeing nothing else but that, may think about the matter. And that sea, the real self, the integral conscious being, the integral force of being, is not ignorant; even the wave is not essentially ignorant, — for it contains within itself all the consciousness it has forgotten and but for that it could not act or endure at all, — but it is self-oblivious, absorbed in its own movement, too absorbed to note anything else than the movement while that continues to preoccupy it. A limited practical self-oblivion, not an essential and binding self-ignorance, is the nature of this exclusive concentration which is yet the root of that which works as the Ignorance.

So too we see that man, though a really indivisible stream of Tapas, of conscious energy in Time, capable of acting in the present only by the sum of his past force of working, creating already his future by his past and his present action, yet lives absorbed in the present moment, lives from moment to moment, and is therefore in this superficial action of consciousness, ignorant of his future and ignorant of his past except for that small part of it which at any moment he may recall to him by memory. He does not, however, live in the past; what he recalls is not the past itself, but only the ghost of it, a conceptual shadow of a reality which is now to him dead, non-existent, no longer in being. But all this is an action of the superficial ignorance. The true consciousness within is not unaware of its past; it holds it there, not necessarily in memory but in being, still active, living, ready with its fruits, and sends it up from time to time in memory or more concretely in result of past action or past causes to the superficial conscious being, — that is indeed the true rationale of what is called Karma. It is or can be aware too of the future, for there is somewhere in the inner being a field of cognition open to future knowledge, a prospective as well as a retrospective Time-sense, Time-vision, Time-perception; something in it lives indivisibly in the three times and contains all their apparent divisions, holds the future ready for manifestation within it. Here, then, in this habit of living in the present, we have a second absorption, a second exclusive concentration which complicates and farther limits the being, but simplifies the apparent course of the action by relating it not to the whole infinite course of Time, but to a definite succession of moments.

Therefore in his superficial consciousness man is to himself dynamically, practically, the man of the moment, not the man of the past who once was but is no longer in existence, nor the man of the future who is not yet in being; it is by memory that he links himself with the one, by anticipation with the other: a continuous ego-sense runs through the three times, but this is a centralising mental construction, not an essential or an extended existence containing what was, is and will be. An intuition of self is behind it, but that is an underlying identity, unaffected by the changes of his personality; in his surface formation of being he is not that but what he is at the moment. Yet all the time this existence in the moment is not the real or the whole truth of his being, but only a practical or pragmatic truth for the purposes of the superficial movement of his life and within its limits. It is a truth, not an unreality, but a truth only in its positive part; in its negative parts it is an ignorance, and this negative ignorance limits and often distorts even the practical truth, so that the conscious life of man proceeds according to an ignorance, a partial, a half-true half-false knowledge, not according to the real truth of himself of which he is oblivious. Yet because his real self is the true determinator and governs all secretly from behind, it is after all a knowledge behind which really determines the formed course of his existence; the superficial ignorance erects a necessary limiting outline and supplies the factors by which the outward colour and turn needed for his present human life and his present moment are given to his consciousness and his action. In the same way and for the same reason man identifies himself solely with the name and form he wears in his present existence; he is ignorant of his past before birth even as of his future after death. Yet all that he forgets is contained, present and effective, in the all-retaining integral consciousness within him.

There is a minor pragmatic use of exclusive concentration on the surface which may also give us an indication in spite of its temporary character. The superficial man living from moment to moment plays, as it were, several parts in his present life and, while he is busy with each part, he is capable of an exclusive concentration, an absorption in it, by which he forgets the rest of himself, puts it behind him for the moment, is to that extent self-oblivious. The man is for the moment the actor, the poet, the soldier or whatever else he may have been constituted and formed into by some peculiar and characteristic action of his force of being, his Tapas, his past conscious energy and by the action which develops from it. Not only is he apt to deliver himself up to this exclusive concentration in a part of himself for the time being, but his success in the action very largely depends on the completeness with which he can thus put aside the rest of himself and live only in his immediate work. Yet all the time we can see that it is the whole man who is really doing the action and not merely this particular part of him; what he does, the way he does it, the elements he brings into it, the stamp he gives to his work depends on his whole character, mind, information, genius, all that the past of him has made him, — and not his past in this life only, but in other lives, and again not only his past, but the past, the present and the predestined future both of himself and the world around him are the determinants of his work. The present actor, poet or soldier in him is only a separative determination of his Tapas; it is his force of being organised for a particular kind of action of its energy, a separative movement of Tapas, which is able, — and this ability is not a weakness, a deficiency, but a great power of the consciousness, — to absorb itself in that particular working to the temporary self-oblivion of the rest of itself, even though that rest is present all the time at the back of the consciousness and in the work itself and is active or has its influence in the shaping of the work. This active self-oblivion of the man in his work and the part he plays, differs from the other, the deeper self-oblivion, in that the wall of separation is less phenomenally and not at all enduringly complete; the mind can dissolve its concentration and go back from its work at any time to the consciousness of the larger self of which this was a partial action. The superficial or apparent man cannot so go back at will to the real man within him; he can only do it to some extent abnormally or supernormally in exceptional conditions of his mentality or, more permanently and completely, as the fruit of a long and arduous self-training, self-deepening, self-heightening, self-expansion. Still he can go back; therefore the difference is phenomenal only, not essential: it is, in essence, in both cases the same movement of exclusive concentration, of absorption in a particular aspect of himself, action, movement of force, though with different circumstances and another manner of working.

This power of exclusive concentration is not confined to absorption in a particular character or type of working of one's larger self, but extends to a complete self-forgetfulness in the particular action in which we happen at the moment to be engaged. The actor in moments of great intensity forgets that he is an actor and becomes the part that he is playing on the stage; not that he really thinks himself Rama or Ravana, but that he identifies himself for the time being with the form of character and action which the name represents and so completely as to forget the real man who is playing it. So the poet forgets himself, the man, the worker, in his work and is for the moment only the inspired impersonal energy which works itself out in formation of word and rhythm; of all else he is oblivious. The soldier forgets himself in the act and becomes the charge and the fury and the slaying. In the same way the man who is overcome by intense anger, forgets himself as it is commonly said, or as it has been still more aptly and forcibly put, becomes anger: and these terms express a real truth which is not the whole truth of the man's being at the time, but a practical fact of his conscious energy in action. He does forget himself, forgets all the rest of himself with its other impulses and powers of self-restraint and self-direction, so that he acts simply as the energy of the passion which preoccupies him, becomes that energy for the time being. This is as far as self-forgetfulness can go in the normal active human psychology; for it must return soon to the wider self-aware consciousness of which this self-forgetfulness is only a temporary movement.

But in the larger universal consciousness there must be a power of carrying this movement to its absolute point, to the greatest extreme possible for any relative movement to reach, and this point is reached, not in human unconsciousness which is not abiding and always refers back to the awakened conscious being that man normally and characteristically is, but in the inconscience of material Nature. This inconscience is no more real than the ignorance of exclusive concentration in our temporary being which limits the waking consciousness of man; for as in us, so in the atom, the metal, the plant, in every form of material Nature, in every energy of material Nature, there is, we know, a secret soul, a secret will, a secret intelligence at work, other than the mute self-oblivious form, the Conscient, — conscient even in unconscious things, — of the Upanishad, without whose presence and informing Conscious-Force or Tapas no work of Nature could be done. What is inconscient there is the Prakriti, the formal, the motional action of the energy absorbed in the working, identified with it, to such an extent as to be bound in a sort of trance or swoon of concentration, unable to go back, while imprisoned in that form, to its real self, to the integral conscious being and the integral force of conscious being which it has put behind it, of which in its ecstatic trance of mere working and energy it has become oblivious. Prakriti, the executive Force, becomes unaware of Purusha, the Conscious-Being, holds him hidden within herself and becomes again slowly aware only with the emergence of consciousness from this swoon of the Inconscience. Purusha indeed consents to assume the apparent form of itself which Prakriti constructs for it; it seems to become the Inconscient, the physical being, the vital being, the mental being: but in all these it remains still in reality itself; the light of the secret conscious Being supports and informs the action of the inconscient or emergingly conscious energy of Nature.

The inconscience is superficial like the ignorance of the waking human mind or the inconscience or subconscience of his sleeping mind, and within it is the All-conscient; it is entirely phenomenal, but it is the complete phenomenon. So complete is it that it is only by an impulsion of evolutionary consciousness emerging into other forms less imprisoned by this inconscient method of working that it can come back to itself, recover in the animal a partial awareness, then in man at his highest some possibility of approach to a first more complete though still superficial initiation of a truly conscious working. But still, as in the case of the superficial and the real man where there is also a similar though lesser inability, the difference is phenomenal only. Essentially, in the universal order of things, the inconscience of material Nature is the same exclusive concentration, the same absorption in the work and the energy as in the self-limitation of the waking human mind, or the concentration of the self-forgetting mind in its working; it is only that self-limitation carried to a farthest point of self-forgetfulness which becomes, not a temporary action, but the law of its action. Nescience in Nature is the complete self-ignorance; the partial knowledge and general ignorance of man is a partial self-ignorance marking in her evolutionary order a return towards self-knowledge: but both are and all ignorance is, when examined, a superficially exclusive self-forgetful concentration of Tapas, of the conscious energy of being in a particular line or section of its movement of which alone it is aware or which alone it seems to be on the surface. The ignorance is effective within the bounds of that movement and valid for its purposes, but phenomenal, partial, superficial, not essentially real, not integral. We have to use the word "real" necessarily in a quite limited and not in its absolute sense; for the ignorance is real enough, but it is not the whole truth of our being and by regarding it by itself even its truth is misrepresented to our outer awareness. In that true truth of itself it is an involved Consciousness and Knowledge evolving back to itself, but it is dynamically effective as an Inconscience and an Ignorance.

This being the root-nature of the Ignorance, a practical truth of a phenomenally but not really dividing, of a limiting and sep-arative conscious energy absorbed in its works to the apparent forgetfulness of its integral and real self, we may answer the questions that arise of the why, the where and the how of this movement. The reason for the Ignorance, its necessity, becomes clear enough once we have seen that without it the object of the manifestation of our world would be impossible, could not be done at all, or not completely, or not in the way in which it should be and is done. Each side of the manifold Ignorance has its justification, which is only a part of the one general necessity. Man, living in his timeless being, could not have thrown himself into the stream of Time with that movement of subjection to its flux from moment to moment which is the nature of his present living. Living in his superconscient or subliminal self, he could not have worked out from the knot of his individual mentality the relations which he has to ravel and unravel with the world about him, or would have to do it in a radically different fashion. Living in the universal self and not in the egoistic separative consciousness, he could not evolve that separate action, personality, outlook from himself as the sole or the initial centre and point of reference which is the contribution of the ego-sense to the world-workings.

He has to put on the temporal, the psychological, the egoistic ignorance in order to protect himself against the light of the infinite and the largeness of the universal, so as to develop behind this defence his temporal individuality in the cosmos. He has to live as if in this one life and put on the ignorance of his infinite past and his future: for otherwise, if the past were present to him, he could not work out his present selected relations with his environment in the way intended; his knowledge would be too great for him, it would necessarily alter the whole spirit and balance and form of his action. He has to live in the mind absorbed by this bodily life and not in the Supermind; for otherwise all these protecting walls of ignorance created by the limiting, dividing, differentiating power of mind would not be built or would become too thin and transparent for his purpose.

That purpose for which all this exclusive concentration we call the Ignorance is necessary, is to trace the cycle of self-oblivion and self-discovery for the joy of which the Ignorance is assumed in Nature by the secret spirit. It is not that all cosmic manifestation would otherwise become impossible; but it would be a quite different manifestation from the one in which we live; it would be confined to the higher worlds of the divine Existence or to a typal non-evolving cosmos where each being lived in the whole light of its own law of nature, and this obverse manifestation, this evolving cycle, would be impossible. What is here the goal would be then the eternal condition; what is here a stage would be the perpetuated type of existence. It is to find himself in the apparent opposites of his being and his nature that Sachchidananda descends into the material Nescience and puts on its phenomenal ignorance as a superficial mask in which he hides himself from his own conscious energy, leaving it self-forgetful and absorbed in its works and forms. It is in those forms that the slowly awaking soul has to accept the phenomenal action of an ignorance which is really knowledge awaking progressively out of the original nescience, and it is in the new conditions created by these workings that it has to rediscover itself and divinely transform by that light the life which is thus labouring to fulfil the purpose of its descent into the Inconscience. Not to return as speedily as may be to heavens where perfect light and joy are eternal or to the supracosmic bliss is the object of this cosmic cycle, nor merely to repeat a purposeless round in a long unsatisfactory groove of ignorance seeking for knowledge and never finding it perfectly, — in that case the ignorance would be either an inexplicable blunder of the All-conscient or a painful and purposeless Necessity equally inexplicable, — but to realise the Ananda of the Self in other conditions than the supracosmic, in cosmic being, and to find its heaven of joy and light even in the oppositions offered by the terms of an embodied material existence, by struggle therefore towards the joy of self-discovery, would seem to be the true object of the birth of the soul in the human body and of the labour of the human race in the series of its cycles. The Ignorance is a necessary, though quite subordinate term which the universal Knowledge has imposed on itself that that movement might be possible, — not a blunder and a fall, but a purposeful descent, not a curse, but a divine opportunity. To find and embody the All-Delight in an intense summary of its manifoldness, to achieve a possibility of the infinite Existence which could not be achieved in other conditions, to create out of Matter a temple of the Divinity would seem to be the task imposed on the spirit born into the material universe.

The ignorance, we see, is not in the secret soul, but in the apparent Prakriti; nor does it belong to the whole of that Prakriti, — it cannot, for Prakriti is the action of the All-conscient, — but arises in some development from its original integrality of light and power. Where does that development take place, in what principle of being does it find its opportunity and starting-point? Not, certainly, in the infinite being, the infinite consciousness, the infinite delight which are the supreme planes of existence and from which all else derives or descends into this obscurer ambiguous manifestation. There it can have no place. Not in the

Supermind; for in the Supermind the infinite light and power are always present even in the most finite workings, and the consciousness of unity embraces the consciousness of diversity. It is on the plane of mind that this putting back of the real self-consciousness becomes possible. For mind is that power of the conscious being which differentiates and runs along the lines of differentiation with the sense of diversity prominent and characteristic and the sense of unity behind it only, not characteristic, not the very stuff of its workings. If by any chance this supporting sense of unity could be drawn back, — it is possessed by mind not in its own separate right, but because it has the Supermind behind it, because it reflects the light of the Supermind of which it is a derivative and secondary power, — if a veil could fall between mind and Supermind shutting off the light of the Truth or letting it come through only in rays diffused, scattered, reflected but with distortion and division, then the phenomenon of the Ignorance would intervene. Such a veil exists, says the Upanishad, constituted by the action of Mind itself: it is in Overmind a golden lid which hides the face of the supramental Truth but reflects its image; in Mind it becomes a more opaque and smoky-luminous coverture. That action is the absorbed looking downward of Mind on the diversity which is its characteristic movement and away from the supreme unity which that diversity expresses, until it forgets altogether to remember and support itself by the unity. Even then the unity supports it and makes its activities possible, but the absorbed Energy is unaware of its own origin and greater, real self. Since Mind forgets that from which it derived, because of absorption in the workings of formative Energy, it becomes so far identified with that Energy as to lose hold even on itself, to become totally oblivious in a trance of work which it still supports in its somnambulist action, but of which it is no longer aware. This is the last stage of the descent of consciousness, an abysmal sleep, a fathomless trance of consciousness which is the profound basis of the action of material Nature.

It must be remembered, however, that when we speak of a partial movement of Consciousness-Force absorbed in its forms and actions, in a limited field of its working, this does not imply any real division of its integrality. The putting of the rest of itself behind it has only the effect of making all that rest occult to the frontal immediately active energy in the limited field of movement, but not of shutting it out of the field; in fact the integral Force is there though veiled by the Inconscience, and it is that integral Force supported by the integral self-being which through its frontal energy does all the work and inhabits all the forms created by the movement. It is to be noted also that in order to remove the veil of the Ignorance the conscious Force of being in us uses a reverse action of its power of exclusive concentration; it quiets the frontal movement of Prakriti in the individual consciousness and concentrates exclusively on the concealed inner being, — on the Self or on the true inner, psychic or mental or vital being, the Purusha, — to disclose it. But when it has done so, it need not remain in this opposite exclusiveness; it can resume its integral consciousness or a global consciousness which includes both being of Purusha and action of Prakriti, the soul and its instruments, the Self and the dynamisms of the Self-Power, *ātmaśakti*: it can then embrace its manifestation with a larger consciousness free from the previous limitation, free from the results of Nature's forgetfulness of the indwelling Spirit. Or it may quiet the whole working it has manifested, concentrate on a higher level of Self and Nature, raise the being to it and bring down the powers of the higher level to transform the previous manifestation: all that is so transformed is still included, but as a part of the higher dynamism and its higher values, in a new and greater self-creation. This is what can happen when the Consciousness-Force in our being decides to raise its evolution from the mental to the supramental level. In each case it is Tapas that is effective, but it acts in a different manner according to the thing that has to be done, according to the predetermined process, dynamism, self-deploying of the Infinite.

But still, even if this is the mechanism of the Ignorance, it may be asked whether it does not remain a mystery how the All-conscient could, though in only a partial action of his conscious energy, succeed in arriving at even this superficial ignorance and

inconscience. Even if it were so, it would be worth-while to fix
the exact action of this mystery, its nature, its limits, so that we
may not be appalled by it and misled from the real purpose it
serves and the opportunity it gives. But the mystery is a fiction of
the dividing intellect which, because it finds or creates a logical
opposition between two concepts, thinks there is a real opposition of the two facts observed and therefore an impossibility
of co-existence and unity between them. This Ignorance is, as
we have seen, really a power of the Knowledge to limit itself,
to concentrate itself on the work in hand, an exclusive concentration in practice which does not prevent the full existence and
working of the whole conscious being behind, but a working
in the conditions chosen and self-imposed on the nature. All
conscious self-limitation is a power for its special purpose, not
a weakness; all concentration is a force of conscious being, not
a disability. It is true that while the Supermind is capable of
an integral, comprehensive, multiple, infinite self-concentration,
this is dividing and limited; it is true also that it creates perverse
as well as partial and, in so far, false or only half-true values
of things: but we have seen the object of the limitation and of
this partiality of knowledge; and the object being admitted, the
power to fulfil it must be admitted also in the absolute force of
the absolute Being. This power of self-limitation for a particular working, instead of being incompatible with the absolute
conscious-force of that Being, is precisely one of the powers
we should expect to exist among the manifold energies of the
Infinite.

The Absolute is not really limited by putting forth in itself
a cosmos of relations; it is the natural play of its absolute being, consciousness, force, self-delight. The Infinite is not limited
by building up in itself an infinite series of interplaying finite
phenomena; rather that is its natural self-expression. The One
is not limited by its capacity for multiplicity in which it enjoys
variously its own being; rather that is part of the true description
of an infinite as opposed to a rigid, finite and conceptual unity.
So too the Ignorance, considered as a power of manifoldly self-
absorbed and self-limiting concentration of the conscious being,

is a natural capacity of variation in his self-conscious knowledge, one of the possible poises of relation of the Absolute in its manifestation, of the Infinite in its series of finite workings, of the One in its self-enjoyment in the Many. The power by self-absorption to become unaware of the world which yet at the same time continues in the being, is one extreme of this capacity of consciousness; the power by absorption in the cosmic workings to become ignorant of the self which all the time is carrying on those workings, is the reverse extreme. But neither really limits the integral self-aware existence of Sachchidananda which is superior to these apparent oppositions; even in their opposition they help to express and manifest the Ineffable.

Chapter XIV

The Origin and Remedy of Falsehood, Error, Wrong and Evil

The Lord accepts the sin and the virtue of none; because knowledge is veiled by Ignorance, mortal men are deluded.

Gita.[1]

They live according to another idea of self than the reality, deluded, attached, expressing a falsehood, — as if by an enchantment they see the false as the true.

Maitrayani Upanishad.[2]

They live and move in the Ignorance and go round and round, battered and stumbling, like blind men led by one who is blind. *Mundaka Upanishad.*[3]

One whose intelligence has attained to Unity, casts away from him both sin and virtue. *Gita.*[4]

He who has found the bliss of the Eternal is afflicted no more by the thought, "Why have I not done the good? Why have I done evil?" One who knows the self extricates himself from both these things. *Taittiriya Upanishad.*[5]

These are they who are conscious of the much falsehood in the world; they grow in the house of Truth, they are the strong and invincible sons of Infinity. *Rig Veda.*[6]

---

[1] V. 15.   [2] VII. 10.   [3] I. 2. 8.   [4] II. 50.   [5] II. 9.   [6] VII. 60. 5.

The first and the highest are truth; in the middle there is false-hood, but it is taken between the truth on both sides of it and it draws its being from the truth.[7]

Brihadaranyaka Upanishad.[8]

IF IGNORANCE is in its nature a self-limiting knowledge oblivious of the integral self-awareness and confined to an exclusive concentration in a single field or upon a conceal-ing surface of cosmic movement, what, in this view, are we to make of the problem which most poignantly preoccupies the mind of man when it is turned on the mystery of his own ex-istence and of cosmic existence, the problem of evil? A limited knowledge supported by a secret All-Wisdom as an instrument for working out within the necessary limitations a restricted world-order may be admitted as an intelligible process of the universal Consciousness and Energy; but the necessity of false-hood and error, the necessity of wrong and evil or their utility in the workings of the omnipresent Divine Reality is less easily admissible. And yet if that Reality is what we have supposed it to be, there must be some necessity for the appearance of these contrary phenomena, some significance, some function that they had to serve in the economy of the universe. For in the complete and inalienable self-knowledge of the Brahman which is necessarily all-knowledge, since all this that is is the Brahman, such phenomena cannot have come in as a chance, an intervening accident, an involuntary forgetfulness or confusion of the Consciousness-Force of the All-Wise in the cosmos or an ugly contretemps for which the indwelling Spirit was not prepared and of which it is the prisoner erring in a labyrinth with the utmost difficulty of escape. Nor can it be an inexplicable

---

[7] The truth of the physical reality and the truth of the spiritual and superconscient reality. Into the intermediate subjective and mental realities which stand between them, falsehood can enter, but it takes either truth from above or truth from below as the substance out of which it builds itself and both are pressing upon it to turn its miscon-structions into truth of life and truth of spirit.

[8] V. 5. 1.

mystery of being, original and eternal, of which the divine All-Teacher is incapable of giving an account to himself or to us. There must be behind it a significance of the All-Wisdom itself, a power of the All-Consciousness which permits and uses it for some indispensable function in the present workings of our self-experience and world-experience. This aspect of existence needs now to be examined more directly and determined in its origins and the limits of its reality and its place in Nature.

This problem may be taken up from three points of view, — its relation to the Absolute, the supreme Reality, its origin and place in the cosmic workings, its action and point of hold in the individual being. It is evident that these contrary phenomena have no direct root in the supreme Reality itself, there is nothing there that has this character; they are creations of the Ignorance and Inconscience, not fundamental or primary aspects of the Being, not native to the Transcendence or to the infinite power of the Cosmic Spirit. It is sometimes reasoned that as Truth and Good have their absolutes, so Falsehood and Evil must also have their absolutes, or, if it is not so, then both must belong to the relativity only; Knowledge and Ignorance, Truth and Falsehood, Good and Evil exist only in relation to each other and beyond the dualities here they have no existence. But this is not the fundamental truth of the relation of these opposites; for, in the first place, Falsehood and Evil are, unlike Truth and Good, very clearly results of the Ignorance and cannot exist where there is no Ignorance: they can have no self-existence in the Divine Being, they cannot be native elements of the Supreme Nature. If, then, the limited Knowledge which is the nature of Ignorance renounces its limitations, if Ignorance disappears into Knowledge, evil and falsehood can no longer endure: for both are fruits of unconsciousness and wrong consciousness and, if true or whole consciousness is there replacing Ignorance, they have no longer any basis for their existence. There can therefore be no absolute of falsehood, no absolute of evil; these things are a by-product of the world-movement: the sombre flowers of falsehood and suffering and evil have their root in the black soil of the Inconscient. On the other hand, there is no such intrinsic obstacle to the absoluteness of Truth and Good: the relativity of truth and error, good and evil is a fact of our experience, but it is similarly a by-product, it is not a permanent factor native to existence; for it is true only of the valuations made by the human consciousness, true only of our partial knowledge and partial ignorance.

Truth is relative to us because our knowledge is surrounded by ignorance. Our exact vision stops short at outside appearances which are not the complete truth of things, and, if we go deeper, the illuminations we arrive at are guesses or inferences or intimations, not a sight of indubitable realities: our conclusions are partial, speculative or constructed, our statement of them, which is the expression of our indirect contact with the reality, has the nature of representations or figures, word-images of thought-perceptions that are themselves images, not embodiments of Truth itself, not directly real and authentic. These figures or representations are imperfect and opaque and carry with them their shadow of nescience or error; for they seem to deny or shut out other truths and even the truth they express does not get its full value: it is an end or edge of it that projects into form and the rest is left in the shadow unseen or disfigured or uncertainly visible. It might almost be said that no mental statement of things can be altogether true; it is not Truth bodied, pure and nude, but a draped figure, — often it is only the drapery that is visible. But this character does not apply to truth perceived by a direct action of consciousness or to the truth of knowledge by identity; our seeing there may be limited, but so far as it extends, it is authentic, and authenticity is a first step towards absoluteness: error may attach itself to a direct or identical vision of things by a mental accretion, by a mistaken or illegitimate extension or by the mind's misinterpretation, but it does not enter into the substance. This authentic or identical vision or experience of things is the true nature of knowledge and it is self-existent within the being, although rendered in our minds by a secondary formation that is unauthentic and derivative. Ignorance in its origin has not this self-existence or this authenticity; it exists by a limitation or absence or abeyance of knowledge, error by a deviation from truth, falsehood by a distortion of truth or its contradiction and denial. But it cannot be similarly said of knowledge that in its very nature it exists only by a limitation or absence or abeyance of ignorance: it may indeed emerge in the human mind partly by a process of such limitation or abeyance, by the receding of darkness from a partial light, or it may have the aspect of ignorance turning into knowledge; but in fact, it rises by an independent birth from our depths where it has a native existence.

Again, of good and evil it can be said that one exists by true consciousness, the other survives only by wrong consciousness: if there is an unmixed true consciousness, good alone can exist; it is no longer mixed with evil or formed in its presence. Human values of good and evil, as of truth and error, are indeed uncertain and relative: what is held as truth in one place or time is held in another place or time to be error; what is regarded as good is elsewhere or in other times regarded as evil. We find too that what we call evil results in good, what we call good results in evil. But this untoward outcome of good producing evil is due to the confusion and mixture of knowledge and ignorance, to the penetration of true consciousness by wrong consciousness, so that there is an ignorant or mistaken application of our good, or it is due to the intervention of afflicting forces. In the opposite case of evil producing good, the happier and contradictory result is due to the intervention of some true consciousness and force acting behind and in spite of wrong consciousness and wrong will or it is due to the intervention of redressing forces. This relativity, this mixture is a circumstance of human mentality and the workings of the Cosmic Force in human life; it is not the fundamental truth of good and evil. It might be objected that physical evil, such as pain and most bodily suffering, is independent of knowledge and ignorance, of right and wrong consciousness, inherent in physical Nature: but, fundamentally, all pain and suffering are the result of an insufficient consciousness-force in the surface being which makes it unable to deal rightly with self and Nature or unable to assimilate and to harmonise itself with the contacts of the universal Energy; they would not exist if in us there were an integral presence of the luminous Consciousness and the divine Force of an integral Being. Therefore the relation of truth to falsehood, of good to evil is not a mutual dependence, but is in the nature of a contradiction as of light and shadow; a shadow depends on light for its existence, but light does not depend for its existence on the shadow. The relation between the Absolute and these contraries of some of its fundamental aspects is not that they are opposite fundamental aspects of the Absolute; falsehood and evil have no fundamentality, no power of infinity or eternal being, no self-existence even by latency in the Self-Existent, no authenticity of an original inherence.

It is no doubt a fact that once truth or good manifests, the conception of falsehood and evil becomes a possibility; for whenever there is an affirmation, its negation becomes conceivable. As the manifestation of existence, consciousness and delight made the manifestation of non-existence, inconscience, insensibility conceivable and, because conceivable, therefore in a way inevitable, for all possibilities push towards actuality until they reach it, so is it with these contraries of the aspects of the Divine Existence. It may be said on this ground that these opposites, since they must be immediately perceivable by the manifesting Consciousness on the very threshold of manifestation, can take rank as implied absolutes and are inseparable from all cosmic existence. But it must first be noted that it is only in cosmic manifestation that they become possible; they cannot pre-exist in the timeless being, for they are incompatible with the unity and bliss that are its substance. In cosmos also they cannot come into being except by a limitation of truth and good into partial and relative forms and by a breaking up of the unity of existence and consciousness into separative consciousness and separative being. For where there is oneness and complete mutuality of consciousness-force even in multiplicity and diversity, there truth of self-knowledge and mutual knowledge is automatic and error of self-ignorance and mutual ignorance is impossible. So too where truth exists as a whole on a basis of self-aware oneness, falsehood cannot enter and evil is shut out by the exclusion of wrong consciousness and wrong will and their dynamisation of falsehood and error. As soon as separateness enters, these things also can enter; but even this simultaneity is not inevitable. If there is sufficient mutuality, even in the absence of an active sense of oneness, and if the separate beings do not transgress or deviate from their norms of limited knowledge, harmony and truth can still be sovereign and evil will have no gate of entry. There is, therefore, no authentic inevitable cosmicity of falsehood and evil even as there is no absoluteness; they are circumstances or results that arise only at a certain stage when separativeness culminates in opposition and ignorance in a primitive unconsciousness of knowledge and a resultant wrong consciousness and wrong knowledge with its content of wrong will, wrong feeling, wrong action and wrong reaction. The question is at what juncture of cosmic manifestation the opposites enter in; for it may be either at some stage of the increasing involution of consciousness in separative mind and life or only after the plunge into inconscience. This resolves itself into the question whether falsehood, error, wrong and evil exist originally in the mental and vital planes and are native to mind and life or are proper only to the material manifestation because inflicted on mind and life there by the obscurity arising from the Inconscience. It may be questioned too whether, if they do exist in supraphysical mind and life, they were original and inevitable there; for they may rather have entered in as a consequence or a supraphysical extension from the material manifestation. Or, if that is untenable, it may be that they arose as an enabling supraphysical affirmation in the universal Mind and Life, a precedent necessity for their appearance in that manifestation to which they more naturally belong as an inevitable outcome of the creative Inconscience.

It was for a long time held by the human mind as a traditional knowledge that when we go beyond the material plane, these things are found to exist there also in worlds beyond us. There are in these planes of supraphysical experience powers and forms of vital mind and life that seem to be the prephysical foundation of the discordant, defective or perverse forms and powers of life-mind and life-force which we find in the terrestrial existence. There are forces, and subliminal experience seems to show that there are supraphysical beings embodying those forces, that are attached in their root-nature to ignorance, to darkness of consciousness, to misuse of force, to perversity of delight, to all the causes and consequences of the things that we call evil. These powers, beings or forces are active to impose their adverse constructions upon terrestrial creatures; eager to maintain their reign in the manifestation, they oppose the increase of light and truth and good and, still more, are antagonistic to the progress of the soul towards a divine consciousness and divine existence. It is this feature of existence that we see figured in the tradition of the conflict between the Powers of Light and Darkness, Good and Evil, cosmic Harmony and cosmic Anarchy, a tradition universal in ancient myth and in religion and common to all systems of occult knowledge.

The theory of this traditional knowledge is perfectly rational and verifiable by inner experience, and it imposes itself if we admit the supraphysical and do not cabin ourselves in the acceptation of material being as the only reality. As there is a cosmic Self and Spirit pervading and upholding the universe and its beings, so too there is a cosmic Force that moves all things, and on this original cosmic Force depend and act many cosmic Forces that are its powers or arise as forms of its universal action. Whatever is formulated in the universe has a Force or Forces that support it, seek to fulfil or further it, find their foundation in its functioning, their account of success in its success and growth and domination, their self-fulfilment or their prolongation of being in its victory or survival. As there are Powers of Knowledge or Forces of the Light, so there are Powers of Ignorance and tenebrous Forces of the Darkness whose work is to prolong the reign of Ignorance and Inconscience. As there are Forces of Truth, so there are Forces that live by the Falsehood and support it and work for its victory; as there are powers whose life is intimately bound up with the existence, the idea and the impulse of Good, so there are Forces whose life is bound up with the existence and the idea and the impulse of Evil. It is this truth of the cosmic Invisible that was symbolised in the ancient belief

of a struggle between the powers of Light and Darkness, Good
and Evil for the possession of the world and the government
of the life of man; — this was the significance of the contest
between the Vedic Gods and their opponents, sons of Darkness
and Division, figured in a later tradition as Titan and Giant
and Demon, Asura, Rakshasa, Pisacha; the same tradition is
found in the Zoroastrian Double Principle and the later Semitic
opposition of God and his Angels on the one side and Satan
and his hosts on the other, — invisible Personalities and Powers
that draw man to the divine Light and Truth and Good or lure
him into subjection to the undivine principle of Darkness and
Falsehood and Evil. Modern thought is aware of no invisible
forces other than those revealed or constructed by Science; it
does not believe that Nature is capable of creating any other
beings than those around us in the physical world, men, beasts,
birds, reptiles, fishes, insects, germs and animalculae. But if there
are invisible cosmic forces physical in their nature that act upon
the body of inanimate objects, there is no valid reason why there
should not be invisible cosmic forces mental and vital in their
nature that act upon his mind and his life-force. And if Mind and
Life, impersonal forces, form conscious beings or use persons to
embody them in physical forms and in a physical world and can
act upon Matter and through Matter, it is not impossible that
on their own planes they should form conscious beings whose
subtler substance is invisible to us or that they should be able to
act from those planes on beings in physical Nature. Whatever
reality or mythical unreality we may attach to the traditional
figures of past human belief or experience, they would then be
representations of things that are true in principle. In that case
the first source of good and evil would be not in terrestrial life
or in the evolution from the Inconscience, but in Life itself, their
source would be supraphysical and they would be reflected here
from a larger supraphysical Nature.

This is certain that when we go back into ourselves very deep
away from the surface appearance, we find that the mind, heart
and sensational being of man are moved by forces not under his
own control and that he can become an instrument in the hands

of Energies of a cosmic character without knowing the origin of his actions. It is by stepping back from the physical surface into his inner being and subliminal consciousness that he becomes directly aware of them and is able to know directly and deal with their action upon him. He grows aware of interventions which seek to lead him in one direction or another, of suggestions and impulsions which had disguised themselves as original movements of his own mind and against which he had to battle. He can realise that he is not a conscious creature inexplicably produced in an unconscious world out of a seed of inconscient Matter and moving about in an obscure self-ignorance, but an embodied soul through whose action cosmic Nature is seeking to fulfil itself, the living ground of a vast debate between a darkness of Ignorance out of which it emerges here and a light of Knowledge which is growing upwards towards an unforeseen termination. The Forces which seek to move him, and among them the Forces of good and evil, present themselves as powers of universal Nature; but they seem to belong not only to the physical universe, but to planes of Life and Mind beyond it.

The first thing that we have to note of importance to the problem preoccupying us is that these Forces in their action seem often to surpass the measures of human relativity; they are in their larger action superhuman, divine, titanic or demoniac, but they may create their formations in him in large or in little, in his greatness or his smallness, they may seize and drive him at moments or for periods, they may influence his impulses or his acts or possess his whole nature. If that possession happens, he may himself be pushed to an excess of the normal humanity of good or evil; especially the evil takes forms which shock the sense of human measure, exceed the bounds of human personality, approach the gigantic, the inordinate, the immeasurable. It may then be questioned whether it is not a mistake to deny absoluteness to evil; for as there is a drive, an aspiration, a yearning in man towards an absolute truth, good, beauty, so these movements, — as also the transcending intensities attainable by pain and suffering, — seem to indicate the attempt at self-realisation of an absolute evil. But the immeasurable is not a sign of absoluteness: for the absolute is not in itself a thing of magnitude; it is beyond measure, not in the sole sense of vastness, but in the freedom of its essential being; it can manifest itself in the infinitesimal as well as in the infinite. It is true that as we pass from the mental to the spiritual, — and that is a passage towards the absolute, — a subtle wideness and an increasing intensity of light, of power, of peace, of ecstasy mark our passing out of our limitations: but this is at first only a sign of freedom, of height, of universality, not yet of an inward absoluteness of self-existence which is the essence of the matter. To this absoluteness pain and evil cannot attain, they are bound to limitation and they are derivative. If pain becomes immeasurable, it ends itself or ends that in which it manifests, or collapses into insensibility or, in rare circumstances, it may turn into an ecstasy of Ananda. If evil became sole and immeasurable, it would destroy the world or destroy that which bore and supported it; it would bring things and itself back by disintegration into non-existence. No doubt the Powers that support darkness and evil attempt by the magnitude of their self-aggrandisement to reach an appearance of infinity, but immensity is all they can achieve and not infinity; or, at most, they are able to represent their element as a kind of abysmal infinite commensurate with the Inconscient, but it is a false infinite. Self-existence, in essence or by an eternal inherence in the Self-existent, is the condition of absoluteness: error, falsehood, evil are cosmic powers, but relative in their nature, not absolute, since they depend for existence on the perversion or contradiction of their opposites and are not like truth and good self-existent absolutes, inherent aspects of the supreme Self-existent.

A second point of questioning emerges from the evidence given for the supraphysical and pre-physical existence of these dark opposites: for that suggests that they may be after all original cosmic principles. But it is to be noted that their appearance does not extend higher than the lower supraphysical life-planes; they are "powers of the Prince of Air", — air being in the ancient symbolism the principle of life and therefore of the mid-worlds where the vital principle is predominant and essential. The adverse opposites are not, then, primal powers of the cosmos, but creations of Life or of Mind in life. Their supraphysical aspects and influences on earth-nature can be explained by the co-existence of worlds of a descending involution with parallel worlds of an ascending evolution, not precisely created by earth-existence, but created as an annexe to the descending world-order and a prepared support for the evolutionary terrestrial formations; here evil may appear, not as inherent in all life, but as a possibility and a pre-formation that makes inevitable its formation in the evolutionary emergence of consciousness out of the Inconscient. However this may be, it is as an outcome of the Inconscience that we can best watch and understand the origin of falsehood, error, wrong and evil, for it is in the return of Inconscience towards Consciousness that they can be seen taking their formation and it is there that they seem to be normal and even inevitable.

The first emergence from the Inconscient is Matter, and in Matter it would seem that falsehood and evil cannot exist, because both are created by a divided and ignorant surface consciousness and its reactions. There is no such active surface organisation of consciousness, no such reactions in material forces or objects: whatever indwelling secret consciousness there may be in them seems to be one, undifferentiated, mute; inertly inherent and intrinsic in the Energy that constitutes the object, it effectualises and maintains the form by the silent occult Idea in it, but is otherwise self-rapt in the form of energy it has created, uncommunicating and inexpressive. Even if it differentiates itself according to the form of Matter in a corresponding form of self-being, *rūpaṁ rūpaṁ pratirūpo babhūva*[9], there is no psychological organisation, no system of conscious actions or reactions. It is only by contact with conscious beings that material objects exercise powers or influences which can be called good or evil: but that good or evil is determined by the contacted being's sense of help or harm, of benefit or injury from them; these values do not belong to the material object but to some Force that uses

---

[9] *Katha Upanishad*, II. 2. 9.

it or they are created by the consciousness that contacts it. Fire warms a man or burns him, but that is as involuntarily he meets it or voluntarily uses it; a medicinal herb cures or a poison kills, but the value of good or evil is brought into action by the user: it is to be observed too that a poison can cure as well as kill, a medicine kill or harm as well as cure or benefit. The world of pure Matter is neutral, irresponsible; these values insisted on by the human being do not exist in material Nature: as a superior Nature transcends the duality of good and evil, so this inferior Nature falls below it. The question may begin to assume a different aspect if we go behind physical knowledge and accept the conclusions of an occult inquiry, — for here we are told that there are conscious influences that attach themselves to objects and these can be good or evil; but it might still be held that this does not affect the neutrality of the object which does not act by an individualised consciousness but only as it is utilised for good or for evil or for both together: the duality of good and evil is not native to the material principle, it is absent from the world of Matter.

The duality begins with conscious life and emerges fully with the development of mind in life; the vital mind, the mind of desire and sensation, is the creator of the sense of evil and of the fact of evil. Moreover, in animal life, the fact of evil is there, the evil of suffering and the sense of suffering, the evil of violence and cruelty and strife and deception, but the sense of moral evil is absent; in animal life there is no duality of sin or virtue, all action is neutral and permissible for the preservation of life and its maintenance and for the satisfaction of the life-instincts. The sensational values of good and evil are inherent in the form of pain and pleasure, vital satisfaction and vital frustration, but the mental idea, the moral response of the mind to these values are a creation of the human being. It does not follow, as might be hastily inferred, that they are unrealities, mental constructions only, and that the only true way to receive the activities of Nature is either a neutral indifference or an equal acceptance or, intellectually, an admission of all that she may do as a divine or a natural law in which everything is impartially admissible. That is indeed one side of the truth: there is an infrarational truth of Life and Matter which is impartial and neutral and admits all things as facts of Nature and serviceable for the creation, preservation or destruction of life, three necessary movements of the universal Energy which are all connectedly indispensable and, each in its own place, of equal value. There is too a truth of the detached reason which can look on all that is thus admitted by Nature as serviceable to her processes in life and matter and observe everything that is with an unmoved neutral impartiality and acceptance; this is a philosophic and scientific reason that witnesses and seeks to understand but considers it futile to judge the activities of the cosmic Energy. There is too a suprarational truth formulating itself in spiritual experience which can observe the play of universal possibility, accept all impartially as the true and natural features and consequences of a world of ignorance and inconscience or admit all with calm and compassion as a part of the divine working, but, while it awaits the awakening of a higher consciousness and knowledge as the sole escape from what presents itself as evil, is ready with help and intervention where that is truly helpful and possible. But, nonetheless, there is also this other middle truth of consciousness which awakens us to the values of good and evil and the appreciation of their necessity and importance; this awakening, whatever may be the sanction or the validity of its particular judgments, is one of the indispensable steps in the process of evolutionary Nature.

But from what then does this awakening proceed? what is it in the human being that originates and gives its power and place to the sense of good and evil? If we regard only the process, we may agree that it is the vital mind that makes the distinction. Its first valuation is sensational and individual, — all that is pleasant, helpful, beneficial to the life-ego is good, all that is unpleasant, malefic, injurious or destructive is evil. Its next valuation is utilitarian and social: all that is considered helpful to the associated life, all that it demands from the individual in order to remain in association and to regulate association for the best maintenance, satisfaction, development, good order of the associated life and its units, is good; all that has in the view of the society a contrary effect or tendency is evil. But thinking mind then comes in with its own valuation and strives to find out an intellectual basis, an idea of law or principle, rational or cosmic, a law of Karma perhaps or an ethical system founded on reason or on an aesthetic, emotional or hedonistic basis. Religion brings in her sanctions; there is a word or law of God that enjoins righteousness even though Nature permits or stimulates its opposite, — or perhaps Truth and Righteousness are themselves God and there is no other Divinity. But, behind all this practical or rational enforcement of the human ethical instinct, there is a feeling that there is something deeper: all these standards are either too narrow and rigid or complex and confused, uncertain, subject to alteration by a mental or a vital change or evolution; yet it is felt that there is a deeper abiding truth and something within us that can have the intuition of that truth, — in other words, that the real sanction is inward, spiritual and psychic. The traditional account of this inner witness is conscience, a power of perception in us half mental, half intuitive; but this is something superficial, constructed, unreliable: there is certainly within us, though less easily active, more masked by surface elements, a deeper spiritual sense, the soul's discernment, an inborn light within our nature.

What then is this spiritual or psychic witness or what is to it the value of the sense of good and evil? It may be maintained that the one use of the sense of sin and evil is that the embodied being may become aware of the nature of this world of inconscience and ignorance, awake to a knowledge of its evil and suffering and the relative nature of its good and happiness and turn away from it to that which is absolute. Or else its spiritual use may be to purify the nature by the pursuit of good and the negation of evil until it is ready to perceive the supreme good and turn from the world towards God, or, as in the Buddhistic ethical insistence, it may serve to prepare the dissolution of the ignorant ego-complex and the escape from personality and suffering. But also it may be that this awakening is a spiritual necessity of the evolution itself, a step towards the growth of the being out of the Ignorance into the truth of the divine unity and the evolution of a divine consciousness and a divine being. For much more than the mind or life which can turn either to good or to evil, it is the soul-personality, the psychic being, which insists on the distinction, though in a larger sense than the mere moral difference. It is the soul in us which turns always towards Truth, Good and Beauty, because it is by these things that it itself grows in stature; the rest, their opposites, are a necessary part of experience, but have to be outgrown in the spiritual increase of the being. The fundamental psychic entity in us has the delight of life and all experience as part of the progressive manifestation of the spirit, but the very principle of its delight of life is to gather out of all contacts and happenings their secret divine sense and essence, a divine use and purpose so that by experience our mind and life may grow out of the Inconscience towards a supreme consciousness, out of the divisions of the Ignorance towards an integralising consciousness and knowledge. It is there for that and it pursues from life to life its ever-increasing upward tendency and insistence; the growth of the soul is a growth out of darkness into light, out of falsehood into truth, out of suffering into its own supreme and universal Ananda. The soul's perception of good and evil may not coincide with the mind's artificial standards, but it has a deeper sense, a sure discrimination of what points to the higher Light and what points away from it. It is true that as the inferior light is below good and evil, so the superior spiritual light is beyond good and evil; but this is not in the sense of admitting all things with an impartial neutrality or of obeying equally the impulses of good and evil, but in the sense that a higher law of being intervenes in which there is no longer any place or utility for these values. There is a self-law of supreme Truth which is above all standards; there is a supreme and universal Good inherent, intrinsic, self-existent, self-aware, self-moved and determined, infinitely plastic with the pure plasticity of the luminous consciousness of the supreme Infinite.

If, then, evil and falsehood are natural products of the Inconscience, automatic results of the evolution of life and mind from it in the processus of the Ignorance, we have to see how they arise, on what they depend for their existence and what is the remedy or escape. In the surface emergence of mental and vital consciousness from the Inconscience is to be found the process by which these phenomena come into being. Here there are two determining factors, — and it is these that are the efficient cause of the simultaneous emergence of falsehood and evil. First, there is an underlying, a still occult consciousness and power of inherent knowledge, and there is also an overlying layer of what might be called indeterminate or else ill-formed stuff of vital and physical consciousness; through this obscure difficult medium the emerging mentality has to force its way and has to impose itself on it by a constructed and no longer an inherent knowledge, because this stuff is still full of nescience, heavily burdened and enveloped with the inconscience of Matter. Next, the emergence takes place in a separated form of life which has to affirm itself against a principle of inanimate material inertia and a constant pull of that material inertia towards disintegration and a relapse into the original inanimate Inconscience. This separated life-form has also to affirm itself, supported only by a limited principle of association, against an outside world which is, if not hostile to its existence, yet full of dangers and on which it has to impose itself, conquer life-room, arrive at expression and propagation, if it wishes to survive. The result of an emergence of consciousness in these conditions is the growth of a self-affirming vital and physical individual, a construction of Nature of life and matter with a concealed psychic or spiritual true individual behind it for which Nature is creating this outward means of expression. As mentality increases, this vital and material individual takes the more developed form of a constantly self-affirming mental, vital and physical ego. Our surface consciousness and type of existence, our natural being, has developed its present character under the compulsion of these two initial and basic facts of the evolutionary emergence.

In its first appearance consciousness has the semblance of a miracle, a power alien to Matter that manifests unaccountably in a world of inconscient Nature and grows slowly and with difficulty. Knowledge is acquired, created out of nothing as it were, learned, increased, accumulated by an ephemeral ignorant creature in whom at birth it is entirely absent or present only, not as knowledge, but in the form of an inherited capacity proper to the stage of development of this slowly learning ignorance. It might be conjectured that consciousness is only the original Inconscience mechanically recording the facts of existence on the brain-cells with a reflex or response in the cells automatically reading the record and dictating their answer; the record, reflex, response together constitute what appears to be consciousness. But this is evidently not the whole truth, for it might account for observation and mechanical action, — although it is not clear how an unconscious record and response can turn into a conscious observation, a conscious sense of things and sense of self, — but does not credibly account for ideation, imagination, speculation, the free play of intellect with its observed material. The evolution of consciousness and knowledge cannot be accounted for unless there is already a concealed consciousness in things with its inherent and native powers emerging little by little. Further, the facts of animal life and the operations of the emergent mind in life impose on us the conclusion that there is in this concealed consciousness an underlying Knowledge or power of knowledge which by the necessity of the life-contacts with the environment comes to the surface.

The individual animal being in its first conscious self-affirmation has to rely on two sources of knowledge. As it is nescient and helpless, a small modicum of uninformed surface consciousness in a world unknown to it, the secret Conscious-Force sends up to this surface the minimum of intuition necessary for it to maintain its existence and go through the operations indispensable to life and survival. This intuition is not possessed by the animal, but possesses and moves it; it is something that manifests of itself in the grain of the vital and physical substance of consciousness under pressure of a need and for the needed occasion: but at the same time a surface result of this intuition accumulates and takes the form of an automatic instinct which works whenever the occasion for it recurs; this instinct belongs to the race and is imparted at birth to its individual members. The intuition, when it occurs or recurs, is unerring; the instinct is automatically correct as a rule, but can err, for it fails or blunders when the surface consciousness or an ill-developed intelligence interferes or if the instinct continues to act mechanically when, owing to changed circumstances, the need or the necessary circumstances are no longer there. The second source of knowledge is surface contact with the world outside the natural individual being; it is this contact which is the cause first of a conscious sensation and sense-perception and then of intelligence. If there were not an underlying consciousness, the contact would not create any perception or reaction; it is because the contact stimulates into a feeling and a surface response the subliminal of a being already vitalised by the subconscious life-principle and its first needs and seekings that a surface awareness begins to form and develop. Intrinsically the emergence of a surface consciousness by force of life contacts is due to the fact that in both subject and object of the contact consciousness-force is already existent in a subliminal latency: when the life-principle is ready, sufficiently sensitive in the subject, the recipient of the contact, this subliminal consciousness emerges in a response to the stimulus which begins to constitute a vital or life mind, the mind of the animal, and then, in the course of the evolution, a thinking intelligence. The secret consciousness is rendered into surface sensation and perception, the secret force into surface impulse.

If this underlying subliminal consciousness were to come itself to the surface, there would be a direct meeting between the consciousness of the subject and the contents of the object and the result would be a direct knowledge; but this is not possible, first, because of the veto or obstruction of the Inconscience and, secondly, because the evolutionary intention is to develop slowly through an imperfect but growing surface awareness. The secret consciousness-force has therefore to limit itself to imperfect renderings in a surface vital and mental vibration and operation and is forced by the absence, holding back or insufficiency of the direct awareness to develop organs and instincts for an indirect knowledge. This creation of an external knowledge and intelligence takes place in an already prepared indeterminate conscious structure which is the earliest formation on the surface. At first this structure is only a minimum formation of consciousness with a vague sensational perception and a response-impulse; but, as more organised forms of life appear, this grows into a life-mind and vital intelligence largely mechanical and automatic in the beginning and concerned only with practical needs, desires and impulses. All this activity is in its initiation intuitive and instinctive; the underlying consciousness is translated in the surface substratum into automatic movements of the conscious stuff of life and body: the mind-movements, when they appear, are involved in these automatisms, they occur as a subordinate mental notation within the predominant vital sense-notation. But slowly mind starts its task of disengaging itself; it still works for the life-instinct, life-need and life-desire, but its own special characters emerge, observation, invention, device, intention, execution of purpose, while sensation and impulse add to themselves emotion and bring a subtler and finer affective urge and value into the crude vital reaction. Mind is still much involved in life and its highest purely mental operations are not in evidence; it accepts a large background of instinct and vital intuition as its support, and the intelligence developed, though always growing as the animal life-scale rises, is an added superstructure.

When human intelligence adds itself to the animal basis, this basis still remains present and active, but it is largely changed, subtilised and uplifted by conscious will and intention; the automatic life of instinct and vital intuition diminishes and cannot keep its original predominant proportion to the self-aware mental intelligence. Intuition becomes less purely intuitive: even when there is still a strong vital intuition, its vital character is concealed by mentalisation, and mental intuition is most often a mixture, not the pure article, for an alloy is added to make it mentally current and serviceable. In the animal also the surface consciousness can obstruct or alter the intuition but, because its capacity is less, it interferes less with the automatic, mechanical or instinctive action of Nature: in mental man when the intuition rises towards the surface, it is caught at once before it reaches and is translated into terms of mind-intelligence with a gloss or mental interpretation added which conceals the origin of the knowledge. Instinct also is deprived of its intuitive character by being taken up and mentalised and by that change becomes less sure, though more assisted, when not replaced, by the plastic power of adaptation of things and self-adaptation proper to the intelligence. The emergence of mind in life brings an immense increase of the range and capacity of the evolving consciousness-force; but it also brings an immense increase in the range and capacity of error. For evolving mind trails constantly error as its shadow, a shadow that grows with the growing body of consciousness and knowledge.

If in the evolution the surface consciousness were always open to the action of intuition, the intervention of error would not be possible. For intuition is an edge of light thrust out by the secret Supermind, and an emergent Truth-Consciousness, however limited, yet sure in its action, would be the consequence. Instinct, if it had to form, would be plastic to the intuition and adapt itself freely to evolutionary change and the change of inner or environing circumstance. Intelligence, if it had to form, would be subservient to intuition and would be its accurate mental expression; its brilliancy would perhaps be modulated to suit a diminished action serving as a minor, not, as it is now, a major function and movement, but it would not be erratic by deviation, would not by its parts of obscurity sink into the false or fallible. But this could not be, because the hold of Inconscience on the matter, the surface substance, in which mind and life have to express themselves, makes the surface consciousness obscure and unresponsive to the light within; it is impelled moreover to cherish this defect, to substitute more and more its own incomplete but better grasped clarities for the unaccountable inner intimations, because a rapid development of the Truth-Consciousness is not the intention in Nature. For the method chosen by her is a slow and difficult evolution of Inconscience developing into Ignorance and Ignorance forming itself into a mixed, modified and partial knowledge before it can be ready for transformation into a higher Truth-Consciousness and Truth-Knowledge. Our imperfect mental intelligence is a necessary stage of transition before this higher transformation can be made possible.

There are, in practical fact, two poles of the conscious being between which the evolutionary process works, one a surface nescience which has to change gradually into knowledge, the other a secret Consciousness-Force in which all power of knowledge is and which has slowly to manifest in the nescience. The surface nescience full of incomprehension and inapprehension can change into knowledge because consciousness is there involved in it; if it were intrinsically an entire absence of consciousness, the change would be impossible: but still it works as an inconscience trying to be conscious; it is at first a nescience compelled by need and outer impact to feeling and response and then an ignorance labouring to know. The means used is a contact with the world and its forces and objects which, like the rubbing of tinders, creates a spark of awareness; the response from within is that spark leaping out into manifestation. But the surface nescience in receiving the response from an underlying source of knowledge subdues and changes it into something obscure and incomplete; there is an imperfect seizure or a misprision of the intuition that answers to the contact: still by this process an initiation of responsive consciousness, a first accumulation of ingrained or habitual instinctive knowledge begins, and there follows upon it first a primitive and then a developed capacity of receptive awareness, understanding, reply of action, previsional initiation of action, — an evolving consciousness which is half-knowledge, half-ignorance. All that is unknown is met on the basis of what is known; but as this knowledge is imperfect, as it receives imperfectly and responds imperfectly to the contacts of things, there can be a misprision of the new contact as well as a misprision or deformation of the intuitive response, a double source of error.

It is evident, in these conditions, that Error is a necessary accompaniment, almost a necessary condition and instrumentation, an indispensable step or stage in the slow evolution towards knowledge in a consciousness that begins from nescience and works in the stuff of a general nescience. The evolving consciousness has to acquire knowledge by an indirect means which does not give even a fragmentary certitude; for there is at first only a figure or a sign, an image or a vibration physical in character created by contact with the object and a resulting vital sensation which have to be interpreted by mind and sense and turned into a corresponding mental idea or figure. Things thus experienced and mentally known have to be related together; things unknown have to be observed, discovered, fitted into the already acquired sum of experience and knowledge. At each step different possibilities of fact, significance, judgment, interpretation, relation present themselves; some have to be tested and rejected, others accepted and confirmed: to shut out error is impossible without limiting the chances of acquisition of knowledge. Observation is the first instrument of the mind, but observation itself is a complex process open at every step to the mistakes of the ignorant observing consciousness; misprision of the fact by the senses and the sense-mind, omission, wrong selection and putting together, unconscious additions made by a personal impression or personal reaction create a false or an imperfect composite picture; to these errors are added the errors of inference, judgment, interpretation of facts by the intelligence: when even the data are not sure or perfect, the conclusions built on them must also be insecure and imperfect.

Consciousness in its acquisition of knowledge proceeds from the known to the unknown; it builds a structure of acquired experience, memories, impressions, judgments, a composite mental plan of things which is of the nature of a shifting and ever modifiable fixity. In the reception of new knowledge, what comes in to be received is judged in the light of past knowledge and fitted into the structure; if it cannot properly fit, it is either dovetailed in anyhow or rejected: but the existing knowledge and its structures or standards may not be applicable to the new object or new field of knowledge, the fitting may be a misfitting or the rejection may be an erroneous response. To misprision and wrong interpretation of facts, there is added misapplication of knowledge, miscombination, misconstruction, misrepresentation, a complicated machinery of mental error. In all this enlightened obscurity of our mental parts a secret intuition is at work, a truth-urge that corrects or pushes the intelligence to correct what is erroneous, to labour towards a true picture of things and a true interpretative knowledge. But intuition itself is limited in the human mind by mental misprision of its intimations and is unable to act in its own right; for whether it be physical, vital or mental intuition, it has to present itself in order to be received, not nude and pure, but garbed with a mental coating or entirely enveloped in an ample mental vesture; so disguised, its true nature cannot be recognised and its relation to mind and its office are not understood, its way of working is ignored by the hasty and half-aware human intelligence. There are intuitions of actuality, of possibility, of the determining truth behind things, but all are mistaken by the mind for each other. A great confusion of half-grasped material and an experimental building with it, a representation or mental structure of the figure of self and things rigid and yet chaotic, half formed and arranged, half jumbled, half true, half erroneous, but always imperfect, is the character of human knowledge.

Error by itself, however, would not amount to falsehood; it would only be an imperfection of truth, a trying, an essay of possibilities: for when we do not know, untried and uncertain possibilities have to be admitted and, even if as a result an imperfect or inapt structure of thought is built, yet it may justify itself by opening to fresh knowledge in unexpected directions and either its dissolution and rebuilding or the discovery of some truth it concealed might increase our cognition or our experience. In spite of the mixture created the growth of consciousness, intelligence and reason could arrive through this mixed truth to a clearer and truer figure of self-knowledge and world-knowledge. The obstruction of the original and enveloping inconscience would diminish, and an increasing mental consciousness would reach a clarity and wholeness which would enable the concealed powers of direct knowledge and intuitive process to emerge, utilise the prepared and enlightened instruments and make mind-intelligence their true agent and truth-builder on the evolutionary surface. But here the second condition or factor of the evolution intervenes; for this seeking for knowledge is not an impersonal mental process hampered only by the general limitations of mind-intelligence: the ego is there, the physical ego, the life-ego bent, not on self-knowledge and the discovery of the truth of things and the truth of life, but on vital self-affirmation; a mental ego is there also bent on its own personal self-affirmation and largely directed and used by the vital urge for its life-desire and life-purpose. For as mind develops, there develops also a mental individuality with a personal drive of mind-tendency, a mental temperament, a mind-formation of its own. This surface mental individuality is egocentric; it looks at the world and things and happenings from its own standpoint and sees them not as they are but as they affect itself: in observing things it gives them the turn suitable to its own tendency and temperament, selects or rejects, arranges truth according to its own mental preference and convenience; observation, judgment, reason are all determined or affected by this mind-personality and assimilated to the needs of the individuality and the ego. Even when the mind aims most at a pure impersonality of truth and reason, a sheer impersonality is impossible to it; even the most trained, severe and vigilant intellect fails to observe the twists and turns it gives to truth in the reception of fact and idea and the construction of its mental knowledge. Here we have an almost inexhaustible source of distortion of truth, a cause of falsification, an unconscious or half-conscious will to error, an acceptance of ideas or facts not by a clear perception of the true and the false, but by preference, personal suitability, temperamental choice, prejudgment. Here is a fruitful seed-plot for the growth of falsehood or a gate or many gates through which it can enter by stealth or by an usurping but acceptable violence. Truth too can enter in and take up its dwelling, not by its own right, but at the mind's pleasure.

In the terms of the Sankhya psychology we can distinguish three types of mental individuality, — that which is governed by the principle of obscurity and inertia, first-born of the

Inconscience, tamasic; that which is governed by a force of passion and activity, kinetic, rajasic; that which is cast in the mould of the sattwic principle of light, harmony, balance. The tamasic intelligence has its seat in the physical mind: it is inert to ideas, — except to those which it receives inertly, blindly, passively from a recognised source or authority, — obscure in their reception, unwilling to enlarge itself, recalcitrant to new stimulus, conservative and immobile; it clings to its received structure of knowledge and its one power is repetitive practicality, but it is a power limited by the accustomed, the obvious, the established and familiar and already secure; it thrusts away all that is new and likely to disturb it. The rajasic intelligence has its main seat in the vital mind and is of two kinds: one kind is defensive with violence and passion, assertive of its mental individuality and all that is in agreement with it, preferred by its volition, adapted to its outlook, but aggressive against all that is contrary to its mental ego-structure or unacceptable to its personal intellectuality; the other kind is enthusiastic for new things, passionate, insistent, impetuous, often mobile beyond measure, inconstant and ever restless, governed in its idea not by truth and light but by the zest of intellectual battle and movement and adventure. The sattwic intelligence is eager for knowledge, as open as it can be to it, careful to consider and verify and balance, to adjust and adapt to its view whatever confirms itself as truth, receiving all that it can assimilate, skilful to build truth in a harmonious intellectual structure: but, because its light is limited, as all mental light must be, it is unable to enlarge itself so as to receive equally all truth and all knowledge; it has a mental ego, even an enlightened one, and is determined by it in its observation, judgment, reasoning, mental choice and preference. In most men there is a predominance of one of these qualities but also a mixture; the same mind can be open and plastic and harmonic in one direction, kinetic and vital, hasty and prejudiced and ill-balanced in another, in yet another obscure and unreceptive. This limitation by personality, this defence of personality and refusal to receive what is unassimilable, is necessary for the individual being because in its evolution, at the stage reached, it has a certain self-expression, a certain type of experience and use of experience which must, for the mind and life at least, govern nature; that for the moment is its law of being, its dharma. This limitation of mind-consciousness by personality and of truth by mental temperament and preference must be the rule of our nature so long as the individual has not reached universality, is not yet preparing for mind-transcendence. But it is evident that this condition is inevitably a source of error and can at any moment be the cause of a falsification of knowledge, an unconscious or half-wilful self-deception, a refusal to admit true knowledge, a readiness to assert acceptable wrong knowledge as true knowledge.

This is in the field of cognition, but the same law applies to will and action. Out of ignorance a wrong consciousness is created which gives a wrong dynamic reaction to the contact of persons, things, happenings: the surface consciousness develops the habit of ignoring, misunderstanding or rejecting the suggestions to action or against action that come from the secret inmost consciousness, the psychic entity; it answers instead to unenlightened mental and vital suggestions, or acts in accordance with the demands and impulsions of the vital ego. Here the second of the primary conditions of the evolution, the law of a separate life-being affirming itself in a world which is not-self to it, comes into prominence and assumes an immense importance. It is here that the surface vital personality or life-self asserts its dominance, and this dominance of the ignorant vital being is a principal active source of discord and disharmony, a cause of inner and outer perturbations of the life, a mainspring of wrong-doing and evil. The natural vital element in us, in so far as it is unchecked or untrained or retains its primitive character, is not concerned with truth or right consciousness or right action; it is concerned with self-affirmation, with life-growth, with possession, with satisfaction of impulse, with all satisfactions of desire. This main need and demand of the life-self seems all-important to it; it would readily carry it out without any regard to truth or right or good or any other consideration: but because mind is there and has these conceptions, because the soul is there and has these soul-perceptions, it tries to dominate mind and get from it by dictation a sanction and order of execution for its own will of self-affirmation, a verdict of truth and right and good for its own vital assertions, impulses, desires; it is concerned with self-justification in order that it may have room for full self-affirmation. But if it can get the assent of mind, it is quite ready to ignore all these standards and set up only one standard, the satisfaction, growth, strength, greatness of the vital ego. The life-individual needs place, expansion, possession of its world, dominance and control of things and beings; it needs life-room, a space in the sun, self-assertion, survival. It needs these things for itself and for those with whom it associates itself, for its own ego and for the collective ego; it needs them for its ideas, creeds, ideals, interests, imaginations: for it has to assert these forms of I-ness and my-ness and impose them on the world around it or, if it is not strong enough to do that, it has at least to defend and maintain them against others to the best of its power and contrivance. It may try to do it by methods it thinks or chooses to think or represent as right; it may try to do it by the naked use of violence, ruse, falsehood, destructive aggression, crushing of other life-formations: the principle is the same whatever the means or the moral attitude. It is not only in the realm of interests, but in the realm of ideas and the realm of religion that the vital being of man has introduced this spirit and attitude of self-affirmation and struggle and the use of violence, oppression and suppression, intolerance, aggression; it has imposed the principle of life-egoism on the domain of intellectual truth and the domain of the spirit. Into its self-affirmation the self-asserting life brings in hatred and dislike towards all that stands in the way of its expansion or hurts its ego; it develops as a means or as a passion or reaction of the life-nature cruelty, treachery and all kinds of evil: its satisfaction of desire and impulse takes no account of right and wrong, but only of the fulfilment of desire and impulse. For this satisfaction it is ready to face the risk of destruction and actuality of suffering; for what it is pushed by Nature to aim at is not self-preservation alone, but life-affirmation and life-satisfaction, formulation of life-force and life-being.

It does not follow that this is all that the vital personality is in its native composition or that evil is its very nature. It is not primarily concerned with truth and good, but it can have the passion for truth and good as it has, more spontaneously, the passion for joy and beauty. In all that is developed by the life-force there is developed at the same time a secret delight somewhere in the being, a delight in good and a delight in evil, a delight in truth and a delight in falsehood, a delight in life and an attraction to death, a delight in pleasure and a delight in pain, in one's own suffering and the suffering of others, but also in one's own joy and happiness and good and the joy and happiness and good of others. For the force of life-affirmation affirms alike the good and the evil: it has its impulses of help and association, of generosity, affection, loyalty, self-giving; it takes up altruism as it takes up egoism, sacrifices itself as well as destroys others; and in all its acts there is the same passion for life-affirmation, the same force of action and fulfilment. This character of vital being and its trend of existence in which what we term good and evil are items but not the mainspring, is evident in subhuman life; in the human being, since there a mental, moral and psychic discernment has developed, it is subjected to control or to camouflage, but it does not change its character. The vital being and its life-force and their drive towards self-affirmation are, in the absence of an overt action of soul-power and spiritual power, Atmashakti, Nature's chief means of effectuation, and without its support neither mind nor body can utilise their possibilities or realise their aim here in existence. It is only if the inner or true vital being replaces the outer life-personality that the drive of the vital ego can be wholly overcome and the life-force become the servant of the soul and a powerful instrumentation for the action of our true spiritual being.

This then is the origin and nature of error, falsehood, wrong and evil in the consciousness and will of the individual; a limited consciousness growing out of nescience is the source of error, a personal attachment to the limitation and the error born of it the source of falsity, a wrong consciousness governed by the life-ego the source of evil. But it is evident that their relative existence is only a phenomenon thrown up by the cosmic Force in its drive towards evolutionary self-expression, and it is there that we have to look for the significance of the phenomenon. For the emergence of the life-ego is, as we have seen, a machinery of cosmic Nature for the affirmation of the individual, for his self-disengagement from the indeterminate mass substance of the subconscient, for the appearance of a conscious being on a ground prepared by the Inconscience; the principle of life-affirmation of the ego is the necessary consequence. The individual ego is a pragmatic and effective fiction, a translation of the secret self into the terms of surface consciousness, or a subjective substitute for the true self in our surface experience: it is separated by ignorance from other-self and from the inner Divinity, but it is still pushed secretly towards an evolutionary unification in diversity; it has behind itself, though finite, the impulse to the infinite. But this in the terms of an ignorant consciousness translates itself into the will to expand, to be a boundless finite, to take everything it can into itself, to enter into everything and possess it, even to be possessed if by that it can feel itself satisfied and growing in or through others or can take into itself by subjection the being and power of others or get thereby a help or an impulse for its life-affirmation, its life-delight, its enrichment of its mental, vital or physical existence.

But because it does these things as a separate ego for its separate advantage and not by conscious interchange and mutuality, not by unity, life-discord, conflict, disharmony arise, and it is the products of this life-discord and disharmony that we call wrong and evil. Nature accepts them because they are necessary circumstances of the evolution, necessary for the growth of the divided being; they are products of ignorance, supported by an ignorant consciousness that founds itself on division, by an ignorant will that works through division, by an ignorant delight of existence that takes the joy of division. The evolutionary intention acts through the evil as through the good; it has to utilise all because confinement to a limited good would imprison and check the intended evolution; it uses any available material and does what it can with it: this is the reason why we see evil coming out of what we call good and good coming out of what we call evil; and, if we see even what was thought to be evil coming to be accepted as good, what was thought to be good accepted as evil, it is because our standards of both are evolutionary, limited and mutable. Evolutionary Nature, the terrestrial cosmic Force, seems then at first to have no preference for either of these opposites, it uses both alike for its purpose. And yet it is the same Nature, the same Force that has burdened man with the sense of good and evil and insists on its importance: evidently, therefore, this sense also has an evolutionary purpose; it too must be necessary, it must be there so that man may leave certain things behind him, move towards others, until out of good and evil he can emerge into some Good that is eternal and infinite.

But how is this evolutionary intention in Nature to fulfil itself, by what power, means, impulsion, what principle and process of selection and harmonisation? The method adopted by the mind of man through the ages has been always a principle of selection and rejection, and this has taken the forms of a religious sanction, a social or moral rule of life or an ethical ideal. But this is an empirical means which does not touch the root of the problem because it has no vision of the cause and origin of the malady it attempts to cure; it deals with the symptoms, but deals with them perfunctorily, not knowing what function they serve in the purpose of Nature and what it is in the mind and life that supports them and keeps them in being. Moreover, human good and evil are relative and the standards erected by ethics are uncertain as well as relative: what is forbidden by one religion or another, what is regarded as good or bad by social opinion, what is thought useful to society or noxious to it, what some temporary law of man allows or disallows, what is or is considered helpful or harmful to self or others, what accords with this or that ideal, what is prompted or discouraged by an instinct which we call conscience, — an amalgam of all these viewpoints is the determining heterogeneous idea, constitutes the complex substance of morality; in all of them there is the constant mixture of truth and half-truth and error which pursues all the activities of our limiting mental Knowledge-Ignorance. A mental control over our vital and physical desires and instincts, over our personal and social action, over our dealings with others is indispensable to us as human beings, and morality creates a standard by which we can guide ourselves and establish a customary control; but the control is always imperfect and it is an expedient, not a solution: man remains always what he is and has ever been, a mixture of good and evil, sin and virtue, a mental ego with an imperfect command over his mental, vital and physical nature.

The endeavour to select, to retain from our consciousness and action all that seems to us good and reject all that seems to us evil and so to re-form our being, to reconstitute and shape ourselves into the image of an ideal, is a more profound ethical motive, because it comes nearer to the true issue; it rests on the sound idea that our life is a becoming and that there is something which we have to become and be. But the ideals constructed by the human mind are selective and relative; to shape our nature rigidly according to them is to limit ourselves and make a construction where there should be growth into larger being. The true call upon us is the call of the Infinite and the Supreme; the self-affirmation and self-abnegation imposed on us by Nature are both movements towards that, and it is the right way of self-affirmation and self-negation taken together in place of the wrong, because ignorant, way of the ego and in place of the conflict between the yes and the no of Nature that we have to discover. If we do not discover that, either the push of life will be too strong for our narrow ideal of perfection, its instrumentation will break and it will fail to consummate and perpetuate itself, or at best a half result will be all that we shall obtain, or else the push away from life will present itself as the only remedy, the one way out of the otherwise invincible grasp of the Ignorance. This indeed is the way out usually indicated by religion; a divinely enjoined morality, a pursuit of piety, righteousness and virtue as laid down in a religious code of conduct, a law of God determined by some human inspiration, is put forward as a part of the means, the direction, by which we can tread the way that leads to the exit, the issue. But this exit leaves the problem where it was; it is only a way of escape for the personal being out of the unsolved perplexity of the cosmic existence. In ancient Indian spiritual thought there was a clearer perception of the difficulty; the practice of truth, virtue, right will and right doing was regarded as a necessity of the approach to spiritual realisation, but in the realisation itself the being arises to the greater consciousness of the Infinite and Eternal and shakes away from itself the burden of sin and virtue, for that belongs to the relativity and the Ignorance. Behind this larger truer perception lay the intuition that a relative good is a training imposed by World-Nature upon us so that we may pass through it towards the true Good which is absolute. These problems are of the mind and the ignorant life, they do not accompany us beyond mind; as there is a cessation of the duality of truth and error in an infinite Truth-Consciousness, so there is a liberation from the duality of good and evil in an infinite Good, there is transcendence.

There can be no artificial escape from this problem which has always troubled humanity and from which it has found no satisfying issue. The tree of the knowledge of good and evil with its sweet and bitter fruits is secretly rooted in the very nature of the Inconscience from which our being has emerged and on which it still stands as a nether soil and basis of our physical existence; it has grown visibly on the surface in the manifold branchings of the Ignorance which is still the main bulk and condition of our consciousness in its difficult evolution towards a supreme consciousness and an integral awareness. As long as there is this soil with the unfound roots in it and this nourishing air and climate of Ignorance, the tree will grow and flourish and put forth its dual blossoms and its fruit of mixed nature. It would follow that there can be no final solution until we have turned our inconscience into the greater consciousness, made the truth of self and spirit our life-basis and transformed our ignorance into a higher knowledge. All other expedients will only be makeshifts or blind issues; a complete and radical transformation of our nature is the only true solution. It is because the Inconscience imposes its original obscurity on our awareness of self and things and because the Ignorance bases it on an imperfect and divided consciousness and because we live in that obscurity and division that wrong knowledge and wrong will are possible: without wrong knowledge there could be no error or falsehood, without error or falsehood in our dynamic parts there could be no wrong will in our members; without wrong will there could be no wrong-doing or evil: while these causes endure, the effects also will persist in our action and in our nature. A mental control can only be a control, not a cure; a mental teaching, rule, standard can only impose an artificial groove in which our action revolves mechanically or with difficulty and which imposes a curbed and limited formation on the course of our nature. A total change of consciousness, a radical change of nature is the one remedy and the sole issue.

But since the root of the difficulty is a split, limited and separative existence, this change must consist in an integration, a healing of the divided consciousness of our being, and since that division is complex and many-sided, no partial change on one side of the being can be passed off as a sufficient substitute for the integral transformation. Our first division is that created by our ego and mainly, most forcefully, most vividly by our life-ego, which divides us from all other beings as not-self and ties us to our ego-centricity and the law of an egoistic self-affirmation. It is in the errors of this self-affirmation that wrong and evil first arise: wrong consciousness engenders wrong will in the members, in the thinking mind, in the heart, in the life-mind and the sensational being, in the very body-consciousness; wrong will engenders wrong action of all these instruments, a multiple error and many-branching crookedness of thought and will and sense and feeling. Nor can we deal rightly with others so long as they are to us others, beings who are strangers to ourselves and of whose inner consciousness, soul-need, mind-need, heart-need, life-need, body-need we know little or nothing. The modicum of imperfect sympathy, knowledge and good-will that the law, need and habit of association engender, is a poor quantum of what is required for a true action. A larger mind, a larger heart, a more ample and generous life-force can do something to help us or help others and avoid the worst offences, but this too is insufficient and will not prevent a mass of troubles and harms and collisions of our preferred good with the good of others. By the very nature of our ego and ignorance we affirm ourselves egoistically even when we most pride ourselves on selflessness and ignorantly even when we most pride ourselves on understanding and knowledge. Altruism taken as a rule of life does not deliver us; it is a potent instrument for self-enlargement and for correction of the narrower ego, but it does not abolish it nor transform it into the true self one with all; the ego of the altruist is as powerful and absorbing as the ego of the selfish and it is often more powerful and insistent because it is a self-righteous and magnified ego. It helps still less if we do wrong to our soul, to our mind, life or body with the idea of subordinating our self to the self of others. To affirm our being rightly so that it may become one with all is the true principle, not to mutilate or immolate it. Self-immolation may be necessary at times, exceptionally, for a cause, in answer to some demand of the heart or for some right or high purpose but cannot be made the rule or nature of life; so exaggerated, it would only feed and exaggerate the ego of others or magnify some collective ego, not lead us or mankind to the discovery and affirmation of our or its true being. Sacrifice and self-giving are indeed a true principle and a spiritual necessity, for we cannot affirm our being rightly without sacrifice or without self-giving to something larger than our ego; but that too must be done with a right consciousness and will founded on a true knowledge. To develop the sattwic part of our nature, a nature of light, understanding, balance, harmony, sympathy, good-will, kindness, fellow-feeling, self-control, rightly ordered and harmonised action, is the best we can do in the limits of the mental formation, but it is a stage and not the goal of our growth of being. These are solutions by the way, palliatives, necessary means for a partial dealing with this root difficulty, provisional standards and devices given us as a temporary help and guidance because the true and total solution is beyond our present capacity and can only come when we have sufficiently evolved to see it and make it our main endeavour.

The true solution can intervene only when by our spiritual growth we can become one self with all beings, know them as part of our self, deal with them as if they were our other selves; for then the division is healed, the law of separate self-affirmation leading by itself to affirmation against or at the expense of others is enlarged and liberated by adding to it the law of our self-affirmation for others and our self-finding in their self-finding and self-realisation. It has been made a rule of religious ethics to act in a spirit of universal compassion, to love one's neighbour as oneself, to do to others as one would have them do to us, to feel the joy and grief of others as one's own; but no man living in his ego is able truly and perfectly to do these things, he can only accept them as a demand of his mind, an aspiration of his heart, an effort of his will to live by a high standard and modify by a sincere endeavour his crude ego-nature. It is when others are known and felt intimately as oneself that this ideal can become a natural and spontaneous rule of our living and be realised in practice as in principle. But even oneness with others is not enough by itself, if it is a oneness with their ignorance; for then the law of ignorance will work and error of action and wrong action will survive even if diminished in degree and mellowed in incidence and character. Our oneness with others must be fundamental, not a oneness with their minds, hearts, vital selves, egos, — even though these come to be included in our universalised consciousness, — but a oneness in the soul and spirit, and that can only come by our liberation into soul-awareness and self-knowledge. To be ourselves liberated from ego and realise our true selves is the first necessity; all else can be achieved as a luminous result, a necessary consequence. That is one reason why a spiritual call must be accepted as imperative and take precedence over all other claims, intellectual, ethical, social, that belong to the domain of the Ignorance. For the mental law of good abides in that domain and can only modify and palliate; nothing can be a sufficient substitute for the spiritual change that can realise the true and integral good because through the spirit we come to the root of action and existence.

In the spiritual knowledge of self there are three steps of its self-achievement which are at the same time three parts of the one knowledge. The first is the discovery of the soul, not the outer soul of thought and emotion and desire, but the secret psychic entity, the divine element within us. When that becomes dominant over the nature, when we are consciously the soul and when mind, life and body take their true place as its instruments, we are aware of a guide within that knows the truth, the good, the true delight and beauty of existence, controls heart and intellect by its luminous law and leads our life and being towards spiritual completeness. Even within the obscure workings of the Ignorance we have then a witness who discerns, a living light that illumines, a will that refuses to be misled and separates the mind's truth from its error, the heart's intimate response from its vibrations to a wrong call and wrong demand upon it, the life's true ardour and plenitude of movement from vital passion and the turbid falsehoods of our vital nature and its dark self-seekings. This is the first step of self-realisation, to enthrone the soul, the divine psychic individual in the place of the ego. The next step is to become aware of the eternal self in us unborn and one with the self of all beings. This self-realisation liberates and universalises; even if our action still proceeds in the dynamics of the Ignorance, it no longer binds or misleads because our inner being is seated in the light of self-knowledge. The third step is to know the Divine Being who is at once our supreme transcendent Self, the Cosmic Being, foundation of our universality, and the Divinity within of which our psychic being, the true evolving individual in our nature, is a portion, a spark, a flame growing into the eternal Fire from which it was lit and of which it is the witness ever living within us and the conscious instrument of its light and power and joy and beauty. Aware of the Divine as the Master of our being and action, we can learn to become channels of his Shakti, the Divine Puissance, and act according to her dictates or her rule of light and power within us. Our action will not then be mastered by our vital impulse or governed by a mental standard, for she acts according to the permanent yet plastic truth of things, — not that which the mind constructs, but the higher, deeper and subtler truth of each movement and circumstance as it is known to the supreme knowledge and demanded by the supreme will in the universe. The liberation of the will follows upon the liberation in knowledge and is its dynamic consequence; it is knowledge that purifies, it is truth that liberates: evil is the fruit of a spiritual ignorance and it will disappear only by the growth of a spiritual consciousness and the light of spiritual knowledge. The division of our being from the being of others can only be healed by removing the divorce of our nature from the inner soul-reality, by abolishing the veil between our becoming and our self-being, by bridging the remoteness of our individuality in Nature from the Divine Being who is the omnipresent Reality in Nature and above Nature.

But the last division to be removed is the scission between this Nature and the Supernature which is the Self-Power of the Divine Existence. Even before the dynamic Knowledge-Ignorance is removed, while it still remains as an inadequate instrumentation of the spirit, the supreme Shakti or Supernature can work through us and we can be aware of her workings; but it is then by a modification of her light and power so that it can be received and assimilated by the inferior nature of the mind, life and body. But this is not enough; there is needed an entire remoulding of what we are into a way and power of the divine Supernature. The integration of our being cannot be complete unless there is this transformation of the dynamic action; there must be an uplifting and change of the whole mode of Nature itself and not only some illumination and transmutation of the inner ways of the being. An eternal Truth-Consciousness must possess us and sublimate all our natural modes into its own modes of being, knowledge and action; a spontaneous truth-awareness, truth-will, truth-feeling, truth-movement, truth-action can then become the integral law of our nature.

END OF THE SECOND BOOK, PART I

Part II

The Knowledge and
the Spiritual Evolution

Chapter XV

Reality and the Integral Knowledge

This Self is to be won by the Truth and by an integral knowledge.
Mundaka Upanishad.[1]

Hear how thou shalt know Me in My totality... for even of the seekers who have achieved, hardly one knows Me in all the truth of My being.
Gita.[2]

THIS THEN is the origin, this the nature, these the boundaries of the Ignorance. Its origin is a limitation of knowledge, its distinctive character a separation of the being from its own integrality and entire reality; its boundaries are determined by this separative development of the consciousness, for it shuts us to our true self and to the true self and whole nature of things and obliges us to live in an apparent surface existence. A return or a progress to integrality, a disappearance of the limitation, a breaking down of separativeness, an overpassing of boundaries, a recovery of our essential and whole reality must be the sign and opposite character of the inner turn towards Knowledge. There must be a replacement of a limited and separative by an essential and integral consciousness identified with the original truth and the whole truth of self and existence. The integral Knowledge is something that is already there in the integral Reality: it is not a new or still non-existent thing that has to be created, acquired, learned, invented or built up by the mind; it must rather be discovered or uncovered, it is a Truth that is self-revealed to a spiritual endeavour: for it is there veiled in our deeper and greater self; it is the very stuff of our own spiritual consciousness, and it is by awaking to it even

[1] III. 1. 5.   [2] VII. 1, 3.

in our surface self that we have to possess it. There is an integral self-knowledge that we have to recover and, because the world-self also is our self, an integral world-knowledge. A knowledge that can be learned or constructed by the mind exists and has its value, but that is not what is meant when we speak of the Knowledge and the Ignorance.

An integral spiritual consciousness carries in it a knowledge of all the terms of being; it links the highest to the lowest through all the mediating terms and achieves an indivisible whole. At the highest summit of things it opens to the reality, ineffable because superconscient to all but its own self-awareness, of the Absolute. At the lowest end of our being it perceives the Inconscience from which our evolution begins; but at the same time it is aware of the One and the All self-involved in those depths, it unveils the secret Consciousness in the Inconscience. Interpretative, revelatory, moving between these two extremes, its vision discovers the manifestation of the One in the Many, the identity of the Infinite in the disparity of things finite, the presence of the timeless Eternal in eternal Time; it is this seeing that illumines for it the meaning of the universe. This consciousness does not abolish the universe; it takes it up and transforms it by giving to it its hidden significance. It does not abolish the individual existence; it transforms the individual being and nature by revealing to them their true significance and enabling them to overcome their separateness from the Divine Reality and the Divine Nature.

An integral knowledge presupposes an integral Reality; for it is the power of a Truth-Consciousness which is itself the consciousness of the Reality. But our idea and sense of Reality vary with our status and movement of consciousness, its sight, its stress, its intake of things; that sight or stress can be intensive and exclusive or extensive, inclusive and comprehensive. It is quite possible, — and it is in its own field a valid movement for our thought and for a very high line of spiritual achievement, — to affirm the existence of the ineffable Absolute, to emphasise its sole Reality and to negate and abolish for our self, to expunge from our idea and sense of reality, the individual being and the cosmic creation. The reality of the individual is Brahman the

Absolute; the reality of the cosmos is Brahman the Absolute: the individual is a phenomenon, a temporal appearance in the cosmos; the cosmos itself is a phenomenon, a larger and more complex temporal appearance. The two terms, Knowledge and Ignorance, belong only to this appearance; in order to reach an absolute superconsciousness both have to be transcended: ego-consciousness and cosmic consciousness are extinguished in that supreme transcendence and there remains only the Absolute. For the absolute Brahman exists only in its own identity and is beyond all other-knowledge; there the very idea of the knower and the known and therefore of the knowledge in which they meet and become one, disappears, is transcended and loses its validity, so that to mind and speech the absolute Brahman must remain always unattainable. In opposition to the view we have put forward or in completion of it, — the view of the Ignorance itself as only either a limited or an involved action of the divine Knowledge, limited in the partly conscious, involved in the inconscient, — we might say from this other end of the scale of things that Knowledge itself is only a higher Ignorance, since it stops short of the absolute Reality which is self-evident to Itself but to mind unknowable. This absolutism corresponds to a truth of thought and to a truth of supreme experience in the spiritual consciousness; but by itself it is not the whole of spiritual thought complete and comprehensive and it does not exhaust the possibilities of the supreme spiritual experience.

The absolutist view of reality, consciousness and knowledge is founded on one side of the earliest Vedantic thought, but it is not the whole of that thinking. In the Upanishads, in the inspired scripture of the most ancient Vedanta, we find the affirmation of the Absolute, the experience-concept of the utter and ineffable Transcendence; but we find also, not in contradiction to it but as its corollary, an affirmation of the cosmic Divinity, an experience-concept of the cosmic Self and the becoming of Brahman in the universe. Equally, we find the affirmation of the Divine Reality in the individual: this too is an experience-concept; it is seized upon not as an appearance, but as an actual becoming. In place of a sole supreme exclusive affirmation negating all else than the transcendent Absolute we find a comprehensive affirmation carried to its farthest conclusion: this concept of Reality and of Knowledge enveloping in one view the cosmic and the Absolute coincides fundamentally with our own; for it implies that the Ignorance too is a half-veiled part of the Knowledge and world-knowledge a part of self-knowledge. The Isha Upanishad insists on the unity and reality of all the manifestations of the Absolute; it refuses to confine truth to any one aspect. Brahman is the stable and the mobile, the internal and the external, all that is near and all that is far whether spiritually or in the extension of Time and Space; it is the Being and all becomings, the Pure and Silent who is without feature or action and the Seer and Thinker who organises the world and its objects; it is the One who becomes all that we are sensible of in the universe, the Immanent and that in which he takes up his dwelling. The Upanishad affirms the perfect and the liberating knowledge to be that which excludes neither the Self nor its creations: the liberated spirit sees all these as becomings of the Self-existent in an internal vision and by a consciousness which perceives the universe within itself instead of looking out on it, like the limited and egoistic mind, as a thing other than itself. To live in the cosmic Ignorance is a blindness, but to confine oneself in an exclusive absolutism of Knowledge is also a blindness: to know Brahman as at once and together the Knowledge and the Ignorance, to attain to the supreme status at once by the Becoming and the Non-Becoming, to relate together realisation of the transcendent and the cosmic self, to achieve foundation in the supramundane and a self-aware manifestation in the mundane, is the integral knowledge; that is the possession of Immortality. It is this whole consciousness with its complete knowledge that builds the foundation of the Life Divine and makes its attainment possible. It follows that the absolute reality of the Absolute must be, not a rigid indeterminable oneness, not an infinity vacant of all that is not a pure self-existence attainable only by the exclusion of the many and the finite, but something which is beyond these definitions, beyond indeed any description either positive or negative. All affirmations and negations are expressive of its aspects, and it is through both a supreme affirmation and a supreme negation that we can arrive at the Absolute.

On the one side, then, presented to us as the Reality, we have an absolute Self-Existence, an eternal sole self-being, and through the experience of the silent and inactive Self or the detached immobile Purusha we can move towards this featureless and relationless Absolute, negate the actions of the creative Power, whether that be an illusory Maya or a formative Prakriti, pass from all circling in cosmic error into the eternal Peace and Silence, get rid of our personal existence and find or lose ourselves in that sole true Existence. On the other side, we have a Becoming which is a true movement of Being, and both the Being and the Becoming are truths of one absolute Reality. The first view is founded on the metaphysical conception which formulates an extreme perception in our thought, an exclusive experience in our consciousness of the Absolute as a reality void of all relations and determinations: that imposes as its consequence a logical and practical necessity to deny the world of relativities as a falsity of unreal being, a Non-Existent (Asat), or at least a lower and evanescent, temporal and pragmatic self-experience, and to cut it away from the consciousness in order to arrive at liberation of the spirit from its false perceptions or its inferior creations. The second view is based on the conception of the Absolute as neither positively nor negatively limitable. It is beyond all relations in the sense that it is not bound by any relativities or limitable by them in its power of being: it cannot be tied down and circumscribed by our relative conceptions, highest or lowest, positive or negative; it is bound neither by our knowledge nor by our ignorance, neither by our concept of existence nor by our concept of non-existence. But neither can it be limited by any incapacity to contain, sustain, create or manifest relations: on the contrary, the power to manifest itself in infinity of unity and infinity of multiplicity can be regarded as an inherent force, sign, result of its very absoluteness, and this possibility is in itself a sufficient explanation of cosmic existence. The Absolute cannot indeed be bound in its nature to manifest a cosmos of relations, but neither can it be bound not to manifest any cosmos. It is not itself a sheer emptiness; for a vacant Absolute is no Absolute, — our conception of a Void or Zero is only a conceptual sign of our mental inability to know or grasp it: it bears in itself some ineffable essentiality of all that is and all that can be; and since it holds in itself this essentiality and this possibility, it must also hold in itself in some way of its absoluteness either the permanent truth or the inherent, even if latent, realisable actuality of all that is fundamental to our or the world's existence. It is this realisable actuality actualised or this permanent truth deploying its possibilities that we call manifestation and see as the universe.

There is, then, in the conception or the realisation of the truth of the Absolute no inherent inevitable consequence of a rejection or a dissolution of the truth of the universe. The idea of an essentially unreal universe manifested somehow by an inexplicable Power of illusion, the Absolute Brahman regarding it not or aloof and not affecting it even as it is unaffected by it, is at bottom a carrying over, an imposing or imputation, *adhyāropa*, of an incapacity of our mental consciousness to That so as to limit it. Our mental consciousness, when it passes beyond its limits, loses its own way and means of knowledge and tends towards inactivity or cessation; it loses at the same time or tends to have no further hold on its former contents, no continuing conception of the reality of that which once was to it all that was real: we impute to absolute Parabrahman, conceived as non-manifest for ever, a corresponding inability or separation or aloofness from what has become or seems now to us unreal; it must, like our mind in its cessation or self-extinction, be by its very nature of pure absoluteness void of all connection with this world of apparent manifestation, incapable of any supporting cognition or dynamic maintenance of it that gives it a reality, — or, if there is such a cognition, it must be of the nature of an Is that is not, a magical Maya. But there is no binding reason to suppose that this chasm must exist; what our relative human consciousness is or is not capable of, is no test or standard of an absolute capacity; its conceptions cannot be applied to an absolute self-awareness: what is necessary for our mental ignorance in order to escape from itself cannot be the necessity of the Absolute which has no need of self-escape and no reason for refusing to cognise whatever is to it cognisable.

There is that unmanifest Unknowable; there is this manifest knowable, partly manifest to our ignorance, manifest entirely to the divine Knowledge which holds it in its own infinity. If it is true that neither our ignorance nor our utmost and widest mental knowledge can give us a hold of the Unknowable, still it is also true that, whether through our knowledge or through our ignorance, That variously manifests itself; for it cannot be manifesting something other than itself, since nothing else can exist: in this variety of manifestation there is that Oneness and through the diversity we can touch the Oneness. But even so, even accepting this co-existence, it is still possible to pass a final verdict and sentence of condemnation on the Becoming and decide on the necessity of a renunciation of it and a return into the absolute Being. This verdict can be based on the distinction between the real reality of the Absolute and the partial and misleading reality of the relative universe.

For we have in this unfolding of knowledge the two terms of the One and the Many, as we have the two terms of the finite and the infinite, of that which becomes and of that which does not become but for ever is, of that which takes form and of that which does not take form, of Spirit and Matter, of the supreme Superconscient and the nethermost Inconscience; in this dualism, and to get away from it, it is open to us to define Knowledge as the possession of one term and the possession of the other as Ignorance. The ultimate of our life would then be a drawing away from the lower reality of the Becoming to the greater reality of the Being, a leap from the Ignorance to the Knowledge and a rejection of the Ignorance, a departure from the many into the One, from the finite into the infinite, from form into the formless, from the life of the material universe into the Spirit, from the hold of the inconscient upon us into the superconscient Existence. In this solution there is supposed to be a fixed opposition, an ultimate irreconcilability in each case between the two terms of our being. Or else, if both are a means of the manifestation of the Brahman, the lower is a false or imperfect clue, a means that must fail, a system of values that cannot ultimately satisfy us. Dissatisfied with the confusions of the multiplicity, disdainful of even the highest light and power and joy that it can reveal, we must drive beyond to the absolute one-pointedness and one-standingness in which all self-variation ceases. Unable by the claim of the Infinite upon us to dwell for ever in the bonds of the finite or to find there satisfaction and largeness and peace, we have to break all the bonds of individual and universal Nature, destroy all values, symbols, images, self-definitions, limitations of the illimitable and lose all littleness and division in the Self that is for ever satisfied with its own infinity. Disgusted with forms, disillusioned of their false and transient attractions, wearied and discouraged by their fleeting impermanence and vain round of recurrence, we must escape from the cycles of Nature into the formlessness and featureless-ness of permanent Being. Ashamed of Matter and its grossness, impatient of the purposeless stir and trouble of Life, tired out by the goalless running of Mind or convinced of the vanity of all its aims and objects, we have to release ourselves into the eternal repose and purity of the Spirit. The Inconscient is a sleep or a prison, the conscient a round of strivings without ultimate issue or the wanderings of a dream: we must wake into the superconscious where all darkness of night and half-lights cease in the self-luminous bliss of the Eternal. The Eternal is our refuge; all the rest are false values, the Ignorance and its mazes, a self-bewilderment of the soul in phenomenal Nature.

Our conception of the Knowledge and the Ignorance rejects this negation and the oppositions on which it is founded: it points to a larger if more difficult issue of reconciliation. For we see that these apparently opposite terms of One and Many, Form and the Formless, Finite and Infinite, are not so much opposites as complements of each other; not alternating values of the Brahman which in its creation perpetually loses oneness to find itself in multiplicity and, unable to discover itself in multiplicity, loses it again to recover oneness, but double and concurrent values which explain each other; not hopelessly incompatible alternatives, but two faces of the one Reality which can lead us to it by our realisation of both together and not only by testing each separately, — even though such separate testing may be a legitimate or even an inevitable step or part of the process of knowledge. Knowledge is no doubt the knowledge of the One, the realisation of the Being; Ignorance is a self-oblivion of Being, the experience of separateness in the multiplicity and a dwelling or circling in the ill-understood maze of becomings: but this is cured by the soul in the Becoming growing into knowledge, into awareness of the Being which becomes in the multiplicity all these existences and can so become because their truth is already there in its timeless existence. The integral knowledge of Brahman is a consciousness in possession of both together, and the exclusive pursuit of either closes the vision to one side of the truth of the omnipresent Reality. The possession of the Being who is beyond all becomings, brings to us freedom from the bonds of attachment and ignorance in the cosmic existence and brings by that freedom a free possession of the Becoming and of the cosmic existence. The knowledge of the Becoming is a part of knowledge; it acts as an Ignorance only because we dwell imprisoned in it, *avidyāyām antare*, without possessing the Oneness of the Being, which is its base, its stuff, its spirit, its cause of manifestation and without which it could not be possible.

In fact, the Brahman is one not only in a featureless oneness beyond all relation, but in the very multiplicity of the cosmic existence. Aware of the works of the dividing mind but not itself limited by it, It finds its oneness as easily in the many, in relations, in becoming as in any withdrawal from the many, from relations, from becoming. Ourselves also, to possess even its oneness fully, must possess it, — since it is there, since all is that, — in the infinite self-variation of the cosmos. The infinity of the multiplicity finds itself explained and justified only when it is contained and possessed in the infinity of the One; but also the infinity of the One pours itself out and possesses itself in the infinity of the Many. To be capable of that outpouring

of its energies as well as not to lose itself in it, not to recoil
defeated from its boundlessness and endlessness of vicissitudes
and differences as well as not to be self-divided by its variations,
is the divine strength of the free Purusha, the conscious Soul in its
possession of its own immortal self-knowledge. The finite self-
variations of the Self in which the mind losing self-knowledge
is caught and dispersed among the variations, are yet not the
denials but the endless expression of the Infinite and have no
other meaning or reason for existence: the Infinite too, while it
possesses its delight of limitless being, finds also the joy of that
very limitlessness in its infinite self-definition in the universe.
The Divine Being is not incapable of taking innumerable forms
because He is beyond all form in His essence, nor by assuming
them does He lose His divinity, but pours out rather in them the
delight of His being and the glories of His godhead; this gold
does not cease to be gold because it shapes itself into all kinds
of ornaments and coins itself into many currencies and values,
nor does the Earth-Power, principle of all this figured material
existence, lose her immutable divinity because she forms herself
into habitable worlds, throws herself out in the hills and hollows
and allows herself to be shaped into utensils of the hearth and
household or as hard metal into the weapon and the engine.
Matter, — substance itself, subtle or dense, mental or material,
— is form and body of Spirit and would never have been created
if it could not be made a basis for the self-expression of the
Spirit. The apparent Inconscience of the material universe holds
in itself darkly all that is eternally self-revealed in the luminous
Superconscient; to reveal it in Time is the slow and deliberate
delight of Nature and the aim of her cycles.

But there are other conceptions of reality, other conceptions
of the nature of knowledge which demand consideration. There
is the view that all that exists is a subjective creation of Mind,
a structure of Consciousness, and that the idea of an objective
reality self-existent, independent of Consciousness, is an illusion,
since we have and can have no evidence of any such independent
self-existence of things. This way of seeing may lead to the affirmation of the creative Consciousness as the sole Reality or to the

denial of all existence and the affirmation of Non-Existence or a nescient Zero as the sole Reality. For, in one view, the objects constructed by consciousness have no intrinsic reality, they are merely structures; even the consciousness that constructs them is itself only a flux of perceptions that assume an appearance of connection and continuity and create a sense of continuous time, but in reality these things have no stable basis as they are only an appearance of reality. This would mean that the reality is an eternal absence at once of all self-conscious existence and of all that constitutes movement of existence: Knowledge would mean a return to that from the appearance of the constructed universe. There would be a double and complete self-extinction, the disappearance of Purusha, the cessation or extinction of Prakriti; for the conscious Soul and Nature are the two terms of our being and comprehend all that we mean by existence, and the negation of both is the absolute Nirvana. What is real, then, must be either an Inconscience, in which this flux and these structures appear, or a Superconscience beyond all idea of self or existence. But this view of the universe is only true of the appearance of things when we regard our surface mind as the whole of consciousness; as a description of the working of that Mind it is valid; there, undoubtedly, all looks like a flux and a construction by an impermanent Consciousness. But this cannot prevail as a whole account of existence if there is a greater and deeper self-knowledge and world-knowledge, a knowledge by identity, a consciousness to which that knowledge is normal and a Being of which that consciousness is the eternal self-awareness; for then the subjective and the objective can be real and intimate to that consciousness and being, both can be something of itself, sides of its identity, authentic to its existence.

On the other hand, if the constructing Mind or Consciousness is real and the sole reality, then the universe of material beings and objects may have an existence, but it is purely subjective-structural, made by Consciousness out of itself, maintained by it, dissolving into it in their disappearance. For if there is nothing else, no essential Existence or Being supporting the creative Power, and there is not, either, a sustaining Void or

Nihil, then this Consciousness which creates everything must itself have or be an existence or a substance; if it can make structures, they must be constructions out of its own substance or forms of its own existence. A consciousness which is not that of an Existence or is not itself an existence, must be an unreality, a perceptive Force of a Void or in a Void raising there unreal structures made of nothing, — a proposition which is not easily acceptable unless all others prove to be invalid. It then becomes apparent that what we see as consciousness must be a Being or an Existence out of whose substance of consciousness all is created.

But if we thus get back to the biune or the dual reality of Being and Consciousness, we can either suppose with Vedanta one original Being or with Sankhya a plurality of beings to whom Consciousness or some Energy to which we attribute consciousness presents its structures. If a plurality of separate original beings alone is real, then, since each would be or create its own world in its own consciousness, the difficulty is to account for their relations in a single identical universe; there must be a one Consciousness or one Energy, — corresponding to the Sankhya idea of a single Prakriti which is the field of experience of many like Purushas, — in which they meet in an identical mind-constructed universe. This theory of things has the advantage of accounting for the multitude of souls and multitude of things and the oneness in diversity of their experience, while at the same time it gives a reality to the separate spiritual growth and destiny of the individual being. But if we can suppose a One Consciousness, or a One Energy, creating a multitude of figures of itself and accommodating in its world a plurality of beings, there is no difficulty in supposing a one original Being who supports or expresses himself in a plurality of beings, — souls or spiritual powers of his one-existence; it would follow also that all objects, all the figures of consciousness would be figures of the Being. It must then be asked whether this plurality and these figures are realities of the one Real Existence, or representative personalities and images only, or symbols or values created by Mind to represent It. This would depend largely on whether it is only Mind as we know it that is in action or a deeper and greater Consciousness, of which Mind is a surface instrument, executrix of its initiations, medium of its manifestations. If it is the former, the universe constructed and seen by Mind can only have a subjective or symbolic or representative reality: if the latter, then the universe and its natural beings and objects can be true realities of the One Existence, forms or powers of its being manifested by its force of being. Mind would be only an interpreter between the universal Reality and the manifestations of its creative Consciousness-Force, Shakti, Prakriti, Maya.

It is clear that a Mind of the nature of our surface intelligence can be only a secondary power of existence. For it bears the stamp of incapacity and ignorance as a sign that it is derivative and not the original creatrix; we see that it does not know or understand the objects it perceives, it has no automatic control of them; it has to acquire a laboriously built knowledge and controlling power. This initial incapacity could not be there if these objects were the Mind's own structures, creations of its self-Power. It may be that this is so because individual mind has only a frontal and derivative power and knowledge and there is a universal Mind that is whole, endowed with omniscience, capable of omnipotence. But the nature of Mind as we know it is an Ignorance seeking for knowledge; it is a knower of fractions and worker of divisions striving to arrive at a sum, to piece together a whole, — it is not possessed of the essence of things or their totality: a universal Mind of the same character might know the sum of its divisions by force of its universality, but it would still lack the essential knowledge, and without the essential knowledge there could be no true integral knowledge. A consciousness possessing the essential and integral knowledge, proceeding from the essence to the whole and from the whole to the parts, would be no longer Mind, but a perfect Truth-Consciousness automatically possessed of inherent self-knowledge and world-knowledge. It is from this basis that we have to look at the subjective view of reality. It is true that there is no such thing as an objective reality independent of consciousness; but at the same time there is a truth in objectivity and it is this, that the reality of things resides in something that is within them and is independent of the interpretation our mind gives to them and of the structures it builds upon its observation. These structures constitute the mind's subjective image or figure of the universe, but the universe and its objects are not a mere image or figure. They are in essence creations of consciousness, but of a consciousness that is one with being, whose substance is the substance of Being and whose creations too are of that substance, therefore real. In this view the world cannot be a purely subjective creation of Consciousness; the subjective and the objective truth of things are both real, they are two sides of the same Reality.

In a certain sense, to use the relative and suggestive phrasing of our human language, all things are the symbols through which we have to approach and draw nearer to That by which we and they exist. The infinity of unity is one symbol, the infinity of the multiplicity is another symbol: again, since each thing in the multiplicity points back to the unity, since each thing that we call finite is a representative figure, a form-front, a silhouette shadowing out something of the infinite, all that defines itself in the universe, — all its objects, happenings, idea-formations, life-formations, — are in their turn each a clue and a symbol. To our subjective mind the infinity of existence is one symbol, the infinity of non-existence is another symbol. The infinity of the Inconscient and the infinity of the Superconscient are two poles of the manifestation of the absolute Parabrahman, and our existence between these two poles and our passage from one to the other are a progressive seizing, a constant interpretation, a subjective building up in ourselves of this manifestation of the Unmanifest. Through such an unfolding of our self-existence we have to arrive at the consciousness of its ineffable Presence and of ourselves and the world and all that is and all that is not as the unveiling of that which never entirely unveils itself to anything other than its own self-light eternal and absolute.

But this way of seeing things belongs to the action of the mind interpreting the relation between the Being and the external Becoming; it is valid as a dynamic mental representation corresponding to a certain truth of the manifestation, but subject to the proviso that these symbolic values of things do not make the things themselves mere significant counters, abstract symbols like mathematical formulae or other signs used by the mind for knowledge: for forms and happenings in the universe are realities significant of Reality; they are self-expressions of That, movements and powers of the Being. Each form is there because it is an expression of some power of That which inhabits it; each happening is a movement in the working out of some Truth of the Being in its dynamic process of manifestation. It is this significance that gives validity to the mind's interpretative knowledge, its subjective construction of the universe; our mind is primarily a percipient and interpreter, secondarily and derivatively a creator. This indeed is the value of all mental subjectivity that it reflects in it some truth of the Being which exists independently of the reflection, — whether that independence presents itself as a physical objectivity or a supraphysical reality perceived by the mind but not perceptible by the physical senses. Mind, then, is not the original constructor of the universe: it is an intermediate power valid for certain actualities of being; an agent, an intermediary, it actualises possibilities and has its share in the creation, but the real creatrix is a Consciousness, an Energy inherent in the transcendent and cosmic Spirit.

There is a precisely opposite view of reality and knowledge which affirms an objective Reality as the only entire truth and an objective knowledge as the sole entirely reliable knowledge. This view starts from the idea of physical existence as the one fundamental existence and the relegation of consciousness, mind, soul or spirit to the position of a temporary outcome of the physical Energy in its cosmic action, — if indeed soul or spirit has any existence. All that is not physical and objective has a lesser reality dependent on the physical and objective; it has to justify itself to the physical mind by objective evidence or a recognisable and verifiable relation to the truth of physical and external things before it can be given a passport of reality. But it is evident that this solution cannot be accepted in its rigour, as it has no integrality in it but looks at only one side of existence, even only one province or district of existence, and leaves all the rest unexplained, without inherent reality, without significance. If pushed to its extreme, it would give to a stone or a plum-pudding a greater reality and to thought, love, courage, genius, greatness, the human soul and mind facing an obscure and dangerous world and getting mastery over it an inferior dependent reality or even an unsubstantial and evanescent reality. For in this view these things so great to our subjective vision are valid only as the reactions of an objective material being to an objective material existence; they are valid only in so far as they deal with objective realities and make themselves effective upon them: the soul, if it exists, is only a circumstance of an objectively real world-Nature. But it could be held, on the contrary, that the objective assumes value only as it has a relation to the soul; it is a field, an occasion, a means for the soul's progression in Time: the objective is created as a ground of manifestation for the subjective. The objective world is only an outward form of becoming of the Spirit; it is here a first form, a basis, but it is not the essential thing, the main truth of being. The subjective and objective are two necessary sides of the manifested Reality and of equal value, and in the range of the objective itself the supraphysical object of consciousness has as much right to acceptance as the physical objectivity; it cannot be *a priori* set aside as a subjective delusion or hallucination.

In fact, subjectivity and objectivity are not independent realities, they depend upon each other; they are the Being, through consciousness, looking at itself as subject on the object and the same Being offering itself to its own consciousness as object to the subject. The more partial view concedes no substantive reality to anything which exists only in the consciousness, or, to put it more accurately, to anything to which the inner consciousness or sense bears testimony but which the outer physical senses do not provide with a ground or do not substantiate. But the outer senses can bear a reliable evidence only when they refer their version of the object to the consciousness and that consciousness gives a significance to their report, adds to its externality its own internal intuitive interpretation and justifies it by a reasoned adherence; for the evidence of the senses is always by itself imperfect, not altogether reliable and certainly not final, because it is incomplete and constantly subject to error. Indeed, we have no means of knowing the objective universe except by our subjective consciousness of which the physical senses themselves are instruments; as the world appears not only to that but in that, so it is to us. If we deny reality to the evidence of this universal witness for subjective or for supraphysical objectivities, there is no sufficient reason to concede reality to its evidence for physical objectivities; if the inner or the supraphysical objects of consciousness are unreal, the objective physical universe has also every chance of being unreal. In each case understanding, discrimination, verification are necessary; but the subjective and the supraphysical must have another method of verification than that which we apply successfully to the physical and external objective. Subjective experience cannot be referred to the evidence of the external senses; it has its own standards of seeing and its inner method of verification: so also supraphysical realities by their very nature cannot be referred to the judgment of the physical or sense mind except when they project themselves into the physical, and even then that judgment is often incompetent or subject to caution; they can only be verified by other senses and by a method of scrutiny and affirmation which is applicable to their own reality, their own nature.

There are different orders of reality; the objective and physical is only one order. It is convincing to the physical or externalising mind because it is directly obvious to the senses, while of the subjective and the supraphysical that mind has no means of knowledge except from fragmentary signs and data and inferences which are at every step liable to error. Our subjective movements and inner experiences are a domain of happenings as real as any outward physical happenings; but if the individual mind can know something of its own phenomena by direct experience, it is ignorant of what happens in the consciousness of others except by analogy with its own or such signs, data, inferences as its outward observation can give it. I am therefore inwardly real to myself, but the invisible life of others has only an indirect reality to me except in so far as it impinges on my own mind, life and senses. This is the limitation of the physical mind of man, and it creates in him a habit of believing entirely only in the physical and of doubting or challenging all that does not come into accord with his own experience or his own scope of understanding or square with his own standard or sum of established knowledge.

This ego-centric attitude has in recent times been elevated into a valid standard of knowledge; it has been implicitly or explicitly held as an axiom that all truth must be referred to the judgment of the personal mind, reason and experience of every man or else it must be verified or at any rate verifiable by a common or universal experience in order to be valid. But obviously this is a false standard of reality and of knowledge, since this means the sovereignty of the normal or average mind and its limited capacity and experience, the exclusion of what is supernormal or beyond the average intelligence. In its extreme, this claim of the individual to be the judge of everything is an egoistic illusion, a superstition of the physical mind, in the mass a gross and vulgar error. The truth behind it is that each man has to think for himself, know for himself according to his capacity, but his judgment can be valid only on condition that he is ready to learn and open always to a larger knowledge. It is reasoned that to depart from the physical standard and the principle of personal or universal verification will lead to gross delusions and the admission of unverified truth and subjective phantasy into the realm of knowledge. But error and delusion and the introduction of personality and one's own subjectivity into the pursuit of knowledge are always present, and the physical or objective standards and methods do not exclude them. The probability of error is no reason for refusing to attempt discovery, and subjective discovery must be pursued by a subjective method of enquiry, observation and verification; research into the supraphysical must evolve, accept and test an appropriate means and methods other than those by which one examines the constituents of physical objects and the processes of Energy in material Nature.

To refuse to enquire upon any general ground preconceived and *a priori* is an obscurantism as prejudicial to the extension of knowledge as the religious obscurantism which opposed in Europe the extension of scientific discovery. The greatest inner discoveries, the experience of self-being, the cosmic consciousness, the inner calm of the liberated spirit, the direct effect of mind upon mind, the knowledge of things by consciousness in direct contact with other consciousness or with its objects, most spiritual experiences of any value, cannot be brought before the tribunal of the common mentality which has no experience of these things and takes its own absence or incapacity of experience as a proof of their invalidity or their non-existence. Physical truth of formulas, generalisations, discoveries founded upon physical observation can be so referred, but even there a training of capacity is needed before one can truly understand and judge; it is not every untrained mind that can follow the mathematics of relativity or other difficult scientific truths or judge of the validity either of their result or their process. All reality, all experience must indeed, to be held as true, be capable of verification by a same or similar experience; so, in fact, all men can have a spiritual experience and can follow it out and verify it in themselves, but only when they have acquired the capacity or can follow the inner methods by which that experience and verification are made possible. It is necessary to dwell for a moment on these obvious and elementary truths because the opposite ideas have been sovereign in a recent period of human mentality, — they are now only receding, — and have stood in the way of the development of a vast domain of possible knowledge. It is of supreme importance for the human spirit to be free to sound the depths of inner or subliminal reality, of spiritual and of what is still superconscient reality, and not to immure itself in the physical mind and its narrow domain of objective external solidities; for in that way alone can there come liberation from the Ignorance in which our mentality dwells and a release into a complete consciousness, a true and integral self-realisation and self-knowledge.

An integral knowledge demands an exploration, an unveiling of all the possible domains of consciousness and experience.

For there are subjective domains of our being which lie behind the obvious surface; these have to be fathomed and whatever is ascertained must be admitted within the scope of the total reality. An inner range of spiritual experience is one very great domain of human consciousness; it has to be entered into up to its deepest depths and its vastest reaches. The supraphysical is as real as the physical; to know it is part of a complete knowledge. The knowledge of the supraphysical has been associated with mysticism and occultism, and occultism has been banned as a superstition and a fantastic error. But the occult is a part of existence; a true occultism means no more than a research into supraphysical realities and an unveiling of the hidden laws of being and Nature, of all that is not obvious on the surface. It attempts the discovery of the secret laws of mind and mental energy, the secret laws of life and life-energy, the secret laws of the subtle-physical and its energies, — all that Nature has not put into visible operation on the surface; it pursues also the application of these hidden truths and powers of Nature so as to extend the mastery of the human spirit beyond the ordinary operations of mind, the ordinary operations of life, the ordinary operations of our physical existence. In the spiritual domain which is occult to the surface mind in so far as it passes beyond normal and enters into supernormal experience, there is possible not only the discovery of the self and spirit, but the discovery of the uplifting, informing and guiding light of spiritual consciousness and the power of the spirit, the spiritual way of knowledge, the spiritual way of action. To know these things and to bring their truths and forces into the life of humanity is a necessary part of its evolution. Science itself is in its own way an occultism; for it brings to light the formulas which Nature has hidden and it uses its knowledge to set free operations of her energies which she has not included in her ordinary operations and to organise and place at the service of man her occult powers and processes, a vast system of physical magic, — for there is and can be no other magic than the utilisation of secret truths of being, secret powers and processes of Nature. It may even be found that a supraphysical knowledge is necessary for the completion of physical knowledge, because the processes of physical Nature have behind them a supraphysical factor, a power and action mental, vital or spiritual which is not tangible to any outer means of knowledge.

All insistence on the sole or the fundamental validity of the objective real takes its stand on the sense of the basic reality of Matter. But it is now evident that Matter is by no means fundamentally real; it is a structure of Energy: it is becoming even a little doubtful whether the acts and creations of this Energy itself are explicable except as the motions of power of a secret Mind or Consciousness of which its processes and steps of structure are the formulas. It is therefore no longer possible to take Matter as the sole reality. The material interpretation of existence was the result of an exclusive concentration, a preoccupation with one movement of Existence, and such an exclusive concentration has its utility and is therefore permissible; in recent times it has justified itself by the many immense and the innumerable minute discoveries of physical Science. But a solution of the whole problem of existence cannot be based on an exclusive one-sided knowledge; we must know not only what Matter is and what are its processes, but what mind and life are and what are their processes, and one must know also spirit and soul and all that is behind the material surface: only then can we have a knowledge sufficiently integral for a solution of the problem. For the same reason those views of existence which arise from an exclusive or predominant preoccupation with Mind or with Life and regard Mind or Life as the sole fundamental reality, have not a sufficiently wide basis for acceptance. Such a preoccupation of exclusive concentration may lead to a fruitful scrutiny which sheds much light on Mind and Life, but cannot result in a total solution of the problem. It may very well be that an exclusive or predominant concentration on the subliminal being, regarding the surface existence as a mere system of symbols for an expression of its sole reality, might throw a strong light on the subliminal and its processes and extend vastly the powers of the human being, but it would not be by itself an integral solution or lead us successfully to the integral knowledge of Reality. In our view the Spirit, the Self is the fundamental reality of existence;

but an exclusive concentration on this fundamental reality to the exclusion of all reality of Mind, Life or Matter except as an imposition on the Self or unsubstantial shadows cast by the Spirit might help to an independent and radical spiritual realisation but not to an integral and valid solution of the truth of cosmic and individual existence.

An integral knowledge then must be a knowledge of the truth of all sides of existence both separately and in the relation of each to all and the relation of all to the truth of the Spirit. Our present state is an Ignorance and a many-sided seeking; it seeks for the truth of all things but, — as is evident from the insistence and the variety of the human mind's speculations as to the fundamental Truth which explains all others, the Reality at the basis of all things, — the fundamental truth of things, their basic reality must be found in some at once fundamental and universal Real; it is that which, once discovered, must embrace and explain all, — for "That being known all will be known": the fundamental Real must necessarily be and contain the truth of all existence, the truth of the individual, the truth of the universe, the truth of all that is beyond the universe. The Mind, in seeking for such a Reality and testing each thing from Matter upwards to see if that might not be It, has not proceeded on a wrong intuition. All that is necessary is to carry the inquiry to its end and test the highest and ultimate levels of experience.

But since it is from the Ignorance that we proceed to the Knowledge, we have had first to discover the secret nature and full extent of the Ignorance. If we look at this Ignorance in which ordinarily we live by the very circumstance of our separative existence in a material, in a spatial and temporal universe, we see that on its obscurer side it reduces itself, from whatever direction we look at or approach it, into the fact of a many-sided self-ignorance. We are ignorant of the Absolute which is the source of all being and becoming; we take partial facts of being, temporal relations of the becoming for the whole truth of existence, — that is the first, the original ignorance. We are ignorant of the spaceless, timeless, immobile and immutable Self; we take the constant mobility and mutation of the cosmic becoming in Time and Space for the whole truth of existence, — that is the second, the cosmic ignorance. We are ignorant of our universal self, the cosmic existence, the cosmic consciousness, our infinite unity with all being and becoming; we take our limited egoistic mentality, vitality, corporeality for our true self and regard everything other than that as not-self, — that is the third, the egoistic ignorance. We are ignorant of our eternal becoming in Time; we take this little life in a small span of Time, in a petty field of Space, for our beginning, our middle and our end, — that is the fourth, the temporal ignorance. Even within this brief temporal becoming we are ignorant of our large and complex being, of that in us which is superconscient, subconscient, intraconscient, circumconscient to our surface becoming; we take that surface becoming with its small selection of overtly mentalised experiences for our whole existence, — that is the fifth, the psychological ignorance. We are ignorant of the true constitution of our becoming; we take the mind or life or body or any two of these or all three for our true principle or the whole account of what we are, losing sight of that which constitutes them and determines by its occult presence and is meant to determine sovereignly by its emergence their operations, — that is the sixth, the constitutional ignorance. As a result of all these ignorances, we miss the true knowledge, government and enjoyment of our life in the world; we are ignorant in our thought, will, sensations, actions, return wrong or imperfect responses at every point to the questionings of the world, wander in a maze of errors and desires, strivings and failures, pain and pleasure, sin and stumbling, follow a crooked road, grope blindly for a changing goal, — that is the seventh, the practical ignorance.

Our conception of the Ignorance will necessarily determine our conception of the Knowledge and determine, therefore, since our life is the Ignorance at once denying and seeking after the Knowledge, the goal of human effort and the aim of the cosmic endeavour. Integral knowledge will then mean the cancelling of the sevenfold Ignorance by the discovery of what it misses and ignores, a sevenfold self-revelation within our consciousness: it will mean the knowledge of the Absolute as the origin of all things; the knowledge of the Self, the Spirit, the Being and of the cosmos as the Self's becoming, the becoming of the Being, a manifestation of the Spirit; the knowledge of the world as one with us in the consciousness of our true self, thus cancelling our division from it by the separative idea and life of ego; the knowledge of our psychic entity and its immortal persistence in Time beyond death and earth-existence; the knowledge of our greater and inner existence behind the surface; the knowledge of our mind, life and body in its true relation to the self within and the superconscient spiritual and supramental being above them; the knowledge, finally, of the true harmony and true use of our thought, will and action and a change of all our nature into a conscious expression of the truth of the Spirit, the Self, the Divinity, the integral spiritual Reality.

But this is not an intellectual knowledge which can be learned and completed in our present mould of consciousness; it must be an experience, a becoming, a change of consciousness, a change of being. This brings in the evolutionary character of the Becoming and the fact that our mental ignorance is only a stage in our evolution. The integral knowledge, then, can only come by an evolution of our being and our nature, and that would seem to signify a slow process in Time such as has accompanied the other evolutionary transformations. But as against that inference there is the fact that the evolution has now become conscious and its method and steps need not be altogether of the same character as when it was subconscious in its process. The integral knowledge, since it must result from a change of consciousness, can be gained by a process in which our will and endeavour have a part, in which they can discover and apply their own steps and method: its growth in us can proceed by a conscious self-transformation. It is necessary then to see what is likely to be the principle of this new process of evolution and what are the movements of the integral knowledge that must necessarily emerge in it, — or, in other words, what is the nature of the consciousness that must be the base of the life divine and how that life may be expected to be formed or to form itself, to materialise or, as one might say, to "realise".

Chapter XVI

The Integral Knowledge
and the Aim of Life;
Four Theories of Existence

When all the desires that cling to the heart are loosed away from it, then the mortal becomes immortal, even here he possesses the Eternal. *Brihadaranyaka Upanishad.*[1]

He becomes the Eternal and departs into the Eternal.
Brihadaranyaka Upanishad.[2]

This bodiless and immortal Life and Light is the Brahman.
Brihadaranyaka Upanishad.[3]

Long and narrow is the ancient Path, — I have touched it, I have found it, — the Path by which the wise, knowers of the Eternal, attaining to salvation, depart hence to the high world of Paradise. *Brihadaranyaka Upanishad.*[4]

I am a son of Earth, the soil is my mother.... May she lavish on me her manifold treasure, her secret riches.... May we speak the beauty of thee, O Earth, that is in thy villages and forests and assemblies and war and battles. *Atharva Veda.*[5]

May Earth, sovereign over the past and the future, make for us a wide world... Earth that was the water on the Ocean and whose course the thinkers follow by the magic of their knowledge, she who has her heart of immortality covered up by the Truth in the supreme ether, may she establish for us light and power in that most high kingdom.

Atharva Veda.[6]

---

[1] IV. 4. 7. [2] IV. 4. 6. [3] IV. 4. 7. [4] IV. 4. 8. [5] XII. 1. 12, 44, 56.
[6] XII. 1. 1, 8.

O Flame, thou foundest the mortal in a supreme immortality for increase of inspired Knowledge day by day; for the seer who has thirst for the dual birth, thou createst divine bliss and human joy.　　　　　　　　　　　　　　　　*Rig Veda.*[7]

O Godhead, guard for us the Infinite and lavish the finite.
　　　　　　　　　　　　　　　　　　　　　　　　Rig Veda.[8]

BUT BEFORE we examine the principles and process of the evolutionary ascent of Consciousness, it is necessary to restate what our theory of integral knowledge affirms as fundamental truths of the Reality and its manifestation and what it admits as effectual sides and dynamic aspects but is unable to accept as sufficient for a total explanation of existence and the universe. For truth of knowledge must base truth of life and determine the aim of life; the evolutionary process itself is the development of a Truth of existence concealed here in an original Inconscience and brought out from it by an emerging Consciousness which rises from gradation to gradation of its self-unfolding until it can manifest in itself the integral reality of things and a total self-knowledge. On the nature of that Truth from which it starts and which it has to manifest must depend the course of the evolutionary development, — the steps of its process and their significance.

First, we affirm an Absolute as the origin and support and secret Reality of all things. The Absolute Reality is indefinable and ineffable by mental thought and mental language; it is self-existent and self-evident to itself, as all absolutes are self-evident, but our mental affirmatives and negatives, whether taken separatively or together, cannot limit or define it. But at the same time there is a spiritual consciousness, a spiritual knowledge, a knowledge by identity which can seize the Reality in its fundamental aspects and its manifested powers and figures. All that is comes within this description and, if seen by this knowledge

---

[7] I. 31. 7.　　[8] IV. 2. 11.

in its own truth or its occult meaning, can be regarded as an expression of the Reality and itself a reality. This manifested reality is self-existent in these fundamental aspects; for all the basic realities are a bringing out of something that is eternal and inherently true in the Absolute; but all that is not fundamental, all that is temporary is phenomenal, is form and power dependent on the reality it expresses and is real by that and by its own truth of significance, the truth of what it carries in it, because it is that and not something fortuitous, not baseless, illusory, a vain constructed figure. Even what deforms and disguises, as falsehood deforms and disguises truth, evil deforms and disguises good, has a temporal reality as true consequences of the Inconscience; but these contrary figures, though real in their own field, are not essential but only contributory to the manifestation and serve it as a temporal form or power of its movement. The universal then is real by virtue of the Absolute of which it is a self-manifestation, and all that it contains is real by virtue of the universal to which it gives a form and figure.

The Absolute manifests itself in two terms, a Being and a Becoming. The Being is the fundamental reality; the Becoming is an effectual reality: it is a dynamic power and result, a creative energy and working out of the Being, a constantly persistent yet mutable form, process, outcome of its immutable formless essence. All theories that make the Becoming sufficient to itself are therefore half-truths, valid for some knowledge of the manifestation acquired by an exclusive concentration upon what they affirm and envisage, but otherwise valid only because the Being is not separate from the Becoming but present in it, constituted of it, inherent in its every infinitesimal atom and in its boundless expansion and extension. Becoming can only know itself wholly when it knows itself as Being; the soul in the Becoming arrives at self-knowledge and immortality when it knows the Supreme and Absolute and possesses the nature of the Infinite and Eternal. To do that is the supreme aim of our existence; for that is the truth of our being and must therefore be the inherent aim, the necessary outcome of our becoming: this truth of our being becomes in the soul a necessity of manifestation, in matter a secret energy, in life an urge and tendency, a desire and a seeking, in mind a will, aim, endeavour, purpose; to manifest what is from the first occult within it is the whole hidden trend of evolutionary Nature.

Therefore we accept the truth on which the philosophies of the supracosmic Absolute take their stand; Illusionism itself, even if we contest its ultimate conclusions, can still be accepted as the way in which the soul in mind, the mental being, has to see things in a spiritual-pragmatic experience when it cuts itself off from the Becoming in order to approach and enter into the Absolute. But also, since the Becoming is real and is inevitable in the very self-power of the Infinite and Eternal, this too is not a complete philosophy of existence. It is possible for the soul in the Becoming to know itself as the Being and possess the Becoming, to know itself as the Infinite in essence but also as the Infinite self-expressed in the finite, the timeless Eternal regarding itself and its works in the founding status and the developing motion of Time-eternity. This realisation is the culmination of the Becoming; it is the fulfilment of the Being in its dynamic reality. This too then must be part of the total truth of things, for it alone gives a full spiritual significance to the universe and justifies the soul in manifestation; an explanation of things that deprives cosmic and individual existence of all significance cannot be the whole explanation or the solution it proposes the sole true issue.

The next affirmation which we put forward is that the fundamental reality of the Absolute is to our spiritual perception a Divine Existence, Consciousness and Delight of Being which is a supracosmic Reality, self-existent, but also the secret truth underlying the whole manifestation; for the fundamental truth of Being must necessarily be the fundamental truth of Becoming. All is a manifestation of That; for it dwells even in all that seem to be its opposites and its hidden compulsion on them to disclose it is the cause of evolution, on Inconscience to develop from itself its secret consciousness, on the apparent Non-Being to reveal in itself the occult spiritual existence, on the insensible neutrality of Matter to develop a various delight of being which must grow, setting itself free from its minor terms, its contrary dualities of pain and pleasure, into the essential delight of existence, the spiritual Ananda.

The Being is one, but this oneness is infinite and contains in itself an infinite plurality or multiplicity of itself: the One is the All; it is not only an essential Existence, but an All-Existence. The infinite multiplicity of the One and the eternal unity of the Many are the two realities or aspects of one reality on which the manifestation is founded. By reason of this fundamental verity of the manifestation the Being presents itself to our cosmic experience in three poises, — the supracosmic Existence, the cosmic Spirit and the individual Self in the Many. But the multiplicity permits of a phenomenal division of consciousness, an effectual Ignorance in which the Many, the individuals, cease to become aware of the eternal self-existent Oneness and are oblivious of the oneness of the cosmic Self in which and by which they live, move and have their being. But, by force of the secret Unity, the soul in becoming is urged by its own unseen reality and by the occult pressure of evolutionary Nature to come out of this state of Ignorance and recover eventually the knowledge of the one Divine Being and its oneness with it and at the same time to recover its spiritual unity with all individual beings and the whole universe. It has to become aware not only of itself in the universe but of the universe in itself and of the Being of cosmos as its greater self; the individual has to universalise himself and in the same movement to become aware of his supracosmic transcendence. This triple aspect of the reality must be included in the total truth of the soul and of the cosmic manifestation, and this necessity must determine the ultimate trend of the process of evolutionary Nature.

All views of existence that stop short of the Transcendence and ignore it must be incomplete accounts of the truth of being. The pantheistic view of the identity of the Divine and the Universe is a truth, for all this that is is the Brahman: but it stops short of the whole truth when it misses and omits the supracosmic Reality. On the other side, every view that affirms the cosmos only and dismisses the individual as a by-product of the cosmic Energy, errs by laying too much emphasis on one apparent factual aspect of the world-action; it is true only of the natural individual and is not even the whole truth of that: for the natural individual, the nature-being, is indeed a product of the universal Energy, but is at the same time a nature-personality of the soul, an expressive formation of the inner being and person, and this soul is not a perishable cell or a dissoluble portion of the cosmic Spirit, but has its original immortal reality in the Transcendence. It is a fact that the cosmic Being expresses itself through the individual being, but also it is a truth that the Transcendental Reality expresses itself through both the individual existence and the Cosmos; the soul is an eternal portion of the Supreme and not a fraction of Nature. But equally any view that sees the universe as existent only in the individual consciousness must very evidently be a fragmentary truth: it is justified by a perception of the universality of the spiritual individual and his power of embracing the whole universe in his consciousness; but neither the cosmos nor the individual consciousness is the fundamental truth of existence; for both depend upon and exist by the transcendental Divine Being.

This Divine Being, Sachchidananda, is at once impersonal and personal: it is an Existence and the origin and foundation of all truths, forces, powers, existences, but it is also the one transcendent Conscious Being and the All-Person of whom all conscious beings are the selves and personalities; for He is their highest Self and the universal indwelling Presence. It is a necessity for the soul in the universe, — and therefore the inner trend of the evolutionary Energy and its ultimate intention, — to know and to grow into this truth of itself, to become one with the Divine Being, to raise its nature to the Divine Nature, its existence into the Divine Existence, its consciousness into the Divine Consciousness, its delight of being into the divine Delight of Being, and to receive all this into its becoming, to make the becoming an expression of that highest Truth, to be possessed inwardly of the Divine Self and Master of its existence and to be at the same time wholly possessed by Him and moved by His Divine Energy and live and act in a complete self-giving and surrender. On this side the dualistic and theistic views of existence which affirm the eternal real existence of God and the Soul and the eternal real existence and cosmic action of the Divine Energy, express also a truth of the integral existence; but their formulation falls short of the whole truth if it denies the essential unity of God and Soul or their capacity for utter oneness or ignores what underlies the supreme experience of the merger of the soul in the Divine Unity through love, through union of consciousness, through fusion of existence in existence.

The manifestation of the Being in our universe takes the shape of an involution which is the starting-point of an evolution, — Matter the nethermost stage, Spirit the summit. In the descent into involution there can be distinguished seven principles of manifested being, seven gradations of the manifesting Consciousness of which we can get a perception or a concrete realisation of their presence and immanence here or a reflected experience. The first three are the original and fundamental principles and they form universal states of consciousness to which we can rise; when we do so, we can become aware of supreme planes or levels of fundamental manifestation or self-formulation of the spiritual reality in which is put in front the unity of the Divine Existence, the power of the Divine Consciousness, the bliss of the Divine Delight of existence, — not concealed or disguised as here, for we can possess them in their full independent reality. A fourth principle of supramental Truth-Consciousness is associated with them; manifesting unity in infinite multiplicity, it is the characteristic power of self-determination of the Infinite. This quadruple power of the supreme existence, consciousness and delight constitutes an upper hemisphere of manifestation based on the Spirit's eternal self-knowledge. If we enter into these principles or into any plane of being in which there is the pure presence of the Reality, we find in them a complete freedom and knowledge. The other three powers and planes of being, of which we are even at present aware, form a lower hemisphere of the manifestation, a hemisphere of Mind, Life and Matter. These are in themselves powers of the superior principles; but wherever they manifest in a separation from their spiritual sources, they undergo as a result a phenomenal lapse into a divided in place of the true undivided existence: this lapse, this separation creates a state of limited knowledge exclusively concentrated on its own limited world-order and oblivious of all that is behind it and of the underlying unity, a state therefore of cosmic and individual Ignorance.

In the descent into the material plane of which our natural life is a product, the lapse culminates in a total Inconscience out of which an involved Being and Consciousness have to emerge by a gradual evolution. This inevitable evolution first develops, as it is bound to develop, Matter and a material universe; in Matter, Life appears and living physical beings; in Life, Mind manifests and embodied thinking and living beings; in Mind, ever increasing its powers and activities in forms of Matter, the Supermind or Truth-Consciousness must appear, inevitably, by the very force of what is contained in the Inconscience and the necessity in Nature to bring it into manifestation. Supermind appearing manifests the Spirit's self-knowledge and whole-knowledge in a supramental living being and must bring about by the same law, by an inherent necessity and inevitability, the dynamic manifestation here of the divine Existence, Consciousness and Delight of existence. It is this that is the significance of the plan and order of the terrestrial evolution; it is this necessity that must determine all its steps and degrees, its principle and its process. Mind, Life and Matter are the realised powers of the evolution and well-known to us; Supermind and the triune aspects of Sachchidananda are the secret principles which are not yet put in front and have still to be realised in the forms of the manifestation, and we know them only by hints and a partial and fragmentary action still not disengaged from the lower movement and therefore not easily recognisable. But their evolution too is part of the destiny of the soul in the Becoming, — there must be a realisation and dynamisation in earth-life and in Matter not only of Mind but of all that is above it, all that has descended indeed but is still concealed in earth-life and Matter.

Our theory of the integral knowledge admits Mind as a creative principle, a power of the Being, and assigns it its place in the manifestation; it similarly accepts Life and Matter as powers of the Spirit and in them also is a creative Energy. But the view of things that makes Mind the sole or the supreme creative principle and the philosophies that assign to Life or Matter the same sole reality or predominance, are expressions of a half-truth and not the integral knowledge. It is true that when Matter first emerges it becomes the dominant principle; it seems to be and is within its own field the basis of all things, the constituent of all things, the end of all things: but Matter itself is found to be a result of something that is not Matter, of Energy, and this Energy cannot be something self-existent and acting in the Void, but can turn out and, when deeply scrutinised, seems likely to turn out to be the action of a secret Consciousness and Being: when the spiritual knowledge and experience emerge, this becomes a certitude, — it is seen that the creative Energy in Matter is a movement of the power of the Spirit. Matter itself cannot be the original and ultimate reality. At the same time the view that divorces Matter and Spirit and puts them as opposites is unacceptable; Matter is a form of Spirit, a habitation of Spirit, and here in Matter itself there can be a realisation of Spirit.

It is true again that Life when it emerges becomes dominant, turns Matter into an instrument for its manifestation, and begins to look as if it were itself the secret original principle which breaks out into creation and veils itself in the forms of Matter; there is a truth in this appearance and this truth must be admitted as a part of the integral knowledge. Life, though not the original Reality, is yet a form, a power of it which is missioned here as a creative urge in Matter. Life, therefore, has to be accepted as the means of our activity and the dynamic mould into which we have here to pour the Divine Existence; but it can so be accepted only because it is a form of a Divine Energy which is itself greater than the Life-force. The Life-principle is not the whole foundation and origin of things; its creative working cannot be perfected and sovereignly fulfilled or even find its true movement until it knows itself as an energy of the Divine Being and elevates and subtilises its action into a free channel for the outpourings of the superior Nature.

Mind in its turn, when it emerges, becomes dominant; it uses Life and Matter as means of its expression, a field for its own growth and sovereignty, and it begins to work as if it were the true reality and the creator even as it is the witness of existence. But Mind also is a limited and derivative power; it is an outcome of Overmind or it is here a luminous shadow thrown by the divine Supermind: it can only arrive at its own perfection by admitting the light of a larger knowledge; it must transform its own more ignorant, imperfect and conflicting powers and values into the divinely effective potencies and harmonious values of the supramental Truth-Consciousness. All the powers of the lower hemisphere with their structures of the Ignorance can find their true selves only by a transformation in the light that descends to us from the higher hemisphere of an eternal self-knowledge.

All these three lower powers of being build upon the Inconscient and seem to be originated and supported by it: the black dragon of the Inconscience sustains with its vast wings and its back of darkness the whole structure of the material universe; its energies unroll the flux of things, its obscure intimations seem to be the starting-point of consciousness itself and the source of all life-impulse. The Inconscient, in consequence of this origination and predominance, is taken now by a certain line of enquiry as the real origin and creator. It has indeed to be accepted that an inconscient force, an inconscient substance are the starting-point of the evolution, but it is a conscious Spirit and not an inconscient Being that is emerging in the evolution. The Inconscient and its primary works are penetrated by a succession of higher and higher powers of being and are made subject to Consciousness so that its obstructions to the evolution, its circles of restriction, are slowly broken, the Python coils of its obscurity shot through by the arrows of the Sun-God; so are the limitations of our material substance diminished until they can be transcended and mind, life and body can be transformed through a possession of them by the greater law of divine Consciousness, Energy and Spirit. The integral knowledge admits the valid truths of all views of existence, valid in their own field, but it seeks to get rid of their limitations and negations and to harmonise and reconcile these partial truths in a larger truth which fulfils all the many sides of our being in the one omnipresent Existence.

At this point we must take a step farther and begin to regard the metaphysical truth we have so stated as a determinant not only of our thought and inner movements but of our life-direction, a guide to a dynamic solution of our self-experience and world-experience. Our metaphysical knowledge, our view of the fundamental truth of the universe and the meaning of existence, should naturally be the determinant of our whole conception of life and attitude to it; the aim of life, as we conceive it, must be structured on that basis. Metaphysical philosophy is an attempt to fix the fundamental realities and principles of being as distinct from its processes and the phenomena which result from those processes. But it is on the fundamental realities that the processes depend: our own process of life, its aim and method, should be in accordance with the truth of being that we see; otherwise our metaphysical truth can be only a play of the intellect without any dynamic importance. It is true that the intellect must seek after truth for its own sake without any illegitimate interference of a preconceived idea of life-utility. But still the truth, once discovered, must be realisable in our inner being and our outer activities: if it is not, it may have an intellectual but not an integral importance; a truth for the intellect, for our life it would be no more than the solution of a thought-puzzle or an abstract unreality or a dead letter. Truth of being must govern truth of life; it cannot be that the two have no relation or interdependence. The highest significance of life to us, the fundamental truth of existence, must be also the accepted meaning of our own living, our aim, our ideal.

There are, roughly, from this viewpoint, four main theories, or categories of theory, with their corresponding mental attitudes and ideals in accordance with four different conceptions of truth of existence. These we may call the supracosmic, the cosmic and terrestrial, the supraterrestrial or other-worldly, and the integral or synthetic or composite, the theories that try to reconcile the three factors, — or any two of them, — which the other views tend to isolate. In this last category would fall our view of our existence here as a Becoming with the Divine Being for its origin and its object, a progressive manifestation, a spiritual evolution with the supracosmic for its source and support, the other-worldly for a condition and connecting link and the cosmic and terrestrial for its field, and with human mind and life for its nodus and turning-point of release towards a higher and a highest perfection. Our regard then must be on the three first to see where they depart from the integralising view of life and how far the truths they stand on fit into its structure.

In the supracosmic view of things the supreme Reality is alone entirely real. A certain illusoriness, a sense of the vanity of cosmic existence and individual being is a characteristic turn of this seeing of things, but it is not essential, not an indispensable adjunct to its main thought-principle. In the extreme forms of its world-vision human existence has no real meaning; it is a mistake of the soul or a delirium of the will to live, an error or ignorance which somehow overcasts the absolute Reality. The only true truth is the supracosmic; or, in any case, the Absolute, the Parabrahman is the origin and goal of all existence, all else is an interlude without any abiding significance. If so, it would follow that the one thing to be done, the one wise and needful way of our being is to get away from all living, whether terrestrial or celestial, as soon as our inner evolution or some hidden law of the spirit makes that possible. True, the illusion is real to itself, the vanity pretends to be full of purpose; its laws and facts, — they are only facts and not truths, empirical and not real realities, — are binding on us so long as we rest in the error. But from any standpoint of real knowledge, in any view of the true truth of things, all this self-delusion would seem to be little better than the laws of a cosmic madhouse; so long as we are mad and have to remain in the madhouse, we are perforce subject to its rules and we must make, according to our temperament, the best or the worst of them, but always our proper aim is to get cured of our insanity and depart into light and truth and freedom. Whatever mitigations may be made in the severity of this logic, whatever concessions validating life and personality for the time being, yet from this viewpoint the true law of living must be whatever rule can help us soonest to get back to self-knowledge and lead by the most direct road to Nirvana; the true ideal must be an extinction of the individual and the universal, a self-annulment in the Absolute. This ideal of self-extinction which is boldly and clearly proclaimed by the Buddhists, is in Vedantic thought a self-finding: but the self-finding of the individual by his growth into his true being in the Absolute would only be possible if both are interrelated realities; it could not apply to the final world-abolishing self-affirmation of the Absolute in an unreal or temporary individual by the annulment of the false personal being and by the destruction of all individual and cosmic existence for that individual consciousness, — however much these errors may go on, helplessly inevitable, in the world of Ignorance permitted by the Absolute, in a universal, eternal and indestructible Avidya.

But this idea of the total vanity of life is not altogether an inevitable consequence of the supracosmic theory of existence. In the Vedanta of the Upanishads, the Becoming of Brahman is accepted as a reality; there is room therefore for a truth of the Becoming: there is in that truth a right law of life, a permissible satisfaction of the hedonistic element in our being, its delight of temporal existence, an effective utilisation of its practical energy, of the executive force of consciousness in it; but, the truth and law of its temporal becoming once fulfilled, the soul has to turn back to its final self-realisation, for its natural highest fulfilment is a release, a liberation into its original being, its eternal self, its timeless reality. There is a circle of becoming starting from eternal Being and ending in it; or, from the point of view of the Supreme as a personal or superpersonal Reality, there is a temporary play, a game of becoming and living in the universe. Here, evidently, there is no other significance of life than the will of the Being to become, the will of consciousness and the urge of its force towards becoming, its delight of becoming; for the individual, when that is withdrawn from him or fulfilled in him and no longer active, the becoming ceases: but otherwise the universe persists or always comes back into manifestation, because the will to become is eternal and must be so since it is the inherent will of an eternal Existence. It may be said that one defect in this view of things is the absence of any fundamental reality of the individual, of any abiding value and significance of his natural or his spiritual activity: but it can be replied that this demand for a permanent personal significance, for a personal eternity, is an error of our ignorant surface consciousness; the individual·is a temporary becoming of the Being, and that is a quite sufficient value and significance. It may be added that in a pure or an absolute Existence there can be no values and significances: in the universe values exist and are indispensable, but only as relative and temporary buildings; there can be no absolute values, no eternal and self-existent significances in a Time-structure. This sounds conclusive enough and it seems that nothing more can be said about the matter. And yet the question remains over; for the stress on our individual being, the demand on it, the value put on individual perfection and salvation is too great to be dismissed as a device for a minor operation, the coiling and uncoiling of an insignificant spiral amid the vast circlings of the Eternal's becoming in the universe.

The cosmic-terrestrial view which we may take next as the exact opposite of the supracosmic, considers cosmic existence as real; it goes farther and accepts it as the only reality, and its view is confined, ordinarily, to life in the material universe. God, if God exists, is an eternal Becoming; or if God does not exist, then Nature, — whatever view we may take of Nature, whether we regard it as a play of Force with Matter or a great cosmic Life or even admit a universal impersonal Mind in Life and Matter, — is a perennial becoming. Earth is the field or it is one of the temporary fields, man is the highest possible form or only one of the temporary forms of the Becoming. Man individually may be altogether mortal; mankind also may survive only for a certain short period of the earth's existence; earth itself may bear life only for a rather longer period of its duration in the solar system; that system may itself one day come to an end or at least cease to be an active or productive factor in the Becoming; the universe we live in may itself dissolve or contract again into the seed-state of its Energy: but the principle of Becoming is eternal, — or at least as eternal as anything can be in the obscure ambiguity of existence. It is indeed possible to suppose a persistence of man the individual as a psychic entity in Time, a continuous terrestrial or cosmic ensouling or reincarnation without any after-life or other-life elsewhere: in that case one may either suppose an ideal of constantly increasing perfection or approach to perfection or a growth towards an enduring felicity somewhere in the universe as the aim of this endless Becoming. But in an extreme terrestrial view this is with difficulty tenable. Certain speculations of human thought have tended in this direction, but they have not taken a substantial body. A perpetual persistence in the Becoming is usually associated with the acceptance of a greater supraterrestrial existence.

In the ordinary view of a sole terrestrial life or a restricted transient passage in the material universe, — for possibly there may be thinking living beings in other planets, — an acceptance of man's mortality and a passive endurance of it or an active dealing with a limited personal or collective life and life-aims are the only choice possible. The one high and reasonable course for the individual human being, — unless indeed he is satisfied with pursuing his personal purposes or somehow living his life until it passes out of him, — is to study the laws of the Becoming and take the best advantage of them to realise, rationally or intuitionally, inwardly or in the dynamism of life, its potentialities in himself or for himself or in or for the race of which he is a member; his business is to make the most of such actualities as exist and to seize on or to advance towards the highest possibilities that can be developed here or are in the making. Only mankind as a whole can do this with entire effect, by the mass of individual and collective action, in the process of time, in the evolution of the race-experience: but the individual man can help towards it in his own limits, can do all these things for himself to a certain extent in the brief space of life allotted to him; but, especially, his thought and action can be a contribution towards the present intellectual, moral and vital welfare and the future progress of the race. He is capable of a certain nobility of being; an acceptance of his inevitable and early individual annihilation does not preclude him from making a high use of the will and thought which have been developed in him or from directing them to great ends which shall or may be worked out by humanity. Even the temporary character of the collective being of humanity does not so very much matter, — except in the most materialist view of existence; for so long as the universal Becoming takes the form of human body and mind, the thought, the will it has developed in its human creature will work itself out and to follow that intelligently is the natural law and best rule of human life. Humanity and its welfare and progress during its persistence on earth provide the largest field and the natural limits for the terrestrial aim of our being; the superior persistence of the race and the greatness and importance of the collective life should determine the nature and scope of our ideals. But if the progress or welfare of humanity be excluded as not our business or as a delusion, the individual is there; to achieve his greatest possible perfection or make the most of his life in whatever way his nature demands will then be life's significance.

The supraterrestrial view admits the reality of the material cosmos and it accepts the temporary duration of earth and human life as the first fact we have to start from; but it adds to it a perception of other worlds or planes of existence which have an eternal or at least a more permanent duration; it perceives behind the mortality of the bodily life of man the immortality of the soul within him. A belief in the immortality, the eternal persistence of the individual human spirit apart from the body is the keyword of this conception of life. That of itself necessitates its other belief in higher planes of existence than the material or terrestrial, since for a disembodied spirit there can be no abiding place in a world whose every operation depends upon some play of force, whether spiritual, mental, vital or material, in and with the forms of Matter. There arises from this view of things the idea that the true home of man is beyond and that the earth-life is in some way or other only an episode of his immortality or a deviation from a celestial and spiritual into a material existence.

But what then is the character, the origin and the end of

this deviation? There is first the idea of certain religions, long persistent but now greatly shaken or discredited, that man is a being primarily created as a material living body upon earth into which a newly born divine soul is breathed or else with which it is associated by the fiat of an almighty Creator. A solitary episode, this life is his one opportunity from which he departs to a world of eternal bliss or to a world of eternal misery either according as the general or preponderant balance of his acts is good or evil or according as he accepts or rejects, knows or ignores a particular creed, mode of worship, divine mediator, or else according to the arbitrary predestining caprice of his Creator. But that is the supraterrestrial theory of life in its least rational form of questionable creed or dogma. Taking the idea of the creation of a soul by the physical birth as our starting-point, we may still suppose that by a natural law, common to all, the rest of its existence has to be pursued beyond in a supraterrestrial plane, when the soul has shaken off from it its original matrix of matter like a butterfly escaped from the chrysalis and disporting itself in the air on its light and coloured wings. Or we may suppose preferably a preterrestrial existence of the soul, a fall or descent into matter and a reascension into celestial being. If we admit the soul's pre-existence, there is no reason to exclude this last possibility as an occasional spiritual occurrence, — a being belonging to another plane of existence may, conceivably, assume for some purpose the human body and nature: but this is not likely to be the universal principle of earth-existence or a sufficient rationale for the creation of the material universe.

It is also sometimes supposed that the solitary life on earth is a stage only and the development of the being nearer to its original glory occurs in a succession of worlds which are so many other stages of its growth, stadia of its journey. The material universe, or earth especially, will then be a sumptuously appointed field created by a divine power, wisdom or caprice for the enacting of this interlude. According to the view we choose to take of the matter, we shall see in it a place of ordeal, a field of development or a scene of spiritual fall and exile. There is too an Indian view which regards the world as a garden of the divine Lila, a play of the divine Being with the conditions of cosmic existence in this world of an inferior Nature; the soul of man takes part in the Lila through a protracted series of births, but it is destined to reascend at last into the proper plane of the Divine Being and there enjoy an eternal proximity and communion: this gives a certain rationale to the creative process and the spiritual adventure which is either absent or not clearly indicated in the other accounts of this kind of soul-movement or soul-cycle. Always there are three essential characteristics in all these varying statements of the common principle: first, the belief in the individual immortality of the human spirit; secondly, as a necessary consequence, the idea of its sojourn on earth as a temporary passage or a departure from its highest eternal nature and of a heaven beyond as its proper habitation; thirdly, an emphasis on the development of the ethical and spiritual being as the means of ascension and therefore the one proper business of life in this world of Matter.

These are the three fundamental ways of seeing, each with its mental attitude towards life, that can be adopted with regard to our existence; the rest are usually midway stations or else variations or composites which attempt to adapt themselves more freely to the complexity of the problem. For, practically, it is impossible for man taken as a race, whatever a few individuals may succeed in doing, to guide his life permanently or wholly by the leading motive of any of these three attitudes, uniquely, to the exclusion of the others' claim upon his nature. A confused amalgam of two or more of them, a conflict or division of his life-motives between them or some attempt at synthesis is his way of dealing with the various impulses of his complex being and the intuitions of his mind to which they appeal for their sanction. Almost all men normally devote the major part of their energy to the life on earth, to the terrestrial needs, interests, desires, ideals of the individual and the race. It could not be otherwise; for the care of the body, the sufficient development and satisfaction of the vital and the mental being of man, the pursuit of high individual and large collective ideals which start from the idea of an attainable human perfection or nearer approach to perfection through his normal development, are imposed upon us by the very character of our terrestrial being; they are part of its law, its natural impulse and rule, its condition of growth, and without these things man could not attain to his full manhood. Any view of our being which neglects, unduly belittles or intolerantly condemns them, is therefore by that very fact, whatever its other truth or merit or utility, or whatever its suitability to individuals of a certain temperament or in a certain stage of spiritual evolution, unfit to be the general and complete rule of human living. Nature takes good care that the race shall not neglect these aims which are a necessary part of her evolution; for they fall within the method and stages of the divine plan in us, and a vigilance for her first steps and for the maintenance of their mental and material ground is a preoccupation which she cannot allow to go into the background, since these things belong to the foundation and body of her structure.

But also she has implanted in us a sense that there is something in our composition which goes beyond this first terrestrial nature of humanity. For this reason the race cannot accept or follow for a very long time any view of being which ignores this higher and subtler sense and labours to confine us entirely to a purely terrestrial way of living. The intuition of a beyond, the idea and feeling of a soul and spirit in us which is other than the mind, life and body or is greater, not limited by their formula, returns upon us and ends by resuming possession. The ordinary man satisfies this sense easily enough by devoting to it his exceptional moments or the latter part of his life when age shall have blunted the zest of his earthly nature, or by recognising it as something behind or above his normal action to which he can more or less imperfectly direct his natural being: the exceptional man turns to the supraterrestrial as the one aim and law of living and diminishes or mortifies as much as possible his earthly parts in the hope of developing his celestial nature. There have been epochs in which the supraterrestrial view has gained a very powerful hold and there has been a vacillation between an imperfect human living which cannot take its large natural expansion and a sick ascetic longing for the celestial life which also does not acquire in more than a few its best pure and happy movement. This is a sign of the creation of some false war in the being by the setting up of a standard or a device that ignores the law of evolutionary capacity or an overstress that misses the reconciling equation which must exist somewhere in a divine dispensation of our nature.

But, finally, there must open in us, as our mental life deepens and subtler knowledge develops, the perception that the terrestrial and the supraterrestrial are not the only terms of being; there is something which is supracosmic and the highest remote origin of our existence. This perception is easily associated by spiritual enthusiasm, by the height and ardour of the soul's aspiration, by the philosophic aloofness or the strict logical intolerance of our intellect, by the eagerness of our will or by a sick disgust in our vital being discouraged by the difficulties or disappointed by the results of life, — by any or all of these motive-forces, — with a sense of the entire vanity and unreality of all else than this remote Supreme, the vanity of human life, the unreality of cosmic existence, the bitter ugliness and cruelty of earth, the insufficiency of heaven, the aimlessness of the repetition of births in the body. Here again the ordinary man cannot really live with these ideas; they can only give at most a greyness and restless dissatisfaction to the life in which he must still continue: but the exceptional man abandons all to follow the truth he has seen and for him they can be the needed food of his spiritual impulse or a stimulus to the one achievement that is now for him the one thing that matters. Periods and countries there have been, in which this view of being has become very powerful; a considerable part of the race has swerved aside to the life of the ascetic, — not always with a real call to it, — the rest adhered to the normal life but with an underlying belief in its unreality, a belief which can bring about by too much reiteration and insistence an unnerving of the life-impulse and an increasing littleness of its motives, or even, by a subtle reaction, an absorption in an ordinary narrow living through a missing of our natural response to the Divine Being's larger joy in cosmic existence and a failure of the great progressive human idealism by which we are spurred to a collective self-development and a noble embrace of the battle and the labour. Here again there is a sign of some insufficiency in the statement of the supracosmic Reality, perhaps an overstatement or a mistaken opposition, a missing of the divine equation, of the total sense of creation and the entire will of the Creator.

That equation can only be found if we recognise the purport of our whole complex human nature in its right place in the cosmic movement, what is needed is to give its full legitimate value to each part of our composite being and many-sided aspiration and find out the key of their unity as well as their difference. The finding must be by a synthesis or an integration and, since development is clearly the law of the human soul, it is most likely to be discovered by an evolutionary synthesis. A synthesis of this kind was attempted in the ancient Indian culture. It accepted four legitimate motives of human living, — man's vital interests and needs, his desires, his ethical and religious aspiration, his ultimate spiritual aim and destiny, — in other words, the claims of his vital, physical and emotional being, the claims of his ethical and religious being governed by a knowledge of the law of God and Nature and man, and the claims of his spiritual longing for the Beyond for which he seeks satisfaction by an ultimate release from an ignorant mundane existence. It provided for a period of education and preparation based on this idea of life, a period of normal living to satisfy human desires and interests under the moderating rule of the ethical and religious part in us, a period of withdrawal and spiritual preparation, and a last period of renunciation of life and release into the spirit. Evidently, if applied as a universal rule, this prescribed norm, this delineation of the curve of our journey, would miss the fact that it is impossible for all to trace out the whole circle of development in a single short lifetime; but it was modified by the theory of a complete evolution pursued through a long succession of rebirths before one could be fit for a spiritual liberation. This synthesis with its spiritual insight, largeness of view, symmetry, completeness did much to raise the tone of human life; but eventually it collapsed: its place was occupied by an exaggeration of the impulse of renunciation which destroyed the symmetry of the system and cut it into two movements of life in opposition to each other, the normal life of interests and desires with an ethical and religious colouring and the abnormal or supernormal inner life founded on renunciation. The old synthesis in fact contained in itself the seed of this exaggeration and could not but lapse into it: for if we regard the escape from life as our desirable end, if we omit to hold up any high offer of life-fulfilment, if life has not a divine significance in it, the impatience of the human intellect and will must end by driving at a short cut and getting rid as much as possible of any more tedious and dilatory processes; if it cannot do that or if it is incapable of following the short cut, it is left with the ego and its satisfactions but with nothing greater to be achieved here. Life is split into the spiritual and the mundane and there can only be an abrupt transition, not a harmony or reconciliation of these parts of our nature.

A spiritual evolution, an unfolding here of the Being within from birth to birth, of which man becomes the central instrument and human life at its highest offers the critical turning-point, is the link needed for the reconciliation of life and spirit; for it allows us to take into account the total nature of man and to recognise the legitimate place of his triple attraction, to earth, to heaven and to the supreme Reality. But a complete solution of its oppositions can be arrived at only on this basis that the lower consciousness of mind, life and body cannot arrive at its full meaning until it is taken up, restated, transformed by the light and power and joy of the higher spiritual consciousness, while the higher too does not stand in its full right relation to the lower by mere rejection, but by this assumption and domination, this taking up of its unfulfilled values, this restatement and transformation, — a spiritualising and supramentalising of the mental, vital and physical nature. The terrestrial ideal, which has been so powerful in the modern mind, restored man and his life on earth and the collective hope of the race to a prominent position and created an insistent demand for a solution; this is the good it has accomplished. But by overdoing and exclusiveness it unduly limited man's scope, it ignored that which is the highest and in the end the largest thing in him, and by this limitation it missed the full pursuit of its own object. If mind were the highest thing in man and Nature, then indeed this frustration might not result; still, the limitation of scope would be there, a narrow possibility, a circumscribed prospect. But if mind is only a partial unfolding of consciousness and there are powers beyond of which Nature in our race is capable, then not only does our hope upon earth, let alone what is beyond it, depend upon their development, but this becomes the one proper road of our evolution.

Mind and life themselves cannot grow into their fullness except by the opening up of the larger and greater consciousness to which mind only approaches. Such a larger and greater consciousness is the spiritual, for the spiritual consciousness is not only higher than the rest but more embracing. Universal as well as transcendent, it can take up mind and life into its light and give them the true and utmost realisation of all for which they are seeking: for it has a greater instrumentality of knowledge, a fountain of deeper power and will, an unlimited reach and intensity of love and joy and beauty. These are the things for which our mind, life and body are seeking, knowledge, power and joy, and to reject that by which all these arrive at their utmost plenitude is to shut them out from their own highest consummation. An opposite exaggeration demanding only some colourless purity of spiritual existence nullifies the creative action of the spirit and excludes from us all that the Divine manifests in its being: it leaves room only for an evolution without sense or fulfilment, — for a cutting off of all that has been evolved is the sole culmination; it turns the process of our being into the meaningless curve of a plunge into Ignorance and return out of it or erects a wheel of cosmic Becoming with only an escape-issue. The intermediary, the supraterrestrial aspiration cuts short the fulfilment of the being above by not proceeding to its highest realisation of oneness and diminishes it below by not allowing a proper amplitude of sense to its presence in the material universe and its acceptance of life in an earthly body. A large relation of unity, an integration, restores the balance, illumines the whole truth of being and links together the steps of Nature.

In this integration the supracosmic Reality stands as the supreme Truth of being; to realise it is the highest reach of our consciousness. But it is this highest Reality which is also the cosmic being, the cosmic consciousness, the cosmic will and life: it has put these things forth, not outside itself but in its own being, not as an opposite principle but as its own self-unfolding and self-expression. Cosmic being is not a meaningless freak or phantasy or a chance error; there is a divine significance and truth in it: the manifold self-expression of the spirit is its high sense, the Divine itself is the key of its enigma. A perfect self-expression of the spirit is the object of our terrestrial existence. This cannot be achieved if we have not grown conscious of the supreme Reality; for it is only by the touch of the Absolute that we can arrive at our own absolute. But neither can it be done to the exclusion of the cosmic Reality: we must become universal, for without an opening into universality the individual remains incomplete. The individual separating himself from the All to reach the Highest, loses himself in the supreme heights; including in himself the cosmic consciousness, he recovers his wholeness of self and still keeps his supreme gain of transcendence; he fulfils it and himself in the cosmic completeness. A realised unity of the transcendent, the universal and the individual is an indispensable condition for the fullness of the self-expressing spirit: for the universe is the field of its totality of self-expression, while it is through the individual that its evolutionary self-unfolding here comes to its acme. But this supposes not only a real being of the individual, but the revelation of our secret eternal oneness with the Supreme and with all cosmic existence. In his self-integration the soul of the individual must awake to universality and to transcendence.

The supraterrestrial existence is also a truth of being; for the material is not the only plane of our existence; other planes of consciousness there are to which we can attain and which have already their hidden links with us: not to reach up to whatever greater regions of the soul are open to us, not to have the experience of them, not to know and manifest their law in ourselves is to fall short of the height and fullness of our being.

But worlds of a higher consciousness are not the only possible scene and habitation of the perfected soul; nor can we find in any unchanging typal world the final or total sense of the Spirit's self-expression in the cosmos: the material world, this earth, this human life are a part of the Spirit's self-expression and have their divine possibility; that possibility is evolutionary and it contains the possibilities of all the other worlds in it, unrealised but realisable. Earth-life is not a lapse into the mire of something undivine, vain and miserable, offered by some Power to itself as a spectacle or to the embodied soul as a thing to be suffered and then cast away from it: it is the scene of the evolutionary unfolding of the being which moves towards the revelation of a supreme spiritual light and power and joy and oneness, but includes in it also the manifold diversity of the self-achieving spirit. There is an all-seeing purpose in the terrestrial creation; a divine plan is working itself out through its contradictions and perplexities which are a sign of the many-sided achievement towards which are being led the soul's growth and the endeavour of Nature.

It is true that the soul can ascend into worlds of a greater consciousness beyond the earth, but it is also true that the power of these worlds, the power of a greater consciousness has to develop itself here; the embodiment of the soul is the means for that embodiment. All the higher powers of Consciousness exist because they are powers of the Supreme Reality. Our terrestrial being has also the same truth; it is a becoming of the One Reality which has to embody in itself these greater powers. Its present appearance is a veiled and partial figure and to limit ourselves to that first figure, to the present formula of an imperfect humanity, is to exclude our divine potentialities; we have to bring a wider meaning into our human life and manifest in it the much more that we secretly are. Our mortality is only justified in the light of our immortality; our earth can know and be all itself only by opening to the heavens; the individual can see himself aright and use his world divinely only when he has entered into greater planes of being and seen the light of the Supreme and lived in the being and power of the Divine and Eternal.

An integration of this kind would not be possible if a spiritual evolution were not the sense of our birth and terrestrial existence; the evolution of mind, life and spirit in Matter is the sign that this integration, this completed manifestation of a secret self contained in it is its significance. A complete involution of all that the Spirit is and its evolutionary self-unfolding are the double term of our material existence. There is a possibility of self-expression by an always unveiled luminous development of the being, a possibility also of various expression in perfect types fixed and complete in their own nature: that is the principle of becoming in the higher worlds; they are typal and not evolutionary in their life principle; they exist each in its own perfection, but within the limits of a stationary world-formula. But there is also a possibility of self-expression by self-finding, a deployment which takes the form and goes through the progression of a self-veiling and an adventure of self-recovery: that is the principle of becoming in this universe of which an involution of consciousness and concealment of the spirit in Matter is the first appearance.

An involution of spirit in the Inconscience is the beginning; an evolution in the Ignorance with its play of the possibilities of a partial developing knowledge is the middle, and the cause of the anomalies of our present nature, — our imperfection is the sign of a transitional state, a growth not yet completed, an effort that is finding its way; a consummation in a deployment of the spirit's self-knowledge and the self-power of its divine being and consciousness is the culmination: these are the three stages of this cycle of the spirit's progressive self-expression in life. The two stages that have already their play seem at first sight to deny the possibility of the later consummating stage of the cycle, but logically they imply its emergence; for if the inconscience has evolved consciousness, the partial consciousness already reached must surely evolve into complete consciousness. It is a perfected and divinised life for which the earth-nature is seeking, and this seeking is a sign of the Divine Will in Nature. Other seekings also there are and these too find their means of self-fulfilment; a withdrawal into the supreme peace or ecstasy, a withdrawal into the bliss of the Divine Presence are open to the soul in earth-existence: for the Infinite in its manifestation has many possibilities and is not confined by its formulations. But neither of these withdrawals can be the fundamental intention in the Becoming itself here; for then an evolutionary progression would not have been undertaken, — such a progression here can only have for its aim a self-fulfilment here: a progressive manifestation of this kind can only have for its soul of significance the revelation of Being in a perfect Becoming.

Chapter XVII

The Progress to Knowledge —
God, Man and Nature

Thou art That, O Swetaketu.   *Chhandogya Upanishad.*[1]

The living being is none else than the Brahman, the whole
world is the Brahman.   *Vivekachudamani.*[2]

My supreme Nature has become the living being and this
world is upheld by it... all beings have this for their source of
birth.   *Gita.*[3]

Thou art man and woman, boy and girl; old and worn thou
walkest bent over a staff; thou art the blue bird and the green
and the scarlet-eyed...   *Swetaswatara Upanishad.*[4]

This whole world is filled with beings who are His members.
                                    Swetaswatara Upanishad.[5]

AN INVOLUTION of the Divine Existence, the spiritual
Reality, in the apparent inconscience of Matter is the
starting-point of the evolution. But that Reality is in its
nature an eternal Existence, Consciousness, Delight of Existence:
the evolution must then be an emergence of this Existence,
Consciousness, Delight of Existence, not at first in its essence
or totality but in evolutionary forms that express or disguise
it. Out of the Inconscient, Existence appears in a first evolutionary form as substance of Matter created by an inconscient
Energy. Consciousness, involved and non-apparent in Matter,
first emerges in the disguise of vital vibrations, animate but

---

[1] VI. 8. 7.   [2] Verse 479.   [3] VII. 5, 6.   [4] IV. 3, 4.   [5] IV. 10.

subconscient; then, in imperfect formulations of a conscient life, it strives towards self-finding through successive forms of that material substance, forms more and more adapted to its own completer expression. Consciousness in life, throwing off the primal insensibility of a material inanimation and nescience, labours to find itself more and more entirely in the Ignorance which is its first inevitable formulation; but it achieves at first only a primary mental perception and a vital awareness of self and things, a life-perception which in its first forms depends on an internal sensation responsive to the contacts of other life and of Matter. Consciousness labours to manifest as best it can through the inadequacy of sensation its own inherent delight of being; but it can only formulate a partial pain and pleasure. In man the energising Consciousness appears as Mind more clearly aware of itself and things; this is still a partial and limited, not an integral power of itself, but a first conceptive potentiality and promise of integral emergence is visible. That integral emergence is the goal of evolving Nature.

Man is there to affirm himself in the universe, that is his first business, but also to evolve and finally to exceed himself: he has to enlarge his partial being into a complete being, his partial consciousness into an integral consciousness; he has to achieve mastery of his environment but also world-union and world-harmony; he has to realise his individuality but also to enlarge it into a cosmic self and a universal and spiritual delight of existence. A transformation, a chastening and correction of all that is obscure, erroneous and ignorant in his mentality, an ultimate arrival at a free and wide harmony and luminousness of knowledge and will and feeling and action and character, is the evident intention of his nature; it is the ideal which the creative Energy has imposed on his intelligence, a need implanted by her in his mental and vital substance. But this can only be accomplished by his growing into a larger being and a larger consciousness: self-enlargement, self-fulfilment, self-evolution from what he partially and temporarily is in his actual and apparent nature to what he completely is in his secret self and spirit and therefore can become even in his manifest existence, is the object of his creation. This hope is the justification of his life upon earth amidst the phenomena of the cosmos. The outer apparent man, an ephemeral being subject to the constraints of his material embodiment and imprisoned in a limited mentality, has to become the inner real Man, master of himself and his environment and universal in his being. In a more vivid and less metaphysical language, the natural man has to evolve himself into the divine Man; the sons of Death have to know themselves as the children of Immortality. It is on this account that the human birth can be described as the turning-point in the evolution, the critical stage in earth-nature.

It follows at once that the knowledge we have to arrive at is not truth of the intellect; it is not right belief, right opinions, right information about oneself and things, — that is only the surface mind's idea of knowledge. To arrive at some mental conception about God and ourselves and the world is an object good for the intellect but not large enough for the Spirit; it will not make us the conscious sons of Infinity. Ancient Indian thought meant by knowledge a consciousness which possesses the highest Truth in a direct perception and in self-experience; to become, to be the Highest that we know is the sign that we really have the knowledge. For the same reason, to shape our practical life, our actions as far as may be in consonance with our intellectual notions of truth and right or with a successful pragmatic knowledge, — an ethical or a vital fulfilment, — is not and cannot be the ultimate aim of our life; our aim must be to grow into our true being, our being of Spirit, the being of the supreme and universal Existence, Consciousness, Delight, Sachchidananda.

All our existence depends on that Existence, it is that which is evolving in us; we are a being of that Existence, a state of consciousness of that Consciousness, an energy of that conscious Energy, a will-to-delight of being, delight of consciousness, delight of energy born of that Delight: this is the root principle of our existence. But our surface formulation of these things is not that, it is a mistranslation into the terms of the Ignorance. Our I is not that spiritual being which can look on the Divine

Existence and say, "That am I"; our mentality is not that spiritual consciousness; our will is not that force of consciousness; our pain and pleasure, even our highest joys and ecstasies are not that delight of being. On the surface we are still an ego figuring self, an ignorance turning into knowledge, a will labouring towards true force, a desire seeking for the delight of existence. To become ourselves by exceeding ourselves, — so we may turn the inspired phrases of a half-blind seer who knew not the self of which he spoke, — is the difficult and dangerous necessity, the cross surmounted by an invisible crown which is imposed on us, the riddle of the true nature of his being proposed to man by the dark Sphinx of the Inconscience below and from within and above by the luminous veiled Sphinx of the infinite Consciousness and eternal Wisdom confronting him as an inscrutable divine Maya. To exceed ego and be our true self, to be aware of our real being, to possess it, to possess a real delight of being, is therefore the ultimate meaning of our life here; it is the concealed sense of our individual and terrestrial existence.

Intellectual knowledge and practical action are devices of Nature by which we are able to express so much of our being, consciousness, energy, power of enjoyment as we have been able to actualise in our apparent nature and by which we attempt to know more, express and actualise more, grow always more into the much that we have yet to actualise. But our intellect and mental knowledge and will of action are not our only means, not all the instruments of our consciousness and energy: our nature, the name which we give to the Force of being in us in its actual and potential play and power, is complex in its ordering of consciousness, complex in its instrumentation of force. Every discovered or discoverable term and circumstance of that complexity which we can get into working order, we need to actualise in the highest and finest values possible to us and to use in its widest and richest powers for the one object. That object is to become, to be conscious, to increase continually in our realised being and awareness of self and things, in our actualised force and joy of being, and to express that becoming dynamically in such an action on the world and ourselves that we and it shall grow more and always yet more towards the highest possible reach, largest possible breadth of universality and infinity. All man's age-long effort, his action, society, art, ethics, science, religion, all the manifold activities by which he expresses and increases his mental, vital, physical, spiritual existence, are episodes in the vast drama of this endeavour of Nature and have behind their limited apparent aims no other true sense or foundation. For the individual to arrive at the divine universality and supreme infinity, live in it, possess it, to be, know, feel and express that alone in all his being, consciousness, energy, delight of being is what the ancient seers of the Veda meant by the Knowledge; that was the Immortality which they set before man as his divine culmination.

But by the nature of his mentality, by his inlook into himself and his outlook on the world, by his original limitation in both through sense and body to the relative, the obvious and the apparent, man is obliged to move step by step and at first obscurely and ignorantly in this immense evolutionary movement. It is not possible for him to envisage being at first in the completeness of its unity: it presents itself to him through diversity, and his search for knowledge is preoccupied with three principal categories which sum up for him all its diversity; himself, — man or individual soul, — God, and Nature. The first is that of which alone he is directly aware in his normal ignorant being; he sees himself, the individual, separate apparently in its existence, yet always inseparable from the rest of being, striving to be sufficient, yet always insufficient to itself, since never has it been known to come into existence or to exist or to culminate in its existence apart from the rest, without their aid and independently of universal being and universal nature. Secondly, there is that which he knows only indirectly by his mind and bodily senses and its effects upon them, yet must strive always to know more and more completely: for he sees also this rest of being with which he is so closely identified and yet from which he is so separate, — the cosmos, world, Nature, other individual existences whom he perceives as always like himself and yet always unlike; for they are the same in nature even to the plant and the animal and yet different in nature. Each seems to go its own way, to be a separate being, and yet each is impelled by the same movement and follows in its own grade the same vast curve of evolution as himself. Finally, he sees or rather divines something else which he does not know at all except quite indirectly; for he knows it only through himself and that at which his being aims, through the world and that at which it seems to point and which it is either striving obscurely to reach and express by its imperfect figures or, at least, founds them without knowing it on their secret relation to that invisible Reality and occult Infinite.

This third and unknown, this *tertium quid*, he names God; and by the word he means somewhat or someone who is the Supreme, the Divine, the Cause, the All, one of these things or all of them at once, the perfection or the totality of all that here is partial or imperfect, the absolute of all these myriad relativities, the Unknown by learning of whom the real secret of the known can become to him more and more intelligible. Man has tried to deny all these categories, — he has tried to deny his own real existence, he has tried to deny the real existence of the cosmos, he has tried to deny the real existence of God. But behind all these denials we see the same constant necessity of his attempt at knowledge; for he feels the need of arriving at a unity of these three terms, even if it can only be done by suppressing two of them or merging them in the other that is left. To do that he affirms only himself as cause and all the rest as mere creations of his mind, or he affirms only Nature and all the rest as nothing but phenomena of Nature-Energy, or he affirms only God, the Absolute, and all the rest as no more than illusions which That thrusts upon itself or on us by an inexplicable Maya. None of these denials can wholly satisfy, none solves the entire problem or can be indisputable and definitive, — least of all the one to which his sense-governed intellect is most prone, but in which it can never persist for long; the denial of God is a denial of his true quest and his own supreme Ultimate. The ages of naturalistic atheism have always been short-lived because they can never satisfy the secret knowledge in man: that cannot be the final Veda because it does not correspond with the Veda within which all mental knowledge is labouring to bring out; from the moment that this lack of correspondence is felt, a solution, however skilful it may be and however logically complete, has been judged by the eternal Witness in man and is doomed; it cannot be the last word of Knowledge.

Man as he is is not sufficient to himself, nor separate, nor is he the Eternal and the All; therefore by himself he cannot be the explanation of the cosmos of which his mind, life and body are so evidently an infinitesimal detail. The visible cosmos too, he finds, is not sufficient to itself, nor does it explain itself even by its unseen material forces; for there is too much that he finds both in the world and in himself which is beyond them and of which they seem only to be a face, an epidermis or even a mask. Neither his intellect, nor his intuitions, nor his feeling can do without a One or a Oneness to whom or to which these world-forces and himself may stand in some relation which supports them and gives them their significance. He feels that there must be an Infinite which holds these finites, is in, behind and about all this visible cosmos, bases the harmony and interrelation and essential oneness of multitudinous things. His thought needs an Absolute on which these innumerable and finite relativities depend for their existence, an ultimate Truth of things, a creating Power or Force or a Being who originates and upholds all these innumerable beings in the universe. Let him call it what he will, he must arrive at a Supreme, a Divine, a Cause, an Infinite and Eternal, a Permanent, a Perfection to which all tends and aspires, or an All to which everything perpetually and invisibly amounts and without which they could not be.

Yet even this Absolute he cannot really affirm by itself and to the exclusion of the two other categories; for then he has only made a violent leap away from the problem he is here to solve, and he himself and the cosmos remain an inexplicable mystification or a purposeless mystery. A certain part of his intellect and his longing for rest may be placated by such a solution, just as his physical intelligence is easily satisfied by a denial of the Beyond and a deification of material Nature; but his heart, his will, the strongest and intensest parts of his being remain without a meaning, void of purpose or justification, or become merely a random foolishness agitating itself like a vain and restless shadow against the eternal repose of the pure Existence or amidst the eternal inconscience of the universe. As for the cosmos, it remains there in the singular character of a carefully constructed lie of the Infinite, a monstrously aggressive and yet really non-existent anomaly, a painful and miserable paradox with false shows of wonder and beauty and delight. Or else it is a huge play of blind organised Energy without significance and his own being a temporary minute anomaly incomprehensibly occurring in that senseless vastness. That way no satisfying fulfilment lies for the consciousness, the energy that has manifested itself in the world and in man: the mind needs to find something that links all together, something by which Nature is fulfilled in man and man in Nature and both find themselves in God, because the Divine is ultimately self-revealed in both man and Nature.

An acceptance, a perception of the unity of these three categories is essential to the Knowledge; it is towards their unity as well as their integrality that the growing self-consciousness of the individual opens out and at which it must arrive if it is to be satisfied of itself and complete. For without the realisation of unity the Knowledge of none of the three can be entire; their unity is for each the condition of its own integrality. It is, again, by knowing each in its completeness that all three meet in our consciousness and become one; it is in a total knowledge that all knowing becomes one and indivisible. Otherwise it is only by division and rejection of two of them from the third that we could get at any kind of oneness. Man therefore has to enlarge his knowledge of himself, his knowledge of the world and his knowledge of God until in their totality he becomes aware of their mutual indwelling and oneness. For so long as he knows them only in part, there will be an incompleteness resulting in division, and so long as he has not realised them in a reconciling unity, he will not have found their total truth or the fundamental significances of existence.

This is not to say that the Supreme is not self-existent and self-sufficient; God exists in Himself and not by virtue of the cosmos or of man, while man and cosmos exist by virtue of God and not in themselves except in so far as their being is one with the being of God. But still they are a manifestation of the power of God and even in His eternal existence their spiritual reality must in some way be present or implied, since otherwise there would be no possibility of their manifestation or, manifested, they would have no significance. What appears here as man is an individual being of the Divine; the Divine extended in multiplicity is the Self of all individual existences.[6] Moreover, it is through the knowledge of self and the world that man arrives at the knowledge of God and he cannot attain to it otherwise. It is not by rejecting God's manifestation, but by rejecting his own ignorance of it and the results of his ignorance, that he can best lift up and offer the whole of his being and consciousness and energy and joy of being into the Divine Existence. He may do this through himself, one manifestation, or he may do it through the universe, another manifestation. Arriving through himself alone, it is possible for him to plunge into an individual immergence or absorption in the Indefinable and to lose the universe. Arriving through the universe alone, he can sink his individuality either in the impersonality of universal being or in a dynamic self of universal Conscious-Force; he merges into the universal self or he becomes an impersonal channel of the cosmic Energy. Arriving through the equal integrality of both and seizing through them and beyond them on all the aspects of the Divine, he exceeds both and fulfils them in that exceeding: he possesses the Divine in his being, even as he is enveloped, penetrated, pervaded, possessed by the Divine Being, Consciousness, Light, Power, Delight, Knowledge; he possesses God in himself and God in the universe. The All-Knowledge justifies to him its creation of himself and justifies by him perfected its creation of the world it has made. All this becomes entirely real and effective by an ascension into a supramental and supreme supernature and the descent of its powers into

---

[6] *eko vaśī sarvabhūtāntarātmā* — *Katha Upanishad*, II. 2. 12.

the manifestation; but even while that consummation is still difficult and distant, the true knowledge can be made subjectively real by a spiritual reflection or reception in mind-life-body Nature.

But this spiritual truth and true aim of his being is not allowed to appear till late in his journey: for the early preparatory business of man in the evolutionary steps of Nature is to affirm, to make distinct and rich, to possess firmly, powerfully and completely his own individuality. As a consequence, he has in the beginning principally to occupy himself with his own ego. In this egoistic phase of his evolution the world and others are less important to him than himself, are indeed only important as aids and occasions for his self-affirmation. God too at this stage is less important to him than he is to himself, and therefore in earlier formations, on the lower levels of religious development, God or the gods are treated as if they existed for man, as supreme instruments for the satisfaction of his desires, his helpers in his task of getting the world in which he lives to satisfy his needs and wants and ambitions. This primary egoistic development with all its sins and violences and crudities is by no means to be regarded, in its proper place, as an evil or an error of Nature; it is necessary for man's first work, the finding of his own individuality and its perfect disengagement from the lower subconscient in which the individual is overpowered by the mass-consciousness of the world and entirely subject to the mechanical workings of Nature. Man the individual has to affirm, to distinguish his personality against Nature, to be powerfully himself, to evolve all his human capacities of force and knowledge and enjoyment so that he may turn them upon her and upon the world with more and more mastery and force; his self-discriminating egoism is given him as a means for this primary purpose. Until he has thus developed his individuality, his personality, his separate capacity, he cannot be fit for the greater work before him or successfully turn his faculties to higher, larger and more divine ends. He has to affirm himself in the Ignorance before he can perfect himself in the Knowledge.

For the initiation of the evolutionary emergence from the

Inconscient works out by two forces, a secret cosmic consciousness and an individual consciousness manifest on the surface.
The secret cosmic consciousness remains secret and subliminal
to the surface individual; it organises itself on the surface by the
creation of separate objects and beings. But while it organises the
separate object and the body and mind of the individual being,
it creates also collective powers of consciousness which are large
subjective formations of cosmic Nature; but it does not provide
for them an organised mind and body, it bases them on the group
of individuals, develops for them a group-mind, a changing yet
continuous group-body. It follows that only as the individuals
become more and more conscious can the group-being also become more and more conscious; the growth of the individual is
the indispensable means for the inner growth as distinguished
from the outer force and expansion of the collective being. This
indeed is the dual importance of the individual that it is through
him that the cosmic spirit organises its collective units and makes
them self-expressive and progressive and through him that it
raises Nature from the Inconscience to the Superconscience and
exalts it to meet the Transcendent. In the mass the collective
consciousness is near to the Inconscient; it has a subconscious,
an obscure and mute movement which needs the individual to
express it, to bring it to light, to organise it and make it effective.
The mass-consciousness by itself moves by a vague, half-formed
or unformed subliminal and commonly subconscient impulse
rising to the surface; it is prone to a blind or half-seeing unanimity which suppresses the individual in the common movement:
if it thinks, it is by the motto, the slogan, the watchword, the
common crude or formed idea, the traditional, the accepted customary notion; it acts, when not by instinct or on impulse, then
by the rule of the pack, the herd-mentality, the type-law. This
mass-consciousness, life, action can be extraordinarily effective
if it can find an individual or a few powerful individuals to
embody, express, lead, organise it; its sudden crowd-movements
can also be irresistible for the moment like the motion of an
avalanche or the rush of a tempest. The suppression or entire
subordination of the individual in the mass-consciousness can

give a great practical efficiency to a nation or a community if the subliminal collective being can build a binding tradition or find a group, a class, a head to embody its spirit and direction; the strength of powerful military states, of communities with a tense and austere culture rigidly imposed on its individuals, the success of the great world-conquerors, had behind it this secret of Nature. But this is an efficiency of the outer life, and that life is not the highest or last term of our being. There is a mind in us, there is a soul and spirit, and our life has no true value if it has not in it a growing consciousness, a developing mind, and if life and mind are not an expression, an instrument, a means of liberation and fulfilment for the soul, the indwelling Spirit.

But the progress of the mind, the growth of the soul, even of the mind and soul of the collectivity, depends on the individual, on his sufficient freedom and independence, on his separate power to express and bring into being what is still unexpressed in the mass, still undeveloped from the subconscience or not yet brought out from within or brought down from the Superconscience. The collectivity is a mass, a field of formation; the individual is the diviner of truth, the form-maker, the creator. In the crowd the individual loses his inner direction and becomes a cell of the mass-body moved by the collective will or idea or the mass-impulse. He has to stand apart, affirm his separate reality in the whole, his own mind emerging from the common mentality, his own life distinguishing itself in the common life-uniformity, even as his body has developed something unique and recognisable in the common physicality. He has, even, in the end to retire into himself in order to find himself, and it is only when he has found himself that he can become spiritually one with all; if he tries to achieve that oneness in the mind, in the vital, in the physical and has not yet a sufficiently strong individuality, he may be overpowered by the mass-consciousness and lose his soul-fulfilment, his mind-fulfilment, his life-fulfilment, become only a cell of the mass-body. The collective being may then become strong and dominant, but it is likely to lose its plasticity, its evolutionary movement: the great evolutionary periods of humanity have taken place in communities where the individual became active, mentally, vitally or spiritually alive. For this reason Nature invented the ego that the individual might disengage himself from the inconscience or subconscience of the mass and become an independent living mind, life-power, soul, spirit, co-ordinating himself with the world around him but not drowned in it and separately inexistent and ineffective. For the individual is indeed part of the cosmic being, but he is also something more, he is a soul that has descended from the Transcendence. This he cannot manifest at once, because he is too near to the cosmic Inconscience, not near enough to the original Superconscience; he has to find himself as the mental and vital ego before he can find himself as the soul or spirit.

Still, to find his egoistic individuality is not to know himself; the true spiritual individual is not the mind-ego, the life-ego, the body-ego: predominantly, this first movement is a work of will, of power, of egoistic self-effectuation and only secondarily of knowledge. Therefore a time must come when man has to look below the obscure surface of his egoistic being and attempt to know himself; he must set out to find the real man: without that he would be stopping short at Nature's primary education and never go on to her deeper and larger teachings; however great his practical knowledge and efficiency, he would be only a little higher than the animals. First, he has to turn his eyes upon his own psychology and distinguish its natural elements, — ego, mind and its instruments, life, body, — until he discovers that his whole existence stands in need of an explanation other than the working of the natural elements and of a goal for its activities other than an egoistic self-affirmation and satisfaction. He may seek it in Nature and mankind and thus start on his way to the discovery of his unity with the rest of his world: he may seek it in supernature, in God, and thus start on his way to the discovery of his unity with the Divine. Practically, he attempts both paths and, continually wavering, continually seeks to fix himself in the successive solutions that may be best in accordance with the various partial discoveries he has made on his double line of search and finding.

But through it all what he is in this stage still insistently seeking to discover, to know, to fulfil is himself; his knowledge of Nature, his knowledge of God are only helps towards self-knowledge, towards the perfection of his being, towards the attainment of the supreme object of his individual self-existence. Directed towards Nature and the cosmos, it may take upon itself the figure of self-knowledge, self-mastery, — in the mental and vital sense, — and mastery of the world in which we find ourselves: directed towards God, it may take also this figure but in a higher spiritual sense of world and self, or it may assume that other, so familiar and decisive to the religious mind, the seeking for an individual salvation whether in heavens beyond or by a separate immergence in a supreme Self or a supreme Non-self, — beatitude or Nirvana. Throughout, however, it is the individual who is seeking individual self-knowledge and the aim of his separate existence, with all the rest, even altruism and the love and service of mankind, self-effacement or self-annihilation, thrown in, — with whatever subtle disguises, — as helps and means towards that one great preoccupation of his realised individuality. This may seem to be only an expanded egoism, and the separative ego would then be the truth of man's being persistent in him to the end or till at last he is liberated from it by his self-extinction in the featureless eternity of the Infinite. But there is a deeper secret behind which justifies his individuality and its demand, the secret of the spiritual and eternal individual, the Purusha.

It is because of the spiritual Person, the Divinity in the individual, that perfection or liberation, — salvation, as it is called in the West, — has to be individual and not collective; for whatever perfection of the collectivity is to be sought after, can come only by the perfection of the individuals who constitute it. It is because the individual is That, that to find himself is his great necessity. In his complete surrender and self-giving to the Supreme it is he who finds his perfect self-finding in a perfect self-offering. In the abolition of the mental, vital, physical ego, even of the spiritual ego, it is the formless and limitless Individual that has the peace and joy of his escape into his own infinity. In the experience that he is nothing and no one, or everything and everyone, or the One which is beyond all things and absolute, it is the Brahman in the individual that effectuates this stupendous merger or this marvellous joining, Yoga, of its eternal unit of being with its vast all-comprehending or supreme all-transcending unity of eternal existence. To get beyond the ego is imperative, but one cannot get beyond the self, — except by finding it supremely, universally. For the self is not the ego; it is one with the All and the One and in finding it it is the All and the One that we discover in our self: the contradiction, the separation disappears, but the self, the spiritual reality remains, united with the One and the All by that delivering disappearance.

The higher self-knowledge begins therefore as soon as man has got beyond his preoccupation with the relation of Nature and God to his superficial being, his most apparent self. One step is to know that this life is not all, to get at the conception of his own temporal eternity, to realise, to become concretely aware of that subjective persistence which is called the immortality of the soul. When he knows that there are states beyond the material and lives behind and before him, at any rate a pre-existence and a subsequent existence, he is on the way to get rid of his temporal ignorance by enlarging himself beyond the immediate moments of Time into the possession of his own eternity. Another step forward is to learn that his surface waking state is only a small part of his being, to begin to fathom the abyss of the Inconscient and depths of the subconscient and subliminal and scale the heights of the superconscient; so he commences the removal of his psychological self-ignorance. A third step is to find out that there is something in him other than his instrumental mind, life and body, not only an immortal ever-developing individual soul that supports his nature but an eternal immutable self and spirit, and to learn what are the categories of his spiritual being, until he discovers that all in him is an expression of the spirit and distinguishes the link between his lower and his higher existence; thus he sets out to remove his constitutional self-ignorance. Discovering self and spirit he discovers God; he finds out that there is a Self beyond the temporal: he comes to the vision of that Self in the cosmic consciousness as the divine Reality behind

Nature and this world of beings; his mind opens to the thought or the sense of the Absolute of whom self and the individual and the cosmos are so many faces; the cosmic, the egoistic, the original ignorance begin to lose the rigidness of their hold upon him. In his attempt to cast his existence into the mould of this enlarging self-knowledge his whole view and motive of life, thought and action are progressively modified and transformed; his practical ignorance of himself, his nature and his object of existence diminishes: he has set his step on the path which leads out of the falsehood and suffering of a limited and partial into the perfect possession and enjoyment of a true and complete existence.

In the course of this progress he discovers step by step the unity of the three categories with which he started. For, first, he finds that in his manifest being he is one with cosmos and Nature; mind, life and body, the soul in the succession of Time, the conscient, subconscient and superconscient, — these in their various relations and the result of their relations are cosmos and are Nature. But he finds too that in all which stands behind them or on which they are based, he is one with God; for the Absolute, the Spirit, the Self spaceless and timeless, the Self manifest in the cosmos and Lord of Nature, — all this is what we mean by God, and in all this his own being goes back to God and derives from it; he is the Absolute, the Self, the Spirit self-projected in a multiplicity of itself into cosmos and veiled in Nature. In both of these realisations he finds his unity with all other souls and beings, — relatively in Nature, since he is one with them in mind, vitality, matter, soul, every cosmic principle and result, however various in energy and act of energy, disposition of principle and disposition of result, but absolutely in God, because the one Absolute, the one Self, the one Spirit is ever the Self of all and the origin, possessor and enjoyer of their multitudinous diversities. The unity of God and Nature cannot fail to manifest itself to him: for he finds in the end that it is the Absolute who is all these relativities; he sees that it is the Spirit of whom every other principle is a manifestation; he discovers that it is the Self who has become all these becomings; he feels that it is the Shakti or

Power of being and consciousness of the Lord of all beings which is Nature and is acting in the cosmos. Thus in the progress of our self-knowledge we arrive at that by the discovery of which all is known as one with our self and by the possession of which all is possessed and enjoyed in our own self-existence.

Equally, by virtue of this unity, the knowledge of the universe must lead the mind of man to the same large revelation. For he cannot know Nature as Matter and Force and Life without being driven to scrutinise the relation of mental consciousness with these principles, and once he knows the real nature of mind, he must go inevitably beyond every surface appearance. He must discover the will and intelligence secret in the works of Force, operative in material and vital phenomena; he must perceive it as one in the waking consciousness, the subconscient and the superconscient: he must find the soul in the body of the material universe. Pursuing Nature through these categories in which he recognises his unity with the rest of the cosmos, he finds a Supernature behind all that is apparent, a supreme power of the Spirit in Time and beyond Time, in Space and beyond Space, a conscious Power of the Self who by her becomes all becomings, of the Absolute who by her manifests all relativities. He knows her, in other words, not only as material Energy, Life-Force, Mind-Energy, the many faces of Nature, but as the power of Knowledge-Will of the Divine Lord of being, the Consciousness-Force of the self-existent Eternal and Infinite.

The quest of man for God, which becomes in the end the most ardent and enthralling of all his quests, begins with his first vague questionings of Nature and a sense of something unseen both in himself and her. Even if, as modern Science insists, religion started from animism, spirit-worship, demon-worship, and the deification of natural forces, these first forms only embody in primitive figures a veiled intuition in the subconscient, an obscure and ignorant feeling of hidden influences and incalculable forces, or a vague sense of being, will, intelligence in what seems to us inconscient, of the invisible behind the visible, of the secretly conscious spirit in things distributing itself in every working of energy. The obscurity and primitive inadequacy of the first perceptions do not detract from the value or the truth of this great quest of the human heart and mind, since all our seekings, — including Science itself, — must start from an obscure and ignorant perception of hidden realities and proceed to the more and more luminous vision of the Truth which at first comes to us masked, draped, veiled by the mists of the Ignorance. Anthropomorphism is an imaged recognition of the truth that man is what he is because God is what He is and that there is one soul and body of things, humanity even in its incompleteness the most complete manifestation yet achieved here and divinity the perfection of what in man is imperfect. That he sees himself everywhere and worships that as God is also true; but here too he has laid confusedly the groping hand of Ignorance on a truth, — that his being and the Being are one, that this is a partial reflection of That, and that to find his greater Self everywhere is to find God and to come near to the Reality in things, the Reality of all existence.

A unity behind diversity and discord is the secret of the variety of human religions and philosophies; for they all get at some image or some side clue, touch some portion of the one Truth or envisage some one of its myriad aspects. Whether they see dimly the material world as the body of the Divine, or life as a great pulsation of the breath of Divine Existence, or all things as thoughts of the cosmic Mind, or realise that there is a Spirit which is greater than these things, their subtler and yet more wonderful source and creator, — whether they find God only in the Inconscient or as the one Conscious in inconscient things or as an ineffable superconscious Existence to reach whom we must leave behind our terrestrial being and annul the mind, life and body, or, overcoming division, see that He is all these at once and accept fearlessly the large consequences of that vision, — whether they worship Him with universality as the cosmic Being or limit Him and themselves, like the Positivist, in humanity only or, on the contrary, carried away by the vision of the timeless and spaceless Immutable, reject Him in Nature and Cosmos, — whether they adore Him in various strange or beautiful or magnified forms of the human ego or for His perfect possession of the qualities to which man aspires, his Divinity revealed to them as a supreme Power, Love, Beauty, Truth, Righteousness, Wisdom, — whether they perceive Him as the Lord of Nature, Father and Creator, or as Nature herself and the universal Mother, pursue Him as the Lover and attracter of souls or serve Him as the hidden Master of all works, bow down before the one God or the manifold Deity, the one divine Man or the one Divine in all men or, more largely, discover the One whose presence enables us to become unified in consciousness or in works or in life with all beings, unified with all things in Time and Space, unified with Nature and her influences and even her inanimate forces, — the truth behind must ever be the same because all is the one Divine Infinite whom all are seeking. Because everything is that One, there must be this endless variety in the human approach to its possession; it was necessary that man should find God thus variously in order that he might come to know Him entirely. But it is when knowledge reaches its highest aspects that it is possible to arrive at its greatest unity. The highest and widest seeing is the wisest; for then all knowledge is unified in its one comprehensive meaning. All religions are seen as approaches to a single Truth, all philosophies as divergent viewpoints looking at different sides of a single Reality, all Sciences meet together in a supreme Science. For that which all our mind-knowledge and sense-knowledge and suprasensuous vision is seeking, is found most integrally in the unity of God and man and Nature and all that is in Nature.

The Brahman, the Absolute is the Spirit, the timeless Self, the Self possessing Time, Lord of Nature, creator and continent of the cosmos and immanent in all existences, the Soul from whom all souls derive and to whom they are drawn, — that is the truth of Being as man's highest God-conception sees it. The same Absolute revealed in all relativities, the Spirit who embodies Himself in cosmic Mind and Life and Matter and of whom Nature is the self of energy so that all she seems to create is the Self and Spirit variously manifested in His own being to His own conscious force for the delight of His various existence, — this is the truth of being to which man's knowledge of Nature and cosmos is leading him and which he will reach when his Nature-knowledge unites itself with his God-knowledge. This truth of the Absolute is the justification of the cycles of the world; it is not their denial. It is the Self-Being that has become all these becomings; the Self is the eternal unity of all these existences, — I am He. Cosmic energy is not other than the conscious force of that Self-existent: by that energy it takes through universal nature innumerable forms of itself; through its divine nature it can, embracing the universal but transcendent of it, arrive in them at the individual possession of its complete existence, when its presence and power are felt in one, in all and in the relations of one with all; — this is the truth of being to which man's entire knowledge of himself in God and in Nature rises and widens. A triune knowledge, the complete knowledge of God, the complete knowledge of himself, the complete knowledge of Nature, gives him his high goal; it assigns a vast and full sense to the labour and effort of humanity. The conscious unity of the three, God, Soul and Nature, in his own consciousness is the sure foundation of his perfection and his realisation of all harmonies: this will be his highest and widest state, his status of a divine consciousness and a divine life and its initiation the starting-point for his entire evolution of his self-knowledge, world-knowledge, God-knowledge.

Chapter XVIII

The Evolutionary Process —
Ascent and Integration

As he mounts from peak to peak... Indra makes him conscious
of that goal of his movement.   *Rig Veda.*[1]

A son of the two Mothers, he attains to kingship in his discoveries of knowledge, he moves on the summit, he dwells in
his high foundation.   *Rig Veda.*[2]

I have arisen from earth to the mid-world, I have arisen from
the mid-world to heaven, from the level of the firmament of
heaven I have gone to the Sun-world, the Light.[3]

                                                  Yajur Veda.[4]

IT IS now possible and necessary, since we have formed a
sufficiently clear idea of the significance of the evolutionary
manifestation in earth-nature and the final turn it is taking
or destined to take, to direct a more understanding regard on
the principles of the process by which it has arrived at its present
level and by which, presumably, with whatever modifications,
its final development, its passage from our still dominant mental ignorance to a supramental consciousness and an integral
knowledge, will be governed and made effective. For we find
that cosmic Nature is constant in its general law of action,
since that depends on a Truth of things which is invariable in
principle although in detail of application abundantly variable.
At the outset, we can easily see that, since this is an evolution

---

[1] I. 10. 2.   [2] III. 55. 7.
[3] The four planes of Matter, Life, pure Mind and Supermind.
[4] 17. 67.

out of a material Inconscience into spiritual consciousness, an evolutionary self-building of Spirit on a base of Matter, there must be in the process a development of a triple character. An evolution of forms of Matter more and more subtly and intricately organised so as to admit the action of a growing, a more and more complex and subtle and capable organisation of consciousness is the indispensable physical foundation. An upward evolutionary progress of the consciousness itself from grade to higher grade, an ascent, is the evident spiral line or emerging curve that, on this foundation, the evolution must describe. A taking up of what has already been evolved into each higher grade as it is reached and a transformation more or less complete so as to admit of a total changed working of the whole being and nature, an integration, must be also part of the process, if the evolution is to be effective.

The end of this triple process must be a radical change of the action of the Ignorance into an action of Knowledge, of our basis of inconscience into a basis of complete consciousness, — a completeness which exists at present only in what is to us the superconscience. Each ascent will bring with it a partial change and modification of the old nature taken up and subjected to a new fundamental principle; the inconscience will be turned into a partial consciousness, an ignorance seeking for more and more knowledge and mastery: but at some point there must be an ascent which substitutes the principle of knowledge, of a fundamental true consciousness, the consciousness of the Spirit, for the inconscience and ignorance. An evolution in the Inconscience is the beginning, an evolution in the Ignorance is the middle, but the end is the liberation of the spirit into its true consciousness and an evolution in the Knowledge. This is actually what we find to be the law and method of the process which has hitherto been followed and by all signs is likely to be followed in her future working by evolutionary Nature. A first involutionary foundation in which originates all that has to evolve, an emergence and action of the involved powers in or upon that foundation in an ascending series, and a culminating emergence of the highest power of all as the agent of a supreme manifestation are the necessary stages of the journey of evolutionary Nature.

An evolutionary process must be by the very terms of the problem to be solved a development, in some first established basic principle of being or substance, of something that that basic principle holds involved in itself or else admits from outside itself and modifies by the admission; for it must necessarily modify by its own law of nature all that enters into it and is not already part of its own nature. This must be so even if it is a creative evolution in the sense of manifesting always new powers of existence that are not native to the first foundation but introduced into it, accepted into an original substance. If, on the contrary, there is already there in involution, — present in the first foundation, but not yet manifested or not yet organised, — the new principle or power of existence that has to be evolved, then, when it appears, it will still have to accept modification by the nature and law of the basic substance: but also it will modify that substance by its own power, its own law of nature. If, further, it is aided by a descent of its own principle already established in its own full force above the field of evolution and pressing down into that field to possess it, then the new power may even establish itself as a dominant element and considerably or radically change the consciousness and action of the world in which it emerges or into which it enters. But its force to modify or change or to revolutionise the law and working of the original substance chosen as the evolutionary matrix will depend upon its own essential potency. It is not likely that it will be able to bring about an entire transformation if it is not itself the original Principle of Existence, if it is only derivative, an instrumental power and not the first puissance.

Here the evolution takes place in a material universe; the foundation, the original substance, the first established all-conditioning status of things is Matter. Mind and Life are evolved in Matter, but they are limited and modified in their action by the obligation to use its substance for their instrumentation and by their subjection to the law of material Nature even while they modify what they undergo and use. For they do transform its substance, first into living substance and then into conscious substance; they succeed in changing its inertia, immobility and inconscience into a movement of consciousness, feeling and life. But they do not succeed in transforming it altogether; they cannot make it altogether alive or altogether conscious: life-nature evolving is bound to death; mind evolving is materialised as well as vitalised; it finds itself rooted in inconscience, limited by ignorance; it is moved by uncontrolled life-forces which drive and use it, it is mechanised by the physical forces on which it has to depend for its own self-expression. This is a sign that neither Mind nor Life is the original creative Power; they, like Matter, are intermediaries, successive and seried instruments of the evolutionary process. If a material energy is not that original Power, then we must seek for it in something above Mind or Life; there must be a deeper occult Reality which has yet to disclose itself in Nature.

An original creative or evolutionary Power there must be: but, although Matter is the first substance, the original and ultimate Power is not an inconscient material Energy; for then life and consciousness would be absent, since Inconscience cannot evolve consciousness nor an inanimate Force evolve life. There must be, therefore, since Mind and Life also are not that, a secret Consciousness greater than Life-Consciousness or Mind-Consciousness, an Energy more essential than the material Energy. Since it is greater than Mind, it must be a supramental Consciousness-Force; since it is a power of essential substance other than Matter, it must be the power of that which is the supreme essence and substance of all things, a power of the Spirit. There is a creative energy of Mind and a creative Life-Force, but they are instrumental and partial, not original and decisive: Mind and Life do indeed modify the material substance they inhabit and its energies and are not merely determined by them, but the extent and way of this material modification and determination are fixed by the inhabitant and all-containing Spirit through a secret indwelling light and force of Supermind, an occult gnosis, — an invisible self-knowledge and all-knowledge. If there is to be an entire transformation, it can only be by the full emergence of the law of the Spirit; its power of Supermind or gnosis must have entered into Matter and it must evolve in Matter. It must change the mental into the supramental being, make the inconscient in us conscious, spiritualise our material substance, erect its law of gnostic consciousness in our whole evolutionary being and nature. This must be the culminating emergence or, at least, that stage in the emergence which first decisively changes the nature of the evolution by transforming its action of Ignorance and its basis of Inconscience.

This movement of evolution, of a progressive self-manifestation of the Spirit in a material universe, has to make its account at every step with the fact of the involution of consciousness and force in the form and activity of material substance. For it proceeds by an awakening of the involved consciousness and force and its ascent from principle to principle, from grade to grade, from power to power of the secret Spirit, but this is not a free transference to a higher status. The law of action, the force of action of each grade or power in its emergence is determined, not by its own free, full and pure law of nature or vim of energy, but partly by the material organisation provided for it and partly by its own status, achieved degree, accomplished fact of consciousness which it has been able to impose upon Matter. Its effectivity is in some sort made up of a balance between the actual extent of this evolutionary emergence and the countervailing extent to which the emergent power is still enveloped, penetrated, diminished by the domination and continuing grip of the Inconscience. Mind as we see it is not mind pure and free, but mind clouded and diminished by an enveloping nescience, mind labouring and struggling to deliver knowledge out of that nescience. All depends upon the more or less involved or more or less evolved condition of consciousness, — quite involved in inconscient matter, hesitating on the verge between involution and conscious evolution in the first or non-animal forms of life in matter, consciously evolving but greatly limited and hampered in mind housed in a living body, destined to be fully evolved by the awakening of the Supermind in the embodied mental being and nature.

To each grade in this series achieved by the evolving Consciousness belongs its appropriate class of existences, — one by one there appear material forms and forces, vegetable life, animals and half-animal man, developed human beings, imperfectly evolved or more evolved spiritual beings: but because of the continuity of the evolutionary process there is no rigid separation between them; each new advance or formation takes up what was before. The animal takes up into himself living and inanimate Matter; man takes up both along with the animal existence. There are furrows left by the transitional process or separating demarcations settled by the fixed habit of Nature: but these distinguish one series from another, serve perhaps to prevent a fall back of what has been evolved, they do not cancel or cut the continuity of the evolution. The evolving Consciousness passes from one grade to another or from one series of steps to another either by an imperceptible process or by some bound or crisis or, perhaps, by an intervention from above, — some descent or ensouling or influence from higher planes of Nature. But, by whatever means, the Consciousness secretly indwelling in Matter, the occult Inhabitant, is able thus to make its way upward from the lower to the higher gradations, taking up what it was into what it is and preparing to take up both into what it will be. Thus, having first laid down a basis of material being, material forms, forces, existences in which it seems to be lying inconscient, though in reality, as we know now, always subconsciently at work, it is able to manifest life and living beings, to manifest mind and mental beings in a material world, and must therefore be able to manifest there Supermind also and supramental beings. Thus has come about the present status of the evolution of which man is the now apparent culmination but not the real ultimate summit; for he is himself a transitional being and stands at the turning-point of the whole movement. Evolution, being thus continuous, must have at any given moment a past with its fundamental results still in evidence, a present in which the results it is labouring over are in process of becoming, a future in which still unevolved powers and forms of being must appear till there is the full and perfect manifestation. The past has been the history of a slow and difficult subconscious working with effects on the surface, — it has been an unconscious evolution; the present is a middle stage, an uncertain spiral in which the human intelligence is used by the secret evolutionary Force of being and participates in its action without being fully taken into confidence, — it is an evolution slowly becoming conscious of itself; the future must be a more and more conscious evolution of the spiritual being until it is fully delivered into a self-aware action by the emergent gnostic principle.

The first foundation in this emergence, the creation of forms of Matter, first of inconscient and inanimate, then of living and thinking Matter, the appearance of more and more organised bodies adapted to express a greater power of consciousness, has been studied from the physical side, the side of form-building, by Science; but very little light has been shed on the inner side, the side of consciousness, and what little has been observed is rather of its physical basis and instrumentation than of the progressive operations of Consciousness in its own nature. In the evolution, as it has been observed so far, although a continuity is there, — for Life takes up Matter and Mind takes up submental Life, the Mind of intelligence takes up the mind of life and sensation, — the leap from one grade of consciousness in the series to another grade seems to our eyes immense, the crossing of the gulf whether by bridge or by leap impossible; we fail to discover any concrete and satisfactory evidence of its accomplishment in the past or of the manner in which it was accomplished. Even in the outward evolution, even in the development of physical forms where the data are clearly in evidence, there are missing links that remain always missing; but in the evolution of consciousness the passage is still more difficult to account for, for it seems more like a transformation than a passage. It may be, however, that, by our incapacity to penetrate the subconscious, to sound the submental or to understand sufficiently a lower mentality different from ours, we are unable to observe the minute gradations, not only in each degree of the series, but on the borders between grade and grade: the scientist who does observe minutely the physical data, has been driven to believe in the continuity of evolution in

spite of the gaps and missing links; if we could observe similarly
the inner evolution, we could, no doubt, discover the possibility
and the mode of these formidable transitions. But still there is
a real, a radical difference between grade and grade, so much
so that the passage from one to another seems a new creation,
a miracle of metamorphosis rather than a natural predictable
development or quiet passing from one state of being to another
with its well-marked steps arranged in an easy sequence.

These gulfs appear deeper, but less wide, as we rise higher
in the scale of Nature. If there are rudiments of life-reaction in
the metal, as has been recently contended, it may be identical
with life-reaction in the plant in its essence, but what might
be called the vital-physical difference is so considerable that
one seems to us inanimate, the other, though not apparently
conscious, might be called a living creature. Between the highest
plant life and lowest animal the gulf is visibly deeper, for it is the
difference between mind and the entire absence of any apparent
or even rudimentary movement of mind: in the one this stuff
of mental consciousness is unawakened though there is a life of
vital reactions, a suppressed or subconscious or perhaps only
submental sense-vibration which seems to be intensely active; in
the other, though the life is at first less automatic and secure in
the subconscious way of living and in its own new way of overt
consciousness imperfectly determined, still mind is awakened, —
there is a conscious life, a profound transition has been made.
But the community of the phenomenon of life between plant
and animal, however different their organisation, narrows the
gulf, even though it does not fill in its profundity. Between the
highest animal and the lowest man there is a still deeper though
narrower gulf to be crossed, the gulf between sense-mind and
the intellect: for however we may insist on the primitive nature
of the savage, we cannot alter the fact that the most primitive
human being has above and beyond the sense-mind, emotional
vitality and primary practical intelligence which we share with
the animals, a human intellect and is capable, — in whatever
limits, — of reflection, ideas, conscious invention, religious and
ethical thought and feeling, everything fundamental of which

man as a race is capable; he has the same kind of intelligence, it differs only in its past instruction and formative training and the degree of its developed capacity, intensity and activity. Still, in spite of these dividing furrows, we can no longer suppose that God or some Demiurge has manufactured each genus and species ready-made in body and in consciousness and left the matter there, having looked upon his work and seen that it was good. It has become evident that a secretly conscious or an inconscient Energy of creation has effected the transition by swift or slow degrees, by whatever means, devices, biological, physical or psychological machinery, — perhaps, having made it, did not care to preserve as distinct forms what were only stepping-stones and had no longer any function nor served any purpose in evolutionary Nature. But this explanation of the gaps is little more than a hypothesis which as yet we cannot sufficiently substantiate. It is probable at any rate that the reason for these radical differences is to be found in the working of the inner Force and not in the outer process of the evolutionary transition; if we look at it more deeply from that inner side, the difficulty of understanding ceases and these transitions become intelligible and indeed inevitable by the very nature of the evolutionary process and its principle.

For if we look, not at the scientific or physical aspects, but at the psychological side of the question and inquire in what precisely the difference lies, we shall see that it consists in the rise of consciousness to another principle of being. The metal is fixed in the inconscient and inanimate principle of matter; even if we can suppose that it has some reactions suggestive of life in it or at least of rudimentary vibrations that in the plant developed into life, still it is not at all characteristically a form of life; it is characteristically a form of matter. The plant is fixed in a subconscient action of the principle of life, — not that it is not subject to matter or devoid of reactions that find their full meaning only in mind, for it seems to have submental reactions that in us are the foundation of pleasure and pain or of attraction and repulsion; but still it is a form of life, not of mere matter, nor is it, so far as we know, at all a mind-conscious being. Man and the animal are both mentally conscious beings: but the animal is fixed in vital mind and mind-sense and cannot exceed its limitations, while man has received into his sense-mind the light of another principle, the intellect, which is really at once a reflection and a degradation of the Supermind, a ray of gnosis seized by the sense-mentality and transformed by it into something other than its source: for it is agnostic like the sense-mind in which and for which it works, not gnostic; it seeks to lay hold on knowledge, because it does not possess it, it does not like Supermind hold knowledge in itself as its natural prerogative. In other words, in each of these forms of existence the universal being has fixed its action of consciousness in a different principle or, as between man and animal, in the modification of a lower by a higher though still not a highest-grade principle. It is this stride from one principle of being to another quite different principle of being that creates the transitions, the furrows, the sharp lines of distance, and makes, not all the difference, but still a radical characteristic difference between being and being in their nature.

But it must be observed that this ascent, this successive fixing in higher and higher principles, does not carry with it the abandonment of the lower grades, any more than a status of existence in the lower grades means the entire absence of the higher principles. This heals the objection against the evolutionary theory created by these sharp lines of difference; for if the rudiments of the higher are present in the lower creation and the lower characters are taken up into the higher evolved being, that of itself constitutes an indubitable evolutionary process. What is necessary is a working that brings the lower gradation of being to a point at which the higher can manifest in it; at that point a pressure from some superior plane where the new power is dominant may assist towards a more or less rapid and decisive transition by a bound or a series of bounds, — a slow, creeping, imperceptible or even occult action is followed by a run and an evolutionary saltus across the border. It is in some such way that the transition from the lower to higher grades of consciousness seems to have been made in Nature.

In fact, life, mind, Supermind are present in the atom, are at work there, but invisible, occult, latent in a subconscious or apparently unconscious action of the Energy; there is an informing Spirit, but the outer force and figure of being, what we might call the formal or form existence as distinguished from the immanent or secretly governing consciousness, is lost in the physical action, is so absorbed into it as to be fixed in a stereotyped self-oblivion unaware of what it is and what it is doing. The electron and atom are in this view eternal somnambulists; each material object contains an outer or form consciousness involved, absorbed in the form, asleep, seeming to be an unconsciousness driven by an unknown and unfelt inner Existence, — he who is awake in the sleeper, the universal Inhabitant of the Upanishads, — an outer absorbed form-consciousness which, unlike that of the human somnambulist, has never been awake and is not always or ever on the point of waking. In the plant this outer form-consciousness is still in the state of sleep, but a sleep full of nervous dreams, always on the point of waking, but never waking. Life has appeared; in other words, force of concealed conscious being has been so much intensified, has raised itself to such a height of power as to develop or become capable of a new principle of action, that which we see as vitality, life-force. It has become vitally responsive to existence, though not mentally aware, and has put forth a new grade of activities of a higher and subtler value than any purely physical action. At the same time, it is capable of receiving and turning into these new life-values, into motions and phenomena of a vibration of vitality, life-contacts and physical contacts from other forms than its own and from universal Nature. This is a thing which forms of mere matter cannot do; they cannot turn contacts into life-values or any kind of value, partly because their power of reception, — although it exists, if occult evidence is to be trusted, — is not sufficiently awake to do anything but dumbly receive and imperceptibly react, partly because the energies transmitted by the contacts are too subtle to be utilised by the crude inorganic density of formed Matter. Life in the tree is determined by its physical body, but it takes up the physical existence and gives it a new value or system of values, — the life-value.

The transition to the mind and sense that appear in the animal being, that which we call conscious life, is operated in the same manner. The force of being is so much intensified, rises to such a height as to admit or develop a new principle of existence, —apparently new at least in the world of Matter, —mentality. Animal being is mentally aware of existence, its own and others, puts forth a higher and subtler grade of activities, receives a wider range of contacts, mental, vital, physical, from forms other than its own, takes up the physical and vital existence and turns all it can get from them into sense values and vital-mind values. It senses body, it senses life, but it senses also mind; for it has not only blind nervous reactions, but conscious sensations, memories, impulses, volitions, emotions, mental associations, the stuff of feeling and thought and will. It has even a practical intelligence, founded on memory, association, stimulating need, observation, a power of device; it is capable of cunning, strategy, planning; it can invent, adapt to some extent its inventions, meet in this or that detail the demand of new circumstance. All is not in it a half-conscious instinct; the animal prepares human intelligence.

But when we come to man, we see the whole thing becoming conscious; the world, which he epitomises, begins in him to reveal to itself its own nature. The higher animal is not the somnambulist, — as the very lowest animal forms still mainly or almost are, — but it has only a limited waking mind, capable of just what is necessary for its vital existence: in man the conscious mentality enlarges its wakefulness and, though not at first fully self-conscious, though still conscious only on the surface, can open more and more to his inner and integral being. As in the two lower ascents, there is a heightening of the force of conscious existence to a new power and a new range of subtle activities; there is a transition from vital mind to reflecting and thinking mind, there is developed a higher power of observation and invention, taking up and connecting data, conscious of process and result, a force of imagination and aesthetic creation, a higher more plastic sensibility, the co-ordinating and interpreting reason, the values no longer of a reflex or reactive but of a mastering, understanding, self-detaching intelligence. As in the lower ascents, so here there is also a widening of the range of consciousness; man is able to take in more of the world and of himself as well as to give to this knowledge higher and completer figures of conscious experience. So, too, there is here also the third constant element of the ascension; mind takes up the lower grades and gives to their action and reaction intelligent values. Man has not only like the animal the sense of his body and life, but an intelligent sense and idea of life and a conscious and observant perception of body. He takes up too the mental life of the animal, as well as the material and bodily; although he loses something in the process, he gives to what he retains a higher value; he has the intelligent sense and the idea of his sensations, emotions, volitions, impulses, mental associations; what was crude stuff of thought and feeling and will, capable only of gross determinations, he turns into the finished work and artistry of these things. For the animal too thinks, but in an automatic way based mainly on a mechanical series of memories and mental associations, accepting quickly or slowly the suggestions of Nature and only awakened to a more conscious personal action when there is need of close observation and device; it has some first crude stuff of practical reason, but not the formed ideative and reflective faculty. The awaking consciousness in the animal is the unskilled primitive artisan of mind, in man it is the skilled craftsman and can become, — but this he does not attempt sufficiently, — not only the artist, but master and adept.

But here we have to observe two particularities of this human and at present highest development, which bring us to the heart of the matter. First, this taking up of the lower parts of life reveals itself as a turning downward of the master eye of the secret evolving spirit or of the universal Being in the individual from the height to which he has reached on all that now lies below him, a gazing down with the double or twin power of the being's consciousness-force, — the power of will, the power of knowledge, — so as to understand from this new, different and wider range of consciousness and perception and nature the lower life and its possibilities and to raise it up, it also, to a higher level, to give it higher values, to bring out of it higher potentialities. And this he does because evidently he does not intend to kill or destroy it, but, delight of existence being his eternal business and a harmony of various strains, not a sweet but monotonous melody the method of his music, he wishes to include the lower notes also and, by surcharging them with a deeper and finer significance, get more delight out of them than was possible in the cruder formulation. Still in the end he lays on them as a condition for his continued acceptance their consent to admit the higher values and, until they do consent, he can deal harshly enough with them even to trampling them under foot when he is bent on perfection and they are rebellious. And that indeed is the true inmost aim and meaning of ethics, discipline and askesis, to lesson and tame, purify and prepare to be fit instruments the vital and physical and lower mental life so that they may be transformed into notes of the higher mental and eventually the supramental harmony, but not to mutilate and destroy them. Ascent is the first necessity, but an integration is an accompanying intention of the spirit in Nature.

This downward eye of knowledge and will with a view to an all-round heightening, deepening and subtler, finer and richer intensification is the secret Spirit's way from the beginning. The plant-soul takes, as we may say, a nervous-material view of its whole physical existence so as to get out of it all the vital-physical intensity possible; for it seems to have some intense excitations of a mute life-vibration in it, — perhaps, though that is difficult for us to imagine, more intense relatively to its lower rudimentary scale than the animal mind and body in its higher and more powerful scale could tolerate. The animal being takes a mentalised sense-view of its vital and physical existence so as to get out of it all the sense-value possible, much acuter in many respects than man's as mere sensation or sense-emotion or satisfaction of vital desire and pleasure. Man, looking downward from the plane of will and intelligence, abandons these lower intensities, but in order to get out of mind and life and sense a higher intensity in other values, intellectual, aesthetic, moral, spiritual, mentally dynamic or practical, — as he terms it; by these higher elements he enlarges, subtilises and elevates his use of life-values. He does not abandon the animal reactions and enjoyments, but more lucidly, finely and sensitively mentalises them. This he does even on his normal and his lower levels, but, as he develops, he puts his lower being to a severer test, begins to demand from it on pain of rejection something like a transformation: that is the mind's way of preparing for a spiritual life still beyond it.

But man not only turns his gaze downward and around him, when he has reached his higher level, but upward towards what is above him and inward towards what is occult within him. In him not only the downward gaze of the universal Being in the evolution has become conscious, but its conscious upward and inward gaze also develops. The animal lives as if satisfied with what Nature has done for it; if there is any upward gaze of the secret spirit within its animal being, it has nothing consciously to do with it, that is still Nature's business: it is man who first makes this upward gaze consciously his own business. For already by his possession of intelligent will, deformed ray of the gnosis though it be, he begins to put on the double nature of Sachchidananda; he is no longer, like the animal, an undeveloped conscious being entirely driven by Prakriti, a slave of the executive Force, played with by the mechanical energies of Nature, but has begun to be a developing conscious soul or Purusha interfering with what was her sole affair, wishing to have a say in it and eventually to be the master. He cannot do it yet, he is too much in her meshes, too much involved in her established mechanism: but he feels, — though as yet too vaguely and uncertainly, — that the spirit within him wishes to rise to yet higher heights, to widen its bounds; something within, something occult, knows that it is not the intention of the deeper conscious Soul-Nature, the Purusha-Prakriti, to be satisfied with his present lowness and limitations. To climb to higher altitudes, to get a greater scope, to transform his lower nature, this is always a natural impulse of man as soon as he has made his place for himself in the physical and vital world of earth and has a little leisure to consider his farther possibilities. It must be so not because of any false and pitiful imaginative illusion in him, but, first, because he is the imperfect, still developing mental being and must strive for more development, for perfection, and still more because he is capable, unlike other terrestrial creatures, of becoming aware of what is deeper than mind, of the soul within him, and of what is above the mind, of Supermind, of spirit, capable of opening to it, admitting it, rising towards it, taking hold of it. It is in his human nature, in all human nature, to exceed itself by conscious evolution, to climb beyond what he is. Not individuals only, but in time the race also, in a general rule of being and living if not in all its members, can have the hope, if it develops a sufficient will, to rise beyond the imperfections of our present very undivine nature and to ascend at least to a superior humanity, to rise nearer, even if it cannot absolutely reach, to a divine manhood or supermanhood. At any rate, it is the compulsion of evolutionary Nature in him to strive to develop upward, to erect the ideal, to make the endeavour.

But where is the limit of effectuation in the evolutionary being's self-becoming by self-exceeding? In mind itself there are grades of the series and each grade again is a series in itself; there are successive elevations which we may conveniently call planes and sub-planes of the mental consciousness and the mental being. The development of our mental self is largely an ascent of this stair; we can take our stand on any one of them, while yet maintaining a dependence on the lower stages and a power of occasional ascension to higher levels or of a response to influences from our being's superior strata. At present we still normally take our first secure stand on the lowest sub-plane of the intelligence, which we may call the physical-mental, because it depends for its evidence of fact and sense of reality on the physical brain, the physical sense-mind, the physical sense-organs; there we are the physical man who attaches most importance to objective things and to his outer life, has little intensity of the subjective or inner existence and subordinates whatever he has of it to the greater claims of exterior reality. The physical man has a vital part, but it is mainly made up of the smaller instinctive and impulsive formations of life-consciousness emerging from the subconscient, along with a customary crowd or round of sensations, desires,

hopes, feelings, satisfactions which are dependent on external
things and external contacts and concerned with the practical,
the immediately realisable and possible, the habitual, the common and average. He has a mental part, but this too is customary,
traditional, practical, objective, and respects what belongs to the
domain of mind mostly for its utility for the support, comfort,
use, satisfaction and entertainment of his physical and sensational existence. For the physical mind takes its stand on matter
and the material world, on the body and the bodily life, on
sense-experience and on a normal practical mentality and its
experience. All that is not of this order, the physical mind builds
up as a restricted superstructure dependent upon the external
sense-mentality. Even so, it regards these higher contents of life
as either helpful adjuncts or a superfluous but pleasant luxury
of imaginations, feelings and thought-abstractions, not as inner
realities; or, even if it receives them as realities, it does not feel
them concretely and substantially in their own proper substance,
subtler than the physical substance and its grosser concreteness,
— it treats them as a subjective, less substantial extension from
physical realities. It is inevitable that the human being should
thus take his first stand on Matter and give the external fact
and external existence its due importance; for this is Nature's
first provision for our existence, on which she insists greatly: the
physical man is emphasised in us and is multiplied abundantly
in the world by her as her force for conservation of the secure, if
somewhat inert, material basis on which she can maintain herself
while she attempts her higher human developments; but in this
mental formation there is no power for progress or only for a
material progress. It is our first mental status, but the mental
being cannot remain always at this lowest rung of the human
evolutionary ladder.

Above physical mind and deeper within than physical sensation, there is what we may call an intelligence of the life-mind,
dynamic, vital, nervous, more open, though still obscurely, to
the psychic, capable of a first soul-formation, though only of
an obscurer life-soul, — not the psychic being, but a frontal
formation of the vital Purusha. This life-soul concretely senses

and contacts the things of the life-world, and tries to realise them here; it attaches immense importance to the satisfaction and fulfilment of the life-being, the life-force, the vital nature: it looks on physical existence as a field for the life-impulses' self-fulfilment, for the play of ambition, power, strong character, love, passion, adventure, for the individual, the collective, the general human seeking and hazard and venture, for all kinds of life-experiment and new life-experience, and but for this saving element, this greater power, interest, significance, the physical existence would have for it no value. This life-mentality is supported by our secret subliminal vital being and is in veiled contact with a life-world to which it can easily open and so feel the unseen dynamic forces and realities behind the material universe. There is an inner life-mind which does not need for its perceptions the evidence of the physical senses, is not limited by them; for on this level our inner life and the inner life of the world become real to us independent of the body and of the symbols of the physical world which alone we call natural phenomena, as if Nature had no greater phenomena and no greater realities than those of gross Matter. The vital man, moulded consciously or unconsciously by these influences, is the man of desire and sensation, the man of force and action, the man of passion and emotion, the kinetic individual: he may and does lay great stress on the material existence, but he gives it, even when most pre-occupied with its present actualities, a push for life-experience, for force of realisation, for life-extension, for life-power, for life-affirmation and life-expansion which is Nature's first impetus towards enlargement of the being; at a highest intensity of this life-impetus, he becomes the breaker of bonds, the seeker of new horizons, the disturber of the past and present in the interest of the future. He has a mental life which is often enslaved to the vital force and its desires and passions, and it is these he seeks to satisfy through the mind: but when he interests himself strongly in mental things, he can become the mental adventurer, the opener of the way to new mind-formations or the fighter for an idea, the sensitive type of artist, the dynamic poet of life or the prophet or champion of a cause. The vital mind is kinetic and therefore a great force in the working of evolutionary Nature.

Above this level of vital mentality and yet more inly extended, is a mind-plane of pure thought and intelligence to which the things of the mental world are the most important realities; those who are under its influence, the philosopher, thinker, scientist, intellectual creator, the man of the idea, the man of the written or spoken word, the idealist and dreamer are the present mental being at his highest attained summit. This mental man has his life-part, his life of passions and desires and ambitions and life-hopes of all kinds and his lower sensational and physical existence, and this lower part can often equibalance or weigh down his nobler mental element so that, although it is the highest portion of him, it does not become dominant and formative in his whole nature: but this is not typical of him in his greatest development, for there the vital and physical are controlled and subjected by the thinking will and intelligence. The mental man cannot transform his nature, but he can control and harmonise it and lay on it the law of a mental ideal, impose a balance or a sublimating and refining influence, and give a high consistency to the multipersonal confusion and conflict or the summary patchwork of our divided and half-constructed being. He can be the observer and governor of his own mind and life, can consciously develop them and become to that extent a self-creator.

This mind of pure intelligence has behind it our inner or subliminal mind which senses directly all the things of the mind-plane, is open to the action of a world of mental forces, and can feel the ideative and other imponderable influences which act upon the material world and the life-plane but which at present we can only infer and cannot directly experience: these intangibles and imponderables are to the mental man real and patent and he regards them as truths demanding to be realised in our or the earth's nature. On the inner plane mind and mind-soul independent of the body can become to us an entire reality, and we can consciously live in them as much as in the body. Thus to live in mind and the things of the mind, to be an intelligence rather than a life and a body, is our highest position, short of spirituality, in the degrees of Nature. The mental man, the man of a self-dominating and self-formative mind and will conscious of an ideal and turned towards its realisation, the high intellect, the thinker, the sage, less kinetic and immediately effective than the vital man, who is the man of action and outer swift life-fulfilment, but as powerful and eventually even more powerful to open new vistas to the race, is the normal summit of Nature's evolutionary formation on the human plane. These three degrees of mentality, clear in themselves, but most often mixed in our composition, are to our ordinary intelligence only psychological types that happen to have developed, and we do not discover any other significance in them; but in fact they are full of significance, for they are the steps of Nature's evolution of mental being towards its self-exceeding, and, as thinking mind is the highest step she can now attain, the perfected mental man is the rarest and highest of her normal human creatures. To go farther she has to bring into the mind and make active in mind, life and body the spiritual principle.

For these are her evolutionary figures built out of the surface mentality; to do more she has to use more amply the unseen material hidden below our surface, to dive inwards and bring out the secret soul, the psyche, or to ascend above our normal mental level into planes of intuitive consciousness dense with light derived from the spiritual gnosis, ascending planes of pure spiritual mind in which we are in direct contact with the infinite, in touch with the self and highest reality of things, Sachchidananda. In ourselves, behind our surface natural being, there is a soul, an inner mind, an inner life-part which can open to these heights as well as to the occult spirit within us, and this double opening is the secret of a new evolution; by that breaking of lids and walls and boundaries the consciousness rises to a greater ascent and a larger integration which, as the evolution of mind has mentalised, so will by this new evolution spiritualise all the powers of our nature. For the mental man has not been Nature's last effort or highest reach, — though he has been, in general, more fully evolved in his own nature than those who have achieved themselves below or aspired above him; she has pointed man to a yet higher and more difficult level, inspired him with the ideal of a spiritual living, begun the evolution in him of a spiritual being. The spiritual man is her supreme supernormal effort of human creation; for, having evolved the mental creator, thinker, sage, prophet of an ideal, the self-controlled, self-disciplined, harmonised mental being, she has tried to go higher and deeper within and call out into the front the soul and inner mind and heart, call down from above the forces of the spiritual mind and higher mind and overmind and create under their light and by their influence the spiritual sage, seer, prophet, God-lover, Yogin, gnostic, Sufi, mystic.

This is man's only way of true self-exceeding: for so long as we live in the surface being or found ourselves wholly on Matter, it is impossible to go higher and vain to expect that there can be any new transition of a radical character in our evolutionary being. The vital man, the mental man have had an immense effect upon the earth-life, they have carried humanity forward from the mere human animal to what it is now. But it is only within the bounds of the already established evolutionary formula of the human being that they can act; they can enlarge the human circle but not change or transform the principle of consciousness or its characteristic operation. Any attempt to heighten inordinately the mental or exaggerate inordinately the vital man, — a Nietzschean supermanhood, for example, — can only colossalise the human creature, it cannot transform or divinise him. A different possibility opens if we can live within in the inner being and make it the direct ruler of life or station ourselves on the spiritual and intuitive planes of being and from there and by their power transmute our nature.

The spiritual man is the sign of this new evolution, this new and higher endeavour of Nature. But this evolution differs from the past process of the evolutionary Energy in two respects: it is conducted by a conscious effort of the human mind, and it is not confined to a conscious progression of the surface nature, but is accompanied by an attempt to break the walls of the Ignorance and extend ourselves inward into the secret principle of our present being and outward into cosmic being as well as upward towards a higher principle. Up till now what Nature had achieved was an enlarging of the bounds of our surface Knowledge-Ignorance; what it attempted in the spiritual endeavour is to abolish the Ignorance, to go inwards and discover the soul and to become united in consciousness with God and with all existence. This is the final aim of the mental stage of evolutionary Nature in man; it is the initial step towards a radical transmutation of the Ignorance into the Knowledge. The spiritual change begins by an influence of the inner being and the higher spiritual mind, an action felt and accepted on the surface; but this by itself can lead only to an illumined mental idealism or to the growth of a religious mind, a religious temperament and some devotion in the heart and piety in the conduct; it is a first approach of mind to spirit, but it cannot make a radical change: more has to be done, we have to live deeper within, we have to exceed our present consciousness and surpass our present status of Nature.

It is evident that if we can live thus deeper within and put out steadily the inner forces into the outer instrumentation or raise ourselves to dwell on higher and wider levels and bring their powers to bear on physical existence, not merely receive influences descending from them, which is all we can now do, there could begin a heightening of our force of conscious being so as to create a new principle of consciousness, a new range of activities, new values for all things, a widening of our consciousness and life, a taking up and transformation of the lower grades of our existence, — in brief, the whole evolutionary process by which the Spirit in Nature creates a higher type of being. Each step could mean a pace, however distant from the goal, or a close approach leading to a larger and more divine being, a larger and more divine force and consciousness, knowledge and will, sense of existence and delight in existence; there could be an initial unfolding towards the divine life. All religion, all occult knowledge, all supernormal (as opposed to abnormal) psychological experience, all Yoga, all psychic experience and discipline are signposts and directions pointing us upon that road of progress of the occult self-unfolding spirit.

But the human race is still weighted by a certain gravitation towards the physical, it obeys still the pull of our yet unconquered earth-matter; it is dominated by the brain-mind, the physical intelligence: thus held back by many ties, it hesitates before the indication or falls back before the too tense demand of the spiritual effort. It has, too, still a great capacity for sceptical folly, an immense indolence, an enormous intellectual and spiritual timidity and conservatism when called out of the grooves of habit: even the constant evidence of life itself that where it chooses to conquer it can conquer, — witness the miracles of that quite inferior power, physical Science, — does not prevent it from doubting; it repels the new call and leaves the response to a few individuals. But that is not enough if the step forward is to be for humanity; for it is only if the race advances that, for it, the victories of the Spirit can be secure. For then, even if there is a lapse of Nature, a fall in her effort, the Spirit within, employing a secret memory, — sometimes represented on the lower side, that of downward gravitation, as an atavistic force in the race, but really the force of a persistent memory in Nature which can pull us either upward or downward, — will call it upward again and the next ascent will be both easier and more lasting, because of the past endeavour; for that endeavour and its impulse and its result cannot but remain stored in the subconscious mind of humanity. Who can say what victories of the kind may have been achieved in our past cycles and how near may be the next ascension? It is not indeed necessary or possible that the whole race should transform itself from mental into spiritual beings, but a general admission of the ideal, a widespread endeavour, a conscious concentration are needed to carry the stream of tendency to its definitive achievement. Otherwise what will be ultimately accomplished is an achievement by the few initiating a new order of beings, while humanity will have passed sentence of unfitness on itself and may fall back into an evolutionary decline or a stationary immobility; for it is the constant upward effort that has kept humanity alive and maintained for it its place in the front of creation.

The principle of the process of evolution is a foundation,

from that foundation an ascent, in that ascent a reversal of consciousness and, from the greater height and wideness gained, an action of change and new integration of the whole nature. The first foundation is Matter; the ascent is that of Nature; the integration is an at first unconscious or half-conscious automatic change of Nature by Nature. But as soon as a more completely conscious participation of the being has begun in these workings of Nature, a change in the functioning of the process is inevitable. The physical foundation of Matter remains, but Matter can no longer be the foundation of the consciousness; consciousness itself will be no longer in its origin a welling up from the Inconscient or a concealed flow from an occult inner subliminal force under the pressure of contacts from the universe. The foundation of the developing existence will be the new spiritual status above or the unveiled soul-status within us; it is a flow of light and knowledge and will from above and a reception from within that will determine the reactions of the being to cosmic experience. The whole concentration of the being will be shifted from below upwards and from without inwards; our higher and inner being now unknown to us will become ourselves, and the outer or surface being which we now take for ourselves will be only an open front or an annexe through which the true being meets the universe. The outer world itself will become inward to the spiritual awareness, a part of itself, intimately embraced in a knowledge and feeling of unity and identity, penetrated by an intuitive regard of the mind, responded to by the direct contact of consciousness with consciousness, taken into an achieved integrality. The old inconscient foundation itself will be made conscious in us by the inflow of light and awareness from above and its depths annexed to the heights of the spirit. An integral consciousness will become the basis of an entire harmonisation of life through the total transformation, unification, integration of the being and the nature.

Chapter XIX

Out of the Sevenfold Ignorance towards the Sevenfold Knowledge

Seven steps has the ground of the Ignorance, seven steps has the ground of the Knowledge.   *Mahopanishad.*[1]

He found the vast Thought with seven heads that is born of the Truth; he created some fourth world and became universal.... The Sons of Heaven, the Heroes of the Omnipotent, thinking the straight thought, giving voice to the Truth, founded the plane of illumination and conceived the first abode of the Sacrifice.... The Master of Wisdom cast down the stone defences and called to the Herds of Light,... the Herds that stand in the secrecy on the bridge over the Falsehood between two worlds below and one above; desiring Light in the darkness, he brought upward the Ray-Herds and uncovered from the veil the three worlds; he shattered the city that lies hidden in ambush, and cut the three out of the Ocean, and discovered the Dawn and the Sun and the Light and the World of Light.
                                                                Rig Veda.[2]

The Master of Wisdom in his first coming to birth in the supreme ether of the great Light, — many his births, seven his mouths of the Word, seven his Rays, — scatters the darknesses with his cry.   *Rig Veda.*[3]

ALL EVOLUTION is in essence a heightening of the force of consciousness in the manifest being so that it may be raised into the greater intensity of what is still unmanifest, from matter into life, from life into mind, from the mind into

---

[1] V. 1.   [2] X. 67. 1–5.   [3] IV. 50. 4.

the spirit. It is this that must be the method of our growth from a mental into a spiritual and supramental manifestation, out of a still half-animal humanity into a divine being and a divine living. There must be achieved a new spiritual height, wideness, depth, subtlety, intensity of our consciousness, of its substance, its force, its sensibility, an elevation, expansion, plasticity, integral capacity of our being, and an assumption of mind and all that is below mind into that larger existence. In a future transformation the character of the evolution, the principle of evolutionary process, although modified, will not fundamentally change but, on a vaster scale and in a liberated movement, royally continue. A change into a higher consciousness or state of being is not only the whole aim and process of religion, of all higher askesis, of Yoga, but it is also the very trend of our life itself, the secret purpose found in the sum of its labour. The principle of life in us seeks constantly to confirm and perfect itself on the planes of mind, vitality and body which it already possesses; but it is self-driven also to go beyond and transform these gains into means for the conscious spirit to unfold in Nature. If it is merely some part of ourselves, intellect, heart, will or vital desire-self, which, dissatisfied with its own imperfection and with the world, strives to get away from it to a greater height of existence, content to leave the rest of the nature to take care of itself or to perish, then such a result of total transformation would not eventuate, — or, at least, would not eventuate here. But this is not the integral trend of our existence; there is a labour of Nature in us to ascend with all ourself into a higher principle of being than it has yet evolved here, but it is not her whole will in this ascension to destroy herself in order that that higher principle may be exclusively affirmed by the rejection and extinction of Nature. To heighten the force of consciousness until it passes from a mental, vital and physical instrumentation into the essence and power of the spirit is the indispensable thing, but that is not the sole object or all the thing to be done.

Our call must be to live on a new height in all our being: we have not, in order to reach that height, to drop back our dynamic parts into the indeterminate stuff of Nature and abide by this liberating loss in a blissful quiescence of the Spirit; that can always be done and it brings a great repose and freedom, but what Nature herself attends from us is that the whole of what we are should rise into the spiritual consciousness and become a manifest and manifold power of the spirit. An integral transformation is the integral aim of the Being in Nature; this is the inherent sense of her universal urge of self-transcendence. It is for this reason that the process of Nature is not confined to a heightening of herself into a new principle; the new height is not a narrow intense pinnacle, it brings with it a widening and establishes a larger field of life in which the power of the new principle may have sufficient play and room for its emergence. This action of elevation and expansion is not confined to an utmost possible largeness in the essential play of the new principle itself; it includes a taking up of that which is lower into the higher values: the divine or spiritual life will not only assume into itself the mental, vital, physical life transformed and spiritualised, but it will give them a much wider and fuller play than was open to them so long as they were living on their own level. Our mental, physical, vital existence need not be destroyed by our self-exceeding, nor are they lessened and impaired by being spiritualised; they can and do become much richer, greater, more powerful and more perfect: in their divine change they break into possibilities which in their unspiritualised condition could not be practicable or imaginable.

This evolution, this process of heightening and widening and integralisation, is in its nature a growth and an ascent out of the sevenfold ignorance into the integral knowledge. The crux of that ignorance is the constitutional; it resolves itself into a manifold ignorance of the true character of our becoming, an unawareness of our total self, of which the key is a limitation by the plane we inhabit and by the present predominant principle of our nature. The plane we inhabit is the plane of Matter; the present predominant principle in our nature is the mental intelligence with the sense-mind, which depends upon Matter, as its support and pedestal. As a consequence, the preoccupation of the mental intelligence and its powers with the material existence as it is shown to it through the senses, and with life as it has been formulated in a compromise between life and matter, is a special stamp of the constitutional Ignorance. This natural materialism or materialised vitalism, this clamping of ourselves to our beginnings, is a form of self-restriction narrowing the scope of our existence which is very insistent on the human being. It is a first necessity of his physical existence, but is afterwards forged by a primal ignorance into a chain that hampers his every step upwards: the attempt to grow out of this limitation of the wholeness, power and truth of the spirit by the materialised mental intelligence and out of this subjection of the soul to material Nature is the first step towards a real progress of our humanity. For our ignorance is not entire; it is a limitation of consciousness, — it is not the complete nescience which is the stamp of the same Ignorance in purely material existences, those which have not only matter for their plane but matter for their dominant principle. It is a partial, a limiting, a dividing and, very largely, a falsifying knowledge; out of that limitation and falsification we have to grow into the truth of our spiritual being.

This preoccupation with life and matter is at the beginning right and necessary because the first step that man has to take is to know and possess this physical existence as well as he can by applying his thought and intelligence to such experience of it as his sense-mind can give to him; but this is only a preliminary step and, if we stop there, we have made no real progress: we are where we were and have gained only more physical elbow-room to move about in and more power for our mind to establish a relative knowledge and an insufficient and precarious mastery and for our life-desire to push things about and jostle and hustle around amid the throng of physical forces and existences. The utmost widening of a physical objective knowledge, even if it embrace the most distant solar systems and the deepest layers of the earth and sea and the most subtle powers of material substance and energy, is not the essential gain for us, not the one thing which it is most needful for us to acquire. That is why the gospel of materialism, in spite of the dazzling triumphs of physical Science, proves itself always in the end a vain and helpless creed, and that too is why physical Science itself with all its achievements, though it may accomplish comfort, can never achieve happiness and fullness of being for the human race. Our true happiness lies in the true growth of our whole being, in a victory throughout the total range of our existence, in mastery of the inner as well as and more than the outer, the hidden as well as the overt nature; our true completeness comes not by describing wider circles on the plane where we began, but by transcendence. It is for this reason that, after the first necessary foundation in life and matter, we have to heighten our force of consciousness, deepen, widen, subtilise it; we must first liberate our mental selves and enter into a freer, finer and nobler play of our mental existence: for the mental is much more than the physical our true existence, because we are even in our instrumental or expressive nature predominantly mind and not matter, mental much rather than physical beings. That growth into the full mental being is the first transitional movement towards human perfection and freedom; it does not actually perfect, it does not liberate the soul, but it lifts us one step out of the material and vital absorption and prepares the loosening of the hold of the Ignorance.

Our gain in becoming more perfect mental beings is that we get to the possibility of a subtler, higher and wider existence, consciousness, force, happiness and delight of being; in proportion as we rise in the scale of mind, a greater power of these things comes to us: our mental consciousness acquires for itself at the same time more vision and power and more subtlety and plasticity, and we are able to embrace more of the vital and physical existence itself, to know it better, to use it better, to give it nobler values, a broader range, a more sublimated action, — an extended scale, higher issues. Man is in his characteristic power of nature a mental being, but in the first steps of his emergence he is more of the mentalised animal, preoccupied like the animal with his bodily existence; he employs his mind for the uses, interests, desires of the life and the body, as their servant and minister, not yet as their sovereign and master. It is as he grows in mind and in proportion as his mind asserts its selfhood and independence against the tyranny of life and matter, that he grows in stature. On one side, mind by its emancipation controls and illumines the life and physicality; on the other, the purely mental aims, occupations, pursuits of knowledge begin to get a value. The mind liberated from a lower control and preoccupation introduces into life a government, an uplifting, a refinement, a finer balance and harmony; the vital and physical movements are directed and put into order, transformed even as far as they can be by a mental agency; they are taught to be the instruments of reason and obedient to an enlightened will, an ethical perception and an aesthetic intelligence: the more this can be accomplished, the more the race becomes truly human, a race of mental beings.

It is this perception of life that was put in front by the Greek thinkers, and it is a vivid flowering in the sunlight of this ideal that imparts so great a fascination to Hellenic life and culture. In later times this perception was lost and, when it came back, it returned much diminished, mixed with more turbid elements: the perturbation of a spiritual ideal imperfectly grasped by the understanding and not at all realised in the life's practice but present with its positive and negative mental and moral influences, and over against it the pressure of a dominant, an inordinate vital urge which could not get its free self-satisfied movement, stood in the way of the sovereignty of the mind and the harmony of life, its realised beauty and balance. An opening to higher ideals, a greater range of life was gained, but the elements of a new idealism were only cast into its action as an influence, could not dominate and transform it and, finally, the spiritual endeavour, thus ill-understood and unrealised, was thrown aside: its moral effects remained, but, deprived of the sustaining spiritual element, dwindled towards ineffectivity; the vital urge, assisted by an immense development of physical intelligence, became the preoccupation of the race. An imposing increase of a certain kind of knowledge and efficiency was the first result; the most recent outcome has been a perilous spiritual ill-health and a vast disorder.

For mind itself is not enough; even its largest play of intelligence creates only a qualified half-light. A surface mental knowledge of the physical universe is a still more imperfect guide; for the thinking animal it might be enough, but not for a race of mental beings in labour of a spiritual evolution. Even the truth of physical things cannot be entirely known, nor can the right use of our material existence be discovered by physical Science and an outward knowledge alone or made possible by the mastery of physical and mechanical processes alone: to know, to use rightly we must go beyond the truth of physical phenomenon and process, we must know what is within and behind it. For we are not merely embodied minds; there is a spiritual being, a spiritual principle, a spiritual plane of Nature. Into that we have to heighten our force of consciousness, to widen by that still more largely, even universally and infinitely, our range of being and our field of action, to take up by that our lower life and use it for greater ends and on a larger plan, in the light of the spiritual truth of existence. Our labour of mind and struggle of life cannot come to any solution until we have gone beyond the obsessing lead of an inferior Nature, integralised our natural being in the being and consciousness, learned to utilise our natural instruments by the force and for the joy of the Spirit. Then only can the constitutional ignorance, the ignorance of the real build of our existence from which we suffer, change into a true and effective knowledge of our being and becoming. For what we are is spirit, — at present using mind predominantly, life and body subordinately, with matter for our original field but not our only field of experience; but this is only at present. Our imperfect mental instrumentation is not the last word of our possibilities; for there are in us, dormant or invisibly and imperfectly active, other principles beyond mind and closer to the spiritual nature, there are more direct powers and luminous instruments, there is a higher status, there are greater ranges of dynamic action than those that belong to our present physical, vital and mental existence. These can become our own status, part of our being, they can be principles, powers and instruments of our own enlarged nature. But for that it is not enough to be satisfied with a vague or an ecstatic ascent into spirit or a formless exaltation through the touch of its infinities; their principle has to evolve, as life has evolved, as mind has evolved, and organise its own instrumentation, its own satisfaction. Then we shall possess the true constitution of our being and we shall have conquered the Ignorance.

The conquest of our constitutional ignorance cannot be complete, cannot become integrally dynamic, if we have not conquered our psychological ignorance; for the two are bound up together. Our psychological ignorance consists in a limitation of our self-knowledge to that little wave or superficial stream of our being which is the conscient waking self. This part of our being is an original flux of formless or only half-formulated movements carried on in an automatic continuity, supported and held together by an active surface memory and a passive underlying consciousness in its flow from moment to moment of time, organised and interpreted by our reason and our witnessing and participating intelligence. Behind it is an occult existence and energy of our secret being without which the superficial consciousness and activity could not have existed or acted. In Matter only an activity is manifest, — inconscient in the outside of things which is all we know; for the indwelling Consciousness in Matter is secret, subliminal, not manifested in the inconscient form and the involved energy: but in us consciousness has become partly manifest, partly awake. But this consciousness is hedged and imperfect; it is bound by its habitual self-limitation and moves in a restricted circle, — except when there are flashes, intimations or upsurgings from the secrecy within us which break the limits of the formation or flow beyond them or widen the circle. But these occasional visitations cannot enlarge us far beyond our present capacities, are not enough to revolutionise our status. That can only be done if we can bring into it the higher undeveloped lights and powers potential in our being and get them consciously and normally into play; for this we must be able to draw freely from those ranges of our being to which they are native but which are at present subconscient or rather secretly intraconscient and circumconscient or else superconscient to us. Or, — the yet more that is also possible, — we must enter into these inner and higher parts of ourselves by an inward plunge or disciplined penetration and bring back with us to the surface their secrets. Or, achieving a still more radical change of our consciousness, we must learn to live within and no longer on the surface and be and act from the inner depths and from a soul that has become sovereign over the nature.

That part of us which we can strictly call subconscient because it is below the level of mind and conscious life, inferior and obscure, covers the purely physical and vital elements of our constitution of bodily being, unmentalised, unobserved by the mind, uncontrolled by it in their action. It can be held to include the dumb occult consciousness, dynamic but not sensed by us, which operates in the cells and nerves and all the corporeal stuff and adjusts their life process and automatic responses. It covers also those lowest functionings of submerged sense-mind which are more operative in the animal and in plant life; in our evolution we have overpassed the need of any large organised action of this element, but it remains submerged and obscurely at work below our conscious nature. This obscure activity extends to a hidden and hooded mental substratum into which past impressions and all that is rejected from the surface mind sink and remain there dormant and can surge up in sleep or in any absence of the mind, taking dream forms, forms of mechanical mind-action or suggestion, forms of automatic vital reaction or impulse, forms of physical abnormality or nervous perturbance, forms of morbidity, disease, unbalance. Out of the subconscious we bring ordinarily so much to the surface as our waking sense-mind and intelligence need for their purpose; in so bringing them up we are not aware of their nature, origin, operation and do not apprehend them in their own values but by a translation into the values of our waking human sense and intelligence. But the risings of the subconscious, its effects upon the mind and body, are mostly automatic, uncalled for and involuntary; for we have no knowledge and therefore no control of the subconscient. It is only by an experience abnormal to us, most commonly in illness or some disturbance of balance, that we can become directly aware of something in the dumb world, dumb but very active, of our bodily being and vitality or grow conscious of the secret movements of the mechanical subhuman physical and vital mind which underlies our surface, — a consciousness which is ours but seems not ours because it is not part of our known mentality. This and much more lives concealed in the subconscience.

A descent into the subconscient would not help us to explore this region, for it would plunge us into incoherence or into sleep or a dull trance or a comatose torpor. A mental scrutiny or insight can give us some indirect and constructive idea of these hidden activities; but it is only by drawing back into the subliminal or by ascending into the superconscient and from there looking down or extending ourselves into these obscure depths that we can become directly and totally aware and in control of the secrets of our subconscient physical, vital and mental nature. This awareness, this control are of the utmost importance. For the subconscient is the Inconscient in the process of becoming conscious; it is a support and even a root of our inferior parts of being and their movements. It sustains and reinforces all in us that clings most and refuses to change, our mechanical recurrences of unintelligent thought, our persistent obstinacies of feeling, sensation, impulse, propensity, our uncontrolled fixities of character. The animal in us, — the infernal also, — has its lair of retreat in the dense jungle of the subconscience. To penetrate there, to bring in light and establish a control, is indispensable for the completeness of any higher life, for any integral transformation of the nature.

The part of us that we have characterised as intraconscient and circumconscient is a still more potent and much more valuable element in the constitution of our being. It includes the large action of an inner intelligence and inner sense-mind, of an inner vital, even of an inner subtle-physical being which upholds and embraces our waking consciousness, which is not brought to the front, which is subliminal, in the modern phrase. But when we can enter and explore this hidden self, we find that our waking sense and intelligence are for the most part a selection from what we secretly are or can be, an exteriorised and much mutilated and vulgarised edition of our real, our hidden being or an up-throw from its depths. Our surface being has been formed with this subliminal help by an evolution out of the Inconscient for the utility of our present mental and physical life on earth; this that is behind is a formation mediating between the Inconscient and the larger planes of Life and Mind which have been created by the involutionary descent and whose pressure has helped to bring about the evolution of Mind and Life in Matter. Our surface responses to physical existence have at their back the support of an activity in these veiled parts, are often responses from them modified by a surface mental rendering. But also that large part of our mentality and vitality which is not a response to the outside world but lives for itself or throws itself out on material existence to use and possess it, our personality, is the outcome, the amalgamated formulation of powers, influences, motives proceeding from this potent intraconscient secrecy.

Again, the subliminal extends itself into an enveloping consciousness through which it receives the shock of the currents and wave-circuits pouring upon us from the universal Mind, universal Life, universal subtler Matter-forces. These, unperceived by us on the surface, are perceived and admitted by our subliminal self and turned into formations which can powerfully affect our existence without our knowledge. If the wall that separates this inner existence from the outer self were penetrated, we could know and deal with the sources of our present mind-energies and life-action and could control instead of undergoing their results. But though large parts of it can be thus known by a penetration and looking within or a freer communication, it is only by going inward behind the veil of superficial mind and living within, in an inner mind, an inner life, an inmost soul of our being that we can be fully self-aware, — by this and by rising to a higher plane of mind than that which our waking consciousness inhabits. An enlargement and completion of our present evolutionary status, now still so hampered and truncated, would be the result of such an inward living; but an evolution beyond it can come only by our becoming conscious in what is now superconscient to us, by an ascension to the native heights of the Spirit.

In the superconscience beyond our present level of awareness are included the higher planes of mental being as well as the native heights of supramental and pure spiritual being. The first indispensable step in an upward evolution would be to elevate our force of consciousness into those higher parts of Mind from which we already receive, but without knowing the source, much of our larger mental movements, those, especially, that come with a greater power and light, the revelatory, the inspirational, the intuitive. On these mental heights, in these largenesses, if the consciousness could succeed in reaching them or maintain and centre itself there, something of the direct presence and power of the Spirit, something even, — however secondary or indirect, — of the Supermind could receive a first expression, could make itself initially manifest, could intervene in the government of our lower being and help to remould it. Afterwards, by the force of that remoulded consciousness, the course of our evolution could rise by a sublimer ascent and get beyond the mental into the supramental and the supreme spiritual nature. It is possible without an actual ascent into these at present superconscient mental planes or without a constant or permanent living in them, by openness to them, by reception of their knowledge and influences, to get rid to a certain extent of our constitutional and psychological ignorance; it is possible to be aware of ourselves as spiritual beings and to spiritualise, though imperfectly, our normal human life and consciousness. There could be a conscious communication and guidance from this greater more luminous mentality and a reception of its enlightening and transforming forces. That is within the reach of the highly developed or the spiritually awakened human being; but it would not be more than a preliminary stage. To reach an integral self-knowledge, an entire consciousness and power of being, there is necessary an ascent beyond the plane of our normal mind. Such an ascent is at present possible in an absorbed superconscience; but that could lead only to an entry into the higher levels in a state of immobile or ecstatic trance. If the control of that highest spiritual being is to be brought into our waking life, there must be a conscious heightening and widening into immense ranges of new being, new consciousness, new potentialities of action, a taking up, — as integral as possible, — of our present being, consciousness, activities and a transmutation of them into divine values which would effect a transfiguration of our human existence. For wherever a radical transition has to be made, there is always this triple movement, — ascent, widening of field and base, integration, — in Nature's method of self-transcendence.

Any such evolutionary change must necessarily be associated with a rejection of our present narrowing temporal ignorance. For not only do we now live from moment to moment of time, but our whole view is limited to our life in the present body between a single birth and death. As our regard does not go farther back in the past, so it does not extend farther out into the future; thus we are limited by our physical memory and awareness of the present life in a transient corporeal formation. But this limitation of our temporal consciousness is intimately dependent upon the preoccupation of our mentality with the material plane and life in which it is at present acting; the limitation is not a law of the spirit but a temporary provision for an intended first working of our manifested nature. If the preoccupation is relaxed or put aside, an extension of the mind effected, an opening into the subliminal and superconscient, into the inner and higher being created, it is possible to realise our persistent existence in time as well as our eternal existence beyond it. This is essential if we are to get our self-knowledge into the right focus; for at present our whole consciousness and action are vitiated by an error of spiritual perspective which prevents us from seeing in right proportion and relation the nature, purpose and conditions of our being. A belief in immortality is made so vital a point in most religions because it is a self-evident necessity if we are to rise above the identity with the body and its preoccupation with the material level. But a belief is not sufficient to alter radically this mistake of perspective: the true self-knowledge of our being in time can come to us only when we live in the consciousness of our immortality; we have to awaken to a concrete sense of our perpetual being in Time and of our timeless existence.

For immortality in its fundamental sense does not mean merely some kind of personal survival of the bodily death; we are immortal by the eternity of our self-existence without beginning or end, beyond the whole succession of physical births and deaths through which we pass, beyond the alternations of our existence in this and other worlds: the spirit's timeless existence is the true immortality. There is, no doubt, a secondary meaning of the word which has its truth; for, corollary to this true immortality, there exists a perpetual continuity of our temporal existence and experience from life to life, from world to world after the dissolution of the physical body: but this is a natural consequence of our timelessness which expresses itself here as a perpetuity in eternal Time. The realisation of timeless immortality comes by the knowledge of self in the Non-birth and Non-becoming and of the changeless spirit within us: the realisation of time-immortality comes by the knowledge of self in the birth and Becoming and is translated into a sense of the persistent identity of the soul through all changes of mind and life and body; this too is not a mere survival, it is timelessness translated into the Time manifestation. By the first realisation we become free from obscuring subjection to the chain of birth and death, that supreme object of so many Indian disciplines; by the second realisation added to the first we are able to possess freely, with right knowledge, without ignorance, without bondage by the chain of our actions, the experiences of the spirit in its successions of time-eternity. A realisation of timeless existence by itself might not include the truth of that experience of persistent self in eternal Time; a realisation of survival of death by itself might still give room for a beginning or end to our existence. But, in either realisation truly envisaged as side and other side of one truth, to exist consciously in eternity and not in the bondage of the hour and the succession of the moments is the substance of the change: so to exist is a first condition of the divine consciousness and the divine life. To possess and govern from that inner eternity of being the course and process of the becoming is the second, the dynamic condition with, as its practical outcome, a spiritual self-possession and self-mastery. These changes are possible only by a withdrawal from our absorbing material preoccupation, — that does not necessitate a rejection or neglect of the life in the body, — and a constant living on the inner and higher planes of the mind and the spirit. For the heightening of our consciousness into its spiritual principle is effectuated by an ascent and a stepping back inward, — both these movements are essential, — out of our transient life from moment to moment into the eternal life of our immortal consciousness; but with it there comes also a widening of our range of consciousness and field of action in time and a taking up and a higher use of our mental, our vital, our corporeal existence. There arises a knowledge of our being, no longer as a consciousness dependent on the body, but as an eternal spirit which uses all the worlds and all lives for various self-experience; we see it to be a spiritual entity possessed of a continuous soul-life perpetually developing its activities through successive physical existences, a being determining its own becoming. In that knowledge, not ideative but felt in our very substance, it becomes possible to live, not as slaves of a blind Karmic impulsion, but as masters, — subject only to the Divine within us, — of our being and nature.

At the same time we get rid of the egoistic ignorance; for so long as we are at any point bound by that, the divine life must either be unattainable or imperfect in its self-expression. For the ego is a falsification of our true individuality by a limiting self-identification of it with this life, this mind, this body: it is a separation from other souls which shuts us up in our own individual experience and prevents us from living as the universal individual: it is a separation from God, our highest Self, who is the one Self in all existences and the divine Inhabitant within us. As our consciousness changes into the height and depth and wideness of the spirit, the ego can no longer survive there: it is too small and feeble to subsist in that vastness and dissolves into it; for it exists by its limits and perishes by the loss of its limits. The being breaks out of its imprisonment in a separated individuality, becomes universal, assumes a cosmic consciousness in which it identifies itself with the self and spirit, the life, the mind, the body of all beings. Or it breaks out upward into a supreme pinnacle and infinity and eternity of self-existence independent of its cosmic or its individual existence. The ego collapses, losing its wall of separation, into the cosmic immensity; or it falls into nothingness, unable to breathe in the heights of the spiritual ether. If something of its movements remains by habit of Nature, yet these also fall away and are replaced by a new impersonal-personal seeing, feeling, action. This disappearance of the ego does not bring with it the destruction of our true individuality, our spiritual existence, for that was always universal and one with the Transcendence; but there is a transformation which replaces the separative ego by the Purusha, a conscious face and figure of the universal being and a self and power of the transcendent Divine in cosmic Nature.

In the same movement, by the very awakening into the spirit, there is a dissolution of the cosmic ignorance; for we have the knowledge of ourselves as our timeless immutable self possessing itself in cosmos and beyond cosmos: this knowledge becomes the basis of the Divine Play in time, reconciles the one and the many, the eternal unity and the eternal multiplicity, reunites the soul with God and discovers the Divine in the universe. It is by this realisation that we can approach the Absolute as the source of all circumstances and relations, possess the world in ourselves in an utmost wideness and in a conscient dependence on its source, and by so taking it up raise it and realise through it the absolute values that converge into the Absolute. If our self-knowledge is thus made complete in all its essentials, our practical ignorance which in its extreme figures itself as wrongdoing, suffering, falsehood, error and is the cause of all life's confusions and discords, will yield its place to the right will of self-knowledge and its false or imperfect values recede before the divine values of the true Consciousness-Force and Ananda. For right consciousness, right action and right being, not in the imperfect human sense of our petty moralities but in the large and luminous movement of a divine living, the conditions are union with God, unity with all beings, a life governed and formed from within outwards in which the source of all thought, will and action shall be the Spirit working through the truth and the divine law which are not built and constructed by the mind of Ignorance but are self-existent and spontaneous in their self-fulfilment, not so much a law as the truth acting in its own consciousness and in a free luminous plastic automatic process of its knowledge.

This would seem to be the method and the result of the conscious spiritual evolution; a transformation of the life of the Ignorance into the divine life of the truth-conscious spirit, a change from the mental into a spiritual and supramental way of being, a self-expansion out of the sevenfold ignorance into the sevenfold knowledge. This transformation would be the natural completion of the upward process of Nature as it heightens the forces of consciousness from principle to higher principle until the highest, the spiritual principle, becomes expressed and dominant in her, takes up cosmic and individual existence on the lower planes into its truth and transforms all into a conscious manifestation of the Spirit. The true individual, the spiritual being, emerges, individual yet universal, universal yet self-transcendent: life no longer appears as a formation of things and an action of being created by the separative Ignorance.

Chapter XX

The Philosophy of Rebirth

An end have these bodies of an embodied soul that is eternal;...
it is not born nor dies nor is it that having been it will not be
again. It is unborn, ancient, everlasting; it is not slain with
the slaying of the body. As a man casts from him his worn-
out garments and takes others that are new, so the embodied
being casts off its bodies and joins itself to others that are new.
Certain is the death of that which is born and certain is the
birth of that which dies....   *Gita.*[1]

There is a birth and growth of the self. According to his actions the embodied being assumes forms successively in many
places; many forms gross and subtle he assumes by force of
his own qualities of nature....   *Swetaswatara Upanishad.*[2]

BIRTH is the first spiritual mystery of the physical universe,
death is the second which gives its double point of perplexity to the mystery of birth; for life, which would otherwise
be a self-evident fact of existence, becomes itself a mystery by
virtue of these two which seem to be its beginning and its end
and yet in a thousand ways betray themselves as neither of these
things, but rather intermediate stages in an occult processus of
life. At first sight birth might seem to be a constant outburst of
life in a general death, a persistent circumstance in the universal
lifelessness of Matter. On a closer examination it begins to be
more probable that life is something involved in Matter or even
an inherent power of the Energy that creates Matter, but able to
appear only when it gets the necessary conditions for the affirmation of its characteristic phenomena and for an appropriate

[1] II. 18, 20, 22, 27.   [2] V. 11, 12.

self-organisation. But in the birth of life there is something more that participates in the emergence, — there is an element which is no longer material, a strong upsurging of some flame of soul, a first evident vibration of the spirit.

All the known circumstances and results of birth presuppose an unknown before, and there is a suggestion of universality, a will of persistence of life, an inconclusiveness in death which seem to point to an unknown hereafter. What were we before birth and what are we after death, are the questions, the answer of the one depending upon that of the other, which the intellect of man has put to itself from the beginning without even now resting in any final solution. The intellect indeed can hardly give the final answer: for that must in its very nature lie beyond the data of the physical consciousness and memory, whether of the race or the individual, yet these are the sole data which the intellect is in the habit of consulting with something like confidence. In this poverty of materials and this incertitude it wheels from one hypothesis to another and calls each in turn a conclusion. Moreover, the solution depends upon the nature, source and object of the cosmic movement, and as we determine these, so we shall have to conclude about birth and life and death, the before and the hereafter.

The first question is whether the before and the after are purely physical and vital or in some way, and more predominantly, mental and spiritual. If Matter were the principle of the universe, as the materialist alleges, if the truth of things were to be found in the first formula arrived at by Bhrigu, son of Varuna, when he meditated upon the eternal Brahman, "Matter is the Eternal, for from Matter all beings are born and by Matter all beings exist and to Matter all beings depart and return", then no farther questioning would be possible. The before of our bodies would be a gathering of their constituents out of various physical elements through the instrumentality of the seed and food and under the influence perhaps of occult but always material energies, and the before of our conscious being a preparation by heredity or by some other physically vital or physically mental operation in universal Matter specialising its action and building the individual through the bodies of our parents, through seed and gene and chromosome. The after of the body would be a dissolution into the material elements and the after of the conscious being a relapse into Matter with some survival of the effects of its activity in the general mind and life of humanity: this last quite illusory survival would be our only chance of immortality. But since the universality of Matter can no longer be held as giving any sufficient explanation of the existence of Mind, — and indeed Matter itself can no longer be explained by Matter alone, for it does not appear to be self-existent, — we are thrown back from this easy and obvious solution to other hypotheses.

One of these is the old religious myth and dogmatic mystery of a God who creates constantly immortal souls out of his own being or else by his "breath" or life-power entering, it is to be presumed, into material Nature or rather into the bodies he creates in it and vivifying them internally with a spiritual principle. As a mystery of faith this can hold and need not be examined, for the mysteries of faith are intended to be beyond question and scrutiny; but for reason and philosophy it lacks convincingness and does not fit into the known order of things. For it involves two paradoxes which need more justification before they can even be accorded any consideration; first, the hourly creation of beings who have a beginning in time but no end in time, and are, moreover, born by the birth of the body but do not end by the death of the body; secondly, their assumption of a ready-made mass of combined qualities, virtues, vices, capacities, defects, temperamental and other advantages and handicaps, not made by them at all through growth, but made for them by arbitrary fiat, — if not by law of heredity, — yet for which and for the perfect use of which they are held responsible by their Creator.

We may maintain, — provisionally, at least, — certain things as legitimate presumptions of the philosophic reason and fairly throw the burden of disproving them on their denier. Among these postulates is the principle that that which has no end must necessarily have had no beginning; all that begins or is created has an end by cessation of the process that created and maintains it or the dissolution of the materials of which it is compounded or the end of the function for which it came into being. If there is an exception to this law, it must be by a descent of spirit into matter animating matter with divinity or giving matter its own immortality; but the spirit itself which so descends is immortal, not made or created. If the soul was created to animate the body, if it depended on the body for its coming into existence, it can have no reason or basis for existence after the disappearance of the body. It is naturally to be supposed that the breath or power given for the animation of the body would return at its final dissolution to its Maker. If, on the contrary, it still persists as an immortal embodied being, there must be a subtle or psychic body in which it continues, and it is fairly certain that this psychic body and its inhabitant must be pre-existent to the material vehicle: it is irrational to suppose that they were created originally to inhabit that brief and perishable form; an immortal being cannot be the outcome of so ephemeral an incident in creation. If the soul remains but in a disembodied condition, then it can have had no original dependence on a body for its existence; it must have subsisted as an unembodied spirit before birth even as it persists in its disembodied spiritual entity after death.

Again, we can assume that where we see in Time a certain stage of development, there must have been a past to that development. Therefore, if the soul enters this life with a certain development of personality, it must have prepared it in other precedent lives here or elsewhere. Or, if it only takes up a ready-made life and personality not prepared by it, prepared perhaps by a physical, vital and mental heredity, it must itself be something quite independent of that life and personality, something which is only fortuitously connected with the mind and body and cannot therefore be really affected by what is done or developed in this mental and bodily living. If the soul is real and immortal, not a constructed being or figure of being, it must also be eternal, beginningless in the past even as endless in the future; but, if eternal, it must be either a changeless self unaffected by life and its terms or a timeless Purusha, an eternal and spiritual Person manifesting or causing in time a stream of changing personality. If it is such a Person, it can only manifest this stream of personality in a world of birth and death by the assumption of successive bodies, — in a word, by constant or by repeated rebirth into the forms of Nature.

But the immortality or eternity of the soul does not at once impose itself, even if we reject the explanation of all things by eternal Matter. For we have also the hypothesis of the creation of a temporary or apparent soul by some power of the original Unity from which all things began, by which they live and into which they cease. On one side, we can erect upon the foundation of certain modern ideas or discoveries the theory of a cosmic Inconscient creating a temporary soul, a consciousness which after a brief play is extinguished and goes back into the Inconscient. Or there may be an eternal Becoming, which manifests itself in a cosmic Life-force with the appearance of Matter as one objective end of its operations and the appearance of Mind as the other subjective end, the interaction of these two phenomena of Life-force creating our human existence. On the other side, we have the old theory of a sole-existing Superconscient, an eternal unmodifiable Being which admits or creates by Maya an illusion of individual soul-life in this world of phenomenal Mind and Matter, both of them ultimately unreal, — even if they have or assume a temporary and phenomenal reality, — since one unmodifiable and eternal Self or Spirit is the only entity. Or we have the Buddhist theory of a Nihil or Nirvana and, somehow imposed upon that, an eternal action or energy of successive becoming, Karma, which creates the illusion of a persistent self or soul by a constant continuity of associations, ideas, memories, sensations, images. In their effect upon the life-problem all these three explanations are practically one; for even the Superconscient is for the purposes of the universal action an equivalent of the Inconscient; it can be aware only of its own unmodifiable self-existence: the creation of a world of individual beings by Maya is an imposition on this self-existence; it takes place, perhaps, in a sort of self-absorbed sleep of consciousness, *suṣupti,*[3] out of which yet all active consciousness and modification of phenomenal becoming emerge, just as in the modern theory our consciousness is an impermanent development out of the Inconscient. In all three theories the apparent soul or spiritual individuality of the creature is not immortal in the sense of eternity, but has a beginning and an end in Time, is a creation by Maya or by Nature-Force or cosmic Action out of the Inconscient or Superconscient, and is therefore impermanent in its existence. In all three rebirth is either unnecessary or else illusory; it is either the prolongation by repetition of an illusion, or it is an additional revolving wheel among the many wheels of the complex machinery of the Becoming, or it is excluded since a single birth is all that can be asked for by a conscious being fortuitously engendered as part of an inconscient creation.

In these views, whether we suppose the one Eternal Existence to be a vital Becoming or an immutable and unmodifiable spiritual Being or a nameless and formless Non-being, that which we call the soul can be only a changing mass or stream of phenomena of consciousness which has come into existence in the sea of real or illusory becoming and will cease to exist there, — or, it may be, it is a temporary spiritual substratum, a conscious reflection of the Superconscient Eternal which by its presence supports the mass of phenomena. It is not eternal, and its only immortality is a greater or less continuity in the Becoming. It is not a real and always existent Person who maintains and experiences the stream or mass of phenomena. That which supports them, that which really and always exists, is either the one eternal Becoming or the one eternal and impersonal Being or the continual stream of Energy in its workings. For a theory of this kind it is not indispensable that a psychic entity always the same should persist and assume body after body, form after form, until it is dissolved at last by some process annulling altogether the original impetus which created this cycle. It is

---

[3] Prajna of the Mandukya Upanishad, the Self situated in deep sleep, is the lord and creator of things.

quite possible that as each form is developed, a consciousness develops corresponding to the form, and as the form dissolves, the corresponding consciousness dissolves with it; the One which forms all, alone endures for ever. Or, as the body is gathered out of the general elements of Matter and begins its life with birth and ends with death, so the consciousness may be developed out of the general elements of mind and equally begin with birth and end with death. Here too, the One who supplies by Maya or otherwise the force which creates the elements, is the sole reality that endures. In none of these theories of existence is rebirth an absolute necessity or an inevitable result of the theory.[4]

As a matter of fact, however, we find a great difference; for the old theories affirm, the modern denies rebirth as a part of the universal process. Modern thought starts from the physical body as the basis of our existence and recognises the reality of no other world except this material universe. What it sees here is a mental consciousness associated with the life of the body, giving in its birth no sign of previous individual existence and leaving in its end no sign of subsequent individual existence. What was before birth is the material energy with its seed of life, or at best an energy of life-force, which persists in the seed transmitted by the parents and gives, by its mysterious infusion of past developments into that trifling vehicle, a particular mental and physical stamp to the new individual mind and body thus strangely created. What remains after death is the same material energy or life-force persisting in the seed transmitted to the children and active for the farther development of the mental and physical life carried with it. Nothing is left of us except what we so transmit to others or what the Energy which shaped the individual by its pre-existent and its surrounding action, by birth and by environment, may take as the result of his life and works into its subsequent action; whatever may

---

[4] In the Buddhist theory rebirth is imperative because Karma compels it; not a soul, but Karma is the link of an apparently continuing consciousness, — for the consciousness changes from moment to moment: there is this apparent continuity of consciousness, but there is no real immortal soul taking birth and passing through the death of the body to be reborn in another body.

help by chance or by physical law to build the mental and vital constituents and environment of other individuals, that alone can have any survival. Behind both the mental and the physical phenomena there is perhaps a universal Life of which we are individualised, evolutionary and phenomenal becomings. This universal Life creates a real world and real beings, but the conscious personality in these beings is not, or at least it need not be, the sign or the shape of consciousness of an eternal nor even of a persistent soul or supraphysical Person: there is nothing in this formula of existence compelling us to believe in a psychic entity that outlasts the death of the body. There is here no reason and little room for the admission of rebirth as a part of the scheme of things.

But what if it were found with the increase of our knowledge, as certain researches and discoveries seem to presage, that the dependence of the mental being or the psychic entity in us on the body is not so complete as we at first naturally conclude it to be from the study of the data of physical existence and the physical universe alone? What if it were found that the human personality survives the death of the body and moves between other planes and this material universe? The prevalent modern idea of a temporary conscious existence would then have to broaden itself and admit a Life that has a wider range than the physical universe and admit too a personal individuality not dependent on the material body. It might have practically to readopt the ancient idea of a subtle form or body inhabited by a psychic entity. A psychic or soul entity, carrying with it the mental consciousness, or, if there be no such original soul, then the evolved and persistent mental individual would continue after death in this subtle persistent form, which must have been either created for it before this birth or by the birth itself or during the life. For either a psychic entity pre-exists in other worlds in a subtle form and comes from there with it to its brief earthly sojourn, or the soul develops here in the material world itself, and with it a psychic body is developed in the course of Nature and persists after death in other worlds or by reincarnation here. These would be the two possible alternatives.

An evolving universal Life may have developed on earth the growing personality that has now become ourselves, before it entered a human body at all; the soul in us may have evolved in lower life-shapes before man was created. In that case, our personality has previously inhabited animal forms, and the subtle body would be a plastic formation carried from birth to birth but adapting itself to whatever physical shape the soul inhabits. Or the evolving Life may be able to build a personality capable of survival, but only in the human form when that is created. This would happen by the force of a sudden growth of mental consciousness, and at the same time a sheath of subtle mind-substance might develop and help to individualise this mental consciousness and would then function as an inner body, just as the gross physical form by its organisation at once individualises and houses the animal mind and life. On the former supposition, we must admit that the animal too survives the dissolution of the physical body and has some kind of soul formation which after death occupies other animal forms on earth and finally a human body. For there is little likelihood that the animal soul passes beyond earth and enters other planes of life than the physical and constantly returns here until it is ready for the human incarnation; the animal's conscious individualisation does not seem sufficient to bear such a transfer or to adapt itself to an other-worldly existence. On the second supposition, the power thus to survive the death of the physical body in other states of existence would only arrive with the human stage of the evolution. If, indeed, the soul is not such a constructed personality evolved by Life, but a persistent unevolving reality with a terrestrial life and body as its necessary field, the theory of rebirth in the sense of Pythagorean transmigration would have to be admitted. But if it is a persistent evolving entity capable of passing beyond the terrestrial stage, then the Indian idea of a passage to other worlds and a return to terrestrial birth would become possible and highly probable. But it would not be inevitable; for it might be supposed that the human personality, once capable of attaining to other planes, need not return from them: it would naturally, in the absence of some greater compelling reason, pursue its existence upon the higher plane to which it had arisen; it would have finished with the terrestrial life-evolution. Only if faced with actual evidence of a return to earth, would a larger supposition be compulsory and the admission of a repeated rebirth in human forms become inevitable.

But even then the developing vitalistic theory need not spiritualise itself, need not admit the real existence of a soul or its immortality or eternity. It might regard the personality still as a phenomenal creation of the universal Life by the interaction of life-consciousness and physical form and force, but with a wider, more variable and subtler action of both upon each other and another history than it had at first seen to be possible. It might even arrive at a sort of vitalistic Buddhism, admitting Karma, but admitting it only as the action of a universal Life-force; it would admit as one of its results the continuity of the stream of personality in rebirth by mental association, but might deny any real self for the individual or any eternal being other than this ever-active vital Becoming. On the other hand, it might, obeying a turn of thought which is now beginning to gain a little in strength, admit a universal Self or cosmic Spirit as the primal reality and Life as its power or agent and so arrive at a form of spiritualised vital Monism. In this theory too a law of rebirth would be possible but not inevitable; it might be a phenomenal fact, an actual law of life, but it would not be a logical result of the theory of being and its inevitable consequence.

Adwaita of the Mayavada, like Buddhism, started with the already accepted belief, — part of the received stock of an antique knowledge, — of supraphysical planes and worlds and a commerce between them and ours which determined a passage from earth and, though this seems to have been a less primitive discovery, a return to earth of the human personality. At any rate their thought had behind it an ancient perception and even experience, or at least an age-long tradition, of a before and after for the personality which was not confined to the experience of the physical universe; for they based themselves on a view of self and world which already regarded a supraphysical consciousness as the primary phenomenon and physical being as only a secondary and dependent phenomenon. It was around these data that they had to determine the nature of the eternal Reality and the origin of the phenomenal becoming. Therefore they admitted the passage of the personality from this to other worlds and its return into form of life upon earth; but the rebirth thus admitted was not in the Buddhistic view a real rebirth of a real spiritual Person into the forms of material existence. In the later Adwaita view the spiritual reality was there, but its apparent individuality and therefore its birth and rebirth were part of a cosmic illusion, a deceptive but effective construction of universal Maya.

In Buddhistic thought the existence of the Self was denied, and rebirth could only mean a continuity of the ideas, sensations and actions which constituted a fictitious individual moving between different worlds, — let us say, between differently organised planes of idea and sensation; for, in fact, it is only the conscious continuity of the flux that creates a phenomenon of self and a phenomenon of personality. In the Adwaitic Mayavada there was the admission of a Jivatman, an individual self, and even of a real self of the individual;[5] but this concession to our normal language and ideas ends by being only apparent. For it turns out that there is no real and eternal individual, no "I" or "you", and therefore there can be no real self of the individual, even no true universal self, but only a Self apart from the universe, ever unborn, ever unmodified, ever unaffected by the mutations of phenomena. Birth, life, death, the whole mass of individual and cosmic experience, become in the last resort no more than an illusion or a temporary phenomenon; even bondage and release can be only such an illusion, a part of temporal phenomena: they amount only to the conscious continuity of the illusory experiences of the ego, itself a creation of the great Illusion, and the cessation of the continuity and the consciousness into the superconsciousness of That which alone

---

[5] The Self in this view is one, it cannot be many or multiply itself; there cannot therefore be any true individual, only at most a one Self omnipresent and animating each mind and body with the idea of an "I".

was, is and ever will be, or rather which has nothing to do with
Time, is for ever unborn, timeless and ineffable.

  Thus while in the vitalistic view of things there is a real universe and a real though brief temporary becoming of individual
life which, even though there is no ever-enduring Purusha, yet
gives a considerable importance to our individual experience
and actions, — for these are truly effective in a real becoming,
— in the Mayavada theory these things have no real importance
or true effect, but only something like a dream-consequence.
For even release takes place only in the cosmic dream or hallucination by the recognition of the illusion and the cessation
of the individualised mind and body; in reality, there is no
one bound and no one released, for the sole-existent Self is
untouched by these illusions of the ego. To escape from the all-
destroying sterility which would be the logical result, we have
to lend a practical reality, however false it may be eventually,
to this dream-consequence and an immense importance to our
bondage and individual release, even though the life of the individual is phenomenal only and to the one real Self both the
bondage and the release are and cannot but be non-existent.
In this compulsory concession to the tyrannous falsehood of
Maya the sole true importance of life and experience must lie in
the measure in which they prepare for the negation of life, for
the self-elimination of the individual, for the end of the cosmic
illusion.

  This, however, is an extreme view and consequence of the
monistic thesis, and the older Adwaita Vedantism starting from
the Upanishads does not go so far. It admits an actual and temporal becoming of the Eternal and therefore a real universe; the
individual too assumes a sufficient reality, for each individual
is in himself the Eternal who has assumed name and form and
supports through him the experiences of life turning on an ever-
circling wheel of birth in the manifestation. The wheel is kept
in motion by the desire of the individual, which becomes the
effective cause of rebirth and by the mind's turning away from
the knowledge of the eternal self to the preoccupations of the
temporal becoming. With the cessation of this desire and of

this ignorance, the Eternal in the individual draws away from the mutations of individual personality and experience into his timeless, impersonal and immutable being.

But this reality of the individual is quite temporal; it has no enduring foundation, not even a perpetual recurrence in Time. Rebirth, though a very important actuality in this account of the universe, is not an inevitable consequence of the relation between individuality and the purpose of the manifestation. For the manifestation seems to have no purpose except the will of the Eternal towards world-creation and it can end only by that will's withdrawal: this cosmic will could work itself out without any machinery of rebirth and the individual's desire maintaining it; for his desire can be only a spring of the machinery, it could not be the cause or the necessary condition of cosmic existence, since he is himself in this view a result of the creation and not in existence prior to the Becoming. The will to creation could then accomplish itself through a temporary assumption of individuality in each name and form, a single life of many impermanent individuals. There would be a self-shaping of the one consciousness in correspondence with the type of each created being, but it could very well begin in each individual body with the appearance of the physical form and end with its cessation. Individual would follow individual as wave follows wave, the sea remaining always the same;[6] each formation of conscious being would surge up from the universal, roll for its allotted time and then sink back into the Silence. The necessity for this purpose of an individualised consciousness persistently continuous, assuming name after name and form after form and moving

---

[6] Dr. Schweitzer in his book on Indian thought asserts that this was the real sense of the Upanishadic teachings and rebirth was a later invention. But there are numerous important passages in almost all the Upanishads positively affirming rebirth and, in any case, the Upanishads admit the survival of the personality after death and its passage into other worlds which is incompatible with this interpretation. If there is survival in other worlds and also a final destiny of liberation into the Brahman for souls embodied here, rebirth imposes itself, and there is no reason to suppose that it was a later theory. The writer has evidently been moved by the associations of Western philosophy to read a merely pantheistic sense into the more subtle and complex thought of the ancient Vedanta.

between different planes backward and forward, is not apparent and, even as a possibility, does not strongly impose itself; still less is there any room for an evolutionary progress inevitably pursued from form to higher form such as must be supposed by a theory of rebirth that affirms the involution and evolution of the Spirit in Matter as the significant formula of our terrestrial existence.

It is conceivable that so the Eternal may have actually chosen to manifest or rather to conceal himself in the body; he may have willed to become or to appear as an individual passing from birth to death and from death to new life in a cycle of persistent and recurrent human and animal existence. The One Being personalised would pass through various forms of becoming at fancy or according to some law of the consequences of action, till the close came by an enlightenment, a return to Oneness, a withdrawal of the Sole and Identical from that particular individualisation. But such a cycle would have no original or final determining Truth which would give it any significance. There is nothing for which it would be necessary; it would be purely a play, a Lila. But if it is once admitted that the Spirit has involved itself in the Inconscience and is manifesting itself in the individual being by an evolutionary gradation, then the whole process assumes meaning and consistence; the progressive ascent of the individual becomes a key-note of this cosmic significance, and the rebirth of the soul in the body becomes a natural and unavoidable consequence of the truth of the Becoming and its inherent law. Rebirth is an indispensable machinery for the working out of a spiritual evolution; it is the only possible effective condition, the obvious dynamic process of such a manifestation in the material universe.

Our explanation of the evolution in Matter is that the universe is a self-creative process of a supreme Reality whose presence makes spirit the substance of things, — all things are there as the spirit's powers and means and forms of manifestation. An infinite existence, an infinite consciousness, an infinite force and will, an infinite delight of being is the Reality secret behind the appearances of the universe; its divine Supermind or

Gnosis has arranged the cosmic order, but arranged it indirectly through the three subordinate and limiting terms of which we are conscious here, Mind, Life and Matter. The material universe is the lowest stage of a downward plunge of the manifestation, an involution of the manifested being of this triune Reality into an apparent nescience of itself, that which we now call the Inconscient; but out of this nescience the evolution of that manifested being into a recovered self-awareness was from the very first inevitable. It was inevitable because that which is involved must evolve; for it is not only there as an existence, a force hidden in its apparent opposite, and every such force must in its inmost nature be moved to find itself, to realise itself, to release itself into play, but it is the reality of that which conceals it, it is the self which the Nescience has lost and which therefore it must be the whole secret meaning, the constant drift of its action to seek for and recover. It is through the conscious individual being that this recovery is possible; it is in him that the evolving consciousness becomes organised and capable of awaking to its own Reality. The immense importance of the individual being, which increases as he rises in the scale, is the most remarkable and significant fact of a universe which started without consciousness and without individuality in an undifferentiated Nescience. This importance can only be justified if the Self as individual is no less real than the Self as cosmic Being or Spirit and both are powers of the Eternal. It is only so that can be explained the necessity for the growth of the individual and his discovery of himself as a condition for the discovery of the cosmic Self and Consciousness and of the supreme Reality. If we adopt this solution, this is the first result, the reality of the persistent individual; but from that first consequence the other result follows, that rebirth of some kind is no longer a possible machinery which may or may not be accepted, it becomes a necessity, an inevitable outcome of the root nature of our existence.

For it is no longer sufficient to suppose an illusory or temporary individual, created in each form by the play of consciousness; individuality can no longer be conceived as an accompaniment of play of consciousness in figure of body which may

or may not survive the form, may or may not prolong its false
continuity of self from form to form, from life to life, but which
certainly need not do it. In this world what we seem at first
to see is individual replacing individual without any continuity,
the form dissolving, the false or transient individuality dissolving
with it, while the universal Energy or some universal Being alone
remains for ever; that might very well be the whole principle of
cosmic manifestation. But if the individual is a persistent reality,
an eternal portion or power of the Eternal, if his growth of consciousness is the means by which the Spirit in things discloses its
being, the cosmos reveals itself as a conditioned manifestation of
the play of the eternal One in the being of Sachchidananda with
the eternal Many. Then, secure behind all the changings of our
personality, upholding the stream of its mutations, there must be
a true Person, a real spiritual Individual, a true Purusha. The One
extended in universality exists in each being and affirms himself
in this individuality of himself. In the individual he discloses
his total existence by oneness with all in the universality. In the
individual he discloses too his transcendence as the Eternal in
whom all the universal unity is founded. This trinity of self-
manifestation, this prodigious Lila of the manifold Identity, this
magic of Maya or protean miracle of the conscious truth of
being of the Infinite, is the luminous revelation which emerges
by a slow evolution from the original Inconscience.

If there were no need of self-finding but only an eternal
enjoyment of this play of the being of Sachchidananda, — and
such an eternal enjoyment is the nature of certain supreme states
of conscious existence, — then evolution and rebirth need not
have come into operation. But there has been an involution of
this unity into the dividing Mind, a plunge into self-oblivion
by which the ever-present sense of the complete oneness is lost,
and the play of separative difference, — phenomenal, because
the real unity in difference remains unabridged behind, — comes
into the forefront as a dominant reality. This play of difference
has found its utmost term of the sense of division by the precipitation of the dividing Mind into a form of body in which
it becomes conscious of itself as a separate ego. A dense and

solid basis has been laid for this play of division in a world of separative forms of Matter by an involution of the active self-conscience of Sachchidananda into a phenomenal Nescience. It is this foundation in Nescience that makes the division secure because it imperatively opposes a return to the consciousness of unity; but still, though effectively obstructive, it is phenomenal and terminable because within it, above it, supporting it is the all-conscient Spirit and the apparent Nescience turns out to be only a concentration, an exclusive action of consciousness tranced into self-forgetfulness by an abysmal plunge into the absorption of the formative and creative material process. In a phenomenal universe so created, the separative form becomes the foundation and the starting-point of all its life-action; therefore the individual Purusha in working out its cosmic relations with the One has in this physical world to base himself upon the form, to assume a body; it is the body that he must make his own foundation and the starting-point for his development of the life and mind and spirit in the physical existence. That assumption of body we call birth, and in it only can take place here the development of self and the play of relations between the individual and the universal and all other individuals; in it only can there be the growth by a progressive development of our conscious being towards a supreme recovery of unity with God and with all in God: all the sum of what we call Life in the physical world is a progress of the soul and proceeds by birth into the body and has that for its fulcrum, its condition of action and its condition of evolutionary persistence.

Birth then is a necessity of the manifestation of the Purusha on the physical plane; but his birth, whether the human or any other, cannot be in this world-order an isolated accident or a sudden excursion of a soul into physicality without any preparing past to it or any fulfilling hereafter. In a world of involution and evolution, not of physical form only, but of conscious being through life and mind to spirit, such an isolated assumption of life in the human body could not be the rule of the individual soul's existence; it would be a quite meaningless and inconsequential arrangement, a freak for which the nature and system of things here have no place, a contrary violence which would break the rhythm of the Spirit's self-manifestation. The intrusion of such a rule of individual soul-life into an evolutionary spiritual progression would make it an effect without cause and a cause without effect; it would be a fragmentary present without a past or a future. The life of the individual must have the same rhythm of significance, the same law of progression as the cosmic life; its place in that rhythm cannot be a stray purposeless intervention, it must be an abiding instrumentation of the cosmic purpose. Neither in such an order can we explain an isolated advent, a one birth of the soul in the human body which would be its first and last experience of the kind, by a previous existence in other worlds with a future before it in yet other fields of experience. For here life upon earth, life in the physical universe is not and cannot be a casual perch for the wanderings of the soul from world to world; it is a great and slow development needing, as we now know, incalculable spaces of Time for its evolution. Human life is itself only a term in a graded series, through which the secret Spirit in the universe develops gradually his purpose and works it out finally through the enlarging and ascending individual soul-consciousness in the body. This ascent can only take place by rebirth within the ascending order; an individual visit coming across it and progressing on some other line elsewhere could not fit into the system of this evolutionary existence.

Nor is the human soul, the human individual, a free wanderer capriciously or lightly hastening from field to field according to its unfettered choice or according to its free and spontaneously variable action and result of action. That is a radiant thought of pure spiritual liberty which may have its truth in planes beyond or in an eventual release, but is not true at first of the earth-life, of life in the physical universe. The human birth in this world is on its spiritual side a complex of two elements, a spiritual Person and a soul of personality; the former is man's eternal being, the latter is his cosmic and mutable being. As the spiritual impersonal person he is one in his nature and being with the freedom of Sachchidananda who has here consented to or willed his involution in the Nescience for a certain round of soul-experience, impossible otherwise, and presides secretly over its evolution. As the soul of personality he is himself part of that long development of the soul-experience in the forms of Nature; his own evolution must follow the laws and the lines of the universal evolution. As a spirit he is one with the Transcendence which is immanent in the world and comprehensive of it; as a soul he is at once one with and part of the universality of Sachchidananda self-expressed in the world: his self-expression must go through the stages of the cosmic expression, his soul-experience follow the revolutions of the wheel of Brahman in the universe.

The universal Spirit in things involved in the Nescience of the physical universe evolves its nature-self in a succession of physical forms up the graded series of Matter, Life, Mind and Spirit. It emerges first as a secret soul in material forms quite subject on the surface to the nescience; it develops as a soul still secret but about to emerge in vital forms that stand on the borders between nescience and the partial light of consciousness which is our ignorance; it develops still farther as the initially conscient soul in the animal mind and, finally, as the more out-wardly conscious, but not yet fully conscient soul in man: the consciousness is there throughout in our occult parts of being, the development is in the manifesting Nature. This evolutionary development has a universal as well as an individual aspect: the Universal develops the grades of its being and the ordered variation of the universality of itself in the series of its evolved forms of being; the individual soul follows the line of this cosmic series and manifests what is prepared in the universality of the Spirit. The universal Man, the cosmic Purusha in humanity, is developing in the human race the power that has grown into humanity from below it and shall yet grow to Supermind and Spirit and become the Godhead in man who is aware of his true and integral self and the divine universality of his nature. The individual must have followed this line of development; he must have presided over a soul-experience in the lower forms of life before he took up the human evolution: as the One was capable of assuming in its universality these lower forms of the plant and animal, so must the individual, now human, have been capable of assuming them in his previous stages of existence. He now appears as a human soul, the Spirit accepting the inner and outer form of humanity, but he is not limited by this form any more than he was limited by the plant or animal forms previously assumed by him; he can pass on from it to a greater self-expression in a higher scale of Nature.

To suppose otherwise would be to suppose that the spirit which now presides over the human soul-experience was originally formed by a human mentality and the human body, exists by that and cannot exist apart from it, cannot ever go below or above it. In fact, it would then be reasonable to suppose that it is not immortal but has come into existence by the appearance of the human mind and body in the evolution and would disappear by their disappearance. But body and mind are not the creators of the spirit, the spirit is the creator of the mind and body; it develops these principles out of its being, it is not developed into being out of them, it is not a compound of their elements or a resultant of their meeting. If it appears to evolve out of mind and body, that is because it gradually manifests itself in them and not because it is created by them or exists by them; as it manifests, they are revealed as subordinate terms of its being and are to be finally taken up out of their present imperfection and transformed into visible forms and instruments of the spirit. Our conception of the spirit is of something which is not constituted by name and form, but assumes various forms of body and mind according to the various manifestations of its soul-being. This it does here by a successive evolution; it evolves successive forms and successive strata of consciousness: for it is not bound always to assume one form and no other or to possess one kind of mentality which is its sole possible subjective manifestation. The soul is not bound by the formula of mental humanity: it did not begin with that and will not end with it; it had a prehuman past, it has a superhuman future.

What we see of Nature and of human nature justifies this view of a birth of the individual soul from form to form until it reaches the human level of manifested consciousness which is its instrument for rising to yet higher levels. We see that Nature develops from stage to stage and in each stage takes up its past and transforms it into stuff of its new development. We see too that human nature is of the same make; all the earth-past is there in it. It has an element of matter taken up by life, an element of life taken up by mind, an element of mind which is being taken up by spirit: the animal is still present in its humanity; the very nature of the human being presupposes a material and a vital stage which prepared his emergence into mind and an animal past which moulded a first element of his complex humanity. And let us not say that this is because material Nature developed by evolution his life and his body and his animal mind, and only afterwards did a soul descend into the form so created: there is a certain truth behind this idea, but not the truth which that formula would suggest. For that supposes a gulf between soul and body, between soul and life, between soul and mind, which does not exist; there is no body without soul, no body that is not itself a form of soul: Matter itself is substance and power of spirit and could not exist if it were anything else, for nothing can exist which is not substance and power of Brahman; and if Matter, then still more clearly and certainly Life and Mind must be that and ensouled by the presence of the Spirit. If Matter and Life had not already been ensouled, man could not have appeared or only as an intervention or an accident, not as a part of the evolutionary order.

We arrive then necessarily at this conclusion that human birth is a term at which the soul must arrive in a long succession of rebirths and that it has had for its previous and preparatory terms in the succession the lower forms of life upon earth; it has passed through the whole chain that life has strung in the physical universe on the basis of the body, the physical principle. Then the farther question arises whether, humanity once attained, this succession of rebirths still continues and, if so, how, by what series or by what alternations. And, first, we have to ask whether the soul, having once arrived at humanity, can go back to the animal life and body, a retrogression which the old popular theories of transmigration have supposed to be an ordinary

movement. It seems impossible that it should so go back with
any entirety, and for this reason that the transit from animal to
human life means a decisive conversion of consciousness, quite
as decisive as the conversion of the vital consciousness of the
plant into the mental consciousness of the animal. It is surely
impossible that a conversion so decisive made by Nature should
be reversed by the soul and the decision of the spirit within
her come, as it were, to naught. It could only be possible for
human souls, supposing such to exist, in whom the conversion
was not decisive, souls that had developed far enough to make,
occupy or assume a human body, but not enough to ensure the
safety of this assumption, not enough to remain secure in its
achievement and faithful to the human type of consciousness.
Or at most there might be, supposing certain animal propensities
to be vehement enough to demand a separate satisfaction quite
of their own kind, a sort of partial rebirth, a loose holding of an
animal form by a human soul, with an immediate subsequent
reversion to its normal progression. The movement of Nature
is always sufficiently complex for us not to deny dogmatically
such a possibility, and, if it be a fact, then there may exist this
modicum of truth behind the exaggerated popular belief which
assumes an animal rebirth of the soul once lodged in man to
be quite as normal and possible as a human reincarnation. But
whether the animal reversion is possible or not, the normal law
must be the recurrence of birth in new human forms for a soul
that has once become capable of humanity.

But why a succession of human births and not one alone?
For the same reason that has made the human birth itself a
culminating point of the past succession, the previous upward
series, — it must be so by the very necessity of the spiritual evolution. For the soul has not finished what it has to do by merely
developing into humanity; it has still to develop that humanity
into its higher possibilities. Obviously, the soul that lodges in a
Caribbee or an untaught primitive or an Apache of Paris or an
American gangster, has not yet exhausted the necessity of human
birth, has not developed all its possibilities or the whole meaning
of humanity, has not worked out all the sense of Sachchidananda

in the universal Man; neither has the soul lodged in a vitalistic European occupied with dynamic production and vital pleasure or in an Asiatic peasant engrossed in the ignorant round of the domestic and economic life. We may reasonably doubt whether even a Plato or a Shankara marks the crown and therefore the end of the outflowering of the spirit in man. We are apt to suppose that these may be the limit, because these and others like them seem to us the highest point which the mind and soul of man can reach, but that may be the illusion of our present possibility. There may be a higher or at least a larger possibility which the Divine intends yet to realise in man, and, if so, it is the steps built by these highest souls which were needed to compose the way up to it and to open the gates. At any rate this present highest point at least must be reached before we can write finis on the recurrence of the human birth for the individual. Man is there to move from the ignorance and from the little life which he is in his mind and body to the knowledge and the large divine life which he can compass by the unfolding of the spirit. At least the opening out of the spirit in him, the knowledge of his real self and the leading of the spiritual life must be attained before he can go definitively and for ever otherwhere. There may too be beyond this initial culmination a greater flowering of the spirit in the human life of which we have as yet only the first intimations; the imperfection of Man is not the last word of Nature, but his perfection too is not the last peak of the Spirit.

This possibility becomes a certitude if the present leading principle of the mind as man has developed it, the intellect, is not its highest principle. If mind itself has other powers as yet only imperfectly possessed by the highest types of the human individual, then a prolongation of the line of evolution and consequently of the ascending line of rebirth to embody them is inevitable. If Supermind also is a power of consciousness concealed here in the evolution, the line of rebirth cannot stop even there; it cannot cease in its ascent before the mental has been replaced by the supramental nature and an embodied supramental being becomes the leader of terrestrial existence.

This then is the rational and philosophical foundation for

a belief in rebirth; it is an inevitable logical conclusion if there exists at the same time an evolutionary principle in the Earth-Nature and a reality of the individual soul born into evolutionary Nature. If there is no soul, then there can be a mechanical evolution without necessity or significance and birth is only part of this curious but senseless machinery. If the individual is only a temporary formation beginning and ending with the body, then evolution can be a play of the All-Soul or Cosmic Existence mounting through a progression of higher and higher species towards its own utmost possibility in this Becoming or to its highest conscious principle; rebirth does not exist and is not needed as a mechanism of that evolution. Or, if the All-Existence expresses itself in a persistent but illusory individuality, rebirth becomes a possibility or an illusory fact, but it has no evolutionary necessity and is not a spiritual necessity; it is only a means of accentuating and prolonging the illusion up to its utmost time-limit. If there is an individual soul or Purusha not dependent on the body but inhabiting and using it for its purpose, then rebirth begins to be possible, but it is not a necessity if there is no evolution of the soul in Nature: the presence of the individual soul in an individual body may be a passing phenomenon, a single experience without a past here or a future; its past and its future may be elsewhere. But if there is an evolution of consciousness in an evolutionary body and a soul inhabiting the body, a real and conscious individual, then it is evident that it is the progressive experience of that soul in Nature which takes the form of this evolution of consciousness: rebirth is self-evidently a necessary part, the sole possible machinery of such an evolution. It is as necessary as birth itself; for without it birth would be an initial step without a sequel, the starting of a journey without its farther steps and arrival. It is rebirth that gives to the birth of an incomplete being in a body its promise of completeness and its spiritual significance.

Chapter XXI

The Order of the Worlds

Seven are these worlds in which move the life-forces that are hidden within the secret heart as their dwelling-place seven by seven. *Mundaka Upanishad.*[1]

May the Peoples of the five Births accept my sacrifice, those who are born of the Light and worthy of worship; may Earth protect us from earthly evil and the Mid-Region from calamity from the gods. Follow the shining thread spun out across the mid-world, protect the luminous paths built by the thought; weave an inviolate work, become the human being, create the divine race.... Seers of truth are you, sharpen the shining spears with which you cut the way to that which is Immortal; knowers of the secret planes, form them, the steps by which the gods attained to immortality. *Rig Veda.*[2]

This is the eternal Tree with its root above and its branches downward; this is Brahman, this is the Immortal; in it are lodged all the worlds and none goes beyond it. This and That are one. *Katha Upanishad.*[3]

IF A spiritual evolution of consciousness in the material world and a constant or repeated rebirth of the individual into an earthly body are admitted, the next question that arises is whether this evolutionary movement is something separate and complete in itself or part of a larger universal totality of which the material world is only one province. This question has already its answer implied in the gradations of the involution which precede the evolution and make it possible; for, if that

---

[1] II. 1. 8. [2] X. 53. 5, 6, 10. [3] II. 3. 1.

precedence is a fact, there must be worlds or at least planes of higher being and they must have some connection with the evolution which has been made possible by their existence. It may be that all they do for us is by their effective presence or pressure on the earth-consciousness to liberate the involved principles of life and mind and spirit and enable them to manifest and assert their reign in material Nature. But it would be in the highest degree improbable that the connection and intervention should cease there; there is likely to be a sustained, if veiled, commerce between material life and the life of the other planes of existence. It is necessary now to look more closely into this problem, regard it in itself and determine the nature and limits of this connection and intercommunication, in so far as it affects the theory of evolution and rebirth in material Nature.

The descent of the Soul into the Ignorance can be thought of as an abrupt precipitation or immediate lapse of a pure spiritual being out of the superconscient spiritual Reality into the first inconscience and the subsequent evolving phenomenal life of material Nature. If that were so, there might be the Absolute above and the Inconscient below, with the material world created out of it, and the issue, the return back would then be a similar abrupt or precipitous transit from a material embodied world-being into the transcendent Silence. There would be no intermediate powers or realities other than Matter and Spirit, no other planes than the material, no other worlds than the world of Matter. But this idea is too trenchant and simple a construction and cannot outlive a wider view of the complex nature of existence.

There are, no doubt, several possible originations of cosmic existence by which such an extreme and rigid world-balancement could have conceivably come into being. There could have been a conception of this kind and a fiat in an All-Will, or an idea, a movement of the soul towards an egoistic material life of the Ignorance. The eternal individual soul urged by some inexplicable desire arising within it can be supposed to have sought the adventure of the darkness and taken a plunge from its native Light into the depths of a Nescience out of which arose this world of Ignorance; or a collectivity of souls may have been so moved, the Many: for an individual being cannot constitute a cosmos; a cosmos must be either impersonal or multipersonal or the creation or self-expression of a universal or infinite Being. This desire may have drawn down an All-Soul with it to build a world based upon the power of the Inconscient. If not that, then the eternally omniscient All-Soul itself may have abruptly plunged its self-knowledge into this darkness of the Inconscience, carrying the individual souls within it to begin their upward evolution through an ascending scale of life and consciousness. Or, if the individual is not pre-existent, if we are only a creation of the All-consciousness or a fiction of the phenomenal Ignorance, either creatrix may have conceived all these myriads of individual beings by the evolution of names and forms out of an original indiscriminate Prakriti; the soul would be a temporary product of the indiscriminate stuff of inconscient force-substance which is the first appearance of things in the material universe.

On that supposition, or on any of them, there could be only two planes of existence: on one side there is the material universe created out of the Inconscient by the blind nescience of Force or Nature obedient perhaps to some inner unfelt Self which governs its somnambulist activities; on the other side there is the superconscient One to which we return out of the Inconscience and Ignorance. Or else we may imagine that there is one plane only, the material existence; there is no superconscient apart from the Soul of the material universe. If we find that there are other planes of conscious being and that there already exist other worlds than the material universe, these ideas might become difficult to substantiate; but we can escape from that annulment if we suppose that these worlds have been subsequently created by or for the evolving Soul in the course of its ascent out of the Inconscience. In any of these views the whole cosmos would be an evolution out of the Inconscient, either with the material universe as its sole and sufficient stage and scene or else with an ascending scale of worlds, one evolving out of the other, helping to grade our return to the original Reality. Our own view has been that the cosmos is a self-graded evolution out of the superconscient Sachchidananda; but in this idea it would be nothing but an evolution of the Inconscience towards some kind of knowledge sufficient to allow, by the annihilation of some primal ignorance or some originating desire, the extinction of a misbegotten soul or an escape out of a mistaken world-adventure.

But such theories either imply a premier importance and originating power of mind or a premier importance of the individual being; both have indeed a great place, but the one eternal Spirit is the original power and the original existence. Idea, conceptively creative, — not the Real-Idea which is Being aware of what is in itself and automatically self-creative by the force of that Truth-awareness, — is a movement of the mind; desire is a movement of life in mind; life and mind then must be pre-existent powers and must have been the determinants of the creation of the material world, and in that case they can equally create worlds of their own supraphysical nature. Or else we must suppose that what acted was not desire in an individual or a universal Mind or Life, but a will in the Spirit, — a will of Being deploying something of itself or of its Consciousness, realising a creative idea or a self-knowledge or an urge of its self-active Force or a turn to a certain formulation of its delight of existence. But if the world has been created, not by the universal Delight of existence, but for the desire of the individual soul, its caprice of an ignorant egoistic enjoyment, then the mental Individual and not the Cosmic Being or a Transcendent Divinity should be the creator and witness of the universe. In the past trend of human thought the individual being has always loomed enormously large in the front plan of things and in the premier dimensions of importance; if these proportions could still be maintained, this origination might conceivably be admitted: for a will towards the life of the Ignorance or an assent to it in the individual Purusha must indeed be part of the operative movement of Consciousness in the involutionary descent of the Spirit into material Nature. But the world cannot be a creation of the individual mind or a theatre erected by it for its own play of consciousness; nor can it have been created solely for the play and the satisfaction or frustration of the ego. As we awake to a sense of the premier importance of the universal and the dependence of the individual upon it, a theory of this kind becomes an impossibility to our intelligence. The world is too vast in its movement for such an account of its working to be credible; only a cosmic Power or a cosmic Being can be the creator and the upholder of the cosmos and it must have too a cosmic and not only an individual reality, significance or purpose.

Accordingly, this world-creating or participating Individual and its desire or assent to the Ignorance must have been awake before the world at all existed; it must have been there as an element in some supracosmic Superconscient from which it comes and to which it returns out of the life of the ego: we must suppose an original immanence of the Many in the One. It becomes then conceivable that a will or an impetus or a spiritual necessity may have stirred, in some transmundane Infinite, in some of the Many which precipitated them downward and compelled the creation of this world of the Ignorance. But since the One is the premier fact of existence, since the Many depend upon the One, are souls of the One, beings of the Being, this truth must determine also the fundamental principle of the cosmic existence. There we see that the universal precedes the individual, gives it its field, is that in which it exists cosmically even though its origin is in the Transcendence. The individual soul lives here by the All-Soul and depends upon it; the All-Soul very evidently does not exist by the individual or depend upon it: it is not a sum of individual beings, a pluralistic totality created by the conscious life of individuals; if an All-Soul exists, it must be the one Cosmic Spirit supporting the one cosmic Force in its works, and it repeats here, modified in the terms of cosmic existence, the primary relation of the dependence of the Many on the One. It is inconceivable that the Many should have independently or by a departure from the One Will desired cosmic existence and forced by their desire the supreme Sachchidananda to descend unwillingly or tolerantly into the Nescience; that would be to reverse altogether the true dependence of things. If the world was directly originated by the will or the spiritual impetus of the Many, which is possible and even probable in a certain sense, there must still have been first a Will in Sachchidananda to that end; otherwise the impetus, — translating here the All-Will into desire, for what becomes desire in the ego is Will in the Spirit, — could not have arisen anywhere. The One, the All-Soul, by whom alone the consciousness of the Individual is determined, must first accept the veil of inconscient Nature before the Individual too can put on the veil of the Ignorance in the material universe.

But once we admit this Will of the supreme and cosmic Being as the indispensable condition of the existence of the material universe, it is no longer possible to accept Desire as the creative principle; for desire has no place in the Supreme or in the All-being. It can have nothing to desire; desire is the result of incompleteness, of insufficiency, of something that is not possessed or enjoyed and which the being seeks for possession or enjoyment. A supreme and universal Being can have the delight of its all-existence, but to that delight desire must be foreign, — it can only be the appanage of the incomplete evolutionary ego which is a product of the cosmic action. Moreover, if the All-consciousness of the Spirit has willed to plunge into the inconscience of Matter, it must be because that was a possibility of its self-creation or manifestation. But a sole material universe and an evolution there out of inconscience into spiritual consciousness cannot be the one solitary and limited possibility of manifestation of the All-being. That could only be if Matter were the original power and form of manifested being and the spirit had no other choice, could not manifest except through Inconscience into Matter as a basis. This would bring us to a materialistic evolutionary Pantheism; we would have to regard the beings who people the universe as souls of the One, souls born here in It and evolving upward through inanimate, animate and mentally developed forms till the recovery of their complete and undivided life in the superconscient Pantheos and its cosmic Oneness would intervene as the end and goal of their evolution. In that case, everything has evolved here; life, mind, soul have arisen out of the One in the material universe by the force of its hidden being, and everything will fulfil itself here in the material universe. There is then no separate plane of the Superconscience, for the Superconscient is here only, not elsewhere; there are no supraphysical worlds; there is no action of supraphysical principles exterior to Matter, no pressure of an already existent Mind and Life upon the material plane.

It has then to be asked what are Mind and Life, and it may be answered that they are products of Matter or of the Energy in Matter. Or else they are forms of consciousness that arise as results of an evolution from Inconscience to Superconscience: consciousness itself is only a bridge of transition; it is spirit becoming partially aware of itself before plunging into its normal trance of luminous superconscience. Even if there proved to be planes of larger Life and Mind, they would only be subjective constructions of this intermediary consciousness erected on the way to that spiritual culmination. But the difficulty here is that Mind and Life are too different from Matter to be products of Matter; Matter itself is a product of Energy, and mind and life must be regarded as superior products of the same Energy. If we admit the existence of a cosmic Spirit, the Energy must be spiritual; life and mind must be independent products of a spiritual energy and themselves powers of manifestation of the Spirit. It then becomes irrational to suppose that Spirit and Matter alone exist, that they are the two confronting realities and that Matter is the sole possible basis of the manifestation of Spirit; the idea of a sole material world becomes immediately untenable. Spirit must be capable of basing its manifestation on the Mind principle or on the Life principle and not only on the principle of Matter; there can then be and logically there should be worlds of Mind and worlds of Life; there may even be worlds founded on a subtler and more plastic, more conscious principle of Matter.

Three questions then arise, interrelated or interdependent: whether there is any evidence or any true intimation of the existence of such other worlds; whether, if they exist, they are of the nature we have indicated, arising or descending in the order and within the rationale of a hierarchical series between Matter and Spirit; if that is their scale of being, are they otherwise quite independent and unconnected, or is there a relation and interaction of the higher worlds on the world of Matter? It is a fact that mankind almost from the beginning of its existence or so far back as history or tradition can go, has believed in the existence of other worlds and in the possibility of communication between their powers and beings and the human race. In the last rationalistic period of human thought from which we are emerging, this belief has been swept aside as an age-long superstition; all evidence or intimations of its truth have been rejected *a priori* as fundamentally false and undeserving of inquiry because incompatible with the axiomatic truth that only Matter and the material world and its experiences are real; all other experience purporting to be real must be either a hallucination or an imposture or a subjective result of superstitious credulity and imagination or else, if a fact, then other than what it purported to be and explicable by a physical cause: no evidence could be accepted of such a fact unless it is objective and physical in its character; even if the fact be very apparently supraphysical, it cannot be accepted as such unless it is totally unexplainable by any other imaginable hypothesis or conceivable conjecture.

It should be evident that this demand for physical valid proof of a supraphysical fact is irrational and illogical; it is an irrelevant attitude of the physical mind which assumes that only the objective and physical is fundamentally real and puts aside all else as merely subjective. A supraphysical fact may impinge on the physical world and produce physical results; it may even produce an effect on our physical senses and become manifest to them, but that cannot be its invariable action and most normal character or process. Ordinarily, it must produce a direct effect or a tangible impression on our mind and our life-being, which are the parts of us that are of the same order as itself, and can only indirectly and through them, if at all, influence the physical world and physical life. If it objectivises itself, it must be to a subtler sense in us and only derivatively to the outward physical sense. This derivative objectivisation is certainly possible; if there is an association of the action of the subtle body and its sense-organisation with the action of the material body and its physical organs, then the supraphysical can become outwardly sensible to us. This is what happens, for example, with the faculty called second sight; it is the process of all those psychic phenomena which seem to be seen and heard by the outer senses and are not sensed inwardly through representative or interpretative or symbolic images which bear the stamp of an inner experience or have an evident character of formations in a subtle substance. There can, then, be various kinds of evidence of the existence of other planes of being and communication with them; objectivisation to the outer sense, subtle-sense contacts, mind contacts, life contacts, contacts through the subliminal in special states of consciousness exceeding our ordinary range. Our physical mind is not the whole of us nor, even though it dominates almost the whole of our surface consciousness, the best or greatest part of us; reality cannot be restricted to a sole field of this narrowness or to the dimensions known within its rigid circle.

If it be said that subjective experience or subtle-sense images can easily be deceptive, since we have no recognised method or standard of verification and a too great tendency to admit the extraordinary and miraculous or supernatural at its face-value, this may be admitted: but error is not the prerogative of the inner subjective or subliminal parts of us, it is also an appanage of the physical mind and its objective methods and standards, and such liability to error cannot be a reason for shutting out a large and important domain of experience; it is a reason rather for scrutinising it and finding out in it its own true standards and its characteristic appropriate and valid means of verification. Our subjective being is the basis of our objective experience, and it is not probable that only its physical objectivisations are true and the rest unreliable. The subliminal consciousness, when rightly interrogated, is a witness to truth and its testimony is confirmed again and again even in the physical and the objective field; that testimony cannot, then, be disregarded when it calls our attention to things within us or to things that belong to planes or worlds of a supraphysical experience. At the same time belief by itself is not evidence of reality; it must base itself on something more valid before one can accept it. It is evident that the beliefs of the past are not a sufficient basis for knowledge, even though they cannot be entirely neglected: for a belief is a mental construction and may be a wrong building; it may often answer to some inner intimation and then it has a value, but, as often as not, it disfigures the intimation, usually by a translation into terms familiar to our physical and objective experience, such as that which converted the hierarchy of the planes into a physical hierarchy or geographical space-extension, turned the rarer heights of subtle substance into material heights and placed the abodes of the gods on the summits of physical mountains. All truth supraphysical or physical must be founded not on mental belief alone, but on experience, — but in each case experience must be of the kind, physical, subliminal or spiritual, which is appropriate to the order of the truths into which we are empowered to enter; their validity and significance must be scrutinised, but according to their own law and by a consciousness which can enter into them and not according to the law of another domain or by a consciousness which is capable only of truths of another order; so alone can we be sure of our steps and enlarge firmly our sphere of knowledge.

If we scrutinise the intimations of supraphysical world-realities which we receive in our inner experience and compare with it the account of such intimations that has continued to come down to us from the beginnings of human knowledge, and if we attempt an interpretation and a summarised order, we shall find that what this inner experience most intimately conveys to us is the existence and action upon us of larger planes of being and consciousness than the purely material plane, with its restricted existence and action, of which we are aware in our narrow terrestrial formula. These domains of larger being are not altogether remote and separate from our own being and consciousness; for, though they subsist in themselves and have their own play and process and formulations of existence and experience, yet at the same time they penetrate and envelop the physical plane with their invisible presence and influences, and their powers seem to be here in the material world itself behind its action and objects. There are two main orders of experience in our contact with them; one is purely subjective, though in its subjectivity sufficiently vivid and palpable, the other is more objective. In the subjective order, we find that what shapes itself to us as a life-intention, life-impulse, life-formulation here, already exists in a larger, more subtle, more plastic range of possibilities, and these pre-existent forces and formations are pressing upon us to realise themselves in the physical world also; but only a part succeeds in getting through and even that emerges partially in a form and circumstance more proper to the system of terrestrial law and sequence. This precipitation takes place, normally, without our knowledge; we are not aware of the action of these powers, forces and influences upon us, but take them as formations of our own life and mind, even when our reason or will repudiates them and strives not to be mastered: but when we go inwards away from the restricted surface consciousness and develop a subtler sense and deeper awareness, we begin to get an intimation of the origin of these movements and are able to watch their action and process, to accept or reject or modify, to allow them passage and use of our mind and will and our life and members or refuse it. In the same way we become aware of larger domains of mind, a play, experience, formation of a greater plasticity, a teeming profusion of all possible mental formulations, and we feel their contacts with us and their powers and influences acting upon our parts of mind in the same occult manner as those others that act upon our parts of life. This kind of experience is, primarily, of a purely subjective character, a pressure of ideas, suggestions, emotional formations, impulsions to sensation, action, dynamic experience. However large a part of this pressure may be traced to our own subliminal self or to the siege of universal Mind-forces or Life-forces belonging to our own world, there is an element which bears the stamp of another origin, an insistent supraterrestrial character.

But the contacts do not stop here: for there is also an opening of our mind and life parts to a great range of subjective-objective experiences in which these planes present themselves no longer as extensions of subjective being and consciousness, but as worlds; for the experiences there are organised as they are in our own world, but on a different plan, with a different process and law of action and in a substance which belongs to a supraphysical Nature. This organisation includes, as on our earth, the existence of beings who have or take forms, manifest themselves or are naturally manifested in an embodying substance, but a substance other than ours, a subtle substance tangible only to subtle sense, a supraphysical form-matter. These worlds and beings may have nothing to do with ourselves and our life, they may exercise no action upon us; but often also they enter into secret communication with earth-existence, obey or embody and are the intermediaries and instruments of the cosmic powers and influences of which we have a subjective experience, or themselves act by their own initiation upon the terrestrial world's life and motives and happenings. It is possible to receive help or guidance or harm or misguidance from these beings; it is possible even to become subject to their influence, to be possessed by their invasion or domination, to be instrumentalised by them for their good or evil purpose. At times the progress of earthly life seems to be a vast field of battle between supraphysical Forces of either character, those that strive to uplift, encourage and illumine and those that strive to deflect, depress or prevent or even shatter our upward evolution or the soul's self-expression in the material universe. Some of these Beings, Powers or Forces are such that we think of them as divine; they are luminous, benignant or powerfully helpful: there are others that are Titanic, gigantic or demoniac, inordinate Influences, instigators or creators often of vast and formidable inner upheavals or of actions that overpass the normal human measure. There may also be an awareness of influences, presences, beings that do not seem to belong to other worlds beyond us but are here as a hidden element behind the veil in terrestrial nature. As contact with the supraphysical is possible, a contact can also take place subjective or objective, — or at least objectivised, — between our own consciousness and the consciousness of other once embodied beings who have passed into a supraphysical status in these other regions of existence. It is possible also to pass beyond a subjective contact or a subtle-sense perception and, in certain subliminal states of consciousness, to enter actually into other worlds and know something of their secrets. It is the more objective order of other-worldly experience that seized most the imagination of mankind in the past, but it was put by popular belief into a gross-objective statement which unduly assimilated these phenomena to those of the physical world with which we are familiar; for it is the normal tendency of our mind to turn everything into forms or symbols proper to its own kind and terms of experience.

This has always been, put into its most generalised terms, the normal range and character of other-worldly belief and experience in all periods of the past of the race; names and forms differ, but the general features have been strikingly similar in all countries and ages. What exact value are we to put upon these persistent beliefs or upon this mass of supernormal experience? It is not possible for anyone who has had these contacts with any intimacy and not only by scattered abnormal accidents, to put them aside as mere superstition or hallucination; for they are too insistent, real, effective, organic in their pressure, too constantly confirmed by their action and results to be so flung aside: an appreciation, an interpretation, a mental organisation of this side of our capacity of experience is indispensable.

One explanation which can be put forward is that man himself creates the supraphysical worlds which he inhabits or thinks he inhabits after death, creates the gods, as ran the ancient phrase, — it is claimed even that God himself was created by man, was a myth of his consciousness, and has now been abolished by man! All these things then may be a sort of myth of the developing consciousness in which it is able to dwell, a captive in its own buildings, and by a kind of realising dynamisation maintain itself in its own imaginations. But pure imaginations they are not, they can only be so treated by us so long as the things they represent, however incorrectly, are not part of our own experience. Yet there may conceivably

be myths and imaginations that are used by the power of the
creative Consciousness-Force to materialise its own idea-forces;
these potent images may take form and body, endure in some
subtly materialised world of thought and react on their creator:
if so, we might suppose that the other worlds are buildings of
this character. But if that were so, if a subjective consciousness
can thus create worlds and beings, it might well be that the
objective world also is a myth of Consciousness or even of our
consciousness, or that Consciousness itself is a myth of the original Nescience. Thus, on this line of thinking, we swing back
towards a view of the universe in which all things assume a
certain hue of unreality except the all-productive Inconscience
out of which they are created, the Ignorance which creates them
and, it may be, a superconscient or inconscient impersonal Being
into whose indifference all finally disappears or goes back and
ceases there.

But we have no proof and there is no likelihood that man's
mind can create in this way a world where none was before, create in *vacuo* without a substance to build in or build on, though it
may well be that it can add something to a world already made.
Mind is indeed a potent agency, more potent than we readily
imagine; it can make formations which effectuate themselves in
our own or others' consciousness and lives and even have an
effect on inconscient Matter; but an entirely original creation in
the void is beyond its possibilities. What we can rather hazard is
that as it grows, man's mind enters into relation with new ranges
of being and consciousness not at all created by him, new to him,
already pre-existent in the All-Existence. In his increasing inner
experience he opens up new planes of being in himself; as the secret centres of his consciousness dissolve their knots, he becomes
able through them to conceive of those larger realms, to receive
direct influences from them, to enter into them, to image them
in his terrestrial mind and inner sense. He does create images,
symbol-forms, reflective shapes of them with which his mind
can deal; in this sense only he creates the Divine Image that he
worships, creates the forms of the gods, creates new planes and
worlds within him, and through these images the real worlds and

powers that overtop our existence are able to take possession of the consciousness in the physical world, to pour into it their potencies, to transform it with the light of their higher being. But all this is not a creation of the higher worlds of being; it is a revelation of them to the consciousness of the soul on the material plane as it develops out of the Nescience. It is a creation of their forms here by a reception of their powers; there is an enlargement of our subjective life on this plane by the discovery of its true relation with higher planes of its own being from which it was separated by the veil of the material Nescience. This veil exists because the soul in the body has put behind it these greater possibilities in order that it might concentrate exclusively its consciousness and force upon its primary work in this physical world of being; but that primary work can have a sequel only by the veil being at least partially lifted or else made penetrable so that the higher planes of Mind, Life and Spirit may pour their significances into human existence.

It is possible to suppose that these higher planes and worlds have been created subsequently to the manifestation of the material cosmos, to aid the evolution or in some sense as a result of it. This is a notion which the physical mind, starting in all its ideas from the material universe as the one thing which it knows, has analysed and can deal with in a beginning of mastery, might easily tend to accept, if obliged to admit a supraphysical existence; it could then keep the material, the Inconscience, as the starting-point and support of all being, as it is undoubtedly the starting-point for us of the evolutionary movement of which the material world is the scene. Our mind could still keep matter and material force as the first existence, — so accepted and cherished by it because it is the first thing that it knows, the one thing that is always securely present and knowable, — and maintain the spiritual and the supraphysical in a dependence upon the assured foundation in Matter.[4] But how then were these other worlds created, by what force, by what instrumentality?

---

[4] There are certain expressions in the Rig Veda which seem to embody this view. Earth (the material principle) is spoken of as the foundation of all the worlds or the seven worlds are described as the seven planes of Earth.

It might be the Life and Mind developing out of the Inconscient which have at the same time developed these other worlds or planes in the subliminal consciousness of the living beings who appear in it. To the subliminal being in life and after death, — for it is the inner being that survives the death of the body, — these worlds might be real because sensible to its wider range of consciousness; it would move in them with that sense of reality, derivative perhaps but convincing, and it would send up its experience of them as belief and imagination to the surface being. This is a possible account, if we accept Consciousness as the real creative Power or agent and all things as formations of consciousness; but it would not give to the supraphysical planes of being the unsubstantiality or less palpable reality which the physical mind would like to attach to them; they would have the same reality in themselves as the physical world or plane of physical experience has in its own order.

If in this or some other way the higher worlds were developed subsequently to the creation of the material world, the primary creation, by a larger secret evolution out of the Inconscient, it must have been done by some All-Soul in its emergence, by a process of which we can have no knowledge and for the purpose of the evolution here, as adjuncts to it or as its larger consequences, so that life and mind and spirit might be able to move in fields of a freer scope with a repercussion of these greater powers and experiences on the material self-expression. But against this hypothesis there stands the fact that we find these higher worlds in our vision and experience of them to be in no way based upon the material universe, in no way its results, but rather greater terms of being, larger and freer ranges of consciousness, and all the action of the material plane looks more like the result and not the origin of these greater terms, derivatory from them, even partly dependent on them in its evolutionary endeavour. Immense ranges of powers, influences, phenomena descend covertly upon us from the Overmind and the higher mental and vital ranges, but of these only a part, a selection, as it were, or restricted number can stage and realise themselves in the order of the physical world; the rest await their time and proper circumstance for revelation in physical term and form, for their part in the terrestrial[5]evolution which is at the same time an evolution of all the powers of the Spirit.

This character of the other worlds defeats all our attempts to give the premier importance to our own plane of being and to our own part in the mundane manifestation. We do not create God as a myth of our consciousness, but are instruments for a progressive manifestation of the Divine in the material being. We do not create the gods, his powers, but rather such divinity as we manifest is the partial reflection and the shaping here of eternal godheads. We do not create the higher planes, but are intermediaries by which they reveal their light, power, beauty in whatever form and scope can be given to them by Nature-force on the material plane. It is the pressure of the Life-world which enables life to evolve and develop here in the forms we already know; it is that increasing pressure which drives it to aspire in us to a greater revelation of itself and will one day deliver the mortal from his subjection to the narrow limitations of his present incompetent and restricting physicality. It is the pressure of the Mind-world which evolves and develops mind here and helps us to find a leverage for our mental self-uplifting and expansion, so that we may hope to enlarge continually our self of intelligence and even to break the prison-walls of our matter-bound physical mentality. It is the pressure of the supramental and spiritual worlds which is preparing to develop here the manifest power of the Spirit and by it open our being on the physical plane into the freedom and infinity of the super-conscient Divine; that contact, that pressure can alone liberate from the apparent Inconscience, which was our starting-point, the all-conscient Godhead concealed in us. In this order of things our human consciousness is the instrument, the intermediary; it is the point in the development of light and power out of the Inconscience at which liberation becomes possible: a greater role than this we cannot attribute to it, but this is great enough, for

[5] Necessarily, by terrestrial we do not mean this one earth and its period of duration, but use earth in the wider root-sense of the Vedantic Prithivi, the earth-principle creating habitations of physical form for the soul.

it makes our humanity all-important for the supreme purpose of evolutionary Nature.

At the same time there are some elements in our subliminal experience which raise a point of question against any invariable priority of the other worlds to the material existence. One such indication is that in the vision of after-death experience there is a persistent tradition of residence in conditions which seem to be a supraphysical prolongation of earth-conditions, earth-nature, earth-experience. Another is that, in the Life-worlds especially, we find formulations which seem to resemble the inferior movements of earth-existence; here are already embodied the principles of darkness, falsehood, incapacity and evil which we have supposed to be consequent upon the evolution out of the material Inconscience. It seems even to be the fact that the vital worlds are the natural home of the Powers that most disturb human life; this is indeed logical, for it is through our vital being that they sway us and they must therefore be powers of a larger and more powerful life-existence. The descent of Mind and Life into evolution need not have created any such untoward developments of the limitation of being and consciousness: for this descent is in its nature a limitation of knowledge; existence and cognition and delight of being confine themselves in a lesser truth and good and beauty and its inferior harmony, and move according to that law of a narrower light, but in such a movement darkness and suffering and evil are not obligatory phenomena. If we find them existing in these worlds of other mind and other life, even though not pervading it but only occupying their separate province, we must either conclude that they have come into existence by a projection out of the inferior evolution, upward from below, by something in the subliminal parts of Nature bursting there into a larger formation of the evil created here, or that they were already created as part of a parallel gradation to the involutionary descent, a gradation forming a stair for evolutionary ascension towards Spirit just as the involutionary was a stair of the descent of the Spirit. In the latter hypothesis the ascending gradation might have a double purpose. For it would contain pre-formations of the good and evil that must evolve in the earth as part of the struggle necessary for the evolutionary growth of the Soul in Nature; these would be formations existing for themselves, for their own independent satisfaction, formations that would present the full type of these things, each in its separate nature, and at the same time they would exercise on evolutionary beings their characteristic influence.

These worlds of a larger Life would then hold in themselves both the more luminous and the darker formations of our world's life in a medium in which they could arrive freely at their independent expression, their own type's full freedom and natural completeness and harmony for good or for evil, — if indeed that distinction applies in these ranges, — a completeness and independence impossible here in our existence where all is mingled in the complex interaction necessary to the field of a many-sided evolution leading towards a final integration. For we find what we call false, dark or evil seems there to have a truth of its own and to be entirely content with its own type because it possesses that in a full expression which creates in it a sense of a satisfied power of its own being, an accord, a complete adaptation of all its circumstances to its principle of existence; it enjoys there its own consciousness, its own self-power, its own delight of being, obnoxious to our minds but to itself full of the joy of satisfied desire. Those life impulses which are to earth-nature inordinate and out of measure and appear here as perverse and abnormal, find in their own province of being an independent fulfilment and an unrestricted play of their type and principle. What is to us divine or titanic, Rakshasic, demoniac and therefore supernatural, is, each in its own domain, normal to itself and gives to the beings that embody these things the feeling of self-nature and the harmony of their own principle. Discord itself, struggle, incapacity, suffering enter into a certain kind of life-satisfaction which would feel itself baulked or deficient without them. When these powers are seen in their isolated working, building their own life-edifices, as they do in those secret worlds where they dominate, we perceive more clearly their origin and reason of existence and the reason also for the hold they have on human life and the attachment of man to his own imperfections, to his life-drama of victory and failure, happiness and suffering, laughter and tears, sin and virtue. Here on earth these things exist in an unsatisfied and therefore unsatisfactory and obscure state of struggle and mixture, but there reveal their secret and their motive of being because they are there established in their native power and full form of nature in their own world and their own exclusive atmosphere. Man's heavens and hells or worlds of light and worlds of darkness, however imaginative in their building, proceed from a perception of these powers existing in their own principle and throwing their influences on him in life from a beyond-life which provides the elements of his evolutionary existence.

In the same way as the powers of Life are self-founded, perfect and full in a greater Life beyond us, so too the powers of Mind, its ideas and principles that influence our earth-being, are found to have in the greater Mind-world their own field of fullness of self-nature, while here in human existence they throw out only partial formations which have much difficulty in establishing themselves because of their meeting and mixture with other powers and principles; this meeting, this mixture curbs their completeness, alloys their purity, disputes and defeats their influence. These other worlds, then, are not evolutionary, but typal; but it is one though not the sole reason of their existence that they provide things that must arise in the involutionary manifestation as well as things thrown up in the evolution with a field of satisfaction of their own significance where they can exist in their own right; this established condition is a base from which their functions and workings can be cast as elements into the complex process of evolutionary Nature.

If we look from this point of view at man's traditional accounts of other-worldly existence, we shall find that mostly they point to worlds of a larger Life liberated from the restrictions and imperfections or incompletenesses of Life in earth-nature. These accounts are evidently built largely by imagination, but there is an element also of intuition and divination, a feeling of what Life can be and surely is in some domain of its manifested or its realisable nature; there is also an element of true subliminal contact and experience. But the mind of man translates what he sees or receives or contacts from other-nature into figures proper to his own consciousness; they are his translations of supraphysical realities into his own significant forms and images and through these forms and images he enters into communication with the realities and can make them to a certain degree present and effective. The experience of an after-death continuance of a modified earth-life may be explained as due to this kind of translation; but it is also explainable partly as the creation of a subjective post-mortal state in which he still lives in figures of habitual experience before he enters into other-worldly realities, partly as a passage through Life-worlds where the type of things expresses itself in formations originative of those to which he was attached in his earthly body or akin to them and therefore exercises a natural attraction on the vital being after its exit from the body. But, apart from these subtler Life-states, the traditional accounts of other-worldly existence contain, though as a rarer more elevated element not included in the popular notion of these things, a higher grade of states of existence which are clearly of a mental and not a vital character and others founded on some spiritual-mental principle; these higher principles are formulated in states of being into which our inner experience can rise or the soul enter. The principle of gradation we have accepted is therefore justified provided we recognise that it is one way of organising our experience and that other ways proceeding from other viewpoints are possible. For a classification can always be valid from the principle and viewpoint adopted by it while from other principles and viewpoints another classification of the same things can be equally valid. But for our purpose the system we have chosen is of the greatest value because it is fundamental and answers to a truth of the manifestation which is of the utmost practical importance; it helps us to understand our own constituted existence and the course of the involution and the evolutionary motion of Nature. At the same time we see that the other worlds are not things quite apart from the material universe and earth-nature, but penetrate and envelop it with their influences and have on it a secret incidence of formative and directive force which is not easily calculable. This organisation of our other-worldly knowledge and experience supplies us with the clue to the nature and lines of action of this incidence.

The existence and influence of other worlds are a fact of primary importance for the possibilities and for the scope of our evolution in terrestrial Nature. For if the physical universe were the only field of manifestation of the infinite Reality and at the same time the field of its whole manifestation, we should have to suppose that, since all the principles of its being from Matter to Spirit are entirely involved in the apparently inconscient Force which is the basis of the first workings of this universe, they are being evolved by it here completely and here solely, without any other aid or pressure except that of the secret Superconscience within it. There would then be a system of things in which the principle of Matter must always remain the first principle, the essential and original determining condition of manifested existence. Spirit might indeed in the end arrive to a limited extent at its natural domination; it might make its basis of physical matter a more elastic instrument not altogether prohibitive of the action of its own highest law and nature or opposed to that action, as it now is in its inelastic resistance. But Spirit would always be dependent upon Matter for its field and its manifestation; it could have no other field: it could not get outside it to another kind of manifestation; and within it also it could not very well liberate any other principle of its being into sovereignty over the material foundation; Matter would remain the one persistent determinant of its manifestation. Life could not become dominant and determinative, Mind could not become the master and creator; their boundaries of capacity would be fixed by the capacities of Matter, which they might enlarge or modify but would not be able to transform radically or liberate. There would be no place for any free and full manifestation of any power of the being, all would be limited for ever by the conditions of an obscuring material formation. Spirit, Mind, Life would have no native field or complete scope of their own characteristic power and principle. It is not easy to believe in the inevitability of this self-limitation if Spirit is the creator and these principles have an independent existence and are not products, results or phenomena of the energy of Matter.

But, given the fact that the infinite Reality is free in the play of its consciousness, it is not bound to involve itself in the nescience of Matter before it can at all manifest. It is possible for it to create just the contrary order of things, a world in which the unity of spiritual being is the matrix and first condition of any formation or action, the Energy at work is a self-aware spiritual existence in movement, and all its names and forms are a self-conscious play of the spiritual unity. Or it might be an order in which the Spirit's innate power of conscious Force or Will would realise freely and directly its own possibilities in itself and not, as here, through the restricting medium of the Life-Force in matter; that realisation would be at once the first principle of the manifestation and the object of all its free and blissful action. It might be an order, again, in which the free play of an infinite mutual self-delight in a multiplicity of beings conscious not only of their concealed or underlying eternal unity but of their present joy of oneness would be the object; in such a system the action of the principle of self-existent Bliss would be the first principle and the universal condition. Again, it might be a world-order in which the Supermind would be the dominant principle from the beginning; the nature of the manifestation would then be a multiplicity of beings finding through the free and luminous play of their divine individuality all the manifold joy of their difference in oneness.

Nor need the series stop here: for we observe that with us Mind is hampered by Life in Matter and finds all the difficulty possible in dominating the resistance of these two different powers and that Life itself is similarly restricted by the mortality, the inertia and the instability of Matter; but evidently there can be a world-order in which neither of these two disabilities forms part of the first conditions of existence. There is the possibility of a world in which Mind would be from the first dominant, free to work upon its own substance or matter as a quite plastic material, or where Matter would be quite evidently the result of the universal Mind-Force working itself out in life. It is that even here in reality; but here the Mind-Force is involved from the beginning, for a long time subconscient, and, even when it has emerged, never in free possession of itself, but subject to its encasing material, while there it would be in possession of itself and master of its material, which would be much more subtle and elastic than in a predominantly physical universe. So too Life might have its own world-order where it would be sovereign, able to deploy its own more elastic and freely variable desires and tendencies, not menaced at every moment by disintegrating forces and therefore occupied chiefly with the care of self-preservation and restricted in its play by this state of precarious tension which limits its instincts of free formation, free self-gratification and free adventure. The separate dominance of each principle of being is an eternal possibility in the manifestation of being, — given always that they are principles distinct in their dynamic power and mode of working, even though one in original substance.

That could make no difference if all this were only a philosophical possibility or a potentiality in the being of Sachchidananda which it never realises or has not yet realised, or, if realised, has not brought within the scope of the consciousness of beings living in the physical universe. But all our spiritual and psychic experience bears affirmative witness, brings us always a constant and, in its main principles, an invariable evidence of the existence of higher worlds, freer planes of existence. Not having bound ourselves down, like so much of modern thought, to the dogma that only physical experience or experience based upon the physical sense is true, the analysis of physical experience by the reason alone verifiable, and all else only result of physical experience and physical existence and anything beyond this an error, self-delusion and hallucination, we are free to accept this evidence and to admit the reality of these planes. We see that they are, practically, different harmonies from the harmony of the physical universe; they occupy, as the word "plane" suggests, a different level in the scale of being and adopt a different system and ordering of its principles. We need not inquire, for our present purpose, whether they coincide in time and space with our own world or move in a different field of space and in another stream of time, — in either case it is in a more subtle substance and with other movements. All that directly concerns us is to know whether they are different universes, each complete in itself and in no way meeting, intercrossing or affecting the others, or are rather different scales of one graded and interwoven system of being, parts therefore of one complex universal system. The fact that they can enter into the field of our mental consciousness would naturally suggest the validity of the second alternative, but it would not by itself be altogether conclusive. But what we find is that these higher planes are actually at every moment acting upon and in communication with our own plane of being, although this action is naturally not present to our ordinary waking or outer consciousness, because that is for the most part limited to a reception and utilisation of the contacts of the physical world: but the moment we either go back into our subliminal being or enlarge our waking consciousness beyond the scope of the physical contacts, we become aware of something of this higher action. We find even that the human being can project himself partially into these higher planes under certain conditions, even while in the body; *a fortiori* must he be able to do it when out of the body, and to do it then completely, since there is no longer the disabling condition of the physical life bound down to the body. The consequences of this relation and this power of transference are of immense importance. On the one side they immediately justify, at any rate as an actual possibility, the ancient tradition of at least a temporary sojourn of the human conscious being in other worlds than the physical after the dissolution of the physical body. On the other side they open to us the possibility of an action of the higher planes on the material existence which can liberate the powers they represent, the powers of life, mind and spirit for the evolutionary intention inherent within Nature by the very fact of their embodiment in Matter.

These worlds are not in their original creation subsequent in order to the physical universe but prior to it, — prior, if not in time, in their consequential sequence. For even if there is an ascending as well as a descending gradation, this ascending gradation must be in its first nature a provision for the evolutionary emergence in Matter, a formative power for its endeavour, contributing to it helpful and adverse elements, and not a mere consequence of the terrestrial evolution; for that is neither a rational probability nor has it a spiritual or dynamic and pragmatic sense. In other words, the higher worlds have not come into being by a pressure from the lower physical universe, — let us say, from Sachchidananda in the physical Inconscience, or else by the urge of his being as it emerges from the Inconscience into Life and Mind and Spirit and experiences the necessity of creating worlds or planes in which those principles shall have a freer play and in which the human soul may strengthen its vital, mental or spiritual tendencies. Still less are they the creations of the human soul itself, whether its dreams or the result of the constant self-projections of mankind in its dynamic and creative being beyond the limits of the physical consciousness. The only thing that man clearly creates in this direction is the reflex images of these planes in his own embodied consciousness and the fitness of his own soul to respond to them, to become aware of them, to participate consciously in the interweaving of their influences with the action of the physical plane. He may indeed contribute the results or projections of his own higher vital and mental action to the action of these planes: but, if so, these projections are, after all, only a return of the higher planes upon themselves, a return from the earth of their powers which have come down from them to the earth-mind, since this higher vital and mental action is itself the result of influences transmitted from above. It is possible also that he can create a certain kind of subjective annexe to these supraphysical planes, or at least to the lower of them, environments of a half-unreal character which are rather self-created envelopes of his conscious mind and life than true worlds; they are the reflections of his own being, an artificial environment corresponding to his attempt during life to image these other worlds, — heavens and hells projected by the image-creating faculty in his human power of conscious being. But neither of these two contributions at all means a total creation of a real plane of being founded and acting on its own separate principle.

These planes or systems are then at least coeval and co-existent with that which presents itself to us as the physical universe. We have been led to conclude that the development of Life, Mind and Spirit in the physical being presupposes their existence; for these powers are developed here by two co-operating forces, an upward-tending force from below, an upward-drawing and downward-pressing force from above. For there is the necessity in the Inconscient of bringing out what is latent within it, and there is the pressure of the superior principles in the higher planes which not only aids this general necessity to realise itself, but may very largely determine the special ways in which it is eventually realised. It is this upward-drawing action and this pressure, this insistence from above, which explain the constant influence of the spiritual, mental and vital worlds upon the physical plane. It is evident that, given a complex universe and seven principles interwoven in every part of its system and naturally therefore drawn to act upon and respond to each other wherever they can at all get at one another, such an action, such a constant pressure and influence, is an inevitable consequence, must be inherent in the very nature of the manifested universe.

A secret continuous action of the higher powers and principles from their own planes upon terrestrial being and nature through the subliminal self, which is itself a projection from those planes into the world born of the Inconscience, must have an effect and a significance. Its first effect has been the liberation of Life and Mind out of Matter; its last effect has been to assist the emergence of a spiritual consciousness, a spiritual will and spiritual sense of existence in the terrestrial being so that he is no longer solely preoccupied with his outermost life or with that and mental pursuits and interests, but has learned to look within, to discover his inner being, his spiritual self, to aspire to overpass earth and her limitations. As he grows more and more inward, his boundaries mental, vital, spiritual begin to broaden, the bonds that held Life, Mind, Soul to their first limitations loosen or snap, and man the mental being begins to have a glimpse of a larger kingdom of self and world closed to the first earth-life. No doubt, so long as he lives mainly on his surface, he can only build a sort of superstructure ideal and imaginative and ideative upon the ground of his normal narrow existence. But if he makes the inward movement which his own highest vision has held up before him as his greatest spiritual necessity, then he will find there in his inner being a larger Consciousness, a larger Life. An action from within and an action from above can overcome the predominance of the material formula, diminish and finally put an end to the power of the Inconscience, reverse the order of the consciousness, substitute the Spirit for Matter as his conscious foundation of being and liberate its higher powers to their complete and characteristic expression in the life of the soul embodied in Nature.

Chapter XXII

Rebirth and Other Worlds; Karma, the Soul and Immortality

He passes in his departure from this world to the physical Self; he passes to the Self of life; he passes to the Self of mind; he passes to the Self of knowledge; he passes to the Self of bliss; he moves through these worlds at will.

Taittiriya Upanishad.[1]

They say indeed that the conscious being is made of desire. But of whatsoever desire he comes to be, he comes to be of that will, and of whatever will he comes to be, he does that action, and whatever his action, to (the result of) that he reaches.... Adhered to by his Karma,[2] he goes in his subtle body to wherever his mind cleaves, then, coming to the end of his Karma, even of whatsoever action he does here, he returns from that world to this world for Karma.

Brihadaranyaka Upanishad.[3]

Equipped with qualities, a doer of works and creator of their consequences, he reaps the result of his actions; he is the ruler of the life and he moves in his journey according to his own acts; he has idea and ego and is to be known by the qualities of his intelligence and his quality of self. Smaller than the hundredth part of the tip of a hair, the soul of the living being is capable of infinity. Male is he not nor female nor neuter, but is joined to whatever body he takes as his own.

Swetaswatara Upanishad.[4]

---

[1] III. 10. 5.   [2] Action, *karma*. In the view expressed in this verse of the Upanishad the Karma or action of this life is exhausted by the life in the world beyond in which its results are fulfilled and the soul returns to earth for fresh Karma. The cause of birth in this world, of Karma, of the soul's passage to other-world existence and its return here is, throughout, the soul's own consciousness, will and desire.
[3] IV. 4. 5, 6.   [4] V. 7-10.

Mortals, they achieved immortality.   *Rig Veda.*[5]

OUR FIRST conclusion on the subject of reincarnation
has been that the rebirth of the soul in successive terrestrial bodies is an inevitable consequence of the original
significance and process of the manifestation in earth-nature;
but this conclusion leads to farther problems and farther results
which it is necessary to elucidate. There arises first the question
of the process of rebirth; if that process is not quickly successive,
birth immediately following death of the body so as to maintain
an uninterrupted series of lives of the same person, if there are
intervals, that in its turn raises the question of the principle
and process of the passage to other worlds, which must be the
scene of these intervals, and the return to earth-life. A third
question is the process of the spiritual evolution itself and the
mutations which the soul undergoes in its passage from birth to
birth through the stages of its adventure.

If the physical universe were the sole manifested world, or
if it were a quite separate world, rebirth as a part of the evolutionary process would be confined to a constant succession of
direct transmigrations from one body to another; death would
be immediately followed by a new birth without any possibility
of an interval, — the passage of the soul would be a spiritual
circumstance in the uninterrupted series of a compulsory, mechanical, material procedure. The soul would have no freedom
from Matter; it would be perpetually bound to its instrument,
the body, and dependent on it for the continuity of its manifested
existence. But we have found that there is a life on other planes
after death and before the subsequent rebirth, a life consequent
on the old and preparatory of the new stage of terrestrial existence. Other planes co-exist with ours, are part of one complex
system and act constantly upon the physical which is their own
final and lowest term, receive its reactions, admit a secret communication and commerce. Man can become conscious of these

[5] I. 110. 4.

planes, can even in certain states project his conscious being into them, partly in life, presumably therefore with a full completeness after the dissolution of the body. Such a possibility of projection into other worlds or planes of being becomes then sufficiently actual to necessitate practically its own realisation, immediately and perhaps invariably following on human earth-life if man is from the beginning endowed with such a power of self-transference, eventual if he only arrives at it by a gradual progression. For it is possible that at the beginning he would not be sufficiently developed to carry on his life or his mind into larger Life-worlds or Mind-worlds and would be compelled to accept an immediate transmigration from one earthly body to another as his only present possibility of persistence.

The necessity for an interregnum between birth and birth and a passage to other worlds arises from a double cause: there is an attraction of the other planes for the mental and the vital being in man's composite nature due to their affinity with these levels, and there is the utility or even the need of an interval for assimilation of the completed life-experience, a working out of what has to be discarded, a preparation for the new embodiment and the new terrestrial experience. But this need of a period of assimilation and this attraction of other worlds for kindred parts of our being may become effective only when the mental and vital individuality has been sufficiently developed in the half-animal physical man; until then they might not exist or might not be active: the life experiences would be too simple and elementary to need assimilation and the natural being too crude to be capable of a complex assimilative process; the higher parts would not be sufficiently developed to lift themselves to higher planes of existence. There can be, then, in the absence of such connections with other worlds, a theory of rebirth which admits only of a constant transmigration; here the existence of other worlds and the sojourn of the soul in other planes are not an actual or at any stage a necessary part of the system. There can be another theory in which this passage is the obligatory rule for all and there is no immediate rebirth; the soul needs an interval of preparation for the new incarnation and new experience. A compromise between the two theories is also possible; the transmigration may be the first rule prevailing while the soul is yet unripe for a higher world-existence; the passage to other planes would be the subsequent law. There may even be a third stage, as is sometimes suggested, in which the soul is so powerfully developed, its natural parts so spiritually alive that it needs no interval, but can immediately resume birth for a more rapid evolution without the retardation of a period of intermittence.

In the popular ideas which derive from the religions that admit reincarnation, there is an inconsistency which, after the manner of popular beliefs, they have been at no pains to reconcile. On the one hand, there is the belief, vague enough but fairly general, that death is followed immediately or with something like immediateness by the assumption of another body. On the other hand, there is the old religious dogma of a life after death in hells and heavens or, it may be, in other worlds or degrees of being, which the soul has acquired or incurred by its merits or demerits in this physical existence; the return to earth intervenes only when that merit and demerit are exhausted and the being is ready for another terrestrial life. This inconsistency would disappear if we admit a variable movement dependent on the stage of evolution which the soul has reached in its manifestation in Nature; all would then turn on the degree of its capacity for entering a higher status than the earthly life. But in the ordinary notion of reincarnation the idea of a spiritual evolution is not explicit, it is only implied in the fact that the soul has to reach the point at which it becomes capable of transcending the necessity of rebirth and returning to its eternal source; but if there is no gradual and graded evolution, this point can be as well reached by a chaotic zigzag movement of which the law is not easily determinable. The definitive solution of the question depends on psychic inquiry and experience; here we can only consider whether there is in the nature of things or in the logic of the evolutionary process any apparent or inherent necessity for either movement, for the immediate transition from body to body or for the retardation or interval before a new reincarnation of the self-embodying psychic principle.

A sort of half necessity for the life in other worlds, a dynamic and practical rather than an essential necessity, arises from the very fact that the different world-principles are interwoven with each other and in a way interdependent and the effect that this fact must have upon the process of our spiritual evolution. But this might be counteracted for a time by the greater pull or attraction of the earth or the preponderant physicality of the evolving nature. Our belief in the birth of an ascending soul into the human form and its repeated rebirth in that form, without which it cannot complete its human evolution, rests, from the point of view of the reasoning intelligence, on the basis that the progressive transit of the soul into higher and higher grades of the earthly existence and, once it has reached the human level, its repeated human birth compose a sequence necessary for the growth of the nature; one brief human life upon earth is evidently insufficient for the evolutionary purpose. In the early stages of a series of human reincarnations, during a period of rudimentary humanity, there is a certain possibility at first sight of an often repeated immediate transmigration, — the repeated assumption of a new human form in a fresh birth immediately the previous body has been dissolved by a cessation or expulsion of the organised Life-energy and the consequent physical disintegration which we call death. But what necessity of the evolutionary process would compel such a series of immediate rebirths? Evidently, it could only be imperative so long as the psychic individuality, — not the secret soul-entity itself but the soul-formation in the natural being, — is little evolved, insufficiently developed, so insufficiently formed that it could not abide except by dependence upon the uninterrupted continuance of this life's mental, vital and physical individuality: unable as yet to persist in itself, discard its past Mind-formation and Life-formation and build after a useful interval new formations, it would be obliged to transfer at once its rudimentary crude personality for preservation to a new body. It is doubtful whether we should be justified in attributing any such entirely insufficient development to a being so strongly individualised that it has got as far as the human consciousness. Even at his lowest normality the human individual is still a soul acting through a distinct mental being, however ill-formed his mind may be, however limited and dwarfed, however engrossed and encased in the physical and vital consciousness and unable or unwilling to detach itself from its lower formations. Yet we may suppose that there is a downward attachment so strong as to compel the being to hasten at once to a resumption of the physical life because his natural formation is not really fit for anything else or at home on any higher plane. Or, again, the life-experience might be so brief and incomplete as to compel the soul to an immediate rebirth for its continuance. Other needs, influences or causes there may be in the complexity of Nature-process, such as a strong will of earthly desire pressing for fulfilment, which would enforce an immediate transmigration of the same persistent form of personality into a new body. But still the alternative process of a reincarnation, a rebirth of the Person not only into a new body but into a new formation of the personality, would be the normal line taken by the psychic entity once it had reached the human stage of its evolutionary cycle.

For the soul personality, as it develops, must get sufficient power over its own nature-formation and a sufficient self-expressive mental and vital individuality to persist without the support of the material body, as well as to overcome any excessive detaining attachment to the physical plane and the physical life: it would be sufficiently evolved to subsist in the subtle body which we know to be the characteristic case or sheath and the proper subtle-physical support of the inner being. It is the soul-person, the psychic being, that survives and carries mind and life with it on its journey, and it is in the subtle body that it passes out of its material lodging; both then must be sufficiently developed for the transit. But a transference to planes of Mind-existence or Life-existence implies also a mind and life sufficiently formed and developed to pass without disintegration and exist for a time on these higher levels. If these conditions were satisfied, a sufficiently developed psychic personality and subtle body and a sufficiently developed mental and vital personality, survival of the soul-person without an immediate new birth would be secured and the pull of the other worlds would become operative. But this by itself would mean a return to earth with the same mental and vital personality and there would be no free evolution in the new birth. There must be an individuation of the psychic person itself sufficient for it not to depend on its past mind and life formations any more than on its past body, but to shed them too in time and proceed to a new formation for new experience. For this discarding of the old and preparation of new forms the soul must dwell for some time between two births somewhere else than on the entirely material plane in which we now move; for here there would be no abiding place for a disembodied spirit. A brief stay might indeed be possible if there are subtle envelopes of the earth-existence which belong to earth but are of a vital or mental character: but even then there would be no reason for the soul to linger there for a long period, unless it is still burdened with an overpowering attachment to the earth-life. A survival of the material body by the personality implies a supraphysical existence, and this can only be in some plane of being proper to the evolutionary stage of the consciousness or, if there is no evolution, in a temporary second home of the spirit which would be its natural place of sojourn between life and life, — unless indeed it is its original world from which it does not return into material Nature.

Where then would the temporary dwelling in the supraphysical take place? what would be the soul's other habitat? It might seem that it ought to be on a mental plane, in mental worlds, both because on man the mental being the attraction of that plane, already active in life, must prevail when there is not the obstacle of the attachment to the body, and because the mental plane should be, evidently, the native and proper habitat of a mental being. But this does not automatically follow, because of the complexity of man's being; he has a vital as well as a mental existence, — his vital part often more powerful and prominent than the mental, — and behind the mental being is a soul of which it is the representative. There are, besides, many planes or levels of world-existence and the soul has to pass through them to reach its natural home. In the physical plane itself or close to it there are believed to be layers of greater and greater subtlety which may be regarded as sub-planes of the physical with a vital and a mental character; these are at once surrounding and penetrating strata through which the interchange between the higher worlds and the physical world takes place. It might then be possible for the mental being, so long as its mentality is not sufficiently developed, so long as it is restricted mainly to the more physical forms of mind and life activity, to be caught and delayed in these media. It might even be obliged to rest there entirely between birth and birth; but this is not probable and could only happen if and in so far as its attachment to the earth-forms of its activity was so great as to preclude or hamper the completion of the natural upward movement. For the post-mortal state of the soul must correspond in some way to the development of the being on earth, since this after-life is not a free upward return from a temporary downward deviation into mortality, but a normal recurrent circumstance which intervenes to help out the process of a difficult spiritual evolution in the physical existence. There is a relation which the human being in his evolution on earth develops with higher planes of exis-tence, and that must have a predominant effect on his internatal dwelling in these planes; it must determine his direction after death and determine too the place, period and character of his self-experience there.

It may be also that he may linger for a time in one of those annexes of the other worlds created by his habitual beliefs or by the type of his aspirations in the mortal body. We know that he creates images of these superior planes, which are often mental translations of certain elements in them, and erects his images into a system, a form of actual worlds; he builds up also desire-worlds of many kinds to which he attaches a strong sense of inner reality: it is possible that these constructions may be so strong as to create for him an artificial post-mortal environment in which he may linger. For the image-making power of the human mind, its imagination, which is in his physical life only an indispensable aid to his acquisition of knowledge and his life-creation, may in a higher scale become a creative force which would enable the mental being to live for a while amid its own images until they were dissolved by the soul's pressure. All these buildings are of the nature of larger Life-constructions; in them his mind translates some of the real conditions of the greater mental and vital worlds into terms of his physical experience magnified, prolonged, extended to a condition beyond physicality: he carries by this translation the vital joy and vital suffering of the physical being into supraphysical conditions in which they have a greater scope, fullness and endurance. These constructive environments must therefore be considered, so far as they have any supraphysical habitat, as annexes of the vital or of the lower mental planes of existence.

But there are also the true vital worlds, — original constructions, organised developments, native habitats of the universal Life-principle, the cosmic vital Anima, acting in its own field and in its own nature. On his internatal journey he may be held there for a period by force of the predominantly vital character of the influences which have shaped his earthly existence, — for these influences are native to the vital world and their hold on him would detain him for a while in their proper province: he may be kept in the grasp of that which held him in its grasp even in the physical being. Any residence of the soul in annexes or in its own constructions could be only a transitional stage of the consciousness in its passage from the physical to the supraphysical state; it must pass from these structures into the true worlds of supraphysical Nature. It may enter at once into the worlds of other-life, or it may remain first, as a transitional stage, in some region of subtle-physical experience whose surroundings may seem to it a prolongation of the circumstances of physical life, but in freer conditions proper to a subtler medium and in some kind of happy perfection of mind or life or a finer bodily existence. Beyond these subtle-physical planes of experience and the life-worlds there are also mental or spiritual-mental planes to which the soul seems to have an internatal access and into which it may pursue its internatal journey; but it is not likely to live consciously there if there has not been a sufficient mental or soul development in this life. For these levels must normally be the highest the evolving being can internatally inhabit, since one who has not gone beyond the mental rung in the ladder of being would not be able to ascend to any supramental or overmental state; or if he had so developed as to overleap the mental level and could attain so far, it might not be possible for him to return so long as the physical evolution has not developed here an organisation of an overmental or supramental life in Matter.

But, even so, the mental worlds are not likely to be the last normal stage of the after-death passage; for man is not entirely mental; it is the soul, the psychic being, and not the mind, that is the traveller between death and birth, and the mental being is only a predominant element in the figure of its self-expression. There must then be a final resort to a plane of pure psychic existence in which the soul would await rebirth; there it could assimilate the energies of its past experience and life and prepare its future. Ordinarily, the normally developed human being, who has risen to a sufficient power of mentality, might be expected to pass successively through all these planes, subtle-physical, vital and mental, on his way to his psychic habitation. At each stage he would exhaust and get rid of the fractions of formed personality-structure, temporary and superficial, that belonged to the past life; he would cast off his mind-sheath and life-sheath as he had already cast off his body-sheath: but the essence of the personality and its mental, vital and physical experiences would remain in latent memory or as a dynamic potency for the future. But if the development of mind were insufficient, it is possible that it would not be able to go consciously beyond the vital level and the being would either fall back from there, returning from its vital heavens or purgatories to earth, or, more consistently, would pass at once into a kind of psychic assimilative sleep co-extensive with the internatal period; to be awake in the highest planes a certain development would be indispensable.

All this, however, is a matter of dynamic probability, and that, though amounting in practice to a necessity, though justified by certain facts of subliminal experience, is still for the reasoning mind not in itself quite conclusive. We have to ask whether there is any more essential necessity for these internatal intervals, or at least any of so great a dynamic power as to lead to an irresistible conclusion. We shall find one such necessity in the decisive part played by the higher planes in the earth-evolution and the relation that it has created between them and the evolving soul-consciousness. Our development takes place very largely by their superior but hidden action upon the earth-plane. All is contained in the inconscient or the subconscient, but in potentiality; it is the action from above that helps to compel an emergence. A continuance of that action is necessary to shape and determine the progression of the mental and vital forms which our evolution takes in material nature; for these progressive movements cannot find their full momentum or sufficiently develop their implications against the resistance of an inconscient or inert and ignorant material Nature except by a constant though occult resort to higher supraphysical forces of their own character. This resort, the action of this veiled alliance, takes place principally in our subliminal being and not on the surface: it is from there that the active power of our consciousness emerges, and all that it realises it sends back constantly into the subliminal being to be stored up, developed and re-emerge in stronger forms hereafter. This interaction of our larger hidden being and our surface personality is the main secret of the rapid development that operates in man once he has passed beyond the lower stages of Mind immersed in Matter.

This resort must continue in the internatal stage; for a new birth, a new life is not a taking up of the development exactly where it stopped in the last, it does not merely repeat and continue our past surface personality and formation of nature. There is an assimilation, a discarding and strengthening and rearrangement of the old characters and motives, a new ordering of the developments of the past and a selection for the purposes of the future without which the new start cannot be fruitful or carry forward the evolution. For each birth is a new start; it develops indeed from the past, but is not its mechanical continuation: rebirth is not a constant reiteration but a progression, it is the machinery of an evolutionary process.

Part of this rearrangement, the discarding especially of past strong vibrations of the personality, can only be effected by an exhaustion of the push of previous mental, vital, physical motives after death, and this internal liberation or lightening of impedimenta must be put through on the planes proper to the motives that are to be discarded or otherwise manipulated, those planes which are themselves of that nature; for it is only there that the soul can still continue the activities which have to be exhausted and rejected from the consciousness so that it can pass on to a new formation. It is probable also that the integrating positive preparation would be carried out and the character of the new life would be decided by the soul itself in a resort to its native habitat, a plane of psychic repose, where it would draw all back into itself and await its new stage in the evolution. This would mean a passage of the soul progressively through subtle-physical, vital and mental worlds to the psychic dwelling-place from which it would return to its terrestrial pilgrimage. The terrestrial gathering up and development of the materials thus prepared, their working out in the earth-life would be the consequence of this internatal resort, and the new birth would be a field of the resultant activity, a new stadium or spiral curve in the individual evolution of the embodied Spirit.

For when we say that the soul on earth evolves successively the physical, the vital, the mental, the spiritual being, we do not mean that it creates them and that they had no previous existence. On the contrary, what it does is to manifest these principles of its spiritual entity under the conditions imposed by a world of physical Nature; this manifestation takes the form of a structure of frontal personality which is a translation of the inner self into the terms and possibilities of the physical existence. In fact we must accept the ancient idea that man has within him not only the physical soul or Purusha with its appropriate nature, but a vital, a mental, a psychic, a supramental, a supreme spiritual being;[6] and either the whole or the greater presence or force of them is concealed in his subliminal

---

[6] *Taittiriya Upanishad.*

or latent and unformulated in his superconscient parts. He has to bring forward their powers in his active consciousness and to awake to them in its knowledge. But each of these powers of his being is in relation with its own proper plane of existence and all have their roots there. It is through them that there takes place the subliminal resort of the being to the shaping influences from above, a resort which may become more and more conscious as we develop. It is logical then that according to the development of their powers in our conscious evolution should be the internatal resort which this nature of our birth here and its evolutionary object and process necessitate. The circumstances and the stages of that resort must be complex and not of the crudely and trenchantly simple character which the popular religions imagine: but in itself it can be accepted as an inevitable consequence of the very origin and nature of the soul-life in the body. All is a closely woven web, an evolution and an interaction whose links have been forged by a Conscious-Force following out the truth of its own motives according to a dynamic logic of these finite workings of the Infinite.

If this view of rebirth and the soul's temporary passage into other planes of existence is correct, both rebirth and the after-life assume a different significance from the colour put on them by the long-current belief about reincarnation and the after-death sojourn in worlds beyond us. Reincarnation is commonly supposed to have two aspects, metaphysical and moral, an aspect of spiritual necessity, an aspect of cosmic justice and ethical discipline. The soul, — in this view or for this purpose supposed to have a real individual existence, — is on earth as a result of desire and ignorance; it has to remain on earth or return to it always so long as it has not wearied of desire and awakened to the fact of its ignorance and to the true knowledge. This desire compels it to return always to a new body; it must follow always the revolving wheel of birth till it is enlightened and liberated. It does not, however, remain always on earth, but alternates between earth and other worlds, celestial and infernal, where it exhausts its accumulated store of merit or demerit due to the enactment of sin or virtue and then returns to the earth and to some kind of terrestrial body, sometimes human, sometimes animal, sometimes even vegetable. The nature of this new incarnation and its fortunes are determined automatically by the soul's past actions, Karma; if the sum of past actions was good, the birth is in the higher form, the life happy or successful or unaccountably fortunate; if bad, a lower form of Nature may house us or the life, if human, will be unhappy, unsuccessful, full of suffering and misfortune. If our past actions and character were mixed, then Nature, like a good accountant, gives us, according to the pitch and values of our former conduct, a well-assorted payment of mixed happiness and suffering, success and failure, the rarest good luck and the severest ill-fortune. At the same time a strong personal will or desire in the past life may also determine our new avatar. A mathematical aspect is often given to these payments of Nature, for we are supposed to incur a precise penalty for our misdeeds, undergo or return the replica or equivalent of what we have inflicted or enacted; the inexorable rule of a tooth for a tooth is a frequent principle of the Karmic Law: for this Law is an arithmetician with his abacus as well as a judge with his code of penalties for long-past crimes and misdemeanours. It is also to be noted that in this system there is a double punishment and a double reward for sin and virtue; for the sinner is first tortured in hell and afterwards afflicted for the same sins in another life here and the righteous or the puritan is rewarded with celestial joys and afterwards again pampered for the same virtues and good deeds in a new terrestrial existence.

These are very summary popular notions and offer no foothold to the philosophic reason and no answer to a search for the true significance of life. A vast world-system which exists only as a convenience for turning endlessly on a wheel of Ignorance with no issue except a final chance of stepping out of it, is not a world with any real reason for existence. A world which serves only as a school of sin and virtue and consists of a system of rewards and whippings, does not make any better appeal to our intelligence. The soul or spirit within us, if it is divine, immortal or celestial, cannot be sent here solely to be put to school for this kind of crude and primitive moral education; if it enters into the Ignorance, it must be because there is some larger principle or possibility of its being that has to be worked out through the Ignorance. If, on the other hand, it is a being from the Infinite plunged for some cosmic purpose into the obscurity of Matter and growing to self-knowledge within it, its life here and the significance of that life must be something more than that of an infant coddled and whipped into virtuous ways; it must be a growth out of an assumed ignorance towards its own full spiritual stature with a final passage into an immortal consciousness, knowledge, strength, beauty, divine purity and power, and for such a spiritual growth this law of Karma is all too puerile. Even if the soul is something created, an infant being that has to learn from Nature and grow into immortality, it must be by a larger law of growth and not by some divine code of primitive and barbaric justice. This idea of Karma is a construction of the smaller part of the human vital mind concerned with its petty rules of life and its desires and joys and sorrows and erecting their puny standards into the law and aim of the cosmos. These notions cannot be acceptable to the thinking mind; they have too evidently the stamp of a construction fashioned by our human ignorance.

But the same solution can be elevated to a higher level of reason and given a greater plausibility and the colour of a cosmic principle. For, first, it may be based on the unassailable ground that all energies in Nature must have their natural consequence; if any are without visible result in the present life, it may well be that the outcome is only delayed, not withheld for ever. Each being reaps the harvest of his works and deeds, the returns of the action put forth by the energies of his nature, and those which are not apparent in his present birth must be held over for a subsequent existence. It is true that the result of the energies and actions of the individual may accrue not to himself but to others when he is gone; for that we see constantly happening, — it happens indeed even during a man's lifetime that the fruits of his energies are reaped by others; but this is because there is a solidarity and a continuity of life in Nature and the individual cannot altogether, even if he so wills, live for himself alone. But, if there is a continuity of his own life by rebirth for the individual and not only a continuity of the mass-life and the cosmic life, if he has an ever-developing self, nature and experience, then it is inevitable that for him too the working of his energies should not be cut off abruptly but must bear their consequence at some time in his continuous and developing existence. Man's being, nature, circumstances of life are the result of his own inner and outer activities, not something fortuitous and inexplicable: he is what he has made himself; the past man was the father of the man that now is, the present man is the father of the man that will be. Each being reaps what he sows; from what he does he profits, for what he does he suffers. This is the law and chain of Karma, of Action, of the work of Nature-Energy, and it gives a meaning to the total force of our existence, nature, character, action which is absent from other theories of life. It is evident on this principle that a man's past and present Karma must determine his future birth and its happenings and circumstances; for these too must be the fruit of his energies: all that he was and did in the past must be the creator of all that he now is and experiences in his present, and all that he is and is doing in the present must be the creator of what he will be and experience in the future. Man is the creator of himself; he is the creator also of his fate. All this is perfectly rational and unexceptionable so far as it goes and the law of Karma may be accepted as a fact, as part of the cosmic machinery; for it is so evident, — rebirth once admitted, — as to be practically indisputable.

There are, however, two riders to this first proposition which are less general and authentic and bring in a doubtful note; for though they may be true in part, they are overstated and create a wrong perspective, because they are put forward as the whole sense of Karma. The first is that as is the nature of the energies so must be the nature of the results, — the good must bring good results, the evil must bring evil results: the second is that the master word of Karma is justice and therefore good deeds must bear the fruit of happiness and good fortune and evil deeds must bear the fruit of sorrow, misery and ill-fortune. Since there must be a cosmic justice which is looking on and controlling in some way the immediate and visible operations of Nature in life, but is not apparent to us in the facts of life as seen by us, it must be present and evident in the totality of her unseen dealings; it must be the subtle and hardly visible, but strong and firm secret thread that holds together the otherwise incoherent details of her dealings with her creatures. If it be asked why actions alone, good or bad deeds alone, should have a result, it might be conceded that good or evil thoughts, feelings, actions have all their corresponding results, but since action is the greater part of life and the test and formulated power of a man's values of being, since also he is not always responsible for his thoughts and feelings, as they are often involuntary, but is or must be held responsible for what he does, as that is subject to his choice, it is mainly his actions that construct his fate; they are the chief or the most forceful determinants of his being and his future. This is the whole law of Karma.

But we have first to observe that a law or chain of Karma is only an outward machinery and cannot be elevated to a greater position as the sole and absolute determinant of the life-workings of the cosmos, unless the cosmos is itself entirely mechanical in its character. It is indeed held by many that all is Law and Process and there is no conscious Being or Will in or behind the cosmos; if so, here is a Law and Process that satisfies our human reason and our mental standards of right and justice and it has the beauty and truth of a perfect symmetry and a mathematical accuracy of working. But all is not Law and Process, there is also Being and Consciousness; there is not only a machinery but a Spirit in things, not only Nature and law of cosmos but a cosmic Spirit, not only a process of mind and life and body but a soul in the natural creature. If it were not so, there could be no rebirth of a soul and no field for a law of Karma. But if the fundamental truth of our being is spiritual and not mechanical, it must be ourself, our soul that fundamentally determines its own evolution, and the law of Karma can only be one of the processes it uses for that purpose: our Spirit, our Self must be greater than its Karma. There is Law, but there is also spiritual freedom. Law and Process are one side of our existence and their reign is over our outer mind, life and body, for these are mostly subject to the mechanism of Nature. But even here their mechanical power is absolute only over body and Matter; for Law becomes more complex and less rigid, Process more plastic and less mechanical when there comes in the phenomenon of Life, and yet more is this so when Mind intervenes with its subtlety; an inner freedom already begins to intervene and, the more we go within, the soul's power of choice is increasingly felt: for Prakriti is the field of law and process, but the soul, the Purusha, is the giver of the sanction, *anumantā*, and even if ordinarily it chooses to remain a witness and concede an automatic sanction, it can be, if it wills, the master of its nature, Ishwara.

It is not conceivable that the Spirit within is an automaton in the hands of Karma, a slave in this life of its past actions; the truth must be less rigid and more plastic. If a certain amount of results of past Karma is formulated in the present life, it must be with the consent of the psychic being which presides over the new formation of its earth-experience and assents not merely to an outward compulsory process, but to a secret Will and Guidance. That secret Will is not mechanical, but spiritual; the guidance comes from an Intelligence which may use mechanical processes but is not their subject. Self-expression and experience are what the soul seeks by its birth into the body; whatever is necessary for the self-expression and experience of this life, whether it intervenes as an automatic outcome of past lives or as a free selection of results and a continuity or as a new development, whatever is a means of creation of the future, that will be formulated: for the principle is not the working out of a mechanism of Law, but the development of the nature through cosmic experience so that eventually it may grow out of the Ignorance. There must therefore be two elements, Karma as an instrument, but also the secret Consciousness and Will within working through the mind, life and body as the user. Fate, whether purely mechanical or created by ourselves, a chain of our own manufacture, is only one factor of existence; Being and its consciousness and its will are a still more important factor.

In Indian astrology which considers all life-circumstances to be Karma, mostly predetermined or indicated in the graph of the stars, there is still provision made for the energy and force of the being which can change or cancel part or much of what is so written or even all but the most imperative and powerful bindings of Karma. This is a reasonable account of the balance: but there is also to be added to the computation the fact that destiny is not simple but complex; the destiny which binds our physical being, binds it so long or in so far as a greater law does not intervene. Action belongs to the physical part of us, it is the physical outcome of our being; but behind our surface is a freer Life-power, a freer Mind-power which has another energy and can create another destiny and bring it in to modify the primary plan, and when the soul and self emerges, when we become consciously spiritual beings, that change can cancel or wholly remodel the graph of our physical fate. Karma, then, — or at least any mechanical law of Karma, — cannot be accepted as the sole determinant of circumstances and the whole machinery of rebirth and of our future evolution.

But this is not all; for the statement of the Law errs by an over-simplification and the arbitrary selection of a limited principle. Action is a resultant of the energy of the being, but this energy is not of one sole kind; the Consciousness-Force of the Spirit manifests itself in many kinds of energies: there are inner activities of mind, activities of life, of desire, passion, impulse, character, activities of the senses and the body, a pursuit of truth and knowledge, a pursuit of beauty, a pursuit of ethical good or evil, a pursuit of power, love, joy, happiness, fortune, success, pleasure, life-satisfactions of all kinds, life-enlargement, a pursuit of individual or collective objects, a pursuit of the health, strength, capacity, satisfaction of the body. All this makes an exceedingly complex sum of the manifold experience and many-sided action of the Spirit in life, and its variety cannot be set aside in favour of a single principle, neither can it be hammered into so many sections of the single duality of ethical good and evil; ethics, the maintenance of human standards of morality, cannot, therefore, be the sole preoccupation of the cosmic Law or the sole principle of determination of the working of Karma. If it is true that the nature of the energy put forth must determine the nature of the result or outcome, all these differences in the nature of the energy have to be taken into account and each must have its appropriate consequence. An energy of seeking for truth and knowledge must have as its natural outcome, — its reward or recompense, if you will, — a growth into truth, an increase in knowledge; an energy used for falsehood should result in an increase of falsehood in the nature and a deeper immersion in the Ignorance. An energy of pursuit of beauty should have as its outcome an increase in the sense of beauty, the enjoyment of beauty or, if so directed, in the beauty and harmony of the life and the nature. A pursuit of physical health, strength and capacity should create the strong man or the successful athlete. An energy put out in the pursuit of ethical good must have as its outcome or reward or recompense an increase in virtue, the happiness of ethical growth or the sunny felicity and poise and purity of a simple and natural goodness, while the punishment of opposite energies would be a deeper plunge into evil, a greater disharmony and perversion of the nature and, in case of excess, a great spiritual perdition, *mahatī vinaṣṭiḥ*. An energy put forward for power or other vital ends must lead to an increase of the capacity for commanding these results or to the development of a vital strength and plenitude. This is the ordinary disposition of things in Nature and, if justice be demanded of her, this surely is justice that the energy and capacity put forward should have in its own kind its fitting response from her. The prize of the race is assigned by her to the swift, the victory in battle to the brave and strong and skilful, the rewards of knowledge to the capable intellect and the earnest seeker: these things she will not give to the good man who is sluggish or weak or skilless or stupid merely because he is righteous or respectable; if he covets these other powers of life, he must qualify for them and put forward the right kind of energy. If Nature did otherwise, she could well be accused of injustice; there is no reason to accuse her of injustice for this perfectly right and normal arrangement or to demand from her a rectification of the balance in a future life so that the good man may be given as a natural reward for his virtue a high post or a large bank-balance or a happy, easy and well-appointed life. That cannot be the significance of rebirth or a sufficient basis for a cosmic law of Karma.

There is indeed in our life a very large element of what we call luck or fortune, which baulks our effort of result or gives the prize without effort or to an inferior energy: the secret cause of these caprices of Destiny, — or causes, for the roots of Fortune may be manifold, — must be no doubt partly sought for in our hidden past; but it is difficult to accept the simple solution that good luck is a return for a forgotten virtuous action in a past life and bad luck a return for a sin or crime. If we see the righteous man suffering here, it is difficult to believe that this paragon of virtue was in the last life a scoundrel and is paying, even after his exemplary conversion by a new birth, for sins he then committed; nor, if the wicked triumphs, can we easily suppose that he was in his last life a saint who has suddenly taken a wrong turn but continues to receive a cash-return for his previous virtue. A total change of this kind between life and life is possible though not likely to be frequent, but to saddle the new opposite personality with the rewards or punishments of the old looks like a purposeless and purely mechanical procedure. This and many other difficulties arise, and the too simple logic of the correlation is not so strong as it claims to be; the idea of retribution of Karma as a compensation for the injustice of life and Nature is a feeble basis for the theory, for it puts forward a shallow and superficial human feeling and standard as the sense of the cosmic Law and is based on an unsound reasoning; there must be some other and stronger foundation for the law of Karma.

Here, as so often, the error comes by our forcing a standard which is the creation of our human mind into the larger, freer and more comprehensive ways of the cosmic Intelligence. In the action attributed to the law of Karma two values are selected out of the many created by Nature, moral good and evil, sin and virtue, and vital-physical good and evil, outward happiness and suffering, outward good fortune and ill-fortune, and it is supposed that there must be an equation between them, the one must be the reward or punishment of the other, the final sanction which it receives in the secret justice of Nature. This collocation is evidently made from the viewpoint of a common vital-physical desire in our members: because happiness and good fortune are what the lower part of our vital being most desires, misfortune and suffering what it most hates and dreads, it proceeds, when it accepts the moral demand upon it for the curbing of its propensities, for self-restraint from doing evil and self-exertion towards doing what is good, to strike a bargain, to erect a cosmic Law which will compensate it for this strenuous self-compulsion and help it by the dread of punishment to adhere to its difficult path of self-denial. But the truly ethical being does not need a system of rewards and punishments to follow the path of good and shun the path of evil; virtue to him is its own reward, sin brings with it its own punishment in the suffering of a fall from his own law of nature: this is the true ethical standard. On the contrary, a system of rewards and punishments debases at once the ethical values of good, turns virtue into selfishness, a commercial bargain of self-interest, and replaces the right motive of abstinence from evil by a baser motive. Human beings have erected the rule of reward and punishment as a social necessity in order to restrain the doing of things harmful to the community and encourage what is helpful to it; but to erect this human device into a general law of cosmic Nature or a law of the supreme Being or the supreme law of existence is a procedure of doubtful value. It is human, but also puerile, to impose the insufficient and narrow standards of our own Ignorance on the larger and more intricate operations of cosmic Nature or on the action of the supreme Wisdom and supreme Good which draws or raises us towards itself by a spiritual power working slowly in ourselves through our inner being and not by a law of temptation and compulsion upon our outer vital nature. If the soul is passing through an evolution by a many-sided and complex experience, any law of Karma or return to action and output of Energy, if it is to fit itself into that experience, must also be complex and cannot be of a simple and exiguous texture or rigid and one-sided in its incidence.

At the same time, a partial truth of fact, not of fundamental or general principle, may be admitted for this doctrine; for although the lines of the action of energy are distinct and independent, they can act together and upon each other, though not by any rigidly fixed law of correspondence. It is possible that in the total method of the returns of Nature there intervenes a strand of connection or rather of interaction between vital-physical good and ill and ethical good and ill, a limited correspondence and meeting-point between divergent dualities not amounting to an inseparable coherence. Our own varying energies, desires, movements are mixed together in their working and can bring about a mixed result: our vital part does demand substantial and external rewards for virtue, for knowledge, for every intellectual, aesthetic, moral or physical effort; it believes firmly in punishment for sin and even for ignorance. This may well either create or else reply to a corresponding cosmic action; for Nature takes us as we are and to some extent suits her movements to our need or our demands on her. If we accept the action of invisible Forces upon us, there may be also invisible Forces in Life-Nature that belong to the same plane of Consciousness-Force as this part of our being, Forces that move according to the same plan or the same power-motive as our lower vital nature. It can be often observed that when a self-assertive vital egoism goes on trampling on its way without restraint or scruple all that opposes its will or desire, it raises a mass of reactions against itself, reactions of hatred, antagonism, unease in men which may have their result now or hereafter, and still more formidable adverse reactions in universal Nature. It is as if the patience of Nature, her willingness to be used were exhausted; the very forces that the ego of the strong vital man seized and bent to its purpose rebel and turn against him, those he had trampled on rise up and receive power for his downfall: the insolent vital force of Man strikes against the throne of Necessity and is dashed to pieces or the lame foot of Punishment reaches at last the successful offender. This reaction to his energies may come upon him in another life and not at once, it may be a burden of consequence he takes up in his return to the field of these Forces; it may happen on a small as well as a large scale, to the small vital being and his small errors as well as in these larger instances. For the principle will be the same; the mental being in us seeking for success by a misuse of force which Nature admits but reacts in the end against it, receives the adverse return in the guise of defeat and suffering and failure. But the promotion of this minor line of causes and results to the status of an invariable absolute Law or the whole cosmic rule of action of a supreme Being is not valid; they belong to a middle region between the inmost or supreme Truth of things and the impartiality of material Nature.

In any case the reactions of Nature are not in essence meant as reward or punishment; that is not their fundamental value, which is rather an inherent value of natural relations and, in so far as it affects the spiritual evolution, a value of the lessons of experience in the soul's cosmic training. If we touch fire, it burns, but there is no principle of punishment in this relation of cause and effect, it is a lesson of relation and a lesson of experience; so in all Nature's dealings with us there is a relation of things and there is a corresponding lesson of experience. The action of the cosmic Energy is complex and the same Forces may act in different ways according to circumstances, to the need of the being, to the intention of the cosmic Power in its action; our life is affected not only by its own energies but by the energies of others and by universal Forces, and all this vast interplay cannot be determined in its results solely by the one factor of an all-governing moral law and its exclusive attention to the merits and demerits, the sins and virtues of individual human beings. Nor can good fortune and evil fortune, pleasure and pain, happiness and misery and suffering be taken as if they existed merely as incentives and deterrents to the natural being in its choice of good and evil. It is for experience, for growth of the individual being that the soul enters into rebirth; joy and grief, pain and suffering, fortune and misfortune are parts of that experience, means of that growth: even, the soul may of itself accept or choose poverty, misfortune and suffering as helpful to its growth, stimulants of a rapid development, and reject riches and prosperity and success as dangerous and conducive to a relaxation of its spiritual effort. Happiness and success bringing happiness are, no doubt, a legitimate demand of humanity; it is an attempt of Life and Matter to catch a pale reflection or a gross image of felicity: but a superficial happiness and material success, however desirable to our vital nature, are not the main object of our existence; if that had been the intention, life would have been otherwise arranged in the cosmic ordinance of things. All the secret of the circumstances of rebirth centres around the one capital need of the soul, the need of growth, the need of experience; that governs the line of its evolution and all the rest is accessory. Cosmic existence is not a vast administrative system of universal justice with a cosmic Law of recompense and retribution as its machinery or a divine Legislator and Judge at its centre. It is seen by us first as a great automatic movement of energy of Nature, and in it emerges a self-developing movement of consciousness, a movement therefore of Spirit working out its own being in the motion of energy of Nature. In this motion takes place the cycle of rebirth, and in that cycle the soul, the psychic being, prepares for itself, — or the Divine Wisdom or the cosmic Consciousness-Force prepares for it and through its action, — whatever is needed for the next step in its evolution, the next formation of personality, the coming nexus of necessary experiences constantly provided and organised out of the continuous flux of past, present and future energies for each new birth, for each new step of the Spirit backward or forward or else still in a circle, but always a step in the growth of the being towards its destined self-unfolding in Nature.

This brings us to another element of the ordinary conception of rebirth which is not acceptable, since it is an obvious error of the physical mind, — the idea of the soul itself as a limited personality which survives unchanged from one birth to another. This too simple and superficial idea of the soul and personality is born of the physical mind's inability to look beyond its own apparent self-formation in this single existence. In its conception, what returns in the reincarnation must be not only the same spiritual being, the same psychic entity, but the same formation of nature that inhabited the body of the last birth; the body changes, the circumstances are different, but the form of the being, the mind, the character, the disposition, temperament, tendencies are the same: John Smith in his new life is the same John Smith that he was in his last avatar. But if that were so, there would be no spiritual utility or meaning at all in rebirth; for there would be the repetition of the same little personality, the same small mental and vital formation to the end of Time. For the growth of the embodied being towards the full stature of its reality, not only a new experience, but a new personality is indispensable; to repeat the same personality would only be helpful if something had been incomplete in its formation of its experience which needed to be worked out in the same cadre of self, in the same building of mind and with the same formed capacity of energy. But normally this would be quite otiose: the soul that has been John Smith cannot gain anything or fulfil itself by remaining John Smith for ever; it cannot achieve growth or perfection by repeating the same character, interests, occupations, types of inner and outer movements for ever. Our life and rebirth would be always the same recurring decimal; it would be not an evolution but the meaningless continuity of an eternal repetition. Our attachment to our present personality demands such a continuity, such a repetition; John Smith wants to be John Smith for ever: but the demand is obviously ignorant and, if it were satisfied, that would be a frustration, not a fulfilment. It is only by a change of outer self, a constant progression of the nature, a growth in the spirit that we can justify our existence.

Personality is only a temporary mental, vital, physical formation which the being, the real Person, the psychic entity, puts forward on the surface, — it is not the self in its abiding reality. In each return to earth the Person, the Purusha, makes a new formation, builds a new personal quantum suitable for a new experience, for a new growth of its being. When it passes from its body, it keeps still the same vital and mental form for a time, but the forms or sheaths dissolve and what is kept is only the essential elements of the past quantum, of which some will but some may not be used in the next incarnation. The essential form of the past personality may remain as one element among many, one personality among many personalities of the same Person, but in the background, in the subliminal behind the veil of the surface mind and life and body, contributing from there whatever is needed of itself to the new formation; but it will not itself be the whole formation or build anew the old unchanged type of nature. It may even be that the new quantum or structure of being will exhibit a quite contrary character and temperament, quite other capacities, other very different tendencies; for latent potentials may be ready to emerge, or something already in action but inchoate may have been held back in the last life which needed to be worked out but was kept over for a later and more suitable combination of the possibilities of the nature. All the past is indeed there, with its accelerated impetus and potentialities for the formation of the future, but all of it is not ostensibly present and active. The greater the variety of formations that have existed in the past and can be utilised, the more rich and multitudinous the accumulated buildings of experience, the more their essential result of capacity for knowledge, power, action, character, manifold response to the universe can be brought forward and harmonised in the new birth, the more numerous the veiled personalities mental, vital, subtle-physical that combine to enrich the new personality on the surface, the greater and more opulent will be that personality and the nearer to the possible transition out of the completed mental stage of evolution to something beyond it. Such a complexity and gathering up of many personalities in one person can be a sign of a very advanced stage of the individual's evolution when there is a strong central being that holds all together and works towards harmonisation and integration of the whole many-sided movement of the nature. But this opulent taking up of the past would not be a repetition of personality; it would be a new formation and large consummation. It is not as a machinery for the persistent renewal or prolongation of an unchanging personality that rebirth exists, but as a means for the evolution of the spiritual being in Nature.

It becomes at once evident that in this plan of rebirth the

false importance which our mind attaches to the memory of past lives disappears altogether. If indeed rebirth were governed by a system of rewards and punishments, if life's whole intention were to teach the embodied spirit to be good and moral, — supposing that that is the intention in the dispensation of Karma and it is not what it looks like in this presentation of it, a mechanical law of recompense and retribution without any reformatory meaning or purpose, — then there is evidently a great stupidity and injustice in denying to the mind in its new incarnation all memory of its past births and actions. For it deprives the reborn being of all chance to realise why he is rewarded or punished or to get any advantage from the lesson of the profitableness of virtue and the unprofitableness of sin vouchsafed to him or inflicted on him. Even, since life seems often to teach the opposite lesson, — for he sees the good suffer for their goodness and the wicked prosper by their wickedness, — he is rather likely to conclude in this perverse sense, because he has not the memory of an assured and constant result of experience which would show him that the suffering of the good man was due to his past wickedness and the prosperity of the sinner due to the splendour of his past virtues, so that virtue is the best policy in the long run for any reasonable and prudent soul entering into this dispensation of Nature. It might be said that the psychic being within remembers; but such a secret memory would seem to have little effect or value on the surface. Or it may be said that it realises what has happened and learns its lesson when it reviews and assimilates its experiences after issuing from the body: but this intermittent memory does not very apparently help in the next birth; for most of us persist in sin and error and show no tangible signs of having profited by the teaching of our past experience.

But if a constant development of being by a developing cosmic experience is the meaning and the building of a new personality in a new birth is the method, then any persistent or complete memory of the past life or lives might be a chain and a serious obstacle: it would be a force for prolonging the old temperament, character, preoccupations, and a tremendous burden hampering the free development of the new personality and its formulation of new experience. A clear and detailed memory of past lives, hatreds, rancours, attachments, connections would be equally a stupendous inconvenience; for it would bind the reborn being to a useless repetition or a compulsory continuation of his surface past and stand heavily in the way of his bringing out new possibilities from the depths of the spirit. If, indeed, a mental learning of things were the heart of the matter, if that were the process of our development, memory would have a great importance: but what happens is a growth of the soul-personality and a growth of the nature by an assimilation into our substance of being, a creative and effective absorption of the essential results of past energies; in this process conscious memory is of no importance. As the tree grows by a subconscient or inconscient assimilation of action of sun and rain and wind and absorption of earth-elements, so the being grows by a subliminal or intraconscient assimilation and absorption of its results of past becoming and an output of potentialities of future becoming. The law that deprives us of the memory of past lives is a law of the cosmic Wisdom and serves, not disserves its evolutionary purpose.

The absence of any memory of past existences is wrongly and very ignorantly taken as a disproof of the actuality of rebirth; for if even in this life it is difficult to keep all the memories of our past, if they often fade into the background or fade out altogether, if no recollection remains of our infancy, and yet with all this hiatus of memory we can grow and be, if the mind is even capable of total loss of memory of past events and its own identity and yet it is the same being who is there and the lost memory can one day be recovered, it is evident that so radical a change as a transition to other worlds followed by new birth in a new body ought normally to obliterate altogether the surface or mental memory, and yet that would not annul the identity of the soul or the growth of the nature. This obliteration of the surface mental memory is all the more certain and quite inevitable if there is a new personality of the same being and a new instrumentation which takes the place of the old, a new mind, a new life, a new body: the new brain cannot be expected to carry in itself the images held by the old brain; the new life or mind cannot be summoned to keep the deleted impressions of the old mind and life that have been dissolved and exist no more. There is, no doubt, the subliminal being which may remember, since it does not suffer from the disabilities of the surface; but the surface mind is cut off from the subliminal memory which alone might retain some clear recollection or distinct impression of past lives. This separation is necessary because the new personality has to be built up on the surface without conscious reference to what is within; as with all the rest of the superficial being, so our surface personality too is indeed formed by an action from within, but of that action it is not conscious, it seems to itself to be self-formed or ready-made or formed by some ill-understood action of universal Nature. And yet fragmentary recollections of past births do sometimes remain in spite of these almost insuperable obstacles; there are even a very few cases of astonishingly exact and full memory in the child-mind. Finally, at a certain stage of development of the being when the inner begins to predominate over the outer and come to the front, past-life memory does sometimes begin to emerge as if from some submerged layer, but more readily in the shape of a perception of the stuff and power of past personalities that are effective in the composition of the being in the present life than in any precise and accurate detail of event and circumstance, although this too can recur in parts or be recovered by concentration from the subliminal vision, from some secret memory or from our inner conscious-substance. But this detailed memory is of minor importance to Nature in her normal work and she makes small or no provision for it: it is the shaping of the future evolution of the being with which she is concerned; the past is put back, kept behind the veil and used only as an occult source of materials for the present and the future.

This conception of the Person and Personality, if accepted, must modify at the same time our current ideas about the immortality of the soul; for, normally, when we insist on the soul's undying existence, what is meant is the survival after death of a definite unchanging personality which was and will always remain the same throughout eternity. It is the very imperfect superficial "I" of the moment, evidently regarded by Nature as a temporary form and not worth preservation, for which we demand this stupendous right to survival and immortality. But the demand is extravagant and cannot be conceded; the "I" of the moment can only merit survival if it consents to change, to be no longer itself but something else, greater, better, more luminous in knowledge, more moulded in the image of the eternal inner beauty, more and more progressive towards the divinity of the secret Spirit. It is that secret Spirit or divinity of Self in us which is imperishable, because it is unborn and eternal. The psychic entity within, its representative, the spiritual individual in us, is the Person that we are; but the "I" of this moment, the "I" of this life is only a formation, a temporary personality of this inner Person: it is one step of the many steps of our evolutionary change, and it serves its true purpose only when we pass beyond it to a farther step leading nearer to a higher degree of consciousness and being. It is the inner Person that survives death, even as it pre-exists before birth; for this constant survival is a rendering of the eternity of our timeless Spirit into the terms of Time.

What our normal demand of survival asks for is a similar survival for our mind, our life, even our body; the dogma of the resurrection of the body attests to this last demand, — even as it has been the root of the age-long effort of man to discover the elixir of immortality or any means magical, alchemic or scientific to conquer physically the death of the body. But this aspiration could only succeed if the mind, life or body could put on something of the immortality and divinity of the indwelling Spirit. There are certain circumstances in which the survival of the outer mental personality representative of the inner mental Purusha could be possible. It could happen if our mental being came to be so powerfully individualised on the surface and so much one with the inner mind and inner mental Purusha and at the same time so open plastically to the progressive action of the Infinite that the soul no longer needed to dissolve the old form of mind and create a new one in order to progress. A similar individualisation, integration and openness of the vital being on the surface would alone make possible a similar survival of the life-part in us, the outer vital personality representative of the inner life-being, the vital Purusha. What would really happen then is that the wall between the inner self and the outer man would have broken down and the permanent mental and vital being from within, the mental and vital representatives of the immortal psychic entity, would govern the life. Our mind-nature and our life-nature could then be a continuous progressive expression of the soul and not a nexus of successive formations preserved only in their essence. Our mental personality and life-personality would then subsist without dissolution from birth to birth; they would be in this sense immortal, persistently surviving, continuous in their sense of identity. This would be evidently an immense victory of soul and mind and life over the Inconscience and the limitations of material Nature.

But such a survival could only persist in the subtle body; the being would still have to discard its physical form, pass to other worlds and in its return put on a new body. The awakened mental Purusha and vital Purusha, preserving the mind-sheath and the life-sheath of the subtle body which are usually discarded, would return with them into a new birth and keep a vivid and sustained sense of a permanent being of mind and life constituted by the past and continuing into the present and future; but the basis of physical existence, the material body, could not be preserved even by this change. The physical being could only endure, if by some means its physical causes of decay and disruption could be overcome and at the same time it could be made so plastic and progressive in its structure and its functioning that it would answer to each change demanded of it by the progress of the inner Person;[7] it must be able to keep

---

[7] Even if Science, — physical Science or occult Science, — were to discover the necessary conditions or means for an indefinite survival of the body, still, if the body could not adapt itself so as to become a fit instrument of expression for the inner growth, the soul would find some way to abandon it and pass on to a new incarnation. The material or physical causes of death are not its sole or its true cause; its true inmost reason is the spiritual necessity for the evolution of a new being.

pace with the soul in its formation of self-expressive personality, its long unfolding of a secret spiritual divinity and the slow transformation of the mental into the divine mental or spiritual existence. This consummation of a triple immortality, — immortality of the nature completing the essential immortality of the Spirit and the psychic survival of death, — might be the crown of rebirth and a momentous indication of the conquest of the material Inconscience and Ignorance even in the very foundation of the reign of Matter. But the true immortality would still be the eternity of the Spirit; the physical survival could only be relative, terminable at will, a temporal sign of the Spirit's victory here over Death and Matter.

Chapter XXIII

Man and the Evolution

The one Godhead secret in all beings, all-pervading, the inner Self of all, presiding over all action, witness, conscious knower and absolute... the One in control over the many who are passive to Nature, fashions one seed in many ways.

Swetaswatara Upanishad.[1]

The Godhead moves in this Field modifying each web of things separately in many ways.... One, he presides over all wombs and natures; himself the womb of all, he is that which brings to ripeness the nature of the being and he gives to all who have to be matured their result of development and appoints all qualities to their workings. *Swetaswatara Upanishad.*[2]

He fashions one form of things in many ways.

Katha Upanishad.[3]

Who has perceived this truth occult, that the Child gives being to the Mothers by the workings of his nature? An offspring from the lap of many Waters, he comes forth from them a seer possessed of his whole law of nature. Manifested, he grows in the lap of their crookednesses and becomes high, beautiful and glorious. *Rig Veda.*[4]

From the non-being to true being, from the darkness to the Light, from death to Immortality.

Brihadaranyaka Upanishad.[5]

A SPIRITUAL evolution, an evolution of consciousness in Matter in a constant developing self-formation till the form can reveal the indwelling Spirit, is then the keynote,

---

[1] VI. 11, 12.   [2] V. 3-5.   [3] II. 2. 12.   [4] I. 95. 4, 5.   [5] I. 3. 28.

the central significant motive of the terrestrial existence. This significance is concealed at the outset by the involution of the Spirit, the Divine Reality, in a dense material Inconscience; a veil of Inconscience, a veil of insensibility of Matter hides the universal Consciousness-Force which works within it, so that the Energy, which is the first form the Force of creation assumes in the physical universe, appears to be itself inconscient and yet does the works of a vast occult Intelligence. The obscure mysterious creatrix ends indeed by delivering the secret consciousness out of its thick and tenebrous prison; but she delivers it slowly, little by little, in minute infinitesimal drops, in thin jets, in small vibrant concretions of energy and substance, of life, of mind, as if that were all she could get out through the crass obstacle, the dull reluctant medium of an inconscient stuff of existence. At first she houses herself in forms of Matter which appear to be altogether unconscious, then struggles towards mentality in the guise of living Matter and attains to it imperfectly in the conscious animal. This consciousness is at first rudimentary, mostly a half subconscious or just conscious instinct; it develops slowly till in more organised forms of living Matter it reaches its climax of intelligence and exceeds itself in Man, the thinking animal who develops into the reasoning mental being but carries along with him even at his highest elevation the mould of original animality, the dead weight of subconscience of body, the downward pull of gravitation towards the original Inertia and Nescience, the control of an inconscient material Nature over his conscious evolution, its power for limitation, its law of difficult development, its immense force for retardation and frustration. This control by the original Inconscience over the consciousness emerging from it takes the general shape of a mentality struggling towards knowledge but itself, in what seems to be its fundamental nature, an Ignorance. Thus hampered and burdened, mental man has still to evolve out of himself the fully conscious being, a divine manhood or a spiritual and supramental supermanhood which shall be the next product of the evolution. That transition will mark the passage from the evolution in the Ignorance to a greater evolution in the Knowledge,

founded and proceeding in the light of the Superconscient and
no longer in the darkness of the Ignorance and Inconscience.
This terrestrial evolutionary working of Nature from Matter
to Mind and beyond it has a double process: there is an outward
visible process of physical evolution with birth as its machinery, — for each evolved form of body housing its own evolved
power of consciousness is maintained and kept in continuity
by heredity; there is, at the same time, an invisible process of
soul evolution with rebirth into ascending grades of form and
consciousness as its machinery. The first by itself would mean
only a cosmic evolution; for the individual would be a quickly
perishing instrument, and the race, a more abiding collective
formulation, would be the real step in the progressive manifestation of the cosmic Inhabitant, the universal Spirit: rebirth is an
indispensable condition for any long duration and evolution of
the individual being in the earth-existence. Each grade of cosmic
manifestation, each type of form that can house the indwelling
Spirit, is turned by rebirth into a means for the individual soul,
the psychic entity, to manifest more and more of its concealed
consciousness; each life becomes a step in a victory over Matter
by a greater progression of consciousness in it which shall make
eventually Matter itself a means for the full manifestation of the
Spirit.

But this account of the process and meaning of the terrestrial creation is at every point exposed to challenge in the mind
of man himself, because the evolution is still half-way on its
journey, is still in the Ignorance, is still seeking in the mind a
half-evolved humanity for its own purpose and significance. It
is possible to challenge the theory of evolution on the ground
that it is insufficiently founded and that it is superfluous as an
explanation of the process of terrestrial existence. It is open
to doubt, even if evolution is granted, whether man has the
capacity to develop into a higher evolutionary being. It is open
also to doubt whether the evolution is likely to go any farther
than it has gone already or whether a supramental evolution, the
appearance of a consummated Truth-Consciousness, a being of
Knowledge, is at all probable in the fundamental Ignorance of

the earthly Nature. Another construction neither teleological nor evolutionary can be put on the workings of the Spirit in the manifestation here, and it may be as well before proceeding farther to formulate succinctly the line of thinking which makes such a construction possible.

Admitting that the creation is a manifestation of the Timeless Eternal in a Time Eternity, admitting that there are the seven grades of Consciousness and that the material Inconscience has been laid down as a basis for the reascent of the Spirit, admitting that rebirth is a fact, a part of the terrestrial order, still a spiritual evolution of the individual being is not an inevitable consequence of any of these admissions or even of all of them together. It is possible to take another view of the spiritual significance and the inner process of terrestrial existence. If each thing created is a form of the manifest Divine Existence, each is divine in itself by the spiritual presence within it, whatever its appearance, its figure or character in Nature. In each form of manifestation the Divine takes the delight of existence and there is no need of change or progress within it. Whatever ordered display or hierarchy of actualised possibilities is necessitated by the nature of the Infinite Being, is sufficiently provided for by the numberless variation, the teeming multitude of forms, types of consciousness, natures that we see everywhere around us. There is no teleological purpose in creation and there cannot be, for all is there in the Infinite: the Divine has nothing that he needs to gain or that he has not; if there is creation and manifestation, it is for the delight of creation, of manifestation, not for any purpose. There is then no reason for an evolutionary movement with a culmination to be reached or an aim to be worked out and effectuated or a drive towards ultimate perfection.

In fact we see that the principles of creation are permanent and unchanging: each type of being remains itself and does not try nor has any need to become other than itself; granting that some types of existence disappear and others come into being, it is because the Consciousness-Force in the universe withdraws its life-delight from those that perish and turns to create others for its pleasure. But each type of life, while it lasts, has its own pattern and remains faithful with whatever minor variations to that pattern: it is bound to its own consciousness and cannot get away from it into other-consciousness; limited by its own nature, it cannot transgress these boundaries and pass into other-nature. If the Consciousness-Force of the Infinite has manifested Life after manifesting Matter and Mind after manifesting Life, it does not follow that it will proceed to manifest Supermind as the next terrestrial creation. For Mind and Supermind belong to quite different hemispheres, Mind to the lower status of the Ignorance, Supermind to the higher status of the Divine Knowledge. This world is a world of the Ignorance and intended to be that only; there need be no intention to bring down the powers of the higher hemisphere into the lower half of existence or to manifest their concealed presence there; for, if they are at all existent here, it is in an occult incommunicable immanence and only to maintain the creation, not to perfect it. Man is the summit of this ignorant creation; he has reached the utmost consciousness and knowledge of which it is capable: if he tries to go farther, he will only revolve in larger cycles of his own mentality. For that is the curve of his existence here, a finite circling which carries the Mind in its revolutions and returns always to the point from which it started; Mind cannot go outside its own cycle, — all idea of a straight line of movement or of progress reaching infinitely upward or sidewise into the Infinite is a delusion. If the soul of man is to go beyond humanity, to reach either a supramental or a still higher status, it must pass out of this cosmic existence, either to a plane or world of Bliss and Knowledge or into the unmanifest Eternal and Infinite.

It is true that Science now affirms an evolutionary terrestrial existence: but if the facts with which Science deals are reliable, the generalisations it hazards are short-lived; it holds them for some decades or some centuries, then passes to another generalisation, another theory of things. This happens even in physical Science where the facts are solidly ascertainable and verifiable by experiment: in psychology, — which is relevant here, for the evolution of consciousness comes into the picture, — its instability is still greater; it passes there from one theory to another before the first is well-founded; indeed, several conflicting theories hold the field together. No firm metaphysical building can be erected upon these shifting quicksands. Heredity, upon which Science builds its concept of life-evolution, is certainly a power, a machinery for keeping a type of species in unchanged being: the demonstration that it is also an instrument for persistent and progressive variation is very questionable; its tendency is conservative rather than evolutionary, — it seems to accept with difficulty the new character that the Life-Force attempts to force upon it. All the facts show that a type can vary within its own specification of nature, but there is nothing to show that it can go beyond it. It has not yet been really established that ape-kind developed into man; for it would rather seem that a type resembling the ape, but always characteristic of itself and not of apehood, developed within its own tendencies of nature and became what we know as man, the present human being. It is not even established that inferior races of man developed out of themselves the superior races; those of an inferior organisation and capacity perished, but it has not been shown that they left behind the human races of today as their descendants: but still such a development within the type is imaginable. The progress of Nature from Matter to Life, from Life to Mind, may be conceded: but there is no proof yet that Matter developed into Life or Life-energy into Mind-energy; all that can be conceded is that Life has manifested in Matter, Mind in living Matter. For there is no sufficient proof that any vegetable species developed into an animal existence or that any organisation of inanimate Matter developed into a living organism. Even if it be discovered hereafter that under certain chemical or other conditions Life makes its appearance, all that will be established by this coincidence is that in certain physical circumstances Life manifests, not that certain chemical conditions are constituents of Life, are its elements or are the evolutionary cause of a transformation of inanimate into animate Matter. Here as elsewhere each grade of being exists in itself and by itself, is manifested according to its own character by its own proper energy, and the gradations above or below it are not origins and resultant sequences but only degrees in the continuous scale of earth-nature.

If it be asked, how then did all these various gradations and types of being come into existence, it can be answered that, fundamentally, they were manifested in Matter by the Consciousness-Force in it, by the power of the Real-Idea building its own significant forms and types for the indwelling Spirit's cosmic existence: the practical or physical method might vary considerably in different grades or stages, although a basic similarity of line may be visible; the creative Power might use not one but many processes or set many forces to act together. In Matter the process is a creation of infinitesimals charged with an immense energy, their association by design and number, the manifestation of larger infinitesimals on that primary basis, the grouping and association of these together to found the appearance of sensible objects, earth, water, minerals, metals, the whole material kingdom. In Life also the Consciousness-Force begins with infinitesimal forms of vegetable life and infinitesimal animalcules; it creates an original plasm and multiplies it, creates the living cell as a unit, creates other kinds of minute biological apparatus like the seed or the gene, uses always the same method of grouping and association so as to build by a various operation various living organisms. A constant creation of types is visible, but that is no indubitable proof of evolution. The types are sometimes distant from each other, sometimes closely similar, sometimes identical in basis but different in detail; all are patterns, and such a variation in patterns with an identical rudimentary basis for all is the sign of a conscious Force playing with its own Idea and developing by it all kinds of possibilities of creation. Animal species in coming into birth may begin with a like rudimentary embryonic or fundamental pattern for all, it may follow out up to a stage certain similarities of development on some or all of its lines; there may too be species that are twy-natured, amphibious, intermediate between one type and another: but all this need not mean that the types developed one from another in an evolutionary series. Other forces than hereditary variation have been at work in bringing about the appearance of new characteristics; there are physical forces such as food, light-rays and others that we are only beginning to know, there are surely others which we do not yet know; there are at work invisible life-forces and obscure psychological forces. For these subtler powers have to be admitted even in the physical evolutionary theory to account for natural selection; if the occult or subconscious energy in some types answers to the need of the environment, in others remains unresponsive and unable to survive, this is clearly the sign of a varying life-energy and psychology, of a consciousness and a force other than the physical at work making for variation in Nature. The problem of the method of operation is still too full of obscure and unknown factors for any at present possible structure of theory to be definitive.

Man is a type among many types so constructed, one pattern among the multitude of patterns in the manifestation in Matter. He is the most complex that has been created, the richest in content of consciousness and the curious ingeniousness of his building; he is the head of the earthly creation, but he does not exceed it. Even as others, so he too has his own native law, limits, special kind of existence, *svabhāva, svadharma*; within those limits he can extend and develop, but he cannot go outside them. If there is a perfection to which he has to arrive, it must be a perfection in his own kind, within his own law of being, — the full play of it, but by observation of its mode and measure, not by transcendence. To exceed himself, to grow into the superman, to put on the nature and capacities of a god would be a contradiction of his self-law, impracticable and impossible. Each form and way of being has its own appropriate way of the delight of being; to seek through the mind the mastery and use and enjoyment of the environment of which he is capable is rightly man the mental being's objective: but to look beyond, to run after an ulterior object or aim of existence, to aspire to surpass the mental stature is to bring in a teleological element into existence which is not visible in the cosmic structure. If a supramental being is to appear in the terrestrial creation, it must be a new and independent manifestation; just as Life and

Mind have manifested in Matter, so Supermind must manifest there and the secret Conscious-Energy must create the necessary patterns for this new grade of its potencies. But there is no sign of any such intention in the operations of Nature.

But if a superior creation is intended, then, certainly, it is not out of man that the new grade, type or pattern can develop; for in that case there would be some race or kind or make of human beings that has already the material of the superman in it, just as the peculiar animal being that developed into humanity had the essential elements of human nature already potential or present in it: there is no such race, kind or type, at most there are only spiritualised mental beings who are seeking to escape out of the terrestrial creation. If by any occult law of Nature such a human development of the supramental being is intended, it could only be by a few in humanity detaching themselves from the race so as to become a first foundation for this new pattern of being. There is no reason to suppose that the whole race could develop this perfection; it cannot be a possibility generalised in the human creature.

If indeed man has evolved in Nature out of the animal, yet now we see that no other animal type shows any signs of an evolution beyond itself; if then there was this evolutionary stress in the animal kingdom, it must have sunk back into quiescence as soon as the object was fulfilled by man's appearance: so too if there is any such stress for a new step in evolution, for self-exceeding, it is likely to subside into quiescence as soon as its object is fulfilled by the supramental being's appearance. But there is no such stress in reality: the idea of human progress itself is very probably an illusion, for there is no sign that man, once emerged from the animal stage, has radically progressed during his race-history; at most he has advanced in knowledge of the physical world, in Science, in the handling of his surroundings, in his purely external and utilitarian use of the secret laws of Nature. But otherwise he is what he always was in the early beginnings of civilisation: he continues to manifest the same capacities, the same qualities and defects, the same efforts, blunders, achievements, frustrations. If progress there has been, it is in a circle, at most perhaps in a widening circle. Man today is not wiser than the ancient seers and sages and thinkers, not more spiritual than the great seekers of old, the first mighty mystics, not superior in arts and crafts to the ancient artists and craftsmen; the old races that have disappeared showed as potent an intrinsic originality, invention, capacity of dealing with life and, if modern man in this respect has gone a little farther, not by any essential progress but in degree, scope, abundance, it is because he has inherited the achievements of his forerunners. Nothing warrants the idea that he will ever hew his way out of the half-knowledge half-ignorance which is the stamp of his kind, or, even if he develops a higher knowledge, that he can break out of the utmost boundary of the mental circle.

It is tempting and not illogical to regard rebirth as the potential means of a spiritual evolution, the factor that makes it possible, but still it is not certain, granting rebirth to be a fact, that this is its significance. All the ancient theories about reincarnation supposed it to be a constant transmigration of the soul from animal to human, but also from human to animal bodies: the Indian idea added the explanation of Karma, of a return for good or evil done, of a result of past will and effort; but there was no suggestion of a progressive evolution from type to higher type, still less of birth into a kind of being that has never yet existed but has still to evolve in the future. If evolution there is, then man is the last stage, because through him there can be the rejection of terrestrial or embodied life and an escape into some heaven or Nirvana. That was the end envisaged by the ancient theories and, since this is fundamentally and unchangeably a world of Ignorance, — even if all cosmic existence is not in its nature a state of Ignorance, — that escape is likely to be the true end of the cycle.

This is a line of reasoning that has a considerable cogency and importance, and it was necessary to state it, even if too briefly for its importance, in order to meet it. For although some of its propositions are valid, its view of things is not complete and its cogency is not conclusive. And first we may without much difficulty get rid of the objection to the teleological element which the idea of a predetermined evolution from inconscience to superconscience, the development of a rising order of beings with a culminating transition from the life of the Ignorance to a life in the Knowledge, brings into the structure of the terrestrial existence. The objection to a teleological cosmos can be based on two very different grounds, — a scientific reasoning proceeding on the assumption that all is the work of an inconscient Energy which acts automatically by mechanical processes and can have no element of purpose in it, and a metaphysical reasoning which proceeds on the perception that the Infinite and Universal has everything in it already, that it cannot have something unaccomplished to accomplish, something to add to itself, to work out, to realise, and there can therefore be in it no element of progress, no original or emergent purpose.

The scientific or materialist objection cannot maintain its validity if there is a secret Consciousness in or behind the apparently inconscient Energy in Matter. Even in the Inconscient there seems to be at least an urge of inherent necessity producing the evolution of forms and in the forms a developing Consciousness, and it may well be held that this urge is the evolutionary will of a secret Conscious-Being and its push of progressive manifestation the evidence of an innate intention in the evolution. This is a teleological element and it is not irrational to admit it: for the conscious or even the inconscient nisus arises from a truth of conscious-being that has become dynamic and set out to fulfil itself in an automatic process of material Nature; the teleology, the element of purpose in the nisus is the translation of self-operative Truth of Being into terms of self-effective Will-Power of that Being, and, if consciousness is there, such a Will-Power must also be there and the translation is normal and inevitable. Truth of Being inevitably fulfilling itself would be the fundamental fact of the evolution, but Will and its purpose must be there as part of the instrumentation, as an element in the operative principle.

The metaphysical objection is more serious; for it seems self-evident that the Absolute can have no purpose in manifestation except the delight of manifestation itself: an evolutionary movement in Matter as part of the manifestation must fall within this universal statement; it can be there only for the delight of the unfolding, the progressive execution, the objectless seried self-revelation. A universal totality may also be considered as something complete in itself; as a totality, it has nothing to gain or to add to its fullness of being. But here the material world is not an integral totality, it is part of a whole, a grade in a gradation; it may admit in it, therefore, not only the presence of undeveloped immaterial principles or powers belonging to the whole that are involved within its Matter, but also a descent into it of the same powers from the higher gradations of the system to deliver their kindred movements here from the strictness of a material limitation. A manifestation of the greater powers of Existence till the whole being itself is manifest in the material world in the terms of a higher, a spiritual creation, may be considered as the teleology of the evolution. This teleology does not bring in any factor that does not belong to the totality; it proposes only the realisation of the totality in the part. There can be no objection to the admission of a teleological factor in a part movement of the universal totality, if the purpose, — not a purpose in the human sense, but the urge of an intrinsic Truth-necessity conscious in the will of the indwelling Spirit, — is the perfect manifestation there of all the possibilities inherent in the total movement. All exists here, no doubt, for the delight of existence, all is a game or Lila; but a game too carries within itself an object to be accomplished and without the fulfilment of that object would have no completeness of significance. A drama without denouement may be an artistic possibility, — existing only for the pleasure of watching the characters and the pleasure in problems posed without a solution or with a forever suspended dubious balance of solution; the drama of the earth evolution might conceivably be of that character, but an intended or inherently predetermined denouement is also and more convincingly possible. Ananda is the secret principle of all being and the support of all activity of being: but Ananda does not exclude a delight in the working out of a Truth inherent in being, immanent in the Force or Will of being, upheld in the hidden self-awareness of its Consciousness-Force which is the dynamic and executive agent of all its activities and the knower of their significance.

A theory of spiritual evolution is not identical with a scientific theory of form-evolution and physical life-evolution; it must stand on its own inherent justification: it may accept the scientific account of physical evolution as a support or an element, but the support is not indispensable. The scientific theory is concerned only with the outward and visible machinery and process, with the detail of Nature's execution, with the physical development of things in Matter and the law of development of Life and Mind in Matter; its account of the process may have to be considerably changed or may be dropped altogether in the light of new discovery, but that will not affect the self-evident fact of a spiritual evolution, an evolution of Consciousness, a progression of the soul's manifestation in material existence. In its outward aspects this is what the theory of evolution comes to, — there is in the scale of terrestrial existence a development of forms, of bodies, a progressively complex and competent organisation of Matter, of Life in Matter, of Consciousness in living Matter; in this scale, the better organised the form, the more it is capable of housing a better organised, a more complex and capable, a more developed or evolved Life and Consciousness. Once the evolutionary hypothesis is put forward and the facts supporting it are marshalled, this aspect of the terrestrial existence becomes so striking as to appear indisputable. The precise machinery by which this is done or the exact genealogy or chronological succession of types of being is a secondary, though in itself an interesting and important question; the development of one form of life out of a precedent less evolved form, natural selection, the struggle for life, the survival of acquired characteristics may or may not be accepted, but the fact of a successive creation with a developing plan in it is the one conclusion which is of primary consequence. Another self-evident conclusion is that there is a graduated necessary succession in the evolution, first the evolution of Matter, next the evolution of Life in Matter, then the evolution of Mind in living Matter, and in this last stage an animal evolution followed by a human evolution. The first three terms of the succession are too evident to be disputable. It may be debated whether there was a succession of man to animal or a simultaneous initial development, man outstripping the animal in Mind-evolution; a theory has even been put forward that man was not the last, but the first and eldest of the animal species. This priority of man is an ancient conception, but it was not universal; it is born of the sense of the clear supremacy of man among earthly creatures, the dignity of this supremacy seeming to demand a priority of birth: but in evolutionary fact the superior is not prior but posterior in appearance, the less developed precedes the more developed and prepares it.

In fact, the idea of the priority of the lower forms of Life is not altogether absent in ancient thinking. Apart from mythical accounts of creation, we find already in ancient and mediaeval thought in India utterances that favour the priority of the animal over man in the time succession in a sense that agrees with the modern evolutionary conception. An Upanishad declares that the Self or Spirit after deciding on life-creation first formed animal kinds like the cow and horse, but the gods, — who are in the thought of the Upanishads powers of Consciousness and powers of Nature, — found them to be insufficient vehicles, and the Spirit finally created the form of man which the gods saw to be excellently made and sufficient and they entered into it for their cosmic functions. This is a clear parable of the creation of more and more developed forms till one was found that was capable of housing a developed consciousness. In the Puranas it is stated that the tamasic animal creation was the first in time. Tamas is the Indian word for the principle of inertia of consciousness and force: a consciousness dull and sluggish and incompetent in its play is said to be tamasic; a force, a Life-energy that is indolent and limited in its capacity, bound to a narrow range of instinctive impulses, not developing, not seeking farther, not urged to a greater kinetic action or a more luminously conscious action, would be assigned to the same category. The animal, in whom there is this less developed force of consciousness, is prior in creation; the more developed human consciousness, in which there is a greater force of kinetic Mind-energy and light of perception, is a later creation. The Tantra speaks of a soul fallen from its status passing through many lacs of births in plant and animal forms before it can reach the human level and be ready for salvation. Here, again, there is implied the conception of vegetable and animal life-forms as the lower steps of a ladder, humanity as the last or culminating development of the conscious being, the form which the soul has to inhabit in order to be capable of the spiritual motive and a spiritual issue out of mentality, life and physicality. This is indeed the normal conception, and it recommends itself so strongly both to reason and intuition that it hardly needs debate, — the conclusion is almost unescapable.

It is against this background of a developing evolutionary process that we have to look at man, his origin and first appearance, his status in the manifestation. There are here two possibilities; either there was the sudden appearance of a human body and consciousness in the earth-nature, an abrupt creation or independent automatic manifestation of reasoning mentality in the material world intervening upon a previous similar manifestation of subconscious life-forms and of living conscious bodies in Matter, or else there was an evolution of humanity out of animal being, slow perhaps in its preparation and in its stages of development, but with strong leaps of change at the decisive points of the transition. The latter theory offers no difficulty: for it is certain that changes of characteristics in the type, though not of the fundamental type itself, can be brought about in species or genus, — indeed this has already been done by man himself and its possibilities are being strikingly worked out on a small scale by experimental Science, — and it may fairly be assumed that the secretly conscious Energy in Nature could effect large-scale operations of the kind and bring about considerable and decisive developments by means of its own creative conventions. The necessary condition for the change from the normal animal to the human character of existence would be a development of the physical organisation which would capacitate a rapid progression, a reversal or turnover of the consciousness, a reaching to a new height and a looking down from it at the lower stages, a heightening and widening of capacity which would enable the being to take up the old animal faculties with a larger and more plastic, a human intelligence, and at the same time or later to develop greater and subtler powers proper to the new type of being, powers of reason, reflection, complex observation, organised invention, thought and discovery. If there is an emergent Consciousness-Force, there would be no difficulty in the transition, the instrument being provided, except the difficulty of the obstruction and resistance of the material Inconscience. The animal has already some of the corresponding qualities on a limited scale, for action only, in a rudimentary organisation crude and simple, with a very inferior scope and plasticity, a narrower and more casual command of the faculty; but especially the working of these faculties is more mechanical, less deliberate, marked with the character of an automatism of Nature-Energy driving an operation of primitive consciousness and not, as in man, of a conscious Energy observing and to a great extent directing and governing and deliberately changing or modifying its own operations. Other animal habits of consciousness are not fundamentally different from man's; all he had to do was to develop and enlarge them on a higher mental level and wherever possible, to mentalise, refine, subtilise, — in brief, to bring to them the enlightenment of his new understanding and intellectual capacity and a power of reasoned control denied to the animal. This change or reversal once effected, the power of the human mind to work upon itself and things, create, know, speculate, would develop in the course of his evolution, even if, as is conceivable, they were at the beginning small in scope, nearer to the animal, still comparatively simple and crude in their action. Such a reversal has been made in each radical transition of Nature: Life-Force emerging turns upon Matter, imposes a vital content on the operations of material Energy while it develops also its own new movements and operations; Life-Mind emerges in Life-Force and Matter and imposes its content of consciousness on their operations while it develops also its own action and faculties; a new greater emergence and reversal, the emergence of humanity, is in line with Nature's precedents; it would be a new application of the general principle.

This theory is therefore easy to accept: its working is intelligible. But the other hypothesis presents considerable difficulties. On the side of consciousness the new manifestation, the human, could be accounted for by an upsurge of concealed Consciousness from the involution in universal Nature. But in that case it must have had some material form already existent for its vehicle of emergence, the vehicle being adapted by the force of the emergence itself to the needs of a new inner creation; or else a rapid divergence from previous physical types or patterns may have brought a new being into existence. But whichever the hypothesis accepted, this means an evolutionary process, — there is only a difference in the method and machinery of the divergence or transition. Or there may have been, on the contrary, not an upsurgence but a descent of mentality from a Mind-plane above us, perhaps the descent of a soul or mental being into terrestrial Nature. The difficulty would then be the appearance of the human body, too complex and difficult an organ to have been suddenly created or manifested; for such a miraculous speed of process, though quite possible on a supraphysical plane of being, does not seem to figure among the normal possibles or potentials of the material Energy. It could only happen there by an intervention of a supraphysical force or law of Nature or by a creator Mind acting with full power and directly on Matter. An action of a supraphysical Force and a creator may be conceded in every new appearance in Matter; each such appearance is at bottom a miracle operated by a secret Consciousness supported by a veiled Mind-Energy or Life-Energy: but the action is nowhere seen to be direct, overt, self-sufficient; it is always superimposed on an already realised physical basis and acts by an extension of some established process of Nature. It is more conceivable that there was an opening of some existing body to a supraphysical influx so that it was transformed into a new body; but no such event can lightly be assumed to have taken place in the past history of material Nature: in order to happen it would seem to need either the conscious intervention of an invisible mental being to form the body he intended to inhabit or else a previous development of a mental being in Matter itself who would be already able to receive a supraphysical power and impose it on the rigid and narrow formulas of his physical existence. Otherwise we must suppose that there was a pre-existent body already so much evolved as to be fitted for the reception of a vast mental influx or capable of a pliable response to the descent into it of a mental being. But this would suppose a previous evolution of mind in body to the point at which such a receptivity would be possible. It is quite conceivable that such an evolution from below and such a descent from above co-operated in the appearance of humanity in earth-nature. The secret psychical entity already there in the animal might have itself called down the mental being, the Mind-Purusha, into the realm of living Matter in order to take up the vital-mental energy already at work and lift it into a higher mentality. But this would still be a process of evolution, the higher plane only intervening to assist the appearance and enlargement of its own principle in terrestrial Nature.

Next, it may be conceded that each type or pattern of consciousness and being in the body, once established, has to be faithful to the law of being of that type, to its own design and rule of nature. But it may also very well be that part of the law of the human type is its impulse towards self-exceeding, that the means for a conscious transition has been provided for among the spiritual powers of man; the possession of such a capacity may be a part of the plan on which the creative Energy has built him. It may be conceded that what man has up till now principally done is to act within the circle of his nature, on a spiral of nature-movement, sometimes descending, sometimes ascending, — there has been no straight line of progress, no indisputable, fundamental or radical exceeding of his past nature: what he has done is to sharpen, subtilise, make a more and more complex and plastic use of his capacities. It cannot truly be said that there has been no such thing as human progress since man's appearance or even in his recent ascertainable history; for however great the ancients, however supreme some of their achievements and creations, however impressive their powers of spirituality, of intellect or of character, there has been in later developments an increasing subtlety, complexity, manifold development of knowledge and possibility in man's achievements, in his politics, society, life, science, metaphysics, knowledge of all kinds, art, literature; even in his spiritual endeavour, less surprisingly lofty and less massive in power of spirituality than that of the ancients, there has been this increasing subtlety, plasticity, sounding of depths, extension of seeking. There have been falls from a high type of culture, a sharp temporary descent into a certain obscurantism, cessations of the spiritual urge, plunges into a barbaric natural materialism; but these are temporary phenomena, at worst a downward curve of the spiral of progress. This progress has not indeed carried the race beyond itself, into a self-exceeding, a transformation of the mental being. But that was not to be expected; for the action of evolutionary Nature in a type of being and consciousness is first to develop the type to its utmost capacity by just such a subtilisation and increasing complexity till it is ready for her bursting of the shell, the ripened decisive emergence, reversal, turning over of consciousness on itself that constitutes a new stage in the evolution. If it be supposed that her next step is the spiritual and supramental being, the stress of spirituality in the race may be taken as a sign that that is Nature's intention, the sign too of the capacity of man to operate in himself or aid her to operate the transition. If the appearance in animal being of a type similar in some respects to the ape-kind but already from the beginning endowed with the elements of humanity was the method of the human evolution, the appearance in the human being of a spiritual type resembling mental-animal humanity but already with the stamp of the spiritual aspiration on it would be the obvious method of Nature for the evolutionary production of the spiritual and supramental being.

It is pertinently suggested that if such an evolutionary culmination is intended and man is to be its medium, it will only be a few especially evolved human beings who will form the new type and move towards the new life; that once done, the rest of humanity will sink back from a spiritual aspiration no longer necessary for Nature's purpose and remain quiescent in its normal status. It can equally be reasoned that the human gradation must be preserved if there is really an ascent of the soul by reincarnation through the evolutionary degrees towards the spiritual summit; for otherwise the most necessary of all the intermediate steps will be lacking. It must be conceded at once that there is not the least probability or possibility of the whole human race rising in a block to the supramental level; what is suggested is nothing so revolutionary and astonishing, but only the capacity in the human mentality, when it has reached a certain level or a certain point of stress of the evolutionary impetus, to press towards a higher plane of consciousness and its embodiment in the being. The being will necessarily undergo by this embodiment a change from the normal constitution of its nature, a change certainly of its mental and emotional and sensational constitution and also to a great extent of the body-consciousness and the physical conditioning of our life and energies; but the change of consciousness will be the chief factor, the initial movement, the physical modification will be a subordinate factor, a consequence. This transmutation of the consciousness will always remain possible to the human being when the flame of the soul, the psychic kindling, becomes potent in heart and mind and the nature is ready. The spiritual aspiration is innate in man; for he is, unlike the animal, aware of imperfection and limitation and feels that there is something to be attained beyond what he now is: this urge towards self-exceeding is not likely ever to die out totally in the race. The human mental status will be always there, but it will be there not only as a degree in the scale of rebirth, but as an open step towards the spiritual and supramental status.

It must be observed that the appearance of human mind and body on the earth marks a crucial step, a decisive change in the course and process of the evolution; it is not merely a continuation of the old lines. Up till this advent of a developed thinking mind in Matter evolution had been effected, not by the self-aware aspiration, intention, will or seeking of the living being, but subconsciously or subliminally by the automatic operation of Nature. This was so because the evolution began from the Inconscience and the secret Consciousness had not emerged sufficiently from it to operate through the self-aware participating individual will of its living creature. But in man the necessary change has been made, — the being has become awake and aware of himself; there has been made manifest in Mind its will to develop, to grow in knowledge, to deepen the inner and widen the outer existence, to increase the capacities of the nature. Man has seen that there can be a higher status of consciousness than his own; the evolutionary oestrus is there in his parts of mind and life, the aspiration to exceed himself is delivered and articulate within him: he has become conscious of a soul, discovered the Self and Spirit. In him, then, the substitution of a conscious for a subconscious evolution has become conceivable and practicable, and it may well be concluded that the aspiration, the urge, the persistent endeavour in him is a sure sign of Nature's will for a higher way to fulfilment, the emergence of a greater status.

In the previous stages of the evolution Nature's first care and effort had to be directed towards a change in the physical organisation, for only so could there be a change of consciousness; this was a necessity imposed by the insufficiency of the force of consciousness already in formation to effect a change in the body. But in man a reversal is possible, indeed inevitable; for it is through his consciousness, through its transmutation and no longer through a new bodily organism as a first instrumentation that the evolution can and must be effected. In the inner reality of things a change of consciousness was always the major fact, the evolution has always had a spiritual significance and the physical change was only instrumental; but this relation was concealed by the first abnormal balance of the two factors, the body of the external Inconscience outweighing and obscuring in importance the spiritual element, the conscious being. But once the balance has been righted, it is no longer the change of body that must precede the change of consciousness; the consciousness itself by its mutation will necessitate and operate whatever mutation is needed for the body. It has to be noted that the human mind has already shown a capacity to aid Nature in the evolution of new types of plant and animal; it has created new forms of its environment, developed by knowledge and discipline considerable changes in its own mentality. It is not an impossibility that man should aid Nature consciously also in his own spiritual and physical evolution and transformation. The urge to it is already there and partly effective, though still incompletely understood and accepted by the surface mentality; but one day it may understand, go deeper within itself and discover the means, the secret energy, the intended operation of the Consciousness-Force within which is the hidden reality of what we call Nature.

All these are conclusions that can be arrived at even from the observation of the outward phenomena of Nature's progression, her surface evolution of being and of consciousness in the physical birth and the body. But there is the other, the invisible factor; there is rebirth, the progress of the soul by ascent from grade to grade of the evolving existence, and in the grades to higher and higher types of bodily and mental instrumentation. In this progression the psychic entity is still veiled, even in man the conscious mental being, by its instruments, by mind and life and body; it is unable to manifest fully, held back from coming to the front where it can stand out as the master of its nature, obliged to submit to a certain determination by the instruments, to a domination of Purusha by Prakriti. But in man the psychic part of the personality is able to develop with a much greater rapidity than in the inferior creation, and a time can arrive when the soul-entity is close to the point at which it will emerge from behind the veil into the open and become the master of its instrumentation in Nature. But this will mean that the secret indwelling spirit, the Daemon, the Godhead within is on the point of emergence; and, when it emerges, it can hardly be doubted that its demand will be, as indeed it already is in the Mind itself when it undergoes the inner psychic influence, for a diviner, a more spiritual existence. In the nature of the earth-life where the Mind is an instrument of the Ignorance, this can only be effected by a change of consciousness, a transition from a foundation in Ignorance to a foundation in Knowledge, from the mental to a supramental consciousness, a supramental instrumentation of Nature.

There is no conclusive validity in the reasoning that because this is a world of Ignorance, such a transformation can only be achieved by a passage to a heaven beyond or cannot be achieved at all and the demand of the psychic entity is itself ignorant and must be replaced by a merger of the soul in the Absolute. This conclusion could only be solely valid if Ignorance were the whole meaning, substance and power of the world-manifestation or if there were no element in World-Nature itself through which there could be an exceeding of the ignorant mentality that still burdens our present status of being. But the Ignorance is only a portion of this World-Nature; it is not the whole of it, not the original power or creator: it is in its higher origin a self-limiting Knowledge and even in its lower origin, its emergence out of the sheer material Inconscience, it is a suppressed Consciousness labouring to find, to recover itself, to manifest Knowledge, which is its true character, as the foundation of existence. In universal Mind itself there are ranges above our mentality which are instruments of the cosmic truth-cognition, and into these the mental being can surely rise; for already it rises towards them in supernormal conditions or receives from them without yet knowing or possessing them intuitions, spiritual intimations, large influxes of illumination or spiritual capacity. All these ranges are conscious of what is beyond them, and the highest of them is directly open to the Supermind, aware of the Truth-Consciousness which exceeds it. Moreover, in the evolving being itself, those greater powers of consciousness are here, supporting Mind-truth, underlying its action which screens them; this Supermind and those Truth-powers uphold Nature by their secret presence: even, truth of Mind is their result, a diminished operation, a representation in partial figures. It is, therefore, not only natural but seems inevitable that these higher powers of Existence should manifest here in Mind as Mind itself has manifested in Life and Matter.

Man's urge towards spirituality is the inner driving of the spirit within him towards emergence, the insistence of the Consciousness-Force of the being towards the next step of its manifestation. It is true that the spiritual urge has been largely other-worldly or turned at its extreme towards a spiritual negation and self-annihilation of the mental individual; but this is only one side of its tendency maintained and made dominant by the necessity of passing out of the kingdom of the fundamental Inconscience, overcoming the obstacle of the body, casting away the obscure vital, getting rid of the ignorant mentality, the necessity to attain first and foremost, by a rejection of all these impediments to spiritual being, to a spiritual status. The other, the dynamic side of the spiritual urge has not been absent, — the aspiration to a spiritual mastery and mutation of Nature, to a spiritual perfection of the being, a divinisation of the mind, the heart and the very body: there has even been the dream or a psychic prevision of a fulfilment exceeding the individual transformation, a new earth and heaven, a city of God, a divine descent upon earth, a reign of the spiritually perfect, a kingdom of God not only within us but outside, in a collective human life. However obscure may have been some of the forms taken by this aspiration, the indication they contain of the urge of the occult spiritual being within to emergence in earth-nature is unmistakable.

If a spiritual unfolding on earth is the hidden truth of our birth into Matter, if it is fundamentally an evolution of consciousness that has been taking place in Nature, then man as he is cannot be the last term of that evolution: he is too imperfect an expression of the Spirit, Mind itself a too limited form and instrumentation; Mind is only a middle term of consciousness, the mental being can only be a transitional being. If, then, man is incapable of exceeding mentality, he must be surpassed and Supermind and superman must manifest and take the lead of the creation. But if his mind is capable of opening to what exceeds it, then there is no reason why man himself should not arrive at Supermind and supermanhood or at least lend his mentality, life and body to an evolution of that greater term of the Spirit manifesting in Nature.

Chapter XXIV

The Evolution of the Spiritual Man

Even as men come to Me, so I accept them. It is my path that men follow from all sides.... Whatever form the worshipper chooses to worship with faith, I set in him firm faith in it, and with that faith he puts his yearning into his adoration and gets his desire dispensed by Me. But limited is that fruit. Those whose sacrifice is to the gods, to elemental spirits, reach the gods, reach the elemental spirits, but those whose sacrifice is to Me, to Me they come. *Gita.*[1]

In these there is not the Wonder and the Might; the truths occult exist not for the mind of the ignorant. *Rig Veda.*[2]

As a seer working out the occult truths and their discoveries of knowledge, he brought into being the seven Craftsmen of heaven and in the light of day they spoke and wrought the things of their wisdom. *Rig Veda.*[3]

Seer-wisdoms, secret words that speak their meaning to the seer. *Rig Veda.*[4]

None knows the birth of these; they know each other's way of begetting: but the Wise perceives these hidden mysteries, even that which the great Goddess, the many-hued Mother, bears as her teat of knowledge. *Rig Veda.*[5]

Made certain of the meaning of the highest spiritual knowledge, purified in their being. *Mundaka Upanishad.*[6]

He strives by these means and has the knowledge: in him this spirit enters into its supreme status.... Satisfied in knowledge, having built up their spiritual being, the Wise, in union with

---

[1] IV. 11; VII. 21-23; IX. 25.   [2] VII. 61. 5.   [3] IV. 16. 3.   [4] IV. 3. 16.
[5] VII. 56. 2, 4.   [6] III. 2. 6.

the spiritual self, reach the Omnipresent everywhere and enter
into the All.   *Mundaka Upanishad.*[7]

IN THE earliest stages of evolutionary Nature we are met by
the dumb secrecy of her inconscience; there is no revelation
of any significance or purpose in her works, no hint of any
other principles of being than that first formulation which is
her immediate preoccupation and seems to be for ever her only
business: for in her primal works Matter alone appears, the sole
dumb and stark cosmic reality. A Witness of creation, if there
had been one conscious but uninstructed, would only have seen
appearing out of a vast abyss of an apparent non-existence an
Energy busy with the creation of Matter, a material world and
material objects, organising the infinity of the Inconscient into
the scheme of a boundless universe or a system of countless universes that stretched around him into Space without any certain
end or limit, a tireless creation of nebulae and star-clusters and
suns and planets, existing only for itself, without a sense in it,
empty of cause or purpose. It might have seemed to him a stupendous machinery without a use, a mighty meaningless movement,
an aeonic spectacle without a witness, a cosmic edifice without
an inhabitant; for he would have seen no sign of an indwelling
Spirit, no being for whose delight it was made. A creation of
this kind could only be the outcome of an inconscient Energy
or an illusion-cinema, a shadow-play or puppet-play of forms
reflected on a superconscient indifferent Absolute. He would
have seen no evidence of a soul and no hint of Mind or Life in
this immeasurable and interminable display of Matter. It would
not have seemed to him possible or imaginable that there could
at all be in this desert universe for ever inanimate and insensible
an outbreak of teeming life, a first vibration of something occult
and incalculable, alive and conscious, a secret spiritual entity
feeling its way towards the surface.

But after some aeons, looking out once more on that vain

[7] III. 2. 4, 5.

panorama, he might have detected in one small corner at least of the universe this phenomenon, a corner where Matter had been prepared, its operations sufficiently fixed, organised, made stable, adapted as a scene of a new development, — the phenomenon of a living Matter, a Life in things that had emerged and become visible: but still the Witness would have understood nothing, for evolutionary Nature still veils her secret. He would have seen a Nature concerned only with establishing this outburst of Life, this new creation, but Life living for itself with no significance in it, — a wanton and abundant creatrix busy scattering the seed of her new power and establishing a multitude of its forms in a beautiful and luxurious profusion or, later, multiplying endlessly genus and species for the pure pleasure of creation: a small touch of lively colour and movement would have been flung into the immense cosmic desert and nothing more. The Witness could not have imagined that a thinking mind would appear in this minute island of life, that a consciousness could awake in the Inconscient, a new and greater subtler vibration come to the surface and betray more clearly the existence of the submerged Spirit. It would have seemed to him at first that Life had somehow become aware of itself and that was all; for this scanty new-born mind seemed to be only a servant of life, a contrivance to help life to live, a machinery for its maintenance, for attack and defence, for certain needs and vital satisfactions, for the liberation of life-instinct and life-impulse. It could not have seemed possible to him that in this little life, so inconspicuous amid the immensities, in one sole species out of this petty multitude, a mental being would emerge, a Mind serving Life still but also making Life and Matter its servants, using them for the fulfilment of its own ideas, will, wishes, — a mental being who would create all manner of utensils, tools, instruments out of Matter for all kinds of utilities, erect out of it cities, houses, temples, theatres, laboratories, factories, chisel from it statues and carve cave-cathedrals, invent architecture, sculpture, painting, poetry and a hundred crafts and arts, discover the mathematics and physics of the universe and the hidden secret of its structure, live for the sake of Mind and its interests, for thought and knowledge, develop into the thinker, the philosopher and scientist and, as a supreme defiance to the reign of Matter, awake in himself to the hidden Godhead, become the hunter after the invisible, the mystic and the spiritual seeker.

But if after several ages or cycles the Witness had looked again and seen this miracle in full process, even then perhaps, obscured by his original experience of the sole reality of Matter in the universe, he would still not have understood; it would still seem impossible to him that the hidden Spirit could wholly emerge, complete in its consciousness, and dwell upon the earth as the self-knower and world-knower, Nature's ruler and possessor. "Impossible!" he might say, "all that has happened is nothing much, a little bubbling of sensitive grey stuff of brain, a queer freak in a bit of inanimate Matter moving about on a small dot in the Universe." On the contrary, a new Witness intervening at the end of the story, informed of the past developments but unobsessed by the deception of the beginning, might cry out, "Ah, then, this was the intended miracle, the last of many, — the Spirit that was submerged in the Inconscience has broken out from it and now inhabits, unveiled, the form of things which, veiled, it had created as its dwelling-place and the scene of its emergence." But in fact a more conscious Witness might have discovered the clue at an early period of the unfolding, even in each step of its process; for at each stage Nature's mute secrecy, though still there, diminishes; a hint is given of the next step, a more overtly significant preparation is visible. Already, in what seems to be inconscient in Life, the signs of sensation coming towards the surface are visible; in moving and breathing Life the emergence of sensitive Mind is apparent and the preparation of thinking Mind is not entirely hidden, while in thinking Mind, when it develops, there appear at an early stage the rudimentary strivings and afterwards the more developed seekings of a spiritual consciousness. As plant-life contains in itself the obscure possibility of the conscious animal, as the animal-mind is astir with the movements of feeling and perception and the rudiments of conception that are the first ground for man the thinker, so man the mental being is sublimated by the endeavour of the evolutionary Energy to develop out of him the spiritual man, the fully conscious being, man exceeding his first material self and discoverer of his true self and highest nature.

But if this is to be accepted as the intention in Nature, there are two questions that put themselves at once and call for a definitive answer, — first, the exact nature of the transition from mental to spiritual being and, when that is given, the process and method of the evolution of the spiritual out of the mental man. It would at first sight seem evident that as each gradation emerges not only out of its precedent grade but in it, as Life emerges in Matter and is largely limited and determined in its self-expression by its material conditions, as Mind emerges in Life-in-Matter and is similarly limited and determined in its self-expression by life-conditions and material conditions, so Spirit too must emerge in a Mind embodied in Life-in-Matter and must be largely limited and determined by the mental conditions in which it has its roots as well as the life-conditions, the material conditions of its existence here. It might even be maintained that, if there has been any evolution of the spiritual in us, it is only as a part of the mental evolution, a special operation of man's mentality; the spiritual element is not a distinct or separate entity and cannot have an independent emergence or a supramental future. The mental being can develop a spiritual interest or preoccupation and may evolve perhaps in consequence a spiritual as well as an intellectual mentality, a fine soul-flower of his mental life. The spiritual may become a predominant trend in some men just as in others there is a predominant artistic or pragmatic trend; but there can be no such thing as a spiritual being taking up and transforming the mental into the spiritual nature. There is no evolution of the spiritual man; there is only an evolution of a new and possibly a finer and rarer element in a mental being. This then is what has to be brought out, — the clear distinction between the spiritual and the mental, the nature of this evolution and the factors which make it possible and inevitable that there should be this emergence of the Spirit in its true distinct character, not remaining, as it now for the most part is in its process or seems to be in its way of appearance, a subordinate or a dominating feature of our mentality, but defining itself as a new power which will finally overtop the mental part and replace it as the leader of the life and nature.

It is quite true that to a surface view Life seems only an operation of Matter, Mind an activity of Life, and it might seem to follow that what we call the soul or spirit is only a power of mentality, soul a fine form of Mind, spirituality a high activity of the embodied mental being. But this is a superficial view of things due to the thought's concentrating on the appearance and process and not looking at what lies behind the process. One might as well on the same lines have concluded that electricity is only a product or operation of water and cloud matter, because it is in such a field that lightning emerges; but a deeper inquiry has shown that both cloud and water have, on the contrary, the energy of electricity as their foundation, their constituent power or energy-substance: that which seems to be a result is, — in its reality, though not in its form, — the origin; the effect is in the essence pre-existent to the apparent cause, the principle of the emergent activity precedent to its present field of action. So it is throughout evolutionary Nature; Matter could not have become animate if the principle of Life had not been there constituting Matter and emerging as a phenomenon of Life-in-Matter; Life-in-Matter could not have begun to feel, perceive, think, reason, if the principle of Mind had not been there behind life and substance, constituting it as its field of operation and emergent in the phenomenon of a thinking life and body: so too spirituality emerging in Mind is the sign of a power which itself has founded and constituted life, mind and body and is now emerging as a spiritual being in a living and thinking body. How far this emergence will go, whether it will become dominant and transform its instrument, is a subsequent question; but what is necessary first to posit is the existence of Spirit as something else than Mind and greater than Mind, spirituality as something other than mentality and the spiritual being therefore as something distinct from the mental being: Spirit is a final evolutionary emergence because it is the original involutionary element and factor. Evolution is an inverse action of the involution: what is an ultimate and last derivation in the involution is the first to appear in the evolution; what was original and primal in the involution is in the evolution the last and supreme emergence.

It is true again that it is difficult for man's mind to distinguish entirely the soul or self or any spiritual element in him from the mental and vital formation in which it makes its appearance; but that is only so long as the emergence is not complete. In the animal mind is not quite distinct from its own life-matrix and life-matter; its movements are so involved in the life-movements that it cannot detach itself from them, cannot stand separate and observe them; but in man mind has become separate, he can become aware of his mental operations as distinct from his life-operations, his thought and will can disengage themselves from his sensations and impulses, desires and emotional reactions, can become detached from them, observe and control them, sanction or cancel their functioning: he does not as yet know the secrets of his being well enough to be aware of himself decisively and with certitude as a mental being in a life and body, but he has that impression and can take inwardly that position. So too at first soul in man does not appear as something quite distinct from mind and from mentalised life; its movements are involved in the mind-movements, its operations seem to be mental and emotional activities; the mental human being is not aware of a soul in him standing back from the mind and life and body, detaching itself, seeing and controlling and moulding their action and formation: but, as the inner evolution proceeds, this is precisely what can, must and does happen, — it is the long-delayed but inevitable next step in our evolutionary destiny. There can be a decisive emergence in which the being separates itself from thought and sees itself in an inner silence as the spirit in mind, or separates itself from the life-movements, desires, sensations, kinetic impulses and is aware of itself as the spirit supporting life, or separates itself from the body-sense and knows itself as a spirit ensouling Matter: this is the discovery of ourselves as the Purusha, a mental being or a life-soul or a subtle self supporting the body. This is taken by many as a sufficient discovery of the true self and in a certain sense they are right; for it is the Self or Spirit that so represents itself in regard to the activities of Nature, and this revelation of its presence is enough to disengage the spiritual element: but self-discovery can go farther, it can even put aside all relation to form or action of Nature. For it is seen that these selves are representations of a divine Entity to which mind, life and body are only forms and instruments: we are then the Soul looking at Nature, knowing all her dynamisms in us, not by mental perception and observation, but by an intrinsic consciousness and its direct sense of things and its intimate exact vision, able therefore by its emergence to put a close control on our nature and change it. When there is a complete silence in the being, either a stillness of the whole being or a stillness behind unaffected by surface movements, then we can become aware of a Self, a spiritual substance of our being, an existence exceeding even the soul-individuality, spreading itself into universality, surpassing all dependence on any natural form or action, extending itself upward into a transcendence of which the limits are not visible. It is these liberations of the spiritual part in us which are the decisive steps of the spiritual evolution in Nature.

It is only through these decisive movements that the true character of the evolution becomes evident; for till then there are only preparatory movements, a pressure of the psychic Entity on the mind, life and body to develop a true soul-action, a pressure of the Spirit or Self for liberation from the ego, from the surface ignorance, a turning of the mind and life towards some occult Reality, — preliminary experiences, partial formulations of a spiritualised mind, a spiritualised life, but no complete change, no probability of an entire unveiling of the soul or self or a radical transformation of the nature. When there is the decisive emergence, one sign of it is the status or action in us of an inherent, intrinsic, self-existent consciousness which knows itself by the mere fact of being, knows all that is in itself in the same way, by identity with it, begins even to see all that to our mind seems external in the same manner, by a movement of identity or by an intrinsic direct consciousness which envelops, penetrates, enters into its object, discovers itself in the object, is aware in it of something that is not mind or life or body. There is, then, evidently a spiritual consciousness which is other than the mental, and it testifies to the existence of a spiritual being in us which is other than our surface mental personality. But at first this consciousness may confine itself to a status of being separate from the action of our ignorant surface nature, observing it, limiting itself to knowledge, to a seeing of things with a spiritual sense and vision of existence. For action it may still depend upon the mental, vital, bodily instruments, or it may allow them to act according to their own nature and itself remain satisfied with self-experience and self-knowledge, with an inner liberation, an eventual freedom: but it may also and usually does exercise a certain authority, governance, influence on thought, life-movement, physical action, a purifying uplifting control compelling them to move in a higher and purer truth of themselves, to obey or be an instrumentation of an influx of some diviner Power or a luminous direction which is not mental but spiritual and can be recognised as having a certain divine character, — the inspiration of a greater Self or the command of the Ruler of all being, the Ishwara. Or the nature may obey the psychic entity's intimations, move in an inner light, follow an inner guidance. This is already a considerable evolution and amounts to a beginning at least of a psychic and spiritual transformation. But it is possible to go farther; for the spiritual being, once inwardly liberated, can develop in mind the higher states of being that are its own natural atmosphere and bring down a supramental energy and action which are proper to the Truth-Consciousness; the ordinary mental instrumentation, life-instrumentation, physical instrumentation even, could then be entirely transformed and become parts no longer of an ignorance however much illumined, but of a supramental creation which would be the true action of a spiritual Truth-Consciousness and Knowledge.

At first this truth of the spirit and of spirituality is not self-evident to the mind; man becomes mentally aware of his soul as something other than his body, superior to his normal mind and life, but he has no clear sense of it, only a feeling of some of its effects on his nature. As these effects take a mental form or a life-form, the difference is not firmly and trenchantly drawn, the soul-perception does not acquire a distinct and assured independence. Very commonly indeed, a complex of half-effects of the psychic pressure on the mental and vital parts, a formation mixed with mental aspiration and vital desires, is mistaken for the soul, just as the separative ego is taken for the self, although the self in its true being is universal as well as individual in its essence, — or just as a mixture of mental aspiration and vital enthusiasm and ardour uplifted by some kind of strong or high belief or self-dedication or altruistic eagerness is mistaken for spirituality. But this vagueness and these confusions are inevitable as a temporary stage of the evolution which, because ignorance is its starting-point and the whole stamp of our first nature, must necessarily begin with an imperfect intuitive perception and an instinctive urge or seeking without any acquired experience or clear knowledge. Even the formations which are the first effects of the perception or urge or the first indices of a spiritual evolution, must inevitably be of this incomplete and tentative nature. But the error so created comes very much in the way of a true understanding, and it must therefore be emphasised that spirituality is not a high intellectuality, not idealism, not an ethical turn of mind or moral purity and austerity, not religiosity or an ardent and exalted emotional fervour, not even a compound of all these excellent things; a mental belief, creed or faith, an emotional aspiration, a regulation of conduct according to a religious or ethical formula are not spiritual achievement and experience. These things are of considerable value to mind and life; they are of value to the spiritual evolution itself as preparatory movements disciplining, purifying or giving a suitable form to the nature; but they still belong to the mental evolution, — the beginning of a spiritual realisation, experience, change is not yet there. Spirituality is in its essence an awakening to the inner reality of our being, to a spirit, self, soul which is other than our mind, life and body, an inner aspiration to know, to feel, to be that, to enter into contact with the greater Reality beyond and pervading the universe which inhabits also our own being, to be in communion with It and union with It, and a turning, a conversion, a transformation of our whole being as a result of the aspiration, the contact, the union, a growth or waking into a new becoming or new being, a new self, a new nature.

In fact, the creative Consciousness-Force in our earth existence has to lead forward, in an almost simultaneous process but with a considerable priority and greater stress of the inferior element, a double evolution. There is an evolution of our outward nature, the nature of the mental being in the life and body, and there is within it, pressing forward for self-revelation because with the emergence of mind that revelation is becoming possible, a preparation at least, even the beginning of an evolution of our inner being, our occult subliminal and spiritual nature. But Nature's major preoccupation must necessarily be still and for a long time the evolution of mind to its greatest possible range, height, subtlety; for only so can be prepared the unveiling of an entirely intuitive intelligence, of Overmind, of Supermind, the difficult passage to a higher instrumentation of the Spirit. If the sole intention were the revelation of the essential spiritual Reality and a cessation of our being into its pure existence, this insistence on the mental evolution would have no purpose: for at every point of the nature there can be a breaking out of the Spirit and an absorption of our being into it; an intensity of the heart, a total silence of the mind, a single absorbing passion of the will would be enough to bring about that culminating movement. If Nature's final intention were other-worldly, then too the same law would hold; for everywhere, at any point of the nature, there can be a sufficient power of the other-worldly urge to break through and away from the terrestrial action and enter into a spiritual elsewhere. But if her intention is a comprehensive change of the being, this double evolution is intelligible and justifies itself; for it is for that purpose indispensable.

This, however, imposes a difficult and slow spiritual advance: for, first, the spiritual emergence has to wait at each step for the instruments to be ready; next, as the spiritual formation emerges, it is mixed inextricably with the powers, motives, impulses of an imperfect mind, life and body, — there is a pull on it to accept and serve these powers, motives and impulses, a downward gravitation and perilous mixture, a constant temptation to fall or deviation, at least a fettering, a weight, a retardation; there is a necessity to return upon a step gained in order to bring up something of the nature which hangs back and prevents a farther step; finally, there is, by the very character of mind in which it has to work, a limitation of the emerging spiritual light and power and a compulsion on it to move by segments, to follow one line or another and leave altogether or leave till later on the achievement of its own totality. This hampering, this obstacle of the mind, life and body, — the heavy inertia and persistence of the body, the turbid passions of the life-part, the obscurity and doubting incertitudes, denials, other-formulations of the mind, — is an impediment so great and intolerable that the spiritual urge becomes impatient and tries rigorously to quell these opponents, to reject the life, to mortify the body, to silence the mind and achieve its own separate salvation, spirit departing into pure spirit and rejecting from it altogether an undivine and obscure Nature. Apart from the supreme call, the natural push of the spiritual part in us to return to its own highest element and status, this aspect of vital and physical Nature as an impediment to pure spirituality is a compelling reason for asceticism, for illusionism, for the tendency to other-worldliness, the urge towards withdrawal from life, the passion for a pure and unmixed Absolute. A pure spiritual absolutism is a movement of the self towards its own supreme selfhood, but it is also indispensable for Nature's own purpose; for without it the mixture, the downward gravitation would make the spiritual emergence impossible. The extremist of this absolutism, the solitary, the ascetic, is the standard-bearer of the spirit, his ochre robe is its flag, the sign of a refusal of all compromise, — as indeed the struggle of emergence cannot end by a compromise, but only by an entire spiritual victory and the complete surrender of the lower nature. If that is impossible here, then indeed it must be achieved elsewhere; if Nature refuses submission to the emerging spirit, then the soul must withdraw from her. There is thus a dual tendency in the spiritual emergence, on one side a drive towards the establishment at all cost of the spiritual consciousness in the being, even to the rejection of Nature, on the other side a push towards the extension of spirituality to our parts of nature. But until the first is fully achieved, the second can only be imperfect and halting. It is the foundation of the pure spiritual consciousness that is the first object in the evolution of the spiritual man, and it is this and the urge of that consciousness towards contact with the Reality, the Self or the Divine Being that must be the first and foremost or even, till it is perfectly accomplished, the sole preoccupation of the spiritual seeker. It is the one thing needful that has to be done by each on whatever line is possible to him, by each according to the spiritual capacity developed in his nature.

In considering the achieved course of the evolution of the spiritual being, we have to regard it from two sides, — a consideration of the means, the lines of development utilised by Nature and a view of the actual results achieved by it in the human individual. There are four main lines which Nature has followed in her attempt to open up the inner being, — religion, occultism, spiritual thought and an inner spiritual realisation and experience: the three first are approaches, the last is the decisive avenue of entry. All these four powers have worked by a simultaneous action, more or less connected, sometimes in a variable collaboration, sometimes in dispute with each other, sometimes in a separate independence. Religion has admitted an occult element in its ritual, ceremony, sacraments; it has leaned upon spiritual thinking, deriving from it sometimes a creed or theology, sometimes its supporting spiritual philosophy, — the former, ordinarily, is the occidental method, the latter the oriental: but spiritual experience is the final aim and achievement of religion, its sky and summit. But also religion has sometimes banned occultism or reduced its own occult element to a minimum; it has pushed away the philosophic mind as a dry intellectual alien, leaned with all its weight on creed and dogma, pietistic emotion and fervour and moral conduct; it has reduced to a minimum or dispensed with spiritual realisation and experience. Occultism has sometimes put forward a spiritual aim as its goal, and followed occult knowledge and experience as an approach to it, formulated some kind of mystic philosophy: but more often it has confined itself to occult knowledge and practice without any spiritual vistas; it has turned to thaumaturgy or mere magic or even deviated into diabolism. Spiritual philosophy has very usually leaned on religion as its support or its way to experience; it has been the outcome of realisation and experience or built its structures as an approach to it: but it has also rejected all aid, — or all impediment, — of religion and proceeded in its own strength, either satisfied with mental knowledge or confident to discover its own path of experience and effective discipline. Spiritual experience has used all the three means as a starting-point, but it has also dispensed with them all, relying on its own pure strength: discouraging occult knowledge and powers as dangerous lures and entangling obstacles, it has sought only the pure truth of the spirit; dispensing with philosophy, it has arrived instead through the heart's fervour or a mystic inward spiritualisation; putting behind it all religious creed, worship and practice and regarding them as an inferior stage or first approach, it has passed on, leaving behind it all these supports, nude of all these trappings, to the sheer contact of the spiritual Reality. All these variations were necessary; the evolutionary endeavour of Nature has experimented on all lines in order to find her true way and her whole way towards the supreme consciousness and the integral knowledge.

For each of these means or approaches corresponds to something in our total being and therefore to something necessary to the total aim of her evolution. There are four necessities of man's self-expansion if he is not to remain this being of the surface ignorance seeking obscurely after the truth of things and collecting and systematising fragments and sections of knowledge, the small limited and half-competent creature of the cosmic Force which he now is in his phenomenal nature. He must know himself and discover and utilise all his potentialities: but to know himself and the world completely he must go behind his own and its exterior, he must dive deep below his own mental surface and the physical surface of Nature. This he can only do by knowing his inner mental, vital, physical and psychic being and its powers and movements and the universal laws and processes of the occult Mind and Life which stand behind the material front of the universe: that is the field of occultism, if we take the word in its widest significance. He must know also the hidden Power or Powers that control the world: if there is a Cosmic Self or Spirit or a Creator, he must be able to enter into relation with It or Him and be able to remain in whatever contact or communion is possible, get into some kind of tune with the master Beings of the universe or with the universal Being and its universal will or a supreme Being and His supreme will, follow the law It gives him and the assigned or revealed aim of his life and conduct, raise himself towards the highest height that It demands of him in his life now or in his existence hereafter; if there is no such universal or supreme Spirit or Being, he must know what there is and how to lift himself to it out of his present imperfection and impotence. This approach is the aim of religion: its purpose is to link the human with the Divine and in so doing sublimate the thought and life and flesh so that they may admit the rule of the soul and spirit. But this knowledge must be something more than a creed or a mystic revelation; his thinking mind must be able to accept it, to correlate it with the principle of things and the observed truth of the universe: this is the work of philosophy, and in the field of the truth of the spirit it can only be done by a spiritual philosophy, whether intellectual in its method or intuitive. But all knowledge and endeavour can reach its fruition only if it is turned into experience and has become a part of the consciousness and its established operations; in the spiritual field all this religious, occult or philosophical knowledge and endeavour must, to bear fruition, end in an opening up of the spiritual consciousness, in experiences that found and continually heighten, expand and enrich that consciousness and in the building of a life and action that is in conformity with the truth of the spirit: this is the work of spiritual realisation and experience.

In the very nature of things all evolution must proceed at first by a slow unfolding; for each new principle that evolves its powers has to make its way out of an involution in Inconscience and Ignorance. It has a difficult task in pulling itself out of the involution, out of the hold of the obscurity of the original medium, against the pull and strains, the instinctive opposition and obstruction of the Inconscience and the hampering mixture and blind obstinate retardations of the Ignorance. Nature affirms at first a vague urge and tendency which is a sign of the push of the occult, subliminal, submerged reality towards the surface; there are then small half-suppressed hints of the thing that is to be, imperfect beginnings, crude elements, rudimentary appearances, small, insignificant, hardly recognisable quanta. Afterwards there are small or large formations; a more characteristic and recognisable quality begins to show itself, first partially, here and there or in a low intensity, then more vivid, more formative; finally, there is the decisive emergence, a reversal of the consciousness, the beginning of the possibility of its radical change: but still much has to be done in every direction, a long and difficult growth towards perfection lies before the evolutionary endeavour. The thing done has not only to be confirmed, secured against relapse and the downward gravitation, against failure and extinction, but opened out into all the fields of its possibilities, its totality of entire self-achievement, its utmost height, subtlety, riches, wideness; it has to become dominant, all-embracing, comprehensive. This is everywhere the process of Nature and to ignore it is to miss the intention in her works and get lost in the maze of her procedure.

It is this process that has taken place in the evolution of religion in the human mind and consciousness; the work done by it for humanity cannot be understood or properly appreciated if we ignore the conditions of the process and their necessity. It is evident that the first beginnings of religion must be crude and imperfect, its development hampered by mixtures, errors, concessions to the human mind and vital part which may often be of a very unspiritual character. Ignorant and injurious and even disastrous elements may creep in and lead to error and evil; the dogmatism of the human mind, its self-assertive narrowness, its intolerant and challenging egoism, its attachment to its limited truths and still greater attachment to its errors, or the violence, fanaticism, militant and oppressive self-affirmation of the vital, its treacherous action on the mind in order to get a sanction for its own desires and propensities, may very easily invade the religious field and baulk religion of its higher spiritual aim and character; under the name of religion much ignorance may hide, many errors and an extensive wrong-building be permitted, many crimes even and offences against the spirit be committed. But this chequered history belongs to all human effort and, if it were to count against the truth and necessity of religion, would count also against the truth and necessity of every other line of human endeavour, against all man's action, his ideals, his thought, his art, his science.

Religion has opened itself to denial by its claim to determine the truth by divine authority, by inspiration, by a sacrosanct and infallible sovereignty given to it from on high; it has sought to impose itself on human thought, feeling, conduct without discussion or question. This is an excessive and premature claim, although imposed in a way on the religious idea by the imperative and absolute character of the inspirations and illuminations which are its warrant and justification and by the necessity of faith as an occult light and power from the soul amidst the mind's ignorance, doubts, weakness, incertitudes. Faith is indispensable to man, for without it he could not proceed forward in his journey through the Unknown; but it ought not to be imposed, it should come as a free perception or an imperative direction from the inner spirit. A claim to unquestioned acceptance could only be warranted if the spiritual effort had already achieved man's progression to the highest Truth-Consciousness total and integral, free from all ignorant mental and vital mixture. This is the ultimate object before us, but it has not yet been accomplished, and the premature claim has obscured the true work of the religious instinct in man, which is to lead him towards the

Divine Reality, to formulate all that he has yet achieved in that direction and to give to each human being a mould of spiritual discipline, a way of seeking, touching, nearing the Divine Truth, a way which is proper to the potentialities of his nature.

The wide and supple method of evolutionary Nature providing the amplest scope and preserving the true intention of the religious seeking of the human being can be recognised in the development of religion in India, where any number of religious formulations, cults and disciplines have been allowed, even encouraged to subsist side by side and each man was free to accept and follow that which was congenial to his thought, feeling, temperament, build of the nature. It is right and reasonable that there should be this plasticity, proper to experimental evolution: for religion's real business is to prepare man's mind, life and bodily existence for the spiritual consciousness to take it up; it has to lead him to that point where the inner spiritual light begins fully to emerge. It is at this point that religion must learn to subordinate itself, not to insist on its outer characters, but give full scope to the inner spirit itself to develop its own truth and reality. In the meanwhile it has to take up as much of man's mentality, vitality, physicality as it can and give all his activities a turn towards the spiritual direction, the revelation of a spiritual meaning in them, the imprint of a spiritual refinement, the beginning of a spiritual character. It is in this attempt that the errors of religion come in, for they are caused by the very nature of the matter with which it is dealing, — that inferior stuff invades the very forms that are meant to serve as intermediaries between the spiritual and the mental, vital or physical consciousness, and often it diminishes, degrades and corrupts them: but it is in this attempt that lies religion's greatest utility as an intercessor between spirit and nature. Truth and error live always together in the human evolution and the truth is not to be rejected because of its accompanying errors, though these have to be eliminated, — often a difficult business and, if crudely done, resulting in surgical harm inflicted on the body of religion; for what we see as error is very frequently the symbol or a disguise or a corruption or malformation of a truth which is lost in the brutal radicality of the operation, — the truth is cut out along with the error. Nature herself very commonly permits the good corn and the tares and weeds to grow together for a long time, because only so is her own growth, her free evolution possible.

Evolutionary Nature in her first awakening of man to a rudimentary spiritual consciousness must begin with a vague sense of the Infinite and the Invisible surrounding the physical being, a sense of the limitation and impotence of human mind and will and of something greater than himself concealed in the world, of Potencies beneficent or maleficent which determine the results of his action, a Power that is behind the physical world he lives in and has perhaps created it and him, or Powers that inform and rule her movements while they themselves perhaps are ruled by the greater Unknown that is beyond them. He had to determine what they are and find means of communication so that he might propitiate them or call them to his aid; he sought also for means by which he could find out and control the springs of the hidden movements of Nature. This he could not do at once by his reason because his reason could at first deal only with physical facts, but this was the domain of the Invisible and needed a supraphysical vision and knowledge; he had to do it by an extension of the faculty of intuition and instinct which was already there in the animal. This faculty, prolonged in the thinking being and mentalised, must have been more sensitive and active in early man, though still mostly on a lower scale, for he had to rely on it largely for all his first necessary discoveries: he had to rely also on the aid of subliminal experience; for the subliminal too must have been more active, more ready to up-surge in him, more capable of formulating its phenomena on the surface, before he learned to depend completely on his intellect and senses. The intuitions that he thus received by contact with Nature, his mind systematised and so created the early forms of religion. This active and ready power of intuition also gave him the sense of supraphysical forces behind the physical, and his instinct and a certain subliminal or supernormal experience of supraphysical beings with whom he could somehow communicate turned him towards the discovery of effective and canalising means for a dynamic utilisation of this knowledge; so were created magic and the other early forms of occultism. At some time it must have dawned on him that he had something in him which was not physical, a soul that survived the body; certain supernormal experiences which became active because of the pressure to know the invisible, must have helped to formulate his first crude ideas of this entity within him. It would only be later that he began to realise that what he perceived in the action of the universe was also there in some form within him and that in him also were elements that responded to invisible powers and forces for good or for evil; so would begin his religio-ethical formations and his possibilities of spiritual experience. An amalgam of primitive intuitions, occult ritual, religio-social ethics, mystical knowledge or experiences symbolised in myth but with their sense preserved by a secret initiation and discipline is the early, at first very superficial and external stage of human religion. In the beginning these elements were, no doubt, crude and poor and defective, but they acquired depth and range and increased in some cultures to a great amplitude and significance.

But as the mental and life development increased, — for that is Nature's first preoccupation in man and she does not hesitate to push it forward at the cost of other elements that will need to be taken up fully hereafter, — there is a tendency towards intellectualisation, and the first necessary intuitive, instinctive and subliminal formations are overlaid with the structures erected by a growing force of reason and mental intelligence. As man discovers the secrets and processes of physical Nature, he moves more and more away from his early recourse to occultism and magic; the presence and felt influence of gods and invisible powers recedes as more and more is explained by natural workings, the mechanical procedure of Nature: but he still feels the need of a spiritual element and spiritual factors in his life and therefore keeps for a time the two activities running together. But the occult elements of religion, though still held as beliefs or preserved but also buried in rites and myths, lose their significance and diminish and the intellectual element increases; finally, where and when the intellectualising tendency becomes too strong, there is a movement to cut out everything but creed, institution, formal practice and ethics. Even the element of spiritual experience dwindles and it is considered sufficient to rely only on faith, emotional fervour and moral conduct; the first amalgam of religion, occultism and mystic experience is disrupted, and there is a tendency, not by any means universal or complete but still pronounced or visible, for each of these powers to follow its own way to its own goal in its own separate and free character. A complete denial of religion, occultism and all that is supraphysical is the last outcome of this stage, a hard dry paroxysm of the superficial intellect hacking away the sheltering structures that are refuges for the deeper parts of our nature. But still evolutionary Nature keeps alive her ulterior intentions in the minds of a few and uses man's greater mental evolution to raise them to a higher plane and deeper issues. In the present time itself, after an age of triumphant intellectuality and materialism, we can see evidences of this natural process, — a return towards inner self-discovery, an inner seeking and thinking, a new attempt at mystic experience, a groping after the inner self, a reawakening to some sense of the truth and power of the spirit begins to manifest itself; man's search after his self and soul and a deeper truth of things tends to revive and resume its lost force and to give a fresh life to the old creeds, erect new faiths or develop independently of sectarian religions. The intellect itself, having reached near to the natural limits of the capacity of physical discovery, having touched its bedrock and found that it explains nothing more than the outer process of Nature, has begun, still tentatively and hesitatingly, to direct an eye of research on the deeper secrets of the mind and the life-force and on the domain of the occult which it had rejected *a priori*, in order to know what there may be in it that is true. Religion itself has shown its power of survival and is undergoing an evolution the final sense of which is still obscure. In this new phase of the mind that we see beginning, however crudely and hesitatingly, there can be detected the possibility of a pressure towards some decisive turn and advance of the spiritual evolution in Nature. Religion, rich but with a certain obscurity in her first infrarational stage, had tended under the overweight of the intellect to pass into a clear but bare rational interspace; but it must in the end follow the upward curve of the human mind and rise more fully at its summits towards its true or greatest field in the sphere of a suprarational consciousness and knowledge.

If we look at the past, we can still see the evidences of this line of natural evolution, although most of its earlier stages are hidden from us in the unwritten pages of prehistory. It has been contended that religion in its beginnings was nothing but a mass of animism, fetishism, magic, totemism, taboo, myth, superstitious symbol, with the medicine-man as priest, a mental fungus of primitive human ignorance, — later on at its best a form of Nature-worship. It could well have been so in the primitive mind, though we have to add the proviso that behind much of its beliefs and practices there may have been a truth of an inferior but very effective kind that we have lost with our superior development. Primitive man lives much in a low and small province of his life-being, and this corresponds on the occult plane to an invisible Nature which is of a like character and whose occult powers can be called into activity by a knowledge and methods to which the lower vital intuitions and instincts may open a door of access. This might be formulated in a first stage of religious belief and practice which would be occult after a crude inchoate fashion in its character and interests, not yet spiritual; its main element would be a calling in of small life-powers and elemental beings to the aid of small life-desires and a rude physical welfare.

But this primitive stage, — if it is indeed such and not, in what we still see of it, a fall or a vestige, a relapse from a higher knowledge belonging to a previous cycle of civilisation or the debased remnants of a dead or obsolete culture, — can have been only a beginning. It was followed, after whatever stages, by the more advanced type of religion of which we have a record in the literature or surviving documents of the early civilised peoples. This type, composed of a polytheistic belief and worship, a cosmology, a mythology, a complexus of ceremonies, practices, ritual and ethical obligations interwoven sometimes deeply into the social system, was ordinarily a national or tribal religion intimately expressive of the stage of evolution of thought and life reached by the community. In the outer structure we still miss the support of a deeper spiritual significance, but this gap was filled in in the greater more developed cultures by a strong background of occult knowledge and practices or else by carefully guarded mysteries with a first element of spiritual wisdom and discipline. Occultism occurs more often as an addition or superstructure, but is not always present; the worship of divine powers, sacrifice, a surface piety and social ethics are the main factors. A spiritual philosophy or idea of the meaning of life seems at first to be absent, but its beginnings are often contained in the myths and mysteries and in one or two instances fully emerge out of them so that it assumes a strong separate existence.

It is possible indeed that it is the mystic or the incipient occultist who was everywhere the creator of religion and imposed his secret discoveries in the form of belief, myth and practice on the mass human mind; for it is always the individual who receives the intuitions of Nature and takes the step forward dragging or drawing the rest of humanity behind him. But even if we give the credit of this new creation to the subconscious mass mind, it is the occultist and mystic element in that mind which created it and it must have found individuals through whom it could emerge; for a mass experience or discovery or expression is not the first method of Nature; it is at some one point or a few points that the fire is lit and spreads from hearth to hearth, from altar to altar. But the spiritual aspiration and experience of the mystics was usually casketed in secret formulas and given only to a few initiates; it was conveyed to the rest or rather preserved for them in a mass of religious or traditional symbols. It is these symbols that were the heart's core of religion in the mind of an early humanity.

Out of this second stage there emerged a third which tried to liberate the secret spiritual experience and knowledge and put it at the disposal of all as a truth that could have a common appeal and must be made universally available. A tendency prevailed, not only to make the spiritual element the very kernel of the religion, but to render it attainable to all the worshippers by an exoteric teaching; as each esoteric school had had its system of knowledge and discipline, so now each religion was to have its system of knowledge, its creed and its spiritual discipline. Here, in these two forms of the spiritual evolution, the esoteric and the exoteric, the way of the mystic and the way of the religious man, we see a double principle of evolutionary Nature, the principle of intensive and concentrated evolution in a small space and the principle of expansion and extension so that the new creation may be generalised in as large a field as possible. The first is the concentrated dynamic and effective movement; the second tends towards diffusion and status. As a result of this new development, the spiritual aspiration at first carefully treasured by a few became more generalised in mankind, but it lost in purity, height and intensity. The mystics founded their endeavour on a power of suprarational knowledge, intuitive, inspired, revelatory and on the force of the inner being to enter into occult truth and experience: but these powers are not possessed by men in the mass or possessed only in a crude, undeveloped and fragmentary initial form on which nothing could be safely founded; so for them in this new development the spiritual truth had to be clothed in intellectual forms of creed and doctrine, in emotional forms of worship and in a simple but significant ritual. At the same time the strong spiritual nucleus became mixed, diluted, alloyed; it tended to be invaded and aped by the lower elements of mind and life and physical nature. It was this mixture and alloy and invasion of the spurious, this profanation of the mysteries and the loss of their truth and significance, as well as the misuse of the occult power that comes by communication with invisible forces, that was most dreaded by the early mystics and prevented by secrecy, by strict discipline, by restriction to the few fit initiates. Another untoward result or peril of the diffusive movement and the consequent invasion has been the intellectual formalisation of spiritual knowledge into dogma and the materialisation of living practice into a dead mass of cult and ceremony and ritual, a mechanisation by which the spirit was bound to depart in course of time from the body of the religion. But this risk had to be taken, for the expansive movement was an inherent necessity of the spiritual urge in evolutionary Nature.

Thus came into being the religions which rely mainly or in the mass on creed and ritual for some spiritual result, but yet hold because of their truth of experience, the fundamental inner reality that was initially present in them and persists so long as there are men to continue or renew it, a means for those who are touched by the spiritual impulse to realise the Divine and liberate the spirit. This development has led farther to a division into two tendencies, catholic and protestant, one a tendency towards some conservation of the original plastic character of religion, its many-sidedness and appeal to the whole nature of the human being, the other disruptive of this catholicity and insistent on a pure reliance on belief, worship and conduct simplified so as to make a quick and ready appeal to the common reason, heart and ethical will. This turn has tended to create an excessive rationalisation, a discrediting and condemnation of most of the occult elements which seek to establish a communication with what is invisible, a reliance on the surface mind as the sufficient vehicle of the spiritual endeavour; a certain dryness and a narrowness and paucity of the spiritual life have been a frequent consequence. Moreover, the intellect having denied so much, cast out so much, has found ample room and opportunity to deny more until it denies all, to negate spiritual experience and cast out spirituality and religion, leaving only intellect itself as the sole surviving power. But intellect void of the spirit can only pile up external knowledge and machinery and efficiency and ends in a drying up of the secret springs of vitality and a decadence without any inner power to save the life or create a new life or any other way out than death and disintegration and a new beginning out of the old Ignorance.

It would have been possible for the evolutionary principle to have preserved its pristine wholeness of movement while pressing on, by an expansion and not a disruption of the wiser ancient harmony, to a greater synthesis of the principle of concentration and the principle of diffusion. In India, we have seen, there has been a persistence of the original intuition and total movement of evolutionary Nature. For religion in India limited itself by no one creed or dogma; it not only admitted a vast number of different formulations, but contained successfully within itself all the elements that have grown up in the course of the evolution of religion and refused to ban or excise any: it developed occultism to its utmost limits, accepted spiritual philosophies of all kinds, followed to its highest, deepest or largest outcome every possible line of spiritual realisation, spiritual experience, spiritual self-discipline. Its method has been the method of evolutionary Nature herself, to allow all developments, all means of communication and action of the spirit upon the members, all ways of communion between man and the Supreme or Divine, to follow every possible way of advance to the goal and test it even to its extreme. All stages of spiritual evolution are there in man and each has to be allowed or provided with its means of approach to the spirit, an approach suited to its capacity, *adhikāra*. Even the primitive forms that survived were not banned but were lifted to a deeper significance, while still there was the pressure to the highest spiritual pinnacles in the rarest supreme ether. Even the exclusive credal type of religion was not itself excluded; provided its affinity to the general aim and principle was clear, it was admitted into the infinite variety of the general order. But this plasticity sought to support itself on a fixed religio-social system, which it permeated with the principle of a graded working out of the human nature turned at its height towards a supreme spiritual endeavour; this social fixity, which was perhaps necessary at one time for unity of life if not also as a settled and secure basis for the spiritual freedom, has been on one side a power for preservation but also the one obstacle to the native spirit of entire catholicity, an element of excessive crystallisation and restriction. A fixed basis may be indispensable, but if settled in essence, this also must be in its forms capable of plasticity, evolutionary change; it must be an order, but a growing order.

Nevertheless, the principle of this great and many-sided religious and spiritual evolution was sound, and by taking up in itself the whole of life and of human nature, by encouraging the growth of intellect and never opposing it or putting bounds to its freedom, but rather calling it in to the aid of the spiritual seeking, it prevented the conflict or the undue predominance which in the Occident led to the restriction and drying up of the religious instinct and the plunge into pure materialism and secularism. A method of this plastic and universal kind, admitting but exceeding all creeds and forms and allowing every kind of element, may have numerous consequences which might be objected to by the purist, but its great justifying result has been an unexampled multitudinous richness and a more than millennial persistence and impregnable durability, generality, universality, height, subtlety and many-sided wideness of spiritual attainment and seeking and endeavour. It is indeed only by such a catholicity and plasticity that the wider aim of the evolution can work itself out with any fullness. The individual demands from religion a door of opening into spiritual experience or a means of turning towards it, a communion with God or a definite light of guidance on the way, a promise of the hereafter or a means of a happier supraterrestrial future; these needs can be met on the narrower basis of credal belief and sectarian cult. But there is also the wider purpose of Nature to prepare and further the spiritual evolution in man and turn him into a spiritual being; religion serves her as a means for pointing his effort and his ideal in that direction and providing each one who is ready with the possibility of taking a step upon the way towards it. This end she serves by the immense variety of the cults she has created, some final, standardised and definitive, others more plastic, various and many-sided. A religion which is itself a congeries of religions and which at the same time provides each man with his own turn of inner experience, would be the most in consonance with this purpose of Nature: it would be a rich nursery of spiritual growth and flowering, a vast multiform school of the soul's discipline, endeavour, self-realisation. Whatever errors Religion has committed, this is her function and her great and indispensable utility and service, — the holding up of this growing light of guidance on our way through the mind's ignorance towards the Spirit's complete consciousness and self-knowledge.

Occultism is in its essence man's effort to arrive at a knowledge of secret truths and potentialities of Nature which will lift him out of slavery to his physical limits of being, an attempt in particular to possess and organise the mysterious, occult, outwardly still undeveloped direct power of Mind upon Life and of both Mind and Life over Matter. There is at the same time an endeavour to establish communication with worlds and entities belonging to the supraphysical heights, depths and intermediate levels of cosmic Being and to utilise this communion for the mastery of a higher Truth and for a help to man in his will to make himself sovereign over Nature's powers and forces. This human aspiration takes its stand on the belief, intuition or intimation that we are not mere creatures of the mud, but souls, minds, wills that can know all the mysteries of this and every world and become not only Nature's pupils but her adepts and masters. The occultist sought to know the secret of physical things also and in this effort he furthered astronomy, created chemistry, gave an impulse to other sciences, for he utilised geometry also and the science of numbers; but still more he sought to know the secrets of supernature. In this sense occultism might be described as the science of the supernatural; but it is in fact only the discovery of the supraphysical, the surpassing of the material limit, — the heart of occultism is not the impossible chimera which hopes to go beyond or outside all force of Nature and make pure phantasy and arbitrary miracle omnipotently effective. What seems to us supernatural is in fact either a spontaneous irruption of the phenomena of other-Nature into physical Nature or, in the work of the occultist, a possession of the knowledge and power of the higher orders or grades of cosmic Being and Energy and the direction of their forces and processes towards the production of effects in the physical world by seizing on possibilities of interconnection and means for a material effectuality. There are powers of the mind and the life-force which have not been included in Nature's present systematisation of mind and life in matter, but are potential and can be brought to bear upon material things and happenings or even brought in and added to the present systematisation so as to enlarge the control of mind over our own life and body or to act on the minds, lives, bodies of others or on the movements of cosmic Forces. The modern admission of hypnotism is an example of such a discovery and systematised application, — though still narrow and limited, limited by its method and formula, — of occult powers which otherwise touch us only by a casual or a hidden action whose process is unknown to us or imperfectly caught by a few; for we are all the time undergoing a battery of suggestions, thought-suggestions, impulse-suggestions, will-suggestions, emotional and sensational suggestions, thought-waves, life-waves that come on us or into us from others or from the universal Energy, but act and produce their effects without our knowledge. A systematised endeavour to know these movements and their law and possibilities, to master and use the power or Nature-force behind them or to protect ourselves from them would fall within one province of occultism: but it would only be a small part even of that province; for wide and multiple are the possible fields, uses, processes of this vast range of little-explored Knowledge.

In modern times, as physical Science enlarged its discoveries and released the secret material forces of Nature into an action governed by human knowledge for human use, occultism receded and was finally set aside on the ground that the physical alone is real and Mind and Life are only departmental activities of Matter. On this basis, believing material Energy to be the key of all things, Science has attempted to move towards a control of mind and life processes by a knowledge of the material instrumentation and process of our normal and abnormal mind and life functionings and activities; the spiritual is ignored as only one form of mentality. It may be observed in passing that if this endeavour succeeded, it might not be without danger for the existence of the human race, even as now are certain other scientific discoveries misused or clumsily used by a humanity mentally and morally unready for the handling of powers so great and perilous; for it would be an artificial control applied without any knowledge of the secret forces which underlie and sustain our existence. Occultism in the West could be thus easily pushed aside because it never reached its majority, never acquired ripeness and a philosophic or sound systematic foundation. It indulged too freely in the romance of the supernatural or made the mistake of concentrating its major effort on the discovery of formulas and effective modes for using supernormal powers. It deviated into magic white and black or into a romantic or thaumaturgic paraphernalia of occult mysticism and the exaggeration of what was after all a limited and scanty knowledge. These tendencies and this insecurity of mental foundation made it difficult to defend and easy to discredit, a target facile and vulnerable. In Egypt and the East this line of knowledge arrived at a greater and more comprehensive endeavour: this ampler maturity can be seen still intact in the remarkable system of the Tantras; it was not only a many-sided science of the supernormal but supplied the basis of all the occult elements of religion and even developed a great and powerful system of spiritual discipline and self-realisation. For the highest occultism is that which discovers the secret movements and dynamic supernormal possibilities of Mind and Life and Spirit and uses them in their native force or by an applied process for the greater effectivity of our mental, vital and spiritual being.

Occultism is associated in popular idea with magic and magical formulae and a supposed mechanism of the supernatural. But this is only one side, nor is it altogether a superstition as is vainly imagined by those who have not looked deeply or at all at this covert side of secret Nature-Force or experimented with its possibilities. Formulas and their application, a mechanisation of latent forces, can be astonishingly effective in the occult use of mind-power and life-power just as it is in physical Science, but this is only a subordinate method and a limited direction. For mind and life forces are plastic, subtle and variable in their action and have not the material rigidity; they need a subtle and plastic intuition in the knowledge of them, in the interpretation of their action and process and in their application, — even in the interpretation and action of their established formulas. An overstress on mechanisation and rigid formulation is likely to result in sterilisation or a formalised limitation of knowledge and, on the pragmatic side, to much error, ignorant convention, misuse and failure. Now that we are outgrowing the superstition of the sole truth of Matter, a swing backward towards the old occultism and to new formulations, as well as to a scientific investigation of the still hidden secrets and powers of Mind and a close study of psychic and abnormal or supernormal psychological phenomena, is possible and, in parts, already visible. But if it is to fulfil itself, the true foundation, the true aim and direction, the necessary restrictions and precautions of this line of inquiry have to be rediscovered; its most important aim must be the discovery of the hidden truths and powers of the mind-force and the life-power and the greater forces of the concealed spirit. Occult science is, essentially, the science of the subliminal, the subliminal in ourselves and the subliminal in world-nature, and of all that is in connection with the subliminal, including the subconscient and the superconscient, and the use of it as part of self-knowledge and world-knowledge and for the right dynamisation of that knowledge.

An intellectual approach to the highest knowledge, the mind's possession of it, is an indispensable aid to this movement of Nature in the human being. Ordinarily, on our surface, man's chief instrument of thought and action is the reason, the observing, understanding and arranging intellect. In any total advance or evolution of the Spirit, not only the intuition, insight, inner sense, the heart's devotion, a deep and direct life-experience of the things of the Spirit have to be developed, but the intellect also must be enlightened and satisfied; our thinking and reflecting mind must be helped to understand, to form a reasoned and systematised idea of the goal, the method, the principles of this highest development and activity of our nature and the truth of all that lies behind it. Spiritual realisation and experience, an intuitive and direct knowledge, a growth of inner consciousness, a growth of the soul and of an intimate soul-perception, soul-vision and a soul-sense, are indeed the proper means of this evolution: but the support of the reflective and critical reason is also of great importance; if many can dispense with it, because they have a vivid and direct contact with inner realities and are satisfied with experience and insight, yet in the whole movement it is indispensable. If the supreme truth is a spiritual Reality, then the intellect of man needs to know what is the nature of that original Truth and the principle of its relations to the rest of existence, to ourselves and the universe. The intellect is not capable by itself of bringing us into touch with the concrete spiritual reality, but it can help by a mental formulation of the truth of the Spirit which explains it to the mind and can be applied even in the more direct seeking: this help is of a capital importance.

Our thinking mind is concerned mainly with the statement of general spiritual truth, the logic of its absolute and the logic of its relativities, how they stand to each other or lead to each other, and what are the mental consequences of the spiritual theorem of existence. But besides this understanding and intellectual statement which is its principal right and share, the intellect seeks to exercise a critical control; it may admit the ecstatic or other concrete spiritual experiences, but its demand is to know on what sure and well-ordered truths of being they are founded. Indeed, without such a truth known and verifiable, our reason might find these experiences insecure and unintelligible, might draw back from them as possibly not founded on truth or else distrust them in their form, if not in their foundation, as affected by an error, even an aberration of the imaginative vital mind, the emotions, the nerves or the senses; for these might be misled, in their passage or transference from the physical and sensible to the invisible, into a pursuit of deceiving lights or at least to a misreception of things valid in themselves but marred by a wrong or imperfect interpretation of what is experienced or a confusion and disorder of the true spiritual values. If reason finds itself obliged to admit the dynamics of occultism, there too it will be most concerned with the truth and right system and real significance of the forces that it sees brought into play; it must inquire whether the significance is that which the occultist attaches to it or something other and perhaps deeper which has been misinterpreted in its essential relations and values or not given its true place in the whole of experience. For the action of our intellect is primarily the function of understanding, but secondarily critical and finally organising, controlling and formative.

The means by which this need can be satisfied and with which our nature of mind has provided us is philosophy, and in this field it must be a spiritual philosophy. Such systems have arisen in numbers in the East; for almost always, wherever there has been a considerable spiritual development, there has arisen from it a philosophy justifying it to the intellect. The method was at first an intuitive seeing and an intuitive expression, as in the fathomless thought and profound language of the Upanishads, but afterwards there was developed a critical method, a firm system of dialectics, a logical organisation. The later philosophies were an intellectual account[8] or a logical justification of what had been found by inner realisation; or they provided, themselves, a mental ground or a systematised method for realisation and experience.[9] In the West where the syncretic tendency of the consciousness was replaced by the analytic and separative, the spiritual urge and the intellectual reason parted company almost at the outset; philosophy took from the first a turn towards a purely intellectual and ratiocinative explanation of things. Nevertheless, there were systems like the Pythagorean, Stoic, and Epicurean, which were dynamic not only for thought but for conduct of life and developed a discipline, an effort at inner perfection of the being; this reached a higher spiritual plane of knowledge in later Christian or Neo-pagan thought-structures where East and West met together. But later on the intellectualisation became complete and the connection of philosophy with life and its energies or spirit and its dynamism was either cut or confined to the little that the metaphysical idea can impress on life and action by an abstract and secondary influence. Religion has supported itself in the West not by philosophy but by a credal theology; sometimes a spiritual philosophy emerges by sheer force of individual genius, but it has not been as in the East a necessary adjunct to every considerable line of spiritual

[8] E.g., the *Gita*.   [9] E.g., the Yoga philosophy of Patanjali.

experience and endeavour. It is true that a philosophic development of spiritual thought is not entirely indispensable; for the truths of spirit can be reached more directly and completely by intuition and by a concrete inner contact. It must also be said that the critical control of the intellect over spiritual experience can be hampering and unreliable, for it is an inferior light turned upon a field of higher illumination; the true controlling power is an inner discrimination, a psychic sense and tact, a superior intervention of guidance from above or an innate and luminous inner guidance. But still this line of development too is necessary, because there must be a bridge between the spirit and the intellectual reason: the light of a spiritual or at least a spiritualised intelligence is necessary for the fullness of our total inner evolution, and without it, if another deeper guidance is lacking, the inner movement may be erratic and undisciplined, turbid and mixed with unspiritual elements or one-sided or incomplete in its catholicity. For the transformation of the Ignorance into the integral Knowledge the growth in us of a spiritual intelligence ready to receive a higher light and canalise it for all the parts of our nature is an intermediate necessity of great importance.

But none of these three lines of approach can by themselves entirely fulfil the greater and ulterior intention of Nature; they cannot create in mental man the spiritual being, unless and until they open the door to spiritual experience. It is only by an inner realisation of what these approaches are seeking after, by an overwhelming experience or by many experiences building up an inner change, by a transmutation of the consciousness, by a liberation of the spirit from its present veil of mind, life and body that there can emerge the spiritual being. That is the final line of the soul's progress towards which the others are pointing and, when it is ready to disengage itself from the preliminary approaches, then the real work has begun and the turning-point of the change is no longer distant. Till then all that the human mental being has reached is a familiarity with the idea of things beyond him, with the possibility of an other-worldly movement, with the ideal of some ethical perfection; he may have made too some contact with greater Powers or Realities which help his mind or heart or life. A change there may be, but not the transmutation of the mental into the spiritual being. Religion and its thought and ethics and occult mysticism in ancient times produced the priest and the mage, the man of piety, the just man, the man of wisdom, many high points of mental manhood; but it is only after spiritual experience through the heart and mind began that we see arise the saint, the prophet, the Rishi, the Yogi, the seer, the spiritual sage and the mystic, and it is the religions in which these types of spiritual manhood came into being that have endured, covered the globe and given mankind all its spiritual aspiration and culture.

When spirituality disengages itself in the consciousness and puts on its distinctive character, it is only at first a small kernel, a growing tendency, an exceptional light of experience amidst the great mass of normal unenlightened human mind, vitality, physicality which forms the outer self and engrosses our natural preoccupation. There are tentative beginnings and a slow evolution and hesitating emergence. An earlier first preliminary form of it creates a certain kind of religiosity which is not the pure spiritual temperament, but is of the nature of mind or life seeking or finding in itself a spiritual support or factor; in this stage man is mostly preoccupied with the utilisation of such contacts as he can get or construct with what is beyond him to help or serve his mental ideas or moral ideals or his vital and physical interests; the true turn to some spiritual change has not come. The first true formations take the shape of a spiritualisation of our natural activities, a permeating influence on them or a direction: there is a preparatory influence or influx in some part or tendency of the mind or life, — a spiritualised turn of thought with uplifting illuminations, or a spiritualised turn of the emotional or the aesthetic being, a spiritualised ethical formation in the character, a spiritualised urge in some life-action or other dynamic vital movement of the nature. An awareness comes perhaps of an inner light, of a guidance or a communion, of a greater Control than the mind and will to which something in us obeys; but all is not yet recast in the mould of that experience. But when these intuitions and illuminations grow in insistence and canalise themselves, make a strong inner formation and claim to govern the whole life and take over the nature, then there begins the spiritual formation of the being; there emerges the saint, the devotee, the spiritual sage, the seer, the prophet, the servant of God, the soldier of the spirit. All these take their stand on one part of the natural being lifted up by a spiritual light, power or ecstasy. The sage and seer live in the spiritual mind, their thought or their vision is governed and moulded by an inner or a greater divine light of knowledge; the devotee lives in the spiritual aspiration of the heart, its self-offering and its seeking; the saint is moved by the awakened psychic being in the inner heart grown powerful to govern the emotional and vital being; the others stand in the vital kinetic nature driven by a higher spiritual energy and turned by it towards an inspired action, a God-given work or mission, the service of some divine Power, idea or ideal. The last or highest emergence is the liberated man who has realised the Self and Spirit within him, entered into the cosmic consciousness, passed into union with the Eternal and, so far as he still accepts life and action, acts by the light and energy of the Power within him working through his human instruments of Nature. The largest formulation of this spiritual change and achievement is a total liberation of soul, mind, heart and action, a casting of them all into the sense of the cosmic Self and the Divine Reality.[10] The spiritual evolution of the individual has then found its way and thrown up its range of Himalayan eminences and its peaks of highest nature. Beyond this height and largeness there opens only the supramental ascent or the incommunicable Transcendence.

This then has been up till now the course of Nature's evolution of the spiritual man in the human mental being, and it may be questioned what is the exact sum of this achievement and its actual significance. In the recent reaction towards the life of the mind in Matter, this great direction and this rare change have been stigmatised as no true evolution of consciousness but rather a sublimated crudity of ignorance deviating from the true human

---

[10] This is the essence of the spiritual ideal and realisation held before us by the *Gita*.

evolution, which should be solely an evolution of life-power, the practical physical mind, the reason governing thought and conduct and the discovering and organising intelligence. In this epoch religion was pushed aside as an out-of-date superstition and spiritual realisation and experience discredited as a shadowy mysticism; the mystic in this view is the man who turns aside into the unreal, into occult regions of a self-constructed land of chimeras and loses his way there. This judgment proceeds from a view of things which is itself bound to pass into discredit, because it depends ultimately on the false perception of the material as alone real and the outward life as alone of importance. But apart from this extreme materialistic view of things, it can be and is still held by the intellect and the physical mind eager for human life-fulfilment, — and that is the prevalent mentality, the dominant modern trend, — that the spiritual tendency in humanity has come to very little; it has not solved the problem of life nor any of the problems with which humanity is at grips. The mystic either detaches himself from life as the other-worldly ascetic or the aloof visionary and therefore cannot help life, or else he brings no better solution or result than the practical man or the man of intellect and reason: by his intervention he rather disturbs the human values, distorts them with his alien and unverifiable light obscure to the human understanding and confuses the plain practical and vital issues life puts before us.

But this is not the standpoint from which the true significance of the spiritual evolution in man or the value of spirituality can be judged or assessed; for its real work is not to solve human problems on the past or present mental basis, but to create a new foundation of our being and our life and knowledge. The ascetic or other-worldly tendency of the mystic is an extreme affirmation of his refusal to accept the limitations imposed by material Nature: for his very reason of being is to go beyond her; if he cannot transform her, he must leave her. At the same time the spiritual man has not stood back altogether from the life of humanity; for the sense of unity with all beings, the stress of a universal love and compassion, the will to spend the energies for the good of all creatures,[11] are central to the dynamic out-flowering of the spirit: he has turned therefore to help, he has guided as did the ancient Rishis or the prophets, or stooped to create and, where he has done so with something of the direct power of the Spirit, the results have been prodigious. But the solution of the problem which spirituality offers is not a solution by external means, though these also have to be used, but by an inner change, a transformation of the consciousness and nature.

If no decisive but only a contributory result, an accretion of some new finer elements to the sum of the consciousness, has been the general consequence and there has been no life-transformation, it is because man in the mass has always deflected the spiritual impulsion, recanted from the spiritual ideal or held it only as a form and rejected the inward change. Spirituality cannot be called upon to deal with life by a non-spiritual method or attempt to cure its ills by the panaceas, the political, social or other mechanical remedies which the mind is constantly attempting and which have always failed and will continue to fail to solve anything. The most drastic changes made by these means change nothing; for the old ills exist in a new form: the aspect of the outward environment is altered, but man remains what he was; he is still an ignorant mental being misusing or not effectively using his knowledge, moved by ego and governed by vital desires and passions and the needs of the body, unspiritual and superficial in his outlook, ignorant of his own self and the forces that drive and use him. His life-constructions have a value as expressions of his individual and collective being in the stage to which they have reached or as a machinery for the convenience and welfare of his vital and physical parts and a field and medium for his mental growth, but they cannot take him beyond his present self or serve as a machinery to transform him; his and their perfection can only come by his farther evolution. Only a spiritual change, an evolution of his being from the superficial

---

[11] *Gita.* The Buddhist elevation of universal compassion, *karuṇā*, and sympathy (*vasudhaiva kuṭumbakam*, the whole earth is my family), to be the highest principle of action, the Christian emphasis on love indicate this dynamic side of the spiritual being.

mental towards the deeper spiritual consciousness, can make a real and effective difference. To discover the spiritual being in himself is the main business of the spiritual man and to help others towards the same evolution is his real service to the race; till that is done, an outward help can succour and alleviate, but nothing or very little more is possible.

It is true that the spiritual tendency has been to look more beyond life than towards life. It is true also that the spiritual change has been individual and not collective; its result has been successful in the man, but unsuccessful or only indirectly operative in the human mass. The spiritual evolution of Nature is still in process and incomplete, — one might almost say, still only beginning, — and its main preoccupation has been to affirm and develop a basis of spiritual consciousness and knowledge and to create more and more a foundation or formation for the vision of that which is eternal in the truth of the spirit. It is only when Nature has fully confirmed this intensive evolution and formation through the individual that anything radical of an expanding or dynamically diffusive character can be expected or any attempt at collective spiritual life, — such attempts have been made, but mostly as a field of protection for the growth of the individual's spirituality, — acquire a successful permanence. For till then the individual must be preoccupied with his own problem of entirely changing his mind and life into conformity with the truth of the spirit which he is achieving or has achieved in his inner being and knowledge. Any premature attempt at a large-scale collective spiritual life is exposed to vitiation by some incompleteness of the spiritual knowledge on its dynamic side, by the imperfections of the individual seekers and by the invasion of the ordinary mind and vital and physical consciousness taking hold of the truth and mechanising, obscuring or corrupting it. The mental intelligence and its main power of reason cannot change the principle and persistent character of human life, it can only effect various mechanisations, manipulations, developments and formulations. But neither is mind as a whole, even spiritualised, able to change it; spirituality liberates and illumines the inner being, it helps mind to communicate with what is higher than itself, to escape even from itself, it can purify and uplift by the inner influence the outward nature of individual human beings: but so long as it has to work in the human mass through mind as the instrument, it can exercise an influence on the earth-life but not bring about a transformation of that life. For this reason there has been a prevalent tendency in the spiritual mind to be satisfied with such an influence and in the main to seek fulfilment in other-life elsewhere or to abandon altogether any outward-going endeavour and concentrate solely on an individual spiritual salvation or perfection. A higher instrumental dynamis than mind is needed to transform totally a nature created by the Ignorance.

Another objection to the mystic and his knowledge is urged, not against its effect upon life but against his method of the discovery of Truth and against the Truth that he discovers. One objection to the method is that it is purely subjective, not true independently of the personal consciousness and its constructions, not verifiable. But this ground of cavil has no great value: for the object of the mystic is self-knowledge and God-knowledge, and that can only be arrived at by an inward and not by an outward gaze. Or it is the supreme Truth of things that he seeks, and that too cannot be arrived at by an outward inquiry through the senses or by any scrutiny or research that founds itself on outsides and surfaces or by speculation based on the uncertain data of an indirect means of knowledge. It must come by a direct vision or contact of the consciousness with the soul and body of the Truth itself or through a knowledge by identity, by the self that becomes one with the self of things and with their truth of power and their truth of essence. But it is urged that the actual result of this method is not one truth common to all, there are great differences; the conclusion suggested is that this knowledge is not truth at all but a subjective mental formation. But this objection is based on a misunderstanding of the nature of spiritual knowledge. Spiritual truth is a truth of the spirit, not a truth of the intellect, not a mathematical theorem or a logical formula. It is a truth of the Infinite, one in an infinite diversity, and it can assume an infinite variety of aspects and

formations: in the spiritual evolution it is inevitable that there
should be a many-sided passage and reaching to the one Truth,
a many-sided seizing of it; this many-sidedness is the sign of the
approach of the soul to a living reality, not to an abstraction or
a constructed figure of things that can be petrified into a dead
or stony formula. The hard logical and intellectual notion of
truth as a single idea which all must accept, one idea or system
of ideas defeating all other ideas or systems, or a single limited
fact or single formula of facts which all must recognise, is an
illegitimate transference from the limited truth of the physical
field to the much more complex and plastic field of life and mind
and spirit.

This transference has been responsible for much harm; it
brings into thought narrowness, limitation, an intolerance of
the necessary variation and multiplicity of viewpoints without
which there can be no totality of truth-finding, and by the
narrowness and limitation much obstinacy in error. It reduces
philosophy to an endless maze of sterile disputes; religion has
been invaded by this misprision and infected with credal dogmatism, bigotry and intolerance. The truth of the spirit is a truth
of being and consciousness and not a truth of thought: mental
ideas can only represent or formulate some facet, some mind-
translated principle or power of it or enumerate its aspects,
but to know it one has to grow into it and be it; without that
growing and being there can be no true spiritual knowledge. The
fundamental truth of spiritual experience is one, its consciousness is one, everywhere it follows the same general lines and
tendencies of awakening and growth into spiritual being; for
these are the imperatives of the spiritual consciousness. But also
there are, based on those imperatives, numberless possibilities
of variation of experience and expression: the centralisation and
harmonisation of these possibles, but also the intensive sole following out of any line of experience are both of them necessary
movements of the emerging spiritual Conscious-Force within us.
Moreover, the accommodation of mind and life to the spiritual
truth, its expression in them, must vary with the mentality of
the seeker so long as he has not risen above all need of such

accommodation or such limiting expression. It is this mental and vital element which has created the oppositions that still divide spiritual seekers or enter into their differing affirmations of the truth that they experience. This difference and variation is needed for the freedom of spiritual search and spiritual growth: to overpass differences is quite possible, but that is most easily done in pure experience; in mental formulation the difference must remain until one can exceed mind altogether and in a highest consciousness integralise, unify and harmonise the many-sided truth of the Spirit.

In the evolution of the spiritual man there must necessarily be many stages and in each stage a great variety of individual formations of the being, the consciousness, the life, the temperament, the ideas, the character. The nature of instrumental mind and the necessity of dealing with the life must of itself create an infinite variety according to the stage of development and the individuality of the seeker. But, apart from that, even the domain of pure spiritual self-realisation and self-expression need not be a single white monotone, there can be a great diversity in the fundamental unity; the supreme Self is one, but the souls of the Self are many and, as is the soul's formation of nature, so will be its spiritual self-expression. A diversity in oneness is the law of the manifestation; the supramental unification and integration must harmonise these diversities, but to abolish them is not the intention of the Spirit in Nature.

Chapter XXV

The Triple Transformation

A conscious being is the centre of the self, who rules past and future; he is like a fire without smoke.... That, one must disengage with patience from one's own body.

Katha Upanishad.[1]

An intuition in the heart sees that truth. *Rig Veda.*[2]

I abide in the spiritual being and from there destroy the darkness born of ignorance with the shining lamp of knowledge.

Gita.[3]

These rays are directed downwards, their foundation is above: may they be set deep within us.... O Varuna, here awake, make wide thy reign; may we abide in the law of thy workings and be blameless before the Mother Infinite. *Rig Veda.*[4]

The Swan that settles in the purity... born of the Truth, — itself the Truth, the Vast. *Katha Upanishad.*[5]

IF IT is the sole intention of Nature in the evolution of the spiritual man to awaken him to the supreme Reality and release him from herself, or from the Ignorance in which she as the Power of the Eternal has masked herself, by a departure into a higher status of being elsewhere, if this step in the evolution is a close and an exit, then in the essence her work has been already accomplished and there is nothing more to be done. The ways have been built, the capacity to follow them has been developed, the goal or last height of the creation is manifest; all that is left is for each soul to reach individually the right stage and turn

[1] II. 1. 12, 13; II. 3. 17. [2] I. 24. 12. [3] X. 11. [4] I. 24. 7, 11, 15.
[5] II. 2. 2.

of its development, enter into the spiritual ways and pass by its own chosen path out of this inferior existence. But we have supposed that there is a farther intention, — not only a revelation of the Spirit, but a radical and integral transformation of Nature. There is a will in her to effectuate a true manifestation of the embodied life of the Spirit, to complete what she has begun by a passage from the Ignorance to the Knowledge, to throw off her mask and to reveal herself as the luminous Consciousness-Force carrying in her the eternal Existence and its universal Delight of being. It then becomes obvious that there is something not yet accomplished, there becomes clear to view the much that has still to be done, *bhūri aspaṣṭa kartvam*; there is a height still to be reached, a wideness still to be covered by the eye of vision, the wing of the will, the self-affirmation of the Spirit in the material universe. What the evolutionary Power has done is to make a few individuals aware of their souls, conscious of their selves, aware of the eternal being that they are, to put them into communion with the Divinity or the Reality which is concealed by her appearances: a certain change of nature prepares, accompanies or follows upon this illumination, but it is not the complete and radical change which establishes a secure and settled new principle, a new creation, a permanent new order of being in the field of terrestrial Nature. The spiritual man has evolved, but not the supramental being who shall thenceforward be the leader of that Nature.

This is because the principle of spirituality has yet to affirm itself in its own complete right and sovereignty; it has been up till now a power for the mental being to escape from itself or to refine and raise itself to a spiritual poise, it has availed for the release of the Spirit from mind and for the enlargement of the being in a spiritualised mind and heart, but not, — or rather not yet sufficiently, — for the self-affirmation of the Spirit in its own dynamic and sovereign mastery free from the mind's limitations and from the mental instrumentation. The development of another instrumentation has begun, but has yet to become total and effective; it has besides to cease to be a purely individual self-creation in an original Ignorance, something supernormal to earth-life that must always be acquired as an individual achievement by a difficult endeavour. It must become the normal nature of a new type of being; as Mind is established here on a basis of Ignorance seeking for Knowledge and growing into Knowledge, so Supermind must be established here on a basis of Knowledge growing into its own greater Light. But this cannot be so long as the spiritual-mental being has not risen fully to Supermind and brought down its powers into terrestrial existence. For the gulf between Mind and Supermind has to be bridged, the closed passages opened and roads of ascent and descent created where there is now a void and a silence. This can be done only by the triple transformation to which we have already made a passing reference: there must first be the psychic change, the conversion of our whole present nature into a soul-instrumentation; on that or along with that there must be the spiritual change, the descent of a higher Light, Knowledge, Power, Force, Bliss, Purity into the whole being, even into the lowest recesses of the life and body, even into the darkness of our subconscience; last, there must supervene the supramental transmutation, — there must take place as the crowning movement the ascent into the Supermind and the transforming descent of the supramental Consciousness into our entire being and nature.

At the beginning the soul in Nature, the psychic entity, whose unfolding is the first step towards a spiritual change, is an entirely veiled part of us, although it is that by which we exist and persist as individual beings in Nature. The other parts of our natural composition are not only mutable but perishable; but the psychic entity in us persists and is fundamentally the same always: it contains all essential possibilities of our manifestation but is not constituted by them; it is not limited by what it manifests, not contained by the incomplete forms of the manifestation, not tarnished by the imperfections and impurities, the defects and depravations of the surface being. It is an ever-pure flame of the divinity in things and nothing that comes to it, nothing that enters into our experience can pollute its purity or extinguish the flame. This spiritual stuff is immaculate and luminous and, because it is perfectly luminous, it is immediately, intimately, directly aware of truth of being and truth of nature; it is deeply conscious of truth and good and beauty because truth and good and beauty are akin to its own native character, forms of something that is inherent in its own substance. It is aware also of all that contradicts these things, of all that deviates from its own native character, of falsehood and evil and the ugly and the unseemly; but it does not become these things nor is it touched or changed by these opposites of itself which so powerfully affect its outer instrumentation of mind, life and body. For the soul, the permanent being in us, puts forth and uses mind, life and body as its instruments, undergoes the envelopment of their conditions, but it is other and greater than its members.

If the psychic entity had been from the beginning unveiled and known to its ministers, not a secluded King in a screened chamber, the human evolution would have been a rapid soul-outflowering, not the difficult, chequered and disfigured development it now is; but the veil is thick and we know not the secret Light within us, the light in the hidden crypt of the heart's innermost sanctuary. Intimations rise to our surface from the psyche, but our mind does not detect their source; it takes them for its own activities because, before even they come to the surface, they are clothed in mental substance: thus ignorant of their authority, it follows or does not follow them according to its bent or turn at the moment. If the mind obeys the urge of the vital ego, then there is little chance of the psyche at all controlling the nature or manifesting in us something of its secret spiritual stuff and native movement; or, if the mind is over-confident to act in its own smaller light, attached to its own judgment, will and action of knowledge, then also the soul will remain veiled and quiescent and wait for the mind's farther evolution. For the psychic part within is there to support the natural evolution, and the first natural evolution must be the development of body, life and mind, successively, and these must act each in its own kind or together in their ill-assorted partnership in order to grow and have experience and evolve. The soul gathers the essence of all our mental, vital and bodily experience and assimilates it for

the farther evolution of our existence in Nature; but this action
is occult and not obtruded on the surface. In the early material
and vital stages of the evolution of being there is indeed no
consciousness of soul; there are psychic activities, but the instrumentation, the form of these activities are vital and physical,
— or mental when the mind is active. For even the mind, so long
as it is primitive or is developed but still too external, does not
recognise their deeper character. It is easy to regard ourselves as
physical beings or beings of life or mental beings using life and
body and to ignore the existence of the soul altogether: for the
only definite idea that we have of the soul is of something that
survives the death of our bodies; but what this is we do not know
because even if we are conscious sometimes of its presence, we
are not normally conscious of its distinct reality nor do we feel
clearly its direct action in our nature.

As the evolution proceeds, Nature begins slowly and tentatively to manifest our occult parts; she leads us to look more
and more within ourselves or sets out to initiate more clearly
recognisable intimations and formations of them on the surface.
The soul in us, the psychic principle, has already begun to take
secret form; it puts forward and develops a soul-personality, a
distinct psychic being to represent it. This psychic being remains
still behind the veil in our subliminal part, like the true mental, the true vital or the true or subtle physical being within
us: but, like them, it acts on the surface life by the influences
and intimations it throws up upon that surface; these form part
of the surface aggregate which is the conglomerate effect of
the inner influences and upsurgings, the visible formation and
superstructure which we ordinarily experience and think of as
ourselves. On this ignorant surface we become dimly aware of
something that can be called a soul as distinct from mind, life or
body; we feel it not only as our mental idea or vague instinct of
ourselves, but as a sensible influence in our life and character and
action. A certain sensitive feeling for all that is true and good and
beautiful, fine and pure and noble, a response to it, a demand
for it, a pressure on mind and life to accept and formulate it
in our thought, feelings, conduct, character is the most usually

recognised, the most general and characteristic, though not the sole sign of this influence of the psyche. Of the man who has not this element in him or does not respond at all to this urge, we say that he has no soul. For it is this influence that we can most easily recognise as a finer or even a diviner part in us and the most powerful for the slow turning towards some aim at perfection in our nature.

But this psychic influence or action does not come up to the surface quite pure or does not remain distinct in its purity; if it did, we would be able to distinguish clearly the soul element in us and follow consciously and fully its dictates. An occult mental and vital and subtle-physical action intervenes, mixes with it, tries to use it and turn it to its own profit, dwarfs its divinity, distorts or diminishes its self-expression, even causes it to deviate and stumble or stains it with the impurity, small-ness and error of mind and life and body. After it reaches the surface, thus alloyed and diminished, it is taken hold of by the surface nature in an obscure reception and ignorant formation, and there is or can be by this cause a still further deviation and mixture. A twist is given, a wrong direction is imparted, a wrong application, a wrong formation, an erroneous result of what is in itself pure stuff and action of our spiritual being; a formation of consciousness is accordingly made which is a mixture of the psychic influence and its intimations jumbled with mental ideas and opinions, vital desires and urges, habitual physical tenden-cies. There coalesce too with the obscured soul-influence the ignorant though well-intentioned efforts of these external parts towards a higher direction; a mental ideation of a very mixed character, often obscure even in its idealism, sometimes even disastrously mistaken, a fervour and passion of the emotional being throwing up its spray and foam of feelings, sentiments, sentimentalisms, a dynamic enthusiasm of the life-parts, eager responses of the physical, the thrills and excitements of nerve and body, — all these influences coalesce in a composite formation which is frequently taken as the soul and its mixed and confused action for the soul-stir, for a psychic development and action or a realised inner influence. The psychic entity is itself free from stain or mixture, but what comes up from it is not protected by that immunity; therefore this confusion becomes possible.

Moreover, the psychic being, the soul-personality in us, does not emerge full-grown and luminous; it evolves, passes through a slow development and formation; its figure of being may be at first indistinct and may afterwards remain for a long time weak and undeveloped, not impure but imperfect: for it rests its formation, its dynamic self-building on the power of soul that has been actually and more or less successfully, against the resistance of the Ignorance and Inconscience, put forth in the evolution upon the surface. Its appearance is the sign of a soul-emergence in Nature, and if that emergence is as yet small and defective, the psychic personality also will be stunted or feeble. It is too, by the obscurity of our consciousness, separated from its inner reality, in imperfect communication with its own source in the depths of the being; for the road is as yet ill-built, easily obstructed, the wires often cut or crowded with communications of another kind and proceeding from another origin: its power to impress what it receives upon the outer instruments is also imperfect; in its penury it has for most things to rely on these instruments and it forms its push to expression and action on their data and not solely on the unerring perceptions of the psychic entity. In these conditions it cannot prevent the true psychic light from being diminished or distorted in the mind into a mere idea or opinion, the psychic feeling in the heart into a fallible emotion or mere sentiment, the psychic will to action in the life-parts into a blind vital enthusiasm or a fervid excitement: it even accepts these mistranslations for want of something better and tries to fulfil itself through them. For it is part of the work of the soul to influence mind and heart and vital being and turn their ideas, feelings, enthusiasms, dynamisms in the direction of what is divine and luminous; but this has to be done at first imperfectly, slowly and with a mixture. As the psychic personality grows stronger, it begins to increase its communion with the psychic entity behind it and improve its communications with the surface: it can transmit its intimations to the mind and heart and life with a greater purity and force; for it is more able to exercise a strong control and react against false mixtures; now more and more it makes itself distinctly felt as a power in the nature. But even so this evolution would be slow and long if left solely to the difficult automatic action of the evolutionary Energy; it is only when man awakes to the knowledge of the soul and feels a need to bring it to the front and make it the master of his life and action that a quicker conscious method of evolution intervenes and a psychic transformation becomes possible.

This slow development can be aided by the mind's clear perception and insistence on something within that survives the death of the body and an effort to know its nature. But at first this knowledge is impeded by the fact that there are many elements in us, many formations which present themselves as soul-elements and can be mistaken for the psyche. In the early Greek and some other traditions about the after-life, the descriptions given show very clearly that what was then mistaken for the soul was a subconscious formation, a subphysical impression-mould or shadow-form of the being or else a wraith or ghost of the personality. This ghost, which is mistakenly called the spirit, is sometimes a vital formation reproducing the man's characteristics, his surface life-mannerisms, sometimes a subtle-physical prolongation of the surface form of the mind-shell: at best it is a sheath of the life-personality which still remains in the front for some time after the departure from the body. Apart from these confusions born of an after-death contact with discarded phantasms or remnants of the sheaths of the personality, the difficulty is due to our ignorance of the subliminal parts of our nature and the form and powers of the conscious being or Purusha which preside over their action; owing to this inexperience we can easily mistake something of the inner mind or vital self for the psychic. For as Being is one yet multiple, so also the same law prevails in ourselves and our members; the Spirit, the Purusha is one but it adapts itself to the formations of Nature. Over each grade of our being a power of the Spirit presides; we have within us and discover when we go deep enough inwards a mind-self, a life-self, a physical self; there is a being of mind, a mental Purusha, expressing something of itself on our surface in the thoughts, perceptions, activities of our mind-nature, a being of life which expresses something of itself in the impulses, feelings, sensations, desires, external life-activities of our vital nature, a physical being, a being of the body which expresses something of itself in the instincts, habits, formulated activities of our physical nature. These beings or part selves of the self in us are powers of the Spirit and therefore not limited by their temporary expression, for what is thus formulated is only a fragment of its possibilities; but the expression creates a temporary mental, vital or physical personality which grows and develops even as the psychic being or soul-personality grows and develops within us. Each has its own distinct nature, its influence, its action on the whole of us; but on our surface all these influences and all this action, as they come up, mingle and create an aggregate surface being which is a composite, an amalgam of them all, an outer persistent and yet shifting and mobile formation for the purposes of this life and its limited experience.

But this aggregate is, because of its composition, a heterogeneous compound, not a single harmonious and homogeneous whole. This is the reason why there is a constant confusion and even a conflict in our members which our mental reason and will are moved to control and harmonise and have often much difficulty in creating out of their confusion or conflict some kind of order and guidance; even so, ordinarily, we drift too much or are driven by the stream of our nature and act from whatever in it comes uppermost at the time and seizes the instruments of thought and action, — even our seemingly deliberate choice is more of an automatism than we imagine; our co-ordination of our multifarious elements and of our consequent thoughts, feelings, impulses, actions by the reason and will is incomplete and a half-measure. In animal being Nature acts by her own mental and vital intuitions; she works out an order by the compulsion of habit and instinct which the animal implicitly obeys, so that the shiftings of its consciousness do not matter. But man cannot altogether act in the same way without forfeiting his prerogative of manhood; he cannot leave his being to be a chaos of instincts and impulses regulated by the automatism of Nature: mind has become conscious in him and is therefore self-compelled to make some attempt, however elementary in many, to see and control and in the end more and more perfectly harmonise the manifold components, the different and conflicting tendencies that seem to make up his surface being. He does succeed in setting up a sort of regulated chaos or ordered confusion in him, or at least succeeds in thinking that he is directing himself by his mind and will, even though in fact that direction is only partial; for not only a disparate consortium of habitual motive-forces but also newly emergent vital and physical tendencies and impulses, not always calculable or controllable, and many incoherent and inharmonious mental elements use his reason and will, enter into and determine his self-building, his nature-development, his life action. Man is in his self a unique Person, but he is also in his manifestation of self a multiperson; he will never succeed in being master of himself until the Person imposes itself on his multipersonality and governs it: but this can only be imperfectly done by the surface mental will and reason; it can be perfectly done only if he goes within and finds whatever central being is by its predominant influence at the head of all his expression and action. In inmost truth it is his soul that is this central being, but in outer fact it is often one or other of the part beings in him that rules, and this representative of the soul, this deputy self he can mistake for the inmost soul-principle.

This rule of different selves in us is at the root of the stages of the development of human personality which we have already had occasion to differentiate, and we can reconsider them now from the point of view of the government of the nature by the inner principle. In some human beings it is the physical Purusha, the being of body, who dominates the mind, will and action; there is then created the physical man mainly occupied with his corporeal life and habitual needs, impulses, life-habits, mind-habits, body-habits, looking very little or not at all beyond that, subordinating and restricting all his other tendencies and possibilities to that narrow formation. But even in the physical man there are other elements and he cannot live altogether as the human animal concerned with birth and death and procreation and the satisfaction of common impulses and desires and the maintenance of the life and the body: this is his normal type of personality, but it is crossed, however feebly, with influences by which he can proceed, if they are developed, to a higher human evolution. If the inner subtle-physical Purusha insists, he can arrive at the idea of a finer, more beautiful and perfect physical life and hope or attempt to realise it in his own or in the collective or group existence. In others it is the vital self, the being of life, who dominates and rules the mind, the will, the action; then is created the vital man, concerned with self-affirmation, self-aggrandisement, life-enlargement, satisfaction of ambition and passion and impulse and desire, the claims of his ego, domination, power, excitement, battle and struggle, inner and outer adventure: all else is incidental or subordinated to this movement and building and expression of the vital ego. But still in the vital man too there are or can be other elements of a growing mental or spiritual character, even if these happen to be less developed than his life-personality and life-power. The nature of the vital man is more active, stronger and more mobile, more turbulent and chaotic, often to the point of being quite unregulated, than that of the physical man who holds on to the soil and has a certain material poise and balance, but it is more kinetic and creative: for the element of the vital being is not earth but air; it has more movement, less status. A vigorous vital mind and will can grasp and govern the kinetic vital energies, but it is more by a forceful compulsion and constraint than by a harmonisation of the being. If, however, a strong vital personality, mind and will can get the reasoning intelligence to give it a firm support and be its minister, then a certain kind of forceful formation can be made, more or less balanced but always powerful, successful and effective, which can impose itself on the nature and environment and arrive at a strong self-affirmation in life and action. This is the second step of harmonised formulation possible in the ascent of the nature.

At a higher stage of the evolution of personality the being of mind may rule; there is then created the mental man who lives predominantly in the mind as the others live in the vital or the physical nature. The mental man tends to subordinate to his mental self-expression, mental aims, mental interests or to a mental idea or ideal the rest of his being: because of the difficulty of this subordination and its potent effect when achieved, it is at once more difficult for him and easier to arrive at a harmony of his nature. It is easier because the mental will once in control can convince by the power of the reasoning intelligence and at the same time dominate, compress or suppress the life and the body and their demands, arrange and harmonise them, force them to be its instruments, even reduce them to a minimum so that they shall not disturb the mental life or pull it down from its ideative or idealising movement. It is more difficult because life and body are the first powers and, if they are in the least strong, can impose themselves with an almost irresistible insistence on the mental ruler. Man is a mental being and the mind is the leader of his life and body; but this is a leader who is much led by his followers and has sometimes no other will than what they impose on him. Mind in spite of its power is often impotent before the inconscient and subconscient which obscure its clarity and carry it away on the tide of instinct or impulse; in spite of its clarity it is fooled by vital and emotional suggestions into giving sanction to ignorance and error, to wrong thought and to wrong action, or it is obliged to look on while the nature follows what it knows to be wrong, dangerous or evil. Even when it is strong and clear and dominant, Mind, though it imposes a certain, a considerable mentalised harmony, cannot integrate the whole being and nature. These harmonisations by an inferior control are, besides, inconclusive, because it is one part of the nature which dominates and fulfils itself while the others are coerced and denied their fullness. They can be steps on the way, but not final; therefore in most men there is no such sole dominance and effected partial harmony, but only a predominance and for the rest an unstable equilibrium of a personality half formed, half in formation, sometimes a disequilibrium or unbalance due to the lack of a central government or the disturbance of a formerly achieved partial poise. All must be transitional until a first, though not a final, true harmonisation is achieved by finding our real centre. For the true central being is the soul, but this being stands back and in most human natures is only the secret witness or, one might say, a constitutional ruler who allows his ministers to rule for him, delegates to them his empire, silently assents to their decisions and only now and then puts in a word which they can at any moment override and act otherwise. But this is so long as the soul-personality put forward by the psychic entity is not yet sufficiently developed; when this is strong enough for the inner entity to impose itself through it, then the soul can come forward and control the nature. It is by the coming forward of this true monarch and his taking up of the reins of government that there can take place a real harmonisation of our being and our life.

A first condition of the soul's complete emergence is a direct contact in the surface being with the spiritual Reality. Because it comes from that, the psychic element in us turns always towards whatever in phenomenal Nature seems to belong to a higher Reality and can be accepted as its sign and character. At first, it seeks this Reality through the good, the true, the beautiful, through all that is pure and fine and high and noble: but although this touch through outer signs and characters can modify and prepare the nature, it cannot entirely or most inwardly and profoundly change it. For such an inmost change the direct contact with the Reality itself is indispensable since nothing else can so deeply touch the foundations of our being and stir it or cast the nature by its stir into a ferment of transmutation. Mental representations, emotional and dynamic figures have their use and value; Truth, Good and Beauty are in themselves primary and potent figures of the Reality, and even in their forms as seen by the mind, as felt by the heart, as realised in the life can be lines of an ascent: but it is in a spiritual substance and being of them and of itself that That which they represent has to come into our experience.

The soul may attempt to achieve this contact mainly through the thinking mind as intermediary and instrument; it puts a psychic impression on the intellect and the larger mind of insight and intuitional intelligence and turns them in that direction.

At its highest the thinking mind is drawn always towards the impersonal; in its search it becomes conscious of a spiritual essence, an impersonal Reality which expresses itself in all these outward signs and characters but is more than any formation or manifesting figure. It feels something of which it becomes intimately and invisibly aware, — a supreme Truth, a supreme Good, a supreme Beauty, a supreme Purity, a supreme Bliss; it bears the increasing touch, less and less impalpable and abstract, more and more spiritually real and concrete, the touch and pressure of an Eternity and Infinity which is all this that is and more. There is a pressure from this Impersonality that seeks to mould the whole mind into a form of itself; at the same time the impersonal secret and law of things becomes more and more visible. The mind develops into the mind of the sage, at first the high mental thinker, then the spiritual sage who has gone beyond the abstractions of thought to the beginnings of a direct experience. As a result the mind becomes pure, large, tranquil, impersonal; there is a similar tranquillising influence on the parts of life: but otherwise the result may remain incomplete; for the mental change leads more naturally towards an inner status and an outer quietude, but, poised in this purifying quietism, not drawn like the vital parts towards a discovery of new life-energies, does not press for a full dynamic effect on the nature.

A higher endeavour through the mind does not change this balance; for the tendency of the spiritualised mind is to go on upwards and, since above itself the mind loses its hold on forms, it is into a vast formless and featureless impersonality that it enters. It becomes aware of the unchanging Self, the sheer Spirit, the pure bareness of an essential Existence, the formless Infinite and the nameless Absolute. This culmination can be arrived at more directly by tending immediately beyond all forms and figures, beyond all ideas of good or evil or true or false or beautiful or unbeautiful to That which exceeds all dualities, to the experience of a supreme oneness, infinity, eternity or other ineffable sublimation of the mind's ultimate and extreme percept of Self or Spirit. A spiritualised consciousness is achieved and the life falls quiet, the body ceases to need and to clamour, the soul itself merges into the spiritual silence. But this transformation through the mind does not give us the integral transformation; the psychic transmutation is replaced by a spiritual change on the rare and high summits, but this is not the complete divine dynamisation of Nature.

A second approach made by the soul to the direct contact is through the heart: this is its own more close and rapid way because its occult seat is there, just behind in the heart-centre, in close contact with the emotional being in us; it is consequently through the emotions that it can act best at the beginning with its native power, with its living force of concrete experience. It is through a love and adoration of the All-Beautiful and All-Blissful, the All-Good, the True, the spiritual Reality of love, that the approach is made; the aesthetic and emotional parts join together to offer the soul, the life, the whole nature to that which they worship. This approach through adoration can get its full power and impetus only when the mind goes beyond impersonality to the awareness of a supreme Personal Being: then all becomes intense, vivid, concrete; the heart's emotion, feeling, spiritualised sense reach their absolute; an entire self-giving becomes possible, imperative. The nascent spiritual man makes his appearance in the emotional nature as the devotee, the bhakta; if, in addition, he becomes directly aware of his soul and its dictates, unites his emotional with his psychic personality and changes his life and vital parts by purity, God-ecstasy, the love of God and men and all creatures into a thing of spiritual beauty, full of divine light and good, he develops into the saint and reaches the highest inner experience and most considerable change of nature proper to this way of approach to the Divine Being. But for the purpose of an integral transformation this too is not enough; there must be a transmutation of the thinking mind and all the vital and physical parts of consciousness in their own character.

This larger change can be partly attained by adding to the experiences of the heart a consecration of the pragmatic will which must succeed in carrying with it, — for otherwise it cannot be effective, — the adhesion of the dynamic vital part which supports the mental dynamis and is our first instrument of outer action. This consecration of the will in works proceeds by a gradual elimination of the ego-will and its motive-power of desire; the ego subjects itself to some higher law and finally effaces itself, seems not to exist or exists only to serve a higher Power or a higher Truth or to offer its will and acts to the Divine Being as an instrument. The law of being and action or the light of Truth which then guides the seeker, may be a clarity or power or principle which he perceives on the highest height of which his mind is capable; or it may be a truth of the divine Will which he feels present and working within him or guiding him by a Light or a Voice or a Force or a divine Person or Presence. In the end by this way one arrives at a consciousness in which one feels the Force or Presence acting within and moving or governing all the actions and the personal will is entirely surrendered or identified with that greater Truth-Will, Truth-Power or Truth-Presence. A combination of all these three approaches, the approach of the mind, the approach of the will, the approach of the heart, creates a spiritual or psychic condition of the surface being and nature in which there is a larger and more complex openness to the psychic light within us and to the spiritual Self or the Ishwara, to the Reality now felt above and enveloping and penetrating us. In the nature there is a more powerful and many-sided change, a spiritual building and self-creation, the appearance of a composite perfection of the saint, the selfless worker and the man of spiritual knowledge.

But, for this change to arrive at its widest totality and profound completeness, the consciousness has to shift its centre and its static and dynamic position from the surface to the inner being; it is there that we must find the foundation for our thought, life and action. For to stand outside on our surface and to receive from the inner being and follow its intimations is not a sufficient transformation; one must cease to be the surface personality and become the inner Person, the Purusha. But this is difficult, first because the outer nature opposes the movement and clings to its normal accustomed poise and externalised way of existence and, in addition, because there is a long way from the surface to the depths in which the psychic entity is veiled from us, and this intervening space is filled with a subliminal nature and nature-movements which are not by any means all of them favourable to the completion of the inward movement. The outer nature has to undergo a change of poise, a quieting, a purification and fine mutation of its substance and energy by which the many obstacles in it rarefy, drop away or otherwise disappear; it then becomes possible to pass through to the depths of our being and from the depths so reached a new consciousness can be formed, both behind the exterior self and in it, joining the depths to the surface. There must grow up within us or there must manifest a consciousness more and more open to the deeper and the higher being, more and more laid bare to the cosmic Self and Power and to what comes down from the Transcendence, turned to a higher Peace, permeable to a greater light, force and ecstasy, a consciousness that exceeds the small personality and surpasses the limited light and experience of the surface mind, the limited force and aspiration of the normal life-consciousness, the obscure and limited responsiveness of the body.

Even before the tranquillising purification of the outer nature has been effected or before it is sufficient, one can still break down the wall screening our inner being from our outer awareness by a strong force of call and aspiration, a vehement will or violent effort or an effective discipline or process; but this may be a premature movement and is not without its serious dangers. In entering within one may find oneself amidst a chaos of unfamiliar and supernormal experiences to which one has not the key or a press of subliminal or cosmic forces, subconscient, mental, vital, subtle-physical, which may unduly sway or chaotically drive the being, encircle it in a cave of darkness, or keep it wandering in a wilderness of glamour, allurement, deception, or push it into an obscure battlefield full of secret and treacherous and misleading or open and violent oppositions; beings and voices and influences may appear to the inner sense and vision and hearing claiming to be the Divine Being or His messengers or Powers and Godheads of the Light or guides of the path to realisation, while in truth they are of a very different character. If there is too much egoism in the nature of the seeker or a strong passion or an excessive ambition, vanity or other dominating weakness, or an obscurity of the mind or a vacillating will or a weakness of the life-force or an unsteadiness in it or want of balance, he is likely to be seized on through these deficiencies and to be frustrated or to deviate, misled from the true way of the inner life and seeking into false paths, or to be left wandering about in an intermediate chaos of experiences and fail to find his way out into the true realisation. These perils were well-known to a past spiritual experience and have been met by imposing the necessity of initiation, of discipline, of methods of purification and testing by ordeal, of an entire submission to the directions of the path-finder or path-leader, one who has realised the Truth and himself possesses and is able to communicate the light, the experience, a guide who is strong to take by the hand and carry over difficult passages as well as to instruct and point out the way. But even so the dangers will be there and can only be surmounted if there is or there grows up a complete sincerity, a will for purity, a readiness for obedience to the Truth, for surrender to the Highest, a readiness to lose or to subject to a divine yoke the limiting and self-affirming ego. These things are the sign that the true will for realisation, for conversion of the consciousness, for transformation is there, the necessary stage of the evolution has been reached: in that condition the defects of nature which belong to the human being cannot be a permanent obstacle to the change from the mental to the spiritual status; the process may never be entirely easy, but the way will have been made open and practicable.

One effective way often used to facilitate this entry into the inner self is the separation of the Purusha, the conscious being, from the Prakriti, the formulated nature. If one stands back from the mind and its activities so that they fall silent at will or go on as a surface movement of which one is the detached and disinterested witness, it becomes possible eventually to realise oneself as the inner Self of mind, the true and pure mental being, the Purusha; by similarly standing back from the life-activities, it is possible to realise oneself as the inner Self of life, the true and pure vital being, the Purusha; there is even a Self of body of which, by standing back from the body and its demands and activities and entering into a silence of the physical consciousness watching the action of its energy, it is possible to become aware, a true and pure physical being, the Purusha. So too, by standing back from all these activities of nature successively or together, it becomes possible to realise one's inner being as the silent impersonal self, the witness Purusha. This will lead to a spiritual realisation and liberation, but will not necessarily bring about a transformation; for the Purusha, satisfied to be free and himself, may leave the nature, the Prakriti, to exhaust its accumulated impetus by an unsupported action, a mechanical continuance not renewed and reinforced or vivified and prolonged by his consent, and use this rejection as a means of withdrawing from all nature. The Purusha has to become not only the witness but the knower and source, the master of all the thought and action, and this can only be partially done so long as one remains on the mental level or has still to use the ordinary instrumentation of mind, life and body. A certain mastery can indeed be achieved, but mastery is not transformation; the change made by it cannot be sufficient to be integral: for that it is essential to get back, beyond mind-being, life-being, body-being, still more deeply inward to the psychic entity inmost and profoundest within us, — or else to open to the superconscient highest domains. For this penetration into the luminous crypt of the soul one has to get through all the intervening vital stuff to the psychic centre within us, however long, tedious or difficult may be the process. The method of detachment from the insistence of all mental and vital and physical claims and calls and impulsions, a concentration in the heart, austerity, self-purification and rejection of the old mind-movements and life-movements, rejection of the ego of desire, rejection of false needs and false habits, are all useful aids to this difficult passage: but the strongest, most central way is to found all such or other methods on a self-offering and surrender of ourselves and of our parts of nature to the Divine

Being, the Ishwara. A strict obedience to the wise and intuitive leading of a Guide is also normal and necessary for all but a few specially gifted seekers.

As the crust of the outer nature cracks, as the walls of inner separation break down, the inner light gets through, the inner fire burns in the heart, the substance of the nature and the stuff of consciousness refine to a greater subtlety and purity, and the deeper psychic experiences, those which are not solely of an inner mental or inner vital character, become possible in this subtler, purer, finer substance; the soul begins to unveil itself, the psychic personality reaches its full stature. The soul, the psychic entity, then manifests itself as the central being which upholds mind and life and body and supports all the other powers and functions of the Spirit; it takes up its greater function as the guide and ruler of the nature. A guidance, a governance begins from within which exposes every movement to the light of Truth, repels what is false, obscure, opposed to the divine realisation: every region of the being, every nook and corner of it, every movement, formation, direction, inclination of thought, will, emotion, sensation, action, reaction, motive, disposition, propensity, desire, habit of the conscious or subconscious physical, even the most concealed, camouflaged, mute, recondite, is lighted up with the unerring psychic light, their confusions dissipated, their tangles disentangled, their obscurities, deceptions, self-deceptions precisely indicated and removed; all is purified, set right, the whole nature harmonised, modulated in the psychic key, put in spiritual order. This process may be rapid or tardy according to the amount of obscurity and resistance still left in the nature, but it goes on unfalteringly so long as it is not complete. As a final result the whole conscious being is made perfectly apt for spiritual experience of every kind, turned towards spiritual truth of thought, feeling, sense, action, tuned to the right responses, delivered from the darkness and stubbornness of the tamasic inertia, the turbidities and turbulences and impurities of the rajasic passion and restless unharmonised kinetism, the enlightened rigidities and sattwic limitations or poised balancements of constructed equilibrium which are the character of the Ignorance.

This is the first result, but the second is a free inflow of all kinds of spiritual experience, experience of the Self, experience of the Ishwara and the Divine Shakti, experience of cosmic consciousness, a direct touch with cosmic forces and with the occult movements of universal Nature, a psychic sympathy and unity and inner communication and interchanges of all kinds with other beings and with Nature, illuminations of the mind by knowledge, illuminations of the heart by love and devotion and spiritual joy and ecstasy, illuminations of the sense and the body by higher experience, illuminations of dynamic action in the truth and largeness of a purified mind and heart and soul, the certitudes of the divine light and guidance, the joy and power of the divine force working in the will and the conduct. These experiences are the result of an opening outward of the inner and inmost being and nature; for then there comes into play the soul's power of unerring inherent consciousness, its vision, its touch on things which is superior to any mental cognition; there is there, native to the psychic consciousness in its pure working, an immediate sense of the world and its beings, a direct inner contact with them and a direct contact with the Self and with the Divine, — a direct knowledge, a direct sight of Truth and of all truths, a direct penetrating spiritual emotion and feeling, a direct intuition of right will and right action, a power to rule and to create an order of the being not by the gropings of the superficial self, but from within, from the inner truth of self and things and the occult realities of Nature.

Some of these experiences can come by an opening of the inner mental and vital being, the inner and larger and subtler mind and heart and life within us, without any full emergence of the soul, the psychic entity, since there too there is a power of direct contact of consciousness: but the experience might then be of a mixed character; for there could be an emergence not only of the subliminal knowledge but of the subliminal ignorance. An insufficient expansion of the being, a limitation by mental idea, by narrow and selective emotion or by the form of the temperament so that there would be only an imperfect self-creation and action and not the free soul-emergence, could easily occur. In the absence of any or of a complete psychic emergence, experiences of certain kinds, experiences of greater knowledge and force, a surpassing of the ordinary limits, might lead to a magnified ego and even bring about instead of an out-flowering of what is divine or spiritual an uprush of the titanic or demoniac, or might call in agencies and powers which, though not of this disastrous type, are of a powerful but inferior cosmic character. But the rule and guidance of the soul brings into all experience the tendency of light, of integration, of harmony and intimate rightness which is native to the psychic essence. A psychic or, more widely speaking, a psycho-spiritual transformation of this kind would be already a vast change of our mental human nature.

But all this change and all this experience, though psychic and spiritual in essence and character, would still be, in its parts of life-effectuation, on the mental, vital and physical level; its dynamic spiritual outcome[6] would be a flowering of the soul in mind and life and body, but in act and form it would be circumscribed within the limitations, — however enlarged, uplifted and rarefied, — of an inferior instrumentation. It would be a reflected and modified manifestation of things whose full reality, intensity, largeness, oneness and diversity of truth and power and delight are above us, above mind and therefore above any perfection, within mind's own formula, of the foundations or superstructure of our present nature. A highest spiritual transformation must intervene on the psychic or psycho-spiritual change; the psychic movement inward to the inner being, the Self or Divinity within us, must be completed by an opening upward to a supreme spiritual status or a higher existence. This can be done by our opening into what is above us, by an ascent of consciousness into the ranges of overmind and supramental nature in which the sense of Self and Spirit is ever unveiled and permanent and in which the self-luminous instrumentation of the Self and Spirit is not restricted or divided as in our mind-nature, life-nature, body-nature. This also the psychic change makes possible; for

[6] The psychic and the spiritual opening with their experiences and consequences can lead away from life or to a Nirvana; but they are here being considered solely as steps in a transformation of the nature.

as it opens us to the cosmic consciousness now hidden from
us by many walls of limiting individuality, so also it opens us
to what is now superconscient to our normality because it is
hidden from us by the strong, hard and bright lid of mind,
— mind constricting, dividing and separative. The lid thins, is
slit, breaks asunder or opens and disappears under the pressure of the psycho-spiritual change and the natural urge of the
new spiritualised consciousness towards that of which it is an
expression here. This effectuation of an aperture and its consequences may not at all take place if there is only a partial psychic
emergence satisfied with the experience of the Divine Reality in
the normal degrees of the spiritualised mind: but if there is any
awakening to the existence of these higher supernormal levels,
then an aspiration towards them may break the lid or operate
a rift in it. This may happen long before the psycho-spiritual
change is complete or even before it has well begun or proceeded
far, because the psychic personality has become aware and has
an eager concentration towards the superconscience. An early
illumination from above or a rending of the upper velamen can
come as an outcome of aspiration or some inner readiness, or it
may even come uncalled for or not called for by any conscious
part of the mind, — perhaps by a secret subliminal necessity or
by an action or pressure from the higher levels, by something
which is felt as the touch of the Divine Being, the touch of the
Spirit, — and its results can be exceedingly powerful. But if it is
brought about by a premature pressure from below, it can be
attended with difficulties and dangers which are absent when
the full psychic emergence precedes this first admission to the
superior ranges of our spiritual evolution. The choice, however,
does not always rest with our will, for the operations of the
spiritual evolution in us are very various, and according to the
line it has followed will be the turn taken at any critical phase
by the action of the Consciousness-Force in its urge towards a
higher self-manifestation and formation of our existence.

   If the rift in the lid of mind is made, what happens is an
opening of vision to something above us or a rising up towards
it or a descent of its powers into our being. What we see by the

opening of vision is an Infinity above us, an eternal Presence or an infinite Existence, an infinity of consciousness, an infinity of bliss, — a boundless Self, a boundless Light, a boundless Power, a boundless Ecstasy. It may be that for a long time all that is obtained is the occasional or frequent or constant vision of it and a longing and aspiration, but without anything further, because, although something in the mind, heart or other part of the being has opened to this experience, the lower nature as a whole is too heavy and obscure as yet for more. But there may be, instead of this first wide awareness from below or subsequently to it, an ascension of the mind to heights above: the nature of these heights we may not know or clearly discern, but some consequence of the ascent is felt; there is often too an awareness of infinite ascension and return but no record or translation of that higher state. This is because it has been superconscient to mind and therefore mind, when it rises into it, is unable at first to retain there its power of conscious discernment and defining experience. But when this power begins to awake and act, when mind becomes by degrees conscious in what was to it superconscient, then there begins a knowledge and experience of superior planes of existence. The experience is in accord with that which is brought to us by the first opening of vision: the mind rises into a higher plane of pure Self, silent, tranquil, illimitable; or it rises into regions of Light or of Felicity, or into planes where it feels an infinite Power or a divine Presence or experiences the contact of a divine Love or Beauty or the atmosphere of a wider and greater and luminous Knowledge. In the return the spiritual impression abides; but the mental record is often blurred and remains as a vague or a fragmentary memory; the lower consciousness from which the ascent took place falls back to what it was, with only the addition of an unkept or a remembered but no longer dynamic experience. In time the ascent comes to be made at will and the consciousness brings back and retains some effect or some gain of its temporary sojourn in these higher countries of the Spirit. These ascents take place for many in trance, but are perfectly possible in a concentration of the waking consciousness or, where that consciousness has become sufficiently psychic, at any unconcentrated moment by an upward attraction or affinity. But these two types of contact with the superconscient, though they can be powerfully illuminating, ecstatic or liberating, are by themselves insufficiently effective: for the full spiritual transformation more is needed, a permanent ascension from the lower into the higher consciousness and an effectual permanent descent of the higher into the lower nature.

This is the third motion, the descent which is essential for bringing the permanent ascension, an increasing inflow from above, an experience of reception and retention of the descending Spirit or its powers and elements of consciousness. This experience of descent can take place as a result of the other two movements or automatically before either has happened, through a sudden rift in the lid or a percolation, a downpour or an influx. A light descends and touches or envelops or penetrates the lower being, the mind, the life or the body; or a presence or a power or a stream of knowledge pours in waves or currents, or there is a flood of bliss or a sudden ecstasy; the contact with the superconscient has been established. For such experiences repeat themselves till they become normal, familiar and well-understood, revelatory of their contents and their significance which may have at first been involved and wrapped into secrecy by the figure of the covering experience. For a knowledge from above begins to descend, frequently, constantly, then uninterruptedly, and to manifest in the mind's quietude or silence; intuitions and inspirations, revelations born of a greater sight, a higher truth and wisdom, enter into the being, a luminous intuitive discrimination works which dispels all darkness of understanding or dazzling confusions, puts all in order; a new consciousness begins to form, the mind of a high wide self-existent thinking knowledge or an illumined or an intuitive or an overmental consciousness with new forces of thought or sight and a greater power of direct spiritual realisation which is more than thought or sight, a greater becoming in the spiritual substance of our present being; the heart and the sense become subtle, intense, large to embrace all existence, to see God, to feel and hear and touch the Eternal, to make a deeper and closer unity of self and the world in a transcendent realisation. Other decisive experiences, other changes of consciousness determine themselves which are corollaries and consequences of this fundamental change. No limit can be fixed to this revolution; for it is in its nature an invasion by the Infinite.

This, effected little by little or in a succession of great and swift definitive experiences, is the process of the spiritual transformation. It achieves itself and culminates in an upward ascent often repeated by which in the end the consciousness fixes itself on a higher plane and from there sees and governs the mind, life and body; it achieves itself also in an increasing descent of the powers of the higher consciousness and knowledge which become more and more the whole normal consciousness and knowledge. A light and power, a knowledge and force are felt which first take possession of the mind and remould it, afterwards of the life-part and remould that, finally of the little physical consciousness and leave it no longer little but wide and plastic and even infinite. For this new consciousness has itself the nature of infinity: it brings to us the abiding spiritual sense and awareness of the Infinite and Eternal with a great largeness of the nature and a breaking down of its limitations; immortality becomes no longer a belief or an experience but a normal self-awareness; the close presence of the Divine Being, his rule of the world and of our self and natural members, his force working in us and everywhere, the peace of the infinite, the joy of the Infinite are now concrete and constant in the being; in all sights and forms one sees the Eternal, the Reality, in all sounds one hears it, in all touches feels it; there is nothing else but its forms and personalities and manifestations; the joy or adoration of the heart, the embrace of all existence, the unity of the spirit are abiding realities. The consciousness of the mental creature is turning or has been already turned wholly into the consciousness of the spiritual being. This is the second of the three transformations; uniting the manifested existence with what is above it, it is the middle step of the three, the decisive transition of the spiritually evolving nature.

If the spirit could from the first dwell securely on the

superior heights and deal with a blank and virgin stuff of mind and matter, a complete spiritual transformation might be rapid, even facile: but the actual process of Nature is more difficult, the logic of her movement more manifold, contorted, winding, comprehensive; she recognises all the data of the task she has set to herself and is not satisfied with a summary triumph over her own complexities. Every part of our being has to be taken in its own nature and character, with all the moulds and writings of the past still there in it: each minutest portion and movement must either be destroyed and replaced if it is unfit, or, if it is capable, transmuted into the truth of the higher being. If the psychic change is complete, this can be done by a painless process, though still the programme must be long and scrupulous and the progress deliberate; but otherwise one has to be satisfied with a partial result or, if one's own scrupulousness of perfection or hunger of the spirit is insatiable, consent to a difficult, often painful and seemingly interminable action. For ordinarily the consciousness does not rise to the summits except in the highest moments; it remains on the mental level and receives descents from above, sometimes a single descent of some spiritual power that stays and moulds the being into something predominatingly spiritual, or a succession of descents bringing into it more and more of the spiritual status and dynamis: but unless one can live on the highest height reached, there cannot be the complete or more integral change. If the psychic mutation has not taken place, if there has been a premature pulling down of the higher Forces, their contact may be too strong for the flawed and impure material of Nature and its immediate fate may be that of the unbaked jar of the Veda which could not hold the divine Soma Wine; or the descending influence may withdraw or be spilt because the nature cannot contain or keep it. Again, if it is Power that descends, the egoistic mind or vital may try to seize on it for its own use and a magnified ego or a hunting after powers and self-aggrandising masteries may be the untoward result. The Ananda descending cannot be held if there is too much sexual impurity creating an intoxicant or degrading mixture; the Power recedes, if there is ambition, vanity or other aggressive form of lower self, the Light if there is an attachment to obscurity or to any form of the Ignorance, the Presence if the chamber of the heart has not been made pure. Or some undivine Force may try to seize hold, not of the Power itself, for that withdraws, but of the result of force it leaves behind in the instrument and use it for the purposes of the Adversary. Even if none of these more disastrous faults or errors should take place, still the numerous mistakes of reception or the imperfections of the vessel may impede the transformation. The Power has to come at intervals and work meanwhile behind the veil or hold itself back through long periods of obscure assimilation or preparation of the recalcitrant parts of Nature; the Light has to work in darkness or semi-darkness on the regions in us that are still in the Night. At any moment the work may be stayed, personally for this life, because the nature is able to receive or assimilate no more, — for it has reached the present limits of its capacity, — or because the mind may be ready but the vital, when faced with a choice between the old life and the new, refuses, or if the vital accepts, the body may prove too weak, unfit or flawed for the necessary change of its consciousness and its dynamic transformation.

Moreover, the necessity of working out the change separately in each part of the being in its own nature and character compels the consciousness to descend into each in turn and act there according to its state and its possibility. If the work were done from above, from some spiritual height, there might be a sublimation or uplifting or the creation of a new structure compelled by the sheer force of the influence from above: but this change might not be accepted as native to itself by the lower being; it would not be a total growth, an integral evolution, but a partial and imposed formation, affecting or liberating some parts of the being, suppressing others or leaving them as they were; a creation from outside the normal nature, by imposition upon it, it could be durable in its entirety only as long as there was a maintenance of the creating influence. A descent of consciousness into the lower levels is therefore necessary, but in this way also it is difficult to work out the full power of the higher principle; there is a modification, dilution, diminution which keeps up an imperfection and limitation in the results: the light of a greater knowledge comes down but gets blurred and modified, its significance misinterpreted or its truth mixed with mental and vital error, or the force, the power to fulfil itself is not commensurate with its light. A light and power of the Overmind working in its own full right and in its own sphere is one thing, the same light working in the obscurity of the physical consciousness and under its conditions is something quite different and, owing to dilution and mixture, far inferior in its knowledge and force and results. A mutilated power, a partial effect or hampered movement is the consequence.

This is indeed the reason of the slow and difficult emergence of the Consciousness-Force in Nature: for Mind and Life have to descend into Matter and suit themselves to its conditions; changed and diminished by the obscurity and reluctant inertia of the substance and force in which they work, they are not able to make a complete transformation of their material into a fit instrument and a changed substance revelatory of their real and native power. The Life-consciousness is unable to effectuate the greatness and felicity of its mighty or beautiful impulses in the material existence; its impetus fails it, its force of effectuation is inferior to the truth of its conceptions, the form betrays the Life-intuition within it which it tries to render into terms of Life-being. The Mind is unable to achieve its high ideas in the medium of Life or Matter without deductions and compromises which deprive them of their divinity; its clarities of knowledge and will are not matched by its force to mould this inferior substance to obey and express it: on the contrary, its own powers get affected, its will is divided, its knowledge confused and clouded by the turbidities of life and the incomprehensiveness of Matter. Neither Life nor Mind succeeds in converting or perfecting the material existence, because they cannot attain to their own full force in these conditions; they need to call in a higher power to liberate and fulfil them. But the higher spiritual-mental powers also undergo the same disability when they descend into Life and Matter; they can do much more, achieve much luminous change, but the modification, the limitation, the disparity between the consciousness that comes in and the force of effectuation that it can mentalise and materialise, are constantly there and the result is a diminished creation. The change made is often extraordinary, there is even something which looks like a total conversion and reversal of the state of consciousness and an uplifting of its movements, but it is not dynamically absolute.

Only the Supermind can thus descend without losing its full power of action; for its action is always intrinsic and automatic, its will and knowledge identical and the result commensurate: its nature is a self-achieving Truth-Consciousness and, if it limits itself or its working, it is by choice and intention, not by compulsion; in the limits it chooses its action and the results of its action are harmonious and inevitable. Again, Overmind is, like Mind, a dividing principle, and its characteristic operation is to work out in an independent formation a selected harmony; its global action enables it indeed to create a harmony whole and perfect in itself or to unite or fuse its harmonies together, to synthetise; but, labouring under the restrictions of Mind, Life and Matter, it is obliged to do it by sections and their joinings. Its tendency of totality is hampered by its selective tendency which is accentuated by the nature of the mental and life material in which it is working here; what it can achieve is separate limited spiritual creations each perfect in itself, but not the integral knowledge and its manifestation. For this reason and because of the diminishing of its native light and power it is unable to do fully what is needed and has to call in a greater power, the supramental force, to liberate and fulfil it. As the psychic change has to call in the spiritual to complete it, so the first spiritual change has to call in the supramental transformation to complete it. For all these steps forward are, like those before them, transitional; the whole radical change in the evolution from a basis of Ignorance to a basis of Knowledge can only come by the intervention of the supramental Power and its direct action in earth-existence.

This then must be the nature of the third and final transformation which finishes the passage of the soul through the

Ignorance and bases its consciousness, its life, its power and form of manifestation on a complete and completely effective self-knowledge. The Truth-Consciousness, finding evolutionary Nature ready, has to descend into her and enable her to liberate the supramental principle within her; so must be created the supramental and spiritual being as the first unveiled manifestation of the truth of the Self and Spirit in the material universe.

Chapter XXVI

The Ascent towards Supermind

Masters of the Truth-Light who make the Truth grow by the Truth.
Rig Veda.[1]

Three powers of Speech that carry the Light in their front ... a triple house of peace, a triple way of the Light.   *Rig Veda.*[2]

Four other worlds of beauty he creates as his form when he has grown by the Truths.
Rig Veda.[3]

He is born a seer with the mind of discernment; an offspring of the Truth, a birth set within in the secrecy, half arisen into manifestation.
Rig Veda.[4]

Possessed of a vast inspired wisdom, creators of the Light, conscious all-knowers, growing in the Truth.   *Rig Veda.*[5]

Beholding the higher Light beyond the darkness we came to the divine Sun in the Godhead, to the highest Light of all.
Rig Veda.[6]

THE PSYCHIC transformation and the first stages of the spiritual transformation are well within our conception; their perfection would be the perfection, wholeness, consummated unity of a knowledge and experience which is already part of things realised, though only by a small number of human beings. But the supramental change in its process carries us into less explored regions; it initiates a vision of heights of consciousness which have indeed been glimpsed and visited, but have yet to be discovered and mapped in their completeness. The

---

[1] I. 23. 5.   [2] VII. 101. 1, 2.   [3] IX. 70. 1.   [4] IX. 68. 5.   [5] X. 66. 1.
[6] I. 50. 10.

highest of these peaks or elevated plateaus of consciousness, the supramental, lies far beyond the possibility of any satisfying mental scheme or map of it or any grasp of mental seeing and description. It would be difficult for the normal unillumined or untransformed mental conception to express or enter into something that is based on so different a consciousness with a radically different awareness of things; even if they were seen or conceived by some enlightenment or opening of vision, another language than the poor abstract counters used by our mind would be needed to translate them into terms by which their reality could become at all seizable by us. As the summits of human mind are beyond animal perception, so the movements of Supermind are beyond the ordinary human mental conception: it is only when we have already had experience of a higher intermediate consciousness that any terms attempting to describe supramental being could convey a true meaning to our intelligence; for then, having experienced something akin to what is described, we could translate an inadequate language into a figure of what we knew. If the mind cannot enter into the nature of Supermind, it can look towards it through these high and luminous approaches and catch some reflected impression of the Truth, the Right, the Vast which is the native kingdom of the free Spirit.

But even what can be said about the intermediate consciousness must perforce be inadequate; only certain abstract generalisations can be hazarded which may serve for an initial light of guidance. The one enabling circumstance here is that, however different in constitution and principle, the higher consciousness is still, in its evolutionary form, in what we can first achieve of it here, a supreme development of elements which are already present in ours in however rudimentary and diminished a figure and power of themselves. It is also a helpful fact that the logic of the process of evolutionary Nature continues, greatly modified in some of the rules of its working but essentially the same, in the ascension of the highest heights as in the lower beginnings; thus we can discover and follow to a certain extent the lines of her supreme procedure. For we have seen something of the nature and law of the transition from intellectual to spiritual mind; from that achieved starting-point we can begin to trace the passage to a higher dynamic degree of the new consciousness and the farther transition from spiritual mind towards Supermind. The indications must necessarily be very imperfect, for it is only some initial representations of an abstract and general character that can be arrived at by the method of metaphysical inquiry: the true knowledge and description must be left to the language of the mystic and the figures, at once more vivid and more recondite, of a direct and concrete experience.

The transition to Supermind through Overmind is a passage from Nature as we know it into Supernature. It is by that very fact impossible for any effort of the mere Mind to achieve; our unaided personal aspiration and endeavour cannot reach it: our effort belongs to the inferior power of Nature; a power of the Ignorance cannot achieve by its own strength or characteristic or available methods what is beyond its own domain of Nature. All the previous ascensions have been effectuated by a secret Consciousness-Force operating first in Inconscience and then in the Ignorance: it has worked by an emergence of its involved powers to the surface, powers concealed behind the veil and superior to the past formulations of Nature, but even so there is needed a pressure of the same superior powers already formulated in their full natural force on their own planes; these superior planes create their own foundation in our subliminal parts and from there are able to influence the evolutionary process on the surface. Overmind and Supermind are also involved and occult in earth-Nature, but they have no formations on the accessible levels of our subliminal inner consciousness; there is as yet no overmind being or organised overmind nature, no supramental being or organised supermind nature acting either on our surface or in our normal subliminal parts: for these greater powers of consciousness are superconscient to the level of our ignorance. In order that the involved principles of Overmind and Supermind should emerge from their veiled secrecy, the being and powers of the Superconscience must descend into us and uplift us and formulate themselves in our being and powers; this descent is a *sine qua non* of the transition and transformation.

It is conceivable indeed that, without the descent, by a secret pressure from above, by a long evolution, our terrestrial
Nature might succeed in entering into a close contact with the
higher now superconscient planes and a formation of subliminal
Overmind might take place behind the veil; as a result a slow
emergence of the consciousness proper to these higher planes
might awake on our surface. It is conceivable that in this way
there might appear a race of mental beings thinking and acting
not by the intellect or reasoning and reflecting intelligence, or not
mainly by it, but by an intuitive mentality which would be the
first step of an ascending change; this might be followed by an
overmentalisation which would carry us to the borders beyond
which lies the Supermind or divine Gnosis. But this process
would inevitably be a long and toilsome endeavour of Nature.
There is a possibility too that what would be achieved might only
be an imperfect superior mentalisation; the new higher elements
might strongly dominate the consciousness, but they would be
still subjected to a modification of their action by the principle
of an inferior mentality: there would be a greater expanded and
illuminating knowledge, a cognition of a higher order; but it
would still undergo a mixture subjecting it to the law of the
Ignorance, as Mind undergoes limitation by the law of Life and
Matter. For a real transformation there must be a direct and
unveiled intervention from above; there would be necessary too
a total submission and surrender of the lower consciousness, a
cessation of its insistence, a will in it for its separate law of action
to be completely annulled by transformation and lose all rights
over our being. If these two conditions can be achieved even now
by a conscious call and will in the spirit and a participation of our
whole manifested and inner being in its change and elevation, the
evolution, the transformation can take place by a comparatively
swift conscious change; the supramental Consciousness-Force
from above and the evolving Consciousness-Force from behind
the veil acting on the awakened awareness and will of the mental
human being would accomplish by their united power the momentous transition. There would be no farther need of a slow

evolution counting many millenniums for each step, the halting and difficult evolution operated by Nature in the past in the unconscious creatures of the Ignorance.

It is a first condition of this change that the mental Man we now are should become inwardly aware and in possession of his own deeper law of being and its processes; he must become the psychic and inner mental being master of his energies, no longer a slave of the movements of the lower Prakriti, in control of it, seated securely in a free harmony with a higher law of Nature. An increasing control of the individual over his own action of nature, a more and more conscious participation in the action of universal Nature, is a marked character, it is indeed a logical consequence, of the evolutionary principle and process. All action, all mental, vital, physical activities in the world are the operation of a universal Energy, a Consciousness-Force which is the power of the Cosmic Spirit working out the cosmic and individual truth of things. But since this creative Consciousness assumes in Matter a mask of inconscience and puts on the surface appearance of a blind universal Force executing a plan or organisation of things without seeming to know what it is doing, the first result is kin to this appearance; it is the phenomenon of an inconscient physical individualisation, a creation not of beings but of objects. These are formed existences with their own qualities, properties, power of being, character of being; but Nature's plan in them and organisation of them have to be worked out mechanically without any beginning of participation, initiation or conscious awareness in the individual object which emerges as the first dumb result and inanimate field of her action and creation. In animal life the Force begins to become slowly conscious on the surface and puts forth the form, no longer of an object, but of an individual being; but this imperfectly conscious individual, although it participates, senses, feels, yet only works out what the Force does in it without any clear intelligence or observation of what is being done; it seems to have no other choice or will than that which is imposed on it by its formed nature. In human mind there is the first appearance of an observing intelligence that regards what is being done and of a will and choice that have become conscious; but the consciousness is still limited and superficial: the knowledge also is limited and imperfect, it is a partial intelligence, a half understanding, groping and empirical in great part or, if rational, then rational by constructions, theories, formulas. There is not as yet a luminous seeing which knows things by a direct grasp and arranges them with a spontaneous precision according to the seeing, according to the scheme of their inherent truth; although there is a certain element of instinct and intuition and insight which has some beginning of this power, the normal character of human intelligence is an inquiring reason or reflective thought which observes, supposes, infers, concludes, arrives by labour at a constructed truth, a constructed scheme of knowledge, a deliberately arranged action of its own making. Or rather this is what it strives to be and partly is; for its knowledge and will are constantly invaded, darkened or frustrated by forces of the being which are half-blind instruments of the mechanism of Nature.

This is evidently not the utmost of which consciousness is capable, not its last evolution and highest summit. A greater and more intimate intuition must be possible which would enter into the heart of things, be in luminous identity with the movements of Nature, assure to the being a clear control of his life or at least a harmony with his universe. It is only a free and entire intuitive consciousness which would be able to see and to grasp things by direct contact and penetrating vision or a spontaneous truth-sense born of an underlying unity or identity and arrange an action of Nature according to the truth of Nature. This would be a real participation by the individual in the working of the universal Consciousness-Force; the individual Purusha would become the master of his own executive energy and at the same time a conscious partner, agent, instrument of the Cosmic Spirit in the working of the universal Energy: the universal Energy would work through him, but he also would work through her and the harmony of the intuitive truth would make this double working a single action. A growing conscious participation of this higher and more intimate kind must be one accompaniment of the transition from our present state of being to a state of Supernature.

A harmonious other-world in which an intuitive mental intelligence of this kind and its control would be the rule, is conceivable; but in our plane of being, owing to the original intention and past history of the evolutionary plan, such a rule and control could with difficulty be stabilised and it is not likely that it could be complete, final and definitive. For an intuitive mentality intervening in a mixed mental, vital, physical consciousness would normally be forced to undergo a mixture with the inferior stuff of consciousness already evolved; in order to act on it, it would have to enter into it and, entering in it, would get entangled in it, penetrated by it, affected by the separative and partial character of our mind's action and the limitation and restricted force of the Ignorance. The action of intuitive intelligence is keen and luminous enough to penetrate and modify, but not large and whole enough to swallow up into itself and abolish the mass of the Ignorance and Inconscience; it could not effect an entire transformation of the whole consciousness into its own stuff and power. Still, even in our present state, a participation of a kind is there and our normal intelligence is sufficiently awake for the universal Conscious-Force to work through it and allow the intelligence and will to exercise a certain amount of direction of inner and outer circumstance, fumbling enough and at every moment dogged by error, capable only of a limited effect and power, not commensurate with the larger totality of her vast operations. In the evolution towards Supernature, this initial power of conscious participation in the universal working would enlarge in the individual into a more and more intimate and extended vision of her workings in himself, a sensitive perception of the course she was taking, a growing understanding or intuitive idea of the methods that had to be followed for a more rapid and more conscious self-evolution. As his inner psychic or occult inner mental being came more to the front, there would be a strengthened power of choice, of sanction, a beginning of authentic free will which would grow more and more effective. But this free will would be mostly in relation to

his own workings of Nature; it would mean only a freer, fuller
and more immediately perceptive control of the motions of his
own being: even there it could not be at first completely free,
so long as it was imprisoned in the limits created by its own
formations or combated by imperfection due to a mixture of the
old and the new consciousness. Still there would be an increasing
mastery and knowledge and an opening to a higher being and a
higher nature.

   Our notion of free will is apt to be tainted with the excessive
individualism of the human ego and to assume the figure of
an independent will acting on its own isolated account, in a
complete liberty without any determination other than its own
choice and single unrelated movement. This idea ignores the
fact that our natural being is a part of cosmic Nature and our
spiritual being exists only by the supreme Transcendence. Our
total being can rise out of subjection to fact of present Nature
only by an identification with a greater Truth and a greater
Nature. The will of the individual, even when completely free,
could not act in an isolated independence, because the individual
being and nature are included in the universal Being and Nature
and dependent on the all-overruling Transcendence. There could
indeed be in the ascent a dual line. On one line the being could
feel and behave as an independent self-existence uniting itself
with its own impersonal Reality; it could, so self-conceived, act
with a great force, but either this action would be still within an
enlarged frame of its past and present self-formation of power
of Nature or else it would be the cosmic or supreme Force that
acted in it and there would be no personal initiation of action, no
sense therefore of individual free will but only of an impersonal
cosmic or supreme Will or Energy at its work. On the other
line the being would feel itself a spiritual instrument and so
act as a power of the Supreme Being, limited in its workings
only by the potencies of the Supernature, which are without
bounds or any restriction except its own Truth and self-law,
and by the Will in her. But in either case there would be, as the
condition of a freedom from the control of a mechanical action
of Nature-forces, a submission to a greater conscious Power or

an acquiescent unity of the individual being with its intention and movement in his own and in the world's existence.

For the action of a new power of being in a higher range of consciousness might, even in its control on outer Nature, be extraordinarily effective, but only because of its light of vision and a consequent harmony or identification with the cosmic and transcendent Will; for it is when it becomes an instrumentation of a higher instead of a lower Power that the will of the being becomes free from a mechanical determinism by action and process of cosmic Mind-Energy, Life-Energy, Matter-Energy and an ignorant subjection to the drive of this inferior Nature. A power of initiation, even of an individual overseeing of world-forces could be there; but it would be an instrumental initiation, a delegated overseeing: the choice of the individual would receive the sanction of the Infinite because it was itself an expression of some truth of the Infinite. Thus the individuality would become more and more powerful and effective in proportion as it realised itself as a centre and formation of the universal and transcendent Being and Nature. For as the progression of the change proceeded, the energy of the liberated individual would be no longer the limited energy of mind, life and body, with which it started; the being would emerge into and put on, — even as there would emerge in him and descend into him, assuming him into it, — a greater light of Consciousness and a greater action of Force: his natural existence would be the instrumentation of a superior Power, an overmental and supramental Consciousness-Force, the power of the original Divine Shakti. All the processes of the evolution would be felt as the action of a supreme and universal Consciousness, a supreme and universal Force working in whatever way it chose, on whatever level, within whatever self-determined limits, a conscious working of the transcendent and cosmic Being, the action of the omnipotent and omniscient World-Mother raising the being into herself, into her Supernature. In place of the Nature of Ignorance with the individual as its closed field and unconscious or half-conscious instrument, there would be a Supernature of the divine Gnosis and the individual soul would be its conscious, open and free field and instrument, a participant in its action, aware of its purpose and process, aware too of its own greater Self, the universal, the transcendent Reality, and of its own Person as illimitably one with that and yet an individual being of Its being, an instrument and a spiritual centre.

A first opening towards this participation in an action of Supernature is a condition of the turn towards the last, the supramental transformation: for this transformation is the completion of a passage from the obscure harmony of a blind automatism with which Nature sets out to the luminous authentic spontaneity, the infallible motion of the self-existent truth of the Spirit. The evolution begins with the automatism of Matter and of a lower life in which all obeys implicitly the drive of Nature, fulfils mechanically its law of being and therefore succeeds in maintaining a harmony of its limited type of existence and action; it proceeds through the pregnant confusion of the mind and life of a humanity driven by this inferior Nature but struggling to escape from her limitations, to master and drive and use her; it emerges into a greater spontaneous harmony and automatic self-fulfilling action founded on the spiritual Truth of things. In this higher state the consciousness will see that Truth and follow the line of its energies with a full knowledge, with a strong participation and instrumental mastery, a complete delight in action and existence. There will be a luminous and enjoyed perfection of unity with all instead of a blind and suffered subjection of the individual to the universal, and at every moment the action of the universal in the individual and the individual in the universal will be enlightened and governed by the rule of the transcendent Supernature.

But this highest condition is difficult and must evidently take long to bring about; for the participation and consent of the Purusha to the transition is not sufficient, there must be also the consent and participation of the Prakriti. It is not only the central thought and will that have to acquiesce, but all the parts of our being must assent and surrender to the law of the spiritual Truth; all has to learn to obey the government of the conscious Divine Power in the members. There are obstinate difficulties in our being, born of its evolutionary constitution, which militate against this assent. For some of these parts are still subject to the inconscience and subconscience and to the lower automatism of habit or so-called law of the nature, — mechanical habit of mind, habit of life, habit of instinct, habit of personality, habit of character, the ingrained mental, vital, physical needs, impulses, desires of the natural man, the old functionings of all kinds that are rooted there so deep that it would seem as if we had to dig to abysmal foundations in order to get them out: these parts refuse to give up their response to the lower law founded in the Inconscient; they continually send up to the conscious mind and life the old reactions and seek to reaffirm them there as the eternal rule of Nature. Other parts of the being are less obscure and mechanical and rooted in inconscience, but all are imperfect and attached to their imperfection and have their own obstinate reactions; the vital part is wedded to the law of self-affirmation and desire, the mind is attached to its own formed movements, and both are willingly obedient to the inferior law of the Ignorance. And yet the law of participation and the law of surrender are imperative; at each step of the transition the assent of the Purusha is needed and there must be too the consent of each part of the nature to the action of the higher power for its change. There must be then a conscious self-direction of the mental being in us towards this change, this substitution of Supernature for the old nature, this transcendence. The rule of conscious obedience to the higher truth of the spirit, the surrender of the whole being to the light and power that come from the Supernature, is a second condition which has to be accomplished slowly and with difficulty by the being itself before the supramental transformation can become at all possible.

It follows that the psychic and the spiritual transformation must be far advanced, even as complete as may be, before there can be any beginning of the third and consummating supramental change; for it is only by this double transmutation that the self-will of the Ignorance can be totally altered into a spiritual obedience to the remoulding truth and will of the greater Consciousness of the Infinite. A long, difficult stage of constant effort, energism, austerity of the personal will, *tapasyā*, has ordinarily to be traversed before a more decisive stage can be reached in which a state of self-giving of all the being to the Supreme Being and the Supreme Nature can become total and absolute. There has to be a preliminary stage of seeking and effort with a central offering or self-giving of the heart and soul and mind to the Highest and a later mediate stage of total conscious reliance on its greater Power aiding the personal endeavour; that integral reliance again must grow into a final complete abandonment of oneself in every part and every movement to the working of the higher Truth in the nature. The totality of this abandonment can only come if the psychic change has been complete or the spiritual transformation has reached a very high state of achievement. For it implies a giving up by the mind of all its moulds, ideas, mental formations, of all opinion, of all its habits of intellectual observation and judgment to be replaced first by an intuitive and then by an overmind or supramental functioning which inaugurates the action of a direct Truth-Consciousness, Truth-sight, Truth-discernment, a new consciousness which is in all its ways quite foreign to our mind's present nature. There is demanded too a similar giving up by the vital of its cherished desires, emotions, feelings, impulses, grooves of sensation, forceful mechanism of action and reaction to be replaced by a luminous, desireless, free and yet automatically self-determining force, the force of a centralised universal and impersonal knowledge, power, delight of which the life must become an instrument and an epiphany, but of which it has at present no inkling and no sense of its greater joy and strength for fulfilment. Our physical part has to give up its instincts, needs, blind conservative attachments, settled grooves of nature, its doubt and disbelief in all that is beyond itself, its faith in the inevitability of the fixed functionings of the physical mind, the physical life and the body, that they may be replaced by a new power which establishes its own greater law and functioning in form and force of Matter. Even the inconscient and subconscient have to become conscient in us, susceptible to the higher light, no longer obstructive to the fulfilling action of the Consciousness-Force, but more and more a mould and lower basis of the Spirit. These things cannot be done so long as either mind, life or physical consciousness are the leading powers of being or have any dominance. The admission of such a change can only be brought about by a full emergence of the soul and inner being, the dominance of the psychic and spiritual will and a long working of their light and power on the parts of the being, a psychic and spiritual remoulding of the whole nature.

A unification of the entire being by a breaking down of the wall between the inner and outer nature, — a shifting of the position and centration of the consciousness from the outer to the inner self, a firm foundation on this new basis, a habitual action from this inner self and its will and vision and an opening up of the individual into the cosmic consciousness, — is another necessary condition for the supramental change. It would be chimerical to hope that the supreme Truth-Consciousness can establish itself in the narrow formulation of our surface mind and heart and life, however turned towards spirituality. All the inner centres must have burst open and released into action their capacities; the psychic entity must be unveiled and in control. If this first change establishing the being in the inner and larger, a Yogic in place of an ordinary consciousness has not been done, the greater transmutation is impossible. Moreover the individual must have sufficiently universalised himself, he must have recast his individual mind in the boundlessness of a cosmic mentality, enlarged and vivified his individual life into the immediate sense and direct experience of the dynamic motion of the universal life, opened up the communications of his body with the forces of universal Nature, before he can be capable of a change which transcends the present cosmic formulation and lifts him beyond the lower hemisphere of universality into a consciousness belonging to its spiritual upper hemisphere. Besides he must have already become aware of what is now to him superconscient; he must be already a being conscious of the higher spiritual Light, Power, Knowledge, Ananda, penetrated by its descending influences, new-made by a spiritual change. It is possible for the spiritual opening to take place and its action to proceed before the psychic is far advanced or complete; for the spiritual influence from above can awaken, assist and complete the psychic transmutation: all that is necessary is that there should be a sufficient stress of the psychic entity for the spiritual higher overture to take place. But the third, the supramental change does not admit of any premature descent of the highest Light; for it can only commence when the supramental Force begins to act directly, and this it does not do if the nature is not ready. For there is too great a disparity between the power of the supreme Force and the capacity of the ordinary nature; the inferior nature would either be unable to bear or, bearing, unable to respond and receive or, receiving, unable to assimilate. Till Nature is ready, the supramental Force has to act indirectly; it puts the intermediary powers of Overmind or Intuition in front, or it works through a modification of itself to which the already half-transformed being can be wholly or partially responsive.

The spiritual evolution obeys the logic of a successive unfolding; it can take a new decisive main step only when the previous main step has been sufficiently conquered: even if certain minor stages can be swallowed up or leaped over by a rapid and brusque ascension, the consciousness has to turn back to assure itself that the ground passed over is securely annexed to the new condition. It is true that the conquest of the Spirit supposes the execution in one life or a few lives of a process that in the ordinary course of Nature would involve a slow and uncertain procedure of centuries or even of millenniums: but this is a question of the speed with which the steps are traversed; a greater or concentrated speed does not eliminate the steps themselves or the necessity of their successive surmounting. The increased rapidity is possible only because the conscious participation of the inner being is there and the power of the Supernature is already at work in the half-transformed lower nature, so that the steps which would otherwise have had to be taken tentatively in the night of Inconscience or Ignorance can now be taken in an increasing light and power of Knowledge. The first obscure material movement of the evolutionary Force is marked by an aeonic graduality; the movement of life-progress proceeds slowly but still with a quicker step, it is concentrated into the figure of millenniums; mind can still further compress the tardy leisureliness of Time and make long paces of the centuries; but when the conscious Spirit intervenes, a supremely concentrated pace of evolutionary swiftness becomes possible. Still, an involved rapidity of the evolutionary course swallowing up the stages can only come in when the power of the conscious Spirit has prepared the field and the supramental Force has begun to use its direct influence. All Nature's transformations do indeed wear the appearance of a miracle, but it is a miracle with a method: her largest strides are taken over an assured ground, her swiftest leaps are from a base that gives security and certainty to the evolutionary saltus; a secret all-wisdom governs everything in her, even the steps and processes that seem to be most unaccountable.

This law of Nature's procedure brings in the necessity of a gradation in the last transitional process, a climbing of degrees, an unfolding of higher and higher states that lead us from the spiritualised mind to Supermind, — a steep passage that could not be accomplished otherwise. There are above us, we have seen, successive states, levels or graded powers of being overtopping our normal mind, hidden in our own superconscient parts, higher ranges of Mind, degrees of spiritual consciousness and experience; without them there would be no links, no helpful intervening spaces to make the immense ascension possible. It is indeed from these higher sources that the secret spiritual Power acts upon the being and by its pressure brings about the psychic transformation or the spiritual change; but in the early stages of our growth this action is not apparent, it remains occult and unseizable. At first what is necessary is that the pure touch of the spiritual force must intervene in mental nature: that awakening pressure must stamp itself upon mind and heart and life and give them their upward orientation; a subtle light or a great transmuting power must purify, refine and uplift their motions and suffuse them with a higher consciousness that does not belong to their own normal capacity and character. This can be done from within by an invisible action through the psychic entity and the psychic personality; a consciously felt descent from above is not indispensable. The presence of the Spirit is there in every living being, on every level, in all things, and because it is there, the experience of Sachchidananda, of the pure spiritual existence and consciousness, of the delight of a divine presence, closeness, contact can be acquired through the mind or the heart or the life-sense or even through the physical consciousness; if the inner doors are flung sufficiently open, the light from the sanctuary can suffuse the nearest and the farthest chambers of the outer being. The necessary turn or change can also be brought about by an occult descent of the spiritual force from above, in which the influx, the influence, the spiritual consequence is felt, but the higher source is unknown and the actual feeling of a descent is not there. A consciousness so touched may be so much uplifted that the being turns to an immediate union with the Self or with the Divine by departure from the evolution and, if that is sanctioned, no question of graduality or steps or method intervenes, the rupture with Nature can be decisive: for the law of departure, once it is made possible, is not or need not be the same as the law of the evolutionary transformation and perfection; it is or can be a leap, a breaking out of bonds rapid or immediate, — the spiritual evasion is secured and its only remaining sanction is the destined fall of the body. But if the transformation of earth life is intended, the first touch of spiritualisation must be followed by an awakening to the higher sources and energies, a seeking for them and an enlargement and heightening of the being into their characteristic status and a conversion of the consciousness to their greater law and dynamic nature. This change must go step by step, till the stair of the ascension is transcended and there is an emergence to those greatest wide-open spaces of which the Veda speaks, the native spaces of a consciousness which is supremely luminous and infinite.

For here there is the same process of evolution as in the rest of the movement of Nature; there is a heightening and widening of the consciousness, an ascent to a new level and a taking up of the lower levels, an assumption and new integration of the existence by a superior power of Being which imposes its own way of action and its character and force of substance-energy on as much as it can reach of the previously evolved parts of nature. The demand for integration becomes at this highest stage of Nature's workings a point of cardinal importance. In the lower grades of the ascension the new assumption, the integration into a higher principle of consciousness, remains incomplete: the mind cannot wholly mentalise life and matter; there are considerable parts of the life-being and the body which remain in the realm of the submental and the subconscient or inconscient. This is one serious obstacle to the mind's endeavour towards the perfection of the nature; for the continued share of the submental, the subconscient and inconscient in the government of the activities, by bringing in another law than that of the mental being, enables the conscious vital and the physical consciousness also to reject the law laid upon them by the mind and to follow their own impulses and instincts in defiance of the mental reason and the rational will of the developed intelligence. This makes it difficult for the mind to go beyond itself, to exceed its own level and spiritualise the nature; for what it cannot even make fully conscious, cannot securely mentalise and rationalise, it cannot spiritualise, since spiritualisation is a greater and more difficult integration. No doubt, by calling in the spiritual force, it can establish an influence and a preliminary change in some parts of the nature, especially in the thinking mind itself and in the heart which is nearest to its own province: but this change is not often a total perfection even within limits and what it does achieve is rare and difficult. The spiritual consciousness using the mind is employing an inferior means and, even though it brings in a divine light into the mind, a divine purity, passion, ardour into the heart or imposes a spiritual law upon the life, this new consciousness has to work within restrictions; for the most part it can only regulate or check the lower action of the life and rigorously control the body, but these members, even if refined or mastered, do not receive their spiritual fulfilment or undergo a perfection and transformation. For that it is necessary to bring in a higher dynamic principle which is native to the spiritual consciousness and by which, therefore, it can act in its own law

and completer natural light and power and impose them upon
the members.

But even this intervention of a new dynamic principle and
this powerful imposition may take long to succeed; for the lower
parts of the being have their own rights and, if they are to
be truly transformed, they must be made to consent to their
own transformation. This is difficult to bring about because the
natural propensity of each part of us is to prefer its own self-
law, its dharma, however inferior, to a superior law or dharma
which it feels to be not its own; it clings to its own consciousness
or unconsciousness, its own impulsions and reactions, its own
dynamisation of being, its own way of the delight of existence.
It clings to them all the more obstinately if that way be a contradiction of delight, a way of darkness and sorrow and pain and
suffering; for that too has acquired its own perverse and opposite
taste, *rasa*, its pleasure of darkness and sorrow, its sadistic or
masochistic interest in pain and suffering. Even if this part of our
being seeks better things, it is often obliged to follow the worse
because they are its own, natural to its energy, natural to its
substance. A complete and radical change can only be brought
about by bringing in persistently the spiritual light and intimate
experience of the spiritual truth, power, bliss into the recalcitrant
elements until they too recognise that their own way of fulfilment
lies there, that they are themselves a diminished power of the
Spirit and can recover by this new way of being their own truth
and integral nature. This illumination is constantly opposed by
the Forces of the lower nature and still more by the adverse
Forces that live and reign by the world's imperfections and have
laid down their formidable foundation on the black rock of the
Inconscience.

An indispensable step towards overcoming this difficulty is
the opening up of the inner being and its centres of action; for
there the task that the surface mind could not achieve begins to
be more possible. The inner mind, the inner life-consciousness
and life-mind, the subtle-physical consciousness and its subtle-
physical mentality, once liberated into action, create a larger,
finer, greater mediating awareness able to communicate with

the universal and with what is above them, able also to bring to bear their power on the whole range of the being, on the submental, on the subconscient mind, on the subconscient life, even on the subconscience of the body: they can, though not wholly enlighten, yet to some extent open, penetrate, work upon the fundamental Inconscience. The spiritual Light, Power, Knowledge, Delight from above can then descend beyond the mind and heart, which are always the easiest to reach and illumine; occupying the whole nature from top to bottom, they can pervade more fully the life and the body and by a still profounder impact shake the foundations of the Inconscience. But even this larger mentalisation and vitalisation from within is still an inferior illumination: it can lessen but it does not get rid of the Ignorance; it assails and compels to recede but it does not overcome the powers and forces that maintain the subtle and secret rule of the Inconscience. The spiritual forces acting through this larger mentalisation and vitalisation can bring in a higher light, strength and joy; but the full spiritualisation, the completest new integration of consciousness, is at this stage still impossible. If the inmost being, the psychic, takes charge, then indeed a deeper mutation, not mental, can make the descent of spiritual force more effective; for the totality of the conscious being will have undergone a preliminary soul-change which emancipates mind, life, body from the snare of their own imperfections and impurities. At this point, a greater spiritual dynamisation, the working of the higher powers of the spiritual Mind and Overmind, can fully intervene: they may indeed have started their work before, though only as influences; but under the new conditions they can uplift the central being towards their own level and commence the last new integration of the nature. These higher powers work already in the human unspiritualised mind, but indirectly and in a fragmentary and diminished action; they are changed into substance and power of mind before they can work, and that substance and power are illumined and intensified in their vibrations, exalted and ecstasised in some of their movements by this entry, but not transformed. But when the spiritualisation begins and, as its greater results manifest themselves, — silence of the mind, the admission of our being into the cosmic consciousness, the Nirvana of the little ego in the sense of universal self, the contact with the Divine Reality, — the interventions of the higher dynamis and our openness to them can increase, they can assume a fuller, more direct, more characteristic power of their working, and this progression continues until some complete and mature action of them is possible. It is then that the turning of the spiritual towards the supramental transformation commences; for the heightening of the consciousness to higher and higher planes builds in us the gradation of the ascent to Supermind, that difficult and supreme passage.

It is not to be supposed that the circumstances and the lines of the transition would be the same for all, for here we enter into the domain of the Infinite: but, since there is behind all of them the unity of a fundamental truth, the scrutiny of a given line of ascent may be expected to throw light on the principle of all ascending possibilities; such a scrutiny of one line is all that can be attempted. This line is, as all must be, governed by the natural configuration of the stair of ascent: there are in it many steps, for it is an incessant gradation and there is no gap anywhere; but, from the point of view of the ascent of consciousness from our mind upwards through a rising series of dynamic powers by which it can sublimate itself, the gradation can be resolved into a stairway of four main ascents, each with its high level of fulfilment. These gradations may be summarily described as a series of sublimations of the consciousness through Higher Mind, Illumined Mind and Intuition into Overmind and beyond it; there is a succession of self-transmutations at the summit of which lies the Supermind or Divine Gnosis. All these degrees are gnostic in their principle and power; for even at the first we begin to pass from a consciousness based on an original Inconscience and acting in a general Ignorance or in a mixed Knowledge-Ignorance to a consciousness based on a secret self-existent Knowledge and first acted upon and inspired by that light and power and then itself changed into that substance and using entirely this new instrumentation. In themselves these grades are grades of energy-substance of the Spirit: for it must not be supposed, because we distinguish them according to their leading character, means and potency of knowledge, that they are merely a method or way of knowing or a faculty or power of cognition; they are domains of being, grades of the substance and energy of the spiritual being, fields of existence which are each a level of the universal Consciousness-Force constituting and organising itself into a higher status. When the powers of any grade descend completely into us, it is not only our thought and knowledge that are affected, — the substance and very grain of our being and consciousness, all its states and activities are touched and penetrated and can be remoulded and wholly transmuted. Each stage of this ascent is therefore a general, if not a total, conversion of the being into a new light and power of a greater existence.

The gradation itself depends fundamentally upon a higher or lower substance, potency, intensity of vibrations of the being, of its self-awareness, of its delight of existence, of its force of existence. Consciousness, as we descend the scale, becomes more and more diminished and diluted, — dense indeed by its coarser crudity, but while that crudity of consistence compacts the stuff of Ignorance, it admits less and less the substance of light; it becomes thin in pure substance of consciousness and reduced in power of consciousness, thin in light, thin and weak in capacity of delight; it has to resort to a grosser thickness of its diminished stuff and to a strenuous output of its obscurer force to arrive at anything, but this strenuousness of effort and labour is a sign not of strength but of weakness. As we ascend, on the contrary, a finer but far stronger and more truly and spiritually concrete substance emerges, a greater luminosity and potent stuff of consciousness, a subtler, sweeter, purer and more powerfully ecstatic energy of delight. In the descent of these higher grades upon us it is this greater light, force, essence of being and consciousness, energy of delight that enter into mind, life, body, change and repair their diminished and diluted and incapable substance, convert it into its own higher and stronger dynamis of Spirit and intrinsic form and force of reality. This can happen because all is fundamentally the same substance, the same consciousness, the same force, but in different forms and powers and degrees of itself: a taking up of the lower by the higher is therefore a possible and, but for our second nature of inconscience, a spiritually natural movement; what was put forth from the superior status is enveloped and taken up into its own greater being and essence.

Our first decisive step out of our human intelligence, our normal mentality, is an ascent into a higher Mind, a mind no longer of mingled light and obscurity or half-light, but a large clarity of the Spirit. Its basic substance is a unitarian sense of being with a powerful multiple dynamisation capable of the formation of a multitude of aspects of knowledge, ways of action, forms and significances of becoming, of all of which there is a spontaneous inherent knowledge. It is therefore a power that has proceeded from the Overmind, — but with the Supermind as its ulterior origin, — as all these greater powers have proceeded: but its special character, its activity of consciousness are dominated by Thought; it is a luminous thought-mind, a mind of Spirit-born conceptual knowledge. An all-awareness emerging from the original identity, carrying the truths the identity held in itself, conceiving swiftly, victoriously, multitudinously, formulating and by self-power of the Idea effectually realising its conceptions, is the character of this greater mind of knowledge. This kind of cognition is the last that emerges from the original spiritual identity before the initiation of a separative knowledge, base of the Ignorance; it is therefore the first that meets us when we rise from conceptive and ratiocinative mind, our best-organised knowledge-power of the Ignorance, into the realms of the Spirit; it is, indeed, the spiritual parent of our conceptive mental ideation, and it is natural that this leading power of our mentality should, when it goes beyond itself, pass into its immediate source.

But here in this greater Thought there is no need of a seeking and self-critical ratiocination, no logical motion step by step towards a conclusion, no mechanism of express or implied deductions and inferences, no building or deliberate concatenation of idea with idea in order to arrive at an ordered sum or outcome of knowledge; for this limping action of our reason is a movement of Ignorance searching for knowledge, obliged to safeguard its steps against error, to erect a selective mental structure for its temporary shelter and to base it on foundations already laid and carefully laid but never firm, because it is not supported on a soil of native awareness but imposed on an original soil of nescience. There is not here, either, that other way of our mind at its keenest and swiftest, a rapid hazardous divination and insight, a play of the searchlight of intelligence probing into the little known or the unknown. This higher consciousness is a Knowledge formulating itself on a basis of self-existent all-awareness and manifesting some part of its integrality, a harmony of its significances put into thought-form. It can freely express itself in single ideas, but its most characteristic movement is a mass ideation, a system or totality of truth-seeing at a single view; the relations of idea with idea, of truth with truth are not established by logic but pre-exist and emerge already self-seen in the integral whole. There is an initiation into forms of an ever-present but till now inactive knowledge, not a system of conclusions from premises or data; this thought is a self-revelation of eternal Wisdom, not an acquired knowledge. Large aspects of truth come into view in which the ascending Mind, if it chooses, can dwell with satisfaction and, after its former manner, live in them as in a structure; but if progress is to be made, these structures can constantly expand into a larger structure or several of them combine themselves into a provisional greater whole on the way to a yet unachieved integrality. In the end there is a great totality of truth known and experienced but still a totality capable of infinite enlargement because there is no end to the aspects of knowledge, *nāstyanto vistarasya me*.

This is the Higher Mind in its aspect of cognition; but there is also the aspect of will, of dynamic effectuation of the Truth: here we find that this greater more brilliant Mind works always on the rest of the being, the mental will, the heart and its feelings, the life, the body, through the power of thought, through the idea-force. It seeks to purify through knowledge, to deliver through knowledge, to create by the innate power of knowledge. The idea is put into the heart or the life as a force to be accepted and worked out; the heart and life become conscious of the idea and respond to its dynamisms and their substance begins to modify itself in that sense, so that the feelings and actions become the vibrations of this higher wisdom, are informed with it, filled with the emotion and the sense of it: the will and the life impulses are similarly charged with its power and its urge of self-effectuation; even in the body the idea works so that, for example, the potent thought and will of health replaces its faith in illness and its consent to illness, or the idea[7] of strength calls in the substance, power, motion, vibration of strength; the idea generates the force and form proper to the idea and imposes it on our substance of Mind, Life or Matter. It is in this way that the first working proceeds; it charges the whole being with a new and superior consciousness, lays a foundation of change, prepares it for a superior truth of existence.

It has here to be emphasised, in order to obviate a natural misconception which can easily arise when the superior power of the higher forces is first perceived or experienced, that these higher forces are not in their descent immediately all-powerful as they would naturally be in their own plane of action and in their own medium. In the evolution in Matter they have to enter into a foreign and inferior medium and work upon it; they encounter there the incapacities of our mind and life and body, meet with the unreceptiveness or blind refusal of the Ignorance, experience the negation and obstruction of the Inconscience. On their own level they work upon a basis of luminous consciousness and luminous substance of being and are automatically effective; but here they have to encounter an already and strongly formed foundation of Nescience, — not only the complete nescience of Matter, but the modified nescience of mind and heart and life. Thus the higher Idea descending into the developed mental intelligence has even there to overcome the barrage of a mass

---

[7] The word expressing the idea has the same power if it is surcharged with the spiritual force; that is the rationale of the Indian use of the *mantra*.

or system of formed ideas which belong to the Knowledge-Ignorance and the will to persistence and self-realisation of these ideas; for all ideas are forces and have a formative or self-effective faculty greater or less according to the conditions, — even reducible to nil in practice when they have to deal with inconscient Matter, but still potential. There is thus ready-formed a power of resistance which opposes or minimises the effects of the descending Light, a resistance which may amount to a refusal, a rejection of the Light, or take the shape of an attempt to impair, subdue, ingeniously modify or adapt or perversely deform the light in order to suit it to the preconceived ideas of the Ignorance. If the preconceived or already formed ideas are dismissed and deprived of their right to persistence, they have still the right of recurrence, from outside, from their prevalence in universal Mind, or they may retire downwards into the vital, physical or subconscient parts and from thence resurge at the least opportunity to repossess their lost domain: for evolutionary Nature has to give this right of persistence to things once established by her in order to bring a sufficient steadiness and solidity to her steps. It is, moreover, the nature and claim of any Force in the manifestation to be, to survive, to effectuate itself wherever possible and as long as possible, and it is therefore that in a world of Ignorance all is achieved not only through a complexus but through a collision and struggle and intermixture of Forces. But for this highest evolution it is essential that all mixture of Ignorance with Knowledge should be abolished; and action and evolution through strife of forces must be replaced by an action and evolution through a harmony of forces: but this stage can only be reached by a last strife and an overcoming of the powers of Ignorance by the powers of Light and Knowledge. In the lower levels of the being, in the heart and life and body, the same phenomenon recurs and on a more intense scale; for here it is not ideas that have to be met but emotions, desires, impulses, sensations, vital needs and habits of the lower Nature; these, since they are less conscious than ideas, are blinder in their response and are more obstinately self-assertive: all have the same or a greater power of resistance and recurrence, or take refuge in the circumconscient universal Nature or in our own lower levels or in a seed-state in the subconscient and from there have the power of new invasion or resurgence. This power of persistence, recurrence, resistance of established things in Nature is always the great obstacle which the evolutionary Force has to meet, which it has indeed itself created in order to prevent a too rapid transmutation even when that transmutation is its own eventual intention in things.

This obstacle will be there, — even though it may progressively diminish, — at each stage of this greater ascent. In order to allow at all to the higher Light an adequate entry and force of working, it is necessary to acquire a power for quietude of the nature, to compose, tranquillise, impress a controlled passivity or even an entire silence on mind and heart, life and body: but even so a continued opposition, overt and felt in the Force of the universal Ignorance or subliminal and obscure in the substance-energy of the individual's make of mind, his form of Life, his body of Matter, an occult resistance or a revolt or reaffirmation of the controlled or suppressed energies of the ignorant nature, is always possible and, if anything in the being consents to them, they can resume dominance. A previously established psychic control is very desirable as that creates a general responsiveness and inhibits the revolt of the lower parts against the Light or their consent to the claims of the Ignorance. A preliminary spiritual transformation will also reduce the hold of the Ignorance; but neither of these influences altogether eliminates its obstruction and limitation: for these preliminary changes do not bring the integral consciousness and knowledge; the original basis of Nescience proper to the Inconscient will still be there needing at every turn to be changed, enlightened, diminished in its extent and in its force of reaction. The power of the spiritual Higher Mind and its idea-force, modified and diminished as it must be by its entrance into our mentality, is not sufficient to sweep out all these obstacles and create the gnostic being, but it can make a first change, a modification that will capacitate a higher ascent and a more powerful descent and further prepare an integration of the being in a greater Force of consciousness and knowledge.

This greater Force is that of the Illumined Mind, a Mind no longer of higher Thought, but of spiritual light. Here the clarity of the spiritual intelligence, its tranquil daylight, gives place or subordinates itself to an intense lustre, a splendour and illumination of the Spirit: a play of lightnings of spiritual truth and power breaks from above into the consciousness and adds to the calm and wide enlightenment and the vast descent of peace which characterise or accompany the action of the larger conceptual-spiritual principle, a fiery ardour of realisation and a rapturous ecstasy of knowledge. A downpour of inwardly visible Light very usually envelops this action; for it must be noted that, contrary to our ordinary conceptions, light is not primarily a material creation and the sense or vision of light accompanying the inner illumination is not merely a subjective visual image or a symbolic phenomenon: light is primarily a spiritual manifestation of the Divine Reality illuminative and creative; material light is a subsequent representation or conversion of it into Matter for the purposes of the material Energy. There is also in this descent the arrival of a greater dynamic, a golden drive, a luminous "enthousiasmos" of inner force and power which replaces the comparatively slow and deliberate process of the Higher Mind by a swift, sometimes a vehement, almost a violent impetus of rapid transformation.

The Illumined Mind does not work primarily by thought, but by vision; thought is here only a subordinate movement expressive of sight. The human mind, which relies mainly on thought, conceives that to be the highest or the main process of knowledge, but in the spiritual order thought is a secondary and a not indispensable process. In its form of verbal thought, it can almost be described as a concession made by Knowledge to the Ignorance, because that Ignorance is incapable of making truth wholly lucid and intelligible to itself in all its extent and manifold implications except through the clarifying precision of significant sounds; it cannot do without this device to give to ideas an exact outline and an expressive body. But it is evident that this is a device, a machinery; thought in itself, in its origin on the higher levels of consciousness, is a perception,

a cognitive seizing of the object or of some truth of things
which is a powerful but still a minor and secondary result of
spiritual vision, a comparatively external and superficial regard
of the self upon the self, the subject upon itself or something
of itself as object: for all there is a diversity and multiplicity
of the self. In mind there is a surface response of perception to
the contact of an observed or discovered object, fact or truth
and a consequent conceptual formulation of it; but in the spiritual light there is a deeper perceptive response from the very
substance of consciousness and a comprehending formulation
in that substance, an exact figure or revelatory ideograph in
the stuff of the being, — nothing more, no verbal representation
is needed for the precision and completeness of this thought-
knowledge. Thought creates a representative image of Truth;
it offers that to the mind as a means of holding Truth and
making it an object of knowledge; but the body itself of Truth
is caught and exactly held in the sunlight of a deeper spiritual sight to which the representative figure created by thought
is secondary and derivative, powerful for communication of
knowledge, but not indispensable for reception or possession
of knowledge.

A consciousness that proceeds by sight, the consciousness of
the seer, is a greater power for knowledge than the consciousness
of the thinker. The perceptual power of the inner sight is greater
and more direct than the perceptual power of thought: it is a
spiritual sense that seizes something of the substance of Truth
and not only her figure; but it outlines the figure also and at
the same time catches the significance of the figure, and it can
embody her with a finer and bolder revealing outline and a larger
comprehension and power of totality than thought-conception
can manage. As the Higher Mind brings a greater consciousness
into the being through the spiritual idea and its power of truth,
so the Illumined Mind brings in a still greater consciousness
through a Truth-sight and Truth-light and its seeing and seizing
power. It can effect a more powerful and dynamic integration;
it illumines the thought-mind with a direct inner vision and
inspiration, brings a spiritual sight into the heart and a spiritual

light and energy into its feeling and emotion, imparts to the life-force a spiritual urge, a truth inspiration that dynamises the action and exalts the life-movements; it infuses into the sense a direct and total power of spiritual sensation so that our vital and physical being can contact and meet concretely, quite as intensely as the mind and emotion can conceive and perceive and feel, the Divine in all things; it throws on the physical mind a transforming light that breaks its limitations, its conservative inertia, replaces its narrow thought-power and its doubts by sight and pours luminosity and consciousness into the very cells of the body. In the transformation by the Higher Mind the spiritual sage and thinker would find his total and dynamic fulfilment; in the transformation by the Illumined Mind there would be a similar fulfilment for the seer, the illumined mystic, those in whom the soul lives in vision and in a direct sense and experience: for it is from these higher sources that they receive their light and to rise into that light and live there would be their ascension to their native empire.

But these two stages of the ascent enjoy their authority and can get their own united completeness only by a reference to a third level; for it is from the higher summits where dwells the intuitional being that they derive the knowledge which they turn into thought or sight and bring down to us for the mind's transmutation. Intuition is a power of consciousness nearer and more intimate to the original knowledge by identity; for it is always something that leaps out direct from a concealed identity. It is when the consciousness of the subject meets with the consciousness in the object, penetrates it and sees, feels or vibrates with the truth of what it contacts, that the intuition leaps out like a spark or lightning-flash from the shock of the meeting; or when the consciousness, even without any such meeting, looks into itself and feels directly and intimately the truth or the truths that are there or so contacts the hidden forces behind appearances, then also there is the outbreak of an intuitive light; or, again, when the consciousness meets the Supreme Reality or the spiritual reality of things and beings and has a contactual union with it, then the spark, the flash or the blaze of intimate truth-perception is lit in its depths. This close perception is more than sight, more than conception: it is the result of a penetrating and revealing touch which carries in it sight and conception as part of itself or as its natural consequence. A concealed or slumbering identity, not yet recovering itself, still remembers or conveys by the intuition its own contents and the intimacy of its self-feeling and self-vision of things, its light of truth, its overwhelming and automatic certitude.

In the human mind the intuition is even such a truth-remembrance or truth-conveyance, or such a revealing flash or blaze breaking into a great mass of ignorance or through a veil of nescience: but we have seen that it is subject there to an invading mixture or a mental coating or an interception and substitution; there is too a manifold possibility of misinterpretation which comes in the way of the purity and fullness of its action. More-over, there are seeming intuitions on all levels of the being which are communications rather than intuitions, and these have a very various provenance, value and character. The infrarational "mystic", so-styled, — for to be a true mystic it is not sufficient to reject reason and rely on sources of thought or action of which one has no understanding, — is often inspired by such communications on the vital level from a dark and dangerous source. In these circumstances we are driven to rely mainly on the reason and are disposed even to control the suggestions of the intuition, — or the pseudo-intuition, which is the more frequent phenomenon, — by the observing and discriminating intelligence; for we feel in our intellectual part that we cannot be sure otherwise what is the true thing and what the mixed or adulterated article or false substitute. But this largely discounts for us the utility of the intuition: for the reason is not in this field a reliable arbiter, since its methods are different, tentative, uncertain, an intellectual seeking; even though it itself really relies on a camouflaged intuition for its conclusions, — for without that help it could not choose its course or arrive at any assured finding, — it hides this dependence from itself under the process of a reasoned conclusion or a verified conjecture. An intuition passed in judicial review by the reason ceases to be an intuition and can only have the authority of the reason for which there is no inner source of direct certitude. But even if the mind became predominantly an intuitive mind reliant upon its portion of the higher faculty, the co-ordination of its cognitions and its separated activities, — for in mind these would always be apt to appear as a series of imperfectly connected flashes, — would remain difficult so long as this new mentality has not a conscious liaison with its suprarational source or a self-uplifting access to a higher plane of consciousness in which an intuitive action is pure and native.

Intuition is always an edge or ray or outleap of a superior light; it is in us a projecting blade, edge or point of a far-off supermind light entering into and modified by some intermediate truth-mind substance above us and, so modified, again entering into and very much blinded by our ordinary or ignorant mind-substance; but on that higher level to which it is native its light is unmixed and therefore entirely and purely veridical, and its rays are not separated but connected or massed together in a play of waves of what might almost be called in the Sanskrit poetic figure a sea or mass of "stable lightnings". When this original or native Intuition begins to descend into us in answer to an ascension of our consciousness to its level or as a result of our finding of a clear way of communication with it, it may continue to come as a play of lightning-flashes, isolated or in constant action; but at this stage the judgment of reason becomes quite inapplicable, it can only act as an observer or registrar understanding or recording the more luminous intimations, judgments and discriminations of the higher power. To complete or verify an isolated intuition or discriminate its nature, its application, its limitations, the receiving consciousness must rely on another completing intuition or be able to call down a massed intuition capable of putting all in place. For once the process of the change has begun, a complete transmutation of the stuff and activities of the mind into the substance, form and power of Intuition is imperative; until then, so long as the process of consciousness depends upon the lower intelligence serving or helping out or using the intuition, the result can only be a survival of the mixed

Knowledge-Ignorance uplifted or relieved by a higher light and force acting in its parts of Knowledge.

Intuition has a fourfold power. A power of revelatory truth-seeing, a power of inspiration or truth-hearing, a power of truth-touch or immediate seizing of significance, which is akin to the ordinary nature of its intervention in our mental intelligence, a power of true and automatic discrimination of the orderly and exact relation of truth to truth, — these are the fourfold potencies of Intuition. Intuition can therefore perform all the action of reason, — including the function of logical intelligence, which is to work out the right relation of things and the right relation of idea with idea, — but by its own superior process and with steps that do not fail or falter. It takes up also and transforms into its own substance not only the mind of thought, but the heart and life and the sense and physical consciousness: already all these have their own peculiar powers of intuition derivative from the hidden Light; the pure power descending from above can assume them all into itself and impart to these deeper heart-perceptions and life-perceptions and the divinations of the body a greater integrality and perfection. It can thus change the whole consciousness into the stuff of Intuition; for it brings its own greater radiant movement into the will, into the feelings and emotions, the life-impulses, the action of sense and sensation, the very workings of the body-consciousness; it recasts them in the light and power of truth and illumines their knowledge and their ignorance. A certain integration can thus take place, but whether it is a total integration must depend on the extent to which the new light is able to take up the subconscient and penetrate the fundamental Inconscience. Here the intuitive light and power may be hampered in its task because it is the edge of a delegated and modified Supermind, but does not bring in the whole mass or body of the identity-knowledge. The basis of Inconscience in our nature is too vast, deep and solid to be altogether penetrated, turned into light, transformed by an inferior power of the Truth-nature.

The next step of the ascent brings us to the Overmind; the intuitional change can only be an introduction to this higher spiritual overture. But we have seen that the Overmind, even when it is selective and not total in its action, is still a power of cosmic consciousness, a principle of global knowledge which carries in it a delegated light from the supramental Gnosis. It is, therefore, only by an opening into the cosmic consciousness that the overmind ascent and descent can be made wholly possible: a high and intense individual opening upwards is not sufficient, — to that vertical ascent towards summit Light there must be added a vast horizontal expansion of the consciousness into some totality of the Spirit. At the least, the inner being must already have replaced by its deeper and wider awareness the surface mind and its limited outlook and learned to live in a large universality; for otherwise the overmind view of things and the overmind dynamism will have no room to move in and effectuate its dynamic operations. When the Overmind descends, the predominance of the centralising ego-sense is entirely subordinated, lost in largeness of being and finally abolished; a wide cosmic perception and feeling of a boundless universal self and movement replaces it: many motions that were formerly egocentric may still continue, but they occur as currents or ripples in the cosmic wideness. Thought, for the most part, no longer seems to originate individually in the body or the person but manifests from above or comes in upon the cosmic mind-waves: all inner individual sight or intelligence of things is now a revelation or illumination of what is seen or comprehended, but the source of the revelation is not in one's separate self but in the universal knowledge; the feelings, emotions, sensations are similarly felt as waves from the same cosmic immensity breaking upon the subtle and the gross body and responded to in kind by the individual centre of the universality; for the body is only a small support or even less, a point of relation, for the action of a vast cosmic instrumentation. In this boundless largeness, not only the separate ego but all sense of individuality, even of a subordinated or instrumental individuality, may entirely disappear; the cosmic existence, the cosmic consciousness, the cosmic delight, the play of cosmic forces are alone left: if the delight or the centre of Force is felt in what was the personal mind, life or body, it is not with a sense of personality but as a field of manifestation, and this sense of the delight or of the action of Force is not confined to the person or the body but can be felt at all points in an unlimited consciousness of unity which pervades everywhere.

But there can be many formulations of overmind conscious-ness and experience; for the Overmind has a great plasticity and is a field of multiple possibilities. In place of an uncentred and unplaced diffusion there may be the sense of the universe in oneself or as oneself: but there too this self is not the ego; it is an extension of a free and pure essential self-consciousness or it is an identification with the All, — the extension or the identification constituting a cosmic being, a universal individual. In one state of the cosmic consciousness there is an individual included in the cosmos but identifying himself with all in it, with the things and beings, with the thought and sense, the joy and grief of others; in another state there is an inclusion of beings in oneself and a reality of their life as part of one's own being. Often there is no rule or governance of the immense movement, but a free play of universal Nature to which what was the per-sonal being responds with a passive acceptance or a dynamic identity, while yet the spirit remains free and undisturbed by any bondage to the reactions of this passivity or this universal and impersonal identification and sympathy. But with a strong influence or full action of the Overmind a very integral sense of governance, a complete supporting or overruling presence and direction of the cosmic Self or the Ishwara can come in and become normal; or a special centre may be revealed or created overtopping and dominating the physical instrument, individual in fact of existence, but impersonal in feeling and recognised by a free cognition as something instrumental to the action of a Transcendent and Universal Being. In the transition towards the Supermind this centralising action tends towards the discovery of a true individual replacing the dead ego, a being who is in his essence one with the supreme Self, one with the universe in extension and yet a cosmic centre and circumference of the specialised action of the Infinite.

These are the general first results and create the normal foundation of the overmind consciousness in the evolved spiritual being, but its varieties and developments are innumerable. The consciousness that thus acts is experienced as a consciousness of Light and Truth, a power, force, action full of Light and Truth, an aesthesis and sensation of beauty and delight universal and multitudinous in detail, an illumination in the whole and in all things, in the one movement and all movements, with a constant extension and play of possibilities which is infinite, even in its multitude of determinations endless and indeterminable. If the power of an ordering overmind Gnosis intervenes, then there is a cosmic structure of the consciousness and action, but this is not like the rigid mental structures; it is plastic, organic, something that can grow and develop and stretch into the infinite. All spiritual experiences are taken up and become habitual and normal to the new nature; all essential experiences belonging to the mind, life, body are taken up and spiritualised, transmuted and felt as forms of the consciousness, delight, power of the infinite existence. Intuition, illumined sight and thought enlarge themselves; their substance assumes a greater substantiality, mass, energy, their movement is more comprehensive, global, many-faceted, more wide and potent in its truth-force: the whole nature, knowledge, aesthesis, sympathy, feeling, dynamism become more catholic, all-understanding, all-embracing, cosmic, infinite.

The overmind change is the final consummating movement of the dynamic spiritual transformation; it is the highest possible status-dynamis of the Spirit in the spiritual-mind plane. It takes up all that is in the three steps below it and raises their characteristic workings to their highest and largest power, adding to them a universal wideness of consciousness and force, a harmonious concert of knowledge, a more manifold delight of being. But there are certain reasons arising from its own characteristic status and power that prevent it from being the final possibility of the spiritual evolution. It is a power, though the highest power, of the lower hemisphere; although its basis is a cosmic unity, its action is an action of division and interaction, an action taking its stand on the play of the multiplicity. Its play is, like that of all Mind, a play of possibilities; although it acts not in the Ignorance but with the knowledge of the truth of these possibilities, yet it works them out through their own independent evolution of their powers. It acts in each cosmic formula according to the fundamental meaning of that formula and is not a power for a dynamic transcendence. Here in earth-life it has to work upon a cosmic formula whose basis is the entire nescience which results from the separation of Mind, Life and Matter from their own source and supreme origin. Overmind can bridge that division up to the point at which separative Mind enters into Overmind and becomes a part of its action; it can unite individual mind with cosmic mind on its highest plane, equate individual self with cosmic self and give to the nature an action of universality; but it cannot lead Mind beyond itself, and in this world of original Inconscience it cannot dynamise the Transcendence: for it is the Supermind alone that is the supreme self-determining truth-action and the direct power of manifestation of that Transcendence. If then the action of evolutionary Nature ended here, the Overmind, having carried the consciousness to the point of a vast illumined universality and an organised play of this wide and potent spiritual awareness of utter existence, force-consciousness and delight, could only go farther by an opening of the gates of the Spirit into the upper hemisphere and a will to enable the soul to depart out of its cosmic formation into Transcendence.

In the terrestrial evolution itself the overmind descent would not be able to transform wholly the Inconscience; all that it could do would be to transform in each man it touched the whole conscious being, inner and outer, personal and universally impersonal, into its own stuff and impose that upon the Ignorance illumining it into cosmic truth and knowledge. But a basis of Nescience would remain; it would be as if a sun and its system were to shine out in an original darkness of Space and illumine everything as far as its rays could reach so that all that dwelt in the light would feel as if no darkness were there at all in their experience of existence. But outside that sphere or expanse of experience the original darkness would still be there and, since all things are possible in an overmind structure, could reinvade the island of light created within its empire. Moreover, since Overmind deals with different possibilities, its natural action would be to develop the separate possibility of one or more or numerous dynamic spiritual formulations to their utmost or combine or harmonise several possibilities together; but this would be a creation or a number of creations in the original terrestrial creation, each complete in its separate existence. The evolved spiritual individual would be there, there might evolve also a spiritual community or communities in the same world as mental man and the vital being of the animal, but each working out its independent existence in a loose relation within the terrestrial formula. The supreme power of the principle of unity taking all diversities into itself and controlling them as parts of the unity, which must be the law of the new evolutionary consciousness, would not as yet be there. Also by this much evolution there could be no security against the downward pull or gravitation of the Inconscience which dissolves all the formations that life and mind build in it, swallows all things that arise out of it or are imposed upon it and disintegrates them into their original matter. The liberation from this pull of the Inconscience and a secured basis for a continuous divine or gnostic evolution would only be achieved by a descent of the Supermind into the terrestrial formula, bringing into it the supreme law and light and dynamis of the Spirit and penetrating with it and transforming the inconscience of the material basis. A last transition from Overmind to Supermind and a descent of Supermind must therefore intervene at this stage of evolutionary Nature.

Overmind and its delegated powers, taking up and penetrating mind and the life and body dependent upon mind, would subject all to a greatening process; at each step of this process a greater power and a higher intensity of gnosis less and less mixed with the loose, diffused, diminishing and diluting stuff of mind could establish itself: but all gnosis is in its origin power of Supermind, so that this would mean a greater and greater influx of a half-veiled and indirect supramental light and power into the nature. This would continue until the point was reached at which Overmind would begin itself to be transformed into Supermind; the supramental consciousness and force would take up the transformation directly into its own hands, reveal to the terrestrial mind, life, bodily being their own spiritual truth and divinity and, finally, pour into the whole nature the perfect knowledge, power, significance of the supramental existence. The soul would pass beyond the borders of the Ignorance and cross its original line of departure from the supreme Knowledge: it would enter into the integrality of the supramental gnosis; the descent of the gnostic Light would effectuate a complete transformation of the Ignorance.

This or something more largely planned on these lines might be regarded as the schematic, logical or ideal account of the spiritual transformation, a structural map of the ascent to the supramental summit, looked at as a succession of separate steps, each accomplished before the passage to the next commences. It would be as if the soul, putting forth an organised natural individuality, were a traveller mounting the degrees of consciousness cut out in universal Nature, each ascent carrying it totally as a definite integer, as a separate body of conscious being, from one state of its existence to the next in order. This is so far correct that a sufficient integration of one status has to be complete before an ascent to the next higher station can be entirely secure: this clear succession might also be the course followed by a few even in the early stages of this evolution, and it might become too a normal process after the whole stair-flight of the evolution had been built and made safe. But evolutionary Nature is not a logical series of separate segments; it is a totality of ascending powers of being which interpenetrate and dovetail and exercise in their action on each other a power of mutual modification. When the higher descends into the lower consciousness, it alters the lower but is also modified and diminished by it; when the lower ascends, it is sublimated but at the same time qualifies the sublimating substance and power. This interaction creates an abundant number of different intermediate and interlocked degrees of the force and consciousness of being, but it also makes it difficult to bring about a complete integration of all the powers under the full control of any one power. For this reason there is not actually a series of simple clear-cut and successive stages in the individual's evolution; there is instead a complexity and a partly determinate, partly confused comprehensiveness of the movement. The soul may still be described as a traveller and climber who presses towards his high goal by step on step, each of which he has to build up as an integer but most frequently re-descend in order to rebuild and make sure of the supporting stair so that it may not crumble beneath him: but the evolution of the whole consciousness has rather the movement of an ascending ocean of Nature; it can be compared to a tide or a mounting flux, the leading fringe of which touches the higher degrees of a cliff or hill while the rest is still below. At each stage the higher parts of the nature may be provisionally but incompletely organised in the new consciousness while the lower are in a state of flux or formation, partly moving in the old way though influenced and beginning to change, partly belonging to the new kind but still imperfectly achieved and not yet firm in the change. Another image might be that of an army advancing in columns which annexes new ground, while the main body is still behind in a territory overrun but too large to be effectively occupied, so that there has to be a frequent halt and partial return to the traversed areas for consolidation and assurance of the hold on the occupied country and assimilation of its people. A rapid conquest might be possible, but it would be of the nature of an encampment or a domination established in a foreign country; it would not be the assumption, total assimilation, integration needed for the entire supramental change.

This entails certain consequences which modify the clear successions of the evolution and prevent it from following the cleanly determined and firmly arranged course which our logical intelligence demands from Nature but seldom gets from her. As Life and Mind begin to appear when the organisation of Matter is sufficient to admit them but the more complex and perfect organisation of Matter comes with the evolution of Life and Mind, as Mind appears when Life is sufficiently organised to admit of a developed vibration of consciousness but Life receives its full organisation and development only after Mind can act upon it, as the spiritual evolution begins when man as Mind is capable of the movements of spirituality but Mind also rises to its own highest perfection by the growth of the intensities and luminosities of the Spirit, so it is with this higher evolution of the ascending powers of the Spirit. As soon as there is a sufficient spiritual development, something of intuition, illumination of the being, the movements of the higher spiritual grades of Consciousness begins to manifest, — sometimes one, sometimes the other or all together, and they do not wait for each power in the series to complete itself before a higher power comes into action. An overmind light and power may descend in some sort, create a partial form of itself in the being and take a leading part or supervise or intervene while the intuitive and illumining Mind and higher Mind are still incomplete; these would then remain in the whole, acting along with the greater Power, often penetrated or sublimated by it or rising into it to form a greater or overmind Intuition, a greater or overmind Illumination, a greater or overmind spiritual Thinking. This intricate action takes place because each descending power by its intensity of pressure on the nature and uplifting effect makes the being already capable of a still higher invasion before that earlier power itself is complete in its self-formation; but also it happens because the work of assumption and transformation of the lower nature can with difficulty be done if a higher and higher intervention does not take place. The Illumination and the higher Thought need the help of the Intuition, the Intuition needs the help of the Overmind to combat the darkness or ignorance in which they labour and to give them their own fullness. Still, it is not possible in the end for the overmind status and integration to be complete until the Higher Mind and the Illumined Mind have been integrated and taken up into the Intuition and the Intuition itself subsequently integrated and taken up into the all-enlarging and all-sublimating overmind energy. The law of the gradation has to be satisfied even in the complexity of the process of evolutionary Nature.

A further cause of complexity arises from the need of integration itself; for the process is not only an ascent of the soul to a higher status, but a descent of the higher consciousness so gained to take up and transform the inferior nature. But this nature has a density of previous formation which resists and obstructs the descent; even when the higher power has broken the barrier and descended and is at work, we have seen that the nature of the Ignorance resists and obstructs the working, that it either strives to refuse transformation altogether or tries to modify the new power into some conformity with its own workings, or even throws itself upon it to seize and degrade and enslave it to its own way of action and lower purpose. Ordinarily, in their task of assumption and assimilation of this difficult stuff of Nature, the higher powers descend first into the mind and occupy the mind-centres because these are nearest to themselves in intelligence and knowledge-power; if they descend first into the heart or into the vital being of force and sensation, as they sometimes do because these happen to be in some individuals more open and call them first, the results are more mixed and dubious, imperfect and insecure than if things happen in the logical order. But, even in its normal working when it takes up the being part by part in the natural order of descent, the descending power is not able to bring about a total occupation and transformation of each before it goes farther. It can only effect a general and incomplete occupation, so that the workings of each remain still partly of the new higher, partly of a mixed, partly of the old unchanged lower order. All the mind in its whole range cannot be transmuted at once, for the mind-centres are not a region isolated from the rest of the being; the mind-action is penetrated by the action of the vital and physical parts, and in those parts themselves are lower formations of mind, a vital mind, a physical mind, and these have to be changed before there can be an entire transformation of the mental being. The higher transforming power has, therefore, to descend, as soon as may be and without waiting for an integral mental change, into the heart so as to occupy and change the emotional nature, and afterwards into the inferior vital centres to occupy and change the whole vital and kinetic and sensational nature, and, finally, into the physical centres so as to occupy and change the whole physical nature. But even this finality is not final, for there are still left the subconscient parts and the inconscient foundation. The intricacy, the interwoven action of these powers and parts of the being is so great that it may almost be said that in this change nothing is accomplished until all is accomplished. There is a tide and ebb, the forces of the old nature receding and again partially occupying their old dominions, effectuating a slow retreat with rear-line actions and return attacks and aggressions, the higher influx occupying each time more conquered territory but imperfectly sure of sovereignty so long as anything is left that has not become part of its luminous regime.

A third complexity is brought in by the power of the consciousness to live in more than one status at a time; especially, a difficulty is created by the division of our being into an inner and an outer or surface nature and the farther intricacy of a secret circumconscient or environmental consciousness in which are determined our unseen connections with the world outside us. In the spiritual opening, it is the awakened inner being that readily receives and assimilates the higher influences and puts on the higher nature; the external surface self, more entirely moulded by the forces of the Ignorance and Inconscience, is slower to awake, slower to receive, slower to assimilate. There is therefore a long stage in which the inner being is sufficiently transformed but the outer is still involved in a mixed and difficult movement of imperfect change. This disparity repeats itself at each step of the ascent; for in each change the inner being follows more readily, the outer limps after, reluctant or else incompetent in spite of its aspiration and desire: this necessitates a constantly repeated labour of assumption, adaptation, orientation, a labour reproduced in new terms always but always the same in principle. But even when the outer and the inner nature of the individual are unified in a harmonised spiritual consciousness, that still more external but occult part of him in which his being mixes with the being of the outside world and through which the outside world invades his consciousness remains a field of imperfection. There is necessarily a commerce here between disparate influences: the inner spiritual influence is met by quite opposite influences strong in their control of the present world-order; the new spiritual consciousness has to bear the shock of the dominant and established unspiritualised powers of the Ignorance. This creates a difficulty which is of capital importance in all stages of the spiritual evolution and its urge towards a change of the nature.

A subjective spirituality can be established which refuses or minimises commerce with the world or is content to witness its action and throw back or throw out its invading influences without allowing any reaction to them or admitting their intrusion: but if the inner spirituality is to be objectivised in a free world-action, if the individual has to project himself into the world and in a sense take the world into himself, this cannot be dynamically done without receiving the world-influences through one's own circumconscient or environmental being. The spiritual inner consciousness has then to deal with these influences in such a way that, as soon as they approach or enter, they become either obliterated and without result or transformed by their very entry into its own mode and substance. Or it may force them to receive the spiritual influence and return with a transforming power on the world they come from, for such a compulsion on the lower universal Nature is part of a perfect spiritual action. But for that the circumconscient or environmental being must be so steeped in the spiritual light and spiritual substance that nothing can enter into it without undergoing this transformation: the invading external influences have not to bring in at all their lower awareness, their lower sight, their lower dynamism. But this is a difficult perfection, because ordinarily the circumconscient is not wholly our own formed and realised self but ourself plus the external world-nature. It is, for this reason, always easier to spiritualise the inner self-sufficient parts than to transform the outer action; a perfection of introspective, indwelling or subjective spirituality aloof from the world or self-protected against it is easier than a perfection of the whole nature in a dynamic, kinetic spirituality objectivised in the life, embracing the world, master of its environment, sovereign in its commerce with world-nature. But since the integral transformation must embrace fully the dynamic being and take up into it the life of action and the world-self outside us, this completer change is demanded of the evolving nature.

The essential difficulty comes from the fact that the substance of our normal being is moulded out of the Inconscience. Our ignorance is a growth of knowledge in a substance of being which is nescient; the consciousness it develops, the knowledge it establishes are always dogged, penetrated, enveloped by this nescience. It is this substance of nescience that has to be transformed into a substance of superconscience, a substance in which consciousness and a spiritual awareness are always there even when they are not active, not expressed, not put into form of knowledge. Till that is done, the nescience invades or encompasses or even swallows up and absorbs into its oblivious darkness all that enters into it; it compels the descending light to compromise with the lesser light it enters: there is a mixture, a diminution and dilution of itself, a diminution, a modification, an incomplete authenticity of its truth and power. Or, at the least, the nescience limits its truth and circumscribes its force, segments its applicability and its range; its truth of principle is barred from a full truth of individual realisation or from an achieved truth of cosmic practice. Thus love as a law of life can affirm itself practically as an inner active principle; but unless it occupies the whole substance of being, the entire individual feeling and action cannot be moulded by the law of love: even if perfected in the individual, it can be rendered unilateral and ineffective by the general nescience which is blind to it and hostile, or it is forced to circumscribe its range of cosmic application. A full action in harmony with a new law of the being is always difficult in human nature; for in the substance of the Inconscience there is a self-protective law of blind imperative Necessity which limits the play of the possibilities that emerge from it or enter into it and prevents them from establishing their free action and result or realising the intensity of their own absolute. A mixed, relative, curbed and diminished play is all that is conceded to them: otherwise they would cancel the frame of Inconscience and violently perturb without effectively changing the basis of the world-order; for none of them have in their mental or vital play the divine power to replace this dark original principle and organise a totally new world-order.

A transformation of human nature can only be achieved when the substance of the being is so steeped in the spiritual principle that all its movements are a spontaneous dynamism and a harmonised process of the Spirit. But even when the higher powers and their intensities enter into the substance of the Inconscience, they are met by this blind opposing Necessity and are subjected to this circumscribing and diminishing law of the nescient substance. It opposes them with its strong titles of an established and inexorable Law, meets always the claim of life with the law of death, the demand of Light with the need of a relief of shadow and a background of darkness, the sovereignty and freedom and dynamism of the Spirit with its own force of adjustment by limitation, demarcation by incapacity, foundation of energy on the repose of an original Inertia. There is an occult truth behind its negations which only the Supermind with its reconciliation of contraries in the original Reality can take up and so discover the pragmatic solution of the enigma. Only the supramental Force can entirely overcome this difficulty of the fundamental Nescience; for with it enters an opposite and luminous imperative Necessity which underlies all things and is the original and final self-determining truth-force of the self-existent Infinite. This greater luminous spiritual Necessity and its sovereign imperative alone can displace or entirely penetrate, transform into itself and so replace the blind Ananke of the Inconscience.

A supramental change of the whole substance of the being and therefore necessarily of all its characters, powers, movements takes place when the involved Supermind in Nature emerges to meet and join with the supramental light and power descending from Supernature. The individual must be the instrument and first field of the transformation; but an isolated individual transformation is not enough and may not be wholly feasible. Even when achieved, the individual change will have a permanent and cosmic significance only if the individual becomes a centre and a sign for the establishment of the supramental Consciousness-Force as an overtly operative power in the terrestrial workings of Nature, — in the same way in which thinking Mind has been established through the human evolution as an overtly operative power in Life and Matter. This would mean the appearance in the evolution of a gnostic being or Purusha and a gnostic Prakriti, a gnostic Nature. There must be an emergent supramental Consciousness-Force liberated and active within the terrestrial whole and an organised supramental instrumentation of the Spirit in the life and the body, — for the body-consciousness also must become sufficiently awake to be a fit instrument of the workings of the new supramental Force and its new order. Till then any intermediate change could be only partial or insecure; an overmind or intuitive instrumentation of Nature could be developed, but it would be a luminous formation imposed on a fundamental and environmental Inconscience. A supramental principle and its cosmic operation once established permanently on its own basis, the intervening powers of Overmind and spiritual Mind could found themselves securely upon it and reach their own perfection; they would become in the earth-existence a hierarchy of states of consciousness rising out of Mind and physical life to the supreme spiritual level. Mind and mental humanity would remain as one step in the spiritual evolution; but other degrees above it would be there formed and accessible by which the embodied mental being, as it became ready, could climb into the gnosis and change into an embodied supramental and spiritual being. On this basis the principle of a divine life in terrestrial Nature would be manifested; even the world of ignorance and inconscience might discover its own submerged secret and begin to realise in each lower degree its divine significance.

Chapter XXVII

The Gnostic Being

A perfect path of the Truth has come into being for our journey
to the other shore beyond the darkness.   *Rig Veda.*[1]

O Truth-Conscious, be conscious of the Truth, cleave out
many streams of the Truth.   *Rig Veda.*[2]

O Flame, O Wine, your force has become conscious; you have
discovered the One Light for the many.   *Rig Veda.*[3]

Pure-white and dual in her largenesses, she follows effectively,
like one who knows, the path of the Truth and diminishes not
its directions.   *Rig Veda.*[4]

By the Truth they hold the Truth that holds all, in the power
of the Sacrifice, in the supreme ether.   *Rig Veda.*[5]

O Immortal, thou art born in mortals in the law of the Truth,
of Immortality, of Beauty.... Born from the Truth, he grows by
the Truth, — a King, a Godhead, the Truth, the Vast.

Rig Veda.[6]

AS WE reach in our thought the line at which the evolution
of Mind into Overmind passes over into an evolution of
Overmind into Supermind, we are faced with a difficulty
which amounts almost to an impossibility. For we are moved to
seek for some precise idea, some clear mental description of the
supramental or gnostic existence of which evolutionary Nature
in the Ignorance is in travail; but by crossing this extreme line
of sublimated Mind the consciousness passes out of the sphere,
exceeds the characteristic action and escapes from the grasp,

---

[1] I. 46. 11.   [2] V. 12. 2.   [3] I. 93. 4.   [4] V. 80. 4.   [5] V. 15. 2.
[6] IX. 110. 4; 108. 8.

of mental perception and knowledge. It is evident indeed that supramental nature must be a perfect integration and consummation of spiritual nature and experience: it would also contain in itself, by the very character of the evolutionary principle, though it would not be limited to that change, a total spiritualisation of mundane nature; our world-experience would be taken up in this step of our evolution and, by a transformation of its parts of divinity, a creative rejection of its imperfections and disguises, reach some divine truth and plenitude. But these are general formulas and give us no precise idea of the change. Our normal perception or imagination or formulation of things spiritual and things mundane is mental, but in the gnostic change the evolution crosses a line beyond which there is a supreme and radical reversal of consciousness and the standards and forms of mental cognition are no longer sufficient: it is difficult for mental thought to understand or describe supramental nature.

Mental nature and mental thought are based on a consciousness of the finite; supramental nature is in its very grain a consciousness and power of the Infinite. Supramental nature sees everything from the standpoint of oneness and regards all things, even the greatest multiplicity and diversity, even what are to the mind the strongest contradictions, in the light of that oneness; its will, ideas, feelings, sense are made of the stuff of oneness, its actions proceed upon that basis. Mental nature, on the contrary, thinks, sees, wills, feels, senses with division as a starting-point and has only a constructed understanding of unity; even when it experiences oneness, it has to act from the oneness on a basis of limitation and difference. But the supramental, the divine life is a life of essential, spontaneous and inherent unity. It is impossible for the mind to forecast in detail what the supramental change must be in its parts of life-action and outward behaviour or lay down for it what forms it shall create for the individual or the collective existence. For the mind acts by intellectual rule or device or by reasoned choice of will or by mental impulse or in obedience to life-impulse; but supramental nature does not act by mental idea or rule or in subjection to any inferior impulse: each of its steps is dictated by an innate spiritual vision, a comprehensive and exact penetration into the truth of all and the truth of each thing; it acts always according to inherent reality, not by the mental idea, not according to an imposed law of conduct or a constructive thought or perceptive contrivance. Its movement is calm, self-possessed, spontaneous, plastic; it arises naturally and inevitably out of a harmonic identity of the truth which is felt in the very substance of the conscious being, a spiritual substance which is universal and therefore intimately one with all that is included in its cognition of existence. A mental description of supramental nature could only express itself either in phrases which are too abstract or in mental figures which might turn it into something quite different from its reality. It would not seem to be possible, therefore, for the mind to anticipate or indicate what a supramental being shall be or how he shall act; for here mental ideas and formulations cannot decide anything or arrive at any precise definition or determination, because they are not near enough to the law and self-vision of supramental nature. At the same time certain deductions can be made from the very fact of this difference of nature which might be valid at least for a general description of the passage from Overmind to Supermind or might vaguely construct for us an idea of the first status of the evolutionary supramental existence.

This passage is the stage at which the supermind gnosis can take over the lead of the evolution from the Overmind and build the first foundations of its own characteristic manifestation and unveiled activities; it must be marked therefore by a decisive but long-prepared transition from an evolution in the Ignorance to an always progressive evolution in the Knowledge. It will not be a sudden revelation and effectuation of the absolute Supermind and the supramental being as they are in their own plane, the swift apocalypse of a truth-conscious existence ever self-fulfilled and complete in self-knowledge; it will be the phenomenon of the supramental being descending into a world of evolutionary becoming and forming itself there, unfolding the powers of the gnosis within the terrestrial nature. This is indeed the principle of all terrestrial being; for the process of earth-existence is the play of an infinite Reality concealing itself first in a succession of obscurely limited, opaque and incomplete half-figures which by their imperfection and character of disguise distort the truth of which they are in labour, but afterwards arriving more and more at half-luminous figures of itself which can become, once there is the supramental descent, a true progressive revelation. The descent from original Supermind, the assumption of evolutionary Supermind is a step which the supramental gnosis can very well undertake and accomplish without changing its own essential character. It can assume the formula of a truth-conscious existence founded in an inherent self-knowledge but at the same time taking up into itself mental nature and nature of life and material body. For the Supermind as the Truth-Consciousness of the Infinite has in its dynamic principle the infinite power of a free self-determination. It can hold all knowledge in itself and yet put forward in formulation only what is needed at each stage of an evolution; it formulates whatever is in accordance with the Divine Will in manifestation and the truth of the thing to be manifested. It is by this power that it is able to hold back its knowledge, hide its own character and law of action and manifest Overmind and under Overmind a world of ignorance in which the being wills on its surface not to know and even puts itself under the control of a pervading Nescience. But in this new stage the veil thus put on will be lifted; the evolution at every step will move in the power of the Truth-Consciousness and its progressive determinations will be made by a conscious Knowledge and not in the forms of an Ignorance or Inconscience.

As there has been established on earth a mental Consciousness and Power which shapes a race of mental beings and takes up into itself all of earthly nature that is ready for the change, so now there will be established on earth a gnostic Consciousness and Power which will shape a race of gnostic spiritual beings and take up into itself all of earth-nature that is ready for this new transformation. It will also receive into itself from above, progressively, from its own domain of perfect light and power and beauty all that is ready to descend from that domain into terrestrial being. For the evolution proceeded in the past by the upsurging, at each critical stage, of a concealed Power from its involution in the Inconscience, but also by a descent from above, from its own plane, of that Power already self-realised in its own higher natural province. In all these previous stages there has been a division between surface self and consciousness and subliminal self and consciousness; the surface was formed mainly under the push of the upsurging force from below, by the Inconscient developing a slowly emergent formulation of a concealed force of the Spirit, the subliminal partly in this way but mainly by a simultaneous influx of the largeness of the same force from above: a mental or a vital being descended into the subliminal parts and formed from its secret station there a mental or a vital personality on the surface. But before the supramental change can begin, the veil between the subliminal and the surface parts must have been already broken down; the influx, the descent will be in the entire consciousness as a whole, it will not take place partly behind a veil: the process will be no longer a concealed, obscure and ambiguous procedure but an open out-flowering consciously felt and followed by the whole being in its transmutation. In other respects the process will be identical, — a supramental inflow from above, the descent of a gnostic being into the nature, and an emergence of the concealed supramental force from below; the influx and the unveiling between them will remove what is left of the nature of the Ignorance. The rule of the Inconscient will disappear: for the Inconscience will be changed by the outburst of the greater secret Consciousness within it, the hidden Light, into what it always was in reality, a sea of the secret Superconscience. A first formation of a gnostic consciousness and nature will be the consequence.

The creation of a supramental being, nature, life on earth, will not be the sole result of this evolution; it will also carry with it the consummation of the steps that have led up to it: for it will confirm in possession of terrestrial birth the Overmind, the Intuition and the other gradations of the spiritual nature-force and establish a race of gnostic beings and a hierarchy, a shining ladder of ascending degrees and successive constituent formations of the gnostic light and power in earth-nature. For the description of gnosis applies to all consciousness that is based upon Truth of being and not upon the Ignorance or Nescience. All life and living beings ready to rise beyond the mental ignorance, but not ready yet for the supramental height, would find in a sort of echelon or a scale with overlapping degrees their assured basis, their intermediate steps of self-formation, their expression of realised capacity of spiritual existence on the way to the supreme Reality. But also the presence of the liberated and now sovereign supramental light and force at the head of evolutionary Nature might be expected to have its consequences in the whole evolution. An incidence, a decisive stress would affect the life of the lower evolutionary stages; something of the light, something of the force would penetrate downwards and awaken into a greater action the hidden Truth-Power everywhere in Nature. A dominant principle of harmony would impose itself on the life of the Ignorance; the discord, the blind seeking, the clash of struggle, the abnormal vicissitudes of exaggeration and depression and unsteady balance of the unseeing forces at work in their mixture and conflict, would feel the influence and yield place to a more orderly pace and harmonic steps of the development of being, a more revealing arrangement of progressing life and consciousness, a better life-order. A freer play of intuition and sympathy and understanding would enter into human life, a clearer sense of the truth of self and things and a more enlightened dealing with the opportunities and difficulties of existence. Instead of a constant intermixed and confused struggle between the growth of Consciousness and the power of the Inconscience, between the forces of light and the forces of darkness, the evolution would become a graded progression from lesser light to greater light; in each stage of it the conscious beings belonging to that stage would respond to the inner Consciousness-Force and expand their own law of cosmic Nature towards the possibility of a higher degree of that Nature. This is at least a strong possibility and might be envisaged as the natural consequence of the direct action of Supermind on the evolution. This intervention would not annul the evolutionary principle, for Supermind has the power of with-holding or keeping in reserve its force of knowledge as well as the power of bringing it into full or partial action; but it would harmonise, steady, facilitate, tranquillise and to a great extent hedonise the difficult and afflicted process of the evolutionary emergence.

There is something in the nature of Supermind itself that would make this great result inevitable. It is in its foundation a unitarian and integralising and harmonic consciousness, and in its descent and evolutionary working out of the diversity of the Infinite it would not lose its unitarian trend, its push to-wards integralisation or its harmonic influence. The Overmind follows out diversities and divergent possibilities on their own lines of divergence: it can allow contradictions and discords, but it makes them elements of a cosmic whole so that they are forced, however unwittingly and in spite of themselves, to contribute their shares to its wholeness. Or we may say that it accepts and even encourages contradictions, but obliges them to support each other's existence so that there may be divergent roads of being and consciousness and experience that lead away from the One and from each other but still maintain themselves on the Oneness and can lead back again each on its own path to the Oneness. That is the secret sense even of our own world of Ignorance which works from the Inconscience but with the un-derlying cosmicity of the overmind principle. But the individual being in such a creation does not possess this secret principle in knowledge and does not base upon it his action. An overmind being here would perceive this secret; but he might still work on his own lines of Nature and law of action, Swabhava, Swad-harma, according to the inspiration, the dynamic control or the inner governance of the Spirit or the Divine within him and leave the rest to their own line in the whole: an overmind creation of knowledge in the Ignorance might therefore be something separate from the surrounding world of Ignorance and guarded from it by the luminous encircling and separating wall of its own principle. The supramental gnostic being, on the contrary, would not only found all his living on an intimate sense and effective realisation of harmonic unity in his own inner and outer life or group-life, but would create a harmonic unity also with the still surviving mental world, even if that world remained altogether a world of Ignorance. For the gnostic consciousness in him would perceive and bring out the evolving truth and principle of harmony hidden in the formations of the Ignorance; it would be natural to his sense of integrality and it would be within his power to link them in a true order with his own gnostic principle and the evolved truth and harmony of his own greater life-creation. That might be impossible without a considerable change in the life of the world, but such a change would be a natural consequence of the appearance of a new Power in Nature and its universal influence. In the emergence of the gnostic being would be the hope of a more harmonious evolutionary order in terrestrial Nature.

A supramental or gnostic race of beings would not be a race made according to a single type, moulded in a single fixed pattern; for the law of the Supermind is unity fulfilled in diversity, and therefore there would be an infinite diversity in the manifestation of the gnostic consciousness although that consciousness would still be one in its basis, in its constitution, in its all-revealing and all-uniting order. It is evident that the triple status of the Supermind would reproduce itself as a principle in this new manifestation: there would be below it and yet belonging to it the degrees of the overmind and intuitive gnosis with the souls that had realised these degrees of the ascending consciousness; there would be also at the summit, as the evolution in Knowledge proceeded, individual beings who would ascend beyond a supermind formulation and reach from the highest height of Supermind to the summits of unitarian self-realisation in the body which must be the last and supreme state of the epiphany of the Creation. But in the supramental race itself, in the variation of its degrees, the individuals would not be cast according to a single type of individuality; each would be different from the other, a unique formation of the Being, although one with all the rest in foundation of self and sense of oneness and in the principle of his being. It is only this general principle of the supramental existence of which we can attempt to form an idea however diminished by the limitations of mental thought and mental language. A more living picture of the gnostic being Supermind only could make; for the mind some abstract outlines of it are alone possible.

The gnosis is the effective principle of the Spirit, a highest dynamis of the spiritual existence. The gnostic individual would be the consummation of the spiritual man; his whole way of being, thinking, living, acting would be governed by the power of a vast universal spirituality. All the trinities of the Spirit would be real to his self-awareness and realised in his inner life. All his existence would be fused into oneness with the transcendent and universal Self and Spirit; all his action would originate from and obey the supreme Self and Spirit's divine governance of Nature. All life would have to him the sense of the Conscious Being, the Purusha within, finding its self-expression in Nature; his life and all its thoughts, feelings, acts would be filled for him with that significance and built upon that foundation of its reality. He would feel the presence of the Divine in every centre of his consciousness, in every vibration of his life-force, in every cell of his body. In all the workings of his force of Nature he would be aware of the workings of the supreme World-Mother, the Supernature; he would see his natural being as the becoming and manifestation of the power of the World-Mother. In this consciousness he would live and act in an entire transcendent freedom, a complete joy of the Spirit, an entire identity with the cosmic Self and a spontaneous sympathy with all in the universe. All beings would be to him his own selves, all ways and powers of consciousness would be felt as the ways and powers of his own universality. But in that inclusive universality there would be no bondage to inferior forces, no deflection from his own highest truth: for this truth would envelop all truth of things and keep each in its own place, in a relation of diversified harmony, — it would not admit any confusion, clash, infringing of boundaries, any distortion of the different harmonies that constitute the total harmony. His own life and the world-life would be to him like a perfect work of art; it would be as if the creation of a cosmic and spontaneous genius infallible in its working out of a multitudinous order. The gnostic individual would be in the world and of the world, but would also exceed it in his consciousness and live in his Self of transcendence above it; he would be universal but free in the universe, individual but not limited by a separative individuality. The true Person is not an isolated entity, his individuality is universal; for he individualises the universe: it is at the same time divinely emergent in a spiritual air of transcendental infinity, like a high cloud-surpassing summit; for he individualises the divine Transcendence.

The three powers which present themselves to our life as the three keys to its mystery are the individual, the cosmic entity and the Reality present in both and beyond them. These three mysteries of existence would find in the life of the supramental being a united fulfilment of their harmony. He will be the perfected and complete individual, fulfilled in the satisfaction of his growth and self-expression; for all his elements would be carried to a highest degree and integrated in some kind of comprehensive largeness. What we are striving towards is completeness and harmony; an imperfection and incapacity or a discord of our nature is that from which inwardly we most suffer. But this is because of our incompleteness of being, our imperfect self-knowledge, our imperfect possession of our self and our nature. A complete self-knowledge in all things and at all moments is the gift of the supramental gnosis and with it a complete self-mastery, not merely in the sense of control of Nature but in the sense of a power of perfect self-expression in Nature. Whatever knowledge of self there would be, would be perfectly embodied in the will of the self, the will perfectly embodied in the action of the self; the result would be the self's complete dynamic self-formulation in its own nature. In the lower grades of gnostic being, there would be a limitation of self-expression according to the variety of the nature, a limited perfection in order to formulate some side, element or combined harmony of elements of some Divine Totality, a restricted selection of powers from the cosmic figure of the infinitely manifold One. But in the supramental being this need of limitation for perfection would disappear; the diversity would not be secured by limitation but by a diversity in the power and hue of the Supernature: the same whole of being and the same whole of nature would express themselves in an infinitely diverse fashion; for each being would be a new totality, harmony, self-equation of the One Being. What would be expressed in front or held behind at any moment would depend not on capacity or incapacity, but on the dynamic self-choice of the Spirit, its delight of self-expression, on the truth of the Divine's will and joy of itself in the individual and, subordinately, on the truth of the thing that had to be done through the individual in the harmony of the totality. For the complete individual is the cosmic individual, since only when we have taken the universe into ourselves, — and transcended it, — can our individuality be complete.

The supramental being in his cosmic consciousness seeing and feeling all as himself would act in that sense; he would act in a universal awareness and a harmony of his individual self with the total self, of his individual will with the total will, of his individual action with the total action. For what we most suffer from in our outer life and its reactions upon our inner life is the imperfection of our relations with the world, our ignorance of others, our disharmony with the whole of things, our inability to equate our demand on the world with the world's demand on us. There is a conflict, — a conflict from which there seems to be no ultimate issue except an escape from both world and self, — between our self-affirmation and a world on which we have to impose that affirmation, a world which seems to be too large for us and to pass indifferently over our soul, mind, life, body in the sweep of its course to its goal. The relation of our course and goal to the world's is unapparent to us, and to harmonise ourselves with it we have either to enforce ourselves upon it and make it subservient to us or suppress ourselves and become subservient to it or else to compass a difficult balance between these two necessities of the relation between the individual personal destiny and the cosmic whole and its hidden purpose. But for the supramental being living in a cosmic consciousness the difficulty would not exist, since he has no ego; his cosmic individuality would know the cosmic forces and their movement and their significance as part of himself, and the Truth-Consciousness in him would see the right relation at each step and find the dynamic right expression of that relation.

For in fact both individual and universe are simultaneous and interrelated expressions of the same transcendent Being; even though in the Ignorance and under its law there is maladjustment and conflict, yet there must be a right relation, an equation to which all arrives but which is missed by our blindness of ego, our attempt to affirm the ego and not the Self one in all. The supramental consciousness has that truth of relation in itself as its natural right and privilege, since it is the Supermind that determines the cosmic relations and the relations of the individual with the universe, determines them freely and sovereignly as a power of the Transcendence. In the mental being even the pressure of the cosmic consciousness overpowering the ego and an awareness of the transcendent Reality might not of themselves bring about a dynamic solution; for there might still be an incompatibility between its liberated spiritual mentality and the obscure life of the cosmic Ignorance which the mind would not have the power to solve or overcome. But in the supramental being, not only statically conscious but fully dynamic and acting in the creative light and power of the Transcendence, the supramental light, the truth light, *rtam jyotiḥ*, would have that power. For there would be a unity with the cosmic self, but not a bondage to the Ignorance of cosmic Nature in its lower formulation; there would on the contrary be a power to act in the light of the Truth on that Ignorance. A large universality of self-expression, a large harmonic universality of world-being would be the very sign of the supramental Person in his gnostic nature.

The existence of the supramental being would be the play of a manifoldly and multiply manifesting truth-power of one-existence and one-consciousness for the delight of one-existence. Delight of the manifestation of the Spirit in its truth of being would be the sense of the gnostic life. All its movements would be a formulation of the truth of the Spirit, but also of the joy of the Spirit, — an affirmation of spiritual existence, an affirmation of spiritual consciousness, an affirmation of spiritual delight of being. But this would not be what self-affirmation tends to be in us in spite of the underlying unity, something egocentric, separative, opposed or indifferent or insufficiently alive to the self-affirmation of others or their demand on existence. One in self with all, the supramental being will seek the delight of self-manifestation of the Spirit in himself but equally the delight of the Divine in all: he will have the cosmic joy and will be a power for bringing the bliss of the Spirit, the joy of being to others; for their joy will be part of his own joy of existence. To be occupied with the good of all beings, to make the joy and grief of others one's own has been described as a sign of the liberated and fulfilled spiritual man. The supramental being will have no need, for that, of an altruistic self-effacement, since this occupation will be intimate to his self-fulfilment, the fulfilment of the One in all, and there will be no contradiction or strife between his own good and the good of others: nor will he have any need to acquire a universal sympathy by subjecting himself to the joys and griefs of creatures in the Ignorance; his cosmic sympathy will be part of his inborn truth of being and not dependent on a personal participation in the lesser joy and suffering; it will transcend what it embraces and in that transcendence will be its power. His feeling of universality, his action of universality will be always a spontaneous state and natural movement, an automatic expression of the Truth, an act of the joy of the Spirit's self-existence. There could be in it no place for limited self or desire or for the satisfaction or frustration of the limited self or the satisfaction or frustration of desire, no place for the relative and dependent happiness and grief that visit and afflict our limited nature; for these are things that belong to the ego and the Ignorance, not to the freedom and truth of the Spirit.

The gnostic being has the will of action but also the knowledge of what is to be willed and the power to effectuate its knowledge; it will not be led from ignorance to do what is not to be done. Moreover, its action is not the seeking for a fruit or result; its joy is in being and doing, in pure state of Spirit, in pure act of Spirit, in the pure bliss of the Spirit. As its static consciousness will contain all in itself and must be, therefore, for ever self-fulfilled, so its dynamis of consciousness will find in each step and in each act a spiritual freedom and a self-fulfilment. All will be seen in its relation to the whole, so that each step will be luminous and joyous and satisfying in itself because each is in unison with a luminous totality. This consciousness, this living in the spiritual totality and acting from it, a satisfied totality in essence of being and a satisfied totality in the dynamic movement of being, the sense of the relations of that totality accompanying each step, is indeed the very mark of a supramental consciousness and distinguishes it from the disintegrated, ignorantly successive steps of our consciousness in the Ignorance. The gnostic existence and delight of existence is a universal and total being and delight, and there will be the presence of that totality and universality in each separate movement: in each there will be, not a partial experience of self or a fractional bit of its joy, but the sense of the whole movement of an integral being and the presence of its entire and integral bliss of being, Ananda. The gnostic being's knowledge self-realised in action will be, not an ideative knowledge, but the Real-Idea of the Supermind, the instrumentation of an essential light of Consciousness; it will be the self-light of all the reality of being and becoming pouring itself out continually and filling every particular act and activity with the pure and whole delight of its self-existence. For an infinite consciousness with its knowledge by identity there is in each differentiation the joy and experience of the Identical, in each finite is felt the Infinite.

An evolution of gnostic consciousness brings with it a transformation of our world-consciousness and world-action: for it takes up into the new power of awareness not only the inner existence but our outer being and our world-being; there is a remaking of both, an integration of them in the sense and power of the spiritual existence. There must come upon us in the change at once a reversal and rejection of our present way of existence and a fulfilment of its inner trend and tendency. For we stand now between these two terms, an outer world of Life and Matter that has made us and a remaking of the world by ourselves in the sense of the evolving Spirit. Our present way of living is at once a subjection to Life-Force and Matter and a struggle with Life and Matter. In its first appearance an outer existence creates by our reactions to it an inner or mental existence; if we shape ourselves at all, it is in most men less by the conscious pressure of a free soul or intelligence from within than by a response to our environment and the world-Nature acting upon us: but what we move towards in the development of our conscious being is an inner existence creating by its knowledge and power its own outer form of living and self-expressive environment of living. In the gnostic nature this movement will have consummated itself; the nature of living will be an accomplished inner existence whose light and power will take perfect body in the outer life. The gnostic being will take up the world of Life and Matter, but he will turn and adapt it to his own truth and purpose of existence; he will mould life itself into his own spiritual image, and this he will be able to do because he has the secret of a spiritual creation and is in communion and oneness with the Creator within him. This will be first effective in the shaping of his own inner and outer individual existence, but the same power and principle will operate in any common gnostic life; the relations of gnostic being with gnostic being will be the expression of their one gnostic self and supernature shaping into a significant power and form of itself the whole common existence.

In all spiritual living the inner life is the thing of first importance; the spiritual man lives always within, and in a world of the Ignorance that refuses to change he has to be in a certain sense separate from it and to guard his inner life against the intrusion and influence of the darker forces of the Ignorance: he is out of the world even when he is within it; if he acts upon it, it is from the fortress of his inner spiritual being where in the inmost sanctuary he is one with the Supreme Existence or the soul and God are alone together. The gnostic life will be an inner life in which the antinomy of the inner and the outer, the self and the world will have been cured and exceeded. The gnostic being will have indeed an inmost existence in which he is alone with God, one with the Eternal, self-plunged into the depths of the Infinite, in communion with its heights and its luminous abysses of secrecy; nothing will be able to disturb or to invade these depths or bring him down from the summits, neither the world's contents nor his action nor all that is around him. This is the transcendence-aspect of the spiritual life and it is necessary for the freedom of the Spirit; for otherwise the identity in Nature with the world would be a binding limitation and not a free identity. But at the same time God-love and the delight of God will be the heart's expression of that inner communion and oneness, and that delight and love will expand itself to embrace all existence. The peace of God within will be extended in the gnostic experience of the universe into a universal calm of equality not merely passive but dynamic, a calm of freedom in oneness dominating all that meets it, tranquillising all that enters into it, imposing its law of peace on the supramental being's relations with the world in which he is living. Into all his acts the inner oneness, the inner communion will attend him and enter into his relations with others, who will not be to him others but selves of himself in the one existence, his own universal existence. It is this poise and freedom in the Spirit that will enable him to take all life into himself while still remaining the spiritual self and to embrace even the world of the Ignorance without himself entering into the Ignorance.

For his experience of cosmic existence will be, by its form of nature and by an individualised centration, that of one living in the universe but, at the same time, by self-diffusion and extension in oneness, that of one who carries the universe and all its beings within him. This extended state of being will not only be an extension in oneness of self or an extension in conceptive idea and vision, but an extension of oneness in heart, in sense, in a concrete physical consciousness. He will have the cosmic consciousness, sense, feeling, by which all objective life will become part of his subjective existence and by which he will realise, perceive, feel, see, hear the Divine in all forms; all forms and movements will be realised, sensed, seen, heard, felt as if taking place within his own vast self of being. The world will be connected not only with his outer but with his inner life. He will not meet the world only in its external form by an external contact; he will be inwardly in contact with the inner self of things and beings: he will meet consciously their inner as well as their outer reactions; he will be aware of that within them of which they themselves will not be aware, act upon all with an inner comprehension, encounter all with a perfect sympathy and sense of oneness but also an independence which is not overmastered by any contact. His action on the world will be largely an inner action by the power of the Spirit, by the spiritual-supramental idea-force formulating itself in the world, by the secret unspoken word, by the power of the heart, by the dynamic life-force, by the enveloping and penetrating power of the self one with all things; the outer expressed and visible action will be only a fringe, a last projection of this vaster single total of activity.

At the same time the universal inner life of the individual will not be confined to an inner pervasive and inclusive contact with the physical world alone: it will extend beyond it through the full realisation of the subliminal inner being's natural connection with other planes of being; a knowledge of their powers and influences will have become a normal element of the inner experience, and the happenings of this world will be seen not solely in their external aspect but also in the light of all that is secret behind the physical and terrestrial creation and movement. A gnostic being will possess not only a truth-conscious control of the realised Spirit's power over its physical world, but also the full power of the mental and vital planes and the use of their greater forces for the perfection of the physical existence. This greater knowledge and wider hold of all existence will enormously increase the power of instrumentation of the gnostic being on his surroundings and on the world of physical Nature.

In the Self-Existence of which Supermind is the dynamic Truth-Consciousness, there can be no aim of being except to be, no aim of consciousness except to be conscious of being, no aim of delight of being other than its delight; all is a self-existent and self-sufficient Eternity. Manifestation, becoming, has in its original supramental movement the same character; it sustains in a self-existent and self-sufficient rhythm an activity of being which sees itself as a manifold becoming, an activity of consciousness which takes the form of a manifold self-knowledge, an activity of force of conscious existence which exists for the glory and beauty of its own manifold power of being, an activity of delight which assumes innumerable forms of delight. The existence and consciousness of the supramental being here in Matter will have fundamentally the same nature, but with subordinate characters which mark the difference between Supermind in its own plane and Supermind working in its manifested power in the earth-existence. For here there will be an evolving being, an evolving consciousness, an evolving delight of existence. The gnostic being will appear as the sign of an evolution from the consciousness of the Ignorance into the consciousness of Sachchidananda. In the Ignorance one is there primarily to grow, to know and to do, or, more exactly to grow into something, to arrive by knowledge at something, to get something done. Imperfect, we have no satisfaction of our being, we must perforce strive with labour and difficulty to grow into something we are not; ignorant and burdened with a consciousness of our ignorance, we have to arrive at something by which we can feel that we know; bounded with incapacity, we have to hunt after strength and power; afflicted with a consciousness of suffering, we have to try to get something done by which we catch at some pleasure or lay hold on some satisfying reality of life. To maintain existence is, indeed, our first occupation and necessity, but it is only a starting-point: for the mere maintenance of an imperfect existence chequered with suffering cannot be sufficient as an aim of our being; the instinctive will of existence, the pleasure of existence, which is all that the Ignorance can make out of the secret underlying Power and Ananda, has to be supplemented by the need to do and become. But what to do and what to become is not clearly known to us; we get what knowledge we can, what power, strength, purity, peace we can, what delight we can, become what we can. But our aims and our effort towards their achievement and the little we can hold as our gains turn into meshes by which we are bound; it is these things that become for us the object of life: to know our souls and to be our selves, which must be the foundation of our true way of being, is a secret that escapes us in our preoccupation with an external learning, an external construction of knowledge, the achievement of an external action, an external delight and pleasure. The spiritual man is one who has discovered his soul: he has found his self and lives in that, is conscious of it, has the joy of it; he needs nothing external for his completeness of existence. The gnostic being starting from this new basis takes up our ignorant becoming and turns it into a luminous becoming of knowledge and a realised power of being. All therefore that is our attempt to be in the Ignorance, he will fulfil in the Knowledge. All knowledge he will turn into a manifestation of the self-knowledge of being, all power and action into a power and action of the self-force of being, all delight into a universal delight of self-existence. Attachment and bondage will fall away, because at each step and in each thing there will be the full satisfaction of self-existence, the light of the consciousness fulfilling itself, the ecstasy of delight of existence finding itself. Each stage of the evolution in the knowledge will be an unfolding of this power and will of being and this joy to be, a free becoming supported by the sense of the Infinite, the bliss of the Brahman, the luminous sanction of the Transcendence.

The supramental transformation, the supramental evolution must carry with it a lifting of mind, life and body out of themselves into a greater way of being in which yet their own ways and powers would be, not suppressed or abolished, but perfected and fulfilled by the self-exceeding. For in the Ignorance all paths are the paths of the Spirit seeking for itself blindly or with a growing light; the gnostic being and life would be the Spirit's self-discovery and its seeing and reaching of the aims of all these paths but in the greater way of its own revealed and conscious truth of being. Mind seeks for light, for knowledge, — for knowledge of the one truth basing all, an essential truth of self and things, but also of all truth of diversity of that oneness, all its detail, circumstance, manifold way of action, form, law of movement and happening, various manifestation and creation; for thinking mind the joy of existence is discovery and the penetration of the mystery of creation that comes with knowledge. This the gnostic change will fulfil in an ample measure; but it will give it a new character. It will act not by the discovery of the unknown, but by the bringing out of the known; all will be the finding "of the self by the self in the self". For the self of the gnostic being will not be the mental ego but the Spirit that is one in all; he will see the world as a universe of the Spirit. The finding of the one truth underlying all things will be the Identical discovering identity and identical truth everywhere and discovering too the power and workings and relations of that identity. The revelation of the detail, the circumstance, the abundant ways and forms of the manifestation will be the unveiling of the endless opulence of the truths of that identity, its forms and powers of self, its curious manifoldness and multiplicity of form bringing out infinitely its oneness. This knowledge will proceed by identification with all, by entering into all, by a contact bringing with it a leap of self-discovery and a flame of recognition, a greater and surer intuition of truth than the mind can reach; there will be an intuition too of the means of embodying and utilising the truth seen, an operative intuition of its dynamic processes, a direct intimate awareness guiding the life and the physical senses in every step of their action and service to the Spirit when they have to be called in as instruments for the effectuation of process in Life and Matter.

A replacement of intellectual seeking by supramental identity and gnostic intuition of the contents of the identity, an omnipresence of Spirit with its light penetrating the whole process of knowledge and all its use, — so that there is an integration between the knower, knowledge and the thing known, between the operating consciousness, the instrumentation and the thing done, while the single self watches over the whole integrated movement and fulfils itself intimately in it, making it a flawless unit of self-effectuation, — will be the character of each gnostic movement of knowledge and action of knowledge. Mind, observing and reasoning, labours to detach itself and see objectively and truly what it has to know; it tries to know it as not-self, independent other-reality not affected by process of personal thinking or by any presence of self: the gnostic consciousness will at once intimately and exactly know its object by a comprehending and penetrating identification with it. It will overpass what it has to know, but it will include it in itself; it will know the object as part of itself as it might know any part or movement of its own being, without any narrowing of itself by the identification or snaring of its thought in it so as to be bound or limited in knowledge. There will be the intimacy, accuracy, fullness of a direct internal knowledge, but not that misleading by personal mind by which we constantly err, because the consciousness will be that of a universal and not a restricted and ego-bound person. It will proceed towards all knowledge, not setting truth against truth to see which will stand and survive, but completing truth by truth in the light of the one Truth of which all are the aspects. All idea and vision and perception will have this character of an inner seeing, an intimate extended self-perception, a large self-integrating knowledge, an indivisible whole working itself out by light acting upon light in a self-executing harmony of truth-being. There will be an unfolding, not as a delivery of light out of darkness, but as a delivery of light out of itself; for if an evolving supramental Consciousness holds back part of its contents of self-awareness behind in itself, it does this not as a step or by an act of Ignorance, but as the movement of a deliberate bringing out of its timeless knowledge into a process of Time-manifestation. A self-illumination, a revelation of light out of light will be the method of cognition of this evolutionary supramental Nature.

As mind seeks for light, for the discovery of knowledge and for mastery by knowledge, so life seeks for the development of its own force and for mastery by force: its quest is for growth, power, conquest, possession, satisfaction, creation, joy, love, beauty; its joy of existence is in a constant self-expression,

development, diverse manifoldness of action, creation, enjoyment, an abundant and strong intensity of itself and its power.
The gnostic evolution will lift that to its highest and fullest expression, but it will not act for the power, satisfaction, enjoyment
of the mental or vital ego, for its narrow possession of itself and
its eager ambitious grasp on others and on things or for its
greater self-affirmation and magnified embodiment; for in that
way no spiritual fullness and perfection can come. The gnostic
life will exist and act for the Divine in itself and in the world,
for the Divine in all; the increasing possession of the individual
being and the world by the Divine Presence, Light, Power, Love,
Delight, Beauty will be the sense of life to the gnostic being. In
the more and more perfect satisfaction of that growing manifestation will be the individual's satisfaction: his power will be
the instrumentation of the power of Supernature for bringing in
and extending that greater life and nature; whatever conquest
and adventure will be there, will be for that only and not for the
reign of any individual or collective ego. Love will be for him the
contact, meeting, union of self with self, of spirit with spirit, a
unification of being, a power and joy and intimacy and closeness
of soul to soul, of the One to the One, a joy of identity and the
consequences of a diverse identity. It is this joy of an intimate
self-revealing diversity of the One, the multitudinous union of
the One and a happy interaction in the identity, that will be for
him the full revealed sense of life. Creation aesthetic or dynamic,
mental creation, life-creation, material creation will have for him
the same sense. It will be the creation of significant forms of the
Eternal Force, Light, Beauty, Reality, — the beauty and truth of
its forms and bodies, the beauty and truth of its powers and
qualities, the beauty and truth of its spirit, its formless beauty
of self and essence.

    As a consequence of the total change and reversal of con-
sciousness establishing a new relation of Spirit with Mind and
Life and Matter, and a new significance and perfection in the
relation, there will be a reversal, a perfecting new significance
also of the relations between the spirit and the body it inhabits.
In our present way of living the soul expresses itself, as best it can

or as badly as it must, through the mind and the vitality, or, more often, allows the mind and the vitality to act with its support: the body is the instrument of this action. But the body, even in obeying, limits and determines the mind's and the life's self-expression by the limited possibilities and acquired character of its own physical instrumentation; it has besides a law of its own action, a movement and will or force or urge of movement of its own subconscious or half-emerged conscious power of being which they can only partially, — and even in that part more by an indirect than by a direct or, if direct, then more by a subconscious than a willed and conscious action, — influence or alter. But in the gnostic way of being and living the will of the Spirit must directly control and determine the movements and law of the body. For the law of the body arises from the subconscient or inconscient: but in the gnostic being the subconscient will have become conscious and subject to the supramental control, penetrated with its light and action; the basis of inconscience with its obscurity and ambiguity, its obstruction or tardy responses will have been transformed into a lower or supporting superconscience by the supramental emergence. Already even in the realised higher-mind being and in the intuitive and overmind being the body will have become sufficiently conscious to respond to the influence of the Idea and the Will-Force so that the action of mind on the physical parts, which is rudimentary, chaotic and mostly involuntary in us, will have developed a considerable potency: but in the supramental being it is the consciousness with the Real-Idea in it which will govern everything. This Real-Idea is a truth-perception which is self-effective; for it is the idea and will of the Spirit in direct action and originates a movement of the substance of being which must inevitably effectuate itself in state and act of being. It is this dynamic irresistible spiritual realism of the Truth-Consciousness in the highest degree of itself that will have here grown conscient and consciously competent in the evolved gnostic being: it will not act as now, veiled in an apparent inconscience and self-limited by law of mechanism, but as the sovereign Reality in self-effectuating action. It is this that will rule the existence with an entire knowledge and power and include in its rule the functioning and action of the body. The body will be turned by the power of the spiritual consciousness into a true and fit and perfectly responsive instrument of the Spirit.

This new relation of the Spirit and the body assumes, — and makes possible, — a free acceptance of the whole of material Nature in place of a rejection; the drawing back from her, the refusal of all identification or acceptance, which is the first normal necessity of the spiritual consciousness for its liberation, is no longer imperative. To cease to be identified with the body, to separate oneself from the body-consciousness, is a recognised and necessary step whether towards spiritual liberation or towards spiritual perfection and mastery over Nature. But, this redemption once effected, the descent of the spiritual light and force can invade and take up the body also and there can be a new liberated and sovereign acceptance of material Nature. That is possible, indeed, only if there is a changed communion of the Spirit with Matter, a control, a reversal of the present balance of interaction which allows physical Nature to veil the Spirit and affirm her own dominance. In the light of a larger knowledge Matter also can be seen to be the Brahman, a self-energy put forth by the Brahman, a form and substance of Brahman; aware of the secret consciousness within material substance, secure in this larger knowledge, the gnostic light and power can unite itself with Matter, so seen, and accept it as an instrument of a spiritual manifestation. A certain reverence, even, for Matter and a sacramental attitude in all dealings with it is possible. As in the Gita the act of the taking of food is spoken of as a material sacrament, a sacrifice, an offering of Brahman to Brahman by Brahman, so also the gnostic consciousness and sense can view all the operations of Spirit with Matter. The Spirit has made itself Matter in order to place itself there as an instrument for the well-being and joy, *yogakṣema*, of created beings, for a self-offering of universal physical utility and service. The gnostic being, using Matter but using it without material or vital attachment or desire, will feel that he is using the Spirit in this form of itself with its consent and sanction for its own purpose. There will be in him a certain respect for physical things, an awareness of the occult consciousness in them, of its dumb will of utility and service, a worship of the Divine, the Brahman in what he uses, a care for a perfect and faultless use of his divine material, for a true rhythm, ordered harmony, beauty in the life of Matter, in the utilisation of Matter.

As a result of this new relation between the Spirit and the body, the gnostic evolution will effectuate the spiritualisation, perfection and fulfilment of the physical being; it will do for the body as for the mind and life. Apart from the obscurity, frailties and limitations, which this change will overcome, the body-consciousness is a patient servant and can be in its large reserve of possibilities a potent instrument of the individual life, and it asks for little on its own account: what it craves for is duration, health, strength, physical perfection, bodily happiness, liberation from suffering, ease. These demands are not in themselves unacceptable, mean or illegitimate, for they render into the terms of Matter the perfection of form and substance, the power and delight which should be the natural outflowing, the expressive manifestation of the Spirit. When the gnostic Force can act in the body, these things can be established; for their opposites come from a pressure of external forces on the physical mind, on the nervous and material life, on the body-organism, from an ignorance that does not know how to meet these forces or is not able to meet them rightly or with power, and from some obscurity, pervading the stuff of the physical consciousness and distorting its responses, that reacts to them in a wrong way. A supramental self-acting self-effectuating awareness and knowledge, replacing this ignorance, will liberate and restore the obscured and spoiled intuitive instincts in the body and enlighten and supplement them with a greater conscious action. This change would institute and maintain a right physical perception of things, a right relation and right reaction to objects and energies, a right rhythm of mind, nerve and organism. It would bring into the body a higher spiritual power and a greater life-force unified with the universal life-force and able to draw on it, a luminous harmony with material Nature and the vast and calm touch of

the eternal repose which can give to it its diviner strength and
ease. Above all, — for this is the most needed and fundamental
change, — it will flood the whole being with a supreme energy
of Consciousness-Force which would meet, assimilate or harmonise with itself all the forces of existence that surround and
press upon the body.

It is the incompleteness and weakness of the Consciousness-
Force manifested in the mental, vital and physical being, its
inability to receive or refuse at will, or, receiving, to assimilate
or harmonise the contacts of the universal Energy cast upon it,
that is the cause of pain and suffering. In the material realm
Nature starts with an entire insensibility, and it is a notable fact
that either a comparative insensibility or a deficient sensibility
or, more often, a greater endurance and hardness to suffering is
found in the beginnings of life, in the animal, in primitive or less
developed man; as the human being grows in evolution, he grows
in sensibility and suffers more keenly in mind and life and body.
For the growth in consciousness is not sufficiently supported by
a growth in force: the body becomes more subtle, more finely
capable, but less solidly efficient in its external energy: man has
to call in his will, his mental power to dynamise, correct and
control his nervous being, force it to the strenuous tasks he
demands from his instruments, steel it against suffering and disaster. In the spiritual ascent this power of the consciousness and
its will over the instruments, the control of spirit and inner mind
over the outer mentality and the nervous being and the body,
increases immensely; a tranquil and wide equality of the spirit to
all shocks and contacts comes in and becomes the habitual poise,
and this can pass from the mind to the vital parts and establish
there too an immense and enduring largeness of strength and
peace; even in the body this state may form itself and meet
inwardly the shocks of grief and pain and all kinds of suffering.
Even, a power of willed physical insensibility can intervene or
a power of mental separation from all shock and injury can be
acquired which shows that the ordinary reactions and the debile
submission of the bodily self to the normal habits of response
of material Nature are not obligatory or unalterable. Still more

significant is the power that comes on the level of spiritual Mind or Overmind to change the vibrations of pain into vibrations of Ananda: even if this were to go only up to a certain point, it indicates the possibility of an entire reversal of the ordinary rule of the reacting consciousness; it can be associated too with a power of self-protection that turns away the shocks that are more difficult to transmute or to endure. The gnostic evolution at a certain stage must bring about a completeness of this reversal and of this power of self-protection which will fulfil the claim of the body for immunity and serenity of its being and for deliverance from suffering and build in it a power for the total delight of existence. A spiritual Ananda can flow into the body and inundate cell and tissue; a luminous materialisation of this higher Ananda could of itself bring about a total transformation of the deficient or adverse sensibilities of physical Nature.

An aspiration, a demand for the supreme and total delight of existence is there secretly in the whole make of our being, but it is disguised by the separation of our parts of nature and their differing urge and obscured by their inability to conceive or seize anything more than a superficial pleasure. In the body-consciousness this demand takes shape as a need of bodily happiness, in our life-parts as a yearning for life-happiness, a keen vibrant response to joy and rapture of many kinds and to all surprise of satisfaction; in the mind it shapes into a ready reception of all forms of mental delight; on a higher level it becomes apparent in the spiritual mind's call for peace and divine ecstasy. This trend is founded in the truth of the being; for Ananda is the very essence of the Brahman, it is the supreme nature of the omnipresent Reality. The Supermind itself in the descending degrees of the manifestation emerges from the Ananda and in the evolutionary ascent merges into the Ananda. It is not, indeed, merged in the sense of being extinguished or abolished but is there inherent in it, indistinguishable from the self of awareness and the self-effectuating force of the Bliss of Being. In the involutionary descent as in the evolutionary return Supermind is supported by the original Delight of Existence and carries that in it in all its activities as their sustaining essence;

for Consciousness, we may say, is its parent power in the Spirit, but Ananda is the spiritual matrix from which it manifests and the maintaining source into which it carries back the soul in its return to the status of the Spirit. A supramental manifestation in its ascent would have as a next sequence and culmination of self-result a manifestation of the Bliss of the Brahman: the evolution of the being of gnosis would be followed by an evolution of the being of bliss; an embodiment of gnostic existence would have as its consequence an embodiment of the beatific existence. Always in the being of gnosis, in the life of the gnosis some power of the Ananda would be there as an inseparable and pervading significance of supramental self-experience. In the liberation of the soul from the Ignorance the first foundation is peace, calm, the silence and quietude of the Eternal and Infinite; but a consummate power and greater formation of the spiritual ascension takes up this peace of liberation into the bliss of a perfect experience and realisation of the eternal beatitude, the bliss of the Eternal and Infinite. This Ananda would be inherent in the gnostic consciousness as a universal delight and would grow with the evolution of the gnostic nature.

It has been held that ecstasy is a lower and transient passage, the peace of the Supreme is the supreme realisation, the consummate abiding experience. This may be true on the spiritual-mind plane: there the first ecstasy felt is indeed a spiritual rapture, but it can be and is very usually mingled with a supreme happiness of the vital parts taken up by the Spirit; there is an exaltation, exultation, excitement, a highest intensity of the joy of the heart and the pure inner soul-sensation that can be a splendid passage or an uplifting force but is not the ultimate permanent foundation. But in the highest ascents of the spiritual bliss there is not this vehement exaltation and excitement; there is instead an illimitable intensity of participation in an eternal ecstasy which is founded on the eternal Existence and therefore on a beatific tranquillity of eternal peace. Peace and ecstasy cease to be different and become one. The Supermind, reconciling and fusing all differences as well as all contradictions, brings out this unity; a wide calm and a deep delight of all-existence are among its first steps of self-realisation, but this calm and this delight rise together, as one state, into an increasing intensity and culminate in the eternal ecstasy, the bliss that is the Infinite. In the gnostic consciousness at any stage there would be always in some degree this fundamental and spiritual conscious delight of existence in the whole depth of the being; but also all the movements of Nature would be pervaded by it, and all the actions and reactions of the life and the body: none could escape the law of the Ananda. Even before the gnostic change there can be a beginning of this fundamental ecstasy of being translated into a manifold beauty and delight. In the mind, it translates into a calm of intense delight of spiritual perception and vision and knowledge, in the heart into a wide or deep or passionate delight of universal union and love and sympathy and the joy of beings and the joy of things. In the will and vital parts it is felt as the energy of delight of a divine life-power in action or a beatitude of the senses perceiving and meeting the One everywhere, perceiving as their normal aesthesis of things a universal beauty and a secret harmony of creation of which our mind can catch only imperfect glimpses or a rare supernormal sense. In the body it reveals itself as an ecstasy pouring into it from the heights of the Spirit and the peace and bliss of a pure and spiritualised physical existence. A universal beauty and glory of being begins to manifest; all objects reveal hidden lines, vibrations, powers, harmonic significances concealed from the normal mind and the physical sense. In the universal phenomenon is revealed the eternal Ananda.

These are the first major results of the spiritual transformation that follow as a necessary consequence of the nature of Supermind. But if there is to be not only a perfection of the inner existence, of the consciousness, of an inner delight of existence, but a perfection of the life and action, two other questions present themselves from our mental viewpoint which have to our human thought about our life and its dynamisms a considerable, even a premier importance. First, there is the place of personality in the gnostic being, — whether the status, the building of the being will be quite other than what we experience as the form and life of the person or similar. If there is a personality and it is in any way responsible for its actions, there intervenes, next, the question of the place of the ethical element and its perfection and fulfilment in the gnostic nature. Ordinarily, in the common notion, the separative ego is our self and, if ego has to disappear in a transcendental or universal Consciousness, personal life and action must cease; for, the individual disappearing, there can only be an impersonal consciousness, a cosmic self: but if the individual is altogether extinguished, no further question of personality or responsibility or ethical perfection can arise. According to another line of ideas the spiritual person remains, but liberated, purified, perfected in nature in a celestial existence. But here we are still on earth, and yet it is supposed that the ego-personality is extinguished and replaced by a universalised spiritual individual who is a centre and power of the transcendent Being. It might be deduced that this gnostic or supramental individual is a self without personality, an impersonal Purusha. There could be many gnostic individuals but there would be no personality, all would be the same in being and nature. This, again, would create the idea of a void or blank of pure being from which an action and function of experiencing consciousness would arise, but without a construction of differentiated personality such as that which we now observe and regard as ourselves on our surface. But this would be a mental rather than a supramental solution of the problem of a spiritual individuality surviving ego and persisting in experience. In the supermind consciousness personality and impersonality are not opposite principles; they are inseparable aspects of one and the same reality. This reality is not the ego but the being, who is impersonal and universal in his stuff of nature, but forms out of it an expressive personality which is his form of self in the changes of Nature.

Impersonality is in its source something fundamental and universal; it is an existence, a force, a consciousness that takes on various shapes of its being and energy; each such shape of energy, quality, power or force, though still in itself general, impersonal and universal, is taken by the individual being as material for the building of his personality. Thus impersonality is in the original undifferentiated truth of things the pure substance of nature of the Being, the Person; in the dynamic truth of things it differentiates its powers and lends them to constitute by their variations the manifestation of personality. Love is the nature of the lover, courage the nature of the warrior; love and courage are impersonal and universal forces or formulations of the cosmic Force, they are the Spirit's powers of its universal being and nature. The Person is the Being supporting what is thus impersonal, holding it in himself as his, his nature of self; he is that which is the lover and warrior. What we call the personality of the Person is his expression in nature-status and nature-action, — he himself being in his self-existence, originally and ultimately, much more than that; it is the form of himself that he puts forth as his manifested already developed natural being or self in nature. In the formed limited individual it is his personal expression of what is impersonal, his personal appropriation of it, we may say, so as to have a material with which he can build a significant figure of himself in manifestation. In his formless unlimited self, his real being, the true Person or Purusha, he is not that, but contains in himself boundless and universal possibilities; but he gives to them, as the divine Individual, his own turn in the manifestation so that each among the Many is a unique self of the one Divine. The Divine, the Eternal, expresses himself as existence, consciousness, bliss, wisdom, knowledge, love, beauty, and we can think of him as these impersonal and universal powers of himself, regard them as the nature of the Divine and Eternal; we can say that God is Love, God is Wisdom, God is Truth or Righteousness: but he is not himself an impersonal state or abstract of states or qualities; he is the Being, at once absolute, universal and individual. If we look at it from this basis, there is, very clearly, no opposition, no incompatibility, no impossibility of a co-existence or one-existence of the Impersonal and the Person; they are each other, live in one another, melt into each other, and yet in a way can appear as if different ends, sides, obverse and reverse of the same Reality. The gnostic being is of the nature of the Divine and therefore repeats in himself this natural mystery of existence.

A supramental gnostic individual will be a spiritual Person, but not a personality in the sense of a pattern of being marked out by a settled combination of fixed qualities, a determined character; he cannot be that since he is a conscious expression of the universal and the transcendent. But neither can his being be a capricious impersonal flux throwing up at random waves of various form, waves of personality as it pours through Time. Something like this may be felt in men who have no strong centralising Person in their depths but act from a sort of confused multi-personality according to whatever element in them becomes prominent at the time; but the gnostic consciousness is a consciousness of harmony and self-knowledge and self-mastery and would not present such a disorder. There are, indeed, varying notions of what constitutes personality and what constitutes character. In one view personality is regarded as a fixed structure of recognisable qualities expressing a power of being; but another idea distinguishes personality and character, personality as a flux of self-expressive or sensitive and responsive being, character as a formed fixity of Nature's structure. But flux of nature and fixity of nature are two aspects of being neither of which, nor indeed both together, can be a definition of personality. For in all men there is a double element, the unformed though limited flux of being or Nature out of which personality is fashioned and the personal formation out of that flux. The formation may become rigid and ossify or it may remain sufficiently plastic to change constantly and develop; but it develops out of the formative flux, by a modification or enlargement or remoulding of the personality, not, ordinarily, by an abolition of the formation already made and the substitution of a new form of being, — this can only occur in an abnormal turn or a supernormal conversion. But besides this flux and this fixity there is also a third and occult element, the Person behind of whom the personality is a self-expression; the Person puts forward the personality as his role, character, *persona*, in the present act of his long drama of manifested existence. But the Person is larger than his personality, and it may happen that this inner largeness overflows into the surface formation; the result is a self-expression of being which can no longer be described by fixed qualities, normalities of mood, exact lineaments, or marked out by any structural limits. But neither is it a mere indistinguishable, quite amorphous and unseizable flux: though its acts of nature can be characterised but not itself, still it can be distinctively felt, followed in its action, it can be recognised, though it cannot easily be described; for it is a power of being rather than a structure. The ordinary restricted personality can be grasped by a description of the characters stamped on its life and thought and action, its very definite surface building and expression of self; even if we may miss whatever was not so expressed, that might seem to detract little from the general adequacy of our understanding, because the element missed is usually little more than an amorphous raw material, part of the flux, not used to form a significant part of the personality. But such a description would be pitifully inadequate to express the Person when its Power of Self within manifests more amply and puts forward its hidden daemonic force in the surface composition and the life. We feel ourselves in presence of a light of consciousness, a potency, a sea of energy, can distinguish and describe its free waves of action and quality, but not fix itself; and yet there is an impression of personality, the presence of a powerful being, a strong, high or beautiful recognisable Someone, a Person, not a limited creature of Nature but a Self or Soul, a Purusha. The gnostic Individual would be such an inner Person unveiled, occupying both the depths, — no longer self-hidden, — and the surface in a unified self-awareness; he would not be a surface personality partly expressive of a larger secret being, he would be not the wave but the ocean: he would be the Purusha, the inner conscious Existence self-revealed, and would have no need of a carved expressive mask or *persona*.

This, then, would be the nature of the gnostic Person, an infinite and universal being revealing, — or, to our mental ignorance, suggesting, — its eternal self through the significant form and expressive power of an individual and temporal self-manifestation. But the individual nature-manifestation, whether strong and distinct in outline or multitudinous and protean but still harmonic, would be there as an index of the being, not as the whole being: that would be felt behind, recognisable but indefinable, infinite. The consciousness also of the gnostic Person would be an infinite consciousness throwing up forms of self-expression, but aware always of its unbound infinity and universality and conveying the power and sense of its infinity and universality even in the finiteness of the expression, — by which, moreover, it would not be bound in the next movement of farther self-revelation. But this would still not be an unregulated unrecognisable flux but a process of self-revelation making visible the inherent truth of its powers of existence according to the harmonic law natural to all manifestation of the Infinite.

All the character of the life and action of the gnostic being would arise self-determined out of this nature of his gnostic individuality. There could be in it no separate problem of an ethical or any similar content, any conflict of good and evil. There could indeed be no problem at all, for problems are the creations of mental ignorance seeking for knowledge and they cannot exist in a consciousness in which knowledge arises self-born and the act is self-born out of the knowledge, out of a pre-existent truth of being conscious and self-aware. An essential and universal spiritual truth of being manifesting itself, freely fulfilling itself in its own nature and self-effectuating consciousness, a truth of being one in all even in an infinite diversity of its truth and making all to be felt as one, would also be in its very nature an essential and universal good manifesting itself, fulfilling itself in its own nature and self-effectuating consciousness, a truth of good one in all and for all even in an infinite diversity of its good. The purity of the eternal Self-existence would pour itself into all the activities, making and keeping all things pure; there could be no ignorance leading to wrong will and falsehood of the steps, no separative egoism inflicting by its ignorance and separate contrary will harm on oneself or harm on others, self-driven to a wrong dealing with one's own soul, mind, life or body or a wrong dealing with the soul, mind, life, body of others, which is the practical sense of all human evil. To rise beyond virtue and sin, good and evil is an essential part of the

Vedantic idea of liberation, and there is in this correlation a self-evident sequence. For liberation signifies an emergence into the true spiritual nature of being where all action is the automatic self-expression of that truth and there can be nothing else. In the imperfection and conflict of our members there is an effort to arrive at a right standard of conduct and to observe it; that is ethics, virtue, merit, *punya*, to do otherwise is sin, demerit, *pāpa*. Ethical mind declares a law of love, a law of justice, a law of truth, laws without number, difficult to observe, difficult to reconcile. But if oneness with others, oneness with truth is already the essence of the realised spiritual nature, there is no need of a law of truth or of love, — the law, the standard has to be imposed on us now because there is in our natural being an opposite force of separateness, a possibility of antagonism, a force of discord, ill-will, strife. All ethics is a construction of good in a Nature which has been smitten with evil by the powers of darkness born of the Ignorance, even as it is expressed in the ancient legend of the Vedanta. But where all is self-determined by truth of consciousness and truth of being, there can be no standard, no struggle to observe it, no virtue or merit, no sin or demerit of the nature. The power of love, of truth, of right will be there, not as a law mentally constructed but as the very substance and constitution of the nature and, by the integration of the being, necessarily also the very stuff and constituting nature of the action. To grow into this nature of our true being, a nature of spiritual truth and oneness, is the liberation attained by an evolution of the spiritual being: the gnostic evolution gives us the complete dynamism of that return to ourselves. Once that is done, the need of standards of virtue, dharmas, disappears; there is the law and self-order of the liberty of the Spirit, there can be no imposed or constructed law of conduct, dharma. All becomes a self-flow of spiritual self-nature, Swadharma of Swabhava.

Here we touch the kernel of the dynamic difference between life in the mental ignorance and life in the gnostic being and nature. It is the difference between an integral fully conscious being in full possession of its own truth of existence and working out that truth in its own freedom, free from all constructed laws,

while yet its life is a fulfilment of all true laws of becoming in
their essence of meaning, and an ignorant self-divided existence
which seeks for its own truth and tries to construct its findings
into laws and construct its life according to a pattern so made.
All true law is the right motion and process of a reality, an energy
or power of being in action fulfilling its own inherent movement
self-implied in its own truth of existence. This law may be inconscient and its working appear to be mechanical, — that is the
character or, at least, the appearance of law in material Nature:
it may be a conscious energy, freely determined in its action by
the consciousness in the being aware of its own imperative of
truth, aware of its plastic possibilities of self-expression of that
truth, aware, always in the whole and at each moment in the
detail, of the actualities it has to realise; this is the figure of the
law of the Spirit. An entire freedom of the Spirit, an entire self-
existent order self-creating, self-effectuating, self-secure in its
own natural and inevitable movement, is the character of this
dynamis of the gnostic Supernature.

    At the summit of being is the Absolute with its absolute
freedom of infinity but also its absolute truth of itself and power
of that truth of being; these two things repeat themselves in the
life of the Spirit in Supernature. All action there is the action
of the supreme Self, the supreme Ishwara in the truth of the
Supernature. It is at once the truth of the being of the self and
the truth of the will of the Ishwara one with that truth, — a
biune reality, — which expresses itself in each individual gnostic
being according to his supernature. The freedom of the gnostic
individual is the freedom of his spirit to fulfil dynamically the
truth of his being and the power of his energies in life; but this is
synonymous with an entire obedience of his nature to the truth
of Self manifested in his existence and to the will of the Divine
in him and all. This All-Will is one in each gnostic individual
and in many gnostic individuals and in the conscious All which
holds and contains them in itself; it is conscious of itself in each
gnostic being and is there one with his own will, and at the same
time he is conscious of the same Will, the same Self and Energy
variously active in all. Such a gnostic consciousness and gnostic

will aware of its oneness in many gnostic individuals, aware of its concordant totality and the meaning and meeting-point of its diversities, must assure a symphonic movement, a movement of unity, harmony, mutuality in the action of the whole. It assures at the same time in the individual a unity and symphonic concord of all the powers and movements of his being. All energies of being seek their self-expression and at their highest seek their absolute; this they find in the supreme Self, and they find at the same time their supreme oneness, harmony and mutuality of united and common self-expression in its all-seeing and all-uniting dynamic power of self-determination and self-effectuation, the supramental gnosis. A separate self-existent being could be at odds with other separate beings, at variance with the universal All in which they co-exist, in a state of contradiction with any supreme Truth that was willing its self-expression in the universe; this is what happens to the individual in the Ignorance, because he takes his stand on the consciousness of a separate individuality. There can be a similar conflict, discord, disparity between the truths, the energies, qualities, powers, modes of being that act as separate forces in the individual and in the universe. A world full of conflict, a conflict in ourselves, a conflict of the individual with the world around him are normal and inevitable features of the separative consciousness of the Ignorance and our ill-harmonised existence. But this cannot happen in the gnostic consciousness because there each finds his complete self and all find their own truth and the harmony of their different motions in that which exceeds them and of which they are the expression. In the gnostic life, therefore, there is an entire accord between the free self-expression of the being and his automatic obedience to the inherent law of the supreme and universal Truth of things. These are to him interconnected sides of the one Truth; it is his own supreme truth of being which works itself out in the whole united truth of himself and things in one Supernature. There is also an entire accord between all the many and different powers of the being and their action; for even those that are contradictory in their apparent motion and seem in our mental experience of them to enter into conflict, fit themselves and their action naturally into each other, because each has its self-truth and its truth of relation to the others and this is self-found and self-formed in the gnostic Supernature.

In the supramental gnostic nature there will therefore be no need of the mental rigid way and hard style of order, a limiting standardisation, an imposition of a fixed set of principles, the compulsion of life into one system or pattern which is alone valid because it is envisaged by mind as the one right truth of being and conduct. For such a standard cannot include and such a structure cannot take up into itself the whole of life, nor can it adapt itself freely to the pressure of the All-life or to the needs of the evolutionary Force; it has to escape from itself or to escape from its self-constructed limits by its own death, by disintegration or by an intense conflict and revolutionary disturbance. Mind has thus to select its limited rule and way of life, because it is itself bound and limited in vision and capacity; but gnostic being takes up into itself the whole of life and existence, fulfilled, transmuted into the harmonic self-expression of a vast Truth one and diverse, infinitely one, infinitely multiple. The knowledge and action of the gnostic being would have the wideness and plasticity of an infinite freedom. This knowledge would grasp its objects as it went in the largeness of the whole; it would be bound only by the integral truth of the whole and the complete and inmost truth of the object, but not by the formed idea or fixed mental symbols by which the mind is caught and held and confined in them so as to lose the freedom of its knowledge. The entire activity also would be unbound by an obligation of unelastic rule or by the obligation of a past state or action or by its compelling consequence, Karma; it would have the sequent but self-guided and self-evolving plasticity of the Infinite acting directly upon its own finites. This movement will not create a flux or chaos, but a liberated and harmonic Truth-expression; there would be a free self-determination of the spiritual being in a plastic entirely conscious nature.

In the consciousness of the Infinite individuality does not break up nor circumscribe cosmicity, cosmicity does not contradict transcendence. The gnostic being living in the consciousness of the Infinite will create his own self-manifestation as an individual, but he will do so as a centre of a larger universality and yet at the same time a centre of the transcendence. A universal individual, all his action would be in harmony with the cosmic action, but, owing to his transcendence, it would not be limited by a temporary inferior formulation or at the mercy of any or every cosmic force. His universality would embrace even the Ignorance around him in its larger self, but, while intimately aware of it, he would not be affected by it: he would follow the greater law of his transcendent individuality and express its gnostic truth in his own way of being and action. His life would be a free harmonic expression of the self; but, since his highest self would be one with the being of the Ishwara, a natural divine government of his self-expression by the Ishwara, by his highest self, and by the Supernature, his own supreme nature, would automatically bring into the knowledge, the life, the action a large and unbound but perfect order. The obedience of his individual nature to the Ishwara and the Supernature would be a natural consonance and indeed the very condition of the freedom of the self, since it would be an obedience to his own supreme being, a response to the Source of all his existence. The individual nature would be nothing separate, it would be a current of the Supernature. All antinomy of the Purusha and the Prakriti, that curious division and unbalance of the Soul and Nature which afflicts the Ignorance, would be entirely removed; for the nature would be the outflowing of the self-force of the Person and the Person would be the outflowing of the supreme Nature, the supramental power of being of the Ishwara. It is this supreme truth of his being, an infinitely harmonic principle, that would create the order of his spiritual freedom, an authentic, automatic and plastic order.

In the lower existence the order is automatic, the binding of Nature complete, her groove firm and imperative: the cosmic Consciousness-Force evolves a pattern of Nature and its habitual mould or fixed round of action and obliges the infrarational being to live and act according to the pattern and in the mould or round made for it. Mind in man starts with this prearranged

pattern and routine, but, as it evolves, it enlarges the design and
expands the mould and tries to replace this fixed unconscious
or half-conscious law of automatism by an order based on ideas
and significances and accepted life-motives, or it attempts an
intelligent standardisation and a framework determined by rational purpose, utility and convenience. There is nothing really
binding or permanent in man's knowledge-structures or his life-
structures; but still he cannot but create standards of thought,
knowledge, personality, life, conduct and, more or less consciously and completely, base his existence on them or, at least,
try his best to frame his life in the ideative cadre of his chosen or
accepted dharmas. In the passage to the spiritual life the supreme
ideal held up is, on the contrary, not law, but liberty in the Spirit;
the Spirit breaks through all formulas to find its self and, if it
has still to be concerned with expression, it must arrive at the
liberty of a free and true instead of an artificial expression, a
true and spontaneous spiritual order. "Abandon all dharmas,
all standards and rules of being and action, and take refuge in
Me alone", is the summit rule of the highest existence held up by
the Divine Being to the seeker. In the seeking for this freedom,
in the liberation from constructed law into law of self and spirit,
in the casting away of the mental control in order to substitute
for it the control of the spiritual Reality, an abandonment of the
lower constructed truth of mind for the higher essential truth of
being, it is possible to pass through a stage in which there is an
inner freedom but a lack of outer order, — an action in the flux
of nature childlike or inert like a leaf lying passive or driven by
the wind or even incoherent or extravagant in outer semblance.
It is possible also to arrive at a temporary ordered spiritual expression of the self which is sufficient for the stage one can reach
for a time or in this life; or it may be a personal order of self-
expression valid according to the norm of what one has already
realised of the spiritual truth but afterwards changing freely by
the force of spirituality to express the yet larger truth that one
goes on to realise. But the supramental gnostic being stands in a
consciousness in which knowledge is self-existent and manifests
itself according to the order self-determined by the Will of the

Infinite in the Supernature. This self-determination according to a self-existent knowledge replaces the automatism of Nature and the standards of Mind by the spontaneity of a Truth self-aware and self-active in the very grain of the existence.

In the gnostic being this self-determining knowledge freely obedient to self-truth and the total truth of Being would be the very law of his existence. In him Knowledge and Will become one and cannot be in conflict; Truth of spirit and life become one and cannot be at variance: in the self-effectuation of his being there can be no strife or disparity or divergence between the spirit and the members. The two principles of freedom and order, which in mind and life are constantly representing themselves as contraries or incompatibles, though they have no need to be that if freedom is guarded by knowledge and order based upon truth of being, are in the supermind consciousness native to each other and even fundamentally one. This is so because both are inseparable aspects of the inner spiritual truth and therefore their determinations are one; they are inherent in each other, for they arise from an identity and therefore in action coincide in a natural identity. The gnostic being does not in any way or degree feel his liberty infringed by the imperative order of his thoughts or actions, because that order is intrinsic and spontaneous; he feels both his liberty and the order of his liberty to be one truth of his being. His liberty of knowledge is not a freedom to follow falsehood or error, for he does not need like the mind to pass through the possibility of error in order to know, — on the contrary, any such deviation would be a departure from his plenitude of the gnostic self, it would be a diminution of his self-truth and alien and injurious to his being; for his freedom is a freedom of light, not of darkness. His liberty of action is not a license to act upon wrong will or the impulsions of the Ignorance, for that too would be alien to his being, a restriction and diminution of it, not a liberation. A drive for fulfilment of falsehood or wrong will would be felt by him, not as a movement towards freedom, but as a violence done to the liberty of the Spirit, an invasion and imposition, an inroad upon his Supernature, a tyranny of some alien Nature.

A supramental consciousness must be fundamentally a Truth-Consciousness, a direct and inherent awareness of the truth of being and the truth of things; it is a power of the Infinite knowing and working out its finites, a power of the Universal knowing and working out its oneness and detail, its cosmicity and its individualities; self-possessed of Truth, it would not have to seek for the Truth or suffer from the liability to miss it as does the mind of the Ignorance. The evolved gnostic being would have entered into this Truth-Consciousness of the Infinite and Universal, and it would be that which would determine for him and in him all his individual seeing and action. His would be a consciousness of universal identity and a consequent or rather inherent Truth-knowledge, Truth-sight, Truth-feeling, Truth-will, Truth-sense and Truth-dynamis of action implicit in his identity with the One or spontaneously arising from his identity with the All. His life would be a movement in the steps of a spiritual liberty and largeness replacing the law of the mental idea and the law of vital and physical need and desire and the compulsion of a surrounding life; his life and action would be bound by nothing else than the Divine Wisdom and Will acting on him and in him according to its Truth-Consciousness. An absence of an imposed construction of law might be expected to lead in the life of the human ignorance, because of the separativeness of the human ego and its smallness, the necessity it feels to impinge on and possess and utilise other life, to a chaos of conflict, license and egoistic disorder; but this could not exist in the life of the gnostic being. For in the gnostic Truth-Consciousness of a supramental being there must necessarily be a truth of relation of all the parts and movements of the being, — whether the being of the individual or the being of any gnostic collectivity, — a spontaneous and luminous oneness and wholeness in all the movements of the consciousness and all the action of the life. There could be no strife of the members; for not only the knowledge and will consciousness but the heart consciousness and life consciousness and body consciousness, what are in us the emotional, vital or physical parts of nature, would be included in this integrated harmony of wholeness and oneness. In our language we might say that the supermind knowledge-will of the gnostic being would have a perfect control of the mind, heart, life and body; but this description could apply only to the transitional stage when the Supernature was remoulding these members into its own nature: once that transition was concluded, there would be no need of control, for all would be one unified consciousness and therefore would act as a whole in a spontaneous integrality and unity.

In a gnostic being there could be no conflict between self-affirmation of the ego and a control by super-ego; for since in his action of life the gnostic individual would at once express himself, his truth of being, and work out the Divine Will, since he would know the Divine as his true self and the source and constituent of his spiritual individuality, these two springs of his conduct would not only be simultaneous in a single action, but they would be one and the same motor-force. This motive power would act in each circumstance according to the truth of the circumstance, with each being according to its need, nature, relation, in each event according to the demand of the Divine Will upon that event: for all here is the result of a complexus and a close nexus of many forces of one Force, and the gnostic consciousness and Truth-Will would see the truth of these forces, of each and of all together, and put forth the necessary impact or intervention on the complex of forces to carry out what was willed to be done through itself, that and no more. In consequence of the Identity present everywhere, ruling everything and harmonising all diversities, there would be no play of a separative ego bent on its own separate self-affirmation; the will of the self of the gnostic being would be one with the will of the Ishwara, it would not be a separative or contrary self-will. It would have the joy of action and result but would be free from all ego-claim, attachment to action or demand of result; it would do what it saw had to be done and was moved to do. In mental nature there can be an opposition or disparity between self-effort and obedience to the Higher Will, for there the self or apparent person sees itself as different from the supreme Being,

Will or Person; but here the person is being of the Being and the opposition or disparity does not arise. The action of the person is the action of the Ishwara in the person, of the One in the many, and there can be no reason for a separative assertion of self-will or pride of independence.

On this fact that the Divine Knowledge and Force, the supreme Supernature, would act through the gnostic being with his full participation, is founded the freedom of the gnostic being; it is this unity that gives him his liberty. The freedom from law, including the moral law, so frequently affirmed of the spiritual being, is founded on this unity of its will with the will of the Eternal. All the mental standards would disappear because all necessity for them would cease; the higher authentic law of identity with the Divine Self and identity with all beings would have replaced them. There would be no question of selfishness or altruism, of oneself and others, since all are seen and felt as the one self and only what the supreme Truth and Good decided would be done. There would be in the action a pervasive feeling of a self-existent universal love, sympathy, oneness, but the feeling would penetrate, colour and move in the act, not solely dominate or determine it: it would not stand for itself in opposition to the larger truth of things or dictate a personally impelled departure from the divinely willed true movement. This opposition and departure can happen in the Ignorance where love or any other strong principle of the nature can be divorced from wisdom even as it can be divorced from power; but in the supermind gnosis all powers are intimate to each other and act as one. In the gnostic person the Truth-Knowledge would lead and determine and all the other forces of the being concur in the action: there would be no place for disharmony or conflict between the powers of the nature. In all action there is an imperative of existence that seeks to be fulfilled; a truth of being not yet manifested has to be manifested or a truth manifesting has to be evolved and achieved and perfected in manifestation or, if already achieved, to take its delight of being and self-effectuation. In the half-light and half-power of the Ignorance the imperative is secret or only half-revealed and the push to fulfilment is an imperfect, struggling, partly frustrated movement: but in the gnostic being and life the imperatives of being would be felt within, intimately perceived and brought into action; there would be a free play of their possibilities; there would be an actualisation in accordance with the truth of circumstance and the intention in the Supernature. All this would be seen in the knowledge and develop itself in act; there would be no uncertain combat or torment of forces at work; a disharmony of the being, a contradictory working of the consciousness could have no place: the imposition of an external standardisation of mechanised law would be entirely superfluous where there is this inherence of truth and its spontaneous working in act of nature. A harmonic action, a working out of the divine motive, an execution of the imperative truth of things would be the law and natural dynamics of the whole existence.

A knowledge by identity using the powers of the integrated being for richness of instrumentation would be the principle of the supramental life. In the other grades of the gnostic being, although a truth of spiritual being and consciousness would fulfil itself, the instrumentation would be of a different order. A higher-mental being would act through the truth of thought, the truth of the idea and accomplish that in the life-action: but in the supramental gnosis thought is a derivative movement, it is a formulation of truth-vision and not the determining or the main driving force; it would be an instrument for expression of knowledge more than for arrival at knowledge or for action, — or it would intervene in action only as a penetrating point of the body of identity-will and identity-knowledge. So too in the illumined gnostic being truth-vision and in the intuitive gnostic being a direct truth-contact and perceptive truth-sense would be the mainspring of action. In the Overmind a comprehensive immediate grasp of the truth of things and the principle of being of each thing and all its dynamic consequences would originate and gather up a great wideness of gnostic vision and thought and create a foundation of knowledge and action; this largeness of being and seeing and doing would be the varied result of an underlying identity-consciousness, but the identity itself

would not be in the front as the very stuff of the consciousness or the very force of the action. But in the supramental
gnosis all this luminous immediate grasp of the truth of things,
truth-sense, truth-vision, truth-thought would get back into its
source of identity-consciousness and subsist as a single body
of its knowledge. The identity-consciousness would lead and
contain everything; it would manifest as an awareness in the
very grain of the being's substance putting forth its inherent
self-fulfilling force and determining itself dynamically in form
of consciousness and form of action. This inherent awareness is
the origin and principle of the working of supramental gnosis;
it could be sufficient in itself with no need of anything to formulate or embody it: but the play of illumined vision, the play
of a radiant thought, the play of all other movements of the
spiritual consciousness would not be absent; there would be a
free instrumentation of them for their own brilliant functioning,
for a divine richness and diversity, for a manifold delight of self-
manifestation, for the joy of the powers of the Infinite. In the
intermediate stages or degrees of the gnosis there might be the
manifestation of various and separate expressions of the aspects
of the divine Being and Nature, a soul and life of love, a soul and
life of divine light and knowledge, a soul and life of divine power
and sovereign action and creation, and innumerable other forms
of divine life; on the supramental height all would be taken up
into a manifold unity, a supreme integration of being and life. A
fulfilment of the being in a luminous and blissful integration of
its states and powers and their satisfied dynamic action would
be the sense of the gnostic existence.

All supramental gnosis is a twofold Truth-Consciousness,
a consciousness of inherent self-knowledge and, by identity of
self and world, of intimate world-knowledge; this knowledge is
the criterion, the characteristic power of the gnosis. But this is
not a purely ideative knowledge, it is not consciousness observing, forming ideas, trying to carry them out; it is an essential
light of consciousness, the self-light of all the realities of being
and becoming, the self-truth of being determining, formulating and effectuating itself. To be, not to know, is the object

of the manifestation; knowledge is only the instrumentation of an operative consciousness of being. This would be the gnostic life on earth, a manifestation or play of truth-conscious being, being grown aware of itself in all things, no longer lost to consciousness of itself, no longer plunged into a self-oblivion or a half-oblivion of its real existence brought about by absorption in form and action, but using form and action with a delivered spiritual power for its free and perfect self-expression, no longer seeking for its own lost or forgotten or veiled and hidden significance or significances, no longer bound, but delivered from inconscience and ignorance, aware of its own truths and powers, determining freely in a movement always concurrent and in tune in every detail with its supreme and universal Reality its manifestation, the play of its substance, the play of its consciousness, the play of its force of existence, the play of its delight of existence.

In the gnostic evolution there would be a great diversity in the poise, status, harmonised operations of consciousness and force and delight of existence. There would naturally appear in time many grades of the farther ascent of the evolutive Supermind to its own summits; but in all there would be the common basis and principle. In the manifestation the Spirit, the Being, while knowing all itself, is not bound to put forth all itself in the actual front of formation and action which is its immediate power and degree of self-expression: it may put forth a frontal self-expression and hold all the rest of itself behind in an unexpressed delight of self-being. That All behind and its delight would find itself in the front, know itself in it, maintain and suffuse the expression, the manifestation with its own presence and feeling of totality and infinity. This frontal formation with all the rest behind it and held in power of being within it would be an act of self-knowledge, not an act of Ignorance; it would be a luminous self-expression of the Superconscience and not an upthrow from the Inconscience. A great harmonised variation would thus be an element in the beauty and completeness of the evolution of the gnostic consciousness and existence. Even in dealing with the mind of ignorance around it, as in dealing with the still lower degrees of the gnostic evolution, the supramental life would use this innate power and movement of its Truth of being: it would relate in the light of that integral Reality its own truth of being with the truth of being that is behind the Ignorance; it would found all relations upon the common spiritual unity, accept and harmonise the manifested difference. The gnostic Light would ensure the right relation and action or reaction of each upon each in every circumstance; the gnostic power or influence would affirm always a symphonic effectuation, secure the right relation of the more developed and the less developed life and impose by its influence a greater harmony on the lower existence.

This would be the nature of the being, life and action of the gnostic individual so far as we can follow the evolution with our mental conception up to that point where it will emerge out of Overmind and cross the border into supramental gnosis. This nature of the gnosis would evidently determine all the relations of the life or group-life of gnostic beings; for a gnostic collectivity would be a collective soul-power of the Truth-Consciousness, even as the gnostic individual would be an individual soul-power of it: it would have the same integration of life and action in unison, the same realised and conscious unity of being, the same spontaneity, intimate oneness-feeling, one and mutual truth-vision and truth-sense of self and each other, the same truth-action in the relation of each with each and all with all; this collectivity would be and act not as a mechanical but a spiritual integer. A similar inevitability of the union of freedom and order would be the law of the collective life; it would be a freedom of the diverse play of the Infinite in divine souls, an order of the conscious unity of souls which is the law of the supramental Infinite. Our mental rendering of oneness brings into it the rule of sameness; a complete oneness brought about by the mental reason drives towards a thoroughgoing standardisation as its one effective means, — only minor shades of differentiation would be allowed to operate: but the greatest richness of diversity in the self-expression of oneness would be the law of the gnostic life. In the gnostic consciousness difference would not lead to discord but to a spontaneous natural adaptation, a sense of complementary plenitude, a rich many-sided execution of the thing to be collectively known, done, worked out in life. For the difficulty in mind and life is created by ego, by separation of integers into component parts which figure as contraries, opposites, disparates: all in which they separate from each other is easily felt, affirmed and stressed; that in which they meet, whatever holds their divergences together, is largely missed or found with difficulty; everything has to be done by an overcoming or an adjustment of difference, by a constructed unity. There is, indeed, an underlying principle of oneness and Nature insists on its emergence in a construction of unity; for she is collective and communal as well as individual and egoistic and has her instrumentation of associativeness, sympathies, common needs, interests, attractions, affinities as well as her more brutal means of unification: but her secondary imposed and too prominent basis of ego-life and ego-nature overlays the unity and afflicts all its constructions with imperfection and insecurity. A farther difficulty is created by the absence or rather the imperfection of intuition and direct inner contact making each a separate being forced to learn with difficulty the other's being and nature, to arrive at understanding and mutuality and harmony from outside instead of inwardly through a direct sense and grasp, so that all mental and vital interchange is hampered, rendered ego-tainted or doomed to imperfection and incompleteness by the veil of mutual ignorance. In the collective gnostic life the integrating truth-sense, the concording unity of gnostic nature would carry all divergences in itself as its own opulence and turn a multitudinous thought, action, feeling into the unity of a luminous life-whole. This would be the evident principle, the inevitable result of the very character of the Truth-Consciousness and its dynamic realisation of the spiritual unity of all being. This realisation, the key to the perfection of life, difficult to arrive at on the mental plane, difficult even when realised to dynamise or organise, would be naturally dynamic, spontaneously self-organised in all gnostic creation and gnostic life.

This much is easily understandable if we regard the gnostic beings as living their own life without any contact with a life of the Ignorance. But by the very fact of the evolution here the gnostic manifestation would be a circumstance, though a decisive circumstance, in the whole: there would be a continuance of the lower degrees of the consciousness and life, some maintaining the manifestation in the Ignorance, some mediating between it and the manifestation in the gnosis; these two forms of being and life would either exist side by side or interpenetrate. In either case the gnostic principle might be expected, if not at once, yet finally to dominate the whole. The higher spiritual-mental degrees would be in touch with the supramental principle now overtly supporting them and holding them together and would be delivered from the once enveloping hold of the Ignorance and Inconscience. As manifestations of the truth of being, though in a qualified and modified degree, they would draw all their light and energy from the supramental gnosis and would be in large contact with its instrumental powers; they would themselves be conscious motive-powers of the Spirit and, although not yet in the full force of their entirely realised spiritual substance, they would not be subjected to a lesser instrumentation fragmented, diluted, diminished, obscured by the substance of the Nescience. All Ignorance rising or entering into the overmind, into the intuitive, into the illumined or higher-mind being would cease to be ignorance; it would enter into the light, realise in that light the truth which it had covered with its darkness and undergo a liberation, transmutation, new state of consciousness and being which would assimilate it to these higher states and prepare it for the supramental status. At the same time the involved principle of the gnosis, acting now as an overt, arisen and constantly dynamic force and no longer only as a concealed power with a secret origination or a veiled support of things or an occasional intervention as its only function, would be able to lay something of its law of harmony on the still existing Inconscience and Ignorance. For the secret gnostic power concealed in them would act with a greater strength of its support and origination, a freer and more powerful intervention; the beings of the Ignorance, influenced by the light of the gnosis through their association with gnostic beings and through the evolved and effective presence of the supramental Being and Power in earth-nature, would be more conscious and responsive. In the untransformed part of humanity itself there might well arise a new and greater order of mental human beings; for the directly intuitive or partly intuitivised but not yet gnostic mental being, the directly or partly illumined mental being, the mental being in direct or part communion with the higher-thought plane would emerge: these would become more and more numerous, more and more evolved and secure in their type, and might even exist as a formed race of higher humanity leading upwards the less evolved in a true fraternity born of the sense of the manifestation of the One Divine in all beings. In this way, the consummation of the highest might mean also a lesser consummation in its own degree of what must remain still below. At the higher end of the evolution the ascending ranges and summits of Supermind would begin to rise towards some supreme manifestation of the pure spiritual existence, consciousness and delight of being of Sachchidananda.

A question might arise whether the gnostic reversal, the passage into a gnostic evolution and beyond it would not mean sooner or later the cessation of the evolution from the Inconscience, since the reason for that obscure beginning of things here would cease. This depends on the farther question whether the movement between the Superconscience and the Inconscience as the two poles of existence is an abiding law of the material manifestation or only a provisional circumstance. The latter supposition is difficult to accept because of the tremendous force of pervasiveness and durability with which the inconscient foundation has been laid for the whole material universe. Any complete reversal or elimination of the first evolutionary principle would mean the simultaneous manifestation of the secret involved consciousness in every part of this vast universal Inconscience; a change in a particular line of Nature such as the earth-line could not have any such all-pervading effect: the manifestation in earth-nature has its own curve and the completion of that curve is all that we have to consider. Here this much might be hazarded that in the final result of the revelatory creation or reproduction of the upper hemisphere of conscious being in the lower triplicity the evolution here, though remaining the same in its degrees and stages, would be subjected to the law of harmony, the law of unity in diversity and of diversity working out unity: it would be no longer an evolution through strife; it would become a harmonious development from stage to stage, from lesser to greater light, from type to higher type of the power and beauty of a self-unfolding existence. It would only be otherwise if for some reason the law of struggle and suffering still remained necessary for the working out of that mysterious possibility in the Infinite whose principle underlies the plunge into the Inconscience. But for the earth-nature it would seem as if this necessity might be exhausted once the supramental gnosis had emerged from the Inconscience. A change would begin with its firm appearance; that change would be consummated when the supramental evolution became complete and rose into the greater fullness of a supreme manifestation of the Existence-Consciousness-Delight, Sachchidananda.

Chapter XXVIII

The Divine Life

O seeing Flame, thou carriest man of the crooked ways into the abiding truth and the knowledge.   *Rig Veda.*[1]

I purify earth and heaven by the Truth.   *Rig Veda.*[2]

His ecstasy, in one who holds it, sets into motion the two births, the human self-expression and the divine, and moves between them.   *Rig Veda.*[3]

May the invincible rays of his intuition be there seeking immortality, pervading both the births; for by them he sets flowing in one movement human strengths and things divine.
                    Rig Veda.[4]

Let all accept thy will when thou art born a living god from the dry tree, that they may attain to divinity and reach by the speed of thy movements to possession of the Truth and the Immortality.   *Rig Veda.*[5]

OUR ENDEAVOUR has been to discover what is the reality and significance of our existence as conscious beings in the material universe and in what direction and how far that significance once discovered leads us, to what human or divine future. Our existence here may indeed be an inconsequential freak of Matter itself or of some Energy building up Matter, or it may be an inexplicable freak of the Spirit. Or, again, our existence here may be an arbitrary fantasy of a supracosmic Creator. In that case it has no essential significance, — no significance at all if Matter or an inconscient Energy is the

---

[1] I. 31. 6.   [2] I. 133. 1.   [3] IX. 86. 42.   [4] IX. 70. 3.   [5] I. 68. 2.

fantasy-builder, for then it is at best the stray description of a
wandering spiral of Chance or the hard curve of a blind Necessity; it can have only an illusory significance which vanishes into
nothingness if it is an error of the Spirit. A conscious Creator
may indeed have put a meaning into our existence, but it must be
discovered by a revelation of his will and is not self-implied in the
self-nature of things and discoverable there. But if there is a self-
existent Reality of which our existence here is a result, then there
must be a truth of that Reality which is manifesting, working
itself out, evolving here, and that will be the significance of our
own being and life. Whatever that Reality may be, it is something
that has taken upon itself the aspect of a becoming in Time, —
an indivisible becoming, for our present and our future carry in
themselves, transformed, made other, the past that created them,
and the past and present already contained and now contain in
themselves, invisible to us because still unmanifested, unevolved,
their own transformation into the still uncreated future. The
significance of our existence here determines our destiny: that
destiny is something that already exists in us as a necessity and
a potentiality, the necessity of our being's secret and emergent
reality, a truth of its potentialities that is being worked out; both,
though not yet realised, are even now implied in what has been
already manifested. If there is a Being that is becoming, a Reality
of existence that is unrolling itself in Time, what that being, that
reality secretly is is what we have to become, and so to become
is our life's significance.

It is consciousness and life that must be the keywords to
what is being thus worked out in Time; for without them Matter
and the world of Matter would be a meaningless phenomenon,
a thing that has just happened by Chance or by an unconscious
Necessity. But consciousness as it is, life as it is cannot be the
whole secret; for both are very clearly something unfinished and
still in process. In us consciousness is Mind, and our mind is
ignorant and imperfect, an intermediate power that has grown
and is still growing towards something beyond itself: there were
lower levels of consciousness that came before it and out of
which it arose, there must very evidently be higher levels to

which it is itself arising. Before our thinking, reasoning, reflecting mind there was a consciousness unthinking but living and sentient, and before that there was the subconscious and the unconscious; after us or in our yet unevolved selves there is likely to be waiting a greater consciousness, self-luminous, not dependent on constructive thought: our imperfect and ignorant thought-mind is certainly not the last word of consciousness, its ultimate possibility. For the essence of consciousness is the power to be aware of itself and its objects, and in its true nature this power must be direct, self-fulfilled and complete: if it is in us indirect, incomplete, unfulfilled in its workings, dependent on constructed instruments, it is because consciousness here is emerging from an original veiling Inconscience and is yet burdened and enveloped with the first Nescience proper to the Inconscient; but it must have the power to emerge completely, its destiny must be to evolve into its own perfection which is its true nature. Its true nature is to be wholly aware of its objects, and of these objects the first is self, the being which is evolving its consciousness here, and the rest is what we see as not-self, — but if existence is indivisible, that too must in reality be self: the destiny of evolving consciousness must be, then, to become perfect in its awareness, entirely aware of self and all-aware. This perfect and natural condition of consciousness is to us a superconscience, a state which is beyond us and in which our mind, if suddenly transferred to it, could not at first function; but it is towards that superconscience that our conscious being must be evolving. But this evolution of our consciousness to a superconscience or supreme of itself is possible only if the Inconscience which is our basis here is really itself an involved Superconscience; for what is to be in the becoming of the Reality in us must be already there involved or secret in its beginning. Such an involved Being or Power we can well conceive the Inconscient to be when we closely regard this material creation of an unconscious Energy and see it labouring out with curious construction and infinite device the work of a vast involved Intelligence and see, too, that we ourselves are something of that Intelligence evolving out of its involution, an emerging consciousness whose emergence cannot stop short on the way until the Involved has evolved and revealed itself as a supreme totally self-aware and all-aware Intelligence. It is this to which we have given the name of Supermind or Gnosis. For that evidently must be the consciousness of the Reality, the Being, the Spirit that is secret in us and slowly manifesting here; of that Being we are the becomings and must grow into its nature.

If consciousness is the central secret, life is the outward indication, the effective power of being in Matter; for it is that which liberates consciousness and gives it its form or embodiment of force and its effectuation in material act. If some revelation or effectuation of itself in Matter is the ultimate aim of the evolving Being in its birth, life is the exterior and dynamic sign and index of that revelation and effectuation. But life also, as it is now, is imperfect and evolving; it evolves through growth of consciousness even as consciousness evolves through greater organisation and perfection of life: a greater consciousness means a greater life. Man, the mental being, has an imperfect life because mind is not the first and highest power of consciousness of the Being; even if mind were perfected, there would be still something yet to be realised, not yet manifested. For what is involved and emergent is not a Mind, but a Spirit, and mind is not the native dynamism of consciousness of the Spirit; Supermind, the light of gnosis, is its native dynamism. If then life has to become a manifestation of the Spirit, it is the manifestation of a spiritual being in us and the divine life of a perfected consciousness in a supramental or gnostic power of spiritual being that must be the secret burden and intention of evolutionary Nature.

All spiritual life is in its principle a growth into divine living. It is difficult to fix the frontier where the mental ceases and the divine life begins, for the two project into each other and there is a long space of their intermingled existence. A great part of this interspace, — when the spiritual urge does not turn away from earth or world altogether, — can be seen as the process of a higher life in the making. As the mind and life become illumined with the light of the Spirit, they put on or reflect something of the divinity, the secret greater Reality, and this must increase until the interspace has been crossed and the whole existence is unified in the full light and power of the spiritual principle. But, for the full and perfect fulfilment of the evolutionary urge, this illumination and change must take up and re-create the whole being, mind, life and body: it must be not only an inner experience of the Divinity but a remoulding of both the inner and outer existence by its power; it must take form not only in the life of the individual but as a collective life of gnostic beings established as a highest power and form of the becoming of the Spirit in the earth-nature. For this to be possible the spiritual entity in us must have developed its own integralised perfection not only of the inner state of the being but of the outgoing power of the being and, with that perfection and as a necessity of its complete action, it must have evolved its own dynamis and instrumentation of the outer existence.

There can undoubtedly be a spiritual life within, a kingdom of heaven within us which is not dependent on any outer manifestation or instrumentation or formula of external being. The inner life has a supreme spiritual importance and the outer has a value only in so far as it is expressive of the inner status. However the man of spiritual realisation lives and acts and behaves, in all ways of his being and acting, it is said in the Gita, "he lives and moves in Me"; he dwells in the Divine, he has realised the spiritual existence. The spiritual man living in the sense of the spiritual self, in the realisation of the Divine within him and everywhere, would be living inwardly a divine life and its reflection would fall on his outer acts of existence, even if they did not pass, — or did not seem to pass, — beyond the ordinary instrumentation of human thought and action in this world of earth-nature. This is the first truth and the essence of the matter; but still, from the point of view of a spiritual evolution, this would be only an individual liberation and perfection in an unchanged environmental existence: for a greater dynamic change in earth-nature itself, a spiritual change of the whole principle and instrumentation of life and action, the appearance of a new order of beings and a new earth-life must be envisaged in our idea of the total consummation, the divine issue. Here the gnostic change assumes a primary importance; all that precedes can be considered as an upbuilding and a preparation for this transmuting reversal of the whole nature. For it is a gnostic way of dynamic living that must be the fulfilled divine life on earth, a way of living that develops higher instruments of world-knowledge and world-action for the dynamisation of consciousness in the physical existence and takes up and transforms the values of a world of material Nature.

But always the whole foundation of the gnostic life must be by its very nature inward and not outward. In the life of the Spirit it is the Spirit, the inner Reality, that has built up and uses the mind, vital being and body as its instrumentation; thought, feeling and action do not exist for themselves, they are not an object, but the means; they serve to express the manifested divine Reality within us: otherwise, without this inwardness, this spiritual origination, in a too externalised consciousness or by only external means, no greater or divine life is possible. In our present life of Nature, in our externalised surface existence, it is the world that seems to create us; but in the turn to the spiritual life it is we who must create ourselves and our world. In this new formula of creation, the inner life becomes of the first importance and the rest can be only its expression and outcome. It is this, indeed, that is indicated by our own strivings towards perfection, the perfection of our own soul and mind and life and the perfection of the life of the race. For we are given a world which is obscure, ignorant, material, imperfect, and our external conscious being is itself created by the energies, the pressure, the moulding operations of this vast mute obscurity, by physical birth, by environment, by a training through the impacts and shocks of life; and yet we are vaguely aware of something that is there in us or seeking to be, something other than what has been thus made, a Spirit self-existent, self-determining, pushing the nature towards the creation of an image of its own occult perfection or Idea of perfection. There is something that grows in us in answer to this demand, that strives to become the image of a divine Somewhat, and is impelled also to labour at the world outside that has been given to it and to remake that too in a greater image, in the image of its own spiritual and mental and vital growth, to make our world too something created according to our own mind and self-conceiving spirit, something new, harmonious, perfect.

But our mind is obscure, partial in its notions, misled by opposite surface appearances, divided between various possibilities; it is led in three different directions to any of which it may give an exclusive preference. Our mind, in its search for what must be, turns towards a concentration on our own inner spiritual growth and perfection, on our own individual being and inner living; or it turns towards a concentration on an individual development of our surface nature, on the perfection of our thought and outer dynamic or practical action on the world, on some idealism of our personal relation with the world around us; or it turns rather towards a concentration on the outer world itself, on making it better, more suited to our ideas and temperament or to our conception of what should be. On one side there is the call of our spiritual being which is our true self, a transcendent reality, a being of the Divine Being, not created by the world, able to live in itself, to rise out of world to transcendence; on the other side there is the demand of the world around us which is a cosmic form, a formulation of the Divine Being, a power of the Reality in disguise. There is too the divided or double demand of our being of Nature which is poised between these two terms, depends on them and connects them; for it is apparently made by the world and yet, because its true creator is in ourselves and the world-instrumentation that seems to make it is only the means first used, it is really a form, a disguised manifestation of a greater spiritual being within us. It is this demand that mediates between our preoccupation with an inward perfection or spiritual liberation and our preoccupation with the outer world and its formation, insists on a happier relation between the two terms and creates the ideal of a better individual in a better world. But it is within us that the Reality must be found and the source and foundation of a perfected life; no outward formation can replace it: there must be the true self realised within if there is to be the true life realised in world and Nature.

In the growth into a divine life the Spirit must be our first preoccupation; until we have revealed and evolved it in our self out of its mental, vital, physical wrappings and disguises, extracted it with patience from our own body, as the Upanishad puts it, until we have built up in ourselves an inner life of the Spirit, it is obvious that no outer divine living can become possible. Unless, indeed, it is a mental or vital godhead that we perceive and would be, — but even then the individual mental being or the being of power and vital force and desire in us must grow into a form of that godhead before our life can be divine in that inferior sense, the life of the infraspiritual superman, mental demi-god or vital Titan, Deva or Asura. This inner life once created, to convert our whole surface being, our thought, feeling, action in the world, into a perfect power of that inner life, must be our other preoccupation. Only if we live in that deeper and greater way in our dynamic parts, can there be a force for creating a greater life or the world be remade whether in some power or perfection of Mind and Life or the power and perfection of the Spirit. A perfected human world cannot be created by men or composed of men who are themselves imperfect. Even if all our actions are scrupulously regulated by education or law or social or political machinery, what will be achieved is a regulated pattern of minds, a fabricated pattern of lives, a cultivated pattern of conduct; but a conformity of this kind cannot change, cannot re-create the man within, it cannot carve or cut out a perfect soul or a perfect thinking man or a perfect or growing living being. For soul and mind and life are powers of being and can grow but cannot be cut out or made; an outer process or formation can assist or can express soul and mind and life but cannot create or develop it. One can indeed help the being to grow, not by an attempt at manufacture, but by throwing on it stimulating influences or by lending to it one's forces of soul or mind or life; but even so the growth must still come from within it, determining from there what shall be made of these influences and forces, and not from outside. This is the first truth that our creative zeal and aspiration have to learn, otherwise all our human endeavour is foredoomed to turn in a futile circle and can end only in a success that is a specious failure.

To be or become something, to bring something into being is the whole labour of the force of Nature; to know, feel, do are subordinate energies that have a value because they help the being in its partial self-realisation to express what it is and help it too in its urge to express the still more not yet realised that it has to be. But knowledge, thought, action, — whether religious, ethical, political, social, economic, utilitarian or hedonistic, whether a mental, vital or physical form or construction of existence, — cannot be the essence or object of life; they are only activities of the powers of being or the powers of its becoming, dynamic symbols of itself, creations of the embodied Spirit, its means of discovering or formulating what it seeks to be. The tendency of man's physical mind is to see otherwise and to turn the true method of things upside down, because it takes as essential or fundamental the surface forces or appearances of Nature; it accepts her creation by a visible or exterior process as the essence of her action and does not see that it is only a secondary appearance and covers a greater secret process: for Nature's occult process is to reveal the being through the bringing out of its powers and forms, her external pressure is only a means of awakening the involved being to the need of this evolution, of this self-formation. When the spiritual stage of her evolution is reached, this occult process must become the whole process; to get through the veil of forces and get at their secret mainspring, which is the Spirit itself, is of cardinal importance. To become ourselves is the one thing to be done; but the true ourselves is that which is within us, and to exceed our outer self of body, life and mind is the condition for this highest being, which is our true and divine being, to become self-revealed and active. It is only by growing within and living within that we can find it; once that is done, to create from there the spiritual or divine mind, life, body and through this instrumentation to arrive at the creation of a world which shall be the true environment of a divine living, — this is the final object that Force of Nature has set before us. This then is the first necessity, that the individual, each individual, shall discover the Spirit, the divine reality within him and express that in all his being and living. A divine life must be first and foremost an inner life; for since the outward must be the expression of what is within, there can be no divinity in the outer existence if there is not the divinisation of the inner being. The Divinity in man dwells veiled in his spiritual centre; there can be no such thing as self-exceeding for man or a higher issue for his existence if there is not in him the reality of an eternal Self and Spirit.

To be and to be fully is Nature's aim in us; but to be fully is to be wholly conscious of one's being: unconsciousness, half consciousness or deficient consciousness is a state of being not in possession of itself; it is existence, but not fullness of being. To be aware wholly and integrally of oneself and of all the truth of one's being is the necessary condition of true possession of existence. This self-awareness is what is meant by spiritual knowledge: the essence of spiritual knowledge is an intrinsic self-existent consciousness; all its action of knowledge, indeed all its action of any kind, must be that consciousness formulating itself. All other knowledge is consciousness oblivious of itself and striving to return to its own awareness of itself and its contents; it is self-ignorance labouring to transform itself back into self-knowledge.

But also, since consciousness carries in itself the force of existence, to be fully is to have the intrinsic and integral force of one's being; it is to come into possession of all one's force of self and of all its use. To be merely, without possessing the force of one's being or with a half-force or deficient force of it, is a mutilated or diminished existence; it is to exist, but it is not fullness of being. It is possible, indeed, to exist only in status, with the force of being self-gathered and immobile in the self; but, even so, to be in dynamis as well as in status is the integrality of existence: power of self is the sign of the divinity of self, — a powerless Spirit is no Spirit. But, as the spiritual consciousness is intrinsic and self-existent, so too this force of our spiritual being must be intrinsic, automatic in action, self-existent and self-fulfilling. What instrumentality it uses, must be part of itself; even any external instrumentality it uses must be made part of itself and expressive of its being. Force of being in conscious action is will; and whatever is the conscious will of the Spirit, its will of being and becoming, that all the existence must be able harmonically to fulfil. Whatever action or energy of action has not this sovereignty or is not master of the machinery of action, carries in it by that defect the sign of an imperfection of the force of being, of a division or disabling segmentation of the consciousness, of an incompleteness in the manifestation of the being.

Lastly, to be fully is to have the full delight of being. Being without delight of being, without an entire delight of itself and all things is something neutral or diminished; it is existence, but it is not fullness of being. This delight too must be intrinsic, self-existent, automatic; it cannot be dependent on things outside itself: whatever it delights in, it makes part of itself, has the joy of it as part of its universality. All undelight, all pain and suffering are a sign of imperfection, of incompleteness; they arise from a division of being, an incompleteness of consciousness of being, an incompleteness of the force of being. To become complete in being, in consciousness of being, in force of being, in delight of being and to live in this integrated completeness is the divine living.

But, again, to be fully is to be universally. To be in the limitations of a small restricted ego is to exist, but it is an imperfect existence: in its very nature it is to live in an incomplete consciousness, an incomplete force and delight of existence. It is to be less than oneself and it brings an inevitable subjection to ignorance, weakness and suffering: or even if by some divine composition of the nature it could exclude these things, it would be to live in a limited scope of existence, a limited consciousness and power and joy of existence. All being is one and to be fully is to be all that is. To be in the being of all and to include all in one's being, to be conscious of the consciousness of all, to be integrated in force with the universal force, to carry all action and experience in oneself and feel it as one's own action and experience, to feel all selves as one's own self, to feel all delight of being as one's own delight of being is a necessary condition of the integral divine living.

But thus to be universally in the fullness and freedom of one's universality, one must be also transcendentally. The spiritual fullness of the being is eternity; if one has not the consciousness of timeless eternal being, if one is dependent on body or embodied mind or embodied life, or dependent on this world or that world or on this condition of being or that condition of being, that is not the reality of self, not the fullness of our spiritual existence. To live only as a self of body or be only by the body is to be an ephemeral creature, subject to death and desire and pain and suffering and decay and decadence. To transcend, to exceed consciousness of body, not to be held in the body or by the body, to hold the body only as an instrument, a minor outward formation of self, is a first condition of divine living. Not to be a mind subject to ignorance and restriction of consciousness, to transcend mind and handle it as an instrument, to control it as a surface formation of self, is a second condition. To be by the self and Spirit, not to depend upon life, not to be identified with it, to transcend it and control and use it as an expression and instrumentation of the self, is a third condition. Even the bodily life does not possess its own full being in its own kind if the consciousness does not exceed the body and feel its physical oneness with all material existence; the vital life does not possess its own full living in its own kind if the consciousness does not exceed the restricted play of an individual vitality and feel the universal life as its own and its oneness with all life. The mentality is not a full conscious existence or activity in its own kind if one does not exceed the individual mental limits and feel a oneness with universal Mind and with all minds and enjoy one's integrality of consciousness fulfilled in their wealth of difference. But one must transcend not only the individual formula but the formula of the universe, for only so can either the individual or the universal existence find its own true being and a perfect harmonisation; both are in their outer formulation incomplete terms of the Transcendence, but they are that in their essence, and it is only by becoming conscious of that essence, that individual consciousness or universal consciousness can come to its own fullness and freedom of reality. Otherwise the individual may remain subject to the cosmic movement and its reactions and limitations and miss his entire spiritual freedom. He must enter into the supreme divine Reality, feel his oneness with it, live in it, be its self-creation: all his mind, life, physicality must be converted into terms of its Supernature; all his thoughts, feelings, actions must be determined by it and be it, its self-formation. All this can become complete in him only when he has evolved out of the Ignorance into the Knowledge and through the Knowledge into the supreme Consciousness and its dynamis and supreme delight of existence; but some essentiality of these things and their sufficient instrumentation can come with the first spiritual change and culminate in the life of the gnostic Supernature.

These things are impossible without an inward living; they cannot be reached by remaining in an external consciousness turned always outwards, active only or mainly on and from the surface. The individual being has to find himself, his true existence; he can only do this by going inward, by living within and from within: for the external or outer consciousness or life separated from the inner Spirit is the field of the Ignorance; it can only exceed itself and exceed the Ignorance by opening into the largeness of an inner self and life. If there is a being of the transcendence in us, it must be there in our secret self; on the surface there is only an ephemeral being of nature, made by limit and circumstance. If there is a self in us capable of largeness and universality, able to enter into a cosmic consciousness, that too must be within our inner being; the outer consciousness is a physical consciousness bound to its individual limits by the triple cord of mind, life and body: any external attempt at universality can only result either in an aggrandisement of the ego or an effacement of the personality by its extinction in the mass or subjugation to the mass. It is only by an inner growth, movement, action that the individual can freely and effectively universalise and transcendentalise his being. There must be for the divine living a transference of the centre and immediate source of dynamic effectuation of the being from out inward; for there the soul is seated, but it is veiled or half veiled and our immediate being and source of action is for the present on the surface. In men, says the Upanishad, the Self-Existent has cut the doors of consciousness outward, but a few turn the eye inward and it is these who see and know the Spirit and develop the spiritual being. Thus to look into ourselves and see and enter into ourselves and live within is the first necessity for transformation of nature and for the divine life.

This movement of going inward and living inward is a difficult task to lay upon the normal consciousness of the human being; yet there is no other way of self-finding. The materialistic thinker, erecting an opposition between the extrovert and the introvert, holds up the extrovert attitude for acceptance as the only safety: to go inward is to enter into darkness or emptiness or to lose the balance of the consciousness and become morbid; it is from outside that such inner life as one can construct is created, and its health is assured only by a strict reliance on its wholesome and nourishing outer sources, — the balance of the personal mind and life can only be secured by a firm support on external reality, for the material world is the sole fundamental reality. This may be true for the physical man, the born extrovert, who feels himself to be a creature of outward Nature; made by her and dependent on her, he would lose himself if he went inward: for him there is no inner being, no inner living. But the introvert of this distinction also has not the inner life; he is not a seer of the true inner self and of inner things, but the small mental man who looks superficially inside himself and sees there not his spiritual self but his life-ego, his mind-ego and becomes unhealthily preoccupied with the movements of this little pitiful dwarf creature. The idea or experience of an inner darkness when looking inwards is the first reaction of a mentality which has lived always on the surface and has no realised inner existence; it has only a constructed internal experience which depends on the outside world for the materials of its being. But to those into whose composition there has entered the power of a more inner living, the movement of going within and living within brings not a darkness or dull emptiness but an enlargement, a rush of new experience, a greater vision, a larger capacity, an extended life infinitely more real and various than the first pettiness of the life constructed for itself by our normal physical humanity, a joy of being which is larger and richer than any delight in existence that the outer vital man or the surface mental man can gain by their dynamic vital force and activity or subtlety and expansion of the mental existence. A silence, an entry into a wide or even immense or infinite emptiness is part of the inner spiritual experience; of this silence and void the physical mind has a certain fear, the small superficially active thinking or vital mind a shrinking from it or dislike, — for it confuses the silence with mental and vital incapacity and the void with cessation or non-existence: but this silence is the silence of the Spirit which is the condition of a greater knowledge, power and bliss, and this emptiness is the emptying of the cup of our natural being, a liberation of it from its turbid contents so that it may be filled with the wine of God; it is the passage not into non-existence but to a greater existence. Even when the being turns towards cessation, it is a cessation not in non-existence but into some vast ineffable of spiritual being or the plunge into the incommunicable superconscience of the Absolute.

In fact, this inward turning and movement is not an imprisonment in personal self, it is the first step towards a true universality; it brings to us the truth of our external as well as the truth of our internal existence. For this inner living can extend itself and embrace the universal life, it can contact, penetrate, englobe the life of all with a much greater reality and dynamic force than is in our surface consciousness at all possible. Our utmost universalisation on the surface is a poor and limping endeavour, — it is a construction, a make-believe and not the real thing: for in our surface consciousness we are bound to separation of consciousness from others and wear the fetters of the ego. There our very selflessness becomes more often than not a subtle form of selfishness or turns into a larger affirmation of our ego; content with our pose of altruism, we do not see that it is a veil for the imposition of our individual self, our ideas, our mental and vital personality, our need of ego-enlargement upon the others whom we take up into our expanded orbit. So far as we really succeed in living for others, it is done by an inner spiritual force of love and sympathy; but the power and field of effectuality of this force in us are small, the psychic movement that prompts it is incomplete, its action often ignorant because there is contact of mind and heart but our being does not embrace the being of others as ourselves. An external unity with others must always be an outward joining and association of external lives with a minor inner result; the mind and heart attach their movements to this common life and the beings whom we meet there; but the common external life remains the foundation, — the inward constructed unity, or so much of it as can persist in spite of mutual ignorance and discordant egoisms, conflict of minds, conflict of hearts, conflict of vital temperaments, conflict of interests, is a partial and insecure superstructure. The spiritual consciousness, the spiritual life reverses this principle of building; it bases its action in the collective life upon an inner experience and inclusion of others in our own being, an inner sense and reality of oneness. The spiritual individual acts out of that sense of oneness which gives him immediate and direct perception of the demand of self on other self, the need of the life, the good, the work of love and sympathy that can truly be done. A realisation of spiritual unity, a dynamisation of the intimate consciousness of one-being, of one self in all beings, can alone found and govern by its truth the action of the divine life.

In the gnostic or divine being, in the gnostic life, there will be a close and complete consciousness of the self of others, a consciousness of their mind, life, physical being which are felt as if they were one's own. The gnostic being will act, not out of a surface sentiment of love and sympathy or any similar feeling, but out of this close mutual consciousness, this intimate oneness. All his action in the world will be enlightened by a truth of vision of what has to be done, a sense of the will of the Divine Reality in him which is also the Divine Reality in others, and it will be done for the Divine in others and the Divine in all, for the effectuation of the truth of purpose of the All as seen in the light of the highest Consciousness and in the way and by the steps through which it must be effectuated in the power of the Supernature. The gnostic being finds himself not only in his own fulfilment, which is the fulfilment of the Divine Being and Will in him, but in the fulfilment of others; his universal individuality effectuates itself in the movement of the All in all beings towards its greater becoming. He sees a divine working everywhere; what goes out from him into the sum of that divine working, from the inner Light, Will, Force that works in him, is his action. There is no separative ego in him to initiate anything; it is the Transcendent and Universal that moves out through his universalised individuality into the action of the universe. As he does not live for a separate ego, so too he does not live for the purpose of any collective ego; he lives in and for the Divine in himself, in and for the Divine in the collectivity, in and for the Divine in all beings. This universality in action, organised by the all-seeing Will in the sense of the realised oneness of all, is the law of his divine living.

It is, then, this spiritual fulfilment of the urge to individual perfection and an inner completeness of being that we mean first when we speak of a divine life. It is the first essential condition of a perfected life on earth, and we are therefore right in making the utmost possible individual perfection our first supreme business. The perfection of the spiritual and pragmatic relation of the individual with all around him is our second preoccupation; the solution of this second desideratum lies in a complete universality and oneness with all life upon earth which is the other concomitant result of an evolution into the gnostic consciousness and nature. But there still remains the third desideratum, a new world, a change in the total life of humanity or, at the least, a new perfected collective life in the earth-nature. This calls for the appearance not only of isolated evolved individuals acting in the unevolved mass, but of many gnostic individuals forming a new kind of beings and a new common life superior to the present individual and common existence. A collective life of this kind must obviously constitute itself on the same principle as the life of the gnostic individual. In our present human existence there is a physical collectivity held together by the common physical life-fact and all that arises from it, community of interests, a common civilisation and culture, a common social law, an aggregate mentality, an economic association, the ideals, emotions, endeavours of the collective ego with the strand of individual ties and connections running through the whole and helping to keep it together. Or, where there is a difference in these things, opposition, conflict, a practical accommodation or an organised compromise is enforced by the necessity of living together; there is erected a natural or a constructed order. This would not be the gnostic divine way of collective living; for there what would bind and hold all together would be, not the fact of life creating a sufficiently united social consciousness, but a common consciousness consolidating a common life. All will be united by the evolution of the Truth-Consciousness in them; in the changed way of being which this consciousness would bring about in them, they will feel themselves to be embodiments of a single self, souls of a single Reality; illumined and motived by a fundamental unity of knowledge, actuated by a fundamental unified will and feeling, a life expressing the spiritual Truth would find through them its own natural forms of becoming. An order there would be, for truth of oneness creates its own order: a law or laws of living there might be, but these would be self-determined; they would be an expression of the truth of a spiritually united being and the truth of a spiritually united life. The whole formation of the common existence would be a self-building of the spiritual forces that must work themselves out spontaneously in such a life: these forces would be received inwardly by the inner being and expressed or self-expressed in a native harmony of idea and action and purpose.

An increasing mechanisation, a standardisation, a fixing of all into a common mould in order to ensure harmony is the mental method, but that would not be the law of this living. There would be a considerable free diversity between different gnostic communities; each would create its own body of the life of the spirit: there would be, too, a considerable free diversity in the self-expression of the individuals of a single community. But this free diversity would not be a chaos or create any discord; for a diversity of one Truth of knowledge and one Truth of life would be a correlation and not an opposition. In a gnostic consciousness there would be no ego-insistence on personal idea and no push or clamour of personal will and interest: there would be instead the unifying sense of a common Truth in many forms, a common self in many consciousnesses and bodies; there would be a universality and plasticity which saw and expressed the One in many figures of itself and worked out oneness in all diversities as the inherent law of the Truth-Consciousness and its truth of nature. A single Consciousness-Force, of which all would be aware and see themselves as its instruments, would act through all and harmonise their action together. The gnostic being would feel a single consonant Force of Supernature acting in all: he would accept its formation in himself and obey or use the knowledge and power it gave him for the divine work, but he would be under no urge or compulsion to set the power and knowledge in him against the power and knowledge of others or affirm himself as an ego striving against other egos. For the spiritual self has its own inalienable joy and plenitude inviolable in all conditions, its own infinity of truth of being: that it feels always in fullness whatever may be the outward formulation. The truth of the Spirit within would not depend on a particular formation; it would have no need, therefore, to struggle for any particular outward formulation and self-affirmation: forms would arise of themselves plastically, in suitable relation to other formulations and each in its own place in the whole formulation. Truth of gnostic consciousness and being establishing itself can find its harmony with all other truth of being around it. A spiritual or gnostic being would feel his harmony with the whole gnostic life around him, whatever his position in the whole. According to his place in it he would know how to lead or to rule, but also how to subordinate himself; both would be to him an equal delight: for the Spirit's freedom, because it is eternal, self-existent and inalienable, can be felt as much in service and willing subordination and adjustment with other selves as in power and rule. An inner spiritual freedom can accept its place in the truth of an inner spiritual hierarchy as well as in the truth, not incompatible with it, of a fundamental spiritual equality. It is this self-arrangement of Truth, a natural order of the Spirit, that would exist in a common life of different degrees and stages of the evolving gnostic being. Unity is the basis of the gnostic consciousness, mutuality the natural result of its direct awareness of oneness in diversity, harmony the inevitable power of the working of its force. Unity, mutuality and harmony must therefore be the inescapable law of a common or collective gnostic life. What forms it might take would depend upon the will of evolutionary manifestation of the Supernature, but this would be its general character and principle.

This is the whole sense and the inherent law and necessity of the passage from the purely mental and material being and life to the spiritual and supramental being and life, that the liberation, perfection, self-fulfilment for which the being in the Ignorance is seeking can only be reached by passing out of his present nature of Ignorance into a nature of spiritual self-knowledge and world-knowledge. This greater nature we speak of as Supernature because it is beyond his actual level of consciousness and capacity; but in fact it is his own true nature, the height and completeness of it, to which he must arrive if he is to find his real self and whole possibility of being. Whatever happens in Nature must be the result of Nature, the effectuation of what is implied or inherent in it, its inevitable fruit and consequence. If our nature is a fundamental Inconscience and Ignorance arriving with difficulty at an imperfect knowledge, an imperfect formulation of consciousness and being, the results in our being, life and action and creation must be, as they now are, a constant imperfection and insecure half result, an imperfect mentality, an imperfect life, an imperfect physical existence. We seek to construct systems of knowledge and systems of life by which we can arrive at some perfection of our existence, some order of right relations, right use of mind, right use and happiness and beauty of life, right use of the body. But what we achieve is a constructed half-rightness mixed with much that is wrong and unlovely and unhappy; our successive constructions, because of the vice in them and because mind and life cannot rest permanently anywhere in their seeking, are exposed to destruction, decadence, disruption of their order, and we pass from them to others which are not more finally successful or enduring, even if on one side or another they may be richer and fuller or more rationally plausible. It cannot be otherwise, because we can construct nothing which goes beyond our nature; imperfect, we cannot construct perfection, however wonderful may seem to us the machinery our mental ingenuity invents, however externally effective. Ignorant, we cannot construct a system of entirely true and fruitful self-knowledge or world-knowledge: our science itself is a construction, a mass, of formulas and devices; masterful in knowledge of processes and in the creation of apt machinery, but ignorant of the foundations of our being and of world-being, it cannot perfect our nature and therefore cannot perfect our life.

Our nature, our consciousness is that of beings ignorant of each other, separated from each other, rooted in a divided ego, who must strive to establish some kind of relation between their embodied ignorances; for the urge to union and forces making for union are there in Nature. Individual and group harmonies of a comparative and qualified completeness are created, a social cohesion is accomplished; but in the mass the relations formed are constantly marred by imperfect sympathy, imperfect understanding, gross misunderstandings, strife, discord, unhappiness. It cannot be otherwise so long as there is no true union of consciousness founded upon a nature of self-knowledge, inner mutual knowledge, inner realisation of unity, concord of our inner forces of being and inner forces of life. In our social building we labour to establish some approach to unity, mutuality, harmony, because without these things there can be no perfect social living; but what we build is a constructed unity, an association of interests and egos enforced by law and custom and imposing an artificial constructed order in which the interests of some prevail over the interests of others and only a half accepted

half enforced, half natural half artificial accommodation keeps
the social whole in being. Between community and community
there is a still worse accommodation with a constant recurrence
of the strife of collective ego with collective ego. This is the best
that we can do and all our persistent readjustments of the social
order can bring us nothing better than an imperfect structure of
life.

It is only if our nature develops beyond itself, if it becomes a
nature of self-knowledge, mutual understanding, unity, a nature
of true being and true life that the result can be a perfection of
ourselves and our existence, a life of true being, a life of unity,
mutuality, harmony, a life of true happiness, a harmonious and
beautiful life. If our nature is fixed in what it is, what it has
already become, then no perfection, no real and enduring happiness is possible in earthly life; we must seek it not at all and
do the best we can with our imperfections, or we must seek it
elsewhere, in a supraterrestrial hereafter, or we must go beyond
all such seeking and transcend life by an extinction of nature and
ego in some Absolute from which this strange and unsatisfactory being of ours has come into existence. But if in us there is a
spiritual being which is emerging and our present state is only an
imperfection or half-emergence, if the Inconscient is a starting-
point containing in itself the potency of a Superconscience and
Supernature which has to evolve, a veil of apparent Nature in
which that greater consciousness is concealed and from which it
has to unfold itself, if an evolution of being is the law, then what
we are seeking for is not only possible but part of the eventual
necessity of things. It is our spiritual destiny to manifest and ·
become that Supernature, — for it is the nature of our true self,
our still occult, because unevolved, whole being. A nature of
unity will then bring inevitably its life-result of unity, mutuality,
harmony. An inner life awakened to a full consciousness and to
a full power of consciousness will bear its inevitable fruit in all
who have it, self-knowledge, a perfected existence, the joy of a
satisfied being, the happiness of a fulfilled nature.

An innate character of the gnostic consciousness and the
instrumentation of Supernature is a wholeness of sight and

action, a unity of knowledge with knowledge, a reconciliation of all that seems contrary in our mental seeing and knowing, an identity of Knowledge and Will acting as a single power in perfect unison with the truth of things; this inborn character of Supernature is the foundation of the perfect unity, mutuality, harmony of its action. In the mental being there is a discord of its constructed knowledge with the real or the whole truth of things, so that even what is true in it is often or is eventually ineffective or only partially effective. Our discoveries of truth are overthrown, our passionate effectuations of truth are frustrated; often the result of our action becomes part of a scheme we did not intend for a purpose whose legitimacy we would not acknowledge, or the truth of the idea is deceived by the actual outcome of its pragmatic success. Even if there is a successful realisation of the idea, yet because the idea is incomplete, an isolated construction of the mind separate from the one and whole truth of things, its success must sooner or later end in disillusionment and a new endeavour. The discordance of our seeing and our notions with the true truth and the whole truth of things, the partiality and superficiality of our mind's deceptive constructions, is the cause of our frustration. But there is also not only a discord of knowledge with knowledge but of will with will and of knowledge with will in the same being, a division and disharmony between them, so that where the knowledge is ripe or sufficient some will in the being opposes it or the will fails it; where the will is powerful, vehement or firmly or forcefully effective, knowledge guiding it to its right use is lacking. All kinds of disparity and maladjustment and incompleteness of our knowledge, will, capacity, executive force and dealing intervene constantly in our action, our working out of life, and are an abundant source of imperfection or ineffectivity. These disorders, defects and disharmonies are normal to a status and energy of Ignorance and can only be dissolved by a greater light than that of mind-nature or life-nature. An identity and authenticity and a harmony of truth with truth are the native character of all gnostic seeing and action; as the mind grows into the gnosis, our mental seeing and action lifted into the gnostic light or visited and ruled by it would begin to partake of this character and, even if still restricted and within limits, must become much more perfect and within these limits effective: the causes of our incapacity and frustration would begin to diminish and disappear. But also the larger existence will invade the mind with the potencies of a greater consciousness and a greater force, a bringing out of new powers of the being. Knowledge is power and act of consciousness, Will is conscious power and conscious act of force of being; both in the gnostic being will reach greater magnitudes than any we now know, a higher degree of themselves, a richer instrumentation: for wherever there is an increase of consciousness, there is an increase of the potential force and the actual power of the existence.

In the terrestrial formulation of Knowledge and Power, this correlation is not altogether apparent because there consciousness itself is concealed in an original Inconscience and the natural strength and rhythm of its powers in their emergence are diminished and disturbed by the discordances and the veils of the Ignorance. The Inconscient there is the original, potent and automatically effective Force, the conscious mind is only a small labouring agent; but that is because the conscious mind in us has a limited individual action and the Inconscient is an immense action of a universal concealed Consciousness: the cosmic Force, masked as a material Energy, hides from our view by its insistent materiality of process the occult fact that the working of the Inconscient is really the expression of a vast universal Life, a veiled universal Mind, a hooded Gnosis, and without these origins of itself it could have no power of action, no organising coherence. Life-Force also in the material world seems to be more dynamic and effective than Mind; our Mind is free and fully powerful in idea and cognition only: its force of action, its power of effectuation outside this mental field is obliged to work with Life and Matter as instruments and, under the conditions imposed on it by Life and Matter, our Mind is hampered and half-effective. But even so we see that Nature-force in the mental being is much more powerful to deal with himself and with Life and Matter than Nature-force in the animal; it is the greater force of consciousness and knowledge, the greater emerged force of being and will that constitute this superiority. In human life itself the vital man seems to have a stronger dynamis of action than the mental man because of his superiority in kinetic life-force: the intellectual tends to be effective in thought but ineffective in power over the world, while the kinetic vital man of action dominates life. But it is his use of Mind that enables him to arrive at a full exploitation of this superiority, and in the end the mental man by his power of knowledge, his science, is able to extend the mastery of existence far beyond what Life in Matter could accomplish by its own agencies or what the vital man could accomplish with his life-force and life-instinct without that increase of effective knowledge. An immensely greater power over existence and over Nature must come when a still greater consciousness emerges and replaces the hampered operations of the mental Energy in our too individualised and restricted force of existence.

A certain fundamental subjection of Mind to Life and Matter and an acceptance of this subjection, an inability to make the law of Mind directly dominant and modify by its powers the blinder law and operations of these inferior forces of being, remains even in the midst of our greatest mental mastery over self and things; but this limitation is not insuperable. It is the interest of occult knowledge that it shows us, — and a dynamic force of spiritual knowledge brings us the same evidence, — that this subjection of Mind to Matter, of the Spirit to a lesser law of Life is not what it at first appears to be, a fundamental condition of things, an inviolable and unalterable rule of Nature. The greatest, most momentous natural discovery that man can make is this that Mind, and still more the force of the Spirit, can in many tried and yet untried ways and in all directions, — by its own nature and direct power and not only by devices and contrivances such as the superior material instrumentation discovered by physical Science, — overcome and control Life and Matter. In the evolution of the gnostic supernature this direct power of consciousness, this direct action of the force of the being, its free mastery and control of Life and Matter, would be consummated and reach their acme. For the greater knowledge of the gnostic being would not be in the main an outwardly acquired or learned knowledge, but the result of an evolution of consciousness and of the force of consciousness, a new dynamisation of the being. As a consequence, he would awake to and possess many things, a clear and complete knowledge of self, a direct knowledge of others, a direct knowledge of hidden forces, a direct knowledge of the occult mechanism of Mind and Life and Matter, which are beyond our present attainment. This new knowledge and action of knowledge would be based on an immediate intuitive consciousness of things and an immediate intuitive control of things; an operative insight, now supernormal to us, would be the normal functioning of this consciousness, and an integral assured effectivity both in the mass of action and in its detail would be the outcome of the change. For the gnostic being would be in unison and communion with the Consciousness-Force that is at the root of everything: his vision and his will would be the channel of the supramental Real-Idea, the self-effective Truth-Force; his action would be a free manifestation of the power and workings of the root Force of existence, the force of an all-determining conscious Spirit whose formulations of consciousness work out inevitably in Mind, Life and Matter. Acting in the light and power of the supramental knowledge, the evolving gnostic being would be more and more master of himself, master of the forces of consciousness, master of the energies of Nature, master of his instrumentation of Life and Matter. In the lesser status, the intermediate stages or formations of the evolving gnostic nature, this power would not be present in its fullness: but in some degree of its activities it would be there; incipient and increasing with the ascent of the scale, it would be a natural concomitant of the growth of consciousness and knowledge.

A new power and powers of consciousness would be, then, an inevitable consequence of an evolution of Consciousness-Force passing beyond Mind to a superior cognitive and dynamic principle. In their essential nature these new powers must have the character of a control of Mind over Life and Matter, of the conscious Life-will and Life-force over Matter, of the spirit over mind, life and matter; they would have the character also of a breaking down of the barriers between soul and soul, mind and mind, life and life: such a change would be indispensable for the instrumentation of the gnostic life. For a total gnostic or divine living would include not only the individual life of the being but the life of others made one with the individual in a common uniting consciousness. Such a life must have for its main constituting power a spontaneous and innate, not a constructed, unity and harmony; this can only come by a greater identity of being and consciousness between individual and individual unified in their spiritual substance, feeling themselves to be self and self of one self-existence, acting in a greater unitarian force of knowledge, a greater power of the being. There must be an inner and direct mutual knowledge based upon a consciousness of oneness and identity, a consciousness of each other's being, thought, feeling, inner and outer movements, a conscious communication of mind with mind, of heart with heart, a conscious impact of life upon life, a conscious interchange of forces of being with forces of being; in any absence or deficiency of these powers and their intimate light there could not be a real or complete unity or a real and complete natural fitting of each individual's being, thought, feeling, inner and outer movements with those of the individuals around him. A growing basis and structure of conscious unanimism, we might say, would be the character of this more evolved life.

Harmony is the natural rule of the Spirit, it is the inherent law and spontaneous consequence of unity in multiplicity, of unity in diversity, of a various manifestation of oneness. In a pure and blank unity there could be indeed no place for harmony, for there is nothing to harmonise; in a complete or a governing diversity there must be either discord or a fitting together of differences, a constructed harmony. But in a gnostic unity in multiplicity the harmony would be there as a spontaneous expression of the unity, and this spontaneous expression presupposes a mutuality of consciousness aware of other consciousness by a direct inner contact and interchange. In infrarational life harmony is

secured by an instinctive oneness of nature and oneness of the
action of the nature, an instinctive communication, an instinctive or direct vital-intuitional sense-understanding by which the
individuals of an animal or insect community are able to co-
operate. In human life this is replaced by understanding through
sense-knowledge and mental perception and communication of
ideas by speech, but the means that have to be used are imperfect
and the harmony and cooperation incomplete. In a gnostic life, a
life of superreason and supernature, a self-aware spiritual unity
of being and a spiritual conscious community and interchange
of nature would be the deep and ample root of understanding:
this greater life would have evolved new and superior means
and powers of uniting consciousness inwardly with consciousness; intimacy of consciousness communicating inwardly and
directly with consciousness, thought with thought, vision with
vision, sense with sense, life with life, body-awareness with
body-awareness, would be its natural basic instrumentation. All
these new powers taking up the old outward instruments and
using them as a subordinate means with a far greater power
and to more purpose would be put to the service of the self-
expression of the Spirit in a profound oneness of being and
life.

An evolution of innate and latent but as yet unevolved
powers of consciousness is not considered admissible by the
modern mind, because these exceed our present formulation
of Nature and, to our ignorant preconceptions founded on a
limited experience, they seem to belong to the supernatural, to
the miraculous and occult; for they surpass the known action
of material Energy which is now ordinarily accepted as the sole
cause and mode of things and the sole instrumentation of the
World-Force. A human working of marvels, by the conscious
being discovering and developing an instrumentation of material
forces overpassing anything that Nature has herself organised,
is accepted as a natural fact and an almost unlimited prospect of
our existence; an awakening, a discovery, an instrumentation of
powers of consciousness and of spiritual, mental and life forces
overpassing anything that Nature or man has yet organised is

not admitted as possible. But there would be nothing supernatural or miraculous in such an evolution, except in so far as it would be a supernature or superior nature to ours just as human nature is a supernature or superior nature to that of animal or plant or material objects. Our mind and its powers, our use of reason, our mental intuition and insight, speech, possibilities of philosophical, scientific, aesthetic discovery of the truths and potencies of being and a control of its forces are an evolution that has taken place: yet it would seem impossible if we took our stand on the limited animal consciousness and its capacities; for there is nothing there to warrant so prodigious a progression. But still there are vague initial manifestations, rudimentary elements or arrested possibilities in the animal to which our reason and intelligence with their extraordinary developments stand as an unimaginable journey from a poor and unpromising point of departure. The rudiments of spiritual powers belonging to the gnostic Supernature are similarly there even in our ordinary composition, but only occasionally and sparsely active. It is not irrational to suppose that at this much higher stage of the evolution a similar but greater progression starting from these rudimentary beginnings might lead to another immense development and departure.

In mystic experience, — when there is an opening of the inner centres, or in other ways, spontaneously or by will or endeavour or in the very course of the spiritual growth, — new powers of consciousness have been known to develop; they present themselves as if an automatic consequence of some inner opening or in answer to a call in the being, so much so that it has been found necessary to recommend to the seeker not to hunt after these powers, not to accept or use them. This rejection is logical for those who seek to withdraw from life; for all acceptance of greater power would bind to life or be a burden on the bare and pure urge towards liberation. An indifference to all other aims and issues is natural for the God-lover who seeks God for His own sake and not for power or any other inferior attraction; the pursuit of these alluring but often dangerous forces would be a deviation from his purpose.

A similar rejection is a necessary self-restraint and a spiritual discipline for the immature seeker, since such powers may be a great, even a deadly peril; for their supernormality may easily feed in him an abnormal exaggeration of the ego. Power in itself may be dreaded as a temptation by the aspirant to perfection, because power can abase as well as elevate; nothing is more liable to misuse. But when new capacities come as an inevitable result of the growth into a greater consciousness and a greater life and that growth is part of the very aim of the spiritual being within us, this bar does not operate; for a growth of the being into Supernature and its life in Supernature cannot take place or cannot be complete without bringing with it a greater power of consciousness and a greater power of life and the spontaneous development of an instrumentation of knowledge and force normal to that Supernature. There is nothing in this future evolution of the being which could be regarded as irrational or incredible; there is nothing in it abnormal or miraculous: it would be the necessary course of the evolution of consciousness and its forces in the passage from the mental to the gnostic or supramental formulation of our existence. This action of the forces of Supernature would be a natural, normal and spontaneously simple working of the new higher or greater consciousness into which the being enters in the course of his self-evolution; the gnostic being accepting the gnostic life would develop and use the powers of this greater consciousness, even as man develops and uses the powers of his mental nature.

It is evident that such an increase of the power or powers of consciousness would be not only normal but indispensable to a greater and more perfect life. Human life with its partial harmony, in so far as that is not maintained by the imposition of a settled law and order on the constituent individuals through a partly willing, partly induced, partly forced or unavoidable acceptance, reposes on the agreement of the enlightened or interested elements in their mind, heart, life-sense, an assent to a composite body of common ideas, desires, vital satisfactions, aims of existence. But there is in the mass of constituting individuals an imperfect understanding and knowledge of the ideas, life-aims, life-motives which they have accepted, an imperfect power in their execution, an imperfect will to maintain them always unimpaired, to carry them out fully or to bring the life to a greater perfection; there is an element of struggle and discord, a mass of repressed or unfulfilled desires and frustrated wills, a simmering suppressed unsatisfaction or an awakened or eruptive discontent or unequally satisfied interests; there are new ideas, life-motives that break in and cannot be correlated without upheaval and disturbance; there are life-forces at work in human beings and their environment that are at variance with the harmony that has been constructed, and there is not the full power to overcome the discords and dislocations created by a clashing diversity of mind and life and by the attack of disrupting forces in universal Nature. What is lacking is a spiritual knowledge and spiritual power, a power over self, a power born of inner unification with others, a power over the surrounding or invading world-forces, a full-visioned and fully equipped power of effectuation of knowledge; it is these capacities missing or defective in us that belong to the very substance of gnostic being, for they are inherent in the light and dynamis of the gnostic nature.

But, in addition to the imperfect accommodation of the minds, hearts, lives of the constituting individuals in a human society, the mind and the life of the individual himself are actuated by forces that are not in accord with each other; our attempts to accord them are imperfect, and still more imperfect is our force to put any one of them into integral or satisfying execution in life. Thus the law of love and sympathy is natural to our consciousness; as we grow in Spirit, its demand on us increases: but there is also the demand of the intellect, the push of the vital force and its impulses in us, the claim and pressure of many other elements that do not coincide with the law of love and sympathy, nor do we know how to fit them all into the whole law of existence or to render any or all of them either justly and entirely effective or imperative. In order to make them concordant and actively fruitful in the whole being and whole life, we have to grow into a more complete spiritual nature; we have, by that growth, to live in the light and force of a higher and larger and more integral consciousness of which knowledge and power, love and sympathy and play of life-will are all natural and ever-present accorded elements; we have to move and act in a light of Truth which sees intuitively and spontaneously the thing to be done and the way to do it and intuitively and spontaneously fulfils itself in the act, and the force, — taking up into that intuitive spontaneity of their truth, into its simple spiritual and supreme normality, the complexity of our forces of being and suffusing with their harmonised realities all the steps of Nature.

It should be evident that no rationalised piecing together or ingenuity of mental construction can accord or harmonise this complexity; it is only the intuition and self-knowledge of an awakened Spirit that can do it. That would be the nature of the evolved supramental being and his existence; his spiritual sight and sense would take up all the forces of the being in a unifying consciousness and bring them into a normality of accorded action: for this accord and concord are the true normality of the Spirit; the discord, the disharmony of our life and nature is abnormal to it although it is normal to the life of the Ignorance. It is indeed because it is not normal to the Spirit that a knowledge within us is dissatisfied and strives towards a greater harmony in our existence. This accord and concord of the whole being, which is natural to the gnostic individual, would be equally natural to a community of gnostic beings; for it would rest on a union of self with self in the light of a common and mutual self-awareness. It is true that in the total terrestrial existence of which the gnostic life would be a part, there would be still continuing within it a life belonging to a less evolved order; the intuitive and gnostic life would have to fit into this total existence and carry into it as much of its own law of unity and harmony as may be possible. Here the law of spontaneous harmony might seem to be inapplicable, since the relation of the gnostic life with the ignorant life around it would not be founded on a mutuality of self-knowledge and a sense of one being and common consciousness; it would be a relation of action of knowledge to action of ignorance. But this difficulty need not be so great as it seems now to us; for the gnostic knowledge would carry in it a perfect understanding of the consciousness of the Ignorance, and it would not be impossible, therefore, for an assured gnostic life to harmonise its existence with that of all the less developed life co-existent with it in the earth-nature.

If this is our evolutionary destiny, it remains for us to see where we stand at this juncture in the evolutionary progression, — a progression which has been cyclic or spiral rather than in a straight line or has at least journeyed in a very zigzag swinging curve of advance, — and what prospect there is of any turn towards a decisive step in the near or measurable future. In our human aspiration towards a personal perfection and the perfection of the life of the race the elements of the future evolution are foreshadowed and striven after, but in a confusion of half-enlightened knowledge; there is a discord between the necessary elements, an opposing emphasis, a profusion of rudimentary unsatisfying and ill-accorded solutions. These sway between the three principal preoccupations of our idealism, — the complete single development of the human being in himself, the perfectibility of the individual, a full development of the collective being, the perfectibility of society, and, more pragmatically restricted, the perfect or best possible relations of individual with individual and society and of community with community. An exclusive or dominant emphasis is laid sometimes on the individual, sometimes on the collectivity or society, sometimes on a right and balanced relation between the individual and the collective human whole. One idea holds up the growing life, freedom or perfection of the human individual as the true object of our existence, — whether the ideal be merely a free self-expression of the personal being or a self-governed whole of complete mind, fine and ample life and perfect body, or a spiritual perfection and liberation. In this view society is there only as a field of activity and growth for the individual man and serves best its function when it gives as far as possible a wide room, ample means, a sufficient freedom or guidance of development to his thought, his action, his growth, his possibility of fullness of being. An opposite idea gives the collective life the first or the sole importance; the existence, the growth of the race is all: the individual has to live for the society or for mankind, or, even, he is only a cell of the society, he has no other use or purpose of birth, no other meaning of his presence in Nature, no other function. Or it is held that the nation, the society, the community is a collective being, revealing its soul in its culture, power of life, ideals, institutions, all its ways of self-expression; the individual life has to cast itself in that mould of culture, serve that power of life, consent only to exist as an instrument for the maintenance and efficiency of the collective existence. In another idea the perfection of man lies in his ethical and social relations with other men; he is a social being and has to live for society, for others, for his utility to the race: the society also is there for the service of all, to give them their right relation, education, training, economic opportunity, right frame of life. In the ancient cultures the greatest emphasis was laid on the community and the fitting of the individual into the community, but also there grew up an idea of the perfected individual; in ancient India it was the idea of the spiritual individual that was dominant, but the society was of extreme importance because in it and under its moulding influence the individual had to pass first through the social status of the physical, vital, mental being with his satisfaction of interest, desire, pursuit of knowledge and right living before he could reach fitness for a truer self-realisation and a free spiritual existence. In recent times the whole stress has passed to the life of the race, to a search for the perfect society, and latterly to a concentration on the right organisation and scientific mechanisation of the life of mankind as a whole; the individual now tends more to be regarded only as a member of the collectivity, a unit of the race whose existence must be subordinated to the common aims and total interest of the organised society, and much less or not at all as a mental or spiritual being with his own right and power of existence. This tendency has not yet reached its acme everywhere, but everywhere it is rapidly increasing and heading towards dominance.

Thus, in the vicissitudes of human thought, on one side the

individual is moved or invited to discover and pursue his own self-affirmation, his own development of mind and life and body, his own spiritual perfection; on the other he is called on to efface and subordinate himself and to accept the ideas, ideals, wills, instincts, interests of the community as his own. He is moved by Nature to live for himself and by something deep within him to affirm his individuality; he is called upon by society and by a certain mental idealism to live for humanity or for the greater good of the community. The principle of self and its interest is met and opposed by the principle of altruism. The State erects its godhead and demands his obedience, submission, subordination, self-immolation; the individual has to affirm against this exorbitant claim the rights of his ideals, his ideas, his personality, his conscience. It is evident that all this conflict of standards is a groping of the mental Ignorance of man seeking to find its way and grasping different sides of the truth but unable by its want of integrality in knowledge to harmonise them together. A unifying and harmonising knowledge can alone find the way, but that knowledge belongs to a deeper principle of our being to which oneness and integrality are native. It is only by finding that in ourselves that we can solve the problem of our existence and with it the problem of the true way of individual and communal living.

There is a Reality, a truth of all existence which is greater and more abiding than all its formations and manifestations; to find that truth and Reality and live in it, achieve the most perfect manifestation and formation possible of it, must be the secret of perfection whether of individual or communal being. This Reality is there within each thing and gives to each of its formations its power of being and value of being. The universe is a manifestation of the Reality, and there is a truth of the universal existence, a Power of cosmic being, an all-self or world-spirit. Humanity is a formation or manifestation of the Reality in the universe, and there is a truth and self of humanity, a human spirit, a destiny of human life. The community is a formation of the Reality, a manifestation of the spirit of man, and there is a truth, a self, a power of the collective being. The individual is a formation of the Reality, and there is a truth of the individual, an individual self, soul or spirit that expresses itself through the individual mind, life and body and can express itself too in something that goes beyond mind, life and body, something even that goes beyond humanity. For our humanity is not the whole of the Reality or its best possible self-formation or self-expression, — the Reality has assumed before man existed an infrahuman formation and self-creation and can assume after him or in him a suprahuman formation and self-creation. The individual as spirit or being is not confined within his humanity; he has been less than human, he can become more than human. The universe finds itself through him even as he finds himself in the universe, but he is capable of becoming more than the universe, since he can surpass it and enter into something in himself and in it and beyond it that is absolute. He is not confined within the community; although his mind and life are, in a way, part of the communal mind and life, there is something in him that can go beyond them. The community exists by the individual, for its mind and life and body are constituted by the mind and life and body of its composing individuals; if that were abolished or disaggregated, its own existence would be abolished or disaggregated, though some spirit or power of it might form again in other individuals: but the individual is not a mere cell of the collective existence; he would not cease to exist if separated or expelled from the collective mass. For the collectivity, the community is not even the whole of humanity and it is not the world: the individual can exist and find himself elsewhere in humanity or by himself in the world. If the community has a life dominating that of the individuals which constitute it, still it does not constitute their whole life. If it has its being which it seeks to affirm by the life of the individuals, the individual also has a being of his own which he seeks to affirm in the life of the community. But he is not tied to that, he can affirm himself in another communal life, or, if he is strong enough, in a nomad existence or in an eremite solitude where, if he cannot pursue or achieve a complete material living, he can spiritually exist and find his own reality and indwelling self of being.

The individual is indeed the key of the evolutionary movement; for it is the individual who finds himself, who becomes conscious of the Reality. The movement of the collectivity is a largely subconscious mass-movement; it has to formulate and express itself through the individuals to become conscious: its general mass-consciousness is always less evolved than the consciousness of its most developed individuals, and it progresses in so far as it accepts their impress or develops what they develop. The individual does not owe his ultimate allegiance either to the State which is a machine or to the community which is a part of life and not the whole of life: his allegiance must be to the Truth, the Self, the Spirit, the Divine which is in him and in all; not to subordinate or lose himself in the mass, but to find and express that truth of being in himself and help the community and humanity in its seeking for its own truth and fullness of being must be his real object of existence. But the extent to which the power of the individual life or the spiritual Reality within it becomes operative, depends on his own development: so long as he is undeveloped, he has to subordinate in many ways his undeveloped self to whatever is greater than it. As he develops, he moves towards a spiritual freedom, but this freedom is not something entirely separate from all-existence; it has a solidarity with it because that too is the Self, the same Spirit. As he moves towards spiritual freedom, he moves also towards spiritual oneness. The spiritually realised, the liberated man is preoccupied, says the Gita, with the good of all beings; Buddha discovering the way of Nirvana must turn back to open that way to those who are still under the delusion of their constructive instead of their real being, — or non-being; Vivekananda, drawn by the Absolute, feels also the call of the disguised Godhead in humanity and most the call of the fallen and the suffering, the call of the self to the self in the obscure body of the universe. For the awakened individual the realisation of his truth of being and his inner liberation and perfection must be his primary seeking, — first, because that is the call of the Spirit within him, but also because it is only by liberation and perfection and realisation of the truth of being that man can arrive at truth of living. A perfected community also can exist only by the perfection of its individuals, and perfection can come only by the discovery and affirmation in life by each of his own spiritual being and the discovery by all of their spiritual unity and a resultant life-unity. There can be no real perfection for us except by our inner self and truth of spiritual existence taking up all truth of the instrumental existence into itself and giving to it oneness, integration, harmony. As our only real freedom is the discovery and disengagement of the spiritual Reality within us, so our only means of true perfection is the sovereignty and self-effectuation of the spiritual Reality in all the elements of our nature.

Our nature is complex and we have to find a key to some perfect unity and fullness of its complexity. Its first evolutionary basis is the material life: Nature began with that and man also has to begin with it; he has first to affirm his material and vital existence. But if he stops there, there can be for him no evolution; his next and greater preoccupation must be to find himself as a mental being in a material life, — both individual and social, — as perfected as possible. This was the direction which the Hellenic idea gave to European civilisation, and the Roman reinforced, — or weakened, — it with the ideal of organised power: the cult of reason, the interpretation of life by an intellectual thought critical, utilitarian, organising and constructive, the government of life by Science are the last outcome of this inspiration. But in ancient times the higher creative and dynamic element was the pursuit of an ideal truth, good and beauty and the moulding of mind, life and body into perfection and harmony by this ideal. Beyond and above this preoccupation, as soon as mind is sufficiently developed, there awakes in man the spiritual preoccupation, the discovery of a self and inmost truth of being and the release of man's mind and life into the truth of the Spirit, its perfection by the power of the Spirit, the solidarity, unity, mutuality of all beings in the Spirit. This was the Eastern ideal carried by Buddhism and other ancient disciplines to the coasts of Asia and Egypt and from there poured by Christianity into Europe. But these motives, burning for a time like dim torchlights in the confusion and darkness created by the barbaric flood that had submerged the old civilisations, have been abandoned by the modern spirit which has found another light, the light of Science. What the modern spirit has sought for is the economic social ultimate, — an ideal material organisation of civilisation and comfort, the use of reason and science and education for the generalisation of a utilitarian rationality which will make the individual a perfected social being in a perfected economic society. What remained from the spiritual ideal was, — for a time, — a mentalised and moralised humanitarianism relieved of all religious colouring and a social ethicism which was deemed all-sufficient to take the place of a religious and individual ethic. It was so far that the race had reached when it found itself hurried forward by its own momentum into a subjective chaos and a chaos of its life in which all received values were overthrown and all firm ground seemed to disappear from its social organisation, its conduct and its culture.

For this ideal, this conscious stress on the material and economic life was in fact a civilised reversion to the first state of man, his early barbaric state and its preoccupation with life and matter, a spiritual retrogression with the resources of the mind of a developed humanity and a fully evolved Science at its disposal. As an element in the total complexity of human life this stress on a perfected economic and material existence has its place in the whole: as a sole or predominant stress it is for humanity itself, for the evolution itself full of danger. The first danger is a resurgence of the old vital and material primitive barbarian in a civilised form; the means Science has put at our disposal eliminates the peril of the subversion and destruction of an effete civilisation by stronger primitive peoples, but it is the resurgence of the barbarian in ourselves, in civilised man, that is the peril, and this we see all around us. For that is bound to come if there is no high and strenuous mental and moral ideal controlling and uplifting the vital and physical man in us and no spiritual ideal liberating him from himself into his inner being. Even if this relapse is escaped, there is another danger, — for a cessation of the evolutionary urge, a crystallisation into a stable comfortable mechanised social living without ideal or outlook is another possible outcome. Reason by itself cannot long maintain the race in its progress; it can do so only if it is a mediator between the life and body and something higher and greater within him; for it is the inner spiritual necessity, the push from what is there yet unrealised within him that maintains in him, once he has attained to mind, the evolutionary stress, the spiritual nisus. That renounced, he must either relapse and begin all over again or disappear like other forms of life before him as an evolutionary failure, through incapacity to maintain or to serve the evolutionary urge. At the best he will remain arrested in some kind of mediary typal perfection, like other animal kinds, while Nature pursues her way beyond him to a greater creation.

At present mankind is undergoing an evolutionary crisis in which is concealed a choice of its destiny; for a stage has been reached in which the human mind has achieved in certain directions an enormous development while in others it stands arrested and bewildered and can no longer find its way. A structure of the external life has been raised up by man's ever-active mind and life-will, a structure of an unmanageable hugeness and complexity, for the service of his mental, vital, physical claims and urges, a complex political, social, administrative, economic, cultural machinery, an organised collective means for his intellectual, sensational, aesthetic and material satisfaction. Man has created a system of civilisation which has become too big for his limited mental capacity and understanding and his still more limited spiritual and moral capacity to utilise and manage, a too dangerous servant of his blundering ego and its appetites. For no greater seeing mind, no intuitive soul of knowledge has yet come to his surface of consciousness which could make this basic fullness of life a condition for the free growth of something that exceeded it. This new fullness of the means of life might be, by its power for a release from the incessant unsatisfied stress of his economic and physical needs, an opportunity for the full pursuit of other and greater aims surpassing the material existence, for the discovery of a higher truth and good and beauty, for the discovery of a greater and diviner spirit which would intervene and use life for a higher perfection of the being: but it is being used instead for the multiplication of new wants and an aggressive expansion of the collective ego. At the same time Science has put at his disposal many potencies of the universal Force and has made the life of humanity materially one; but what uses this universal Force is a little human individual or communal ego with nothing universal in its light of knowledge or its movements, no inner sense or power which would create in this physical drawing together of the human world a true life-unity, a mental unity or a spiritual oneness. All that is there is a chaos of clashing mental ideas, urges of individual and collective physical want and need, vital claims and desires, impulses of an ignorant life-push, hungers and calls for life satisfaction of individuals, classes, nations, a rich fungus of political and social and economic nostrums and notions, a hustling medley of slogans and panaceas for which men are ready to oppress and be oppressed, to kill and be killed, to impose them somehow or other by the immense and too formidable means placed at his disposal, in the belief that this is his way out to something ideal. The evolution of human mind and life must necessarily lead towards an increasing universality; but on a basis of ego and segmenting and dividing mind this opening to the universal can only create a vast pullulation of unaccorded ideas and impulses, a surge of enormous powers and desires, a chaotic mass of unassimilated and intermixed mental, vital and physical material of a larger existence which, because it is not taken up by a creative harmonising light of the Spirit, must welter in a universalised confusion and discord out of which it is impossible to build a greater harmonic life. Man has harmonised life in the past by organised ideation and limitation; he has created societies based on fixed ideas or fixed customs, a fixed cultural system or an organic life-system, each with its own order; the throwing of all these into the melting-pot of a more and more intermingling life and a pouring in of ever new ideas and motives and facts and possibilities call for a new, a greater consciousness to meet and master the increasing potentialities of existence and harmonise them. Reason and Science can only help by standardising, by fixing everything into an artificially arranged and mechanised unity of material life. A greater whole-being, whole-knowledge, whole-power is needed to weld all into a greater unity of whole-life.

A life of unity, mutuality and harmony born of a deeper and wider truth of our being is the only truth of life that can successfully replace the imperfect mental constructions of the past which were a combination of association and regulated conflict, an accommodation of egos and interests grouped or dovetailed into each other to form a society, a consolidation by common general life-motives, a unification by need and the pressure of struggle with outside forces. It is such a change and such a reshaping of life for which humanity is blindly beginning to seek, now more and more with a sense that its very existence depends upon finding the way. The evolution of Mind working upon Life has developed an organisation of the activity of Mind and use of Matter which can no longer be supported by human capacity without an inner change. An accommodation of the egocentric human individuality, separative even in association, to a system of living which demands unity, perfect mutuality, harmony, is imperative. But because the burden which is being laid on mankind is too great for the present littleness of the human personality and its petty mind and small life-instincts, because it cannot operate the needed change, because it is using this new apparatus and organisation to serve the old infraspiritual and infrarational life-self of humanity, the destiny of the race seems to be heading dangerously, as if impatiently and in spite of itself, under the drive of the vital ego seized by colossal forces which are on the same scale as the huge mechanical organisation of life and scientific knowledge which it has evolved, a scale too large for its reason and will to handle, into a prolonged confusion and perilous crisis and darkness of violent shifting incertitude. Even if this turns out to be a passing phase or appearance and a tolerable structural accommodation is found which will enable mankind to proceed less catastrophically on its uncertain journey, this can only be a respite. For the problem is fundamental and in putting it evolutionary Nature in man is confronting herself with a critical choice which must one day be solved in the true sense if the race is to arrive or even to survive. The evolutionary nisus is pushing towards a development of the cosmic Force in terrestrial life which needs a larger mental and vital being to support it, a wider Mind, a greater wider more conscious unanimised Life-Soul, Anima, and that again needs an unveiling of the supporting Soul and spiritual Self within to maintain it.

A rational and scientific formula of the vitalistic and materialistic human being and his life, a search for a perfected economic society and the democratic cultus of the average man are all that the modern mind presents us in this crisis as a light for its solution. Whatever the truth supporting these ideas, this is clearly not enough to meet the need of a humanity which is missioned to evolve beyond itself or, at any rate, if it is to live, must evolve far beyond anything that it at present is. A life-instinct in the race and in the average man himself has felt the inadequacy and has been driving towards a reversal of values or a discovery of new values and a transfer of life to a new foundation. This has taken the form of an attempt to find a simple and ready-made basis of unity, mutuality, harmony for the common life, to enforce it by a suppression of the competitive clash of egos and so to arrive at a life of identity for the community in place of a life of difference. But to realise these desirable ends the means adopted have been the forcible and successful materialisation of a few restricted ideas or slogans enthroned to the exclusion of all other thought, the suppression of the mind of the individual, a mechanised compression of the elements of life, a mechanised unity and drive of the life-force, a coercion of man by the State, the substitution of the communal for the individual ego. The communal ego is idealised as the soul of the nation, the race, the community; but this is a colossal and may turn out to be a fatal error. A forced and imposed unanimity of mind, life, action raised to their highest tension under the drive of something which is thought to be greater, the collective soul, the collective life, is the formula found. But this obscure collective being is not the soul or self of the community; it is a life-force that rises from the subconscient and, if denied the light of guidance by the reason, can be driven only by dark massive forces which are powerful but dangerous for the race because they are alien to the conscious evolution of which man is the trustee and bearer. It is not in this direction that evolutionary Nature has pointed mankind; this is a reversion towards something that she had left behind her.

Another solution that is attempted reposes still on the materialistic reason and a unified organisation of the economic life of the race; but the method that is being employed is the same, a forced compression and imposed unanimity of mind and life and a mechanical organisation of the communal existence. A unanimity of this kind can only be maintained by a compression of all freedom of thought and life, and that must bring about either the efficient stability of a termite civilisation or a drying up of the springs of life and a swift or slow decadence. It is through the growth of consciousness that the collective soul and its life can become aware of itself and develop; the free play of mind and life is essential for the growth of consciousness: for mind and life are the soul's only instrumentation until a higher instrumentation develops; they must not be inhibited in their action or rendered rigid, unplastic and unprogressive. The difficulties or disorders engendered by the growth of the individual mind and life cannot be healthily removed by the suppression of the individual; the true cure can only be achieved by his progression to a greater consciousness in which he is fulfilled and perfected.

An alternative solution is the development of an enlightened reason and will of the normal man consenting to a new socialised life in which he will subordinate his ego for the sake of the right arrangement of the life of the community. If we inquire how this radical change is to be brought about, two agencies seem to be suggested, the agency of a greater and better mental knowledge, right ideas, right information, right training of the social and civic individual and the agency of a new social machinery which will solve everything by the magic of the social machine cutting humanity into a better pattern. But it has not been found in experience, whatever might have once been hoped, that education and intellectual training by itself can change man; it only provides the human individual and collective ego with better information and a more efficient machinery for its self-affirmation, but leaves it the same unchanged human ego. Nor can human mind and life be cut into perfection, — even into what is thought to be perfection, a constructed substitute, — by any kind of social machinery; matter can be so cut, thought can be so cut, but in our human existence matter and thought are only instruments for the soul and the life-force. Machinery cannot form the soul and life-force into standardised shapes; it can at best coerce them, make soul and mind inert and stationary and regulate the life's outward action; but if this is to be effectively done, coercion and compression of the mind and life are indispensable and that again spells either unprogressive stability or decadence. The reasoning mind with its logical practicality has no other way of getting the better of Nature's ambiguous and complex movements than a regulation and mechanisation of mind and life. If that is done, the soul of humanity will either have to recover its freedom and growth by a revolt and a destruction of the machine into whose grip it has been cast or escape by a withdrawal into itself and a rejection of life. Man's true way out is to discover his soul and its self-force and instrumentation and replace by it both the mechanisation of mind and the ignorance and disorder of life-nature. But there would be little room and freedom for such a movement of self-discovery and self-effectuation in a closely regulated and mechanised social existence.

There is the possibility that in the swing back from a mechanistic idea of life and society the human mind may seek refuge in a return to the religious idea and a society governed or sanctioned by religion. But organised religion, though it can provide a means of inner uplift for the individual and preserve in it or behind it a way for his opening to spiritual experience, has not changed human life and society; it could not do so because, in governing society, it had to compromise with the lower parts of life and could not insist on the inner change of the whole being; it could insist only on a credal adherence, a formal acceptance of its ethical standards and a conformity to institution, ceremony and ritual. Religion so conceived can give a religio-ethical colour

or surface tinge, — sometimes, if it maintains a strong kernel of
inner experience, it can generalise to some extent an incomplete
spiritual tendency; but it does not transform the race, it cannot
create a new principle of the human existence. A total spiritual
direction given to the whole life and the whole nature can alone
lift humanity beyond itself. Another possible conception akin
to the religious solution is the guidance of society by men of
spiritual attainment, the brotherhood or unity of all in the faith
or in the discipline, the spiritualisation of life and society by the
taking up of the old machinery of life into such a unification
or inventing a new machinery. This too has been attempted
before without success; it was the original founding idea of
more than one religion: but the human ego and vital nature
were too strong for a religious idea working on the mind and by
the mind to overcome its resistance. It is only the full emergence
of the soul, the full descent of the native light and power of the
Spirit and the consequent replacement or transformation and
uplifting of our insufficient mental and vital nature by a spiritual
and supramental Supernature that can effect this evolutionary
miracle.

At first sight this insistence on a radical change of nature
might seem to put off all the hope of humanity to a distant
evolutionary future; for the transcendence of our normal human
nature, a transcendence of our mental, vital and physical being,
has the appearance of an endeavour too high and difficult and
at present, for man as he is, impossible. Even if it were so, it
would still remain the sole possibility for the transmutation of
life; for to hope for a true change of human life without a change
of human nature is an irrational and unspiritual proposition; it
is to ask for something unnatural and unreal, an impossible
miracle. But what is demanded by this change is not something
altogether distant, alien to our existence and radically impossible; for what has to be developed is there in our being and not
something outside it: what evolutionary Nature presses for, is
an awakening to the knowledge of self, the discovery of self, the
manifestation of the self and spirit within us and the release of
its self-knowledge, its self-power, its native self-instrumentation.

It is, besides, a step for which the whole of evolution has been a preparation and which is brought closer at each crisis of human destiny when the mental and vital evolution of the being touches a point where intellect and vital force reach some acme of tension and there is a need either for them to collapse, to sink back into a torpor of defeat or a repose of unprogressive quiescence or to rend their way through the veil against which they are straining. What is necessary is that there should be a turn in humanity felt by some or many towards the vision of this change, a feeling of its imperative need, the sense of its possibility, the will to make it possible in themselves and to find the way. That trend is not absent and it must increase with the tension of the crisis in human world-destiny; the need of an escape or a solution, the feeling that there is no other solution than the spiritual cannot but grow and become more imperative under the urgency of critical circumstance. To that call in the being there must always be some answer in the Divine Reality and in Nature.

• The answer might, indeed, be only individual; it might result in a multiplication of spiritualised individuals or even, conceivably though not probably, a gnostic individual or individuals isolated in the unspiritualised mass of humanity. Such isolated realised beings must either withdraw into their secret divine kingdom and guard themselves in a spiritual solitude or act from their inner light on mankind for what little can be prepared in such conditions for a happier future. The inner change can begin to take shape in a collective form only if the gnostic individual finds others who have the same kind of inner life as himself and can form with them a group with its own autonomous existence or else a separate community or order of being with its own inner law of life. It is this need of a separate life with its own rule of living adapted to the inner power or motive force of the spiritual existence and creating for it its native atmosphere that has expressed itself in the past in the formation of the monastic life or in attempts of various kinds at a new separate collective living self-governed and other in its spiritual principle than the ordinary human life. The monastic life is in its nature an association of other-worldly seekers, men whose whole attempt is to find and realise in themselves the spiritual reality and who form their common existence by rules of living which help them in that endeavour. It is not usually an effort to create a new life-formation which will exceed the ordinary human society and create a new world-order. A religion may hold that eventual prospect before it or attempt some first approach to it, or a mental idealism may make the same endeavour. But these attempts have always been overcome by the persistent inconscience and ignorance of our human vital nature; for that nature is an obstacle which no mere idealism or incomplete spiritual aspiration can change in its recalcitrant mass or permanently dominate. Either the endeavour fails by its own imperfection or it is invaded by the imperfection of the outside world and sinks from the shining height of its aspiration to something mixed and inferior on the ordinary human level. A common spiritual life meant to express the spiritual and not the mental, vital and physical being must found and maintain itself on greater values than the mental, vital, physical values of the ordinary human society; if it is not so founded, it will be merely the normal human society with a difference. An entirely new consciousness in many individuals transforming their whole being, transforming their mental, vital and physical nature-self, is needed for the new life to appear; only such a transformation of the general mind, life, body nature can bring into being a new worthwhile collective existence. The evolutionary nisus must tend not merely to create a new type of mental beings but another order of beings who have raised their whole existence from our present mentalised animality to a greater spiritual level of the earth-nature.

Any such complete transformation of the earth-life in a number of human beings could not establish itself altogether at once; even when the turning-point has been reached, the decisive line crossed, the new life in its beginnings would have to pass through a period of ordeal and arduous development. A general change from the old consciousness taking up the whole life into the spiritual principle would be the necessary first step; the preparation for this might be long and the transformation itself once begun proceed by stages. In the individual it might after a certain point be rapid and even effect itself by a bound, an evolutionary saltus; but an individual transformation would not be the creation of a new type of beings or a new collective life. One might conceive of a number of individuals thus evolving separately in the midst of the old life and then joining together to establish the nucleus of the new existence. But it is not likely that Nature would operate in this fashion, and it would be difficult for the individual to arrive at a complete change while still enclosed in the life of the lower nature. At a certain stage it might be necessary to follow the age-long device of the separate community, but with a double purpose, first to provide a secure atmosphere, a place and life apart, in which the consciousness of the individual might concentrate on its evolution in surroundings where all was turned and centred towards the one endeavour and, next, when things were ready, to formulate and develop the new life in those surroundings and in this prepared spiritual atmosphere. It might be that, in such a concentration of effort, all the difficulties of the change would present themselves with a concentrated force; for each seeker, carrying in himself the possibilities but also the imperfections of a world that has to be transformed, would bring in not only his capacities but his difficulties and the oppositions of the old nature and, mixed together in the restricted circle of a small and close common life, these might assume a considerably enhanced force of obstruction which would tend to counterbalance the enhanced power and concentration of the forces making for the evolution. This is a difficulty that has broken in the past all the efforts of mental man to evolve something better and more true and harmonious than the ordinary mental and vital life. But if Nature is ready and has taken her evolutionary decision or if the power of the Spirit descending from the higher planes is sufficiently strong, the difficulty would be overcome and a first evolutionary formation or formations would be possible.

But if an entire reliance upon the guiding Light and Will and a luminous expression of the truth of the Spirit in life are to be the law, that would seem to presuppose a gnostic world, a world in which the consciousness of all its beings was founded on this basis; there it can be understood that the life-interchange of gnostic individuals in a gnostic community or communities would be by its very nature an understanding and harmonious process. But here, actually, there would be a life of gnostic beings proceeding within or side by side with a life of beings in the Ignorance, attempting to emerge in it or out of it, and yet the law of the two lives would seem to be contrary and to offend against each other. A complete seclusion or separation of the life of a spiritual community from the life of the Ignorance would then seem to impose itself: for otherwise a compromise between the two lives would be necessary and with the compromise a danger of contamination or incompleteness of the greater existence; two different and incompatible principles of existence would be in contact and, even though the greater would influence the lesser, the smaller life would also have its effect on the greater, since such mutual impact is the law of all contiguity and interchange. It might even be questioned whether conflict and collision would not be the first rule of their relation, since in the life of the Ignorance there is present and active the formidable influence of those forces of Darkness, supporters of evil and violence, whose interest it is to contaminate or destroy all higher Light that enters into the human existence. An opposition and intolerance or even a persecution of all that is new or tries to rise above or break away from the established order of the human Ignorance, or if it is victorious, an intrusion of the lower forces into it, an acceptance by the world more dangerous than its opposition, and in the end an extinction, a lowering or a contamination of the new principle of life, have been a frequent phenomenon of the past; that opposition might be still more violent and a frustration might be still more likely if a radically new light or new power were to claim the earth for its heritage. But it is to be supposed that the new and completer light would bring also a new and completer power. It might not be necessary for it to be entirely separate; it might establish itself in so many islets and from there spread through the old life, throwing out upon it its own influences and filtrations, gaining upon it, bringing to it a help and illumination which a new aspiration in mankind might after a time begin to understand and welcome.

But these are evidently problems of the transition, of the evolution before the full and victorious reversal of the manifesting Force has taken place and the life of the gnostic being becomes as much as that of the mental being an established part of the terrestrial world-order. If we suppose the gnostic consciousness to be established in the earth-life, the power and knowledge at its disposal would be much greater than the power and knowledge of mental man, and the life of a community of gnostic beings, supposing it to be separate, would be as safe against attack as the organised life of man against any attack by a lower species. But as this knowledge and the very principle of the gnostic nature would ensure a luminous unity in the common life of gnostic beings, so also it would be sufficient to ensure a dominating harmony and reconciliation between the two types of life. The influence of the supramental principle on earth would fall upon the life of the Ignorance and impose harmony on it within its limits. It is conceivable that the gnostic life would be separate, but it would surely admit within its borders as much of human life as was turned towards spirituality and in progress towards the heights; the rest might organise itself mainly on the mental principle and on the old foundations, but, helped and influenced by a recognisable greater knowledge, it would be likely to do so on lines of a completer harmonisation of which the human collectivity is not yet capable. Here also, however, the mind can only forecast probabilities and possibilities; the supramental principle in Supernature would itself determine according to the truth of things the balance of a new world-order.

A gnostic Supernature transcends all the values of our normal ignorant Nature; our standards and values are created by ignorance and therefore cannot determine the life of Supernature. At the same time our present nature is a derivation from Supernature and is not a pure ignorance but a half-knowledge; it is therefore reasonable to suppose that whatever spiritual truth there is in or behind its standards and values will reappear in the higher life, not as standards, but as elements transformed, uplifted out of the ignorance and raised into the true harmony of a more luminous existence. As the universalised spiritual individual sheds the limited personality, the ego, as he rises beyond mind to a completer knowledge in Supernature, the conflicting ideals of the mind must fall away from him, but what is true behind them will remain in the life of Supernature. The gnostic consciousness is a consciousness in which all contradictions are cancelled or fused into each other in a higher light of seeing and being, in a unified self-knowledge and world-knowledge. The gnostic being will not accept the mind's ideals and standards; he will not be moved to live for himself, for his ego, or for humanity or for others or for the community or for the State; for he will be aware of something greater than these half-truths, of the Divine Reality, and it is for that he will live, for its will in himself and in all, in a spirit of large universality, in the light of the will of the Transcendence. For the same reason there can be no conflict between self-affirmation and altruism in the gnostic life, for the self of the gnostic being is one with the self of all, — no conflict between the ideal of individualism and the collective ideal, for both are terms of a greater Reality and only in so far as either expresses the Reality or their fulfilment serves the will of the Reality, can they have a value for his spirit. But at the same time what is true in the mental ideals and dimly figured in them will be fulfilled in his existence; for while his consciousness exceeds the human values so that he cannot substitute mankind or the community or the State or others or himself for God, the affirmation of the Divine in himself and a sense of the Divine in others and the sense of oneness with humanity, with all other beings, with all the world because of the Divine in them and a lead towards a greater and better affirmation of the growing Reality in them will be part of his life-action. But what he shall do will be decided by the Truth of the Knowledge and Will in him, a total and infinite Truth that is not bound by any single mental law or standard but acts with freedom in the whole reality, with respect for each truth in its place and with a clear knowledge of the forces at work and the intention in the manifesting Divine Nisus at each step of cosmic evolution and in each event and circumstance.

All life for the achieved spiritual or gnostic consciousness must be the manifestation of the realised truth of Spirit; only what can transform itself and find its own spiritual self in that greater Truth and fuse itself into its harmony can be accorded a life-acceptance. What will so survive the mind cannot determine, for the supramental gnosis will itself bring down its own truth and that truth will take up whatever of itself has been put forth in our ideals and realisations of mind and life and body. The forms it has taken there may not survive, for they are not likely to be suitable without change or replacement in the new existence; but what is real and abiding in them or even in their forms will undergo the transformation necessary for survival. Much that is normal to human life would disappear. In the light of gnosis the many mental idols, constructed principles and systems, conflicting ideals which man has created in all domains of his mind and life, could command no acceptance or reverence; only the truth, if any, which these specious images conceal, could have a chance of entry as elements of a harmony founded on a much wider basis. It is evident that in a life governed by the gnostic consciousness war with its spirit of antagonism and enmity, its brutality, destruction and ignorant violence, political strife with its perpetual conflict, frequent oppression, dishonesties, turpitudes, selfish interests, its ignorance, ineptitude and muddle could have no ground for existence. The arts and the crafts would exist, not for any inferior mental or vital amusement, entertainment of leisure and relieving excitement or pleasure, but as expressions and means of the truth of the Spirit and the beauty and delight of existence. Life and the body would be no longer tyrannous masters demanding nine-tenths of existence for their satisfaction, but means and powers for the expression of the Spirit. At the same time, since the matter and the body are accepted, the control and the right use of physical things would be a part of the realised life of the Spirit in the manifestation in earth-nature.

It is almost universally supposed that spiritual life must necessarily be a life of ascetic spareness, a pushing away of all that is not absolutely needed for the bare maintenance of the body; and this is valid for a spiritual life which is in its nature and intention a life of withdrawal from life. Even apart from that ideal, it might be thought that the spiritual turn must always make for an extreme simplicity, because all else would be a life of vital desire and physical self-indulgence. But from a wider standpoint this is a mental standard based on the law of the Ignorance of which desire is the motive; to overcome the Ignorance, to delete the ego, a total rejection not only of desire but of all the things that can satisfy desire may intervene as a valid principle. But this standard or any mental standard cannot be absolute nor can it be binding as a law on the consciousness that has arisen above desire; a complete purity and self-mastery would be in the very grain of its nature and that would remain the same in poverty or in riches: for if it could be shaken or sullied by either, it would not be real or would not be complete. The one rule of the gnostic life would be the self-expression of the Spirit, the will of the Divine Being; that will, that self-expression could manifest through extreme simplicity or through extreme complexity and opulence or in their natural balance, — for beauty and plenitude, a hidden sweetness and laughter in things, a sunshine and gladness of life are also powers and expressions of the Spirit. In all directions the Spirit within determining the law of the nature would determine the frame of the life and its detail and circumstance. In all there would be the same plastic principle; a rigid standardisation, however necessary for the mind's arrangement of things, could not be the law of the spiritual life. A great diversity and liberty of self-expression based on an underlying unity might well become manifest; but everywhere there would be harmony and truth of order.

A life of gnostic beings carrying the evolution to a higher supramental status might fitly be characterised as a divine life; for it would be a life in the Divine, a life of the beginnings of a spiritual divine light and power and joy manifested in material Nature. That might be described, since it surpasses the mental human level, as a life of spiritual and supramental supermanhood. But this must not be confused with past and present ideas of supermanhood; for supermanhood in the mental idea consists of an overtopping of the normal human level, not in kind but in degree of the same kind, by an enlarged personality, a magnified and exaggerated ego, an increased power of mind, an increased power of vital force, a refined or dense and massive exaggeration of the forces of the human Ignorance; it carries also, commonly implied in it, the idea of a forceful domination over humanity by the superman. That would mean a supermanhood of the Nietzschean type; it might be at its worst the reign of the "blonde beast" or the dark beast or of any and every beast, a return to barbaric strength and ruthlessness and force: but this would be no evolution, it would be a reversion to an old strenuous barbarism. Or it might signify the emergence of the Rakshasa or Asura out of a tense effort of humanity to surpass and transcend itself, but in the wrong direction. A violent and turbulent exaggerated vital ego satisfying itself with a supreme tyrannous or anarchic strength of self-fulfilment would be the type of a Rakshasic supermanhood: but the giant, the ogre or devourer of the world, the Rakshasa, though he still survives, belongs in spirit to the past; a larger emergence of that type would be also a retrograde evolution. A mighty exhibition of an overpowering force, a self-possessed, self-held, even, it may be, an ascetically self-restrained mind-capacity and life-power, strong, calm or cold or formidable in collected vehemence, subtle, dominating, a sublimation at once of the mental and vital ego, is the type of the Asura. But earth has had enough of this kind in her past and its repetition can only prolong the old lines; she can get no true profit for her future, no power of self-exceeding, from the Titan, the Asura: even a great or supernormal power in it could only carry her on larger circles of her old orbit. But what has to emerge is something much more difficult and much more simple; it is a self-realised being, a building of the spiritual self, an intensity and urge of the soul and the deliverance and sovereignty of its light and power and beauty, — not an egoistic supermanhood seizing on a mental and vital domination over humanity, but the sovereignty of the Spirit over its own instruments, its possession of itself and its possession of life in the power of the spirit, a new consciousness in which humanity itself shall find its own self-exceeding and self-fulfilment by the revelation of the divinity that is striving for birth within it. This is the sole true supermanhood and the one real possibility of a step forward in evolutionary Nature.

This new status would indeed be a reversal of the present law of human consciousness and life, for it would reverse the whole principle of the life of the Ignorance. It is for the taste of the Ignorance, its surprise and adventure, one might say, that the soul has descended into the Inconscience and assumed the disguise of Matter, for the adventure and the joy of creation and discovery, an adventure of the Spirit, an adventure of the Mind and Life and the hazardous surprises of their working in Matter, for the discovery and conquest of the new and the unknown; all this constitutes the enterprise of life and all this, it might seem, would cease with the cessation of the Ignorance. Man's life is made up of the light and the darkness, the gains and losses, the difficulties and dangers, the pleasures and pains of the Ignorance, a play of colours moving on a soil of the general neutrality of Matter which has as its basis the nescience and insensibility of the Inconscient. To the normal life-being an existence without the reactions of success and frustration, vital joy and grief, peril and passion, pleasure and pain, the vicissitudes and uncertainties of fate and struggle and battle and endeavour, a joy of novelty and surprise and creation projecting itself into the unknown, might seem to be void of variety and therefore void of vital savour. Any life surpassing these things tends to appear to it as something featureless and empty or cast in the figure of an immutable sameness; the human mind's picture of heaven is the incessant repetition of an eternal monotone. But this is a misconception; for an entry into the gnostic consciousness would be an entry into the Infinite. It would be a self-creation bringing out the Infinite infinitely into form of being, and the interest of the Infinite is much greater and multitudinous as well as more imperishably delightful than the interest of the finite. The evolution in the Knowledge would be a more beautiful and glorious manifestation with more vistas ever unfolding themselves and more intensive in all ways than any evolution could be in the

Ignorance. The delight of the Spirit is ever new, the forms of beauty it takes innumerable, its godhead ever young and the taste of delight, *rasa*, of the Infinite eternal and inexhaustible. The gnostic manifestation of life would be more full and fruitful and its interest more vivid than the creative interest of the Ignorance; it would be a greater and happier constant miracle.

If there is an evolution in material Nature and if it is an evolution of being with consciousness and life as its two key-terms and powers, this fullness of being, fullness of consciousness, fullness of life must be the goal of development towards which we are tending and which will manifest at an early or later stage of our destiny. The Self, the Spirit, the Reality that is disclosing itself out of the first inconscience of life and matter, would evolve its complete truth of being and consciousness in that life and matter. It would return to itself, — or, if its end as an individual is to return into its Absolute, it could make that return also, — not through a frustration of life but through a spiritual completeness of itself in life. Our evolution in the Ignorance with its chequered joy and pain of self-discovery and world-discovery, its half-fulfilments, its constant finding and missing, is only our first state. It must lead inevitably towards an evolution in the Knowledge, a self-finding and self-unfolding of the Spirit, a self-revelation of the Divinity in things in that true power of itself in Nature which is to us still a Supernature.

THE END

Glossary and Index

GLOSSARY OF SANSKRIT TERMS

*As far as possible definitions have been made using
Sri Aurobindo's own words.*

acitti — the Ignorance; unconsciousness; the non-perceiving principle in our consciousness. (cf. *citti*)

adevī māyā — undivine *māyā*.

adhikāra — capacity; something in the immediate power of a man's nature that determines by its characteristics his right to this or that way of Yoga.

adhyakṣa — presiding control; presiding person or presence.

adhyāropa — imposition.

advaita (Adwaita) — Monism; the monistic school of Vedanta.

advaitin (Adwaitin) — one who follows the school of *advaita*; Vedantic Monist.

ādyā śakti (Adya Shakti) — original and identical Power; the Supreme Consciousness and Power above the universe; the Transcendent Mother.

agni — fire; the god of Fire; the flame of the Divine Will or Force of consciousness working in the worlds.

ahaṅkāra — ego-sense; ego-idea; the subjective principle by which the *puruṣa* is induced to identify himself with *prakṛti* and her activities.

akṣara (Akshara) — the immutable, the immobile, the silent and inactive Self. (cf. *kṣara*)

ānanda — Bliss, Delight, Beatitude; the essential principle of delight; a self-delight which is the very nature of the transcendent and infinite existence.

ānandamaya (puruṣa) — Bliss-Self of the Spirit.

anirvacanīya — inexplicable and ineffable; not conceivable or expressible by the reason.

anīśa — not lord; subject (to Nature).

anṛtasya bhūreḥ — an abundant falsehood. (Rig Veda 7.60.5.)

anumantā — the giver of the sanction.

aparārdha — the lower hemisphere; the lower half of world existence. (cf. *parārdha*)

apraketam salilam — sea of Inconscience. (Rig Veda 10.129.3.)

aśanāyā mṛtyuḥ — the Hunger which is Death. (Brihadaranyaka Upanishad 1.2.4.)

asat — Non-Being; the negation of all existence. (cf. *sat*)

asura — Titan; adversary of the gods; hostile being of the mentalised vital plane.

aśvattha (Ashwattha) — fig-tree, symbol of the cosmic manifestation.

ātman — Self; Spirit; the original and essential nature of our existence; in relation to the individual the Supreme is our own true and highest self, *ātman*. (cf. *brahman*)

ātmaśakti (Atmashakti) — Self-power; soul power and spiritual power.

avidyā — the Ignorance; the Ignorance of oneness; the consciousness of Multiplicity; the relative and multiple consciousness. (cf. *vidyā*)

avidyāyām antare — within the Ignorance. (Katha Upanishad 1.2.5; Mundaka Upanishad 1.2.8.)

bālavat — as if a child; a state of pure, happy and free irresponsibility of action.

bhakta — a lover and devotee of the Divine.

bhayānaka — the terrible; one of the eight forms of emotional aestheticism in Sanskrit Rhetoric.

bhūri aspaṣṭa kartvam — there is made clear the much that has still to be done.

bībhatsa — the horrible or repellent; one of the eight forms of emotional aestheticism in Sanskrit Rhetoric.

brahmaloka — world of the *brahman* in which the soul is one with the infinite existence and yet in a sense still a soul able to enjoy differentiation in the oneness.

brahman — the Absolute; the Spirit; the Supreme being; the Reality; the Eternal; the One besides whom there is nothing else existent; in relation to the universe the Supreme is *brahman*, the one Reality which is not only the spiritual, material and conscious substance of all the ideas and forces and forms of the universe, but their origin, support and possessor, the cosmic and supracosmic Spirit. (cf. *ātman*)

brahmavidyā — the science of knowing the *brahman*.

bṛhat (Brihat) — the Vast, Wide or Large; the vast self-awareness.

buddhigrāhyam atīndriyam — beyond perception by the sense but seizable by the perceptions of the reason. (Gita 6.21.)

caitya puruṣa (Chaitya Purusha) — psychic entity; individual soul.

cit (Chit) — pure Consciousness; the free and all-creative self-awareness of the Absolute.

cit-śakti (Chit-Shakti) — consciousness-force; the integral conscious-power of the supreme Being.

cit-tapas (Chit-Tapas) — consciousness-force; pure energy of Consciousness.

citti — the Knowledge; the truth-perceiving conscious vision and knowledge. (cf. *acitti*)

deva — god; godhead.

devānām adabdha-vratāni — the unbroken laws of working of the gods.

dharma — law; standard of Truth or rule or law of action; means literally that which one lays hold of and which holds things together, the law, the norm, the rule of nature, action and life.

ekātma-pratyaya-sāram — Whose substance is certitude of One Self.

eko vasī sarvabhūtāntarātmā — one calm and controlling Spirit within all creatures. (Katha Upanishad 2.2.12.)

gītā — short form for *śrimad-bhagavadgītā*; the Song Celestial, being the spiritual teachings of Sri Krishna to Arjuna on the battlefield of Kurukshetra, given as an episode in the Indian epic, the Mahabharata.

goloka — world of Love, Beauty and Ananda full of spiritual radiances; the Vaishnava heaven of eternal Beauty and Bliss.

haṭhayogin — one who practises *haṭhayoga*, the use of the body for the opening of the divine life on all its planes.

hṛdya samudra — Ocean of the Heart.

iśvara (Ishwara) — Lord; Master; God; the Divine.

iśvara-śakti (Ishwara-Shakti) — the dual principle of the Lord and his executive Power.

iti iti — it is this, it is this. (cf. *neti neti*)

jaḍavat — like a thing inert in the hands of Nature; outwardly inert and inactive, moved by circumstance or forces, but not self-mobile.

jīvātman — individual self; the self of the living creature; the Spirit individualised and upholding the living being in its evolution from birth to birth.

jugupsā — shrinking, contraction; self-protecting recoil; the feeling of repulsion caused by the sense of a want of harmony between one's own limited self-formation and the contacts of the external with a consequent recoil of grief, fear, hatred, discomfort, suffering.

kālī — the dark face of the Universal Mother, the Divine Shakti.

karma — action, work; the power which by its continuity and development as a subjective and objective force determines the nature and eventuality of the soul's repeated existences.

karuṇa — the sorrowful; one of the eight forms of emotional aestheticism in Sanskrit Rhetoric.

karuṇā — compassion.

kṣara (Kshara) — the mobile or mutable; the soul that immediately informs the action, the mutations, the successive becomings of Nature. (cf. *akṣara*)

līlā — play, game; the cosmic play.

mahat — the essential and original matrix of consciousness in Nature out of which individuality and formation come; the vast cosmic principle of Force.

mahatī vinaṣṭiḥ — great is the perdition. (Kena Upanishad 2.5.)

manas — mind; the sense mind.

manomaya (puruṣa) — the mental being; mental self; soul in mind.

manomayaḥ prāṇa-śarīra-netā — the mental being, leader of the life and body. (Mundaka Upanishad 2.2.7.)

mantra — sacred syllable, name or mystic formula; expressive sound symbol.

manu — the Thinker; the mental being in a terrestrial body.

māra — conscious Devil or self-existent principle of evil.

māyā — phenomenal consciousness; creative consciousness; signified originally in the Veda the comprehensive and creative knowledge, wisdom that is from of old; afterwards taken in its second and derivative sense, cunning, magic, Illusion.

māyāvāda — Illusionism.

māyāvādin — an advocate of *māyāvāda*.

mukti — liberation; freedom of the soul.

nara — the human being. (cf. *nārāyaṇa*)

nārāyaṇa — a name of Vishnu, who, as the God in man, lives constantly associated in a dual unity with *nara*, the human being.

nāstyanto vistarasya me — there is no end to my self-extension. (Gita 10.19.)

neti neti — it is not this, it is not that.

nirguṇa (brahman) — the Eternal without qualities; the Impersonal Divine. (cf. *saguṇa*)

nirvāṇa — liberating annihilation; extinction, not necessarily of all being, but of being as we know it; extinction of ego, desire and egoistic action and mentality.

nivṛtti (Nivritti) — calm; holding back from action; the soul's involution into the passivity. (cf. *pravṛtti*)

pāpa — sin; demerit.

parabrahman — supreme being; supracosmic Divine; the spaceless and timeless Absolute.

paramātman — the supreme Self; the Absolute.

parā prakṛti (Para Prakriti) — the supreme Nature; the original and eternal nature of the Spirit; the infinite, timeless conscious power of the self-existent being out of which all existences in the cosmos are manifested.

para puruṣa (Para Purusha) — the supreme soul; God; the Self containing and enjoying both the stillness and the movement, but conditioned and limited by neither of them.

parārdha — the higher hemisphere; the upper half of world existence. (cf. *aparārdha*)

parātpara — a higher than the highest; the Supreme beyond the Most High.

piśāca (Pishacha) — demon; hostile being of the lower vital plane.

piśācavat — as the wild and disordered soul; as the unbound vital being, the divine maniac or else the divine demoniac.

pradhāna — first substance; the first state or arrangement of matter and its essential principle.

prajñā — the all-wise Intelligence; the universal intelligence.

prājna — the Self situated in deep sleep; the Master of Wisdom and Knowledge.

prajñāna — apprehending consciousness; the consciousness that cognizes all things as objects confronting its observation; in the divine mind it is knowledge regarding things as their source, possessor and witness.

prakṛti (Prakriti) — Nature; the Lord's executive force; Nature-Soul; the Energy, the Will-in-Power executive in the universe. (cf. *puruṣa*; cf. also *māyā*, *śakti*)

prāṇa — life; life-energy; the life-force in the nervous system; vital dynamis or kinesis.

prāṇamaya puruṣa (Pranamaya Purusha) — life-soul; the vital being; the being behind the Force of Life.

pravṛtti (Pravritti) — activity; movement and impulsion and kinesis; impetus towards action and works; the soul's evolution into the action. (cf. *nivṛtti*)

prithivī (Prithivi) — earth; the Earth-Principle.

puṇya — virtue; merit.

puruṣa (Purusha) — the Conscious Being; Conscious Soul; essential being supporting the play of *prakṛti*; a Consciousness — or a Conscient — behind, that is the lord, witness, knower, enjoyer, upholder and source of sanction for Nature's works; the true or spiritual Person. (cf. *prakṛti*)

puruṣa-prakṛti (Purusha-Prakriti) — Soul-Nature; Soul supporting Nature (even in their separation the two are one and inseparable).

puruṣottama (Purushottama) — the Supreme; the highest *puruṣa*; the Supreme Conscious Being; the supreme divine Person. (same as *para puruṣa*)

Rajasic — of the nature of *rajas*, the force of kinesis which translates in quality as struggle and effort, passion and action.

rākṣasa (Rakshasa) — giant; hostile being of the middle vital plane.

Rakshasic — of the *rākṣasa*, gigantic.

rasa — sap; essence; taste; the taste of delight.

ṛṣi (Rishi) — seer; sage.

ṛta-cit — Truth-Consciousness.

ṛtam (Ritam) — the Right; ordered truth of active being; truth of knowledge and action. (cf. *satyam*)

ṛtam jyotiḥ — the truth light.

ṛtam satyam bṛhat — the Right, the Truth, the Vast.

ṛtasya bṛhate — to or for the vastness of Truth.

rūpam rūpam pratirūpo babhūva — it shapes itself to form and form. (Katha Upanishad 2.2.9.)

saccidānanda (Sachchidananda) — Existence (*sat*) — Consciousness (*cit*) — Bliss (*ānanda*); a trinity of absolute existence, self-awareness and self-delight; the Divine Being.

sadanam ṛtasya — the seat of the Truth.

sad brahman — the pure Existent; Existence pure, indefinable, infinite, absolute.

sādharmya — identity in nature; becoming of one law of being and action with the Divine.

sādharmya mukti — liberation by assumption of the Divine Nature.

sādhunām rājyam — the reign of the saints.

sādṛśya — likeness (to the Divine).

saguṇa (*brahman*) — the Eternal with infinite qualities; the personal Divine. (cf. *nirguṇa*)

śakti (Shakti) — Energy; Force; Will; Power; Conscious-Force; Soul-Force; the self-existent, self-cognitive, self-effective Power of the Lord which expresses itself in the workings of *prakṛti*. (cf. *māyā; prakṛti*)

sālokya mukti — liberation by conscious existence in one world of being with the Divine.

samādhi — inner trance; yoga-trance.

samam brahma — the equal *brahman*.

sāmrājya — outward empire, the control by the subjective consciousness of the outer activities and environment.

sāṅkhya — a system of philosophy and spiritual practice: the analysis, the enumeration and discriminative setting forth of the principles of our being; the abstract and analytical realisation of truth.

Sankhyas — those who follow the system of the *sāṁkhya*, the analytic thinkers.

samnyāsin (Sannyasin) — an ascetic; one who renounces the world.

sat — being; existence; the thing that truly is. (cf. *asat*)

Sattwic — of the nature of *sattva*, the force of equilibrium, which translates in quality as good and harmony and happiness and light.

satyam — Truth; truth of being. (cf. *ṛtam*)

satyam ṛtam — the Truth, the Right.

śiva (Shiva) — one of the Gods of the Hindu trinity, the Destroyer.

soma — the sacred wine, it represents the intoxication of the divine delight of being. (cf. *ānanda*)

śruti — hearing; inspiration; knowledge received by the hearing of the Truth; inspired Revelation.

sthāṇu — stable.

sūkṣma deha — subtle body.

sūkṣma dṛṣti — subtle vision.

sūkṣma indriya — subtle organ.

śūnya — void; Nothingness.

suṣupti — deep sleep; the sleep-state.

svabhāva (Swabhava) — principle of self-becoming; nature; the essential nature and self-principle of being in each becoming; spiritual temperament, essential character.

svadharma (Swadharma) — own law of action.

svārājya (Swarajya) — self-rule; empire of oneself.

svarūpa — self-form; form of essential being; true essence and nature.

sve dame ṛtasya — the own home of the Truth.

syād vā na syād vā — may be or may not be.

tama āsīt tamasā gūḍham — darkness veiled within darkness.

tamas — the principle of inertia of consciousness and force; the force of inconscience, which translates in quality as obscurity and incapacity and inaction.

Tamasic — governed by the principle of obscurity and inertia (*tamas*).

tantra — a yogic system based on the principle of Consciousness-Power (conceived of as the Mother) as the Supreme Reality.

Tantric, Tantrik — pertaining to *tantra*; one who follows the discipline of *tantra*.

tapas — literally "heat"; any kind of energism, askesis, austerity of conscious force acting upon itself or its object; power; the Divine Force; the essential principle of energy; energism of consciousness.

tapasyā — effort; energism; askesis; austerity of the personal will; the law of energy increasing through compression.

tathāstu — Let it be so.

titikṣā — endurance; the bearing firmly of all contacts pleasant or unpleasant, not being overpowered by that which is painful, not being carried away by that which is pleasant; the facing, enduring and conquest of all shocks of existence.

tucchyena — by infinitesimal fragmentation.

turīyam dhāma — the fourth placing or poise of existence.

turīyam svid — a certain Fourth.

unmattavad — as one inconsequent in thought and impulse; in a God-possessed frenzy careless of itself and the world.

upaniṣad (Upanishad) — literally inner knowledge, that which enters into the final truth and settles in it; each of a class of philosophic writings posterior to the Vedas.

vaiṣṇava (Vaishnava) — pertaining to *viṣṇu*; a devotee of *viṣṇu*.

vasudhaiva kuṭumbakam — the whole earth is my family.

vāyu — air; wind; breath; the Lord of Life; the substantial will and energy in the cosmos working out into determined form and action and conscious dynamis of being.

veda — "the book of the Knowledge", the earliest Indian Scripture.

vedānta — "the culmination of the *veda*"; a system of philosophy and spiritual discipline based on the Upanishads.

vidyā — the Knowledge; Knowledge in its highiest spiritual sense; the consciousness of Unity. (cf. *avidyā*)

viṣṇu (Vishnu) — one of the Gods of the Hindu trinity, the Preserver.

viśvamānava — the universal man.

vṛndāvana (Vrindavan) — the *vaiṣṇava* heaven of eternal Beauty and Bliss.

Yoga — Union; the union of the soul with the immortal being and consciousness and delight of the Divine; a methodised effort towards self-perfection by the expression of the potentialities latent in the being and a union of the human individual with the universal and transcendent Existence.

yogakṣema — getting and having of good; well-being and joy.

yogamāyā (Yoga-Maya) — the power of Brahman's Consciousness-Force put out in self-manifestation.

yogin — one who practises *yoga*; one established in spiritual realisation.

INDEX

A

Absolute, (the), 84–85, 87–88, 340,
    372, 391–402 *passim*, 494–97,
    662–67 *passim*, 686–88, 1036
  and contraries, 625
    See also Contradictions
  and determinations, 337
  and limitation, 494, 618
  and Man and Nature, 718–19
  and Power (dynamis), 327–28, 476
  and qualities, 350–52
  and the divine soul, 165–66
  and the relative (relativities), 85,
    340, 342, 391–97 *passim*, 400–
    02 *passim*
  and the universe, 666
  fundamental cognition of, 330
  indeterminability of, 332–33, 349–50
  supracosmic view of, 696–97
  the Will of, 483–84
    See also Brahman; *cf.* Reality
Absoluteness, 629
Absolutism, 663, 893
Action,
  and limitations, 478–79
  and the Universal Energy, 959
  based on the Self, 348–49
  essence of life, 73–74
  of the Gnostic being, 1013–14,
    1017, 1035–46 *passim*, 1068–
    69, 1104
  of the Infinite, 348–49
  of the liberated man, 478–79
  resultant of the energy of the be-
    ing, 843–44
  subordinate to being, 1060–61
    See also Activity; Karma; *cf.* Will
Activity,
  and passivity, 594–600
Actuality(ies), 346, 454, 499
Adoration,
  approach to the Reality through,
    938
Adwaita,
  and rebirth, 782–85
  true (real), 37, 166
    See also Mayavada; Monism

Aesthetic creation, 1022
Aesthetic reception of things, 118–19
Affirmation(s), 663–64
  and negations, 36–37, 431–37,
    495–96; *see also* Negation(s)
Aggregation, 200, 200*fn*, 215–18 *pas-
    sim*, 260
  law of, 254
Agni, 168–69
Agnosticism, 14, 16, 590
Ahankara, 90
Aims,
  as binding, 1018–19
  of life, 685–711
Air, 630
Akshara (Purusha), 597
All, the, 37–38
    See also Reality, omnipresent
All-Bliss (All-Delight), 104–05, 422–23
    cf. Delight
All-Knowledge, 518
    cf. Omniscience
All-Soul, 801
    cf. One, the
All-Will, 1036
Altruism, 654, 1067, 1087
Ananda, 869, 1027–29
  and pain, 517, 630, 1027
  denial of, 264
  descent of, and sexual impurity,
    950–51
    See also Bliss; Delight
Anger, 611
Anima, 1095
Animal(s), 739, 741
  and intuition and instinct, 637–40
    passim, 932
  and man, 743–44, 871–73 *passim*
  and soul, 793–94
  ego-sense in the lower animal, 540
  its faculties relative to man, 872–
    73
  mentalised animal enjoyments,
    745–46
  rebirth as, 794
Animal life, 192, 959
  and Consciousness-Force, 959
  and evil, 632

E

H

8 88 8 8 8 8 8 8 88888

and the divine soul, 166
reconciliation, 667–69, 771
See also Unity, and multiplicity
Oneness, 352, 356–58, 588–90
and sameness, 1048
and the Overmind, 1007
instinctive, in infrarational life,
1079
with others, 655
spiritual, 946–47, 967, 996
See also Unity
Oppositions (opposites), 6–8, 33–34,
54–56, 221, 299, 338–81 *passim*,
394–403 *passim*, 620–57 *passim*
See also Contradictions; Dualities
Order, 1039–41
and the gnostic collective life,
1070
and theories of creation, 316–23
passim
Outer consciousness, 1065
See also Surface consciousness
Outer life,
shaped by inner, 723, 1014–15
Outer nature, 244, 996
purification of, 940–42
cf. Lower nature
Outer..., *see* Surface...
Overmind, 250*fn*, 251*fn*, 293–94,
325–29 *passim*, 616, 953, 957–58,
974, 986–92, 1045
action of, 953, 973–74, 990–91
and contradictions, 1007
and possibility, 295–301 *passim*,
303, 326, 334, 990–91
and Supermind, 293–94, 957–58,
991–92
and the cosmic consciousness,
987–88
and the physical consciousness,
952
descent of, 987–92 *passim*
harmony of, 300, 490
in gnosis, 1045
powers descending from, 812
views of creation, 325–29
cf. Cosmic Mind; Spiritual mind;
Universal mind
Overmind law, 303
Overmind Maya, 286–305 *passim*
Oversoul, 293, 583

P

Pain, 102–04, 107, 117, 261–63, 624,
630, 972, 1026–27, 1063–64
and Ananda (delight), 630, 1027
clinging to, 972
not an absolute, 630
See also Suffering; *cf.* Imperfection
Pain and pleasure,
and Ananda (delight), 517
and indifference (insensitivity),
and delight (Ananda), 113–20
passim, 236–38 *passim*
Pantheism, 689
materialistic evolutionary, 802
Para-Prakriti, 367
Para Purusha, 529*fn*
Parabrahman, 529*fn*; *see also* Absolute
Paramatman, 529*fn*
Passivity, 594–600
cf. Brahman, dual consciousness
Patanjali, 914*fn*
Peace,
and ecstasy, 1028–29
of the gnostic being, 1016
Percipient, perception, percept, 457–
500
Perfection, 175, 213–14, 230, 1058,
1069, 1072–74 *passim*, 1085–90
passim
of man (human), 33
of the nature and mind, 971
of the physical being, 1025–26
relative, and divine, 410–14
secret of, 1087
strivings towards, 1058
Person, the (the true, spiritual, etc.
Person), 239–41, 369–70, 725,
788, 933, 1010–11, 1031–34
and personality, 790, 850–57 *passim*
and the Impersonal, 297
cf. Ishwara; Mental person; Psychic
entity; Purusha
Persona, 1032–33
Personal Divine (Deity), 143, 369
Personality, 47, 103, 369–70, 766,
932–36
and character, 1032–33
and memory, 522, 541
and rebirth, 780–96 *passim*, 849–
51
and the gnostic individual, 1029–
33

OTHER TITLES BY SRI AUROBINDO

Sri Aurobindo
Rebirth and Karma

REBIRTH AND KARMA by Sri Aurobindo
In-depth study of the concepts of rebirth, karma and the higher lines of karma. One of the best introductions to this area we have ever found.
LOTUS PRESS   ISBN 0-941524-63-9   190 pp pb $9.95

THE LIFE DIVINE by Sri Aurobindo
The Life Divine is Sri Aurobindo's major philosophical exposition, spanning more than a thousand pages and integrating the major spiritual directions of mankind into a coherent picture of the growth of the spiritual essence of man through diverse methods, philosophies and spiritual practices.

LOTUS PRESS   ISBN 0-941524-62-0   1113 pp hb $39.95
LOTUS PRESS   ISBN 0-941524-61-2   1113 pp pb $29.95

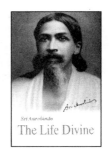

Sri Aurobindo
The Life Divine

Sri Aurobindo
The Integral Yoga
Sri Aurobindo's Teaching and Method of Practice

THE INTEGRAL YOGA
Sri Aurobindo's Teaching and Method of Practice
by Sri Aurobindo (compilation)

"These carefully selected excerpts from the writings of Sri Aurobindo provide a wonderfully accessible entre into the writings of one of the great masters of spiritual synthesis." Ram Dass

LOTUS PRESS   ISBN 0-941524-76-0   416 pp pb $14.95

SYNTHESIS OF YOGA, US EDITION by Sri Aurobindo
In *The Synthesis of Yoga* Sri Aurobindo unfolds his vision of an integral yoga embracing all the powers and activities of man. First, he reviews the three great yogic paths of Knowledge, Works and Love, along with Hatha Yoga, Raja Yoga and Tantra, and then integrates them all into a great symphony. "Truth of philosophy is of a merely theoretical value unless it can be lived, and we have therefore tried in the *The Synthesis of Yoga* to arrive at a synthetical view of the principles and methods of the various lines of spiritual self-discipline and the way in which they can lead to an integral divine life in the human existence".

Sri Aurobindo
The Synthesis of Yoga

LOTUS PRESS   ISBN 0-941524-66-3   899 pp hb $34.95
LOTUS PRESS   ISBN 0-941524-65-5   889 pp pb $29.95

Available from your local bookseller or
Lotus Press, PO Box 325, Twin Lakes, WI 53181 • 262-889-8561
www.lotuspress.com • email: lotuspress@lotuspress.com

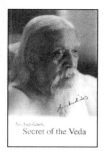

SECRET OF THE VEDA by Sri Aurobindo

In this ground-breaking book, Sri Aurobindo has revealed the secret of the Veda and illustrated his method with numerous translations of the ancient hymns. *Secret of the Veda* has been acclaimed by scholars and yogins as the ultimate key to revealing the hidden sense and secret inner meanings of the original spiritual revelation of the Veda. The *Rig Veda* provides an inner spiritual and psychological practice to achieve realization. It is the foundation upon which the Upanishads were later developed. *Now in its first US edition.*

Secret of the Veda | LOTUS PRESS   ISBN 0-914955-19-5   581 pp pb $19.95

ESSAYS ON THE GITA by Sri Aurobindo

The *Bhagavad Gita* stands alone in the spiritual tradition of humanity by being at the same time a Scripture, a teaching , a poetic utterance and a practical guidebook to the problems of life in the world. For this reason, the Gita is a powerful aid to anyone who wants to integrate the life of the Spirit with the issues of life in the world. It does not "cut the knot" but systematically works to untie it. In so doing, it helps us clarify the issues alive within ourselves. Sri Aurobindo understood these issues and in his famous *Essays on the Gita* he was able to reveal many subtle and hidden aspects of the teaching of the Gita. He entered into the spirit of the original and created a commentary that has stood

Essays on the Gita

the test of time in its lucidity and value for anyone wishing to truly understand the *Bhagavad Gita*. *Essays on the Gita* has been widely acclaimed for opening up the deeper sense of the *Bhagavad Gita*. *Now in its first US edition.*

LOTUS PRESS   ISBN 0-914955-18-7   588 pp pb $19.95

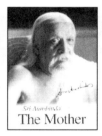

THE MOTHER by Sri Aurobindo

Sri Aurobindo has created, in this small book, a powerful guide to the practice of spirituality in life. To discover this gem is to gain a constant companion whose guidance remains forever meaningful. Its power of expression and meaning are so concentrated and far reaching that many have called it "Matri Upanishad", the Upanishad of the Mother. Sri Aurobindo's Matri Upanishad is the text which reveals this power and energy of creation in its universal and personal sense, providing both truth of philosophy and truth of yogic experience at one and the same time. *Now in its first US edition.*

The Mother

LOTUS PRESS   ISBN 0-941524-79-5   62 pp pb $3.95

SAVITRI: A LEGEND AND A SYMBOL by Sri Aurobindo

Savitri is an inner guidebook for the soul. These mantric verses imbue even the body with potent spiritual resonance. In this epic spiritual poem, Sri Aurobindo reveals his vision of mankind's destiny within the universal evolution. He sets forth the optimistic view that life on earth has a purpose, and he places our travail within the context of this purpose: to participate in the evolution of consciousness that represents the secret thread behind life on earth. Sri Aurobindo's verses describe the origin of the universe, the appearance of sentient beings and the stages of evolution, as well as speak to many of mankind's unanswered questions concerning pain and death. *Now in its first US edition.*

Savitri
A Legend and a Symbol

LOTUS PRESS   ISBN 0-941524-80-9   816 pp pb $24.95

Available from your local bookseller or
Lotus Press, PO Box 325, Twin Lakes, WI 53181 • 262-889-8561
www.lotuspress.com • email: lotuspress@lotuspress.com

Sri Aurobindo
The Upanishads

THE UPANISHADS by Sri Aurobindo
with Sanskrit text, English translation
and Sri Aurobindo's commentary

The Upanishads clearly rank with the greatest spiritual and philosophical writings of mankind. They have been revered for their beauty of expression and for the philosophical issues they address in a way that can benefit all, regardless of the particular religious or spiritual tradition one follows. They are considered to be a universal body of expression of mankind's highest aspirations and seeking for truth. While many have undertaken to translate the Upanishads, Sri Aurobindo's work deserves a special place. Sri Aurobindo brought more than just a scholarly effort to this work. Rather, he informed it with experience and spiritual practice, which allows him to enter into the spirit of the Upanishads and communicate it to us.

LOTUS PRESS   ISBN 0-914955-23-3   466 pp pb $17.95

Sri Aurobindo
Hymns to the Mystic Fire

HYMNS TO THE MYSTIC FIRE by Sri Aurobindo
with Sanskrit text, English translation and
Sri Aurobindo's commentary

Sri Aurobindo unlocked the hidden secret of the veda. In this book, he illustrates the "key" he found by translating all the Hymns to Agni from the Rig Veda. Agni is the "mystic fire" of the Rig Veda and has the largest number of hymns dedicated to any one concept. Included for reference are the actual Sanskrit text of each hymn. The "Doctrine of the Mystics" reveals the underlying philosophical, psychological and spiritual truths experienced by the sages.

LOTUS PRESS   ISBN 0-914955-22-5   502 pp pb $17.95

THE IDEAL OF HUMAN UNITY by Sri Aurobindo
While humanity has made many attempts at achieving unity, most of these were founded on the basis of some form of "uniformity". Sri Aurobindo points out that such an attempt to create unity through uniformity is bound to fail. He therefore puts before us a wider and more embracing formula, "unity with diversity". He explores the potential for human oneness founded on a basis of freedom and respect between people, while allowing the infinite diversity of human thought, religion, culture and lifestyle to manifest in all its wonderful and colorful forms.

LOTUS PRESS   ISBN 0-914955-43-8   460 pp pb $17.95

Sri Aurobindo
The Ideal of Human Unity

THE HUMAN CYCLE: THE PSYCHOLOGY OF SOCIAL DEVELOPMENT by Sri Aurobindo
Sri Aurobindo develops the overview of mankind's evolution to show that societies pass through a series of stages, starting from the "symbolic", moving to the "typal and conventional", evolving to the "individualist" and finally ending in the "subjective". Each of these stages has characteristic elements that determine how the social structures are developed and how individuals view their own purpose and activity in life. As a result of this review, Sri Aurobindo indicates that we are approaching a new spiritual age of humanity which is the fulfillment of the seeking of all religious and philosophical leaders of the ages.

LOTUS PRESS   ISBN 0-914955-44-6   280 pp pb $14.95

Sri Aurobindo
The Human Cycle
The Psychology of Social Development

Available from your local bookseller or
Lotus Press, PO Box 325, Twin Lakes, WI 53181 • 262-889-8561
www.lotuspress.com • email: lotuspress@lotuspress.com